Freshfields Bruckhaus Deringer

on

Financial Services: Investigations and Enforcement

Third Edition

Freshfields Bruckhaus Deringer

on

Financial Services: Investigations and Enforcement

Third Edition

Freshfields Bruckhaus Deringer

Bloomsbury Professional

Published by
Bloomsbury Professional Ltd, Maxwelton House, 41–43 Boltro Road,
Haywards Heath, West Sussex, RH16 1BJ

© Bloomsbury Professional Ltd 2014

Bloomsbury Professional is an imprint of Bloomsbury Publishing Plc

British Library Cataloguing-in-Publication Data.
A catalogue record for this book is available from the British Library.

ISBN 978 1 78043 126 0

While every care has been taken to ensure the accuracy of this work, no responsibility for loss or damage occasioned to any person acting or refraining from action as a result of any statement in it can be accepted by the authors, editors or publishers.

Typeset by Phoenix Photosetting, Chatham, Kent
Printed and bound in Great Britain by CPI Group (UK) Ltd, Croydon, CR0 4YY

Foreword by Lord Turnbull

Since the second edition of this highly useful volume was published in 2005, the financial services industry has undergone perhaps the greatest shock in its history. The recent global financial crisis has been the severest in living memory and has had an impact that will reverberate for many years.

One of the clearest effects of the crisis has been on financial regulation. The depth and impact of the crisis has led to significant changes in regulation around the world, not least in the United Kingdom. There have been several new Acts of Parliament; the composition and structure of the bodies responsible for financial regulation have changed; for the banking sector the Approved Persons Regime is to be replaced by a Senior Persons Regime which will define responsibilities more closely and hence provide a clearer basis for enforcement; and an increasing number of areas are being drawn into the regulatory framework. Perhaps most unsurprisingly, there has been a sharp swing away from the idea of non-enforcement-led regulation in favour of a regime that has been using enforcement quite aggressively as a tool.

These are some of the principal changes that have taken place in response to the crisis, all of which make the third edition of this book timely. Some of these changes were probably inevitable, given the widespread view that regulators were both complaisant and complacent before the crisis. However, there will be many practitioners who believe that the pendulum may have swung too far the other way, a view that is not without its adherents beyond the industry. As I write, parts of the regulatory environment are being examined, for example whether the enforcement regime fully meets best practice in the separation of investigation, prosecution and judgement. There are also concerns that earlier publicity around Warning Notices could cause grave damage, particularly to small businesses, that turn out to be innocent.

There are fears that the dial may have moved too far towards enforcement action after the fact, as opposed to early supervisory intervention. There is also the question of whether enforcement action may now be more likely to be used in respect of conduct of business or market abuse because enforcement lies within the Financial Conduct Authority rather than with the Prudential Regulation Authority. Enforcement actions can be complex, costly and take a long time. Sometimes supervisory action can produce a more effective result for all concerned.

Given these conditions, this book is more useful than ever, providing excellent commentary on the new trends in regulation. In this fluid climate, it is hard to imagine that practitioners will have to wait as long for the fourth edition of this excellent volume as they have for the third.

Lord Turnbull
April 2014

Lord Turnbull KCB CVO is a past Secretary to the Cabinet and Permanent Secretary to HM Treasury. He was a member of the Parliamentary Commission on Banking Standards. He is a non-executive director of British Land, Prudential and Frontier Economics.

Preface

When we published the last edition of this work, in October 2005, the boom in financial services was near its peak. Whilst regulatory enforcement was a real issue, particularly for firms who found themselves on the wrong side of the regulator, the relationship between the regulator and the regulated community was on the whole much less challenging than it is today and the political environment was more benign.

The growth, since the financial crisis, of public mistrust of financial services firms and those who work in them, coupled with the realities of systemic risk, have led to a more contentious style of regulation. Well publicised cases of significant mis-selling and other serious misconduct within some firms have tended to reinforce those perceptions. In this environment, the need for enforcement to play a sufficiently high profile role to act as a 'credible deterrent' against misconduct has led to soaring fines. Cultural change is seen as the solution, but all acknowledge that that will take some years and in the meantime heavy handed enforcement is likely to continue.

At the time of the last edition, the FSA had introduced reforms to the enforcement system which made the process fairer for those who sought to contest liability whilst at the same time introducing a structured system of inducements for early settlement. The settlement system has proven to be very important, with the great majority of cases being resolved at an early stage and relatively few disputes being taken through the formal stages of the enforcement process. More recently, however, firms have been pressed towards accepting increasingly unpalatable outcomes, sometimes causing significant damage to the business. The further the regulators push firms, the more the pendulum risks swinging back towards a more actively contested environment. The FSA encouraged its enforcement division to be 'bold' and to test the limits of its statutory powers. The regulator has increasingly done so, but too often without the limits of those powers actually being tested by a regulated community which has not felt able or willing to do so. We are not convinced the balance is right, and although the political environment currently is intolerant of firms challenging the regulator, it seems to us that a certain amount of challenge is a sign of a healthy system.

Recent reforms have made a number of significant structural changes to regulation, not least dividing the work of the FSA into the FCA and the PRA and introducing new statutory objectives, including the FCA's competition objective, which will guide the regulators' policy and use of their powers. We expect the

Preface

PRA to be less active as an enforcement regulator, but its powers will nonetheless be important to understand.

Looking ahead, we foresee the disputes between firms and regulators moving increasingly upstream, as the regulators attempt to persuade or force firms to adapt their business models to avoid risks crystallising, rather than waiting for problems to arise. This leads into different, less charted territory with fewer statutory powers in reality being exercised and considerable risk of unintended consequences. Senior management may be increasingly exposed in that environment, as they are stretched between their regulatory duties (and the potential for personal liability) and their primary duty to their firm.

Whilst creating scope for different kinds of disputes, we do not think this will lessen the focus on enforcement. Fines for retail misconduct are likely to grow to similar levels as those recently seen in the wholesale market. Senior management will increasingly be in the firing line, particularly in the light of the new regime for senior bankers introduced by the Financial Services (Banking Reform) Act 2013. The criminal law is becoming increasingly relevant to financial services enforcement and may over time lead to the development of a parallel white collar regime in a similar way to other jurisdictions. The increasing focus on competition in financial services markets also complicates the picture. All of this makes it challenging for firms to navigate the problems that inevitably arise from time to time, so as to protect the business whilst acting appropriately with regulators, customers and other stakeholders.

In this edition, we have maintained our approach of seeking to provide a comprehensive but practical guide to the enforcement aspects of the regulatory regime. The introduction of two regulators has somewhat complicated the picture, and we have tried to cover the powers and policy of both in a way that does not overly complicate the text. We have introduced a new chapter on regulatory intervention in markets, to deal with the upstream disputes which are increasingly important and the competition elements of the regime. We have also introduced a new chapter on multi-jurisdictional investigations, reflecting the increasing amount of cooperation and coordination between global regulators. The book has been very substantially revised and we hope that it will remain current for as long as the previous edition.

We would like to acknowledge the enormous amount of work which has gone into producing this edition, from the entirety of the Financial Institutions Disputes Group team in London, listed on the Acknowledgements page, as well as partners and other colleagues from our Non-Contentious Regulatory, Employment and Anti-Trust practices. Without their efforts, this edition would not have been possible.

David Scott and Simon Orton

1 April 2014

Acknowledgements

The editorial team has consisted of:
Tim Cave
Richard Chalk
Sharon Grennan
Mark Kalderon
Simon Orton
Sarah Parkes
Raj Parker
Piers Reynolds
Christopher Robinson
Ali Sallaway
David Scott
James Smethurst
Ian Taylor

Encompassing our contentious and non-contentious regulatory practice.
Thanks are also due to the following people who contributed to the text of this edition of the book:
Maria Banks
Nigel Best
Anthea Bowater
Neil Boyd
Michelle Bramley
Dan Butler
Chris Chapman
Divvika Choksi
Tom Clark
Rhys Corbett
Jennifer Devlin
Neil Donovan
Kitty Edwards
Piers Elliot
Hannah Fairbairn
Oliver Harland
Oliver Hayes
Philip Henderson

Acknowledgements

Daren Hlaing
Natalie Kearney
Edward Levene
Tom Luck
Andrew Marsh
Martin McElwee
Lauren McGuirl
Craig Montgomery
Chris Morris
Joseph Ninan
Andrew Norman
Jason Oliver
Elisabeth Overland
Jo Pagan
Sarah Robinson
Rebecca Sambrook
Louise Steel
Niall Stewart
Thomas Storer
Kevin Whibley

Contents

Contents

Section B   Investigations

Contents

Section C   Enforcement

Chapter 8   Disciplinary sanctions and other
regulatory action against firms

Contents

Section E   Specific Topics

Contents

Glossary of key terms

This section contains a simple glossary of certain key terms used in this book. For a detailed glossary of terms used in the PRA or FCA Handbooks (the Authorisation, Supervision, Enforcement and Decision Procedure and Penalties manuals), see the PRA or FCA Handbook, Glossary of Definitions.

Appointed representative
A person who contracts with an authorised person to carry on certain activities set out in the Financial Services and Markets Act 2000 (Appointed Representatives) Regulations 2001, SI 2001/1217, for which the authorised person takes responsibility, and who is thereby an exempt person, under the FSMA 2000, s 39.

Approved person
A person approved by the FCA or PRA under the FSMA 2000, s 59 to carry out a function of a firm which is specified by the FCA or PRA as a controlled function.

Authorised person
A person authorised by the FCA or PRA to carry on regulated activities under the FSMA 2000. In particular, this includes: (i) a person who has a Part 4A permission; (ii) an incoming firm; and (iii) a UCITS qualifier: see the FSMA 2000, s 31.

The Bank
The Bank of England.

City Code
The City Code on Takeovers and Mergers issued by the Panel on Takeovers and Mergers.

Code of market conduct
The Code which the FCA is required to issue under the FSMA 2000, s 119 to give guidance to those determining whether or not behaviour amounts to market abuse: see the FCA Handbook at MAR 1.

Code of practice for approved persons
The code of practice which the FCA and PRA are required to issue under the FSMA 2000, s 64 for the purpose of helping to determine whether an approved person's conduct complies with a Statement of Principle: see the FCA or PRA Handbook at APER.

Compensation Scheme or FSCS
The Financial Services Compensation Scheme established under the FSMA 2000, s 213 for compensating persons in cases where authorised persons (and appointed representatives) are unable, or likely to be unable, to satisfy claims against them.

Competent authority	The FCA in its capacity as UK Listing Authority for the purposes of the FSMA 2000, Part 6 (Official Listing) or the equivalent authority in another EEA state. The same phrase may also refer to a body acting as the relevant financial sector regulator in an EU Member State, as defined in European legislation, including the PRA and FCA in the UK.
Complaints commissioner	The person appointed by the Regulators to hear and determine complaints in accordance with the complaints scheme.
Complaints scheme	The scheme for the determination of complaints (usually relating to procedural and jurisdictional matters) made against the PRA, FCA and FPC under the Financial Services Act 2012, s 84(1)(a).
Compulsory jurisdiction	The jurisdiction of the FOS to which firms are compulsorily subject: see the FCA Handbook at DISP 2.
Controlled function	Those functions relating to the carrying on of regulated activities by authorised persons that are specified by the Regulators under the FSMA 2000, s 59 and which are required to be carried out by an approved person: see the FCA Handbook at SUP 10A.4.4 R and the PRA Handbook at SUP 10B.4.3 R.
Controller	A person who, in very broad terms, holds more than 10% of the shares of an undertaking or its parent, or is entitled to exercise or control the exercise of more than 10% of the voting power of the undertaking or its parent, or is able to exercise a significant influence over the management of the undertaking or its parent: for details: see the FSMA 2000, s 422. When used in relation to a UK insurance intermediary, cases where a person holds 20% or more of the shares of a firm or other undertaking.
Decision Making Committee or DMC	An executive body of the PRA, which decides whether or not the PRA will give a statutory notice. A DMC performs a function equivalent to the RDC in the context of the FCA. A DMC must include at least one person who has not been directly involved in the development of the case being considered: see the FSMA 2000, s 395(2).
Decision notice	A notice which the FCA or PRA is required under the FSMA 2000 to issue when deciding to take certain types of disciplinary or enforcement action (or certain decisions relating, broadly, to authorisation or approval under the FSMA 2000). It represents the PRA's or FCA's final decision, and may embody settlement terms: see the FCA Handbook at DEPP 2 Annex 1.

Dual-regulated	Firms or individuals that have met both PRA and FCA' conditions for authorisation, and are regulated by both authorities.
ECHR	European Convention on Human Rights.
Exempt person	A person who is exempt from the general prohibition in respect of particular regulated activities: see the FSMA 2000, s 417(1).
FCA-regulated	Firms that are only required to meet FCA conditions for authorisation and are regulated by the FCA for both prudential and conduct purposes.
Final notice	A notice which the FCA or PRA is required to issue under the FSMA 2000, s 390 when taking certain types of disciplinary or enforcement action.
Financial Conduct Authority or FCA	The UK regulator that supervises the conduct of all firms conducting regulated financial services business in the UK. The FCA's objectives mean that it focuses on protecting consumers, the integrity of the UK financial markets and effective competition. It supervises regulatory compliance of listed companies, brings enforcement action for market abuse and can pursue criminal prosecutions.
Financial Ombudsman Service or FOS	The Financial Ombudsman Service, and the ombudsmen appointed under it.
Financial Policy Committee or FPC	The Bank of England committee responsible for dealing with systematic risks in the UK financial system through macro-prudential regulation.
Financial Services Act 2012 or FS Act 2012	This legislation enacts changes to the existing legislation (primarily the FSMA 2000) and enacts new provisions necessary to facilitate the reforms in the reglatory regime that came into force on 1 April 2013.
Financial Services Authority or FSA	The primary regulator of the UK financial services sector between 2001 and 1 April 2013.
Financial Services (Banking Reform) Act 2013 or FS(BR)A 2013	This legislation received Royal Assent in December 2013 but, at the time of writing the implementation dates have not been announced. Amongst other changes, this legislation introduces concurrent competition powers for the FCA and amendments to the FSMA 2000 affecting regulatory enforcement, including, introducing a new senior persons regime, extended liability for senior persons and extends the limiation period for enforcement action to six years.

Financial Services and Markets Act 2000 or FSMA 2000	This is the main legislation governing the constitution, functions and powers of the Regulators in the UK and setting out the framework for regulation of firms. The FSMA 2000 has been amended including by the Financial Services Act 2010 and Financial Services Act 2012 (FS Act 2012) and is supplemented by multiple statutory instruments.
Financial Services Register	The public register of authorised persons, authorised unit trusts, authorised OEICs, recognised schemes, recognised investment exchanges, recognised clearing houses, individuals subject to a prohibition order and approved persons (among others) which the FCA is required to maintain under the FSMA 2000, s 347.
Firm	An authorised person. This term is used to refer to all financial institutions conducting regulated financial services business in the UK.
Fit and proper	The fundamental test applicable to determine whether a firm or person is suitable to be authorised to be involved in regulated activities.
General prohibition	The prohibition under the FSMA 2000, s 19 against a person carrying on a regulated activity unless he is an authorised person or an exempt person.
Incoming firm	A firm primarily regulated in another EEA state that conducts regulated financial services business in the UK either by notifying the home and host state regulators to use passport rights under the Single Market Directives or by obtaining an additional 'top-up' permission from the UK regulators.
Market abuse	Behaviour which falls within the FSMA 2000, s 118.
Notice of discontinuance	A notice which the FCA or the PRA is required to issue if it decides not to take the action proposed in a warning notice or the action to which a decision notice relates: see the FSMA 2000, s 389.
OEIC	Open-Ended Investment Company.
Part 4A permission	Permission to carry on regulated activities given by the PRA or FCA under the FSMA 2000, Pt 4A.
Principles for businesses	The 11 high-level rules that prescribe the fundamental standards applicable to authorised persons/firms: see the PRA or FCA Handbook at PRIN.
Private warning	An informal warning given by the PRA or FCA as an alternative to taking formal disciplinary or enforcement action.

Prohibition order	An order made by the PRA or FCA under FSMA 2000, s 56, prohibiting a person from performing specified functions.
Prudential Regulation Authority or PRA	The UK regulator responsible for the micro-prudential regulation of specified categories of firms – broadly deposit takers, insurers and significant investment firms.
Recognised clearing house or RCH	A clearing house in relation to which the FSA has issued a recognition order under the FSMA 2000, s 290 which remains in force.
Recognised investment exchange or RIE	An investment exchange in relation to which the FSA has issued a recognition order under the FSMA 2000, s 290 which remains in force.
Regulated activities	Those activities specified in accordance with the FSMA 2000, s 22 in Pt II of the Financial Services and Markets Act 2000 (Regulated Activities) Order 2001, SI 2001/544 (as amended) the carrying on of which requires authorisation or exemption under the FSMA 2000.
The Regulators	The FCA and the PRA, unless otherwise stated.
Regulatory Decisions Committee or RDC	A Committee of the FCA Board responsible for taking certain enforcement decisions (such as issuing warning notices and decision notices).
Regulatory objectives	The regulatory objectives of the FCA and PRA as set out in the FSMA 2000. For example, the FCA's objectives of market integrity, competition and the protection of consumers, specified in the FSMA 2000, ss 1C–1E.
Restitution order	An order made by the Regulators or the court under the FSMA 2000, ss 382–386, requiring a person to pay compensation for losses and/or disgorge any gains it has made as a result of a regulatory breach or market abuse.
Senior Person	A person approved by the FCA or PRA to hold a senior management function at a deposit-taker or dual-regulated investment firm under the senior persons regime introduced by the FS(BR)A 2013.
Single Market Directives	The Banking Consolidation Directive, the Third Non-Life Insurance Directives, the Markets in Financial Instrument Directive, the Insurance Mediation Directive, UCITS Directive, the Payment Services Directive, and the Second Electronic Money Directive.

Statements of principle for approved persons	The high-level principles made by the PRA and FCA under the FSMA 2000, s 64, which prescribe the fundamental standards applicable to approved persons: see the PRA and FCA Handbook at APER.
Supervisory notice	A notice which the FCA or PRA is required to issue when it proposes or decides to take certain types of action: see the FCA Handbook at DEPP 2 Annex 2.For a list of supervisory notices, see the FSMA 2000, s 395(13).
Threshold Conditions	The fundamental requirements for authorisation under the FSMA 2000, found in Sch 6: see the Handbooks at COND.
Top-up permission	An additional permission granted to an incoming firm or a UCITS qualifier to carry on a regulated activity not covered by its authorisation under the passport notifications procedures in the FSMA 2000, Sch 3, 4 and/or 5.
Tribunal	The Upper Tribunal (Chancery and Tax Chamber), an independent tribunal to which certain FCA and PRA decisions may be referred for fresh consideration.
UCITS qualifier	A firm which is the operator, trustee or depositary of a scheme recognised under the FSMA 2000, s 264 and authorised under the FSMA 2000, Sch 5.
UK Listing Authority or UKLA	The FCA in its capacity as the UK's competent authority for listing.
UK regulated firm	An authorised person that is primarily regulated in the UK.
Variation of permission	The FCA's or PRA's powers to vary a firm's permission.
Voluntary jurisdiction	The jurisdiction of the Ombudsman in which authorised or unauthorised persons participate voluntarily by contract.
Warning notice	A notice which the FCA or PRA is required under the FSMA 2000 to issue when it proposes to take certain types of disciplinary or enforcement action (or certain decisions relating, broadly, to authorisation or approval under the FSMA 2000): see the FCA Handbook at DEPP 2 Annex 1.
Withdrawal of approval	The PRA's and FCA's powers under the FSMA 2000, s 63, to withdraw a person's approval.

Table of Statutes

All references are to paragraph numbers.

Table of Statutes

Table of Statutes

Table of Statutes

Table of Statutes

Table of Statutory Instruments

All references are to paragraph numbers.

Table of Cases and Regulatory Decisions

All references are to paragraph numbers.

Table of Cases and Regulatory Decisions

S

FINANCIAL SERVICES AUTHORITY AND FINANCIAL CONDUCT AUTHORITY FINAL NOTICES

Table of Cases and Regulatory Decisions

Table of PRA and FCA Materials

This table contains references to sections of the Handbooks and guides published by the Regulators. All references are to paragraph numbers.

Table of PRA and FCA Materials

Table of PRA and FCA Materials

Table of PRA and FCA Materials

Section A
Introduction to the Regulatory Regime

Chapter 1   An introduction to the UK and European regulatory authorities

OVERVIEW

1.1   Since 1 April 2013, the UK regulatory regime involves two main institutions acting as regulators; the Prudential Regulatory Authority (PRA) to regulate prudential issues at banks, insurers and the most significant investment firms; and, the Financial Conduct Authority (FCA) to regulate prudential issues at other firms and conduct issues for all firms. In addition, the Financial Policy Committee (the FPC) of the Bank of England (the Bank) oversees macro-prudential risks.

1.2   This structure was introduced as a means of replacing the Financial Services Authority (FSA), which had since 1 October 2001 had been the unified prudential and conduct regulator of the UK financial services sector.

1.3   Although primarily a book about investigations and enforcement by the regulators in the UK, we cannot ignore the increasingly important role of EU institutions in shaping the regulatory regime in the UK, encouraging convergence of regulation between EU Member States and promoting co-operation and co-ordination between national regulators.

1.4   This chapter contains:

*   an overview of the UK regulatory regime, the regulators, their roles, objectives and regulatory philosophy; and

*   an overview of the European influence on UK regulation – the sources of EU law, the key bodies in the European System of Financial Supervision, the interaction between national regulators and European bodies, the

tendency for EU law to encourage convergence and the effect of EU law on enforcement in the UK.

UK REGULATORY FRAMEWORK

Introduction

1.5 The diagram below shows the key players in the UK regulatory regime.

UK regulatory structure

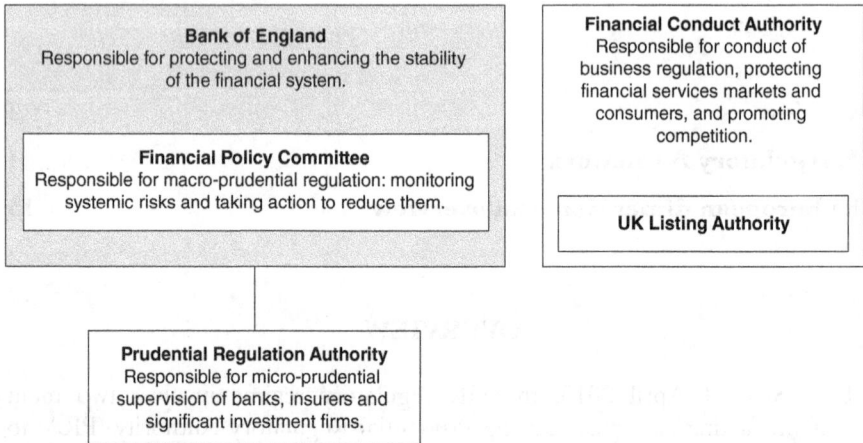

Bank of England
Responsible for protecting and enhancing the stability of the financial system.

Financial Policy Committee
Responsible for macro-prudential regulation: monitoring systemic risks and taking action to reduce them.

Financial Conduct Authority
Responsible for conduct of business regulation, protecting financial services markets and consumers, and promoting competition.

UK Listing Authority

Prudential Regulation Authority
Responsible for micro-prudential supervision of banks, insurers and significant investment firms.

1.6 The reasons for the changes to the regulatory regime in 2013 and the objectives and approach of each of the key players will be described briefly below.

How did this regime come about?

1.7 In the wake of the financial crisis of 2007–2009, the incoming coalition government in the UK took the view that the existing 'tripartite' system, under which regulatory responsibility was split between the FSA, the Bank and HM Treasury, had failed. In particular, the FSA's responsibility was thought to be too wide, ranging from prudential regulation of the largest banks to conduct regulation of the smallest investment adviser. In addition, the Bank had responsibility for financial stability but no tools to carry out that role. Crucially, there was a 'regulatory underlap' between the roles of the FSA and the Bank, with no mechanism to turn concerns about the stability of the system as a whole into concrete action. And finally, it was not clear who was in charge in a crisis. The design of the current regulatory system is intended to address these problems.

1.8 The main changes are, first, the separation of prudential responsibility from conduct regulation, and second, the giving of new powers to the Bank through a Financial Policy Committee for 'macro-prudential supervision' – ie supervision of the stability of the financial system as a whole.

1.9   The regime is created by the Financial Services Act 2012, which amends the Financial Services and Markets Act 2000 (FSMA 2000), the Bank of England Act 1998 and other relevant legislation. The FSMA 2000 as amended therefore is the primary legislation governing financial services in the UK.

Prudential Regulatory Authority (PRA)

What is the PRA?

1.10   The PRA is established as a subsidiary of the Bank and its constitution is prescribed by law[1]. It is responsible for prudential regulation of all deposit-takers, including banks, building societies and credit unions, as well as insurers and a small number of major investment firms that could present significant risks to UK financial stability. The firms that are subject to regulation by the PRA are sometimes referred to as dual-regulated firms (as well as PRA-authorised firms) because their conduct is also subject to regulation by the FCA.

1 FSMA 2000, Sch 1ZB.

What are the objectives of the PRA?

1.11   In discharging its general functions of making rules, codes, guidance and statements of policy, the PRA must, as far as is reasonably possible, act in a way which advances its general objective[1], and, where appropriate, its insurance objective.

1 FSMA 2000, s 2B(1).

1.12   The PRA's general objective is to promote the safety and soundness of dual-regulated firms[1]. In particular, it seeks to ensure that the business of these firms does not have an adverse effect on UK financial stability, and to minimise the adverse effect that the failure of a firm is expected to have on UK financial stability. However, it is explicitly not the PRA's role to ensure that no firm fails[2]. The PRA's general objective also requires the PRA to seek to ensure that the conduct of core banking business activities that are ring-fenced does not have an adverse effect on the continuity of core banking services in the UK.

1 FSMA 2000, s 2B(2).
2 FSMA 2000, s 2G.

1.13   For insurers, the PRA has the additional objective of contributing to the securing of an appropriate degree of protection for those who are or may become policyholders[1].

1 FSMA 2000, s 2C(2).

1.14   When exercising its functions, the PRA must also, so far as is reasonably possible, as a secondary objective, facilitate effective competition in the markets for services provided by dual-regulated firms[1] as well as to the general principles of good regulation:

- the need for the regulators to use resources economically and efficiently[2];

- the principle that any burden or restriction imposed by a regulator should be proportionate to the benefits;

- the desirability of medium and long term sustainable growth in the UK's economy;

- the principle that consumers are responsible for their own decisions;

- the responsibilities of senior management to ensure compliance of those subject to FSMA 2000 requirements;

- the desirability of exercising its functions in a way that recognises differences in the nature and objectives of businesses carrying out regulated business;

- the desirability of publishing information about those persons subject to requirements under FSMA 2000 or requiring those persons to publish information as a means of advancing a regulator's objectives; and

- the principle that regulators should exercise their functions as transparently as possible.

1 FSMA 2000, s 2H(1).
2 See the FSMA 2000, s 3B for this and the other regulatory principles applicable to both the PRA and FCA.

What is the regulatory approach of the PRA?

1.15   The PRA has been in place since 1 April 2013 but, at the time of writing, has not revealed its approach by publicised enforcement action. Nevertheless, the PRA has published papers on its approach[1].

1 'The Prudential Regulation Authority's Approach to Banking Supervision', April 2013 and the equivalent document relating to insurance supervision.

1.16   There is an emphasis on supervisory judgement by both the PRA and FCA. The PRA, in particular, is said to be more willing to make forward-looking judgements based on its assessment of future risks and not merely on whether a firm complies with prudential rules today[1]. This suggests that the PRA will place great reliance on the high level standards expounded in the Principles for Businesses and the Threshold Conditions, and not merely require compliance with (for example) specific capital or liquidity rules.

1 'The Prudential Regulation Authority's Approach to Banking Supervision', April 2013, for example at paras 9 and 40 but multiple references.

1.17   In carrying out its supervisory responsibilities, the PRA uses a risk analysis framework, and a 'proactive intervention framework' which is intended to ensure that the PRA responds to emerging risks at an early stage.

1.18   In most circumstances the PRA will prefer informal methods of promoting its objectives and supervisory measures to enforcement action[1]. The PRA has the power, however, to bring enforcement action in relation to prudential matters falling within the scope of its objectives, and has published a statement of policy on aspects of its investigations and enforcement powers[2], which are discussed in more detail in **CHAPTERS 4, 5** and **11**. There are likely to be incidents and matters that interest both the PRA and FCA when a combination of conduct and prudential/systems issues arise, but it is likely to be the FCA that takes the lead in the majority of investigations and enforcement actions. Even when a decision is taken to conduct an investigation or disciplinary action, the PRA may choose to outsource the investigation to independent advisors or the FCA enforcement staff, who have greater experience in investigations and enforcement.

1 'The Prudential Regulation Authority's Approach to Banking Supervision', April 2013, para 199 ff.
2 The statement of policy can be found online at: http://www.bankofengland.co.uk/publications/ Documents/other/pra/approachenforcement.pdf.

Financial Conduct Authority (FCA)

What is the role of the FCA?

1.19   The FCA is the second main regulator in the UK regime. It took on many of the FSA's regulatory functions and powers and, as with the PRA, its constitution is prescribed in the FSMA 2000[1].

1 FSMA 2000, Sch 1ZA.

1.20   It is responsible for regulating the conduct of business of all authorised firms, and for prudential regulation for the firms that are not dual-regulated. It is also responsible for the authorisation and regulation of electronic money institutions[1] and authorised payment institutions[2]. From April 2014, it will regulate all consumer credit businesses, previously licensed and regulated by the Office of Fair Trading (OFT). In addition, it has functions as the UK listing authority, has responsibility for enforcing the market abuse regime and is a prosecutor for criminal offences under the FSMA 2000 and other financial crime offences to advance its objectives.

1 Under the Electronic Money Regulations 2011, SI 2011/99.
2 Under the Payment Services Regulations 2009, SI 2009/209.

What are the objectives of the FCA?

1.21   The FCA's strategic objective is to ensure that relevant markets work well[1]. It also has three operational objectives:

- securing an appropriate degree of protection for consumers (defined extremely widely to include all users of regulated financial services)[2];

- protecting and enhancing the integrity of the UK financial system[3]; and,

- promoting effective competition in the interests of consumers[4].

1 FSMA 2000, s 1B(2).

2 FSMA 2000, s 1C.
3 FSMA 2000, s 1D.
4 FSMA 2000, s 1E.

1.22   In discharging its general functions of making rules, codes and guidance the FCA must, so far as is reasonably possible, act in a way which is compatible with its strategic objective and advances at least one of the operational objectives[1]. The FCA must also, so far as is consistent with advancing either the consumer protection or integrity operational objective, discharge its general functions in a way which promotes effective competition in the interests of consumers[2].

1 FSMA 2000, s 1B.
2 FSMA 2000, s 1B(4).

1.23   The picture is further complicated by requiring the FCA to have regard to the following factors when exercising its functions in pursuit of its objectives:

• the regulatory principles set out above for the PRA see para **1.14** above; and

• the importance of taking action to minimise the risk of a business carried on by a firm or a recognised investment exchange being used for a purpose connected with financial crime[1].

1 FSMA 2000, s 1B(5).

1.24   The general functions of the FCA include making general guidance, such as the policy and approach set out in the FCA Enforcement Guide, and the general policy and approach on enforcement set out in the FCA Handbook and elsewhere. In addition, the FCA will select its priorities for current enforcement and use its investigation and enforcement powers in pursuit of its objectives[1]. Therefore, it is important to bear these regulatory objectives in mind when considering the likely reaction of the FCA, for example, to notifications of potential breaches, the business strategy and products of a firm and information provided to the FCA.

1 FCA Enforcement Guide at EG 2.6 ff.

What is the regulatory approach of the FCA?

1.25   Some notable features of the developing FCA philosophy as described in the FCA policy approach[1] are:

• fair treatment of consumers[2];

• a focus on wholesale misconduct[3];

• proactive supervision and early intervention[4];

• a focus on senior management responsibility[5];

• credible deterrence[6]; and

• the competition lens.

1 As expounded in the FSA's 'Journey to the Financial Conduct Authority' paper, October 2012.
2 See, for example, FSA's 'Journey to the Financial Conduct Authority', pp 25–28.
3 For example, FSA's 'Journey to the Financial Conduct Authority', p 31.
4 For example, FSA's 'Journey to the Financial Conduct Authority', p 30.
5 For example, FSA's 'Journey to the Financial Conduct Authority', p 37.
6 For example, FSA's 'Journey to the Financial Conduct Authority', pp 37–38.

Fair treatment of consumers

1.26 The key to the FCA's supervisory approach can be found in its analysis of past regulatory failures:

'The regulatory model ... failed ... in the UK [and] globally. The standard orthodoxy ... was that people make rational decisions when given sufficient information; that markets are self-correcting organisms; and ... that if you oversee the distribution channels ... the right products get to the right people. All three orthodoxies failed.'[1]

1 Martin Wheatley, FCA Chief Executive, January 2012.

1.27 The statutory definition of consumers, which sets the consumer protection objective in context, is broad and is not confined to the traditional definition of retail consumers[1]. The definition includes any person who:

- directly or indirectly uses, has used or may use regulated financial services;

- directly or indirectly has invested or may invest in financial instruments; or

- has rights or interests related to regulated financial services or financial instruments.

1 FSMA 2000, s 1G.

1.28 The scope of this definition encompasses those who interact only indirectly with firms, such as investors in pension funds and collective investment schemes or the 'end consumers' of products put together by wholesale firms for distribution into the retail market. The breadth of the definition means that many activities typically viewed as institutional or wholesale market business could come to be scrutinised by reference to the protection of the ultimate consumer.

1.29 This sort of thinking represents a further development of a regulatory philosophy that was previously present in the FSA's 'treating customers fairly' initiative. The FCA aims to engage with the basic root causes of bad consumer outcomes. For example, the FCA will ask probing questions about a firm's business model and its future business plans, and the FCA focuses strongly on a firm's culture and governance to ensure that they are based on a foundation of fair treatment of customers.

1.30 Rather than assuming that consumers will make logical decisions given access to appropriate and clear information and basing regulatory policy on that assumption, the FCA's policy, risk and research unit will conduct studies of common consumer behaviour and adapt regulation with this in mind. With a wide definition of 'consumers' in mind, this focus need not relate to what was traditionally thought of as retail consumers.

A focus on wholesale misconduct

1.31 By wholesale misconduct, the FCA means a much wider range of regulatory breaches than market abuse, which has typically been a target for enforcement activity. The FCA has moved away from an assumption that transactions in the wholesale market are between sophisticated parties and should not be scrutinised. A belief in the inter-connectedness of retail and wholesale markets and that misconduct in the wholesale market can damage the reputation of the financial services sector as a whole mean that the FCA has a greater interest in wholesale market conduct than has been the case in the past. The FCA has stated that it will look at the relative sophistication of the parties entering into a wholesale transaction and whether misconduct in a wholesale market has the potential to lead indirectly to detriment to retail consumers.

Proactive supervision and early intervention

1.32 The FCA aims to identify and tackle problems early with the aim of avoiding consumer detriment rather than responding once the damage has been done. To pursue this objective, more resources will be devoted to thematic work, and accordingly fewer supervisors will be allocated to specific firms. But where potential issues are identified there will be more in-depth, structured work with the firms concerned.

1.33 The FCA has a large toolkit to deal with potential issues at an early stage, including product intervention powers, the ability to remove misleading advertisements and powers to intervene by varying, restricting or suspending a firm's permission to conduct business. These powers are discussed in **CHAPTERS 15** and **16**.

A focus on senior management responsibility

1.34 The FCA aims to improve culture and governance within firms to rebuild confidence in financial institutions and reduce the risk of further scandals in the future. The FCA believes that a firm's culture is led by example from senior management and that individuals holding those positions should be held responsible for a firm's regulatory breaches caused by management failings. As a result, the FCA will consider whether to take enforcement action against any individuals in senior management positions whenever it is considering enforcement action against a firm.

1.35 The focus on senior management responsibility is likely to be all the more acute in relation to regulatory breaches by deposit-taking institutions following the implementation of the Financial Services (Banking Reform) Act 2013. The definition of misconduct for the purposes of bringing disciplinary actions against senior managers at banks has been significantly extended. In new provisions of the FSMA 2000, ss 66A(5) and 66B(5), a senior manager of a bank can be liable to regulatory sanctions if the firm has breached a requirement and the senior manager is responsible for the activities of the bank in which the contravention took place, unless that person can show that he took reasonable steps to prevent the breach. Therefore, the burden of proof will be reversed for some disciplinary actions involving senior managers of banks. This, in theory, will make it easier for the Regulators to hold management liable for breaches of firms.

Credible deterrence

1.36 The FCA will continue to devote substantial resources to enforcement action, seeking to impose high financial penalties and pursue criminal prosecutions where appropriate to create a credible deterrent to misconduct. The level of financial penalties has risen dramatically in recent years and now that the regulators use percentages of relevant business revenue as a starting point for financial penalties[1], this trend is likely to continue.

1 See **CHAPTER 8**.

The competition lens

1.37 The FCA's statutory objectives and duties set out above, place competition at the heart of the FCA's work. We consider this in more detail in **CHAPTER 15**. The FCA's ambitions in this respect are indicated clearly by the fact that, even since coming into being, it has successfully petitioned the government for additional competition powers, and the Financial Services (Banking Reform) Act 2013 gives it powers equivalent to the generalist competition authorities to enforce against anticompetitive agreements and abuse of a dominant position. This is in addition to the market study powers already contemplated before this new power was proposed. Moreover, the FCA is investing in skills and expertise in the areas of behavioural economics and competition that will influence its approach to market-wide or sectoral issues. The developing expertise of the FCA is likely to mean that the FCA will conduct a different kind of analysis and consider different types of intervention from those under the FSA regime, in order to meet the objective of ensuring that markets work for the benefit of consumers. In the past, the FSA focused much of its supervisory and enforcement resources on analysing compliance with regulatory obligations, typically those at the point of sale. Looking at particular retail products or markets through a competition lens, with the FCA's intervention powers available, could result in a broader, more creative use of the FCA's powers, including its rule-making powers, to achieve better outcomes for consumers. The FCA is likely to look at both market structures (including market shares, barriers to entry and exit, and barriers to switching) and indications of competitive outcomes (such as profitability and innovation) in order to assess whether markets appear to be working competitively.

Co-ordination between the PRA and FCA

1.38   Recognising the need for co-ordination between the PRA and FCA for the regulatory regime to function effectively, there is a statutory duty for the PRA and FCA to co-ordinate the exercise of their respective functions, in addition to any requirements to co-operate in specific circumstances[1]. Each of the PRA and FCA must consult the other regulator if there is a risk of impinging on the other's regulatory objectives and seek information and advice when the other would be expected to have information or expertise on a particular matter, provided that co-ordination is compatible with the advancement of that regulator's objectives and the burden of co-operation does not outweigh the benefits.

1   FSMA 2000, s 3D.

1.39   This general duty of co-ordination will apply equally to investigations and enforcement by either regulator and, for example, could be important if potential regulatory breaches fall into areas of potential interest to both regulators. An example might be accounting irregularities at a large retail financial institution that give rise to concerns of adequate financial resources, of interest to the PRA, and consumer protection concerns, of primary interest to the FCA. The PRA and FCA have signed a memorandum of understanding to govern the co-ordination of their activities[1].

1   And are required to co-ordinate their activities under the FSMA 2000, s 3E.

1.40   Co-ordination between the PRA and FCA is particularly important in the area of investigations and enforcement because the FCA is expected to take the lead in most enforcement action and, when the PRA is considering disciplinary action, the PRA is likely to outsource the investigation to the more experienced FCA enforcement staff.

Financial Policy Committee (FPC)

What is the role of the FPC?

1.41   The Financial Policy Committee (FPC) of the Bank is tasked with macro-prudential regulation. Although it has an important role in the regulatory regime as a whole, it is not a 'regulator' of specific firms and individuals conducting financial services business in the UK and, therefore, references to the 'Regulators' later in this book refer to the PRA and FCA (but not the FPC) unless otherwise stated.

The scope of the UK regime

Firms to which the regime applies: authorisation and permission

1.42   At the most basic level, there are two types of firms: those that are within the regime and those that are outside it. Firms within the regime are allowed to carry on particular regulated activities and are in principle subject to the Regulators' supervision under the FSMA 2000 and to the Regulators' rules as set out in their Handbooks (the Handbooks)[1]. Firms outside the regime are not allowed to carry on regulated activities (it is a criminal offence for them to do so[2]) and although there are a number of provisions under the FSMA 2000 applicable to such unregulated firms, these are primarily prohibitions with criminal or quasi-criminal penalties for breach (for example, market abuse). Such firms are not generally subject to the Regulators' rules or to their regulatory powers[3].

1 There is a separate regulatory regime for authorised payment institutions and electronic money institutions under the Payment Services Regulations 2009 and the Electronic Money Regulations 2011, respectively.
2 Note that it is not a criminal offence for an authorised firm to carry on additional activities outside the scope of its regulatory 'permission', although it may be liable to regulatory enforcement action for doing so: see para **2.115** ff below.
3 There are various exceptions where the Regulators can exercise their regulatory powers in relation to those who are unregulated. For example, the market abuse regime (see **CHAPTER 17** below) applies to all persons whether or not regulated under the FSMA 2000 and the FCA's powers as UK Listing Authority (see **CHAPTER 20** below) apply to listed companies whether or not they are regulated. Firms which are unregulated can also in some instances become involved in an investigation relating to a regulated firm. Note also that where the FSMA 2000 contains criminal prohibitions, an unregulated firm could be subject to the FCA's actions as a criminal prosecuting authority (see **CHAPTER 18** below).

1.43   So far as those within the regime are concerned, the FSMA 2000 differentiates in a number of respects between different classes of firms authorised to carry on regulated activities. The key distinction is between those whose authorisation is derived from a permission granted by the PRA or FCA under the FSMA 2000[1] and those who are authorised or licensed in another EEA Member State and whose authorisation is derived from the Directives for incoming firms, as outlined in paras **1.73** ff below[2]. The term 'firms' is used throughout this book to refer to all financial services institutions conducting regulated activities in the UK.

1 Additionally, in some instances, an exemption from authorisation may be granted by or under the FSMA 2000.
2 Most notably, 'intervention' takes the form of a variation of the firm's permission, so that different provisions are required for incoming firms that do not have a 'permission': see **CHAPTER 16**.

1.44   The way that firms are brought within the regime is, for most firms, via the permission system. Whilst a detailed analysis of the system for obtaining permissions is beyond the scope of this book, a very brief introduction is worthwhile.

1.45   The permission system is found at the FSMA 2000, Pt 4A. The permission is tailored specifically to the firm, by means of the Regulators' ability to assess what is required for that firm and will involve: first, giving permission for more or fewer regulated activities[1] than the firm has applied for; second, describing each regulated activity in the way appropriate to that particular firm; and third, imposing limitations or requirements on the firm's permission. The Regulators' primary concerns in doing so are to ensure that the firm satisfies, and will continue to satisfy, certain basic criteria known as the threshold conditions[2].

The firm emerges from this process with a single 'Part 4A permission' and, as a result, is automatically authorised under the FSMA 2000.

1   Those activities which constitute 'regulated activities' are set out in the Financial Services and
    Markets Act 2000 (Regulated Activities) Order 2001, SI 2001/544 (as amended).
2   The threshold conditions are described in more detail at para **2.4** ff.

1.46   A Part 4A permission is the route for obtaining authorisation for firms incorporated in the UK or in non-EEA overseas jurisdictions. A firm incorporated in another EEA state has the choice of incorporating a UK subsidiary which will obtain a separate authorisation through a Part 4A permission or obtaining authorisation through the mechanisms set up in the EU Single Market Directives[1].

1   It is not possible for a firm established in another EEA state to apply for authorisation through a
    Part 4A permission, because of the fundamental principle of EU financial services legislation that
    a firm must be authorised in the place where it has its head office. Firms based elsewhere in the
    EEA may conduct regulated business in the UK using rights under EU treaties and Directives ie
    the right to passport referred to at paras **1.74** ff below.

1.47   Certain persons, however, are exempt from authorisation under the FSMA 2000, including appointed representatives[1] who contract with an authorised firm to carry out certain types of business and for whom the firm takes full responsibility[2]; recognised investment exchanges and clearing houses[3]; and certain international organisations such as the World Bank, the European Bank for Reconstruction and Development and the European Investment Bank[4].

1   FSMA 2000, s 39.
2   Accordingly a firm may be disciplined where it fails adequately to monitor its appointed
    representatives.
3   FSMA 2000, s 285.
4   FSMA 2000, s 38 and see the Financial Services and Markets Act 2000 (Exemption) Order 2001,
    SI 2001/1201.

Individuals working for firms

1.48   In addition to the authorisation regime applicable to firms carrying on regulated activities, the FSMA 2000 contains a statutory regime[1] for the approval of certain individuals working for authorised firms. The system of individual approval is backed by its own enforcement and disciplinary powers and a separate body of requirements applicable to approved individuals[2].

1   Under the FSMA 2000, ss 59, 59A and 59B.
2   In addition to the approved persons regime in place at the time of writing, there are proposals
    for a new senior persons regime for senior persons at banks, building societies and credit unions
    (see paras **2.51** ff below). The FCA will consult on consequent changes to the approved persons
    regime, which may apply to the financial services sector as a whole rather than to banks and other
    deposit takers alone.

THE EUROPEAN DIMENSION – AN OVERVIEW

Introduction

1.49   The role of EU legislation and the influence of European bodies is becoming increasingly important for the regulation of firms in the UK. Here we provide an introductory explanation, including:

- EU legislation in the financial services arena;

- the European System of Financial Supervision, its key players and their functions;

- interaction between national competent authorities and the European bodies;

- how EU legislation promotes convergence; and

- how EU legislation affects enforcement.

EU legislation in the financial services arena

1.50   Since taking office in 2009, Michel Barnier, the Commissioner for the Internal Market and Services, has pushed through reforms affecting investment funds, credit rating agencies, market infrastructure and banking to name but a few. A considerable reform agenda in the wake of the financial crisis from 2008 was carried out, however, even before the impact of EU legislation affected UK regulation. For example, the Markets in Financial Instruments Directive (Directive 2004/39/EC) (MiFID) was implemented in the UK by the FSA (the UK regulator at the time) by copying out substantive provisions from this Directive to form part of the Conduct of Business Sourcebook.

1.51   In particular, EU legislation has an impact on investigations and enforcement against firms operating in the UK by introducing regulatory requirements on UK firms, governing how firms authorised in one Member State are regulated when they conduct business in another Member State, requiring national regulators to take action in certain circumstances and specifying the functions and powers of EU institutions with roles in the financial services arena. It is, therefore, worth considering the nature and effect of the different legislation and other measures emanating from the EU in this introductory section.

1.52   The EU measures affecting financial services can be categorised briefly in the following way:

- level 1 measures – these measures are the framework legislation in a particular area. They can be implemented by either Regulations, which are directly applicable in Member States without the need for national legislation to implement them, or Directives, which require implementing measures in each Member State;

- level 2 measures – these are the technical measures designed to supplement level 1 measures by clarifying elements of interpretation for implementation of the level 1 measures. These are adopted and implemented in the form of Regulations;

- level 3 measures – these are guidance and recommendations on technical issues arising from the level 1 and level 2 measures. Strictly speaking they are not binding on Member States but an inconsistent approach taken by a Member State or its competent authorities could indicate a breach of EU law.

1.53   All three may have an impact on regulation in the UK whether as a measure directly applicable to firms and individuals conducting business in the UK, by requiring the UK to implement its own legislation or by standards or guidance that indicates how EU measures should be interpreted.

1.54   The effect of the substantial financial services reform agenda from the EU is further concentration of lawmaking at the EU level, reinforced by the creation of the European System of Financial Supervision (ESFS) and the European Supervisory Authorities (ESAs) who are responsible for level 2 measures, leaving little room to manoeuvre for differing national implementation. The European Commission (the Commission) has tended to introduce financial services legislation in the form of Regulations because they have a more harmonising effect than Directives, which require national transposition, whereas Regulations are directly applicable and require no transposition time to implement into the legislation of Member States.

1.55   The role of the EU in primary and secondary legislation in the financial services space is increasing. Member States play a role in the development and negotiation of EU legislation through representation in the Council and Member State's regulators (known as competent authorities in the EU) are represented in the European Supervisory Authorities (ESAs).

The European System of Financial Supervision (ESFS)

1.56   In 2010, in response to the financial crisis which exposed important failures in financial supervision, the EU established the ESFS, composed of three sectoral ESAs, working with an overarching body and the national competent authorities:

Sectoral ESAs

- The European Banking Authority (EBA)

- The European Insurance and Occupational Pensions Authority (EIOPA)

- The European Securities and Markets Authority (ESMA)

Oversight body

- The European Systemic Risk Board (ESRB)

Competent authorities

- the competent authorities (ie national regulators in the Member States)

The ESAs were established to:

- improve the functioning of the internal market, including in particular a sound, effective and consistent level of regulation and supervision;

- protect depositors, investors, policyholders, consumers and other beneficiaries;

- ensure the integrity, efficiency and orderly functioning of financial markets;

- safeguard the stability of the financial system; and

- strengthen international supervisory co-ordination.

1.57 In order to meet these objectives, each ESA is required to contribute to ensuring the coherent, efficient and effective application of relevant EU law.

1.58 The ESRB is intended to be an EU body with macro-prudential oversight. Its role is to contribute to the prevention and mitigation of systemic risks to the EU's financial stability by means of ex-ante warnings and recommendations.

The example of ESMA

1.59 The EBA, EIOPA and ESMA have similar powers set out in EU legislation and we consider the legislative provisions relating to ESMA by way of example. ESMA's powers are outlined in Regulation 1095/2010[1]. The types of powers can be divided into three categories: direct supervision; decision making/regulatory powers; and decision making which overrides national competent authorities' decisions.

1 Regulation 1095/2010 ([2010] OJ L331/84) on establishing a European Supervisory Authority (European Securities and Markets Authority).

1.60 The direct supervisory powers of ESMA relate to credit rating agencies, trade repositories' data[1], identifying and managing systemic risks[2], undertaking peer reviews of competent national authorities[3], recommending action to the Commission when a competent authority has breached EU law[4] and co-ordinating the college of supervisors[5].

1 Regulation 648/2012 ([2012] OJ L201/1) on OTC derivatives, central counterparties and trade repositories, Article 73.
2 Regulation 1095/2010, Articles 22(1)(b) and 23.
3 Regulation 1095/2010, Articles 8(1)(e) and 30.
4 Regulation 1095/2010, Article 17.
5 Regulation 1095/2010, Articles 8(1)(i) and 21.

1.61 ESMA develops guidelines and recommendations[1] and drafts the regulatory technical standards (delegated acts)[2] and implementing technical standards (implementing acts)[3] that supplement the level 1 measures.

1 Regulation 1095/2010, Articles 8(1)(a), 8(2)(c) and 16.
2 Regulation 1095/2010, Articles 8(1)(a), 8(2)(a) and 10.
3 Regulation 1095/2010, Articles 8(1)(a), 8(2)(b) and 15.

1.62   In some instances ESMA will have powers that override those of the Member States' competent authorities. ESMA can restrict or prohibit certain financial activities[1], settle disputes between competent authorities[2], make a decision on a specific market participant when a competent authority is in breach of EU law[3] and in emergency situations. ESMA's decisions on compliance take precedence over those of competent authorities[4].

1 Regulation 1095/2010, Article 19.
2 Regulation 1095/2010, Article 19.
3 Regulation 1095/2010, Article 17.
4 Regulation 1095/2010, Article 18.

1.63   The ESAs also have a role in ensuring the convergent application of rules across Member States and will facilitate the exchange of information and agreements among national authorities to ensure this. If needed, they will also mediate and settle disputes between national authorities.

1.64   The ESAs therefore will have a much greater influence on national authorities than was the case under the previous Lamfalussy Committees[1]. The ESAs play an active role in ensuring a common supervisory culture is adopted in all Member States and will, as part of this, monitor the application and enforcement of EU legislation by national authorities to ensure a consistent approach. As a last resort, they can adopt decisions that are binding on national authorities, including where an authority has incorrectly applied EU legislation.

1 The three level 3 committees were the Committee of European Banking Supervisors (CEBS), the Committee of European Securities Regulators (CESR), and the Committee of European Insurance and Occupational Pensions Supervisors (CEIOPS). The new ESAs have more extensive powers than the original committees such as: the ability to draft technical standards that are legally binding; ability to launch a fast track procedure to ensure consistent application of EU law; powers in resolving disagreements between national authorities; ability to enter into administrative arrangements with supervisory authorities, international organisations and the administrations of third countries.

The role of the ESAs in EU law-making

1.65   One of the most important powers of the ESAs is their ability to advise the Commission on the drafting of regulatory technical standards. The process by which this advice is consulted on, drafted, finalised and then passed to the Council and the European Parliament (the Parliament) for scrutiny and approval is still evolving.

1.66   Level 1 measures set out the framework covered by the legislation. Occasionally, at this early stage, ESMA or another ESA may be asked for technical advice by the Commission as it develops its legislative proposal.

1.67   However, the ESAs have a greater role in drafting level 2 measures, known as delegated acts and implementing acts (these measures are supposed to be technical in nature not involving decisions on policy). At level 3, the ESAs develop guidelines and recommendations with a view to establishing consistent, efficient and effective supervisory practices within the ESFS, and to ensure the common, uniform and consistent application of EU law.

1.68   An example of ESMA's role in law-making is the regulation governing OTC derivatives, central counterparties and trade repositories (EMIR), which provides for a number of technical standards to be provided by ESMA. ESMA consulted widely on various aspects of the technical standards before drawing up final drafts which were passed to the Commission to consider for three months before adoption. Under the ESMA Regulation, the Parliament and the Council have one month to scrutinise these measures before final adoption and entry into force. During this process, the Parliament threatened to reject some of the measures proposed by ESMA.

1.69   As a consequence, both the Council and the Parliament may be wary of delegating tasks to ESMA in the future, which may lead to more prescriptive level 1 legislation and require fewer level 2 measures from ESAs and the Commission.

1.70   In turn this will require regular review of adopted legislation which will have to go through the lengthy co-decision procedure before it can be amended. Level 2 standards on the other hand can be revised more quickly, making legislation more adaptable in the future.

1.71   ESMA and the other supervisory authorities will continue to be key players in the process however and remain responsible for a large proportion of technical work set out in level 1 legislation. It is also likely that the ESAs will begin work on technical aspects of legislation before the level 1 texts are finalised.

1.72   The Commission will conduct periodic reviews of the ESAs and ESRB, which are likely to resolve some of the ambiguities about their powers and operations, such as:

- the ESAs' role in emergency situations;

- strengthening of the consumer protection mandate;

- the composition of the stakeholder groups within the ESAs (lack of retail representation in particular);

- the ability to ban products/services;

- co-ordination and convergence across national supervisory authorities;

- the scope for further direct supervision (currently CRAs, trade repositories but possible extension to benchmark administrators); and

- financing and resources of the individual authorities.

Interaction between national competent authorities and European bodies

1.73   National competent authorities, such as the PRA and FCA in the UK, have to interact both with other competent authorities and with the European bodies. To illustrate this, we consider how cross-border firms are regulated. We also consider trends in EU law-making that promote convergence between activities of national competent authorities in their regulation and enforcement within each Member State to encourage a more consistent approach to enforcement of EU law whether competent authorities are co-ordinating their activities or acting independently.

Who regulates a cross-border firm?

1.74 Day-to-day regulation and supervision of UK-based institutions rests with the FCA and/or the PRA as explained above.

1.75 Firms based outside the UK are able to conduct regulated activities in the UK, in some cases without going through the full application process for a Part 4A permission. MiFID and the other single market directives[1] allow firms incorporated elsewhere in the EEA to provide investment services and carry out specified regulated activities from a UK branch or across EEA borders on the basis of home Member State authorisation for the same activities. Relevant firms are 'passported' to conduct business in another Member State by notifying both its home and the host Member State competent authority. This avoids the need for a full Part 4A permission.

1 The single market directives are: Insurance Mediation Directive (2002/92/EC); Banking Directive (2006/48/EC); Third Non-Life Insurance Directive (92/49/EEC); Consolidated Life Assurance Directive (2002/83/EC); Markets in Financial Instruments Directive (2004/39/EC); UCITS Directive (85/611/EEC); and Reinsurance Directive (2005/68/EC).

1.76 Passported firms remain regulated by the authority in their home Member State for all organisation and prudential matters. However, a host state authority does have certain supervisory responsibilities for the compliance of a branch of an incoming EEA firm with certain MiFID requirements. In particular, operational matters (such as a number of conduct of business requirements) are regulated by the competent authority in the host Member State for activities of the branch carried on within the host country. In all other cases, the home Member State regulates operational matters too.

1.77 EEA-based financial services firms that wish to conduct a regulated activity in the UK for which they do not have home state authorisation, or that fall outside the scope of the single market directives (but within the UK regime) will need to apply for an additional or top-up permission to supplement their home state authorisation. Firms conducting regulated activities in the UK using passport rights or a top-up permission are referred to collectively as 'incoming firms'.

1.78 Colleges of supervisors form a key aspect of the supervision of the largest cross-border financial institutions. Information sharing and co-operation between national regulators are central to the operation of the Colleges, but the ESAs will also participate.

1.79 Third country firms (ie firms established outside the EEA) are not captured by the passporting regime and the access of third country firms to the

EEA markets is not generally harmonised. This means that national regimes apply to the authorisation and supervision of these firms. This will, however, change to some extent in the future. The Commission's proposals to replace MiFID (which were agreed by the European Parliament in February 2014 and are likely to come into effect in 2016) include a uniform third country regime based on third country equivalence and reciprocal treatment of EEA firms. To provide services to retail investors, an EEA branch would be required to be set up, but third country firms would then be able to passport their services and activities to eligible counterparties and professional investors in other Member States. ESMA will play a key role in the authorisation process of such firms.

How does recent EU legislation promote convergence?

1.80   With new EU legislation often taking the form of directly applicable Regulations rather than Directives, both at level 1 (eg the European Market Infrastructure Regulation (EMIR)[1], the Market Abuse Regulation (MAR)[2] and the Markets in Financial Instruments Regulation (MiFIR) and at the point of the more detailed Level 2 technical standards, there is much less scope for detailed rule making or introducing additional, more onerous requirements at a national level as no implementation is required. The ESAs also play a major part in developing the technical standards necessary for the implementation of new EU legislation.

1 Regulation 648/2012 ([2012] OJ L201/1) on OTC derivatives, central counterparties and trade repositories.
2 At the time of writing, the text of this Regulation has not been published in the Official Journal because it will be finalised with MiFIR to ensure consistency of definitions.

1.81   Additionally, the level 3 guidance published by the ESAs (in particular ESMA) and the Commission, including in the form of Question and Answers, may replace detailed guidance at a national level or lead to competent authorities being less willing to provide their own guidance that could run the risk of being interpreted differently from guidance issued by an ESA. For example, it is not clear whether the FCA will update its Code of Market Conduct once MAR comes into force or if the Code of Market Conduct will then cease to exist, leaving firms to consider guidance published at the EU level instead. Member States, however, have declined to apply or follow guidance from ESMA, on occasion, in particular, in relation to the scope of the market making exemption under the short selling regulation[1].

1 Regulation 236/2012 ([2012] OJ L86/1) on short selling and certain aspects of credit default swaps.

How do recent EU developments affect enforcement?

1.82   Existing information sharing and co-ordination between competent authorities and arrangements for joint supervision of cross-border financial institutions mean that there is already a significant risk of a regulatory issue in one EU Member State giving rise to investigations in other Member States, or indeed a jurisdiction outside the EU.

1.83   Recent EU legislative proposals recognise that the role of enforcement will continue primarily to sit with national authorities rather than the ESAs or other European bodies. However, the recent legislative trend gives competent authorities less discretion in interpreting EU legislation and when a regulatory requirement under EU law has been breached. In addition, the Commission has considered how to further harmonise enforcement policy across the EU through the range of powers available to competent authorities. Under the laws of EU Member States, competent authorities have different investigatory powers, sanctions available, publicity surrounding enforcement and policy to use the powers available. Rather than promulgating EU legislation on the topic of regulatory enforcement, the Commission will incorporate provisions to promote harmonisation in this area into EU legislation as it is reviewed or created. Two examples are given below.

1.84   MiFIR and MiFID 2, to replace MiFID, exemplify the approach of reinforcing the role and powers of competent authorities. It contains a list of investigative powers and sanctions that must be available to competent authorities as a minimum toolkit. However, ESMA could also play a role in harmonising the enforcement approach across the EU. In particular, in co-operation with ESMA, competent authorities will in certain circumstances be able to ban specific products, practices or services where they threaten investor protection, financial stability or the orderly functioning of markets. ESMA will also take any steps necessary to co-ordinate actions by competent authorities for products that are considered risky from the point of view of investor protection or financial stability.

1.85   The powers of national regulators will also be reinforced under MAR, both in the powers they have to access information needed to detect market abuse and to sanction such abuse. For example, regulators will be able to obtain telephone and data records from telecoms operators if there is a reasonable suspicion that market abuse has occurred, and obtain access to private premises and documents in certain circumstances. Also, the range of administrative sanctions that must be available to competent authorities is specified, including a minimum level for the maximum penalty.

1.86   In addition to harmonising enforcement and sanctioning powers of competent authorities, ESMA has recognised that the regulatory approach to enforcement needs to be harmonised to create a level playing field for firms established in different Member States[1]. It is proposed that ESMA periodically publish comparative data showing the enforcement outcomes in Member States to highlight differences in the use of enforcement sanctions across the EU, furthering the objective of creating a level playing field for firms set up in any Member State to provide financial services in any part of the EU.

1 ESMA press release 2012–272 dated 26/04/2012.

1.87   So, on the one hand, future EU law will ensure that competent authorities, such as the PRA and FCA, have the powers they need to investigate and enforce compliance with EU legislation. However, on the other hand, the ESAs will have a significant influence on the way that competent authorities operate and in their co-operation with each other to promote a common supervisory culture across the EU, furthering the objective of creating a level playing field for firms set up in any Member State to provide financial services in any part of the EU.

Chapter 2   The UK regime in more detail

OVERVIEW

2.1   **CHAPTER 1** explained the UK regulatory framework, the objectives and functions of the key players, and set the UK regime in the wider context of the European financial services sector, which has its own institutions, legislation and standards that heavily influence the UK regulatory regime.

2.2   This chapter will focus on the way that firms within the UK regime are regulated. It will explain the regulatory obligations of firms and individuals in the UK financial services sector, the key sources of those obligations and how to interpret the provisions of the Handbooks where the Regulators' rules appear, and the breaches that could give rise to regulatory enforcement action.

THE FUNDAMENTAL REQUIREMENTS APPLICABLE TO FIRMS

2.3   The regulatory regime involves certain fundamental conditions and broad principles applicable to firms on an ongoing basis[1]. These conditions and principles underlie and permeate every aspect of the regulatory structure. They are directly relevant to some of the enforcement and disciplinary issues discussed here and, more generally, are important in understanding how the enforcement regime works.

1 Some of these requirements do not apply to incoming firms.

2.4 The UK regime in more detail

The threshold conditions

2.4 The conditions referred to above are the 'threshold conditions' prescribed in the FSMA 2000, Sch 6[1]. When giving or varying a firm's permission (or imposing or varying conditions or requirements applied to its permission[2]), the PRA and FCA are required to ensure that the firm will satisfy, and continue to satisfy, the threshold conditions in relation to all regulated activities for which the firm has, or will have, permission[3]. The Regulators have to ensure that the firm not only complies with these conditions at the outset but that it continues to comply with them. Each Regulator has its own set of threshold conditions which apply depending on whether the firm is FCA-only regulated or dual-regulated.

1 See also the Financial Services and Markets Act 2000 (Variation of Threshold Conditions) Order 2001, SI 2001/2507 (as amended by the Financial Services and Markets Act 2000 (Variation of Threshold Conditions) (Amendments) Order 2005, SI 2005/680).
2 See further in **CHAPTER 16** below.
3 FSMA 2000, s 55B(3).

2.5 There are a number of threshold conditions that apply to all firms. These can be summarised as follows[1]:

- *location of offices*: a UK incorporated firm must have both its head office and its registered office in the UK or, if it has no registered office but has its head office in the UK, it must carry out business there[2];

- *suitability*: the firm must satisfy the Regulators (or, in the case of an FCA-regulated firm, the FCA) that it is a fit and proper person, for example, that it complies with requirements imposed by the relevant Regulator and that those who manage the firm's affairs have adequate skills and experience and have acted with probity[3];

- *effective supervision*: the firm must be capable of being effectively supervised by the Regulators (or, in the case of an FCA-regulated firm, the FCA) having regard to all circumstances, including the nature of any regulatory activity it seeks to carry on, the complexity of any products it provides, the way the business is organised, whether the firm is subject to consolidated supervision and whether being a member of a group or governed by overseas legislation is likely to prevent the relevant Regulator's effective supervision. In addition, if the firm has 'close links' (as defined) with another person, then the relevant Regulator must be satisfied that those links are not likely to prevent the Regulator's effective supervision of the firm[4]; and

- *appropriate resources*: the resources of the firm must be appropriate in relation to the regulated activities it seeks to carry on. This includes both financial resources and non-financial resources, such as skilled management[5]. For dual-regulated firms, this condition is included within the requirement for business to be conducted in a prudent manner.

1 For a more detailed explanation of the threshold conditions, see the FSMA 2000, s 55B and Sch 6, and the Handbooks at COND.
2 See FSMA 2000, Sch 6, paras 2B, 4C and 5C. Note that the location of a firm that is dual-regulated is a condition for which the PRA rather than the FCA is responsible.

3 FSMA 2000, Sch 6, paras 2E, 3D, 4E and 5E.
4 FSMA 2000, Sch 6, paras 2C, 3B, 4F and 5F.
5 FSMA 2000, Sch 6, paras 2D and 3C. Note that dual-regulated firms must satisfy the PRA of their financial and non-financial resources and the FCA of their non-financial resources.

2.6   An additional threshold condition that applies only to FCA regulated firms is:

• *business model:* the firm's strategy for doing business must be suitable for carrying on its regulated activities and compatible with continuing to conduct business in a sound and prudent manner[1].

1 FSMA 2000, Sch 6, paras 2F and 3E. Note that the PRA will also assess the business model of a dual-regulated firm and has separate guidance on this.

2.7   Firms that are dual-regulated are required to comply with the following extra threshold conditions:

• *legal status:* where a firm is carrying on insurance or deposit-taking, it is required to have a specified legal status[1]; and

• *business to be conducted in a prudent manner:* this is the equivalent to the FCA threshold condition, of 'appropriate resources'. Dual-regulated firms must conduct their business in a prudent manner and have appropriate financial and non-financial resources. An example of a matter that is relevant in determining whether the firm satisfies the condition is the effect that the firm's failure or being closed to new business might have on the stability of the UK financial system. If the firm is carrying on insurance, the firm is 'closed to new business' if it has ceased to effect contracts of insurance or has substantially reduced the number of such contracts[2].

1 FSMA 2000, Sch 6, paras 4B and 5B.
2 FSMA 2000, Sch 6, paras 4D and 5D.

To whom and to what do the threshold conditions apply?

2.8   The threshold conditions relate to all firms that apply for and have a Part 4A permission. They apply to all of such a firm's regulated activities, wherever they are conducted[1]. The threshold conditions have limited or no application to EEA firms that conduct business in the UK by passporting rather than having a Part 4A permission.

1 See the Handbook at COND 1.1A.7.

How are the threshold conditions relevant to enforcement?

2.9   The threshold conditions are, in the enforcement context, directly relevant to the Regulators' 'own initiative' powers[1]. They are also potentially relevant to the Regulators' enforcement powers.

1 These powers are to vary a firm's permission: see **CHAPTER 16** below.

2.10 The threshold conditions most relevant in practice relate to financial resources and suitability. The threshold condition on financial resources has been used in cases in which firms have failed to maintain adequate professional indemnity insurance and where they have been in financial deficit for sustained periods. However, it is the threshold condition on suitability – the question whether a firm is fit and proper to be carrying on its regulated activities – that is most relevant to enforcement. The question whether the firm is fit and proper can arise in many situations, for example in relation to issues about the firm's systems and controls, the supervision or training of staff, or about the firm's response to a regulatory problem.

The Principles for Businesses

2.11 The second set of fundamental requirements applicable to firms is the Principles for Businesses. They differ from the threshold conditions in that, instead of being conditions laid down by the FSMA 2000, they are high-level rules made by the Regulators[1]. Although they are not linked to the threshold conditions in legal terms, the Regulators regard the Principles as expressing, among other things, the main dimensions of the 'fit and proper' standard in the threshold condition on suitability[2] and they clearly also overlap with other threshold conditions. Being able, willing and organised to abide by the Principles is therefore a critical factor when a firm applies for authorisation and breaching them may call into question whether an authorised firm is still fit and proper[3].

1 Primarily under the FSMA 2000, ss 137A and 137G. Note that the PRA applies only Principles 1 to 4, 8 and 11. At the time of writing, the Principles for Businesses appear in both the PRA and FCA Handbooks. During 2014 and 2015, the PRA will re-write the PRA Handbook to create the PRA Rulebook based on the existing PRA Handbook. The first consultation includes a proposal to replace the Principles for Businesses with nine fundamental rules, based on the six existing Principles for Businesses that it applies, plus three new rules requiring that dual-regulated firms operate prudently; prepare resolution plans; and, do not knowingly or recklessly provide the PRA with information that is false or misleading in a material particular: see the Bank of England and PRA consultation (CP 2/14) 'The PRA Rulebook'. This chapter will focus on the current Principles for Businesses but the proposed new provisions for the PRA Rulebook should also be borne in mind.
2 See the Handbook at PRIN 1.1.4.
3 See the Handbook at PRIN 1.1.4.

The Principles

2.12 With that brief introduction, the Principles are as follows:

- *Principle 1:* a firm must conduct its business with integrity;
- *Principle 2:* a firm must conduct its business with due skill, care and diligence;
- *Principle 3:* a firm must take reasonable care to organise and control its affairs responsibly and effectively, with adequate risk management systems[1];
- *Principle 4:* a firm must maintain adequate financial resources;
- *Principle 5:* a firm must observe proper standards of market conduct[2];

* *Principle 6:* a firm must pay due regard to the interests of its customers and treat them fairly[3];

* *Principle 7:* a firm must pay due regard to the information needs of its clients, and communicate information to them in a way which is clear, fair and not misleading;

* *Principle 8:* a firm must manage conflicts of interest fairly, both between itself and its customers and between a customer and another client;

* *Principle 9:* a firm must take reasonable care to ensure the suitability of its advice and discretionary decisions for any customer who is entitled to rely upon its judgement;

* *Principle 10:* a firm must arrange adequate protection for clients' assets when it is responsible for them; and

* *Principle 11:* a firm must deal with its Regulators in an open and co-operative way, and must disclose to the PRA and FCA appropriately anything relating to the firm of which the PRA and FCA, respectively, would reasonably expect notice[4].

1   This tends to be the Principle that is used most often in an enforcement context.
2   This Principle is especially relevant in cases of market misconduct.
3   This Principle forms the basis of the FSA's 'treating customers fairly' (or 'TCF') project (see **Chapter 13** below).
4   Principle 11 is directly relevant to how a firm must respond when a regulatory problem arises. There are two components: notification of matters to the Regulators (discussed [in detail] at para **3.42** ff below) and co-operation with the Regulators (discussed in detail at para **4.24** ff below).

How are the Principles applied?

2.13   The Principles are binding rules made by the Regulators and firms must comply with them. They are, however, expressed in very broad terms and no detailed explanation of what each involves accompanies them. This is deliberate. Although the regulatory regime involves a large volume of detailed rules and guidance applicable to particular aspects of firms' businesses, complying with all the specific requirements is not necessarily sufficient. The Principles sit above the detailed rules[1]. Their generality ensures that they cover new or unforeseen situations and situations where no need for guidance was foreseen. This is viewed as an important aspect of regulation. It recognises that the market moves more quickly than the Regulators and allows the Regulators to let firms develop new products and markets, knowing that the regulatory regime is sufficiently adaptable to apply to them. It also means that the rulebook does not have to address every issue that may arise in every area of business.

1   They are, however, often interrelated with the detailed rules. For example, many of the Conduct of Business rules clearly fall within the scope of one or more of the Principles and there is an overlap between Principle 3 and the Handbooks at SYSC (Senior Management Arrangements, Systems and Controls), between Principle 4 and the PRA Handbook at GENPRU, BIPRU and INSPRU (Prudential Sourcebook) and between Principle 5 and the Code of Market Conduct (see **Chapter 17** below).

2.14 In determining whether a Principle has been breached, it is necessary to look at the standard of conduct required by the Principle in question, and for the Regulator to show that the firm was at fault in some way[1]. For example, Principles 3 and 9 require the taking of reasonable care, Principles 6 and 7 refer to paying due regard: hence, the Regulator must show that the firm has failed to take reasonable care, pay due regard, and so on[2]. It is clear that each Principle is drawn up so as to incorporate a (certain but undefined) standard of practice. However, firms must recognise that many of the concepts are so broadly drawn that non-compliance risks being more easily judged with the benefit of hindsight.

1 See the Handbooks at PRIN 1.1.7.
2 But note that breach of the Principles does not give rise to a right of action for private individuals under the FSMA 2000, s 138D: see the Handbook at PRIN 3.4.4.

2.15 Firms need to have the Principles squarely in mind when considering how to react when a regulatory problem arises. For example:

- the firm's obligations under Principles 6, 7 and 8 require it to consider the interests of its customers[1];

- the firm may be required, under Principle 11, to notify the problem to the PRA or FCA[2];

- the firm must, under Principle 11, co-operate with the Regulators[3]; and

- the firm's obligations under Principle 3 may require it to consider the position of any employees involved and the implications for its systems and controls[4].

1 This is discussed in more detail at para **2.50** ff below.
2 This is discussed in more detail at para **3.42** ff below.
3 This is discussed in more detail at para **4.24** ff below.
4 This is discussed in more detail at para **3.120** ff below.

Obligations to clients and customers

2.16 Principles 6–10 require firms to pay attention to the needs of their clients or customers. The extent of the obligation will vary according to the particular circumstances including the nature of the client concerned. There are two reasons for this. First, what constitutes, for example, 'due regard' or 'fairly', will depend upon the situation in each particular case, including the nature of the client[1]. Second, Principles 6, 8 and 9[2] refer to customers, rather than clients. Customers, in this context, means clients who are not eligible counterparties[3].

1 See the Handbooks at PRIN 1.2.1.
2 The same point is to some extent true of Principle 7. The only requirement of Principle 7 relating to eligible counterparties is that a firm must communicate information in a way that is not misleading: see the Handbooks at PRIN 3.4.1.
3 See the Handbooks at PRIN 1.2.2. For an explanation of the categorisation of clients, see the FCA Handbook at COBS 3.4–3.6.

2.17 There is a clear distinction in the Principles, and the Handbooks more generally, between obligations of firms when conducting business with different categories of client. Generally, there are lesser obligations on firms when dealing with professional clients and eligible counterparties than with retail customers. This is a general feature of the regulatory system[1] although transactions with professional clients are likely to receive greater scrutiny from the FCA than they have in the past.

1 See, for example, the FCA Handbook at the Conduct of Business Sourcebook.

To whom and to what types of business do the Principles apply?

2.18   The Principles apply to a different extent to UK regulated firms, other group members of UK regulated firms and incoming firms.

2.19   UK regulated firms are subject to the Principles in relation to the conduct of their regulated activities in the UK and, in certain respects, beyond the UK[1]. In addition:

- Principles 3 and 4 also apply to the firm's unregulated activities[2]; and

- Principle 11 applies with respect to activities wherever they are carried on[3] and, in addition, it applies, so far as it relates to informing the PRA or FCA, with respect to the firm's unregulated activities[4]. Therefore, the firm's obligation to the PRA and FCA to deal with regulators in an open and co-operative way includes other regulators with recognised jurisdiction, whether in the UK or not, and the firm's obligation to report applies equally to its unregulated activities.

1 For the detailed rules on territorial application, see the Handbooks at PRIN 3.3.1 and see also the explanation at PRIN 1.1.6. Broadly, Principles 4 and 11 apply with respect to activities wherever they are carried on; Principles 1, 2 and 3 apply in a prudential context with respect to activities wherever they are carried on but more generally with respect to activities carried on from a UK establishment; Principle 5 applies to activities everywhere if they have, broadly, a negative impact on confidence in the UK financial system or were carried on from a UK establishment, and Principles 6–10 apply, generally speaking, to activities carried on from a UK establishment.
2 In the case of Principle 3, only in a prudential context: see the Handbooks at PRIN 3.2.3.
3 See the Handbooks at PRIN 3.3.1. Misleading foreign regulators may therefore breach the Principles.
4 See the Handbooks at PRIN 3.2.3.

2.20   Other group members of a UK regulated firm are relevant to Principle 3 (organisation and control, but only in a prudential context), Principle 4 (assessing the adequacy of the firm's financial resources), and Principle 11 (but only in so far as relates to informing the PRA or FCA)[1].

1 See the Handbooks at PRIN 3.2.3.

2.21   Incoming firms are, generally speaking, subject to the Principles in relation to the same activities as UK regulated firms but only in so far as responsibility for the matter in question is not reserved by European legislation to the firm's home state regulator[1].

1 See the Handbooks at PRIN 3.1.1 and SUP 13A, Annex 2 for guidance on the reservation of responsibility to a home state regulator.

THE FUNDAMENTAL REQUIREMENTS APPLICABLE TO INDIVIDUALS

2.22   It is not only firms that are regulated by the PRA and FCA. There is also a statutory regime for the approval of individuals working for authorised firms. Since some degree of personal responsibility applies to virtually every regulatory problem, it is relevant to understand the fundamental requirements applicable to individuals and briefly to review the way in which individuals are regulated.

2.23   As will be clear from the commentary below (see para **2.53** ff), the Financial Services (Banking Reform) Act 2013 (FS(BR)A 2013) introduces a significant structural change for the regulation of individuals working at certain institutions, broadly speaking UK banks, building societies, credit unions and dual-regulated investment firms. (The Treasury has power to extend the scope to include certain non-UK firms.) The changes include a new 'senior persons' regime and a proposed set of rules for individual standards applying to a wide range of employees at those firms. At the time of writing, the relevant provisions of the FS(BR)A 2013 are not in force and a commencement date is not known. In addition, it is unclear how the new rules for individual standards will differ from current provisions applicable to approved persons. Further, it is unclear whether the Regulators will extend aspects of the senior persons regime to the approved persons regime that will continue to apply to employees of firms not covered by the FS(BR)A 2013 changes. In the context of individuals, this chapter sets out to explain the approved persons regime as it is in force at the time of writing and then explain the changes introduced by the FS(BR)A 2013 and, to the extent possible, comment on the new regime overall.

Brief introduction to approved persons

2.24   Under the FSMA 2000, persons performing certain functions (known as 'controlled functions') for regulated firms in relation to their regulated activities are, broadly, required to be approved by the PRA or FCA for the performance of the particular function[1]. For dual-regulated firms, certain controlled functions are overseen by the PRA and others by the FCA with the intention that there is no overlap or duplication between the controlled functions governed by each of the Regulators. It is for the PRA or FCA, as appropriate, to specify what the controlled functions are, within the parameters set by the FSMA 2000.

1 Firms are obliged, broadly, to take reasonable care to ensure that no person performs a controlled function in relation to a regulated activity of the firm unless the PRA or FCA, as appropriate, approves the performance by the person of the particular controlled function: see the FSMA 2000, s 59(1) and (2). Breach by the firm can lead to a damages claim by a private person who suffers loss as a result: FSMA 2000, s 71. It could also lead to disciplinary and/or enforcement proceedings against the firm and/or the persons concerned.

2.25   Controlled functions fall into three broad categories[1]:

- those involving the exercise of a significant influence on the conduct of the firm's affairs;

- those involving dealing with the firm's customers; and

- those involving dealing with the property of customers.

1 FSMA 2000, s 59. A full list of controlled functions can be found in the Handbooks at SUP 10A.4.4.

2.26   The basic criterion for the approval of a particular person to perform a particular controlled function is that the PRA or FCA is satisfied he is a fit and proper person to perform the function to which the application relates[1]. If the Regulator is not so satisfied, it will refuse approval[2]. The test of 'fit and proper' is thus critical not only for the authorisation of firms but also for the approval of individuals. As with firms, the obligation to be fit and proper is a continuing one: if the PRA or FCA considers that an approved person is not fit and proper, it may withdraw approval[3]. However, as will be seen, the test is interpreted differently for individuals than it is for firms[4].

1 FSMA 2000, s 61(1). Note that the question is not whether the applicant is fit and proper, but whether, on the balance of probabilities, the Regulator is satisfied that he is fit and proper.
2 The FCA website sets out a list of persons for whom it has refused applications for approval and gives brief details of the reasons: 'Approved persons – refusals of applications'.
3 FSMA 2000, s 63.
4 Where a firm knows that a person is not fit and proper, it should not apply for the person's approval and it may be disciplined if it does so.

2.27   As a result of being an approved person, an individual is subject to the Statements of Principle and Code of Practice for approved persons[1] and is also amenable to regulatory disciplinary proceedings for misconduct[2].

1 FSMA 2000, s 64 and see para **2.31** ff.
2 FSMA 2000, s 66, although amendments introduced by the FS(BR)A 2013 cast the net wider so that other employees of certain dual-regulated deposit takers and investment firms may also be subject to disciplinary actions as discussed in more detail at para **2.53** ff and in **CHAPTER 9** below.

2.28   In addition to being able, through the granting and withdrawal of approvals, to ensure that only appropriate people exercise 'controlled functions' in relation to a firm's regulated activities, the Regulators have the rather broader power to prohibit any person, whether approved or not, from performing particular functions[1]. The basis for imposing a prohibition order again depends on whether the person is fit and proper to perform functions in relation to a regulated activity carried on by an authorised person.

1 FSMA 2000, s 56 and see para **9.86** ff below.

The test of fit and proper

2.29   As outlined above, approval is subject to a test of whether a person is fit and proper. The Regulators have given guidance as to the considerations that they take into account[1]. The three primary considerations (being the most important considerations albeit not the only ones) are:

- honesty[2], integrity[3], and reputation[4];

33

2.29 The UK regime in more detail

- competence and capability; and

- financial soundness.

1 See, generally, the Handbooks at FIT.
2 In *Hoodless and Blackwell v FSA (2003) FSMT 007*, the Tribunal held that two tests have to be fulfilled before a person is found to be dishonest. First, there is an objective test: the person's conduct must be dishonest by the ordinary standards of reasonable and honest people. Second, there is a subjective test: the person must realise that any relevant action would be dishonest by the aforementioned standards. It is not a defence that the person himself has low standards and does not consider dishonest, conduct which would offend others. See also *Cox v FSA (2003) FSMT 003* where the Tribunal held that, other than a single lapse, the applicant had an otherwise 'unblemished' career. However, the lapse was continuing in that the applicant still owed money to the Inland Revenue. The Tribunal indicated that when the money was repaid, a subsequent application could (successfully) be made. The FSA argued that defrauding the Inland Revenue showed dishonesty, but this was not accepted by the Tribunal which considered that a single incident of dishonesty, 'provided that it is not of overwhelming gravity', will not necessarily be a bar to returning to the financial services industry.
3 In *Hoodless and Blackwell v FSA (2003) FSMT 007*, 'integrity' was defined as: 'moral soundness, rectitude and steady adherence to a moral code'. A person will lack integrity if he is unable to distinguish between what is honest or dishonest by ordinary standards. The Tribunal also distinguished conduct which might show a lack of reasonable skill and care and that which showed a lack of integrity, accepting that mistakes could be made: 'even by relatively experienced and conscientious people'.
4 From the refusals of applications for approval that have been published, it seems that a person's lack of honesty, integrity and reputation has been the most important factor leading to refusal.

2.30 Each is the subject of detailed guidance which is applied in general terms but is expressly not exhaustive of the matters that could lead to a person being declared not fit and proper to perform a particular function for a particular firm[1].

1 See the Handbooks at FIT 1.3.3.

2.31 A person does not fail to be fit and proper simply because his conduct falls within one or more of the matters listed in the guidance. If a matter comes to the Regulators' attention which suggests that the person might not be fit and proper, the Regulator will take into account how relevant and how important that matter is[1].

1 See the Handbooks at FIT 1.3.4.

Statements of Principle and Code of Practice for approved persons

2.32 At the time of writing, the FSMA 2000[1] empowers the Regulators to issue Statements of Principle with respect to the conduct expected of approved persons and requires the Regulators, on issuing such Statements of Principle, also to issue a Code of Practice for the purpose of helping to determine whether or not conduct complies with the Statements of Principle.

1 FSMA 2000, s 64. When the FS(BR)A 2013 comes into force, the Regulators will no longer be required to publish a Code of Practice but, as discussed at para **2.53** below, will publish rules for the conduct of senior persons and other employees at certain firms (or possibly all firms), which may, in many respects, reflect the content of the existing Code of Practice for approved persons.

2.33   There are seven Statements of Principle, four of which apply to all approved persons and three of which apply only to persons approved to perform significant influence functions (which, broadly, means senior management functions), with a corresponding Code of Practice. These are outlined below.

What are the Statements of Principle?

2.34   The Statements of Principle are the fundamental, high-level principles applicable to approved persons in the day-to-day performance of their 'controlled functions', breach of which can give rise to disciplinary or other enforcement consequences for the individual[1].

1   See para **2.123** ff. Note that breach does not of itself give rise to any right of action by persons affected or affect the validity of any transaction: FSMA 2000, s 64(8).

What conduct is subject to the Statements of Principle?

2.35   The Statements of Principle do not apply to all conduct of all employees working for authorised firms. They only apply to approved persons[1] but do apply to all 'accountable' functions (ie FCA or PRA controlled functions) carried out by those individuals in relation to regulated activities[2].

1   Although, additionally, certain requirements and standards could apply to all employees of certain dual-regulated firms from 2015: see further at para **2.52** ff below.
2   See the Handbooks at APER 1.1A.2.

What is the Code of Practice?

2.36   The Code of Practice is the Code which the Regulators are required to issue for the purpose of determining whether a person's conduct complies with the Statements of Principle[1]. Under the FSMA 2000, the Code of Practice must specify:

- conduct which, in the Regulators' opinion, complies with the Statements of Principle;

- conduct which, in the Regulators' opinion, does not comply; and

- factors which, in the Regulators' opinion, are to be taken into account in determining whether or not a person's conduct complies.

1   FSMA 2000, s 64(2).

2.37   In fact, the current Code of Practice describes conduct that is non-compliant and those factors to be taken into account in determining whether or not conduct complies, but the Regulators have not specified any conduct which does comply with the Statements of Principle[1]. In addition, included with the Code of Practice are various pieces of 'guidance' that are expressly not part of the Code and do not have binding force.

1   The closest is at APER 4.3.4, which relates to Statement of Principle 3 and indicates that compliance with the Code of Market Conduct will tend to show compliance with this Principle.

2.38 The Code is only an aid to interpreting the Statements of Principle. It has evidential effect: it may be relied upon so far as it tends to establish whether or not conduct complies with a Statement of Principle[1]. The fact that an approved person's conduct was of a type specified in the Code as not complying with a particular Statement of Principle is not therefore determinative that the conduct breached the relevant Statement of Principle. It will, however, be strong evidence that the conduct did not comply. Equally, if the Code did specify conduct which in the Regulators' view complied with the Statements of Principle, that would not provide an absolute safe harbour for approved persons who conducted themselves in that way, although, again, it would be strong evidence that they had complied and indeed it would be difficult for the Regulators to take action against them in that situation.

1 FSMA 2000, s 64(7) and see the Handbooks at APER 3.1.5.

2.39 The Code is not exhaustive of the conduct that may contravene the Statements of Principle. The fact that a person's conduct is not proscribed by or mentioned in the Code does not necessarily mean it complies with the Statements of Principle. Conduct needs to be measured against the Statements themselves, using the Code as an indication of the types of conduct which the Regulators regard as unacceptable.

2.40 Three additional points are relevant in applying the Code. First, it is the Code of Practice in issue at the time when the conduct occurred that is relevant in assessing whether the person complied with the Statement of Principle[1]. Having said that, since the Code is not exhaustive, the Statements of Principle may be breached even if the conduct concerned was not expressly prohibited under the Code at the relevant time.

1 FSMA 2000, s 64(7) and see the Handbooks at APER 3.1.2.

2.41 Second, as to whether there has been any breach of a Statement of Principle, to the extent that the Statements impose particular standards, for example to take reasonable care or exercise due skill, care and diligence, then it may be necessary to look beyond the Code in order to understand what the applicable standard of behaviour was and whether the person's conduct fell below that standard. How the Regulators approach such issues is discussed at para **2.123** ff below. In addition, the significance of conduct that is specified in the Code as tending to show compliance or to show a breach is assessed in the light of all the circumstances, including the circumstances of the particular case, the characteristics of the particular controlled function and the behaviour to be expected in that function[1].

1 See the Handbooks at APER 3.1.3.

2.42 Third, as to the consequence of any breach, a breach of a Statement of Principle is capable of leading to disciplinary action, but not every breach will do so. An important question is: what are the circumstances in which individuals will, in practice, be disciplined for breaches? The Regulators can only take action where it appears to them appropriate in all the circumstances to do so. In addition, as may be clear from the way in which the Code is framed, an element of personal culpability is required. What, precisely, this means is discussed at para **9.13** below.

The Statements

Statement of Principle 1 – integrity

2.43   An approved person must act with integrity in carrying out his controlled function. Conduct outlawed under the Code[1] includes: deliberately misleading clients, the firm or the Regulators; deliberately recommending unsuitable investments; deliberately failing to correct misunderstandings of the customer, the firm or the Regulators; deliberately preparing inaccurate or inappropriate records; deliberately misusing assets or confidential information of a client or the firm; deliberately designing transactions so as to disguise regulatory breaches; or deliberately failing to disclose conflicts of interest. The use of the word 'deliberately' in each case reflects the fact that this Statement of Principle is directed at integrity.

1 See the Handbooks at APER 4.1.

Statement of Principle 2 – acting with due skill, care and diligence

2.44   An approved person must act with due skill, care and diligence in carrying out his controlled function. Some of the instances of non-compliant conduct specified by the Code[1] are similar to those applicable to Statement of Principle 1, save that in each case the emphasis is on doing something without reasonable grounds or failing to do something which ought to have been done. This reflects the difference between a lack of integrity (which it seems from the above involves proof of deliberate misconduct) and a failure to take reasonable care. Additional areas covered include failing to realise that misconduct is occurring[2]; and undertaking, recommending or providing advice on transactions without a reasonable understanding of the risk exposure to a customer[3] or the firm.

1 See the Handbooks at APER 4.2.
2 This will be especially relevant for senior management.
3 This is likely to be especially relevant in mis-selling cases.

Statement of Principle 3 – proper standards of market conduct

2.45   An approved person must observe proper standards of market conduct in carrying out his controlled function. The Code[1] makes clear that a factor to be taken into account is whether the person, or his firm, complied with the Code of Market Conduct[2] or other relevant market codes and exchange rules. Compliance with those codes or rules will tend to show compliance with this Statement of Principle. Accordingly, where the FCA (being the lead Regulator for market conduct issues) brings disciplinary action against an individual for market misconduct, the FCA may also allege a breach of this Statement of Principle[3].

1 See the Handbooks at APER 4.3.
2 See the FCA Handbook at MAR Chapter 1, and see para **17.260**.
3 See **CHAPTER 17** for the position on market misconduct.

2.46 This leaves open two questions. First, whether the Statement of Principle is capable of being breached in a situation where there is no code or set of rules applicable to the particular market. It is thought that, in principle, the answer is that it is, particularly given the wide wording of the Statement of Principle 1. Second, whether the Statement of Principle is capable of being breached where the conduct falls within the scope of a market code or rule but does not amount to a breach of that code or rule. The answer to this is that it cannot be ruled out that a breach of the Statement of Principle would still have been committed, particularly if the reason why the applicable market code or rule had not been breached was technical or unmeritorious. The Code provides that compliance with applicable market codes or rules will tend to show compliance with the Statement of Principle, but this falls short of providing a safe harbour[1].

1 A similar issue arises in the context of market abuse and is discussed at para **17.256** ff.

Statement of Principle 4 – dealings with Regulators

2.47 An approved person must deal with all Regulators in an open and co-operative way and must disclose appropriately any information of which the PRA or FCA would reasonably expect notice.

2.48 The requirements of this Statement of Principle and the Code of Practice[1] are considered in more detail at para **3.42** ff (so far as relates to reporting) and para **4.24** ff below (so far as relates to co-operating). It should be apparent that this Statement of Principle broadly parallels the firm's obligation under Principle 11, taking into account that in many situations the individual's disclosure obligation should be limited to making the appropriate report internally, rather than reporting direct to the PRA or FCA.

1 See the Handbooks at APER 4.4.

Statement of Principle 5 – organising the business

2.49 An approved person performing a significant influence function must take reasonable steps to ensure that the business of the firm for which he is responsible in his controlled function is organised so that it can be controlled effectively. Conduct which the Code indicates the Regulators regard as non-compliant[1] includes failing to take reasonable steps to: (a) apportion responsibilities for all areas of the business within his control; (b) apportion responsibilities clearly (including implementing confusing or uncertain reporting lines; authorisation levels or job descriptions); or (c) ensure that suitable people are responsible for those aspects of the business under the person's control (including failing properly to review staff, giving undue weight to financial performance when considering suitability or allowing managerial vacancies to remain without arranging suitable cover). The business strategy in the area is also relevant: if the strategy is to enter high-risk areas, then the degree of control and strength of monitoring reasonably required will be that much higher[2].

1 See the Handbooks at APER 4.5. Note also the guidance accompanying the Code of Practice: see the Handbooks at APER 4.5.10–4.5.15.
2 See, for example *Peter Cummings final notice (12/09/12)*.

Statement of Principle 6 – managing the business

2.50 An approved person performing a significant influence function must exercise due skill, care and diligence in managing the business of the firm for which he is responsible in his controlled function. The Code of Practice[1] refers to an individual: failing to take reasonable steps adequately to inform himself about the affairs of the business for which he is responsible; delegating authority without reasonable grounds for believing the person delegated to have the necessary capacity, competence, knowledge, seniority or skill; failing to take reasonable steps to maintain an appropriate understanding of the matters delegated; and failing to supervise and monitor adequately the persons delegated to. Relevant factors to be taken into account include the competence, knowledge, seniority and past performance of the delegate[2].

1 See the Handbooks at APER 4.6.
2 Note also the guidance accompanying the Code of Practice: see the Handbooks at APER 4.6.11–4.6.14.

Statement of Principle 7 – compliance with regulatory requirements

2.51 An approved person performing a significant influence function must take reasonable steps to ensure that the business of the firm for which he is responsible in his controlled function complies with the relevant requirements and standards of the regulatory system. Non-compliant conduct includes[1] failing to take reasonable steps to: (a) implement adequate and appropriate systems of control; (b) monitor compliance with the relevant requirements and standards; (c) obtain information about the reason why actual or suspected significant breaches may have arisen; or (d) review and, if appropriate, improve systems following the identification of significant breaches.

1 See the Handbooks at APER 4.7. Note also the guidance accompanying the Code of Practice: see the Handbooks at APER 4.7.11–4.7.14.

The 'senior persons' regime

2.52 The Parliamentary Commission on Banking Standards (the Commission), which published its report on professional culture and standards in the UK banking sector in June 2013, made recommendations concerning the approval and obligations of senior managers at banks and other deposit takers, and strengthening sanctioning powers for serious failures in those roles.

2.53 The FS(BR)A 2013 amends the regulatory framework set out in the FSMA 2000 to implement these recommendations, although supplementary Handbook changes in relation to approval and conduct of individuals working in the financial services sector are left to consultation and rule-making by the Regulators. The commencement date for the relevant legislative provisions has not, at the time of writing, been announced. Until the commencement date, the approved person regime, as described above, will apply to individuals holding 'controlled functions' at all firms. In addition to the date when the legislation comes into force, there are other uncertainties as to which individuals at which firms will be affected and the extent of the changes to the Regulators' rules governing standards of conduct. The legislative changes primarily relate to individuals working at UK-incorporated dual-regulated deposit takers and investment firms (collectively referred to as banking firms in this book), but not insurers. The relevant changes include:

- for senior managers of banking firms, the existing approved persons regime will be replaced with a 'senior persons' regime. Banking firms will need to obtain approval for 'senior persons'. A 'senior person' is a person carrying out a designated senior management function with responsibility for (or taking or participating in decisions concerning) an aspect of a banking firm's affairs that involves, or might involve, a risk of serious consequences for the banking firm, or for business or for other interests in the UK. Although a wide range of individuals could be categorised as senior persons, the Regulators are likely to designate only the most senior positions, or positions with a key influence on the soundness of a banking firm, as senior management functions;

- other more junior employees of banking firms, who would broadly have fallen within the approved persons regime, will be vetted and certified annually by the banking firm itself as fit and proper to hold that position;

- a relevant banking firm seeking approval for a senior manager has a statutory responsibility to vet that person's qualifications, training, competence and personal characteristics to satisfy itself that the person is suitable for the role[1]. The approval application for these persons will have to be accompanied by a written statement of their responsibilities[2] and, when they cease to perform their role, they will have to prepare a handover certificate stating how they have fulfilled those responsibilities. Regulatory approval for them to act as senior managers may be time-limited or subject to conditions[3];

- following a successful enforcement action against a banking firm for serious failings, the Regulators will be able to exercise disciplinary powers, broadly speaking, against senior persons responsible for the relevant functions at the time, unless those persons can show that they took reasonable steps to prevent the failings[4]. The important point is that the burden of proof is reversed. Other heads of misconduct for which approved persons can face disciplinary action are extended to all employees at these firms;

- the existing Principles and Code for approved persons will be replaced with a new set of rules to apply to the conduct of senior persons and other employees at banking firms. The Regulators may decide to change the approved persons regime so that these new standards and requirements also apply to approved persons at firms other than banking firms;

- the time limit for the Regulators to take disciplinary action against individuals will be increased to six years (from three years)[5];

- a senior person at a banking firm (except credit unions) will also be potentially liable for a new criminal offence of reckless misconduct in the management of a bank if, broadly speaking, a decision which they make causes the institution for which they work to fail and their conduct is viewed as falling far below what is reasonably expected of a person in their position[6].

1 FS(BR)A 2013, s 21.
2 FS(BR)A 2013, s 20.
3 FS(BR)A 2013, s 23.
4 FSMA 2000, s 66A(5) and (6) and s 66B(5) and (6), as inserted by the FS(BR)A 2013, s 32(2).
5 FSMA 2000, s 66, as amended by the FS(BR)A 2013, s 28.
6 FS(BR)A 2013, s 36.

2.54 The Regulators will consult on implementation of the new regulatory regime for senior persons in 2014, with a view to introducing the senior persons regime in 2015. At the same time, the Regulators intend to consider the implications of these changes for the approved persons regime more generally.

THE REGULATORY TOOLKIT

2.55 What powers do the Regulators have to promote or enforce compliance with the obligations placed on firms and individuals? Enforcement and discipline are not the Regulators' only means of achieving their regulatory objectives. The FSMA 2000 and the Handbooks give the Regulators a broad range of powers and functions to enable them to do so. The Regulators refer to these as their 'regulatory toolkit'. Understanding briefly what these tools are helps to place the enforcement and disciplinary regime into perspective. As part of this, it is helpful to look briefly at the Regulators' general approach to supervision.

2.56 The Regulators' tools are wide-ranging in their nature and effect. Some allow the Regulators to influence the industry as a whole[1]; others are designed to influence the behaviour of consumers in general[2]. The protection of consumers is a recurrent theme as well as one of the FCA's prescribed operational objectives. Five of the eleven Principles for Businesses relate specifically to how firms deal with their clients[3]. Another important part of the regime is the publicly available Register, which the FCA is required to keep[4], of those who are, broadly, authorised, approved[5] or recognised under the FSMA 2000, and those against whom a prohibition order has been made. Consumers and others should therefore readily be able to ascertain whether they are dealing with someone who is entitled to carry on regulated activities.

2.56 The UK regime in more detail

1 For example, the training and competence regime, the ability to make rules, market monitoring, sector-wide projects (for example, the work carried out on particular 'themes', such as money laundering, and anti-bribery systems and controls) and the Regulators' liaison with overseas regulators.
2 For example, ensuring proper disclosure to consumers, complaints handling mechanisms, the ombudsman service, and the issuing of public statements by the FCA to try to influence the behaviour of consumers and firms.
3 The importance of keeping consumers in mind when dealing with a regulatory issue is discussed at **CHAPTER 13** below.
4 FSMA 2000, s 347. Access to the Register is available on the FCA's website.
5 Approved persons are those individuals who have been approved by the PRA or FCA: see para **2.23** ff.

2.57 The Regulators also have tools to influence the behaviour of individual firms. These include: authorisation; the policing of the regulatory perimeter (ie the requirement to be authorised to carry out regulated activities); the supervision of firms; and the ability to impose conditions and restrictions on a firm's permission[1]; as well as investigatory and enforcement powers. The ability to vet firms and individuals at the point of entry is particularly important and operates on the basis that 'prevention is better than cure'. In practice, the Regulators also address compliance issues by making their concerns clear to firms and by issuing private warnings[2] without resorting to their formal enforcement process.

1 This refers to the Regulators' 'own initiative' powers, described more fully in **CHAPTER 16** below.
2 See para **8.27** ff.

2.58 Investigation, enforcement and discipline are therefore only a part, albeit an important part, of the overall armoury available to the Regulators for ensuring regulatory compliance and, more broadly, the fulfilment of their regulatory objectives. This broader context is relevant when considering how the PRA or FCA is likely to react in a particular situation.

INTRODUCING THE HANDBOOKS

2.59 It should already be clear that the FSMA 2000, notwithstanding its length, provides little more than a framework for the regulatory regime. The detailed rules are to be found in the Handbooks[1], to which reference is frequently made throughout this book. However, not everything contained in the Handbooks is binding on firms and individuals. A substantial proportion of the content is no more than non-binding guidance. Other provisions are of evidential value. Yet further provisions comprise the Regulators' policy on how they will act. The precise nature of the provision in question therefore requires some thought.

1 In the case of the PRA, there is also a PRA Rulebook, which, at the time of writing, primarily contains materials relating to capital adequacy but the PRA intends to re-write text from the PRA Handbook to develop the PRA Rulebook over the first few years of the PRA's operation. Some of the detailed provisions are also to be found in secondary legislation made under the FSMA 2000. Secondary legislation is generally less relevant in the enforcement context, but certain statutory instruments are relevant and reference to them is made where appropriate.

2.60   Why is this relevant in a book about enforcement? When a problem arises, firms need to understand the precise nature and effect of the rules concerned, not only the specific rules that may have been breached in the particular situation, but also those rules which prescribe how the firm and the Regulators should act in the context of the ensuing regulatory investigation and enforcement proceedings. Is the rule binding? If not, does it matter that the firm has not complied? Do the Regulators have to act in the way stated in their policy? It can readily be seen that an understanding of how the Handbooks work underlies an understanding of the regime.

2.61   The main powers that the Regulators have to make the rules and other provisions contained in the Handbooks are described below. An explanation is also provided as to how the nature of each rule or provision is identified in the Handbooks, and the effect of rules made under the various statutory rule-making provisions.

2.62   The Regulators have the following main statutory powers and duties under the FSMA 2000 to make the provisions of the Handbooks:

- power to make general rules;
- power to make specific types of rules;
- duty to issue codes;
- power to make evidential or other non-binding provisions;
- power to give guidance;
- duty to publish policy and procedures.

Each of these is considered in turn. Further information can be found in the Reader's Guide to the Handbooks and in the Handbooks at GEN[1].

1 Note that the provisions of the Handbooks are to be given a purposive interpretation: see the Handbooks at GEN 2.2.1. The purpose of any provision is to be gathered first and foremost from the text of the provision in question and its context: Handbooks at GEN 2.2.2.

General rules

2.63   The Regulators have a general rule-making power under the FSMA 2000, ss 137A and 137G, allowing them to make such rules applying to authorised persons, in respect of both their regulated and unregulated activities, as appear to the Regulators to be necessary or expedient for the purpose of protecting the interests of consumers.

2.64   These provisions form the basis of a significant proportion of the Handbooks, including the Principles for Businesses[1].

1 See para **2.11** ff.

2.65   Unless the rule specifies otherwise, rules normally have binding effect[1] and breach can give rise to the regulatory consequences discussed in this book[2]. These rules are denoted by 'R' in the Handbooks.

2.65   The UK regime in more detail

1 See the Handbooks, Reader's Guide, Chapter 6. Precisely what effect the rule has will depend upon the language that is used. For example, is it expressed in mandatory language?
2 The Regulators can also waive or modify the application of rules to specific firms: see the FSMA 2000, s 138A and the Handbooks at SUP Chapter 8.

Specific types of rules

2.66   The Regulators have also been empowered to make specific types of rules applicable to certain areas. Examples include client money rules[1], price stabilising rules[2] and financial promotion rules[3]. Again, unless the rule specifies otherwise, such rules normally have binding effect and breaches can give rise to the regulatory consequences discussed in this book. These rules are also denoted by 'R' in the Handbooks[4].

1 FSMA 2000, s137B.
2 FSMA 2000, s 137Q.
3 FSMA 2000, s 137R.
4 In addition, various provisions of the FSMA 2000 empower the Regulators to give directions or impose other requirements (for example, as to the manner in which applications for Part 4A permission are to be made: FSMA 2000, s 55U(1)). Such directions or other requirements are denoted by 'D' in the Handbooks. They are binding. See further the Handbooks, Reader's Guide, Chapter 6.

2.67   The Statements of Principle for approved persons[1] also constitute binding rules. These are denoted by 'P' in the Handbooks.

1 FSMA 2000, s 64.

Codes

2.68   The two notable examples of codes issued by the Regulators are:

•   the Code of Practice for approved persons[1]; and

•   the Code of Market Conduct[2] that must be issued by the FCA.

1 FSMA 2000, s 64 required the Regulators to publish this code but the FS(BR)A 2013 amends the FSMA 2000 so that the PRA and FCA 'may' make rules for the conduct of individuals in the future: see para **2.35** ff above.
2 FSMA 2000, s 119: see para **17.21** below.

2.69   The Code of Practice for approved persons is discussed above. Provisions of the Code are denoted by 'E' in the Handbooks, indicating that they are of evidential effect.

2.70   The Code of Market Conduct is discussed in detail at para **17.21** ff below. The effect of the Code of Market Conduct is twofold[1]:

•   in so far as it provides that behaviour does not amount to market abuse, that behaviour is taken as not amounting to market abuse. To that extent, the

Code is binding, and such provisions are denoted in the FCA Handbook by the letter 'C'[2];

- otherwise, the Code may be relied upon in so far as it indicates whether or not behaviour amounts to market abuse. To that extent, it is not binding but is only of evidential effect, and such provisions are denoted in the FCA Handbook by the letter 'E'[3].

1 FSMA 2000, s 122.
2 See the Handbooks, Reader's Guide, Chapter 6.
3 See the Handbooks, Reader's Guide, Chapter 6.

Evidential or other non-binding provisions

2.71 In addition to the evidential effect of the Codes, the FSMA 2000[1] allows the Regulators to prescribe rules which have evidential effect. Such rules do not stand on their own, but relate to other binding rules and indicate examples of compliance and contravention.

1 FSMA 2000, s 138C.

2.72 These rules have a non-binding effect. In other words, contravention of the rule does not of itself give rise to regulatory consequences. However, contravention of the rule may indicate that some other rule has been contravened, and that contravention may give rise to regulatory consequences. Compliance with or contravention of these rules creates a rebuttable presumption that the other rule has been complied with or contravened[1].

1 See the Handbooks, Reader's Guide, Chapter 6.

2.73 Where a Regulator creates such rules:

- it must state in the rule that contravention does not give rise to the consequences specified under the FSMA 2000[1];

- the rule must also state either that its contravention may be relied upon as tending to establish contravention of some other, specified rule or that compliance with the rule may be relied upon as tending to establish compliance with some other, specified rule[2]; and

- it denotes this type of rule in the Handbooks by using the letter 'E'.

1 FSMA 2000, s 138C(1).
2 FSMA 2000, s 138(2).

Guidance

2.74 The Regulators may also give guidance[1] consisting of information and advice relating to the operation of the FSMA 2000 and the rules, any matters relating to the Regulators' functions, for the purpose of meeting their regulatory objectives, or in relation to other matters where the Regulators consider it desirable to give information or advice. The relevant provisions are denoted by the letter 'G'[2]. Additionally, urgent or temporary guidance is published in separate 'Guidance Notes'. Information that is not contained within the Handbooks or a Guidance Note is not guidance unless it says so.

1 FSMA 2000, s 139A.
2 Guidance may also be given to firms individually under the FSMA 2000, s 139A: see the discussion in the Handbooks at SUP Chapter 9.

2.75 This guidance is entirely non-binding, and has no evidential effect, in that following it or failing to follow it does not in itself have any disciplinary consequences, nor is there a presumption that departing from guidance is indicative of a breach of the relevant rule[1]. Having said that, where a person acts in accordance with guidance in the circumstances contemplated by that guidance, then the Regulators are likely to proceed on the footing that the person has complied with the aspects of the rule or other requirement to which the guidance relates. Guidance cannot, however, affect any rights that third parties might have.

1 See the Handbooks, Reader's Guide, Chapter 6.

2.76 On the face of it, therefore, it would seem that, in the context of enforcement, guidance can only be used by the firm in its defence and not by the Regulators against it. However, this is probably too hasty an assumption. First, even if guidance cannot be expressly cited by the Regulators in support of enforcement action, it is an aid to the Regulators' views about the proper application of a rule and therefore the way in which the Regulators will approach a particular set of facts. Second, the fact that a particular standard or practice is referred to in guidance makes it at least more likely that that standard will generally be followed. Since good industry practice is undoubtedly likely to be relevant to the interpretation of some principles and rules, guidance will therefore, at least at one remove, be relevant to the application of those principles and rules and to the firm's exposure to enforcement action. Guidance cannot therefore be ignored. The practical result seems to be that the firms should normally follow guidance unless there is some good reason to the contrary.

Policy and procedures

2.77 The provisions of the Handbooks outlined thus far primarily concern the behaviour of firms. Various provisions of the FCA Handbook at DEPP, the FCA enforcement guide (not strictly part of the FCA Handbook) and the PRA's statements of policy relate to the Regulators' behaviour in the context of enforcement. To what extent do these bind the Regulators?

2.78 The Regulators are required, under the FSMA 2000, to publish a statement of their policy on the exercise of various of their powers, including (in the enforcement context):

• policy on the imposition, and amount, of penalties against approved persons for misconduct[1] and against firms for contraventions of the FSMA 2000 or the Regulators' rules[2];

- in its capacity as UK Listing Authority, the FCA's policy on the imposition, and amount, of penalties against issuers or applicants and their directors[3];

- the FCA's policy on the imposition, and amount, of penalties for market abuse[4]; and

- policy on the conduct of interviews where the PRA or FCA direct that an overseas regulator may attend and take part[5].

1 FSMA 2000, s 69 and see **CHAPTER 9** below.
2 FSMA 2000, s 210 and see **CHAPTER 8** below.
3 FSMA 2000, s 93 and see **CHAPTER 20** below.
4 FSMA 2000, s 124 and see **CHAPTER 17** below.
5 FSMA 2000, s 169(9) and see **CHAPTERS 4** and **7** below.

2.79   In each of the first three cases, the Regulators are required to have regard to their policy when exercising or deciding whether to exercise the relevant power. The policy is thus binding on the Regulators[1]. However, each policy statement tends to be worded very broadly, generally making clear that the Regulators will have regard to all the relevant circumstances of the case including a non-exhaustive list of factors[2]. As a result, it is in practice likely to be difficult for a firm to complain that the Regulators did not follow their policy in the particular case. Statements of policy are denoted in the Handbooks by the letter 'G' and, in the case of the PRA, are published separately on the PRA website.

1 It is not clear whether the policy is the only factor to which the Regulators are allowed to 'have regard': this is a matter of statutory interpretation. If it is, then the policy is strictly binding. If it is not, then whilst the Regulators must 'have regard to' it, that could include considering it and deciding to afford it no weight as a relevant factor in their decision how to act.
2 See, for example, the FCA Handbook at DEPP 6.4.1 (criteria for determining whether to impose a penalty or issue a public censure), DEPP 6.5A (factors relevant to the amount of fines) and the Statement of PRA's Policy on the imposition and amount of financial penalties under the Act.

2.80   The FSMA 2000 also requires the Regulators to determine and publish their procedure in one respect, namely in relation to the giving of supervisory notices and warning/decision notices[1]. This procedure is expressly binding. The Regulators must follow their stated procedure[2] and they could in principle be challenged if they failed to do so. These statements of procedure are denoted in the FCA Handbook by the letter 'G' and, for the PRA, are set out in its 'Statement of PRA's Policy on Statutory Notices and the Allocation of Decision-making Under the Act'.

1 FSMA 2000, s 395(1).
2 FSMA 2000, s 395(9). Note, however, that a failure to do so does not affect the validity of the Regulators' action: FSMA 2000, s 395(11).

2.81   Beyond complying with these specific requirements imposed on them under the FSMA 2000, the Regulators have provided a great deal of information as to how they will exercise their other powers, for example the circumstances when injunctions or restitution orders will be appropriate (in the FCA Enforcement Guide) or the giving of private warnings (both in the FCA Enforcement Guide and the PRA's statements of policy). This additional information constitutes general guidance under the FSMA 2000, s 139B rather than formal guidance on rules and, to emphasise this, the FCA Enforcement Guide, where most of this additional information is to be found in the context of the FCA, is expressly not part of the FCA Handbook.

CONDUCT GIVING RISE TO ENFORCEMENT

What types of conduct by firms give rise to enforcement?

2.82 The processes and consequences discussed in this book all arise from a regulatory breach of some description. The purpose of the following paragraphs is to outline different types of conduct that may give rise to enforcement action. It should be noted that the Regulators do not pursue a 'zero tolerance' approach to enforcement, but take a 'risk based' approach to deciding how to deploy their enforcement resources.

2.83 Types of conduct fall broadly into four categories:

- breaches of the FSMA 2000;

- breaches of specific rules or regulations made by the Regulators or HM Treasury under their powers granted by the FSMA 2000;

- breaches of the Principles for Businesses; and

- conduct giving rise to concerns of failure to be fit and/or proper;

2.84 Within those categories, the following are worth highlighting separately:

- issues arising abroad with implications in the UK;

- issues arising in a firm's unregulated business; and

- breach of the perimeter.

Breaches of the FSMA 2000

2.85 The top level of regulation is the FSMA 2000 itself. It contains a number of prohibitions, breach of which may have regulatory consequences. The prohibitions can be divided into three types:

- those which have criminal law consequences;

- those which have the specific consequences provided for in the FSMA 2000; and

- those which have no specified consequences.

Breaches with criminal law consequences

2.86 For provisions of the FSMA 2000 that give rise to a criminal offence[1], (where the FCA will often act as the prosecuting authority[2]), the FCA will have the power to investigate first and then decide what action to take. That action may not be limited to a criminal prosecution. The breach may also give rise to regulatory enforcement action where the person concerned is an authorised firm or approved person, because the breach would not only be a potential criminal offence but would also probably amount to a contravention of a requirement imposed by or under the FSMA 2000. This is one of the key phrases used to describe the circumstances which may trigger disciplinary or other enforcement action and is discussed further below. The breach may also cast doubt on whether the firm or person concerned is fit and proper, again with potential enforcement consequences.

1 For example, the general prohibition, unlawful financial promotion, making misleading statements and insider dealing (under the Criminal Justice Act 1993, Pt V).
2 This is discussed in **CHAPTER 18** below.

Breaches with specified consequences

2.87 As to those provisions in the FSMA 2000 which give rise to specified consequences, examples include:

- failing without reasonable excuse to comply with an information gathering requirement, which is punishable as contempt of court[1]; and

- breach of the market abuse provisions, which gives rise to liability to a civil penalty[2].

1 FSMA 2000, s 177(2) and see para **4.80**, n 3 below.
2 FSMA 2000, s 123 and see **CHAPTER 17** below.

2.88 Again, the specified consequences are only part of the picture, particularly for those within the regulated community. The breach is likely also to amount to the contravention of a requirement imposed by or under the FSMA 2000, and could also cast doubt on whether the firm or a person concerned is fit and proper, in each case potentially giving rise to regulatory concerns and disciplinary or other action appropriate to address those concerns.

Breaches with no specified consequences

2.89 Despite the absence of specified consequences, the breach is likely to amount to the contravention of a requirement by or under the FSMA 2000, and could also cast doubt on whether the firm or a person concerned is fit and proper. As a result, it could give rise to disciplinary or other enforcement action as described below for breaches of specific rules.

Breaches of specific rules

2.90 At the level below the FSMA 2000, there are a large number of specific rule-making powers allowing the Regulators, or in some instances HM Treasury, to make specific rules or regulations applicable to firms generally or specific types of firms or parts of firms' businesses.

2.91 Although the relevant rule is not imposed directly by the FSMA 2000, its breach could give rise to regulatory consequences under the FSMA 2000. This is because the FSMA 2000 prescribes various criteria for the exercise of the Regulators' enforcement powers and these criteria are, generally speaking, capable of being fulfilled by a breach of a rule or regulation imposed indirectly, by the Regulators or HM Treasury under their statutory powers, rather than directly by the FSMA 2000. They include in particular the following:

- circumstances suggesting the breach of specific rules, which may allow the Regulators to invoke their formal investigative powers[1];

- the breach of a requirement imposed by or under the FSMA 2000: the key phrase, discussed in detail below;

- the breach of a requirement imposed by or under any other Act whose contravention constitutes an offence which the FCA has the power to prosecute under the FSMA 2000, which may allow the FCA to impose or apply for a restitution order or to apply for a civil injunction[2];

- failure to satisfy the threshold conditions, including failing to be fit and proper, which may allow the Regulators to vary or cancel the firm's permission[3]; and

- it being desirable to act in order to protect the interests of consumers or potential consumers, which may enable the Regulators to vary or cancel the firm's permission or impose similar action in relation to an incoming firm[4].

1 FSMA 2000, s 168 and, for a detailed discussion, see para **4.68** ff below.
2 FSMA 2000, ss 380, 382 and 384: see **CHAPTER 8** below.
3 FSMA 2000, s 55J and see paras **16.32** ff and **16.252** ff below. For a discussion of the threshold conditions, and the test of fit and proper, see para **2.4** ff and **2.28** ff above.
4 FSMA 2000, ss 55J and 194 and see paras **16.48** ff and **16.85** ff below.

2.92 The Regulators will, in certain types of emergency situations, excuse conduct that would otherwise amount to a breach of their rules[1].

1 For details, see the Handbooks at GEN 1.3.

2.93 Certain specific types of breaches may have additional or alternative types of consequences. For example, there are specific powers relating to listed companies[1] and market abuse[2] which are discussed in separate chapters of this book.

1 See **CHAPTER 20** below.
2 See **CHAPTER 17** below.

Contravention of a requirement imposed by or under the FSMA 2000

2.94 This is the phrase which appears most often in the enforcement provisions of the FSMA 2000. Where a firm contravenes a requirement imposed on it by or under the FSMA 2000, it could be susceptible to:

- disciplinary action[1];

- a restitution order[2];

- a civil injunction[3]; and

- the imposition of intervention action on an incoming firm[4].

1 FSMA 2000, ss 205, 206 and 206A and see para **8.8** ff below.
2 FSMA 2000, ss 382 and 384 and see para **8.100** ff below.
3 FSMA 2000, s 381 and see para **8.138** ff below.
4 FSMA 2000, s 194 and see **CHAPTER 15** below.

2.95   In considering whether the firm has contravened a requirement imposed on it by or under the FSMA 2000, there are two main questions. First, what constitutes a 'requirement imposed by or under the FSMA 2000' and, second, when will such a requirement have been contravened.

Meaning of requirement by or under the FSMA 2000

2.96   The FSMA 2000 does not provide any definition of the phrase, leaving some scope for uncertainty. Certain propositions can however be made.

2.97   First, it certainly includes breaches of requirements imposed directly by the FSMA 2000. In principle, this should include any provision of the FSMA 2000 which imposes a requirement on an authorised person to do something or not to do something. An example would be the requirement that authorised firms must take reasonable care not to allow a person to perform a controlled function unless the person is approved by the Regulators to carry out that function[1]. The use of the word 'must' indicates that the provision is mandatory. This may be important in determining whether the particular provision amounts to a 'requirement' for these purposes.

1 FSMA 2000, s 59(1).

2.98   Second, the phrase extends to requirements imposed by the Regulators where the FSMA 2000 not only empowers the Regulators to make the relevant rules but also specifically imposes a requirement on a person to comply with them. An example would be the rules relating to auditors and actuaries[1]. In that case, the requirement is probably one imposed directly under the FSMA 2000, namely the statutory requirement to comply with those rules made by the Regulators.

1 FSMA 2000, s 340.

2.99   Third, the phrase certainly includes to some extent rules and regulations derived indirectly from the FSMA 2000, in other words the rules of the Regulators[1] and the regulations of any other body, such as HM Treasury, made under powers granted under the FSMA 2000. To the extent that those rules or regulations impose requirements on firms, they will amount to requirements imposed under the FSMA 2000.

1 Or the UKLA's Listing Rules.

2.100   In relation to such provisions, the more difficult question may be whether the particular provision amounts to a 'requirement'. The different wording of s 138D[1] suggests that there is a distinction between a 'rule' and a 'requirement'. As has already been seen[2], the Regulators have the power to make various types of rules and other provisions, and the effect of any particular provision depends upon its type and the nature of the wording used. Thus:

- the Regulators can make rules which are only of evidential effect[3], breach of which should not of itself amount to contravention of a requirement;

- the Regulators can and do give guidance[4], which is non-binding and should not therefore amount to a requirement, the contravention of which would attract enforcement consequences;

- the most difficult area concerns those rules which do not amount to evidential provisions or guidance but which are not expressed in such a way as to indicate that they amount to a requirement. Some rules are not expressed in mandatory language and, as indicated above, the FSMA 2000 seems to distinguish between rules and requirements. There does therefore seem to be scope for PRA or FCA rules not to amount to a requirement for these purposes. Whether a particular rule falls within this category will depend primarily upon the precise wording used; and

- the Principles for Businesses are rules made by the Regulators under the FSMA 2000[5] and the above therefore applies equally to them.

1 Contravention of a 'rule' may give rise to a damages claim for breach of statutory duty, for private persons only: see **CHAPTER 19** below.
2 See the discussion of the Handbooks at para **2.59** ff above.
3 FSMA 2000, s 138C.
4 For example, the FSMA 2000, s 139A.
5 See the Handbooks, Reader's Guide, Chapter 6.

2.101 Fourth, it seems that prohibitions in the FSMA 2000 which attract criminal law consequences also fall within the phrase 'requirement imposed by or under the FSMA 2000'. The word 'requirement' is a broad one and does not differentiate between any particular types of prohibition, for example criminal, civil or regulatory. Furthermore, the FSMA 2000 seems to contemplate, in the provisions relating to injunctions and restitution orders[1], that such requirements are included.

1 FSMA 2000, ss 380, 382 and 384: see **CHAPTER 8** below. The definition of 'relevant requirement' in relation to the Regulators distinguishes between: (i) requirements imposed by or under the FSMA 2000; and (ii) requirements imposed by or under any other Act which the FCA has the power to prosecute under the FSMA 2000. It must have been intended that criminal prohibitions under the FSMA 2000 would be included in the former; otherwise, they would be excluded from the definition of 'relevant requirement' (which cannot have been intended).

2.102 Finally, the FSMA 2000 specifically provides[1] that, where a firm carries on a regulated activity otherwise than in accordance with its permission, it is taken to have contravened a requirement imposed on it by the Regulators under the FSMA 2000.

1 FSMA 2000, s 20.

When will such a requirement have been contravened?

2.103 Many PRA and FCA rules or other applicable requirements impose strict obligations, which will be contravened simply when there is a failure to comply. Take, for example, an obligation on a firm to make a periodic report to the Regulators on a particular matter. If the firm fails to make the relevant report by the time prescribed, it will clearly have contravened the requirement.

2.104 Some other types of rules do not impose strict obligations, but instead require the firm or an approved person to, for example, 'take reasonable care' or 'pay due regard'. Examples include the Principles for Businesses[1], the Statements of Principle for approved persons[2] and the firm's obligation not to employ a prohibited person[3]. In those cases, assessing whether the firm has contravened the requirement is more complicated and requires the Regulator to consider whether the firm (or approved person) has met the standard required of it.

1 See the discussion on Principles for Businesses at para **2.11** ff above.
2 See para **2.33** ff above.
3 FSMA 2000, s 56(6).

Breaches of the Principles for Businesses

2.105 On a more general level, as has been seen, firms are subject to the Principles for Businesses, which are deliberately drafted at a high level of generality[1]. The Principles are rules made by the Regulators under the FSMA 2000. A breach will therefore amount to a breach of a requirement imposed on the firm under the FSMA 2000 and is not different from a breach of any other PRA or FCA rule[2]. Serious breaches of the Principles may carry wider consequences than other rule breaches because the Principles are said to embody the main elements of the 'fit and proper' standard. Hence, breaches of the Principles may indicate that the firm is not suitable to carry on particular regulated activities and thus lead to variation or cancellation of permission[3].

1 There are also regulatory general principles applicable to approved persons, namely the Statements of Principle.
2 Breaching a Principle makes a firm liable to disciplinary sanctions: see the Handbooks at PRIN 1.1.7.
3 See **CHAPTER 16** below.

2.106 Is it appropriate for the Regulators to subject firms to an additional 'charge' of breach of the Principles, where there is already a clear charge of a breach of a particular rule? Principle 2 is a good example: failing to act with due skill, care and diligence could be added to almost any charge sheet, giving the appearance that the firm had committed a further breach in addition to the breach of one or more specific rules. For example, if a firm is accused of producing inaccurate or misleading marketing material in relation to a particular product, should it also face a charge of breach of Principle 2, that it failed to act with due skill, care and diligence?

2.107 Also, if the firm shows that it did not, technically, breach the relevant rules regarding marketing material, or even that those rules did not apply in the specific circumstances, should the Regulators still be able to charge it for breaching Principle 2[1]? In other words, should the Principles be used by the Regulators to subject a firm to regulatory consequences in circumstances where no particular regulatory breach could otherwise be identified[2] or where there were no applicable regulations[3]? It is here that the Regulators' use of Principles as a basis for enforcement action causes real concern, particularly where that enforcement action is perceived as an attempt to improve market practices in an area where there was previously no clear benchmark as to acceptable standards.

1   In *Legal & General v FSA (2003) FIN 0022*, L&G highlighted to the Tribunal that the FSA had not alleged a breach of particular rules but had instead proceeded under more general standards, including SIB Principle 2. The Tribunal agreed with the FSA that the general standards are formed by obligations which are the subject of the more specific rules. Further, the Tribunal stated that 'the [Regulator] is free to rely on whichever rule or rules reflect what they perceive to be the gravity and extent of the alleged mischief. It would be undesirable, and potentially oppressive to an applicant, for [the Regulator] to be required to "clutter the indictment" unnecessarily with a whole range of extra charges. The omission of a particular charge from a case is not to be taken as a concession that [the Regulator] accepts that there has not been a breach' (para 27). However, in this particular case, the FSA accepted that reliance on General Principle 2 was a fallback provision which did not add to its case (para 41).
2   Such as where the misconduct is a new form of breach not contemplated by the rules.
3   In *Hoodless Brennan & Partners plc final notice (17/12/03)* a breach was based solely on breaches of principles for businesses. This is not a novel position now. Most enforcement actions involve breaches of Principles and detailed rules but there are a significant number, particularly for mis-selling, that rely on breaches of Principles alone.

2.108 The Regulators may bring enforcement actions based on breaches of Principles for Businesses alone or in combination with breaches of specific rules. The Regulators' policy[1] is that it will be appropriate in cases to discipline on the basis of breach of the Principles alone. Examples include where there is no detailed rule which prohibits the behaviour but it clearly contravenes a Principle, or where a firm has committed a number of breaches of detailed rules which, individually, may not merit disciplinary action but the cumulative effect of which indicates the breach of a Principle. In any case, it is for the Regulators to show that the firm has been at fault in some way, as indicated by the terms of each Principle[2]. There are links between the Principles and the Regulators' rules, for example, many of the Conduct of Business Sourcebook rules derive from one or more Principles for Businesses[3], so that breach of a rule may also mean that a Principle has been breached. In the past, most enforcement action was brought for a combination of Principle and rule breaches but enforcement actions are now generally based on breaches of Principles alone[4].

1   See the Handbooks at DEPP 6.2.14 and FCA Enforcement Guide at EG 2.19.
2   For example, some of the Principles require firms to 'take reasonable care'; others require them to 'pay due regard', etc.
3   Many examples could be given. To take only three, see the FCA Handbook at COBS 6.1E.2, COBS 2.3.3 and COBS 3.7.6, which all refer to a firm's obligations under specific Principles. Other rules that interrelate with the Principles include the detailed rules in SYSC (Senior Management Arrangements, Systems and Controls) and MAR 1 (Code of Market Conduct).
4   See, for example, the high profile enforcement actions involving: *Coöperatieve Centrale Raiffeisen-Boerenleenbank BA (Rabobank) final notice (29/10/13)*; *JPMorgan Chase Bank, NA final notice*

(18/09/13); Prudential Assurance Company Limited final notice (27/03/13); and Barclays Bank plc final notice (27/06/13).

2.109 The broad scope of the Principles for Businesses gives rise to a concern that the Regulators could bring enforcement action for a breach of a Principle alone for conduct by a firm that complied with detailed rules and met what the firm thought were the Regulators' expectations of conduct at the time. The Regulators do, however, recognise that the application of Principles should be reasonably predictable, so that firms are not held liable for conduct or omissions that the firm could not reasonably have predicted were in breach of a Principle[1]. There remains a tension, however, between the Regulators' stated intention to use the Principles to bring enforcement actions and the need to ensure reasonable predictability in the application of the Principles (see para **8.15** ff below for further discussion).

1 FCA Enforcement Guide at EG 2.20.

Failure to be fit and proper

2.110 The concept of fitness and propriety – that is, that authorised firms are fit and proper to carry on regulated business – is the bedrock of the regulatory system and the foundation for the suitability criterion that is one of the threshold criteria underlying the firm's authorisation[1].

1 FSMA 2000, s 55B and Sch 6. Fitness and propriety is also relevant to individuals, although its meaning is different in that context: see **2.28** ff above.

2.111 With one exception, a failure to be fit and proper does not of itself give rise to regulatory enforcement consequences, but:

- the circumstances which give rise to the failure to be fit and proper may amount to a breach of a specific rule for which the usual disciplinary and other enforcement consequences would be applicable, and in particular could well amount to the breach of one or more of the Principles; and

- the situation could certainly be investigated by the Regulators[1].

1 Either as circumstances suggesting the breach of a specific rule (see para **5.20** ff below) or on the basis there was 'good reason' to investigate the firm's business (see para **5.11** ff below).

2.112 The one exception is that it could lead to the Regulators imposing conditions or restrictions on the firm by the variation of its permission or the cancellation of its permission[1].

1 See **CHAPTER 16**.

Issues arising in a firm's unregulated business

2.113 Issues arising in the firm's unregulated business may have regulatory implications, broadly because:

- the issue may amount to the breach of a rule notwithstanding the fact that it occurred in the firm's unregulated business. The FSMA 2000[1] allows the

2.113 The UK regime in more detail

Regulators to make rules in relation to the carrying on by firms of not only regulated activities but also unregulated activities. This applies only where the rule concerned indicates that it applies to unregulated activities[2]; and

• more generally, the conduct may give rise to concerns about whether the firm is fit and proper or whether it complies with the Principles for Businesses in relation to its regulated business or may be relevant to the adequacy of the firm's resources or other prudential matters.

1 FSMA 2000, ss 137A and 137G.
2 See the Handbooks at GEN 2.2.17.

2.114 The possible regulatory consequences would depend upon the circumstances but in principle any of those outlined in this book could be relevant.

Breach of the perimeter

2.115 Breach of the perimeter (also referred to as 'breach of the general prohibition') refers to the carrying on of a regulated activity without authorisation[1]. The Regulators have broad powers of investigating and dealing with breaches of the perimeter, including the power to bring civil proceedings to prevent the breach and prosecution for the criminal offence committed. In addition, any transactions entered into are unenforceable against the other party, who is entitled to recover any money or other property transferred under the agreement and compensation for any loss[2]. A detailed discussion of these powers is outside the scope of this book, since it is not on the whole an issue for the regulated community.

1 For which there is a 'general prohibition' under the FSMA 2000, s 19. There is an exception for 'exempt persons' who do not require authorisation.
2 FSMA 2000, ss 26 and 28. In certain circumstances, agreements made by regulated firms through unregulated third parties can also be unenforceable: FSMA 2000, s 27.

2.116 One question for firms is whether they commit the criminal offence of breaching the general prohibition if they carry on an activity for which they do not have permission. This question arises from the nature of the authorisation process. Firms apply for, and receive, permission to carry on particular regulated activities. Once they receive permission, they are 'authorised persons' for the purposes of the FSMA 2000. However, they are not permitted to carry on other regulated activities outside their permission. Thus, for example, a firm with permission to carry on particular types of investment business (only) is not permitted also to carry on insurance business.

2.117 The answer is that since the firm is an 'authorised person' for the purposes of the FSMA 2000, it would not commit a criminal breach of the general prohibition. The FSMA 2000 makes clear[1] that in this situation the firm has contravened a requirement by or under the FSMA 2000[2], but has not committed an offence, is not liable to transactions being void or unenforceable and is not subject to civil damages claims for breach of statutory duty[3]. However, the firm has clearly committed a regulatory breach, with the same potential consequences as any other breach of specific rules or regulations, and may also have breached the Principles for Businesses and caused the PRA or FCA to have doubts about whether it is fit and proper.

1 FSMA 2000, s 20.
2 See para **2.96** ff above.
3 In practice, a private person will normally have a right of action under the FSMA 2000, s 138D: see para **19.19** ff.

What types of conduct by individuals give rise to enforcement?

2.118 There will be frequent examples where the same incident constitutes both a breach by a firm and misconduct by an individual. Regulatory problems do not arise in a vacuum. If 'the firm' has done or omitted to do something, and so committed a breach, at some level this is almost bound to have been caused by the acts or omissions of particular individuals. Those in the frame might include, for example, not only the particular salesman who mis-sold the investment to a consumer, but also the back office staff who failed to notice the consumer had not returned the relevant form, the internal audit staff who did not pick up the same problem on their periodic review the following week, the training department whose courses had not been sufficient to make the salesman aware of his responsibilities, the line manager who took three months to refer the consumer's complaint to the relevant department and the compliance officer who investigated the matter and identified only that there had been a problem with the sale of the investment but not the other matters outlined above and decided that the specific issue could be resolved without needing to tell the FCA (as the Regulator primarily interested in protecting the interests of consumers).

2.119 Not all of these individuals will have done anything wrong. Indeed, some of them may not even be amenable to the Regulators' discipline[1], but the example illustrates the number of people who may in some way be culpable and the complexities involved in assigning blame.

1 Some of them may not be approved persons or employees of banking firms to which the provisions of the FS(BR)A 2013 will apply, ie personally approved under the FSMA 2000: see above para **2.22** ff for a brief explanation of the regime.

2.120 The FSMA 2000 leaves the question of when individuals are to be subjected personally to enforcement action largely in the hands of the Regulators. As has already been seen, it is left to the Regulators to determine, subject to broad statutory criteria, which functions are to be 'controlled functions' which may be performed only by people approved to do so, and to issue Statements of Principle, a Code of Practice and other rules as to the conduct to be expected of such persons. It is also left to the Regulators to determine their policy on the imposition of penalties against individuals[1]; in other words the circumstances when they will seek to discipline individuals, and to decide in each case whether it is appropriate to do so[2]. These aspects are considered in more detail in **CHAPTER 9** below, but an outline is provided here of the types of acts which could give rise to enforcement action against individuals, both approved persons and others.

1 FSMA 2000, s 69(1)(a).
2 FSMA 2000, s 66(1)(b).

2.121 There are five general bases upon which the Regulators can, or will be able to, take enforcement action against individuals – three are applicable at the time of writing and the other two are introduced by the FS(BR)A 2013. These grounds are:

- failure of an approved person to comply with a Statement of Principle[1], which could lead to disciplinary action, an injunction[2] and/or a restitution order[3];

- failure to comply with a rule[4], which could lead to disciplinary action, an injunction and/or a restitution order;

- being knowingly concerned in a contravention by an authorised person[5], which could lead to disciplinary action, an injunction and/or a restitution order;

- a Senior Person's liability for the regulatory breaches of a firm[6];

- not being a fit and proper person to perform functions in relation to a firm's regulated activities, which could lead to the PRA or FCA withdrawing the person's approval[7] or imposing a prohibition order[8].

1 FSMA 2000, s 66(2)(a) and (2A)(a). See also **CHAPTER 9** below.
2 FSMA 2000, s 380. See also **CHAPTER 9**.
3 FSMA 2000, s 382. See also **CHAPTER 9**.
4 FSMA 2000, ss 66A(2) and 66B(2) as introduced by the FS(BR)A 2013, s 32(2), and see **CHAPTER 9** below.
5 FSMA 2000, s 66(2)(b) and (2A)(b), which will be superseded by the FSMA 2000, ss 66A(3) and 66B(3) as introduced by the FS(BR)A 2013, s 32(2). See also **CHAPTER 9** below.
6 FSMA 2000, ss 66A(5) and 66B(5) as introduced by the FS(BR)A 2013. See also **CHAPTER 9** below.
7 FSMA 2000, s 63 and see **CHAPTER 9** below.
8 FSMA 2000, s 56.

2.122 Note that these conditions apply to different categories of person: the first to approved persons only; the second and third are extended to a potentially wider category of employees at certain deposit takers and investment banking firms; the fourth only to senior managers at those deposit takers and investment banking firms; and the fifth, where prohibitions are concerned, to any person working in the UK financial services sector. Each of these is considered in turn below[1].

1 In addition, there are other bases for taking specific types of enforcement action, such as market abuse (see **CHAPTER 17** below), criminal prosecutions for offences under the FSMA 2000 (see **CHAPTER 18** below) and action against directors of listed companies (see **CHAPTER 20** below).

Failure to comply with a Statement of Principle

2.123 A failure by an approved person to comply with a Statement of Principle can in some circumstances give rise to disciplinary action for misconduct by the Regulators against the individual and could also lead to an injunction or restitution order being imposed[1]. In addition, it could be relevant to demonstrating that the person was not a fit and proper person to be carrying out a controlled function, in which case it could lead to his approval being withdrawn or to a prohibition order being made against him[2].

1 FSMA 2000, s 66(2)(a) or (2A)(a) defines this as misconduct for which disciplinary action can be brought but the PRA and FCA can also obtain an injunction or restitution order on the basis that the failure to comply with a Statement of Principle constitutes the contravention of a requirement by or under the FSMA 2000. See para **9.131** ff below for a discussion of injunctions and restitution orders.
2 For a discussion of withdrawal of approval and prohibition orders, see paras **9.68** and **9.99** below.

2.124   The Statements of Principle for approved persons are only of evidential effect. This means that it will often not be clear whether the individual's conduct did amount to a breach.

Breach of a rule imposed by the PRA or FCA

2.125   When the FS(BR)A 2013 comes into force, this ground will supersede and encompass the ground mentioned in the previous paragraphs for employees to whom rules rather than principles apply. The Regulators will make rules for the conduct of senior persons and other employees at banking firms (ie potentially a wider range of individuals than are currently approved persons at banking firms). The existing Statements of Principles and Code may continue to apply to approved persons at other firms or new rules may be introduced for those individuals as well. The Regulators will be able to bring disciplinary action against any person who breaches a rule that applies to him[1]. Note that disciplinary action under these provisions can be brought for breaches of rules, rather than breaches of guidance or evidential provisions. In addition to disciplinary action, the Regulators will be able to obtain injunctions and restitution orders for any breaches of these rules[2].

1 FSMA 2000, ss 66A(2) and 66B(2) as introduced by the FS(BR)A 2013, s 32(2).
2 Under the FSMA 2000, ss 380 and 382 on the basis that breaches of the rules are contraventions of requirements under the FSMA 2000. See also para **9.131** ff below for a discussion of injunctions and restitution orders.

Knowingly concerned in a contravention by the relevant authorised person

2.126   In many instances, an approved person may be susceptible to disciplinary or other enforcement action, such as an injunction or restitution order[1], because of his involvement in a regulatory breach committed by the firm. The FS(BR)A 2013 extends this basis for disciplinary action to senior persons and 'other employees' (potentially all employees) of banking firms as well as approved persons at other firms. The test used is whether he was knowingly concerned in a contravention by the relevant firm of a requirement imposed on that firm by or under the FSMA 2000[2]. The meaning of 'requirement imposed by or under the FSMA 2000' has been considered at para **2.96** ff. It will be considered here when a person's actions will amount to being knowingly concerned in such a contravention.

2.126 The UK regime in more detail

1 The Regulators can obtain injunctions under the FSMA 2000, s 380 and restitution orders under the FSMA 2000, s 382 against a person who is knowingly concerned in a firm's contravention of a requirement under the FSMA 2000. See para **9.131** ff for a discussion of injunctions and restitution orders.
2 FSMA 2000, s 66(2)(b) and (2A)(b), which will be replaced by the FSMA 2000, ss 66A(3) and 66B(3) when the FS(BR)A 2013 comes into force.

2.127 On the face of it, the phrase is unclear[1]. For example, is it enough that the individual knows about the relevant actions or omissions which amounted to a breach? Or does he also have to know that those actions did or could constitute a breach and is it sufficient that, for example, he had line responsibility for what happened, and perhaps knew that it was happening? Or should have known that it was happening? Or does he need to be actively involved?

- first, ignorance of the law is no defence. Hence, it is irrelevant whether the person had any knowledge that the matters amounted to a breach. The person is not to be judged on the facts as he believed them to be, but on the law as it is;

- second, it seems that actual knowledge of the facts is required, although in the criminal law context wilful blindness is capable of being sufficient. It is not therefore clear whether the fact that a person should have known, but did not know, about the relevant matters, in a situation where he had deliberately shut his eyes to the obvious, would make him liable to disciplinary action under this limb (although his lack of knowledge may of course amount to a breach of a Statement of Principle or other rule, for which, if the principle or rule applied to him, he could be disciplined if he should have had knowledge);

- third, it seems that mere knowledge will not be sufficient; some sort of actual involvement in the contravention must be established;

- fourth, it appears from criminal law authority that the person must be aware of the true nature of the conduct in which he was involved, although he need not be aware of the precise details.

1 Although the concept of 'knowingly concerned' is also well known in criminal legislation. The criminal law cases demonstrate that a fairly broad test has been applied, at least in the criminal law context. Note, however, that: (i) the second and third points above are obiter dicta and therefore not strictly binding, albeit they are strongly persuasive given the seniority of the judge concerned; and (ii) it may be that the Tribunal or the courts will take a different approach in the context of the FSMA 2000.

This phrase is therefore a reasonably broad one, although its precise meaning is unclear. The third of the above points may give some indication that those with managerial responsibility but who were not directly or actively involved in the matter would not be regarded as having been 'knowingly concerned' in it, but caution should be exercised in following this line of argument. Where a person has both the relevant knowledge of the facts and the personal responsibility for carrying out a task, which he fails to carry out and this leads to, or exacerbates a breach, that person is more likely to be found to be knowingly concerned in the breach or, separately, face disciplinary action for failing to meet his own regulatory obligations.

Senior manager's liability for firm's breach

2.128 This is a new condition for disciplinary actions introduced by the FS(BR)A 2013, applying only to senior persons at banking firms[1]. The PRA or FCA can bring disciplinary action under this head if:

- the person has at any time been a senior manager at a relevant firm (dual-regulated deposit taker or investment firm);

- there has at that time been (or continued to be) a contravention of a requirement by that firm; and

- the senior manager was at that time responsible for the management of any of the firm's activities in relation to which the contravention occurred.

1   FS(BR)A 2013, s 32(2) of this legislation introduces the FSMA 2000, ss 66A(5) and 66B(5).

2.129   A person is not guilty of misconduct under this head if he can show that he took such steps as a person in his position could reasonably be expected to take to avoid the contravention occurring or continuing.

2.130   This effectively reverses the burden of proof in the disciplinary proceedings against an individual. Assuming that a disciplinary action is successful against a firm, or a firm settles an enforcement action, the individual responsible for managing that business unit or a particular aspect of the business could be prima facie liable for the firm's breaches in that area unless he can demonstrate that he took reasonable steps to avoid the breaches. By its nature, this head requires less knowledge of the facts underlying the firm's breaches than a person who is 'knowingly concerned' in a firm's breaches but, in principle, allows a competent senior manager to avoid liability.

2.131   Although the specified conditions can give rise to disciplinary action, they will not by themselves give rise to injunctions or restitution orders against the individual, for which the Regulators need to show a contravention of a requirement under the FSMA 2000 by that individual or that he was knowingly concerned in a contravention by a firm[1]. However, withdrawal of approval or prohibition may still result if the individual is not 'fit and proper' (see para **2.132** below).

1   See the FSMA 2000, ss 380 and 382 and para **9.131** ff below for a discussion of injunctions and restitution orders.

Failure to be a fit and proper person

2.132   The need for an individual to be fit and proper is central to an approved person being granted approval by the PRA or FCA to carry on controlled functions. Equally, where the PRA or FCA considers that a person lacks fitness or propriety, it may take action to withdraw his approval or make a prohibition order against him. The test of fit and proper in the context of individuals has been considered at para **2.29** ff above.

the person has at any time been a loser or manager of a share in that client is held a deposit taker or investment firm;

Those that at that time been determined or been composition of the registration by that firm; and

wherever there was at that time responsible for the management of any of the firm's activities in which the contravention occurred.

(MiFID r 2.3.7R, etc.; see also similar provisions on IPRU 2007 amended)

2.129   A person is not guilty of misconduct unless he is all the can show that, case such act as a person, his position could reasonably be expected to being to avoid the contravention occurring or continuing.

2.130   The incident shows that the burden of proof on the authority's shoulders has to meet by that. Assuming that a disciplinary action is one could apply section or a fact of action to contravene or not on the individual responsible by showing that his/her some parts that aspect of the matter could be put in liable, for several breaches to that a matter he can demonstrate that the authority's cannot satisfied as to the breaches. But in that case the breach requires less than the kind of the free nature of being able — the matter responsible is ... a likely comprised of a man's conduct but the principle shows a more common nature of a would like able.

2.131   Although the ... these conditions apply such as to disciplinary action they will not be themselves give rise to quotations of restitution orders because the sanction for which the regulator need to show a contravention or an enrichment under the SSAU 2000 by that individual for the person is knowingly contributed in a contravention by virtue. However, while a level of approval or prohibition may still result in the individual is fit and proper. See para 2.132 below.

(see pp 130, 135 below 2000 and ITU 9.1.14 below and Chapter 4 prohibition order on that matter.)

Failure to be a fit and proper person

2.132   The other was an individual comes in conflict, the authority may approve a person, grant approval under IRK or IKA or IKA or refuse by compelled by certain requirements under the IKA of IKA. conduct to approve those firm's complexity to a cancellation of authority its approval or such a prohibited order. Depending on the loss of fit and proper in the context of individual see the discussion at pp 2.20 ff above as well.

Section B
Investigations

Chapter 3   Steps to take when an issue arises

INTRODUCTION

3.1   The purpose of this chapter is to review some of the legal and practical points that arise when a matter comes to the firm's attention, raising issues that may be of concern to the regulator. As will be seen, the firm is likely to be under a duty to the Financial Conduct Authority (FCA) and/or the Prudential Regulation Authority (PRA) (collectively, the Regulators) to take certain immediate steps, such as notifying the appropriate regulator. Beyond this, though, it may be prudent for the firm to act in a particular way to protect its own interests as well as the interests of, among others, its employees, its customers and its market counterparties.

3.2   Whether the firm needs to take any action and, if so, what action it should take, depends upon the nature and seriousness of the particular problem. But a number of points should at least be considered in most cases. The primary issues that arise at the outset include:

- whether the firm should investigate;

- whether the firm should report the problem;

- how the firm should deal with its customers or its market counterparties;

- whether the firm should be taking any action internally (for example, to remedy any defects in procedures and to deal with any employees);

3.2 Steps to take when an issue arises

- whether the problem potentially gives rise to criminal proceedings; and

- taking care over document creation and retention.

These are addressed in turn below, after considering two initial points, namely, first, the scope of those matters that are likely to be of concern to the Regulators and, second, the question of how the problem was discovered.

3.3   The guiding principle of an open and co-operative relationship between the firm and the Regulators[1], as well as the Regulators' policy of proactive supervision and early intervention[2], drives much of the discussion below. This approach is fundamental to the UK regulatory regime and needs to be borne in mind throughout. Moreover, the firm's response to the regulatory problem is of itself a part of the firm's systems and controls. Handling the problem properly is an important part of demonstrating that the firm takes reasonable care to organise and control its affairs responsibly and effectively[3]. In addition, the firm's approach to handling problems when they arise, and the Regulators' perception of how the firm tends to address such problems (including the extent to which it is perceived to have co-operated with the FCA), have a significant bearing on whether the Regulators will decide that enforcement action needs to be taken[4] and will also be relevant to the severity of any enforcement action that is taken[5]. It should also be remembered that the FCA views senior management as being responsible for the firms systems and controls, including the steps which are taken by the firm when a regulatory problem arises[6]. Enforcement action can, and has, been taken against senior management for failing to ensure that appropriate systems and controls are in place to comply with the regulatory rules and standards in such circumstances[7].

1   Principle 11, Principles for Businesses: see para **2.12** ff above and paras **3.43**, **4.25** ff and **4.133** below.
2   See paras **1.15** ff and **1.26** ff above.
3   Principle 3, Principles for Businesses: see para **2.12** above.
4   See Enforcement Guide at EG 2.33 ('Co-operation'), in which the FCA set out some of the factors it considers important in deciding whether to refer a matter to enforcement.
5   Co-operating with the Regulators has benefits for firms in the sense that a firm can receive credit within the disciplinary process. For a fuller discussion, see para **8.83**.
6   See para **1.34**.
7   See para **9.26**.

What types of matters will concern the Regulators?

3.4   The first issue is to identify those types of problems that potentially raise regulatory concerns. The scope of matters that may be of concern will become evident from, among other things, the discussion of the firm's reporting obligations that follows in para **3.44** ff below, but, briefly, the Regulators' approach is to cast its net wide and firms therefore need to do the same. The matters that may be of regulatory concern include breaches of specific rules as well as principles[1] which are drafted at a high level of generality and thus cover a wide range of matters. Examples of conduct likely to concern the Regulators include conduct giving rise to concerns about:

- whether particular persons are fit and proper to be involved in the firm's regulated activities[2];

- the firm's integrity or standards of market conduct or those of its employees[3];

- the firm's internal supervision or controls[4]; or

- how the firm has dealt with its customers, particularly consumers[5].

1 Breach of one of the Principles for Businesses or, for approved persons, the Statements of Principle, can have disciplinary or other enforcement consequences: see paras **2.105** ff and **2.123** above. For a detailed discussion of the Principles for Businesses see para **2.11** ff above and, of the Statements of Principle, see para **2.31** ff above.
2 As to the meaning of fit and proper in relation to individuals, see para **2.28** above. This would include anything relevant to their integrity, their training or competence to carry out the job and their financial soundness.
3 See Principles 1 and 5, Principles for Businesses. The approved persons regime is now split between the FCA and the PRA. The FCA specifies customer-dealing functions, while the PRA specifies all-governing functions. In relation to conduct of employees, see Statements of Principle 1 and 3 for approved persons and the FCA Handbook at COBS.
4 See Principle 3, Principles for Businesses, Statements of Principle 5–7 for approved persons, and the Handbooks at SYSC.
5 See Principles 6–9, Principles for Businesses and Statements of Principle 1 and 2 for approved persons, and the Handbooks at COBS. See also the discussion at para **3.94** ff below.

3.5   These examples are little more than illustrative. In assessing whether the matter is potentially of interest to the Regulators, firms need to have in mind all of their obligations and the standards expected of them and senior management in the light of the Principles for Businesses and Statements of Principle for approved persons, as well as those matters that the Regulators have indicated need to be reported to them[1].

1 See para **3.43** ff below.

How was the problem discovered?

3.6   How the firm reacts initially will depend to some extent on how the problem was discovered, and in particular whether it was the firm or the Regulators who became aware of the problem first.

3.7   There are many ways that a regulatory issue can come to light. The firm might become aware of it, when a specific 'incident' occurs, from the reports (formal or informal) of an employee, through regular or specific internal audit or compliance checks, from customer complaints, from complaints by a market counterparty, or even from market activity or rumour. The Regulators, for their part, could also pick up the issue in a variety of ways. Examples include from information obtained on a visit to the firm, in the course of reviewing an issue relating to another firm, or on receiving a report from another regulator. The Regulators could also pick up a story in the press or receive a customer complaint. The FCA takes a proactive approach to identifying problems early on and visits firms on both a regular or sample basis to gather information as well as using themed visits to investigate practices in a section of the market[1].

1 See para **4.36**.

3.8 Steps to take when an issue arises

3.8   As will be seen[1], if it is the firm that discovers the problem, it will need quickly to consider notifying the FCA or PRA. Obviously, if it was one of the Regulators that discovered the problem first, then this will not be an issue, but there will instead be other issues to confront, not least how to explain why the problem went unnoticed by the firm. Even where the firm discovers the problem first, the Regulators will want to know how it discovered the problem and whether it could have done so earlier. This may be relevant to what enforcement action it is appropriate to take[2]. The best position, from the firm's point of view, is for its systems or controls to have identified the problem as early as possible.

1 See para **3.43** ff below.
2 See, for example, the FCA Enforcement Guide at EG 8.9(8) (policy on variation of permission: see para **16.120** below). The answer may also give rise to questions about the firm's systems and controls.

SHOULD THE FIRM INVESTIGATE?

3.9   The firm will normally be faced at the outset with a limited amount of information about the problem and the obvious question is whether it should carry out further investigations and, if it should, what ought to be the procedure for those investigations. The following will be reviewed:

- the reasons why the firm should investigate;

- who should investigate; and

- how the investigation should be carried out.

Why investigate?

3.10   It is difficult to assess the seriousness of the problem, and therefore what action, if any, needs to be taken, before the firm has a proper understanding of what the problem involves. Equally, if it is necessary to contact the FCA or PRA, or indeed any other regulators, then the firm will want to ensure that it understands the problem and can demonstrate to the Regulator that it has the matter properly in hand. However, problems which may seem at first to be minor or one-dimensional can turn out to have wider consequences, or be part of a wider problem, and may therefore need to be treated more seriously than it appeared initially. Action may be required across a broad front, including not only in relation to the Regulator, but also potentially involving customers, staff, systems, market counterparties, the firm's insurers, sometimes the police and even the press. It is therefore imperative for the firm to get to the root of the problem as quickly as possible and to make some kind of assessment as to its implications. Moreover, taking proper steps to investigate when a problem arises is likely to be viewed as relevant to whether the firm's systems and controls are adequate. A failure to take proper steps to investigate may, particularly, impact on the Regulators' view of the firm's compliance department[1].

1 The importance of reviewing the reasons for significant breaches and assessing the implications for the firm's systems is also reflected in the Code of Practice applicable to Statement of Principle 7: see the Handbooks at APER 4.7 and para **2.50** above.

3.11 If a firm fully considers a problem when it arises, depending on the seriousness of the matter it will be likely to reduce the prospect that a regulatory investigation will result, and may reduce the cost of dealing with the problem, maximise the prospect of a successful outcome and in some circumstances enhance the firm's relationship with the Regulators. When assessing how to approach the Regulators, the firm should be aware of its obligation to act openly and co-operatively but consider carefully the possible disadvantages as well as the advantages of being more co-operative than necessary (for example, by waiving legal privilege over documents). If an investigation results, such an investigation is likely to be inquisitorial and possibly adversarial (depending upon whether the investigation results in enforcement action being proposed). Moreover, a problem may give rise to criminal and civil liability as well as regulatory consequences.

3.12 Carrying out a proper review of the problem and its implications can, however, be time consuming. Even where the firm needs or wishes to carry out an exhaustive internal review, this does not mean that it can delay taking any action whatsoever until that process has been completed. Some action may need to be taken promptly and there is clearly a trade off between, on the one hand, understanding the problem fully and thus being in a position to assess properly what action is appropriate, and, on the other hand, reacting, and being seen to react, with the proper expedition.

Who should investigate?

3.13 The first question is how an internal investigation should be structured and, particularly, who should carry it out? Whilst there are attractions in allowing internal audit or compliance to carry out an internal review, and this is often part of their normal role, it is important to recognise the potential risks of an internal investigation that is not properly structured. Primarily, any report produced by internal audit or compliance, and their notes (even handwritten notes) of any discussions they have with the staff involved, could be at risk of disclosure not only to the FCA or PRA but also to other parties, for example if legal proceedings arose from the matter[1]. Equally, if management, understandably, take steps to interview the staff involved as soon as the problem comes to light, and do so without consulting the legal department, they may create documents which could be liable to be disclosed. Documents of this nature, particularly those created at an early stage when there is not yet a full understanding of the problem, can often cause problems later, however innocuous they may seem at the time they are written.

1 Issues relating to the disclosure of documents are considered in more detail at paras **3.136** ff and **10.51** ff below.

3.14 In addition, it is important to recognise that reporting lines and compliance structures can sometimes be viewed by the Regulators as having played some part in the problem. Of particular interest to the Regulators will be whether a firm's internal supervision and controls can be seen to have some

3.14 Steps to take when an issue arises

bearing on the problem having arisen[1]. The firm would be well advised to ensure that the review, whoever conducts it, is able to cast an objective eye over the possibility of such issues arising. The integrity of the process is absolutely critical if it is to bear the scrutiny of the Regulators.

1 See, for example, the FCA Handbook at DEPP 6.2.1(d)G and DEPP 6.5A.2(7)(c)G. The likely impact of ineffective systems and controls on the level of a fine that is subsequently imposed is considered at para **8.61** ff below. Subsequent improvements in a firm's systems and controls are likely to be viewed positively as is also shown in that paragraph.

3.15 There are, therefore, often strong reasons for involving internal or external legal counsel at an early stage, to advise in respect of the appropriate conduct of the investigation including document creation and the applicability of legal professional privilege over such documents[1] as well as to ensure the integrity and independence of the process.

1 See further para **3.142** ff below.

How should the investigation be carried out?

3.16 Four issues are considered here, namely:

- the scope of the investigation;
- gathering together and reviewing the documents;
- investigating employees; and
- interviewing employees.

3.17 As a preliminary point, the firm should keep careful track of what steps it has taken and, if appropriate, the reasons why it decided not to take particular steps, so that it can explain the extent of its investigation to the Regulators if it is asked to do so.

The scope of the investigation

3.18 One of the first points is to decide upon the scope of the investigation. This will depend upon the nature and seriousness of the matter concerned: not every minor breach requires an exhaustive investigation aimed at identifying any underlying systemic causes. Equally though, the Regulators will expect the firm (and especially its senior management[1]) to have considered whether there are any wider implications, particularly since, among other things, this is relevant to whether the firm needs to notify the Regulators[2]. It also allows the firm to consider how the problem can be prevented from recurring[3].

1 See para **9.22** ff below.
2 See para **3.42** ff below. The need to identify any wider implications is reinforced by the Regulators' requirements in respect of firms' internal complaints handling procedures: see the Handbooks at DISP and see **CHAPTER 11** below.
3 This is a relevant issue for the Regulators: see para **3.117** ff below.

Gathering together and reviewing the documents

3.19   The firm should consider gathering together, at an early stage, all the potentially relevant documents. These will include:

- the working files of any members of staff or department involved, including back office files, compliance or internal audit files and the files of any person to whom any relevant person reported;

- material stored electronically, including e-mails and documents on the hard drives of the people concerned; and

- tapes of telephone conversations on the lines of those people involved.

To the extent that any of this material relates to specific employees, there may be additional points to consider, discussed at para **3.21** below.

3.20   Gathering the material together allows the firm to ensure that none of the evidence is destroyed or tampered with[1]. It also allows the firm to react promptly to requests by the Regulators for documents or information and thus to be seen to have the matter under control. Also it assists the firm in carrying out its own review, and ensuring that the scope of its review is appropriate.

1 This may be a criminal offence: see para **3.138** below.

3.21   There are a number of practical points to consider. In particular:

- it is important to preserve files intact, as the order of the file may be relevant and this will also assist in demonstrating that it has not been tampered with and that documents have not been removed;

- careful consideration needs to be given as to whether electronic documents have been deleted or should be retrieved[1];

- a record should be kept of where each file was found; and

- a record should be kept of the chain of custody of each file, again to allow the firm to address any questions about whether it has been tampered with.

1 Accordingly, any electronic destruction policy should also be stopped; the firm should ensure that it does not destroy anything and preserves all documents: see para **3.136** ff below.

3.22   Once the documents have been gathered together, the firm, or its representatives, will want to review them as part of its internal review. Among other things, this allows the firm to identify those documents that could or should be withheld from the Regulators if there is an investigation[1], so that the firm is ready and able to respond swiftly to any requests from the Regulators.

1 Primarily, this means legally privileged material but may also include documents that are covered by a duty of banking confidence: see paras **5.56** ff and **5.60** ff below.

Investigating employees

3.23   In reality, any question about what the firm has done involves reviewing the activities of one or more employees, not only those who were directly involved, but also others who may have been involved less directly or may have relevant evidence, for example back office staff or a person to whom an employee under suspicion reported. The firm may wish to ensure at an early stage that it has identified all the relevant people, so that it is in a position to assess whether or not their conduct should be reviewed and whether or not they are likely to have relevant documents or other evidence. Steps can also then be taken, for example, to obtain evidence or secure their future co-operation, if any of those people is likely to be unavailable to the firm in the future for any reason. Given the FCA's focus on the responsibility of senior management for a firm's regulatory failings[1], it is important that the firm's list of relevant people includes all those in the supervisory chain for the employee concerned including the SIF[2] responsible for the relevant business area.

1 See para **1.34**.
2 Significant Influence Function, see para **1.77**.

3.24   In some cases, it may be appropriate, whilst the firm reviews the activities of the relevant employees, to take immediate action to suspend suspect-employees or remove them from sensitive positions[1]. This is a matter of common sense, particularly where the circumstances suggest that the breach may result from some deliberate action by an employee. But it may also be viewed by the Regulators as a positive step taken by the firm in response to the breach, in order to protect its customers, to ensure that the breach is not repeated in the short term and protect the evidence.

1 In so far as it takes any disciplinary action, the firm should ensure that it complies with the terms of any disciplinary procedure in conjunction with the guidance contained in the ACAS Code of Practice 1 – Disciplinary and Grievance Procedures (April 2009). This should reduce the risk of a dismissed employee successfully claiming that he has been unfairly dismissed or, in the event that the claim is successful, reduce the risk of a Tribunal finding an employer to have unreasonably failed to follow the Code and increasing the award by up to 25%.

3.25   Three issues are worth further consideration:

(1) whether or not material relating to employees recorded in the ordinary course of the firm's business has been lawfully recorded;

(2) whether or not adequate arrangements are in place that allow the firm to review that material once a problem comes to light;

(3) the extent to which a more intrusive investigation can be made into a particular individual after a problem comes to light.

The first two issues will be discussed together, and some practical guidance provided, and then the third issue will be considered. The same English legal issues[1] arise in relation to all three questions, but the importance of the legal issue differs according to the question.

1 Certain legal obligations may apply throughout the EU although they may be implemented differently in each country. For example, the Data Protection Act 1998 was intended to implement the EU Data Protection Directive (95/46/EC). Note that the draft European General Data Protection Regulation (which will supersede this Directive) was unveiled on 25 January 2012. At the time of writing the Regulation was going through the first reading stage at the European Parliament. The European Parliament, the European Council and the European Commission would like to see the Regulation adopted before the European Parliament elections and the

next rotation of the Commissioners in 2014. If this happens in the intended time frame, the Regulation is likely to become directly applicable in Member States in 2016. However the privacy laws of other EU states do not necessarily reflect the provisions of the 1998 Act. This issue could be relevant if, for example, a telephone call was taped at an overseas branch of the firm. How the firm acts where it is required under the UK legislation to provide information to the Regulators when asked to do so, but is constrained by applicable overseas law from doing so, is a particularly difficult problem in practice. See further para **5.69** below. There may also be applicable overseas legal considerations, for example data protection legislation applies throughout the EU and in some other countries and many other states have their own privacy laws.

Material recorded in the ordinary course of business

3.26   Firms regularly monitor and store e-mails and tapes of telephone conversations and indeed often do so under regulatory obligations. But the interception and recording of communications, including both e-mails and telephone calls, by the firm, even within its own private telecommunications system, may have other legal implications. In particular, firms need to have in mind the Data Protection Act 1998[1], the Regulation of Investigatory Powers Act 2000[2] and the employee's possible right under the Human Rights Act 1998 to respect for privacy in connection with family life and correspondence[3]. The firm's ability not only to record the material, but also to review the material recorded may be restricted[4].

1   Recording, reviewing and using tapes of telephone calls, CCTV and e-mails relating to employees, among other things, may amount to the processing of personal data about a data subject (ie, the employee) under the Data Protection Act 1998, in which case the firm, as a data controller, must comply with the eight Data Protection Principles and the other provisions of the Data Protection Act 1998. In the current context, the firm will be concerned to ensure data is acquired and stored fairly and lawfully. It will also be necessary to consider whether the data subject must be informed about the firm's activities, or whether exemptions under the Act may be relied upon. Failure to comply with the requirements under the 1998 Act may give rise to enforcement action by the Information Commissioner (including the issue of a monetary penalty notice of up to £500,000 for a serious contravention of the Data Protection Act and the instigation of criminal proceedings) or a claim for damages by the employee. For a more detailed discussion, see Jay, *Data Protection: Law and Practice* (4th edn, 2012).
2   The Regulation of Investigatory Powers Act 2000, s 1(3) prohibits the interception of communications on a private telecommunications system and makes it actionable at the suit of the sender, recipient or intended recipient. But interceptions are permitted if they fall within the Telecommunications (Lawful Business Practice) (Interception of Communications) Regulations 2000, SI 2000/2699: see para **3.27**, n 2 below.
3   The right to respect for privacy, and the question whether the employee has such a right against the firm is discussed at para **3.29** ff below.
4   Most of these hurdles can be overcome if the employee has consented to the monitoring operation. 'Consent' is defined for these purposes in the Data Protection Directive (95/46/EC).

3.27   The firm therefore needs to have appropriate arrangements in place to ensure that the recording and review of material does not contravene the applicable requirements. In broad terms, those arrangements need to include:

• an understanding on the part of employees that their e-mails and telephone calls are monitored, stored and reviewed for various purposes, including to ascertain regulatory compliance, and, preferably, their consent to this;

• a clear and internally available policy on the use of e-mails, the telephone[1] and computers for private purposes, so as to ensure, among other things, that employees have no expectation of a right to privacy other than that which has been indicated;

- the waiver by employees of any rights to privacy in respect of material recorded, including any private conversations, e-mails or electronic documents created or held;

- if practical, employees' consent more generally to their conduct being investigated in other ways by the firm, for example by reviewing the contents of their desks, offices and hard drives, and monitoring them by CCTV, without prior notice; and

- ensuring e-mails and telephone calls are monitored and recorded for the sole purpose of[2]:

    – establishing the existence of facts; and/or

    – ascertaining compliance with applicable regulatory practices or procedures; and/or

    – preventing or detecting crime.

1 It may be appropriate to make a telephone line available specifically for private calls which will not be monitored or recorded.
2 These are the relevant purposes permitted under the Lawful Business Practice Regulations: see para **3.26**, n 2 above.

3.28   In reviewing the material once the problem comes to light, the firm should ensure that the information is used and disclosed only to the extent[1]:

- covered by the employee's consent; or

- that it is necessary to do so in order to comply with a legal obligation; or

- that it is necessary to do so for the firm's own legitimate interests[2].

The firm also needs to take care if it wishes to use for some other purpose information which it has come across during an investigation carried out for a particular purpose.

1 These are the relevant conditions of the First Data Protection Principle and are provided in order to give some indication of the parameters of permitted processing. For a more detailed discussion of this and the other requirements of the Data Protection Act 1998, see Jay, *Data Protection: Law and Practice* (4th edn, 2012).
2 This last condition may only be relied upon where no unwarranted prejudice to the data subject's privacy is caused. Since the issues of 'prejudice' and whether that prejudice is 'unwarranted' will depend upon the circumstances, it will normally be preferable to seek consent where it is practical to do so.

A more intrusive investigation?

3.29   The firm may wish to go further than simply reviewing the material that it already has relating to the particular employee. It may wish to conduct a more intrusive investigation, for example by checking the contents of the employee's office or desk, including locked cupboards or drawers, reviewing the hard drive on his computer, or monitoring his telephone. Some of these steps may need to be taken late at night. To what extent is the firm limited in its ability to take this kind of action?

3.30 The main limitation is the employee's possible ECHR right to respect for privacy[1]. Whilst the ECHR rights apply primarily as between, broadly, public authorities and private individuals or companies, it cannot be ruled out that courts and employment tribunals will start to apply those rights horizontally, for example such as to create a direct right of respect for privacy as between employer and employee[2]. ECHR inspired developments have led to attempts to establish an English law concept of privacy[3]. Moreover, whether or not an employee has a directly enforceable right to privacy as against his employer, the employee may seek to raise ECHR based arguments (for example relating to the way evidence was collected) before a court or tribunal subsequently considering whether he was fairly dismissed or whether it was appropriate for the FCA or PRA to take action against him. A court or tribunal is required under the Human Rights Act 1998 to act in a way that is compatible with the ECHR and this may well involve it considering such arguments if they are raised. In this way, the ECHR rights may effectively be enforceable horizontally.

1 ECHR, Art 8.
2 For a discussion, see Lester and Pannick, *Human Rights Law and Practice* (3rd edn, 2009), at para 2.6.3, n 3.
3 See *Douglas v Hello! Ltd [2000] EWCA Civ 353, [2001] QB 967* where the Court of Appeal used the action of breach of confidence to uphold the claimants' right to privacy; and *Campbell v Mirror Group Newspapers Ltd [2004] UKHL 22, [2004] 2 AC 457, HL.*

3.31 Assuming the employee has a right to privacy as against the employer, this includes a right to privacy at work and could be infringed by, for example, the tapping of a telephone at work, or monitoring e-mail and internet usage[1]. But the right is not an absolute one. It can be interfered with provided this is done in accordance with the law, for a legitimate aim and is necessary in a democratic society for certain specified purposes[2]. The test of necessity requires there to be a pressing social need for the interference and for the means employed to be proportionate to the legitimate aim pursued[3]. The key for the firm is thus to ensure that the investigation is carried out in a way that is proportionate to the legitimate aim sought to be achieved[4].

1 See, for example, the high profile case of *Halford v United Kingdom [1997] ECHR 32, (1997) 24 EHRR 523* as applied in *Valenzuela Contreras v Spain (1998) 28 EHRR 483.* In this regard, see the subsequent Regulation of Investigating Powers Act 2000 as applied in *Valenzuela Contreras v Spain (1998) 28 EHRR 483.* See also *Copland v United Kingdom [2007] All ER (D) 32 (Apr),* in which ECHR ruled that a UK college breached an employee's right to privacy by monitoring, collecting and storing information relating to her telephone, e-mail and internet usage – since the employer did not have a policy. Although note that Regulation of Investigating Powers Act 2000 and the Lawful Business Practice Regulations were not considered as neither were in force at the time.
2 These are the interests of national security, public safety or the economic well-being of the country, the prevention of disorder or crime, the protection of health or morals or the protection of the rights and freedoms of others: ECHR, Art 8(2).
3 See Lester and Pannick, *Human Rights Law and Practice* (3rd edn, 2009), at para 3.16.
4 The firm also needs to ensure that the consents discussed at para **3.27** ff above are in place.

3.32 Steps to take when an issue arises

3.32 Precisely what this means will depend upon the situation. Difficult questions include whether the firm can listen to ostensibly private telephone calls, and read private e-mails, and whether it can undertake in secret other particularly intrusive forms of investigation, such as going through someone's desk, locked cupboards and hard drive late at night. Answers to these questions cannot be given in the abstract, since the relevant issues such as legitimate aim, pressing social need and proportionality depend to such a large extent on the particular situation. In general terms, the firm will probably not be entitled to obtain and review material from a source which the employee would reasonably expect to be private[1], at least not without consent.

1 For example, a telephone which was specifically designated for private calls: see *Halford v United Kingdom [1997] ECHR 32, (1997) 24 EHRR 523*. In *Copland v United Kingdom [2007] All ER (D) 32 (Apr)*, the claimant had been given no warning that her phone calls would be monitored and therefore had a reasonable expectation as to the privacy of the calls made from her work telephone.

3.33 An additional limitation is found in the statutory restrictions outlined at para **3.26** above, which limit the purposes for which the firm can obtain material about its employees and impose requirements on the way in which it uses and handles that material. The points discussed at paras **3.26** and **3.27** above therefore apply equally in this context[1].

1 The firm may also wish to have regard to the guidance on the monitoring of employees contained in Part 3 of the Employment Practices Data Protection Code, published in June 2005 by the Information Commissioner. The Code constitutes guidance as to good practice under the Data Protection Act 1998, s 51(3)–(6). The Data Protection Act does not prevent an employer from monitoring workers, but such monitoring must be done in a way which is consistent with the Act, and any adverse impact on workers must be justified by the benefits to the employer and others. The Code is designed to help employers determine when this might be the case by carrying out an impact assessment. This will involve identifying the purpose behind the monitoring, any likely adverse impact of the monitoring, any alternatives available, the obligations that arise from the monitoring and judging whether the monitoring is justified.

Interviewing employees

3.34 There are a number of issues to consider when the firm comes to interview an employee. The following will be considered:

• whether the employee should be invited to take independent legal advice;

• who should carry out the interview; and

• the conduct of the interview.

3.35 Only interviews that are held as part of the firm's investigation into the matter and not disciplinary hearings held to decide what action to take in relation to the particular employee, are considered here. Different considerations will be relevant to the latter[1].

1 For a discussion of disciplinary hearings, see *Harvey on Industrial Relations and Employment Law* (looseleaf). Employers should be mindful of the guidance in the ACAS Code of Practice. The statutory disciplinary and grievance procedure set out in Sch 2 to the Employment Act 2002 was

repealed by the Employment Act (EA) 2008 and replaced by the (non-statutory) ACAS Code of Practice. The EA 2008 and the ACAS Code came into force on 6 April 2009. Under transitional provisions, the EA 2002 statutory procedure still applies in limited circumstances: to any dismissal that took place on or before 5 April 2009; or to any dismissal that took place after that date but for which the first/second stage of the process (the grievance put into writing/a meeting held to discuss issue) had taken place prior to 6 April 2009.

Independent legal advice

3.36 Should the employee be independently represented at the interview? It is difficult to provide any absolute rule. If the individual asks to bring a lawyer to the interview, it may be imprudent as well as counter-productive to refuse[1]. Beyond this, if there is a real, rather than purely technical, risk of the employee facing a criminal prosecution, or a real risk that his interests and those of the firm will conflict, the firm should make clear to the individual that he may wish to take his own legal advice. It is then a matter for the employee whether or not he wishes to do so[2]. Depending upon the nature of the issue, its seriousness and the evidence available, some regulators may expect individuals to have separate representation.

1 In contrast, at a disciplinary hearing, the employee is entitled to be accompanied (but not represented) by a fellow worker or trade union official under the Employment Relations Act 1999.
2 See para **4.182** below for a discussion of the issue of representation in the context of interviews carried out by the Regulators.

Who should carry out the interview?

3.37 Careful consideration should be given to who carries out the interview and whether legally qualified staff or outside counsel should be involved. The interview, and any notes (including manuscript notes) of it, are unlikely to be legally privileged and protected from disclosure to third parties[1] and the Regulators[2] unless the interview has been carried out by a lawyer. Even if the interview has been carried out by a lawyer, this is no guarantee that the documents generated as a result of the interview will be protected from disclosure. The specific requirements of legal privilege must be satisfied in order for it to apply[3].

1 Third parties who may have an interest in obtaining such material would include not only customers, but also any other parties who may in any way have been involved in, or affected by, the transaction and who might seek to claim from any firm any losses or expenses they have incurred as result: see **CHAPTER 19** below generally and especially at para **19.78** ff.
2 The Regulators are (see **CHAPTER 10** below) normally entitled to interview the employee themselves. The Regulators cannot require the firm to produce or disclose legally privileged material: FSMA 2000, s 413 and see para **5.56** ff below. Note that the FSMA 2000 contains its own definition of legal privilege for these purposes which may not cover, among other things, without prejudice material.
3 See para **4.153**. For a further discussion of this decision, see para **4.153**, n 2 and para **4.155**, n 1.

3.38 It is normally good practice for an interview to be conducted by two people, to split the tasks of asking questions and taking notes, to help ensure that all the relevant points are properly covered, and to ensure that the process is witnessed so that any allegations subsequently made by the employee as to what transpired can properly be rebutted.

3.39 Steps to take when an issue arises

The conduct of the interview

3.39   How the interview is conducted will depend very much upon the circumstances, but it is possible to make some general points:

- the in-house lawyer should clearly notify the employee being interviewed that the lawyer only acts for the firm and not for the employee as an individual[1];

- the person conducting the interview should ensure he understands in advance what questions he will ask and consider carefully what documents he will show to the person being interviewed;

- in the employment law context, it is good practice to tell the employee in advance why he is being interviewed, so that he has a chance to prepare. In the context of an investigation, whether this will be appropriate and/or practicable will depend upon the circumstances;

- at the outset, the purpose of the interview may need to be explained and whether it is privileged[2];

- if appropriate, it should be made clear to the employee that he has no right to control the use that is made of the information disclosed at the interview, which is a matter purely for the firm[3]; and

- a detailed note of the interview should be taken[4].

1   This is known as an 'Upjohn Warning' and is a practice stemming from the US Supreme Court case *Upjohn Company v United States, 449 US 383 (1981)* in order to reduce any conflict arising from a firm and its employees, directors or officers having differing interests and indeed different legal representation in the context of an internal investigation. It also makes it clear that any legal privilege protecting documents created as a result of the investigation belongs solely to the firm and not to the employee being interviewed.
2   Among other things, it is sensible to make clear that the interview is not a disciplinary hearing but that information obtained in it may be used for the purpose of disciplinary proceedings, if they should result.
3   If the interview is legally privileged, it is generally the firm's privilege and not that of the employee. For a further discussion, see para **4.167** ff below. See eg *Ford, R (on the application of) v The Financial Services Authority [2011] EWHC 2583 (Admin)* (where there was found to be joint privilege of the company and a director).
4   In some circumstances, it may be appropriate to agree that the employee may comment on the note.

3.40   If the firm has notified the FCA – pursuant to Principle 11 or otherwise[1] – that it is interviewing an employee or employees in connection with its investigation into the matter, the FCA may request that the interview(s) be conducted in accordance with requirements that it stipulates or even seek to impose conditions on the conduct of such interviews. In particular, those requirements or conditions are likely to concern the manner in which information obtained by the firm in the course of the interview is recorded and, where appropriate[2], how that information is subsequently to be communicated to the FCA. That is particularly the case when the FCA has concerns that the matter has criminal implications, and desires that a complete record of the interviewee's recollections is preserved.

1   As to which, see para **2.12** ff.

2 That is, if it is information that the FCA might reasonably expect would be provided to it
   (Principle 11) and subject to any questions of privilege.

3.41   Historically, the provision to the regulator of a note of the interview
has in practice sufficed to meet this concern. However, there are signs that the
FCA is seeking to take an increasingly interventionist approach in the early
stages of a firm's investigation. This may include a requirement that the firm
tapes interviews with employees. While there is generally no legal bar to a firm
recording an interview with an employee, the 'chilling' effect such an approach
is likely to have may hinder the progress of the firm's investigation. In addition,
there are issues of fairness for the firm's employees. A firm will wish carefully to
consider whether it will itself record an interview with an employee and provide
that recording to the FCA. In that event, the statutory protections[1] afforded to
interviewees in the context of compelled interviews (which would typically be
tape-recorded)[2] would not be available to the interviewed employee.

1 Principally the FSMA 2000, s 174.
2 See para **4.190** below.

SHOULD THE FIRM REPORT THE PROBLEM?

3.42   If the problem is not already known to the FCA or PRA, or if their
understanding is partial or mistaken, the firm and its senior management need to
think quickly about whether to report it to them. Both regulated firms and their
employees who are approved persons owe extensive duties of disclosure to the
Regulators, breach of which is treated extremely seriously.

3.43   The following paragraphs consider:

- the scope of the firm's obligations to report to the Regulators;

- the obligation of individual employees to do so;

- the potential consequences of not complying with these obligations;

- the obligations which there may, in some circumstances, be to report to other
  bodies; and

- how to notify the Regulators.

The firm's obligation to report

3.44   The firm's basic reporting obligation, contained in Principle 11, is to
disclose to the Regulators appropriately anything relating to the firm of which the
Regulators would reasonably expect notice[1]. This is a wide obligation and has to
some extent been fleshed out by rules contained in the Handbooks[2].

1 Principle 11, FCA and PRA Principles for Businesses; see para **2.12** above. In addition to the
   obligation to report, Principle 11 also contains an obligation to be open and co-operative, which
   is considered at paras **4.25** ff and **4.133** below.
2 See the Handbooks at SUP 15.3.

3.45 Steps to take when an issue arises

3.45 Principle 11 requires a firm to deal with its regulators (generally the FCA or PRA) in an open and cooperative way and to disclose to the appropriate regulator anything relating to the firm of which the regulator would reasonably expect notice[1].

1 See para **4.28** ff.

3.46 The firm's obligation of disclosure under Principle 11 is not limited to its regulated activities and matters relating to the firm's non-regulated activities or affecting other group companies may be notifiable to the Regulators[1]. Incoming firms are also generally required to comply with Principle 11 in the same way as UK regulated firms, in so far as responsibility for the matter in question is not reserved to the firm's home state regulator[2]. Even where a particular matter does not fall within the specific rules, the firm must still consider whether it should notify the Regulators pursuant to its general obligation under Principle 11[3].

1 The potential relevance of issues arising in a firm's unregulated business to the Regulators' enforcement roles is discussed at para **2.113** above.
2 See para **2.21** above and, in relation to incoming firms, para **3.46**, n 2 above.
3 See the *JPMorgan Chase Bank NA final notice (18/9/13)*, the *Prudential Assurance Company Limited final notice (27/3/13)* and the *Goldman Sachs International final notice (9/9/10)*. In each of these cases the firm received significant fines for failing to satisfy its general obligation under Principle 11.

3.47 Compliance with Principle 11 includes, but is not limited to, giving the appropriate regulator notice of the following[1]:

- any proposed restructuring, reorganisation or business expansion which could have a significant impact on the firm's risk profile or resources;

- any significant failure in the firm's systems or controls, including those reported to the firm by the firm's auditor;

- any action which a firm proposes to take which would result in a material change in its capital adequacy or solvency.

1 See the Handbooks at SUP 15.3.7.

3.48 In addition, the firm must notify the appropriate regulator immediately:

- if it becomes aware, or has information which reasonably suggests, that a matter having serious regulatory impact has or may have occurred or may occur in the foreseeable future[1];

- of breaches of rules and other requirements in or under the FSMA 2000[2];

- of civil, criminal or disciplinary proceedings against the firm[3];

- of fraud, errors and other irregularities[4]; and

- of events relating to its insolvency, bankruptcy and winding up[5].

Each of these are discussed in further detail below.

1 See the Handbooks at SUP 15.3.1.
2 See the Handbooks at SUP 15.3.11.
3 See the Handbooks at SUP 15.3.15.

3.49   As to the form and manner of the notification, see para **3.95** ff below.

Matters having a serious regulatory impact

3.50   Matters having a serious regulatory impact include[1]:

- the firm failing to satisfy one or more of the threshold conditions[2];

- any matter which could have a significant adverse impact on the firm's reputation;

- any matter which could affect the firm's ability to continue to provide adequate services to its customers and which could result in serious detriment to a customer of the firm; or

- any matter in respect of the firm which could result in serious financial consequences to the UK financial system or to other firms.

1 See the Handbooks at SUP 15.3.1.
2 For a discussion of the threshold conditions, see para **2.4** ff above.

3.51   Applying this requirement may not, however, be straightforward. Three points may in particular be made. First, the test has both subjective and objective limbs, only one of which needs to be satisfied in order to trigger the obligation to notify. The subjective limb requires the firm to notify the appropriate regulator where it is actually aware of the matter, whereas the objective limb requires the firm to notify the appropriate regulator where it 'has information which reasonably suggests' the problem. This means that, in assessing whether the firm properly complied with its reporting obligation, the question can be asked 'should the firm have appreciated?' (as opposed to 'did the firm actually know?').

3.52   Second, the rule places a heavy onus on firms to try to predict what the future consequences of a particular event may be. Whilst, in theory, the firm should be judged by reference to what consequences of a particular matter were foreseeable at the relevant time, there may in practice be a temptation to judge what consequences were foreseeable by reference to what actually happened and it may be difficult for firms to show otherwise.

3.53   Third, this is exacerbated by the broad terms of each of the four categories of consequences set out in para **3.50** above. The Regulators have not provided any guidance on the second, third or fourth categories. There is plenty of room for disagreement over whether something had a significant adverse impact on the firm's reputation or affected its ability to continue to provide adequate services to its customers, let alone whether it was foreseeable that one of these consequences might occur.

Breaches of rules and other requirements under the FSMA 2000

3.54 Breaches of rules and other requirements under the FSMA 2000 include[1]:

- a significant breach of a rule (which includes one of the Principles for Businesses[2]) or a Statement of Principle[3];

- a breach of any requirement imposed by the FSMA 2000 or by regulations or orders made under the FSMA 2000 by HM Treasury (except if the breach is a criminal offence, in which case the next point applies);

- the bringing of a prosecution for, or a conviction of, any offence under the FSMA 2000; or

- breaches of certain other directly applicable regulations[4] by (or against) the firm, or any of its directors, officers, employees, approved persons or appointed representatives.

1 See the Handbooks at SUP 15.3.11R.
2 For an explanation, see para **2.11** ff above.
3 See para **2.31** ff above.
4 Such as the MiFID Regulation or AIFMD UK regulation: see the Handbooks at SUP 15.3.11(1)(d)–(h).

3.55 This is another extremely broad provision, requiring the firm to blow the whistle on itself, its employees and a limited range of others, in a variety of situations. A number of points can be made in considering how it applies.

3.56 First, it requires the firm to report breaches of the Regulators' rules, but only those which are 'significant'[1]. It is important to recognise that the Regulators' views on the significance of a particular breach may not always be the same as the views of the firm and in practice the question for the firm will be whether the Regulators are likely to view the breach as significant.

1 Significance is to be determined by reference to the potential financial losses to customers or the firm, the frequency of the breach, implications for the firm's systems and controls and if there were delays in identifying or rectifying the breach. See the Handbooks at SUP 15.3.12G.

3.57 Second, the obligation is to make a notification immediately after the firm becomes aware, or has information which reasonably suggests, that a breach has occurred or may have occurred or may occur in the foreseeable future. Thus, whilst there may be scope for the firm to make further enquiries, and in the meantime not to notify the Regulators, where it only has a 'suspicion' that there may have been a breach, as soon as the information available to it reaches the state of 'reasonably suggesting' there may have been a breach, it must immediately notify. In that situation, it is not entitled first to take further steps to investigate the matter to decide whether or not there has been a breach. If it did so, decided that a breach had occurred, and then notified the Regulators, it could be in breach of this rule[1]. Technically, it would be in breach of the rule even if it investigated and, after investigating the matter, decided there had been no breach or offence and there was therefore nothing to report to the Regulators, but the likelihood of this coming to the Regulators' attention, or of the Regulators taking action, must be rather lower.

1   See also the discussion at para **3.74** ff below.

3.58   Third, the Regulators require relatively specific information to be provided to them on the notification, which may not always sit easily with the obligation to notify immediately the information which reasonably suggests that a breach may have occurred. It may be difficult in practice for firms to provide the information which the Regulators are asking for when making the first notification, given the early stage at which the notification has to be made. Often this means that the first notification will be a form of 'heads up' to the Regulators, letting them know that the firm is investigating further and will revert with further information.

3.59   Fourth, the rule is sufficiently wide to enable the Regulators to charge the firm with breach of this rule where a problem arises which the firm did not know about, but in the Regulators' view should have known about and prevented. In that type of situation, the Regulators may be more concerned with management, systems and controls issues, but it may be that a breach of this rule will also be alleged. Whether the firm had breached the rule would depend upon the nature of the information available to it at the time and whether it reasonably suggested that the particular breach might occur (even if at the time it did not in fact consider that a breach might occur).

Civil, criminal or disciplinary proceedings against the firm

3.60   Civil, criminal or disciplinary proceedings include[1]:

- civil proceedings are brought against the firm and the amount of the claim is significant in relation to the firm's financial resources or its reputation;

- any action is brought against the firm under the FSMA 2000, ss 71 or 138D[2];

- disciplinary measures or sanctions have been imposed on the firm by any statutory or regulatory authority, professional organisation or trade body (other than the Regulators) or the firm becomes aware that one of those bodies has started an investigation into its affairs;

- the firm is prosecuted for, or convicted of, any offence involving fraud or dishonesty or any penalties are imposed on it for tax evasion; or

- it is a trustee of an occupational pension scheme and is removed as trustee by a court order.

1   See the Handbooks at SUP 15.3.15R. Firms also have an obligation to report to the FCA immediately in certain circumstances where the conduct of certain employees is called into question: see para **3.124** ff below. See also SUP 15.3.16G.
2   As to actions for damages which the FSMA 2000 allows investors to bring arising from the breach by the firm of certain requirements under the FSMA 2000 or the FCA or PRA rules: see para **19.19** ff below.

3.61   Steps to take when an issue arises

3.61   The firm is required to report to the Regulators the fact that another regulator (for example, an overseas regulator) has started an investigation into the firm's affairs[1]. There is nothing in the rule to confine it to those situations where the investigation could involve or impact on matters occurring in the firm's UK operations. Nor is the firm entitled to wait until the enquiry concludes.

1 See **CHAPTER 7**.

Fraud, errors and other irregularities

3.62   Fraud, errors and other irregularities include the following events, if they are significant[1]:

- the firm becomes aware that an employee may have committed a fraud against one of its customers;

- the firm becomes aware that a person, whether or not employed by it, may have committed a fraud against it;

- the firm considers that any person, whether or not employed by it, is acting with intent to commit a fraud against it;

- the firm identifies irregularities in its accounting or other records, whether or not there is evidence of fraud; or

- the firm suspects that one of its employees may be guilty of serious misconduct concerning his honesty or integrity and which is connected with the firm's regulated activities or ancillary activities[2].

1 See the Handbooks at SUP 15.3.17R.
2 This corresponds to the types of situations where the Regulators may need to consider withdrawing the approval of an approved person or making a prohibition order against any person: see **CHAPTER 9** below.

3.63   The Regulators have provided guidance on the meaning of 'significant' in the context of this rule and as to when an event will be regarded as being significant. In determining whether a matter is significant, the firm should have regard to[1]:

- the size of any monetary loss or potential monetary loss to itself or customers (either in terms of a single incident or a group of similar or related incidents);

- the risk of reputational loss to the firm; and

- whether the incident or a pattern of incidents reflects weaknesses in the firm's internal controls.

1 See the Handbooks at SUP 15.3.18G.

Insolvency, bankruptcy and winding up

3.64   Events relating to its insolvency, bankruptcy and winding up include[1]:

- the calling of a meeting to consider a resolution for winding up the firm; or

- an application to dissolve the firm or to strike it off the Register of Companies; or

- the presentation of a petition for the winding up of the firm; or

- the making of, or any proposals for the making of, a composition or arrangement with any one or more of its creditors; or

- an application for the appointment of an administrator or trustee in bankruptcy to the firm; or

- the appointment of a receiver to the firm (whether an administrative receiver or a receiver appointed over particular property); or

- an application for an interim order against the firm under the Insolvency Act 1986, s 252; or

- if the firm is a sole trader: an application for a sequestration order on the firm; or the presentation of a petition for bankruptcy; or

- anything equivalent to the above events occurring in respect of the firm in a jurisdiction outside the United Kingdom.

1 See the Handbooks at SUP 15.3.21 and SUP 15.3.18–15.3.20G.

Does the firm have to report to the Regulators known misconduct of others?

3.65   There is no general obligation under English law, including under the FSMA 2000, to report the misconduct of others[1]. Firms are required under the Regulators' rules outlined above to report certain types of breaches or conduct by their employees, directors, officers and appointed representatives[2]. Beyond this, there are certain, very limited whistleblowing obligations mentioned at para **3.92** ff below. The wider whistleblowing obligations that exist under the Proceeds of Crime Act 2002 are considered at para **3.93** ff below.

1 However, different rules apply where the conduct of others falls within the Proceeds of Crime Act 2002; see para **3.93** ff below.
2 See, for example, the Handbooks at SUP 15.3.17R outlined at para **3.52** ff above.

Reports to other regulators

3.66   Principle 11 extends to require the firm to co-operate with its other regulators, for example, exchanges or overseas regulators, and it could be treated by the Regulators as having committed a UK regulatory breach if it failed to do so[1]. A failure to comply with its obligations to other regulators could also be relevant to whether the firm was a fit and proper person[2]. The extent of the obligation to report to other regulators depends on the situation and the obligations that the firm has to the other regulator. But the lack of formal reporting obligations to another regulator may not of itself be determinative. Situations can be envisaged which the Regulators would regard as being so serious that any responsible firm would report them to all its regulators, whatever its formal obligations.

3.66 Steps to take when an issue arises

1 See, for example, *Credit Suisse First Boston International (formerly Credit Suisse Financial Products) final notice (11/12/02)* where the firm misled Japanese tax and regulatory authorities and was fined £4 million by the FSA for doing so (following the imposition of similar sanctions by the Japanese authorities: as to which see Credit Suisse Group Press Release FSA/PN/124/2002.
2 For an explanation of fitness and propriety in relation to firms, see para **2.28** ff above.

The individual's obligation to report

3.67   The individual's obligation to report is the duty to deal with the Regulators and other relevant regulators in an open and co-operative way and to disclose appropriately any information of which the Regulators would reasonably expect notice[1]. At the time of writing, this obligation applies to approved persons. Following the implementation of the Financial Services (Banking Reform) Act 2013, it is anticipated that equivalent obligations will apply to senior persons and certain other employees of firms, as well as individuals who remain classified as approved persons. The obligations under the current regime are described below.

1 Statement of Principle 4: see the Handbooks at APER 2.1A.3P and APER 2.1B.3P and para **2.46** ff above. For a discussion of the nature and effect of the Statements of Principle and Code of Practice for Approved Persons, see para **2.31** ff above.

3.68   The Code of Practice[1] applicable to Statement of Principle 4 provides some assistance in determining whether or not conduct complies with this principle[2]. It describes three types of conduct which, in the Regulators' opinion, do not comply with Statement of Principle 4 and sets out factors to be taken into account in determining whether or not a person's conduct complies. One of these three types of conduct relates to approved persons generally, one relates to those who are responsible within the firm for reporting to the Regulators, and the third relates to co-operation with the Regulators, rather than the obligation to report, and is not therefore relevant here[3]. The following paragraphs therefore consider, first, the obligation so far as relates to individuals generally and, second, so far as it relates to those responsible for reporting to the Regulators. Finally, whether any individuals have obligations to report to other regulators is considered. Whether or not an individual has an obligation to report a matter to the Regulators, if he does so that report may well be protected under the Public Interest Disclosure Act 1998, so that the firm must not discipline him or subject him to any detriment as a result[4].

1 Handbooks at APER 4.4 and para **2.35** ff above.
2 The Code of Practice is only evidential guidance: see para **2.37** ff above.
3 This is discussed at para **4.47** ff below.
4 See the discussion at para **4.53** below. The Regulators believe that firms should ordinarily be the first port of call for disclosures by employees and therefore encourage firms to adopt and publicise appropriate internal procedures: see the Handbooks at SYSC 4.2.1. The FCA also have a dedicated telephone line and e-mail address for disclosures. Note that the FCA has indicated it will regard as a serious matter any evidence that a firm had acted to the detriment of a worker who made a protected disclosure: this could call into question the fitness and propriety of the firm or relevant members of its staff: see the FCA Handbook at SYSC 18.2.3G.

The obligation on approved persons generally

3.69   An approved person's conduct does not, in the Regulators' opinion, comply with the Statement of Principle if he fails to report promptly in accordance with the firm's internal procedures or, if none exists, direct to the Regulators, information which it would be reasonable to assume would be of material significance to the Regulators, whether in response to questions or otherwise[1].

1 Handbooks at APER 4.4.3 E and 4.4.4 E.

3.70   Matters to be taken into account in determining the person's compliance or otherwise with the Statement of Principle are[1]:

- the likely significance to the Regulators of the information which it was reasonable for the individual to assume;
- whether the information related to the individual himself or to his firm; and
- whether any decision not to report the matter internally was taken after reasonable enquiry and analysis of the situation.

Each is considered briefly below.

1 Handbooks at APER 4.4.6 E.

3.71   The emphasis is therefore on reporting internally within the firm and the Code seems to indicate that the person is, in the normal course, only expected to report direct to the Regulators if there are no relevant internal procedures. Having said that, the provision is a negative one as it explains when a person's conduct fails to comply with his obligations. It does not positively indicate that a person's conduct will comply if he reports internally and there may therefore be circumstances when he will not be absolved from responsibility by virtue of having done so[1]. As ever, the focus needs to be on the broad Statement of Principle and not purely on the detailed provisions of the Code. Moreover, there may be situations where the Regulators can treat a person as though he was responsible for reporting the matter to the Regulators, and therefore measure his conduct against the matters set out at para **3.95** ff below, even though he did not have that responsibility within the firm. In particular, the Regulators have indicated that if a person takes steps to influence the decision so as not to report to the Regulators or acts in a way that is intended to obstruct the reporting of the information to the Regulators, the Regulators will, in respect of that information, view him as one of those who has taken on responsibility for the decision of whether or not to report that matter to the Regulators[2].

1 Such circumstances ought to be relatively rare, particularly given the three factors to be taken into account.
2 Handbooks at APER 4.4.5 E.

3.72   It should be remembered that the FCA believes that senior management should be held responsible for a firm's regulatory breaches caused by management failings[1]. Senior management who are involved in a matter are particularly at risk of being held accountable for the decision whether to report to the Regulators.

1 See para **1.34** above.

3.73   The obligation is to report, whether in answer to questions or otherwise. In other words, the individual cannot wait until he is asked about the matter, but must take steps to volunteer information where appropriate.

3.74   Steps to take when an issue arises

Likely significance of the information

3.74   The first of the three factors to be taken into account in determining whether or not the person's conduct complied with Statement of Principle 4 is the likely significance to the Regulators of the information which it was reasonable for the person to assume. This may be a difficult test to apply in practice. It requires the Regulators to assess what it was reasonable for the person to assume at the time about how the Regulators would judge the significance of the information. The test is primarily an objective one. It is necessary to look at what it was reasonable for the person to assume, not at what he did assume. Equally, though, it would be wrong for the Regulators to judge the person's behaviour by reference to what the Regulators regard as the significance of the information. There may also be room for a more subjective element. Arguably, the question of what it was reasonable for the person to assume about what the Regulators would regard as significant requires regard to be had to the circumstances of the particular person concerned. In other words, the level of knowledge about the Regulators' practices which it is reasonable for some approved persons to have may be different from that of others: compare, for example, a compliance officer with a sales person. It seems that the test is, in this way, tailored to some extent to the particular person.

Whether the information related to the person or the firm

3.75   The second factor is self-explanatory. The implication is that it will be more egregious for a person to withhold information relating to his own personal position.

Whether any decision not to report was taken after reasonable enquiry and analysis

3.76   The third factor provides some protection for individuals. If the person makes a reasonable decision, having undertaken reasonable enquiries or taken professional advice, then this will be a factor in his favour, even if the decision was, on the Regulators' view, the wrong one. But if he does not undertake reasonable enquiries and analysis or does not make a reasonable decision, then this may be a factor against him.

Approved persons responsible for reporting to the Regulators

3.77   An approved person who is one of those responsible within the firm for reporting matters to the Regulators[1] fails, in the Regulators' opinion, to comply with the Statement of Principle if he fails promptly to inform the Regulators of information of which he is aware and which it would be reasonable to assume would be of material significance to the Regulators, whether in response to questions or otherwise[2].

1   This may include those who take steps to influence that decision or obstruct the reporting: see para **3.67** above.
2   Handbooks at APER 4.4.7E.

3.78   Matters to be taken into account in determining the person's compliance or otherwise with the Statement of Principle are[1]:

- the likely significance of the information to the Regulators which it was reasonable for the person to assume[2]; and

- whether any decision not to inform the Regulators was taken after reasonable enquiry and analysis of the situation[3].

1   Handbooks at APER 4.4.8E.
2   This is discussed at para **3.69** above.
3   This is discussed at para **3.76** above.

3.79   The key here is that those responsible within the firm for reporting matters to the Regulators (or who assume such responsibility) are personally responsible to the Regulators if they do not do so. There are two points to note in this regard.

3.80   First, if several people have responsibility within the firm for making reports to the Regulators, no express distinction is drawn between the person responsible for reporting the particular matter, or deciding not to do so, and those who were not involved in the decision at all. In principle, if any of them has committed a breach of the Statement of Principle, it should be only the person who actually took the decision that led to the breach who will ultimately be held responsible for that breach. The Regulators' general policy[1], that personal culpability is a key element in deciding whether an individual should be held responsible, should help to ensure that this is the case.

1   See para **7.16** ff below.

3.81   Second, and most important, those responsible for making reports to the Regulators need to have this personal obligation constantly in mind, particularly where there is pressure from within the firm not to report a particular matter for some reason.

Disclosure to other regulators

3.82   The duty on individuals extends to openness and co-operation with other regulators, for example exchanges or overseas regulators[1]. The Regulators regard individuals as having breached their duties to them if they fail to co-operate or be open with other relevant bodies. The extent of the duty to be open and co-operate with other regulators, and what this requires to be reported to the relevant regulator, will depend upon the situation and the individual's obligations to the relevant regulator. The lack of any formal obligations to the other regulator may not in itself be determinative. Some issues may be sufficiently serious that the Regulators would expect any responsible regulated person to report them, whatever his formal obligations.

1   For the purpose of Statement of Principle 4, regulators in addition to the FCA and the PRA are those which have recognised jurisdiction in relation to regulated activities and a power to call for information from the approved person in connection with his accountable function or in connection with the business for which he is responsible. This may include an exchange or an overseas regulator: see Handbooks at APER 4.4.2AG and 4.4.2BG.

3.83 Steps to take when an issue arises

3.83 Failure to be open and co-operative with other regulators could give rise to disciplinary consequences[1], could impact on the Regulators' view of whether the person remained fit and proper[2], and potentially gives rise to additional enforcement consequences[3].

1 See, for example, the action detailed in para **9.98**, n 3 below. In that case, prohibition orders were issued against two individuals who had deliberately attempted to mislead Japanese regulatory authorities.

2 The question whether a person demonstrates a readiness and willingness to comply with the applicable legal, regulatory and professional requirements and standards is a factor to be taken into account.

3 The withdrawal of his approval or the issue of a prohibition order against him: see also **CHAPTER 9** for a more general discussion of these potential consequences.

Consequences of not reporting to the Regulators

3.84 To understand the importance for firms and individuals of complying with these obligations, it is worth briefly reviewing the potential consequences of failing to do so. If the firm or individual fails to report a matter to the Regulators (or internally when obliged to do so), then this may have a number of consequences:

- it may have an effect on the Regulators' approach to the investigation;

- it may be more likely that the Regulators will bring enforcement proceedings for the original breach;

- it will be relevant to the Regulators' decision as to the size of the enforcement penalty and as to what other regulatory response is appropriate for the original breach;

- the firm and/or the approved person may be liable to enforcement or other regulatory action for the failure to report; and

- there may, in some situations, be a risk of criminal liability for misleading the Regulators.

Each of these is considered in turn.

Effect on the Regulators' approach to the investigation

3.85 In the short term, a failure to fully co-operate with the Regulators, including a failure to report the problem to them, is almost bound to compound the original problem and affect the way the Regulators choose to handle the case. It may make the Regulators suspicious of the firm, as a result not trusting the firm to investigate matters itself. The potential practical effect from the firm's perspective is to lessen the firm's ability to maintain any control over the process, and potentially to increase the burden of the investigation[1].

1 For a discussion of the reasons for and benefits of co-operating with the Regulators in the context of its investigation, see para **4.24** ff below.

More likely that the FCA will bring enforcement proceedings

3.86   One of the factors to be taken into account by the FCA in deciding whether to bring disciplinary proceedings for a particular breach is whether the breach was brought to its attention and, if so, how quickly, effectively and completely[1]. Failure to report the matter properly may therefore make it more likely that the firm will face enforcement action in relation to the original problem.

1   See the FCA Handbook at DEPP 6.2.1(2)(a)G and para **8.24** ff below.

It may affect the sanction imposed for the original breach

3.87   Similarly, whether the firm brought the misconduct to the FCA's attention is one of the factors to be taken into account by the FCA in determining the proper disciplinary or other regulatory response to any breach[1]. Failure to do so is likely to result in an increased penalty or in a more severe regulatory response than would otherwise have been the case.

1   See, for example, the FCA Handbook at DEPP 6.5A.3(2)(a) and (b) G and para **8.66** ff below (relevant to the size of the fine to be imposed), FCA Enforcement Guide at EG 8.9(8) and para **16.215** below (relevant to whether it is appropriate to use the own-initiative power as a matter of urgency).

The failure to report may have its own disciplinary consequences

3.88   Furthermore, the failure to report is in itself a regulatory breach[1], which could result in enforcement action or to an additional disciplinary charge being brought. It could also impact on the Regulators' view of whether the firm or individual was fit and proper, potentially exposing them to other types of regulatory enforcement action[2].

1   Namely, as appropriate, breach of Principle 11 of the Principles for Businesses, Statement of Principle 4 of the Statements of Principle for approved persons, or the specific rules outlined at paras **3.45** to **3.68** above in relation to firms. For an example of a firm being fined for taking internal disciplinary action but failing to report the matter to the former-FSA, see Andrew Richard Holt, Douglas Carr and Nicholson Barber (24 July 2000, SFA Board Notice 550).
2   In relation to the firm, the variation or cancellation of its permission (see **CHAPTER 16** below); in relation to the individual, the withdrawal of his approval or the making of a prohibition order (see **CHAPTER 7** below). In reality these are unlikely to be under consideration save in a very serious case.

Potential criminal liability

3.89   The FSMA 2000 prescribes various criminal offences which relate to the provision of information to the Regulators including the offence of knowingly or recklessly providing false or misleading information to the Regulators in purported compliance with a requirement imposed by or under the FSMA 2000[1]. A failure to provide information to the Regulators is not of itself a criminal offence, but for example, deliberately or recklessly misleading the Regulators by providing one piece of information whilst withholding another could be a criminal offence[2].

3.89   Steps to take when an issue arises

1 FSMA 2000, s 398(1) and see para **5.79** ff below.
2 This would also probably be a breach of the Regulators' rules: see para **3.83** ff above.

Obligations to report to other bodies

3.90   In some situations, the firm may be under an obligation to report a matter to bodies other than the Regulators. This could arise either in relation to the firm's own conduct or in relation to the conduct of others (for example, its employees) of which it is aware.

Reporting the firm's conduct to other bodies

3.91   As outlined at paras **3.65** ff and **3.67** ff above, the Regulators regard both firms and approved persons as under an obligation to be open and co-operative with any other applicable regulators, for example stock exchanges or overseas regulators. Moreover, it is obviously possible for conduct which gives rise to a regulatory issue in the UK also to raise regulatory concerns in other jurisdictions in which the firm does business or vice versa[1]. There may indeed be reporting obligations in those other jurisdictions in those circumstances. From a practical perspective, if the firm concludes that it has obligations to report to another regulator, it needs to bear in mind that regulators are increasingly communicating with one another (as explained in **CHAPTER 7**). It will therefore need to take care to avoid a situation where something it should have reported to one regulator is reported to that regulator by another regulator. In the majority of circumstances it should provide the same information to each relevant regulator[2].

1 See, for example, the note to para **3.66** above.
2 In some circumstances, however, this may not be appropriate such as where the degree of protection applying to the disclosure that will be provided by the other regulator may render the disclosure unnecessarily discloseable to third parties in any likely or concurrent civil litigation. What civil litigation may arise at the same time as a regulatory problem is considered at **CHAPTER 19** below.

Reporting the conduct of others

3.92   Whilst there is no general whistleblowing obligation under English law, there are certain well-known exceptions, for example in relation to money laundering and terrorism[1]. As explained at para **3.66** above, the firm may owe obligations to report the conduct of other persons to other regulators in the UK or other jurisdictions.

1 See para **3.93** ff below.

3.93   Under the Proceeds of Crime Act 2002 (POCA 2002), those working in the 'regulated sector'[1] (which includes all firms) are obliged to report any knowledge or suspicion of money laundering to the authorities[2]. The obligation to report money laundering is onerous, and covers the laundering of proceeds generated from any criminal act, no matter how small the sums involved, how minor the crime or when it took place[3]. Therefore, firms and their employees may find themselves in a position where they are required to report their clients, other parties or even themselves, to the authorities or otherwise risk committing an offence. Additionally, an objective or 'negligence' test in the legislation ensures that those in the regulated sector act proficiently when dealing with potentially reportable matters. Simply failing to report where there are reasonable grounds for knowing or suspecting money laundering is an offence, even if the person concerned genuinely had no suspicion of money laundering. Firms therefore tend to opt to report in many situations rather than risk committing any of the offences even if there is little value to the authorities.

1 See the POCA 2002, Sch 9.
2 The Serious Organised Crime Agency in the UK. In addition, to the obligation to report and offence for failing to do so, the breadth of the offences under the POCA 2002 can mean that firms are also at risk of committing money laundering in certain situations, see the POCA 2002, ss 327–329.
3 This applies retrospectively, such that the practices of a client that were non-compliant some years ago may be reportable.

3.94   There is a substantial body of terrorism legislation in the UK[1] which mirrors many of the obligations in the general money laundering regime in respect of funds and property for use by terrorists, as well as the proceeds of terrorist activities. Firms are required to report suspicions or knowledge of terrorist funding to the authorities. However, it is generally much more difficult for firms to identify terrorist funds or proceeds. Whilst more typical money laundering aims to cleanse proceeds with a criminal origin, terrorist finance instead employs funds from many different and legitimate sources, for criminal or terrorist ends. The breadth of the legislation[2] also means that the activities of groups not conventionally associated with terrorism, such as various political interest groups, may be caught which increases the burden on firms when monitoring accounts.

1 See the Terrorism Act 2000; Terrorism Act 2006; Counter-Terrorism Act 2008; Terrorist Asset-Freezing etc Act 2010; Terrorism Prevention and Investigation Measures Act 2011; Al-Qaida (Asset-Freezing) Regulations 2011, SI 2011/2742; Al-Qaida (United Nations Measures) (Overseas Territories) Order 2012, SI 2012/1757; and Afghanistan (United Nations Measures) (Over-seas Territories) Order 2012, SI 2012/1758.
2 Terrorism Act 2000, s 1 (as amended by the Terrorism Act 2006, s 34) sets out the definition of terrorism.

HOW TO NOTIFY THE REGULATORS

Making notifications under specific rules

3.95   Notifications to the Regulators are required[1] to be in writing, in English, and to give the firm's Firm Reference Number, unless the notification rule states otherwise or the notification relates solely to Principle 11 and not to one of the specific rules. Details of how to make the notification are found in the Handbooks at SUP 15.7.4R–15.7.9G. Notifications can be made by post, hand delivery, fax, e-mail, or online submission via the FCA's or PRA's website[2]. A notification not made in compliance with the rules is considered invalid and the firm may therefore be in breach of the notification requirement[3].

3.95 Steps to take when an issue arises

1 Handbooks at SUP 15.7.1R.
2 See the Handbooks at SUP 15.7.5BR. The FCA website is www.fca.org.uk and the PRA website is www.bankofengland.co.uk/pra/.
3 Handbooks at SUP 15.7.15G.

3.96 In some urgent cases, though, it seems that written notification may not be enough[1]. Firms are required to have regard to the urgency and significance of a matter and, if appropriate, to notify their usual supervisory contact at the appropriate regulator by telephone or other prompt means before submitting a written notification[2]. Oral notifications should be given directly to the firm's usual supervisory contact at the appropriate regulator. It is unlikely to be sufficient to leave a message with another person or on a voicemail system.

1 Handbooks at SUP 15.7.2G.
2 Handbooks at SUP 15.3.2G.

Making notifications under Principle 11

3.97 Notifications under Principle 11[1], rather than under one of the specific rules, may be made to the Regulators orally or in writing, although the Regulators may request written confirmation of a matter. The Regulators regard it as the firm's responsibility to ensure that matters are properly and clearly communicated to it[2] and suggest that a firm provide a written notification if the matter is complex or if it may require the Regulators to take action. The point made above about notifications in urgent cases applies equally. Moreover, in most cases, it will be in the firm's interests to ensure that a record exists of the notification and that the record has been prepared by it, rather than only by a staff member of one of the Regulators.

1 Handbooks at SUP 15.3.10G.
2 See further, at para **3.101** ff below.

Who makes the notification?

3.98 From the Regulators' point of view, they are entitled to rely on any information they receive from a firm and to consider any notification as having been made by a person authorised to do so[1]. The firm therefore needs to consider having in place procedures to ensure that only appropriate employees make notifications to the Regulators and that senior management is kept informed and involved in the decision making process as necessary[2].

1 Handbooks at SUP 15.7.3G.
2 Where the firm is a member of a group which includes more than one firm, it may be possible for it to make a notification on behalf of all the members of the group: see the Handbooks at SUP 15.7.8G. Nevertheless, the obligation to make the notification remains the responsibility of the individual firm itself.

When should the notification be made?

3.99 Whilst not expressly stated in this context[1], it would be prudent for the firm to assume that it is the firm's responsibility to ensure delivery of the notification to the Regulators within the requisite time. It may therefore be sensible to keep a proof of delivery, for example, a proof of posting, a fax transmission report, an electronic confirmation of receipt for an e-mail or a time-stamped receipt in respect of a courier delivery to the Regulators[2].

With regard to the timing of the notification, the Regulators have specified that if the rule requires notification to be made within a specified period, the firm must give the notification so as to be received by the Regulators no later than the end of that period[3]. The Regulators have also given guidance that if the rule does not require notification to be made within a specified period, the firm should act reasonably in deciding when to notify[4].

1   This point is expressly made in the Regulators' reporting rules: see the Handbooks at SUP 16.3.16G.
2   See the FCA Handbook at SUP 15.7.5AR, and PRA Handbook at SUP 15.7.5BR. Where the firm makes a notification by e-mail or fax, it should have already obtained an appropriate address or number from the appropriate regulator: see the Handbooks at SUP 15.7.9G.
3   See the Handbooks at SUP 15.7.10R. If the end of the period falls on a day which is not a business day, the notification must be given so as to be received by the Regulators no later than the first business day after the end of that period.
4   Handbooks at SUP 15.7.11G.

3.100   Principle 11 does not expressly require a notification under it to be given within a specific time, but instead specifies that a firm must disclose to the regulator 'appropriately' anything relating to the firm of which that regulator would reasonably expect notice[1]. The Regulators have indicated that the timing of the notification will depend on the event that has occurred[2], but that they expect firms to discuss relevant matters with them at an early stage, before making any internal or external commitments. The latter part of that sentence is particularly significant. Although, as will be seen, the Regulators expect firms to take action to address issues which arise, and not to wait for the Regulators to do so, it is clear that they expect to be notified in appropriate circumstances before the firm takes any action, whether that action is internal (for example, disciplining employees or remedying systems) or external (for example, compensating customers).

1   However, see the Handbooks at SUP 15.3.10G (regarding communications with the Regulators in accordance with Principle 11), which states that the firm should have regard to the guidance in SUP 15.7.2G in respect of providing important information promptly.
2   Handbooks at SUP 15.3.9G.

The contents of the report to the Regulators

3.101   Where the firm is under an obligation to report, what should be the content of its report? It is difficult to do more than state a few general propositions.

3.102   First, in some instances where the firm is notifying in accordance with a specific rule, the Regulators' guidance indicates what information the Regulators expect to be notified to them (see for example rules 2 and 3 above[1]). In such cases, the firm should comply with the guidance as far as possible.

1   See para **3.54** ff above.

3.103 Steps to take when an issue arises

3.103 Second, it will generally be better to provide the Regulators promptly with an indication that there is a potential problem which the firm is investigating, and some information about the nature of the problem, than to present it with the results of a report which has taken some time to produce relating to a problem of which the Regulators were not until then aware. One of the Regulators' first questions will be when this first came to the firm's notice and why it was not brought to their attention. The Regulators will expect the firm to investigate internally and, if satisfied that it is doing so in a responsible manner and keeping them informed as to the progress, they will be likely, depending upon the circumstances, be content not to intervene. The Regulators are likely to only carry out their own investigation when the firm's investigation is complete and where they consider that some matters will require further or independent inquiry.

3.104 Third, the firm must not provide the Regulators with incomplete information which might be false or misleading. Doing so could constitute a criminal offence[1]. In addition, the Regulators have made a rule requiring firms to take reasonable steps to ensure that all information they give to the Regulators is both factually accurate (or, in the case of estimates and judgements, fairly and properly based after appropriate enquires) and complete (in that it should include anything of which the Regulators would reasonably expect notice)[2]. There is precedent (albeit somewhat dated) for a compliance officer being disciplined for providing information in the course of an interview with the regulator which was false, misleading or inaccurate in a material particular. It was held that it was his duty, as compliance officer, to ensure the correctness of the answers which he gave in the course of his interviews. Instead, by casting himself to some extent in the role of 'fencing advocate', he had provided information which was patently wrong in certain material particulars[3].

1 See paras **3.89** below.
2 See the Handbooks at SUP 15.6.1R. If a firm is unable to obtain such information, then it should inform the appropriate regulator that the scope of the information provided is, or may be, limited: see the Handbooks at SUP 15.6.3G. In addition, firms are required to notify the Regulators immediately if they become aware, or have information which reasonably suggests, that they have or may have provided the appropriate regulator with information which was or may have been false, misleading or inaccurate or may have changed in a material particular: see the Handbooks at SUP 15.6.4R.
3 Capel-Cure Myers Management Ltd, Pattison and Nead (SFA Board Notice 446, 10/97). The report stresses that no aspect of the proceedings reflected on his integrity. See also the FSA's final notice against David John Marriott dated 2 September 2010, in which a former chief executive of two insurance intermediary firms was fined for misusing client money and providing false and deliberately misleading information to the FSA.

HOW SHOULD THE FIRM DEAL WITH ITS CUSTOMERS?

3.105 The protection of consumers is one of the Regulators' key regulatory objectives under the FSMA 2000[1] and an important factor in many of the decisions the Regulators takes in the enforcement context. Firms also owe duties to the Regulators under the Principles for Businesses as regards to their actions in dealing with their customers, both consumers and others such as market counterparties[2]. The following paragraphs consider, first, the Regulators' requirements on how a firm should deal with its customers when a regulatory problem arises and, second, what in practice this requires the firm to do.

1 For a discussion of the Regulators' regulatory objectives, see para **1.11** and **1.21** ff above.
2 Principles 6–10 of the Principles for Businesses: see para **2.12** above.

What are the firm's obligations to act in the interests of customers?

3.106 Firms owe their customers certain general regulatory obligations outlined below. In addition, the way that the firm treats its customers may have specific regulatory and legal implications. Each of these is considered in turn below.

3.107 As a practical matter, particularly in less serious cases, if the firm is seen to be taking all the appropriate steps to address the problem that has arisen, which would include dealing properly with its customers, then the Regulators may be prepared to deal with the matter solely within the supervisory relationship and without the need for the enforcement division to become involved.

The firm's general obligations to its customers

3.108 The Principles for Businesses require firms to[1]:

- pay due regard to the interests of customers and treat them fairly[2];

- pay due regard to the information needs of clients and communicate information to them in a way which is clear, fair and not misleading[3]; and

- manage conflicts of interest fairly, both between themselves and their customers and between a customer and another client[4].

'Customers' means, in this context, clients which are not eligible counterparties[5]. These duties do not, therefore, apply to all of the firm's customers (since they do not apply to eligible counterparties), but they are not confined to, for example, consumers[6].

1 See para **2.12** above.
2 Principles for Businesses, Principle 6.
3 Principles for Businesses, Principle 7.
4 Principles for Businesses, Principle 8.
5 See the Handbooks at PRIN 1.2.2G and, in relation to Principle 7, see the Handbooks at PRIN 3.4.1R. For the rules on classifying customers, see the FCA Handbook at COBS 3 and at **Chapter 10**.
6 'Consumers' has a broad definition under the FSMA 2000, s 425A and includes those who are 'contemplating' whether to use a firm's services.

3.109 Failure to comply with these obligations, including Principles 6, 7 and 8, would in itself constitute a regulatory offence capable of leading to disciplinary proceedings and sanctions[1]. In addition, in a serious case it could give rise to sufficient concerns about the firm to cause the Regulators to exercise their power to vary or cancel the firm's permission[2]. How far do the obligations extend?

1 The use of the Principles as the basis for disciplinary action is discussed at para **2.105** ff above.
2 See generally **CHAPTER 16**.

3.110 It is difficult to give any definitive guidance on the extent of the firm's duties to its customer, but some general comments can be made[1]. First, the extent of the duty may depend in part upon the nature of the customer concerned because, for example, what is involved in paying 'due regard' will depend upon the circumstances.

1 See **CHAPTER 13**.

3.111 Second, a key question is whether the firm should offer some kind of redress to its customers and, if so, how that should be done. This is discussed in more detail at para **13.57** ff below. For present purposes, it is worth noting that the starting point in considering what, if any, redress the firm should offer to its customers should generally be, first, whether there has been a breach of any rule and second, if so, what consequences that breach has caused for customers, particularly in terms of loss. The firm may well wish to go beyond its strict legal responsibilities, for example, by offering compensation where there is no strict legal duty to do so[1], and the question of whether 'fairness' (within the meaning of Principle 6) requires it to do this must be judged from case to case. Often, this course of action will be appropriate in order to reduce negative publicity, avoid an increased level of complaints and reduce the risk of enforcement action for the original breach[2].

1 There may, conceivably, be circumstances in which the factors referred to mean the firm is not required to go as far as its strict legal responsibilities. However, such circumstances will be rare.
2 For example, *Chase de Vere Financial Services plc final notice (17/12/03)* offered all customers who had invested in products promoted by a misleading direct offer promotion the opportunity to withdraw at no cost.

3.112 Third, a difficult question is whether the firm can use the same sort of defensive strategy which it might want to adopt if it were a defendant to possible civil proceedings, such as not volunteering information and facts which are unhelpful to it unless and until necessary in the legal process. In principle, such action could be regarded as inappropriate to the extent of breaching the Principles, although this would depend upon the circumstances of the case and the nature of the customer concerned. For example, action which may be appropriate in dealing with a customer of equal commercial strength may be viewed rather differently as against a consumer.

What action should the firm consider taking?

3.113 In general terms, when a problem arises which affects customers, the firm needs to take, and to be seen to be taking, steps to look after the interests of those customers, particularly but not solely where consumers are involved.

Precisely what steps need to be taken will depend upon the circumstances, but these will generally include:

- keeping customers informed;

- safeguarding customers' interests, for example, by taking steps to secure assets, to remedy the problem or to ensure that no further losses are suffered; and

- identifying or taking steps to identify what losses have been suffered and either paying compensation or at least reassuring customers that compensation will be paid in due course.

WHAT OTHER INTERNAL ACTION SHOULD THE FIRM TAKE?

3.114   Firms are primarily responsible for managing themselves. It is for the firm to take the steps which it needs to take to deal with all of the issues to which a particular regulatory breach gives rise, and not for the regulator to have to tell the firm what to do. The Regulators will thus want to see not only that the firm has investigated the matter, and that it is dealing appropriately both with its regulator and with any customers affected, but also that it has taken all the appropriate internal steps to address the consequences of the issue[1].

1   The Code of Practice for Approved Persons suggests that these matters are relevant to compliance with the Statements of Principle by those exercising 'significant influence functions' (see para **2.31** ff above). In particular: (a) failing to review the competence, knowledge, skills and performance of staff to assess their suitability to fulfil their duties despite evidence that their performance is unacceptable may indicate a breach of Statement of Principle 5 (see the Handbooks at APER 4.5.9(1)E and 4.5.14G); and (b) failing to take reasonable steps to ensure that procedures and systems of control are reviewed and, if appropriate, improved following the identification of significant breaches may indicate a breach of Statement of Principle 7 (see the Handbooks at APER 4.7.7E and 4.7.13G).

3.115   Taking the appropriate internal steps may require the firm to consider a number of issues, including particularly the following:

- What steps should the firm take to ensure the problem will not recur?

- How should the firm deal with any employees who were involved?

- Should the firm be taking any legal action (against employees or third parties)?

- Should the firm notify its insurers?

3.116   It is the first two of these issues that are of primary interest to the Regulators and these are discussed in detail below. The third, taking legal action, could in some circumstances be of relevance to the Regulators, for example if financial fraud were involved, if customers would be entitled to money which the firm has the right to recover on their behalf, or if legal claims are contemplated which might affect the solvency of the firm. The fourth point, notifying the firm's insurers, particularly its professional indemnity insurers, is an important practical consideration which should not be overlooked[1]. It may also be relevant to the Regulators, particularly if a failure to notify resulted in the firm being unable, because it then had no insurance coverage, to pay compensation to customers[2]. The failure to notify could potentially amount to a failure by the firm to conduct its business with due skill, care and diligence in breach of Principle 2, for which there could be regulatory consequences not only against the firm[3] but also against any individuals involved who were approved persons[4] (or certain other employees of a firm).

1 Particularly if there is a risk of civil claims which may be covered by the firm's indemnity insurance, for example claims for breach of statutory duty, negligence or breach of contract or trust (see **CHAPTER 19**). Firms are prohibited from obtaining insurance that would have the effect of indemnifying them against financial penalties imposed by the Regulators, see the Handbooks at GEN 6. However, insurance may still cover the costs of defending enforcement action and any costs that they may be ordered to pay to the FCA or PRA.

2 This could result in claims being made against the Financial Services Compensation Scheme: see the Handbooks at COMP. The financial resources of the firm, taking into account any insurance cover, is a relevant factor for the FCA in considering whether to take urgent action: see the FCA Enforcement Guide at EG 8.9(5) and see para **16.117** ff below.

3 The consequences of breaching the Principles are discussed at para **2.105** ff above.

4 The individual may have been 'knowingly concerned' in the firm's breach or may have breached a Statement of Principle: see para **2.118** ff above and para **9.15** ff below.

Taking steps to ensure the problem will not recur

3.117   The Regulators are likely to be interested not just in the particular breach that occurred but also more generally in the reasons why it occurred. It will want to see that the firm has considered, and addressed, any specific weaknesses in its systems or controls which allowed the problem to arise and also any more general issues that the problem highlights, such as systems and controls more generally, compliance culture or the need for further employee training on compliance issues[1]. The firm therefore needs to ensure that it thinks about these wider issues and does not focus purely on the specific breach.

1 See for example *Aon Limited final notice (8/1/09)*. Aon was fined for failings in its anti bribery and corruption systems and controls. The FSA stated that the pro-active determination of Aon Ltd's senior management to identify past issues and improve the firm's systems and controls in this area since the discovery of its failings in 2007 was a model of best practice that other firms may wish to adopt.

Why does this matter?

3.118   The firm's response to the regulatory issue may itself be relevant in assessing whether it has appropriate systems and controls in place[1]. On a practical level, if the firm can show, at the time when it reports the problem to the Regulators or shortly thereafter, that it has put a stop to the conduct in question, has assessed whether there are any wider implications and has taken, or is in the process of taking, the necessary steps to address those implications, then this may help to lessen the risk that the problem is elevated from the supervisory relationship to the Regulators' enforcement divisions and thus allow the matter to be addressed informally. The extent to which this is the case will depend upon the nature and seriousness of underlying issue. The key point here is for the firm to show that it is in control, that it is investigating properly and keeping the Regulators fully informed, and that it intends to take whatever action needs to be taken to address the implications of the problem.

1 As noted at para **3.114**, n 1 above, this is also relevant to compliance with Statement of Principle 7 by those exercising 'significant influence' functions.

3.119 Where the problem is referred to a Regulator's enforcement division, the firm's conduct generally following discovery of the problem will be relevant to the decisions, such as whether or not to take formal enforcement action against the firm for the breach[1] and, if so, the extent of the relevant punishment and whether to exercise as a matter of urgency its own-initiative power to vary the firm's permission[2]. The firm does, however, also need to bear in mind that the existence of wider, systemic issues increases the nature and seriousness of the problem in the FCA's eyes[3] and makes it more likely that the FCA will exercise its formal disciplinary or other enforcement powers and that any disciplinary sanction it imposes will be greater.

1 See the FCA Handbook at DEPP 6.2.1(2)(a) and (b)G, and DEPP 6.5A.3(2)(a) and (b)G and see para **8.19** ff below.
2 Or to intervene in an incoming firm. See the FCA Enforcement Guide, EG 8.9(8) and para **16.216** ff below.
3 See, for example, the FCA Handbook at DEPP 6.2.1(1)G.

What steps should the firm take?

3.120 What steps are required to be taken by the firm will depend upon the circumstances. They include:

- preventing the conduct from continuing;

- assessing whether any deficiencies in systems or controls gave rise to or contributed to the problem (or failed to pick up that the problem had occurred), and then remedying those deficiencies;

- considering the position of any employees involved, not only from a disciplinary perspective but also from the perspective of whether they had been properly trained or require further training;

- considering whether the problem highlights any issues regarding the level of oversight and supervision being provided by management, and addressing those issues; and

- considering whether the firm has suitable policies and procedures in place to escalate such matters to the attention of senior management, where appropriate.

Dealing with employees

3.121 It is rare that a regulatory breach occurs without an individual being involved who has taken or failed to take some kind of action, whether

3.121 Steps to take when an issue arises

inadvertently or deliberately. Most cases therefore potentially give rise to questions about the conduct of particular individuals. Whilst it may in some cases be clear that the individual has deliberately flouted the rules, and in other cases it may be equally clear that the error was inadvertent, it may in many cases not be so simple. The issue of whether the firm should support the individual concerned can make dealing with the personnel implications of possible regulatory breaches something of a minefield. Although it is not the purpose of this book to address the employment law issues[1], there are some important issues to consider in the regulatory context. How will the Regulators expect the firm to be approaching these issues? Can the firm wait for the Regulators to investigate and decide on the position of the individual? Or does it need to take some kind of action itself?

1 For a detailed discussion, see *Harvey on Industrial Relations and Employment Law*, Looseleaf, at DI[1351] ff.

3.122 In answering these questions, the following paragraphs will consider:

- why this is important to the Regulators;

- what the firm is required to do; and

- requirements in relation to taking disciplinary action against employees (where the firm decides that such action should be taken).

Why is this important to the Regulators?

3.123 The Regulators expect firms, under Principle 3[1], to take reasonable care to organise and control their affairs responsibly. They expect management to take responsibility for what happens in firms[2]. Also, the Regulators expect firms to review the suitability of those who act for them if something happens to make a fresh look appropriate[3]. Each of these points is illustrative of a general regulatory concern to see that firms take appropriate internal steps to review the activities of their employees and, if appropriate, take disciplinary or other action against them and do not simply wait for the Regulators to take steps or to require the firm to do so. The Regulators may, however, in some circumstances expect to be consulted before the firm takes action[4].

1 Principle 3 of the Principles for Businesses: see para **2.12** above.
2 This is one of the principles of good regulation: see para **1.14** above. It is also reflected directly in the Code of Practice for Approved Persons: see para **3.114**, n 1 above.
3 Handbooks at SYSC 3.2.14G.
4 See para **3.40** ff above. In any event, the Regulators will often need to be notified of the matter under Principle 11: for a case where a firm was fined for not doing so, see *Andrew Richard Holt, Douglas Carr and Nicholson Barber* (24 July 2000, SFA Board Notice 550).

What is the firm required to do?

3.124 Where there is a particular employee involved, one of the Regulators' first questions to the firm is often to ask what the firm intends to do about him or her. This can be a difficult area in practice.

3.125 The starting point is that the firm needs to have taken, or be in the course of taking, appropriate steps to investigate the problem, including, where necessary, the role of particular individuals. This is discussed at para **3.9** ff above, together with various points to consider in investigating and interviewing employees. The firm may initially be able to satisfy the Regulators' enquiries by reassuring the Regulators that such investigations are still underway. Depending upon the situation, it may also be appropriate for the firm to suspend the particular employee or at least remove him from any sensitive positions, pending the outcome of the investigation[1]. The firm plainly needs to have in place terms and conditions of employment that allow it to take appropriate action against its employees[2].

1 In some cases, a firm will consider it more beneficial to keep the employee on the premises at work and put him in an alternative role so as to maintain his co-operation and access to him during the investigation.
2 Such as an express power of suspension, or appointment to an alternative position, pending the outcome of an investigation where breach of any regulatory obligation is alleged or suspected; and an express power to dismiss summarily where the employee breaches a regulatory obligation/ ceases to be fit and proper. Other provisions which will help protect the firm include appropriate restrictive covenants (including, for example, the protection of confidential information) and clear provisions regarding the treatment of bonuses and share options in respect of employees who are dismissed.

3.126 Eventually, though, the firm needs to decide what, if any, disciplinary action to take. This can present difficulties. The firm needs to consider very carefully the nature and seriousness of the disciplinary charges which are merited against the individual. The Regulators may have their own view of the seriousness of the matter. If the firm's action against its employee is too lenient, then it may indicate to the Regulators that the firm does not take the matter sufficiently seriously. If it is too strong, then it may indicate to the Regulators that the firm regards the matter as more serious than the Regulators had anticipated. This could also potentially be used by the Regulators in any regulatory proceedings against the firm in which the seriousness of the matter is a relevant factor[1]. But it may be difficult for the firm to control the outcome of its disciplinary process in the way that this may suggest. If the firm is to have, and be seen to have, a fair and reasonable disciplinary process, then that process will need to be based on a judgement of the merits of the charges against the individual, and not on what the firm wishes to achieve vis-à-vis its regulator.

1 The seriousness of the matter is relevant to most of the FCA's enforcement decisions. Examples include deciding whether or not to take disciplinary action (see the FCA Handbook at DEPP 6.2.1(1)G), whether to impose a fine or a public statement (FCA Handbook at DEPP 6.4.2G), the amount of any fine (FCA Handbook at DEPP 6.5A G) and whether to apply for an injunction (see The FCA Enforcement Guide at EG 10.3).

3.127 Another difficult question is at what point in time the firm must consider whether disciplinary action is merited against its employee. There may in practice be pressure from the Regulators for the firm to undertake its internal disciplinary process before the Regulators conclude their own investigation[1]. As already indicated, there can be a tendency for the Regulators to make reference in disciplinary charges to action already taken by the employer and this may cause

3.127 Steps to take when an issue arises

a concern that action taken by the employer will worsen the employee's position before the Regulator. In some situations, there may be merit in the firm waiting until the regulatory investigation is complete because the Regulators will have access to sources of information external to the firm and additional information may emerge which casts further light on the matter.

1 In principle, the timing ought to be irrelevant to the Regulators, provided that, in appropriate cases, steps have been taken to remove the employee from any sensitive positions. The Regulators should be able to decide whether to bring regulatory disciplinary charges against the employee based on the evidence and then to seek to prove those charges based on that evidence.

3.128 One important question which will apply in all cases where an approved person's employment (or that of certain other employees) is suspended or terminated will be how the firm should notify that fact to the Regulators and the form of the employee's reference. Where an employee ceases to perform a controlled function[1], the firm must notify the FCA and/or PRA[2] within seven business days by submitting a completed Form C[3]. However, if the firm has reasonable grounds for believing that it will submit a qualified Form C, then it has an obligation to notify the FCA and/or PRA of that fact as soon as practicable and ideally within one business day of becoming aware of those facts. A Form C will be qualified[4] if the information it contains:

- relates to the fact that the firm has dismissed, or suspended, the FCA or PRA-approved person from its employment; or

- relates to the resignation by the FCA or PRA-approved person while under investigation by the firm, the FCA, PRA, or any other regulatory body; or

- otherwise reasonably suggests that it may affect the FCA's or PRA's assessment of the FCA or PRA-approved person's fitness and propriety.

Accordingly, the firm will be obliged to disclose a suspected misconduct issue even where the relevant employee has resigned before the issue has been investigated or has been fully understood by the firm. The firm will also have to consider what information it should include in the former employee's reference.

1 Even where the cessation is only intended to be temporary, for example, where the employee has been suspended.
2 Depending upon whether the person is an 'FCA-approved person' and/or a 'PRA-approved person': see further the FCA Handbook at SUP 10A.14 and the PRA Handbook at SUP 10B.12.
3 FCA Handbook at SUP 10A.14.8R and SUP 10A, Annex 6R, and the PRA Handbook at SUP 10B.12.10 and SUP 10B Annex 6R.
4 FCA Handbook at SUP 10A.14.10R and the PRA Handbook at SUP 10B.12.12R.

DOES THE PROBLEM POTENTIALLY GIVE RISE TO CRIMINAL PROCEEDINGS?

3.129 If, in the circumstances, there is a risk that the breach may have involved the commission of criminal offences by the firm or its employees, then the firm's dealings with the Regulators may be more complicated and, in addition, the firm needs to be particularly aware of the potential for conflict between its interests and those of the relevant members of staff.

3.130 We outline here some of the main areas of potential criminal conduct in this context and then briefly consider what steps the firm might consider taking in those circumstances[1].

1 A more detailed discussion of criminal prosecutions, including the practical issues that arise, can be found at **CHAPTER 18** below.

Relevant types of criminal offences

3.131 Areas which potentially give rise to issues about criminal liability include:

- breach of the perimeter;
- unlawful financial promotions[1];
- money laundering[2];
- insider dealing[3];
- bribery;
- fraud;
- misleading statements and practices;
- provision of false or misleading information to the Regulators, an investigator appointed by the Regulators, or the firm's auditor or actuary;
- deliberate destruction of documents; or
- acting in breach of a prohibition order[4].

1 Financial promotions are considered in more detail at para **13.26** ff below.
2 The Proceeds of Crime Act 2002 is considered in more detail at para **3.93**.
3 Insider dealing is considered in more detail at para **17.47** below.
4 The circumstances in which the Regulators may decide to impose a prohibition order are considered at para **9.96** ff below.

3.132 Under the FSMA 2000, s 400, if an offence committed by the firm was committed with the consent or connivance of an officer of the firm, or is attributable to neglect on that officer's part, then the officer (as well as the firm) is guilty of the offence and may be prosecuted and punished accordingly.

Steps to take where criminal offences may be involved

3.133 If the firm suspects that it or one of its employees may have committed a criminal offence, then it will need to consider whether to report that to the Regulators. Under the Regulators' specific notification rules[1], the obligation to report in respect of criminal offences arises only where the firm becomes aware, or has information which reasonably suggests, that a criminal prosecution or conviction may occur. The simple fact that certain actions had occurred which may constitute a criminal offence should not, without more, fall within this. However, the specific notification rules do not supplant the firm's general duties to the Regulators[2] to report matters of which they would expect notice and it cannot therefore be ruled out that the Regulators would expect to be notified, depending upon the circumstances, for example if the matter also had other regulatory implications. The firm must also be open and co-operative with the Regulators in its investigation of the matter[3].

1 See para **3.54** ff above.
2 Principle 11, Principles for Businesses: see para **3.45** ff above.
3 Principle 11: see para **4.25** ff below.

3.134 The firm is not entitled to withhold information from the Regulators on the ground of the privilege against self-incrimination. The privilege applies only in certain respects to information obtained from a witness in interview and to the use of information once obtained[1]. It does not prevent the information from being obtained, nor does it allow the firm to refuse to provide it.

1 It prevents the use of self-incriminating statements in criminal proceedings or proceedings for market abuse. This is discussed at para **5.68** ff below.

3.135 If there is a real risk that an employee will be prosecuted for a criminal offence, then the firm should probably advise the employee that he should consider obtaining independent legal advice[1].

1 This is discussed in more detail at para **3.36** above.

TAKING CARE ABOUT DOCUMENT DESTRUCTION AND CREATION

3.136 As with any other situation which may potentially be contentious, from the time when the firm discovers a potential problem it needs to bear in mind the need to take particular care about the documents it creates and destroys[1].

1 There are no general rules as to what a firm's document retention policy should be (although the Regulators have certain record keeping requirements relating to specific types of records). It will be advisable to adopt, disseminate and implement a consistent policy. Moreover, it will be beneficial to keep a record of where documents have come from, by whom they were created and when they were created.

Document destruction

3.137 Normal document destruction processes, including erasing e-mails and the destruction of tapes of relevant telephone lines, should be stopped immediately. It is important that an appropriately worded notice is disseminated and preserved, so that the firm can later demonstrate that it took appropriate steps to inform the relevant people[1].

1 For an example of a structured document management policy, see the FSA's 'Records Management Policy and Standards – RMPS'.

3.138 Why does this matter? It is a criminal offence[1] for any person who knows or suspects that an investigation is being or is likely to be conducted by the Regulators or the Secretary of State under Pt 11 of the FSMA 2000 to:

- falsify, conceal, destroy or otherwise dispose of a document which he knows or suspects is or would be relevant to such an investigation; or

- cause or permit the falsification, concealment, destruction or disposal of such a document,

unless he shows that he had no intention of concealing facts disclosed by the documents from the investigator.

1 FSMA 2000, s 177(3).

3.139 The offence is potentially very broad. It applies to a person who no more than suspects that an investigation is likely to be conducted, and to documents which the person suspects would be relevant to that investigation. It applies not only to the person who takes the action, but also to any person who causes or permits someone else to do so.

3.140 In addition, if the criminal offence is investigated by another authority, then there are other, parallel offences that may be applicable[1].

1 For example, a similar offence applies in relation to investigations by the Serious Fraud Office: Criminal Justice Act 1987, s 2(16).

3.141 Moreover, on a practical level, if it subsequently appeared that documents had been destroyed after the matter came to the firm's attention, this could cause embarrassment, and suspicion, with the Regulators and the Tribunal, as well as with the court if any legal proceedings were to result. A court could draw negative inferences and, in some cases, may refuse to give the firm the benefit of any doubt or to draw any inference in its favour[1].

1 See Hollander, *Documentary Evidence* (11th edn, 2012), from 11.24.

Document creation

3.142 The firm also needs to take care not to create, so far as possible, additional documents which might be prejudicial to it. There are broadly two concerns, namely that:

- such material might be disclosable to the FCA, PRA, or indeed to other regulators, in the context of any regulatory investigation which ensues[1]; and

- the material, either in the Regulators' hands or in the firm's hands, might be disclosable to third parties who might bring legal proceedings against the firm arising from the problem[2].

1 The extent of the information that the Regulators, or an investigator appointed by either, can require to be produced is discussed in **Chapter 4** below.
2 The risks of disclosure of material are discussed in detail at para **4.145** ff below.

3.143 In order to illustrate this, it may be helpful to explain what sorts of documents are likely to cause concern. The firm will of course have created documents in the course of its business which relate to the problem, for example records of transactions, records of checks carried out, and internal memos and e-mails created during the ordinary course of business. Those documents will contain the primary facts relating to the problem. They will form the basis for

3.143 Steps to take when an issue arises

the Regulators' investigation and any enforcement action, and may also form the basis for any legal claim brought by any third party. In general, there is no question of withholding them[1].

1 There are certain categories of documents which the Regulators cannot require to be disclosed to them, namely documents protected by legal professional privilege and, in some circumstances, documents in relation to which the firm owes a banker's duty of confidence: see para **5.55** ff below.

3.144 The concern therefore primarily arises in relation to documents that the firm creates after the problem has arisen. Examples include:

- material produced in order to assist the Regulators, for example explanations of the firm's procedures, schedules of likely investor losses, and so on. There may be some difficult tensions between seeking to assist the Regulators in this way and trying to ensure that the firm does not produce material that would expose it to claims from third parties;

- reports containing opinions or conclusions, even provisional ones, as to the reasons for problems, responsibility for those problems and how to rectify them; and

- notes of early meetings with potential witnesses, particularly where the full scope of the problem was still unknown and/or people had not yet had the opportunity to refresh their memories from the documents.

3.145 However, as indicated, certain types of documents may be protected from disclosure, particularly those which are legally privileged. If it is necessary to produce any material, then consideration should be given as to whether it should be structured in such a way as to try to ensure that the material is protected. Simply copying a document to a lawyer is unlikely to be sufficient[1].

1 For a more detailed discussion, see para **4.153** ff below.

3.146 Whatever the extent to which a document is perceived as harmless at the time it is written, it is impossible to predict all the situations in which it could come to be scrutinised and with hindsight the firm may wish it had not been produced. Whilst in some situations it may be necessary to produce material of this nature, in many situations it is not, and it should be avoided if possible.

3.147 Documents which may need to be disclosed can be produced in many ways. They include not only physical documents but also e-mails which, on many systems, are stored even when deleted and thus capable of retrieval, and telephone calls on taped lines. All methods of document creation should be avoided, even to the extent of staff being warned to avoid discussing the problem on taped lines[1].

1 Accordingly, staff should be educated as to the risks of document creation. When documents are created, those creating them should remember that they may be provided to the Regulators or used in court and draft accordingly. Similarly, communications that are intended to be privileged should, where possible, be kept separate from other communications so that there is no risk that they are inadvertently disclosed. Care should also be taken that they are not distributed to an unnecessarily wide range of parties, particularly (without checking carefully) to those jurisdictions where the rules of document production and legal privilege may be very different.

3.148   Finally, firms need to bear in mind that the risk of being required to disclose material should not be assessed purely in the UK context. If overseas regulators, customers or market counterparties are involved, then there may be similar considerations in other jurisdictions and the types of material that must be disclosed and rules of legal privilege may be very different in those other jurisdictions.

Chapter 4   FCA and PRA powers of information gathering

INTRODUCTION

A brief overview

4.1   This chapter outlines the powers of the FCA and PRA to gather information in the event that a potential regulatory issue is identified. The Regulators share many of the same powers to gather information on a formal or informal basis and to conduct investigations in respect of a firm. The FCA has set out guidance on the use of its information gathering powers in the FCA Enforcement Guide at EG 3. There is no equivalent Enforcement Guide for the PRA, although it is likely that the PRA will take into account similar considerations to those set out in EG 3 of the FCA's enforcement guide in the FCA Handbook at SUP 2[1].

---

1   The provisions of SUP 2 are likely to be incorporated into the PRA's own Rulebook as it is developed with the addition of provisions requiring firms to co-operate with and provide reasonable assistance to the PRA: see Bank of England and PRA Consultation Paper C 2/14 'The PRA Rulebook'.

4.2   As explained in **CHAPTER 1**, it is likely that the FCA will take the lead in the majority of information requests and investigations. Even when a decision is taken by the PRA to make an information request or commence an investigation, the PRA may choose to outsource the investigation to independent advisors or to FCA enforcement staff, who have greater experience in these areas. This chapter therefore focuses principally on the FCA's information gathering powers. The information gathering powers exercisable by the PRA only are outlined in para **4.110** below.

4.3   Potential issues can come to the FCA's attention in a variety of ways. These include reporting by firms, enquiries from other regulators, complaints or enquiries from customers, reports or issues relating to other firms, whistleblowing by actuaries or auditors or from the FCA's own enquiries or monitoring visits to the firm[1]. As seen in **CHAPTER 3** above, if the FCA is not already aware of a potential problem which comes to light, then the firm may have to report the matter to it.

1 See FCA Enforcement Guide at EG 2.17.

4.4 If the FCA wishes to gain a deeper understanding of a problem, it has a variety of powers it can use to obtain information. Each power is exercisable in specific situations, allowing certain categories of material to be obtained from certain people. Broadly, four forms of power exist. First, the FCA can use its informal (ie non-statutory) powers to require firms to provide information to it. Second, in some circumstances, the FCA can exercise its formal (ie statutory) powers to require information to be provided to it. Third, the FCA has formal powers enabling it to initiate an investigation by appointing a formal investigator who conducts an investigation and reports to it. Fourth, the FCA has formal powers to require a firm to commission a report by a skilled person or to require a firm to appoint a skilled person to collect or update information. This chapter addresses the first and second of these forms of power. The FCA's powers of investigation are outlined in **CHAPTER 5**. The FCA's powers to require a firm to commission a report by a skilled person or to require a firm to appoint a skilled person to collect or update information are outlined in **CHAPTER 6**. The powers exercisable by the PRA only are outlined in para **4.110** below.

4.5 The FCA regards all these powers as fact-finding in nature. In other words, the FCA must first obtain the facts relating to a problem and then decide how to act in light of those facts. The FCA's information gathering and investigation powers are therefore central to the exercise of all of its enforcement functions[1].

1 'Making use of the information we gather, from a wide variety of sources, we will identify risks sooner and tolerate lower levels of risk. This means we will step in earlier, and act faster, when we identify problems that could harm consumers or the integrity of the market': Martin Wheatley, FCA Chief Executive-Designate in 'Journey to the FCA', October 2012.

4.6 Four principles underpin the FCA's approach to enforcement[1]. First, the FCA expects to maintain an open and co-operative relationship with firms. Second, it will exercise its powers in a manner that is transparent, proportionate, responsive to the issue in question and consistent with its publicly stated policies. Third, the FCA will seek to ensure the fair treatment of those involved in any particular case. Fourth, it will aim to change the behaviour of those who are the subject of its actions, so as to deter future non-compliance by others, to eliminate any financial gain or benefit arising from non-compliance and, where appropriate, to remedy any harm caused by the non-compliance. Whether the firm can challenge the FCA if it fails to act in accordance with these policies will be discussed in **CHAPTER 21** below. At para **4.223** ff below, the use the FCA can make of the information it obtains will be discussed.

1 These principles are set out in the FCA Enforcement Guide at EG 2.2 and mirror the four principles which underpinned the approach of the FSA to enforcement. As noted in para **4.1** above, there is no equivalent Enforcement Guide for the PRA. The guidance set out in the FCA Enforcement Guide and outlined in this chapter should therefore be taken to apply to the FCA only.

4.7   The guiding principle of an open and co-operative relationship between firm and regulator[1] drives much of the discussion on how the firm should deal with the FCA once a regulatory problem has arisen. This approach is fundamental to the UK regulatory regime, has advantages for the firm as well as the FCA, and needs to be borne in mind throughout.

1 The Handbooks, Principle 11, Principles for Businesses: see paras **2.12** above and **4.24** ff, **4.50** and **4.133** below.

INFORMATION GATHERING POWERS

The range of powers available

4.8   The following paragraphs outline the formal and informal powers available to the Regulators to require the provision of information:

- the informal power to obtain information from firms by requesting their co-operation and assistance (see para **4.24** ff);

- the formal power to make a request for information from firms (see para **4.68** ff); and

- the power to obtain a search warrant to search and seize documents (see paras **4.88** ff below).

4.9   These powers are also exercisable by the PRA.

4.10   The range of information gathering powers exercisable by the Regulators are:

Informal powers (exercisable by both Regulators):

Principle 11	to require firms to co-operate under Principle 11, without resorting to the use of the Regulators' formal powers;
The Supervision rules	powers under the Supervision rules to require specific types of co-operation and assistance from firms;
Statement of Principle 4	to require approved persons to co-operate;

The formal information gathering powers (exercisable by both Regulators):

FSMA 2000, s 165	to require firms, and certain others, to provide information in relation to any matter relevant to the exercise of the Regulators' formal functions;
FSMA 2000, s 166	to require a firm to commission a report by a skilled person (this is addressed in **CHAPTER 6**);

4.10 FCA and PRA powers of information gathering

FSMA 2000, s 166A	where a firm has contravened a regulatory requirement to collect and keep up to date information, to require the firm to appoint, or the Regulator itself to appoint, a skilled person to collect or update information (this is addressed in **CHAPTER 6**);
FSMA 2000, s 169	to require the provision of information under the FSMA 2000, s 165 or conduct an investigation at the request of an overseas regulator (this is addressed in **CHAPTER 5**);
FSMA 2000, s 176	to obtain a warrant to enter premises to search and seize documents and information; and

The PRA's formal information gathering powers (exercisable only by the PRA)

FSMA 2000, s 165A	to require firms, and certain others, to provide information in relation to the stability of one or more aspects of the UK financial system.

4.11 In addition, the FCA has various other information gathering powers that are exercisable in specific circumstances, for example to:

- require the provision of information[1] (or commence an investigation[2]) in connection with short selling; and

- require the provision of information in connection with various applications made to it[3].

1 FSMA 2000, s 131E and the FCA Enforcement Guide at EG 3.15A and 3.15B.
2 FSMA 2000, s 131FA and the FCA Enforcement Guide at EG 3.15C and 3.15D.
3 See, for example, the FSMA 2000, ss 55U (relating to applications for Part 4A permissions) and 289 (relating to applications for recognition by exchanges). These powers are not reviewed here because they do not arise in the enforcement context. Note that these powers are exercisable by both the FCA and PRA.

4.12 Before each of the formal and informal powers in the above table are explained, the Regulators' policies will first be addressed.

When will the FCA use its formal or informal powers?

4.13 As will be seen, the firm has an obligation to co-operate with, and assist, the FCA under Principle 11[1], which is interpreted broadly by the FCA and the Supervision rules that amplify Principle 11[2]. In many instances this will be sufficient to enable the FCA to obtain the information that it needs without resorting to its formal powers[3].

1 The Handbooks at Principle 11, Principles for Businesses. For a detailed discussion of the obligation to co-operate under Principle 11, see para **4.24** ff below.
2 See para **4.41** ff below.
3 See the Handbooks at SUP 2.1.6.

4.14   The FCA therefore usually only needs to use its formal powers where this relationship breaks down, where the nature and seriousness of the matter is such that it should not be handled within the informal context or, alternatively, where there are other particular circumstances that require the use of the FCA's formal powers. Thus, although the FCA has a wide range of formal information gathering and investigation powers under the FSMA 2000, it will often be able to address any issues without the need to resort to those powers.

4.15   The FCA Handbook contains limited guidance as to when the FCA will use its formal as opposed to its informal powers. The FCA's starting point when determining whether to use its formal or informal powers is that if information received by it raises a regulatory concern, it may need to make further enquiries. The nature of those enquiries depends upon the nature and seriousness of its concerns and upon the attitude of the firm or individual concerned.

4.16   The types of matters that may give rise to further enquiries could include any matter concerning a firm's business and relate to the FCA's performance of its statutory functions.

4.17   In some instances the FCA may exercise its formal or informal powers or carry out an investigation where the matter has been referred to it by another regulator, but that regulator has no powers over the parties concerned. Equally, the FCA may exercise its formal or informal powers or conduct investigations in parallel with other authorities, or, if it considers that another authority is better placed to take action, the FCA may refer certain issues to that other authority for consideration.

How the FCA's policy on the use of its powers is implemented in practice

4.18   A number of points may be made in respect of how the FCA determines when to use its formal powers in practice.

4.19   First, the FCA has made clear that many issues can appropriately be addressed without the need for formal disciplinary or other enforcement action, but within the relationship that exists between the firm and its supervisors. Where this happens, it is unlikely that the FCA will need to use its formal powers[1]. Some cases, on the other hand, will be sufficiently serious so as to require the conduct of an effective and thorough investigation with the FCA using its formal powers[2].

1 Where they are to be used, the power used will often be that of requiring the firm to commission a report: see the FCA Enforcement Guide at EG 3.4 and **CHAPTER 6** below.

4.19 FCA and PRA powers of information gathering

2 See the FCA Enforcement Guide at EG 3. In any particular case, the FCA will decide which powers, or combination of powers, are most appropriate to use having regard to all the circumstances: see the FCA Enforcement Guide at EG 3.1.

4.20   Second, it is the FCA's general policy to use its enforcement powers in a manner that is transparent, proportionate and consistent with its publicly stated policies and to seek to ensure the fair treatment of those who are subject to the exercise of its enforcement powers[1]. It is likely that the FCA will adopt the same approach in exercising its information gathering powers. The policy of proportionality, in other words that the exercise of the FCA's information gathering powers should be proportionate to the concerns to which the issue gives rise, is important for firms and, as discussed at **CHAPTER 21**, if the FCA seeks to use its powers disproportionately, then it may be possible for the firm to challenge its actions. The need for fair treatment is also important, but it is unclear that this would, for example, require the FCA to accept assistance tendered voluntarily without resorting to its formal powers.

1 See the FCA Enforcement Guide at EG 2.2(2) and (3) and see para **1.21** ff above.

4.21   Third, the FCA is required by the principles of good regulation[1] to have regard to the need to use its resources in the most efficient and economic way when, among other things, deciding its policy. Whilst this probably does not give firms the right to complain about how the FCA chooses to act in a particular case[2], the FCA should, in general terms, be pressured to act in a cost-effective manner and to allocate its resources according to its policy objectives[3].

1 These are discussed at para **1.14** above.
2 See the discussion at para **1.26** ff above.
3 As discussed at para **8.21** ff below, in deciding when to take enforcement action, the FCA takes account of its wider policy objectives.

4.22   Fourth, the formal powers give rise to serious potential liability for failure to comply. However, the statutory tests that the Regulators need to overcome to exercise their formal powers present a fairly low hurdle. In response to concerns that the formal powers could be used to mount fishing expeditions where there was slim, or no, evidence of wrongdoing, the FSA confirmed that it would not use those powers on a speculative basis[1] and it is expected that the Regulators will take the same approach.

1 See the FSA's Response to Consultation Paper 17 'Financial services regulation: enforcing the new regime', para 92.

Does the PRA have a policy regarding the use of its formal and informal powers?

4.23   As foreshadowed above in this chapter, there is no separate Enforcement Guide in respect of the PRA. However, in the PRA's approach to banking supervision published in April 2013, it is noted that although the PRA will in the first instance co-operate with firms in seeking to obtain information, it will not hesitate in using the formal powers of information gathering available to it where it considers them to be an appropriate means of achieving its desired supervisory outcomes[1].

1 See the Bank of England publication 'The Prudential Regulatory Authority's approach to banking supervision' (April 2013) (http://www.bankofengland.co.uk/publications/Documents/praapproach/bankingappr1304.pdf), para 96.

The informal information gathering powers

4.24   Once an issue which raises regulatory concerns comes to the FCA's attention, the FCA is likely, often without using any of its formal powers, to ask the firm to provide it with information about the problem. How should the firm respond to such a request? There are likely to be three main considerations. First, the scope of the firm's obligations to co-operate with the FCA under Principle 11 of the Principles for Businesses and the Supervision rules; second, the obligations of the firm's employees to co-operate with the FCA under Statement of Principle 4 of the Statements of Principle and Code of Practice for Approved Persons; and third, the practical consequences of assisting or refusing to assist the FCA. These are considered in turn below. Finally, the guidance the FCA has provided encouraging firms to share with it any reports commissioned by the firms themselves are reviewed below.

Principle 11

4.25   The firm has a general obligation under Principle 11 of the FCA's Principles for Businesses[1] to co-operate with the FCA[2], the scope of which is the subject of guidance in the FCA Handbook. Note that the same obligation also appears at Principle 11 of the PRA's Principles for Businesses.

1 See the Handbooks at PRIN 2.1.1 and see further para **2.12** above.
2 Note that Principle 11 requires firms to co-operate with the PRA also.

4.26   The FCA's policy, however, is that it will generally use its formal powers to require the production of documents and the provision of information, rather than relying on Principle 11, for reasons of fairness, transparency and efficiency, although this will not always be the case[1]. The FCA has said that it will make it clear to a person whether it requires them to produce information under the FCA's formal powers or whether the provision of information is purely voluntary[2].

1 See the FCA Enforcement Guide at EG 4.8. There are, however, circumstances in which the FCA considers it appropriate to deviate from this standard practice, for example: (i) for suspects in criminal or market abuse investigations, the FCA may prefer to question that person on a voluntary basis, possibly under caution; (ii) in the case of third parties with no professional connection with the financial services industry, such as victims of alleged fraud or misconduct, the FCA will usually seek information voluntarily; and (iii) in some cases where the FCA is asked by overseas regulators to obtain documents on their behalf, the FCA will consider with the overseas regulator the most appropriate method of obtaining evidence for use in their country.
2 See the FCA Enforcement Guide at EG 4.9.

4.27   In addition, the FCA does not rely upon Principle 11 to require firms to provide a great deal of information where it is not conducting a formal investigation. Where the FCA relies upon Principle 11, there may be little option but to co-operate and the maintenance of a close mutual relationship with the FCA may be the most effective way for the firm to have some control over the process. Co-operating with the FCA in an investigation may also be of benefit to the firm if a question later arises of whether (and what) enforcement action should be taken following the investigation, as credit may be given to the firm for its co-operation[1].

1 The FCA has indicated that it will be inclined to give credit to firms and individuals who assist the FCA in conducting its enquiries quickly and efficiently. The FCA will consider each case on its merits and there are no hard and fast rules as to when credit is given; however, there are instances where the FCA has not taken enforcement action in respect of an issue as a result of the firm's or individual's response to the issue: see the section of the FCA's website (www.fca.org.uk) entitled 'The benefits to firms and individuals of cooperating with the FCA'. See further paras **4.55** ff and **8.22** ff below.

4.28   Under Principle 11, a firm is required to deal with the FCA in an open and co-operative manner and must disclose to the FCA appropriately anything relating to the firm of which the FCA would reasonably expect notice[1].

1 The equivalent provision for individuals is set out at Statement of Principle 4 of the Code of Practice for Approved Persons: see the Handbooks at APER 2.1A.3 and para 2.46 ff above. Note that both Principle 11 and Statement of Principle 4 apply in respect of both the FCA and PRA.

4.29   This has two limbs. First, the need to deal with the FCA in an open and co-operative manner; and, second, the requirement to give the FCA notice of matters that arise. The first of these limbs is considered here. The scope of a firm's obligations under the second limb is discussed at para **3.44** ff above.

4.30   The FCA has provided detailed guidance on the co-operation that it expects from firms under Principle 11. Although this guidance appears in the Supervision section of the FCA Handbook[1] and is phrased primarily in the language of supervision, as has been seen, many regulatory issues may be dealt with in that context and, in addition, it applies in the enforcement context as well[2]. Broadly, the FCA expects to rely upon Principle 11 in order to obtain the information that it needs from firms in many situations (although not generally when it is conducting a formal investigation). The FCA considers that Principle 11 sets out the basic degree of co-operation that firms should provide and has attempted to demonstrate to firms the benefits of compliance[3].

1 See the Handbooks at SUP 2.3.
2 See the FCA Enforcement Guide at EG 2.3 and 2.4 and the Handbooks at SUP 2.1.8.
3 See the section of the FCA's website (www.fca.org.uk) entitled 'The benefits to firms and individuals of cooperating with the FCA'. The equivalent provision for individuals is set out at Statement of Principle 4 of the Code of Practice for Approved Persons: see the FCA Handbook at APER 2.1A.3 and see also para **4.47** below.

What information and co-operation can a firm be required to provide?

4.31   The FCA Handbook states that, in complying with Principle 11, the FCA considers that a firm should[1]:

- make itself readily available for meetings with the FCA;

- give the FCA reasonable access to any records, files, tapes or computer systems which are within the firm's possession or control[2] and provide any facilities which the FCA may reasonably request;

- produce to the FCA specified documents, files, tapes, computer data or other material in the firm's possession or control as reasonably requested;

- print information in the firm's possession or control which is held on computer or on microfilm or otherwise convert it into a readily legible document or other record which the FCA may reasonably request;

- permit the FCA to copy documents or other materials on the firm's premises at the firm's reasonable expense and remove such copies and hold them elsewhere or provide any copies as reasonably requested; and

- answer truthfully, fully and promptly all reasonable questions which are put to it by the FCA.

1 See the Handbooks at SUP 2.3.3. Note that the FCA may also make such requests in order to assist other regulators and may pass on information to those other regulators without having notified the firm: see the Handbooks at SUP 2.3.11 and para **5.34** ff below in respect of overseas regulators.
2 Such material may, of course, relate to the firm's customers, employees or market counterparties.

4.32   It should also take reasonable steps to ensure that its employees, agents and appointed representatives, and any other members of its group and their employees and agents, provide the same assistance[1].

1 See the Handbooks at SUP 2.3.4.

4.33   This is subject to the statutory limitations on the documents the FCA can require firms to produce, in particular, documents falling within the statutory test for legal privilege[1]. The FCA has also indicated that it would not normally use Principle 11 to seek information protected by the (rather limited) statutory protection for banking confidentiality in circumstances where this statutory protection would prevent the FCA obtaining the information using its formal powers[2].

1 FSMA 2000, s 413 and see the Handbooks at SUP 2.2.3 and the discussion at para **5.56** below.
2 See the Handbooks at SUP 2.2.3 and see also para **5.60** ff below.

4.34   The FCA can also conduct an investigation by carrying out 'mystery shopping' in relation to a firm, its agents or appointed representatives, approaching them in the role of a potential retail customer, and can record any telephone calls or meetings held. It can do this to establish a firm's normal practices in a way which would not be possible by other means[1].

1 See the Handbooks at SUP 2.4 and see also para **13.26** below. Note that this power is not exercisable by the PRA.

4.35 FCA and PRA powers of information gathering

Can the FCA require information or co-operation to be provided on demand under Principle 11?

4.35 The FCA can seek access to premises without notice, although it has said that this will only be appropriate 'on rare occasions'[1]. No guidance is given as to when this is likely to be appropriate or as to what information or documents the FCA might seek access when conducting such a visit. There is also a specific rule[2] that requires firms to permit the FCA, or its representatives, to have access to their premises with or without notice. Whether the FCA can properly demand immediate assistance will depend upon the circumstances in the particular case, especially given the right to privacy under the ECHR[3]. This is discussed further at para **5.67** below.

1 See the Handbooks at SUP 2.3.2. If a firm considers that there is a possibility that the FCA may exercise this power, it should ensure that its employees (including its receptionists who will be likely to be the first point of contact with the FCA) are instructed on how to deal with such an investigation.
2 See paras **4.39** and **4.41** ff below.
3 If the firm has such a right: see para **5.67** below.

4.36 The FCA may seek assistance in a variety of ways. For example, it may seek to organise a meeting at its offices or elsewhere. Alternatively, it may seek information or documents over the telephone, at meetings, or in writing (including by e-mail)[1]. The FCA may also make a visit to the firm, whether on a regular or sample basis, for a special purpose such as a theme visit, or when it has a particular reason for visiting the firm[2].

1 See the Handbooks at SUP 2.3.1.
2 The Handbooks at SUP 2.3.1 set out that the FCA will need to have access to a firm's documents, personnel and business premises to carry out a visit.

4.37 A theme visit is not a formal investigation into a particular firm, but is a method by which the FCA gathers information on practices in a section of the market, particularly where it has concerns, but has insufficient information to determine whether its concerns warrant some kind of regulatory action, and if so, how it should proceed. Whilst the FCA is not conducting an investigation into a specific firm, firms should be aware that if the FCA concludes that such concerns are substantiated, it may seek to conduct a formal investigation into one of those firms which it visited during a theme visit and may use the information that it gathered. In addition, if the FCA decides to take enforcement action because of the level of its concern following a series of theme visits, it is likely that that action will be against the firms that took part in the theme visit. Theme visits, or similar types of informal industry-wide investigations, have, for example, been conducted into the sale of mortgage endowments, the handling of conflicts of interest and aspects of financial promotion.

4.38 The FCA's guidance confirms that there is little that it cannot ask of a firm, even without exercising its formal powers. The guidance outlined at para **4.30** above is not expressed in mandatory language (the word 'should' is used, instead of 'must'), and therefore it does not strictly seem to be binding[1]. However, it does show the level of co-operation which the FCA expects from firms and, if firms do not comply, then they will be at risk of being found to have breached Principle 11, with the potential consequences outlined at para **4.57** below. Whether a lack of co-operation is sufficient to amount to a breach of Principle 11 will depend upon the circumstances of the particular case[2]. In order for firms to receive credit as part of the disciplinary process, there will have to be 'evidence of further pro-active co-operation'[3]. What may amount to pro-active co-operation is set out at para **8.84** below.

1 See the discussion at para **2.74** ff above.
2 There is a separate question of whether the firm's co-operation with the FCA is sufficient to entitle the firm to 'credit' in any disciplinary process. This is considered at para **8.84** ff below. As will be seen, it will require more than simply providing information so as not to breach Principle 11.
3 See the section of the FCA's website (www.fca.org.uk) entitled 'The benefits to firms and individuals of cooperating with the FCA'.

4.39   The extent of the co-operation which the FCA will expect, including the ability to require access to a firm's premises without notice (despite the fact that the FCA has not given proper guidance as to when such access will be appropriate or as to what information the FCA may seek during such a visit), and the obligation for firms to take reasonable steps to ensure that companies within the same group, or their employees or agents, comply, all add up to a set of powers which can, in practice, be very intrusive. The firm will only have a limited ability to challenge the use of Principle 11 in this way[1].

1 For a discussion of how a firm might challenge the use of the FCA's powers, see para **5.51** ff and **Chapter 21** below.

Co-operation from other parties

4.40   In many instances, the FCA considers it necessary to obtain information from parties other than the person under investigation, for example, its counterparties or advisers. If those parties are regulated firms, they are required to co-operate with the FCA under Principle 11[1]. The FCA also obtains information from other regulatory bodies (both in the UK and elsewhere) and has entered into memoranda of understanding with many such bodies so as to facilitate the exchange of information[2]. The firm under investigation may not know that the FCA has obtained information from these other sources and, indeed, the FCA may seek to prevent parties from disclosing to the firm under investigation that they have received requests for information from the FCA.

1 See para **4.32** ff above. In some cases, where the firm has obtained legal advice upon which it relies or, for example, a report by its lawyers on the matters under investigation, the FCA will ask to see such advice so as to confirm its substance. Legally privileged material should only be provided to the FCA if the firm agrees and whilst, as a matter of law, the firm may be entitled to withhold such material, in practice the firm will in some cases nonetheless wish to provide it to the FCA.
2 For example, the FCA has entered into such memoranda of understanding with HMRC, the Institute of Chartered Accountants in England and Wales, the Institute of Chartered Accountants of Scotland, the Institute of Chartered Accountants in Ireland, the Solicitors Regulation Authority, the Law Society of Northern Ireland, the Law Society of Scotland, the Institute and Faculty of Actuaries and the Association of Chartered Certified Accountants. Where information may be exchanged, the firm should consider whether the exchange of information is permissible and, for example, whether the exchange may contravene provisions of the Human Rights Act 1998 or the Data Protection Act 1998.

4.41   FCA and PRA powers of information gathering

Supervision rules

4.41   In addition, a firm has two specific obligations under the FCA's Supervision rules[1], namely to:

- permit the FCA or its representatives to have access, with or without notice, during reasonable business hours to any of the firm's business premises in relation to the discharge of the FCA's functions under the FSMA 2000 or its obligations under the short selling regulation[2] and to take reasonable steps to ensure that its agents, suppliers under material outsourcing arrangements[3] and appointed representatives give that permission in relation to their premises[4]; and

- take reasonable steps to ensure that each of its suppliers under material outsourcing arrangements deals in an open and co-operative way with the FCA in the discharge of its functions under the FSMA 2000 in relation to the firm[5].

1   See the Handbooks at SUP 2.3.
2   The short selling regulation is Regulation 236/2012 ([2012] OJ L86/1) on short selling and certain aspects of credit default swaps.
3   'Material outsourcing' means outsourcing services of such importance that weakness, or failure, of the services would cast serious doubt upon the firm's continuing satisfaction of the threshold conditions (set out in the FSMA 2000, Sch 6) or compliance with the Principles for Businesses: see the Glossary to the Handbooks.
4   See the Handbooks at SUP 2.3.5.
5   Handbooks at SUP 2.3.7.

4.42   Note that both of these obligations also apply under the PRA's own Supervision rules.

4.43   As will be seen, these obligations are sufficiently broad in scope to allow the FCA to conduct an intrusive investigation into the firm, and the firm has limited ability to object to or challenge the process.

4.44   The two specific obligations contained within the FCA's Supervision rules are different in nature from the guidance as to the application of Principle 11 set out above because they have the status of FCA rules. Hence, a failure to comply would, on the face of it, amount to a regulatory contravention.

4.45   The scope of these two obligations requires comment. First, the FCA has given no guidance as to those circumstances in which it will exercise what potentially can be a very intrusive right to demand immediate access to a firm's premises (although it has said that it will normally expect to give reasonable notice[1]) and the rule itself provides no limitations or conditions as to the right. Nonetheless, the FCA's duties as a public body may impose some limitations as to what action it can take and, as a result, the person concerned may be able to object if the FCA behaves unreasonably. This is discussed further at para **5.65** below.

1   Handbooks at SUP 2.3.6.

4.46   Second, the FCA has said[1] that the obligation relating to material outsourcing arrangements requires the firm, when it appoints or renews the appointment of a supplier under a material outsourcing arrangement, to satisfy itself that the terms of its contract require the supplier to give the FCA access to premises and co-operate with it in the same way as the firm (save that the co-operation the firm is expected to procure from the supplier is similar to that expected of the firm but does not extend to matters outside the scope of the FCA's functions in relation to the firm). The firm must therefore ensure that there are appropriate terms in the relevant outsourcing agreements. But which outsourcing arrangements will be material outsourcing arrangements? The answer may not always be clear. The FCA has said that a supplier under a material outsourcing arrangement is one that supplies services of such importance that weakness, or failure, of the function would cast doubt on the firm's continuing satisfaction of the threshold conditions or compliance with the Principles for Businesses[2]. This is not an easy test to apply and there may be a risk of the question whether a particular contractor was such a supplier being judged with hindsight.

1   Handbooks at SUP 2.3.8–SUP 2.3.9.
2   See the definition of 'material outsourcing' in the Glossary to the Handbooks.

Statement of Principle 4

4.47   Employees of a firm who are approved persons[1] owe a general obligation to the FCA under Statement of Principle 4 of the Statements of Principle and Code of Practice for Approved Persons (the 'Code of Practice')[2] in similar terms to the firm's obligation under Principle 11. Under Statement of Principle 4, an approved person must deal with the FCA and other regulators in an open and co-operative way and must disclose appropriately any information of which the FCA would reasonably expect notice. Note that the same obligation appears under Statement of Principle 4 of the PRA's Statements of Principle and Code of Practice for Approved Persons.

1   For a brief introduction to 'approved persons', see para **2.23** ff above.
2   For an explanation of the Statements of Principle for approved persons and the Code of Practice, see para **2.31** ff above.

4.48   As with Principle 11, there are two limbs to this obligation. First, notifying the FCA or others of relevant matters that come to light (discussed at para **3.67** above). Second, co-operating with the FCA.

4.49   So far as the duty to co-operate with the FCA is concerned, the Code of Practice provides[1] that, in the FCA's view, conduct which does not comply with Statement of Principle 4 includes the failure by an approved person without good reason:

- to inform a regulator of information of which the approved person is aware when questioned by that regulator;

- to attend an interview or answer questions put by a regulator, despite a request or demand being made; or

- to supply a regulator with appropriate documents or information following a request or requirement to do so and within the time limit attaching to the request or requirement.

1 See the Handbooks at APER 4.4.3 and APER 4.4.9.

4.50 This differs from the firm's obligation under Principle 11 in that it specifically envisages the individual being able to claim that a good reason may exist for not co-operating with the FCA. No indication is given as to what may constitute a good reason. In particular, the extent to which an individual may successfully claim that he was simply obeying orders from more senior employees is not clear. However, the obligation is obviously wide and its lack of specificity merely highlights this.

4.51 It is important to recognise the effect of this provision of the Code of Practice. The Code of Practice is of evidential effect only. In other words, failure to comply with this provision tends to indicate that the person's conduct failed to comply with the Statement of Principle, but it is not determinative of that. The failure to comply with the provision of the Code of Practice does not of itself constitute a regulatory breach. In addition, the Code of Practice is not exhaustive of the implications of Statement of Principle 4. Approved persons therefore need to have in mind the broad Statement of Principle, and not focus purely on the specific guidance in the Code of Practice. These issues are discussed in more detail at para **2.35** ff above. The FCA considers that Statement of Principle 4 sets out the minimum degree of co-operation that individuals should provide[1].

1 See the section of the FCA's website entitled 'The benefits to firms and individuals of cooperating with the FCA'. This is the same in relation to the equivalent Principle for firms as stated at para **4.30** above.

4.52 There is in this area scope for divergent interests as between the firm and its employees[1]. When the FCA asks the firm to provide documents or information or to attend a meeting, it will in practice be addressing those requests at particular individuals from the firm, many of whom will be approved persons (or other individuals holding senior management functions). If the firm fails to comply (or instructs the individual not to comply because, for example, it wishes to take a tough stance against its regulator for its own reasons) it could be argued by the FCA that the individual was personally in breach of the Statement of Principle. Whether the individual committed a breach may depend upon whether the FCA regards him as having had 'good reason' for not complying in view of the instructions he received from the firm[2]. There is also a separate question whether, if he did commit a breach, he would be disciplined for that breach. This depends upon the application of the FCA's policy on when it will discipline individuals personally, which broadly is based on personal culpability, and whether it is appropriate in the circumstances for the FCA to take action against the individual[3].

1 In a serious case, this could result in the employee needing to obtain his own legal advice.

2 The effect of the Public Interest Disclosure Act 1998 (discussed at para **4.53** below) may, in certain circumstances, provide an argument that such instructions would not constitute 'good reason' for not reporting to the FCA.

3 This is discussed in detail at para **9.5** ff below.

4.53   If an individual disobeys a firm's instructions and assists the FCA, then the firm needs to be careful not to discipline him or subject him to any detriment as a result of that. Where no ulterior purpose exists for the disclosure[1], the individual is likely to be protected under the Public Interest Disclosure Act 1998[2]. The FCA will regard as a serious matter any evidence that a firm has acted to the detriment of an individual because that individual made a protected disclosure under the Public Interest Disclosure Act 1998 about matters relevant to the functions of the FCA[3]. The FCA has also stated that any such evidence could call into question the fitness and propriety of the firm or relevant members of its staff, and could therefore affect the firm's continuing satisfaction of the threshold conditions or an individual's status as an approved person (or senior person or other employee)[4].

1 *Street v Derbyshire Unemployed Workers' Centre [2004] EWCA Civ 964, [2004] 4 All ER 839.*

2 The FCA is a 'prescribed person' to whom employees may disclose certain types of information with the protection of the Act: see the Public Interest Disclosure (Prescribed Persons) Order 1999, SI 1999/1549 (as amended by the Financial Services Act 2012 (Consequential Amendments and Transitional Provisions) Order 2013, SI 2013/472). Also included on the list are the Director of the Serious Fraud Office, the Information Commissioner and the Treasury. The list does not include the ombudsman (as to which, see **CHAPTER 14** below), the Tribunal (as to which, see **CHAPTER 12** below) or the Complaints Commissioner (as to which, see **CHAPTER 21** below). The types of information which may be disclosed include: (i) that a criminal offence has been committed; and (ii) a failure to comply with a legal obligation: Employment Rights Act 1996, s 43B(1). The FCA has set out guidance on whistleblowing under the Public Interest Disclosure Act 1998 in the FCA Handbook at SYSC 18. See further the discussion at para **3.68** above.

3 See the Handbooks at SYSC 18.2.3.

4 See the Handbooks at SYSC 18.2.3.

Duties of other employees

4.54   Although other employees are not subject to a requirement to co-operate with the regulator, their actions are not entirely clear of regulatory consequences. First, as shown, the firm's own obligation extends to taking reasonable steps to ensure that its employees comply[1]. The firm may therefore be at risk of committing a regulatory breach if the employee does not co-operate with the FCA. At least, the firm may need to consider, and be seen to consider, taking disciplinary action against the individual or requiring him to submit to further training. Second, the individual's conduct could in a serious case have regulatory consequences against him personally because it could impact on the FCA's view if it later came to consider whether he is a fit and proper person[2].

1 See para **4.32** above.

2 One of the relevant considerations would be whether the person was candid and truthful in all his dealings with the regulator and whether he demonstrated a readiness and willingness to comply with the requirements and standards of the regulatory system: see the FCA Handbook at FIT 2.1.3(13).

Practical issues in assisting the Regulators when they exercise their informal powers

4.55 For a variety of reasons outlined below, it will normally be in the firm's interests 'voluntarily' to provide the co-operation and assistance that the Regulator seeks, although in some situations the firm may want the Regulator to impose a formal requirement on it.

4.56 First, as will be seen, the Regulators have wide-ranging formal powers to obtain information from the firm and can reach the decision to exercise those powers without great difficulty. Those powers include interviewing employees, requesting documents, e-mails, electronic records and tapes of telephone lines, requiring the firm to procure auditors' reports, and even approaching the firm's bankers or solicitors for information. But a wide-ranging or unfocused regulatory investigation is likely to require a significant amount of the firm's management's time and to cause a corresponding disruption to its business. The firm will often prefer to provide information informally and to maintain a close and co-operative relationship with the Regulator in order to assist it in focusing its enquiries, thereby minimising unnecessary cost and disruption. In co-operating with a regulator, however, the firm will need to consider carefully any requirements that the Regulator wants to impose on the firm, for example, when the firm interviews its own employees (discussed at para **3.40** ff above). Voluntary co-operation by the firm is also attractive from the Regulators' point of view, since it enables it to use its resources more effectively.

4.57 Second, if the firm does not provide the Regulators with the necessary co-operation and assistance, it risks committing a regulatory breach, with, broadly, the same consequences as discussed at para **3.84** ff above in relation to failing to notify the Regulators of a matter which ought to be reported to the FCA. In addition, if the firm or any person knowingly or recklessly provides false or misleading information to the Regulators in purported compliance with a requirement imposed by or under the FSMA 2000[1], they may commit a criminal offence[2]. This should cover the provision of information under Principle 11 as well[3].

1 Or by the short selling regulation: see the FSMA 2000, s 398(1).
2 FSMA 2000, s 398(1).
3 See para **4.31** ff above for a fuller description of a firm's obligations under Principle 11. In extreme cases, the FCA may seek to cancel a firm's Part 4A permission where it does not comply with its obligations under Principle 11, such as in the FCA's Final Notice 2013 (26/07/13) in which the FCA cancelled the Part 4A permission of the firm in question in response to, amongst other things, the firm's failure to be open and co-operative in its dealings with the FCA and consequently its failure to comply with Principle 11.

4.58 Third, in some situations, there may be reasons why the firm would want to be the subject of a formal investigation or be required formally to provide information, rather than providing information to the Regulators solely under Principle 11. For example, as outlined below, the firm may be concerned about its obligations of confidentiality to other parties. Or there may come a stage when, from the firm's perspective, the (limited) protections that it has in the context of a formal investigation, for example, being notified of its scope, greater legal certainty as to the extent of the powers being exercised against it, and a statutory protection against self-incrimination[1], make it preferable to be subjected to a formal investigation[2].

1 There is no express statutory protection against self-incrimination in relation to statements tendered voluntarily, or pursuant to a request under Principle 11 or Statement of Principle 4. See the FCA Handbook at SUP 2.2.5 and the FCA Enforcement Guide at EG 3.1A and the discussion at para **4.204** ff below.
2 The FCA's policy (discussed at para **4.26** ff above) of generally using its statutory powers to conduct investigations should minimise the frequency of this occurring. However, there are still occasions when the FCA conducts investigations using Principle 11.

4.59   The question of whether Principle 11 will override the firm's obligations of confidentiality requires further comment. The firm is likely to owe duties of confidence to its clients, the precise scope of which will depend on its terms of business or, to the extent they are silent, the terms that the law implies in the particular circumstances of the relationship. Sometimes, it will be clear from the language used in the firm's terms of business that the firm can provide confidential information to the regulator without any formal requirement being imposed on it. In many cases, however, this will not be clear and the question will then arise as to whether the duty will allow the disclosure to be made. A disclosure made under a legal obligation will normally be permitted[1]. It is less clear that a voluntary disclosure to a regulator would be permitted. It is likely that it would[2], although this will depend upon the circumstances.

1 To the extent that the duty of confidence is the banker's duty of confidence (discussed at para **5.60**), that duty does not preclude disclosure of confidential information under compulsion of law: see *Tournier v National Provincial and Union Bank of England [1924] 1 KB 461*. So far as other duties of confidence are concerned, it is likely, although by no means certain, that the scope of the duty would be interpreted so as to permit disclosures required by law (in the present context, although relating to employees rather than customers, see *Re A Company's Application [1989] Ch 477*) or, if not, and therefore the disclosure is potentially in breach, there may be a sufficient public interest to justify the disclosure (see Denning MR in *Initial Services Ltd v Putterill [1967] EWCA Civ J0628-4, [1968] 1 QB 396*). For a discussion of the balance of public interest in the context of banking supervision, see *Price Waterhouse v BCCI Holdings (Luxembourg) SA [1992] BCLC 583* (Millet LJ). The precise answer in any case will depend upon the circumstances.
2 Given the statutory scheme of regulation, and the existence of Principle 11 (see para **2.12** above), most disclosures said to be voluntary could be classed as made under compulsion of law. Even where this does not apply, the points made at para **4.59**, n 2 above about the need to interpret the scope of the duty of confidence in the particular case and in relation to the public interest are relevant.

4.60   One concern will be that taking such a stance could be regarded by the Regulators as a failure to co-operate and therefore a breach of Principle 11. However, it ought to be possible to make clear to the Regulators that the firm would prefer a formal investigation, together with the firm's wish to co-operate within the context of that formal investigation, without unduly risking breaching Principle 11[1].

1 Note that the FCA will not bring disciplinary proceedings against a person for a breach of Principle 11, or any of the other Principles for Businesses, for choosing not to attend a purely voluntary interview or to answer questions at such an interview, although there may be circumstances in which an adverse inference may be drawn from the reluctance of a person to participate in a voluntary interview: see the FCA Enforcement Guide at EG 4.10.

4.61 Finally, there will be a number of practical and mechanical issues to consider when providing material to a Regulator. These are discussed at para **4.109** ff below. They are also relevant in the context of formal investigations.

Firm-commissioned reports

4.62 The FCA has recognised that firms may themselves at times want to commission an internal investigation or report from an external law firm or other advisor for a variety of reasons, for example, for disciplinary purposes, to promote good management or to address operational and risk control issues[1]. The FCA considers that such reports can be helpful for the FCA in circumstances where enforcement action is anticipated or under way[2]. It therefore encourages firms to consider discussing with the FCA whether to commission such a report, and the scope of what any such report should cover, in circumstances where a potential regulatory issue has been identified[3]. The FCA has emphasised that the potential use and benefit of a firm-commissioned report will be greater if the FCA has been involved in discussions around its scope and purpose[4].

1 See the FCA Enforcement Guide at EG 3.17.
2 FCA Enforcement Guide at EG 3.1A and EG 3.18.
3 FCA Enforcement Guide at EG 3.20.
4 FCA Enforcement Guide at EG 3.21.

4.63 The FCA has made clear that work done or commissioned by a firm cannot fetter the FCA's ability to use its statutory powers to gather information and to commence a formal enforcement investigation[1]. A firm-commissioned report may, however, assist the FCA in determining what action to take, or may narrow the scope of the issues in question, which may ultimately reduce the amount of investigative work needed to be carried out by the FCA and the firm[2].

1 FCA Enforcement Guide at EG 3.19.
2 FCA Enforcement Guide at EG 3.19.

4.64 It is not always the case that the FCA will prefer a firm to commission a report before it starts an investigation because this could, in some circumstances, be damaging to an FCA investigation – for example, in criminal investigations where alerting the suspects could have adverse consequences[1] (see the FCA Enforcement Guide at EG 3.23). Also note that the FCA may not want a firm to undertake its own investigation or commission an investigation without agreement on certain aspects, for example how evidence will be obtained and recorded (see, for example, the discussion at paras **3.40** and **3.41** above).

1 FCA Enforcement Guide at EG 3.23.

4.65 The FCA has also made clear that if it is to rely on the firm's report, it expects that the firm should be prepared to provide both the report itself and the underlying material on which the report is based, including notes of any interviews conducted[1]. Where reports or notes are prepared by legal advisors, the firm must carefully consider with its advisors whether the communications may be protected by legal professional privilege (see para **4.153** ff below for

---

a more detailed discussion of legal professional privilege). Although the FCA cannot compel the production of 'protected items' under the FSMA 2000, s 413, its preference would be to receive such materials and it has noted that it is not uncommon for there to be disagreement with firms about the scope of the protection offered for 'protected items'[2].

1 FCA Enforcement Guide at EG 3.26.
2 FCA Enforcement Guide at EG 3.27.

4.66 There may be circumstances in which the FCA would accept an oral briefing rather than a written report. However, the FCA has stated that it considers that the greatest mutual benefit for both the firm and the FCA is most likely to flow from disclosure of the written report itself and any supporting papers[1]. The FCA has made clear that any reluctance by a firm to provide underlying materials may devalue the usefulness of the report and require the FCA to undertake additional enquiries[2].

1 FCA Enforcement Guide at EG 3.27.
2 FCA Enforcement Guide at EG 3.27.

4.67 Any information provided to the FCA is likely to fall within the confidentiality provisions in the FSMA 2000, s 348 (see para **4.224** ff above for a more detailed discussion of the confidentiality provisions)[1]. Further, where a firm is prepared to provide privileged material to the FCA in the context of a firm-commissioned report, the FCA accepts that the firm may wish to limit the waiver of privilege and impose conditions on the use of the materials disclosed[2]. However, the FCA has warned that it will not accept any condition that would purport to restrict its ability to use the information provided in the exercise of its statutory functions[3]. The exercise of such functions means that there is a risk, particularly in circumstances where there may be related criminal proceedings, that the FCA will need to use a firm's privileged documents and that, in certain circumstances, onward disclosure of the documents could occur. Firms should therefore consider carefully with their legal advisors the provision of privileged material.

1 FCA Enforcement Guide at EG 3.30.
2 FCA Enforcement Guide at EG 3.28.
3 FCA Enforcement Guide at EG 3.29.

The formal information gathering powers

4.68 The FCA has formal information gathering powers (also available to the PRA), which allow it to obtain information itself in certain situations without initiating a formal investigation and appointing an investigator. Indeed, as will be seen, the FCA does not even have to suspect that any regulatory breach has been committed in order to exercise these powers. They are simply information gathering powers.

4.69 The powers are:

• the formal power under the FSMA 2000, s 165 to obtain information or documents by notice in writing[1];

4.69 FCA and PRA powers of information gathering

- the formal power under the FSMA 2000, s 166 to require a firm to commission a report by a skilled person[2]. This is addressed in **CHAPTER 6**;

- where a firm has contravened a regulatory requirement to collect and keep up to date information, the formal power under the FSMA 2000, s 166A to require the firm to appoint, or itself appoint, a skilled person to collect or update information. This is also addressed in **CHAPTER 6**[3];

- the formal power under the FSMA 2000, s 169 either to require the provision of information under the FSMA 2000, s 165 or to conduct an investigation, each at the request of an overseas regulator; and

- the power to obtain a warrant to enter and search premises for documents or information with the assistance of the police[4].

1 FSMA 2000, s 165.
2 FSMA 2000, s 166.
3 FSMA 2000, s 166A.
4 FSMA 2000, s 176.

4.70 The above powers are also exercisable by the PRA in respect of dual-regulated firms. The PRA also has an additional power to obtain information or documents relevant to the stability of the UK financial system by notice in writing, which is addressed at para **4.112** below[1].

1 FSMA 2000, s 165A.

4.71 The following paragraphs look at the FCA's power to obtain information or documents by notice in writing, including the circumstances when the relevant power may be exercised, the FCA's policy on when it will be exercised, what information may be sought, the relevant procedure and the practical issues that are likely to arise for firms.

FSMA 2000, s 165

4.72 Under the FSMA 2000, s 165, the FCA has a general information gathering power that applies whether or not a formal investigation is already taking place[1]. This allows the FCA to obtain information or documents relating to any matter, subject to narrow limitations.

1 See also the FCA Enforcement Guide at EG 3.2 and EG 3.3.

4.73 The FCA may, to the extent that it is reasonably required in connection with the exercise of its functions under the FSMA 2000[1], either:

- by notice, in writing, require a firm[2] to provide or produce specified information or documents, or information or documents of a specified description, before the end of such reasonable period as may be specified and at such a place as may be specified[3]; or

- through an officer, member of staff or agent of the FCA, with written authorisation to do so, require a firm to provide or produce without delay[4] specified information or documents or information or documents of a specified description (in which case there will be no requirement for a written notice to be given)[5].

1 FSMA 2000, s 165(4).
2 Or one of the other persons in relation to whom the power can be exercised: see para **4.76** below. As to the manner in which such written notice must be given, see the Financial Services and Markets Act 2000 (Service of Notices) Regulations 2001, SI 2001/1420.
3 FSMA 2000, s 165(1) and (2).
4 This has been taken to mean without unjustified or unreasonable delay.
5 FSMA 2000, s 165(3) and (9) and see the FCA Enforcement Guide at EG 3.3.

4.74   The FCA may require that information is provided in such form as it may reasonably require[1]. It may also require the information or documents to be verified or authenticated in such manner as it may reasonably require[2]. This might include requiring information to be verified on oath in appropriate circumstances.

1 FSMA 2000, s 165(5).
2 FSMA 2000, s 165(6).

4.75   Various ancillary provisions applicable more generally are discussed at para **4.119** ff below.

4.76   The information gathering power set out in the FSMA 2000, s 165 applies primarily in relation to authorised persons[1], but also extends to:

- a person who was at any time, but has ceased to be, an authorised person[2];

- a person 'connected with' an authorised person – that is, broadly, a member of the same group or partnership, a controller of an authorised person or the various types of connected persons listed in the FSMA 2000, Sch 15, Pt I[3];

- a recognised investment exchange[4];

- a person 'connected with' a recognised investment exchange – this has the same meaning as outlined above, namely a member of the same group or partnership, a controller of a recognised investment exchange or the various types of connected persons listed in the FSMA 2000, Sch 15, Pt I[5]; and

- an operator, trustee or depositary of a collective investment scheme recognised under the FSMA 2000, s 272, who is not an authorised person[6].

1 See the definition of 'authorised persons' at the FSMA 2000, s 31.
2 FSMA 2000, s 165(8).
3 FSMA 2000, s 165(7)(a) and (11). Broadly, this covers officers, managers, employees and agents. It specifies different types of person depending upon the precise legal relationship of the authorised person concerned.
4 FSMA 2000, s 165(7)(c).
5 FSMA 2000, s 165(7)(d) and (11). The introduction of a power to obtain documents and information from persons connected with recognised investment exchanges was one of the legislative changes made by the Financial Services Act 2012.
6 FSMA 2000, s 165(7)(b).

4.77   Both the FCA and the PRA may use the information gathering power set out in the FSMA 2000, s 165 to obtain information or documents from authorised persons (including any person who was at any time, but has ceased to be, an authorised person) and persons connected with authorised persons. Only the FCA (and not the PRA), however, may use this power to obtain information or documents from recognised investment exchanges, persons connected with recognised investment exchanges and operators, trustees and depositaries of collective investment schemes[1].

1 FSMA 2000, s 165(7).

4.78 The FCA's power under the FSMA 2000, s 165 is a general one, although mainly confined to firms and those connected with firms. The only criterion for its use is that the information is reasonably required in connection with the FCA's functions under the FSMA 2000[1]. There is no need for any link between the regulatory concern which leads the FCA to seek the information and the firm asked to provide the information. A firm could therefore be asked to provide information where the FCA was concerned about an issue relating to another firm, or even where there was no regulatory concern in an enforcement sense, but rather the information was needed by the FCA in connection with another of its statutory functions.

1 FSMA 2000, s 165(4).

4.79 As indicated above, the power overlaps substantially with Principle 11, but it does have wider repercussions in terms of connected persons and also allows the FCA to require that, for example, information is verified or authenticated; it may be beyond the firm's duty under Principle 11 to do so.

When will the s 165 power be exercised?

4.80 The FCA has made clear that this power can be used to support both its supervisory and enforcement functions[1]. In practice, if the FCA seeks information from an authorised firm, it can probably obtain it pursuant to the firm's general obligations under Principle 11[2]. If the firm is for some reason unwilling to co-operate, then the FCA may need to make a formal requirement under this provision in order to use the sanctions which are available for non-compliance[3]. Indeed, in some situations, the firm may prefer to be subjected to a formal request under this provision[4].

1 See the FCA Enforcement Guide at EG 3.2.
2 Principle 11 extends to requiring firms to take reasonable steps to ensure that certain types of connected people provide information to the FCA: see para **4.32** above and the Handbooks at SUP 2.3.4.
3 In particular, the possibility of having the firm punished for contempt of court (FSMA 2000, s 177(1) and (2) and the FCA Enforcement Guide at EG 4.11) or of obtaining a warrant allowing the police to enter the firm's premises so as to obtain the information (FSMA 2000, s 176 and the FCA Enforcement Guide at EG 4.28). See further para **5.75** ff below.
4 See the discussion at para **4.55** above.

4.81 To the extent that the FCA seeks information from a person who is not an authorised firm, for example, a connected person or a firm that used to be authorised, it may find that the information will not be provided voluntarily, perhaps because the relevant firm is not able legally to provide it, and that the formal power needs to be used.

What information can the FCA require the firm to provide?

4.82   Given the wide meaning of information and documents[1], and the (rather broad) sole criterion that the information or documents be reasonably required by the FCA in connection with its exercise of its functions under the FSMA 2000, there is little that the FCA could not request within the scope of this section[2]. A request could cover any type of document or other record containing information, as well as requiring people to provide information which is not recorded, for example, their recollections or knowledge[3].

1 See para **4.99** ff below.
2 See the exceptions outlined at para **4.105** below.
3 A difficult question in practice is whether this can include a person's opinions: for example, could the FCA successfully ask for a compliance report to be produced regarding a particular issue? It seems doubtful that such a request will fall within this provision, but such a report may be something that the FCA would accordingly seek to request under Principle 11: see para **4.31** above.

4.83   The FCA could also call meetings by requiring information to be provided in a particular form (orally) at a particular time and place. Whether they could interview a person under this provision is less clear[1]. Generally, the difference between a meeting and an interview may be one that is more of emphasis than of substance, although one distinction is that it is not clear whether the FCA could insist upon tape recording a meeting held under this provision. Various practical issues for firms to consider in relation to interviews, as well as the FCA's policy on conducting interviews, are set out at para **4.180** ff below.

1 On the face of it, the provision is broad enough to include an interview. However, (i) the FSMA 2000 specifically refers to 'attending and answering questions' where interviews are envisaged: see, for example, ss 171 to 173, and (ii) the statutory privilege against self-incrimination is not stated to apply to requests under this section: see para **4.207** below.

4.84   There are two types of information which firms cannot be required to produce, namely legally privileged material[1] and, with various exceptions, information which is subject to a banker's duty of confidentiality[2]. In addition, there may be particular grounds for objecting to complying with a particular request. Whether the firm can object and how it might do so, and the consequences of failing to comply, are discussed at para **5.75** ff below.

1 FSMA 2000, s 413 and see para **5.56** ff below. Note that the FSMA 2000 effectively contains its own definition of legal privilege for these purposes.
2 FSMA 2000, s 175(5) and see para **5.60** ff below.

The procedure for making a formal request under the FSMA 2000, s 165

4.85   The procedure for making a formal request under s 165 is a simple one[1]. The FSMA 2000 allows the FCA to impose its requirement by notice in writing. All that the FCA need do, therefore, is to notify the firm or other person in writing[2] of the information or documents that they are required to provide or produce and the time and place of provision or production[3].

1 There is no prescribed procedure as to how the FCA should internally reach the decision as to whether to make a formal request under this provision and the FSMA 2000 does not provide for the person subject to the information request to refer the decision to the Tribunal.
2 As to the manner in which written notices must be given, see the Financial Services and Markets Act 2000 (Service of Notices) Regulations 2001, SI 2001/1420.
3 FSMA 2000, s 165(1), (2) and (10).

4.86 The FCA may also require information or documents to be provided under s 165 without delay and without giving any written notice in certain circumstances[1].

1 FSMA 2000, s 165(3) and see para **4.73** above.

FSMA 2000, s 169

4.87 Under the FSMA 2000, s 169, the FCA may also exercise the information gathering power under s 165[1], or appoint an investigator to investigate any matter[2], at the request of an overseas regulator. This power is also exercisable by the PRA. The use of formal information gathering and investigative powers at the request of an overseas regulator is addressed in more detail in **CHAPTER 5**.

1 FSMA 2000, s 169(1)(a). Note that it is not clear whether the exercise of the FCA's information gathering power under the FSMA 2000, s 165 at the request of an overseas regulator would always fulfil the criterion under the FSMA 2000 that the information is reasonably required in connection with the exercise of the FCA's functions under the FSMA 2000 (see para **5.17** below for further detail on this criterion).
2 FSMA 2000, s 169(1)(b).

FSMA 2000, s 176

4.88 Under the FSMA 2000, s 176 the Regulators or an investigator appointed by the PRA or FCA can apply to a magistrate for a warrant to enter and search premises for the purpose of gathering evidence. The warrant can only be executed with the attendance and under the supervision of the police. This procedure is often referred to as a 'dawn raid', although a warrant can be executed at any time of day or night. Dawn raids are often associated with criminal prosecutions, partly because of the need for the Regulators to obtain the assistance of the police, but the Regulators can and will use this power in a wider range of cases, not just when a criminal offence is suspected (see para **4.92** ff below).

4.89 A warrant can authorise a police officer:

- to enter the premises specified in the warrant[1];

- to search the premises and take possession of any documents or information of the kind for which the warrant was issued or take any other steps that may appear to be necessary for preserving them or preventing interference with them[2];

- to take copies of or extracts from such documents or information[3];

- to require any person on the premises to provide an explanation of documents or information of the relevant kind or to state where it may be found[4]; and

- to use such force as may be reasonably necessary[5].

1 FSMA 2000, s 176(5)(a).
2 FSMA 2000, s 176(5)(b).
3 FSMA 2000, s 176(5)(c).
4 FSMA 2000, s 176(5)(d).
5 FSMA 2000, s 176(5)(e).

4.90 Employees of a Regulator (or an investigator appointed under the FSMA 2000, ss 167–168 (explained in **CHAPTER 5**) can exercise the same powers pursuant to the warrant provided that they are accompanied by, and under, the supervision of the police officer authorised in the warrant.

4.91 A brief outline follows of when search and seizure warrants may be used by the Regulators, certain aspects of a search, how a firm can challenge those executing the warrant and some practical guidance for firms.

When will the Regulators use their s 176 powers?

4.92 The Regulators can give evidence that one of three sets of conditions have been met to apply for a search warrant.

4.93 The first[1] is where:

- a person on whom an information requirement (explained above) has been imposed has failed (wholly or in part) to comply with it; and

- that documents or information required are on the premises specified in the warrant.

1 FSMA 2000, s 176(2).

4.94 The second[1] is where:

- the premises specified in the warrant are premises of an authorised person or an appointed representative;

- there are on the premises documents or information in relation to which an information requirement could be imposed; and

- if such a requirement were to be imposed it would not be complied with or the documents or information would be removed, tampered with or destroyed.

1 FSMA 2000, s 176(3).

4.95 The third[1] is:

- an offence of insider dealing, market manipulation or various offences in the FSMA 2000, for which the maximum sentence on conviction on indictment is two years or more, has been (or is being) committed by any person;

- there are on the premises specified in the warrant documents or information relevant to whether that offence has been (or is being) committed;

- there are on the premises documents or information in relation to which an information requirement could be imposed; and

- if such a requirement were to be imposed it would not be complied with or the documents or information would be removed, tampered with or destroyed.

1 FSMA 2000, s 176(4).

4.96   An application for a search warrant can be based on any one of these sets of conditions and a search warrant can be obtained as the first stage of an information gathering process or, later on, following an information requirement or the appointment of investigators.

4.97   The use of search warrants is mentioned briefly in FCA guidance[1] but this does not add anything to the statutory provisions and there is no PRA guidance on the use of the FSMA 2000, s 176.

1 FCA Enforcement Guide at EG 4.28–4.29.

4.98   In practice, search warrants are used sparingly and usually in the context of potential market abuse or criminal offences. They are, however, draconian and can cause significant business disruption whilst underway.

What information can the Regulators obtain and what is protected?

4.99   As with the other information gathering powers, the scope of hard copy and electronic documents and information that the Regulators can access is broad (and the definitions are discussed in more detail at paras **4.121** ff below).

4.100   Again, broadly speaking, privileged documents are protected from a search warrant under the FSMA 2000, s 413. In practice, however, it may be more difficult to protect privileged documents from inspection and seizure in the heat of a dawn raid than in response to an information requirement unless external counsel and/or internal legal staff work quickly to identify potential privileged material in the course of the raid.

4.101   There are additional powers for the search team to take material that is privileged or potentially privileged in part if it is impracticable to separate privileged and non-privileged material at the time[1]. This is not a licence to retain privileged material but to remove the material to sift through later, when privileged material can be identified and returned. Use of this 'seize and sift' power is more likely with large volumes of documents, especially electronic, and the firm's team may be able to reduce the volume of this material significantly by practical means of quickly sorting through the material to separate some of the privileged material from the rest.

1 Criminal Justice and Police Act 2001, ss 50–64.

How will the search be conducted?

4.102   The scope of the search is restricted by the terms of the warrant. Beyond this, the requirements and safeguards applicable to police searches under the Police and Criminal Evidence Act 1984, ss 15(5)–(8) and 16(3)–(12) must be observed and Code B of the associated Codes of Practice applies in the same way as for other search warrants executed by the police. So, for example, the search team must consider whether taking copies and images of documents and data is a satisfactory alternative to taking the originals when removal of a large volume of material may impact on the continuity of business[1].

1   Police and Criminal Evidence Act 1984, Code of Practice B, para 7.7.

4.103   It should be noted that a warrant does not authorise the search team to interview employees beyond asking questions about the existence and location of documents. The search team can ask employees to give interviews voluntarily, under caution or using compulsory powers as at other times in the information gathering or investigation process, so the nature of any interview needs to be clarified at the time of a request.

4.104   Within these limitations, the search team has a broad discretion to determine the course and extent of the raid. It may, therefore, be possible for the firm or its legal advisers to influence the order in which locations are searched for documents, electronic documents are copied and employees are asked about documents, which could help to manage logistics of responding to the raid and minimise business disruption.

How can a firm challenge a decision to seize privileged documents or any other aspect of the search?

4.105   A firm can challenge the issue of a search warrant or the conduct of the search team in executing the warrant if they exceed their powers. However, this is unlikely to give the firm an effective remedy because the search will continue even if the firm indicates that it will apply for judicial review.

4.106   What is more likely to be an effective method of challenging particular aspects of the search is informal discussion with the search team as part of an ongoing dialogue about the conduct of the search and documents protected by privilege. For this to have a chance of success it is important for the firm's in-house or external legal advisers to understand the terms of the warrant and discuss the scope of the search at the outset, identify areas where privileged material is most likely to exist and, by shadowing members of the search team, identify documents that are potentially privileged. If the search team proposes to remove or restrict access to documents, equipment or part of the building, the firm or its advisers should explain the potential impact on business continuity and, if possible, suggest an alternative that would give the search team access to the same information in a way that has a lower impact on the business.

4.107 Which documents are covered by privilege is one of the most common points of contention. The search team may bring an independent lawyer with them to determine disputes over privilege there and then or, if they cannot be determined at the time, to keep the documents over which privilege is claimed separate from other documents to determine issues of privilege after the search.

Practical guidance for firms

4.108 Many firms will have procedures and guidelines in place for reception, security and legal/compliance staff, and training for the relevant staff in place in advance of a dawn raid, however, it will be how the situation is managed on the day that will determine how well the firm mitigates the effects and potential disruption to its business.

4.109 Here, some practical suggestions for handling a dawn raid are listed, but this guidance is by no means exhaustive.

- **Check the warrant:** It is important to check the terms of a warrant carefully and take a copy of it for reference. Simple checks could identify a flaw in the warrant that would prevent its immediate use, for example, check the date of issue[1], that the authorised person matches the identity of the person at the premises, and that the correct name for the corporate entity and address of the premises are stated in or encompassed by the warrant. Other information, such as the statutory provisions under which the warrant is made will inform the firm and its legal advisors of the scope of the powers that can be used in executing the warrant. Here it is assumed that the warrant has been obtained by the PRA or FCA under the FSMA 2000, s 176 but other authorities, such as the Serious Fraud Office, and UK and European competition authorities can also obtain search warrants. The description of the documents and information sought will assist in-house and external counsel in assessing the limits of the search and potentially the underlying issues that are being investigated.

- **Assemble a team:** It is important to quickly assemble a legal team at least as large as the search team executing the warrant. The firm's legal team will need to shadow each member of the search team. The firm's reception or security staff should keep the search team in reception until a person from the firm arrives to co-ordinate the firm's response to the raid (the firm's co-ordinator). The search team will usually wait for a short time (for example, 20 or 30 minutes) for the firm's co-ordinator and the rest of the team unless there is a need for urgency. Even if the search team will not wait any longer and reception or security allow the search team into the rest of the building, the search team should be escorted at all times.

- **Suspend document destruction:** The firm will need to suspend its routine destruction of documents, including overwriting of electronic back-ups of electronic data and recordings of telephone calls. This should be done immediately to avoid any allegations of attempts to destroy or conceal documents from the search team, which can constitute a criminal offence[2].

- **Manage internal and external communications:** The firm's co-ordinator should check with the search team co-ordinator before contacting any employees in the business teams targeted by the raid. Providing that the search team co-ordinator does not object, the firm's co-ordinator should contact the head of the team involved and prepare a message for employees within the relevant teams. Employees in those business teams may need to know of the raid and should be asked to co-operate and deal professionally with the search team. Employees may need to be warned not to sign anything without checking with in-house or external counsel first and should be told that they can request legal advice if they are interviewed by a member of the search team. A firm will usually be required to keep a raid confidential whilst it is ongoing, however, it may be advisable to inform any public relations or corporate communications staff so that they are not taken unaware if they are contacted by the media.

- **Keep detailed records of the activities of the search team:** In addition to a copy of the warrant, the firm's co-ordinator should try to establish the purpose of the search and general nature of the issues being investigated from the person executing the warrant. The names and positions of all members of the search team should be noted and the firm's legal team should keep detailed notes of their actions throughout the raid. The firm's team should keep detailed notes of documents reviewed, copied or taken, questions put to employees and answers given. That way, the search team's co-ordinator can be presented with a list to acknowledge the documents taken. The firm should keep a full copy of all documents and data taken or copied, which will help if it comes to preparing the firm's defence or responding to further document requests.

- **Clearly identify privileged material and challenge its inspection/seizure:** The firm's team needs to try to identify potentially privileged documents or their general location near the start of the raid and inform the search team. The firm's team should also try to inspect folders or potential documents in advance of the search team member who they are shadowing to identify additional documents that may be privileged. The firm's co-ordinator should ask the search team co-ordinator to acknowledge the claim of privilege and, if it is not agreed at the time, ask that the relevant documents are put to one side to discuss later or put into a sealed envelope held by the firm's external legal advisers (or independent lawyer, if present) until the dispute over privilege is resolved. The issues become more complex when only part of a document is privileged but it may be possible to agree redaction of privileged material from documents that are otherwise pertinent, and all documents that are not relevant to the search or are wholly privileged should be returned.

- **Warn employees of criminal offences:** Obstructing the lawful exercise of rights under a warrant[3], tipping off third parties of the raid[4] concealing or destroying documents[5] and deliberately or recklessly providing false or misleading information to the search team[6] could all give rise to criminal liability for an individual employee. Therefore, relevant employees should be warned to co-operate with requests provided that they are within the scope of the warrant, provide accurate information and truthful answers to questions and to refrain from sending e-mails or other communications about the raid to colleagues or external parties that could tip off a person who was not otherwise aware of the raid or its nature.

- **Follow up after the raid:** There may be obvious further steps to take following the raid, such as dealing with disputes over privilege, any challenges to the execution of the warrant or conduct of the investigating team. In addition, it is important to collate all of the notes from the firm's team and copies of documents taken or copied by the investigating team to analyse the nature of the raid and whether the firm needs to initiate its own investigation (discussed in **CHAPTERS 3** and **7**. This may be the first time that the firm knows of a potential regulatory breach, or potential market abuse or insider dealing by an employee in which case the firm will want to stay a step ahead of the Regulator in the investigation. If the firm was aware of the potential issue, then it should consider carefully whether it has met its reporting obligations (discussed at paras **3.42** ff above).

1 A warrant must be exercised within three months of issue: see the Police and Criminal Evidence Act 1984, s 16(3).
2 FSMA 2000, s 177(4).
3 FSMA 2000, s 177(6).
4 Proceeds of Crime Act 2002, s 342.
5 FSMA 2000, s 165A(2).
6 FSMA 2000, s 165A(3) and (4).

Powers exercisable by the PRA only

FSMA 2000, s 165A

4.110 Under the FSMA 2000, s 165A, the PRA has a specific information-gathering power to obtain information concerning the stability of one or more aspects of the UK financial system, whether or not a formal investigation is taking place[1]. This power is broadly analogous to the Regulators' power under s 165 within a narrower scope but requires greater formalities (discussed further below)[2].

1 FSMA 2000, s 165A(1), (3).
2 See para **4.114** ff.

4.111 The section is applicable only to a defined class of persons or those connected with them, such as for example, a person who is responsible for the management of a relevant investment fund or any person providing a service to an authorised person[1].

1 FSMA 2000, s 165A(2).

4.112 The PRA may, to the extent that it is, or might be, relevant to the stability of one or more aspects of the UK financial system, serve a notice on a service provider or a person connected with a service provider to provide information or documents that the PRA considers are, or might be, relevant to the stability of one or more aspects of the UK financial system, if it considers that either:

- the way in which the service (or any part of it) is being provided; or

- failure to provide the service (or any part of it)

poses, or would be likely to pose, a serious threat to the stability of the UK financial system[1].

1   FSMA 2000, s 165A(3) and (4).

4.113   Time limits, the form of information provided and provisions regarding the verification of certain information are the same as those contained in the FSMA 2000, s 165[1].

1   See para **4.72** ff above and the FSMA 2000, s 165A(5), (6) and (7).

4.114   The procedure for making a formal request under the FSMA 2000, s 165A is more complicated than the procedure in respect of s 165. The FSMA 2000 requires that the PRA serve a warning notice upon the person before exercise of its s 165A power[1]. Such warning notice must contain the reasons for which the PRA intends to exercise its s 165A power and specify a reasonable period within which the recipient can make representations to the PRA[2]. The PRA must then decide within a reasonable period whether it wishes to exercise its s 165A power[3].

1   FSMA 2000, s 165B(1).
2   FSMA 2000, s 165B(2).
3   FSMA 2000, s 165B(3).

4.115   The PRA may also require information or documents to be provided under the FSMA 2000, s 165A without delay and without giving any warning notice under s 165B(1) in certain circumstances, although it cannot dispense with the requirement to give a written notice if exercising its power under s 165A[1].

1   FSMA 2000, s 165B(4).

4.116   If the PRA issues a notice under the FSMA 2000, s 165A, the notice must contain reasons for the exercise of its power and the PRA must accordingly prepare a statement of policy with respect to the exercise of that power that has been approved by HM Treasury[1].

1   FSMA 2000, s 165B(5), (6) and (7).

4.117   In practice it is likely that persons served with a warning notice will co-operate with the PRA and provide it with the information sought without the need for the PRA to issue a formal s 165A notice.

PRACTICAL GUIDANCE FOR FIRMS DEALING WITH THE FCA

4.118   The following paragraphs review:

- certain general points applicable to all formal requests for information from the FCA (or PRA); and

- guidance for firms in dealing with a formal information request.

4.119 FCA and PRA powers of information gathering

General points applicable to all formal information requests

4.119 The FSMA 2000 and the FCA Handbook contain various ancillary provisions applicable to all of the formal information gathering powers outlined at para **4.68** ff above, as well as the investigation powers considered in **CHAPTER 5**. The ancillary provisions provide practical guidance for firms when dealing with information requests and investigations and are as follows:

- the meaning of 'documents' and 'information';
- requiring copies or explanations of documents;
- requiring an explanation of where a document is located;
- documents in the possession of third parties;
- the effect on liens;
- documents that need not be provided;
- in respect of information requests from the FCA, the timeframe within which a firm must provide information and documents; and
- for how long the FCA may retain documents that have been produced to it.

4.120 Each of these issues is considered in turn below, followed by a brief discussion of FCA interviews. The detailed analysis of the scope of the information gathering and investigation powers needs to be read against these ancillary provisions.

The meaning of documents and information

4.121 The FSMA 2000 contains many references to 'documents' and 'information'. 'Document' includes information recorded in any form and, in relation to information recorded otherwise than in legible form, references to its production include references to producing a copy of the information in legible form or in a form from which it can readily be produced in visible and legible form[1]. In other words, 'document' includes information held electronically, including e-mails or other electronic material, information stored on microfiche and tapes, for example, of telephone calls. If asked to produce information which is stored electronically or, for example, stored on microfiche, the firm must produce the information in legible form.

1 FSMA 2000, s 417(1).

4.122 The FSMA 2000 provides no definition of 'information'. It ought to follow from the definition of 'documents' that 'information' means information not recorded in any form. In other words, it would include a person's knowledge.

Copies or explanations of documents

4.123 Where a document is produced in response to a requirement, the person to whom it is produced may take copies or extracts or require the person producing it, or any relevant person, to provide an explanation of it[1]. Notably, this is not confined to the person producing the document but allows the FCA (or the PRA or an investigator) to ask a different person[2] for an explanation of it.

1 FSMA 2000, s 175(2).
2 The categories of 'relevant person' who can be required to provide an explanation will, broadly, be employees, directors (including proposed directors), controllers, auditors, accountants, actuaries and lawyers (or persons who formerly held these positions): see the FSMA 2000, s 175(7). In most cases, the explanation will be required from an employee at interview.

Location of documents not produced

4.124 If a person who is required to produce a document fails to do so, he may be required to state, to the best of his knowledge and belief, where the document is located[1].

1 FSMA 2000, s 175(3). This does not apply to 'protected items': as to which, see para **5.56** ff below.

Documents in the possession of third parties

4.125 If the FCA (or the PRA or an investigator) has the power to require a person to produce a document, but it appears that the document is in the possession of a third person, that power may be exercised in relation to the third person[1]. Third parties holding documents, but who are not otherwise within the scope of the information gathering or investigation power used, may therefore nonetheless be required to produce documents.

1 FSMA 2000, s 175(1).

The effect on liens

4.126 If a person claims a lien on a document, its production pursuant to one of the formal information gathering or investigation powers does not affect the lien[1].

1 FSMA 2000, s 175(6).

Exceptions to the requirements to produce information and/or documents

4.127 There are two statutory exceptions to the requirement to produce documents and information. First, a firm cannot be required to produce, disclose or permit the inspection of a 'protected item' which broadly means a legally privileged communication[1]. However, a lawyer can be required to furnish the name and address of his client[2]. Second, there is a restriction on the disclosure of documents in relation to which the person owes a banker's obligation of confidence[3], with certain, fairly wide exceptions. There is no equivalent protection for other forms of business, such as the insurance broker's duties of confidentiality to policyholders.

4.127   FCA and PRA powers of information gathering

1   FSMA 2000, s 413. For a detailed discussion, see para **5.56** ff below. Note that the FSMA 2000
    effectively contains its own definition of legal privilege for these purposes.
2   FSMA 2000, s 175(4). This could, for example, be relevant in a money laundering enquiry.
3   FSMA 2000, s 175(5). For a detailed discussion, see para **5.60** ff below.

4.128   In addition, there may be specific reasons for objecting to the production
of information or documents in the circumstances of the particular case. This is
discussed at para **5.55** ff below.

The timeframe within which a firm must provide information and documents

4.129   The FCA has said that firms should respond to information and
document requests from the FCA in a timely manner, so as to meet any deadlines.
The FCA has stated that it will not usually agree to an extension of time for
complying with a requirement once it a request has been issued[1].

1   See the FCA Enforcement Guide at EG 4.15 and EG 4.16. Note that this guidance appears in
    the FCA Enforcement Guide and therefore applies only to information requests from the FCA,
    although it is suggested that firms should deal with any information requests in a similarly timely
    manner.

Retention of documents by the FCA

4.130   The FCA may retain documents produced to it in the context of a
formal information request or a formal investigation for as long as it considers
necessary for its information gathering or investigation purposes[1]. The original
documents themselves may be retained by the FCA rather than merely copies[2].
In addition, if the FCA reasonably believes that any document(s) may have to
be produced in legal proceedings and might otherwise be unavailable for those
proceedings, it may retain the relevant document(s) until the conclusion of those
legal proceedings[3].

1   FSMA 2000, s 175(2A).
2   FSMA 2000, s 175(2A).
3   FSMA 2000, s 175(2B).

Guidance for firms in dealing with a formal information request

4.131   If the firm is faced with a formal request for information from the FCA
or a formal investigation, or is asked to provide information in the context of
an investigation into another firm, what general approach should it take in its
dealings with the FCA? Are there any steps it can take to ease the process of
providing documents to the FCA (or the PRA or an investigator)? Are there any
risks in preparing additional documents for the FCA? What steps should be taken
before individuals are interviewed? How are interviews conducted? Some of the
practical issues that arise and how the firm might address them are outlined here,
namely:

●   being open and co-operative with the FCA;

- practical steps to take when providing documents;

- the risks of producing material for, or in, an investigation; and

- practical steps to take in relation to interviews.

4.132 In general, when dealing with the FCA in the context of a formal information request or an investigation, the firm needs to be well organised and have a clear view of its position and what it wishes to achieve. It is often sensible to nominate a single point of contact with the FCA, to ensure that all aspects are properly co-ordinated, and to maintain a dialogue. Meetings with the FCA should generally be preceded by an agenda and, where appropriate, a minute agreed with the FCA[1]. As discussed below, the firm will generally wish to co-operate with the FCA, but in a manner consistent with legitimately protecting its position.

1 See *Deakin, Roe, Harrison, Ridings GB and Glenbow Financial Management Ltd v FSA [2005] UKFSM FSM014*, in which it was stated that it would be 'better practice for all concerned' for these steps to be taken in more formal meetings.

The general approach: being open and co-operative with the FCA

4.133 The importance of maintaining an open and co-operative relationship with the FCA, and what this may require of the firm, has been discussed at para **4.55** ff above. A formal information request or the commencement of a formal investigation does not excuse the firm from its obligations under Principle 11 to co-operate with the FCA[1], nor does it necessarily prevent an open and co-operative relationship from continuing. The firm can still co-operate with the FCA within the context of the formal information request or the formal investigation and, as demonstrated by much of the discussion that follows, in most situations it will probably be in the firm's interests to do so[2]. The discussion that follows thus also applies in relation to the PRA and investigators[3].

1 The consequences of non-compliance with Principle 11 are outlined at para **5.82**.
2 The same practical factors as are discussed at para **4.55** ff above will equally apply in the context of a formal information request or formal investigation.
3 See also the discussion in **CHAPTER 6** on the FCA using its statutory powers to obtain information under the FSMA 2000, ss 166 and 166A.

Practical steps to take when providing documents

What documents does the FCA really want?

4.134 When faced with a wide-ranging or unspecific request for documents from the FCA or PRA or an investigator, the first question will often be to ask what documents are really sought. Often, a wide, formal request is issued to ensure that all of the primary documents are captured. It may be that the width of the request is intended as a safety net, that some or much of the documentation it covers is immaterial and that it imposes an unnecessary burden both on the firm and on the FCA. By maintaining a dialogue with the FCA or PRA or an investigator, the firm may be able to agree sensible limits on the categories of documents that are to be provided or, for example, to provide material on a rolling basis in order to lessen the burden on resources.

Reviewing documents to remove those that need not be provided

4.135 Firms will often want to review the material that falls within the FCA's, PRA's or investigator's request before providing it. Why would the firm do this? There are three main considerations.

4.136 First, legally privileged material is generally protected from disclosure to the FCA[1] as well as to third parties in the context of any legal proceedings. But if privileged material is disclosed to the FCA, there is a risk of that material losing the protection as a result and being susceptible to disclosure to a third party who brings legal proceedings against the firm[2]. If the particular document disclosed is part of a chain of documents, then the risk may extend to the whole chain. This is quite apart from the more direct prejudice that the firm could suffer by making available to the FCA sensitive material which it did not need to disclose.

1 The firm cannot be required by the FCA to disclose legally privileged material: see para **5.56** below.
2 The issue is whether the firm has, by providing it to the FCA, waived its legal privilege in the particular material, so that it is no longer protected from disclosure. This is considered in more detail at para **4.153** ff below.

4.137 Second, the firm may owe duties of confidentiality to third parties which are overridden only if the firm is required to provide the relevant information to the FCA[1]. If the firm provides the FCA with information confidential to customers or others which it is not obliged to provide to the FCA, either because the material is outside the strict terms of the FCA's request or because it can properly be withheld, for example because it is covered by an obligation of banking confidence[2], then the firm may expose itself to claims if the third party suffers loss as a result.

1 The nature and extent of the firm's obligations of confidentiality will depend upon the particular circumstances. For example, some confidentiality undertakings allow the voluntary disclosure of information to the FCA, whereas others only allow the disclosure of information when 'required' by the FCA. This is discussed in more detail at paras **4.59** above and **4.160** below.
2 In some situations, the firm may not be required to produce documents which are subject to an obligation of banking confidence: see para **5.60** ff below.

4.138 Third, there is a more practical consideration, namely that the firm may want to know what documents and information it is providing to the FCA (or to the PRA or an investigator). Among other things, this enables the firm to anticipate and therefore deal more effectively with any questions that arise from the material. It also allows witnesses to prepare themselves to answer questions at any interviews[1].

1 This is discussed further at para **4.180** ff below.

4.139 Whether the FCA (or the PRA or an investigator) will allow the firm a timetable for providing the material that will enable it to review the documents may be another matter. Certainly, the first two of the considerations outlined above should be good reason for the firm to ask for sufficient time. There may, however, be other issues putting pressure on the timetable. The firm's best option will normally be to discuss the matter with the FCA (or the PRA or an investigator).

Keeping track of what has been provided

4.140 A practical consideration that is easy to overlook is the need for the firm to keep track of what material it has provided to the FCA (or to the PRA or an investigator). This can be done by indexing and numbering the material and taking copies. This enables the firm to deal more effectively with requests that it receives for explanations or for further material arising from documents that have been provided, and enables witnesses to prepare themselves to answer questions at any interview. It also enables the firm to deal with any dispute that may arise over what material has been provided to the FCA. Finally, it may help the firm to deal with the results of the FCA's investigation if it knows precisely what material has been provided, for example, if the FCA places undue reliance on certain material and ignores other material that would shed a different light on the situation.

Providing tapes of telephone calls, copies of e-mails etc

4.141 Difficult logistical issues may arise when the firm needs to identify the relevant material from a large source, for example locating relevant e-mails and other documents held on a computer system or identifying the relevant telephone calls on tapes. Where material produced over a substantial period needs to be reviewed, significant resources can be required to identify the relevant material, copy it and, so far as telephone calls are concerned, prepare transcripts. The practical considerations outlined above in favour of reviewing material, where possible, before providing it to the FCA, apply equally to the provision of such material. Again, it is often important for the firm to maintain a constructive dialogue with the FCA to ensure that unnecessarily wide requests are minimised and to manage the FCA's expectations on timing.

The extent of any search for material

4.142 In practice, judgements often have to be formed on the extent of the search that is appropriate to identify the material responsive to the FCA's requests. It is difficult to be absolutely sure that all relevant information within the categories requested by the FCA has been identified. This issue arises particularly in relation to electronic information. Typically, an enormous amount of data is stored on a firm's electronic archives; the question is how far the firm needs to go to search its systems in any particular case. Searches for relevant e-mails can be hugely time consuming, involving a combination of data restoration, electronic searching and then physical review; searches of other types of electronic data can be even more challenging. In many cases, it will be appropriate to discuss the difficulties with the FCA and agree a basis upon which to proceed.

4.143   FCA and PRA powers of information gathering

4.143   In deciding how to proceed, issues to be considered include:

- the timeframe for any search;

- the range of data, for example, whether the search should be limited to e-mails or should cover other types of electronic data as well;

- the identities of the individuals by reference to whom searches should be conducted;

- any key words to be used for electronic searching;

- whether the search should include deleted items; and

- overall, the scope and likely cost of undertaking the searches relative to the significance of the matter and the likely result.

Providing disclosure electronically to the FCA

4.144   In many cases, much of the information that the FCA requests will be stored electronically and it may be that providing information to the FCA in electronic form would be simpler and would assist both the firm and the FCA. From the firm's perspective, this may reduce the amount of time needed to produce the relevant material[1] and may also create an electronic database, which could be of considerable benefit if the firm later contests the FCA's charges[2]. From the FCA's perspective, there may be attractions in handling documents electronically, particularly if a large volume of material is involved. The FCA will generally permit electronic disclosure (and in many cases will construct a searchable electronic database itself). However, the precise terms of disclosure must be agreed with the FCA and typically the firm's IT experts should liaise with those at the FCA to agree how this should be done.

1   Although, for the reasons indicated at para **4.135** ff above, it is still advisable to review the material before providing it to the FCA.
2   For example, by responding to a draft investigation report or making representations to the RDC: see **CHAPTER 12** below.

The risks of producing material to the FCA

4.145   As has been highlighted at para **3.142** ff above, firms need to be careful not to produce additional documentary material during the investigation and enforcement process which could be disclosable to third parties in any legal proceedings which might be brought against the firm, or indeed which the firm might wish to bring. The primary concern is to ensure that the firm does not unnecessarily increase its potential exposure to civil claims by third parties by producing material which, if any third party does bring a claim against the firm, will need to be disclosed under the Civil Procedure Rules[1] and is likely to assist the third party in establishing that claim and/or prejudicial to the firm. Equally, it would not wish to produce material which would assist a third party in defeating a claim brought by the firm.

1   Or the rules of any other jurisdiction in which such claims may be brought.

4.146 These concerns relate not so much to the records which the firm creates in the normal course of its business, which will mostly be disclosable in any event, but to any further material produced after the problem came to light, which for example:

- takes a position inconsistent with that which the firm adopts in the legal proceedings;

- indicates how the firm interprets the facts and whether it believes it acted wrongly; or

- assesses what losses were suffered as a result of the firm's errors.

4.147 Why does this matter? If legal proceedings are brought against the firm, it will be for the claimant to prove that the firm's actions amounted to a breach of its duties and that he suffered loss as a result. Documents of this nature can make that task considerably easier or can harm the firm's defence, for example by reducing the credibility of its evidence. Often, a firm will not know the full facts at the outset of the investigation and could therefore wrongly interpret the information initially available to it. Material which may seem relatively harmless, particularly at a time when the firm is focusing on the regulatory aspects of the problem, could thus prejudice the firm's defence to any civil claims subsequently made against it. Equally, if the firm takes proceedings against a third party, they could assist the third party in resisting the claims brought by the firm.

4.148 Since the firm is likely to need to produce material in order to co-operate with its regulator and to respond properly to the investigation process, it is important to understand what material can be required to be disclosed to third parties and whether documents can be produced in a way that will reduce the risk of disclosure. Of course, a copy of the relevant material may be not only in the firm's hands, but also in the FCA's hands and it may be that the third party will try to obtain a copy from the FCA[1]. What are the risks and what are the firm's options? In the following paragraphs[2]:

- first, the basic rules on the disclosure of documents are outlined;

- second, four types of material that can cause particular difficulty are considered, namely:

  - communications with or from compliance officers;

  - communications with the firm's employees;

  - without prejudice communications; and

  - information provided to the FCA (or to the PRA or an investigator);

- third, whether the same material can be obtained by the third party from the FCA is reviewed; and

- finally, some practical steps the firm can take to reduce the risks are outlined.

1 For a further discussion, see para **4.174** ff below.

4.148 FCA and PRA powers of information gathering

2 The discussion that follows relates to English legal proceedings. Documents may also need to be produced in proceedings in other jurisdictions (for example, where the firm is listed in the US) in which case different rules may apply.

The basic rules on the disclosure of documents

4.149 Material that is relevant to a civil legal claim made against or by the firm could be disclosable to the third party, unless in the circumstances the material is protected by the doctrine of legal professional privilege. Precisely what this means requires further explanation.

4.150 The question whether material is disclosable in the context of a particular civil claim depends upon the relevance of the material to the claim. If the firm relies on the document, if the document adversely affects its case, or if it supports or adversely affects the third party's case then, in principle, and subject to the discussion that follows, it falls within the firm's disclosure obligations[1]. In addition, the court can order the disclosure of particular documents or classes of documents that may be relevant[2].

1 See Civil Procedure Rules, Pt 31, r 31.6.
2 See Civil Procedure Rules, Pt 31, r 31.12.

4.151 The fact that a document was created in the context of a regulatory enforcement process does not, by itself, provide grounds for withholding disclosure. It has been argued, in *Kaufmann v Credit Lyonnais Bank*[1], that such documents should be protected under a general category of public interest immunity, as there is a public interest in promoting the candid provision of information between the regulator and the regulated. That argument was rejected because such immunity is not necessary for the proper functioning of the regulatory regime. It is a requirement for firms to be open and co-operative with their regulators and to give disclosure of relevant information. The prospect of subsequent disclosure should not deter firms from meeting such obligations – compliance with the rules being their primary motivation. There is, therefore, no general rule that will protect material that has been produced for, or by, the regulator from being disclosed. This does not preclude a claim of public interest immunity based upon the contents of a particular document.

1 [1995] CLC 300.

4.152 Since no general immunity is likely to apply to such material, the question of whether a particular document will be disclosable will primarily depend[1] upon whether it will be protected from disclosure by the doctrine of legal professional privilege. Whether material will be considered to be legally privileged will depend upon who produced it and for what purpose.

1 As indicated above, there may still be scope for public interest immunity to apply to particular documents: see Civil Procedure Rules, Pt 31, r 31.19.

4.153 Very broadly[1], material will only be protected by the doctrine of legal privilege if it was produced as a confidential communication with a lawyer in his professional capacity and was sent or received for the purposes of seeking or giving legal advice ('legal advice privilege')[2], or was produced for the sole or dominant purpose of ongoing or contemplated legal proceedings ('litigation privilege')[3]. In addition, documents that were properly created on a 'without prejudice' basis are generally speaking protected in the same way[4]. How legal privilege will be likely to apply in four common situations is considered below. Six general points may first, however, be usefully made[5].

1   For a more detailed analysis of legal privilege, see Passmore, *Privilege* (3rd edn, 2013); Matthews and Malek, *Disclosure* (4th edn, 2012) and Hollander, *Documentary Evidence* (11th edn, 2012).

2   In *Three Rivers District Council v Governor and Company of the Bank of England (No 6) [2004] UKHL 48, [2005] 1 AC 610*, the House of Lords approved the decision in *Balabel v Air India [1988] EWCA Civ J0316-8, [1988] 1 Ch 317 at 330*, where Taylor LJ stated that: 'legal advice is not confined to telling the client the law; it must include advice as to what should prudently and sensibly be done in the relevant legal context'. Lord Brown stated at 120 'I would go so far as to state as a general principle that the general process by which a client seeks and obtains his lawyer's assistance in the presentation of his case for the purposes of any formal inquiry – whether concerned with public law or private law issues, whether adversarial or inquisitorial in form, whether held in public or private, whether or not directly affecting his rights or liabilities – attracts legal advice privilege'. The dicta of the law lords suggest that advice given by lawyers to clients in inquiries should be covered by legal advice privilege as long as the advice (even if it does not directly relate to legal matters) is directly related to the lawyer's performance of his professional duty as legal adviser to the client.

3   For proceedings to be contemplated, there must be a 'real likelihood' that they will arise and not a 'mere possibility' or a 'general apprehension' that they will arise for this form of privilege to apply: see *USA v Philip Morris and BAT [2004] EWCA (Civ) 330, [2004] 1 CLC 811* (where tobacco litigation was held to be anticipated but not to be 'reasonably in prospect'). Accordingly, it is not sufficient for future litigation to be more likely than not. The Court of Appeal has held that litigation is contemplated if it is reasonably in prospect or could well give rise to litigation in the future: see *Westminster International BV v Dornoch Ltd [2009] EWCA Civ 1323*.

4   See para **4.147** above.

5   The discussion here is limited to various points that may be particularly relevant. For a more detailed analysis of legal privilege, see the works referred to at n 1 above.

4.154   First, communications that have taken place between a firm or its lawyers and third parties[1], for example in which information was sought from those third parties, are unlikely to be legally privileged unless they were produced for the sole or dominant purpose of ongoing or contemplated legal proceedings[2]. This is an important limitation in practice.

1   Such as skilled persons see para **6.26** ff below. See para **5.26** below for consideration of who will constitute a third party. Presently, in some circumstances, even an employee of the firm may be a third party for this purpose.

2   A report prepared by accountants for a firm's legal adviser is therefore unlikely to be privileged unless litigation is in contemplation: see *Price Waterhouse v BCCI Holdings (Luxembourg) SA [1992] BCLC 583, CA*. Communications with third parties who are purely acting as an agent of the client or of the solicitor and that are produced for the purpose of providing the information may, however, be covered by legal advice privilege and therefore be privileged irrespective of whether any proceedings are contemplated.

4.155   Second, and linked to the above, 'legal advice privilege' will apply if the communication is between the firm's 'lawyers' and their 'client'. Legal advice privilege does not apply to legal advice given by someone other than a member of the legal profession[1]. The definition of client is more problematic. In some instances, it presently is possible that the client will not be the firm as a whole, but only a subdivision of it, such as a committee that has been appointed to deal with the FCA's investigation[2] and therefore, interviews of the firm's employees may not be protected under 'legal advice' privilege (but in appropriate circumstances could be protected under 'litigation privilege'). Firms must therefore consider which employees are likely to constitute the client for these purposes[3]. The nomination of a group of people as the 'client' (for example, in the external lawyer's client care letter) may not be accepted by the court where this is seen as artificially widening the client entity.

1 See *R (on the application of Prudential Plc) v Special Commissioner of Income Tax [2013] UKSC 1, [2013] 2 WLR 325* where legal advice given by accountants in relation to a tax avoidance scheme was not protected by legal advice privilege.

2 See *Three Rivers District Council v Governor and Company of the Bank of England (No 5) [2003] EWCA Civ 474* where the Court of Appeal held that legal advice privilege would not apply to communications with employees of the Bank of England who were simply witnesses. Legal advice privilege was held only to apply to communications with the unit within the Bank that was created to manage the Bank's conduct of the relevant public inquiry. Although the decision of the Court of Appeal was queried before the House of Lords (and, as is especially evident from the dictum of Lord Carswell, was not approved by them), it was not overturned by the House of Lords in *Three Rivers District Council v Governor and Company of the Bank of England (No 6) [2004] UKHL 48, [2005] 1 AC 610*.

3 Accordingly, where there is doubt as to who will be held to be the client, it is better to route all communications with external lawyers through the firm's in-house lawyer.

4.156 Third, the purpose for which the document was produced is critical. Material produced internally to enable the firm to take legal advice may well be privileged[1]. Material produced in the context of the firm's defence to regulatory enforcement proceedings may also be privileged, although this is less clear for reasons discussed below at para **4.159**. But it may be difficult to produce information requested by the FCA during its investigation in a way that is legally privileged, if producing it for the FCA is the main purpose behind the document. Again, this is likely in practice to be a significant limitation on the firm's ability to rely on the doctrine of legal privilege in this context. Material produced for commercial purposes will generally not be legally privileged.

1 Legal advice has been interpreted fairly widely to include all communications within the continuum aimed to keep the solicitor and client informed. However, as is evident from para **4.155** above, the definition of the client may now be difficult to ascertain conclusively. Furthermore, it is questionable whether internal communications within the firm that do not involve a lawyer but which, for example, are aimed at collecting information for submission to a lawyer, would fall within the statutory protection for legal privilege (whatever their status under the general law): see para **5.58** below.

4.157 Fourth, a difficult question yet to be decided by the courts is whether 'litigation privilege' covers material produced for regulatory proceedings in the same way as material produced for legal proceedings in court. To the extent that there is any authority on the answer, it is that proceedings before a tribunal exercising judicial or quasi-judicial functions which are adversarial in nature are 'legal proceedings' for these purposes, but that a purely administrative fact-finding process is not.

4.158 If this is the correct test, it seems clear that the FCA's investigation is not a legal proceeding, and firms should therefore treat with care the production of documents in that context, particularly documents involving third parties[1]. Proceedings before the Tribunal[2] are almost certainly legal proceedings and material produced for the purposes of those proceedings should therefore be privileged, provided it fulfils the other requirements for legal privilege.

1 Such as reports produced by skilled persons: see **CHAPTER 6** below.
2 For a discussion of the Tribunal, and what matters can be referred to it, see **CHAPTER 12** below.

4.159 Whether proceedings before the Regulatory Decisions Committee[1] are legal proceedings is more difficult[2] and produces uncertainty in practice[3]. It should, though, be possible to minimise the risks caused by this uncertainty by ensuring that many documents are protected either by legal advice privilege or by litigation privilege (if they are produced with possible Tribunal proceedings primarily in mind), and other documents may properly be without prejudice and therefore gain similar protection[4].

1 For an explanation, see para **10.25** ff below.
2 The FSMA 2000 indicates that, for some purposes, the issue of a warning notice constitutes 'proceedings' (see, for example, ss 66(5)(b) and 389(3)). Accordingly, the consideration of a case by the Regulatory Decisions Committee may be viewed as quasi-judicial.
3 See para **10.127** ff below.
4 See the discussion at para **4.169** below.

4.160 Fifth, a document that is legally privileged will not necessarily remain privileged forever[1]. The privilege in a document can in principle be waived by the firm and once this has been done it no longer attracts the same protection. The concern is that the provision of a document to one third party, for example the FCA, could cause privilege to be waived generally, thus entirely destroying the protection.

1 Although the basic legal principle is that a document that is privileged remains privileged.

4.161 Where privileged material is to be produced by one party to another within a confidential relationship then, provided that the documents are voluntarily provided for a limited purpose and upon the express basis that privilege is not waived, privilege should still apply as against third parties[1]. Consequently, where material is disclosed to the FCA, there is a good argument that this principle ensures that the material will remain privileged as against any other party, including any third parties who might bring civil claims against the firm. This is because the disclosure to the FCA will have been made within the confines of the confidentiality obligation imposed by the FSMA 2000[2]. Firms should therefore record when communicating with the FCA that, despite the limited disclosure that has taken place to the FCA, any material is disclosed upon the express basis that privilege is not waived.

1 The limited purpose underlying the disclosure of the documents and the express basis by which privilege will not be waived should be made clear when the material is provided to the FCA. See *City of Gotha v Sothebys [1997] EWCA Civ J0619-13, [1998] 1 WLR 114; B v Auckland District Law Society [2003] UKPC 38, [2003] 2 AC 736, PC and Berezovsky v Hine [2011] EWCA Civ 1089.*
2 FSMA 2000, s 348: see para **4.226** ff below. This seems also to have been the government's view: see the Economic Secretary to HM Treasury in Standing Committee (23/11/99) where the Financial Services and Markets Bill was debated. However, whilst this is thought to be the better argument, it is not clear that it will succeed because the FSMA 2000 also allows the FCA

to disseminate information in certain situations, for example to other regulators. It is possible that a court could take the view that the provision of information to the FCA sufficiently impacts on its confidentiality to destroy any privilege. Indeed, the expectation that the information would be disclosed by the regulator was one of the points considered by Arden J to indicate the lack of public interest immunity in *Kaufmann*.

4.162   Sixth, even if the material does remain privileged as against third parties notwithstanding its disclosure to the FCA, the FCA will generally speaking (see para **4.226** ff below) be able to use it in Tribunal or certain court proceedings[1]. If the Tribunal or court hearing is held in public as is likely to be the case, then the information is no longer likely to be confidential and, as a result, privilege will be lost and so the material will not be protected from disclosure[2].

1 The ability to refer in Tribunal or court proceedings to documents that are otherwise protected could also, in certain circumstances, allow the FCA to bypass the statutory confidentiality restrictions outlined at para **4.226** ff below.
2 Publicity during the court process is considered at para **19.12** below. The same question is considered in relation to Tribunal hearings at para **12.37** below.

Types of material that can cause particular difficulty

Communications with or from compliance officers

4.163   Compliance staff are often involved when regulatory problems arise and indeed this is usually part of their normal role. However, the production of documents by compliance officers can cause a number of problems. First, it is important to understand from the outset that documents created by compliance staff in the course of their routine compliance function, even if such staff are legally qualified, are unlikely to be legally privileged[1].

1 But if a legally qualified compliance officer produces a document, the purpose of which is to give legal advice to the firm, then that document may be legally privileged.

4.164   Second, if the compliance department investigates the matter once the problem comes to light, it is likely that neither the documents which they produce in the context of their investigation, for example notes of interviews with other staff, nor their report, will be legally privileged[1]. Such reports and documents can in practice be particularly damaging[2]. If the reason, or one of the reasons[3], for having the compliance department investigate and produce a report is to enable the firm to address the compliance issues arising from the problem, then the investigation is unlikely to be privileged and, as a result, it is unlikely that any material produced will be protected from disclosure. This applies even more so if the purpose of the investigation is to assess the commercial implications of the matter.

1 Subject to the same exception articulated above.
2 See the discussion at para **4.116** above.
3 See *Waugh v British Railways Board [1980] AC 521, HL* in which an accident report was held to have been produced not only in anticipation of litigation but also for the purpose of railway operation and safety. This was held as insufficient for a claim to privilege.

4.165   In order to be privileged, the document must be produced either in response to a request from a legal advisor to enable him to provide legal advice[1] or in relation to existing or contemplated litigation. In either case, there will be issues as to whether the particular document does fall within the scope of, as applicable, legal advice privilege or litigation privilege and the answer will depend very much upon the circumstances. As a practical matter it may assist if it was demonstrable on the face of the report that it was produced for the requisite purpose[2]. Generally, it may assist that a lawyer was instructed before the report was prepared and was involved in determining its parameters and that the report is addressed to him and not to the firm.

1   Such legal advice could be requested from an external or internal lawyer. It could also include legal advice from a compliance officer who is legally qualified provided that the provision of such advice is the main purpose of the investigation. In practice it may be difficult to demonstrate that the purpose of the investigation is to enable the compliance officer to provide legal advice to the firm. Generally, care must be exercised in relying upon legal advice privilege: see *Price Waterhouse v BCCI Holdings (Luxembourg) SA [1992] BCLC 583*. Care must also be taken to ensure that the advice is requested by the 'client': see para **4.155** above.

2   This will not, though, be conclusive: see *Waugh v British Railways Board [1980] AC 521, HL*. Nonetheless, it may be helpful to mark documents 'legally privileged – created to obtain legal advice and for legal proceedings', where appropriate.

Communications between the firm and its employees

4.166   The firm's communications with its employees may also cause difficulties. The decision by the Court of Appeal in the BCCI[1] litigation means that legal advice privilege[2] can only apply to communications between lawyers and those employees within the firm who can be said to be their 'client'[3]. Who will be considered to be the 'client' is uncertain[4]. In practice, this has a significant effect on a firm's ability to collect information from its employees (for example, by interviewing them and making notes of interviews) in a way that is protected from disclosure. Where feasible, it may be advisable to establish in advance who exactly constitutes the client. This ought to be done early on in the process so that those handling the investigation know the scope of the protection from disclosure. It will also be appropriate to consider internal processes for the gathering of information and for the creation of preparatory documents in relation to the investigation so that they will not be disclosable in subsequent litigation.

1   See *Three Rivers District Council v Governor and Company of the Bank of England (No 5) [2003] EWCA Civ 474*.

2   At the investigation stage, 'litigation privilege' is unlikely to apply: see para **4.153** ff above.

3   It is uncertain whether and, if so, how this decision will apply to the 'protected items' regime under the FSMA 2000: see para **5.56** ff below.

4   In *Three Rivers District Council v Governor and Company of the Bank of England (No 5) [2003] EWCA Civ 474*, the Court of Appeal gave no guidelines as to how to decide whether an employee of the firm is the client. See para **4.133**.

4.167   Where communications are held to be privileged, the privilege will be that of the firm and not of the employee[1]. Accordingly it will only be for the firm to decide whether to waive the privilege and disclose the communication, for example, to the FCA. Even if the information may be damaging to the employee, he will be likely to have no general right to prevent its disclosure[2]. The employee, for his part, will be likely to be bound by a duty of confidentiality that may prevent

him from disclosing the privileged communication[3] and may also not be required
to disclose it under the FSMA 2000[4].

1   For a further discussion, see Matthews and Malek, *Disclosure* (4th edn, 2012).
2   This is subject to any specific confidentiality restriction existing in the particular circumstances.
    From an employment law perspective, the firm might consider specifically advising the employee
    that the firm may disclose information provided and may rely on it in disciplinary proceedings:
    see the discussion at para **4.29** above.
3   Note that this is limited in scope. The facts which the employee reports to the firm are unlikely
    of themselves to be legally privileged, although the employee may owe a duty of confidence
    which prevents him from disclosing them to any other party (other than the regulator: see *Re a
    Company's Application [1989] Ch 477*). It is only the communication for the privileged purpose that
    is protected. Note also that the firm's ability to prevent or redress an unauthorised disclosure to
    the FCA may be limited by the Public Interest Disclosure Act 1998: see para **4.53** above.
4   FSMA 2000, s 413 and see the discussion at para **5.56** ff below.

4.168   Additionally, some communications between firm and employee are
in any event not made for a privileged purpose and will not be protected from
disclosure. It is difficult to provide any definitive guidance as to precisely where
the line is drawn. Broadly, in so far as the firm communicates with its employee
as its agent, there ought to be no difficulty. But where the firm and the employee
are in a hostile stance as against one another, communications between them are
unlikely to be privileged. An example is where the firm interviews an employee
for disciplinary purposes, in which case that interview is unlikely to be privileged.
The firm could be required to disclose what was said and any notes of the
interview could also be required to be disclosed.

Without prejudice communications

4.169   The enforcement process may involve settlement discussions between
the firm and the FCA[1] and, separately, the matter may give rise to disputes
between the firm and other parties which the firm wishes to settle. In order to
reach settlements, the firm may wish to provide information to the FCA or, if
relevant, to a third party and/or to make admissions about its conduct. To what
extent can any such material generated be used against the firm subsequently if a
third party seeks to bring civil claims against it[2]? Generally speaking, discussions
that are genuinely[3] aimed at settlement will be treated as 'without prejudice' and
therefore protected as if they are legally privileged, subject to various limitations[4].

1   For details, see para **10.42** ff below.
2   A separate question arises as to whether that material can be used against the firm in any Tribunal
    proceedings (if a settlement is not, ultimately, reached with the FCA). This is considered at para
    12.85 below. Note that without prejudice communications are not protected under the FSMA
    2000 in the same way as legally privileged material: see para **5.56** ff below. Hence, there is
    nothing, on the face of it, to prevent the FCA, the Tribunal or the ombudsman from requiring
    the firm to disclose such material. However, the Enforcement Guide at 5.9 states that: 'The FCA
    would expect to hold any settlement discussions on the basis that neither FCA staff nor the person
    concerned would seek to rely against the other on any admissions or statements made if the
    matter is considered subsequently by the RDC or the Tribunal'.
3   The fact that a document is marked 'without prejudice' does not conclusively or automatically
    render it privileged. A court may seek to ascertain for itself whether the document concerned
    was genuinely a negotiating document: see *Buckinghamshire County Council v Moran [1989] EWCA
    Civ J0213-1, [1990] Ch 623*, and *South Shropshire District Council v Amos [1986] EWCA Civ J0725-5,*

[1986] 1 WLR 1271. However, the rule does not only apply to admissions: 'At a meeting of that sort the discussions between the parties' representatives may contain a mixture of admissions and half-admissions against a party's interest, more or less confident assertions of a party's case, offers, counter-offers, and statements ... about future plans and possibilities' per Robert Walker LJ in *Unilever plc v Proctor and Gamble Co [1999] EWCA Civ J1028-16, [2000] I WLR 2436*.

4 See *Rush & Tompkins Ltd v Greater London Council [1989] 1 AC 1280* and, for the limitations, *Muller v Linsley & Mortimer [1996] PNLR 74, CA* and *Unilever plc v Proctor and Gamble Co [1999] EWCA Civ J1028-16, [2000] I WLR 2436*. For a more general discussion, see Hollander, *Documentary Evidence* (11th edn, 2012).

Information provided to the FCA or the investigator

4.170 Communications between the firm and the FCA or an investigator are not generally legally privileged and, as already discussed[1], are not protected from disclosure by any general class of public interest immunity. In principle, therefore, any material that the firm produces for submission, and actually provides, to the FCA or an investigator may be capable of being required to be disclosed to third parties[2]. Disclosure may also be more likely given that the FCA has indicated that it intends to be increasingly transparent in its processes and it considers disclosure to be key to transparency[3]. The FCA will continue and further the FSA's Code of Practice on Regulatory Transparency (the Code)[4]. The Code means that the FCA will proactively disclose information about firms where each of the following principles is met:

- the FCA believes that the disclosure of information, on balance, serves rather than harms the public interest;

- the disclosure of the information meets the FCA's standards of economy, efficiency and effectiveness; and

- the disclosure of the information would not infringe any statutory restrictions, including those set by the FSMA 2000.

1 See para **4.151** above.
2 This is by no means an absolute rule and there may be circumstances when the document would be protected. For example, the document may contain confidential information which the firm received from the FCA and which is protected under FSMA 2000, s 348 (see para **4.226** ff below). Alternatively, it may, in some circumstances, be possible for the document to be legally privileged.
3 The FCA confirmed in its Discussion Paper (DP13/1) on 'Transparency' that it continues to view the Code as a valuable tool but intends to go further than the Code.
4 DP 13/1 takes account of and draws lessons from the FSA's 2009 discussion paper 'Transparency as a Regulatory Tool' (DP 08/3). DP13/1 indicates that the FCA will continue to engage with the industry to establish how best transparency may be achieved and presented.

4.171 There are two additional points to note. First, the firm is likely to have a copy not only of the final document provided to the FCA but also of any drafts that were produced[1]. Those drafts would in principle also be disclosable documents. It may, however, be possible to produce them in a way that makes them legally privileged, for example if they were produced for the purpose of obtaining legal advice on the information that should be provided to the FCA. Care therefore needs to be taken.

1 Indeed, many computer systems store each version of a document automatically.

4.172 Second, the firm may have provided information to the FCA in interviews between the FCA and the firm's employees and the firm will often have copies of transcripts of the interviews[1]. Such transcripts could potentially be required to be disclosed to a third party, even if the interview was held compulsorily[2], save to the extent that they contain information which is protected under the FSMA 2000[3].

1 See para **4.168** above.
2 See *Wallace Smith Trust Co Ltd v Deloitte Haskins & Sells [1996] EWCA Civ J0710-5, [1997] 1 WLR 257* (Simon Brown LJ at 23-24), applied in *British & Commonwealth Holdings plc v Barclays de Zoete Wedd [1998] All ER (D) 491.*
3 FSMA 2000, s 348: see para **4.165** ff above. Note that this is limited in its effect in this context: the mere fact that the firm provides information to the FCA does not confer on that information a protection against disclosure from the firm to third parties. Note also that it may be possible for a court to order the transcripts to be disclosed with any protected parts redacted: see *Re Galileo Group Ltd, Elles v Hambros Bank Ltd [1999] Ch 100 and Real Estate Opportunities Ltd v Aberdeen Asset Managers Jersey Ltd [2007] EWCA Civ 197, [2007] 2 All ER 791.* See para **4.175** below for a discussion as to how the confidentiality restrictions under the FSMA 2000 interrelate with the disclosure obligations under the Civil Procedure Rules.

4.173 In some situations, the firm will produce information to the FCA in relation to the FCA's enquiries into another firm or person. Where the firm does so, there is a different concern, namely whether that can give rise to libel proceedings against the firm. A communication with the FCA where the FCA seeks evidence for its enforcement functions is probably protected by an absolute privilege against use in libel proceedings, but it is not clear whether information spontaneously (and perhaps maliciously) proffered to the regulator would do so[1].

1 See *Mahon v Rahn (No 2) [2000] EWCA Civ J0608-10, [2000] 1 WLR 2150.*

Can the third party obtain material from the FCA?

4.174 The FCA's files could potentially contain a great deal of information that may assist a third party seeking to bring a claim against the firm. The FCA may have a report from its investigator, possibly transcripts of interviews and the various documents which the firm and any other parties involved have produced for it or for the investigator. It will also have other material produced in the enforcement process which followed the investigation, such as a draft investigation report[1], the recommendation to the Regulatory Decisions Committee of what action to take, and the underlying material on which the recommendation is based[2]. Each of these documents could help the third party show that breaches were committed by the firm. The FCA may also have produced other material, such as schedules of investor losses, which could be of use to the third party in proving its losses. Is there a risk of the third party being able to obtain access to the FCA's documents in order to sue the firm?

1 Previously known as a 'preliminary findings letter'.
2 The production of these documents is considered at para **10.91** ff below.

4.175 The answer is that there is a risk, but generally speaking it is a low risk. The court does have the power to order a person that is not party to the legal proceedings, like the FCA, to give disclosure of documents in certain situations[1].

However, material of this nature is likely to be protected under the FSMA 2000 as confidential information obtained by the FCA in the discharge of its functions which relates to the business or affairs of any person². Where this is the case, since the FSMA 2000 does not expressly give the court any ability to override this confidentiality restriction³, and since it would therefore be a criminal offence for a person to disclose such information⁴, it is very unlikely that a court could order the FCA to give disclosure⁵. Note, however, that even if there are no formal legal proceedings, a third party may, in some circumstances, be able to obtain information under the Freedom of Information Act 2000⁶.

1 The power exists if one of the parties to the proceedings can demonstrate to the court that the FCA has documents which are likely to support his case or adversely affect the firm's case and that the disclosure is necessary in order to dispose fairly of the claim and save costs: see the Civil Procedure Rules, Pt 31, r 31.17. It is also possible that the court may summons FCA staff members to appear before it: see the Civil Procedure Rules, Pt 34.
2 FSMA 2000, s 348: see para **4.226** ff below.
3 However, an individual can request information from the FCA under the Data Protection Act 1998. But, in *Durant v FSA [2004] FSR 28, [2003] EWCA Civ 1746*, the Court of Appeal held that the Data Protection Act 1998 only entitled an individual to access to data held about himself and gave the examples of medical history and salary details. The Information Commissioner in 'The Durant case and its impact on the interpretation of the Data Protection Act 1998' (4/10/04) states that where a public authority is in doubt as to whether information actually relates to the person concerned, it should take into account whether or not the information requested would have an adverse impact on the individual. If so, then the information does relate to him. The Information Commissioner has published further guidance on personal data: see 'What is personal data? – A quick reference guide' (12/12/2012) and 'Determining what is personal data' (12/12/2012).
4 See para **4.236** below.
5 See *BCCI v Price Waterhouse (Bank of England intervening) [1998] Ch 84, [1997] 4 All ER 781* (Laddie J); *Re Galileo Group Ltd; Elles v Hambro Bank Ltd [1999] Ch 100, [1998] 1 All ER 545* (Lightman J); *Barings plc v Coopers & Lybrand [2000] EWCA Civ J0505-5, [2000] 1 WLR 2353*; and *Rowell v Pratt [1938] AC 101*.
6 The Freedom of Information Act 2000 (FOIA 2000) came fully into force on 1 January 2005 and gives individuals, firms and third parties the right to request and receive certain information from public authorities (the FCA is a public authority for the purposes of this Act). However, not all information held by the FCA is disclosable. Two broad categories of exemption exist: absolute exemptions and qualified exemptions. In many situations, material held by the FCA will be protected from disclosure under the FOIA 2000 by an absolute exemption. Absolute exemptions cover various types of information, including that provided in confidence (FOIA 2000, s 41), where disclosure is prohibited by any other Act (FOIA 2000, s 44) (eg the FSMA 2000, s 348) and personal information (FOIA 2000, s 40). If the information falls within an absolute exemption, the FCA has no obligation to confirm or deny that the information even exists. Where an absolute exemption is unavailable, the qualified exemption relating to commercially sensitive information (FOIA 2000, s 43) may apply or the qualified exemption relating to where disclosure would be likely to prejudice the exercise by any public authority of its functions for the purpose of ascertaining whether regulating action is justified (FOIA 2000, s 31). If the information comes under a qualified exemption head, the FCA can disclose it provided disclosure is in the public interest (FOIA 2000, s 17(3)), which will depend on the facts of each case.
   The First-tier Tribunal (Information Rights) (FTTIR) (or the Information Commissioner as it was until 17 January 2010) has sought to interpret some of these exceptions narrowly. In *FSA v Information Commissioner (EA/2008/0061) (FS50147637)* the Information Tribunal rejected submissions by the FSA that disclosure of documents containing its analysis or preliminary views on a matter would have an adverse effect on the FSA's ability to carry out its functions. In these circumstances, the FSA could not rely on the FOIA 2000, ss 31 and 43. However, the Information Tribunal and the FTTIR have upheld the FSA's decision to withhold information requested on grounds of the potential prejudice to the commercial interest of regulated firms: *FSA v IC [2009]*

4.175   FCA and PRA powers of information gathering

UKIT EA/2008/0061 (16 February 2009); FSA v IC [2008] UKIT EA/2008/0047 (23 December 2008); FS50467752 (26 March 2013). Even though disclosure is prohibited when the FSMA 2000, s 348 applies (see *Rowland v FSA UKIT EA/2008/0075 and FS50438560*), the Information Tribunal has interpreted the relevant criteria restrictively, such that only information strictly covered by s 348 may be withheld on this ground (*FSA v Commissioner (Appeal EA/2007/0093 and 0100 (13 October 2008)*). The courts have been critical of the Information Tribunal's approach to the law of confidence in particular: see Eady J's comments in *Secretary of State for the Home Office v British Union for the Abolition of Vivisection [2008] EWHC 892 (QB), [2009] 1 WLR 636.*

4.176   There are some important caveats. First, if the material has been used in open court, for example in Tribunal proceedings[1], then it is unlikely to be confidential any more and will not therefore be protected from disclosure[2]. This may be an important caveat in practice, because civil legal proceedings may follow the conclusion of the regulatory enforcement process. Second, it is likely that the statutory protection does not preclude a court from ordering disclosure of the material by a person where that disclosure would be permitted under the Gateway Regulations[3].

1   Publicity in the Tribunal process is considered at para **12.37** ff below.
2   FSMA 2000, s 348(4): see para **4.230** below.
3   The Financial Services and Markets Act 2000 (Disclosure of Confidential Information) Regulations 2001 (the 'Gateway Regulations'), SI 2001/2188 as amended by FSMA 2000 (Disclosure of Confidential Information) (Amendment) Regulations 2012, SI 2012/3019: see para **4.234** below. This is the implication of the authorities cited at para **4.175**, n 5 above, particularly *Rowell v Pratt [1938] AC 101*, although the point has not been directly decided. Note that the Gateway Regulations (para 5) allow the disclosure of information for the purposes of civil proceedings arising by or under the FSMA 2000. On its own, this might seem to encompass breach of statutory duty claims under s 138D, but s 349(1) makes clear that the disclosure is only permitted when made for the purpose of enabling the carrying out of a public function. It is unclear whether claims by investors under s 138D would fulfil this criterion. For a further discussion of the Gateway Regulations, see para **4.234** below (and see in particular n 4).

What can the firm do to reduce the risk of disclosure?

4.177   Three main steps can be taken by the firm to reduce the risk of disclosure. First, whilst the firm will not be able to influence the nature of the material that the FCA may produce which might be disclosable, it will have control over the nature and scope of the material that it produces. The risk of producing damaging material which might need to be disclosed to third parties will need to be borne in mind and weighed up against the need to provide material to the FCA and the terms by which such material should be produced and provided. It may also be possible to pass some information orally, rather than in writing, in some circumstances. In practice, to ensure that the FCA is aware of the need to consider whether an exemption under the Freedom of Information Act 2000 applies, firms will often label material as 'commercially sensitive' and, if appropriate, 'confidential'[1].

1   See para **4.175**, n 6 above for further information on absolute and qualified exemptions.

4.178   Second, the firm needs to consider structuring the production of material in such a way as to ensure that it is legally privileged. This will not always be possible but should at least be considered.

4.179   Third, if a privileged document is to be provided to the FCA, then it may assist the firm in maintaining a claim to privilege over the material if it tries to agree in advance with the FCA the terms upon which the document is provided. If it is possible, in the particular circumstances, to agree what restrictions should apply to its use, then that should assist[1].

1 See para **4.161** above.

Practical steps to take in relation to interviews

4.180   From the perspective of individuals within the firm, being interviewed by the FCA is often one of the most difficult parts of the process. Some practical guidance relating to interviews, both voluntary interviews and compulsory ones[1] are outlined here, and, in particular, the following points will be addressed:

- preparing for the interview;

- who should attend the interview?

- how will the interview be conducted?

- will there be a record of the interview?

- can the interviewee inform the company of the substance of the interview?

1 Note that statements made in voluntary interviews do not attract the (limited) statutory protection against self-incrimination: see paras **4.58** above and **4.204** ff below.

Preparing for the interview

4.181   It is important that individuals who are to be interviewed prepare themselves thoroughly for the interview. This should include reviewing the relevant documents, refreshing their memories and familiarising themselves fully with the main issues and areas regarding which they are likely to be questioned. The firm may therefore decide to ask the FCA what topics the interview is likely to cover. Particularly, when a significant period of time has elapsed since the relevant events, the FCA will often accede to such a request. Firms should also remember that, apart from the FCA's initial scoping visit which is considered at para **5.50** below, formal interviews are likely to be the firm's first opportunity to comment upon the FCA's understanding of the facts, refute any misconceptions and begin to develop the themes of its defence.

Who should attend the interview?

4.182   Although the FSMA 2000 does not require it, the FCA allows individuals to be accompanied by a legal adviser if they so wish[1]. This gives rise to two questions. First, whether a legal adviser should attend the interview and, second, if so, then which legal adviser?

1 See the FCA Enforcement Guide, EG 4.20.

4.183   If the individual is concerned about his own personal position, for example because he may have committed a criminal offence or is likely to be charged with misconduct, then he will potentially increase his exposure by not having a legal adviser present. Where the individual is less likely to be viewed by the FCA as being personally culpable, and is being interviewed more in the position of a witness who has relevant information, then it will be less necessary for a legal adviser to be present. Nonetheless, this can often be helpful, to provide general support and subsequently to give an objective view of the interview.

4.184   As to who should attend, the difficult question is whether the firm's lawyers, whether members of the legal or compliance[1] department or outside counsel, can or should attend or whether the individual should be personally represented[2]. The FCA's view is not clear from its guidance, but where a conflict of interests is possible, it is likely to ask the lawyer who attends the interview whether he does so on behalf of the interviewee or the firm. The FCA has also highlighted the fact that, in some circumstances, firms may not realise that conflicts could exist between the interests of the firm and those of the employee[3]. Situations where the lawyer advises both the witness and his employer have been identified as needing particular care.

1   In some circumstances, it may be possible for this role to be fulfilled by the firm's compliance officer, if he is legally qualified or if the FCA is willing to allow a non-legal adviser to be present. This will not, though, always be appropriate, particularly where the compliance officer is also a potential witness.
2   Where the individual could be held to be personally culpable (particularly when criminal liability is in issue), it may be advisable to offer the interviewee separate legal representation as well as to attempt to have a representative of the firm attending the interview. Firms should not force individuals only to be represented by their own legal adviser in case a conflict of interests subsequently arises.
3   The FSA has also noted that where a firm's systems and controls are under investigation, the firm's general counsel can, in some instances, be too closely aligned to the processes under scrutiny to bring an 'objective mind' to the process.

4.185   Why is this relevant? Even if there has, until this point, been no conflict between the interests of the firm and those of the individual, there may be a possibility that a conflict will arise in the future, for example if the firm then wishes to take disciplinary action against the individual. Information may emerge at the interview which suggests that such action is appropriate. This could place a lawyer who has attended the interview on behalf of both parties in a difficult position. Unless it was made clear that he was only acting for the firm, he could also be disqualified from acting for either party[1]. The formal interview may therefore be the stage at which the individual will need to obtain separate legal advice, particularly if that individual is likely to be viewed by the FCA or the investigator as a suspect as much as a witness.

1   See the *SRA Code of Conduct* (2011) Version 7, at O(3.7). The adviser will therefore need to be clear as to whom he is advising. As indicated above, it is unclear that the FCA will necessarily allow a lawyer who only represents the firm to attend the interview and investigators are likely to seek to clarify at the commencement of the interview who the lawyer is representing.

How will the interview be conducted?

4.186   Where appropriate[1], the FCA will explain to the individual what use can be made of the answers in proceedings against them[2]. The FCA will also, in a subsequent voluntary interview, explain the limited use that can be made of the individual's previous answers in the compulsory interview in criminal proceedings or proceedings for market abuse conducted against the person[3]. At the outset of the interview, the FCA will generally indicate when breaks will occur[4]. Generally, at least two representatives of the FCA will be present at the interview although more than two may be present if, for example, the matter is complex or the questions are likely to relate to different areas[5]. The interview will normally be tape recorded and will subsequently be transcribed. A copy of the transcript will be forwarded to the interviewee together with one of the sets of tapes of the interview so that the interviewee can agree the transcript. It should also be remembered that the FCA may request a further interview with a person where new issues need to be raised[6] or where further clarification of issues is needed.

1   See the FCA Enforcement Guide, EG 4.20.
2   The consequences of non-compliance with formal requests are discussed at para **5.75** ff below.
3   See FCA Enforcement Guide, EG 4.22. The FCA will not warn an individual who has been previously interviewed under caution and then wishes to conduct a compulsory interview to the same extent: see FCA Enforcement Guide, EG 4.23 and para **4.180**, n 1 above.
4   CDs are used to record interviews and in practice breaks occur every 40 minutes or so. If, at any point, the interviewee feels tired, he should always ask for a break.
5   See para **5.25** below as to whether a representative of an overseas regulator may be allowed to participate.
6   For example, as a result of other interviews.

4.187   How the interview is conducted will depend very much upon the circumstances[1]. Some general points can be made about how the individual might respond to questions, namely:

- regardless of the tone that is adopted by the interviewer (which may range from being light-hearted to being aggressive), the interviewee should adopt a polite but 'to the point' approach;

- he should answer only within his own knowledge;

- he should listen and take time before answering a question[2];

- he should answer only the exact question that has been asked and should not speculate[3];

- he should ask the questioner to break up multiple questions or rephrase a question that has been phrased in a manner which is not clear;

- he should ask for time to consider the answer, where needed;

- where an answer may relate to legal advice that has been given, the interviewee should ask for the chance to confer with the person accompanying him, so as to consider whether he can and should disclose information that may be legally privileged; and

- he should generally not answer questions about documents that he has not seen until he has properly considered them[4].

1 Additional considerations, outlined at para **4.210** ff below, arise when a person is interviewed under caution for the purpose of obtaining evidence for use in criminal proceedings.
2 The length of a pause before answering a question should not be reflected in the transcript.
3 If the interviewee does not know the answer to the question, the correct response will be to state that he does not know the answer. To many questions a simple 'yes' or 'no' will be enough.
4 Generally, it will be better that the interviewee does not take documents to the interview. However, if this does happen, those documents should have already been disclosed to the FCA and should not be annotated. Where the FCA produces documents during an interview, for example, to ask for the interviewee's comments on them, the interviewee (or his adviser) should ask for a copy. Where a document is presented to an interviewee, he should take time to read it. Even a document which might, at first sight, seem familiar, may be in draft form or annotated.

4.188 The individual does not have the right to refuse to answer a question on the ground that to do so might incriminate him. The (fairly limited) protection against self-incrimination applicable to mandatory interviews is described at para **4.204** ff below. In summary, the FCA cannot use the transcript of a mandatory interview in evidence in criminal or market abuse proceedings against that particular witness and no question can be raised at those proceedings in relation to the responses given at interview. Despite this protection, the transcript of a mandatory interview may be used in evidence:

- in proceedings brought by the FCA to show that the witness lied, either at the mandatory interview or subsequently, in court;

- in any proceedings (whether criminal or civil, including proceedings for market abuse) brought against a different individual or possibly the firm; and/or

- in any other regulatory proceedings against the individual other than market abuse proceedings (or criminal proceedings).

4.189 Generally, the FCA must act fairly[1]. This can only be judged properly on the circumstances of each case. Nonetheless, it may be possible for lengthy questioning, particularly revisiting what was already covered by compulsory questioning, to be unfair and oppressive[2].

1 See *Re Pergamon Press Ltd [1970] EWCA Civ J0713-2, [1971] Ch 388*. This was in a slightly different context, but the same principles ought to apply.
2 See for example *Re an Inquiry into Mirror Group Newspapers plc [2000] Ch 194*. Again, this was in a slightly different context, but it is considered that the same principles apply.

Will there be a record of the interview?

4.190 A record is kept of interviews, and the individual will be given a copy of it. Where the interview is tape-recorded, the person interviewed will be given a copy of the audio tape of the interview and where a transcript is made, the person will be given a copy of the transcript[1]. As regards voluntary interviews, the investigator will always make a record if the interviewee is the subject of the investigation and in other cases may make a record. If a record is made, the FCA will give a copy of it to the person interviewed[2].

Requesting information from particular types of person

4.191 The breadth of the information gathering armoury available to the FCA, either directly or through investigators appointed by it, and the array of people against whom it may be deployed, should be apparent from the discussion above. The purpose of the following paragraphs is to discuss some of the particular issues which are likely to arise as a result of the imposition of these powers on three particular categories of person, namely:

- third parties unconnected to the firm;

- the firm's solicitors, bankers, brokers, claims managers, auditors and actuaries; and

- other members of the same group as the firm, and particularly overseas members.

Third parties unconnected to the firm

4.192 The principal point to have in mind is the breadth of possible involvement of unconnected third parties, whether or not they carry on any regulated business. Third parties can be involved to a varying extent in each of the four types of formal investigation outlined at para **5.11** ff below, including being required in some instances not only to produce documents or information, but also to answer questions, potentially even on oath. If they produce a document, then they can be required to provide an explanation of it. If they fail to comply with a requirement, they could be subject to proceedings for contempt of court or to a warrant to search their premises[1].

1 See para **5.75** ff below.

4.193 In addition, although on the face of it the FCA's general information gathering power can only be exercised against authorised persons and those connected with them, if it appears that a document is in the possession of a third person then that power may be exercised in relation to that third person. An unregulated third party, unconnected with any authorised person but for some reason holding documents for an authorised person, could therefore be required by the FCA to produce the relevant documents.

The firm's solicitors, bankers, brokers, claims managers, auditors and actuaries

4.194 The firm's solicitors, bankers, brokers, claims managers, auditors and actuaries (and those of other group members) may be required to provide documents, or information, in exactly the same way as the firm, in any of the ss 167, 168 or 169 investigations outlined in **CHAPTER 5**[1].

4.194 FCA and PRA powers of information gathering

1 They are included as 'connected persons' for the purpose of the FSMA 2000, ss 167, 168(1), 168(4) or 169 investigations (see para **5.18**, n 3 below and the FSMA 2000, Sch 15, Pt II). In relation to s 168(1) or (4) investigations, a third party could be involved as a person who is neither the subject of the investigation nor a person connected with such a person, and, in relation to s 168(2) investigations, a third party could be involved as a person who may be able to give relevant information.

4.195 There are, however, some limitations:

- many of the records of, or correspondence with, solicitors, but by no means necessarily all, will be covered by the doctrine of legal professional privilege and will be 'protected items' under the FSMA 2000, which a person cannot be required to produce, disclose or permit the inspection of[1];

- the doctrine of legal professional privilege[2] may also protect work carried out by other professionals (for example, accountants or actuaries) in circumstances where the dominant purpose of their work was to assist the lawyers for actual or contemplated legal proceedings, and in some situations may also protect communications with other third parties; and

- there is a limited protection for banking secrecy[3].

1 FSMA 2000, s 413 and see the discussion at para **5.56** ff below. Note: (i) a lawyer can nonetheless be required to furnish the name of his client; and (ii) legal privilege effectively has its own definition under the FSMA 2000 for this purpose.
2 See para **4.145** above.
3 See para **5.60** ff below.

4.196 There is nothing to prevent the FCA from requiring, for example, auditors or solicitors (subject to legal privilege) to produce their working papers, even though some of these documents would not normally be disclosable to their own client[1].

1 See *Chantrey Martin & Co v Martin [1953] 2 QB 286*.

Other members of the firm's group

Why might other group members be relevant?

4.197 The requirements that can be imposed on firms to provide information and documents either to the FCA or to an investigator can also be imposed on a wide range of connected persons, including other companies within the same group as the firm. Indeed, the FCA regards the obligation on firms under Principle 11 to co-operate with it as extending to taking reasonable steps to ensure that other group companies co-operate with it[1]. Many of these other group companies may, however, be based overseas and therefore hold any relevant documents overseas.

1 See para **4.32** above.

Can the FCA require overseas companies to provide information to it?

4.198 As shown, the provisions are extremely wide. Why should an overseas company with little to do with the group's UK regulated business (or as an entirely unconnected third party) be subjected to the application of UK extra-territorial regulatory jurisdiction purely because, for example, the FCA believes the information to be reasonably required in connection with its functions in the UK, even where the FCA is not alleging that the UK firm has been involved in any regulatory contravention[1]?

1 This would be a possible application of the FSMA 2000, s 165.

4.199   There is a general principle of English law that legislation is not intended to have effect overseas unless Parliament has made clear in the legislation that it intended it to do so[1]. The FSMA 2000 does not expressly authorise or prevent the FCA, or an investigator appointed by it, from exercising its powers in order to require the provision of information held overseas, whether by a group company or by an unconnected third party. The FSMA 2000 does envisage the investigation powers applying to overseas bodies that are authorised persons, for example incoming firms[2], and to other bodies that commit specific contraventions such as breach of the perimeter[3]. But there is nothing to suggest that the investigation powers apply in respect of documents held overseas, or that they apply against connected overseas companies or wholly unconnected third parties based overseas. It is, thus, unclear what approach a court would take.

1 See, for example, *Re A B & Co [1900] 1 QB 541* (Lindley MR at 544) and *A-G for Alberta v Huggard Assets Ltd [1953] AC 420, PC*. Similarly, save in exceptional circumstances, a court will not require a foreign bank which is not a party to an action to produce documents outside the jurisdiction concerning business transacted outside the jurisdiction: see *McKinnon v Donaldson, Lufkin and Jenrette Securities Corpn [1986] Ch 482*.
2 See, for example, the intervention powers in Pt XIII (discussed in **CHAPTER 16** below). This is perhaps comparable with the position under the Insolvency Act 1986, s 221 which allows overseas companies to be wound up; hence Parliament was taken to have intended that the court's powers under s 236 could be used to require the production of documents held overseas: see *Re Mid East Trading Ltd, Lehman Bros Inc v Phillips [1998] 1 All ER 577*.
3 FSMA 2000, s 168(2).

Is the firm able to provide the information?

4.200   Providing information from connected companies overseas may cause problems. For example, the non-UK firm may owe obligations of confidentiality to customers or as a matter of law in its home jurisdiction, which under the relevant applicable law may or may not be overridden by the imposition of requirements extra-territorially from the UK. There may therefore be an important legal or practical bar to it providing the information. By way of example, this can be a particular issue for a firm that is connected with a bank in a jurisdiction with strict banking secrecy laws. It may not be open to the overseas bank to release information to the UK institution or to the FCA. Indeed, to do so could be a criminal offence. But it is quite possible for the overseas bank to have information relevant to a regulatory enquiry in the UK, for example if funds used in a trade suspected of constituting market abuse were sourced from an account at the bank, or if that account was the destination of the proceeds of a particular investment which was the subject of an investigation. Similarly, data protection laws in some jurisdictions might be breached by the disclosure of the information, and in some cases this would be a criminal offence. The firm's exposure to breaches of the law overseas does not, though, necessarily give it grounds under English law for refusing to comply with the requirements imposed on it[1].

1 See *A v B Bank (Bank of England intervening) [1993] QB 311*: an injunction restraining the bank in New York was not a 'reasonable excuse' for non-compliance with a notice under the Banking Act 1987, s 39 requiring the production of documents. A similar issue arises in the context of freezing orders: see *Baltic Shipping Co v Translink Shipping Ltd [1995] 1 Lloyd's Rep 673* and see Gee, *Commercial injunctions* (5th edn), from p [289].

How might the firm address these issues?

4.201 In practice, the firm is likely to want to assist the FCA to the extent that it can do so because:

- the FCA has made clear in its guidance on the obligation of co-operation under Principle 11[1] that it expects firms to take reasonable steps to ensure that group companies co-operate with it (although it has not specified that this includes overseas companies); and

- if the FCA does have difficulty obtaining information about a firm's business because of its group structure, this could, in a serious case, cast doubt on whether the firm continues to satisfy the threshold conditions, because of its close links with others[2], and could amount to grounds for the FCA to vary the firm's permission or even, in a particularly serious case, to cancel it.

1 See para **4.32** above.
2 The close links threshold condition: see para **2.5** above.

4.202 However, bearing in mind the differences in regulation and legislation in different jurisdictions which affect privilege and confidentiality of documents (this is addressed in more detail in **CHAPTER 7**), the firm may want to request that the FCA makes an official request for mutual assurance from the relevant overseas regulator.

4.203 As ever, the answer will often be a practical one of maintaining a close and open relationship with the FCA and the investigator, which may allow such problems to be resolved by discussion. For example, the FCA may be able to obtain the information that it seeks through mutual assistance with the regulator or other authority in the relevant overseas jurisdiction.

Can the FCA compel information from a person who is suspected of a criminal offence?

4.204 The FCA can compel information to be provided by a person suspected of a criminal offence. There is no right under the FSMA 2000 or the ECHR to refuse to provide information or to answer a question required under compulsion in the investigation stage of the process on the ground of self-incrimination, but there are limitations on the uses which can be made of the answer. In accordance with the decision of the European Court of Human Rights in the case of *Ernest*

Saunders[1], the FSMA 2000 draws a distinction between the requirement that can be imposed upon a person to provide information and the use to which the information obtained in that way may be put.

1   *Saunders v United Kingdom (1996) 2 BHRC 358*. See also *Attorney General's Reference (No 7 of 2000) [2001] EWCA Crim 888, [2001] 1 WLR 1879*.

4.205   Generally, a statement made by a person to an investigator in compliance with an information requirement[1] is admissible in evidence in any proceedings (whether criminal or civil, and subject to any procedural rules relating to the admissibility of evidence). However, such statements are not admissible in criminal proceedings or proceedings for market abuse[2] against the person who made the statement, in that:

- no evidence relating to the statement may be adduced; and

- no question relating to it may be asked

by or on behalf of the prosecution or the FCA, unless evidence relating to it is adduced or a question relating to it is asked in the proceedings by, or on behalf of, the person who gave it[3]. This is subject to the exception that the statement may be used in criminal proceedings for perjury or for the criminal offences under the FSMA 2000 of providing false or misleading information to the FCA.

1   That is a requirement to provide information imposed by an investigator under the FSMA 2000, ss 171, 172, 173 or 175: see s 174(5) (amended by (3A) additional power conferred by s 172/3 when investigating information exchanges)). This provision does not, therefore, cover all statements made to the FCA: see para **4.207** below.
2   The application of this provision in the context of market abuse is considered at para **17.142** ff below.
3   FSMA 2000, s 174.

4.206   The protection is limited. If the FCA cannot use the statement in the criminal proceedings, then it can still use it in order to obtain evidence by other means which it can use in those proceedings. The FSA previously made it clear that it would use what it regards as its fact finding powers in this way[1] and there is no reason for the FCA to depart from this. In addition, the privilege relates only to statements; it does not prevent the use of any documents[2].

1   See Consultation Paper 17 ('Enforcing the New Regime'), December 1998, para 68. Contrast the implied undertaking against the collateral use of information obtained on disclosure or through a freezing order: see *A-G for Gibraltar v May [1998] EWCA Civ J1106-21, [1999] 1 WLR 998*. In addition, an express undertaking against collateral use is normally required in respect of a freezing order. For further discussion, see Gee, *Commercial Injunctions* (5th edn, 2004), at Ch 18.
2   See *A-G's Reference (No 7) of 2001 (29 March 2001, unreported), CA*.

4.207   It is possible for individuals to be required to provide, or voluntarily provide, a statement in circumstances where this statutory protection against use would not apply. For example, an employee or officer of an authorised person could be required to provide information orally to the FCA under s 165[1], and that requirement would have statutory force, but any statement provided would not attract the protection of s 174 as it would not be made in compliance with an 'information requirement' for this purpose[2]. Equally, an individual could be asked to attend a meeting with the FCA or provide a statement without the FCA using its formal powers and, if an approved person would need to comply because of his obligations under Statement of Principle 4[3]. Again, this would not attract the protection of s 174. The same point could be made in relation to other employees of an authorised person, who could effectively be compelled to attend an interview because of the firm's obligations under Principle 11 and the regulatory expectation that those who work for authorised firms should be willing to co-operate with the regulator. Similarly, a statement provided entirely voluntarily would not fall within s 174. Nonetheless, the statutory protection reflects the position under the ECHR in accordance with the decision in *Saunders*. If the FCA tried to adduce in evidence a statement made under compulsion, to which s 174 did not apply, the ECHR may provide a means for the individual to try to have it excluded. It would, though, be difficult to argue that a statement provided entirely voluntarily (for example, by a person who had no obligation to co-operate with the FCA) should be excluded. It may also be possible to agree with the FCA in advance of an interview that the interview should be treated as a compelled interview, even though that is not strictly the case, and that it should therefore attract the protection of s174[4].

1 See para **4.72** ff above.
2 See para **4.205**, n 1 above.
3 See para **2.11** above.
4 See *Financial Services Authority v Asset L I Inc (trading as Asset Land Investment Inc) [2013] EWCH 178 (Ch), [2013] WLR (D) 54*, at para 29.

4.208 It is not only individuals who may attract criminal liability under the FSMA 2000. The firm itself may have committed a criminal offence. While companies are in principle entitled to claim privilege against self incrimination, it is difficult to see how a firm could be protected by s 174 as practice statements will always actually be made by an officer or employee. Can a statement made by an employee or officer of the firm be used in evidence in criminal proceedings against the firm? There is no English or ECHR authority on this point, although its logic has been recognised by at least one member of the House of Lords[1]. In principle, companies have human rights in the same way as individuals and the *Saunders* protection should therefore apply to a company, whatever the limitations on the wording of s 174. Equally, companies can only act through individuals. Therefore, if the right is to have any value in the corporate context, the company ought to be able to claim the privilege against self-incrimination in relation to statements made by its officers or employees. It is not clear whether the FCA accepts this. The court has power under s 78 of the Police and Criminal Evidence Act 1984 to ensure that any trial is fair and respects Article 6 of the ECHR.

1 *Rio Tinto Zinc Corpn v Westinghouse Electric Corpn; Re Westinghouse Electric Corpn Uranium Contract Litigation MDL Docket No 235 (No 1) and (No 2) [1978] AC 547*, per Lord Fraser at 652, and see also Lord Wilberforce at 617 and Viscount Dilhorne at 632. It was unnecessary to decide the point in that case and the House of Lords declined to do so, although there were some indications that upholding such a claim would be stretching English Law. See also the Court of Appeal in *Sociedade Nacional de Combustiveis de Angola UEE v Lundqvist [1990] EWCA Civ J0131-5, [1991] 2 QB 310*, and, more recently, *Kensington International Ltd v Republic of Congo [2007] EWCA Civ 1128, [2008] 1 WLR 1144*, where the court declined to answer the question in the context of the Fraud Act 2006.

4.209 Individual employees or officers being prosecuted for a criminal offence cannot claim to exclude statements from the company or other officers or employees on the grounds of privilege against self-incrimination[1].

1 See *Gavin v Domus Publishing Ltd [1989] Ch 335*; *Tate Access Floors Inc v Boswell [1991] Ch 512*.

The FCA's procedure for obtaining information where a criminal offence is suspected

4.210 The FCA has indicated[1] that, when its inquiries lead it to consider the institution of criminal proceedings against a person who has been required to answer questions under compulsion, fairness to the person concerned means that he should be given an opportunity voluntarily to answer the FCA's questions so that his answers can be put to the criminal court in any subsequent prosecution. The FCA therefore will ordinarily afford a potential defendant an opportunity to submit voluntarily to an interview under caution conducted in accordance with the requirements of the Criminal Procedure and Investigations Act 1996 and the Police and Criminal Evidence Act 1984[2].

1 See Consultation Paper 17 ('Enforcing the new regime'), para 69, and the FCA's Response to Consultation Paper 17 at para 99.
2 See the FCA Enforcement Guide, EG 4.21.

4.211 It is important to note that this interview is voluntary on the part of the individual. This is consistent with the Police Code of Conduct, which makes clear that an interview under caution cannot take place once a police officer reaches the conclusion that there is sufficient evidence for a successful prosecution. The reason for this is that it is wrong for adverse inferences to be drawn from a person choosing to remain silent once that point has been passed[1]. The FCA could, however, probably still use its formal powers to compel an interview[2], for example as part of the continuing regulatory investigation.

1 See *R v Pointer [1997] Crim LR 676*, *R v Gayle [1999] EWCA Crim J0218-36, [1999] 2 CrAppR 130*, and *R v Odeyimi [1999] Crim LR 828*.
2 See *R v Director of Serious Fraud Office, ex p Smith [1993] AC 1, HL*.

4.212 If the person does agree to be interviewed on a voluntary basis[1], he will be warned of his right to remain silent and the consequences of doing so and will be informed that he is entitled to have a legal adviser present. If the person has already been interviewed by the FCA under its compulsory powers, he will be provided with the transcript or other record of the compulsory interview and an explanation of the difference between the two types of interviews[2]. He will also be told of the limited use that can be made of his previous answers, as outlined above. The interview will be subject to the safeguards of PACE Code C[3].

1 See the FCA Enforcement Guide, EG 4.21.
2 FCA Enforcement Guide, EG 4.22.
3 FCA Enforcement Guide, EG 4.21 and for details, see Archbold (2013), at 15–425.

4.213 What will happen if an interviewee fails to attend such an interview or it seems likely to the FCA that the interviewee will not attend? Investigators appointed by the FCA have no powers of arrest. However, the FCA has adopted the FSA's previous agreement with the Association of Chief Police Officers[1], that the police will provide assistance where it appears likely that a request by the FCA for a voluntary interview will prejudice an ongoing investigation or risk the destruction of evidence, or dissipation of assets, or where the interviewee fails to attend a voluntary interview[2]. Given that the FCA will need to provide the police with sufficient information in order to enable them to consider the request for assistance[3], it is likely that the FCA will need to provide the police with confidential information relating to the firm or person but the FCA considers that such information may be disclosable under reg 4 of the Gateway Regulations[4]. Although the FCA will be responsible for the investigation of the offence, practical factors, such as the interviewee's length of detention and whether to grant bail, will be the responsibility of the police[5]. Where a person has been arrested and is being detained by the police, he may be interviewed by the FCA if the Custody Sergeant so permits. A representative of the police will attend the interview so as to ensure the interview's compliance with PACE[6].

1 See the 'Memorandum of Understanding between the Association of Chief Police Officers and the FSA' concluded on 03/08/05. The Memorandum is intended to record the best practice for co-operation between the police and the FSA (now FCA) but is not expressed so as to limit the action that can be taken.
2 For example, powers of arrest were used in July 2013 in relation to the Libor fixing investigations: *Financial Times* (15/7/13). The power to arrest exists in cases of suspected market abuse, insider dealing, money laundering or illegal deposit taking. Where the police do provide the FCA with assistance, they will be reimbursed in relation to any 'incidental expenses incurred': see the Memorandum of Understanding between the Association of Chief Police Officers and the FSA concluded on 3/08/05 at para 12.1.
3 An example of the format of a request for an arrest can be found at Annex 1 to the Memorandum of Understanding between the Association of Chief Police Officers and the FSA concluded on 03/08/05. The example includes a section where the FSA (now FCA) is to provide evidence that reasonable grounds exist for suspecting that an arrestable offence (within the meaning of PACE, s 24(1)) has been committed and that reasonable grounds exist for suspecting that the individual has committed an offence in relation to which he is guilty. Such evidence, for example, may include transcripts of interviews or of telephone conversations. The pro forma envisages that the request should be made by the investigator and approved by the relevant person within the Enforcement Division who has overall managerial responsibility for the conduct of the case: see the Memorandum of Understanding between the Association of Chief Police Officers and the FSA concluded on 03/08/05 at section 7.
4 Financial Services and Markets Act 2000 (Disclosure of Confidential Information) Regulations 2001, SI 2001/2188 as amended by FSMA 2000 (Disclosure of Confidential Information) (Amendment) Regulations 2012, SI 2012/3019.
5 The police will monitor whether conditions for continued detention are met, but the FCA will decide whether the suspect should be charged or summonsed and will do so according to its internal processes and guidelines for instituting proceedings: see the Memorandum of Understanding between the Association of Chief Police Officers and the FSA concluded on 03/08/05 at para 10.1.
6 As with other interviews conducted by the FCA, the interview will be tape recorded: see the Memorandum of Understanding between the Association of Chief Police Officers and the FSA concluded on 03/08/05 at section 9.

What are the consequences of refusing to answer questions?

4.214 It is always possible for a person to refuse to answer a question, whatever the consequences, so it is worth briefly examining the consequences of doing so.

If a person refuses to answer questions in response to a compulsory requirement by the FCA, the primary consequence is that a court, if it decides he has done so without reasonable excuse, may treat him as though he had committed a contempt of court[1]. It could therefore fine or even imprison him. There may, in some situations, be a reason for refusing to answer questions, for example if, contrary to the policy outlined above, a person against whom the FCA intended to bring a criminal prosecution was required to submit to a further compulsory interview. In those circumstances, the person would need to argue that he had a 'reasonable excuse' for not complying. These and some other possible consequences of failing to provide information to the FCA are outlined at para **5.75** ff below.

1 Pursuant to the FSMA 2000, s 177.

Can the FCA investigate firms' unregulated business?

4.215 Although, for the most part, the FCA is likely to be interested chiefly in a firm's regulated business, there is nothing to prevent the FCA from asking the firm questions about its unregulated business, or non-UK business, or even from exercising its compulsory powers to require the firm to provide such information, if this information is relevant to the discharge of the FCA's functions. On 1 April 2013, the FCA acquired the power to oversee and direct certain unregulated parent undertakings where that is desirable and appropriate[1]. This was accompanied by the power to make rules requiring such qualified parent undertakings to provide information and documents of a specific description[2]. The FCA has not yet made such rules and it is expected that it will utilise the ad hoc powers described below where appropriate[3].

1 FSMA 2000, Pt 12A.
2 FSMA 2000, s 192J.
3 The Bank of England has expressly said that it will adopt this approach in its February 2013 consultation paper: 'Proposed statutory statements of policy in respect of the Bank of England's supervision of financial market infrastructures'.

Why is unregulated business relevant to the FCA?

4.216 Information relating to unregulated business could be relevant to the FCA in a number of respects, particularly regarding UK regulated firms[1]. A number of examples follow.

1 In the context of parent undertakings, the FCA has set out a non-exhaustive list of possible scenarios in which the FCA may consider exercising its powers of direction (in appendix 1 to FSA PS13/5 – The New FCA Handbook).

4.217 First, the conduct of the firm's unregulated activities may be relevant to whether it continues to fulfil the threshold conditions. The threshold conditions that are likely to be particularly relevant are, first, the need for adequate resources and, second, suitability (that the firm is a fit and proper person to be carrying on regulated business). The considerations relevant to suitability are set out at para **2.28** ff above. As will be seen, those are very general considerations, not in any way confined to the firm's regulated business or indeed its UK business.

4.218   Second, the conduct of the firm's unregulated activities may be relevant to whether it has failed to comply with any of the Principles for Businesses. As discussed at para **2.18** ff above, the scope of application of the Principles varies depending upon the Principle concerned and whether the firm is a UK firm or an incoming firm. However, it can be seen that the firm's activities overseas and/or its unregulated business may be relevant to whether it complies with the Principles.

4.219   More generally, issues which occur in the firm's unregulated, or non-UK, business may cause the FCA to ask questions about the firm's conduct of its regulated business. For example, issues might arise which raise questions about the firm's internal organisation, its controls and risk management systems and the training which it gives to its staff. These may lead naturally to the FCA wanting to know whether there are similar issues in its regulated activities.

4.220   Finally, the FCA has power under the FSMA 2000 to make rules applying to the carrying on by authorised persons of unregulated activities if this appears to it necessary or expedient for the purpose of protecting the interests of consumers[1].

1   FSMA 2000, s 138(1). Rules are to be interpreted as not applying to a firm with respect to the carrying on of unregulated activities unless and then only to the extent that a contrary intention appears: see the FCA Handbook at GEN 2.2.17.

How could the FCA investigate non-regulated business?

4.221   The FCA could invoke various powers in order to investigate such matters. For example it could use:

- the general information gathering power under s 165[1], on the basis that the information is reasonably required in connection with the exercise of its functions under the FSMA 2000;

- the power to commence an investigation under s 167[2], on the basis it appears to the FCA there is 'good reason to do so', which expressly applies to investigating a part of the business of an authorised person which does not consist of carrying out regulated activities; or

- the power to commence an investigation under s 168(4)[3], on the basis, among other things, that there are circumstances suggesting that an authorised person has contravened one of the Principles for Businesses or that an approved person (or other individual) is not a fit and proper person to be working in the financial services sector.

1   See para **4.72** above.
2   See para **5.11** below.
3   See para **5.20** below.

Should the firm volunteer information regarding its non-regulated business?

4.222   A difficult question for the firm is whether it should volunteer information to the FCA as to problems it is having with an unregulated activity, on the basis that this is information of which the FCA would reasonably expect notice under Principle 11[1]. The FCA has made clear that Principle 11, in so far as it relates to informing the FCA, applies equally to unregulated activity[2]. Indeed, the FCA rules on the circumstances that need to be notified to it are not confined to regulated business, nor do they contain any particular territorial limits[3]. The answer is, therefore that the firm may need to notify the FCA of something that has happened that relates to its non-regulated activities. Whether a notification is required, and if so the extent of the notification, will depend upon the precise circumstances in the case.

1 Principle 11, Principles for Businesses: see para **3.44** ff above.
2 See para **2.19** above.
3 For a detailed discussion of what information needs to be notified to the FCA, see the FCA Handbook at SUP 2 and para **3.44** ff above.

USE OF INFORMATION OBTAINED BY THE FCA

4.223 The following paragraphs consider various issues relating to the use that the FCA can make of information that it has obtained regarding firms and others, and in particular:

- Can the FCA disclose to others information that it has obtained?

- Could such information be used in criminal proceedings?

Can the FCA disclose information to others that it has obtained?

4.224 The FSMA 2000 contains a general prohibition on the disclosure of confidential information obtained under the FSMA 2000[1], breach of which is a criminal offence. This is, however, subject to various exceptions outlined below. The following paragraphs consider the prohibition and its exceptions before looking at whether the firm has any ability to object to information being passed on in this way.

1 FSMA 2000, s 348. This is similar to the prohibitions that existed before.

4.225 The question of whether the FCA can be forced to disclose to third parties, for example those who wish to bring legal claims against the firm, information which it has regarding a firm is considered at para **4.174** ff above.

The prohibition on the disclosure of confidential information

4.226 Discussion of the prohibition can, for simplicity, be broken down as follows:

- To whom does the prohibition apply?

- To what information does it apply?

- What does it prevent?

175

4.226 FCA and PRA powers of information gathering

- What are the exceptions?

- What are the penalties for breach[1]?

1 The FSA has previously published a memorandum summarising its understanding of how the prohibition on the disclosure of confidential information applies: see: 'The Protection of Regulatory Information under English Law'.

To whom does the prohibition apply?

4.227 The prohibition applies to 'primary recipient[s]' or 'any person who obtains the information directly or indirectly from a primary recipient' (collectively defined herein as 'any recipient').

4.228 'Primary recipient' means: the FCA (including in its capacity as the UK Listing Authority); the PRA; the Secretary of State; any person who is or has been employed by any of the foregoing, any person who is or has been engaged to provide services to them; or a person appointed to collect or update information or provide a report under s 166[1]. 'Expert' includes a person appointed to carry out an investigation by the FCA, PRA, or the Secretary of State under the FSMA 2000, Pt 11 or who has been appointed by the FCA under the FSMA 2000, s 97. This will include an investigator appointed under any of the powers discussed at para **5.10** ff below or in relation to an investigation into a listed company under **CHAPTER 20** below[2].

1 See **CHAPTER 6**.
2 Previously it was not clear whether an investigator appointed to carry out an investigation into a collective investment scheme could be a primary recipient unless he was also an FSA employee. The Financial Services Act 2012 introduced a further catch-all provision encompassing any person engaged to provide services to the FCA, under which such an investigator now appears to be covered.

4.229 No express need exists for the person who obtains the information directly or indirectly from the primary recipient to have any knowledge that the information is covered by these provisions. The lack of knowledge, and suspicion, may, however, be relevant to whether that person has committed a criminal offence in breaching the prohibition[1].

1 See para **4.236** below and see also para **4.230**, n 2 below.

To what information does it apply?

4.230 The prohibition applies to 'confidential information', defined as information which:

- relates to the business or other affairs of any person[1]; and

- is received by the primary recipient for the purposes of, or in the discharge of, any functions of the FCA, the PRA, or the Secretary of State under any provision made by, or under, the FSMA 2000[2]; and

- is not prevented from being confidential information, either:

- because it has been made available to the public by such disclosure, or use, as is not prohibited under the prohibition[3]; or

- because it is in the form of a summary, or collection, of information so framed that it is not possible to ascertain from it information relating to any particular person.

1 This should be sufficiently wide to include the business or affairs of a person other than the person under investigation: see *BCCI v Price Waterhouse (Bank of England intervening) [1998] Ch 84, [1997] 4 All ER 781*, at 791 (Laddie J).

2 It was thought that whether the information was received for this purpose depended upon the intention of the primary recipient: see *BCCI v Price Waterhouse (Bank of England intervening) [1998] Ch 84, [1997] 4 All ER 781*, at 791 (Laddie J). But this was disapproved by the Court of Appeal in *Barings plc v Coopers & Lybrand [2000] EWCA Civ J0505-5, [2000] 1 WLR 2353* in which Lord Woolf MR indicated that the offence would only be committed if the person concerned had knowledge of the circumstances which meant that the prohibition applies to the information.

3 This exception is important in practice, given that documents will no longer be confidential once they have been referred to in Tribunal proceedings in public: Tribunal proceedings are normally held in public (see para **12.37** below). Alternatively, documents may be referred to in a public hearing in a civil court, for example on an application for an injunction or restitution order, and, again, will be likely to lose their confidentiality as a result. When documents are put before a court to be read in evidence, the onus will be on the person presenting them to contest that they should not enter the public domain: see *Barings plc v Coopers & Lybrand [2000] EWCA Civ J0505-5, [2000] 1 WLR 2353* (Woolf MR).

4.231 It is immaterial whether or not the information was received by virtue of a requirement to provide it imposed by or under the FSMA 2000[1], and whether it was received for other purposes as well as the purposes outlined above[2].

1 Information provided 'voluntarily' or under Principle 11 will therefore be covered.
2 FSMA 2000, s 348(3).

What does it prevent?

4.232 The prohibition prevents the disclosure of the confidential information. Disclosure means providing it to someone who did not already have it. Hence, there is no disclosure of information when it is transmitted to a person who already had knowledge of it[1]. In addition, the so-called Gateway Regulations outlined below place restrictions on the purposes for which information may be disclosed and allow restrictions to be placed on the purposes for which information disclosed may be used[2]. Finally, where the disclosure of information is prohibited, it seems that a court could not order the relevant person to disclose the information[3].

1 See *Real Estate Opportunities Ltd v Aberdeen Asset Managers Jersey Ltd [2007] EWCA Civ 197, [2007] 2 All ER 791*.
2 This is permitted by the FSMA 2000, s 349.
3 See the discussion at para **4.175** above.

What exceptions exist?

4.233 Confidential information may be disclosed with the consent of the person from whom the primary recipient has obtained it and, if different, the person to whom it relates[1].

1 This will be widely construed and will be likely, for example, to include, the consent of those customers of a firm to whose affairs the information relates: see *BCCI v Price Waterhouse (Bank of England intervening) [1998] Ch 84, [1997] 4 All ER 781, at 796* (Laddie J).

4.234 In addition, the FSMA 2000[1] allows the disclosure of information which is made to facilitate the carrying out of a public function[2] and is permitted by regulations (known as the 'Gateway Regulations') made by HM Treasury. Both of these conditions need to be complied with before confidential information can be disclosed[3]. The Gateway Regulations[4] are complex and, in very broad terms, the disclosures that they permit include the following:

- by the FCA, PRA, Bank of England, Secretary of State, or HM Treasury[5], to any person for the purpose of assisting, or enabling them to discharge, any of their public functions[6];

- the sharing of information among the FCA, PRA, or Bank of England for the purpose of discharging public functions[7] (see para **1.37** ff);

- to the FCA, PRA, Bank of England, Secretary of State, or HM Treasury, by any recipient for the purpose of assisting, or enabling them to discharge, any of their public functions[8];

- by any recipient for the purposes of criminal investigations or proceedings, whether in the UK or elsewhere (including proceedings under Parts 2, 3 or 4 of the Proceeds of Crime Act 2002[9])[10];

- broadly, by any recipient[11] for the purposes of, among other things, civil proceedings arising under or by virtue of the FSMA 2000[12] (and certain other legislation)[13], proceedings before the Tribunal, any other civil proceedings to which the FCA is (or is proposed to be) party, proceedings under the Company Directors Disqualification Act 1986 and certain proceedings under the Insolvency legislation[14];

- to comply with an European Community obligation[15];

- in relation to so-called 'single market information'[16], disclosures to certain limited bodies, in some circumstances subject to further conditions, and disclosures by the same categories of bodies for certain purposes[17]; and

- in relation to information that is not subject to restrictions under the directives, disclosures by a recipient to a range of bodies for the purposes of enabling, or assisting, them to discharge specified functions[18], or by any of those bodies, to any person, for the purpose of discharging the same functions[19], or to various disciplinary bodies, broadly, for the purposes of disciplinary proceedings initiated, or which could be initiated by them[20] and by each disciplinary body to any person for the same purposes[21].

1 FSMA 2000, s 349.
2 This is defined in the FSMA 2000, s 349(5).
3 There is no requirement to inform the person, to whom the information relates, of the disclosure. Contrast the position where the police wish to disclose confidential information: 'In order to safeguard the interests of the individual, it is, in my judgement, desirable that where the police are minded to disclose, they should, as in this case, inform the person affected of what they propose to do in such time as to enable that person, if so advised, to seek assistance from

the court. In some cases, that may not be practicable or desirable, but in most cases that seems to me to be the course that should be followed': *Woolgar v Chief Constable of the Sussex Police [1999] EWCA Civ J0526-12, [2000] 1 WLR 25*, at 18 (Kennedy LJ).

4 Financial Services and Markets Act 2000 (Disclosure of Confidential Information) Regulations 2001, SI 2001/2188 as amended by FSMA 2000 (Disclosure of Confidential Information) (Amendment) Regulations 2012, SI 2012/3019.

5 Including an employee of, or auditor, or expert instructed by these bodies.

6 Gateway Regulations, reg 3(1)(a)–(c). This will be subject to any applicable 'directive restrictions' – ie restrictions under the Markets in Financial Instruments Directive, the Banking Consolidation Directive, art 30, the Third Life Insurance Directive, art 15, the Third Non-Life Insurance Directive, art 16, the UCITS Directive, art 50, and the Listing Particulars Directive, art 107: see the Gateway Regulations, reg 3(3).

7 Gateway Regulations, reg 3(1)(d). Including an employee of, or auditor, or expert instructed by these bodies. The points in para **4.228**, n 2 also apply.

8 Gateway Regulations, reg 3(2). Including an employee of, or auditor, or expert instructed by these bodies. The points in para **4.228**, n 2 also apply.

9 See para **3.93** above and see the Gateway Regulations, reg 12C.

10 Gateway Regulations, reg 4. 'Criminal investigation' means an investigation of any crime, including an alleged or suspected crime, and an investigation of whether a crime may have been committed: see the Gateway Regulations, reg 2.

11 The rules relating to those to whom such information can be disclosed are complex: see the Gateway Regulations, reg 5.

12 The FCA has stated that it does consider that a claim of negligence by a customer against a firm or of misrepresentation will arise 'under or by virtue of' the FSMA 2000: see 'The Protection of Regulatory Information under English Law' at http://www.fsa.gov.uk/pubs/mou/equivalence/equivalence-memorandum.pdf.

13 This appears to be a broad phrase, capable of encompassing not only proceedings brought by the FCA (for example, for an injunction or a restitution order: see para **8.99** ff below), but potentially also proceedings for breach of statutory duty under the FSMA 2000, s 138D (see para **19.18** ff below). Note that in order for the gateway to apply, the disclosure must be made for the purpose of facilitating the carrying out of a public function: FSMA 2000, s 349(1)(a). It is not clear whether this would always exclude the use of the gateway in relation to private civil law claims: in *Melton Medes v Securities and Investments Board [1995] Ch 317*, it seems to have been accepted by Lightman J that this may be relevant to the SIB's (the old name of the FSA) responsibilities for the protection of investors and for the maintenance of proper standards of integrity and fair dealing. The same argument could be made in relation to the FCA (depending upon the circumstances).

14 Gateway Regulations, reg 5.

15 Gateway Regulations, reg 6.

16 That is, confidential information received by the FCA in the course of the discharge of its functions as a competent authority under EU legislation. The gateway also encompasses information received under the UCITS Directive.

17 Gateway Regulations, regs 8–10.

18 Gateway Regulations, reg 12(1)(a). The bodies concerned include (amongst others) recognised investment exchanges and clearing houses, the Takeover Panel, the Society of Lloyd's, designated professional bodies, skilled persons (see para **6.18** ff below), persons appointed to conduct statutory investigations (see para **5.10** ff below), auditors or actuaries, overseas regulators, the FOS (see **CHAPTER 14**), and the Pensions Ombudsman. The functions specified in relation to each have been widely drawn. For a full list, see the Gateway Regulations, Schs 1 and 2. Disclosure is also permitted for the purposes of any proceedings under the Proceeds of Crime Act 2002, Pt 2 or under the Proceeds of Crime Act 2002 more generally: see the Gateway Regulations, regs 4 and 12C, respectively. Note the limitations on the confidential information to which reg 12 applies: see the Gateway Regulations, reg 11.

19 Gateway Regulations, reg 12(2).

20 Gateway Regulations, reg 12(1)(b). The disciplinary proceedings concerned include those relating to (amongst others): (i) the exercise of professional duties by barristers, solicitors, auditors, accountants, valuers or actuaries; and (ii) the discharge of duties by officers or servants of the Crown, the FCA, the Takeover Panel and various other bodies.

21 Gateway Regulations, reg 12(3). Where information is to be disclosed to an overseas regulatory authority outside the EU, the FCA will only be likely to disclose confidential information where there is a co-operation agreement in place and the rules of the overseas regulator are likely to ensure that the information will be afforded equivalent guarantees of professional secrecy as are provided under the FSMA 2000, the Gateway Regulations and the single market directives. See the section of the FCA's website (www.fca.org.uk) entitled 'Institutions assessed by the FCA Equivalence Committee to be subject to Equivalent Professional Secrecy Obligations since N2'.

4.235 The Gateway Regulations allow information to be disclosed subject to conditions on how that information will be used[1]. Where such a condition is imposed, the relevant person will commit a criminal offence if he discloses the information in breach of that condition without the consent of the person who disclosed it to him[2].

1 Gateway Regulations, reg 7. Note that such conditions cannot be placed on the FCA, the Secretary of State, HM Treasury or the Bank of England.
2 FSMA 2000, s 352(3) and the Gateway Regulations, reg 7.

What are the penalties for breach?

4.236 Breach of the prohibition against disclosure, or of any restrictions on use imposed under the Gateway Regulations, constitutes a criminal offence[1] unless the person proves that[2]:

- he did not know and had no reason to suspect that the information was confidential information; and

- he took all reasonable precautions and exercised all due diligence to avoid committing the offence.

1 FSMA 2000, s 352(1). As of the date of writing, there have been no significant publicised prosecutions for breaching the prohibition as to disclosure.
2 FSMA 2000, s 352(6).

4.237 It is not clear from the FSMA 2000 whether the above two defences are alternative or whether the defendant has to prove both. It is preferable to regard them as alternatives[1].

1 Although there are contradictory commentaries on this point, the case of *Financial Services Authority v Information Commissioner [2009] EWHC 1548 (Admin)* suggests that the two defences are alternative. This is supported by the explanatory notes and more logical, since they are dealing with different situations.

4.238 Breach of the prohibition does not confer a personal cause of action in favour of those whose consent to the disclosure was required[1].

1 See *Melton Medes Ltd v Securities and Investments Board [1995] Ch 137.*

Can the firm object to the FCA providing information to others?

4.239 The FCA's decision to provide information to another regulator is not one in which the firm has any right to become involved. Indeed, the firm will not normally know about disclosure between the FCA and any other regulators or prosecuting authorities. It is therefore very rare that the firm can object.

4.240 In one situation, the Human Rights Act 1998 may provide grounds for a firm to object to the FCA providing particular information to an overseas regulator. That is where the relevant overseas regulator does not provide equivalent ECHR protections for the firm or individual employees[1]. In such situations, it may be objectionable on ECHR grounds for the FCA to provide the particular information to the overseas regulator, but this will very much depend on the precise circumstances. For example, if an overseas jurisdiction does not recognise the privilege against self-incrimination, then it may arguably be wrong for the FCA to provide a regulator in that jurisdiction with a record of an interview with an individual who may have committed a criminal offence there.

1 Accordingly, see the section of the FCA's website (www.fca.org.uk) entitled 'Institutions assessed by the FCA Equivalence Committee to be subject to Equivalent Professional Secrecy Obligations since N2'.

Use of information in criminal proceedings

4.241 Generally speaking, a statement made by a person to the FCA in response to the exercise of its compulsory investigation powers[1] may not be used in criminal proceedings against that person, except for proceedings relating to perjury or in relation to the provision of false or misleading statements to the FCA. The statement may, however, be used to obtain evidence from other parties which can be used in the proceedings[2].

1 The statutory protection will not, however, encompass all of the compulsory investigation powers and does not apply to statements that have been tendered voluntarily: see para **4.207** above. It also will not prevent other evidence (for example, documentary evidence) that has been compulsorily obtained from a person from being used against him.
2 For a more detailed discussion see para **4.204** ff above.

4.242 Since the FCA regards its investigation powers as being fact finding powers, in many cases it will likely in practice try to obtain the strongest possible evidence by whatever means and then consider what action will be appropriate for it to take and what evidence will be admissible in support of such action.

Chapter 5   Enforcement investigations

INTRODUCTION

5.1   The Regulators have powers corresponding to those previously held by the Financial Services Authority to carry out investigations.

5.2   This chapter outlines those formal powers of investigation under the FSMA 2000, addressing the grounds on which a firm might object to the use of those powers, the steps to take if it wishes to do so and the consequences of not complying with requests made in exercise of these powers.

5.3   The focus of this chapter is mainly on investigations under the FSMA 2000[1] that do not concern breaches of the perimeter (the criminal offence of carrying on regulated activities without authorisation or exemption under the FSMA 2000)[2].

1 The FCA has other statutory powers of investigation, for example, under the Payment Services Regulations 2009, SI 2009/209 and the Electronic Money Regulations 2011, SI 2011/99.
2 If a firm acts beyond the scope of its permission, that may also give rise to regulatory consequences.

5.4   The FSMA 2000 provides a reasonably detailed framework for the Regulators' extensive investigation powers. The FCA's policy on the use of those powers is in the FCA Enforcement Guide at EG Chapter 3 and at other parts of the FCA Handbook, as specified below. No equivalent policy guidance has been provided by the PRA. As a result, only FCA policy is set out below.

5.5   The Regulators will work closely together and, where separate investigations are appropriate, the FCA and the PRA will seek to co-ordinate them. Each Regulator must, however, decide cases and any consequential enforcement or disciplinary actions separately.

THE RANGE OF POWERS AVAILABLE

5.6   The range of formal investigation powers outlined in this chapter is as follows:

Section 167	To investigate the nature, conduct or state of the business, an aspect of that business or the ownership or control of a recognised investment exchange, an authorised person or an appointed representative.
Section 168(1) and (4)	To investigate specific contraventions, offences and other matters.
Section 168(2)	To investigate certain serious criminal or regulatory offences relating to financial services, including insider dealing, market abuse, breach of the general prohibition, unlawful financial promotion, misleading statements or misleading impressions.
Section 169	To conduct an investigation at the request of an overseas regulator.

5.7   These powers are available to the Regulators, save that the PRA may not conduct an investigation in relation to a recognised investment exchange. In addition, the Secretary of State may also exercise certain of these powers[1]. Where this is the case, a reference to the Regulators should be read to encompass a reference to the Secretary of State.

1   Namely, the powers under the FSMA 2000, s 167 in relation to a recognised investment exchange, and the FSMA 2000, s 168 investigation powers for investigations commenced as a result of s 168 (1) or (2).

5.8   The statutory scheme is complicated and allows for either Regulator to gather information itself and to commence a formal investigation and also to appoint investigators in a variety of circumstances. Precisely what information can be demanded and from whom will differ depending upon the ground for the formal investigation.

5.9   Nonetheless, in broad terms, the Regulators can ask the firm to disclose almost any relevant information within its possession, however it has been recorded. This includes documents and records, e-mails, material on its computer system and tapes of telephone calls. It can also interview people and ask for explanations of documents to be given. The mechanism used is the appointment of an investigator to conduct a factual enquiry. In exercise of this appointment, investigators are required to act fairly[1].

1   *Re Pergamon Press Ltd* [1971] 1 Ch 388 at 394.

FORMAL INVESTIGATIONS

5.10   In the following paragraphs, each of the formal investigation powers is reviewed in turn. At paras **5.38** ff the procedure for conducting a formal investigation and practical guidance for firms in dealing with formal investigations is also reviewed.

FSMA 2000, s 167 – general investigations into firms and appointed representatives

When may an investigation be commenced?

5.11   Where it appears that there is good reason for doing so, the Regulators[1] may appoint one or more competent persons to conduct an investigation on its behalf into[2]:

- the nature, conduct or state of the business of an authorised person or of an appointed representative; or

- a particular aspect of that business; or

- the ownership or control of a recognised investment exchange[3]; or

- the ownership or control of an authorised person.

1   This power may also be exercised by the PRA. In addition, the FCA and the Secretary of State have the power to appoint investigators to conduct an investigation into a recognised investment exchange.
2   FSMA 2000, s 167(1). See also the FCA Enforcement Guide at EG Chapter 2, which describes the criteria the FCA must take into account in deciding if there are grounds to investigate.
3   As noted above, this power is not exercisable by the PRA.

5.12   For these purposes, 'business' includes any part of a business even if it does not consist in the carrying out of regulated activities[1]. The investigation could therefore be carried out wholly, or partly, into the firm's unregulated or overseas business.

1   FSMA 2000, s 167(5).

5.13   Although the power is primarily aimed at authorised persons, it is wider in two respects. First, the investigator may, if he thinks it necessary for the purposes of his investigation, also investigate the business of a person who is, or has at any relevant time been, either: (a) a member of the same group[1] as the person under investigation; or (b) a partnership of which that person is

5.13 Enforcement investigations

a member[2], in which case the investigator must give that other person written notice of his decision[3].

1 FSMA 'Group' is defined in the FSMA 2000, s 421.
2 This will not, therefore, extend to a member of the same partnership in respect of its non-partnership business.
3 FSMA 2000, s 167(2) and (3).

5.14 Second, the power may be exercised in relation to a former authorised person (or former appointed representative), but only in relation to business carried on at any time when he was an authorised person (or appointed representative), or in relation to the ownership, or control, of the former authorised person during the same period[1].

1 FSMA 2000, s 167(4).

When will the power be exercised?

5.15 The FCA has indicated that it will rely on this power where it has general concerns about a firm, an appointed representative, or a recognised investment exchange, but the circumstances do not, at that stage, suggest any specific breach or contravention[1].

1 See the FCA Enforcement Guide at EG 3.8.

5.16 The Regulators must give the person who is subject of the investigation written notice of the appointment of an investigator[1].

1 FSMA 2000, s 170(2).

The scope of the power

5.17 The breadth of the activities that can be investigated under this power is notable. This is because many of the factors which may impact on the business of an authorised person – including its financial state and the financial risks of its business generally, the way in which it is controlled and the manner in which it conducts its business – could relate to matters outside a firm's regulated activities. They may relate to non-regulated activities, activities abroad or to the way in which other group companies control the firm or conduct their own businesses. At its widest interpretation, an investigation could probably extend to the non-regulated business of a company in the same group as a company that used to be an authorised person.

What information can the firm be asked to provide?

5.18 In outline[1], an investigator appointed under the FSMA 2000, s 167 may require[2]:

- the person who is the subject of the investigation, or any connected person[3], to meet with the investigator and answer questions or otherwise to provide such information as the investigator may require; or

- any person to produce at a specified time and place any specified documents or documents of a specified description.

1 This topic is dealt with more fully in **Chapter 4** in relation to the Regulators' information gathering powers.
2 FSMA 2000, s 171.
3 Whether a person is a connected person is set out in the FSMA 2000, s 171(4).

5.19   The above requirements may only be imposed insofar as the investigator reasonably considers that the requirement is relevant to the purposes of the investigation[1].

1 FSMA 2000, s 171(3).

FSMA 2000, s 168(1) and (4) – investigations into certain criminal or regulatory offences

When can an investigation be commenced?

5.20   The Regulator may appoint one or more investigators to conduct an investigation on its behalf where circumstances suggest a criminal or regulatory offence may have been committed[1]. This includes the following circumstances:

- failing, without reasonable excuse, to comply with any requirement to provide information to an investigator[2];

- falsifying, concealing, destroying or disposing of any document known to be or likely to be relevant to the investigation (or causing or permitting the same)[3];

- providing false or misleading information either knowingly or recklessly to the investigator[4] or to the firm's auditors or actuaries[5];

- offences in relation to notification of changes in control over authorised persons[6]; or

- in relation to Treaty firms[7], criminal offences under the FSMA 2000, Sch 4.

1 FSMA 2000, s 168(1).
2 FSMA 2000, s 177(1) and (2).
3 FSMA 2000, s 177(3).
4 FSMA 2000, s 177(4) and the FSMA 2000, s 398(1).
5 FSMA 2000, s 346.
6 FSMA 2000, s 191F.
7 Ie a person whose head office is situated in an EEA state other than the United Kingdom: FSMA 2000, Sch 4, para 1.

5.21   If it appears that there are circumstances suggesting that one of the regulatory contraventions or offences listed below has been committed, the Regulators may appoint one or more investigators to conduct an investigation on its behalf[1]. The contraventions are[2]:

- a breach of the FSMA 2000, s 20: the carrying on of a regulated activity other than in accordance with the firm's permission[3];

5.21 Enforcement investigations

- an offence under the Money Laundering Regulations[4];

- an offence under the Counter-Terrorism Act 2008, Sch 7;

- a contravention of one of either of the Regulator's rules, including the Principles for Businesses;

- a contravention by a recognised investment exchange of the recognition requirements within the meaning of the FSMA 2000, Pt 18;

- a lack of fitness and propriety in an individual to perform functions in relation to a regulated activity carried on by an authorised or exempt person;

- a breach by an individual or firm in relation to the application of a prohibition order;

- a breach by an authorised or exempt person, or a person to whom the general prohibition does not apply, by failing to take reasonable care to ensure no regulated function of his is carried out by a person prohibited under a prohibition order[5];

- failure by an authorised person to ensure that no person performs a controlled function under an arrangement entered into to carry out a regulated activity, unless authorised for that controlled activity by the Regulator[6];

- a lack of fitness and propriety in an individual approved by either Regulator for the purpose of carrying out a controlled function under s 59;

- an individual has performed a controlled function where that individual is not approved or should not be so;

- misconduct by an approved person (or certain other employees of a firm, see para **2.52** ff);

- contravention of any provision under the FSMA 2000 for the purposes of implementing the Markets in Financial Instruments Directive 2004/39/EC;

- contravention of any provision made by the Alternative Investment Fund Managers Regulations 2013[7]; or

- contravention of a qualifying EU provision specified by the Treasury by order.

1 FSMA 2000, s 168(4). This power may also be exercised by the PRA. The Secretary of State does not have any parallel power to investigate: s 168(6)(b).
2 FSMA 2000, s 168(4)(a)–(k).
3 This is the equivalent of breaching the general prohibition against businesses carrying on regulated activities without authorisation (although it does not give rise to a criminal offence).
4 This refers to the Money Laundering Regulations 2007, SI 2007/2157: see reg 1(2).
5 Ie breach of the FSMA 2000, s 56(6).
6 Ie breach of the FSMA 2000, s 59(1) or (2).
7 SI 2013/1773.

When will the power be exercised?

5.22 Before it proceeds with an investigation, the FCA will satisfy itself that there is good reason to investigate under the statutory provisions that give the FCA powers to appoint investigators. If the statutory test is met, it will decide whether to carry out an investigation after considering all the relevant circumstances[1].

1 FCA Enforcement Guide at EG 2.10.

5.23 In cases involving both general and specific concerns, the FCA may choose to appoint investigators under both the FSMA 2000, s 167 (in respect of the general concerns) and s 168 (in respect of the specific concerns) at the outset. The FCA may also choose to extend an appointment of investigators under s 167 to cover matters under s 168 as well[1].

1 FCA Enforcement Guide at EG 3.9.

The scope of the power

5.24 The hurdle for the use of this power is a low one: it need only to 'appear' to the Regulators that there are 'circumstances suggesting' a person 'may' be guilty of an offence[1]. A person or firm is therefore likely to have difficulty in challenging the appointment of an investigator on the ground that the statutory test has not been met. Whether the person or firm will subsequently be able to challenge the investigator's use of his powers is a separate question, which is considered at **CHAPTER 21** below.

1 FSMA 2000, s 168(1).

What information can the firm be required to provide?

5.25 In outline[1], an investigator appointed under s 168(1) or (4) has the same powers as an investigator appointed under s 167 plus an additional power to require a person who is neither the subject of the investigation nor a person connected with that person to meet with the investigator, or otherwise to provide such information as the investigator may require for the purposes of the investigation[2].

1 This topic is dealt with more fully in **CHAPTER 4** in relation to the Regulators' information
   gathering powers.
2 FSMA 2000, s 172(1) and (2).

5.26 The test for whether a requirement should be imposed on an unconnected third party focuses on the reasons for obtaining the information from the third party, such that the requirement must be 'necessary' or 'expedient'[1] for the purposes of the investigation[2]. This test is different from the test an investigator applies for imposing a requirement on the firm or a connected person, which focuses on whether the requirement is relevant to the purposes of the investigation. Whilst neither 'necessary' nor 'expedient' expressly requires the investigator to consider whether the material is relevant to the investigation, this must be implicit because it cannot be necessary or expedient for the purposes of the investigation to obtain information which is irrelevant.

1 FSMA 2000, s 172(3).

2 The requirement for material to be 'necessary' or 'expedient' will give a margin of discretion to the investigator: see Lord Diplock in *Secretary of State for Defence v Guardian Newspapers Ltd [1985] AC 339, [1984] 3 All ER 601*. Precisely what will be 'necessary' will depend upon the circumstances. It will 'lie somewhere between "indispensable" on the one hand and "useful" or "expedient" on the other': see Lord Griffiths in *Re an Inquiry under the Company Securities (Insider Dealing) Act 1985 [1988] AC 660, [1988] 1 All ER 203.*

FSMA 2000, s 168(2) – investigations into certain serious criminal or regulatory offences

When can an investigation be commenced?

5.27   The Regulators may appoint an investigator under the FSMA 2000, s 168(2) to conduct an investigation on its behalf if it appears to it that there are circumstances suggesting that any of the following offences may have been committed[1]:

- a person has falsely described or held himself out to be authorised or exempt in relation to a regulated activity[2];

- a person gives a false or misleading statement or creates a false or misleading impression[3];

- the criminal offences of insider dealing[4];

- a breach of the general prohibition[5];

- a contravention of the restrictions on financial promotion[6]; or

- any market abuse[7].

1 As noted above, this power may also be exercised by the Secretary of State.
2 FSMA 2000, s 24(1).
3 Financial Services Act 2012, Pt 7.
4 Under the Criminal Justice Act 1993, Pt V.
5 The criminal offence of breaching the general prohibition against carrying on regulated activities without being authorised or exempt: see the FSMA 2000, ss 19 and 23.
6 FSMA 2000, ss 21 and 238.
7 FSMA 2000, Pt 8.

5.28   This is the most serious of the investigation procedures. In contrast with the other forms of investigation, the subject of an investigation under the FSMA 2000, s 168(2) will not generally be notified of the investigation, at least in the first instance[1]. Furthermore, an investigator appointed under s 168(2) has the widest powers to obtain information from the widest range of people.

1 FSMA 2000, s 170(3). See also the FCA Enforcement Guide at EG 4.3.

When will the power be exercised?

5.29   Leaving aside market abuse and insider dealing, which are discussed separately in **CHAPTER 17**, investigations under the FSMA 2000, s 168(2) are primarily aimed at situations where people are carrying out unauthorised business in some way. The main aim in exercising s 168(2) powers in such circumstances is to protect the interests of consumers[1]. The Regulators will therefore need to consider at an early stage whether it should take urgent enforcement action, as well as continuing its fact finding investigation.

1 FCA Enforcement Guide at EG 2.13 (and EG 2.12–2.14 generally).

What information can the firm be required to provide?

5.30   In outline[1], an investigator appointed under the FSMA 2000, s 168(2) may require any person whom he considers is, or may be, able to give information which is, or may be, relevant to the investigation[2] to:

- meet with an investigator and answer questions or otherwise provide such information as the investigator may require for the purposes of the investigation;

- produce specified documents, or documents of a specified description which appear to the investigator to relate to any matter relevant to the investigation; or

- give the investigator all assistance in connection with the investigation which the person is reasonably able to give.

1 This topic is dealt with more fully in **CHAPTER 4** in relation to the Regulators' information gathering powers.
2 FSMA 2000, s 173.

5.31   The powers afforded by the provision are different from those that apply to the FSMA 2000, ss 167 and 168(1) and (4) investigations, primarily because the s 168(2) powers are expressed not by reference to the person under investigation, but instead by reference to those persons who may hold relevant information. The rationale is that, in an investigation of this nature, it may not be clear (at least at the outset) who will be the person under investigation. Rather, it may be that the investigation relates to a general situation.

5.32   At its widest, a person whom an investigator considers 'may be able' to give information which 'may be relevant to the investigation' could be required to give 'all assistance' with the investigation. This is a very low hurdle for an investigator and gives him broad discretion as to what assistance he can require.

5.33   There are, however, some limitations. An investigator can only require reasonable assistance, which means that he cannot place unreasonable demands on people, whether as to the time they are to expend or as to the expense that they must incur in preparation for the questions or in any other respect[1]. Also if, for whatever reason, the person concerned does not have legal representation, then that is a factor to be taken into account in determining what is reasonable[2].

1 See *Re Mirror Group plc [1999] 3 WLR 583, at 601.*
2 See *Re Mirror Group plc [1999] 3 WLR 583, at 604.*

5.34   Enforcement investigations

FSMA 2000, s 169 – investigations at the request of an overseas regulator

When can an investigation be commenced?

5.34   A regulator may, at the request of an overseas regulator, exercise its s 165 information gathering power or appoint an investigator to investigate any matter[1].

1 FSMA 2000, s 169(1). In respect of the FCA, see also the FCA Enforcement Guide at EG 3.12 and DEPP 7.2.1.

When will the power be exercised?

5.35   The FCA has provided limited guidance as to when it will accede to requests from overseas regulators. The FCA must consider whether the exercise of that power is necessary to comply with any Community obligation[1]. If no Community obligation requires the FCA to assist the overseas regulator, it will first consider whether it is able to assist without using its formal powers, for example, by obtaining the information voluntarily[2]. Where this is not possible, various considerations[3] the FCA may take into account include whether or not:

- corresponding assistance would be given to a UK regulatory authority;

- the case concerns a breach of law where there is no close parallel in the UK or asserts a jurisdiction not recognised by the UK;

- the case is serious and the importance of it to persons in the UK;

- it would be in the public interest to give the assistance sought;

- the overseas regulator will contribute to the FCA's costs.

1 FSMA 2000, s 169(3) and see the FCA Enforcement Guide at EG 3.13. 'Community obligation' refers to EU legal requirements and is a phrase derived from the European Communities Act 1972.
2 FCA Enforcement Guide at EG 3.15.
3 FSMA 2000, s 169(4) and (5) and see the FCA Enforcement Guide at EG 3.14–3.15.

5.36   Given the increasing importance of co-operation between regulators and the international nature of many financial services businesses, firms should expect that the FCA will increasingly use this power in order to obtain information for the purposes of overseas investigations[1]. The extent to which the FCA will be willing to assist overseas regulators may, in practice, largely depend upon its relationship with the relevant regulator. Crucially, this is not something that the firm is likely to be able to influence, except by showing a willingness to provide the information voluntarily, or unless there are particular reasons why the overseas investigation should not be carried on here which will be convincing to the FCA[2].

1 In 2012/2013, the FSA received over 855 formal requests from overseas regulators for assistance relating to investigations or enforcement action.
2 For example, if the safeguards of the Human Rights Act 1998, such as the privilege against self-incrimination, were not available in the overseas jurisdiction, that might be grounds for the firm to seek to prevent certain information from being passed to the overseas body.

What information can the firm be required to provide?

5.37   An investigator appointed under the FSMA 2000, s 169 has identical powers to an investigator appointed as a result of s 168(1). The Regulator may direct an investigator to permit a representative of the overseas regulator to attend and take part in any interviews[1], subject to the Regulator being satisfied that any information obtained by the overseas regulator as a result of the interview will be subject to the same safeguards against disclosure as apply under the FSMA 2000[2].

1 FSMA 2000, s 169(7).
2 FSMA 2000, s 169(8). See also the FSMA 2000, s 131FA and the FCA Enforcement Guide at EG 4.25.

THE PROCEDURE FOR INVESTIGATIONS

How is the investigation started?

5.38   An investigation is commenced by the appointment of an investigator under one of the statutory powers outlined above. The Regulators will usually appoint as investigator one of its own staff[1].

1 This is permitted under the FSMA 2000, s 170(5).

Is the person under investigation notified of the investigation?

5.39   The Regulator is required to give written notice of the appointment of an investigator to the person who is the subject of the investigation[1], subject to the two exceptions set out in the following paragraphs[2]. Where a notice is given, it must specify the provisions under which, and as a result of which, the investigator is appointed and the reason for his appointment. The person who is the subject of the investigation will therefore normally be informed at the outset of the nature of, and reasons for, the investigation. There is, however, no specific requirement for him to be informed of the scope of the investigation, although that information will normally be encompassed within the above.

1 FSMA 2000, s 170(4).
2 See para **5.40** ff below.

5.40   The first exception to the requirement to give written notice is where the investigation is commenced under the FSMA 2000, s 168(2)[1]. The rationale is that, in an investigation of this nature, it may not be clear (at least at the outset) who will be the person under investigation. Rather, it may be that the investigation relates to a general situation. Once it becomes clear who the persons under investigation are, the FCA will normally notify them when it proceeds to exercise its statutory powers to require them to provide information, provided that such notification will not, in the FCA's view, prejudice its ability to conduct the investigation effectively[2].

1 FSMA 2000, s 170(3)(b) – ie an investigation relating to circumstances described in para **5.27** above.
2 FCA Enforcement Guide at EG 4.3.

5.41   In practice, the firm may become aware of the nature of such an investigation when it is first asked to provide information to the investigator. However, this will not necessarily be the same as giving proper notice to the person under investigation. Moreover, the policy outlined above does not preclude the FCA from choosing to obtain information from others, even if it knows exactly who is the subject of the investigation. It is difficult to see why the FCA should not give the person notice at the time when his identity becomes apparent, save where reasons exist to believe that giving him notice might prejudice the conduct of the investigation.

5.42   The second exception to the requirement to give written notice is that, under a s 168(1) or (4) investigation, the Regulator does not need to notify the person under investigation if it believes that the notice would be likely to result in the investigation being frustrated[1]. Neither Regulator has provided any indication of what it would regard as frustrating, or likely to frustrate, an investigation. It could, however, include situations where there are issues about document destruction, misleading information being provided, or concerns that serious fraud or criminal misconduct have been committed. There only has to be a belief (not a 'reasonable belief' or 'reasonable grounds for believing'), that the notice 'would be likely' to result in the investigation being frustrated.

1 FSMA 2000, s 170(3)(a).

5.43   An individual or firm who is aggrieved about the decision not to notify him does not have any particular means of challenging the decision and in any case is likely only to know about it after the event. It may be possible to make a formal complaint[1], although this is unlikely to be of real benefit in relation to the substantive action arising from the investigation, or the point could be made before the Tribunal if the final enforcement decision is referred to the Tribunal[2].

1 See **CHAPTER 14** below.
2 See **CHAPTER 12** below.

Is the investigation made public?

5.44   The FCA will not normally make public the fact that it is or is not investigating a particular matter[1]. As a result, publicity should generally not attach during the investigatory phase. However, the FCA can[2], subject to the restriction on disclosure of confidential information in the FSMA 2000, s 348, make a public announcement that it has commenced an investigation where such announcement is desirable to: (1) maintain public confidence in the financial system or the market; (2) protect consumers or investors; (3) prevent widespread malpractice; (4) help the investigation itself, for example by bringing forward witnesses; or (5) maintain the smooth operation of the market. A public announcement should be made only in exceptional circumstances, such as where the investigation is the subject of public concern, speculation or rumour. The FCA should consider the potential prejudice to the subject of the investigation before making any public announcement[3]. The FCA may also make a public announcement that it has not commenced, nor does it intend to commence, an investigation in the context of a takeover bid[4].

1   FCA Enforcement Guide at EG 6.1.
2   FCA Enforcement Guide at EG 6.3 and 6.4.
3   For example, in April 2013 the FCA publicised the commencement of an FCA enforcement investigation into IT failures at RBS.
4   The decision to issue a public announcement in this context should follow discussion between the FCA and the Takeover Panel. See the FCA Enforcement Guide at EG 6.2.

5.45   Further, the FCA may, in tandem with conducting its investigation, take some other regulatory action which may be made public. For example, this may include where the FCA makes use of its urgent own-initiative or intervention powers[1] or when it has applied to the court for a civil injunction or restitution order[2].

1   See paras **16.115** ff and **16.215** below.
2   See paras **16.165** ff and **16.111** ff below.

5.46   The FCA will not normally publish details of the information found or conclusions reached during an investigation. However, in exceptional circumstances the FCA may, subject to the restriction on disclosure of confidential information in the FSMA 2000, s 348, publish the information found or the conclusions reached during the investigation, in particular where the fact of the FCA's investigation has been made public and it concludes that the concerns that prompted the investigation were unwarranted[1].

1   FCA Enforcement Guide at EG 6.6.

5.47   Where an investigation gives rise to the commencement of enforcement proceedings, as a result of changes to the FSMA 2000 introduced by the Financial Services Act 2012, the matter is likely to become public after a Warning Notice is issued[1].

1   See para **10.108** below.

How is the investigation conducted?

5.48   Once a formal investigation has been commenced, the person appointed as the investigator has broad statutory powers for gathering information from the person under investigation and also from various third parties. As set out in para **5.8** above, the extent of the powers available in any case depends upon the statutory provision under which the investigation was commenced.

5.49   The Regulators may give directions to the investigator to control the scope of the investigation, the period during which it is to be conducted, the manner in which it is to be conducted and how it is to be reported[1]. In particular, such directions may confine or extend the scope of the investigation, discontinue or limit steps to be taken in the investigation, or require the investigator to provide the Regulators with interim reports[2]. No guidance has been given as to the use of such directions.

5.49 Enforcement investigations

1 FSMA 2000, s 170(7).
2 FSMA 2000, s 170(8).

Scoping discussions

5.50   The FCA's policy is to use 'scoping discussions' at the outset of formal investigations in order to help focus its investigations. These discussions will usually be the first meeting between the investigators, the firm and its representatives. They allow the FCA to give the firm an overview of its investigation process and an indication of its concerns. They are also an opportunity for the FCA to seek to identify key individuals, information and documents so that the subsequent investigation can be properly focused and so that the investigators can gain an understanding of the firm's business early on in the investigation[1]. Whilst such meetings can be relatively informal, they may have significant implications for how the investigation will be conducted and appropriate care must be given as to what points are made during these discussions and their accuracy.

1 FCA Enforcement Guide at EG 4.12.

5.51   Points that firms should consider discussing at any scoping discussions include:

- the extent to which the FCA intends to repeat work already carried out in the course of an internal investigation/a skilled person's report;

- the likely timing for production of documents, including producing documents in stages and the prioritisation of certain documents;

- the likely timing for any interviews;

- the format requirements for any documents to be produced electronically;

- whether the FCA is presently minded to pursue individuals as well as the firm; and

- principal communications channels for ongoing dialogue.

Changes to the scope or conduct of the investigation

5.52   If the Regulator issues a direction changing the scope or conduct of the investigation and, in its opinion, the person subject to investigation is likely to be significantly prejudiced by not being made aware of it, the person must be given written notice of the change[1]. This is subject to the same two exceptions as the requirement to notify the commencement of the investigation[2]. The FCA has given limited guidance on how it will apply this in practice, indicating that significant prejudice might include being subjected to unnecessary costs of dealing with an aspect of the investigation which the FCA no longer intends to pursue or where a person may inadvertently incriminate himself by not knowing of the change in scope[3]. The statutory test gives the Regulators a substantial amount of discretion as to whether a particular change needs to be notified. The FCA's views on what is likely significantly to prejudice the person under investigation may be rather different from the views of the person under investigation. However, it is clear from the provision that it is the FCA's views that count and it may be difficult to challenge a decision by the FCA not to notify a change in a particular case[4].

1   FSMA 2000, s 170(9). For the manner in which written notices are to be given, see the Financial Services and Markets Act 2000 (Service of Notices) Regulations 2001, SI 2001/1420.
2   FSMA 2000, s 170(3) and see the FCA Enforcement Guide at EG 4.2 and 4.3.
3   FCA Enforcement Guide at EG 4.1.
4   There is no right to refer such a matter to the Tribunal and, in any event, the firm is unlikely to be aware of it until afterwards. As to the possible options open to the firm, see **CHAPTER 21** below.

5.53   The FCA contemplates that there may be circumstances where it has appointed an investigator under the FSMA 2000, s 167 but circumstances subsequently come to light to suggest that one of the specific regulatory or criminal offences may have been committed, in which case it may decide to extend the appointment to cover one of the s 168 powers[1]. In that case, there could be a desire on the FCA's part to extend the investigation because an investigator appointed under one of the s 168 powers can obtain a greater scope of information from a wider class of people.

1   FCA Enforcement Guide at EG 3.9.

5.54   However, the FCA has not stated what it will do where the opposite is true. Whilst it would seem fair for the FCA to narrow the scope of its investigation and the investigatory powers at its disposal, there is nothing in the FSMA 2000 to require the FCA to do so and there is a clear disadvantage for the FCA to narrow its investigatory powers voluntarily.

OBJECTING TO THE FCA'S USE OF INVESTIGATION POWERS

5.55   Some of the common reasons for seeking to object to the FCA's use of its investigation powers include the following:

- the material requested is protected by legal privilege;

- the material is the subject of a duty of banking confidentiality;

- the firm wishes to co-operate and should not be subjected to the exercise of a formal power;

- the request is contrary to the FCA's stated policy, unreasonable, oppressive or disproportionate;

- providing the information might incriminate an individual or the firm; and

- providing the information would give rise to difficulties for the firm in another jurisdiction.

The material is protected by legal privilege

5.56 Section 413 of the FSMA 2000 provides that a person may not be required to produce, disclose or permit the inspection of 'protected items'. 'Protected items' are:

- communications between a professional legal adviser and his client (or a person representing his client) made: (i) in connection with the giving of legal advice to the client; or (ii) in connection with, or in contemplation of, legal proceedings and for the purposes of those proceedings; or

- communications between any of the above persons and any other person made in connection with, or in contemplation of, legal proceedings and for the purposes of those proceedings; or

- items: (i) enclosed with or referred to in any of the above communications; (ii) made in connection with the giving of legal advice to the client or in connection with, or in contemplation of, legal proceedings and for the purposes of those proceedings; and (iii) in the possession of a person entitled to possession of them[1].

1 It is not wholly clear what this is intended to cover but, under the general law, a non-privileged document will not become a privileged document simply because it is enclosed with a privileged document: see *Ventouris v Mountain [1991] 1 WLR 607*.

5.57 Communications or items will not be 'protected items' if they are held with the intention of furthering a criminal purpose[1].

1 FSMA 2000, s 413(4).

5.58 This complex provision broadly mirrors the doctrine of legal professional privilege and allows firms to decline to provide or disclose documents which are protected under it. However, it still is uncertain whether these provisions reflect precisely the current common law position regarding the extent of legal professional privilege[1]. Since the FSMA 2000 effectively contains its own definition of what is legally privileged, firms need to take care in relying upon this provision. In particular, the statutory definition is unclear in some respects and will need to be clarified by the courts. Importantly, the provision is static whereas the law develops constantly[2]. Accordingly, in considering whether a particular document created, or to be created, will be protected from disclosure under the FSMA 2000 it must be measured as against this provision (properly construed) and not against the common law doctrine.

1 In some respects it seems to be wider than the common law position. In others, it may be narrower. For example, it may not protect 'without prejudice' communications, which the law normally treats as being privileged. Moreover, it is not clear whether internal communications within the firm that have been created for the purposes of obtaining legal advice would be protected, and it is not clear whether the FSMA 2000, s 413 extends to protecting communications that would be regarded as being protected by common interest privilege. However, note that in *R v Special Commissioner of Income Tax, ex p Morgan Grenfell & Co Ltd [2002] UKHL 21, [2003] 1 AC 563*, the House of Lords held that legal professional privilege is to be considered a fundamental human right and that any attempt by statute to curtail that right must expressly be stated or appear by necessary implication.

2   For example, it remains to be seen whether the interpretation given to the common law by the Court of Appeal in *Three Rivers* (*Three Rivers District Council v The Bank of England [2004] EWCA Civ 218*) will also apply to these provisions.

5.59   Section 413 of the FSMA 2000 prevents the Regulators from requiring any person to produce, disclose or permit the inspection of a protected item. In most cases, a document will not cease to be a protected item because it is in the hands of a third party[1]. Should the Regulator obtain materials that are potentially protected communications in which the subject of the investigation participated/ privileged at common law, in circumstances in which it is not clear that privilege has been properly waived (for example, where the item is provided voluntarily by a third party), it should discuss this with the subject of the investigation before the material is considered by the investigators or relied on in the course of regulatory activity. Absent such a discussion, the subject of the investigation may bring an action against the Regulator to prevent the use of such materials[2].

1   The tests under the FSMA 2000, s 413(2)(a)–(b) are unaffected by whether the communications between the specified parties are held by them or by others. Items which are protected items as a result of s 413(2)(c) will only continue to be protected items if they are held by a third party if the third party is entitled to possess them.
2   In *R (Ford) v The Financial Services Authority [2011] EWHC 2583 (Admin), [2012] 1 All ER 1238*, the FSA was provided with two documents which were the claimant's privileged materials. The claimant instituted judicial review proceedings and the High Court ordered that the FSA may not rely on the content of the privileged documents in its regulatory proceedings. See also *R (Ford) v The Financial Services Authority [2012] EWHC 997 (Admin)*. Although not cited, the case appears to apply in the financial services regulatory context the principle in *Goddard v Nationwide Building Society [1987] QB 670, CA* that court will restrain a litigant from making use of privileged material.

The material is the subject of a duty of banking confidentiality

5.60   Confidentiality does not generally provide a basis for declining to produce material to the FCA. However, the FSMA 2000 does contain a limited protection for materials subject to a banker's duty of confidence[1]. This is a qualified duty of confidence which a bank owes its customers[2]. What amounts to a 'bank' for these purposes is unclear, but it seems not to be limited to those institutions that are authorised to carry on a banking business[3]. Where a banker's duty exists, it extends to all information obtained in the course of acting as banker for the customer[4].

1   FSMA 2000, s 175(5). The protection of the banker's duty of confidence by legislation is not new. For example, similar protection was introduced into the Financial Services Act 1986 by the Companies Act 1989.
2   See *Tournier v National Provincial and Union Bank of England [1924] 1 KB 461*.
3   The view of the Financial Law Panel was that the substance, rather than form, of the relationship will be key: see Financial Law Panel Discussion Paper, 'Legal Uncertainties in the Secondary Debt Market', January 1997. Banking Services: Law and Practice, Report by the Review Committee (Chairman: Professor R B Jack) (February 1989), Cm 622 also reviewed in some detail the operation of *Tournier*, but did not address the question of what constituted a 'bank'.
4   In this respect, it is wider than the normal duty of confidentiality which might apply to information which one person receives from another. It could include information which the bank receives about his customer from a third party because he is the customer's banker, subject to the requirement that such information was obtained in the course of the person acting 'as a banker'.

5.61 Enforcement investigations

5.61 The qualifications to the banker's duty of confidence are that it does not preclude the disclosure of information[1]:

- under the compulsion of law;

- where there is a duty to the public to disclose;

- where the interests of the bank require disclosure; or

- where the disclosure is made with the express or implied consent of the customer.

1 See *Tournier v National Provincial and Union Bank of England [1924] 1 KB 461*. For a more detailed discussion, see Toulson and Phipps, *Confidentiality* (3rd edn, 2012), at Ch 12.

5.62 The protection afforded under the FSMA 2000 is also subject to the following exceptions[1]:

- the person who owes the duty of confidence is the person under investigation or a member of that person's group;

- the person to whom the duty of confidence is owed is the person under investigation or a member of that person's group;

- the person to whom the duty of confidence is owed consents to its disclosure or production; or

- the imposition of the requirement with respect to such information or document has been specifically authorised by the Regulators.

1 FSMA 2000, s 175(5).

5.63 The protection afforded by the FSMA 2000 is therefore extremely limited as it only applies to third parties outside of the group of the subject of the investigation. Moreover, through the fourth exception, it can readily be overcome.

The firm wishes to co-operate and should not be subjected to the exercise of a formal power

5.64 Whilst this may be an important practical objection, it is one which may best be made to the FCA itself in the context of a good working relationship. It is difficult to see any legal basis for making an objection on this ground, particularly since the FCA's policy makes clear that, in some instances, for example due to the seriousness of the matter, the FCA will want to use its compulsory powers irrespective of whether the firm is willing to provide information voluntarily. In addition, firms usually prefer the Regulators to compel the production of information under their statutory powers since this usually avoids data protection and confidentiality issues which a firm may face if it were to provide the information voluntarily.

The request is contrary to the Regulator's policy, unreasonable, oppressive or disproportionate

5.65   Such objections may be remediable through the mechanism of judicial review. Whether any objection or challenge is available, and on what basis, will depend very much upon the circumstances of the particular case. This is a complex area and a detailed discussion is beyond the scope of this book. The following paragraphs provide a brief outline of the general considerations in this area.

5.66   Public law bodies owe duties to those affected by their decisions, the scope of which may encompass these sorts of objections. If, for example, the FCA decided to take a particular course of action based on irrelevant considerations, or perhaps different considerations from those set out in the FCA Handbook, or acted in a way that was objectively wholly unreasonable, then the decision may be susceptible to challenge. More generally, the Regulators have to act fairly[1]. In addition, the FCA has indicated that it will use powers, including its enforcement powers, in a proportionate manner[2].

1   See *Re Pergamon Press Ltd [1971] Ch 388* but note that all the rules of natural justice probably do not apply at the investigation stage: see *Herring v Templeman [1973] 3 All ER 569*; *Norwest Holst v Secretary of State for Trade [1978] 1 Ch 201*; and *Moran v Lloyd's [1981] 1 Lloyd's Rep 423*.
2   See the FCA's principles for good regulation and the FCA Enforcement Guide at EG 2.2(2).

5.67   The Regulators must also act in a way that is ECHR compatible. Article 8 of the Convention contains a right to respect for privacy, which applies to individuals, even within the workplace, but it is not yet clear whether it applies to companies[1]. The right is not an absolute one but can be overridden provided this is done in accordance with the law, for a legitimate aim and is necessary in a democratic society for various specified reasons. The test of necessity requires the Regulator to consider whether there is in the particular case a pressing social need for the interference and whether the means employed are proportionate to the aim pursued. This will normally enable the Regulator or an investigator to carry out its investigation, but it requires the Regulator or the investigator to consider the extent of the intrusion that is merited in the particular case and may therefore provide some parameters for the conduct of investigations. The need for proportionality in particular is likely to form the basis for individuals, and perhaps firms, to challenge or object to the use of the investigation powers on human rights grounds.

1   See *R v Broadcasting Standards Commission, ex p BBC [2000] EWCA Civ 116, [2000] 3 All ER 989*, the Court of Appeal held that a company had the right to complain under the Broadcasting Act 1996 that its privacy had been infringed, albeit whilst expressly not commenting on the application of the ECHR, Art 8.

Providing the information might incriminate an individual or the firm

5.68   Self-incrimination is not a basis for refusing to provide information under the FSMA 2000[1]. However, there are limitations on the use that can be made of self-incriminating statements that are obtained using compulsory powers[2]. It is not yet clear whether a statement by an individual employee attracts privilege against self-incrimination in the context of potential criminal proceedings against the company for whom he works.

1 This follows from, among others: *Bank of England v Riley [1992] Ch 475*; *Re London United Investments plc [1992] 2 All ER 842, CA*; and *R v Hertfordshire County Council, ex p Green Environmental Industries Ltd [2000] UKHL 11, [2000] 1 All ER 773.*
2 FSMA 2000, s 174.

Providing the information would give rise to difficulties for the firm in another jurisdiction

5.69   A problem which can arise in practice is that the provision of information to the Regulator would potentially expose the firm to civil or criminal sanctions for breach of applicable overseas requirements, for example banking secrecy laws or data protection legislation. To what extent does this enable the firm to refuse to comply? Whilst the answer will always depend upon the circumstances, the courts have not always been sympathetic to such concerns[1] and the firm will often therefore need to find a pragmatic solution, usually in discussion with the Regulator.

1 See for example, *A v B Bank Ltd (Bank of England intervening) [1992] 1 All ER 778.*

HOW TO OBJECT

5.70   In the first instance, it may be worth raising the objection with the Regulators since the manner in which a request has been framed may be the result of a lack of understanding of the situation on their part. Failing this, trying to make good the objection presents a number of difficulties, not least because the FSMA 2000 contains no procedure for appealing against the exercise of these investigation powers. The firm has no right of recourse to the Tribunal in this regard.

5.71   There are, however, three possible options for a firm:

* refuse to comply with the request;

* make a complaint under the statutory complaints procedure; and/or

* bring a legal challenge to the FCA's, or the investigator's, decision to impose the requirement.

Refusing to comply with the request

5.72   Whilst it may be appropriate in some cases, refusing to comply with a request is an uncertain, high-risk strategy. As set out in para **5.76** below, such conduct could give rise to a court process in which the court may impose a fine or even a custodial sanction if it considers that there was no reasonable excuse for the failure to comply with the statutory requirement. Crucially, a person who refuses to comply with a statutory requirement will not know at the time of the refusal if a court will consider that there was a reasonable excuse for such conduct.

Making a complaint

5.73   In practice, it is unlikely to provide a means for avoiding responding to a request for information. It is much more likely to be used as a means for making a complaint about the FCA's behaviour, and perhaps seeking some compensation, after the event. The complaints procedure, and the potential remedies which it provides, is considered at **CHAPTER 21** below.

Challenging the FCA in court

5.74   If the firm or individual wishes to take action which could prevent the FCA from pursuing its request, then this is likely to be the applicable route. The procedure for bringing legal proceedings against the FCA or PRA to challenge its decisions is outlined in **CHAPTER 21** below.

THE CONSEQUENCES OF NOT COMPLYING WITH FORMAL REQUESTS

5.75   If the firm, or indeed any person, is subjected to a formal request for information from the FCA, or an investigator appointed by it, in the exercise of powers under the FSMA 2000, failure to comply could have a number of potentially serious consequences, as outlined below.

Contempt of court

5.76   The primary consequence is that the person on whom the requirement was imposed could be punished by a court as though he were in contempt of court[1]. This means he could be fined or, in a serious case, imprisoned. To seek such a punishment, the Regulators, or the person appointed to investigate, must certify to the court that the person has not complied with a requirement imposed under the FSMA 2000, Pt 11. The court will then consider whether the firm failed to comply and whether it lacked a reasonable excuse for the failure.

1 FSMA 2000, s 177(1) and (2). Note that this provision does not apply to failures in relation to the provision of information under Principle 11.

5.77   One important question will be who, precisely, is the person on whom the requirement was imposed[1]? It may not be the firm, or solely the firm, since these requirements can be imposed on a range of 'connected persons', including employees, officers and directors. Even if the requirement was imposed on the firm, rather than an individual, an individual may not be absolved from responsibility. The FSMA 2000 allows the court, where dealing with a body corporate, to treat not only the company but also any director or officer as being in contempt[2]. The meaning of the word 'officer' is not entirely clear, but it may include to some extent those who exercise managerial functions or are responsible for maintaining accounts or other records[3]. There is therefore scope for personal liability for certain of those involved in a firm's default.

1 For example, where an investigator writes to the firm's compliance director requesting information, is that a request imposed on him or on the firm? In most situations, unless otherwise specified, it would be natural to expect that it had been imposed on the firm, not on the individual.

2 FSMA 2000, s 177(2). It has been held that a director or officer who is aware of the requirement is under a duty to take reasonable steps to ensure it is obeyed and if he wilfully failed to take those steps then, unless he reasonably believed some other director or officer was taking them, could be punished for contempt: *A-G for Tuvalu v Philatelic Distribution Corpn Ltd [1990] 2 All ER 216* (Woolf LJ). It seems that the mere fact that the person is a director is not in itself sufficient: see *Director General of Fair Trading v Buckland [1990] 1 All ER 545*.

3 'Officer' in relation to a limited liability partnership means a member of the limited liability partnership. Whilst there is no general definition of the word 'officer' in the context of the FSMA 2000, s 177, the FSMA 2000, s 400 defines 'officer' (for the purposes of that section) as meaning a director, member of the committee of management, chief executive, manager, secretary or other similar officer, or a person purporting to act in any such capacity, and an individual who is a controller. 'Manager' is defined in the FSMA 2000, s 423 to include, very broadly, those who exercise managerial functions or are responsible for maintaining accounts or other records.

5.78 The court cannot impose a penalty if it considers that the person had a 'reasonable excuse' for his failure to comply. However, this point is only relevant when the application for contempt is being considered and it would therefore be unsafe to rely on it, save for in fairly exceptional circumstances[1].

1 Cases in which a similar exception has been considered include the following: a journalist argued that he had a 'reasonable excuse' under the Financial Services Act 1986, s 178 for refusing to disclose his sources relying by analogy on the Contempt of Court Act 1981, s 10: *Re an Inquiry under the Company Securities (Insider Dealing) Act 1985 [1988] AC 660, HL*. An overseas injunction restraining compliance was not a 'reasonable excuse' under the Banking Act 1987, s 39: *A v B Bank Ltd (Bank of England intervening) [1992] 1 All ER 778*. But a direction under the Insolvency Rules that a s 236 interview should not be made available to the SFO could amount to a 'reasonable excuse': *Re Arrows Ltd [1992] Ch 545*, although preserving the confidentiality of documents belonging to foreign residents was not a reasonable excuse – see *Omega Group Holdings Ltd v Kozeny [2004] EWHC 189 Comm*. Unfair questioning may amount to a 'reasonable excuse': *Re Mirror Group Newspapers plc [2000] Ch 194*. See also *Re London United Investments plc [1992] 2 All ER 842, CA*.

Criminal offences

5.79 It is a criminal offence for a person knowingly or recklessly to provide information which is false or misleading in a material particular, in purported compliance with a requirement imposed under the FSMA 2000[1]. It is likely that the deliberate provision of partial information which was true but misleading (whilst withholding another piece of information that would provide the full picture) could be sufficient to constitute the offence.

1 FSMA 2000, s 177(4) and s 398(1). This will include providing false or misleading information, even though that provision is in compliance with the firm's obligations under Principle 11: see para **4.25** ff above.

5.80 It is difficult to see that a simple failure to comply with a requirement to provide information could, without more, amount to a criminal offence.

5.81   To the extent that a firm commits any criminal offence, then any officer who consented to or connived in that conduct, or to whose neglect it is attributable, could personally be prosecuted for a criminal offence[1].

1   FSMA 2000, s 400.

Other regulatory consequences

5.82   A firm's failure to provide information could also have regulatory consequences, either because the failure amounted to a breach of Principle 11, for which the FCA could discipline the firm and/or any approved persons (or certain other employees of a firm) who were involved[1], or because it demonstrated that the firm, or relevant individuals, were not fit and proper, which could lead to wider regulatory repercussions, such as the use of own initiative powers[2] or the withdrawal of an individual's approval[3].

1   For example, see the *Towry Investment Management Limited final notice (14/9/11)* (fine imposed for providing incorrect information to the FSA even though Towry was not seeking to deliberately mislead the FSA). Also see para **9.15** below for a discussion of disciplinary action against individuals for being knowingly concerned in regulatory contraventions of firms.
2   See CHAPTER 16 below.
3   See para **16.122** below.

Warrants

5.83   Finally, the FCA may be able to obtain a warrant to enter the relevant premises and seize the material[1]. The Regulators expect authorised persons to grant access voluntarily as part of their duty to co-operate under Principle 11 and a specific rule exists to require this[2].

1   FSMA 2000, s 176.
2   See the Handbooks at SUP 2.3.5R.

5.84   As discussed at paras **4.88** ff above, the FSMA 2000 only allows forced access to premises if a warrant is first obtained from a magistrate. Certain conditions must be satisfied for a warrant to be granted[1]. If granted, a warrant will authorise the police (or an FCA investigator, under supervision and in the company of the police) to[2]:

- enter the premises;

- search the premises and take possession of any documents or information appearing to be relevant to the warrant or take, in relation to any such documents or information, any other steps which may appear to be necessary for preserving or preventing interference with them;

- take copies of or extracts from any documents or information appearing to be relevant;

- require any person on the premises to provide an explanation of any such document or information, or to state where it may be found; and

- use such force as may be reasonably necessary.

5.84 Enforcement investigations

1 FSMA 2000, s 176(2)–(4).
2 FSMA 2000, s 176(5) and see the FCA Enforcement Guide at EG 4.29.

5.85 It should be noted that the power to obtain a warrant is, in certain situations, available pre-emptively where there are grounds for believing that information would not be provided if it were requested.

5.86 It is a criminal offence intentionally to obstruct the exercise of any rights conferred by a warrant[1]. The firm will, however, have a legitimate interest in protecting any legally privileged material[2]. Therefore, whilst the firm will be unlikely to have the opportunity to review its files to identify privileged documents before the warrant is executed, it may wish to assert a claim to privilege in relation to files which it believes could contain privileged material. This will place Regulators on notice of the issue and a mechanism will need to be found for ascertaining whether privileged material that can be withheld exists[3].

1 FSMA 2000, s 177(6).
2 Legally privileged material will clearly be protected, but the extent and basis of that protection is not entirely clear. In particular, compare the FSMA 2000, s 413 and the Police and Criminal Evidence Act 1984, s 19(6). The former precludes the firm from being required to produce, disclose, or permit the inspection of certain classes of privileged material. The latter applies a test of whether the constable has 'reasonable grounds for believing' material to be legally privileged and may involve a different test of legal privilege. See also *R v Chesterfield Justices, ex p Bramley [2000] QB 576.*
3 'It is desirable that any potential dispute about privilege should be resolved before the material is considered by investigators and relied upon in the course of regulatory activity.' *R (Ford) v The Financial Services Authority [2011] EWHC 2583 (Admin), [2012] 1 All ER 1238* at para 13.

USE OF INFORMATION IN CRIMINAL PROCEEDINGS

5.87 Since the FCA regards its investigation powers as being fact finding powers, in many cases it will be likely in practice to try to obtain all the facts by using its statutory powers and then consider what action will be appropriate for it to take and what evidence will be admissible in support of such action.

5.88 Generally speaking, a statement made by a person to the FCA in response to the exercise of its compulsory investigation powers may not be used in criminal proceedings against that person, except for proceedings relating to perjury or in relation to the provision of false or misleading statements to the Regulators[1]. The statement may, however, be used to obtain evidence from other parties which can be used in the proceedings[2].

1 The statutory protection will not encompass all of the compulsory investigation powers and does not apply to statements that have been tendered voluntarily: see para **4.207** above. Any evidence that, for the purposes of the FSMA 2000, s 174(1), is 'evidence relating' to a statement that falls within the FSMA 2000, s 174(1) is protected. However, the protection will not prevent other evidence that has been compulsorily obtained from a person from being used against him.
2 For a more detailed discussion see para **4.204** ff above.

WHAT ACTION CAN THE REGULATORS TAKE AS A RESULT OF AN INVESTIGATION?

5.89   The main purpose of the investigation is for the Regulator to gather the facts relating to the problem so that it can decide what regulatory action should be taken. It is important to realise that the investigation does not necessarily lead to disciplinary charges being brought[1]. Rather, there is a whole range of options for enforcement action open to the Regulators. This includes the following:

- institute disciplinary proceedings;

- vary or cancel a firm's permission;

- withdraw an approved person's approval;

- impose a prohibition order on an individual;

- issue, or apply for a restitution order;

- apply for a civil injunction;

- start insolvency proceedings in relation to the firm;

- prosecute certain offences;

- provide information to another regulatory or prosecuting authority whether in the UK or overseas; and

- commence proceedings for market abuse.

1   For example, the FCA could decide to take no action at all or to issue an informal private warning: see para **8.27** ff below.

5.90   The powers of the Regulators, the basis for the decision as to whether to pursue any of the options above and the procedure for taking that decision are described in **CHAPTERS 8–11**.

5.91   In some instances, the Regulators will decide that the results of the investigation will not merit taking any action at all. Where this happens, the FCA's policy is that it will confirm this to the person concerned as soon as it considers it appropriate to do so having regard to the circumstances of the case[1].

1   FCA Enforcement Guide at EG 4.6.

Chapter 6   Skilled persons' reports

OVERVIEW

6.1   Skilled persons' reports have become an increasingly used and increasingly costly part of the regulatory toolkit. Whereas 64 reports were commissioned in total during 2005–2008[1], in recent years more than 90 have been commissioned annually[2]. The most expensive reports each year currently tend to cost £3–4m each, although a single report has cost as much as £40m[3]. The trend in the increasing use and cost of skilled persons' reports is likely to continue.

1 FSA Annual reports, 2005/2006, 2006/2007, 2007/2008.
2 FSA Annual reports, 2010/2011, 2011/2012, 2012/2013. In contrast, the most expensive report between 2005–2008 cost £1.1m.
3 FSA Annual reports, 2010/2011, 2011/2012, 2012/2013.

6.2   There has also been a trend towards skilled persons' reports resulting in enforcement action against firms and senior individuals. Even where they do not result in an enforcement outcome, skilled persons' reports can still have significant implications for firms and senior management. For instance, they may recommend changes to governance structures, reporting lines or Board composition, all of which can be expensive and disruptive to implement.

6.3   This chapter considers:

- the scope of the power;

- who may exercise the power?

- who may the power be exercised against?

- when is the power exercised?

- the scope of the report;

- selection of the skilled person;

- appointment of the skilled person;

- assisting the skilled person;

- the reporting process;

- practical issues for firms;

- dealing with the skilled person's report; and

- the use of skilled persons under the FSMA 2000, s 166A.

THE SCOPE OF THE POWER

6.4   The power under the FSMA 2000, s 166 to require a skilled person's report is extremely broad and the threshold for exercising the power is very low: a skilled person may be appointed to provide a report on any matter about which the Regulator has required or could require a person to provide information or produce documents[1].

1   FSMA 2000, s 166(1).

WHO MAY EXERCISE THE POWER?

6.5   The power may be exercised by the FCA, PRA or, in certain circumstances, by the Bank[1].

1   FSMA 2000, Sch 17A, para 12.

WHO MAY THE POWER BE EXERCISED AGAINST?

6.6   Any firm who is, or was at the relevant time, carrying on a business and falls within one of the categories below can be the subject of a skilled person's report:

- an authorised person (A)[1], a recognised investment exchange (B)[2] or a recognised clearing house (C)[3]; and

- any member of A, B or C's group[4] or a partnership of which A, B or C is a member.

1 FSMA 2000, s 166(2).
2 FSMA 2000, s 166(10).
3 FSMA 2000, Sch 17A, para 12.
4 'Group' is defined in the FSMA 2000, s 421.

WHEN IS THE POWER EXERCISED?

6.7   Using a skilled person to produce a report has an obvious attraction from a Regulator's perspective for the following reasons:

- the cost of the report falls on the firm[1]. There is therefore little downside to a Regulator in deciding to require a skilled person's report;

- the Regulator can direct the focus of the report, both at the outset and through a continuing dialogue with the skilled person;

- the report itself will be considered independent and authoritative;

- the skilled person can be asked to provide a purely factual report or to provide one which includes its judgements and recommendations about an aspect of the firm's business;

- the report will in many instances allow a Regulator to consider whether to commence an enforcement investigation. Where such a step is taken, it is likely that the report will reduce significantly the amount of additional work required by the enforcement investigation team.

1 Where the skilled person is appointed by the firm, the contract between the firm and the skilled person will govern the payment of the skilled person's fees. Where the skilled person is appointed by a Regulator, the rules in the Handbooks at FEES 3.1.1 and 3.2.7 provide that the firm will be required to pay the fees that the skilled person invoices within 30 days of the invoice being provided to the Regulator.

6.8   This might suggest that the Regulators will require a skilled person's report at almost every opportunity. However, despite the recently increased numbers of reports, that is not the case.

6.9   The policy on the Regulators' use of skilled persons' reports is set out in the Handbooks in the Supervision Manual at SUP 5[1]. Before deciding to require a skilled person's report, a Regulator must consider whether it is appropriate to exercise the power and must have regard, on a case-by-case basis, to all relevant factors[2]. This includes having regard to the alternative regulatory tools available, such as[3]:

- obtaining what is required without using any specific statutory powers (for example, by a visit from a Regulator's staff or a request for information on an informal basis);

6.9 Skilled persons' reports

- requiring information from firms and others, including under the FSMA 2000, s 165; and

- appointing investigators to carry out an investigation under the FSMA 2000, ss 167 or 168.

1 Save for a small number of FCA-specific provisions, SUP 5 applies equally to the FCA and PRA.
2 See the Handbooks at SUP 5.3.3.
3 Handbooks at SUP 5.3.5.

6.10 Although the Regulator is required to have regard to the cost to the firm of the skilled person's report[1], it is clear that little weight is placed on this factor for large firms. For instance, skilled persons' reports commissioned in 2012/13 for interest rate hedging products – which involved an analysis of a very high number of individual transactions with counterparties – have cost one firm £40m and another 13 firms an average of £7.8m each[2].

1 Handbooks at SUP 5.3.8.
2 FSA Annual report, 2012/2013, Appendix 6.

6.11 Before the Regulator finally makes its decision and notifies the firm of the requirement to commission a report, it will normally contact the firm to discuss its likely requirements[1]. Given the potentially significant and disruptive outcomes of skilled persons' reports, firms ought to discuss with the Regulator at this stage (if not before) whether a skilled person's report is strictly necessary in the circumstances and, if so, what is the required scope of the report.

1 See the Handbooks at SUP 5.4.2.

THE SCOPE OF THE REPORT

6.12 According to the Handbook guidance, reports may be used for a variety of purposes, including[1]:

- diagnostic – to identify, assess and measure risks;

- monitoring – to track the development of identified risks, where these arise;

- preventative – to limit or reduce identified risks and so prevent them from crystallising or increasing; and

- remedial – to respond to risks when they have crystallised.

1 Handbooks at SUP 5.3.1.

6.13 In practice, however, more important than the categorisation of the report's purpose is the question of the scope of the work that the skilled person will undertake to prepare his report and whether the scope is proportionate to what the Regulator intends to achieve from the report. The scope of the work to be carried out impacts not only on the cost of having the skilled person produce the report, which will be for the firm to bear, but also on the amount of management time involved and other disruption to the firm's business. Moreover, the nature of the issue that the skilled person is asked to consider has an important bearing on the potential implications of the report for the firm and on how the firm deals with the skilled person[1].

1 For example, in the context of suspected mis-selling, there may be a great deal of difference between a report that is aimed at assessing whether mis-selling took place and one aimed at assessing how any compensation should be assessed and distributed, assuming that mis-sales took place.

6.14 The most significant parameters that affect the cost and potential burden of the report and the potential exposure to the firm are:

- whether the report will be purely factual or whether the skilled person will make judgements, express opinions and give recommendations;

- the period the report is to cover;

- the level of detail required in the final report;

- the categories of documents that the skilled person will review;

- whether the skilled person will conduct any interviews;

- the deadline for the skilled person to provide the report to the Regulator; and

- the skilled person's budget for the report.

6.15 The Regulator will, in most cases, discuss the scope of the report with the firm before it makes its decision to require the production of a report[1]. It may also hold a tripartite meeting involving the firm, the Regulator and the (proposed) skilled person[2]. The firm should take advantage of opportunities to discuss the scope of the work with the Regulator and the skilled person. To the extent possible, the matters set out above should be agreed with the Regulator before the skilled person starts work.

1 See the Handbooks at SUP 5.4.2.
2 Handbooks at SUP 5.4.4.

SELECTION OF THE SKILLED PERSON

6.16 The prospective skilled person must appear to the Regulator to have the skills necessary to make a report on the matter concerned[1]. Depending on the precise nature of the report required, the person appointed could be, for example, a lawyer, compliance consultant, accountant, actuary, IT specialist or any other professional with relevant business, technical or technological skills[2].

1 FSMA 2000, s 166(6) and the Handbooks at SUP 5.4.7.
2 Handbooks at SUP 5.4.7.

6.17 In deciding whether a particular person is appropriate, the Regulator will consider a variety of factors, including whether the person has the necessary skills and any relevant specialist knowledge, his ability to complete the report on time, whether there is any potential conflict of interest and whether he has sufficient detachment to provide an objective opinion[1]. The FCA has designated a panel of skilled persons as appropriate to produce reports[2]. The Regulators expect that only members of this panel will be appointed as a skilled person, regardless of who makes the appointment[3].

1 Handbooks at SUP 5.4.8.
2 See http://www.fca.org.uk/your-fca/documents/skilled-person-panel--1-april-2013. The panel was developed so that the Regulators could use the new power under the FSMA 2000, s 166 to appoint a skilled person directly and comply with the European Procurement Directive and the Public Contracts Regulations 2006, SI 2006/5.
3 See http://www.fca.org.uk/about/what/regulating/how-we-supervise-firms/reports-by-skilled-persons; http://www.bankofengland.co.uk/pra/Pages/supervision/activities/reportsskilledpersons.aspx.

APPOINTMENT OF THE SKILLED PERSON

6.18   The Financial Services Act 2012 introduced a new power under the FSMA 2000, s 166 for the Regulator to appoint a skilled person itself. This is in addition to the existing power which enables a Regulator to require the firm to contract with a skilled person who has been nominated or approved by the Regulator[1].

1 FSMA 2000, s 166(3).

6.19   There is no restriction on when a Regulator may choose to appoint a skilled person itself. The Handbooks provide a non-exhaustive list of examples of when the FCA may appoint the skilled person itself rather than require a firm to do so, including[1]:

- to provide a report or information that is urgently required;

- to assert a greater degree of control over the appointment and oversight of the skilled person due to the sensitive nature of the matter concerned; and

- to assert a greater degree of control over the appointment and oversight of the skilled person in circumstances where more than one firm is the subject of the same report or information required.

1 See the Handbooks at SUP 5, Annex 1.

6.20   No examples have been provided for when the PRA may appoint a skilled person itself.

6.21   Apart from a difference in the appointment and the reporting processes, there are not any significant differences between the process for the Regulator to appoint a skilled person and where the skilled person is appointed by the firm.

6.22   The Handbooks do not provide any guidance as to the contractual terms on which the Regulator will enter into a contract with the skilled person. However, where a firm appoints the skilled person, the firm is required to include certain terms in favour of the Regulator in the contract with the skilled person[1]. These requirements include that:

- the skilled person is required and permitted during and after the course of his appointment:

  - to co-operate with the Regulator in the discharge of its functions under the FSMA 2000 in relation to the firm[2]; and

  - to report to the relevant Regulator various specified categories of matters which the skilled person reasonably believes to be relevant to the Regulator[3]. This will be applicable, for instance, in circumstances where the skilled person becomes aware of an issue falling outside the strict terms of his appointment;

- the Regulator is allowed to enforce the above requirements directly against the skilled person[4]; and

- the contract is governed by the laws of a part of the UK.

1 Handbooks at SUP 5.5.1.
2 Handbooks at SUP 5.5.2 contains guidance as to what such co-operation should include. SUP 5.5.4 states that this may involve direct communication between the Regulator and the skilled person, but also envisages that the firm will generally be kept informed of what information passes between the skilled person and the Regulator where the skilled person is appointed by the firm.
3 For details, see SUP 5.5.1.
4 This should be possible under the Contracts (Rights of Third Parties) Act 1999: see the Handbooks at SUP 5.5.6. Certain specific requirements to ensure that this can be done are found at SUP 5.5.5(2) and (3).

6.23   The contract must also require the skilled person to prepare the report within the time specified and must waive any duty of confidentiality the skilled person may otherwise owe the firm that might limit the provision of information or opinion by the skilled person to the Regulator[1]. Confidential information which a skilled person obtains relating to a person's business or affairs will be covered by the statutory confidentiality restrictions, which apply both to the skilled person and to the Regulator[2].

1 Handbooks at SUP 5.5.1(3). See also the FSMA 2000, s 353 and the Financial Services and Markets Act 2000 (Disclosure of Information by Prescribed Persons) Regulations 2001, SI 2001/1857.
2 FSMA 2000, s 348 and the Handbooks at SUP 5.6.1. The skilled person will be a 'primary recipient' and will therefore commit a criminal offence if he improperly discloses confidential information which he obtains relating to the firm's business or affairs. See **4.226** ff above. Banking confidentiality and legal privilege will also apply: see SUP 5.6.2 and see respectively paras **5.60** ff and **5.56** ff above.

6.24   The Regulator will ask the firm to give it a copy of the draft contract before it has been finalised with the skilled person and, if so, may inform the firm of any matters that it considers require clarification or discussion before the contract is entered into[1].

1 See the Handbooks at SUP 5.5.7. Whilst the guidance is not stated in absolute terms, since the contract with the skilled person will dictate the scope and methodology of the report, the Regulator will wish to review the draft contract.

6.25   In practice, a firm should seek to include the following in its contract with a skilled person[1]:

6.25 Skilled persons' reports

- whether the report should be solely factual or should set out the facts and provide an opinion on them;

- whether any relevant documents should be appended to the report or only summarised within it;

- whether interim reports will be required;

- whether updates as to how the investigation is progressing are to be provided;

- whether there are means to ensure that the costs are controlled;

- whether drafts of the report will be provided; and

- whether any other parties will receive a copy of the report.

1 Handbooks, SUP 5.5.2: the firm should also permit the skilled person to provide the Regulator (should it so request) with (i) information relating to the planning and progress of the report; (ii) relevant documents, and (iii) copies of any drafts that have been provided to the firm.

ASSISTING THE SKILLED PERSON

6.26 Firms are required to provide all reasonable assistance to any skilled person that has been appointed[1]. Reasonable assistance will include giving access during reasonable business hours to the firm's accounting and other records (in whatever form), providing such information and explanations as the skilled person reasonably considers to be necessary or desirable for the performance of his duties, and permitting him to obtain directly from the firm's auditors such information as he reasonably considers to be necessary or desirable for the proper performance of his duties[2]. A firm will be expected to provide such assistance in a timely manner[3].

1 Handbooks, SUP 5.5.9 ff. The firm would not, though, need to provide information or documents protected under the FSMA 2000, s 413 as being, broadly, legally privileged (see para **5.56** ff) and, in certain circumstances, it may be possible to withhold information or documents protected by a duty of banking confidentiality (see the FSMA 2000, s 175(5), SUP 5.6.2 and para **5.60** ff above). See also para **6.23** above.
2 See the Handbooks at SUP 5.5.11.
3 Handbooks at SUP 5.4.3. Adherence to the timetable can obviously be affected by how the firm, or its advisers, deals with the skilled person. If the skilled person becomes aware that the report may not be delivered in time, he will be obliged to inform the Regulator and the firm as soon as possible: SUP 5.4.12.

6.27 Reasonable assistance will also include taking reasonable steps to ensure that, when reasonably required by the skilled person, its appointed representatives waive any duty of confidentiality and provide the same reasonable assistance to the skilled person[1].

1 Handbooks at SUP 5.5.10.

6.28 A failure to co-operate with the skilled person is probably a breach of Principle 11[1]. Moreover, if, in purported compliance with a requirement imposed by a Regulator, a firm knowingly or recklessly provides information which was false or misleading in a material particular, then the firm would be guilty of a criminal offence[2]. Thus, where a firm knowingly or recklessly provides false or misleading information to a skilled person which is then set out in the skilled person's report that the firm provides to the Regulator, the firm would also be guilty of a criminal offence.

1 The Handbooks, Principles for Businesses, Principle 11. For a description of the Principle 11 obligation and the consequences of its breach, see para **4.25** ff above.
2 FSMA 2000, s 177(4).

6.29   Any person who provides, or has provided, services to the firm in relation to the subject matter of the skilled person's report is under a duty to provide the skilled person with all such assistance as he may reasonably require[1]. This is enforceable by injunction[2]. Neither the FSMA 2000 nor the Handbook rules explain who bears the cost of this assistance, but, often, it will in practice be the firm that does so.

1 FSMA 2000, s 166(7). Co-operation will also, for example, be expected from the firm's suppliers under material outsourcing arrangements: SUP 5.5.13.
2 FSMA 2000, s 166(8).

6.30   There is no indication of precisely what assistance it is reasonable for the skilled person to require and so this may be the subject of some debate. Whilst a service-provider to the firm may, for example, be willing to spend a relatively small amount of time explaining the firm's systems, the way in which particular funds have been valued or the rationale for particular controls, auditors or actuaries may take a different view if the skilled person wants access to their own files and working papers, which may be the property of the auditor or the actuary, not of his client, and which he may therefore properly withhold from his client[1].

1 See *Chantrey Martin & Co v Martin [1953] 2 QB 286* and *Gomba Holdings UK Ltd v Minories Finance Ltd [1988] 1 WLR 1231.*

THE REPORTING PROCESS

6.31   If a skilled person is appointed by the Regulator itself, the skilled person will report 'directly' to the Regulator[1]. It remains to be seen how this guidance will be applied in practice. It would be highly surprising if it results in the firm not seeing the report. It seems that the more likely approach would be that, in circumstances in which a report is urgently required, the report is provided to the Regulator and the firm at the same time so that the provision of the report to the Regulator is not delayed by waiting for the firm to provide its comments.

1 The Handbooks at SUP 5.4.10A.

6.32   If the skilled person is appointed by the firm, the skilled person will normally report to the Regulator 'through' the firm. As such, the skilled person would provide the report to the firm and the firm would then provide it to the Regulator. The firm will usually be provided with a draft of the report and given the opportunity to provide the skilled person with written comments before a final version is produced for the Regulator[1].

1 Handbooks at SUP 5.4.10.

6.33   The Regulator may require the report to be in such form as is specified in the notice, although in substantial or complex cases, the Regulator may monitor progress and re-focus the report if necessary[1]. While the report is being prepared, the Regulator may discuss matters relevant to the report with the skilled person. Such discussions may also involve the firm[2].

1 Handbooks at SUP 5.5.4.
2 Handbooks at SUP 5.4.11. For example, such discussions may concern whether, in light of the information that has been gathered, the scope of the report should be changed.

6.34   When the report has been finalised, the Regulator may organise a tripartite meeting with the firm and the skilled person to discuss the report's conclusions. The Regulator may also decide to meet the skilled person without the firm being present to discuss the final report[1].

1 Handbooks at SUP 5.4.13.

PRACTICAL ISSUES FOR FIRMS

6.35   The proposal to appoint a skilled person will raise a number of practical questions for the firm. Issues which the firm may need to consider include:

• Can the firm avoid the appointment?

• Can the firm control the scope of the report?

• Are any staff resource issues likely to arise?

• Is there a risk of prejudicial material being created?

• Should the firm obtain a 'parallel' expert report?

6.36   Each of these is considered in turn below.

Can the firm avoid the appointment?

6.37   Given the potentially significant and disruptive potential outcomes of skilled persons' reports, firms ought to discuss with the Regulator at an early stage whether in fact a skilled person's report is necessary in the circumstances. Possible alternative means to provide the Regulator with a report outside of the formal skilled person's regime could be, for example, by commissioning an internal report or by the firm commissioning a report from its own advisers who are familiar with its business.

Can the firm control the scope of the report?

6.38   If faced with a request for a report which appears to ask the wrong questions or which appears unfocused in its objectives, unrealistically wide in its scope or otherwise disproportionate, the first step for the firm is to seek to have the scope of the report narrowed. Too broad a scope may stem from a lack of understanding of the firm's business by the Regulator. Through discussions, it may be possible to reach agreement on the nature of the report that is really required to meet the Regulator's objectives (in the event that it has been decided that a skilled person's report is required).

6.39   Although the firm may raise its concerns, ultimately the scope of the report is the decision of the Regulator. If the firm has a fundamental disagreement with the Regulator's assessment as to the need for, or scope of, the report, the only remedy likely to be available to the firm will be to institute judicial review proceedings against the Regulator: see further **CHAPTER 21** below. However, this is not likely to be a potential remedy, save in rare circumstances.

Are any staff resource issues likely to arise?

6.40   The firm's obligation to assist the skilled person has been outlined at para **6.26** ff above. Depending on the issues within scope, providing the necessary assistance may entail significant time from the firm's employees and relevant management. Among other things, the skilled person may need assistance with accessing the firm's computer systems or understanding the firm's documents, procedures, policies and processes. If there are likely to be difficulties in providing staff resource to assist the skilled person, it may be worth raising this with the Regulator, particularly if it may impact on the timing of producing the report.

Is there a risk of prejudicial, disclosable material being produced?

6.41   The skilled person's report, and any discussions the firm has with the skilled person and documents the firm provides to him, will clearly be disclosable to the Regulator. Such material could also be disclosable to third parties who might bring civil claims against the firm arising from the same matter. The potential disclosure implications of the investigation process are considered more generally at para **4.145** above. There are three primary points to note for present purposes.

6.42   First, relevant documents will exist not only in the firm's hands but also in the hands of the skilled person and the Regulator. Documents which the firm has are unlikely to be protected from disclosure to third parties, unless they are legally privileged[1]. Documents held by the skilled person or the Regulator are, however, likely to be protected from disclosure under the FSMA 2000, unless they are made publicly available, for example, in Tribunal proceedings held in public[2].

1 The meaning of legal privilege is considered at para **4.153** ff. A firm should consider how best to protect its privilege position as against third parties in respect of any privileged information that it discloses to the skilled person and/or the Regulator.
2 The skilled person will be a 'primary recipient' under the FSMA 2000, s 348 and confidential information which he obtains in the discharge of his functions will therefore be strictly protected under the FSMA 2000, subject to the Gateway Regulations, SI 2001/2188: see para **4.226** ff above.

6.43   Second, the firm should take care in relation to the documents that it creates for the skilled person and in its discussions with the skilled person. Since the firm is required to co-operate fully with the skilled person, this consideration is most relevant for matters that could create a potential litigation risk for the firm that is unconnected or only peripherally connected to the scope of the skilled person's report. For matters that fall directly within the scope of the report, it will be difficult in practice to do much to lessen the risk posed by the creation of damaging material. However, it may, for example, be possible to avoid creating particularly damaging written material and instead provide the skilled person with an oral briefing on the relevant subject. The skilled person may decide not to report on that matter at all or in less detail than that disclosed[1].

1 Of course, if the skilled person produces notes of the oral briefing, there will be a risk that those notes will be disclosable.

6.44   Third, although the general practice is for the firm to be provided with a copy of the skilled person's report, once the report is in the hands of the firm, the firm may be required to disclose this in any ensuing litigation[1]. Moreover, the skilled person himself could potentially be required to give evidence in such litigation[2].

1 Provided that the information contained within it is not protected under the FSMA 2000, s 348: see para **4.226** ff above.
2 Subject to the same proviso.

Should the firm obtain a parallel expert report?

6.45   The skilled person's report will potentially have a significant effect, not only in terms of the firm's exposure to regulatory action but also in relation to its potential civil liability. As set out above, a report could result in enforcement action, alterations in governance structures, reporting lines, board composition or have other implications and consequences. Reports can also be used to enable the Regulator to assess the extent of losses suffered by customers.

6.46   Whether or not the skilled person is required to express opinions, make judgements or recommendations, the appropriate next steps following the skilled person's report will be a matter for discussion with the Regulator. The firm may wish to commission a parallel expert report so that it can consider privately with its expert the most appropriate next steps, and enable the firm to advocate its position to the Regulator.

6.47   The second expert would act purely for the firm and it may be possible for his work to be structured so as to be protected by legal privilege, in whole or in part, and thus be protected from disclosure both to the Regulator and to third parties. The expert's role would be to assist the firm in its dealings with the Regulator and the skilled person, particularly in technical areas where experts might disagree. There is a cost involved, in that the firm must pay for the skilled person and the expert to carry out broadly the same work, but this may be outweighed by the benefits in large or complex cases[1]. Moreover, where the aim of the report is to evaluate a matter of opinion (for example, whether the firm has acted in accordance with market practice), a second report may help the firm to raise, with greater credibility, questions about the results of a report with which it disagrees.

1 For example, in *Legal & General Assurance Society Ltd v FSA (2003) FIN 0022*, the existence of a second report commissioned privately by the firm at the same time as a tripartite report was being produced was an important factor in enabling the firm to challenge the results of the tripartite report.

6.48   Where the firm does commission its own report and its results differ from the skilled person's report, the firm may consider whether the experts should meet to discuss the reasons for the difference. That meeting is likely to be of most use before any decision is taken by the Regulator to recommend enforcement action[1].

1 The decision by the Regulator on whether or not to recommend enforcement action is considered at para **10.86** ff below.

DEALING WITH THE REPORT

6.49   Given the reasons why skilled person's reports are commissioned, it is likely that the resulting report will indicate matters which the Regulator may want the firm to address. The firm should consider carefully not only at the reporting stage but also during the course of the skilled person's exercise any remedial action that should be taken.

6.50   If, before the final report is prepared, the firm considers that it is likely to disagree with part of the skilled person's report, the firm should seek to discuss the matter with the skilled person. If the matter cannot be resolved and the points on which the firm disagrees are contained in the final report, the firm should consider setting out its reasons for the disagreement in writing and sending them to the Regulator at the same time as the final report is provided. This will be easier to do if the firm has commissioned a second report, as discussed at para **6.45** ff above.

6.51   There are two main reasons for taking issue with any part of the report with which the firm disagrees. First, the report may lead to enforcement action against the firm. If the firm does not promptly rebut the points made in the report with which it disagrees, it may later be regarded as having initially accepted them, notwithstanding the contents of any subsequent representations. For the firm to have any prospect of persuading the enforcement staff not to recommend action on the basis of a report containing damaging findings, then it will need to provide cogent reasons for disputing the report. Second, in certain circumstances, there may be a risk of the report needing to be disclosed in litigation with third parties[1] and, again, it may be important that the firm immediately indicated that it disagreed with its content.

1 See para **6.41** ff above.

THE USE OF SKILLED PERSONS UNDER THE FSMA 2000, S 166A

6.52   The Financial Services Act 2012 introduced a new power under the FSMA 2000, s 166A which, in contrast to the FSMA 2000, s 166, can only be exercised when the Regulator considers that the firm has contravened a requirement to collect and keep certain information[1] up to date. In such circumstances, a skilled person can be appointed to collect or update the information. As such, the power under the FSMA 2000, s 166A is purely remedial and should be scoped accordingly.

1   This is information of a description specified in any rule made by the FCA or PRA under the FSMA 2000. See the FSMA 2000, ss 166A and 419.

6.53   The considerations relating to the selection and appointment of the skilled person, and the duties of the firm and others towards the skilled person, under this power will be similar to those discussed above.

Chapter 7 Handling multi-jurisdictional investigations

INTRODUCTION

7.1 This chapter focuses on the key issues that need to be considered when handling a cross-border or multi-jurisdictional investigation.

7.2 In the aftermath of the financial crisis, financial services regulators around the world have adopted a more interventionist approach to their regulation of firms. Regulatory investigations and enforcement actions have proliferated and now increasingly involve criminal as well as anti-trust authorities.

7.3 Regulators across jurisdictions (whether civil or criminal) are increasingly exchanging information and in some cases co-ordinating and co-operating in relation to investigations. In 2012/2013 the Financial Conduct Authority (FCA) (and its predecessor, the Financial Services Authority) received 855 formal requests for assistance from overseas regulators[1]. In 2012 the US Securities and Exchange Commission (SEC) made 718 requests of overseas regulators and received 450 requests[2]. This pattern has been repeated by other regulators. France's financial markets regulator, AMF, closed 43 investigations in 2012 that were opened in response to requests for international assistance[3], and over the same period

7.3   Handling multi-jurisdictional investigations

the Hong Kong Securities and Futures Commission dealt with 112 overseas enforcement-related requests and made 146 requests of overseas regulators[4].

1   FSA/FCA Enforcement Annual Performance Account for 2012/2013 at p 31.
2   SEC 2012 Annual Performance Report.
3   AMF Facts & Figures 2012.
4   See http://www.sfc.hk/web/annualreport2012-13/EN/operational-review/regulatory-collaboration. html).

7.4   This trend towards regulatory co-operation and co-ordination is set to continue. The International Organization of Securities Commission (IOSCO), which regulates more than 95% of the world's securities markets, has reinforced its standard on cross-border co-operation and adopted measures to encourage 28 non-signatory members to sign the IOSCO Multilateral Memorandum of Understanding (MMoU) on co-operation and exchange of information which was established in 2002[1].

1   See www.iosco.org/news/pdf/IOSCONEWS299.pdf. The MMoU currently has a total of 97 signatories out of a total of 125 eligible IOSCO members.

7.5   The MMoU facilitates cross-border investigation of market misconduct and enhances global regulation and enforcement by providing a vehicle through which securities regulators share investigative material, such as beneficial ownership information, securities and derivatives transaction records and bank and brokerage records. It also sets out specific requirements for the exchange of information, ensuring that no domestic banking secrecy, blocking laws or regulations prevent the provision of enforcement information among securities regulators[1].

1   In 2006, 520 requests for assistance were made pursuant to the MMoU while in 2012 2,374 requests were made.

7.6   Within the EU, provisions for the exchange of information and co-operation and co-ordination are also being enhanced, for example in the Market Abuse Regulation and MiFID 2[1].

1   Neither of these instruments have been published in the Official Journal at the time of writing but see for example arts 17–23 of the proposed Market Abuse Regulation adopted by the European Parliament on 10/09/2013, proposed to replace Directive EC 2003/6, and arts 83–85 of MiFID II adopted by the European Commission on 20/10/2011, proposed to replace Directive 2004/39.

7.7   Increased levels of multi-jurisdictional regulatory co-ordination and co-operation significantly impact how firms should handle regulatory inquiries as well as any internal investigations that they may need to conduct. A co-ordinated approach across jurisdictions is vital to the successful management of any issue that has a cross-border dimension.

7.8   At the outset of any investigation it is therefore vital to plan for the differences in regulatory and jurisdictional regimes that are likely to be involved. These differences need to be managed throughout the investigation.

7.9   A firm should devise a co-ordinated international strategy for a cross-border investigation based on an assessment of the following key factors:

- *understand the regulators involved*: identify the relevant regulators and understand the scope of their regulatory powers;

- *identify the party conducting the investigation*: identify the entity within the firm that should conduct the investigation, based both on regulatory requirements and the need to protect legal privilege and confidentiality;

- *best practices*: manage issues such as legal privilege and confidentiality, data protection obligations and employee-related issues; these factors must be considered when structuring the investigation, including who may be involved in conducting it and where documents should be located;

- *communications with regulators*: consider self-reporting obligations in the jurisdictions at issue, expectations for voluntary self-reporting, and the collateral consequences for other jurisdictions if self-reporting is required or strategically preferred in any one jurisdiction;

- *public disclosure*: evaluate disclosure obligations in various jurisdictions, including the need for announcements to the market and/or disclosures in public filings;

- *resolution*: analyse the forms of resolution available and consider the impact of reaching a resolution in one jurisdiction on ongoing investigations in other jurisdictions.

7.10   Given the resources and powers of US regulators and their inclination to exercise extra-territorial jurisdiction, firms have tended to be most concerned about their position in the US. However, regulatory activity is flourishing elsewhere in the world, as non-US regulators acquire enhanced powers and increasingly seek to impose substantial sanctions[1]. Moreover, non-US regulators are unlikely to accept that their enquiries or concerns are or should be of lesser import for firms than those of their US counterparts. This means that firms need increasingly to be aware of their potential exposure outside the US and develop a strategy that has regard to the potential interests of all regulators (whether civil or criminal), wherever they are located around the world.

1   See for example the FCA Press Release FCA/PN/88/2013 of the £137 million fine imposed on JP Morgan for failings related to its Chief Investment Office concerning the 'London Whale' trades.

7.11   In practice, a firm might decide to make separate self-reports in multiple jurisdictions and then proactively manage the resulting regulatory climate. This will mean not only choosing which regulator to approach first, but developing a clear plan as to which other regulators might have an interest in the matter and defining an approach to them so that the firm's exposure is controlled.

7.12   Consideration will also have to be given to PR and capital market announcements. Again, these may need to be co-ordinated so that they are done on a simultaneous basis internationally to avoid the damaging consequences of prolonged media attention and potential impact on share price that might be caused by providing disclosure to multiple regulators on a rolling basis.

7.13 Handling multi-jurisdictional investigations

7.13 Given that regulators are increasingly sharing information with each other, a firm must therefore ensure that it deals with regulators in a consistent fashion. Indeed, a co-ordinated approach across jurisdictions is vital to the success of any cross-border investigation and in some cases it may even be possible to conclude a single, global resolution with multiple regulators.

THE REGULATORS AND THEIR POWERS

7.14 The first area that needs to be addressed in any cross-border or multi-jurisdictional regulatory inquiry or investigation is to identify and understand which regulators are likely to be involved in the issue, both immediately and as it progresses, and what action those regulators may wish to take.

7.15 Regulatory investigations, and the enforcement sanctions that may follow, can have a significant financial effect on a firm as well as on its business reputation. In the current climate of growing regulatory focus on market conduct, as well as enhanced co-operation between national authorities, firms need to be acutely aware of the processes that financial services and other regulators adopt when they carry out their investigations and enforcement actions.

7.16 In recent years regulators have started to work together in some cases to jointly investigate and resolve international problems[1]. However, regulators are often driven by their own political agendas and tensions can sometimes arise over which regulator or regulators will take the lead role in co-ordinating a cross-border matter. This in turn can lead to various challenges for firms including, for example, how to respond to different regulators' powers and dealing with multiple and sometimes overlapping requests for information from different regulators and on different timescales.

1 Recent examples include: (i) the investigations and subsequent settlements with Barclays, UBS and RBS over attempts to manipulate LIBOR involved the US SEC, Department of Justice and UK FSA (and in the case of UBS, the Swiss Financial Market Supervisory Authority). Regulators in Asia also continue to conduct investigations in relation to LIBOR related issues; (ii) US and UK authorities investigations and subsequent settlement with JP Morgan in relation to the 'London Whale' trading losses.

Who are the regulators in the key financial markets?

7.17 This section summarises the main financial services regulators in key financial markets.

France

7.18 The Autorité des Marchés Financiers (AMF) has primary responsibility for regulation of the financial services sector in France, excluding the insurance sector[1]. The AMF is equipped with extensive investigative and sanctions powers and has four main areas of responsibility: (i) regulation; (ii) authorisation; (iii) supervision; and (iv) enforcement. The AMF consists of two separate bodies: the

Board and the Sanctions Commission, which has the exclusive power to impose penalties and sanctions. The Commission has 12 members, none of whom are members of the Board.

1 Article L621 of the *Code monétaire et financier* (the CMF). The AMF is responsible for issuers, credit institutions authorised to provide investment services, investment firms, investment management companies, investment advisers, direct sellers and rating agencies etc.

7.19   The Sanctions Commission may impose sanctions or penalties on: (i) professional entities that are under the supervision of the AMF, for any breach of professional obligations established by law, regulations or rules of professional conduct approved by the AMF; (ii) natural persons (individuals) under the authority of or acting on behalf of such entities; and (iii) any other person who commits, or attempts to commit, market abuse, insider trading or the disclosure of false or misleading information.

7.20   Where the facts of a case suggest that a criminal offence has been committed, the Board of the AMF must hand the matter over to the Public Prosecutor and pass on its inspection or investigation report[1].

1 Article L 621-20-1 of the CMF.

7.21   The French Prudential Supervisory Authority (ACP) is an independent regulatory body created in January 2010 following the merger of the regulators of the banking and insurance sectors[1]. The ACP's main function is to ensure stability in the financial system and protect bank's customers and insurance policyholders. The ACP has investigative, administrative, sanctioning powers, and the ability to impose professional sanctions and fines of up to €100m.

1 For further information, see: http://www.acap.banque-france.fr.

Germany

7.22   Since 2002, the Federal Financial Supervisory Authority (Bundesanstalt für Finanzdienstleistungsaufsicht (the BaFin) has been the central regulator for the financial services sector in Germany which supervises all firms and ensures compliance with and enforces the rules of the German Securities Trading Act (WpHG), the Securities Acquisition and Takeover Act (WpÜG), and the Securities Prospectus Act (VerkaufprospektG).

7.23   BaFin has powers to investigate breaches of regulatory rules, make orders or demands, including to partially or completely liquidate a business or require firms to remove managers[1].

1 See section 1 ff of the Act Establishing the Federal Financial Supervisory Authority (FinDAG).

7.24   BaFin does not have the authority to prosecute criminal offences; it may only impose fines for administrative purposes. Instead, exclusive jurisdiction for criminal prosecutions lies with the prosecutor's offices within Germany's Federal States.

7.25   Handling multi-jurisdictional investigations

Hong Kong

7.25   The Securities and Futures Commission (the SFC) has overall responsibility for the regulation and development of Hong Kong listed securities and futures markets[1].

1   The SFC derives its regulatory powers from the Securities and Futures Ordinance (the SFO) (Cap 571). Introduced in 2003, this is the main piece of legislation in Hong Kong dealing with the securities and futures markets.

7.26   The SFC licenses individuals and companies who provide financial services to the public. It also polices and investigates the conduct of regulated activities, any misconduct on the Hong Kong securities and futures markets and mismanagement of listed companies and has broad supervisory and investigatory powers over licensed corporations, listed companies and companies and persons trading on the Hong Kong markets.

7.27   In addition, the Hong Kong Monetary Authority (the HKMA) maintains monetary and banking stability and remains the frontline regulator for banks.

7.28   The Commercial Crimes Bureau of the Hong Kong Police Force investigates high-value economic crimes. However, the Prosecutions Division of the Department of Justice is responsible for initiating and conducting the prosecution of all such cases, including indictable offences under the Securities and Futures Ordinance.

Italy

7.29   There is no single regulator with comprehensive jurisdiction over the financial services sector in Italy. The Italian regulatory system is based on combined supervision by a number of independent authorities and government entities.

7.30   The principal financial services regulators are Commissione Nazionale per la Società e la Borsa (Consob) (the regulator for financial services, capital markets and the stock exchange); Banca d'Italia (Bank of Italy), which supervises the banking system and the stability of financial intermediaries; and Instituto per la Vigilanza sulle Assicurazioni Private e di Interesse Collettivo (ISVAP), which regulates the insurance sector.

7.31   In addition, public prosecutors (Pubblico Ministero) in Italy frequently become involved in financial services related investigations, with the Milan Public Prosecutor being particularly active. All regulatory breaches which are considered to be criminal offences in Italy will be prosecuted by the Pubblico Ministero.

Japan

7.32   The principal financial services regulators in Japan are the Japan Financial Services Agency (the JFSA) and the Securities and Exchange

Surveillance Commission (the SESC). The JFSA is primarily responsible for stabilising financial markets and protecting investors by inspecting and supervising firms such as banks, securities firms and insurance companies. The SESC, like the JFSA, is responsible for protecting investors and maintaining the integrity of the Japanese securities market. It focuses on surveillance and inspection and its enforcement powers are exercised by the JFSA. Although the SESC is supervised by the JFSA, its autonomy is highly respected.

7.33   The Public Prosecutors Office (Kensatsu Cho) has significant investigative and prosecutorial powers relating to criminal offences. The prosecutors decide whether or not to prosecute and often initiate and complete investigations involving bribery and high-value financial crime independently of the police. Special Investigative Departments within the District Public Prosecutor's Offices in Osaka, Nagoya and Tokyo tend to deal with the headline-making financial investigations. In addition to prosecution, the Kensatsu Cho supervises the execution of judgments by the judiciary.

Spain

7.34   The Securities Markets Commission or Comisión Nacional del Mercado de Valores (the CNMV) is the key regulatory authority that conducts investigations in Spain. It is responsible for the supervision, inspection, and discipline of the securities market. In general, the CNMV is entitled to exercise its oversight and supervision powers and impose sanctions on: (i) governing bodies of official and unofficial secondary markets (with the exception of the Bank of Spain); (ii) Spanish investment firms and non-EU investment firms which operate in Spain; (iii) securities issuers; (iv) credit institutions; and (v) investment services firms operating in Spain and authorised by another EU member state. The CNMV is also entitled to request information from any firm domiciled in Spain or operating in the Spanish market.

7.35   The Bank of Spain is responsible for monetary policy and the stability of the financial system. It supervises the solvency, performance and specific regulatory compliance of credit institutions, savings banks, credit co-operative banks, branches of foreign credit institutions, specialised credit institutions and electronic money issuers and can pursue and impose sanctions on credit institutions for certain infringements.

7.36   The Insurance General Directorate monitors firms operating in the insurance and pension fund markets and is responsible for the orderly functioning and development of those markets.

7.37   The Public Prosecution Service (Ministerio Fiscal) is the only prosecuting body in Spain and participates in all stages of criminal proceedings. Within the Ministerio Fiscal, the Special Prosecutor's Office against Corruption and Organised Crime investigates and prosecutes economic crimes with the support of technical experts and a special police unit.

The Netherlands

7.38 The Autoriteit Financiële Markten or the Netherlands Authority for the Financial Markets (AFM) is the principal conduct regulator of the Dutch financial markets. The AFM supervises firms that provide savings, loans, investments, securities and insurance products and services. In addition, the Dutch central bank, De Nederlandsche Bank (DNB) plays an important role and focuses on the solvency of firms, including securities brokers, credit institutions and insurance companies.

7.39 In relation to criminal proceedings, the Openbaar Ministerie (OM) is the sole criminal prosecuting body in the Netherlands. OM decide whether to bring a case to court and are ultimately responsible for the investigation of any criminal activity.

UK

7.40 For the purposes of investigations and enforcement action, the principal regulator is the FCA which deals with conduct regulation, however the PRA also has the power to investigate and bring disciplinary action for matters within its prudential remit. (See **CHAPTERS 5** and **8–11** for more detail on FCA and PRA powers of investigation and enforcement.)

7.41 In addition, the Serious Fraud Office investigates and prosecutes serious or complex fraud[1] including bribery and corruption and fraud, and in recent years it has focused its attention on a number of investigations involving firms[2].

1 Under the Criminal Justice Act 1987.
2 At the time of writing, the SFO is currently conducting investigations into the alleged manipulation of the LIBOR benchmarks and has arrested a number of individuals in connection with that investigation. It is also conducting an investigation in conjunction with US authorities in relation to Barclays' £8bn recapitalisation in 2008 with Qatari investment.

US

7.42 The financial services regulatory regime in the United States is complex, fragmented and in a state of transition. There are multiple regulators at the state and federal level, often with overlapping responsibilities, but no single regulator with overarching responsibility for regulation of financial services. The key regulators are discussed in the following paras **7.43–7.46**.

7.43 The Federal Reserve (the Fed) which shares supervisory and regulatory responsibility for US banking institutions with the Office of the Comptroller of the Currency (the OCC), the Federal Deposit Insurance Corporation.

7.44 The Securities and Exchange Commission (the SEC) is the agency principally responsible for the enforcement of US federal securities laws, which are intended to preserve the integrity of the securities markets and to protect investors. The SEC can exercise its enforcement powers against issuers registered with the SEC, their officers and employees, registered broker-dealers, and members of self-regulatory organisations (SROs). The most important SRO for present purposes is the Financial Industry Regulatory Authority (FINRA), which is charged by the SEC with regulating the activities of brokerage firms. FINRA can exercise its powers against its member firms and their associated persons.

7.45 The Commodities and Futures Trading Commission (the CFTC) is responsible for regulation of the wholesale futures markets. The CFTC takes enforcement actions against individuals and firms registered with the CFTC, those who are engaged in commodity futures and options trading on designated domestic exchanges, and those who improperly market futures and options contracts.

7.46 The Department of Justice (the DOJ) plays an important role in enforcing the federal securities laws when conduct constitutes a criminal offence. The DOJ, together with its investigative arm the Federal Bureau of Investigation (the FBI) and its prosecutorial arm the US Attorneys' Offices (the USAO), exercises very broad jurisdiction to prosecute violations of federal laws (including securities laws).

7.47 In addition to the federal regulators identified above, there is also a significant amount of regulatory activity at the state level. The US has no uniform regulation of the insurance sector at the federal level. Instead, responsibility for regulation of insurance companies rests with insurance commissioners or departments in each of the 50 states, such as the New York State Insurance Department. (Similarly, state-licensed and state-chartered banks and firms are subject to regulation at the state level, eg by the New York Department of Financial Services[1].)

1 The New York Department of Financial Services agreed a US$ 340 million settlement with Standard Chartered Bank in August 2012 for breaches of US sanctions after having threatened to revoke its New York State Banking licence. Subsequent settlements of US$ 327 million were also reached in December 2012 with Office of Foreign Assets Control, (OFAC) the Federal Reserve Bank of New York, the DOJ and the New York County District Attorney's Office relating to past violations of sanctions laws. See http://www.standardchartered.com/en/news-and-media/news/global/10-12-2012-final-settlement-us.html.

7.48 Finally, each state has an Attorney General with broad investigative powers and statutory authority to protect consumers (and in some instances investors) from fraud. In recent years they have played an increasingly active role in investigations.

Powers of regulators

7.49 Regulators typically have broad powers to request information and documents from firms operating within their jurisdiction (and sometimes from firms outside their jurisdictions) and to interview employees. Firms should be aware of the potential sanctions for any failure to co-operate with a regulatory investigation which, as discussed below, can often be severe.

Motivations for investigations

7.50   Regulators may open an investigation for a variety of reasons, sometimes as a result of complaints received from a whistleblower within the organisation, an investor, competitor or customer or because of the regulators' gathering of market intelligence and daily monitoring of financial markets. For example, the UKLA in the UK conducts its own monitoring of share price movements and if a listed company's share price drops sharply following any announcement, the company often receives a letter of enquiry. Regulators will also usually investigate referrals from the media and from other regulators or law enforcement agencies.

7.51   Finally, a firm may also report an issue itself to a regulator in order to comply with reporting obligations in certain jurisdictions or in a pre-emptive move to seek leniency (discussed further at para **7.82** ff).

Levels of regulatory scrutiny

7.52   Historically, the US regulatory and prosecutorial authorities have been the most active. They are better resourced and tend to adopt a more aggressive approach than equivalent agencies in many other countries. US regulators have comparatively high rates of enforcement and prosecution. However, non-US regulators are starting to become increasingly active.

7.53   European regulators, in particular, have become increasingly active since the 2008 financial crisis. The UK FCA has been keen to emphasise that enforcement forms a key part of its 'credible deterrence strategy'. It now has a large and active Enforcement Division and is obtaining settlements with firms that are on a par with its US counterparts[1]. France's AMF and Italy's Consob also emphasise that enforcement is an important part of their activities although they have yet to impose the level of sanctions seen in the UK and US[2].

1 See for example JP Morgan 'London Whale' settlement referenced at para **7.10**, n 1 above.
2 For example in Italy, the law on Public Savings quintupled all administrative fines provided for by the Legislative Decree No 58 of 24 February 1998 as subsequently amended (Financial Law Consolidated Act). The Law on Public Savings also doubled criminal sanctions. Administrative sanctions can reach millions of euros and in market abuse cases sanctions can reach up to €25 million and up to 12 years' imprisonment.

Investigation tools

7.54   Most regulators have a broad range of investigation tools at their disposal. These often include powers to:

- search premises and seize documents;

- require document production;

- make information requests; and

- compel individuals to attend interviews with regulators.

Extra-territorial powers

7.55   The extent to which regulators will attempt to operate extra-territorially varies between jurisdictions and depends on the existence of any mutual legal assistance arrangements between jurisdictions (discussed further at para **7.59** ff below).

7.56   European and Hong Kong regulators are generally restricted to operating within their territorial jurisdiction and can usually only operate extra-territorially through the co-operation of the relevant authorities in other countries. However, certain acts taking place overseas may still fall within the jurisdiction of a European regulator, either because they have an effect in the jurisdiction (for example, insider trading and market abuse in relation to securities listed on a jurisdiction's stock exchange regardless of where the issue or conduct takes place) or because they fall within legislation that has extra-territorial application (for example, the UK Bribery Act 2010 imposes criminal liability for any act of bribery committed anywhere in the world by any body or person associated with the body, where the body is incorporated in the UK or carries on business or part of its business in the UK; or Italy's Decree 231 which establishes 'quasi criminal' liability over foreign corporations and banks even where they do not have a branch or office in Italy, as long as some business is transacted in Italy).

7.57   US regulators have broad authority to issue subpoenas seeking documents and information located in the United States and abroad, even where compliance would conflict with local law. Failure to comply with a US administrative subpoena can trigger injunctive proceedings, sizeable (daily) fines and/or a finding of civil or criminal contempt. In *United States v Bank of Nova Scotia*[1], for example, a US court held a Bahamian bank's Miami agency in contempt after it refused to comply with a federal grand jury subpoena, even though disclosure of the subpoenaed materials would have violated Bahamian bank secrecy laws.

1   *In Re Grand Jury Proceedings Bank of Nova Scotia Nos 83-5708, 84-5198. 740 F.2d 817 (1984).*

7.58   The US DOJ has also demonstrated a willingness to operate extra-territorially in connection with its investigation into tax evasion by US citizens holding assets in Swiss bank accounts. The DOJ reached a landmark settlement with UBS in 2009 in which UBS agreed to pay US$ 780 million for assisting US citizens to commit tax evasion[1] and on 29 August 2013 the DOJ issued a joint statement with the Swiss Federal Department of Finance announcing a program aimed at reaching similar settlements with other Swiss banks[2].

1   DOJ Press Release dated 17 November 2009: 'Justice Department & IRS Announce Results of UBS Settlement & Unprecedented Response in Voluntary Tax Disclosure Program'.
2   DOJ Press Release dated 29 August 2013: 'United States and Switzerland Issue Joint Statement Regarding Tax Evasion Investigations'.

Mutual legal assistance and sharing of information between regulators

7.59   Regulators within the EEA often actively assist, request assistance and share information with other EEA regulators within the framework of their supervisory role as well as in the course of investigations.

7.60   Outside the EEA, there are a number of multilateral agreements providing for the provision of assistance and exchange of information and documents between countries, such as the International Organization of Securities Commissions Multilateral Memorandum of Understanding concerning the consultation and co-operation and the exchange of information.

7.61   Many countries also enter into bi-lateral agreements and Memoranda of Understanding (MOUs) with foreign regulators to foster co-operation and information sharing. MOUs do not typically create binding legal obligations and are subject to domestic laws but, despite this, there is an increasing trend in cross-border regulatory co-operation.

7.62   Some regulators may try to obtain documents directly from entities located abroad. In certain circumstances, it may be advisable to ask foreign regulators to make document requests through local regulators. For example, US regulators often prefer to obtain information and materials directly from a subpoenaed entity and are often reluctant to pursue mutual assistance. However, as discussed below, providing documents through a local regulator can help to avoid data protection issues when providing documents from European entities to countries (such as the US) that are regarded as having insufficient data privacy safeguards to comply with European legal standards. If complying with a foreign regulator's request for information and/or documents would require an entity to violate the laws of its home jurisdiction, it may be necessary to insist that the foreign regulator use mutual assistance.

7.63   Providing documents through a local regulator may also help with negotiating the scope of document requests as there may be greater ability to negotiate a more limited request for documents and information with local regulators. However, entities should take care when deciding whether to encourage a foreign regulator to pursue mutual assistance channels as doing so may trigger an investigation by regulators in other jurisdictions not previously involved in the inquiry.

7.64   It is important to understand the willingness (or not) of regulators to obtain documents through mutual assistance channels. Many regulators prefer to obtain documents directly from the required entity to avoid complications of pursuing mutual assistance. However, the approach may differ even between regulators within the same jurisdiction. For example, in Italy Consob will frequently seek co-operation from other regulators whereas public prosecutors are more reluctant to pursue this route.

7.65   It is increasingly common for regulators in different jurisdictions to work together on investigations which impact a number of jurisdictions. For example, as noted in para **7.58** above, US and Swiss regulators have been working together for a number of years to identify potential tax evasion by US citizens holding assets in Switzerland. In recent years there have also been numerous investigations into the fixing of LIBOR and EURIBOR rates. As a result of these investigations, the FCA issued significant fines to Barclays[1], RBS[2] and Rabobank[3] and its largest ever fine to UBS[4]. In the press-releases announcing the fines the FSA acknowledged the '*significant cross-border*' nature of the investigations and thanked numerous regulators based in the US, Switzerland, Singapore, the Netherlands and Japan.

1   FSA Press Release FSA/PN/070/2012: 'Barclays fined £59.5 million for significant failings in relation to LIBOR and EURIBOR'.
2   FSA Press Release FSA/PN/011/2013: 'RBS fined £87.5 million for significant failings in relation to LIBOR'.
3   FCA Press Release FCA/PN/100/2013: 'FCA fines Rabobank £105 million for serious LIBOR-related misconduct'.
4   FSA Press Release FSA/PN/116/2012: 'UBS fined £160 million for significant failings in relation to LIBOR and EURIBOR'.

Sanctions for failure to co-operate

7.66   The sanctions for failing to co-operate with regulatory investigations will understandably vary according to the nature of the investigation and the severity of the failure. The approach to sanctioning also varies from jurisdiction to jurisdiction and regulator to regulator. However, there is a recent global trend towards regulators imposing more severe sanctions for failures to co-operate.

7.67   Failure to co-operate with informal or voluntary investigations may not lead to any formal sanctions but it is likely to damage a firm's relationship with its regulators, and the fact of a firm's unwillingness to co-operate may in fact lead to closer scrutiny if a regulator believes a firm has something to hide.

7.68   Regulators often impose fines by way of sanction for failure to co-operate with investigations. US regulators have historically led the way in imposing hefty fines on entities for failing to co-operate with investigations. In 2004 the SEC imposed a (then) record US$ 10 million fine on Bank of America Securities for its failure to fully co-operate with a federal investigation into potential improper trading at the bank's securities unit. A statement from the SEC noted 'we will not tolerate unreasonable delay in responding to our inquiries and will act aggressively to protect the integrity of the Commission's investigative processes'[1].

1   SEC Press Release dated 10 March 2004: 'SEC Brings Enforcement Action against Banc of America Securities for Repeated Document Production Failures during a Pending Investigation'.

7.69   European regulators are now beginning to catch up with their US counterparts. Principle 11 of the UK Regulators Principles for Business sets out the requirement that a firm must:

'deal with its regulators in an open and cooperative way, and must disclose to the appropriate regulator appropriately anything relating to the firm of which that regulator would reasonably expect notice'.

The wording of Principle 11 is intentionally widely drafted and takes into account the activities of other members of a firm's group[1] and activities elsewhere in the world outside the UK[2]. The FCA underlined the seriousness of Principle 11 breaches when the FCA fined JP Morgan £137.6 million in September 2013 for breaches in connection with losses sustained from the 'London Whale' trades[3]. Approximately £60 million of this total fine was imposed in relation to the breach of Principle 11 and the FCA's finding that:

'During the first half of 2012, JPMorgan failed to be open and co-operative with the FCA in that it concealed the extent of the losses as well as numerous serious and significant issues regarding the risk situation in the relevant synthetic credit portfolio'.

In addition, and discussed in more detail in para **7.84** below, in 2010 the FSA fined Goldman Sachs £17.5 million, in part because of failing to provide the FSA with appropriate information in relation to an SEC investigation into a synthetic collateralised debt obligation structured by Goldman Sachs[4].

1 See the Handbooks at PRIN 1.1.5G and 3.2.3R.
2 See the Handbooks at PRIN 1.1.6G and 3.3.1R.
3 FCA Press Release FCA/PN/88/2013: 'JPMorgan Chase Bank N.A. fined £137,610,000 for serious failings relating to its Chief Investment Office's 'London Whale' trades'.
4 FSA Press Release FSA/PN/141/2010: 'FSA fines Goldman Sachs International £17.5 million for weaknesses in controls resulting in failure to provide FSA with appropriate information'.

7.70 Certain regulators also have powers to issue criminal sanctions for non-compliance. For example, failure to comply with a request by either the Hong Kong SFC or the HKMA for production of documents, provision of information or participation in an examination under the SFO without reasonable excuse is a criminal offence[1]. Refusal to co-operate with, or disclosure of inaccurate, incomplete or misleading information to, the French AMF is a criminal offence punishable by up to two years' imprisonment and/or a fine. Similarly, providing Consob in Italy with false documents/information or fraudulently concealing them from Consob is a criminal offence punishable by one to four years' imprisonment. In Spain, failure to co-operate with the CNMV can result in a fine of up to 2 per cent of an entity's equity capital.

1 In 2009 two people were convicted of failing to co-operate with SFC investigations and were sentenced to serve a further one month's imprisonment concurrently with sentences of market manipulation, see *SFC Annual Report 2009–10.*

INTERNAL INVESTIGATIONS AND COMMUNICATING WITH REGULATORS

Internal investigations

7.71 Firms often take steps to conduct voluntary internal investigations into certain issues prior to regulatory involvement. Conducting internal investigations in this manner is not only good corporate governance but also enables a firm to make an informed decision as to whether an issue triggers a regulatory requirement to self-report (as exists in the UK in relation to financial services related regulatory breaches which must be reported to the Regulators and in relation to offences under the Proceeds of Crime Act 2002 which must be reported to the National Crime Agency)[1] or whether it should consider voluntarily reporting an issue to a regulator. For example, in certain jurisdictions, incentives such as leniency may be available in return for early self-reporting.

1   For example, in the UK, firms are expected to discuss relevant matters with the Regulators at an early stage, and before making any internal or external commitments (SUP 15.3.9G). The supervisory approach places reliance on firms and their senior management to ensure timely and proactive communication with the Regulators. The need for early communication is crucial since a firm cannot know exactly how or within what timescale the appropriate regulator will deal with any issue, or what steps it may take in response to being notified (see *Prudential plc FCA final notice (27/03/2013)*). See **CHAPTER 3** for more detail.

7.72   A firm will usually wish to maintain a pro-active relationship with its regulators and conducting a voluntary investigation may be a highly effective way to manage regulatory interest in a particular area.

7.73   In many instances, voluntary internal investigations can (at least initially) be conducted discreetly to avoid adverse publicity relating to the matter. Should the matter subsequently become subject to publicity, the perceived swift action of the firm in investigating the issue at an early stage can be critical to both the public and regulatory reaction to the issue.

Who should conduct the investigation?

7.74   A cross-border investigation should have one single point of management and control, so it is important at the outset to determine the jurisdiction that will lead the investigation and the individual who will be accountable for it. This will be key to the overall strategic direction of the investigation as well as its operational management.

7.75   It is critical to ensure that any internal investigation is conducted impartially. Ideally, the controlling person or body responsible for the investigation should lie outside line management. However, this can create issues, as it may be difficult to say at the outset whether line management (possibly senior) had any responsibility for the issues that are to be investigated.

7.76   If line management has to be the sponsor of the investigation process, it may be appropriate to provide support using some independent party (such as an external adviser, an audit committee or a senior independent or non-executive director) to give it the necessary degree of impartiality. An investigation conducted by a person or body not perceived to be neutral will, regardless of the actual result and the quality of work, have little value for external stakeholders. Damage to a firm's reputation over a perceived attempt to conceal wrongdoing could ultimately prove more harmful than the potential wrongdoing itself.

7.77 Although larger firms may have the resources in-house to conduct investigations internally, there are a number of reasons why it may be advisable to engage external legal advisers to co-ordinate the process particularly in the context of cross-border investigations. External legal advisers will be experienced not only in conducting interviews and interpreting facts but will often be able to provide (or procure) legal advice specific to the relevant jurisdictions and provide the benefit of their experience of dealing with the relevant regulators. In civil law systems engaging external legal advisers will also provide a greater degree of privilege protection over the investigation itself[1].

1 In civil law jurisdictions internal legal advisers may not be regarded as having the appropriate degree of independence to satisfy the related concept of confidentiality which fulfils similar functions to privilege under the common law system.

7.78 It is important to allocate sufficient resources to an investigation which will often be conducted under considerable time constraints. It may require the review of large volumes of documentation and the interviewing of many employees, often within a relatively short time frame. Appropriate expertise also needs to be available in multiple jurisdictions so that the investigation can be conducted as efficiently as possible. Co-ordinating investigations globally also creates additional logistical issues, such as ensuring that teams working in multiple jurisdictions are acting in a consistent manner and are regularly updating each other as to their findings. External legal advisers may be best placed to provide the necessary resources required to do this. In addition specialist forensic IT and accounting skills will often be required to assist in gathering and reviewing documents and evidence.

How to conduct the investigation

7.79 It is important to clearly define the scope of an investigation. An investigation that is too narrow or superficial risks being of little value or being characterised as an attempt by management to 'paper over the cracks' whilst an overly broad and unwieldy investigation will be time consuming, an unnecessary drain on resources and may not be completed to the required level of detail. The importance of clearly defining the scope of an investigation is particularly acute where issues are raised that may affect multiple jurisdictions. The entity conducting the investigation will need to ensure that all potentially relevant jurisdictions are investigated whilst avoiding raising unnecessary concerns in jurisdictions where issues do not arise.

7.80 It is usually good practice for the entity that has responsibility for the investigation to establish written terms of reference defining the scope of the investigation. However, whilst it is important for the scope of the investigation to be clearly defined, the process should not be so inflexible that it ignores matters of concern that come to light as a result of the investigation but which technically fall outside the agreed scope. It is critical for corporate governance purposes that matters of concern are appropriately addressed and, if necessary, reported to the regulators once an entity becomes aware of such matters having arisen.

7.81   It is also crucial that the entity with responsibility for conducting the investigation is granted sufficient authority to enable it to achieve its purpose. Internal investigations are often of a sensitive nature and employees under investigation can be defensive of their actions, particularly if they are perceived to be (or believe they may be perceived to be) in any way responsible for potential issues. A responsible senior officer with sufficient authority within the firm should be appointed to oversee the investigation to ensure that employees appreciate the serious nature of the investigation and provide appropriate assistance to the individuals conducting the investigation.

The culture and benefits of self-reporting

7.82   The thresholds triggering reporting obligations will vary between jurisdictions and between regulators. When making a decision not to self-report in a jurisdiction where there is no mandatory obligation to do so, a firm should take steps to ensure that it will not be in breach of any of its reporting obligations across all relevant jurisdictions.

7.83   Firms should proceed on the basis that self-reporting in one jurisdiction effectively constitutes self-reporting in all relevant jurisdictions. It is not uncommon for conduct giving rise to a potential reporting obligation to be relevant to and/or fall within the regulatory remit of a number of regulators in different jurisdictions. Given the increasing levels of communication and co-operation between regulators, it should be assumed that it will not be possible to contain a decision to self-report to a particular jurisdiction and it will often simply not be feasible for an entity to co-operate with regulators in one jurisdiction without assisting regulators in another.

7.84   The danger of failing to self-report in all relevant jurisdictions was highlighted by the FSA's 2010 decision to fine Goldman Sachs International (GSI) £17.5 million for weaknesses in controls resulting in failure to provide the FSA with appropriate information[1]. The fine related to an SEC investigation into a synthetic collateralised debt obligation called Abacus structured by Goldman Sachs & Co (GSI's US affiliate). The FSA found that GSI did not have effective systems and controls in place to ensure that relevant information about the SEC investigation was shared between relevant Goldman Sachs entities and, in particular, to ensure that GSI's compliance department was made aware of the SEC investigation so that it could consider whether any notifications needed to be made to the FSA in compliance with GSI's UK regulatory reporting obligations.

1   FSA Press Release FSA/PN/141/2010: '*FSA fines Goldman Sachs International £17.5 million for weaknesses in controls resulting in failure to provide FSA with appropriate information.*'

7.85   The decision to self-report should therefore be considered for all potentially relevant jurisdictions. However, this can give rise to tension given the divergent approaches taken by agencies in different jurisdictions both in terms of the expectations upon entities to self-report and the potential benefits to be gained from self reporting.

7.86   Handling multi-jurisdictional investigations

7.86   For example, regulators in the US expect firms to self-report. Not only can regulators offer substantial reductions in sanctions to firms that self-report at an early stage, failing (in the eyes of the regulators) to self-report at an appropriate time may also invoke closer regulatory scrutiny in the future. By contrast, regulators in Italy do not expect firms to self-report and there is little to be gained in terms of leniency by self-reporting. So in a situation where a firm has to deal with issues involving both jurisdictions, there will be a considerable tension between the US and Italian business operations in determining what is best for the firm as a whole in terms of self-reporting.

7.87   These decisions require complex decision-making and careful strategic planning especially as the decision as to whether to self-report often needs to be taken at a very early stage if UK regulators may be involved.

7.88   Firms will also need to act swiftly if they wish to take advantage of any benefits that may be available for early self-reporting. The importance of this initial decision to self-report is further emphasised by the fact that once the decision has been made, it is impossible to back-track. The decision should therefore be considered thoroughly with the benefit of legal advice for each relevant jurisdiction.

7.89   The appendix to this chapter, following para **7.172** below, sets out the requirements for self-reporting in a number of key financial markets.

Ongoing communications with regulators

7.90   Once a matter has been reported to a regulator (or regulators) a firm may appoint its general counsel, compliance officer, or a member of senior management to be the contact point with the regulators and to manage those communications on an ongoing basis. It is often preferable to manage communications with the regulators in conjunction with external counsel, whose specialist skills and familiarity with the regulators can be invaluable.

7.91   Regulators will also usually require a firm's senior management to have some oversight of any ongoing investigation. In general, this demonstrates the firm's commitment to the process, provides accountability and allocates responsibility for implementing any remedial steps. Regulators will also want to be informed of the scope, methodology and progress of any ongoing investigation and to be kept informed of material action taken in relation to employees and counterparties.

PROVIDING DOCUMENTS AND INFORMATION TO REGULATORS

7.92   Many regulators have broad powers to compel the production of documents. As noted above, there are significant sanctions for failing to co-operate with regulatory investigations and regulators typically also have specific sanctions for failing to provide documents. For example, in Germany BaFin has coercive powers and can compel the production of documents; it can impose fines of up to €250,000 and administrative fines of €150,000 for failure to comply with its requests. In Italy failure to comply with Consob requests for production of documents or information will result in sanctions of up to €200,000.

Obtaining and preserving evidence

7.93   Firms need to take steps at an early stage to preserve evidence in all relevant jurisdictions. The inferences that will be drawn by the courts and/or regulators from the destruction of evidence are often far worse than the reality of those documents being produced.

7.94   It is important, therefore, to ensure from the start that all employees involved in an investigation appreciate the importance of document preservation. Most regulators can (and will) bring criminal charges against individuals who falsify, conceal or dispose of documents that are relevant to an investigation.

7.95   The first step will be to establish the scope of the investigation so that all relevant material can be identified. If an external investigation is already underway this will likely be done in dialogue with regulators. Once this has been established, a list of relevant employees should be compiled and document preservation notices should be issued in respect of hard copy and electronic documents as well as any recorded telephone calls.

7.96   Depending upon the scope of relevant data it may be advisable to engage external IT consultants to set up a single document database and facilitate the review process. An electronic database makes it easier to conduct searches of documents (for example, by using key word or date range parameters) to identify relevant material. This can speed up the review process and enable quick and comprehensive responses to be given to queries raised by regulators. It will also enable the investigations team to maintain an audit trail of disclosures provided to which regulators. Consideration may also need to be given to converting documents in local languages into one common language (often English).

7.97   Another issue that is of frequent concern is where to locate the database. Careful consideration will need to be given to this having regard to the specific facts of the investigation, the requirements for disclosure and scope of legal privilege protection in the various jurisdictions that are involved.

Negotiability of document/information requests

7.98   In many instances it may be possible to negotiate with regulators both as to the scope and timing of compliance with requests for documents and information. The ability to negotiate such matters will vary from regulator to regulator. It is advisable to discuss methods of data collection and processing with investigators at an early stage as the use of key word searching (as opposed to wholesale disclosure) may further limit the volume of documents to be disclosed. In addition, the timing and method of returning documents should be discussed prior to disclosure.

7.99   It may also be possible in certain circumstances for an entity to try to limit the volume of documents/information to be disclosed to regulators on the basis of privilege, business secrecy and the protection of employees' personal data. Document disclosure with regulators also needs to be conducted with a view to mitigating the risk of disclosure in civil litigation at a later stage (especially where there is a risk that claimants in subsequent civil litigation will ask regulators for information).

7.100   In some jurisdictions (such as the UK and Hong Kong) where documents and/or information sought by a regulator are legally privileged and the entity wishes to provide the documents or information to the regulators, it may be possible to negotiate with the regulators that the information and/or documents will be provided on the basis of a limited waiver of privilege only for the purpose of the investigation. However, as most regulators have the right or obligation to disclose material obtained to other regulators, there is no guarantee that the privilege will not be considered waived or the information will not leak out, so that confidentiality and any privilege protection will be lost.

7.101   Local advice should be obtained on the prospects of negotiating any document or information requests and the timing of negotiations may also be important. For example, in Italy it is often possible in practice to negotiate with Consob over the timing of compliance with requests for documents and information. However, once an order for disclosure has been issued, there is no room for negotiation as to scope. In light of this, any discussions need to take place at the very early stages of the investigation.

7.102   US regulators frequently issue very broad subpoenas and request compliance within short time periods. However, they are often willing to negotiate more reasonable parameters and rolling production schedules. In these circumstances, it may be helpful for an entity to highlight the magnitude of potential documents caught by the subpoena as regulators may not have properly considered the practicalities of complying with their request.

7.103   Finally, regulatory relationships need to be managed particularly carefully where asymmetries of information arise when dealing with multiple requests from multiple regulators. Consideration needs to be given as to how this may impact relationships with regulators who have not been provided information or not provided information at the same time as other regulators.

Data protection

7.104   Data protection issues have become an increasingly important consideration when dealing with requests for documents from overseas regulators. Cross-border investigations often need to deal with the variations in data protection regimes in different jurisdictions. These issues are usually time consuming and administratively burdensome and can often be an unwelcome distraction from the actual investigation.

7.105 There are inherent tensions between the competing interests of regulatory investigations and data protection law. Balancing legal principles which are designed to control the disclosure of sensitive personal data with the need to quickly investigate relevant (and often highly sensitive) matters can be difficult.

7.106 Much of the law in this area is derived from European legislation. However, data protection regimes do differ even between EU member states as the EU Data Protection Directive (the Directive) is very general in its terms and the latitude given to member states in interpreting and implementing the Directive into national law has led to significant differences between national regimes.

7.107 The Directive prescribes a minimum level of safeguarding of personal data, therefore member states have the ability to impose stricter rules when creating their own legislation. Set out below is a summary of the issues arising from a firm's obligations under the UK data protection regime. It should be noted that although the UK's data protection regime is derived from the Directive, a number of countries in the EU (whose regimes are also derived from the Directive) are significantly more stringent than the UK regime. For example, in Italy particular data protection breaches can constitute a criminal offence[1]. Local advice should therefore be obtained before undertaking cross-border data transfers.

1 Unlawful data processing can result in imprisonment for between six months and three years (see section 167 of the Legislative Decree no 196 of 30 June 2003); untrue declarations and notifications submitted to the DPA may lead to imprisonment of between six months and three years (see section 168 of the Legislative Decree no 196 of 30 June 2003); and failure to provide minimum security measures can result in imprisonment of up to two years (see section 169 of the Legislative Decree no 196 of 30 June 2003).

Issues arising from a firm's obligations under the UK data protection regime

7.108 Firms located in the UK have obligations pursuant to the Data Protection Act (DPA) 1998 in respect of personal data relating to employees and clients. The DPA 1998 implements the Directive[1].

1 The European Commission published a draft General Data Protection Regulation (Proposed Regulation) on 25 January 2012. The adoption is proposed in 2014 with the regulation coming into force in 2015. Discussions regarding the proposed regulation are still ongoing. If the Proposed Regulation is adopted into EU law, it will replace the various pieces of national legislation that implement the Directive (including the DPA 1998) by introducing a uniform set of data privacy laws that would have automatic and direct legal effect in the UK and all other member states.

7.109 The DPA 1998 aims to protect individuals whose 'personal data' is held or processed by 'data controllers'.

7.110   The term 'personal data' covers any information that relates to an identified or identifiable individual[1]. There has been considerable debate in the UK as to the broad scope of this definition[2], which has led to the Information Commissioner issuing guidance on the scope of personal data. This guidance states that the data controller needs to take into account whether or not the information is capable of having an adverse impact on the individual's privacy. Given the apparent breadth of the scope of 'personal data' and continuing uncertainty as to its precise boundaries, UK data controllers need to proceed on the assumption that any data relating to an individual is 'personal data' and be mindful of obligations in respect of that data pursuant to the DPA 1998.

1 DPA 1998, s 1(1).
2 See in particular the Court of Appeal's controversial interpretation in *Durant v Financial Services Authority [2003] EWCA Civ 1746*, followed by the High Court in *Johnson v Medical Defence Union [2004] EWHC 2509 (Ch)*.

7.111   The term 'data controller' covers any party who independently, jointly or in common with others, determines the purposes for which and the manner in which any personal data is processed. The Directive defines 'data processors' as third parties who process data on behalf of data controllers. The importance of the distinction between 'control' and 'processing' is that only 'data controllers' are required to comply with the DPA 1998, and the DPA 1998 holds 'data controllers' responsible for the actions of any 'data processors' acting on their behalf.

7.112   The term 'processing' has been observed by the Information Commissioner to be very wide; its 'Guide to Data Processing'[1] states that 'it is difficult to think of anything an organisation might do with data that would not be processing'[2].

1 As issued by the Information Commissioner on 1 October 2009.
2 The Court of Appeal has also acknowledged the breadth of this concept. See *Campbell v MGN [2003] 1 QB 633* at 646 as affirmed by the House of Lords *[2005] 4 All ER 793* and the European Court of Justice in *MGN v United Kingdom (ECHR Case No 39401/04)*.

7.113   The main obligation on UK data controllers is to comply with a series of data protection principles. When involved in either internal or external investigations, data controllers will need to ensure the fair and lawful processing of 'personal data'.

7.114   Processing of 'personal data' will be fair and lawful if:

(a) conducted with the prior consent of the relevant individuals;

(b) conducted in pursuit of legitimate interests where this does not cause unwarranted prejudice to the privacy interests of the affected individuals;

(c) it is necessary for compliance with a non-contractual legal obligation; or

(d) it is necessary for the administration of justice.

Data collection

7.115   The collection of either employee or client data for the purposes of an internal or regulatory investigation will need to comply with the DPA 1998's requirement for fair and lawful processing.

Consent of the data subject(s)

7.116   Consent to collection of data can only validly be provided where the data subject has been properly informed. Employees may have been informed of such collection either in their employment contract or as a result of subsequent notices issued. It should be made clear to employees what type of communications may be collected and why. As regards client consent to collect data, this may be set out in its engagement letter or in subsequent notices issued and should be examined to ensure that collection of data for the purposes of carrying out an investigation has been obtained.

Legitimate interests

7.117   Where employee or client consent has not been obtained, it may be possible to justify the collection on the basis of there being a 'legitimate interest'. The 'legitimate interests' can be those of either the firm itself or another group company. The impact of collection on the privacy interests of employees and client must be balanced with any 'legitimate interests' on which the firm may seek to rely. This balancing of interests means that, in practice, it is sensible to build safeguards into the collection process to protect the privacy of data subjects (for example by not collecting more data than is strictly necessary).

Administration of justice

7.118   The collection of data may be permitted where a court order or subpoena requires a firm to provide such information. The collected data should be limited to only that required in order to comply with the order or subpoena.

Legal obligation

7.119   Firms may also have a legal obligation to collect certain data (for example for the purposes of notifying any suspicious financial transactions). As above, the data collected should be limited to only that information which is necessary to meet the firm's statutory obligations.

Intra-group sharing

7.120   Where a firm is required to share collected data with another group company, it will again need to ensure that it has complied with its obligations to process data fairly and lawfully. The grounds for fair and lawful collection of data as set out above (ie consent, legitimate interests, administration of justice and legal obligation) apply equally to intra-group sharing. The key practical issue is to

245

ensure that no more data is shared than is strictly necessary. There are additional complications involved where an intra-group transfer involves the transfer of data from an EEA entity to a non-EEA entity (see further below).

Restrictions imposed on the transfer of data outside the EEA

7.121   The DPA 1998 provides that personal data must not be transferred to a country or territory outside the EEA unless that country or territory ensures an adequate level of protection for the rights and freedoms of data subjects in relation to the processing of personal data.

7.122   This can cause significant issues for European data controllers, as compliance with document/information requests from regulators may require the data controller to transfer documents and/or information to a country that does not ensure an adequate level of protection. At present, findings of 'adequacy' have only been made in respect of a relatively small number of countries[1].

1   Among others, findings of adequacy have been made in relation to Switzerland, Canada, Argentina, Guernsey, Jersey, the Isle of Man, Andorra, Israel (with certain limitations) and the Faroe Islands (with certain limitations).

7.123   The US is not currently deemed to have an adequate level of protection and as a result, complying with requests for documents and/or information from US regulators can cause data protection issues. Generally, personal data can still be transferred to companies in the US providing those companies have signed up to certain 'safe harbour' principles agreed between the US government and the European Commission in 2000. US companies can sign up to the safe harbour regime by agreeing to adhere to certain standards when processing data which provides similar safeguards to those set out in the DPA 1998. However, US companies in certain sectors (including financial services) do not currently qualify for the safe harbour list.

7.124   One possible option is to anonymise personal data by redacting documents prior to providing them to foreign regulators. However, in practice, given the breadth of the definition of 'personal data', redaction may severely limit the usefulness of the documents that are being requested by the regulator.

7.125   In practice this leads to tensions within multinational firms or groups. For example, if a US firm regulated by the SEC receives a request for documents located in its UK group company, the UK group company may not be able to assist the US firm in complying with that request without breaching its obligations under the DPA 1998.

Exemptions available under the data protection regime

7.126   The export of data to a country or territory outside the EEA which does not have adequate levels of protection is still possible providing that an exception to the general prohibition on exporting data applies. Set out below are a number of exceptions that may be relevant in the context of cross-border regulatory investigations.

Consent of the data subject(s)

7.127 Where personal data relates to the employees of a data controller, it may be possible to obtain express consent. However, this may not be possible where the personal data of third parties is concerned. Consent must be freely given and can be withdrawn by the data subject at any time[1].

1 Indeed there is a question as to whether an employee can ever 'freely' give consent in response to a request from his employer.

7.128 It is usually advisable for data controllers to obtain the consent of data subjects wherever practicable but this consent should not be relied upon as the sole basis of an otherwise prohibited transfer.

Appropriate contractual arrangements

7.129 It is possible to transfer data to a non-EEA based entity using an approved form of contract between the UK data controller and the recipient entity to protect the rights of the data subject. The European Commission has approved model sets of clauses for such transfers. The guidance from the UK Information Commissioner is that parties cannot amend any of the model clauses but are free to include other clauses provided they do not contradict the model clauses.

7.130 In practice it is very unlikely that a non-EEA regulator will agree to enter into a contract that mirrors the European Commission's model clauses as this will severely restrict the use of any information received and US regulators have frequently refused to enter into model clause contracts for this very reason.

Public interest

7.131 This criterion will usually only be satisfied in circumstances where the transfer is deemed necessary for the purposes of national security, tax collection or preventing or detecting a crime.

7.132 In *Re Bernard L Madoff Investment Securities LLC*[1], the High Court ordered the transfer of personal data from the UK to the US on the basis that the transfer was necessary for reasons of substantial public interest (to investigate the alleged fraud perpetrated by Mr Madoff).

1 *Re Bernard L Madoff Investment Securities LLC and Re Madoff Securities International Ltd [2009] EWHC 442 (Ch).*

7.133 However, whether a transfer is truly necessary for reasons of substantial public interest will depend entirely on the specific circumstances of the proposed transfer. Determining whether a transfer will definitely be caught by this exclusion is not therefore straightforward. It is not advisable for a firm to rely on this exclusion without (at the very least) legal advice to that effect or, in the majority of cases, a court judgment confirming that the transfer is indeed necessary. Given that obtaining a court judgment is an expensive and time consuming exercise, in many circumstances it is advisable to seek to rely on an alternative exception.

Necessary in connection with legal proceedings

7.134   There are exemptions on transfers that are necessary for: (a) the purpose of or in connection with legal proceedings; and (b) for the purpose of obtaining legal advice. These exceptions are unlikely to be of assistance in practice in these circumstances as regulatory investigations are not 'legal proceedings' as envisaged by the DPA 1998. In addition, although an entity may be able to provide documents to its legal advisers for the purposes of seeking advice in connection with a regulatory investigation, this will not enable documents to be provided to the regulator.

Transfers via UK regulators

7.135   The exemptions set out above are therefore unlikely to be particularly satisfactory as a means for transferring data to a non-EEA regulator. Therefore, in this scenario, it is advisable to encourage the foreign regulator to liaise with its UK counterpart and, if possible, ask the UK counterpart to issue a request for the documents and/or information sought by the foreign regulator. The UK data controller then has a legal compulsion to provide documents to its UK regulator who can then, providing there is an MoU in place between the two countries, share documents with the foreign regulator.

7.136   Providing documents through the FCA is fast becoming the best practice approach for UK data controllers required to provide documents to foreign regulators in jurisdictions without sufficient data protection safeguards. The steps to be taken in such circumstances will vary on a case-by-case basis and will in large part depend on the familiarity of the foreign regulator with this process. It is important to identify whether an MoU exists between the two countries pursuant to which the documents can be passed between regulators. If an MoU is in place a firm should then contact the FCA to advise it that the entity will be asking the foreign regulator to request documents through the FCA to avoid a potential breach of the DPA 1998. The FCA is relatively familiar with these requests, however the foreign regulator may not be familiar with this process and so may require some persuasion to adopt this approach. In these situations, it is often helpful to have some form of legal opinion confirming the likelihood of a potential breach of the DPA 1998 unless documents are obtained through the FCA which can be shared with the foreign regulator. It will also be crucial to work closely with local counsel who can leverage relationships with the local regulator to help facilitate the process.

New EU Data Protection Regulation

7.137 A new EU-wide Data Protection Regulation has been proposed which will be directly effective in member states and replace the Directive (and hence also the implementing legislation in individual member states such as the DPA 1998). The full text of the new Regulation has (at the time of printing) not yet been finalised and is not expected to come into force until 2015. The new Regulation is intended to be broader than existing legislation and will expressly apply to data controllers headquartered outside Europe. The draft Regulation also contains an even broader definition of 'personal data' and regulators will have new powers to impose large fines for breaches of up to 2 per cent of global turnover. There are also express provisions to make international data transfers easier, such as the increased recognition of binding corporate rules and the use of EU Model International Data Transfer Agreements. Until the final text of the Regulation is published the full implications remain uncertain. The provisions aimed at making international data transfers easier may assist firms facing multi-jurisdictional investigations. However, given the heavy potential sanctions for breaching the new Regulation, firms will need to ensure that they have sufficient safeguards in place to avoid any potential breaches.

Blocking statutes

7.138 Blocking statutes can be a particular cause for concern in cross-border investigations because these laws commonly restrict or prevent the disclosure of information for foreign disclosure purposes.

7.139 For example, Article 271(1) of the Swiss Penal Code has developed into a de facto blocking statute that frequently obstructs international disclosure. The Swiss courts have interpreted Article 271(1), which prohibits official acts on Swiss territory on behalf of a foreign state, sufficiently broadly to encompass the taking of evidence for foreign proceedings. As a result, the gathering and compilation of evidence (including the collection of documents, taking of witness depositions and creation of written witness statements) are all considered official acts that can only be performed by Swiss authorities.

7.140 Article 271(1) also prohibits the facilitation of unauthorised acts on Swiss territory. As a result, anyone who facilitates another party to breach this provision may be criminally liable, regardless of the nature and extent of the assistance given. Therefore, as a general rule, in judicial or administrative matters, the collection of evidence must be done through official channels and processes for requesting legal assistance.

7.141 The French Penal Law No 80-538 also prohibits the 'requesting, seeking or disclosing [of] ... documents or information ... for the purposes of constituting evidence in view of foreign judicial or administrative proceedings'[1]. Breach of the Penal Code is punishable by a €18,000 fine and/or six months' imprisonment.

1 Statute N° 80-538 of July 16, 1980.

7.142 However, blocking statutes are sometimes disregarded or afforded little weight by the courts and regulators of other jurisdictions. In *Colombia Pictures Industries v Bunnell*[1], the US court required the disclosure of certain data stored on computers in the Netherlands to be produced and stated that:

> 'foreign blocking statutes do not deprive an American court of the power to order a party subject to its jurisdiction to produce evidence even though the act of production may violate that statute'.

1 *C Cal, 2007.*

7.143 The English courts have also recently adopted a similarly dismissive approach to French Law No 678 of 26 July 1968 as amended (the French Blocking Statute). In *National Grid Electricity plc v ABB Ltd*[1] certain French defendants sought to resist an order for disclosure on the basis that compliance would place them in breach of the French Blocking Statute. Roth J held, without deciding that disclosure would breach the French Blocking Statute, that prosecution of the French defendants was 'virtually inconceivable' and therefore ordered disclosure against them.

1 *[2013] EWHC 822 (Ch).*

7.144 This approach creates difficulties for firms subject to blocking statute restrictions who are faced with the choice of breaching the blocking statute or failing to comply with an order of a foreign court and/or a request from a foreign regulator.

7.145 Disclosure of financial documents and information from certain jurisdictions may also be limited as a result of banking secrecy rules. For example, banking secrecy is prevalent in jurisdictions such as Switzerland, Singapore and Luxembourg and firms bound by banking secrecy rules are usually prohibited from providing information and documents without obtaining a waiver from the individual or entity to whom such secrecy obligations are owed.

7.146 When a firm is located in or has documents in a jurisdiction with a blocking statute or banking secrecy obligations and is faced with a document request from a foreign court or regulator, the best course of action is to seek to persuade the foreign court or regulator to follow the Hague Convention on taking of evidence. There may, however, be some reluctance by foreign courts and/or regulators to follow the Hague Convention so it is important to seek to be proactive and try (with the assistance of local legal counsel) to provide alternative methods of complying with foreign requests whilst minimising the risk of contravening the blocking statute. For example, it may be possible (although not risk free) to seek to make employees or directors available to the court and/or regulator as witnesses.

7.147 Finally it is also important to consider other national laws that may affect disclosure obligations, such as banking regulations, employment laws, confidentiality laws and trade secrecy laws as they may also be relevant to any legal analysis of the risks of providing any disclosure requested by regulators.

Privilege

7.148 In the UK, legal professional privilege (whether advice, litigation or common interest) and the privilege against self-incrimination are substantive rights. These privileges enable a company[1] or individual to resist compulsory process requiring the production of documents or provision of oral evidence. These rights can be relied on unless overridden by statute.

1 In some jurisdictions, such as Australia, a company can not claim privilege against self-incrimination. However, this is available to companies in the UK.

7.149 Consideration of privilege issues and their interplay with the provision of documents or information to the UK Regulators are dealt with in detail at para **4.136** ff and **5.56** ff above.

7.150 In a cross-border investigation it is important to bear in mind that other jurisdictions have different concepts of privilege or client confidentiality: some jurisdictions recognise privilege in a similar way to the UK but apply it differently; others do not recognise privilege but protect documents through a concept of lawyers' professional confidentiality. These differences may give rise to different levels of protection both for documents which already exist and those which come into existence as a result of an investigation.

7.151 Whether privilege or similar rights may be relied on to resist the disclosure of documents to regulators needs to be examined on a jurisdiction, regulator and power specific basis with the assistance of local counsel. These jurisdictional differences are relevant considerations when deciding:

- how to obtain information during the course of an investigation;

- where to store information gathered in response to an internal or external investigation or enforcement action;

- whether a regulator can compel production of material protected elsewhere; and

- whether to waive privilege protection by volunteering information to a particular regulator.

Privilege, or protection, in other jurisdictions

Common law jurisdictions

7.152 Many common law jurisdictions provide privilege protection for legal advice and work product in a similar manner to the UK. For example, legal professional privilege – both legal advice privilege and litigation privilege – is recognised in Hong Kong on very similar bases to the UK. Although the existence of relevant privileged documents must be disclosed, the documents themselves are protected from production to regulators. Similarly, numerous other commonwealth (and former commonwealth) jurisdictions, such as Australia, adopt very similar privilege rules to the UK.

7.153 Handling multi-jurisdictional investigations

7.153 The US concepts of attorney-client privilege and attorney work product protection are similar to legal professional privilege in the UK – legal advice privilege and litigation privilege – although they are applied in a different way. Therefore, despite the similarities of these concepts, it cannot safely be assumed that a document that attracts privilege under UK law would necessarily attract privilege under US law (and vice versa) so it is important to obtain local law advice.

Civil law jurisdictions

7.154 Many civil law jurisdictions (for example, France, Germany, Italy and Japan) do not recognise the concept of legal professional privilege as understood in the UK. Civil law jurisdictions often instead protect lawyer-client relationships through professional secrecy obligations. These obligations typically protect any legal advice and communications between lawyers and their clients.

7.155 Civil law often prevents the seizure and inspection of material held by lawyers, and regulators are often prohibited from inspecting lawyers' offices. Breach of such obligations by lawyers constitutes a criminal offence in numerous jurisdictions (including France and Italy). Where documents are held by the client the position is more complicated and rules vary between jurisdictions; some jurisdictions (such as France and Italy) protect documents covered by professional secrecy that are held by the client, other jurisdictions (for example Japan and Germany[1]) do not.

1 However, note that in Germany, if the relevant lawyer-client material is in the sole possession of in-house counsel it *may* be protected in certain circumstances.

7.156 The position for in-house legal counsel also differs from jurisdiction to jurisdiction. For example, in France and Italy the advice and correspondence of in-house counsel is not protected by professional secrecy rules as in-house counsel are not typically members of the Bar and not subject to the rules and ethics of the Bar. In civil law jurisdictions, in-house counsel, as employees of the firm, are also often not considered to be independent.

7.157 Generally speaking, professional confidentiality will be lost if material is disclosed to a third party. However, the disclosure of confidential material to a regulator will often not constitute a waiver of confidentiality as regulators will frequently be under a duty to keep information confidential that has been obtained by them in the course of an investigation. There are, however, carve-outs to this rule that permit regulators to disclose information to other regulators or prosecutors (such as the UK gateway regulations)[1]. In practice, however, there is a risk that once a regulator has possession of the information it may become available to a third party and entities should give careful consideration to this before providing privileged documents to regulators.

1 The Financial Services and Markets Act 2000 (Disclosure of Confidential Information) Regulations 2001, SI 2001/2188.

OTHER PRACTICAL CONSIDERATIONS

Employee issues

7.158 Firms will usually need to take steps to secure ongoing and future co-operation of any employees involved in the issue under investigation. If the investigation involves potential employee misconduct, consideration may need to be given as to whether employees need separate legal representation. This is likely to be particularly important in cases where there are potential criminal implications such as insider trading, cartel-related or bribery offences. Firms will also need to consider whether it is necessary to take any internal disciplinary action against employees for any misconduct, although where possible, disciplinary action should not usually take place until after the investigation has been concluded. It is also important to ensure that a firm continues to have access to any ex-employees who can assist in defending any ongoing investigation. In the event that a relevant individual is no longer employed by the firm it may be appropriate to enter into a co-operation agreement that requires the ex-employee to co-operate in any ongoing investigation.

7.159 Where an investigation has commenced as a result of a whistleblower's report, firms also need to take steps to ensure that the whistleblower is adequately protected from retaliation. A number of jurisdictions, including the US, the UK and Japan, have legal protection for whistleblowers. Some jurisdictions have gone even further, introducing financial incentives for whistleblowers. In the US for example, the Dodd-Frank Act rewards whistleblowers for reporting suspected securities or commodities trading violations to the SEC and the CFTC. The UK OFT also has the power to pay up to £100,000 to informants in cartel cases. These reward schemes are likely to lead to an increase in the number of whistleblowers coming forward to regulators.

Public relations

7.160 Adverse media coverage arising from an investigation can be very damaging to a firm, in some instances more so than the regulatory response. It is important, therefore, to put in place a public relations strategy that is implemented consistently by the firm in all relevant jurisdictions. This may include co-ordinating press-conferences in different jurisdictions to ensure that accurate and consistent information is given to the media and, if possible, agreeing with the regulators what will be said and when.

7.161 It is often helpful to have a central point of decision making within the firm as this ensures consistency and credibility. External PR support may be engaged to co-ordinate the flow of information and ensure that no misleading information is given to the market or regulators that may result in even more serious consequences for the firm. It is important to ensure that legal counsel are involved with the drafting of press-releases to ensure that no third parties' rights are violated and that the message presented to the market and/or regulators is balanced and accurate. An appropriate person should be appointed as the primary point of contact for press and this should be communicated to employees and other members of the investigation team to ensure that the message presented to the press is consistent and controlled.

PUBLIC DISCLOSURE REQUIREMENTS

7.162   Firms will also need to consider carefully whether any potential disclosures need to be made to meet capital market requirements such as announcements to the markets and disclosures in public filings. Failure to handle this issue could result in accusations of a lack of transparency. When a firm has shares listed on different exchanges, it is important to ensure that notifications to all relevant exchanges are made having regard to local rules and are co-ordinated where possible both in terms of timing and detail. Any announcements to the market should be carefully worded to ensure that the information provided is both accurate and sufficiently detailed to meet the firm's disclosure requirements. However, this can be a delicate balancing act as it will generally be in the firm's interest not to say more than it has to in order to meet its regulatory requirements, particularly when an investigation is at an early stage.

LITIGATION RISKS

7.163   In some cases a regulatory investigation and enforcement action may result in follow on criminal litigation by regulators or civil litigation by third parties or regulatory action by other regulators. A common concern is whether documents disclosed to a regulator can be obtained by individuals engaged in private litigation through third-party disclosure requests. Documents provided to a regulator as part of any settlement or leniency application in which an entity admits to certain conduct will be of particular concern as they may prejudice ongoing or potential litigation with third parties.

7.164   The UK courts have traditionally provided protection for such documents, however, the position is less clear following the European Court of Justice's ruling in *Pfleiderer*[1] which suggests that courts may have discretion to require the production of such documents despite the protections afforded.

1 *Pfleiderer AG v Bunderskartellamt (C-360/09)* European Court of Justice (Grand Chamber), 14 June 2011. The test established in *Pfleiderer* was applied (for the first time by a national court) in *Amtsgericht Bonn, Beschluss vom 18/01/2012 (51 Gs 53/09)*. In *Amtsgericht* the court refused to use its discretion to require the disclosure of leniency documents held by the German Federal Cartel Office.

7.165   Applications from litigants usually focus on communications between the firm in question and the relevant regulator rather than the regulator's internal papers (which a firm will not have a right to access). One frequently-used solution to this issue is to therefore avoid making such admissions or providing prejudicial evidence in written communications with the relevant regulator. Where a particular regulator requires an admission from the firm based on its internal findings, this can be communicated by an oral presentation from the firm's lawyers to the relevant regulator setting out their findings based on their own privileged notes. The regulator can then create its own notes of the presentation for its records which will usually be protected from disclosure.

7.166   There is a real risk, however, that documents prepared by a firm during the course of a regulatory investigation and enforcement process have to be disclosed to third parties in subsequent litigation. This approach is particularly common in the US and findings by regulators (or admissions) of regulatory breach are frequently used by claimants in support of civil claims. However, such a finding or admission is, of course, only one element of any civil claim and the claimant will still have to prove that the amount and extent of the loss suffered by the claimant related to the regulatory breach.

RESOLUTION

7.167   Some regulators (such as the UK FCA) now have formalised settlement processes that provide for discounts where settlements are concluded at an early stage. Careful consideration needs to be given to whether admissions may need to be made as part of the settlement process and some regulators (such as in the UK or US) may insist that a firm or person who has been disciplined agrees not to dispute the facts and matters contained in the enforcement notice or settlement order as a condition to agreeing the settlement.

7.168   In the US, the DOJ frequently makes use of deferred prosecution agreements where firms agree to pay a fine and have their prosecution deferred and subsequently dismissed as long as certain conditions relating to the settlement are fulfilled. Deferred prosecution agreements are also due to be implemented in the UK by the Serious Fraud Office in early 2014.

7.169   Other regulators (such as BaFin in Germany and the regulators in Italy) do not encourage settlement as a matter of public policy although in practice it is sometimes possible to reach informal agreements where the firm accepts a sanction in return for regulatory action being discontinued.

7.170   As noted in para **7.3** ff above, it is becoming increasingly common for regulators in different jurisdictions to co-operate in relation to investigations. This has led in recent years to a number of cases where firms have reached so-called global settlements with regulators. For example, at the same time that Barclays announced its settlement with the FSA in relation to allegations of manipulation of LIBOR, similar settlements were announced by the DOJ and CFTC[1]. Rabobank announced a $1 billion global settlement with regulators and prosecutors for serious LIBOR-related misconduct that included the DOJ, CFTC, FCA, Japanese Financial Services Agency, De Nederlandische Bank and the Dutch Public Prosecutor's Office[2]. Similarly, in respect of the 'London Whale' investigation, JP Morgan reached a global settlement with the FCA, the SEC, the OCC and the Federal Reserve[3].

1   FSA Press Release FSA/PN/070/2012: 'Barclays fined £59.5 million for significant failings in relation to LIBOR and EURIBOR'. Global settlements in relation to the manipulation of LIBOR have also been entered into by ICAP, see FCA Press Release FCA/PN/90/2013; RBS (see FSA Press Release FSA/PN/011/2013) and UBS (see FSA Press Release FSA/PN/116/2012).
2   FCA Press Release FCA/PN/100/2013: 'Rabobank fined £105 million for serious LIBOR-related misconduct; see also DOJ Press Release (http://www.justice.gov/opa/pr/2013/October/13-crm-1147.html) and CFTC Order (http://www.cftc.gov/ucm/groups/public/@lrenforcementactions/documents/legalpleading/enfrabobank102913.pdf); Dutch Public Prosecutor's Office Press Release (http://www.om.nl/algemene_onderdelen/uitgebreid_zoeken/@161679/rabobank-pays-dutch/) and De Nederlandsche Bank (http://www.dnb.nl/en/news/news-and-archive/persberichten-2013/dnb298704.jsp) and Japanese Financial Services Agency Press Release (http://www.fsa.go.jp/en/news/2013/20131029-1.html).
3   FCA Press Release FCA/PN/88/2013: 'JPMorgan Chase Bank N.A. fined £137,610,000 for serious failings relating to its Chief Investment Office's 'London Whale' trades'.

7.171   When considering entering into settlement negotiations with one or more regulators in the context of a cross-border investigation it is important to try to achieve a co-ordinated settlement involving all regulators where possible. This has the advantage of minimising negative publicity and potential impact on a firm's share price. Where possible, agreement should also be reached as to which regulator will take the lead on settlement.

7.172   However, where it is not possible to reach a globally co-ordinated settlement, consideration will also need to be given to the impact that settlement with one or more regulators has in relation to any ongoing investigations or regulatory proceedings with other regulators or any potential litigation. In particular, careful consideration will need to be given to whether the settlement negotiations or settlement agreements may be admissible in proceedings with other regulators.

APPENDIX 1 TO CHAPTER 7: OBLIGATION TO SELF-REPORT REGULATORY BREACHES IN DIFFERENT JURISDICTIONS

Is there an obligation to self-report regulatory breaches?

United Kingdom

Yes, under Principle 11 of the FCA's Principles for Businesses, firms must openly cooperate with the appropriate regulator (the FCA or PRA) and disclose anything relating to the firm of which that regulator would reasonably expect notice. Generally, Principle 11 requires the firm to co-operate with the FCA and PRA as well as overseas regulators.

Under Statement of Principle 4, there is a similar obligation on those individuals who are approved persons. According to the FCA and PRA Handbook (combined view), individuals who do not have responsibility for the firm's communications with the FCA and/or PRA will satisfy their personal duty by internal reporting within the firm. A breach of one of these principles may lead to enforcement action and makes it more likely that the FCA will bring proceedings in respect of the original breach (that was not reported) and increases the chance of greater penalty for the original breach.

Germany

No, in principle there is no general obligation to self-report regulatory breaches. The legislation only imposes a duty to disclose information upon request by the BaFin.

Nevertheless, there are specific obligations to report certain risks for mandatory solvency and suspicions of market abuse or insider dealing. However, in practice firms normally self-report breaches to the BaFin, but only when it is about to officially start an investigation.

France

No, there is no such general obligation. However, there are reporting obligations in certain specific areas (for instance, financial intermediaries are under an obligation to notify any suspicious transactions).

Italy

No, in principle there is no general obligation to self-report breaches, and statutes only impose the duty to disclose information upon request by the relevant regulators or with specific regard to suspicious transactions in the context of market abuse and anti-money laundering rules.

However, the board of statutory auditors of listed companies and financial intermediaries, whose role is to supervise the firm's compliance with applicable laws, is under an obligation to notify Consob of any irregularities found in the context of its supervisory activity.

US

No, statutory or other regulatory obligations to self-report to the SEC or to the DOJ are relatively rare.

However, as a matter of practice, the SEC and DOJ encourage prompt self-reporting in appropriate cases, and the timeliness of any such disclosure is a factor considered when determining whether to take further action.

The decision whether to self-report evidence of wrongdoing is a finely-balanced one, various factors should be considered including the scope or nature of the conduct in question, the seniority of personnel involved, and the costs and potential consequences of self-reporting. The decision to self-report should generally be made after consulting with experienced counsel.

By contrast, FINRA imposes self-reporting requirements on its members in a very broad range of circumstances. For example, a self-reporting obligation is triggered by the finding of a violation by an external body, including a violation of any securities law or regulation, any rule of any governmental agency or financial business. There is also a parallel obligation to self-report violations where the member has concluded on its own that a violation has occurred.

Japan

No, there is no general obligation under Japanese law for companies to self-report regulatory violations.

However, the Banking Act, the FIEA and the Insurance Business Law (the *IBL*) contain requirements for firms to report certain activities. For example, a bank or an insurance company is required to report to the JFSA within 30 days after it becomes aware that its employees or officers have breached laws or regulations.

The Netherlands

Yes, under the Dutch Financial Supervision Act, firms are obliged to self-report certain incidents to regulators. These include controlled and ethical conduct of business as further specified in law. There is an obligation to self-report when these rules of controlled and ethical conduct of business are breached.

Furthermore, the Dutch Corporate Governance Code requires companies to put in place whistle-blowing procedures for employees, enabling them to report irregularities of a general, operational or financial nature to the chairman of the supervisory board or to an officer especially designated for such purpose.

Spain

No, in general there is no such obligation under Spanish law.

258

Section C
Enforcement

Chapter 8   Disciplinary sanctions and other regulatory action against firms

INTRODUCTION

8.1   The Regulators' investigations into a particular matter may reveal more than just a breach of regulatory requirements for which the firm and perhaps also one or more of its officers or employees could, or should, be held culpable. Other issues that may be uncovered include that losses have been caused to a number of investors, that there are continuing breaches and, in some cases, that there are other matters of more general regulatory concern, such as a systemic failure within the firm or matters impacting on market confidence or consumer protection. Whilst these may be interrelated as the various consequences of the same problem, each gives rise to concerns of a different nature and may need to be addressed separately. The Regulators have the ability to take a range of enforcement actions, aimed at addressing different types of concern, and any particular course of action can generally either be taken alone or in combination with another action, depending upon what is appropriate in the circumstances of the case. For example, it may be appropriate both to fine the firm and to require it to pay restitution to customers. Also, the Regulators (or another body) may seek to take action separately, at different times, so that the conclusion of the process relating to one type of enforcement action does not necessarily represent the conclusion of all the possible consequences that may arise from the matter[1].

1   The FCA may decide to use its own-initiative powers as set out at **CHAPTER 16** below, civil action may result (whether in the UK or elsewhere) as set out in **CHAPTER 19** below, or criminal action may result as explained in **CHAPTER 18** below. Alternatively another regulator such as the SEC or an EU regulator may decide that the breach is also within its jurisdiction (for a discussion of multi-jurisdictional investigations please see **CHAPTER 7**). For an example of concurrent regulatory action in more than one jurisdiction, see *Barclays Bank plc final notice (27/6/12)*.

8.2 Disciplinary sanctions and other regulatory action against firms

8.2 This chapter discusses the different types of regulatory action that the Regulators can take against firms. The focus here will be on the substance of each type of enforcement action: what it is and when it can be imposed. The procedure for taking action is considered generally in **CHAPTERS 10** and **11** below, although particular points to note regarding the process in respect of each power, will be highlighted here.

8.3 In particular, there will be a review of the Regulators' powers:

- to take disciplinary action against firms (para **8.8** ff);

- to order restitution to be made to investors or to apply to the court for such an order (para **8.100** ff);

- to apply to the court for civil injunctions (para **8.138** ff).

8.4 Although the Regulators share many of the same powers to impose disciplinary sanctions on firms, it is likely that the FCA will be the more active of the Regulators in the enforcement sphere, and this expectation would appear to be borne out by the guidance each of the Regulators has issued on the subject. Each has published separate guidance on the use of its enforcement powers: the FCA has gone into some detail in setting out its guidance in the FCA Handbook and the FCA Enforcement Guide; the PRA has merely issued a 'Statement of the PRA's Policy on the Imposition and Amount of Financial Penalties under the Act' (the 'Penalty Statement')[1] and a 'Statement of the PRA's Policy on the Imposition of Suspensions or Restrictions under the Act and the Period for which they are to have Effect' (the 'Suspension/Restriction Statement')[2]. The Penalty Statement and the Suspension/Restriction Statement constitute the minimum level of guidance required from the PRA under the FSMA 2000.

1 The Penalty Statement is contained in the PRA's Policy Statement on 'The Prudential Regulation Authority's approach to enforcement: statutory statements of policy and procedure', April 2013 at Appendix 2.
2 PRA's Policy Statement on 'The Prudential Regulation Authority's approach to enforcement: statutory statements of policy and procedure', Appendix 3.

8.5 The Regulators have three additional general powers not covered in this chapter, namely:

- to discipline and/or exercise other enforcement powers against approved persons and other individuals working for firms, considered in **CHAPTER 9** below;

- to vary or cancel a firm's permission, give directions or intervene in an incoming firm, considered in **CHAPTER 16** below; and

- to prosecute various criminal offences, considered in **CHAPTER 18** below.

8.6 The Regulators also have various specific powers, for example:

- the FCA's power to require the withdrawal or amendment of a financial promotion (which can be with immediate effect), considered in **CHAPTER 15**;

- the FCA's power to intervene in the market to ban the sale of particular products, or require the imposition of particular features or terms, considered in **Chapter 15**;

- the FCA's power to deal with cases of market misconduct, considered in **Chapter 17** below;

- the FCA in its capacity as UK Listing Authority in relation to listed companies, applicants for listing, directors and former directors, considered in **Chapter 20** below;

- the FCA's power in relation to regulated collective investment schemes[1];

- the Regulators' power to disqualify, censure and penalise auditors and actuaries[2];

- the Regulators' power in relation to the Lloyd's insurance market[3];

- the FCA's power in relation to recognised investment exchanges and recognised clearing houses[4]; and

- the FCA's power in relation to professionals and designated professional bodies[5].

1 The FSMA 2000 contains separate provision for investigation and enforcement in relation to authorised unit trusts and other regulated collective investment schemes. These are set out in Pt 17 of the FSMA 2000. It should be noted that the FSMA 2000 does not contain detailed provisions relating to authorised open-ended investment companies, but enables rules relating to them to be made, see: the Open-Ended Investment Companies Regulations 2001, SI 2001/1228.
2 FSMA 2000, ss 345 and 345A.
3 FSMA 2000, Pt 19.
4 FSMA 2000, Pt 18 and see the FCA Handbook at REC Chapter 4. The enforcement powers of the recognised investment exchanges in relation to their members are briefly considered in para **17.205** ff below.
5 FSMA 2000, Pt 20 and see the FCA Handbook at PROF Chapter 3.

8.7   In the vast majority of cases, disciplinary action is available only against firms and individuals working for firms. The Regulators have no general ability to take disciplinary action against those who are not part of the regulated community. However, they have certain powers that apply to the wider community, for example the FCA can make applications for injunctions and restitution orders, bring criminal prosecutions as well as imposing fines and restitution orders for market abuse.

DISCIPLINARY ACTION

Introduction

8.8   The following paragraphs review the Regulators' powers to take disciplinary action against firms and their policy and practice on the use of those powers. In common with many other aspects of the regime, the FSMA 2000 provides only the basic framework for the Regulators' powers, allowing the Regulators to take action in certain situations but leaving it to the Regulators to determine when in practice it will be appropriate to do so.

8.9 Disciplinary sanctions and other regulatory action against firms

8.9   In some instances, the Regulators will address non-compliance without recourse to disciplinary action[1]. The FCA has published a policy on when it will take formal action and on what action it will take[2], which should be considered by any firm facing the possibility of such action. As outlined at para **8.25** ff below, the implementation of that policy depends in part on the objectives important to the FCA at the particular point in time; however, since the onset of the financial crisis in 2008 it is far more likely that the FCA will take disciplinary action where it has the power to do so. The PRA has issued less policy guidance in this area and will be less focused on enforcement than the FCA.

1 FCA Enforcement Guide at EG 7.1 and see para **8.27** ff below.
2 This policy is found in the FCA Enforcement Guide at EG Chapter 7.

8.10   Although this chapter is mainly concerned with firms (ie authorised persons), examples of disciplinary action taken against others are included insofar as they are relevant.

What disciplinary powers do the Regulators have?

8.11   The FSMA 2000 allows the Regulators to impose a fine and/or publicly censure a firm, and/or suspend or restrict that person's permission to carry on regulated activities, as disciplinary measures. In addition, the Regulators may, in some circumstances, issue informal private warnings to firms rather than taking formal disciplinary action. As will be seen, these warnings do carry potential regulatory consequences. The circumstances when the FCA will issue a private warning, and the potential consequences, are discussed at para **8.27** ff below.

8.12   The statutory powers may be exercised by the 'appropriate Regulator'[1], which in summary refers to the PRA in relation to:

- a breach of a requirement imposed by the PRA under the FSMA 2000, such as those contained in the PRA Handbook;

- the performance of controlled functions by non-approved persons, where the approval in question falls to be given by the PRA or the PRA has made a prohibition order;

- breaches of certain EU provisions, specified by the Treasury[2], where the Treasury has also designated the PRA as the 'appropriate regulator'; and

- criminal offences where the PRA is the Regulator with the power to prosecute the offence[3];

and otherwise refers to the FCA.

1 'Appropriate regulator' is defined under the FSMA 2000, s 204A(3)–(7).
2 Under SI 2013/419.
3 Such offences are set out in the FSMA 2000, s 401(3A).

8.13   If the appropriate Regulator considers that a firm has contravened a relevant requirement, it may:

- publish a statement to that effect[1]; and/or

- impose a penalty in respect of the contravention, of such amount as they consider appropriate[2]; and/or

- suspend or restrict any permission to carry on a regulated activity[3].

1 FSMA 2000, s 205.
2 FSMA 2000, s 206(1).
3 FSMA 2000, s 206A.

8.14   The primary question is thus normally whether the firm has contravened a requirement imposed by or under the FSMA 2000[1], in other words, broadly breached one of the Regulators' rules or a requirement imposed under regulations made under the FSMA 2000 or directly by the legislation. It is important to appreciate that this includes not only breaches of specific rules but also breaches of the Principles for Businesses, which are wide-ranging in their potential application[2]. The Principles for Businesses are rules, breach of which can give rise to disciplinary action.

1 For a detailed discussion of what is encompassed within this phrase, see para **2.94** ff above.
2 The Principles for Businesses are discussed at para **2.12** ff above.

8.15   The Regulators can bring enforcement action for breach of the Principles alone, breach of the detailed rules in the Handbooks alone, or a combination of the two. In the past, most enforcement action was brought for a combination of Principle and rule breaches but increasingly enforcement actions are based on breaches of Principles alone[1]. The FCA's policy is to bring enforcement actions for breaches of Principles alone where there is no detailed rule that prohibits the behaviour but it clearly contravenes a Principle, or where a firm has committed a number of breaches of detailed rules which, individually, may not merit disciplinary action but the cumulative effect of which indicates the breach of a Principle[2].

1 See for example, the high profile enforcement actions involving *Coöperatieve Centrale Raiffeisen-Boerenleenbank BA (Rabobank) final notice (29/10/2013)*, *JPMorgan Chase Bank, NA final notice (18/09/2013)*, *Prudential Assurance Company Limited final notice (27/03/2012)* and *Barclays Bank plc final notice (27/06/13)*.
2 Handbooks at DEPP 6.2.14 and FCA Enforcement Guide at EG 2.19.

8.16   The broad scope of the Principles gives rise to a concern that the Regulators could use current guidance, policy or stated expectations of conduct to bring enforcement action for a breach of a Principle alone for conduct that complied with detailed rules and met what the firm thought were the Regulators' expectations of conduct at the time. This raises an issue of fairness: the Regulators should not be able to use hindsight to hold firms liable for conduct that met regulatory standards and firms should not have to second guess and comply with future regulatory standards in order to avoid enforcement action. The Regulators do, however, recognise that the application of Principles should be reasonably predictable, so that firms are not held liable for conduct or omissions that the firm could not reasonably have predicted fell below regulatory standards[1]. There is also an onus on the Regulator bringing the enforcement action to show that the firm is at fault and fell below the standards required to meet the relevant

Principle at the time of the conduct[2]. There remains a tension, however, between the Regulators' stated intention to use the Principles to bring enforcement actions for misconduct and the need to ensure reasonable predictability in the application of the Principles. This is particularly the case when the Regulators are considering enforcement action for new products or activities for which there are no specific rules. Firms should bear these points in mind when faced with an enforcement action alleging breaches of Principles alone.

1   FCA Enforcement Guide at EG 2.20.
2   The Handbooks at PRIN 1.1.7 and DEPP 6.2.15.

8.17   The provisions outlined here form the framework for the imposition of disciplinary sanctions against firms. A key question is when in practice the Regulators are likely to take such action and how they determine the amount of any penalty. The Regulators have set out their policy with respect to the imposition and amount of penalties and are required to have regard to the policy in force at the time the contravention occurred[1].

1   FSMA 2000, s 210.

When will the Regulators take disciplinary action?

8.18   Discipline, and indeed enforcement action more generally, is only one of a number of actions available to the Regulators to address a particular regulatory issue[1]. Not every rule breach will lead to the Regulators taking disciplinary action against the relevant firm. This section considers the Regulators' policy in two key respects, namely:

- when will formal disciplinary action be appropriate? and

- in the case of the FCA, when will it give an informal private warning?

1   FCA Enforcement Guide at EG 7.1.

8.19   The Regulators' policy on what disciplinary sanctions to impose, in those cases where formal action is appropriate, is considered separately at para **8.36** ff below.

When will formal disciplinary action be appropriate?

The PRA

8.20   The PRA has not issued any detailed guidance as to when it will seek to discipline a firm. It is thought that the factors applied by the FCA, discussed below, are likely also to be relevant to the PRA, and a firm faced with the potential of a PRA enforcement action should therefore be considering the same sort of factors. However, it is likely that forward-looking, non-disciplinary steps will generally be the PRA's preferred course of action. This should mean that disciplinary action (which is inherently after the event) should be considerably less common than for the FCA.

The FCA

8.21   In deciding whether or not to take formal disciplinary action for conduct appearing to the FCA to be a breach, the FCA considers the full circumstances of the case, including an extensive list of potentially relevant factors set out in the FCA Handbook at DEPP 6.2.1 and 6A.2.1. The FCA will undertake a reasonably broad analysis of the situation to decide whether in all the circumstances formal disciplinary action is appropriate. Some issues may be able to be addressed by the firm's supervisors without the need for formal action and, in others, a private warning may be given[1]. Many of the factors listed at DEPP 6.2.1 and 6A.2.1 are similar to those which the FCA will consider in deciding what form of sanction to impose (see para **8.45** ff below). Accordingly the FCA may consider the same aspect of a firm's conduct when addressing both questions: whether to take action, and what action to take.

1 FCA Enforcement Guide at EG 7.10. Private warnings are considered at para **8.27** ff below.

8.22   The list of factors includes[1]:

- the nature, seriousness and impact of the suspected breach, which can include whether the breach was deliberate or reckless; the duration and frequency of the breach; and the amount of benefit gained or loss avoided as a result of the breach;

- the conduct of the firm after the breach, which can include the degree of co-operation; how quickly and completely the firm brought the breach to the attention of the FCA; and the remedial steps taken in respect of the breach such as compensating consumers for their losses, disciplining staff involved and addressing any systemic failures;

- the previous disciplinary record and compliance history of the person, which can include whether the firm has previously undertaken not to do a particular act or engage in a particular behaviour; and whether the FCA has previously requested the firm to take remedial action or the FCA has used its own initiative powers;

- FCA guidance and other published materials;

- action taken by the FSA or FCA in previous similar cases; and

- action taken by other domestic or international regulatory authorities, in particular whether the other authority's action would be adequate to address the FCA's concerns.

1 FCA Handbook at DEPP 6.2.1.

8.23   It is important to appreciate that the FCA will not decline to take any action simply because another regulatory authority claims jurisdiction. The FCA will examine all the circumstances of the case and consider whether the other regulator's action would adequately address the FCA's concerns or whether it should take action itself[1]. It recognises that sometimes it may be appropriate for both authorities to be involved[2]. Where overseas regulators are involved, both the

8.23   Disciplinary sanctions and other regulatory action against firms

FCA and the overseas regulator may have an interest in taking action to protect their own regulatory standards and fulfil their objectives.

1   FCA Handbook at DEPP 6.2.1(6) and 6.2.20.
2   FCA Handbook at DEPP 6.2.21.

8.24   Firms may therefore be involved in multiple investigations and enforcement proceedings arising from the same problem. The FCA is continuing to develop operating arrangements with other regulatory authorities (both within the UK and overseas), with a view to ensuring that cases are approached in a co-ordinated, effective and efficient manner and that those who are the subject of investigations or potential disciplinary action are treated fairly[1]. It is also involved in similar international initiatives[2].

1   See the FCA Handbook at DEPP 6.2.21. Other UK regulators with which the FCA deals include the recognised investment exchanges and clearing houses, the Society of Lloyd's, relevant designated professional bodies, the Department for Business, Innovation and Skills, the PRA, the Serious Fraud Office and the police, to name but a few.
2   Multi-jurisdictional investigations and enforcement action are discussed in detail in **CHAPTER 7** above.

8.25   It is clear that the FCA has not abandoned the risk-based approach which was historically employed by the FSA, and that it will target products and sectors of the market it considers to be particularly important at the relevant point in time[1]. Accordingly, rather than pursuing a 'zero-tolerance' regime or focusing on the volume of enforcement action, the FCA adopts a thematic approach in order to send messages to the market, encourage changes in the market's behaviour, promote market confidence and protect consumers.

1   See the FCA's Risk Outlook for 2013.

8.26   Irrespective of which areas are regarded as a particular priority at any time, in accordance with its statutory objectives, the FCA is always likely to prioritise cases that involve serious market misconduct, financial crime or consumer harm. The FCA is not likely to decide against disciplinary action in cases where third parties, particularly consumers, have been prejudiced to a significant degree or in significant numbers (at least without steps being taken to protect and/or compensate them). Where enforcement action is concentrated on a particular sector of the market, the FCA recognises that drawing the public's attention to that sector may have a disproportionate and harmful effect on consumer confidence and therefore the FCA may seek to limit the damage where possible and as appropriate (for example, where the FCA considers that the danger to consumers only arises from a minority of firms). The way in which the FCA pursues its enforcement activities can therefore have an impact on firms beyond those directly affected by the FCA's action.

When will the FCA give an informal private warning?

8.27   In some situations, despite having concerns about the behaviour of a firm (or individual), the FCA may decide that it is not appropriate to bring formal disciplinary action. For instance, this may be the case where the matter giving cause for concern is only minor or where full and immediate remedial action has been taken by the firm. In those situations, the FCA may give the firm a private warning to make it aware that it has come close to being subject to formal disciplinary action.

What is a private warning?

8.28   A private warning is a warning to the firm that it came close to being subjected to formal action. A private warning requires that the FCA identifies and explains its concerns about a person's conduct and/or procedures, and tells the subject of the warning that the FCA has seriously considered formal steps to impose a penalty or censure[1].

1 FCA Enforcement Guide at EG 7.11.

What benefits does a private warning have?

8.29   There are clear benefits in the FCA being able to issue private warnings. Primarily, the system has a flexibility that allows the FCA to deal informally with more minor or inconsequential breaches that do not merit formal action but that require some sort of acknowledgement that there has been wrongdoing. Usually, this benefits both the FCA, which is spared the cost of taking formal enforcement action for minor breaches, and the firm, which is not subjected to formal action.

What is the effect of the private warning?

8.30   The private warning does not have any formal effect; it is evidence of the fact that the FCA had cause for concern, but it is not a determination by the FCA as to whether the recipient has breached the FCA's rules[1]. However, it is important to recognise that the private warning is not wholly free from regulatory consequences: as the FCA makes clear, it forms part of the firm's compliance history. As such it may influence the FCA's decision whether to commence disciplinary action in the future. Although it may not be relied upon in determining whether a breach has taken place, if a firm has previously been told via a private warning of the FCA's concerns on an issue, then this can be an aggravating factor for the level of a penalty imposed for a similar issue that is the subject of later FCA action[2]. In other words, it is relevant in deciding whether or not a future breach merits disciplinary action[3], but not in proving that the breach occurred. When considering the future breach, the FCA will have to assess the significance of the private warning, including its age (although a long-standing warning may still be relevant), and several private warnings may be relevant cumulatively even though they relate to separate areas of the firm's business or different subsidiaries of the same parent; for example if they show concerns about the compliance culture or the senior management team[4].

1 FCA Enforcement Guide at 7.15. The use of the word 'determination' is deliberate. It is a determination that triggers the ECHR fair trial guarantees.

8.30 Disciplinary sanctions and other regulatory action against firms

2 FCA Enforcement Guide at EG 7.15.
3 As was the case in *Catalyst Investment Group Limited final notice (30/09/13)*.
4 FCA Enforcement Guide at EG 7.16/17.

8.31   The private warning may also have other less tangible effects. The fact that it recites the FCA's view that there has been cause for concern may raise difficult questions about whether it must be disclosed to others; for example, the firm's other regulators or its insurers. The practical effect may be that such other parties will take the view that a breach has been committed. There may also be a risk of civil claims being brought against the firm[1], which could result in the disclosure of the otherwise 'private' warning.

1 FSMA 2000, s 138D and more generally at **CHAPTER 19** below.

8.32   This can be particularly problematic for approved persons[1], who will have an unsubstantiated adverse entry on their regulatory record. If they are dual registered, they may need to disclose it to their other regulator. It could also potentially affect their future employment prospects in a similar way to a reference or Form C which sets out concerns about an individual's fitness and propriety.

1 Also, senior persons, and possibly other individuals, in the regime introduced by the Financial Services (Banking Reform) Act 2013 and associated consultations.

What practical steps can the firm take?

8.33   When issuing a private warning, the FCA will invite the firm to comment on the warning if it wishes to do so[1]. That response will also form part of the compliance history[2]. If the firm feels that there are good reasons why the private warning was not merited, or could be misinterpreted in the future, then it is important to respond appropriately to try to ensure that the compliance history reflects a more balanced view. In practice, where the proposed wording of a private warning may give rise to serious unintended consequences, the FCA may be receptive to considering this with the firm.

1 FCA Enforcement Guide at EG 7.19.
2 FCA Enforcement Guide at EG 7.15.

Can a private warning be challenged?

8.34   Since private warnings are a non-statutory measure which the FCA views as no different to any other communication which criticises or expresses concern about a firm's conduct, the firm to which a private warning is issued has no right to intervene in the process or to refer the matter to the Tribunal. In theory, one might be able to press the FCA into taking formal action, so that the firm can vindicate itself before the Tribunal, but this will usually involve greater risks as well as significant costs and it is hard to imagine when that would be a prudent course to follow. Other theoretical challenges include judicial review, or by bringing a complaint before the independent complaints commissioner as set out at **CHAPTER 21** below. In practice, neither of these is likely to take place. The opportunity of discussing the private warning with the FCA and subsequently the ability to comment on the private warning provide the best means of mitigating its potential effect.

How long does a private warning last?

8.35   The FCA Handbook is silent on when an informal warning will cease to form part of the compliance history, although it does indicate that warnings may be 'long-standing'[1]. Equally, there is no specific provision allowing the firm to apply to the FCA to have the warning revoked or varied, and there is no provision enabling the FCA to do so. The implication is that the warning is likely to remain permanently on the FCA's database. There may, however, be scope in practice for seeking to agree with the FCA at the time the warning is given that it will only remain on the database for a particular period of time or asking for it to be removed after a particular period has elapsed. Certainly, as the FCA has indicated, the relevance of the warning should normally diminish over time[2].

1   FCA Enforcement Guide at EG 7.16.
2   FCA Enforcement Guide at EG 7.16.

What disciplinary sanction will be imposed?

8.36   The following paragraphs review three key issues regarding the disciplinary sanction to be imposed, namely:

- choosing which sanction to impose;

- the contents of a public censure; and

- determining the amount of a fine.

8.37   The key question of when firms will be given credit for co-operation will also be examined.

8.38   Reference will be made to the FCA's policy and approach, for which there is more detailed guidance, but key points from the PRA's published guidance will be highlighted where available.

Choosing which sanction to impose

The FCA

8.39   As already seen, the Regulators can impose a fine, a public censure or a suspension or restriction. Before looking at how the FCA chooses which to impose, it is worth briefly reviewing the purpose of each.

8.40   Clearly, the publication of a censure or statement of misconduct can have a serious effect on a firm's business, brand and reputation. They also allow the FCA to highlight the standards of conduct that it expects and demonstrate that those standards are being effectively enforced. The FCA believes that this helps to maintain confidence in the financial system and promotes public awareness of the standards that it expects. The requirement of public awareness means that public censures are drafted so as to have an impact on the market and to be noticed by the press and consumers. Accordingly, the FCA considers the timing of such censures to be important and will try to ensure that important censures are not published over holiday periods and that two important censures do not coincide so that their impact is not diminished. Censures are invariably accompanied by an FCA press release.

8.41   Financial penalties are seen as having similar aims in that they are meant to deter firms from committing contraventions, help deter others[1] and demonstrate generally the benefits of compliant behaviour[2]. The difference is that the financial aspect of the penalty tends to receive more attention. In practice, the FCA has rarely used its power to issue a public censure without simultaneously imposing a fine and this should be regarded as the norm. Those rare cases where a public censure has been imposed without a fine have typically been where the firm has had insufficient resources: for example, in the case of Cattles Ltd the FSA stated that it would have imposed a 'substantial financial penalty' on the company had it not been the subject of a scheme of arrangement with its creditors (although the company's former finance director was fined for his involvement in the breach)[3].

1   The deterrent effect of a fine will be considered to be particularly relevant where the breach occurs in an area where the FCA is placing greater emphasis (*Sun Life Insurance Company of Canada (UK) Limited final notice (18/10/12)*). The FCA believes that in order to achieve credible deterrence senior managers within firms must be held to account (speech by Tracey McDermott, the FCA's Director of Enforcement & Financial Crime (18/6/13); see also *Peter Cummings final notice (12/9/12)*.
2   FCA Handbook at DEPP 6.1.2.
3   *Cattles Ltd final notice (28/3/12)*.

8.42   Firms are not able to insure themselves against the costs of such fines although they may still take insurance against the legal costs of dealing with enforcement action[1]. Insurance may also cover the costs of paying compensation to customers.

1   Handbooks at GEN Chapter 6.

8.43   In an enhancement to the powers previously conferred on the FSA, the Regulators may now also impose a suspension or restriction of a firm's permission to carry out regulated activities[1], for example by limiting a firm's activities so that it may only sell certain products or carry out certain services. This sanction may also be applied to approved persons (and certain other individuals), in respect of which see **CHAPTER 9**. The Regulators may decide to take such measures in addition to, or instead of, imposing a fine or a public censure. In reaching this decision the FCA will take into account the factors it would consider when considering whether to impose a financial penalty or public censure[2]. The maximum length of a suspension or restriction that can be imposed on a firm is 12 months[3]; the FCA retains the discretion to decide on the length of the period of suspension or restriction subject to this statutory limit. The FCA also has the discretion to delay the start of a suspension or restriction[4].

1   FCA Handbook at DEPP 6A.1.2.
2   FCA Handbook at DEPP 6A.2.2.
3   FSMA 2000, s 206A(3).
4   FCA Handbook at DEPP 6A.3.3. Note that the list of factors to be taken into account in such a determination is non-exhaustive.

8.44   The FCA's early settlement discount scheme applies to the imposition of a suspension or restriction. Discounts will be applied to the period of suspension or restriction in the same way as to financial penalties, ie a 30% discount would see a 10-month suspension or restriction reduced to 7 months. The early settlement discount scheme is discussed in detail at para **10.45** ff below.

8.45   Against that background, therefore, how does the FCA decide which sanction to impose? Since the imposition of a fine will nearly always be made public, the real decision is not whether to impose one or the other but whether to impose only a public censure or both a fine and a public censure. At the same time as making this decision, the FCA will also normally determine whether or not to impose the additional sanction of a suspension or restriction[1]. In reaching that decision, the FCA will consider its statutory objectives[2] and all the circumstances of the case. The FCA Handbook sets out at DEPP 6.4.2 an extensive (though non-exhaustive) list of factors which are likely to be relevant to the FCA's assessment of whether a fine or public censure should be imposed. These include[3]:

- whether or not deterrence may be effectively achieved by issuing a public censure;

- if the firm has made a profit or avoided loss as a result of the breach, a financial penalty may be more appropriate;

- if the breach is more serious in nature or degree, a financial penalty may be more appropriate on the basis that the sanction should reflect the seriousness of the breach;

- if the firm has brought the breach to the attention of the FCA, a public censure may be more appropriate;

- if the firm has admitted the breach and provides full and immediate co-operation to the FCA and takes steps to ensure that those who have suffered loss due to the breach are fully compensated for those losses, a public censure may be more appropriate;

- if the firm has a poor disciplinary record or compliance history, a financial penalty may be more appropriate;

- the FCA's aim is to achieve a consistent approach to the imposition of sanctions and may consider its approach to similar previous cases; and

- the impact on the firm concerned may result in the FCA agreeing to issue a public censure rather than impose a financial penalty, although, this will only be considered in exceptional cases.

1 FCA Handbook at DEPP 6A.2.1. Note that at the time of writing the FCA has yet to impose a suspension or restriction on a firm.
2 See para **1.21** ff above. For example the protection of consumers objective will be relevant in cases of misselling (*Lloyds Banking Group final notice (15/2/13)*) and the reduction of financial crime objective will be relevant in cases of inadequate anti-money laundering controls (*Coutts & Company final notice (23/3/12)*).
3 FCA Handbook at DEPP 6.4.2. This list is expressly non-exhaustive.

8.46 Disciplinary sanctions and other regulatory action against firms

8.46 As already indicated, the FCA also has the power to impose a suspension or restriction as a disciplinary measure. Since its introduction in 2010, this power has never been used in practice. However, it remains an option for the FCA in appropriate cases. As a matter of policy, the FCA will impose a restriction or suspension in addition to a fine where it believes that such action will be a more effective and persuasive deterrent than the imposition of a financial penalty alone[1]. This is more likely in high-profile cases where the FCA believes that it is necessary to take direct and visible action in relation to a particular breach. While the FCA will usually (if taking such action) suspend or restrict a firm from carrying out activities directly linked to the breach, in certain circumstances it may take such action in relation to activities which are not so linked, for example when a firm's relevant business no longer exists or has been restructured[2]. Again, the FCA Handbook sets out (at DEPP 6A.2.3) a list of factors that will militate in favour of a suspension or restriction, including any previous disciplinary action taken against the firm, any failure to carry out agreed remedial measures and whether the firm's competitive position in the market has improved as a result of the breach.

1 FCA Handbook at DEPP 6A.2.3.
2 FCA Handbook at DEPP 6A.2.4.

8.47 In the past, the FSA would only issue a public censure without a fine in exceptional cases[1]. Such exceptional cases could include where a firm has negligible net assets, or would be unable to meet its financial resources requirements as a result of a fine[2]. In the future, the FCA may impose a suspension or restriction on a firm in addition to a public censure and in place of a fine.

1 See para **8.41** above and the FCA's very rare use of public censures without taking other action.
2 As in *Gracechurch Investments Limited (In Liquidation) final notice (20/12/12)*. Where a firm is in such difficulties, the FCA will probably also consider it necessary to use its own-initiative powers. See also *Cattles Ltd final notice (28/3/12)*, discussed at para **8.41** above.

The PRA

8.48 The PRA has the same disciplinary powers as the FCA, exercisable by the PRA where it is the appropriate regulator under the FSMA 2000, s 204A. Similarly, therefore, the PRA must consider in each case what (if any) is the appropriate punishment[1]. When considering whether to impose a penalty[2], the PRA may have regard to certain general principles including the need to act in a way which advances the statutory objectives of the PRA, the desirability of encouraging and upholding high standards of behaviour and the need to ensure that disciplinary measures: (i) properly reflect the seriousness of the breach; (ii) are proportionate to the breach; (iii) are effective in deterring the person who committed the breach and others from committing similar or other breaches; and (iv) are in the public interest.

1 The PRA's policy is set out in the Penalty Statement and the Suspension/Restriction Statement in 'The Prudential Regulation Authority's approach to enforcement', April 2013, Appendices 2 and 3.
2 See the Penalty Statement in 'The Prudential Regulation Authority's approach to enforcement', April 2013, at Appendix 2, para 2.

8.49   In determining whether it will take action for a penalty, the PRA must consider all relevant facts and circumstances of the case. The Penalty Statement sets out factors that may be relevant for this purpose, which include the following[1]:

- the impact (or potential impact) of the misconduct on the stability of the financial system;

- the seriousness of the breach of the PRA's regulatory requirements, including for example whether it was deliberate or reckless and its potential impact on the advancement of the PRA's statutory objectives;

- the extent of the firm's responsibility for the breach;

- the conduct of the firm after the breach was committed, including for example the firm's degree of co-operation and the effectiveness of any remedial action;

- the previous disciplinary and/or supervisory record of the person (including: any previous enforcement/regulatory action by the PRA, the FCA and/ or any predecessor regulators; private warnings; previous undertakings by the person to act in a particular way and their compliance with it; and the general supervisory record of the person or specific aspects of it relevant to the behaviour in question);

- relevant guidance/information provided by the PRA, FCA and/or any predecessor regulators, which were in force at the time of the behaviour in question; and

- any relevant action by other domestic and/or international regulatory authorities (including whether, if such agencies are taking or propose to take relevant action for the behaviour in question, it is necessary or desirable for the PRA also to take its own separate action, including action for a penalty).

1 Penalty Statement in 'The Prudential Regulation Authority's approach to enforcement', April 2013, at Appendix 2, para 3.

8.50   These are very similar to the factors considered by the FCA[1], save for the first factor (impact on the stability of the financial system), which reflects the different focus of the PRA.

1 See para **8.45** above.

8.51   The PRA's policy on the imposition and period of suspensions or restrictions of permissions of authorised firms under the FSMA 2000, ss 66 and 206A is set out in this Suspensions/Restrictions statement. In deciding whether it will impose a suspension or restriction, or a penalty or public censure (or any combination of these measures), the PRA will consider the overall impact and deterrent effect of the disciplinary measures and ensure the impact of those measures is appropriate and proportionate to the breach in question[1].

1 See the Suspension/Restriction Statement, para 13.

8.52   When considering whether to impose a suspension or restriction, the

8.52 Disciplinary sanctions and other regulatory action against firms

PRA must have regard to certain considerations[1], which are similar to the considerations in the Penalty Statement described at para **8.49** ff above. The Suspension/Restriction Statement also sets out factors to which the PRA may have regard when determining the period of the suspension or restriction that is appropriate for the breach concerned[2], including the possible impact of a suspension or restriction on the person in breach and the potential for such a measure to have a wider impact on any other persons or the stability of the financial system. At the date of writing, the practical application of these policies has yet to be seen.

1 See the Suspension/Restriction Statement, paras 2–6.
2 See the Suspension/Restriction Statement, paras 10 and 11.

The contents of a public censure

8.53 Firms will commonly take a close interest in the precise contents of the public censure and the press release that will typically accompany it[1]. Firms must also be careful where they are not the target of the action but are affected by it, such as when action is taken against a present or former employee, since details of what happened at the firm and of its internal procedures may be given[2]. It is important to view the censure and press release in their wider context in order to assess their potential impact. For example:

- they may impact on the firm's reputation and that of other parties, for example its advisers[3];

- they could amount to a finding against the firm, which could lead to claims by third parties, make the firm liable to a restitution order, increase the firm's susceptibility to adverse findings by the FOS[4], and potentially prejudice any claim the firm may have against its insurers[5]; or

- they could cause the firm difficulties with overseas regulators[6].

1 See para **10.194** ff below for a description of the publicity that is likely to arise on the issue of a final notice.
2 For example, in *Sachin Surendra Karpe and Jaspreet Singh Ahuja final notices (27/6/12)* the notices related to the individuals' withdrawal of approval but the firm and its internal procedures were described in detail.
3 See para **10.149** ff below for the rights of third parties considered to be prejudiced by an FCA notice (and also for the position where the FCA does not consider that the third party has been prejudiced).
4 See **CHAPTER 14** below.
5 See also the discussion at para **3.116** above.
6 For an example of an FSA finding based on misconduct occurring abroad, see *Barclays Bank plc final notice (27/6/12)*.

8.54 The firm may want to try, to the extent it is able, to ensure that the censure does not contain statements which are unnecessary from the Regulator's perspective, but have a significant collateral impact on the firm. Furthermore, the firm may wish to seek to agree wording that places the breaches in perspective, for example, by recording those areas where no breach has been found. To what extent does the firm have any input in the contents of the censure?

8.55   The Handbooks give little guidance as to how the contents of a public censure are determined. Where a public censure is issued, whether or not in conjunction with a fine, the public censure will take the form of a final notice issued together with a press release (although, as explained in **CHAPTER 10**, the Regulator does have the power to, and does, publicise warning notices and decision notices, not merely final notices)[1].

1 See **CHAPTER 10** for a description of the enforcement procedure which also sets out what facts and matters are likely to be included in the notices, and see para **10.194** ff below for the publicity that is likely to arise.

8.56   In those rare cases where the Regulator has issued a warning notice proposing only a public censure, and not also a fine or a suspension or restriction, it may be imprudent to dispute the wording of the public censure too far in practice since a decision notice imposing a fine may be issued after the relevant decision-making body has considered the firm's representations[1]. Also, if the firm were to refer the decision to impose a public censure to the Tribunal based on objections to the wording of the proposed statement, there may be a risk of the Tribunal deciding that a fine would be more appropriate[2].

1 FSMA 2000, s 388(2) and see para **10.164** below.
2 FSMA 2000, s 133(5) and see para **12.152** ff below.

8.57   In practice, there is some scope for discussing the terms of the censure with the relevant Regulator and, in particular, to seek to ensure that it does not contain unnecessarily damaging material and in some circumstances to include wording that places the breaches in context[1]. Public censures (whether or not accompanied by fines, suspensions or restrictions) tend to set out the background to and facts underlying the misconduct, the rules or requirements that have been breached, the factors considered when deciding whether to impose a sanction and the form of the sanction (and, where a fine is imposed, factors determining the amount of the fine)[2]. In some instances, the Regulator will use the censure (sometimes in conjunction with its press release) to clarify its interpretation of its rules for the benefit of other firms. It should be noted, however, that the FCA appears less willing than the FSA to engage in detailed discussion of a warning notice and so firms should not enter such discussions believing that the whole document is up for negotiation.

1 For example, see: *Hargreaves Lansdown Asset Management Limited final notice (2/6/04)* stating that: 'For the avoidance of all doubt, the FSA's reasons for the action do not include any allegation against HLAM concerning the structuring, management or pricing of any constituent share of the SGP, nor collusive behaviour'.
2 How final notices tend to be set out is considered in more detail at para **10.192** below.

Determining the amount of a fine

8.58   The Regulators are required[1] to issue a statement of their policy for the imposition and amount of fines imposed on firms and to have regard to that statement when exercising or deciding whether to exercise their powers.

1 FSMA 2000, s 210. The FCA's statement of policy is set out in the FCA Handbook DEPP 6.5 to DEPP 6.5D and the PRA's statement of policy is set out in the 'The Prudential Regulation Authority's approach to enforcement', April 2013, at Appendix 2.

8.59   Disciplinary sanctions and other regulatory action against firms

8.59   When deciding whether to impose a fine and the amount of any fine, the Regulator concerned will need to consider the purpose for imposing the fine. Should the fine have the aim of punishing, censuring or deterring? All factors are likely to be relevant. However, given that even a large fine is unlikely to make a significant financial difference to a large firm, the focus is often on censure[1] and the fine's deterrent effect both on that firm and the market generally. The FCA has now begun to impose penalties as high as those in the US, and it is clear that the significant increase in fines in recent years has been intended to improve the deterrent effect and ensure that significant enforcement actions remain newsworthy[2].

1   As is evident from the length and detail of the final notices that accompany fines.
2   In the period April–December 2012, for example, the FSA imposed fines totalling £286.8 million (which included the £59.5 million fine issued to Barclays and the £160 million fine issued to UBS for misconduct relating to the submission of LIBOR and EURIBOR rates). See *Barclays Bank plc final notice (27/6/12)* and *UBS AG final notice (19/12/12)*. The FCA's fine of £137.6 million (approximately US$220 million) against JP Morgan in 2013 was similar to the fines imposed concurrently by the US Securities and Exchange Commission and the US Federal Reserve (each US$200 million) (see *JPMorgan Chase Bank, NA final notice (18/09/13)*).

8.60   Finally, although the size of a fine is likely to make the newspaper headlines, in circumstances where consumers have suffered loss the fine may be accompanied by the announcement of an offer of redress. In many such cases, the likely amount of redress will be greater than the amount of the fine[1].

1   See, for example, *Swinton Group Limited final notice (16/7/13)* where the fine was £7.38 million but redress was estimated at £11.2 million.

How does the FCA determine the amount of the fine?

8.61   The FCA has published a fining policy that provides a detailed account of the factors relevant to determining the appropriate level of a fine. Generally, the FCA does not adopt a tariff of penalties for different kinds of contravention[1] because there will be few cases in which all the circumstances will be the same. However, the FCA does aim to ensure consistency for the amount of fines in similar cases. The fining policy is stated to be of assistance in achieving that desired outcome.

1   There is an exception for breaches arising from the late submission of returns which is not covered here but the relevant FCA policy can be found in the FCA Handbook at DEPP 6.6.

8.62   The current regime governing financial penalties came into force on 6 March 2010. For any breaches which occurred prior to this date, the FCA will apply the previous penalty framework (which was less methodical than the approach described below). For any breaches arising prior to 6 March 2010 and continuing after that date, the FCA will apply the current penalty framework to the part of the breach occurring after 6 March 2010.

8.63   The FCA's methodology for calculating fines is based on a five-step framework[1], which is as follows:

- step 1: disgorgement;

- step 2: the seriousness of the breach;

- step 3: mitigating and aggravating factors;

- step 4: deterrence; and

- step 5: settlement discount.

1   FCA Handbook at DEPP 6.5A.

8.64   Each of the five steps is discussed below. Note, this framework is varied for fines for market abuse (discussed in **CHAPTER 17**) and breaches of the Listing Rules, Prospectus Rules, Listing Principles and other breaches of Part 6 of the FSMA 2000 (discussed in **CHAPTER 20**) respectively.

Step 1: Disgorgement

8.65   The FCA will first consider whether it should deprive the firm of any financial benefit derived directly from the breach in question, including any profit made or loss avoided, to the extent such benefit can be identified and quantified. Interest will normally be charged on any such benefit. Where a firm agrees to carry out a redress programme to compensate those who have suffered loss as a result of the breach, or where the FCA decides to impose a redress programme, the FCA will take this into consideration. In such cases the final penalty might not include a disgorgement element, or the disgorgement element might be reduced[1].

1   FCA Handbook at DEPP 6.5A.1. See also *Swinton Group Limited final notice (16/7/13)*.

Step 2: Seriousness of breach

8.66   The FCA will determine a base figure that will be used as a starting point to determine the appropriate level of any fine[1]. This base figure will then be adjusted to reflect the seriousness of the breach, in order to arrive at a fine that is appropriate to punish the firm in question and to deter others from similar conduct.

1   FCA Handbook at DEPP 6.5A.2(1).

8.67   The FCA will use either the amount of 'relevant revenue' for the relevant period or an 'appropriate alternative', which is indicative of the harm or potential harm that the breach may have caused, to determine the base figure[1]. The FCA will then take a percentage of the base figure and that will form the basis of the penalty (the base fine). The FCA will categorise any breaches as belonging to one of five levels to determine the percentage used to arrive at the base fine (ranging from 0 to 20% (see further below)[2], depending on the FCA's assessment of the nature, impact and seriousness of the relevant breach).

1   FCA Handbook at DEPP 6.5A.2(2) and DEPP 6.5A.2(1).
2   Level 1 – 0%; level 2 – 5%; level 3 – 10%; level 4 – 15%; and level 5 – 20%. See the FCA Handbook at DEPP 6.5A.2(3).

8.68   Disciplinary sanctions and other regulatory action against firms

Relevant revenue or appropriate alternative?

8.68   What approach the FCA will take to calculating relevant revenue (or an appropriate alternative) is potentially an important area of debate in any enforcement case, as it could have a very significant impact on the level of the fine. The question of what is the right approach to adopt will depend on the circumstances of the case.

8.69   The FCA retains the discretion to use an 'appropriate alternative' means of determining the base figure where it considers that revenue is not an appropriate indicator of the harm or potential harm that a firm might cause[1]. What might be considered an appropriate alternative will vary according to the facts of a particular case. The FSA took the position that it was difficult to predict in advance what the relevant alternative measure may be in a particular case and therefore declined to set out prospectively the alternative measures that would be used[2]. Recent enforcement actions have shown how an alternative might be used: for example, in cases concerning systems and controls for holding client money, the relevant measure will usually relate to the amount of client money held by the firm during the period of the breach (averaged over the period). Where the FCA does decide to use this approach, it is clear that the base figure will usually be determined as a percentage of the appropriate alternative (with the particular percentage used depending upon the seriousness of the breach)[3].

1   FCA Handbook at DEPP 6.5A.2.
2   See FSA Policy Statement (PS10/4) 'Enforcement financial penalties – feedback on CP09/19'.
3   See the FCA Handbook at DEPP 6.5A.2(13). However, the FCA is not obliged to use the 0–20% range when using the 'appropriate alternative'. In one case it employed a 0–100% range in order to ensure that the penalty properly reflected the seriousness of the breach. See *Exillon Energy plc final notice (26/4/2012)*. See also *JPMorgan Chase Bank, NA final notice (18/09/13)*, where revenue was not considered an appropriate indicator of the harm or potential harm of the firm's breach of Principle 11.

Assessing the seriousness of the breach

8.70   Once a base figure has been determined (either using the relevant revenue or an appropriate alternative), the FCA will assess the seriousness of any breaches. The FCA Handbook sets out at DEPP 6.5A.2 an extensive, though non-exhaustive, list of factors which:

- relate to the impact of the breach;

- relate to the nature of the breach;

- show whether the breach was deliberate; and

- show whether the breach was reckless[1].

1   FCA Handbook at DEPP 6.5A.2(5).

8.71   In terms of impact, the FCA will consider factors including the benefit gained, or intended to be gained, by the firm; any loss, or risk of loss, to individual consumers or consumers as a whole; and the inconvenience or distress caused to consumers. The impact of any breaches is likely to be considered significant if the FCA determines that substantial losses to consumers were caused by breaches of regulations[1]. However, it is clear that breaches which give rise to the risk of such losses will also be viewed as particularly serious[2].

1 FCA Handbook at DEPP 6.5A.2(5).
2 See *JP Morgan Securities Ltd final notice (25/5/10)*, where the FSA issued a fine of £33.32 million in respect of continued failings by a firm to segregate client money in a trust account. No customers sustained any losses as a result of the breach, but the fact that clients would have been severely prejudiced in an insolvency scenario due to the absence of a trust was cited by the FSA as a factor of particular seriousness.

8.72   In considering the nature of any breaches, the FCA will consider, amongst other factors, the rules which have been breached; the frequency of breaches; whether the firm's senior management was aware of the breaches; and whether the breaches revealed serious or systemic weaknesses in the firm's systems and internal controls[1].

1 FCA Handbook at DEPP 6.5A.2(7).

8.73   The FCA's consideration of whether any breaches can be viewed as deliberate will be informed by a number of factors, such as whether the firm's senior management intended or foresaw that the likely or actual consequences of their actions or inaction would result in a breach; whether management sought to conceal their misconduct or reduce the risk that it might be discovered; and whether the breach was repeated.

8.74   In assessing recklessness, the FCA will consider the extent to which the firm's senior management or responsible individuals appreciated or were aware that there was a risk of breach and they failed to mitigate this risk or check whether they were acting in accordance with the firm's procedures. The extent to which senior management were or were not aware of any breaches will be important to the FCA[1].

1 FCA Handbook at DEPP 6.5A.2(9).

Determination of percentage level to be applied to Base Figure

8.75   Following an assessment of the factors described above, the FCA will categorise any breaches on a scale of 1 to 5. Each level relates to a different percentage to be applied to the base figure. Where 'relevant revenue' is used, Level 1 is 0%; Level 2 is 5%; Level 3 is 10%; Level 4 is 15%; and Level 5 is 20%[1].

1 FCA Handbook at DEPP 6.5A.2(3).

8.76   Generally, a breach will be categorised as level 4 or 5 if:

- it caused a significant loss or risk of loss to individual consumers;

- it revealed serious or systemic weaknesses in the firm's procedures, management systems or internal controls;

- the firm failed to conduct its business with integrity; or

- it was deliberate or reckless[1].

1 FCA Handbook at DEPP 6.5A.2(11). See also *Swinton Group Limited final notice (16/7/13)*.

8.77   A breach will be more likely to be categorised as within levels 1–3 if it was committed negligently or inadvertently, with little risk of loss to consumers or profit to the firm, and if the breach does not indicate any widespread problem or systemic weakness within the firm[1].

1 FCA Handbook at DEPP 6.5A.2(12).

Step 3: Mitigating and aggravating factors

8.78   If the FCA decides that the seriousness of any breaches is such that a fine is an appropriate sanction, then it will consider whether there are mitigating or aggravating factors that warrant an increase or decrease in the overall penalty. Any adjustment will be a percentage adjustment[1]. The level to which any adjustment is made will depend on the FCA's overriding opinion on their findings under the investigation. The FCA Handbook sets out at DEPP 6.5A(3) a number of factors (again, the list is non-exhaustive), which may be relevant in determining any adjustment. These include the conduct of the firm in bringing (or failing to bring) the breach to the FCA's attention; the degree of co-operation shown by the firm during the investigation of the breach; any remedial steps taken since the identification of the breach; and whether the firm had previously been told about the FCA's concerns in relation to the issue in question.

1 FCA Handbook at DEPP 6.5A.3(1).

Step 4: Deterrence

8.79   The FCA may then increase the amount of the financial penalty if it considers the amount arrived at following the application of Steps 1 to 3 is insufficient to deter the firm from committing further or similar breaches. An increase may occur if the FCA does not consider that the penalty meets its objective of credible deterrence or where previous FCA action for similar breaches has failed to improve the industry standards. If the FCA considers it likely that similar breaches will be committed by the firm in question or by other firms in the future in the absence of an increase in the fine, it may wish to use the case to send a clear warning to the industry[1].

1 FCA Handbook at DEPP 6.5A.4.

Step 5: Settlement discount

8.80   The FCA will apply a settlement discount to reflect the stage at which the FCA and the firm reach an agreement. This early settlement discount scheme[1] allows for the application of a fixed discount to the fine, excluding any disgorgement calculated at Stage 1 above, that would otherwise be imposed by the FCA for the breach in question. The settlement discount scheme is described at para **10.45** ff below. The amount of the discount will depend on how early in the enforcement process settlement is reached: the aim is to encourage firms to settle with the FCA early and therefore avoid some of the time and costs that might otherwise be incurred by both sides.

1   FCA Handbook at DEPP 6.7.

8.81   The FCA will therefore apply the four steps set out above to determine the appropriate level of the fine. That number will then be reduced by a fixed percentage, the amount of which will depend upon the stage at which settlement is reached[1] (bearing in mind that any disgorgement figure reached at Step 1 (see paras **8.65** and **8.89**) cannot be subject to discount).

1   FCA Handbook at DEPP 6.7.3. See para **10.46** and **CHAPTER 10** more generally for the FCA's approach to settlement.

8.82   The firm may ask the FCA for permission to pay the fine by instalments[1]. The FCA will only agree to such a request where the firm has produced verifiable evidence that serious financial hardship or other financial difficulties will result if such a form of payment is not permitted. In other cases, fines are generally payable within 14 days of the date that the firm receives the final notice.

1   See *Xcap Securities PLC final notice (31/05/013)* for a fine of £120,900 that was allowed to be paid in six monthly instalments.

Credit for co-operation

8.83   As discussed in **CHAPTER 3** above, when faced with a regulatory problem, a firm needs to consider, for example, what steps it should take to investigate, whether to report the problem, how the firm should deal with its customers or its market counterparties and whether it should be taking any action internally. How the firm handles these matters will be taken into account by the FCA when it considers:

- whether or not to take formal disciplinary action[1]; and

- what the outcome should be, including the level of fine or length/extent of any suspension or restriction on a firm's permission[2]; and

- the content of the public censure.

1   For other factors in this regard see para **8.22** ff above.
2   In respect of the choice and magnitude of sanctions see para **8.39** ff above.

8.84   The firm may therefore get 'credit' for co-operating with the FCA, for which purpose there must be 'evidence of proactive co-operation'[1].

1   See the section of the FCA's website entitled 'The benefits to firms and individuals of co-operating with the FCA'.

8.85   In this context, the following should be noted. First, to get credit for co-operation, firms need to demonstrate that they are proactively addressing the regulatory problems. The FCA has stated that proactive co-operation will be likely to result in reduced charges or lighter sanctions (including a 'significant discount in the level of the fine') being applied[1]. The FCA has indicated that the following types of co-operation will be relevant when the FCA staff consider whether to take disciplinary action, and if so, the appropriate sanction[2]:

- how quickly the firm (or individual) notified the FCA (or another relevant regulator) of the problem and whether the problem was brought to the FCA's attention at the earliest opportunity;

- what action was taken once the problem was identified, what action was then taken to investigate the nature and source of the problem and the degree of co-operation with the FCA shown during the investigation;

- whether the firm has done everything possible to fix the problem once it was identified and what the likelihood is of the problem recurring;

- what steps were taken to find out whether customers have been financially disadvantaged and how promptly redress is to be/was offered;

- whether senior management actively and meaningfully participated in efforts to address and remedy the issue;

- whether the facts underlying the issue are quickly agreed with the FCA and whether the basis upon which enforcement action can be concluded is similarly agreed quickly;

- how promptly the firm reacts to requests for information and provides information that has not been directly requested (or may be information that the FCA may not otherwise be aware of); and

- how the firm communicates any lessons that it learns to the appropriate staff and the likelihood that the same type of contravention will recur if no disciplinary action is taken.

1 The level of co-operation that is afforded will also be likely to be referred to in the final notice or press release as is illustrated by the examples given on the section of the FCA's website entitled 'The benefits to firms and individuals of co-operating with the FCA'. For example, the FCA has stated that 'the firm received a significant discount in the level of the fine that we would otherwise, but for the cooperation, have imposed'.
2 See para **4.24** ff above and the section of the FCA's website entitled 'The benefits to firms and individuals of co-operating with the FCA'.

8.86   In practice, the FCA tends to look for evidence that a firm did more than it was required to do as a matter of law and regulation, if the steps taken by the firm are to be considered as mitigating factors. In some instances, the firm's co-operation may result in its supervisors not seeing the need to refer a matter to the FCA's enforcement division[1]. The FCA has provided various examples of this on its website[2]. However, co-operation does not necessarily mean acceptance of the FCA's view of there having been breaches, nor does it mean acceptance of any proposed penalty. A firm or individual can contest regulatory charges without forfeiting the right to credit for co-operation if it is eventually established that the firm has committed a breach[3].

1 However, in some circumstances, 'the misconduct [will be] so serious that no amount of co-operation or other mitigating conduct can justify a decision not to bring any enforcement action at all'. See the section of the FCA's website entitled 'The benefits to firms and individuals of co-operating with the FCA'.
2 See the section of the FCA's website entitled 'The benefits to firms and individuals of co-operating with the FCA'.
3 See *Card Protection Plan Limited final notice (14/11/12)*, where the firm received credit for co-operation despite disputing the FSA's allegations at every stage.

8.87 A final notice may note that the FCA imposed a lower level of fine (or less severe sanction of another kind) than would have otherwise been the case owing to the co-operation that the firm showed, any remedial action taken and the stage in the enforcement proceedings at which the firm chose to settle with the FCA[1]. The FCA's website sets out an example of a case when it reduced the level of a fine as a result of the firm providing what the FCA regarded as 'the model type of co-operation' and acceptance of responsibility[2].

1 FCA Handbook at DEPP 6.7.
2 See the section of the FCA's website entitled 'The benefits to firms and individuals of co-operating with the FCA'. The steps taken included the positive response of the firm's senior management once the problem was identified; the conduct of an independent review into the firm's compliance arrangements; the instruction of independent reporting accountants to establish whether mis-selling had taken place and whether, as a result, customers had lost out; accepting the findings of a sample review; taking steps to ensure that redress was paid where due and in cases of mis-selling, erring on the side of the customer where there were doubts to whether a mis-sale occurred. The FCA has taken a range of other mitigating factors into account in the past when setting the level of fine in particular cases, such as the taking of disciplinary action against the employees involved in the breach; the appointment of a third party to conduct either a substantive investigation or a review of relevant systems and controls; and taking steps to ensure that similar problems cannot arise in future. See for example *UBS AG final notice (25/11/12)*, *Policy Administration Services final notice (1/7/13)* and *Lloyds Banking Group final notice (15/2/13)*.

How does the PRA determine the amount of the fine?

8.88 The PRA follows a similar five step framework for calculating the amount of the fine to be imposed on firms as the FCA (see para **8.61** ff above). Each of the five steps are discussed below.

Step 1: Disgorgement

8.89 The PRA follows the same approach as the FCA (outlined at para **8.65** above) in that it will seek to deprive the firm of any financial benefit derived from the breach, where this is quantifiable.

Step 2: Seriousness of breach

8.90 In addition to having regard to the seriousness of the breach to determine a base figure for a penalty (see the FCA's approach to step 2 at para **8.66** above), the PRA also considers the size and financial position of the firm.

8.91 Where the PRA considers that revenue is a suitable indicator of the size and financial position of the firm, it may calculate the penalty by reference to the firm's total revenue or revenue for a certain business unit or area, usually during its last business year (ie the financial year preceding the date when the breach ended). The PRA follows a similar policy to the FCA in applying the appropriate percentage to the firm's relevant revenue depending on the nature, extent, scale and gravity of the breach[1]. However, the PRA does not specify fixed percentages that correspond to levels of seriousness. Instead, generally the more serious and widespread the breach, and the greater the threat of the behaviour in question to the advancement of the PRA's statutory objectives, the higher the percentage of relevant revenue that the PRA will use as the basis for a fine. This is balanced against the requirement that the penalty will be appropriate and proportionate to the particular breach[2].

1 Penalty Statement, paras 18–23.
2 Penalty Statement, footnote 26.

8.92 The PRA has provided a non-exhaustive list of factors it may take into account when considering the seriousness of the breach. These include[1]:

- the effect or potential effect of the breach on the advancement of the PRA's statutory objectives;

- the duration or frequency of the breach in relation to the nature of the requirements contravened;

- whether the breach was deliberate or reckless;

- whether the breach forms part of a course or pattern of non-compliant behaviour. For example, consistently late, inaccurate or inadequate reporting; and

- whether the breach reveals serious or systematic weaknesses or potential weaknesses in the firm's business model, financial strength, governance, risk or management systems and internal controls relating to all or part of its business[2].

1 Penalty Statement, para 21.
2 The timely, accurate and complete submission of reports by firms required under the PRA's rules is of significant importance to the PRA. Therefore, in addition to the factors set out above, the PRA gives guidance on other considerations which may be relevant where the PRA is deciding whether to impose a penalty on a firm for late or incomplete submission reports. These include: (i) the length of time after the due date the report is submitted and the implications or potential implications of the default; (ii) the nature and extent of any omissions, inaccuracies or incomplete information in the report; (iii) any repeated failures to submit accurate and complete reports or to do so on time; and (iv) any failure or persistent failure fully, promptly and adequately to engage with the PRA's supervisors in connection with the preparation and/or submission of reports.

Step 3: Mitigating and aggravating factors

8.93 The PRA will have regard to a number of mitigating and aggravating factors, which may increase or decrease the base figure of the fine, many of which are similar to those published by the FCA, as discussed in para **8.78** above[1]. The principal difference between the two sets of factors relates to the performance of controlled functions without approval, in that the PRA explicitly states that it will regard the withdrawal or rejection of any previous application for the individual in question to perform the same or a similar significant influence function, or a controlled function, as aggravating the seriousness of the breach.

1　Penalty Statement, paras 24 and 26.

Step 4: Deterrence

8.94　The circumstances in which the PRA may make an upward adjustment to the penalty to ensure an adequate deterrent effect are the same as for the FCA, see para **8.79** above.

Step 5: Settlement discount

8.95　The PRA's settlement process (including its approach to settlement discounts) is explained at para **11.35** ff.

What happens to the money paid as fines?

8.96　The Regulators are required[1] to pay any amounts received in fines over to the Treasury, net of 'enforcement costs' (ie the expenses incurred in connection with the exercise of their enforcement powers or the recovery of financial penalties)[2]. The Regulators operate a scheme for ensuring that any sums retained as enforcement costs are applied for the benefit of firms[3].

1　The Regulators are also prohibited from taking into account the expenses which they have incurred or expect to incur in discharging their functions when setting the amount of a fine. See the FSMA 2000, Sch 1ZA, para 19, Sch 1ZB, para 27.
2　FSMA 2000, Sch 1ZA, para 20 and Sch 1ZB, para 28.
3　FSMA 2000, Sch 1ZA, para 21 and Sch 1ZB, para 29.

Practical guidance for firms subject to a fine

8.97　If the firm is to have any real ability to discuss with the Regulators the amount of the fine that is appropriate, it will need to put together reasons why a lower fine should be imposed and evidence to support those reasons. Precisely what those reasons are will depend upon the circumstances of the particular case. However, the Regulators will be considering the criteria outlined at paras **8.70** and **8.92** above, so they will normally form the focus of the firm's response. In particular, the firm will want to give careful consideration to how it will seek to define certain key areas of its engagement with the Regulators, namely:

- the scope of the business, which was involved in or culpable for the breach;

- the relevant period during which the breach was committed or ongoing; and

- in light of the previous two factors, how the relevant revenue might most appropriately be calculated.

8.98　The firm will also want to consider whether relevant revenue should be used as a starting point for the calculation of the fine, or whether a more favourable outcome might be obtained by arguing for an appropriate alternative. It must be borne in mind, though, that the Regulators are not limited to the 0–20% range when using the 'appropriate alternative', and may even impose a fine of 100% of this figure if they deem it to be appropriate in the circumstances. The aim is to reach an outcome which reflects the harm (or risk of harm) caused by the breach.

8.99 Any engagement with the Regulators concerning the amount of a fine will therefore have to deal with the issue of the seriousness of the breach, and the firm will need to put forward a reasoned argument in favour of the percentage it believes ought to be used. For example, if the breach resulted in only minimal harm being suffered, and a low risk of potential harm, then it would be open to the firm to argue that this ought to be reflected in the level of the financial penalty. In addition to the factors relating to the firm, it may be useful to compile evidence about previous fines levied in similar situations and evidence, sometimes including expert evidence, on the seriousness or otherwise of the firm's breaches. Finally, in the light of the express policy to use fines for deterrent purposes, there may be scope for challenging the imposition of a fine that was wholly disproportionate to the breach, but justified primarily by the need to make an example out of the firm[1].

1 The basis for such a challenge could be the ECHR right to property in Article 1 of the First Protocol to the Convention. This requires a fair balance to be struck between the demands of the general interest of the community and the requirements of the protection of the individual's fundamental rights. The requisite balance will not be found if the person concerned has had to bear an 'individual and excessive burden': see *Lithgow v United Kingdom (1986) 8 EHRR 329 and Piron v France (2002) 34 EHRR 14.*

RESTITUTION

Introduction

8.100 The Regulators have the same powers under the FSMA 2000 to make a restitution order. Which of the PRA and FCA is able to exercise this power in a particular case, will depend on which is the 'appropriate regulator' in respect of the breach concerned. In general, the FCA is the 'appropriate regulator' for a restitution order against a firm, except where the matter concerns[1]:

- a breach of a requirement imposed by the PRA under the FSMA 2000, such as those contained in the PRA Handbook;

- the performance of controlled functions by non-approved persons, where the approval in question falls to be given by the PRA or the PRA has made a prohibition order;

- breaches of certain EU provisions, specified by the Treasury[2], where the Treasury has also designated the PRA as the 'appropriate regulator'; and

- criminal offences where the PRA is the Regulator with the power to prosecute the offence[3].

1 FSMA 2000, s 382(11)–(14).
2 Under SI 2013/419.
3 Such offences are set out in the FSMA 2000, s 401(3A).

8.101   The Regulators can, in certain circumstances, secure compensation for investors who have suffered losses arising from a regulatory breach by a firm or sometimes by others. The Regulators usually do this either by agreeing redress with the firm when imposing disciplinary action, but they can also do this by making a restitution order themselves, or by applying to the court for a restitution order to be made. From the Regulators' perspective, whether this is appropriate in the particular case will depend upon a number of considerations including their statutory objectives, for example, the FCA is responsible for securing appropriate protection for consumers. From the firm's perspective too, there could be advantages as well as disadvantages in being subject to a restitution order. For example, in some situations that may assist the firms more efficiently to compensate large numbers of disgruntled customers.

8.102   The FSA rarely exercised this power in practice (other than in perimeter cases: enforcing the perimeter is now the responsibility of the FCA). Instead, redress was dealt with in other ways, discussed at **CHAPTER 15**. Going forward, it is likely that the FCA will prefer to take disciplinary action and agree how to secure redress at the same time as part of the overall settlement reached with the firm; or in some cases redress may be agreed first (with the question of whether any disciplinary action is appropriate left to be decided in due course). In some cases, the amount of redress will be easy to establish and customers can be paid promptly but in other cases, such as in difficult cases of mis-selling, the firm will need to work closely with the FCA in drawing up a redress methodology[1].

1 See para **13.55** ff below.

8.103   The following paragraphs review the Regulators' powers to make and apply for restitution orders, and consider, in particular:

- What is a restitution order?
- When can the Regulators make or apply for a restitution order?
- How do the Regulators make or apply for a restitution order?
- How is restitution calculated and distributed? and
- How should the firm approach the question of a restitution order?

8.104   In certain circumstances, a restitution order can be made against a person who works for a firm. The availability of restitution orders against individuals is considered at para **9.131** ff below. Restitution orders can also be made in the context of market abuse. To the extent that there are differences in the rules or policy, these are considered at para **17.245** ff below.

What is a restitution order?

8.105   A restitution order can be summarised as an order made either by the Regulators or by the court requiring a person either to compensate those who have suffered loss from a regulatory breach or to disgorge profits that should not have been made.

Restitution orders made by the Regulators

8.106 The appropriate Regulator may make a restitution order if satisfied that a firm has contravened a relevant requirement[1], or been knowingly concerned in the contravention of such a requirement[2] and:

- profits have accrued to the firm as a result of the contravention; or

- one or more persons have suffered loss or been otherwise adversely affected as a result of the contravention;

in which case either the PRA or FCA (as the case may be) may require the firm, in accordance with such arrangements as either the PRA or FCA considers appropriate, to pay to the appropriate person[3] or distribute among the appropriate persons such amount as appears to either the PRA or FCA to be just having regard to:

- the profits appearing to either the PRA or FCA to have accrued, and/or

- the extent of the loss or other adverse effect.

1 For the purpose of this subsection 'Relevant requirement' means: (a) a requirement imposed by or under the FSMA 2000 or by a qualifying EU provision specified, or of a description specified, for the purposes of subsection 384(7) by the Treasury by order; or (b) a requirement which is imposed by or under any other Act and whose contravention constitutes an offence mentioned in s 402(1); or (c) a requirement imposed by the Alternative Investment Fund Managers Regulations 2013.
2 FSMA 2000, s 384(1).
3 In other words, the person or persons to whom the profits are attributable or who have suffered the loss or other adverse effects.

8.107 The FCA may also make a restitution order if it is satisfied that a person (the person concerned) has engaged in market abuse or has required or encouraged another person to engage in behaviour which, if engaged in by the person concerned, would amount to market abuse, and:

- profits have accrued to the person concerned as a result of the market abuse; or

- one or more persons have suffered loss or been otherwise adversely affected as a result of the market abuse[1].

1 FSMA 2000, s 384(2)–(3).

Restitution orders made by the court

8.108 The court's power to make a restitution order[1] is very similar to the Regulators' powers as set out at para **8.106** above. The differences are as follows:

- there must first be an application to the court either by either the PRA or FCA or by the Secretary of State[2];

- the court can make a restitution order against any person, not only a firm. It could therefore order restitution to be paid by:

  - an approved person,

- an exempt person,

- any other firm or individual, who is knowingly concerned in a contravention by a firm[3], or

- any other person[4] who contravenes a requirement by or under the FSMA 2000 or a requirement which the FCA or the Secretary of State has the power to prosecute;

- the court orders the person concerned to pay either the PRA or FCA such sum as appears to the court to be just (having regard to the same matters as are set out at para **8.106** above) and directs either the PRA or FCA how to pay or distribute the money, which either the PRA or FCA must then do[5].

1 FSMA 2000, s 382.
2 The Secretary of State can make an application in relation to the contravention of a requirement imposed by or under the FSMA 2000 whose contravention constitutes a criminal offence which the Secretary of State has the power to prosecute under the FSMA 2000, s 382(9)(b). The Secretary of State has parallel powers to prosecute offences under the FSMA 2000, s 401(2).
3 For the meaning of the phrase 'knowingly concerned', see the discussion at para **8.110** below.
4 Examples of contraventions which could be committed by unregulated persons include breach of the general prohibition (FSMA 2000, s 19), unlawful financial promotion (FSMA 2000, s 21), or failing to provide information or documents when required to do so (FSMA 2000, s 177).
5 FSMA 2000, s 382(2) and (3).

When can the Regulators make or apply for a restitution order?

Requirement for a regulatory breach

8.109 The starting point is that there must have been a regulatory breach of the type described at para **8.106** above. An admission by the firm that it committed a breach, made for example in order to settle the PRA or FCA's disciplinary proceedings against it, or an adverse finding against it, could thus form the basis for making a restitution order.

Persons knowingly concerned in the breach

8.110 A restitution order may be made not only against the firm or person who committed the breach but also (or alternatively) against any other person[1] who was knowingly concerned in the contravention. This means that if the firm that committed the breach has insufficient resources to compensate investors, another firm with greater resources that was involved, albeit less directly, may be required to do so or the order could be made against both. Two issues are critical and the answer to both is unclear.

1 Whether or not a firm – if the restitution order is made by the court. A restitution order may only be made by the FCA (see para **8.106** above) against a firm (save in cases of market abuse: see para **17.245** ff below).

8.111 First, although there is some authority on the meaning of the phrase 'knowingly concerned'[1], precisely what it encompasses is not clear, and recent authority on the issue is limited. Examples of third parties whom courts have held to be, or indicated were, knowingly concerned include: the firm's solicitors[2], an associated firm that knowingly received funds from the relevant transactions[3], the firm's managing director[4], and the firm's servants and agents[5]. However, the implications of the test are not limited to these examples: whether a person is knowingly concerned will depend to a large extent upon his knowledge of the facts that constitute the breach committed by the firm.

1 See para **2.126** ff above. The cases cited arise from the Banking Act 1987 (now repealed) which contains the predecessors to the current statutory provisions and uses the same language in relation to injunctions. For a discussion of injunctions, see para **8.138** ff below.
2 See *FSA v Martin [2005] EWCA Civ 1422*.
3 See *SIB v Pantell [1989] 2 All ER 673*.
4 See *SIB v Scandex Capital Management A/S [1998] 1 All ER 514*.
5 See *SIB v Vandersteen Associates NV [1991] BCLC 206*.

8.112   Second, a restitution order will not be made in every case where the statutory test is satisfied. It is a matter within the discretion of the Regulators or the court, as appropriate. A key issue is therefore whether it is appropriate in the circumstances to make the third party pay restitution. No guidance is given on how the discretion to make orders against those knowingly concerned will be exercised, but courts have suggested that they may make less stringent orders against third parties than against the firm that committed the breach and have also suggested that it might be appropriate to link the two so that, for example, the third party is required to pay if the firm does not do so[1].

1 See *SIB v Pantell (No 2) [1993] 1 All ER 134*.

Disgorging gains

8.113   Restitution orders can be made not only to compensate investors for their losses but also to require the firm to disgorge gains it should not have made[1]. The purpose of this is to discourage non-compliant behaviour by ensuring that firms do not benefit from it.

1 FSMA 2000, ss 382(2)(a) and 384(5)(a).

8.114   The FSMA 2000 envisages such profits being repaid to those to whom those profits are attributable. This can cause difficulty in practice. In some situations, it will be clear that a profit is attributable to a particular identifiable person, for example if a commission is wrongly taken on the sale of a particular financial product; in other cases, it may be clear that the profit is attributable to a particular person, but less clear that that person should benefit by receiving the profit because it would constitute a windfall gain. Of most difficulty are those cases where the profit cannot sensibly be attributed to any particular person.

8.115   The FCA Handbook does not contain any guidance as to how these issues are to be addressed. Where there are real difficulties in assessing to whom profits should be paid, or it is otherwise inappropriate for a restitution order to be made, the firm can be deprived of its profits by an alternative means, namely by a fine being levied of sufficient amount to cancel out the profits[1].

1   The amount of any profits made is a relevant factor in determining the amount of any fine: see para **8.65** above.

Other adverse effects

8.116   Restitution orders can be made to address not only losses suffered but also 'other adverse effects' of the contravention. It is not entirely clear what this envisages. The effects of the contravention could include non-financial effects, such as damage to reputation or, bearing in mind that this relates primarily to consumers, stress. Losses may also have been suffered that are indirect or impossible to quantify precisely. However, the phrase makes it clear that the discretion of the Regulators and the court to order restitution extends beyond those cases where investors can demonstrate that they have suffered what a court would regard as loss for which it could award damages. In other words, the Regulators and the court can bypass technical arguments about whether loss can be proved, and focus instead on how it is appropriate for them to exercise their discretion in the particular case.

Repayment of money only

8.117   Although the phrase 'restitution' may suggest otherwise, a restitution order can only require the repayment of money. It cannot, for example, be used to secure the return of securities or other investments wrongly transferred. In such circumstances, an injunction may be an appropriate remedy[1].

1   See para **8.138** ff below.

The effect of a restitution order

8.118   So far as the firm is concerned, the effect of a restitution order, once made, is to bind the firm to make the payment for distribution by either the PRA or FCA, as the case may be. The question of how this obligation can be enforced is considered at para **8.130** ff below. The effect so far as customers are concerned is rather different. From their perspective, the payment is effectively ex gratia and does not prevent them bringing their own proceedings to recover losses they have suffered in respect of the same matter[1], although it is likely that the FOS or court would take into account payments already made to them in assessing damages[2]. In practice, customers are unlikely to bring proceedings unless they consider the compensation they have received significantly fails to address their recoverable losses. Nothing in the FCA Handbook entitles the firm to require customers to settle all their claims when they receive restitution. But, equally, nothing expressly precludes it and it may be worth considering and raising with the FCA (or the PRA) in an appropriate case.

1   Where the restitution order is made by the court, the FSMA 2000 specifically provides that nothing in the statutory provision affects the right of any person other than the Regulators or the

Secretary of State to bring proceedings in respect of the same matter: FSMA 2000, s 382(7) and (in respect of market abuse) s 383(9). There is no similar express provision in relation to restitution orders made by the Regulators. The meaning and effect of this provision is considered in more detail at para **19.73** ff below.
2   This is discussed in more detail at para **19.73** ff below.

What is the FCA's policy on making or applying for a restitution order?

8.119   The following paragraphs consider the circumstances in which it may be appropriate for the FCA to make a restitution order and alternatively when it might apply to the court in order to secure such redress for consumers. Although the FCA has given detailed guidance on this particular issue, the PRA has published no equivalent statements of policy.

8.120   Clearly, it is neither the FCA's role nor an appropriate use of its resources to secure restitution in respect of every regulatory breach[1]. In many cases, the effects of the breach will be confined to market counterparties or other large customers of the firm, who will have the sophistication and resources to pursue legal remedies for themselves. In other cases, the effect will be limited to a small number of consumers, who could either agree compensation with the firm or use the FOS[2]. The number of cases where it will be appropriate for the FCA to exercise its power to seek restitution will therefore be limited.

1   Although the powers outlined in para **2.58** ff above are available to both the PRA and the FCA, in practice (and for the reasons outlined below) restitution is more likely to be sought by the FCA.
2   The ombudsman scheme is discussed in **CHAPTER 14** below.

8.121   In deciding whether to make such an order the FCA will consider all the relevant circumstances of the case, in particular: whether identifiable persons have suffered quantifiable losses (or the firm has made quantifiable profits that are owed to identifiable persons); the number of persons who have suffered loss and the extent of those losses; whether the persons who have suffered losses are in a position to bring civil proceedings on their own behalf; and the costs that would be incurred by the FCA in securing redress and whether these costs are justified by the benefit that would result from such action[1].

1   FCA Enforcement Guide at EG 11.3.

8.122   A restitution order is therefore likely only to be contemplated in those cases where large numbers of consumers have suffered significant losses, or where the losses suffered are significant overall, but relatively small individually. Market professionals are likely to be regarded as being able to pursue their own remedies. If a breach affects a relatively small number of consumers, the FCA may take the view that the matter can be more effectively handled by each customer individually with the firm or through the FOS.

8.123   The FCA's power to make a restitution order and its power to apply to court for a restitution order overlap to a large extent in those cases where a firm is involved (or in a case of market abuse[1]). However, the FCA expects firms to comply with the FCA's requirements and does not therefore foresee the need for the additional force of court orders except in rare cases. In cases where it is appropriate to exercise its powers to obtain restitution from firms it will therefore first use its administrative powers before considering taking court action[2]. However, the FCA may choose to combine an application for a restitution order with another application, for example, if the FCA wishes to apply to court for an injunction against the same firm or is prosecuting a firm for conducting regulated business, the FCA may apply for a restitution order at the same time[3].

1 See para **17.232** ff below.
2 FCA Enforcement Guide at EG 11.4.
3 FCA Enforcement Guide at EG 11.5.

How do the Regulators make or apply for a restitution order?

8.124 The following paragraphs consider five procedural issues relating to restitution orders, namely:

- how do the Regulators or the court obtain the information it needs to consider whether an order should be made?

- how do the Regulators make a restitution order?

- how do the Regulators apply to the court for a restitution order?

- is there a risk of publicity arising from a restitution order?

- how is a restitution order enforced?

How do the Regulators or the court obtain the information required?

8.125 In order to consider whether to make a restitution order and, if so, the terms and amount of the order, the Regulators and, if appropriate, the court, will need evidence not only of the regulatory breach but also of the amount of the losses caused by the breach, the profits the firm made from the breach and the identity of those who suffered loss and those to whom any profits are attributable. This may go substantially beyond the evidence that would otherwise be required, for example, for any disciplinary proceedings. However, the Regulators have a wide range of information-gathering and investigative powers exercisable where authorised firms, among others, commit regulatory breaches[1]. In addition:

- firms have extensive duties of co-operation with the Regulators which enable the Regulators to obtain much of the information that they need without using any formal powers[2];

- the Regulators have a general power to require firms to provide information to them[3]; and

8.125 Disciplinary sanctions and other regulatory action against firms

- the Regulators may require a firm to obtain a report from a skilled person[4], not only to determine any profits or losses but also to determine their distribution.

1 These are considered in **CHAPTER 4** above. For a list, see paras **4.10** and **4.11** above.
2 Principle 11, Principles for Businesses: see para **4.25** ff above.
3 FSMA 2000, s 165: see para **4.68** ff above.
4 FSMA 2000, s 166: see **CHAPTER 6** above. See also the FCA Enforcement Guide at EG 11.7.

8.126 To a large extent the court will base its decision upon the evidence which the appropriate regulator puts before it and any evidence which the firm provides in response. The court does however also have its own fact-finding powers[1] in connection with an application for a restitution order. It may require the person concerned to supply it with such accounts or other information as it may require for any one or more of the following purposes:

- to establish what, if any, profits have accrued to the person as a result of the contravention;

- to establish whether any person or persons have suffered any loss or adverse effect as a result of the contravention and, if so, the extent of that loss or adverse effect; and

- to determine how any amounts are to be paid or distributed;

and it may require any accounts or other information supplied to be verified in such manner as it may direct.

1 FSMA 2000, s 382(4) and (5).

How do the Regulators make a restitution order?

8.127 Where the Regulators seek to impose a restitution order against a firm, they must follow the warning/decision notice procedure considered in **CHAPTER 10** below[1]. The firm will have the right to discuss the proposed restitution order with the FCA or the PRA and ultimately can refer the matter to the Tribunal for determination. In addition:

- the warning notice must specify the amount which the FCA or PRA proposes to require the firm to pay or distribute[2];

- the decision notice must[3]:

  - state the amount that the firm is to pay or distribute,

  - identify the person or persons to whom that amount is to be paid or among whom it is to be distributed, and

  - state the arrangements in accordance with which the payment or distribution is to be made.

1 FSMA 2000, ss 385 and 386.
2 FSMA 2000, s 385(2).
3 FSMA 2000, s 386(2).

How do the Regulators apply to the court for an order?

8.128 An application for a restitution order[1] is made by the appropriate regulator issuing a claim form in the High Court under the Civil Procedure Rules[2]. It will, of course, be possible for the firm to oppose the application.

1 As to the FCA's internal decision-making process, it is for the Chairman of the RDC to decide whether an application for a restitution order is appropriate (see the FCA Enforcement Guide at EG 11.1A), although others may decide in urgent cases (for details, see footnote 1 to para **8.159** below).
2 For a more detailed explanation of the procedure, see the Civil Procedure Rules, Pt 7.

Is there a risk of publicity?

8.129 There is certainly a risk of publicity, but whether there will be publicity will vary from case to case. Civil proceedings for a restitution order will often be public as soon as they commence[1]. The FCA will generally consider it appropriate to publish details of successful applications to the court for restitution orders if, for example, publicising them could protect and inform consumers and maintain market confidence. The FCA may decide not to publicise a restitution order in some cases, where for example, publication could damage confidence in the financial system or undermine market integrity in a way that would be prejudicial to the interests of consumers[2].

1 FCA Enforcement Guide at 6.15.
2 FCA Enforcement Guide at 6.16.

How is a restitution order enforced?

8.130 The FSMA 2000 does not contain any specific provision for the enforcement of restitution orders. Enforcement is therefore a matter of general principle. As a result, if a person fails to comply with an order made by the appropriate regulator:

- this is likely to constitute the contravention of a requirement imposed by or under the FSMA 2000, potentially giving rise to disciplinary and other regulatory enforcement proceedings[1];

- the appropriate regulator could apply to the court for an injunction to require the firm to remedy the contravention and to prevent it from dissipating its assets[2];

- it may cause the FCA to doubt whether the firm remains fit and proper to perform regulated activities, which could lead to its permission being varied or even cancelled[3]; and

- it could give rise to concerns about the firm's solvency, which might lead the FCA to consider exercising its insolvency powers[4].

1 For a discussion of this phrase and its potential consequences, see para **2.94** ff above.
2 Applications to court for injunctions are discussed at para **8.138** ff below.
3 These issues are discussed in **CHAPTER 16** below.
4 These powers are not covered by this book but are set out in the FCA Enforcement Guide at EG Chapter 13.

8.131   If a firm fails to comply with an order made by the court, each of the above could apply. In addition, whether or not the person concerned is a firm, the court could enforce the restitution order in the same way as any other court order.

How is restitution calculated and distributed?

8.132   The starting point lies in the statutory provisions[1] that enable the Regulators or the court to order the payment of such sum as appears to be just, having regard to the amount of the profits which have accrued to the firm and/ or the amount of the losses or other adverse effects that have been suffered. Two points are notable:

- the amount awarded is within the discretion of, as appropriate, the appropriate regulator or the court applying the test set out above, and need not correlate directly with the actual amount of profits and losses; and

- the amount awarded is in practice likely to be linked with the method of distribution, because in many cases the overall figure will simply amount to the sum of the restitution payable to individual investors. The position may be different where profits are being disgorged, since the amount of the profit may be a defined figure and the main issue is how that amount should be distributed.

1   FSMA 2000, ss 382(2) and 384(5).

8.133   It is for the appropriate regulator or the court (as applicable) to determine how the restitution payments are distributed[1]. The payment can only be distributed among those to whom the profits which the firm wrongfully made are attributable or who suffered the loss or other adverse effect. Neither regulator has given any guidance on how this is to work in practice. The expectation must be that the payment will be distributed in such a way as to compensate each person for their loss or to pay them the profits attributable to them. The practical issues discussed at para **8.132** ff above also arise here[2].

1   FSMA 2000, ss 382(3) and 384(5): see para **8.106** ff above.
2   See also para **8.114** above.

Can the compensated person object?

8.134   Since both the amount of compensation and its distribution may be determined to achieve a fair and reasonable result, rather than the result that most closely parallels the legal claims of each customer, there is a risk of a particular customer not receiving the amount to which he believes he is entitled. However, there is no express right for any customer to become involved in the process of making a restitution order, either before the appropriate regulator or before the court; in any event, he is unlikely to want to object until after the order has been made and the terms are made known to him. At that stage, there are two options. First, if the restitution order was made by the appropriate regulator, the customer may be able to apply to have it judicially reviewed[1]. Second, he can accept the payment and then take legal action for the remainder of his claim[2].

1 Judicial review is briefly outlined in **Chapter 21** below.
2 Also see para **8.118** above. He may also be able to bring a claim for the remainder before the ombudsman: see **Chapter 14** below.

How should the firm approach the question of a restitution order?

8.135 Clearly, firms will ordinarily want to avoid being made subject to a restitution order; indeed, in some cases, the figures involved may be so significant, or the firm may feel sufficiently strongly about the issue as a matter of principle, that the firm will want to resist the restitution order and try to avoid liability altogether. In addition, the firm may be concerned about the risk of customers making further claims, or trying to obtain a double recovery. However, there may be practical reasons for agreeing to give redress, whether through a restitution or by another means (eg an agreement with the regulator):

- it may be possible to achieve full and final settlement of all claims at the same time;

- in the long run it may prove cheaper than dealing with large numbers of individual claims, brought either in the courts or via the FOS;

- being seen to pay restitution quickly and fairly may allow the firm to repair any reputational damage; and

- being seen to be co-operating with the appropriate regulator and taking appropriate steps to protect the interests of customers may assist the firm in any disciplinary proceedings arising from the same matter[1].

1 In respect of co-operation generally, see para **8.83** ff above.

8.136 A firm's aim will often be to work with the appropriate regulator to agree a basis upon which restitution can be paid and distributed to customers and others. It will be important to find a practical solution to the real difficulties of calculating restitution. Also, in some instances, the firm may want to be seen to be offering restitution at an early stage and taking the lead in assessing what payments should be made.

8.137 In addition to the powers to make or apply for restitution orders, the FCA has a power under the FSMA 2000, ss 404 and 404A to require the establishment of a consumer redress scheme for one or more firms (discussed at para **13.72** ff below). The FCA's powers to make a restitution order and to require the payment of redress to consumers overlap to a certain extent. Indeed, it is likely that the objective of ss 404 and 404A could be achieved via the use of a restitution order together with the appointment of a skilled person under s 166, whose task it would be to identify the individual consumers to whom restitution is due. More important, in practice, is whether the FCA will use these powers at all or whether it will seek to resolve redress issues by reaching agreement with the relevant firms, either on its own or as part of an overall settlement with the firm of a disciplinary action.

INJUNCTIONS

Introduction

8.138   The Regulators may seek an injunction against a firm on application to the court. The PRA has the same powers as the FCA under the FSMA 2000 and the same conditions as those outlined at para **8.100** ff above are used in the FSMA 2000 to determine which is the appropriate regulator to seek an injunction from the court.

8.139   In some situations, the Regulators may need to prevent a firm from continuing to carry on an activity in breach of regulatory requirements or freeze its assets in order to protect the interests of consumers. Although the Regulators need not go to court to intervene in the business of firms[1], they cannot exercise those powers against those who are outside the regulated community. Alternatively, they may consider that their own powers against those who are regulated carry insufficient weight, because the penalties for non-compliance are inadequate. In such situations, the FSMA 2000 allows the Regulators to seek an injunction from the court. The following paragraphs consider:

- the types of injunctions that can be obtained and the grounds on which they can be granted (para **8.143** ff);

- the circumstances when the Regulators will seek an injunction (para **8.156** ff); and

- the procedure involved, including any attendant publicity (para **8.158** ff).

1 They can do this by varying a firm's permission (or imposing an equivalent restriction on an incoming firm): see **CHAPTERS 10** and **16** below.

8.140   There is a separate provision enabling the FCA to apply for an injunction in cases of market abuse. This is considered at para **17.227** ff below.

8.141   The FCA has additional powers to apply for injunctions under the Unfair Terms in Consumer Contracts Regulations 1999 or, in the context of insurance, an injunction in relation to an incoming firm at the request of an overseas regulator in certain specified circumstances relating to the EU First Life and First Non-life Insurance Directives[1]. These powers are not reviewed here. The FCA's policy can be found in the FCA Enforcement Guide at EG 10.11.

1 FSMA 2000, s 198.

8.142   An injunction may also be granted upon application by the Secretary of State, relating to the contravention of requirements by or under the FSMA 2000 that constitute a criminal offence which the Secretary of State has the power to prosecute under the FSMA 2000[1].

1 FSMA 2000, s 380(1) and (6)(b).

What types of injunctions can be obtained?

8.143   There are broadly three different types of injunctions, namely:

- to restrain contraventions of regulations;
- to require breaches to be remedied; and
- to secure assets.

8.144   The grounds upon which each can be obtained are outlined in turn below. As the FCA is more likely to exercise this power and has issued more guidance on the use of injunctions, it is the FCA's approach to seeking an injunction on these grounds which is considered below.

8.145   Whilst a detailed discussion of injunctive relief as a general matter would be inappropriate in this context, two points are worth highlighting at the outset:

- injunctive relief is discretionary, that is, the court is not obliged to grant an injunction simply because the appropriate regulator establishes that the statutory grounds have been met; and

- in many cases, an injunction is initially applied for on an interim basis. Although the purpose of an interim injunction is theoretically only to preserve the position pending a full trial as to whether or not an injunction should be granted (effectively allowing either the appropriate regulator to investigate properly an urgent matter which has been brought to its attention), in practice the matter may never proceed to a full trial. The granting of an interim injunction may therefore tend to dispose of the matter.

8.146   In determining an application for an interim injunction the court is involved in a balancing exercise[1], taking into account, among other things, the prospects of the appropriate regulator ultimately being successful[2] and the consequences of granting or refusing interim relief. The court will make the order that appears to be most just in all the circumstances; however, in practice it is likely to be reasonably receptive to either the appropriate regulator's views on the need for an interim injunction, particularly if the purpose of seeking the injunction is to protect consumers or markets[3].

---

1   See Spry, *Equitable Remedies* (8th edn, 2010) at pp 508–510.
2   The claimant need only show that there is a serious issue to be tried in favour of a final injunction: see *American Cyanamid Co v Ethicon Ltd [1975] AC 396*, but a higher or different test may be required to be satisfied in cases of mandatory injunctions and freezing orders: see paras **8.150** and **8.152** below. Note that in cases where the grant or refusal of an interim injunction will have the practical effect of putting an end to the action, the court may be more willing to give detailed consideration to the evidence and the prospects of the claim: see *Cayne v Global Natural Resources plc [1984] 1 All ER 225*.
3   Note that the court has a discretion not to require a cross-undertaking in damages from the FCA and is likely not to do so: See *FSA v Sinaloa Gold plc and Barclays Bank plc [2013] UKSC 11*; also *SIB v Lloyd-Wright [1993] 4 All ER 210*, applying *Kirklees Metropolitan Borough Council v Wickes Building Supplies Ltd [1992] 3 All ER 717, Re Highfield Commodities Ltd [1984] 3 All ER 884* and *F Hoffmann-La Roche & Co AG v Secretary of State for Trade and Industry [1974] 2 All ER 1128, HL*.

Restraining contraventions

8.147 If, on the application of the appropriate regulator or the Secretary of State, the court is satisfied that[1]:

- there is a reasonable likelihood that any person will contravene a relevant requirement[2]; or

- any person has contravened a relevant requirement and there is a reasonable likelihood that the contravention will continue or be repeated;

then the court may make an order restraining the contravention[3].

1 FSMA 2000, s 380(1).
2 For the purpose of this section, 'relevant requirement' means (in relation to an application by the appropriate Regulator) a requirement which (a) is imposed by or under the FSMA 2000 or by a qualifying EU provision specified, or of a description specified, for the purposes of subsection 380(6) by the Treasury by order; or (b) which is imposed by or under any other Act and whose contravention constitutes an offence mentioned in s 402(1) of the FSMA 2000; or is imposed by the Alternative Investment Fund Managers Regulations 2013; or (in relation to an application by the Secretary of State) a requirement which is imposed by or under the FSMA 2000 and whose contravention constitutes an offence which the Secretary of State has power to prosecute under the FSMA 2000.
3 For an example of such an order, see para 33 of *Scotts Private Client Services Limited final notice (9/6/04)*.

8.148 Where such an injunction is breached, the person will not only be liable for contravening the relevant requirement but may also be in contempt of court[1].

1 The effect of this extra sanction is especially evident on individuals, who if found to be in contempt of court may be imprisoned: see para **5.76** above.

8.149 There are several points to note here:

- the FCA (or PRA, as the case may be) will need to substantiate the existence of the reasonable likelihood. Quite what the court will require will depend upon the circumstances[1]: it may be sufficient that the firm has refused to respond positively to a request by the appropriate regulator for an undertaking not to take particular action. The court may be reluctant to grant an injunction where a significant period of time has passed since prior contraventions;

- in applications for an interim injunction where there is a real issue as to whether or not a particular activity is legitimate, the court may prefer to order an expedited trial rather than preventing someone from carrying on what may turn out to be a lawful business[2];

- the FSMA 2000 provides that the injunction is to restrain the contravention but does not specify against whom it can be made. An injunction is ordinarily likely only to be needed against the person who commits or is intending to commit the relevant breach. However, it is possible to envisage a situation where an injunction may be appropriate against others including persons who are not members of the regulated community.

1 See, for example, *SIB v Vandersteen Associates NV [1991] BCLC 206*, where Harman J accepted that there was a reasonable likelihood of future contraventions without discussion of the test. Vandersteen was a Belgian company that had been cold-calling UK investors.

2 When exercising its wide discretion under ss 380 and 382 of the FSMA 2000, it the court is obliged to consider all the circumstances that bear upon the fairness of the order to be made. See *FSA v Shepherd [2009] Lloyd's Rep FC 631*.

Requiring breaches to be remedied

8.150 If, on the application of the appropriate regulator or the Secretary of State, the court is satisfied that[1]:

- any person has contravened a relevant requirement[2]; and

- there are steps which could be taken for remedying the contravention, including mitigating its effect;

then the court may make an order requiring that person, and any other person who appears to have been knowingly concerned in the contravention, to take such steps as the court may direct to remedy it, including mitigating its effect[3].

1 FSMA 2000, s 380(2).
2 See para **8.147**, n 2 for the definition of 'relevant requirement' applicable to the FSMA 2000, s 380(2).
3 This is similar to the earlier power under the Financial Services Act 1986, s 61(1)(c) although there was previously no reference to 'mitigating [the] effect' of the contravention. See also the Financial Services Act 1986, s 6(2).

8.151 Several points require further comment:

- such an injunction could be used in a variety of situations. It is likely to require more than simply the payment of money (as that could often be accomplished by a restitution order[1]) – for example, it might order securities to be transferred[2] or other steps to be taken[3]. The FSMA 2000 provides that references to remedying a contravention include references to mitigating its effect[4], giving the court flexibility to address situations where, strictly speaking, the breach is incapable of being remedied[5];

- an interim injunction requiring the firm to take steps in relation to a particular transaction would effectively dispose of the matter, as the relevant steps would have been taken before the case came to trial. The courts recognise that this may be the effect of interim injunctions that require positive steps to be taken[6], and this may be important in deciding whether an interim injunction is appropriate;

- an injunction may be granted not only against the person who committed the breach but also against any person who was knowingly concerned in it. The same issue arises in the context of restitution orders and is considered at para **8.110** ff above. It is irrelevant whether the third party profited from the contravention, though this may be relevant to the exercise of the court's discretion[7].

1 In the context of the Financial Services Act 1986, it was held that an injunction should be directed to individual transactions, rather than to secure compensation for investors as a class (for which a restitution order would now be the appropriate remedy): see *SIB v Pantell (No 2) [1993] 1 All ER 134, CA*.

2 For this reason, it may prove to be an important tool in the context of market misconduct. For the FCA to obtain such an order, the investor concerned would need to consent to it and, for example, would need to return the shares or money which he had obtained; it therefore operates as a form of 'statutory recession': see *SIB v Pantell (No 2) [1993] 1 All ER 134, CA.*

3 It may be possible for the FCA to obtain an interim payment for investors, on the basis that an interim payment is a step to mitigate the effect of the contravention: see *Securities and Investment Board v Scandex Capital Management A/S [1998] 1 All ER 514.*

4 FSMA 2000, s 380(5).

5 This addresses doubts expressed by Scott LJ in *SIB v Pantell (No 2) [1993] 1 All ER 134* based on the wording of the Financial Services Act 1986, s 61(1). See also *FSA v Martin [2005] EWCA Civ 1422* and *FSA v Watkins [2011] EWHC 1976* where, after granting the FSA summary judgment on its claim concerning an illegal land banking scheme, Proudman J ruled that it was also appropriate to make a declaration that the individual in question had purported to operate a collective investment scheme. Such additional relief would be useful to investors and the general public as well as the FSA.

6 These are known as mandatory injunctions: for further discussion, see *Equitable Remedies,* Spry (8th edn, 2010) at pp 556–560.

7 See Scott LJ in *SIB v Pantell (No 2) [1993] 1 All ER 134* at 144 and Steyn LJ at 148. See also Lloyd LJ in *FSA v Martin [2005] EWCA Civ 1422* at 38.

8.152 If, on the application of the appropriate regulator or the Secretary of State, the court is satisfied that any person may have[1]:

- contravened a relevant requirement[2]; or

- been knowingly concerned in the contravention of such a requirement;

then the court may make an order restraining the person from disposing of, or otherwise dealing with, any assets of his[3] which it is satisfied he is reasonably likely to dispose of or otherwise deal with.

1 FSMA 2000, s 380(3).

2 See para **8.147**, n 2 for the definition of 'relevant requirement' applicable to the FSMA 2000, s 380(2).

3 In *FSA v Fitt [2004] EWHC 1669 (Ch)*, a freezing injunction was granted not only over assets that belonged to the person but also over assets belonging to clients over which the person had a power of attorney. The extent of the freezing order went beyond the court's jurisdiction under the FSMA 2000, s 380(3), but was considered to be appropriate under court's jurisdiction under the Supreme Court Act 1981 [since renamed the Senior Courts Act 1981], s 37(1) to grant orders on the basis of what is 'just and convenient'.

8.153 Such injunctions may be granted with worldwide effect.

8.154 A number of points should be made:

- this is a freezing order – it does not in itself grant any substantive remedy, but will normally be made ancillary to some other proceedings, in order to secure the person's assets to ensure that he is not able to dissipate them and thereby defeat potential claims arising from the breach[1]. It could, for example, be used to protect the assets from which restitution might be made to investors[2];

- the injunction will normally be sought on an interim basis, often urgently, and if granted will usually stay in place until the trial of the substantive matter. The test normally applied by the courts is whether there is a good arguable case that the firm will incur liability, a real risk that its assets might otherwise be dissipated such that any award or judgment would go unsatisfied, and that it is just and convenient to grant the injunction[3]. It is unclear whether the same test will be applied in relation to statutory injunctions under this provision;

- the injunction can be granted not only against the person who committed the breach but also against a person who was knowingly concerned in it[4];

- such an injunction will prevent other creditors recovering their debts. A freezing order will need to be set aside or varied if it is to allow creditors to recover their debts. The appropriate regulator may oppose such a variation if it would have the effect of preferring certain creditors over others.

1 The provision enables an injunction to be made only in relation to a contravention which has already taken place. However, the FCA may ask the court to grant an injunction in the exercise of its inherent jurisdiction where it has evidence showing that there is a reasonable likelihood that a person will commit a breach and that this will result in the dissipation of assets belonging to investors: see the FCA Enforcement Guide at EG 10.5.

2 See the FCA Enforcement Guide at EG 10.3(5). The FCA also suggests that it could be used to safeguard funds containing client assets, but whether that is right would depend upon whether the assets were the firm's assets or the client's assets, because the provision refers to 'assets of his' (ie the firm's). A freezing order may nonetheless be available under the court's inherent jurisdiction: see para **8.153** above.

3 For further discussion, see Gee, *Commerical Injunctions* (6th edn, 2013).

4 This is discussed further at paras **8.110** ff and **8.151** above. The position of individuals is described at paras **9.123** to **9.131** ff below. It is notable that in *FSA v Martin [2005] EWCA Civ 1422* the injunction was also granted against a third party who was arguably knowingly concerned.

What is the Regulators' policy on seeking an injunction?

8.155 The PRA has issued no guidance on its approach to seeking injunctions. Accordingly, the following paragraphs are concerned with the policy of the FCA in this area.

8.156 In deciding whether to seek an injunction, the FCA applies a broad test of whether it will be the most effective means of dealing with its concerns[1]. The FCA will consider all relevant circumstances and take into account a wide range of factors, including the nature and seriousness of the contravention; whether other steps could be taken to remedy the contravention; and whether the conduct has ceased and consumers are adequately protected[2]. In any case where, in the FCA's view, any potential exercise of its power may affect the timetable or outcome of a takeover bid, the FCA will consult the Takeover Panel before taking any steps and give due weight to its views[3].

1 FCA Enforcement Guide at EG 10.3.
2 For a full list, see the FCA Enforcement Guide at EG 10.3.
3 FCA Enforcement Guide at EG 10.3(11).

8.157 The power to apply for an injunction, particularly against a firm, overlaps in various respects with the FCA's own powers; where this is the case, the FCA will consider the relative effectiveness of the other powers available to it compared with injunctive relief. For example, breach of an injunction amounts to contempt of court and is punishable accordingly, and the FCA may feel that this additional weight is needed in order to ensure the firm's compliance. In practice, injunctions are most commonly used to prevent and address perimeter breaches by unauthorised firms[1] which includes protecting client assets, but they may also be used to provide a remedy to those affected by market misconduct[2] and in support of proceedings for restitution orders or other significant civil claims from investors[3].

1 For a brief explanation of perimeter breaches, see para **2.115** above. In practice, most, if not all, injunctions have been made where the perimeter has been breached. See, for example, the freezing order granted against Da Vinci Invest Ltd and others: FSA Press Release FSA/ PN/077/2011.
2 This is addressed in more detail in **CHAPTER 17** below.
3 For a discussion of restitution orders, see para **8.100** ff above.

Procedure for making an application to the court

8.158 An application for an injunction[1] is made by issuing a claim form in the High Court under the Civil Procedure Rules. It will, of course, be possible for the firm to oppose the application[2]. The appropriate regulator may, in appropriate cases, obtain an urgent interim injunction without giving notice to the firm. This will be especially relevant where the injunction is to restrain the disposal of assets or further market abuse. In such cases, there will be a further hearing shortly afterwards at which the firm will have the opportunity to be heard.

1 Before the FCA makes an application to the court, it must reach a decision that such an application is appropriate in the particular case. The FCA has indicated that a decision to begin (or discontinue) such proceedings will be made by the RDC Chairman (see **CHAPTER 10** above) or, in an urgent case and if the Chairman is not available, a Deputy Chairman and where possible, but subject to the need to act swiftly, one other RDC member. In an exceptionally urgent case, the decision could be taken by a senior FCA staff member. For details, see the FCA Enforcement Guide at EG 10.1A.
2 For a more detailed analysis of the procedure, see the Civil Procedure Rules, Pt 7.

8.159 There is no specific prohibition against the appropriate regulator publicising the fact that it is applying for, or has obtained, an injunction. Indeed, the claim form commencing the civil action against the firm will normally be a public document. Moreover, the FCA has indicated that, in line with its general policy, it will normally publish details of successful applications to the court for injunctions and the results of most such applications are generally summarised in press releases[1]. In some circumstances, such as where the perimeter has been breached, the FCA may regard it as particularly important to publicise the injunction to ensure that consumers are aware of the position. However, there may be situations where the PRA or FCA decides not to publicise the injunction, or does not do so immediately[2], for example where this might damage market confidence or undermine market integrity in a way which would be prejudicial to the interests of consumers.

1 See the FCA Enforcement Guide at EG 6.16.
2 Where the matter arises in the context of a takeover bid, and in the FCA's view publication may affect the timetable or outcome of the bid, it will consult the Takeover Panel over the timing of publication and give due weight to its views: see the FCA Enforcement Guide at EG 6.18 .

8.160 This policy does not distinguish between interim injunctions and final injunctions, but it does suggest that interim injunctions will usually be made public. Where publication would be unfair or inappropriate, or there is no good reason for publication, it may be possible for the firm to seek restrictions on publication from the court at the time when it grants the injunction. At the very least, the PRA or FCA could be pressed to justify the need for publication in the case. In any event, the hearing of the application for an injunction may itself be held in public.

Chapter 9 Disciplinary sanctions and other regulatory action against individuals

INTRODUCTION

9.1   Whilst the regulatory regime operates primarily at the level of firms, it is not confined to firms. At the time of writing, the primary mechanism for bringing those who work for firms personally within the regime is the approved persons regime, described briefly at para **2.24** ff above. Approved persons are in general terms regulated by the FCA, or the PRA, or both. The approved person can be disciplined by a Regulator for misconduct or, in more serious cases, their approval for one or more functions could be withdrawn. Not all employees are, however, required to be approved persons. Whether approved persons or other employees, they can be prohibited from being involved with regulated firms if their conduct demonstrates that they are not fit and proper. As mentioned at para **2.53** ff above, the Financial Services (Banking Reform) Act 2013 (FS(BR)A 2013) will introduce a new senior persons regime for individuals holding senior management functions at deposit takers and dual-regulated investment firms (collectively referred to as 'banking firms' here), when it comes into force[1]. The Regulators will publish rules to govern the conduct of senior persons and will grant approval for individuals holding relevant functions, whilst continuing to grant approval for approved persons at non-banking firms. The Regulators will be able to bring disciplinary actions against approved persons, senior persons and other employees of banking firms for any breaches of rules that apply to them, or for being knowingly concerned in a firm's contraventions, and there is an additional ground on which the Regulators may bring a disciplinary action against senior persons as distinct from other individuals working in the financial services sector. Both the FCA and the PRA can also fine individuals who carry on a controlled function without approval. In some instances, restitution orders and injunctions can be made against individual employees of firms either instead of, or as well as, the relevant firm. Finally, all employees of firms (and in many cases individuals not working for firms) may be subject to sanctions under the FSMA 2000 in so far as they commit (or are involved in) market abuse[2], are knowingly concerned in breaches of the listing rules[3], or where they commit one of the criminal offences under the FSMA 2000[4].

1   At the time of writing, a commencement date has not been announced.
2   For further discussion see **CHAPTER 17** below.
3   See **CHAPTER 20** below.
4   See **CHAPTER 18** below.

9.2   Since the various enforcement powers available against those who work for firms are aimed at addressing different concerns, they are not mutually exclusive and thus may be used separately or in combination. By way of illustration, if an approved person caused the firm to commit a serious regulatory breach and then tried to conceal assets and destroy incriminating evidence, his conduct could potentially give rise to disciplinary action, the withdrawal of his approval, the making of a prohibition order, a civil injunction and prosecution for criminal offences. The purpose of and basis for the exercise of each power would be different. The various enforcement powers outlined in this chapter therefore need to be viewed not in isolation but as part of an overall scheme to allow the Regulators to take appropriate enforcement action in relation to the activities of those who work for firms.

9.3   Under the FS(BR)A 2013 regime, senior persons will require approval from one or both Regulators in the same way as approved persons at other firms. In addition, banking firms will themselves certify more junior employees as suitable to hold their positions. The Regulators have not published guidance as to the application of the senior persons regime or the firm-certification of other employees, but it is likely that banking firms will have to certify at least those other employees who hold positions equivalent to approved persons at other firms, if not all employees other than senior persons. These more junior employees, although certified by their employer, do not hold a formal 'approval' from the FCA or PRA. The term 'approved persons' will be referred to broadly in this chapter so that, when using this term, it will also include senior persons at banking firms where appropriate. A broader category of 'other banking firm employees' will also be referred to where applicable. This chapter will review:

- the enforcement action that can be taken against approved persons, and other employees at banking firms, namely disciplinary action and the withdrawal of approval of approved persons;

- action the Regulators can take against individuals performing controlled functions without approval;

- prohibition orders; and

- the application of injunctions and restitution orders to individuals.

9.4   This chapter considers the powers and approach of each of the Regulators in respect of the above points. As with **CHAPTER 8**, however, the focus is on the FCA, which is expected to continue to be the more active Regulator in enforcement. Indeed, at the time of writing, the PRA has not concluded enforcement action against any firm or individual, and has published only limited material on its approach to enforcement. By contrast, the FCA and its predecessor have increasingly turned their attention to holding individuals accountable for failings at financial institutions. However, as yet, the FCA has not published its guidance on the senior persons regime or the changes that will need to be made to its Handbook or the FCA Enforcement Guide following implementation of the FS(BR)A 2013.

DISCIPLINARY ACTION AGAINST EMPLOYEES OF FIRMS

Introduction

9.5   The following paragraphs will review the Regulators' powers to take disciplinary action against approved persons and other banking firm employees and their policies on when and how they use those powers in practice. In particular, the following will be considered:

- What disciplinary powers do the Regulators have?

- When will the Regulators seek to discipline an employee?

- What disciplinary sanction will be imposed?

- What is the procedure?

- What publicity will there be?

9.6   As discussed in **CHAPTER 8** above, the FSMA 2000 allows each Regulator to determine when in practice it will be appropriate for it to take disciplinary action. In many respects, therefore, it is the Regulators' policies on when they will take formal action and what action they will take that will be of primary interest.

9.7   The Regulators' policy on taking disciplinary action against approved persons and other banking firm employees overlaps in some respects with their policy on taking disciplinary action against firms, outlined at **CHAPTER 8** above. Reference is made to **CHAPTER 8** where appropriate below.

What disciplinary powers do the Regulators have?

9.8   Both the Regulators can impose a fine on an approved person or other banking firm employee, publicly censure him, impose restrictions on his performance of controlled functions[1] (if applicable) and, in the case of approved persons only, withdraw or suspend his approval. In addition, the Regulators will in some circumstances issue informal private warnings to individuals[2]. Whilst these warnings do not amount to formal disciplinary action, they are not free from regulatory consequences. The circumstances in which the Regulators will issue a private warning, the nature of a private warning and the consequences, are discussed at para **8.27** ff above. The focus here will be on formal disciplinary action.

1 FSMA 2000, s 66(3).
2 See the FCA Enforcement Guide at EG 7.10, in the case of private warnings imposed by the FCA, and the 'Statement of the PRA's Policy on the imposition and amount of financial penalties under the Act' (April 2013), (PRA penalty statement), p 3, n 9, in the case of private warnings imposed by the PRA.

9.9   The FCA may take disciplinary action against a person if[1]:

- it appears to the FCA they are guilty of 'misconduct', that is:

    – an approved person or other banking firm employee has failed to comply with a rule applicable to him; or

    – an approved person or other banking firm employee has been knowingly concerned in a contravention by his firm of a requirement imposed by or under the FSMA 2000 or certain EU provisions specified by the Treasury[2]; or

    – a senior person of a banking firm was, at the relevant time responsible for those activities in relation to which the firm's contravention occurred or continued, and is unable to show he took reasonable steps to prevent it[3];

    and

- the FCA is satisfied that it is appropriate in all the circumstances to take action against him.

1 FSMA 2000, s 66(1).
2 These are specified in SI 2013/419.
3 Senior persons also face potential criminal liability in the extreme situation where management decisions cause the failure of a banking firm (FS(BR)A 2013, s 36). Three elements must be present for the offence to be committed. The first is that a senior person takes a decision (or agrees to it being taken or fails to do what he can to prevent it) and that decision causes the insolvency of the bank or another financial institution in its group. The second is that the senior person is aware at the time that the decision could cause that insolvency. And third, his conduct in relation to the decision must 'fall far below' what could reasonably be expected of a person in his position. A person found guilty of this offence faces a fine and/or up to seven years' imprisonment. Proving that a senior person's behaviour fell far below the expected standard is likely to be a major hurdle for the prosecution in all but the most egregious cases. Similarly it will often not be easy to prove that a particular decision was the cause of a bank's insolvency – in many cases the insolvency will be caused by the coincidence of a number of different factors, none of which would have caused the insolvency on its own.

9.10   This test also applies to disciplinary action taken by the PRA[1].

1 It is immaterial for the purposes of disciplinary action by the FCA or PRA which Regulator granted the individual's approval: see the FSMA 2000, s 66(1).

9.11   The FSMA 2000 imposes an additional requirement that the Regulators may not take action after the end of the period of three years (or six years if the misconduct takes place after the FS(BR)A 2013 comes into force) beginning with the first day on which the Regulator knew of the misconduct, unless proceedings in respect of it against the approved person concerned were begun before the end of that period[1]. There is therefore a three-year (or six-year) limitation period for bringing proceedings for misconduct. Time starts to run when the Regulator knows of the misconduct, which includes having information from which the misconduct can reasonably be inferred[2]. The proceedings start when a warning notice is issued under FSMA 2000, s 67(1)[3].

1 FSMA 2000, s 66(4). The FS(BR)A 2013, s 28 changes this limitation period to six years for conduct after the date on which this legislation comes into force. In contrast there is no limitation period for imposing a prohibition order: see para **9.111** below.
2 FSMA 2000, s 66(5)(a). The Tribunal has found that time starts to run for the purposes of limitation when the FCA has sufficient knowledge of misconduct, or such knowledge can be inferred so as 'to justify an investigation. Mere suspicion is not enough, nor is any general impression that misconduct may have taken place' – *Jeffery v FCA, FS/2010/0039*, para 337.
3 FSMA 2000, s 66(5)(b).

Timing of misconduct

9.12   At the time of writing, the Regulators can only take such action against a person in relation to his conduct while he was an approved person. This includes both current and former approved persons. Thus, a person who is not and has not been an approved person, because he does not carry out a 'controlled function' for which he requires approval by the FCA or PRA, is not within the scope of the Regulators' disciplinary powers. However, as discussed in para **2.35** ff the Statements of Principle apply not only to the performance by approved persons of controlled functions, but also to their performance of other functions which relate to the carrying on of regulated activities by their firms[1]. As such, an approved person can breach a Statement of Principle, and therefore be disciplined for that breach, in respect of activities he has carried on which are not controlled functions.

1 FCA Handbook at APER 1.1A.2(2); PRA Handbook at 1.1B.2(2); FSMA 2000, s 64(1B)(b).

9.13   By the same token, under the provisions introduced by the FS(BR)A 2013, disciplinary action can be brought against a senior person only in relation to the firm's breaches that took place whilst he was responsible for the relevant aspect of that firm's business as a senior person. Equally, a person could be subject to disciplinary action for being knowingly concerned in the firm's breach only by reference to their position (and knowledge and conduct) at the relevant time.

Failure to comply with a Statement of Principle or rule

9.14   At the time of writing, the Regulators can bring disciplinary action against approved persons for breaches of the Statements of Principle for Approved Persons, but not generally against other individuals for breaches of these principles or other rules[1]. The Statements of Principle are outlined at para **2.12** ff above, with an explanation of the Code of Practice issued by the

Regulators to help determine whether or not a person's conduct has complied with a Statement of Principle. An important point to keep in mind is that it is the Statements of Principle, not the Code of Practice, that are paramount. The Code of Practice only has evidential effect[2].

1 FSMA 2000, s 66(2)(a) and (2A)(a) although there are circumstances in which the Regulators can commence civil or criminal proceedings against an individual who is not an approved person, such as for market abuse (see **CHAPTER 17** below).
2 The effect of the Code of Practice is discussed in more detail at para **2.32** ff above.

9.15 The FS(BR)A 2013 extends the regime by enabling the Regulators to make 'rules' applicable to individuals, not just the Statements of Principle. Correspondingly, the grounds for disciplinary action relate to breaches of such rules. The Regulators will be able to bring disciplinary action against an approved person or another banking firm employee who breaches a rule applicable to him[1]. This is broader than a breach of a Statement of Principle by an approved person. These new rules could be extended to approved persons at non-banking firms or the existing Statements of Principle could continue to apply to those individuals. In either case, breaches by approved persons will still constitute misconduct for which the Regulators can bring disciplinary action.

1 FSMA 2000, ss 66A(2) and 66B(2) introduced by the FS(BR)A 2013.

Knowingly concerned in a contravention

9.16 The meaning of 'knowingly concerned in a contravention' is discussed at para **2.126** ff above. The question whether a person has been knowingly concerned in a contravention depends in part upon his knowledge at the relevant time. The meaning of 'contravention of a requirement imposed by or under the FSMA 2000' is considered at para **2.94** ff above.

9.17 This category of 'misconduct' for which disciplinary action can be brought is amended by the FS(BR)A 2013, which applies it both to approved persons at non-banking firms and to employees of banking firms (including senior persons) who are knowingly concerned in that firm's contravention of requirements under the FSMA 2000 or qualifying EU measures specified by the Treasury[1].

1 FSMA 2000, ss 66A(3) and 66B(3), which will come into force with the FS(BR)A 2013, although, at the time of writing, a commencement date has not been announced.

Misconduct by senior persons

9.18 The FS(BR)A 2013 introduces a new category of 'misconduct' as a basis for disciplinary action that applies only to senior persons at banking firms[1]. The conditions for this category of misconduct are met when:

- the person has been, at any time, a senior person at a banking firm;

- there has at that time been (or continued to be) a contravention of a requirement by that banking firm; and

- the senior person was, at that time, responsible for the management of any of the firm's activities in relation to which the contravention occurred or continued.

1   The FS(BR)A 2013 introduces the FSMA 2000, ss 66A(5) and 66B(5).

9.19   A person is not guilty of misconduct under this head if he can show that he took such steps as a person in his position could reasonably be expected to take to avoid the contravention occurring or continuing.

9.20   This reverses the burden of proof for senior persons. A finding that a banking firm has breached principles or rules (whether that finding appears in a final notice following a settlement or a contested process) will, prima facie, give rise to a presumption of misconduct on the part of one or more senior persons responsible for that area of the business. The statements of responsibility that banking firms must prepare for each senior person are likely to make it easier for the Regulators to identify which senior person is responsible for management of the firm's activities in relation to which the contravention occurred. The onus will then be on the relevant senior person to show that he took reasonable steps to avoid or put a stop to the regulatory breaches. It will therefore be critical for senior persons to be able readily to show how they exercise proper oversight over the activities for which they are responsible, so as to avoid breaches from occurring, and the steps taken to investigate and remediate issues which arise.

Appropriate in all the circumstances to take action

9.21   Each Regulator is required[1] to prepare and issue a statement of its policy with respect to the imposition and amount of penalties and the period for which suspensions or restrictions are to have effect and, in the case of any particular contravention, to have regard to the policy in force at the time the contravention occurred when exercising, or deciding whether to exercise, its powers. The Regulators' policies in this regard are discussed below[2]. However, the FSMA 2000 imposes the additional requirement that the Regulator concerned must be satisfied that it is appropriate in all the circumstances to take action against the person. Therefore it is clear that the mere fact that 'misconduct' can be attributed to an individual does not of itself mean that disciplinary action against an individual will result. This reflects what is one of the more difficult questions in this context, namely, in what circumstances should the Regulator look to punish an individual instead of, or in addition to, the firm?

1   FSMA 2000, s 69.
2   See para **9.23** ff.

When will the Regulators seek to discipline an employee?

9.22   It is rare that the firm commits a breach without one or more persons working for the firm having had some sort of involvement in that breach[1]. As has been seen, the FSMA 2000 gives the Regulators a broad discretion to decide when such persons should be disciplined, provided that one of the definitions of 'misconduct' is met, by requiring the Regulator to be satisfied that it is appropriate in all the circumstances to take disciplinary action.

1 See the example given at para **2.118** above.

What is the FCA's policy?

9.23   At the time of writing, the FCA's policy is that the primary responsibility for ensuring compliance with the firm's regulatory obligations rests on the firm itself[1] although there has over time been a shift in emphasis with a greater focus being placed on whether members of senior management have discharged their duties. Normally, the firm will be the FCA's main focus. However, in some cases, it may not be appropriate to hold the firm responsible for the actions of those who work for it, for example where the firm can show it took all reasonable steps to prevent the breach. In other cases, it may be appropriate to take action against both the firm and an individual, for example, where the firm failed to take reasonable care to maintain proper systems and controls and an approved person with responsibility for the relevant business had failed in their management or oversight of the business, or, alternatively, where an approved person took advantage of the lack of systems and controls for his own ends[2].

1 FCA Handbook at DEPP 6.2.4.
2 FCA Handbook at DEPP 6.2.5 in which the FCA gives the example of where the approved person took advantage of the deficiencies by front running orders or misappropriating assets.

9.24   At the time of writing, the FCA has not published guidance on when it will bring disciplinary action against senior persons or other banking firm employees. The FCA's existing broad guidance as to when it will be appropriate to take disciplinary action against approved persons, (which might inform the FCA's development of guidance as to its approach to disciplinary actions under the new regime, except against senior persons as described in para **9.18** above) is as follows:

- the FCA may take disciplinary action against an approved person where there is evidence of personal culpability, which means either that the behaviour was deliberate or that it was below the standard which would be reasonable in all the circumstances at the time of the conduct concerned[1];

- in determining whether it is appropriate to take disciplinary action the FCA may consider these other factors[2]:

  - the approved person's position and responsibilities, with the likelihood of the FCA's taking action increasing with the level of seniority of the person concerned;

  - whether action against the firm, rather than the approved person, would be a more appropriate regulatory response[3]; and

  - whether disciplinary action would be a proportionate response to the nature and seriousness of the breach by the approved person[4];

- the FCA will not discipline approved persons on the basis of holding them responsible for the acts of others, provided there has been appropriate delegation and supervision. In particular, it will not take action against an approved person exercising a 'significant influence function'[5] simply because a regulatory failure has occurred in an area of business for which he is responsible[6]. The FCA will only consider that such a person may have breached Statements of Principle 5 to 7[7] if his conduct was below the standard it was reasonable to expect in all the circumstances at the time of such conduct[8]. An approved person will not be in breach if he has exercised due and reasonable care when assessing information, has reached a reasonable conclusion and has acted on it[9]; and

- in assessing whether a person has breached a Statement of Principle, the FCA will take into account the context in which the conduct occurred, including the precise circumstances of the individual case, the characteristics of the particular controlled function and the behaviour to be expected in that function[10].

1 FCA Handbook at DEPP 6.2.4 and the PRA Handbook at APER 3.1.4(1). See also the FCA Enforcement Guide at EG 2.31: 'The FCA will not pursue senior managers where there is no personal culpability'.
2 FCA Handbook at DEPP 6.2.6.
3 In *UBS AG final notice (25/11/2012)* the FCA identified a number of failings of management to investigate and challenge the activities of a rogue trader, who was subsequently imprisoned for his actions. The firm was disciplined for weaknesses in its systems and controls and failing to conduct its business with due skill, care and diligence, but individual members of management were not.
4 FCA Enforcement Guide at EG 2.32: 'The FCA recognises that cases against individuals are very different in their nature from cases against corporate entities and the FCA is mindful that an individual will generally face greater risks from enforcement action, in terms of financial implications, reputation and livelihood than would a corporate entity.'
5 Broadly, equivalent to senior management. See para **9.29** ff below.
6 Although this policy cannot apply to the liability of senior persons under the new category of misconduct (described at para **9.18** above), which is fundamentally based on the rationale of holding senior management responsible for a firm's contravention on the basis that he was responsible for that area of the business, whether or not he has direct personal culpability for the contravention.
7 The Statements of Principle applicable to those exercising significant influence functions: see para **2.49** ff above.
8 FCA Handbook at DEPP 6.2.7. See also the FSA report 'The failure of the Royal Bank of Scotland' (December 2011), p 353: The 'Enforcement Division does not have the power to take action simply because a failure occurs in an area for which an individual is responsible (ie there is no requirement of strict liability). It cannot, therefore, take action against the CEO of a firm simply on the grounds that there were a number of failures at the firm, even though the CEO is ultimately responsible for the actions of the firm … [To] take enforcement action Enforcement Division needs to have clear evidence of personal culpability. Nor can it take action just because a decision is made which subsequently proves to be a wrong decision. In order to succeed in enforcement action, it needs to prove that the individual's action or decision, when viewed without the benefit of hindsight, was below reasonable standards at the time it was taken.'
9 FCA Handbook at DEPP 6.2.8.
10 FCA Handbook at APER 3.1.3. See also para **2.41** ff above.

9.25   The FCA's policy for bringing disciplinary action against senior persons for 'misconduct' is likely to differ from the policy set out above. This is primarily because the senior persons regime is based on the rationale that the individuals holding senior positions at the most significant firms should be held responsible for rule breaches by those firms unless they can show they took reasonable steps. In principle, there ought still to be scope for the FCA to take personal culpability into account when deciding whether to proceed with such disciplinary action but the balance may be somewhat different.

What does the FCA's policy mean?

9.26   In considering what this policy means, it may be helpful to consider the position of approved persons generally before looking at some additional factors relevant to those approved persons who exercise 'significant influence' functions. And, although the FCA policy on disciplining senior persons has not been published at the time of writing, the underlying rationale for the senior persons regime and what effect this might have on the FCA's policy for disciplinary action against senior persons is considered below.

Approved persons generally

9.27   Whilst the question of whether an individual was personally culpable, and therefore should be subject to disciplinary proceedings, may seem to be a subjective test, taking into account the person's state of mind, the FCA has made it plain that an objective test may be used. As outlined above, by personal culpability, the FCA means either that the behaviour was deliberate or that the person's conduct was below the standard of behaviour which the FCA would reasonably expect from a person carrying out their particular functions. Whether behaviour was deliberate is clearly subjective, since it depends on the intentions of the person. It may be difficult to argue that deliberate misconduct (in the sense of acting deliberately and in the knowledge that the actions constituted, or would cause, a breach[1]) should not be punished. Among other things, it may cast doubt on the integrity of the person and whether he is fit and proper to be an approved person at all.

1   It is not, though, clear that this is what the FCA means by 'behaviour [that] was deliberate' in the FCA Handbook at DEPP 6.2.4. An alternative interpretation would be that the test is whether the actions were deliberate, irrespective of whether the person had any knowledge that the consequences might constitute a breach.

9.28   The other question is whether the person's conduct fell below the applicable standard. This is an objective test, and it would be quite possible for a person to fail that test without any reference being made to his state of mind at the relevant time. Indeed, a person could fall below the applicable standard whilst acting with the best of intentions. Thus, for example, if a person made an error and unwittingly caused a breach, he may be 'personally culpable' within this policy if his conduct fell below the standard reasonably to be expected of him[1].

1   See for example *Cheick Tidjane Thiam final notice (27/3/2013)*.

Those exercising significant influence functions

9.29   The discussion above applies equally to those exercising significant influence functions, but there are some additional factors. The person exercising a significant influence function is less likely to have been directly involved. Rather, the question is often whether the breach was able to occur because of failures in the systems and controls, or failures in supervision, in the area for which that person was responsible[1]. In considering whether such a person should be disciplined personally, it is necessary to consider, first, whether he has been knowingly concerned in a rule breach by the firm, or has breached a Statement of Principle or other rule and, second, whether it is appropriate for the FCA to take action against him.

1 See for example, *Pottage v FSA, FS/2010/33*, discussed below at para **9.33**, n 3.

9.30   As to the first question, whether there has been a breach, unless the person had some active involvement in the breach, it is less likely he will have been knowingly concerned in it[1]. The question is therefore often whether he committed a breach of any of the Statements of Principle. Statements of Principle 5 to 7, which are those additional Principles applicable to persons exercising significant influence functions, each contain an objective standard ('reasonable steps', 'due skill, care and diligence', 'reasonable care'). In considering whether a person complied with that standard, the FCA takes into account factors such as the nature, scale and complexity of the business, the role and responsibility of the person concerned and the knowledge that he had or should have had of the regulatory concerns in the business under his control[2].

1 See for example, *Peter Cummings final notice (12/09/12)*, discussed below at para **9.33**, n 3, in which Mr Cummings was found to have been knowingly concerned in his firm's breach of Principle 3. For a discussion of 'knowingly concerned', see para **2.126** ff above.
2 See para **2.41** above.

9.31   Again, therefore, an objective test is applied. The difficulty lies in predicting how this works in practice. Most regulatory issues which were not caused deliberately, as well as many that were, are capable at some level of being attributed to a systemic failure of some description, for example a failure of controls, a lack of training or an unclear compliance manual. It is then but a short step to an arguable case that a person exercising a significant influence function fell below the applicable standard in allowing that failure to occur.

9.32   The second question, whether it is appropriate to take disciplinary action, thus remains important: this is discussed at para **9.21** above.

9.33   The culpability of senior managers also needs to be viewed against the general policy[1] of devolving regulatory responsibility from the FCA to those who manage firms. From the FCA's point of view, this is more efficient and may result in less intervention in firms' businesses. But the corollary is that the FCA has been increasingly clear that it wants senior management to take, and be seen to take, responsibility for the firm[2]. Enforcement action has been taken against senior management in a number of cases[3].

9.33 Disciplinary sanctions and other regulatory action against individuals

1 The principle of responsibility of those who manage firms is outlined at para **1.34** above.
2 See also the FCA Enforcement Guide at EG 2.31 and 2.32: 'The FCA is committed to ensuring that senior managers of firms fulfil their responsibilities'. One way the FCA has attempted to achieve this is through the increased use of attestations, in which the FCA requires a senior individual to confirm that his or her firm complies with certain regulatory requirements specified in the attestation.
3 Two disciplinary actions by the FSA against senior individuals at major firms illustrate this in particular:

   - In a decision overturned by the Tribunal in April 2012 (*Pottage v FSA, FS/2010/33*), the FSA fined John Pottage, the former head of UK Wealth Management at UBS, £100,000 for breach of Statement of Principle 7. Statement of Principle 7 requires that a person performing a significant influence function take reasonable steps to ensure that the firm for which he is responsible complies with regulatory rules and standards. The FSA had claimed that Mr Pottage failed to initiate a comprehensive review of systems and controls at the firm early enough to identify and remediate deficiencies in the firm's risk management framework, when a number of operational and compliance issues arose between September 2006 and July 2007. The Tribunal disagreed, finding that Mr Pottage took reasonable steps to deal with these issues, and should not reasonably be expected to have ordered a comprehensive review earlier.
   - In September 2012, the FSA fined Peter Cummings £500,000 and prohibited him from performing a significant influence function in a bank, building society, investment or insurance firm for breaching Statement of Principle 6, and being knowingly concerned in the breach of Principle 3 by his firm, HBOS (*Peter Cummings final notice (12/09/12)*). Statement of Principle 6 requires a person performing a significant influence function to exercise due skill, care and diligence in managing the business of the firm for which he is responsible, while Principle 3 requires firms to take reasonable care to organise and control their affairs responsibly and effectively, and implement adequate risk management systems. Mr Cummings had been the chief executive of the Corporate Division of the bank, and had presided over the aggressive expansion of this division without taking reasonable steps to mitigate the high risks of its business, and without ensuring that it managed adequately high value transactions under stress.

   Similarly, the FCA has increased its attention in market abuse cases on senior individuals at large institutions, rather than merely those who enter into abusive transactions: see, for example, *Andrew Osborne final notice (15/2/12)*, *Caspar Jonathan William Agnew final notice (3/10/11)* and the *Ian Hannam decision notice (27/2/12)*. The latter notice was referred to the Tribunal, which had yet to publish its decision at the time of writing.

Senior persons

9.34   The senior persons regime is proposed to cover a narrower range of individuals than approved persons at banking firms at the time of writing, but it is intended to cover individuals holding responsibility for the key activities and risks faced by the firm. The firm will prepare a statement of responsibility for each senior person when they apply for approval but these statements will also enable the Regulators to identify the individual with responsibility for an area of the business in which a regulatory issue has arisen. The Statements of Principle for Approved Persons will not apply to senior persons who will be governed by a new set of banking standards rules intended to set out more clearly the Regulators' expectations of conduct.

9.35   Two main objectives for the senior persons regime were stated by the Parliamentary Commission on Banking Standards[1]. First, to encourage greater clarity of responsibility and improve corporate governance at banking firms. Second, to establish beyond doubt individual responsibility to provide a sound basis for the Regulators to impose remedial requirements or take enforcement action against individuals when a serious problem occurs. The intention is not to discourage collective decision making or delegation of decision-making where appropriate, but means that it will be easier to identify one or more individual with overall responsibility for a particular activity or risk that is the subject of a contravention, despite collective or delegated decision-making.

1 Parliamentary Commission on Banking Standards report 'Changing banking for good' (June 2013), Vol 1, para 98 and Vol 2, para 616.

9.36   In the past, enforcement action against senior managers at banks has been viewed as difficult, in part because of the lack of clear responsibility for particular decisions under the matrix and other governance structures at large institutions, but also because of the need to show personal culpability by an individual. The reversal of the burden of proof for the category of misconduct applicable only to senior persons is intended, with the other changes, to make enforcement action against senior managers easier in the event of a serious contravention by the firm[1]. A senior person will need to be able to show what steps he took to avoid or stop the firm's contravention and meet his defined responsibilities. The meaning of this defence will need to be clarified over time, and particularly the extent to which it requires the senior person to show he took steps directed specifically at the issue that has arisen (or that are sufficient to show adequate management and oversight overall). What is clear, though, is that the structures through which the senior person exercises management and oversight will become 'increasingly' important, to enable senior persons to carry out their duties without fear of inappropriate blame. The extension of the limitation period for enforcement action against individuals from three to six years is intended to allow the Regulators sufficient time to complete any enforcement action against the firm before going on to consider whether to take enforcement action against one or more senior persons based on the firm's contravention.

1 Parliamentary Commission on Banking Standards report 'Changing banking for good' (June 2013), Vol 2, para 1116, box 21.

Other banking firm employees

9.37   Employees at banking firms who are not designated as senior persons will be subject to the same banking standards rules as senior persons. Although these employees will not need approval from the Regulators, the firm itself has a statutory obligation to vet the employees and certify to the Regulators that they are fit and proper to hold their positions. As part of this certification, it will be down to a firm to provide adequate training to ensure that employees understand the rules that apply to them.

9.38   The scope of this licensing regime has not been defined at the time of writing but is intended to extend beyond the category of individuals who were classified as approved persons at banking firms, although the most junior administrative staff would fall outside the licensing regime. The rationale for firm certification of these employees is to allow the Regulators to focus resources on approval of senior persons who are the real senior decision-makers.

9.39   Disciplinary sanctions and other regulatory action against individuals

9.39   As explained above (see paras **9.15** and **9.17**), these other banking firms employees can face disciplinary action for breaching rules that apply to them or for being knowingly concerned in a firm's contravention in the same way as senior persons or approved persons at other firms[1]. Employees make the decisions of a firm and the liability for being knowingly concerned in a firm's breach ensures that those individuals can be held responsible for the relevant decisions and actions of banking firms.

1 See para **2.126** above.

What is the PRA's policy?

9.40   The PRA has issued little guidance as to when it will seek to discipline an approved person, beyond its statutory statement of policy referred to at para **9.21** above. However, the Code of Practice for Approved Persons contained in the PRA Handbook makes clear that a person will only be in breach of a Statement of Principle – and therefore liable to disciplinary action – where he is personally culpable, that is where his conduct was deliberate or fell below that which would be reasonable in all the circumstances[1]. Again, the PRA will develop a policy for bringing action against senior persons under the new legislative provisions but, in other respects, much of the discussion at para **9.23** ff above applies equally to disciplinary action by the PRA.

1 See the Handbooks at APER 3.1.4A(1).

9.41   The PRA has also stated that its preference is to use its statutory powers to secure remedial action before a person's activities become a disciplinary matter[1]. Nevertheless, it emphasises the personal responsibility of senior management to run their firms prudently[2]. The factors the PRA will consider in assessing whether it is appropriate to take disciplinary action against an approved person include[3]:

- the impact of the person's behaviour on the PRA's ability to advance its objectives, including the behaviour of other persons in his firm over whom the person should exercise control, and therefore whether this behaviour casts doubt on the person's fitness and propriety to be an approved person; and

- the person's behaviour towards the PRA, including the level of co-operation and openness of the person with the PRA, and the appropriateness of his response to concerns raised by the PRA.

1 'The Prudential Regulation Authority's approach to banking supervision' (April 2013), para 93; 'The Prudential Regulation Authority's approach to insurance supervision' (April 2013), para 103.
2 PRA penalty statement, para 7.
3 'The Prudential Regulation Authority's approach to banking supervision' (April 2013), para 95; 'The Prudential Regulation Authority's approach to insurance supervision' (April 2013), para 105.

What disciplinary sanction will be imposed?

9.42   Where formal disciplinary action is appropriate, each Regulator has powers to:

- impose a fine of such amount as it considers appropriate; and/or

- for up to two years[1], suspend the person's approval to perform any controlled functions, or impose limitations or restrictions on the person's performance of such functions; and/or

- publish a statement of the person's misconduct[2].

1 FSMA 2000, s 66(3A).
2 FSMA 2000, s 66(3).

9.43 The purpose of each sanction, how the Regulators choose which sanction to impose, and the contents of any statement of misconduct that they choose to publish, are discussed in the context of firms in **CHAPTER 8** above. That discussion applies equally to individuals. In addition, the PRA has stated that it will take into account the following additional factors when considering specifically whether to impose a financial penalty against an individual[1]:

- the nature of the significant influence function performed by the individual, and his role and responsibilities;

- whether the person's behaviour calls into question his fitness and propriety; and

- whether the imposition of a penalty, together with any other sanction, would be an appropriate and effective response to the person's behaviour.

1 PRA penalty statement, para 8.

How do the Regulators determine the amount of a fine?

9.44 The Regulators both follow a similar five-step methodology for calculating the amount of the fine to be imposed on individuals[1] as that for fines imposed on firms, described in **CHAPTER 8** above, albeit that the steps are modified as follows[2].

1 Firms are prohibited from indemnifying employees against financial penalties imposed by a Regulator: see the Handbooks at GEN 6.1.4A and GEN 6.1.5. However, a firm can indemnify an employee or director against the costs of defending himself against FCA or PRA enforcement action or against any costs he may be ordered to pay a Regulator: see GEN at 6.1.7.
2 The procedure used by the FCA for the calculation of the amount of the fine to be imposed on individuals in market abuse cases differs from that outlined here, and is described in para **17.186** ff below.

Step 1: Disgorgement

9.45 Both Regulators will seek to deprive the person of any financial benefit derived from the breach, where this is quantifiable. They may also add interest[1].

1 FCA Handbook at DEPP 6.5B.1; PRA penalty statement, para 17. The FCA states that it will 'ordinarily' charge interest on the benefit; the PRA states that it will determine whether interest should be payable 'on a case by case basis'.

Step 2: Seriousness of breach

Relevant income

FCA

9.46 The FCA will then calculate the person's 'relevant income'. This is the total remuneration received by the person from his employment at the time of the breach, including salary, bonus and other benefits, for the duration of the breach. If the breach lasted less than 12 months, the relevant income is that received during the 12 months preceding the breach. If the person occupied the relevant job for less than 12 months, his income is scaled up pro rata to be the equivalent of 12 months' income[1].

1 FCA Handbook at DEPP 6.5B.2.

PRA

9.47 By contrast, the PRA will ordinarily calculate the 'relevant income' as the individual's annual income, including salary, bonus and other benefits, during the tax year preceding the date the breach ended (or, where the breach is continuing, a figure based on the individual's income in the previous and/or current tax year)[1].

1 PRA penalty statement, para 20.

Assessing the seriousness of the breach

FCA

9.48 The FCA will then determine the proportion of the person's relevant income to impose as a fine, by assessing the seriousness of the breach he has committed. As with firms, the FCA Handbook sets out a non-exhaustive list of factors the FCA is likely to consider, grouped into four categories[1], namely factors:

- relating to the impact of the breach, including:
    - the benefit gained by the individual from the breach;
    - the effect, such as financial losses, which the breach caused others; and
    - whether the breach had an effect on particularly vulnerable people;
- relating to the nature of the breach, including:
    - the frequency of the breach;
    - whether financial crime occurred or could have occurred in connection with the breach;
    - whether the person failed to act with integrity, or abused a position of trust; and
    - the individual's seniority, prominence within the industry, and experience;

- indicating that the breach was deliberate, including

  - whether the individual foresaw or intended the consequences of his breach;

  - whether he intended to benefit financially from the breach;

  - whether he knew that his actions contravened his firm's internal procedures; and

  - whether he attempted to conceal his breach; and

- indicating that the breach was reckless, including:

  - where the individual knew that there was a risk that his actions might result in a breach, but failed to attempt to mitigate the risk, or to check whether these actions were in accordance with his firm's internal procedures.

1   FCA Handbook at DEPP 6.5B.2(7)–(11).

PRA

9.49   The PRA also sets out in its statement of policy (as referred to in para **9.21** above) a non-exhaustive list of factors it may take into account when considering the seriousness of the breach, and therefore the proportion of the person's relevant income to impose as a fine. These include[1]:

- the seniority or experience of the individual and the extent of his responsibility for the breach, and for the business area affected by the breach;

- whether the individual failed to act with integrity, abused a position of trust or breached a professional code of conduct; and

- the factors described at para **8.92** above.

1   PRA penalty statement, para 21.

Determining the base level of the fine

FCA

9.50   The FCA will then use its assessment of the seriousness of the breach to categorise the misconduct into one of five levels. Each level corresponds to a fixed percentage, increasing in 10% increments from 0% for the least serious, level 1 breach, to 40% for the most serious, level 5 breach[1]. This percentage is multiplied by the relevant income, described in para **9.46** above, to arrive at the base level of the fine, which is then adjusted in accordance with steps 3–5, described below. A breach is likely to fall within levels 1–3 of severity where:

- the individual received no benefit for the breach;

- there was little or no loss or risk of loss caused to consumers, investors or other market users;

9.50 Disciplinary sanctions and other regulatory action against individuals

- the breach had little or no effect on the orderliness of or confidence in the markets; and

- the breach arose inadvertently, or out of negligence[2].

1 FCA Handbook at DEPP 6.5B.2(5): level 1 – 0%; level 2 – 10%; level 3 – 20%; level 4 – 30%; and level 5 – 40%.
2 FCA Handbook at DEPP 6.5B.2(13).

9.51 Conversely, the breach is likely to fall within levels 4–5 where:

- it caused significant loss or risk of loss;

- it enabled the commission of financial crime (whether or not a crime did in fact result from the breach);

- the individual abused a position of trust or failed to act with integrity;

- the individual occupied a prominent position in the industry; and

- the breach was committed deliberately or recklessly[1].

1 FCA Handbook at DEPP 6.5B.2(12).

PRA

9.52 The PRA follows a similar policy of applying a percentage to the individual's relevant income to determine the base level of the fine. However, it does not specify fixed percentages that correspond to levels of seriousness, but instead follows the guidance described in para **8.91** ff above.

Step 3: Mitigating and aggravating factors

FCA

9.53 The FCA may then apply a percentage increase or decrease to the base level of the fine determined under step 2 (but not the disgorgement element of the fine calculated under step 1), to take into account factors which aggravate or mitigate the breach. The factors which the FCA may take into account are similar for both individuals and firms found to have committed misconduct, and are discussed in para **8.78** above. In addition, the FCA may take into account whether the individual agreed to undertake training following his breach as a possible mitigating factor[1].

1 FCA Handbook at DEPP 6.5B.3.

PRA

9.54 The PRA may also take into account the mitigating and aggravating factors described at para **8.93** above in deciding whether to increase or decrease the base figure of the fine.

Step 4: Deterrence

9.55   Each Regulator may increase the amount of the penalty if it considers that it would not sufficiently deter the individual or others from committing similar breaches. In addition to those factors discussed at para **9.79** ff, which apply equally to the imposition of penalties by the FCA[1] and the PRA[2] on individuals, the FCA may also increase the penalty where, for example, the individual has a low income but owns significant assets, such that a penalty based on his income would be an insufficient deterrent.

1 FCA Handbook at DEPP 6.5B.4(1).
2 PRA penalty statement, paras 27 and 28.

Step 5: Settlement discount

9.56   The individual may receive a discount on the penalty (but not on any element of disgorgement calculated under step 1) in return for settling with a Regulator at an early stage in the enforcement process[1]. The principles are the same as those for firms, and are discussed by reference to the FCA at para **8.80** ff. The settlement discount scheme applies equally to settlements with the PRA. The stages and applicable discounts are the same as those set out for the FCA at para **10.46**, with the sole exception that the PRA defines 'Stage 1', that is the stage at which a 30% settlement discount applies, as the time from the PRA's commencement of an enforcement investigation until it has communicated to the individual the nature of the case against him, has allowed what the PRA considers to be a reasonable time for the individual to respond, and has allowed a reasonable opportunity for the parties to reach a settlement agreement[2].

1 FCA Handbook at DEPP 6.5B.5; PRA penalty statement, para 29.
2 'Statement of the PRA's settlement decision-making procedure and policy for the determination of the amount of penalties and the period of suspensions or restrictions in settled cases', (PRA settlement policy), para 28.

9.57   Given the impact that enforcement action can have on an individual's career, individuals have been much more likely than firms to forgo some or all of the settlement discount available and contest cases, either before the RDC or by referring the decision to the Tribunal. This process is discussed in detail in **Chapters 10** and **12**.

Reduction in penalty for financial hardship

9.58   The Regulators may reduce the amount of a fine if the individual discloses verifiable evidence that payment of the fine would cause him serious financial hardship[1].

1 FCA Handbook at DEPP 6.5D.1; PRA penalty statement, paras 30–36.

How do the Regulators determine the length of a suspension or restriction?

9.59   As noted at para **9.42** above, the Regulators may suspend or restrict a person's approvals to perform controlled functions for up to two years. Senior persons at banking firms, as well, as approved persons at other firms, hold approvals granted by the Regulators. Approval for a senior person can be granted subject to conditions or a time limit, and such a condition or time limit can be imposed or varied subsequently using supervisory powers. In addition, the Regulators' power to impose a suspension or restriction as a result of a disciplinary action applies both to approved persons at non-banking firms and senior persons (collectively, approved persons).

9.60   Factors which the FCA may take into account in determining the appropriate length of the restriction or suspension are as follows[1]:

- the need to deter the individual and others from committing further breaches;
- the seriousness of the breach, which may include consideration of the factors described at para **9.48** above;
- aggravating and mitigating factors, which may include those factors described at para **8.78** above;
- the impact of the suspension or restriction on the individual, including the earnings he would be expected to lose from not being able to carry on the suspended or restricted activity, and whether the suspension or restriction would cause him serious financial hardship; and
- the impact of the suspension or restriction on other persons, such as the extent to which consumers may suffer loss or inconvenience as a result.

1 FCA Handbook at DEPP 6A.3.

9.61   Factors which the PRA may take into account in determining the appropriate length of the restriction or suspension are[1]:

- the factors set out at para **9.49** above;
- aggravating or mitigating factors, including those set out at **8.93** above;
- the impact of a suspension or restriction on the individual, including whether this would be likely to cause the individual serious financial hardship; and
- the potential for the measures to have a wider impact, including on persons other than the individual in breach, and on the stability of the financial system.

1 'Statement of the PRA's policy on the imposition of suspensions or restrictions under the act and the period for which they are to have effect', (PRA policy on suspensions and restrictions), paras 9 and 10.

9.62   Both the FCA and the PRA may agree to impose a reduced period of suspension or restriction in return for early settlement of enforcement action by the individual. The applicable percentage reduction depends on the stage at which the settlement agreement is reached, and is the same as that for financial penalties, discussed at para **8.80** ff.

What is the procedure?

9.63   Where a Regulator seeks to take disciplinary action, the warning/decision notice procedure applies[1]. The procedure is considered in detail in **CHAPTER 10** below in the case of the FCA, and in **CHAPTER 11** below, in the case of the PRA. Among other things, the person has the right to refer the matter to the Tribunal. As noted at para **9.57** above, individuals have been more likely to refer cases to the Tribunal than firms.

1 FSMA 2000, s 67.

What publicity will there be?

9.64   The question of publicity is discussed in **CHAPTER 10** below. That discussion applies to individuals as it does to firms. Generally, it is the Regulators' policy to publish decision notices and final notices[1]. The FCA is also now able to publish details of warning notices it has issued, although it will not ordinarily identify the individual in this statement[2]. The contents of any public censure are considered at para **8.53** ff above.

1 See in particular, para **10.180** below.
2 See para **10.108** below.

Withdrawal of approval

9.65   The process of granting approval to persons to carry out certain specified functions for firms, known as 'controlled functions', has been outlined at para **2.24** ff above. The need for a person carrying out certain functions to be specifically approved in this way is driven primarily by consumer protection considerations. Thus, the Regulators' power to withdraw a person's approval in certain circumstances, is also aimed primarily at protecting consumers. Approval is required for senior persons holding specified management functions at banking firms and approved persons at other firms. The following issues in relation to withdrawal of approval are considered below:

- On what grounds can the Regulators withdraw a person's approval?

- When will the Regulators seek to do so in practice?

- What is the effect of the Regulators withdrawing approval?

- What is the procedure for the Regulators to do so?

- Practical issues for firms.

9.66   As noted at para **9.2** above, the withdrawal of approval may be used in conjunction with other enforcement powers. For example, it may be appropriate to discipline an approved person in order to punish him for his act of misconduct and additionally, to withdraw his approval in order to ensure that he cannot continue to perform his controlled function. He may also carry out other controlled functions, approval for which may also need to be withdrawn. But even this does not prevent him from carrying out other, non-controlled functions for the same or another firm. If a Regulator wishes to prevent him from doing so, then it will need to make a prohibition order against him. Both Regulators have expressly indicated that they may need to consider using these other powers as well as withdrawing approval[1]. Even where a Regulator has already established the person's misconduct, it will still need to establish a lack of fitness and propriety in order to withdraw his approval[2].

1 FCA Enforcement Guide at EG 9.23 and PRA Settlement policy, para 6.
2 For an example of a case where the FSA withdrew an individual's approval, without also imposing a prohibition order or disciplinary sanctions, see *Kathleen Hales final notice (9/10/08)*.

9.67 The FCA may withdraw an approval given either by itself or by the PRA. The PRA may withdraw an approval given by itself, but may only withdraw an approval given by the FCA where it relates to a significant influence function performed in relation to a dual-regulated firm carrying on a regulated activity[1]. Before one Regulator withdraws an approval given by the other Regulator, it must consult that other Regulator[2].

1 FSMA 2000, s 63(1A).
2 FSMA 2000, s 63(1C).

On what grounds can the Regulators withdraw a person's approval?

9.68 The criterion for withdrawing approval mirrors that for granting approval, namely whether or not the person is a fit and proper person to perform the relevant function[1]. The sole ground for withdrawing approval is thus that the Regulator considers that the person in respect of whom the approval was given is not a fit and proper person to perform the function to which the approval relates[2].

1 FSMA 2000, s 61(1) and see para **2.132** above.
2 FSMA 2000, ss 63(1) and 63(1A)(b).

9.69 'Fit and proper' is a broad test[1]. The withdrawal of approval is thus aimed at addressing broad concerns about a person's suitability to be involved in the relevant activities on the firm's behalf. Withdrawal of approval is different in nature and purpose to the disciplinary powers available to punish particular breaches. The concerns that lead to a finding that a person is not fit and proper may arise from a particular rule breach and, as will be seen, the seriousness of the breach will in that situation be a relevant factor. In the case of senior persons, the firm employing the person is required to consider, at least once a year, whether there are any grounds on which the Regulators could withdraw the person's approval and notify the Regulators if this is the case[2].

1 The meaning of fit and proper in the context of individuals is outlined at para **2.29** ff above.
2 FSMA 2000, s 63(2A) introduced by the FS(BR)A 2013, s 25.

9.70 The main difference between the withdrawal of approval and the granting of approval[1] lies in the burden of proof. When a firm proposes an individual to the Regulator for approval, it is for the individual and his firm to prove that he is fit and proper to be approved[2]. Where a Regulator proposes to withdraw the individual's approval (or impose a prohibition order on him), it is for that Regulator to prove that the individual is no longer fit and proper[3].

1 Described briefly at para **2.26** ff above.
2 See the Handbooks at SUP 10A.13.15 and 10B.11.15. See also *Cox v FSA (2003) FSMT 003*, para 2.
3 *Hoodless and Blackwell v FSA (2003) FSMT 007*, para 20.

9.71 The differing burden of proof has led to an anomaly in practice. The problem occurs when the FCA[1] is investigating an individual and for whatever reason, he has left his controlled function and then seeks approval for a new controlled function; for example, at another firm. The person may have left after being disciplined by his previous firm, but this will not necessarily be the case. By the time that the person applies for a new approval, the existence of the investigation concerning him may mean that the FCA is on notice that he may not be fit and proper[2]. However, until that investigation is concluded, those concerns will not be proven. In these circumstances, the FCA is in a difficult position. It has unconfirmed concerns about an individual and a duty to protect consumers[3], but a firm is seeking approval for that individual and in doing so is seeking to show that he is fit and proper. This problem has occurred on a number of occasions when the FCA's predecessor has refused to grant approval in such circumstances[4]. The Tribunal has confirmed that the FCA may do so, but the existence of an investigation should not in itself lead to the conclusion that the person is not fit and proper[5].

1 At the time of writing, no enforcement action has been taken by the PRA, however the discussion contained in this paragraph would in principle also apply to investigations and approvals being considered by the PRA.
2 See **CHAPTER 10** below for a description of the circumstances in which the FSA will investigate a firm or individual.
3 FSMA 2000, s 1C.
4 See *Rayner & Townsend v FSA (2004) FSMT 009*, para 85, where both applicants sought approval while they were under investigation. One applicant was refused and one was accepted. The Tribunal was told that the FSA's system had not picked up the fact that the individual whose application was accepted was under investigation.
5 *Thomas v FSA (2004) FSMT 010.*

9.72 However, a colleague of the individual seeking the approval may also be under investigation for the same matter and the colleague may not have left his controlled function at the original firm. The FCA may have the same concerns as to his fitness and propriety, but is unlikely to apply for the withdrawal of his approval until it has reached a decision as to those concerns because of the differing burden of proof. Accordingly, two people who are in the same position may be treated differently merely because one has left his original job[1].

1 *Thomas v FSA (2004) FSMT 010*, para 86.

When will a Regulator seek to withdraw approval?

9.73   The statutory ground for withdrawing approval provides no more than a framework. It does not expressly oblige a Regulator to withdraw approval in every case where lack of fitness and propriety is made out (although, as discussed below, this is likely to be the result), and instead leaves it to the Regulator's discretion as to when the power should be exercised.

9.74   The question of whether a person is fit and proper is assessed against a wide range of factors and, in contrast with the question whether a person has committed a particular rule breach, is largely a matter of judgement for the Regulator. Fitness and propriety is, though, fundamental to the regulatory regime. As a result, as indicated above, it is perhaps unlikely that the Regulator would reach a finding of lack of fitness and propriety and yet take no action. It may be more likely for the Regulator to address lesser concerns by restricting or suspending a person's approvals, as described in para **9.59** ff, reserving to the more serious cases the sanction of withdrawal of approval, which may have a greater impact on the relevant person's employment prospects.

9.75   The PRA has not published separate guidance as to the factors it will take into account in considering whether to withdraw approval[1], however, the FCA has published some guidance beyond the factors considered in an application for approval. The FCA has stated that it will take into account all relevant circumstances of the case, including[2]:

- whether the person has the qualifications, training and competence prescribed in the FCA's rules in relation to the particular function in question[3];

- the criteria for assessing fitness and propriety outlined at para **2.29** ff above. These broadly fall under three heads, namely: (i) honesty, integrity and reputation; (ii) competence and capability; and (iii) financial soundness;

- whether and to what extent the person has failed to comply with rules applicable to him, has been knowingly concerned in a contravention by the relevant firm of a requirement imposed on the firm under the FSMA 2000, or has failed to comply with a directly applicable EU regulation[4];

- whether the person has engaged in market abuse;

- the relevance, materiality and length of time since the occurrence of any matters indicating unfitness;

- the severity of the risk which the person poses to consumers and confidence in the financial system;

- the person's disciplinary record and compliance history; and

- the nature of the particular controlled function which the person performs, the nature and activities of the firm concerned, and the markets in which the person operates.

1 FSMA 2000, s 63(2) states that the Regulators may take into account any matter which could be taken into account in considering an application for approval under s 60 in respect of the performance of the function to which the approval relates.
2 FCA Enforcement Guide at EG 9.9.
3 The FCA Enforcement Guide singles this out by prescribing as a potentially relevant factor the matters set out in the FSMA 2000, s 61(2). Qualifications, training and competence are specified in that provision. See also the FCA Handbook at TC.
4 This equates with misconduct by approved persons for which the FSMA 2000 allows the FCA to take disciplinary action, as discussed at para **9.12** ff above. The fact that the relevant misconduct or breach may have been a mistake which could have been made by a relatively experienced and conscientious person may suggest that it should not lead to the withdrawal of a person's approval (see para 49 of the Tribunal's decision in *Hoodless and Blackwell v FSA (2003) FSMT 007*).

9.76   There may be other relevant matters, for example providing false or misleading information or failing to disclose material considerations on application forms such as details of criminal convictions. Where there are such other matters, the FCA will consider whether the conduct or matter is relevant to the question of whether the person is fit and proper for the particular controlled function[1]. The FCA may also have regard to the cumulative effect of a number of factors each of which may not be sufficient grounds to withdraw approval when considered in isolation[2].

1 FCA Enforcement Guide at EG 9.12 and 9.13.
2 FCA Enforcement Guide at EG 9.10.

What is the effect of a Regulator withdrawing approval?

9.77   The practical effect of withdrawal of approval is to prevent the person from carrying out the particular controlled function or functions to which the relevant approval related. As discussed in para **9.89** ff below, the Regulators can fine the individual if he continues to carry out the controlled function after his approval has been withdrawn. Furthermore, an obligation is imposed on firms[1] to take reasonable care to ensure that no unapproved person performs a controlled function in relation to its regulated activities, either when employed by the firm or when working for it under contracting arrangements[2]. If the firm fails to take reasonable care, then the Regulators may take enforcement action against it[3].

1 FSMA 2000, s 59(1) and (2). The firm concerned will be notified of the withdrawal of approval: FSMA 2000, s 63(3), (4) and (6).
2 This might include freelancers or outsourcing.
3 The firm may also be exposed to civil actions for damages, primarily by private persons: FSMA 2000, s 71 and see para **19.24** ff below.

9.78   The withdrawal of approval does not, however, prevent the person from continuing to work for the firm, in relation to any controlled functions for which his approval has not been withdrawn or any other functions not prescribed by the Regulators as controlled functions. However, as the Tribunal has acknowledged, the withdrawal of a person's approval may have the practical effect that the person 'cannot work in any responsible capacity in the financial services industry'[1].

1 See para 8 of the Tribunal's decision in *Hoodless and Blackwell v FSA (2003) FSMT 007*.

9.79 A further likely consequence is that the withdrawal of approval will be publicised, following the Regulators' general approach to the publication of enforcement action, discussed in the context of the FCA at para **10.179** ff below[1].

1 In addition, the Financial Services register includes information about approved persons: see the FSMA 2000, s 347.

9.80 Once approval has been withdrawn, the person concerned cannot perform the relevant controlled function until a new approval is obtained. If the firm believes that the person has remedied the matters that caused concern and should be regarded as fit and proper to carry out one or more controlled functions, then a new application for approval could be made on his behalf. This is likely to be difficult where the matter of concern related to his honesty or integrity, but perhaps less so where it was a matter of qualifications, training or competence. The Regulators have given no indication of any specific considerations or factors that they will take into account in relation to such an application. The application would, therefore, be considered in the same way as any other application for approval[1]. It may be that the Regulators would have in mind similar factors as are relevant to applications to remove a prohibition order[2].

1 See para **2.26** ff above, the FCA Handbook at SUP 10A and the PRA Handbook at SUP 10B.
2 FCA Enforcement Guide at EG 9.19 and paras **9.126** ff below.

What is the procedure for withdrawing approval?

9.81 The procedure where a Regulator wishes to withdraw a person's approval is the warning/decision notice procedure discussed in detail in **CHAPTERS 10** and **11** below[1]. Among other things, there will be a right to refer the matter to the Tribunal for determination.

1 FSMA 2000, s 63(3) and (4).

9.82 There are two particular points to note. First, warning notices, decision notices and final notices relating to withdrawals of approval must be given by the Regulator not only to the person concerned but also to the person on whose application the approval was given, and the person by whom the person's services are retained, if not the same person[1]. In other words, the firm for whom the person performs one or more controlled functions must be notified and, if the person is employed by another body which contracts with the firm, then that body must also be notified. Each of those parties has the right to refer the matter to the Tribunal[2].

1 FSMA 2000, ss 63(3), (4) and (6); and 390(1).
2 FSMA 2000, s 63(5). In the case of *Hoodless and Blackwell v FSA (2003) FSMT 007*, one of the applicants was successful in his challenge (see para **2.29**, nn 2 and 3 above and para **12.15**, n 2 below for further discussion).

9.83 Second, the final notice will specify the date on which the decision to withdraw approval takes effect[1].

1 FSMA 2000, s 390(7)(b). For a discussion of final notices, see para **10.188** ff below.

Practical issues for firms

9.84   How should the firm deal with an employee against whom a Regulator has brought proceedings for the withdrawal of approval? This can cause real tensions because on the one hand, the firm may wish to be seen to take proactive steps to remove from any sensitive positions those employees whose conduct is questionable but, on the other hand, will not wish to expose itself to claims by its employees, for example for breach of contract[1]. This will be an ongoing issue because the regulatory process could take several months, perhaps longer. It may also be the case that the employee will seek to defend himself against the Regulator's action by stating that the firm was partly or totally to blame for his lack of fitness or propriety[2].

1 The FCA expects firms to be aware of the possible effects on their contractual relationships with contractors and employees that withdrawal of approval might have: see the FCA Enforcement Guide at EG 9.28.
2 For example, the employee may state that he had inadequate training or supervision. Alternatively, the employee may allege that such impropriety was commonplace or well known within the firm. Such allegations may cause questions to be raised about the firm's systems and controls. See, for example, *Sachin Karpe v FSA, FS/2010/0019*.

9.85   The firm has a number of options, including:

• standing by the employee and supporting him in the regulatory process;

• taking no view on the merits of the action being taken by the Regulator against the employee but suspending him pending the outcome of the regulatory process, provided the firm's terms and conditions of employment allow it to do so;

• moving the employee out of a sensitive position and providing him with other work, provided he consents or the terms and conditions of employment allow the firm to do so[1];

• where the firm considers that the employee's apparent lack of fitness and propriety can be remedied by further training, it may consider moving the employee from his position and retraining him[2]; and

• taking its own disciplinary action against the employee without awaiting the outcome of the regulatory process.

1 If the employee does not consent, this could constitute a serious breach of contract entitling the employee to treat himself as having been constructively dismissed.
2 Again, this may entitle the employee to treat himself as having been constructively dismissed if he does not consent.

9.86   Which option is appropriate will depend upon the precise circumstances. In many situations the Regulator will expect to see the firm taking its own decision on what disciplinary action is merited and not awaiting the outcome of the regulatory process. It may not therefore be appropriate for the firm to take an entirely neutral stance[1].

1 This is discussed in more detail at para **3.24** ff above.

9.87   Depending on what course of action the firm takes, there may be a risk of Employment Tribunal proceedings being commenced by the employee against the firm whilst the regulatory proceedings are still pending. The interaction of the two can cause difficulty in practice. For example, the employee may not wish to provoke the firm into taking an overtly hostile stance against him which could reflect on its involvement in the regulatory proceedings. Also, from the firm's perspective, it needs to consider whether any of the evidence which it would want to use to defend itself against the employee would impact negatively on the Regulator's view of the firm[1].

1 For example, if the evidence will be that the employee was well known to be questionable, or was largely left to his own devices, then this may cause questions to be raised about management or about the firm's systems and controls.

POWER TO IMPOSE A PENALTY FOR PERFORMING CONTROLLED FUNCTIONS WITHOUT APPROVAL

9.88   As mentioned in para **2.24**, n 1, firms are required to take reasonable care to ensure that persons without an approval from a Regulator do not perform controlled functions in relation to the firms' regulated activities, and the Regulators may take enforcement action against firms which contravene this requirement. The Regulators are also empowered to fine individuals who perform controlled functions without approval. If the individual has been performing an FCA-controlled function without approval, the FCA holds this power; where he has been performing a PRA-controlled function without approval, it is the PRA which may impose a fine[1].

1 FSMA 2000, s 63A(5A).

On what grounds can the Regulators impose a fine?

9.89   A Regulator must be satisfied as to two conditions before it may impose a fine[1]:

- the individual has performed without approval a controlled function under an arrangement entered into by an authorised person or that person's contractor, in relation to the person's carrying on of a regulated activity; and

- at the time he was performing the controlled function without approval, he knew, or could be reasonably expected to have known, that he was performing a controlled function without approval.

1 FSMA 2000, s 63A(1).

9.90   The Regulator may only take action within a three-year (or six-year) limitation period[1], beginning on the day it knew that the individual was performing a controlled function without approval (or had information from which this knowledge could be reasonably inferred), and ending on the day it gives a warning notice to the person concerned in respect of the action[2].

1   FS(BR)A 2013, s 28 changes this limitation period to six years for this conduct after this legislation comes into force.
2   FSMA 2000, s 63A(3)–(5).

When will the Regulators exercise their power?

9.91   Both Regulators have published guidance as to the factors which will influence their decision as to whether to take action. The PRA's guidance[1] is substantially the same as that of the FCA, which has stated that it will take into account[2]:

- whether, had the person performing the controlled function been approved, he would have committed misconduct under which the FCA could have taken disciplinary proceedings, and if so, the seriousness of the misconduct;

- the length of time for which the person performed the controlled function without approval;

- whether the person is an individual;

- the seniority of the individual, such that the more senior the individual concerned, the greater the likelihood of action[3]; and

- the extent to which a firm is culpable for the person's carrying on of a controlled function without approval, for example where a firm decided that the individual did not need to obtain approval, and it was reasonable for the individual to rely on the firm's judgement.

1   PRA penalty statement, para 9.
2   FCA Handbook at DEPP 6.2.9A.
3   The PRA does not include this in its list of factors it will take into account when considering whether to impose a fine. Given that all PRA-controlled functions are also significant influence functions, it is likely that any person who may be the subject of such action by the PRA will be occupying a senior role. The PRA also adds to the list set out in para **8.22** above whether such action 'is or is likely to be an appropriate and effective regulatory response to the misconduct in question'.

9.92   In this last point, the FCA appears to recognise a tension between its power to impose a penalty against the individual himself, and the fact that a person cannot become approved on his own initiative, but only on the application of the firm (unless he is a sole trader). Consequently, where an individual who has carried on a controlled function without approval was employed by a firm, it is likely that the latter will also bear some responsibility for the individual's actions.

9.93   The Regulators have also provided guidance on when they will expect to be satisfied that the person could reasonably be expected to have known that he was performing a controlled function without approval. Again, the guidance issued by the PRA[1] is similar to that of the FCA, which has stated that it will take into account where[2]:

- the person has previously performed a similar role, for which he has been approved;

- a firm has previously applied for approval for the person to perform the same or a similar controlled function;

- the person's seniority and experience is such that he can reasonably be expected to have known that he was performing a controlled function without approval; and

- the responsibilities associated with the person's role were clear.

1 PRA penalty statement, para 9(d).
2 FCA Handbook at DEPP 6.2.9A(2).

How do the Regulators determine the amount of the fine?

9.94 The five-step procedure outlined at para **9.44** ff above applies[1]. When determining the seriousness of the breach at step 2 of the procedure, in addition to those factors discussed at paras **9.48** and **9.49** above, the FCA may also consider[2]:

- whether the individual also committed misconduct while performing the controlled function without approval, including whether the FCA would have had the power to take disciplinary action against him, had he been approved; and

- the factors noted at para **9.93** above which indicate the extent to which the person could reasonably have been expected to have known that he was performing a controlled function without approval.

1 FCA Handbook at DEPP 6.5B; PRA penalty statement, para 12 ff.
2 FCA Handbook at DEPP 6.5B.2(9)(p)–(r).

9.95 The PRA has also indicated that it may take into account the factors noted at para **9.49** above when assessing the seriousness of the breach[1].

1 PRA penalty statement, para 21(k).

9.96 A mitigating or aggravating factor which the FCA may take into account at step 3, in addition to those factors discussed at para **8.78** above, is whether the individual's employer or another firm had previously withdrawn an application for the individual to perform the same or a similar controlled function, or has had such an application rejected by the FCA[1]. The PRA takes into account relevant previous applications and rejections for any controlled function, whether to the FCA, PRA or the FSA[2].

1 FCA Handbook at DEPP 6.5B.3(n).
2 PRA penalty statement, para 25(g).

9.97 The FCA considers that a breach of the FSMA 2000, s 63A is likely to fall within levels 1–3 of the five-level categorisation of the amount of the fine discussed at para **9.50** ff above where the individual's only misconduct was to perform a controlled function without approval[1].

1 FCA Handbook at DEPP 6.5B.2(13)(e).

What is the procedure?

9.98 The warning/decision notice procedure applies[1]. This is considered further in **CHAPTER 10** below. The individual has the right to refer the matter to the Tribunal[2].

1 FSMA 2000, s 63B.
2 FSMA 2000, s 63B(5).

PROHIBITION ORDERS

9.99 The Regulators have the power to make a prohibition order against a person[1], preventing him from being involved in either regulated activities generally, or certain specific types of activities. This power is, broadly speaking, aimed at protecting consumers and markets. The following paragraphs consider:

- What is a prohibition order?

- On what grounds can a prohibition order be made?

- When will a Regulator seek a prohibition order?

- What is the procedure for doing so?

- What is the effect of the prohibition order?

- Is the making of an order publicised?

- Can an order be varied or revoked?

1 FSMA 2000, s 56.

9.100 As with the Regulators' other enforcement powers, prohibition orders may be used by the FCA or PRA concurrently with taking other action, such as disciplining or withdrawing the approval of an approved person or prosecuting an individual for a criminal offence[1].

1 See the FCA Enforcement Guide at EG 9.23 and the PRA policy on suspensions and restrictions, para 6. For example, in *Christian Littlewood final notice (31/5/12)* and *Angie Littlewood final notice (31/5/12)*, the FSA imposed prohibition orders on two individuals after they had been convicted of insider dealing offences.

What is a prohibition order?

9.101 A prohibition order is an order prohibiting an individual from performing[1]:

- a specified function;

- any function falling within a specified description; or

- any function.

1 FSMA 2000, s 56(2).

9.102 Disciplinary sanctions and other regulatory action against individuals

9.102 The order may relate to[1]:

- a specified regulated activity, any regulated activity falling within a specified description, or all regulated activities; and/or

- firms generally or within a specified class of firms;

and can be made in relation to regulated activities carried on by an exempt person, or a professional firm under the FSMA 2000, Pt 20[2].

1 FSMA 2000, s 56(3).
2 FSMA 2000, s 56(3A).

9.103 The FSMA 2000 therefore gives the Regulators a significant degree of flexibility to prescribe the extent to which the person is prohibited. A prohibition order can be used either as a rather blunt tool, to prevent a person from working in regulated financial services business generally, or as a more sophisticated instrument, to prevent him from working in particular areas or for particular types of firms. For example, a Regulator could prohibit the person from working in a particular type of business (for example, insurance), or on particular types of products (for example, derivatives), or in particular types of roles[1]. Thus, the Regulators can make a prohibition order as narrow or almost as broad as circumstances require. Generally, prohibition orders which have previously been imposed by the FSA and FCA relate to any regulated activity carried on by an authorised person, exempt person or [FSMA 2000, Pt 20] professional firm. However, in a small number of instances the order is narrower[2]. In some cases the FCA has imposed different forms of prohibition order in respect of different persons involved in the same misconduct[3].

1 See for example, *David Thornberry final notice (29/3/12)*, which prohibited Mr Thornberry from performing the compliance oversight functions at any authorised or exempt firm.
2 For example, the order contained in the *Ian Jones final notice (21/9/11)*, prohibits Mr Jones from performing controlled functions in relation to the promotion of unregulated collective investment schemes.
3 See for example, *Jonathan Edwards final notice (15/8/11)*, *Stephen Hunt final notice (15/8/11)* and *Gary Forster final notice (15/8/11)*, in which different partial prohibition orders were imposed on three executives of an investment advisory firm.

9.104 The power is clearly a fairly draconian one. Not only does it allow the Regulators to impose requirements relating to persons who would not otherwise be directly accountable to the FCA or the PRA, it also potentially impacts seriously on the livelihood of the person concerned. This is not, therefore, a power to be exercised lightly or routinely. The FCA, in particular, seems to recognise this in its policy on when it will exercise the power, as outlined at para **9.108** ff below.

9.105 As the above may indicate, it is not entirely clear whether a prohibition order can extend to prohibiting the person from carrying out any activities whatsoever for firms, whether or not those activities relate to the firm's regulated business. In other words, it is unclear whether a person can be prohibited from working for a firm in its unregulated business. The FSMA 2000 is ambiguous[1]. HM Treasury seemed at the time the FSMA 2000 was introduced to take the narrower view[2]; the FCA now seems to take the wider view[3].

1 Compare 'any function' in the FSMA 2000, s 56(2) and the list of functions at s 56(3). It is not clear whether s 56(3) qualifies s 56(2) or is merely illustrative of the orders that can be made. See also the extent of the firm's duty to take reasonable care not to engage a prohibited person: s 56(6). Note also the test for making a prohibition order (see para **9.106** ff below).
2 'Functions in relation to any regulated activities': Explanatory Notes to the FSMA 2000, para 134. For comparison see the statement by the Financial Secretary to HM Treasury in Standing Committee, 26 October 1999: 'it [may] make an order prohibiting someone from working in the financial services industry at all'.
3 An order may prevent the person 'from being employed' by any authorised firm: see the FCA Enforcement Guide at EG 9.4.

On what grounds can a prohibition order be made?

9.106 The FCA may impose a prohibition order if it appears to it that a person is not a fit and proper person to perform functions in relation to a regulated activity carried on by an authorised person, exempt person or Part 20 professional firm[1]. The PRA, on the other hand, may make a prohibition order if it appears to it that a person is not fit and proper to perform functions in relation to a regulated activity carried on by a dual-regulated firm, or by a person who is exempt in relation to a PRA-regulated activity carried on by that person[2].

1 FSMA 2000, s 56(1).
2 FSMA 2000, s 56(1A).

9.107 As will be seen, the meaning of fit and proper in this context is that outlined at para **2.29** ff above. Candidates for approval as a senior person or approved person must be 'fit and proper' to hold controlled functions and, in addition, certain firms must certify additional specified categories of employees as 'fit and proper' to hold their positions[1]. Also, it is clearly relevant to the question as to whether the firm is fit and proper that it has honest employees who adhere to proper standards[2].

1 FSMA 2000, s 63F introduced by the FS(BR)A 2013, s 29.
2 See para **2.29** above.

When will the Regulators seek a prohibition order?

9.108 The PRA has not published guidance as to when it will seek a prohibition order, and at the time of writing had not exercised its power to do so. This section therefore focuses on the FCA's exercise of its power to impose prohibition orders.

9.109 The FCA has indicated that it may exercise the power to make a prohibition order where it considers that an individual presents such a risk to consumers, or to confidence in the market generally that it is necessary either to prevent him from carrying out any function in relation to regulated activities, or from being employed by any firm, or to restrict the functions which he may carry out or the type of firm by which he may be employed. The stress is thus on addressing a risk to consumers or to market confidence, and the power is one which is envisaged to be used only in serious situations[1]. Whether or not the individual intends to carry on the functions to be prohibited in the future is not relevant to the question of whether a prohibition order should be imposed. As with when the FCA considers whether to take disciplinary action, it seems that the FCA may make a prohibition order 'in order to send out messages to the financial services industry and to the public about unacceptable conduct in the financial markets and in order to deter others'[2].

1 FCA Enforcement Guide at EG 9.1, EG 9.5 and EG 9.8.
2 *R v Financial Services Authority, ex p Davies [2004] 1 WLR 185*, per Mummery LJ at 192.

9.110 In deciding whether to make a prohibition order, the FCA will consider[1] all the relevant circumstances, including whether any other enforcement action should be taken or has been taken against the individual by the FCA or by other enforcement agencies or professional bodies[2]. The factors which the FCA will take into account differ to some extent dependent upon the nature of the person against whom it is considering making the order. They are outlined below.

1 FCA Enforcement Guide at EG 9.3.
2 See *Blunden and Stevens (10/11/03)* for prohibition orders that were made for reasons involving another regulator.

9.111 It should also be noted that unlike the Regulators' powers to take disciplinary action against an individual, there is no limitation period for imposing a prohibition order[1]. Where a Regulator wishes to take disciplinary action against an individual, but the period for taking that action has elapsed, it may decide to impose a prohibition order instead[2].

1 Paragraph **9.11** above sets out the limitation period applicable to disciplinary action against individuals.
2 In *R v Financial Services Authority, ex p Davies [2004] 1 WLR 185*, the FSA issued warning notices, proposing to impose prohibition orders where the limitation period for taking disciplinary action had elapsed. The individuals concerned unsuccessfully contested the issue of the notices on the basis that the FSA should not be able to circumvent a statutory time bar by taking a different form of action.

9.112 Where the FCA considers making a prohibition order, but decides not to do so, it may consider issuing a private warning to the person concerned, to notify him that this was under active consideration[1]. For a discussion of the nature and effect of private warnings, see para **8.28** ff above. Alternatively, the person against whom the FCA was considering making a prohibition order may undertake to the FCA not to perform certain functions in the future[2]. The circumstances in which the FCA will be prepared to accept such an undertaking rather than issue a prohibition order are unclear.

1 FCA Enforcement Guide at EG 7.13. The PRA has also suggested that it may use private warnings as an alternative to enforcement action: see the 'Statement of the PRA's Policy on the imposition and amount of financial penalties under the Act' (April 2013), (PRA penalty statement), p 3, n 9.
2 See for example, *Peter Sprung final notice (23/2/10)*.

Prohibition orders against approved persons

9.113 The Regulators' power to withdraw approval from an approved person whom it considers is no longer fit and proper to be carrying on the particular function to which the approval relates has already been reviewed[1]. That power is exercisable on a very similar ground to the power to issue a prohibition order, namely a failure to be fit and proper. A prohibition order does, however, have more serious consequences for the person concerned, because of its wider scope and the more serious, criminal consequences of breach. It may therefore be appropriate to make a prohibition order as well as withdrawing approval. Before considering either sanction, however, the FCA will consider whether disciplinary action would be an adequate means of achieving its statutory objectives[2].

1 See para **9.65** ff above.
2 See for example, *Peter Sprung final notice (23/2/10)*.

9.114 In deciding whether to exercise the power against an approved person, the FCA may consider the same factors as are relevant for determining whether to withdraw the person's approval, discussed at para **9.75** ff[1] above.

1 FCA Enforcement Guide at EG 9.9.

9.115 Prohibition orders are likely to be used against approved persons where the person's conduct is such that a wider scope of prohibition is required than could be accomplished solely by the withdrawal of approval. In practice, the FCA and FSA have often imposed prohibition orders in addition to the withdrawal of approval.

Prohibition orders against others

9.116 The Regulators' power to make a prohibition order extends beyond approved persons[1]. It includes both those working for firms but not carrying out controlled functions and those not working for regulated firms. It also includes individuals who are exempt persons. In other instances, the person will have been an approved person at the time that the relevant misconduct took place, but owing to disciplinary action by the firm, or other circumstances, will not be approved when the Regulator seeks the prohibition order.

1 FSMA 2000, s 56(1) and (1A). See also the FCA Enforcement Guide at EG 9.15–9.18, and, for example, the prohibition order imposed on Stefan Chaligné, who was not an approved person: *Chaligné, Sejean and Diallo v FSA, FS/2011/0001, FS/2011/0002 and FS/2011/0005*, para 94.

9.117 Broadly, the FCA will consider the severity of the risk posed by the relevant person when deciding whether to make a prohibition order against someone other than an approved person[1]. The FCA will consider all the relevant circumstances of the case, which may include the factors referred to at para **9.75** above. It should be noted that where the individual is not an approved person, the FCA will not be able to withdraw his approval or, unless he is a banking firm employee, take other disciplinary action such as imposing a fine[2]. In such circumstances, the FCA may consider itself forced to issue a prohibition order.

1 FCA Enforcement Guide at EG 9.17.
2 However, directors of listed companies may be sanctioned by the UKLA in respect of certain breaches even if they are not approved persons, see para **20.103** ff below. The FCA may also sanction persons who are not approved as a result of market misconduct: **CHAPTER 17** below.

9.118 Disciplinary sanctions and other regulatory action against individuals

What is the procedure for imposing a prohibition order?

9.118 Where the FCA or PRA wish to make a prohibition order, the warning/ decision notice procedure applies and there is a right to refer the matter to the Tribunal[1]. The procedure for issuing warning and decision notices is discussed in detail in **CHAPTERS 10** and **11** below and the procedure for references to the Tribunal in **CHAPTER 12** below[2].

1 FSMA 2000, s 57.
2 The FCA is obliged to consult with the PRA before issuing a warning notice, where it proposes to prohibit an individual from performing a function in relation to a regulated activity carried on by a PRA-authorised person or a person who is exempt in relation to a PRA-regulated activity which it carries on (FSMA 2000, s 57(6) and (7)). In all circumstances, the PRA must consult the FCA before it issues a warning notice in which it proposes to impose a prohibition order (FSMA 2000, s 57(8)).

9.119 Specific points to note in this context are as follows:

• the warning notice must set out the terms of the proposed prohibition[1];

• the decision notice must[2]:

  – name the individual to whom the prohibition applies;

  – set out the terms of the order; and

  – be given to the individual named in the order.

1 FSMA 2000, s 57(2).
2 FSMA 2000, s 57(4).

9.120 There is no specific requirement for the firm to be provided with a copy of the warning and decision notice[1], although it is likely it will be provided with a copy as a third party named in the notice to whom it is prejudicial[2]. Where a Regulator seeks both to withdraw an approved person's approval and to prohibit him, it is likely that the two will be run in tandem, although there is no such requirement.

1 Contrast the position in relation to withdrawal of approval: see para **9.82** above.
2 FSMA 2000, s 393 and see para **10.150** ff below.

What is the effect of the prohibition order?

9.121 A prohibition order has two primary effects. First, it is a criminal offence for a person to perform or agree to perform a function in breach of a prohibition order[1], subject to the defence of showing that the person took all reasonable precautions and exercised all due diligence to avoid committing the offence[2].

1 FSMA 2000, s 56(4). Contrast this with the effect of withdrawing a person's approval: see para **9.77** ff above.
2 FSMA 2000, s 56(5).

9.122 Second, firms are obliged to take reasonable care to ensure that no function of theirs in relation to the carrying on of a related activity is performed by a person who is prohibited from performing that function by a prohibition order[1]. The FCA or PRA may consider taking disciplinary action against a firm that breaches this provision[2]. The FCA regards a search of the Financial Services register as an essential part of the firm's statutory duty of taking reasonable care. Where the search does not reveal a record of the prohibition order, it will only consider taking action where the firm had access to additional information indicating that a prohibition order had been made[3].

1 FSMA 2000, s 56(6).
2 In the case of the FCA, see the FCA Enforcement Guide at EG 9.24.
3 FCA Enforcement Guide at EG 9.24.

9.123 In addition, to the extent that the firm breaches its statutory duty, a private person who suffers loss as a result may have a civil claim against it[1].

1 FSMA 2000, s 71. Such civil claims are considered at para **19.24** below.

9.124 Finally, if it appears to a Regulator that there are circumstances suggesting that an individual may have performed or agreed to perform a function in breach of a prohibition order, or a firm may have breached its statutory duty described above, then it can initiate a formal investigation under the FSMA 2000, s 168(4)[1].

1 This is discussed in detail in **CHAPTERS 10** and **11** below.

Will the making of an order be publicised?

9.125 The FCA is required to maintain on its public register in relation to each prohibition order that has been made, at least the name of the individual against whom it has been made and details of the effect of the prohibition order[1]. The FCA generally also publicises the final notice relating to the imposition of the order[2], and the PRA has stated that it intends to do the same[3]. Where the PRA decides to impose an order, the PRA is required to provide the FCA with at least the name of the individual concerned and details of the effect of the order, so that the FCA may update the Financial Services register[4]. In the case of prohibition orders imposed by the FCA, once its decision to impose the order is no longer open to review, the FCA will consider what additional information about the circumstances of the order it is appropriate to include on the register[5]. The FCA will balance any possible prejudice to the person concerned against the interests of consumer protection. The FCA will normally maintain the entry on the Financial Services register while the prohibition order remains in effect and for six years after it is revoked[6]. The question of publication following successful enforcement action is discussed generally at para **10.195** below.

1 FSMA 2000, s 347(1)(g) and (2)(f). In practice this information is set out on the list of prohibited individuals.
2 FSA Enforcement Guide at EG 6.8 and 6.8B.
3 'Statement of the PRA's approach to publicity of regulatory action', para 14.
4 FSMA 2000, s 347A(1)(b).
5 Where the FCA publishes the relevant final notice, brief details of the reasons for issuing the prohibition order are also set out.
6 FCA Enforcement Guide at EG 6.19. See also para **9.130** below.

Can an order be varied or revoked?

9.126 Most prohibition orders remain effective without time limit. It is therefore important that the FSMA 2000 allows the Regulator which has made a prohibition order, on the application of the individual named in the order, to vary or revoke the order[1]. The FCA has also stated that it may indicate in the decision or final notice that it would be minded to revoke the order on the application of the individual after a specified number of years, provided no new evidence emerges that the person is not fit and proper. However, such an indication is no guarantee that an application will be successful[2]. When considering whether to grant or refuse such an application, the FCA will take into account all the relevant circumstances, including various factors outlined in the FCA Enforcement Guide[3].

1 FSMA 2000, s 56(7).
2 FCA Enforcement Guide at EG 9.6. See also *Stuart Unwin final notice (25/4/12)*, para 1.4, in which rather than specifying a time after which it would consider an application for revocation, the FSA stated that it 'would be minded to revoke the Prohibition Order, on Mr Unwin's application, in the event that Mr Unwin is able to demonstrate to the satisfaction of the FSA that he has taken adequate steps to remedy his lack of competence and capability'.
3 FCA Enforcement Guide at EG 9.19. See also *Jonathan Townrow final notice (28/1/13)* and *Townrow v FSA, FS/2012/0007* for an example of the reasons the FCA may consider in refusing an application for the revocation of a prohibition order.

9.127 If the person wishes to perform a controlled function, then the relevant firm will also need to apply for him to be approved to act in that capacity[1].

1 FCA Enforcement Guide at EG 9.21. The process of approval is discussed briefly at paras **2.24** ff above. Details can be found in the FCA Handbook at SUP 10A, and in the PRA Handbook at SUP 10B.

9.128 An important question is when in practice the Regulators will consider varying or revoking a prohibition order. The PRA has not published guidance as to when it will consider varying or revoking a prohibition order it has imposed. However, the FCA has indicated that it will generally only grant an application to vary a prohibition order if it is satisfied that the proposed variation will not result in a recurrence of the risk to consumers or to confidence in the financial system that resulted in the order being made. The FCA has also indicated that it will not revoke a prohibition order unless it is satisfied that the person is fit to carry out functions in relation to regulated activities generally or those specific activities which were prohibited[1]. In either case, therefore, the concerns that gave rise to the making of the order must have been dispelled or, in the case of a variation, must not be prejudiced[2].

1 FCA Enforcement Guide at EG 9.22.
2 The circumstances under which the Regulators must consult each other before revoking or varying a prohibition order are similar to those set out at para **9.118**, n 2 in relation to the imposition of such orders (FSMA 2000, s 56(7A) and (7C)).

9.129 As to the procedure for assessing the application:
- if the Regulator decides to grant the application, it gives the applicant a written notice[1], which is neither a warning or decision notice nor a supervisory notice;

- if it proposes to refuse the application, then the warning notice/decision notice procedure applies[2].

1 FSMA 2000, s 58(2).
2 FSMA 2000, s 58(3) and (4). For a detailed explanation, see **CHAPTERS 10** and **11** below.

9.130 If a successful application is made to vary the order, then a note of the variation will be made on the Financial Services register. If a successful application to revoke the order is made, then a note will be made on the register to the effect that the order has been revoked and the reasons for the revocation of the order[1]. As noted above, the FCA will normally maintain an annotated record of revoked prohibition orders for a period of six years from the date of the revocation, after which period the record will be removed from the register. The effect of this is potentially to prolong the stigma of a prohibition order for some years after the order has been revoked.

1 FCA Enforcement Guide at EG 6.19. The FCA is entitled under the FSMA 2000 to remove the entry but indicates at EG 6.19(2) that it will not immediately do so. If it does not remove the entry, this information is required to be placed on the register by the FSMA 2000, s 347(4).

INJUNCTIONS AND RESTITUTION ORDERS AGAINST INDIVIDUALS

Introduction

9.131 The availability of injunctions and restitution orders is considered in detail in **CHAPTER 8** above. The purpose of the following paragraphs is to outline briefly their applicability to individuals personally. Whilst the FSMA 2000 does allow injunctions and restitution orders to be made against individuals, the FCA and the FSA have in practice used these powers rarely. The powers are, however, used more regularly against individuals than firms, mostly in perimeter enforcement cases. Where a person breaches a court order, he will be in contempt of court. The consequences of being held to be in contempt of court are dealt with at para **5.76** ff above.

Injunctions

9.132 The FSMA 2000 allows the court, on application by the 'appropriate regulator', to make three types of injunctions[1], namely:

- to restrain a contravention;
- to remedy a contravention; and
- to secure assets.

1 FSMA 2000, s 380 and see para **8.138** ff above.

9.133 The 'appropriate regulator' is in general the FCA for injunctions against individuals, except where the matter concerns[1]:

- a breach of a requirement imposed by the PRA under the FSMA 2000, such as those contained in the PRA Handbook;

- breaches of certain EU provisions, specified by the Treasury[2], where the Treasury has also designated the PRA as the 'appropriate regulator'; and

- criminal offences where the PRA is the Regulator with the power to prosecute the offence[3].

1 FSMA 2000, s 380(8)–(11).
2 Under SI 2013/419.
3 Such offences are set out in the FSMA 2000, 401(3A), and include contravention of a prohibition order imposed by the PRA.

Restraining contraventions

9.134 The FSMA 2000 does not specify against whom an injunction to restrain a contravention can be made[1]. In principle, it could be made not only against the firm that would commit the contravention but also, where appropriate, against any individual, for example an employee or officer, who needs to be restrained in order to ensure that the contravention does not take place. Indeed, where the FCA is dealing with perimeter breaches by corporate bodies, it may often seek an injunction not only against the corporate body but also against those individuals who are involved. Save for perimeter breaches, though, the expectation is that it will ordinarily be sufficient to restrain the firm. Employees or officers are likely to be personally restrained only where there is some good reason for doing so. An injunction could in principle also be sought against an approved person who would otherwise fail to comply with a Statement of Principle or a senior person who does not comply with a rule applicable to him[2].

1 FSMA 2000, s 380(1).
2 The failure to comply would probably amount to the contravention of a 'relevant requirement' under s 380(1) and (6), which includes a requirement imposed by or under the FSMA 2000: see paras **2.101**, n 1 and **8.154** ff, n 2 above.

Remedying contraventions

9.135 An injunction to require a person to take steps to remedy or mitigate the effect of a contravention can be made against the person who committed the contravention (which could include a firm that committed a regulatory breach but also any employee who has failed to comply with a rule (or Statement of Principle) applicable to him[1]) and also against any person who appears to have been knowingly concerned in the firm's contravention[2]. The use of the phrase 'knowingly concerned' allows an injunction to be made against an employee or officer who, in broad terms, was knowingly involved in the breach[3]. But again, it will be comparatively rare that it is appropriate for the court to make an injunction against the employee or officer personally. An example of when it might be appropriate would be where a particular step that needs to be taken is required to be taken by the individual personally, for example because he has transferred to himself or a body controlled by him, assets which should be returned to the customer.

1 See para **8.147** ff above.
2 FSMA 2000, s 380(2).
3 The meaning of 'knowingly concerned' is considered at para **2.126** ff above.

Securing assets

9.136 An injunction to secure assets can be made against the person that committed the contravention[1] and also against any person knowingly concerned in a firm's contravention[2]. The purpose of an injunction of this nature is to secure assets in support of some other proceedings, to ensure that the relevant person does not dissipate his assets in order to defeat any judgment that might be made against him[3].

1 This includes not only a firm that has committed a regulatory breach but also an approved person who has failed to comply with a Statement of Principle: see para **8.147** ff above.
2 FSMA 2000, s 380(3)(b).
3 This is discussed in more detail at para **8.152** ff above.

Restitution orders

9.137 Restitution orders can be made either by the Regulators or by the court. The same conditions as those outlined at para **8.106** ff above are used in the FSMA 2000 to determine which Regulator is the 'appropriate regulator' to impose a restitution order. Save in cases of market abuse[1], the Regulators can only make a restitution order against a firm (ie an authorised person) or recognised investment exchange[2].

1 This is considered separately in **CHAPTER 17** below.
2 FSMA 2000, s 384(1).

9.138 The court can, however, make a restitution order against any person who commits a contravention, whether or not a firm[1] (this could, for example, include an employee who has failed to comply with a rule (or a Statement of Principle) applicable to him[2]). It can also make a restitution order against any person who was knowingly concerned in the contravention[3]. However, an order against an individual is unlikely to be a more efficient or effective means for securing compensation for consumers, save perhaps for certain perimeter enforcement cases, and is therefore unlikely normally to be in prospect.

1 FSMA 2000, s 382(1).
2 See para **8.147** ff above.
3 FSMA 2000, s 382(1). See also, more generally, the discussion of restitution orders at paras **8.100** ff above.

Chapter 10   FCA enforcement process

INTRODUCTION

An overview of Chapter 10

10.1   This chapter reviews the FCA's procedure where it wishes to impose disciplinary sanctions or take certain other enforcement action. It reviews the process that applies from the conclusion of the FCA's investigation until the question of disciplining the firm, or imposing the relevant sanction, is resolved by mutual agreement, finally determined by the FCA, or is referred to the Tax and Chancery Chamber of the Upper Tribunal (the Tribunal)[1]. The procedure that applies to cases referred to the Tribunal is reviewed in **CHAPTER 12** below. (Throughout this chapter for ease of reference the assumption is that it is a 'firm' facing disciplinary proceedings. However, an individual may equally be subject to the enforcement process.)

1 The Tribunal assumed the role previously held by the Financial Services and Markets Tribunal (FSMT) when the latter was abolished on 6 April 2010.

10.2   The question of whether the FCA will impose a disciplinary sanction must not be viewed in isolation. As has been seen[1], a regulatory breach may give rise to a range of potential consequences, only some of which are disciplinary in nature. The range of enforcement action that the FCA can take, and the circumstances when the FCA is likely to consider taking it, including its policy on the form or level of disciplinary action, is considered mainly in **CHAPTERS 8** and **9** above. The following paragraphs concentrate on the process.

1 A list of the actions the FCA can take is set out at para **5.89** above.

Other situations where the same procedure applies

10.3   The procedure outlined in this chapter, known as the warning/decision notice procedure, applies not only where the FCA wishes to take disciplinary action against firms and individuals who may have breached its rules, but also where the FCA seeks to take any of the following measures[1]:

- impose a restitution order[2];

- cancel a firm's permission otherwise than at its request[3];

- impose a prohibition order against an individual[4];

- withdraw the approval of an approved person or senior person[5];

- impose a sanction for market abuse[6];

- revoke the authorisation or, as appropriate, recognition of a unit trust scheme[7], an open-ended investment company[8], or a recognised collective investment scheme[9];

- disqualify an auditor or actuary[10];

- make a disapplication order in respect of a professional firm[11]; and

- decline applications to revoke or vary certain requirements, directions or orders that have already been imposed[12].

1   The warning/decision notice procedure also applies in certain non-enforcement situations, such as when the FCA proposes to refuse an application for Part 4 permission (see the FSMA 2000, ss 55V and 55X).
2   FSMA 2000, s 385 and see para **8.100** ff above.
3   FSMA 2000, s 55Z and see para **16.122** ff below.
4   FSMA 2000, s 57 and see para **9.99** ff above.
5   FSMA 2000, s 63 and see para **9.65** ff above. See para **2.52** ff above for an explanation of senior persons.
6   FSMA 2000, ss 126 and 127, and see para **17.155** ff below.
7   FSMA 2000, s 255.
8   FSMA 2000, s 262 and the Open-Ended Investment Companies Regulations 2001, SI 2001/1228.
9   FSMA 2000, s 280.
10   FSMA 2000, s 345 and see para **8.6** above.
11   FSMA 2000, s 331. As of the date of writing, this power has not been exercised: see the section of the FCA's Financial Services Register entitled 'Disapplication of Exemption', available at http://www.fsa.gov.uk/register/home.do.
12   FSMA 2000, ss 58, 200, 260, 269 or 331.

10.4   Most of the above measures are considered in detail elsewhere in this book. Where appropriate, reference is made to the warning/decision notice procedure outlined here and any specific points (for example, in relation to the contents of such notices or the identity of those on whom they must be served) are highlighted.

10.5   The above list is not, however, an exhaustive description of all the circumstances when the FCA can take enforcement action. An alternative procedure, known as the supervisory notice procedure, applies to certain other courses of action which the FSMA 2000 allows the FCA to take. The supervisory notice procedure is discussed in detail in para **16.130** ff below in the context of variations of permission, but is also applicable to other types of action[1]. Again, where the supervisory notice procedure is to be followed when taking a particular course of action, this is made clear in this book's discussion of the relevant action.

1 For a full list, see para **16.131** below.

10.6   Separate procedures, outlined in **CHAPTER 20** below, apply when the FCA exercises certain powers in relation to listed companies[1]. In this context, the FCA acts in accordance with the powers afforded to it under the FSMA 2000, Pt 6.

1 In practice, as is outlined in **CHAPTER 20** below, these procedures are very similar to those discussed here.

10.7   The procedures outlined in this chapter do not, amongst other things, apply to the FCA's decisions as to whether to exercise its information gathering and investigatory powers[1], to prosecute criminal offences[2], or to apply to the courts for injunctions, restitution[3] or insolvency orders[4]. The procedure that applies to each of these decisions is set out in this book where the action itself is considered. In addition, a modified procedure applies in relation to fines for the late submission of reports to the FCA[5].

1 These are discussed in **CHAPTERS 4** and **5** above.
2 This is outlined in **CHAPTER 18** below.
3 Injunctions and restitution orders are discussed in **CHAPTER 8** above.
4 Insolvency orders are not reviewed in this book. The FCA's powers in respect of insolvency are discussed in the FCA's Enforcement Guide at EG, Chapter 13.
5 For details, see the FCA Handbook at DEPP 6.6.1G–6.6.5G.

OUTLINE OF THE PROCEDURE

10.8   Before looking at the procedure in detail, it may be helpful to give an overview of how it works. The procedure is summarised in the diagram below. There are seven parts to the process, five of which are covered in this chapter.

10.9   The initial phase, which is outlined in **CHAPTERS 4** and **5** above, is the fact-finding investigation which will be undertaken by the FCA (or by an investigator on its behalf) when it becomes aware that a regulatory issue has arisen. The primary purpose of the investigatory stage is to give the FCA a proper understanding of the facts, so that it is in a position to assess properly what regulatory action should be taken.

10.10   The next phase (and the first phase covered in detail in this chapter) is the issue, by the FCA, of a Stage 1 Letter, inviting the firm to enter into settlement discussions. The Stage 1 Letter is issued at the latest at the same time as the preliminary findings letter (see para **10.11** below). The significance of a Stage 1 Letter is that the firm is given a reasonable period following the letter (typically 28 days) in which to reach a settlement. If the matter is settled within that period (the Stage 1 settlement period), the firm receives the maximum permitted discount

10.10 FCA enforcement process

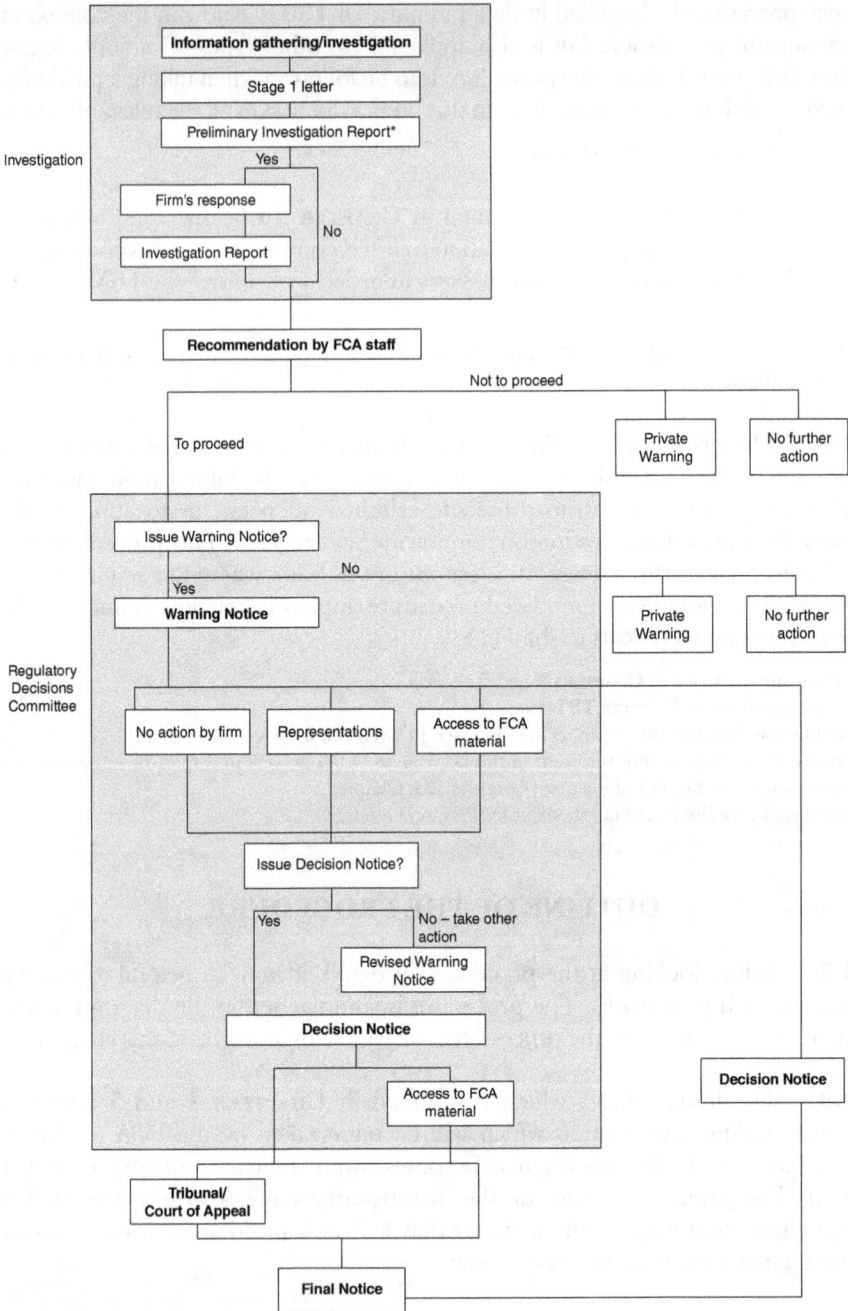

Investigation

- Information gathering/investigation
- Stage 1 letter
- Preliminary Investigation Report*
  - Yes
    - Firm's response
    - Investigation Report
  - No

Recommendation by FCA staff

- Not to proceed
  - Private Warning
  - No further action
- To proceed

Regulatory Decisions Committee

- Issue Warning Notice?
  - No
    - Private Warning
    - No further action
  - Yes
    - Warning Notice
      - No action by firm
      - Representations
      - Access to FCA material
    - Issue Decision Notice?
      - Yes
      - No – take other action
        - Revised Warning Notice
      - Decision Notice
        - Access to FCA material

Decision Notice

Tribunal/ Court of Appeal

Final Notice

* Not always done

(30%) (see para **10.46** below). A Stage 1 letter may be preceeded by discussions between the firm and the FCA, in which the parties may explore the extent to which there is common ground between the parties, and the potential scope for settlement. In some cases, the FCA may provide to the firm a draft warning notice, along with the Stage 1 letter. The FCA may continue to investigate the matter after the issue of the Stage 1 Letter.

10.11 The third phase (and the second phase covered in detail in this chapter) arises where the FCA's investigation is nearing its conclusion. During this phase, the FCA may issue a preliminary findings letter, normally annexing a Preliminary Investigation Report (PIR)[1], giving the firm an opportunity to agree with, dispute, or correct the facts as the FCA then sees them. Having done so, and having considered the response, the FCA staff concerned will decide whether or not to make a recommendation to the decision-making body in order to set the enforcement process in motion. In some circumstances, no preliminary findings letter will be issued[2].

1 FCA Enforcement Guide at EG 4.30.
2 This includes where: (a) the firm consents not to receive a preliminary findings letter; (b) the FCA determines that it is not practicable to send a preliminary findings letter in light of public policy considerations, including the need for urgent action in the interests of consumer protection or reducing financial crime; or (c) the FCA believes that no useful purpose would be achieved in sending a preliminary findings letter. See the FCA Enforcement Guide at EG 4.31.

10.12 The fourth phase (also covered in this chapter)[1] is the consideration of the recommendation and, if appropriate, the issue of a 'warning notice' by the FCA, a decision which, in most cases, will be made by a body called the Regulatory Decisions Committee (RDC)[2]. As set out below, whilst the RDC is a committee of the FCA, it is separate from the enforcement staff who investigated the matter. It is the RDC that decides whether to commence the enforcement process by issuing a warning notice, informing the firm that the FCA proposes to take a particular course of action against it and giving it the opportunity: (i) to review the material on which the FCA relied and any secondary material which, in the FCA's opinion, might undermine the FCA's decision[3]; and (ii) make representations.

1 See para **10.96** ff below.
2 The RDC was created as the decision-making body for disciplinary actions brought by the Financial Services Authority. During the passage of the Financial Services (Banking Reform) Act 2012 through Parliament, amendments were tabled that would have replaced the RDC with an independent decision making body for decisions of the PRA and FCA but independent of both. These proposals were withdrawn but there will be a review of the RDC, which may lead to changes to the decision-making process for both the FCA and PRA.
3 FSMA 2000, s 394.

10.13 The fifth phase (also covered in this chapter)[1] takes place after representations have been made. Then the RDC reaches a decision on what is the appropriate action to take and if it decides that it should continue with the action that was previously proposed, it will issue a 'decision notice'. If it proposes to take a different course of action, then it may need to discontinue the action that was commenced and issue another warning notice. Once a decision notice has been issued, although the matter has been decided so far as the FCA is concerned, it has still not been finally determined from the firm's point of view, as the firm has the right to refer the matter for consideration by the Tribunal.

1 See para **10.162** ff below.

10.14   The next phase may therefore be a reference to the Tribunal, which is an independent Superior Court of Record run by the Ministry of Justice as part of HM Courts & Tribunals Service. The nature of the Tribunal and the procedure for appearing before it are reviewed in **CHAPTER 12** below. It is important to appreciate that the Tribunal is not an appellate body, but a tribunal of first instance, that is able to consider all the evidence, whether or not it was originally available to the FCA, and in the majority of cases can reach its own decision as to what action it is appropriate for the FCA to take. As such, the Tribunal can potentially increase, as well as decrease, the sanction that was originally to be imposed. In some cases (other than disciplinary cases) the Tribunal has a more limited mandate (see para **12.151**). In some circumstances, there may be a right of appeal from the Tribunal, but only on points of law.

10.15   The final phase[1], and the fifth phase covered in detail by this chapter, is what happens when the action proposed by the FCA takes effect, either because the firm has elected not to refer the matter to the Tribunal, or because the Tribunal has reached a decision and any appeals from it have been disposed of. At this stage, the FCA issues a 'final notice' and the action takes effect.

1 See para **10.188** ff below.

10.16   Very little of this process is set out in the FSMA 2000 and this allows the FCA some flexibility as to how the process should take effect. For example, the FSMA 2000 does not require the FCA to issue a preliminary findings letter. The FSMA 2000 only contains the underlying framework which requires warning notices, decision notices and final notices to be issued in certain circumstances and provides that certain decisions require a separation of functions within the FCA. It also provides some protections for those firms that are subjected to the process. The details of the procedure are to be found in the FCA's rules and, in particular, in the Decision Procedure and Penalties Manual (DEPP) and the Enforcement Guide (EG).

10.17   Although the procedure consists of a number of phases, and in complex or contested cases is likely to take a long time to complete, it does not always need to be lengthy and complicated[1]. The procedure has to fit a range of different scenarios applying to the entire regulated community, from individual IFAs to international investment banks, from insurers to listed companies and from single issue problems to complex disputes involving several firms and/or individuals and large numbers of consumers. Before turning to these phases, the following paragraphs first set out the nature of the enforcement procedure followed by the FCA.

1 For cases completed during 2012/13, the FSA has reported the average length of those cases, from the date of referral to enforcement to the conclusion of the case, as a result of: (a) settlement (19.6 months); (b) subsequent referral to the RDC (37.8 months); and (c) subsequent to referral to the Tribunal (50.1 months). See the Financial Services Authority's Enforcement Annual Performance Account 2012/13, para 55.

NATURE OF THE PROCEDURE

What is the regime designed to achieve?

10.18   The form of the disciplinary process was the subject of a great deal of debate in the consultation process which preceded the FSMA 2000. Two main concerns arose. First, a tension was seen to arise between the need for an efficient and effective process from the point of view of the FSA (as it then was) and the need for the process to be fair from the point of view of those subjected to it. Second, the process had to comply with the European Convention on Human Rights (ECHR) fair trial guarantees implemented in the UK by the Human Rights Act 1998.

Impact of the Human Rights Act 1998

10.19   The Human Rights Act 1998 requires public bodies, such as the FCA, to act in a way that is ECHR compatible. That includes, among other things, the right under Article 6(1), where a person's civil rights and obligations or any criminal charge against him are being determined, to a fair trial within a reasonable time by an independent and impartial tribunal established by law[1]. It has since become accepted that FCA enforcement proceedings involve the determination of firms' civil rights and obligations, attracting this protection[2].

1   For an outline of the safeguards that this involves, see para **10.25** ff below.
2   See for example, *König v Germany (1978) 2 EHRR 170, Le Compte, Van Leuven and De Meyere v Belgium (1982) 4 EHRR 1, Albert and Le Compte v Belgium (1983) 5 EHRR 533* and *Benthem v Netherlands (1986) 8 EHRR 1. In R v Securities and Futures Authority, ex p Fleurose [2002] IRLR 297*, it was common ground that Article 6(1) applied to the disciplinary proceedings in question.

10.20   Moreover, certain types of enforcement proceedings have been held to constitute the determination of a 'criminal charge' for ECHR purposes, requiring the application of various additional safeguards under Article 6(2) and (3)[1]. Whether a particular matter will amount to a civil matter or the determination of a 'criminal charge' depends upon three main factors taken into account by the ECHR[2], namely:

- how the matter is characterised under English law (if it is described as 'criminal', that will normally be determinative; however, if it is described as 'civil', this will only be a factor to be taken into account);

- the nature of the offence, including whether it overlaps with criminal law and, significantly in this context, whether the offence can be committed by people generally or only by particular groups of people; and

- the nature and level of penalty.

1   For a brief outline of some of the main safeguards involved, see para **17.18** ff below.
2   See in particular, *Engel v Netherlands (1976) 1 EHRR 647* and, for a further discussion, see *Human Rights Practice, (loose-leaf)* Simor and Emmerson, June 2000, at para 6.046.

10.21   In *R v Securities and Futures Authority, ex p Fleurose*[1], the Court of Appeal held that disciplinary proceedings under the pre-FSMA regime were not criminal for

ECHR purposes. The main reasons for reaching that conclusion apply equally under the FSMA 2000[2]. However, the issue is assessed on a case-by-case basis and, as was recognised in *Fleurose*, there may be some disciplinary proceedings whose characteristics are so akin to criminal proceedings that the concept of fairness requires more or less the same protections in both. For example, the Financial Services and Markets Tribunal (FSMT, the predecessor to the Tribunal) held that market abuse is a criminal charge within the meaning of Article 6 of the ECHR[3].

1 *[2002] IRLR 297*. See also *Han & Yau v Commissioners of Customs and Excise [2001] EWCA Civ 1048* and *Official Receiver v Stern [2001] EWCA Civ 111, [2000] 1 WLR 2230*, which were both examined by the Court of Appeal.
2 Primarily, that the fines imposed are recoverable as a civil debt, and that the regime applies not to society as a whole, but only to those who have 'volunteered' to be subject to it.
3 See *Davidson v FSA (2006)*. The FSMT held that the civil burden of proof (balance of probabilities, rather than beyond reasonable doubt) should apply, but that the standard was flexible in its application – thus the more serious the allegation, the stronger the evidence needed by the FCA to establish the case. This reflects the common-law position that the more serious the allegation the more cogent is the evidence required to overcome the unlikelihood of what is alleged (see *In re Dellow's Will Trusts [1964] 1 WLR 451* at 455 and *In re H (Minors) [1996] AC 563* at 586). However, the House of Lords has expressly disapproved of this 'sliding scale' standard of proof. See: *In re B (Children) (Care Proceedings: Standard of Proof) [2009] 1 AC 11 (HL)*, and *In re D [2008] 1 WLR 1499 (HL)*.

10.22 The system that was devised to resolve that tension gives the FCA the ability, and authority, to take enforcement decisions, but only after it complies with four important safeguards. First, the decisions themselves are not to be taken by the FCA staff responsible for the investigation[1] but are instead placed in the hands of a separate body, the RDC, which, although answerable to the FCA Board, is otherwise intended to be independent from the FCA[2]. Second, the system was intended to place a heavy emphasis on the settlement of cases and includes discounts for early settlement, and scope for mediation[3]. Third, it allows the decision to be reviewed in its entirety by a wholly independent tribunal, the Tribunal, which has a wide remit and, whose primary task is to decide what action it is appropriate for the FCA to take in the particular case. It can also make recommendations about the FCA's procedures[4]. Fourth, the decision does not take effect until the Tribunal process (and any subsequent right of appeal) is exhausted or the firm has foregone the opportunity to take advantage of it. The firm's ability to have its case reviewed in its entirety by the Tribunal was also seen as ensuring that the process would fulfil the ECHR fair trial guarantees[5].

1 Note that certain decisions are taken by FCA staff, including when settlements are implemented: see para **10.56** ff below.
2 For a detailed discussion of the RDC, see para **10.25** ff below.
3 See the discussion of the penalty discount scheme for early settlement in para **10.46** ff below, and the discussion of the mediation scheme in para **10.60** ff below.
4 For a detailed discussion of the Tribunal process, see **CHAPTER 12** below.
5 These are outlined at para **12.26** ff below.

10.23 The FSMA 2000 provides the framework and the FCA's rules fill in the details. Whilst the two were developed in tandem, there is nothing to prevent the FCA from amending its rules in the future to create a different structure as long as it complies with the statutory framework.

10.24   The enforcement process was subject to a fundamental review in 2005 (the Enforcement Process Review), as a result of criticisms of the FSA's procedures by the Tribunal in *Legal & General Assurance Society Ltd v FSA*[1]. The recommendations of the review, all of which were accepted by the FSA, were published in July 2005[2].

1   *Legal & General Assurance Society Ltd v FSA [2005] All ER (D) 154 (Jan)*.
2   FSA Consultation Paper (CP05/11) 'Enforcement process review – Handbook changes'.

THE REGULATORY DECISIONS COMMITTEE

10.25   The FCA's procedure in relation to the giving of warning and decision notices is required to ensure, among other things, that the decision which gives rise to the obligation to issue the notice is taken by a person who is not directly involved in establishing the evidence upon which that decision is based, or by two or more persons, at least one of whom was not directly involved in establishing the evidence on which the decision is based[1].

1   FSMA 2000, s 395(2). The decision must be made: (a) by a person not directly involved in establishing the evidence on which the decision is based; or, (b) by two or more persons who include a person not directly involved in establishing that evidence. Where the FSMA 2000 requires the supervisory notice procedure to be followed (see para **10.5** above), rather than the warning/decision notice procedure, an exception to this rule may be available where the FCA considers that it is necessary to depart from the rule in order to advance one or more of its operational objectives: see paras **16.135** and **16.218** below and the FSMA 2000, s 395(3).

10.26   The FCA's procedures therefore need to ensure that a separation of functions exists, between those within the FCA who investigate and the independent person, or persons, involved in taking the resulting enforcement decisions. The requirement for a separation of functions should not only be seen as a statutory requirement with which the FCA needs to comply, but also as an important part of ensuring that the regulated community sees the procedure as being fair and thereby increasing the likelihood of settlement[1]. The FCA's answer to this is the Regulatory Decisions Committee (RDC)[2], which was created to take most of the decisions that involve the giving of warning and decision notices (as well as certain other notices known as supervisory notices which are discussed in more detail in **CHAPTER 16** below)[3].

1   See the discussion at para **10.18** ff above.
2   Although, as mentioned above, the RDC process will undergo an independent review in 2014.
3   For a full list of those decisions for which the RDC is solely responsible, see the FCA Handbook at DEPP 2.5.7G–2.5.8G and 2.5.10G.

10.27   The RDC is a committee of the FCA Board empowered to exercise certain regulatory powers on its behalf. It is accountable to the FCA Board for the decisions that it takes[1], but is not involved in establishing the underlying evidence. It is not a judicial body, but rather an administrative decision-making body.

1   FCA Handbook at DEPP 3.1.1G, and para **10.30** below.

10.28   The RDC is outside the FCA's management structure[1] and is supported by its own legal advisers and administrative staff, the RDC Office, who are also separate from those members of the FCA staff involved in conducting investigations and making recommendations to the RDC[2].

1 See the FCA Handbook at DEPP 3.1.2G, although it is accountable to the FCA Board as is stated at para **10.30** below.
2 FCA Handbook at DEPP 3.1.3G.

Who are the RDC members and how are they appointed?

10.29   RDC members are current and recently retired practitioners who possess financial services industry skills and knowledge and also some non-practitioners[1]. The RDC consists of[2]:

- a Chairman, who is employed by the FCA[3] and is appointed by the FCA Board; and

- one or more Deputy Chairmen and a panel of other members, appointed by the FCA Board. They are not employees of the FCA.

All members are appointed for fixed periods. They may be removed by the FCA Board but only in the event of misconduct or incapacity[4].

1 Biographies of each member of the RDC are available on the FCA's website at: http://www.fca.org.uk/about/structure/committees/rdc-biographies.
2 FCA Handbook at DEPP 3.2.2G.
3 FCA Handbook at DEPP 3.1.2G.
4 FCA Handbook at DEPP 3.1.2G(2).

To whom does the RDC report?

10.30   The RDC is accountable to the FCA Board[1] in respect of its procedures, policies and general arrangements, while retaining its independence in relation to its individual decisions. Although the FCA Board will not intervene in individual RDC decisions, the FCA Board is, nevertheless, ultimately responsible for ensuring that the RDC is adequately briefed on relevant FCA policies[2].

1 FCA Handbook at DEPP 3.1.1G.
2 The Enforcement Process Review called for regular briefings to the RDC on the FCA's policies.

Is the RDC independent?

10.31   The RDC fulfils the statutory requirement for the separation of functions within the FCA, in that it is not directly involved in obtaining the evidence upon which its decisions are based. This is all that is required by the FSMA 2000.

The procedure of the RDC

10.32   The RDC will either meet as a full committee or in panels[1]. At present, each meeting must include the Chairman or a Deputy Chairman, who will chair the meeting, and at least two other members. The composition and size of the panels, and the pattern of their meetings may vary depending on the nature of the particular matter under consideration and is a matter for the Chairman or Deputy[2]. Such flexibility is to allow for the composition of the most suitable panels to consider particular cases.

1 FCA Handbook at DEPP 3.2.2G.
2 In situations where the issuance of a warning notice, decision notice or supervisory notice is deemed 'straightforward', or the issuance of a supervisory notice is deemed urgent, the Chairman or Deputy Chairman may take the decision alone or with one or more other RDC members. See the FCA Handbook at DEPP 3.3 and 3.4. For more information concerning supervisory notices, see also para **16.130** ff below.

10.33 In cases where representations are made to the RDC by affected parties, it is usual for the warning notice panel to be supplemented at the decision notice stage by additional members of the RDC who have not previously considered the matter[1]. If no representations are made, the warning notice and decision notice panels will usually be the same.

1 FCA Handbook at DEPP 3.2.3G.

10.34 The RDC will seek to avoid inviting a member to join a panel to consider a matter in which the member has a potential conflict of interest[1]. Members of the RDC are required to declare any potential conflicts of interest to the Chairman, and to the RDC Office[2] and, where the Chairman considers it reasonable and appropriate, will be required to stand down from considering any particular matter. The Chairman is also required to declare any conflicts of interest and must do so to the Chairman of the FCA. Similarly, the Deputy Chairman of the RDC must disclose any potential conflict to the Chairman of the RDC, or if unavailable, the Chairman of the FCA[3]. It is notable that any such conflicts will not be declared to the firm concerned, and are only addressed within the RDC, although disclosures of, and steps taken to manage, potential conflicts will be recorded by the RDC Office[4].

1 FCA Handbook at DEPP 3.2.4G.
2 For example, members may have shares in a listed company against whom action is being considered.
3 FCA Handbook at DEPP 3.2.5G.
4 FCA Handbook at DEPP 3.2.6G.

10.35 Meetings of the RDC are held in private[1], and are conducted in the manner that the RDC considers suitable so as to enable it to determine fairly and expeditiously the matters under consideration[2]. There is, therefore, flexibility in the procedure that can be adopted in RDC meetings, subject to the overriding requirement for fairness. As is noted below, a record will be kept of RDC meetings, although usually firms will have no means of gaining access to these records[3].

1 FCA Handbook at DEPP 3.2.1G.
2 FCA Handbook at DEPP 3.2.7G.
3 Firms may consider such records to be relevant given that they will show how the members of the RDC have voted and whether any particular issues were raised.

10.36 The RDC may require FCA staff to attend its meetings to provide: additional information about the matter; to explain any aspect of the FCA staff recommendation or accompanying papers; or, information as to the FCA's priorities and policies, including the FCA's view as to correct interpretation of the law[1]. The staff may, for example, present the RDC with the previous disciplinary record of the firm and may also draw to its attention the general compliance history of the firm. The RDC may not, however, consider the previous disciplinary record of the firm for the purpose of establishing a breach that has occurred subsequently, although the firm's compliance history may be relevant to the decision whether to take action and, if so, what sanction should be imposed in a disciplinary case[2], and that would clearly be the purpose of drawing it to the RDC's attention. Such communications between the RDC and FCA enforcement staff will be recorded and disclosed to the firm[3].

1 FCA Handbook at DEPP 3.2.10G.
2 See for example, the list of matters relevant to the FCA's decision as to the nature of the disciplinary action (if any), in the FCA Handbook at DEPP 6.2.1G(3) and the FCA Handbook at DEPP 6.4.2G(6), and the list of matters relevant to the amount of a fine to be levied against a firm, the FCA Handbook at DEPP 6.5A.3G(2)(i), discussed further in para **8.61** ff above.
    From a firm's perspective it would be preferable for this information to be withheld from the RDC, when it considers whether to issue a warning notice, until the RDC reaches a view on whether or not the alleged breaches took place. There will otherwise be the risk that the information will improperly influence the RDC or, at least, undermine the perceived fairness of the process.
3 FCA Handbook at DEPP 3.2.14G(4).

10.37 In reaching its decisions the RDC will apply relevant statutory provisions by considering the overall context of the matter itself. The RDC will therefore give consideration to not only the relevant facts and applicable law but also to the FCA's own priorities and policies, including those that are set out in the FCA Handbook[1]. Thus, for example, where the FCA Handbook sets out the FCA's policy on a particular matter, such as whether to take disciplinary action against an individual, or as to the amount of a fine, the RDC is likely to apply the same policy. The RDC will also take into account the FCA's own policies with regards to matters of legal interpretation.

1 FCA Handbook at DEPP 1.2.7G.

10.38 Each member of the RDC present is entitled to vote on the matter under consideration, and the Chairman of the meeting will have a casting vote if that is required[1].

1 FCA Handbook at DEPP 3.2.8G.

10.39 In relation to each decision, the RDC Office keeps a record of the meetings and representations (if any) and materials considered by the decision-makers[1]. The RDC Office is also required to record and fully document all disclosures of potential conflicts of interest and the steps that were taken to manage them[2]. These requirements were intended to improve the accountability of the RDC. However, in practice firms are not generally given access to such records save where they relate to substantive communications between the enforcement staff and the RDC or are records of representations made to the RDC[3].

1 FCA Handbook at DEPP 1.2.8G.
2 See para **10.34** above.
3 See the discussion at para **10.122** below.

10.40 Finally, the RDC Office which has its own small dedicated legal function, is responsible for finalising warning notices and drafting decision notices[1].

1 See the FCA Handbook at DEPP 2.2.3G(3) in relation to warning notices, and the FCA Handbook at DEPP 2.3.1G(3) in relation to decision notices.

THE PROCEDURE IN DETAIL

Phase 1 – fact finding investigation

10.41 As outlined in para **10.9** ff above, phase 1 (the FCA's fact-finding investigation) is outlined in **CHAPTERS 4–6**.

Phase 2 – the Stage 1 Letter

10.42 The next phase (and the first phase covered in this chapter) is the issue, by the FCA, of a Stage 1 Letter, inviting the firm to enter into settlement discussions. The settlement of disciplinary and other regulatory enforcement issues has always been an important part of the regulatory regime. This remains the case and the present regime is intended to facilitate this process.

10.43 Settlement discussions are informal discussions, held on a 'without prejudice' basis with the intention that the firm and the FCA come to an agreement as to how to conclude the enforcement process. In practice, questions of settlement often arise early in the enforcement process and settlement discussions may be initiated at any stage of the enforcement process if both parties agree[1], even before the FCA's investigation has been concluded. However, the FCA has stated that it will only engage in settlement discussions once it has a sufficient understanding of the nature and gravity of the suspected misconduct to make a reasonable assessment of the appropriate outcome[2]. For that reason, the FCA are unlikely to entertain an offer to enter into settlement discussions before the issuance of a Stage 1 Letter[3].

1 FCA Enforcement Guide at EG 5.6.
2 FCA Enforcement Guide at EG 5.7.
3 For discussion of the Stage 1 Letter, see para **10.69** ff below.

10.44 Whenever the question of settlement is considered, therefore, the firm must evaluate whether it is in a position to conduct settlement discussions, given the level of its own understanding of what has occurred, and, in addition, whether discussions with the FCA staff are likely to be fruitful at that stage, in light of their understanding of the case and expectations. For example, the firm may need to consider whether discussions would be more productive once the investigation has been concluded and a report produced or even at a later stage, once the RDC has considered the matter and has issued a warning notice[1]. In some cases, settlement discussions may be appropriate after a decision notice has been issued, for example, where the firm does not wish to dispute the issue of liability but strongly disagrees with the level of sanction or the precise wording of the decision notice. As this indicates, what is appropriate will vary from case to case.

1 Typically, it is only once the warning notice has been issued that the firm knows precisely what is alleged against it and what sanction is proposed. However, in the context of settlement discussions, the firm may wish to ask the FCA to produce a draft warning notice, which can form the basis of any discussions.

10.45 Incentives for early settlement exist, involving a scale of discounts of penalties[1], with the discounts varying in accordance with the stage at which the settlement is reached[2].

1 For the purpose of the settlement discount scheme, 'penalties' means financial penalties, periods of suspension or periods of restriction that would be imposed upon a firm or individual following a finding of a breach. See the FCA Handbook at DEPP 6.7 and the FCA Enforcement Guide at EG 5.14.
2 FCA Handbook at DEPP 6.7 and FCA Enforcement Guide at EG 5.14–5.19A.

10.46 For this purpose, an enforcement case is split into three stages and varying levels of discount apply to settlements reached at each of the stages detailed below[1]:

- Stage 1 – 30% discount: This discount is available in the period from commencement of investigation until the end of the period for a firm to reach agreement as to the amount of the penalty following the issuance of the Stage 1 Letter (Stage 1). The Stage 1 Letter is intended to demonstrate that the FCA has a sufficient understanding of the nature and gravity of the breach to make a reasonable assessment of the appropriate penalty and may include a draft statutory notice detailing the alleged rule breaches and proposed penalty[2]. Given the objective of the Stage 1 Letter, the timing of a Stage 1 Letter will vary from case to case but the latest point at which a Stage 1 Letter may be issued is when the FCA staff issues the PIR[3]. The Stage 1 Letter will then permit the firm reasonable opportunity, typically 28 days, to reach agreement as to the amount of the penalty;

- Stage 2 – 20% discount: This discount is available in the period from the end of Stage 1 until the date on which a firm makes its written representations in response to a warning notice, or the date on which the period of time for making such written representations expires;

- Stage 3 – 10% discount: This discount is available in the period from the end of Stage 2 until the giving of a decision notice.

1 For discussion of how settlement discounts affect calculation of financial penalties, see paras **8.80** ff and **8.95** above.
2 FCA Enforcement Guide at EG 5.17.
3 FCA Enforcement Guide at EG 5.18.

10.47 There are two potential practical difficulties with this system. First, if the FCA issues a Stage 1 Letter before the PIR (and the Stage 1 Letter does not fully set out all the evidence against the firm), or is unrealistic in its own expectations (for example, by putting forward charges that are unsupported by the evidence), then firms may be deprived of the opportunity of reaching an early settlement and benefiting from the discount. Accordingly, in exceptional cases where a settlement should have been reached but, because of unreasonable FCA behaviour, was not reached, there may be an element of 'backtracking' the discount[1]. Second, if the process is to work properly, the FCA must be disciplined when setting levels of penalty and must ensure that an appropriate settlement is not lost solely because a high starting figure is put forward as a basis for negotiation, rather than a proper figure at which the FCA is prepared to settle.

1 FCA Handbook at DEPP 6.7.4G.

10.48 The firm should also recognise that a negotiated settlement with the FCA is different from settlement in the commercial sense. In light of the FCA's statutory objectives and its accountability to Parliament (discussed at **CHAPTER 1** above), the bargaining power of the firm with the FCA is very different to what it would be when negotiating settlement with a commercial counterparty. For that reason, the best opportunity a firm may have to reduce any penalty against it may be to agree to early settlement.

10.49 In practice, the vast majority of enforcement actions against firms have been settled at Stage 1. Enforcement actions to date show that individuals tend to feel a lesser need than firms to reach a settlement with the FCA, especially where they feel the need to be fully vindicated so as to preserve their reputation or to ensure that they can continue to work within the industry.

Does the firm have to take part in settlement discussions?

10.50 There is no requirement upon the firm to engage in settlement discussions with the FCA. Such a requirement would not sit easily with the consensual nature of the settlement process. Having said that, there are, generally speaking, strong reasons militating in favour of at least exploring the possibility of settlement with the FCA including not only the discounts for early settlement but also avoiding the substantial cost and management time which is likely to be involved when pursuing a case to its conclusion.

With whom are settlement discussions held?

10.51 The discussions are held with FCA staff[1], rather than with the RDC. Any decision by the FCA to settle will be taken by two members of the FCA's senior management, one of whom will be at least director of division level and the other of whom will be of at least head of department level (referred to in the FCA Handbook as the 'settlement decision makers')[2]. Settlement discussions will usually be with the enforcement staff who carried out the investigation into the firm, and it is possible that the FCA settlement decision makers may be involved in settlement discussions with the firm[3]. It is difficult to give guidance in the abstract on the nature of the settlement discussions and as to how the firm should approach them. This will very much depend on the nature of the breach alleged, the action that the FCA proposes to take, the level of the firm's understanding of the problem, the significance and potential implications of the matter for the firm and what it seeks to achieve in the settlement discussions, and finally, its relationship with the regulator and more particularly the enforcement staff involved.

1 FCA Handbook at DEPP 5.1.
2 See the FCA Handbook at DEPP 5.1.1G(3). A settlement decision maker will not have been directly involved in establishing the evidence on which the decision is based (DEPP 5.1.1G(4)). Also see the FCA Enforcement Guide at EG 5.5.
3 FCA Handbook at DEPP 5.1.5G.

Can the firm be candid with the FCA in its settlement discussions?

10.52 The FCA and the firm will generally agree that any discussions take place on a without prejudice basis and that neither party may subsequently rely on admissions or statements made in the context of the discussions or documents recording the discussions[1]. No publicity should normally result.

1 FCA Handbook at DEPP 5.1.4G.

10.53 Where the FCA and the firm agree that the discussions should be held on a without prejudice basis, this gives a certain amount of protection to the discussions. The doctrine of 'without prejudice' protects the firm in two ways. First, it means that any admissions made in the discussions cannot subsequently be used against it in regulatory proceedings. Second, it gives the discussions a protection similar to that which applies where legal privilege exists. This broadly means that the firm cannot be required to disclose documents relating to the discussions to any third party[1]. This is significant because, as already highlighted[2], firms need to have in mind the risk of creating unattractive documents which could be useful to third parties who may wish to bring legal proceedings against the firm arising from the same matter. Documents that are genuinely without prejudice should mostly be protected[3]. A court will, however, want to see that documents labelled as being 'without prejudice' are properly so called[4]. That should not be a problem in the disciplinary context.

1 This is the position in a civil court. If the question of whether a document should be disclosed is considered in a regulatory context, note that without prejudice communications are not specifically protected under the FSMA 2000: see para **5.58** above.
2 See para **4.145** ff above.
3 See *Rush & Tomkins Ltd v Greater London Council [1989] AC 1280, HL, Unilever plc v Proctor & Gamble Co [2001] 1 All ER 783, CA* and *Muller v Linsley & Mortimer [1996] PNLR 74, CA*, and see the discussion at at para **4.169** above.
4 See for example, *Buckinghamshire County Council v Moran [1989] 2 All ER 225, CA; South Shropshire District Council v Amos [1987] 1 All ER 340, CA; The Prudential Assurance Company Ltd v HE Prudential Insruance Company of America [2002] EWHC 2809 (Ch).*

10.54 There are various caveats to this protection[1]. Matters that have been disclosed to the regulator in the context of without prejudice discussions will inevitably remain in the regulator's mind and if they give rise to any additional points that are seen to need to be addressed, then the FCA may well, subsequently, seek to deal with those points. Second, the firm's admissions may form the basis of the terms that are finally agreed and may therefore be outlined in the decision notice and the subsequent final notice that is published by the FCA, in which case they will become publicly known. Any admissions of breaches could then form the basis of civil claims brought by third parties[2].

1   See the discussion at para **4.169** above.
2   See para **10.75** below and, generally, **CHAPTER 19** below.

What happens if a settlement is reached?

10.55   The following factors should be contemplated when addressing the final terms of any settlement agreement:

* whether the agreement is in full and final settlement. If it is, whether it will only relate to the parties concerned[1], the period of time that has been investigated and the specific third parties believed to be prejudiced;

* when the FCA intends to impose the proposed sanction and the period the firm will have to pay[2];

* the wording of any final notice[3] and accompanying press release[4];

* whether the agreement should expressly provide that the settlement agreement is to be confidential.

1   Third parties, such as employees, will generally have some involvement in any breach, and possibly the right to make representations before any decision notice is issued. Alternatively, for example, a market counterparty or appointed representative may also be involved.
2   See para **10.192** below.
3   See para **10.192** ff below.
4   See para **10.195** below.

10.56   If the FCA staff and firm are able to agree terms, that will not automatically be the end of the matter. The settlement must be approved by the FCA taking the formal decision to issue the statutory notice that contains its terms. The decision to issue that notice is taken by the FCA's settlement decision makers[1]. This process does not, however, involve the RDC[2]. Further, third parties who have been accorded rights on the issue of the warning notice may make representations on the form of the decision notice. These representations are considered by the executive decision-makers who have decided on the settlement.

1   See para **10.51** above. At least one, and sometimes both, settlement decision makers are from the Enforcement division. In particularly important cases the managing directors, the Chief Executive and even the FCA Board could become involved. See FCA Handbook at DEPP 5.1.1G.
2   The FCA Handbook states in relation to settlements (at DEPP 5.1.8 G(2)) that 'if the proposed action by the FCA has been submitted to the RDC for consideration, it will be for the RDC to decide: … (b) if representations have been made in response to a warning notice … whether to proceed to give a decision notice …'. Elsewhere, however, DEPP 5 suggests that the FCA's settlement decision makers will decide on any settlement, even one that is entered into after representations have been made in response to a warning notice (see DEPP 5.1.3G, 5.1.6G(1), and 5.1.7G(1)). In practice, the FCA may involve the RDC internally before agreeing to any settlement entered into after the stage at which representations have been made in response to a warning notice.

10.57 To ensure consistency between settlements reached and decisions made by the RDC, regular discussions are supposed to be held between the settlement decision makers and the RDC.

10.58 In reaching a settlement with the FCA, the firm must keep in mind the other potential regulatory consequences that may arise from the same matter. If it admits a breach in order to settle a disciplinary case, will it find that the admission is used as the basis for the imposition of a restitution order or a prohibition order against one of its employees? It will be important, so far as is possible, to bring an end to all potential regulatory consequences at the same time.

What happens if a settlement cannot be reached?

10.59 If the FCA staff and the firm cannot reach settlement then, in some circumstances, it is possible that the matter may proceed to mediation[1]. Alternatively, or where mediation has failed, it will proceed to the decision notice stage[2] after the person has made representations to the RDC (if this has not already been done).

1 See para **10.60** ff below.
2 See para **10.162** ff below.

The opportunity to mediate

10.60 Mediation is a non-binding dispute resolution process, frequently used in commercial litigation situations to aid parties to reach settlement in a quick and cost-effective way. It involves a neutral third party appointed by third parties, who acts as a mediator and engages in shuttle diplomacy between the parties. The mediator does not evaluate each party's case. He is there purely to facilitate discussions (on the basis of agreed terms negotiated between the parties and delimited in a mediation agreement that is signed by the FCA, the firm or individual and the selected mediator) and to help the parties to reach an agreed settlement. The FCA allows mediation to be used in appropriate cases[1].

1 See the FCA Handbook at DEPP 5.1.9G and the FCA Enforcement Guide at EG 5.20–5.21. The detailed information formerly provided in the FCA Handbook at DEC Appendix 1 has not been duplicated in either the DEPP or FCA Enforcement Guide. However, some basic guidance on mediation is also available on the FCA's website at: http://www.fca.org.uk/firms/being-regulated/enforcement/how-we-enforce-the-law/settlement-mediation.

When can mediation take place?

10.61 Mediation is intended to supplement the informal settlement discussions likely to take place between the person concerned and the FCA enforcement staff where the parties consider that the involvement of a neutral mediator may facilitate further progress. Although mediation may take place at any time during the enforcement process, the FCA considers that it is most likely to be of use in the period following the issue of the warning notice since, at that point, the firm will have access to the material upon which the RDC has relied in its decision to commence disciplinary proceedings[1]. From the firm's point of view, it may not want to mediate before a warning notice has been issued, since it may not be aware of the exact extent of the allegations that it faces or the precise facts that underlie those allegations[2]. Mediation is generally only available once during the enforcement process and this means that the firm will have to make a difficult decision as to when to propose mediation.

1 See para **10.118** ff below.
2 For example, where the evidence pointing to the breach has come from a third party. See para **10.74** below for consideration of how the FCA's use of material that has not yet been disclosed to the firm may similarly impact on the firm's ability to reply to a preliminary findings letter.

Does the firm always have the right to mediate?

10.62 Neither party is obliged to submit a case for mediation, since mediation is a consensual process. There are certain categories of case where the FCA consider that mediation is not appropriate. Aside from these categories, however, it appears from the wording of the rules and the FCA's guidance that the FCA is likely to at least consider entry into mediation discussions in most other circumstances[1].

1 The section on mediation on the FCA's website indicates that there are relatively few disciplinary cases in which mediation will not be available, the notable exceptions being cases involving allegations of criminal conduct and those requiring urgent action, such as injunctive relief.

What effect does mediation have on the enforcement process?

10.63 If the firm has not yet made its representations to the RDC, then it will want to await the outcome of the settlement discussions and/or mediation before doing so. The firm may therefore wish to seek an extension to the period for making written representations[1].

1 See para **10.144** ff below.

Confidentiality in the mediation process

10.64 Mediation is generally conducted on a 'without prejudice' basis. Matters disclosed in, and documents created for the purposes of, the mediation cannot therefore be referred to in the public domain[1], and matters disclosed by one party to the mediator in confidence will not be disclosed to the other party without consent. After the mediation, such matters retain the confidential status that they had in the mediation itself.

1 Such matters may not be disclosed in court save as is required by law.

10.65 There are, however, two exceptions:

- if any information indicating potentially criminal conduct is disclosed to the mediator, the mediator will not be required to keep that information confidential (and may choose to terminate the mediation); and

- the terms of any settlement that has been reached will, if approved by the FCA, be incorporated in a decision notice and subsequently a final notice, which is likely to be made public.

What are the possible outcomes?

10.66 The mediation will have one of two outcomes, either a proposal for settlement will be agreed between the parties, or there will be no agreed proposal:

- if no agreed proposal is reached, the mediation will be terminated and the case will be returned to the point that was reached in the enforcement process prior to commencement of the mediation; or

- if a settlement proposal is agreed, it will be considered by the firm and the FCA's decision makers[1], who will decide whether to enter into the settlement.

1 FCA Handbook at DEPP 5.1.

10.67 If a settlement proposal is agreed, it will generally be preferable for the exact terms of the settlement agreement to be reached as soon as possible[1]. For example, although the firm may have agreed to a particular level of sanction, it may not have been aware of the level of publicity that the FCA was contemplating[2].

1 If this is not possible immediately after the mediation has ended, heads of terms could be agreed as an alternative.
2 The publicity that will be likely to accompany a sanction imposed by the FCA is considered at para **10.194** ff below.

Phase 3 – conclusion of the investigation and referral to the RDC

10.68 Before the RDC is given the opportunity to decide what action will be appropriate for the FCA to take, the fact-finding investigation must conclude and result in the FCA enforcement staff making a decision to refer the matter to the RDC and to request the issuance of a warning notice[1]. This is effectively the first stage of the decision-making process. As will be seen, the firm under consideration may have a limited opportunity to have some input at this stage so as to try to prevent the matter from progressing. There are three parts to this process:

- the issue of a preliminary findings letter and a Preliminary Investigation Report (PIR) by the FCA's investigators, and the opportunity to respond;

- the FCA's decision as to whether or not to recommend to the RDC that action be taken; and

- the FCA's recommendation that is made to the RDC.

These are considered in turn below.

1 Where the FCA only seeks to impose a financial penalty for the late submission of a report, in most cases it will not be necessary for the FCA to appoint an investigator, since the fact of the breach will be clear, or to send the firm concerned a preliminary findings letter. See the FCA Handbook at DEPP 6.6.1G–6.6.5G, and the FCA Enforcement Guide at EG 2.35.

Preliminary findings letter

10.69   A preliminary findings letter is a letter that may be sent to the firm under investigation by the FCA investigators and will normally annex the investigators' PIR. These documents will set out and analyse those parts of the evidence that have been gathered which the FCA considers to be relevant[1], outline key elements of the FCA's legal analysis of the case, and summarise the conclusions that the investigators are minded to reach. It will invite the person concerned to comment upon the contents.

1 The preliminary findings letter and/or PIR is likely to include excerpts from key documents and passages from transcripts of any interviews that have taken place.

10.70   A preliminary findings letter, and a PIR, will often be issued before the FCA investigators consider whether to recommend to the RDC that enforcement action should be taken[1].

1 FCA Enforcement Guide at EG 4.30–4.33.

Will the firm receive a preliminary findings letter in every case?

10.71   There is no statutory requirement for the FCA to produce a preliminary findings letter or a PIR. Both were devised as part of the FCA's detailed rules in relation to the procedure for taking enforcement action[1]. The FCA Handbook states that the FCA investigators will generally send the firm a preliminary findings letter unless: (a) the firm agrees not to receive one; (b) it is not practicable to do so; or (c) no useful purpose would be served in doing so[2]. In many cases, FCA enforcement staff do produce a preliminary findings letter. In some circumstances, the FCA may decide to proceed straight to issuing a draft warning notice, particularly where the firm has indicated a desire to settle the case at an early stage[3]. Since the focus of the preliminary findings letter will be to confirm the facts that have been uncovered by the investigation, in order to ensure so far as possible that action is not taken as a result of an incorrect understanding of the facts, the preliminary findings letter (or its final version) is presented to the RDC in most cases where one has been produced[4].

1 The extent to which the FCA is able to decide how exactly the procedure is to be operated is explained in para **10.16** above.
2 FCA Enforcement Guide at EG 4.31.
3 See para **10.96** below.
4 See para **10.91** ff below.

What should the firm do when it receives a preliminary findings letter?

10.72   Where such a letter, with or without a PIR, is issued, the firm will be given a reasonable period, normally 28 days, to comment upon it[1]. The firm will therefore have an opportunity to respond and would be well advised to make use of that opportunity and, at the very least, to consider the wording of the preliminary findings letter very carefully. For a variety of reasons, the firm will need to take particular care over precisely what is contained in the preliminary findings letter, how it is presented and what it accepts as being correct. The firm may later regret having agreed to statements which seemed to be innocuous at the time, but are subsequently used against them.

1   See the FCA Enforcement Guide at EG 4.32. Where the firm does wish to respond, it must do so within the period that is specified (unless an extension is agreed). The FCA is expressly not obliged to take into account a response that is received outside the period.

10.73   The preliminary findings letter/PIR may seem to be innocuous because much of it will be factual and, rather than setting out the FCA's conclusions, will only set out their preliminary findings. However, care should be taken in reviewing its contents. First, even areas of the report that purport only to be a recitation of agreed facts may in reality be opinion or disputed facts[1]. Second, the report may attempt to construct links between unrelated facts or to 'fill in' the gaps between them. Third, it will be necessary for the firm to ensure that it is clear what areas of the report contain facts that are admitted and what other areas represent the FCA's opinion with which the firm disagrees. Finally, the preliminary findings letter and PIR (whether in draft or final form) are likely to be the RDC's main evidential basis when considering whether to issue a warning notice[2].

1   For example, there may be a difference between 'failing' to do something and 'not doing' the same thing. The first may imply that there was some kind of duty or obligation, and therefore introduces a conclusion, whereas the second may not.
2   See para **10.91** ff below.

10.74   One area that has led to significant difficulty in practice has been the inclusion in the preliminary findings letter or the PIR of evidence that is not otherwise available to the firm (for example, information obtained from third parties)[1]. Although the firm will have access to all the materials that it has disclosed to the FCA and to the transcripts of interviews that have been conducted with its employees, it is likely that it will not have access to documents disclosed to the FCA by other firms, or to transcripts of interviews that the FCA has conducted with others, including, potentially, the firm's ex-employees. Where such materials are referred to in the report and conclusions are reached as a result of them, the firm may find it difficult to refute them. For example, the FCA may use a quote from such a transcript out of context. However, since the firm may not have access to that transcript, it may find it difficult to address the quote. What should the firm do when confronted with the use of such evidence in a report? First, it should make best use of all the evidence to which it does have access (which may also mean pointing to evidence that the FCA has not sought to gather or persons that have not been interviewed) and second, it should, at the beginning of its response, make it clear that the FCA cannot expect it to provide a full response to allegations that arise from such evidence until that evidence is made available to the firm.

1   It is important to remember that the FCA will not, at this stage, have disclosed to the firm all relevant material that it will have received as a result of the investigation. The FCA's obligation to disclose such material will only arise once the warning notice has been issued: see para **10.118** ff below.

10.75   In reviewing the letter and the PIR, the firm will need to be alert to the potential for claims by other parties who were involved or affected. Amongst other things, a breach of FCA rules can give rise to a claim for breach of statutory duty on the part of private customers who suffer loss[1] and it may also enable the FCA to make a restitution order[2]. The firm could also, as a result, incur civil liability to others, for example, corporate clients or market counterparties[3]. It is important to bear in mind in this context that the preliminary findings letter, the PIR and the firm's response could be disclosed in any civil proceedings that may subsequently arise[4]. If the firm is seen, in its response, or by its lack of response, to accept the facts as alleged by the FCA, it may make it difficult to argue in subsequent legal proceedings that those facts were in fact wrong. Equally, misguided comments in the firm's response could increase its potential exposure to third parties. It will always be difficult to predict, or control, the circumstances when the preliminary findings letter, and any response, will reappear.

1   FSMA 2000, s 138D (among others). Such claims are discussed at para **19.18** ff below.
2   See para **8.100** ff above.
3   Generally, see **CHAPTER 19** below.
4   This is discussed in more detail at para **4.145** ff above.

10.76   The response gives the firm their last opportunity to comment on the FCA's understanding of the facts, refute any misconceptions, and also to develop the themes of its defence before the matter is considered by the RDC and a warning notice issued[1]. The principal aim will therefore be to try to ensure that the matter is not referred to the RDC[2]. It will be apparent from the receipt of the preliminary findings letter that there is a real prospect of FCA enforcement proceedings against the firm. As will be seen, once those proceedings are initiated with the issue of a warning notice, the firm will have a great deal of work to do within a fairly limited time, and it may therefore be prudent for the firm to start the work that will be needed to be done to respond to the warning notice once it receives the preliminary findings letter.

1   Prior opportunities will have arisen at the FCA's scoping discussions (see para **5.50** ff above) and during the FCA's formal interviews of the firm's employees (see para **4.180** ff above).
2   How the FCA staff will take the decision as to whether or not to refer the matter to RDC is considered at para **10.87** ff below.

To whom is the firm's response sent?

10.77   The response is sent to the FCA staff, or often the enforcement investigation team, who issued the preliminary findings letter. The RDC is not involved at this stage.

What happens to the response?

10.78   The FCA staff will take into account the response in considering whether to recommend that enforcement action should be initiated provided that they receive it within the required period[1].

1   FCA Enforcement Guide at EG 4.32.

Are the preliminary findings letter and response confidential?

10.79 The contents of the preliminary findings letter, and the firm's response to it are likely, in general, to be protected by the confidentiality restrictions under the FSMA 2000[1] and should not therefore in general be disclosed outside the FCA. However, some exceptions may apply.

1 FSMA 2000, s 348: this is discussed in detail at para **4.224** ff above.

10.80 First, the FCA may pass information onto other regulators, for example, exchanges or overseas regulators, particularly, but by no means only, where the FCA is carrying out its investigation in order to assist those other regulators[1]. The FCA is permitted to disclose information to other parties under the Gateway Regulations which permit the disclosure of information which is otherwise subject to the statutory confidentiality restrictions[2].

1 The extent to which the FCA is likely to co-operate in providing information to other regulators is considered at para **5.34** ff above.
2 For an explanation of the Gateway Regulations: see para **4.234** ff above.

10.81 Second, there is a possibility that third parties will obtain disclosure of the preliminary findings letter and the PIR, and the response to it, from the firm itself in the context of civil proceedings brought by the third party against the firm[1]. These documents could potentially be of relevance and value to the third party as they will contain preliminary findings by the FCA and the firm's initial reaction to those findings.

1 Again this will be subject to the application of the FSMA 2000, s 348 since the report may contain 'confidential information' relating to the business or other affairs of a third party which the firm has received as a result of the FCA's use of its investigatory powers: see para **4.224** ff above. See also para **19.78** ff below.

10.82 Third, if the information in the preliminary findings letter and the PIR, and the firm's response, comes into the public domain, for example, as a result of Tribunal proceedings which will be likely to take place in public[1], then it will cease to be confidential and the statutory protection will fall away[2]. The result will be that the documents could then become disclosable in any civil proceedings. If, therefore, the disciplinary proceedings are decided in the Tribunal, the statutory protection may be only temporary.

1 The question of what publicity will be likely to arise during Tribunal proceedings is considered at para **12.37** below.
2 The protection of the FSMA 2000, s 348 applies only to 'confidential information'. Information will not be confidential if it has been made available to the public by virtue of being disclosed in any circumstances in which, or for any purposes by which, disclosure is not precluded by s 348: see the FSMA 2000, s 348(4)(a).

Is there a risk of publicity during the investigation stage?

10.83 The FCA will not normally make public the fact that it is or is not investigating a particular matter[1]. As a result, publicity should generally not attach during the investigatory phase. However, the FCA can[2], subject to the restriction on disclosure of confidential information in s 348 of the FSMA 2000, make a public announcement that it has commenced an investigation where such announcement is desirable to: (1) maintain public confidence in the financial system or the market; (2) protect consumers or investors; (3) prevent widespread malpractice; (4) help the investigation itself, for example by bringing forward witnesses; or (5) maintain the smooth operation of the market. A public announcement should be made only in exceptional circumstances, such as where the investigation is the subject of public concern, speculation or rumour, and the FCA should consider the potential prejudice to the subject of the investigation before making any public announcement[3]. The FCA may also make a public announcement that it has not commenced, nor does it intend to commence, an investigation in the context of a takeover bid[4].

1 FCA Enforcement Guide at EG 6.1.
2 FCA Enforcement Guide at EG 6.3 and 6.4.
3 For example, in April 2013 the FCA publicised the commencement of an FCA enforcement investigation into IT failures at RBS. Further, in October 2013 the FCA publicised the commencement of an investigation relating to trading on the foreign exchange market.
4 The decision to issue a public announcement in this context should follow discussion between the FCA and the Takeover Panel. See the FCA Enforcement Guide at EG 6.2.

10.84 Further, the FCA may, in tandem with conducting its investigation, have taken some other regulatory action which may have been made public, depending upon the circumstances in which the action was taken and the FCA's application of its policy as to when to publicise such action. For example, this may include where the FCA has made use of its urgent own-initiative or intervention powers[1] or when it has applied to the court for a civil injunction or restitution order[2].

1 See para **16.215** ff below.
2 See respectively, paras **8.138** ff and **8.100** ff above.

Whether to refer the matter to the RDC

10.85 Once the FCA staff, or the investigator, has concluded the investigation and, where appropriate, has issued a preliminary findings letter, and waited for and considered any response, the next question will be whether the matter should be referred to the RDC[1] for a decision as to what, if any, disciplinary action should be taken. The FCA staff can also decide at this stage to take no further action.

1 For a list of those decisions for which the RDC is responsible, see the FCA Handbook at DEPP 2.5.7G–2.5.8G and 2.5.10G. Where the RDC is not responsible for a decision, FCA staff will make decisions under executive procedures, following a procedure broadly similar (although less formal and structured) than the RDC procedure: see the FCA Handbook at DEPP 4.1, in particular DEPP 4.1.13G. For simplicity, and because all the relevant enforcement powers involve the RDC, reference is made only to the RDC.

Who takes the decision whether to refer the matter to the RDC?

10.86 The FCA Handbook[1] states that the FCA staff will, if they consider that enforcement action is appropriate, recommend that a warning notice is given.

Presently, the decision is taken by the case's project sponsor after consultation with the enforcement staff who were responsible for the investigation and an FCA in-house lawyer. The legal review of the case must be conducted by a lawyer who has not been part of the investigation and who can therefore provide an objective view[2]. Members of senior management are consulted during the investigation stage, and prior to referral to the RDC, to the extent that a case is deemed to be high impact, precedent setting or which requires a significant commitment of FCA resources. (In practice, members of senior management can also be consulted at other stages in an enforcement action.) The combination of FCA senior management involvement in certain cases and an independent legal review of all cases prior to referral to the RDC is designed to ensure an objective analysis of the relative merits of the case and to provide a check on the process.

1 FCA Handbook at DEPP 2.2.1G.
2 See the FCA Enforcement Guide at EG 2.36. In complex cases, this role could be performed by outside counsel.

How is the decision taken?

10.87 The FCA Handbook gives little detail about how the FCA staff take the decision whether to recommend that enforcement action be initiated. Clearly, they will have to consider the facts uncovered by the investigation, the response to the preliminary findings letter if one was produced, and then decide what action is likely to be appropriate in the light of those facts. Additionally, the FCA staff will have regard to the FCA's policy as to when enforcement action should be pursued. This will include whether the action is merited under the FCA's risk based approach which is described at para **8.25** ff above. The FCA Handbook suggests[1] that, in order to make a recommendation, the FCA staff have to consider that enforcement action is appropriate. If they cannot positively recommend the action, then no action should be taken.

1 FCA Handbook at DEPP 2.2.1G.

Does the FCA have any options other than recommending that enforcement action be taken?

10.88 The FCA staff may decide, as a result of the investigation, to take no further action, for example, if it appears to them that no breaches have been committed. Alternatively, although they may have concerns about the firm's behaviour, they may decide that it is not appropriate in all the circumstances to bring formal disciplinary action. Examples given in the FCA Handbook[1] include where the breach is minor in nature or degree, or the firm has taken immediate and full remedial action[2]. In such circumstances, the FCA staff may decide not to recommend enforcement action but may nonetheless issue a private warning in order to let the firm know that it has come close to taking formal enforcement action. If that is the case, the FCA should write to the relevant firm stating that it is minded to issue a private warning and invite comments. Private warnings will be approved by a head of department or more senior members of FCA staff.

1 FCA Enforcement Guide at EG 7.10–7.19.
2 For a fuller consideration of the factors that are likely to be considered by the FCA, see **Chapters 8, 9** and **16**.

Is the firm informed of the FCA staff's recommendation?

10.89 Where the FCA's decision is to make a recommendation that disciplinary action be taken the firm will, in due course, hear about the decision if it is issued with a warning notice. Where the FCA decides not to take any further action, the FCA will in practice notify the person under investigation that the investigation has been concluded[1].

1 See the discussion at para **5.91** above.

Will there be any publicity when the FCA enforcement staff finish their investigation?

10.90 The FCA will not normally publish details of the information found or conclusions reached during an investigation. However, in exceptional circumstances the FCA may, subject to the restriction on disclosure of confidential information in s 348 of the FSMA 2000, publish the information found or the conclusions reached during the investigation, in particular where the fact of the FCA's investigation has been made public and it concludes that the concerns that prompted the investigation were unwarranted[1]. The circumstances in which the FCA may make public the fact that it is investigating a matter are considered in para **10.83** ff above. If the FCA does not publish details of the information found or conclusions reached during an investigation, it is nevertheless likely to publish information about the matter if and when a warning notice is issued (see para **10.108** ff below).

1 FCA Enforcement Guide at EG 6.6.

The recommendation by the FCA staff to the RDC

What is contained in the recommendation?

10.91 The FCA Handbook does not prescribe what should be contained in the recommendation that is made by enforcement staff to the RDC. However, the recommendation is likely to set out the background to the case, a summary of the FCA's analysis of the conduct that is in issue, the relevant rules and guidance, the position that the firm will be likely to take on being issued with the warning notice[1], the firm's compliance history and the FCA's policy on the suggested sanction (and examples of sanctions that have already been imposed in relation to similar misconduct). The RDC is therefore likely to be aware, from the outset, of matters relevant to the issue of sanction, such as the person's previous compliance history[2]. Attached to the recommendation are likely to be excerpts from key pieces of evidence as well as documents such as the investigation report (if one was produced), the firm's reply, the skilled person's report (again, if one was produced)[3] and the firm's reply to that document. To the extent relevant, the recommendation will also be accompanied by legal submissions on the case[4]. Most importantly, the RDC will also receive a draft warning notice prepared by the FCA which it will be able to amend as necessary when it reaches its decision as to what action to take or whether to take any action.

1   This may, for example, be evident from the firm's response to the preliminary findings letter.
2   This may give rise to certain issues, as discussed at para **10.36** above.
3   For more detail on skilled person's reports, see **CHAPTER 6** above.
4   The FCA Enforcement Division will not provide legal advice to the RDC, only submissions. To the extent the RDC requires legal advice it has its own small dedicated legal function which may amongst other things assist the RDC in considering the case and underlying material and provide legal advice where required. See the FCA Handbook at DEPP 3.1.3G.

Does the firm receive a copy of the recommendation?

10.92   In all but extremely rare cases the firm will receive the FCA's recommendation and/or case review paper once the RDC has decided to issue a warning notice. The recipient of a warning notice would expect to receive the recommendation in accordance with its rights of access to relevant materials relied upon by the FCA in deciding to issue a statutory notice[1]. Any legal or policy points that the FCA enforcement staff wish to make will therefore be disclosed to the firm[2].

1   FSMA 2000, s 394. For more detail on the the right to access material held by the FCA, see para **10.118** ff below.
2   The only exception to this is the comparative penalty material which is not yet public (and will contain confidential information about third parties) and rare cases where material would be protected by public interest immunity (for example, very sensitive material about informants or whistleblowers).

A Notice of Discontinuance

10.93   The FCA may discontinue the enforcement action at any stage, by issuing a Notice of Discontinuance. A Notice of Discontinuance must simply identify the proceedings that are being discontinued[1] and state that the FCA may publish such information about the matter as it considers appropriate, if the person to whom it is given consents (and a similar statement must appear where the notice is copied to a third party[2]). The FCA staff will send the Notice of Discontinuance to the person concerned (and to any third party who was provided with a copy of the warning or decision notice). The Notice of Discontinuance does not require the agreement of the RDC but the RDC will be notified of any decision to discontinue[3].

1   FSMA 2000, ss 389(3) and 391(2) and (3).
2   See para **10.94** below.
3   FCA Handbook at DEPP 3.2.26.

10.94 Information relating to a Notice of Discontinuance can only be published by the FCA with the consent of the person concerned and, in so far as relevant to a third party, the consent of any third party to whom that notice is copied[1].

1 FSMA 2000, s 391(2) and (3). Note that the FSMA 2000 does not as such prohibit the publication of information about the Notice of Discontinuance without the consent of the firm concerned (or the third party). It says that the Notice of Discontinuance must state that information may be published if the person consents.

10.95 In cases where the *FCA* has publicised the fact that a warning notice has been issued, and the FCA subsequently decides not to take any further action, or where it publishes a decision notice and the firm succeeds on a reference to the Tribunal, the FCA's Enforcement Guide makes clear that the FCA will clarify on its website that the warning notice or the decision notice no longer applies, normally by publishing a Notice of Discontinuance[1].

1 FCA Enforcement Guide at EG 6.10C.

Phase 4 – Issue of a warning notice

10.96 Once the FCA staff have decided to make a recommendation that enforcement action should be taken, the RDC will have to decide whether or not to accept that recommendation and accordingly whether or not to issue a warning notice. The following paragraphs review the process from that point to the next formal stage, which is when the RDC is charged with deciding whether or not to issue a decision notice, and in particular considers:

- the options that are open to the RDC when considering the FCA staff recommendation and how it reaches its decision;

- if the RDC does decide to proceed, the nature of the warning notice which it is required to issue;

- the firm's rights following issue of the warning notice and, in particular:

  - the right of access to the FCA's material; and

  - the right to make representations;

- what rights third parties may have on issue of the warning notice; and

- whether the FCA can conduct further investigations following the conclusion of the representations.

10.97 It should be noted at the outset that the RDC stage, including the process of making written and oral submissions to the RDC, and the RDC considering the evidence and making a decision whether to issue a decision notice (and if so the form of that notice) takes many months. The FSA's Annual Performance Account 2012/13 included, in respect of cases concluded during 2012/13, data on the average period of time taken to complete the case. This data refers to the period from the date of referral to enforcement to the conclusion of the case (as opposed to from the issue of the warning notice to the conclusion of the case), but nevertheless provides an indication of the time periods for the key phases of the enforcement process. This period varied from an average of just over a year and a half for cases that were settled, to just over three years for cases that were referred to the RDC (indicating that the RDC process typically takes some 18 months), to just over four years for cases referred to the Tribunal[1].

1 See the Financial Services Authority's Enforcement Annual Performance Account 2012/13, para 55.

The RDC's consideration of the FCA staff's recommendation

10.98 As has been indicated above, the first step taken by the RDC will be to consider whether or not to accept the recommendation from the FCA staff that enforcement action should be taken[1]. The RDC may decide:

- to take no further action, with or without a private warning being issued[2]; or

- to send a warning notice to the firm or individual.

1 This decision is taken by an RDC panel generally comprising the Chairman or Deputy and two others: see para **10.32** above. In addition, in straightforward cases (such as simple cases involving threshold conditions) the warning notice decision may be taken by the Chairman or Deputy alone or with one other: see the FCA Handbook at DEPP 3.3.1G–3.3.3G.
2 See the FCA Handbook at DEPP 2.2.3G. In 2012/13, 10.5% of cases (excluding threshold conditions cases) investigated by the FSA concluded without any further action being taken. In an additional 25 cases, the FSA decided to issue private warnings – expressions of concern as to the behaviour of a firm or individual – whilst stopping short of recommending formal disciplinary action. See the FSA Enforcement Annual Performance Account 2012/13 at paras 48 and 49. For a fuller discussion of private warnings, see para **8.27** ff above.

How does the RDC decide whether or not to take the proposed action?

10.99 The RDC will make decisions with regard to the facts, law, and FCA priorities and policies (including on matters of legal interpretation)[1]. The FCA's policy as to when it will take enforcement action in particular circumstances against firms is outlined in **CHAPTER 8** above. The FCA's policy on taking other types of enforcement action is outlined where the relevant action is considered in this book[2].

1 See the FCA Handbook at DEPP 1.2.7G. The FCA staff are likely to have outlined the FCA's policy in their recommendation to the RDC: see para **10.91** above.
2 Action against individuals is considered at **CHAPTER 9** above, the FCA's own initiative powers are considered at **CHAPTER 16** and criminal prosecutions are considered at **CHAPTER 18**. Action taken against listed companies is considered at **CHAPTER 20** and action in relation to market misconduct is set out at **CHAPTER 17** below.

Is the firm able to make submissions as to the recommendation?

10.100 The conclusion of the investigation, the recommendation by the FCA staff and the consideration by the RDC as to whether to issue a warning notice are internal processes, in relation to which the firm has no right to be involved. Accordingly, there is no provision which allows the subject of the process to make submissions on the substance of the FCA staff's recommendation, either at the point at which the FCA is considering whether to make the recommendation or when the RDC decides what to do as a result of that recommendation. In practice, the FCA's recommendation to the RDC is likely to be based on the information in the FCA's preliminary findings letter (if one was issued), and the firm will have been provided with a reasonable opportunity in which to reply to the preliminary findings letter (see para **10.72** above).

When does the firm find out the RDC's decision?

10.101 If the RDC decides not to take any further action then, where the FCA has previously informed the person that he is under investigation, it will communicate the RDC's decision promptly to the person concerned[1]. If the RDC accepts the FCA staff recommendation, the person concerned will be informed of the result when it receives the warning notice.

1 FCA Handbook at DEPP 2.2.4G.

The issue of a warning notice

10.102 A warning notice is a notice that the FSMA 2000 requires the FCA to issue when it proposes to take various types of enforcement action, including disciplinary measures such as fining or making a public statement in respect of a firm[1]. This is an important part of the process and, as will be seen, the firm then will have various rights to obtain information and to try to influence the RDC's decision as to whether to take the action proposed.

1 FSMA 2000, s 67(1) (for disiplinary action against individuals) or s 207 (for firms). Various other types of enforcement action to which this process applies are listed at para 10.3 above, together with the statutory provision from which each is derived.

10.103 In cases where enforcement action is to be taken against more than one person in relation to the same underlying facts, the FCA may address the same warning notice to multiple parties[1] or issue separate notices to the individual parties[2].

1 For example, this may be the case where the RDC decides that action should be taken against a firm and an employee, or multiple employees and not the firm (such as in *Yamazaki/Okazaki/ McKibbin/Oda/Morota/Titterington final notice (29/1/04)*). In some instances, the consolidation of the offences committed by multiple parties will not be appropriate and will only serve to tarnish them unnecessarily. Where this is the case, this should be addressed in the firm's representations to the RDC. Other similar problems can apply such as when third parties are involved in the process: see para **10.149** ff below.
2 For an example of separate notices that have been issued against different legal entities within the same group, and an employee, see the *Prudential and Tidjane Thiam final notices (27/03/13)*.

What must a warning notice contain?

10.104 A warning notice must[1]:

- be in writing;

- state the action which the FCA proposes to take;

- give reasons for the proposed action;

- explain whether the firm has a right of access to the FCA's material[2] and if so what material and whether any secondary material exists to which it must be allowed access; and

- state that the firm is entitled to make representations to the FCA, and specify a reasonable period for making those representations[3].

In addition, the FSMA 2000 imposes specific requirements with regard to warning notices that relate to specific types of regulatory action[4].

1 See the FCA Handbook at DEPP 2.2.1G–2.2.5G and FSMA 2000, s 387. The final bullet point is found in the FCA Handbook, rather than the statutory provision.
2 This is discussed in more detail at para **10.118** ff below.
3 FCA Handbook at DEPP 3.2.14C(4) provides that the recipient of a warning notice may request an extension of the time allowed for making representations, and that such a request must normally be made within seven days of the notice being given. This is discussed in more detail at para **10.137** ff below.
4 See for example, the FSMA 2000, ss 67(2) (fines against individuals), 67(3) (public statements relating to individuals), 207(3) (fines against firms), and 207(2) (public statements about firms).

10.105 The warning notice will set out precisely what action the FCA proposes to take against the firm concerned (for example the amount of any fine and the terms of the public statement that the FCA proposes to make) and what breaches are alleged[1]. As a result, it will be of real assistance in finally setting out the case the firm has to meet. The firm will be in a position to assess the significance or otherwise of the matter to its business and accordingly will be able to take any decisions as to how to proceed.

1 If the firm has not been served with a preliminary findings letter, this is likely to be the first point at which the person is presented with the FCA's allegations after they were briefly summarised in the FCA's formal request for information.

When does the firm receive the warning notice?

10.106 The FCA Handbook does not specify precisely at what point a warning notice will be sent to the person who is the subject of it but it is generally sent soon after the RDC has made the decision to proceed with the disciplinary action. Detailed rules exist as to how the FCA must serve such notices and as to when they will be determined as having been received[1].

1 See the Financial Services and Markets Act 2000 (Service of Notices Regulations) 2001, SI 2001/1420 and Financial Services and Markets Act 2000 (Service of Notices Regulations) (Amendment) 2005, SI 2005/274.

Can the firm challenge the warning notice?

10.107 The firm to whom the warning notice is issued has no opportunity or right to challenge the RDC's decision to issue it. However, the notice does not, of itself, have any effect. Rather, the person has the right to make representations to the RDC in relation to matters contained within the warning notice, with a view to influencing the RDC's decision as to whether to proceed with the enforcement process by issuing a decision notice[1] and ultimately the firm has the right to refer any enforcement action set out in a decision notice to the Tribunal[2].

1 For a discussion of decision notices, see para **10.162** ff below.
2 There is no right to obtain a judicial review of the decision to issue a warning notice (see the decision in *R (on the application of Davies) v Financial Services Authority [2004] 1 WLR 185)*. The court held that if judicial review of a decision not to issue a warning notice was generally available, it would bypass the statutory scheme. In *R (on the application of Willford) v Financial Services Authority [2013] EWCA Civ 677* the High Court approved the decision in *Davies* but nevertheless quashed a decision notice as the reasoning in the decision notice was inadequate. This was overturned by the Court of Appeal.

Is there any risk of publicity?

10.108 As a result of changes to the FSMA 2000 brought about by the Financial Services Act 2012 (the FS Act 2012), the FCA may, in respect of certain warning notices publish such information about the matter to which the notice relates as the FCA considers appropriate (a 'warning notice statement')[1]. There remains a statutory prohibition against the publication of the actual warning notice itself by either the FCA or a person to whom it is given or copied[2].

1 FSMA 2000, s 391(1).
2 FSMA 2000, s 391(1)(a) and (1ZA).

10.109 As a matter of policy, the FCA consider that it will normally be appropriate to publish a warning notice statement identifying the FCA's concerns[1]. In making the decision to publish a warning notice statement, the FCA staff may recommend publication of a warning notice statement, but it is the RDC that will decide whether it is appropriate in all the circumstances to publish a warning notice statement[2]. In deciding, the RDC will have regard to: (i) whether a warning notice statement is appropriate to enable consumers, firms and market users to understand the nature of the FCA's concerns; (ii) whether it is also appropriate to identify the subject of the warning notice; (iii) the representations concerning publication made by the persons to whom the warning notice is given or copied; and (iv) whether any grounds as set out in the FSMA 2000, s 391 prohibit publication[3].

1 See FCA Policy Statement (PS13/9) 'Publishing information about enforcement warning notices', at pp 8–10 and the FCA Enforcement Guide at EG 6.7E(1).
2 See the FCA Handbook at DEPP 3.2.14AG and 3.2.14BG. For the purposes of DEPP 3.2.14AG–3.2.14GG, references to the RDC are considered to be references to the Chairman of the RDC panel which issued the warning notice, or if he is unavailable, either the Chairman or Deputy Chairman of the RDC. See the FCA Handbook at DEPP 3.2.14HG.
3 See the FSMA 2000, s 391(1ZB). Broadly, the FCA can publish warning notice statements where the FCA proposes to censure, fine or suspend a firm or individual. The power to publish warning notices does not apply to non-disciplinary outcomes. In respect of warning notices in relation to non-disciplinary outcomes, the FCA and the subject of the warning notice remain prohibited from publishing either the warning notice or any details concerning it (see the FSMA 2000, s 391(1ZA)).

10.110 The FCA consider that in the case of individuals, the potential harm caused by identification in a warning notice statement would normally exceed the benefits of early transparency. However, the FCA may still identify the individual in certain circumstances, including where: (i) it is not possible to describe the FCA's concerns without identifying the individual; (ii) it is necessary to avoid the mis-identification of other individuals; (iii) it would help protect consumers or investors; (iv) it is necessary to maintain public confidence in the financial system or market; or (v) it is desirable to quash market rumours[1].

1   FCA Enforcement Guide at EG 6.7E(2).

10.111 The FCA may not publish information in respect of a warning notice where the information would be: (a) unfair to the person with respect to whom the action was taken (or was proposed to be taken); (b) prejudicial to the interests of consumers; or, (c) detrimental to the stability of the UK financial system[1]. In determining whether publication would be unfair, the FCA will have regard to a number of factors including: (i) whether the person implicated in the warning notice is a firm or individual; (ii) the size of the firm; and (iii) the extent to which the firm or individual have been made aware of the case against them in the course of the investigation[2].

1   See the FSMA 2000, s 391(6), the FCA Handbook at DEPP 3.2.14BG and the FCA Enforcement Guide at EG 6.7A–6.7J.
2   Enforcement Guide at EG 6.7E(3).

10.112 The RDC must consult the person to whom the warning notice is given or copied if it proposes to publish a warning notice statement. The proposed wording of the Warning Notice Statement to be given by the FCA should be settled by the RDC and then sent to the recipient. The proposed warning notice statement will specify the time allowed for the recipient to respond in writing to the RDC[1]. This will normally be 14 days, although an extension may be requested (normally within 7 days of the proposed warning notice Statement being given). The RDC will not normally permit a response to a warning notice Statement to be made in person[2].

1   The written representations should detail how potential unfairness may arise from the publication of the warning notice statement and that the damage incurred would be disproportionate. See the FCA Enforcement Guide at EG 6.7F.
2   See the FSMA 2000, s 391(1)(c) and the FCA Handbook at DEPP 3.2.14CG.

10.113 The RDC should consider the response (if any) by the recipient and decide whether it is appropriate in all the circumstances to publish the warning notice statement[1]. Where the RDC decides that the FCA should not publish a warning notice statement, the RDC staff will notify the relevant parties of that decision. Where the RDC considers that a warning notice Statement should be published, the RDC will notify the relevant parties and FCA staff in writing of the decision, settle the wording, and the FCA will make arrangements for its publication[2].

1   FCA Handbook at DEPP 3.2.14EG.
2   See the FCA Handbook at DEPP 3.2.14EG–3.2.14GG and FCA Enforcement Guide at EG 6.7G. The warning notice statement will include a brief summary of the facts which gave rise to the warning notice but not normally the nature and level of the proposed disciplinary sanctions. See the FCA Enforcement Guide at EG 6.7H.

10.114 The firm to whom the warning notice is given or copied may not publish any details concerning the notice unless the FCA has published those details[1]. The FSMA 2000 does not specify any particular penalty or consequence for a breach of this provision. If the person who is the subject of the process publishes information about the warning notice in breach of the prohibition, it is likely to have contravened a requirement imposed on it by, or under, the FSMA 2000 and as a result may in theory be exposed to regulatory enforcement action[2].

1 FSMA 2000, s 391(1)(b).
2 For a discussion of this test, and the possible consequences, see para **2.94** ff above. As of the date of writing, there is no evidence that anyone has been pursued for breaching this prohibition, whether in relation to a warning, or any other notice to which the prohibition applies. In some circumstances, the recipient of the warning notice may feel compelled to publish information relating to it, for example, as a result of its disclosure obligations if it is a listed company. For a discussion as to what to do in such circumstances, see para **10.181**, n 2 below.

What is the effect of receiving a warning notice?

10.115 In itself, the warning notice has no effect in respect of the firm which is the subject of the enforcement action. It is merely the first stage in the enforcement process and, because it is a pre-requisite under the FSMA 2000, the FCA cannot take enforcement action unless it is issued[1].

1 However, certain types of enforcement action do not require the issue of a warning notice: see para **10.7** above.

10.116 The issue of the notice will, however, afford the firm to whom it is issued a number of options and rights, in particular:

- to have access to certain of the FCA's documents;
- to make representations to the RDC;
- to enter into settlement discussions with the FCA; and
- in some situations to try to resolve the matter through mediation.

Each of these is considered in turn below.

10.117 In some circumstances, third parties may have the right to receive a copy of the warning notice and, if so, may also have a right of access to the FCA's documents. Third party rights and their potential implications on the main recipient of a warning notice are discussed at para **10.149** ff below.

The right of access to the FCA's material

When is the firm entitled to access the FCA's documents?

10.118 A firm which has been issued with a warning notice[1] will usually have a right to access certain documents that the FCA has received during the course of its investigation[2]. The right will be triggered by the issue of the warning notice and the warning notice is required to state whether the recipient does have a right of access to relevant materials under the FSMA 2000, s 394[3]. Although it will not arise in relation to all warning notices provided for by the FSMA 2000, it will arise in the vast majority of cases[4].

1 A similar right will arise upon the issue of a decision notice: see para **10.172** below.
2 FSMA 2000, s 394. The RDC will take the decision as to whether to refuse access to FCA material relevant to the warning notice. See the FCA Handbook at DEPP 1.2.6G(3).
3 FSMA 2000, s 387(1)(d). See para above.
4 Cases which are excluded include where a warning notice is required to be issued where a firm has applied to vary or revoke action that has already been taken by the FCA. For a list of those cases where there will be a right of access to the FCA's documents, see the FSMA 2000, s 392.

What documents is the firm entitled to review?

10.119 The FCA is required to allow the firm access to certain types of material, in particular[1]:

- the material upon which the FCA (being the RDC) relied in taking the decision which gave rise to the obligation to give the warning notice (in other words, the decision by the RDC to propose that enforcement action should be taken). This can be described as 'primary material'; and

- any secondary material which, in the FCA's opinion, might undermine that decision. Accordingly, secondary material means[2] other material that has not been included within the above 'primary material', but which was considered by the RDC in reaching the decision or was obtained by the FCA staff in connection with the matter, but which was not considered by the RDC in reaching that decision[3].

1 FSMA 2000, s 394(1).
2 FSMA 2000, s 394(6).
3 See the Explanatory Notes to FSMA, produced by HM Treasury, para 693.

10.120 The firm's entitlement is subject to various exceptions which allow the FCA to refuse access to certain categories of material, in particular:

- material which was intercepted under a warrant that was issued under the interception of communications legislation or which may indicate that such a warrant was issued or that material has been intercepted in such a way[1];

- material that is covered by the statutory protection for legal privilege[2], in which case the FCA must give the firm written notice of the existence of the item and its decision not to allow the person access to it[3];

- material relating to a case involving a different person and which was taken into account by the RDC in this case only for the purposes of comparison with other cases[4]; or

- if, in the RDC's opinion, to allow the firm access to the material[5]:

  – would not be in the public interest; or

  – would not be fair having regard to: (i) the likely significance of the material to the firm in relation to the matter in respect of which it has been given the warning notice; and (ii) the potential prejudice to the commercial interests of another person which would be caused by the material's disclosure.

1   FSMA 2000, s 394(2) and (7)(a).
2   FSMA 2000, ss 394(2), (7)(c) and 413. For a detailed discussion, see para **5.56** ff above. Note that FSMA 2000 effectively contains its own definition of legal privilege for this purpose, which does not equate in all respects with the common law definition.
3   FSMA 2000, s 394(2), (4) and (7)(c).
4   FSMA 2000, s 394(2)(a) and (b). Such material ought to be taken into account, only for the purposes of assessing the appropriate sanction or punishment, and not in order to ascertain whether the person committed the breach.
5   FSMA 2000, s 394(3). If the FCA refuses to allow access to material on this basis, it must give the firm written notice of the refusal and the reasons for it: FSMA 2000, s 394(5).

10.121 These provisions setting out the firm's rights to access the FCA's material are complex. The scope of the FCA's obligation to provide access to material, and precisely what material will be accessible by the person, requires closer analysis. Firms need to be aware that the statutory provisions that permit access to the FCA's documents are not all embracing. Material may be taken into account by the RDC without the firm having any right to see or comment upon it. It is only in the Tribunal that the firm has a wider right of access to the documents[1].

1   This may depend upon what applications are made to the Tribunal with regard to disclosure, and the Tribunal's views in the particular case: see further para **12.73** ff below.

Primary material

10.122 The obligation to provide access to the material upon which the FCA relied is relatively straightforward. The obligation applies to the regulator that gives the warning notice and this should be read as referring to the RDC, since it is the RDC that will make, upon the FCA's behalf, the decision as to whether to issue the warning notice. One point that is unclear is the meaning of the word 'material'. The word 'material' is not defined in the FSMA 2000 (the words 'information' and 'documents' are more commonly used). It seems to derive from the Criminal Procedure and Investigations Act 1996[1], in which context it is defined as referring to material of all kinds and in particular includes information and objects[2]. Material is not, therefore, limited to documentary material[3]. Any legal advice upon which the RDC relied is not required to be disclosed[4].

1   'In broad terms we are persuaded that a case may be made for aligning the requirement [to provide access] more closely to the rules on disclosure that apply in criminal cases': Economic Secretary to HM Treasury in Standing Committee (9/12/99).
2   Criminal Procedure and Investigations Act 1996, s 2(4). The same issue, of whether non-documentary material should be provided, should not arise in the context of a criminal prosecution, because there is a duty on the prosecutor to record material which consists of information not recorded in any form: see para 4.1, Code of Practice issued under Pt II, Criminal Procedure and Investigations Act 1996. For a discussion more generally, see Archbold 2013, at **CHAPTER 18** below.
3   This appears to be supported by para 4.1 of the Code of Practice, which refers to 'material which … consists of information which is not recorded in any form'.
4   This is discussed further at para **10.127** below.

Secondary material

10.123 A limited amount of secondary material must be provided. The test is set out above. It is fairly complicated and, notably, it is not simply a test of 'relevance'[1]. It also provides the FCA with a degree of discretion as to what material should be provided[2]. There is therefore scope for material to exist which, although it may be relevant to the decision, was not relied upon by the RDC in taking the decision, and in the FCA's view does not undermine that decision. That material could be of interest and relevance to the firm but could fall outside the scope of the access provisions.

1 This is deliberate. There were concerns that a test of 'relevance' would result in a 'bureaucratic and unhelpful' disclosure process, given the large amount of information which the FCA is likely to have about firms, for example from its supervisory relationship: see Economic Secretary to HM Treasury in Standing Committee (9/12/99).
2 At least at this stage: the firm may be able to obtain access to the material in the Tribunal, see paras **10.131** ff and **12.73** ff below.

10.124 One document to which the firm may wish to have access is the FCA recommendation to the RDC that led to the warning notice being issued[1]. This record should have been kept by the RDC Office[2]. Moreover, the firm may wish to obtain information about the conduct of the meeting, as distinct from the material that was relied upon by the RDC in reaching its decision at the meeting, for example:

- whether any conflicts of interest were declared and how they were dealt with;

- the basis upon which the decision was made, and by whom; and

- whether any member of the FCA staff was present at the meeting (and what oral representations were made by the FCA to the RDC).

1 See para **10.91** ff above.
2 See para **10.39** above and the FCA Handbook at DEPP 1.2.8G.

10.125 As set out above, the firm is entitled to receive copies of all material provided by the FCA enforcement staff to the RDC. The RDC Office, with its own legal function is also required to document all meetings between the RDC and FCA enforcement staff and provide a copy of that record to the firm or individual concerned. Therefore, to the extent that the FCA recommendation is made at a meeting between the FCA enforcement staff and the RDC the firm will receive a record of that. However, it is unlikely that the firm will receive any record of RDC meetings at which neither the FCA staff nor the firm were present, for example when the RDC members meet to deliberate on their decision[1].

1 See para **10.35** ff above.

The exceptions

10.126 The four exceptions to the access provisions have been outlined above. Whilst the FCA must notify the person where material exists but is being withheld as a result of two of the exceptions[1], the FSMA 2000 does not require it to do so where the material falls within the other two exceptions[2]. The fact that some of this material exists may not therefore be known to the firm, at least pending a possible application for disclosure in any Tribunal proceedings that are brought[3].

1 Namely, legally privileged material and material that has been withheld on the basis that access would not be in the public interest or would be unfair: see para **10.120** above.
2 Namely, material intercepted under a warrant, and material relating to others and used for the purposes of comparison: see para **10.120** above.
3 See para **12.92** below.

10.127 One point deserves particular attention. Any legal advice which the RDC or the FCA has obtained does not need to be disclosed. Importantly, the statutory definition as to what legally privileged material may be withheld[1] is drawn widely, and not only includes legal advice privilege but also what is known as litigation privilege. Broadly this is defined as including correspondence with third parties for the purposes of legal proceedings. The FSMA 2000 does not define 'legal proceedings' or the degree of connection that is needed for the material to be 'in connection with' such proceedings. From the perspective of the firm against which the enforcement action is being taken[2], it is clearly important that 'legal proceedings' do not only encompass civil claims but also regulatory proceedings[3].

1 FSMA 2000, s 413 and see the discussion at para **5.56** ff above.
2 Note that the converse of this could be that certain of the material which the FCA has obtained could potentially be classified as having been obtained for the purposes of 'legal proceedings' and the FCA could therefore seek to argue that such material could properly be withheld. This could include witness statements and expert reports which the FCA has commissioned to assist it in determining whether there has been a regulatory breach. However, this may of itself be insufficient to enable the FCA to claim privilege over such material. It would also need to overcome the dominant purpose test applied in relation to claims for litigation privilege, ie that the material had been produced for the dominant purpose of prosecuting or defending the proceedings and not for some other purpose (for example, the FCA exercising its function of investigating or of considering whether the conduct merited enforcement action). (See *Waugh v British Railways Board [1979] 2 All ER 1169*.)
3 In some specific respects, the FSMA 2000 clearly anticipates that there are 'proceedings' when a warning notice is issued: see, for example, the FSMA 2000, ss 66(4) and (5) and 389(2) and (3). For a more detailed discussion of legal privilege, see paras **4.136**, **4.149** ff and a more general discussion at para **5.56** above. For the meaning of proceedings' in this context, see para **4.157** above.

10.128 So far as expert reports are concerned, such reports may often be at the hub of the FCA's case. For example, where the rule concerned requires the firm to have complied with a particular standard, such as to 'take reasonable care' or 'pay due regard', an important issue will be what the requisite standard was and whether the person's actions fell below that standard. In considering the answer to these types of questions, the RDC may well rely upon the report of an expert. It appears to have been envisaged in the parliamentary debates that such reports would be disclosable and indeed one of the issues debated was what amendments would be required to ensure that any reports detrimental to the FCA's case would also be disclosed[1]. Nonetheless, it may be arguable, depending upon how the production of such reports was structured by the FCA, that such reports could constitute 'protected items' under the FSMA 2000 and as a result would not need to be disclosed.[2]

1 See Economic Secretary to HM Treasury in Standing Committee (9/12/99).

2 However, see *Re Barings plc, Secretary of State for Trade and Industry v Baker [1998] Ch 356* in which the court held that a person under investigation was entitled to see the expert report on which a decision to bring proceedings (in that case directors disqualification proceedings) was brought where there was a statutory duty for the report to be delivered. Due to the statutory obligation, the expert report could not be said to have been created in anticipation of litigation and therefore be protected by litigation privilege. In the absence of a claim of public interest immunity, the expert report could not be withheld from being disclosed. The Commercal Court in *West London Pipeline and Storage Ltd v Total UK Ltd [2008] EWHC 1729 (Comm)* subsequently considered the *Re Barings* decision and noted that in order for the purposes of the report to be deemed irrelevant for privilege purposes, there must be a statutory duty to report and not just a duty to investigate.

Who decides what material should be given to the firm?

10.129 The FCA Handbook provides that it is the RDC, rather than the FCA staff, who will be responsible for any decision that is taken in connection with the issue of a warning or decision notice, to refuse access to any material within the possession of the FCA staff[1]. In other words, it is for the RDC to decide whether any particular material is to fall within one of the exceptions and whether it should therefore be withheld. The FCA Handbook does not, however, make it clear who will take the more general decision as to what material falls within the scope of primary and secondary material to which the FCA is obliged to provide access. This is generally a decision taken by the FCA staff who have the requisite resources and knowledge to make such a decision.

1 FCA Handbook at DEPP 1.2.6G.

How does the firm obtain access to the material?

10.130 In practice, the FCA sends the firm photocopies of the material in question at the same time as the warning notice is issued, or soon thereafter. Given the very limited time available for the firm to respond to the warning notice, as discussed below[1], the period will need to be no more than a few days, and access to the documents should therefore be requested immediately on receipt of the warning notice if they have not already been provided.

1 See para **10.143** below.

What action can the firm take if it believes that it is entitled to additional material?

10.131 The right of access to material is not supported by an express right to challenge the extent of the material that has been provided. As with much of the enforcement process, there is an unwritten assumption that the FCA will comply with its statutory and other obligations. If the FCA does not comply with its duties properly, or narrowly construes what material it is obliged to disclose, the firm is unlikely to be aware of the existence of certain categories of material which are being withheld by the FCA[1]. The firm therefore needs to think carefully about what other material might exist in order to be in a position to challenge any disclosure statements made by the FCA[2].

1 See para **10.126** ff above.
2 The FCA has in the past failed to provide material that undermined the reasons for the action that is proposed.

10.132 So, what can the firm do if it suspects that additional material exists which, for some reason, has not been disclosed? A number of options are open to it:

- it can discuss the matter with the FCA staff, to see whether the issue can be clarified or resolved on an informal basis;

- it can raise the issue directly with the RDC; and

- if the matter cannot be resolved, it could consider bringing proceedings for a judicial review of the FCA's decision not to provide the relevant material[1], make a complaint against the FCA[2], or take no action for the time being, with the intention of raising the non-provision of material if, or when, the matter as a whole comes to be heard before the Tribunal[3].

The firm does not have the right to refer the question of whether the FCA should disclose the additional material to the Tribunal, at least, until it refers the enforcement action as a whole to the Tribunal following the issue of a decision notice[4].

1 For a further discussion of judicial review, see para **21.16** ff below.
2 The complaints procedure is discussed at para **21.44** ff below.
3 See **CHAPTER 12** below.
4 See para **10.171** ff below.

10.133 A firm may also be able to obtain further potentially relevant information by making a request for information under the Freedom of Information Act (FOIA) 2000. FOIA 2000 creates a general right of access, subject to certain exemptions, to information held by public bodies such as the FCA[1].

1 For a detailed discussion of the Freedom of Information Act 2000, see *The Law of Freedom of Information*, John Macdonald QC (2009).

Should the firm request access to the FCA's material?

10.134 There will rarely be a good reason for the firm not to ask for access to the FCA's material or, at least, to inspect the documents so as to obtain a better understanding of the FCA's case. Whether the firm should ask for copies of the documents may be a more difficult question, particularly where some of the documents may potentially be harmful. There may be a risk that the firm will be required, in the context of any civil proceedings that may subsequently be brought against it by third parties arising from the same matter, to disclose documents that it has obtained from the FCA[1]. This will need to be borne in mind if real concerns exist about the possibility of significant claims being brought by third parties. The answer may therefore depend upon balancing, in the particular case, the importance of defending the regulatory enforcement proceedings against the likelihood of claims being brought by third parties[2]. These problems only arise insofar as the firm takes copies or makes notes of the FCA's material. If there are serious risks, it may be possible to inspect the FCA's files without taking copies or making notes so as to avoid these issues arising. Firms should bear in mind that, in practice, it is likely that during the course of RDC proceedings the FCA will serve documents on the firm, so the firm may find it difficult to avoid receiving copies of *any* of the material on which the FCA seeks to rely.

1   For a further discussion, see para **4.145** ff above. This will be subject to the statutory restrictions on the disclosure of confidential information: see paras **4.226** ff above and **10.136** ff below.
2   If the firm decides not to obtain copies of the documents at the warning notice stage, it will have another opportunity to do so at the decision notice stage and, again, if the matter is referred to the Tribunal, although the same issues regarding the risk of disclosure to others will arise at each stage.

10.135 The primary disadvantage to the firm of not exercising its right to access the material is likely to be that it will not be in a position to engage as fully as possible in the process of making representations to the RDC, which takes place between the issue of the Warning and decision notices. This could have the effect of impeding the settlement of the dispute or could make it more likely that a decision notice will be issued with a higher or more serious form of sanction than the person might otherwise have received. Ultimately, the firm may not have as strong a position as it would otherwise have had before the Tribunal if it subsequently decides to refer the matter to the Tribunal.

What use can the firm make of the FCA's material?

10.136 From the firm's perspective, the FCA's material will primarily assist it in making representations to the RDC and, more generally, to prepare its defence to the regulatory proceedings. To the extent that the material contains confidential information that the FCA has obtained from a third party, or that relates to the business or affairs of a third party[1], such material may be covered by the statutory prohibition against disclosure and, as a person receiving the information directly or indirectly from the FCA, the firm may be guilty of committing a criminal offence if it subsequently discloses that information in breach of the statutory prohibition[2]. Beyond this, no express limitation exists as to the uses that the person can make of the material, although it is possible that a court would imply a restriction that it cannot be used for any purpose other than for the preparation of the firm's defence to the regulatory proceedings[3].

1   Such a third party may not only be a market counterparty but may more likely be an ex-employee who was involved in the commission of the breach.
2   FSMA 2000, s 348. For a more detailed explanation, see paras **4.226** ff and **4.236** ff above.
3   For example, unused prosecution material disclosed in criminal proceedings is subject to an implied undertaking that it cannot be used for any purpose other than in the conduct of the defence: *Taylor v Serious Fraud Office [1999] 2 AC 177, HL.*

The right to make representations

Why should the firm make representations?

10.137 The warning notice will set out the timeframe within which the firm is able to make representations to the RDC[1]. Whilst there is no requirement for the firm to make representations, in the vast majority of cases the firm should do so. This stage represents the last opportunity for a firm to influence the process (and the first before the RDC) ahead of the issuance of a decision notice. Further, where the RDC receives no response or representations by the time the decision to issue a decision notice is to be made, it may regard the allegations or matters in the warning notice as being undisputed and give a decision notice accordingly[2].

Whilst the firm's unwillingness to make representations to the RDC ought not to prejudice its position before the Tribunal[3], the firm should also consider that this is the last opportunity to make representations in the enforcement process ahead of any subsequent referral to the Tribunal – an expensive, time consuming and public process[4].

Therefore, whilst there may be cases when the firm will prefer not to make representations at this stage, these are likely to be exceptional. For example, firms may take the view that, in cases where a warning notice statement has already been published, a key reason for making representations to the RDC (the desire to avoid the FCA publicly sanctioning the firm) falls away; some firms may in that situation choose to keep any arguments to themselves pending a hearing before the Tribunal.

1 See FSMA 2000, s 387. A warning notice must specify that a recipient is entitled to make representations in response to the warning notice and those responses should be received within a reasonable period of no less than 14 days of the receipt of the warning notice. The recipient can apply for an extension of the deadline, see FSMA 2000, s 387(3) and the FCA Handbook at DEPP 3.2.16G and 1.2.6G. See also para **10.144** ff below.
2 FCA Handbook at DEPP 2.3.2G.
3 See the FCA Handbook at DEPP 2.3.2G. The fact the RDC is entitled, by virtue of this provision of the FCA's rules, to regard the matter as undisputed should not of itself affect the Tribunal in its determination of what action it is appropriate for the FCA to take.
4 The procedure that applies to cases referred to the Tribunal is reviewed in **CHAPTER 12** below.

How are representations made?

10.138 Representations can be made in writing, orally, or both. In practice, in many cases, the firm will want both to make written representations and to meet the RDC in order to present its case in person. Written representations must be sent to the RDC Office.

If the firm wishes to make oral representations, it should notify the RDC Office of this in writing at the address stated in the warning notice, specifying the matters as to which it wishes to make the oral representations, an estimate of how much time the representations are likely to take, and the names of any legal representatives that have been appointed to attend[1].

1 As to the firm's ability to appoint a legal representative: see para **10.139** ff below.

10.139 As regards the procedure for making oral representations[1]:

• the RDC may specify the place where the representations will be received[2];

• the representations will be received in private[3];

- the firm may appoint a representative (who may be a lawyer) to attend the meeting and make, or assist it in making, the representations[4];

- the RDC may limit the type, length and content of any representations[5];

- the meeting will be recorded[6]; and

- the RDC may ask the firm or its representative to provide additional information in writing after the meeting[7].

1 See the FCA Handbook at DEPP 3.2.17G–3.2.21G. Oral representations will generally be heard by the warning notice panel (usually consisting of the Chairman or Deputy plus two others) which will normally be supplemented by two new members at the decision notice stage. If no representations are made, the warning notice and the decision notice panels will usually be the same.
2 In most cases, this will be at the FCA's offices.
3 FCA Handbook at DEPP 3.2.1G.
4 FCA Handbook at DEPP 3.2.19G.
5 FCA Handbook at DEPP 3.2.18G.
6 See the FCA Handbook at DEPP 1.2.8G. The RDC will produce a tape recording of the meeting, a copy of which the firm may request.
7 FCA Handbook at DEPP 3.2.20G.

10.140 In practice, the FCA staff members responsible for the investigation are present at the oral representations and it is normal practice that they will present the FCA's case. The main focus of the meeting is, however, on the firm providing its oral representations to the RDC. The precise procedure to be adopted is determined on a case by case basis by the Chairman or Deputy Chairman sitting on the panel. The procedure is not as formal as, for example, a court process. In advance of the meeting, the RDC Office (see para **10.28** above) will liaise with the parties to ensure that all relevant documents are available to all parties at the meeting, and to advise all parties of the structure and timeframes for the meeting.

10.141 The representations meeting takes place around a series of tables. The order in which representations are made, and the structure of any meeting, is a matter for the RDC to determine. In practice, the RDC seeks to ensure that the meeting provides all parties with a fair opportunity properly to present their case. The firm may wish to provide a skeleton argument to the RDC, outlining the points that the firm intends to make. The RDC will have read the firm's written representations in advance of the meeting, so it is unlikely to be necessary or desirable to repeat those representations full; the firm may prefer to use the meeting as an opportunity to develop particular points. The firm will be given an opportunity to present its oral submissions, the FCA will present its case, and the firm will have an opportunity to respond to the FCA's submissions. The FCA may decide simply to assert its view in relation to the alleged misconduct, rather than engaging with arguments advanced by the firm (for example, if the FCA is enforcing for breaches of Principles, and considers the points made by the firm to be overly legalistic or technical in nature). Parties granted third party rights will also be entitled to make submissions, should they wish to do so. Any party may be represented by counsel at the hearing, although parties are entitled to appear without representation. It is possible to submit statements from factual or expert witnesses to support the firm's submissions, and for witnesses to make oral statements to the RDC. The RDC members present may pose questions at any point, but there is no cross-examination of witnesses or of individuals making representations. Naturally, the firm should be prepared for the likely areas of questioning. Should the RDC find it necessary to meet with or discuss the matter with the FCA staff, the other relevant parties will be given the opportunity to be present at any further meeting or respond accordingly to those discussions[1].

1 FCA Handbook at DEPP 3.2.2 1G.

What should the representations contain?

10.142 The content of the representations will depend entirely upon the situation and it is impossible to give much guidance in the abstract. Neither the FSMA 2000 nor the FCA's rules prescribe any limitations on the nature or content of the representations that can be made, although, as has already been noted[1], the RDC may limit the type, length and content of oral representations. The overriding consideration for the firm will be that the representations will be its main opportunity to have input into the process, short of going through the full Tribunal procedure. The firm will therefore want to stress, as much as possible, the main points of its defence, with a view to influencing the RDC's decision. The areas that it might want to consider covering include:

- key factual points that the firm has made in its response to the preliminary findings letter;

- the reasons why the firm believes it did not breach the relevant rules or regulations and, in particular, where appropriate, the firm's case on what standard of market practice applied at the time and why its conduct did not fall below that standard;

- why the proposed sanction or other action is inappropriate or disproportionate;

- what steps the firm has taken since the problem arose, such as in dealing with its customers and the FCA and addressing any internal issues; and

- any particular complaints or issues that the firm has about the FCA's procedures and how they were implemented in the case.

1 See para **10.139** above.

Within what period must the firm make its representations?

10.143 When it decides whether to issue a warning notice, the RDC will give a reasonable period for the firm to make representations. The period, which cannot be less than 14 days, is stated in the warning notice[1].

1 FSMA 2000, s 387(2) and FCA Handbook at DEPP 1.2.6G(1).

Can the firm ask for an extension of time?

10.144 The recipient of the warning notice may request an extension of the time for making representations, for example to provide time for settlement discussions, or where the matter is particularly complicated and the firm had little idea of what was going to be alleged against it until it received the warning notice, and the firm needs to review the FCA's material before it can prepare its representations. The firm may also have had no control, and no warning, as to the timing of the warning notice. It may be received at a particularly busy time of year, or at a time when key people are away[1].

Such a request must normally be made within seven days of the notice being given[2]. The Chairman or Deputy Chairman of the RDC will decide whether to allow an extension, and may take into account any comments from the FCA staff involved in relation to the matter in question[3]. Firms should proceed on the cautious assumption that they will have only 14 days to respond.

1   The FCA has granted extensions of time, but the maximum extension has tended to be a further 28 days.
2   FCA Handbook at DEPP 3.2.16G(1).
3   FCA Handbook at DEPP 3.2.16G(2) and 1.2.6G(1).

10.145   The need for the request to be made within seven days of receipt of the warning notice needs to be borne in mind. This can cause difficulty in practice as it may often not be apparent until the process of preparing the representations is well under way that additional time is required. The FCA's rules do not expressly allow firms to apply for an extension outside the seven-day period.

The person concerned will promptly be notified of its decision whether to grant an extension[1]. An extension may, for example, be appropriate if mediation is taking place[2].

1   FCA Handbook at DEPP 3.2.16G.
2   See para **10.63** above.

10.146   No guidance is given within the rules as to what factors the RDC will take into account in deciding whether or not to accede to a request for an extension of time[1]. The warning notice will not explain the basis upon which the RDC came to its original decision on the period granted for submission of representations[2]. The person concerned will not, therefore, be able to address whatever concerns gave rise to the original decision on the period that was considered to be reasonable. Reasons for requesting an extension of time are therefore likely to relate primarily to the firm, such as the availability to it of relevant people, the amount of preparatory work that will need to be done and the time that will be likely to be necessary to review the FCA's material.

In exceptional cases where the firm can show on reasonable grounds that it did not receive the warning notice to which a decision notice has been issued, or that it had reasonable grounds for not responding to it within the specified period, the RDC may permit it to make representations before it takes the decision whether to issue a Notice of Discontinuance[3] or a further decision notice[4].

1   The rationale for the reduction in the period for making written representations from 28 to 14 days in the FS Act 2012 was to reduce the overall time taken to complete enforcement actions. The legislation having been amended in this way, the FCA may now be reluctant to grant extensions of time. The FSA has also stated (in its report 'The 'End to End' Review of the Enforcement

Process', July 2004) , prior to the reduction in the period from 28 to 14 days, that it envisaged that extensions of time will only be given in 'exceptional circumstances' so as to ensure that the enforcement process does not take too long: see also John Tiner FSA Enforcement Conference speech (6/9/04). There are seven days to request an extension of time to make representations, which will be decided by the Chairman or Deputy Chairman of the RDC (FCA Handbook at DEPP 3.2.16G).

2 Contrast a supervisory notice: see para **16.152** ff below.

3 See the FCA Handbook at DEPP 2.3.4G. Such a Notice of Discontinuance will be issued if the RDC, having heard the representations, decides that the action should not be taken: see para **10.165** below.

4 That type of decision notice would probably be issued under the rules discussed at para **10.183** ff below.

Are the firm's written representations discloseable to third parties?

10.147 The question of whether material that is produced by the firm and which is given to the RDC is discloseable to third parties in legal proceedings brought in relation to the same matter is considered at para **4.170** ff above.

10.148 Where the FCA has given a copy of the warning notice to a third party and that party has exercised its right to make representations, the RDC is likely to disclose each party's representations to the other, at least insofar as it is relevant for the other party to see the representations so as to have an opportunity of addressing any points made. If there is a reason why the firm does not consider this to be appropriate, it should give that reason to the RDC on submitting the representations.

What rights will other parties have?

10.149 The FCA must in certain circumstances give a copy of a warning notice to a third party[1] and that third party will then have various statutory rights. The relevant provisions are outlined below.

1 FSMA 2000, s 393.

The right to receive a copy of a warning notice

10.150 The obligation to provide a third party with a copy of the warning notice may arise in relation to many, but not all, warning notices[1]. In relation to such warning notices, a copy of the notice must be given to a third party if any of the reasons contained in the warning notice:

- identifies[2] the third party (being a person other than the person to whom the notice was given); and

- in the opinion of the FCA is prejudicial[3] to that person.

There is no requirement to give the person a copy of the notice if the FCA has given him a separate warning notice in relation to the same matter or gives him such a notice at the same time[4].

1 It applies in relation to those types of warning notice that are listed at the FSMA 2000, s 392. These are the same warning notices that rise to the right of access to the FCA's documents: see para **10.118** ff above.
2 See the decision of the Tribunal in relation to the reference made by Sir Philip Watts (the former chairman of Shell) in *Sir Philip Watts v FSA FSMT Case 020* (13/09/05). The Tribunal declined to interpret the concept of 'identified' broadly. The fact that an individual, who is not named in the final notice, might generally be known to have been associated with matters referred to in the warning notice is not sufficient to confer third party rights on that person. However, the Tribunal declined to adopt the FCA's proposal that in order to have third party rights an individual must actually be named in the notice.
3 Such 'prejudice' is likely to arise from the wording of the warning notice and the impact that it may have on the person's reputation. Although the third party will not be censured (because, to impose censure, the FCA would need to take enforcement action against that party), its involvement in the breach, although blameless, may, for example, somehow impact upon its reputation or may leave it open to civil claims from third parties.
4 FSMA 2000, s 393(2).

10.151 The FCA Handbook does not set out examples of when, in practice, the FCA will serve a copy of a warning notice on a third party. The decision in any particular case will be made by the RDC[1] unless the decision is made in relation to a matter where a settlement has been agreed. In settlement cases the decision is made by the settlement decision makers[2] who, as already discussed, will be FCA staff members.

1 FCA Handbook at DEPP 1.2.6G(2).
2 FCA Handbook at DEPP 1.2.5G and 1.2.6G.

10.152 For example, assume a firm, 'X Co', breaches a regulatory rule by mispricing an investment belonging to a customer and then by selling it to another firm, 'Y Co'. One of X Co's traders, T, will have actually carried out the pricing and the trading. In such a situation, questions could clearly arise, not only in relation to X Co (Why did this happen? Who was responsible for authorising the mispricing and the trade? Were X Co's systems and controls adequate?) but also in relation to T (Were his actions deliberate? Was he aware of the rules? Did he personally benefit from the breach?) and even Y Co (Why was it involved? What did it know? Have its obligations to its investors been fulfilled?). A warning notice proposing disciplinary action against X Co alleging, say, that its controls were inadequate, will be likely to identify T and perhaps even Y Co when setting out the reasons for taking the action. It may also be prejudicial to them in that the resolution of the matter between X Co and the FCA, may involve reaching findings or admissions that will adversely affect them. For example, it may find that there has been a breach by T, of which Y Co (or one of its employees) was (or should have been) aware. Whilst such findings or admissions will be unlikely to bind Y Co and T[1], they could, in practice, expose them to, or affect their position in, regulatory proceedings or civil claims brought by third parties, as well as affecting their reputation.

1 See para **19.89** ff below.

10.153 In such a situation, the FCA will also be obliged to serve a copy of the notice on Y Co and T unless it contemporaneously issues them with a separate warning notice, or has already done so. The involvement of third parties in the decision-making process has, in practice, given rise to complications. For example, the FCA may have already started disciplinary proceedings against Y Co and T. If it then serves a notice on X Co which must be copied to Y Co and T then, as will be seen, Y Co and T will have a right to participate in the proceedings against X Co. This may become particularly difficult at the decision notice stage[1] or if settlement discussions or mediation takes place[2]. The FCA may therefore want to wait until its investigations into all three have been completed before proceeding against all at the same time. However, in some situations it will not be able to do this, particularly given the statutory three year limitation period that applies to proceedings conducted against individuals for misconduct[3].

1 See the discussion at para **10.166** ff below.
2 See the discussion at para **10.42** ff above.
3 FSMA 2000, ss 66 and 91.

10.154 In practice, third party rights have been recognised in a number of situations, including: where action was taken against a firm's employee (whether or not related action was also taken against the firm)[1], where different breaches were committed by different parties in relation to the same or similar underlying facts[2], where the breaches were directed against specific third parties such as counterparties[3], where the breaches occurred when the firm formed part of another firm's group but subsequently ceased to form part of that group[4], where the breach relates to the firm's failure to exercise properly its responsibility in relation to a third party[5], and where the implication of the firm's breach was that a third party adviser had also breached its regulatory obligations[6].

1 See, for example, *Antony Blunden final notice (10/11/03)*. The individual's former firm was issued with a copy of the notice despite the fact that it had already been disciplined in relation to the relevant breaches, both by the Japanese regulator (see Credit Suisse Group press release (29/7/99)) and the FSA (see *Credit Suisse First Boston International final notice (11/12/02)*).
2 For example, when prohibition orders were issued against two stockbrokers who worked at the same firm (one of whom was its Chief Executive), the firm received copies of the notices and, since the underlying breaches were different but related, the individuals were issued with copies of each other's notices: see *Barry Scott and Lata Gaur final notices (6/3/03)*. Note that the process will not always be reciprocal. For example, when the FSA censured a firm and fined its former CEO, the firm was issued with the notice that was served on the CEO, but the opposite did not occur: see *Keith Rutter and the Underwriter Insurance Company Limited final notices (29/11/04)*.
3 See for example, *Reto Moser final notice (6/1/03)*, which resulted from the failures of an individual. Both his employer and a firm for which he was the customary point of contact were served with copies of the notices.
4 See for example, *Capita Trust Company final notice (20/10/04)*, where the firm's breaches occurred between 1997 and 2002. In 2001, it was sold as a going concern by the Royal & Sun Alliance Group plc. The latter was issued with a copy of the notice despite the fact that the firm being disciplined no longer formed part of its group.
5 For example, *Sesame Limited final notice (1/10/04)* related to the firm's failure to monitor adequately the selling practices of an appointed representative. Although no disciplinary action was taken against the appointed representative, it was issued with a copy of the notice.
6 For example, *Prudential Plc final notice (27/03/2013)*, in which Prudential's sponsor was granted third party rights.

10.155 What is also evident from the above is that the test of what may be prejudicial to a person will potentially be very wide. It is difficult to see why it should be limited to matters that could have a regulatory impact on the person, or even to matters that may have a financial impact. A matter likely to affect a person's reputation adversely could be prejudicial to him as could a matter that could potentially affect his liability to third parties. However, it is the RDC's (or, in the case of a settlement, the FCA's) view of whether a matter is prejudicial to that person that matters for these purposes[1].

1 The same test is used in relation to whether a decision notice should be copied to a third party, and a decision by the FCA not to provide a copy of the decision notice may be challenged in the Tribunal: see para **10.177** below.

10.156 The notice does not need to be given to the third party if the RDC (or, in the case of a settlement, FCA) considers that it is impracticable to do so[1]. No indication is provided as to what the FCA regards this as meaning. However, this should be interpreted as relating to the practicability of issuing the notice and not as to the likely consequences.

1 FSMA 2000, s 393(7).

10.157 In practice, affording rights to third parties in relation to proposed enforcement action is a difficult area because it can complicate the decision-making process, particularly where there is pressure to settle. For example, whereas the firm against whom the action is to be taken may wish to settle, the third party may be concerned about the impact of the decision on it and, in some cases, may even be prepared to refer the matter to the Tribunal[1]. If so, the FCA would be unable to take the proposed action despite the fact that an agreement has been reached with the firm that is to be disciplined. The RDC (or settlement decision maker) is only obliged to involve the third party at the warning notice stage if the notice relates to a matter that prejudices the third party in *its* opinion[2]. It thus has considerable discretion, (the extent of which has been considered by the Tribunal[3]). However, as will be seen, that is not the end of the story, because the third party may still have the right to refer the matter to the Tribunal once the decision notice or final notice is issued, and the effect of that would be to delay, or potentially even prevent, the settlement. In some instances, third parties will only become aware of potential prejudice when the relevant final notice has been issued and in those cases, the damage is likely already to have been done. In addition, in many cases third parties will be unwilling to take the step of referring a case to the Tribunal notwithstanding the prejudice caused to them by a decision notice or final notice. If these problems are to be avoided, and the rights of third parties are not to be over-ridden in the rush to a settlement, it is incumbent upon the FCA and parties attempting to reach a settlement to be cautious about the potential effect on third parties[4].

1 See **Chapter 12** below. Individuals may in practice be less likely to accept a settlement than firms.
2 FSMA 2000, s 393(1).
3 See *Sir Philip Watts v FSA FSMT Case 020 (13/09/05)*.
4 See FCA Enforcement Guide at EG 5.11–5.13 in relation to the rights of third parties on settlement.

Rights to become involved in the process

10.158 A third party provided with a copy of a warning notice has four rights:

- the right to make representations to the FCA in relation to publication of information about the matter to which the warning notice relates, if the FCA proposes to make such a public statement[1].

- the right to make representations to the FCA within the reasonable period specified on the notice, which must be not less than 14 days[2];

- a right of access to the FCA's material on the same basis as the person to whom the warning notice was given[3], but only in so far as the material which the FCA is required to disclose relates to the matter which identifies the third party[4] (and the notice must explain the effect of this provision[5]); and

- the right to be given a Notice of Discontinuance where that is served on the person on whom the warning notice was served[6].

As will be seen, the third party will have further rights at the decision notice stage.

1 FSMA 2000, s 391(1)(c) and FCA Handbook at DEPP 3.2.14CG–3.2.14EG.
2 FSMA 2000, s 393(3). For a discussion of the process of making representations, see para **10.137** ff above. The same provisions of the FCA Handbook apply to the third party: see the FCA Handbook at DEPP 2.4.1G and 3.2.15G–3.2.21G. There is no express statutory limitation as to the issues on which the third party may make representations, but in practice this is likely to be limited to the matter which identifies or affects him.
3 See para **10.118** ff above.
4 FSMA 2000, s 393(12).
5 FSMA 2000, s 393(13).
6 FSMA 2000, s 393(14). Notices of discontinuance are discussed at para **10.93** ff below.

Further investigations or further action by the FCA

10.159 If the process of making representations gives rise to new issues that the FCA wishes to investigate, or which lead it to believe that other action may be required, to what extent can it take additional steps? There are two separate questions. The first is whether the FCA, having heard the firm's representations, can take a different kind of action against the firm from that which was originally proposed in the warning notice or further action in addition to that which was proposed in the warning notice. The answer to this is that it can, but that it may need to issue another warning notice[1]. It may, however, first need to obtain further information, particularly if information was supplied to it by the firm upon a without prejudice basis with the result that it cannot be relied upon by the FCA against the firm[2].

1 This is considered at para **10.164** below.
2 See the discussion at para **10.54** above.

10.160 The second question is whether, in the light of the representations made, the FCA can conduct further investigations into the matter. There is nothing to prevent the FCA from doing so. It is the FCA that controls the timetable and, provided that the RDC is content to allow it, the FCA can conduct further investigations and put further material before the RDC for use at the decision notice stage[1]. In undertaking the further investigations, the FCA has to be careful not to misuse any information that has been provided in confidence or on a without prejudice basis[2].

1 Note, however, that the RDC may not, after a warning notice has been issued, meet with, or discuss the matter with, the FCA staff conducting the investigation, without the subject of the investigation and any relevant third parties being present or otherwise having the opportunity to respond (see the FCA Handbook at DEPP 3.2.21G).
2 See the discussion at para **10.54** above.

10.161 When, in practice, will the FCA do this? In practice this may depend on the RDC's response to the matters within the warning notice and the representations. The RDC may take some time to deliberate and ask for further work to be done by the FCA enforcement staff, prior to reaching a decision[1].

1 The RDC may, following oral representations, ask for additional written information from enforcement and from other parties that were present at the oral representations meeting (see the FCA Handbook at DEPP 3.2.21G).

Phase 5 – the issue of a decision notice

Considering the representations made by the firm

10.162 Assuming that no settlement has been reached, the next step is for the RDC to consider the written and any oral representations and then to decide whether it should take:

- the action it proposed in its warning notice; or

- some other action; or

- no action.

The RDC considers the question of what action the FCA should take by reference to the FCA's policy on when to take the relevant action, in the same way as it takes the decision to issue a warning notice[1]. Where the question of whether there was a breach depends on market standards, the standards in question will be those that applied when the alleged breach occurred. In such cases, expert evidence as to what standards applied may be necessary. Following representations, the FCA staff may prepare a similar form of recommendation as to whether the RDC should decide to issue a decision notice/Notice of Discontinuance in the same way as they did in respect of the RDC's decision as to whether to issue a warning notice[2].

1 See para **10.99** above.
2 The contents of the FCA's recommendation to the RDC as to whether to issue a warning notice is considered at para **10.91** above.

10.163 If the RDC decides to take the action specified in the warning notice, it must issue a decision notice[1] that states the reasons for the decision to take the action that is being proposed, including the reasons why the firm's representations have been rejected[2]. The process for doing so, and the effect of the notice, is discussed in detail below.

1 So far as disciplinary action is concerned, see the FSMA 2000, ss 208 (for firms) and 67(4) (for individuals). Equivalent provisions exist in relation to the other enforcement action which involves the warning/decision notice procedure: for the relevant references, see para **10.3** above.
2 Whilst there is no statutory requirement that the decision notice contain details of why the firm or individual's representations were rejected, the RDC has faced criticism from the Court of Appeal for the failure of decision notices to do so (see *R (on the application of Christopher Willford) v FSA [2013] EWCA Civ 677*).

10.164 If the RDC decides to take some other action, there are two possibilities, depending upon what action it wishes to take:

- if the action it decides to take is under the same part of the FSMA 2000 as the action proposed in the warning notice, then the RDC may simply issue a decision notice[1]. This would allow the RDC, having originally proposed, say, a fine, to issue a greater or smaller fine, or a public censure, but will not allow it to decide to cancel or vary the firm's permission or require the firm to pay restitution;

- otherwise, the RDC must discontinue the action to which the original warning notice applied, by issuing a Notice of Discontinuance[2], and then by issuing a new warning notice in relation to the action now proposed.

1 FSMA 2000, s 388(2).
2 See para **10.93** ff above.

10.165 If the RDC decides to take no action, it must give a Notice of Discontinuance to the person to whom the warning notice was given[1] and to any third party to whom a copy of the warning notice was given (see para **10.93** above)[2].

1 FSMA 2000, s 389. It does not need to do so if the discontinuance of the proceedings results in the granting of an application made by the firm to whom the warning or decision notice was issued: see the FSMA 2000, s 389(2). This could apply, for example, if the FCA originally decided not to accede to the firm's request to vary or revoke action which it has already taken, and therefore has issued a warning notice, but has subsequently decided to accede to that request.
2 FSMA 2000, s 393(14).

The decision notice

10.166 A decision notice is the notice that the FSMA 2000 requires the FCA to issue if it decides to take any of various courses of action[1] following the issue of a warning notice. Normally, such a notice will be issued because the RDC has decided to take the action proposed in the warning notice, but it may alternatively decide to take a more limited range of action other than that proposed in the warning notice[2]. In some circumstances, and with the person's consent, a decision notice may be issued without any related warning notice having been issued[3].

1 See the list at para **10.3** above.
2 See para **10.164** above.
3 See para **10.183** ff below.

10.167 Although the issuance of a decision notice signifies that the FCA, through the RDC[1], has reached a decision that the sanction or action it proposed is appropriate, the action itself is not imposed at this stage. As will be seen, the firm retains a right to refer the decision notice to the Tribunal, which can look at the case afresh, and the action specified will not be imposed until the Tribunal has determined the matter and a final notice[2] has been issued.

1 Although the decision reflected in the decision notice will normally have been made by the RDC, it may, for example, also follow a decision made by the FCA following settlement discussions: see para **10.56** ff above.
2 See para **10.188** ff below.

What must a decision notice contain?

10.168 A decision notice must[1]:

- be in writing;

- give the FCA's reasons for the decision to take the action to which the notice relates;

- explain whether the firm has a right of access to the FCA's material and if so, what this means and whether there is any secondary material to which the firm must be allowed access[2]; and

- give an indication of any right the firm has to have the matter referred to the Tribunal and the procedure on such a reference[3].

1 FSMA 2000, s 388(1).
2 For a discussion of the right of access to the FCA's material, and of the meaning of secondary material, see para **10.123** ff above. The discussion there applies equally in the context of a decision notice. As to whether the firm would wish to exercise the right at the decision notice stage, see para **10.171** below.
3 See para **10.173** below. As to whether the firm should refer the matter to the Tribunal, see para **10.182** below.

10.169 In addition to the statutory requirement under the FSMA 2000 to state the reasons for the decision to take the action specified, a decision notice should also explain why the RDC rejected the representations made by the recipient of the notice. The FSA was criticised for failing to explain the reasons why the firm's representations were rejected in the Legal & General case in 2003[1]. Further, in a more recent case, the recipient of a decision notice challenged the notice as failing to set out the RDC's reasons for rejecting the representations made by the subject of the regulatory action. The claimant succeeded at first instance, but failed on appeal, although it remains clear that the RDC should properly explain its reasoning in any decision notice[2].

1 This followed criticism of previous practice. In the Tribunal's view, Legal & General was 'justified in feeling aggrieved by, among other things, the lack of any explanation of the reasons why its representations were rejected': see *Legal & General Assurance Society Ltd v FCA [2003] FIN 0022*. As a result, the FCA's Report on the Enforcement Process (July 2005) recommended that such explanations should be provided.
2 *R (on the application of Christopher Willford) v FSA [2013] EWCA Civ 677* (on appeal from the High Court decision in *R (C) v Financial Services Authority [2012] EWHC 1417 (Admin)*). The recipient of the decision notice challenged the notice by way of judicial review (as opposed to exercising his right to refer the decision notice to the Tribunal). The High Court permitted a judicial review,

since it would have been prejudicial to the recipient of the notice to have to decide whether to refer the matter to the Tribunal (which might increase the penalty) without knowing the reasoning for the conclusion reached by the RDC.

The High Court quashed the decision notice, and referred the matter back to the RDC to re-consider. The Court of Appeal overturned the decision of the High Court but were critical of the RDC's reasoning in the decision notice: (Pill LJ (at 75): '*I agree that the appeal should be allowed but would expect a clearer and more focussed approach by RDCs. It is the quality of the reasoning rather than its length that is important*'.)

When does the firm receive the decision notice?

10.170 The firm receives the decision notice when the RDC (or FCA) decides to take the action which gives rise to an obligation under the FSMA 2000 to issue a decision notice[1]. The delivery of a decision notice to the firm may be a number of months after the firm has made its representations to the RDC. There are detailed rules on the service and receipt of statutory notices[2].

1 FSMA 2000 contains varying requirements on the timing for provision of a decision notice. For example, s 208 requires one to be provided without delay, whereas s 67 is silent on the point.
2 See the FSMA 2000 (Service of Notices) Regulations 2001, SI 2001/1420. Among other things, the regulations make provision for when a notice is to be treated as having been received.

What is the effect of receiving a decision notice?

10.171 Although termed a 'decision notice', the notice is not the final step in the enforcement process. The decision notice records the conclusions of the RDC concerning the conduct of the firm and that the action proposed by the FCA is appropriate in the circumstances. However, the action proposed does not occur at the time the decision notice is issued.

10.172 The decision notice gives the firm two rights. First, the firm has a right of access to the FCA's material, on the same basis as the right which arose upon issue of the warning notice[1]. The decision notice does not necessarily need to be based solely on the material available to the RDC at the warning notice stage together with the firm's representations. The FCA may in the meantime have continued to obtain or create further material, for example, it may have obtained further evidence which refutes points made by the firm in its representations. In practice, the firm should already have received this material to the extent it was provided to the RDC (although there is no continuing disclosure obligation in the FSMA 2000 requiring the FCA to provide such material to the firm on an ongoing basis). Any additional material (for example, material that was not provided to the RDC and which might undermine the FCA's case) may be relevant to the firm's assessment of whether to refer the case to the Tribunal and it may therefore wish to exercise its right of access before making that decision.

1 For a detailed discussion, see para **10.118** ff above.

10.173 Second, the firm has a right to refer the case to the Tribunal, so that the case can be heard and determined in an independent and public forum. A detailed discussion of the nature of the Tribunal, and the procedure for Tribunal proceedings, is found in **CHAPTER 12** below. It is only if the firm decides not to take this step, which it normally has 28 days to do[1], or for some reason does not do so within the requisite period, that the FCA will issue a further notice, the final notice[2], and the action set out in the decision notice will take effect. In the meantime, the FCA cannot take the relevant action[3].

1 For the detailed rules, see para **12.42** ff below.
2 See para **10.188** ff below.
3 FSMA 2000, s 133A(4).

What rights do third parties have?

10.174 In the same way as for a warning notice[1], the decision notice must be copied to a third party if one of the reasons set out in the notice relates to a matter which identifies a person other than the firm to whom the notice is given and in the opinion of the FCA is prejudicial to that third party[2]. In addition, if the decision notice was preceded by a warning notice, a copy must be given to each person to whom the warning notice was copied[3]. This is subject to the same exceptions as for warning notices[4] and applies to the same types of notices[5].

1 See para **10.150** ff above.
2 FSMA 2000, s 393(4).
3 FSMA 2000, s 393(5).
4 See paras **10.150** and **10.156** above.
5 See footnote 1 to para **10.150** above.

10.175 A third party to whom a copy of a decision notice is given has a right of access to the FCA's material in the same way as the person to whom the decision notice was given, but only in so far as the material relates to the matter which identifies the third party[1]. The copy of the notice must be accompanied by a description of the right of access[2].

1 FSMA 2000, s 393(12). For a discussion of the right of access to FCA material, see para **10.118** ff above.
2 FSMA 2000, s 393(13).

10.176 The third party also has the right to refer the matter to the Tribunal, but limited to[1]:

• the decision in question, so far as it is based on the reason which identifies him and is prejudicial to him; or

• any opinion expressed by the FCA in relation to him.

1 FSMA 2000, s 393(9).

10.177 A person who alleges that a copy of the decision notice should have been given to him, but was not, may also refer that alleged failure to the Tribunal, as well as either of the two matters outlined above[1].

1 FSMA 2000, s 393(11).

10.178 Whilst introducing an element of fairness to third parties, these provisions have the practical effect of introducing an element of uncertainty so far as the person primarily subject to the enforcement proceedings is concerned. In particular, the FCA Handbook does not prevent the third party challenging the decision notice where the firm which is the subject of the enforcement proceedings accepts it and elects not to refer the matter to the Tribunal. Similarly, a third party can prevent a matter from being disposed of, even where the firm and the FCA reach an agreed settlement[1].

1   Once the decision notice is referred to the Tribunal, it will not take effect until the reference, and any appeal, has been finally disposed of: FSMA 2000, s 133A(4). There is nothing in the FSMA 2000 to restrict the effect of this in cases where it is a third party who refers the matter to the Tribunal. The problem is illustrated by the following example: On 20 December 2002, the FCA issued decision notices to a firm and two of its directors. The directors referred the matter to the Tribunal but the firm did not. Following consideration of the matter by the Tribunal, the FCA's proposed action against one of the directors was upheld. Accordingly, the FCA was only able to issue final notices against that director and the firm, a year later, on 17 December 2003: see *Hoodless Brennan and Partners Plc/Sean Blackwell final notices (17/12/03)* and *Hoodless and Blackwell v FCA (2003) FSMT 007.*

Publicity

10.179 The FCA must publish such information about the matter to which the decision notice relates as the FCA considers appropriate[1], and in such manner as the FCA considers appropriate[2]. The FCA may not, however, publish information in respect of a decision notice where the information would be: (a) unfair to the person with respect to whom the action was taken (or was proposed to be taken); (b) prejudicial to the interests of consumers; or, (c) detrimental to the stability of the UK financial system[3].

1   FSMA 2000, s 391(4).
2   FSMA 2000, s 391(7). The FCA may decide not to publish a decision or final notice against one party where a related enforcement action is proceeding in parallel against another party. In these circumstances, the FCA may refrain from publishing any notice pending the conclusion of the parallel enforcement action. See for example *Peter Cummings final notice (12/09/12)* and *Bank of Scotland Plc final notice (dated 9/3/12, but published on the FSA website 19/10/2012).*
3   See the FSMA 2000, s 391(6) and FCA Enforcement Guide at EG 6.9.
      Where the final notice relates to behaviour in the context of a takeover bid, and the FCA believes that publicity may affect the timetable or outcome of that bid, the FCA will consult the Takeover Panel and give due weight to its views: see the FCA Enforcement Guide at EG 6.18.

10.180 The FCA's normal policy is to publish decision notices if the firm decides to refer the matter to the Tribunal[1]. However, the FCA may also publish a decision notice before a firm has decided whether to refer the matter to the Tribunal if the FCA considers that there is a compelling reason to do so (for example to preserve market confidence or protect consumers)[2]. If the FCA intends to publish, it will give advance notice to the firm and to any third party to whom a copy of the notice is given, and will consider any representations made[3]. If the FCA publishes a decision notice, and the firm successfully refers the matter to the Tribunal, the FCA will make clear on its website that the decision notice no longer applies[4].

1   FCA Enforcement Guide at EG 6.8.
2   FCA Enforcement Guide at EG 6.8

3   See FCA Enforcement Guide at EG 6.8. The FCA has indicated in its guidance on publication
    in the FCA Enforcement Guide at EG 6.8 that reputational damage will not be a sufficient
    reason to not publish. The FCA's guidance at EG 6.8 also states that the FCA will not decide
    against publication solely because a person asks for confidentiality when they refer a matter to the
    Tribunal. However, publication by the FCA in these circumstances would effectively negate the
    Tribunal's discretionary power to order that Tribunal proceedings should be in private (because
    publication of the decision notice would make render meaningless any privacy order by the
    Tribunal). A firm referring a decision notice to the Tribunal, and seeking to avoid publicity, should
    therefore seek an undertaking from the FCA that it will not publish the decision notice pending
    an order from the Tribunal in relation to privacy. In the *Swift Trade case [2011] EWHC 2766
    (Admin)* the High Court rejected an application by the recipient of the decision notice for an order
    prohibiting the publication of the decision notice on grounds of unfairness and under Article 8
    ECHR (right to respect for private and family life).
4   The FCA will normally do this by publishing a Notice of Discontinuance. See FCA Enforcement
    Guide at EG 6.10C.

10.181 The firm or individual to whom the decision notice is given or copied
may not publish the notice or any details concerning the notice unless the FCA
has published the notice or those details[1]. The FSMA 2000 does not specify any
particular penalty or consequence for a breach of this provision. If the firm
publishes the decision notice, or information about the decision notice, in breach
of the prohibition, it is likely to have contravened a requirement imposed on
it by, or under, the FSMA 2000 and as a result may be exposed to regulatory
enforcement action[2].

1   FSMA 2000, s 391(1A).
2   For a discussion of this test, and the possible consequences, see para **2.94** ff above. As of the
    date of writing, there is no evidence that anyone has been pursued for breaching this prohibition,
    whether in relation to a decision, or any other notice to which the prohibition applies. In some
    circumstances, a listed company may feel that its disclosure obligations under the Listing Rules
    make it necessary to announce the existence of the decision notice. For example, one listed
    company announced the fact that a decision notice had been issued, the FCA had decided to
    impose a financial penalty upon it for contraventions of the Listing Rules, the decision by the
    company's Board of Directors to refer the matter to the Tribunal and the fact that the Board did
    not believe that these facts would have a significant effect on the company's financial position: see
    My Travel Group plc trading update, November 2004.

Should the firm accept the decision notice?

10.182 Whether or not the firm should accept the decision notice or appeal
against it to the Tribunal will depend very much upon the particular circumstances.
The factors relevant to that consideration are set out in **CHAPTER 12** below.

Issuing a further decision notice

10.183 After issuing a decision notice the FCA may[1], with the consent of the
firm, issue a further decision notice proposing different action be taken. The
further decision notice should be issued before the FCA takes the action specified
in the original decision notice and the firm will have the same right as with the
original decision notice to refer the matter to the Tribunal. The firm may also
have a right of access to the FCA's material[2].

1 FSMA 2000, s 388(3)–(5).
2 It is not clear whether the original decision notice falls away; this may depend upon the circumstances when the further decision notice is issued.

10.184 Where a further decision notice is to be issued, the FCA has prescribed the following procedure[1]:

- the FCA staff will recommend to the RDC that the further decision notice is given, either before or after obtaining the firm's consent[2];

- the RDC will consider whether the action proposed is appropriate in the circumstances;

- if it considers that the action proposed is not appropriate, and it decides not to issue the further decision notice, the original decision notice will stand and the firm's rights in relation to that notice will not be affected; and

- if the RDC considers that the action proposed is appropriate, it will issue the further decision notice, subject to the firm's consent being, or having been, obtained.

1 FCA Handbook at DEPP 2.3.5G.
2 The FCA will normally require consent to be in writing: see the FCA Handbook at DEPP 2.3.6G.

10.185 The FCA Handbook does not give any indication as to when it will make use of this procedure[1]. However, it could be appropriate in a number of situations. For example, it could be used to allow discussions between the FCA and the firm to continue after a decision notice has been issued and for the case to be settled before a decision is made whether to refer the case to the Tribunal. It could also be used where the FCA decides to take some other action which would require the issue of a further warning notice[2], and neither the firm nor the FCA want to waste further time going through a second warning notice procedure and waiting a further 14 days for the period for representations to expire. In that situation, the firm may consent to cutting short the procedure, but without prejudice to its right to refer the second decision notice to the Tribunal. The FSMA 2000 here provides a certain amount of flexibility which is useful in practice.

1 The FCA has made use of this power: see, for example *Evolution Beeson Gregory Limited/Christopher Potts final notice (12/11/04)* and *Cantor Index Limited final notice (30/12/04)*.
2 For the limitations on the action which can be taken in a decision notice, in the light of the warning notice given: see para **10.164** above.

10.186 Third parties identified in, and who may be prejudiced by, the decision notice may be entitled to receive a copy and would then have additional rights[1].

1 See para **10.174** above. An example of this in practice is shown in *Robert Stevens final notice (10/11/03)* where the further decision notice was also served on the individual's former firm.

Phase 6 – reference to the Tribunal

10.187 As discussed in para **10.173** above, the firm may refer the RDC's decision to the Tribunal. The nature of the Tribunal and the procedure for appearing before it are reviewed in **CHAPTER 12** below.

Phase 7 – issue of a final notice

10.188 The final stage is for the FCA to issue a final notice giving effect to the regulatory action which is being imposed.

When is a final notice issued?

10.189 A final notice is issued in two situations[1]:

- where the RDC has issued a decision notice and the matter has not been referred to the Tribunal within the requisite period, the FCA must, on taking the action to which the decision notice relates, give the firm, and any person to whom the decision notice was copied, a final notice; or

- where the FCA has given a person a decision notice and the matter has been referred to the Tribunal, the FCA must give the firm, and any person to whom the decision notice was copied, a final notice on taking action in accordance with any directions given by the Tribunal, or the court on an appeal from the Tribunal.

1 FSMA 2000, s 390(1) and (2).

10.190 The final notice is therefore issued when the FCA makes the public statement or issues the fine or restitution order, and so on. This can only be done once the Tribunal process has been exhausted or the firm concerned has not availed itself of the opportunity to refer the matter to the Tribunal[1].

1 As to how the FCA is required to issue statutory notices, and the date when a notice is treated as having been received, see the Financial Services and Markets Act 2000 (Service of Notices) Regulations 2001, SI 2001/1420.

10.191 If the FCA decides for some reason not to take the action referred to in a decision notice, then it must issue a Notice of Discontinuance[1]. For a discussion of Notices of Discontinuance, see para **10.93** ff above.

1 FSMA 2000, s 389(1).

What must a final notice contain?

10.192 Like the decision notice, the final notice will[1] set out the facts and matters to which the notice relates and also the terms of, as appropriate, the statement, order, financial penalty (including any discount on the financial penalty) or other action being taken. The final notice will also include details of the date on which the action is to take effect. In relation to a financial penalty, it must state when it is to be paid (which must not be less than 14 days beginning with the date on which the final notice is given), and how it will be recovered if not paid. In relation to a public statement, it will set out the terms of the statement and give details of the manner in which, and date upon which, it will be published. Final notices (like decision notices and warning notices) often include quotes from the material that has been gathered, or from the transcripts of interviews that have been conducted.

1 For the detailed requirements, see the FSMA 2000, s 390(3)–(7).

To whom must a final notice be given?

10.193 The final notice must be given to the person to whom the FCA gave the decision notice and also to any person to whom the decision notice was copied[1].

1 FSMA 2000, s 390(1) and (2).

Publicity

10.194 Once a final notice has been issued, the FCA is under a duty[1] to publish such information about the matter to which the final notice relates as it considers appropriate, and in such manner as the FCA considers appropriate[2]. It may not, however, publish information in respect of a final notice where the information would be: (a) unfair to the person with respect to whom the action was taken (or was proposed to be taken); (b) prejudicial to the interests of consumers; or, (c) detrimental to the stability of the UK financial system[3]. There is a statutory duty to publish and therefore an expectation that the FCA will publish information about regulatory action at the conclusion of the regulatory process. This reflects the fact that, generally speaking, the publication of successful enforcement action is seen as an important aspect of the FCA's regulatory objectives, highlighting the regulatory requirements and standards, demonstrating that they are being effectively enforced, and thereby helping to maintain confidence in the financial system, promoting public awareness and contributing towards consumer protection[4].

1 FSMA 2000, s 391(4) and see the FCA Handbook at EG 6.8. Where the final notice relates to behaviour In the context of a takeover bid, and the FCA believes that publicity may affect the timetable or outcome of that bid, the FCA will consult the Takeover Panel and give due weight to its views: see FCA Enforcement Guide at EG 6.18.
2 FSMA 2000, s 391(7). Also see para **10.179**, n 2 above.
3 See the FSMA 2000, s 391(6) and FCA Enforcement Guide at EG 6.9.
    Where the final notice relates to behaviour in the context of a takeover bid, and the FCA believes that publicity may affect the timetable or outcome of that bid, the FCA will consult the Takeover Panel and give due weight to its views: see the FCA Enforcement Guide at EG 6.18.
4 FCA Enforcement Guide at EG 6.8 and 6.10.

10.195 Final notices are usually accompanied by an FCA press release on its website[1]. Where the FCA has decided to issue a prohibition order against an individual, the FCA will consider what additional information about the circumstances of the prohibition order to include on the FCA's Financial Services Register[2]. Finally, the FCA may refer to the enforcement action in its annual report.

1 See the FCA Enforcement Guide at EG 6.8B and 6.19. The Financial Services Register is a public record of all bodies (including individuals) that the FCA regulates.
2 See the FCA Enforcement Guide at EG 6.8B. The FCA considers that the press release is non-negotiable since the firm may issue a press release itself. However, in the past there have been occasions when the FCA has agreed to negotiate the wording of the press release as part of the settlement process. The press release will also be approved by the RDC Chairman or relevant Deputy.

COSTS

10.196 The FSMA 2000 provides[1] that the FCA, in determining its policy with respect to the amount of penalties to be imposed by it under the FSMA 2000, must take no account of the expenses which it incurs, or expects to incur, in discharging its functions. In other words, the cost of enforcement is borne by the regulated community as a whole, by means of the annual fees payable to the FCA, and not by individual firms.

1 FSMA 2000, Sch 1, Pt 3, para 19.

10.197 In certain circumstances, costs orders may be made by the Tribunal in relation to the costs incurred in the specific case before the Tribunal, although the normal rule is that there is no order for costs in the Tribunal. This issue is discussed in more detail at para **12.167** ff below[1].

1 See the Tribunal Procedure (Tribunal) Rules 2008, SI 2008/2698, r 10(3).

10.198 In some situations, firms will agree to pay the legal costs of an employee who is the subject of an investigation or enforcement process. It is not thought that there is any objection to this, and indeed it is a relatively usual practice[1].

1 Firms may not pay a fine levied by the FCA against the employee personally, since this would remove much of the deterrent effect of imposing the fine. See GEN 6.1.4A.

Chapter 11 PRA enforcement process

INTRODUCTION

11.1 This chapter considers the procedure followed by the PRA where it wishes to take enforcement action. Since, at the time of writing, the PRA has not yet concluded any publicised enforcement action, the position outlined in this chapter is based solely on the material published by the PRA regarding its enforcement process. The PRA's policies and guidance on its decision-making procedure and other aspects of its disciplinary and enforcement powers are contained in the appendices to the PRA's April 2013 Policy Statement titled 'The Prudential Regulation Authority's approach to enforcement: statutory statements of policy and procedure' (the April 2013 Statement). This statement is (at the time of writing) the only PRA policy document/official guidance relating to the PRA's enforcement process (although they are likely to be incorporated into a PRA Rulebook as it is developed over the first few years of the PRA's operation), and its contents are light in detail when compared with the policies and guidance published by the FCA on its own enforcement procedure[1] (see **CHAPTER 10**).

1 These are contained in FCA Handbook at DEPP and the FCA Enforcement Guide.

11.2   The policies included in the April 2013 Statement include the PRA's policies on statutory notices and the allocation of decision-making (the Notice and Decision Making Statement)[1], the imposition of financial penalties by the PRA (the Penalty Statement)[2], suspensions and restrictions[3], the PRA's settlement procedure (the Settlement Statement)[4] and the PRA's approach to the publicity of regulatory action (the Publicity Statement)[5].

1 The 'Statement of the PRA's policy on statutory notices and the allocation of decision-making under the Act' is contained at Appendix 1 of the April 2013 Statement.
2 The 'Statement of the PRA's policy on the imposition and amount of financial penalties under the Act' is contained at Appendix 2 of the April 2013 Statement.
3 The 'Statement of the PRA's policy on the imposition of suspensions or restrictions under the Act and how the period for which they are to have effect' is contained at Appendix 3 of the April 2013 Statement.
4 The 'Statement of the PRA's settlement decision-making procedure and policy for the determination of the amount of penalties and the period of suspensions or restrictions in settled cases' is contained at Appendix 4 of the April 2013 Statement.
5 The 'Statement of the PRA's approach to publicity of regulatory action' is contained at Appendix 5 of the April 2013 Statement.

11.3   It is possible that in practice the PRA may adopt aspects of the FCA enforcement process, particularly when there are gaps in its own (published) process. The PRA's enforcement procedure is similar to that of the FCA, and this chapter should be read in conjunction with **CHAPTER 10** which contains general advice for firms and individuals in relation to the FCA enforcement process. The only notable point where the PRA enforcement procedure diverges from that of the FCA is in relation to the decision-making body that decides whether it is appropriate to issue the relevant statutory notice, which in the PRA procedure is called a Decision Making Committee.

THE INITIAL STAGES OF THE ENFORCEMENT PROCESS

11.4   The types of conduct that give rise to enforcement by the PRA against firms and/or individuals are outlined in **CHAPTERS 2, 8** and **9**. Conduct which could give rise to PRA enforcement may come to the PRA's attention through a variety of means, including through the use of the PRA's information gathering and investigatory powers (see **CHAPTERS 4** and **5**).

11.5   During an enforcement investigation (up to the stage where a decision is taken to issue a warning notice) the PRA will not normally make public the fact that it is investigating a particular matter, the identity of a firm or individual under investigation, or any of the investigation findings[1]. However, taking into account the extent to which any publicity would assist the investigation (for example by bringing forward witnesses), or deter more widespread breaches, the PRA may determine it is appropriate to make a public announcement regarding the matter[2]. In making this determination the PRA will need to take into account any potential prejudice, risk of unfairness or disproportionate damage that may be caused to any persons who may be a subject of the investigation or to third parties[3]. The PRA's power in this respect is similar to the FCA's power (see para **10.83** ff above)[4]. In circumstances where the existence of a PRA investigation has been made public and the PRA subsequently concludes no further action is warranted or the action it proposes to take is materially different to that in the public domain, it '*may*' take reasonable steps to publicise the fact[5].

1 PRA's Publicity Statement, para 5.
2 PRA's Publicity Statement, para 6.
3 PRA's Publicity Statement, para 7.
4 As noted in para **10.83**, n 3, the FCA made use of their power to publicise enforcement investigations in April 2013 in an investigation into IT failures at RBS.
5 PRA's Publicity Statement, para 8.

11.6   Where the PRA's investigation is sufficiently advanced, the PRA will generally produce an investigation report containing written details of its findings[1]. This report will set out the evidence uncovered and the extent to which the evidence is indicative that one or more of the PRA's regulatory requirements have been breached[2], and may be similar in form to the Preliminary Investigation Report produced by the FCA (see **CHAPTER 10**).

1 PRA's Settlement Statement, para 11.
2 See the statement on enforcement policies on the PRA section of the Bank of England website, which refers in particular to the outsourcing of enforcement investigations (http://www.bankofengland.co.uk/pra/Pages/supervision/regulatoryaction/enforcement.aspx).

11.7   The PRA will then determine what action it proposes to take as a result of the investigation, including (but not limited to) the use of the PRA's enforcement powers. If the PRA staff consider that action requiring a warning notice is appropriate, they will make a recommendation to a PRA decision-making body (known as a Decision Making Committee) that the notice should be given[1].

1 PRA's Notice and Decision Making Statement, paras 17 and 41.

SELECTION OF THE DECISION MAKING COMMITTEE

11.8   Decisions as to whether the PRA will give a statutory notice (such as a warning or decision notice) will be made by a committee of individuals called a Decision Making Committee (DMC). The DMCs will also take decisions associated with a statutory notice, such as decisions to: set or extend time for making representations; give copies of the notice to any third party; grant access to PRA material relevant to a notice under the FSMA 2000, s 394; and to publicise the notice[1].

1 PRA's Notice and Decision Making Statement, para 11.

11.9   The DMC differs in both name and composition from the decision-making body used in the FCA enforcement process, the Regulatory Decisions Committee (RDC). A DMC will be made up of individuals selected from the PRA's management[1], whilst the FCA's RDC is outside of the FCA's management structure (although it is a committee of the FCA Board (see paras **10.25** ff above for further detail on the RDC). The PRA have explained this approach by stating that: 'To embed the PRA's forward-looking and judgement-led approach, decisions will be taken by the executive, who will have a detailed knowledge and understanding of the operation of firm's business and the risks that they may pose to the PRA's objectives'[2].

1 PRA's Notice and Decision Making Statement, para 32 states that all DMC members are PRA employees and part of its executive management structure other than the members of the Regulatory Sub-Committee of the PRA board where some members will be non-executives.
2 The joint Bank of England and FSA Consultation Paper CP 12/39 dated December 2012.

11.10 A DMC will usually be composed of at least three members who will include a chairman, although the size may vary depending on the nature of the matter[1]. In certain urgent cases where the PRA considers, in order to advance any of its objectives, it is necessary to take a decision before a recommendation can be made to the appropriate DMC, a decision can be made by two individuals of at least the same level of seniority as the individuals who would have comprised the DMC. In this case, at least one of these two people will be independent of establishing the evidence on which the decision is based[2]. Further details on the nature and procedures of the DMCs are set out at paras 32–40 of the PRA's Notice and Decision Making Statement.

1 The DMC composition needs to secure that statutory decisions are taken by two or more persons who include a person not directly involved in establishing the evidence on which that decision is based (FSMA 2000, s 395(2)).
2 PRA's Notice and Decision Making Statement, paras 70–71.

11.11 The proposed DMC process raises some questions about the independence of the PRA's decision-making procedure. Whilst FCA enforcement decisions will continue to be made using the RDC process (which is intended to provide a decision-making body independent from the enforcement team and FCA management) (see **CHAPTER 10**), the DMC process will involve enforcement decisions being taken by PRA employees. The PRA addressed concerns about the independence of the DMC process by stating that although a DMC may include an individual who had been involved in handling the case before it reached the DMC, there will be at least two further individuals on the DMC who were not involved in the casework[1]. This approach is in line with the FSMA 2000, s 395 which states that statutory decisions can be made by two or more persons including a person not directly involved in establishing the relevant evidence.

1 The PRA's April 2013 policy document on its Approach to Enforcement stated that the decision-making framework is 'fair and proportionate' and will involve 'at least one person who has not been directly involved in the development of the case being considered', and that the members 'of the committees [are] suitable and capable of reaching proportionate decisions'.

11.12 The PRA has four levels of DMC responsible for the issue of statutory notices, each one of varying seniority[1]. The choice of which level of DMC will take any given decision will be determined by the category of firm and likely impact of the decision. Firms are divided into five categories reflecting each firm's impact on the PRA's objectives[2]. The PRA also considers the category of the statutory decision. Statutory decisions are divided into three categories (Type A, Type B and Type C) depending on the potential impact of the decision on: (i) the relevant firm's ability to carry out its business; and (ii) on the PRA's objectives[3]. In summary, the more significant the firm and the greater the decision's impact, the more senior the composition of the DMC[4].

1 These are: (i) the PRA Board excluding the FCA CEO; (ii) the Supervision, Risk and Policy Committee; (iii) the Supervision and Assessment Panel; and (iv) the Panel of Heads of Departments and Managers. See the PRA's Notice and Decision Making Statement, para 10.
2 The five categories of impact are set out in the PRA's approach to banking supervision and the PRA's approach to insurance supervision.
3 Type A Decisions are those decisions which the PRA expects to have a significant impact on a firm's ability to carry out its business effectively or which could have a significant impact on its objectives. Type C Decisions are decisions which the PRA expects to have a low impact on a firm's ability to carry on its business effectively or on its objectives, or to which a precedent has already been sent. See the PRA's Notice and Decision Making Statement, para 15.
4 PRA's Notice and Decision Making Statement, para 16.

11.13 A diagram showing the PRA's decision making framework can be seen below.

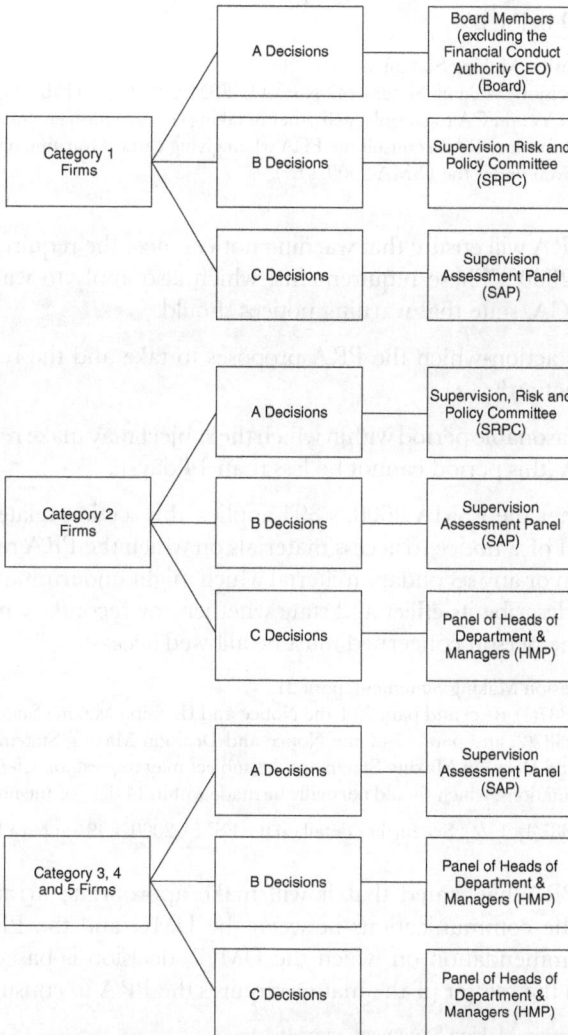

WARNING NOTICES

11.14 Where the PRA has made a recommendation that action requiring a warning notice is appropriate, the relevant DMC (selected in the manner described above) will[1]:

- consider whether the material on which the recommendation is based is adequate to support it (the decision maker may seek additional information regarding the recommendation);

- take into consideration the FCA's views on the issue if the PRA is required to consult the FCA[2];

- satisfy itself that the action recommended is appropriate in all the circumstances;

- decide whether to give the notice and settle the terms of any notice; and

- consider whether it is desirable to publicise any details about the notice (see para **11.19** below).

1 Notice and Decision Making Statement, para 20.
2 Notice and Decision Making Statement, para 44. FSMA 2000, s 415B contains provisions requiring the PRA and FCA to consult each other in taking certain enforcement action, including the requirement for the PRA to consult the FCA when giving certain warning or decision notices (such as those given under the FSMA 2000, s 67).

11.15 The PRA will ensure that warning notices meet the requirements set out in the FSMA 2000[1]. These requirements, which also apply to warning notices issued by the FCA, state that warning notices should:

- set out the action which the PRA proposes to take and the reasons for the proposed action[2];

- specify a reasonable period within which the subject may make representations to the PRA (this period cannot be less than 14 days)[3];

- state whether the FSMA 2000, s 394 applies (this section relates to the right of a subject of a notice to access materials on which the PRA relied in taking the decision or any secondary material which might undermine that decision) and if so, describe its effect and state whether any secondary material exists to which the person concerned must be allowed access[4].

1 Notice and Decision Making Statement, para 21.
2 FSMA 2000, s 387(1)(a)–(c) and para 7 of the Notice and Decision Making Statement.
3 FSMA 2000, s 387(2) and para 47 of the Notice and Decision Making Statement. Under s 49 of the Notice and Decision Making Statement the subject may request an extension of time for making representations, which should normally be made within 14 days of the notice being given.
4 FSMA 2000, s 387(1)(d)–(e). See further detail on the FSMA 2000, s 394 at para **10.118** ff above.

11.16 The PRA has stated that it will make appropriate arrangements for disclosure of the communications between the DMC and the PRA staff who made the recommendation on which the DMC's decision is based, and of the FCA's views on the matter (if the matter requires the PRA to consult the FCA)[1].

1 Notice and Decision Making Statement, para 46.

11.17 When giving the warning notice, the PRA will specify a time within which the recipient is required to indicate whether he/she wishes to make oral representations to the DMC[1]. If the recipient indicates they wish to make oral representations, the PRA will arrange a suitable date for a meeting at which the DMC will hear such representations (and those of any third party who has the right to make representations). At this hearing the DMC may ask for comments from any party if it feels these may help its understanding of the case. The PRA staff may provide the DMC with a written response to the oral representations within seven days of the hearing but (save in exceptional circumstances) the DMC will not, whilst a matter is ongoing, meet with PRA staff responsible for the case after the PRA has given a warning notice, without other relevant parties being present or otherwise having the opportunity to respond.

1 The procedure for representations is set out at the Notice and Decision Making Statement, paras 47–63.

11.18 In some circumstances, third parties may have the right to receive a copy of the warning notice and, if so, may also have a right of access to PRA materials[1]. These rights derive from the FSMA 2000, ss 393 and 394, and their potential implications on the main recipient of a warning notice, are discussed at para **10.149** ff above.

1 Notice and Decision Making Statement, para 31.

PUBLICITY REGARDING WARNING NOTICES

11.19 The rules around publicity regarding warning notices are the same for the PRA as for the FCA (see para **10.108** ff above)[1]. The general position is that neither the PRA nor the person to whom a warning notice is given or copied may publish the notice[2]. However, in relation to certain categories of warning notice[3], the PRA may publish such information as it considers appropriate about the matter after consulting the persons to whom the notice was given or copied[4]. The PRA will consider representations made to it by such persons, which should normally be made in writing and should contain detailed information (with reference to the test in the FSMA 2000, s 391) as to why it would not be appropriate for the PRA to publish details of the notice[5].

1 A paper published by the Treasury in June 2011 ('A new approach to financial regulation: the blueprint for reform') stated at para 2.106 that the Government envisaged the new power enabling Regulators to disclose the fact that a warning notice has been issued would be used mainly by the FCA (to 'support its strong enforcement function and contribute to the strategy of credible deterrence').
2 FSMA 2000, s 391(1)(a).
3 The categories of warning notice to which the power applies are set out in the FSMA 2000, s 391(IZB). Paragraph **10.132**, n 1 contains further detail on this.
4 FSMA 2000, s 391(1)(c) and paras 9 and 15 of the Publicity Statement. Note also that, under the FSMA 2000, s 391(1)(b), persons to whom a warning notice is given or copied may not publish any details concerning the notice unless the PRA has published those details.
5 Publicity Statement, para 16.

11.20 The decision whether to publish any details concerning a warning notice will be made by the same committee which took the decision to issue the notice[1].

11.20 PRA enforcement process

In determining whether it is appropriate to publish such details, factors for the PRA to consider include whether the publicity enhances financial stability, signals unacceptable behaviour to firms and prevents more widespread breaches of its regulatory requirements. The PRA will not publish information if it would be unfair to the persons concerned or prejudicial to the safety and soundness of PRA-authorised persons or (in a case relevant to the PRA's insurance objective[2]) to securing the appropriate degree of protection for policyholders[3]. However the PRA will not normally decide against publication solely because it is claimed that publication could have a negative impact on a person's reputation[4].

1 Publicity Statement, para 19.
2 FSMA 2000, s 2C.
3 Publicity Statement, paras 10–11 and the FSMA 2000, s 391(6A).
4 Publicity Statement, para 17.

11.21 The PRA has stated that information they publish in relation to warning notices will normally include details as to the identity of the firm or individual concerned, a brief summary of the facts relied on by the PRA and a statement that the warning notice is not a final decision[1].

1 Publicity Statement, para 21.

11.22 After it has published any information regarding a warning notice, the PRA will on request review the notice and any related press release published on its website to determine whether (at the time of the request) continued publication is appropriate, or whether the published information should be removed or amended[1]. In determining whether this is appropriate, the PRA will take into account various factors including whether it has continuing concerns in respect of the person, how much time has passed since publication and any representations made by the person[2].

1 Publicity Statement, para 24.
2 Publicity Statement, para 25.

DECISION NOTICES

11.23 If the PRA receives no representations or response to the warning notice within the period specified in that notice (in which case the PRA will regard the contents of the warning notice as undisputed), the PRA will issue a decision notice[1].

1 Notice and Decision Making Statement, paras 26 and 64.

11.24 If the PRA does receive representations to the warning notice, the relevant DMC[1] will consider whether it is appropriate to issue a decision notice. In deciding whether it is appropriate to give the decision notice, the DMC will review the material before it, consider any representations made (and any comments by PRA staff in respect of those representations) and take into consideration the FCA's views on the issue (if the FSMA 2000 requires the PRA to do so)[2].

1 The Notice and Decision Making Statement, para 24 states that, unless the DMC decides otherwise, the same DMC that issued the warning notice will determine whether to issue the

decision notice and settle the terms of any notice including whether, and in what form, to publicise the decision notice.

2 Notice and Decision Making Statement, para 23. As noted above, the FSMA 2000, s 415B contains provisions requiring the PRA to consult the FCA when giving certain decision notices (such as those given under the FSMA 2000, ss 67, 207 and 386).

11.25 If the DMC decides that the PRA should not give a decision notice it will notify the relevant parties of the decision in writing[1]. If the DMC decides that the PRA should issue a decision notice then the PRA will distribute the decision notice to all relevant parties (including any third parties if appropriate[2]), and the DMC will consider whether it is desirable to publicise the notice (see further on this at para **11.32** below)[3].

1 Notice and Decision Making Statement, para 68.
2 In some circumstances, third parties may have the right to receive a copy of the decision notice and, if so, may also have a right of access to PRA materials. These rights, which derive from the FSMA 2000, ss 393 and 394, and their potential implications on the main recipient of a decision notice are discussed at para **10.174** ff above.
3 Notice and Decision Making Statement, paras 66–67.

11.26 Decision notices issued by the PRA will need to meet the requirements set out for decision notices in the FSMA 2000[1]. These requirements, which also apply to decision notices issued by the FCA, state that decision notices should:

- state the PRA's reasons for the decision to take the action to which the notice relates[2];

- include a brief summary of how the PRA has dealt with the key representations made during the enforcement process[3];

- state whether the FSMA 2000, s 394 applies (this section relates to the right of a subject of a notice to access materials on which the PRA relied and any secondary material which might undermine that decision)[4]; and

- give an indication of any right of the subject to refer the matter to the Tribunal and the procedure for such a reference[5].

1 Notice and Decision Making Statement, para 25.
2 FSMA 2000, s 388(1)(b) and para 7 of the Notice and Decision Making Statement.
3 Notice and Decision Making Statement, para 66.
4 FSMA 2000, s 388(1)(c)–(d). See further comment on the FSMA 2000, s 394 at para **10.118** ff above.
5 FSMA 2000, s 388(1)(e).

11.27 As in the FCA enforcement process, the subject will normally have 28 days after receipt of the decision notice to make a referral to the Upper Tribunal, even if it has not previously made any response or representations to the PRA during the enforcement process. A detailed discussion of the nature of the Tribunal, and the procedure for Tribunal proceedings, is found in **CHAPTER 12**.

11.28 In exceptional circumstances, a person who has received a decision notice (or against whom action detailed in the warning notice has taken effect) may show on reasonable grounds that the person to whom the notice relates did not receive the warning notice or that he had reasonable grounds for not responding within the specified period. In such circumstances, if the DMC considers it appropriate, and the person to whom the notice relates gives their consent, it may decide to revoke the decision notice and the matter may be considered afresh or it may decide to give a further decision notice[1].

1   Notice and Decision Making Statement, para 29.

11.29   Following the giving of a decision notice, but before the PRA takes action to which the notice relates, the PRA may give the person concerned a further decision notice relating to a different action concerning the same matter, if that person consents[1].

1   FSMA 2000, s 388(3)–(4) and the Notice and Decision Making Statement, para 30 (which contains the procedure which will apply in these circumstances).

11.30   PRA staff responsible for recommending action to a DMC will continue to assess the appropriateness of the proposed action in light of any new information or representations received. It may be that they decide it is not appropriate to take the action proposed in a warning notice, or the action to which a decision notice relates, and in such circumstances the PRA must (except in certain limited circumstances) give a notice of discontinuance to the person to whom the notice was given[1].

1   FSMA 2000, s 389(1) and the Notice and Decision Making Statement, para 69. FSMA 2000, s 389(2) states that notices of discontinuance should not be given where the discontinuance of proceedings results in the granting of an application made by the person to whom the notice was given.

FINAL NOTICES

11.31   If the PRA has given a person a decision notice and the matter is not referred to the Tribunal within the required period, the PRA must, on taking the action to which the decision notice relates, give the person concerned and any person to whom the decision notice was copied a final notice[1]. A final notice must also be issued where the matter is referred to the Tribunal and the Tribunal (or higher court) directs that it be given[2]. The PRA has not published any statement on the procedure around the issuing of final notices, but final notices issued by the PRA must set out the terms of the action the PRA is taking[3] (as with a final notice issued by the FCA (see para **10.192** above).

1   FSMA 2000, s 390(1).
2   FSMA 2000, s 390(2)–(3).
3   FSMA 2000, s 390 (3)–(7) and the Notice and Decision Making Statement, para 7.

PUBLICITY REGARDING DECISION AND FINAL NOTICES

11.32   As for the FCA (see **CHAPTER 10**), the PRA must publish such information as it considers appropriate about the matters to which a decision notice and final notice relate[1]. However, as with warning notices (see para **11.19** ff above), the PRA may not publish information concerning a decision or final notice which would be unfair to the persons concerned, prejudicial to the safety and soundness of PRA-authorised persons or prejudicial to securing the appropriate degree of protection for policyholders[2].

1 FSMA 2000, s 391 and the Publicity Statement, para 12.
2 FSMA 2000, s 391 and the Publicity Statement, para 13.

11.33 The decision as to whether to publish any details concerning a decision or final notice will be made by the same committee which took the decision to issue the notice[1]. As with warning notices, when it proposes to publish details of a decision or final notice, the PRA will consider any representations made to it by the subject of the notice and any person to whom the notice is copied[2].

1 Publicity Statement, para 20.
2 Publicity Statement, para 15. As noted above at para **11.19**, such representations should normally be made in writing and should contain detailed information (with reference to the test in the FSMA 2000, s 391) as to why it would not be appropriate for the PRA to publish details of the notice.

11.34 Publicity relating to decision and final notices will generally include placing the relevant notice on the PRA's website[1]. As with warning notices, the PRA will on request review the notice and any related press release published on its website to determine whether (at the time of the request) continued publication is appropriate, or whether they should be removed or amended[2].

1 Publicity Statement, para 22. Paragraph 23 of the Publicity Statement also states that, in relation to final notices, the PRA should also consider what matters it should notify to the FCA for inclusion on the FCA's public register under the FSMA 2000, s 347A.
2 Publicity Statement, para 24. As noted in relation to warning notices, in determining whether this is appropriate, the PRA will take into account various factors including whether it has continuing concerns in respect of the person, how much time has passed since publication and any representations made by the person.

SETTLEMENT

11.35 The PRA's 'Statement of the PRA's settlement decision-making procedure and policy for the determination of the amount of penalties and the period of suspensions or restrictions in settled cases'[1] (the Settlement Statement) sets out the PRA's policy on the settlement of enforcement action by the PRA.

1 The 'Statement of The PRA's approach to enforcement' is contained at Appendix 4 of the April 2013 Statement.

11.36 CHAPTER 10 considered how settlement operated in the FCA enforcement regime; most of the issues discussed in that chapter with regards to settlement (such as when settlement discussions will take place, whether the firm has to take part in settlement discussions and whether the firm can be candid in its settlement discussions) will also be relevant when considering settlement in relation to a PRA enforcement action.

11.37 PRA enforcement process

11.37 It is, however, worth noting the following points which apply to the PRA settlement process in particular:

- settlement discussions in PRA enforcement actions will normally be conducted by one or more of the investigators appointed by the PRA and/or any members of the PRA's staff responsible for the conduct of the matter[1]; and

- a summary of the case and the terms of the in-principle settlement will be sent to the appropriate DMC, which will consider the settlement and either:

  - endorse it by deciding to give the relevant statutory notices based on the terms of the settlement (any decision by the DMC to conclude a binding settlement agreement must be unanimous[2]); or

  - will decline the proposed settlement[3].

1 Settlement Statement, para 17.
2 Settlement Statement, paras 21–23.
3 Notice and Decision Making Statement, paras 74–81 set out the PRA procedure in relation to decision makers involved in settlement decision making.

11.38 Where the PRA proposes to impose a financial penalty or a suspension or restriction and a settlement has been negotiated by the parties and approved by the DMC, the person concerned will be entitled to a reduction in the amount (or, if a suspension or restriction, the period) of the relevant sanction[1]. As with the FCA settlement discount scheme, the settlement discount applied by the PRA depends on the stage the enforcement process has reached when the settlement discussions are concluded. For these purposes, an enforcement case is split into four stages (as in the FCA settlement procedure):

- in the period from the commencement of an enforcement investigation by the PRA until the PRA has communicated to the subject of its investigation the essential nature of the case against him and allowed him what it considers to be a reasonable opportunity to understand it, and has allowed what it considers to be a reasonable opportunity for the parties to reach a settlement agreement[2] (Stage 1), the penalty should be discounted by 30%;

- in the period from the end of Stage 1 until the expiry of the period (including any extensions of it) for making written representations in response to the giving of a warning notice or, if sooner, the date on which such representations are received by the PRA (Stage 2), the penalty should be discounted by 20%;

- in the period from the end of Stage 2 until the giving of a decision notice (Stage 3), the penalty should be discounted by 10%;

- in the period after the end of Stage 3, including any proceedings before the Tribunal and any subsequent appeals (Stage 4), there is no discount to the penalty.

1 Settlement Statement, paras 26–29.
2 The PRA has not (at the time of writing) issued guidance on what a reasonable period is for these purposes. It is possible that they may follow the example of the FCA, which considers that 28 days will normally be the timeframe for a reasonable opportunity to reach agreement before the expiry of Stage 1: see FCA Enforcement Guide at EG 5.19.

11.39 Where a binding settlement of an enforcement action by the PRA can be concluded and a disciplinary measure is to be imposed by the PRA, that decision will usually give rise to a statutory obligation on the PRA to give the person concerned the requisite statutory notices (the fact that the matter is settled will not alter this obligation)[1]. If this involves the issue of a final notice, the PRA is in practice likely to publish the notice.

1 Notice and Decision Making Statement, para 73.

CO-ORDINATION BETWEEN THE FCA AND PRA

11.40 As noted above, the PRA and FCA are required to consult with each other in taking certain enforcement action, including when giving certain warning or decision notices such as those given under the FSMA 2000, s 67 (disciplinary powers relating to individuals)[1].

1 FSMA 2000, s 415B.

11.41 The Memorandum of Understanding between the FCA and PRA (the MOU)[1] contains details regarding the co-ordination of enforcement actions. This notes that, in respect of dual-regulated firms, each Regulator will consult with the other in advance of issuing warning and decision notices[2], and will notify the other before issuing any press release relating to an enforcement action involving a dual-regulated firm (or a member of a group of a dual-regulated firm)[3]. The MOU requires senior officials from the FCA and PRA responsible for enforcement and legal intervention to meet quarterly to discuss potential and on-going enforcement actions against relevant firms[4].

1 FSMA 2000, Sch 17A requires the regulators to maintain a memorandum describing how they will co-ordinate their functions.
2 MOU, para 43.
3 MOU, Annex 1, para 27.
4 MOU, para 47.

11.42 Certain misconduct by dual-regulated firms or individuals may result in breaches of the rules and requirements of the FCA or other domestic or overseas regulatory or law enforcement agencies (as well as those of the PRA[1]). In such scenarios it is possible that the PRA and the FCA (as well as such other agencies) could each undertake an investigation, make a decision and take enforcement action in respect of their own regulatory objectives for what some may consider to be the same misconduct[2]. The PRA will determine whether it is appropriate for it to investigate and take enforcement or other action in respect of the misconduct, and in appropriate cases, the PRA in conjunction with the FCA and/or any other relevant agencies will determine whether any joint or co-ordinated investigation and enforcement or other action is required[3].

1 FCA Enforcement Guide at EG 2.15A notes that a joint investigation could arise where misconduct adversely affects both regulators' statutory objectives.
2 Penalty Statement, para 3(h).
3 Penalty Statement, para 3(h). Section 46 of the MOU notes that if a regulator decides to carry out an investigation in relation to a dual-regulated person, the Regulators will (wherever practicable) consider whether or not the investigation should be co-ordinated jointly.

11.43   PRA enforcement process

11.43   In response to concerns raised about the possibility of the PRA enforcing standards of conduct that could mean that person facing action by both Regulators for the same issue, or that standards imposed by the Regulators could diverge over time and even conflict, the PRA has stated that it is entirely appropriate that, if there is potential misconduct relating to both prudential and conduct issues, for both the PRA and FCA to apply different standards, or to express standards differently, given their different statutory objectives. The PRA believes that 'the duty to co-ordinate, and to consult each other on policy changes, should ensure the PRA and FCA do not introduce conflicting requirements'[1].

1 PRA Policy Statement PS1/13 'Regulatory reform: amendments to the Prudential Regulation Authority Handbook' dated March 2013, paras 2.10–2.12.

11.44   Where separate PRA and FCA investigations are appropriate, the two agencies will seek to co-ordinate their investigations[1]; however, the PRA and FCA must 'decide cases and any consequential enforcement or disciplinary actions separately'[2].

1 FCA Enforcement Guide at EG 4.35 states that in cases where the FCA and PRA pursue investigations into different aspects of the same misconduct, the FCA will attempt to ensure that the person concerned is not prejudiced or unduly inconvenienced by the fact that there are two investigatory authorities.
2 The April 2013 Statement at p 4.

HOW MUCH USE WILL THE PRA MAKE OF ITS ENFORCEMENT POWERS?

11.45   Although the commentary above indicates a willingness on the part of the PRA to be involved in enforcement actions even where the misconduct in question may fall within the remit of the FCA, statements published by the Treasury, FCA and PRA indicate that PRA enforcement actions could be a rare occurrence[1]. The PRA intends to take a forward-looking approach to prudential issues (requiring remedial action to be taken in advance of problems emerging) and disciplinary actions should on this basis be relatively infrequent. The PRA's enforcement powers may only be employed where other measures such as directions or restrictions imposed by the PRA are ignored by a firm. The Treasury has stated that in practice most enforcement action is taken with respect to conduct regulation and the Government therefore expects the FCA to make greater use of enforcement powers than the PRA[2].

1 Examples of such statements include:
   (A) The October 2012 Bank of England and FSA paper on 'The PRA's approach to banking supervision', which stated at para 198 that: 'The PRA's preference will be to use its powers to secure ex ante, remedial action, given its approach of intervening early to address emerging risk. If successful, application of this approach should mean that enforcement actions are rare'.
   (B) A Treasury White Paper published in June 2011 on 'A new approach to financial regulation: the blueprint for reform' made a similar point, stating that: 'While the PRA will have the same powers as the FCA to impose penalties on authorised persons, it is expected that under the PRA's approach disciplinary actions will be relatively rare'.
   (C) See also the paper published by The Bank of England and the FSA in May 2011 on 'The Bank of England, Prudential Regulation Authority – Our approach to banking supervision'.
2 Treasury paper published in February 2011 on 'A new approach to financial regulation: building a stronger system'.

Chapter 12   The Tribunal and appeals

INTRODUCTION

12.1   One of the primary protections for firms subject to enforcement action is the ability to require a regulator to prove its case before the Upper Tribunal (Tax and Chancery Chamber) (known as 'the Tribunal'). Decisions of both the PRA and the FCA can be referred to the Tribunal. It is anticipated that the majority of enforcement action will be conducted by the FCA, and that the majority of referrals to the Tribunal will be referrals of FCA decisions. In light of that expectation, and of the fact that referrals of both FCA and PRA decisions to the Tribunal follow the same process, reference is made to the FCA throughout this chapter. The commentary is, however, relevant to both bodies unless otherwise indicated[1].

1 The Tribunal Procedure (Upper Tribunal) (Amendment No 2) Rules 2013, SI 2013/606, provide for references against more than one regulator in one case.

12.2   The Tribunal has an important role in the regulatory structure in providing a possible means of recourse for a firm or individual aggrieved by a particular decision which the FCA has taken regarding it[1]. Furthermore, as Tribunal decisions are published, a body of precedent is building up which helps to define the parameters within which the FCA can operate and can thereby affect the FCA's approach in cases more generally[2]. The Tribunal therefore forms a key part of the checks and balances on the FCA's actions under the FSMA 2000.

12.2   The Tribunal and appeals

1 See **CHAPTER 21** below for other means of recourse.
2 As at October 2013, over 100 decisions of the Tribunal (in its various guises) had been published. The Tribunal itself has used its previous decisions as precedent, including those made under the previous regime: see, for example, *Stephen Robert Allen v FSA FS/2012/0019*, where the Tribunal followed *Legal & General Assurance Soc Ltd v FSA [2005] UKFSM FSM011, Stefan Chaligné, Patrick Sejean and Cheickh Tidiane Diallo v FSA, FS/2011/0001, 0002 and 0003 and Jabre v FSA (Case 036, August 2006)* and distinguished *James Parker v FSA [2006] UKFSM FSM037* on the facts.

12.3   This chapter reviews the Tribunal process, including the procedure for referring cases to the Tribunal, the Tribunal process that follows the reference and the practical issues that arise; the conduct of the hearing itself; the Tribunal's decision; and the limited options open to the firm, or indeed the FCA, where it disagrees with the Tribunal's decision, namely to obtain a review of the decision by the Tribunal or to appeal on a point of law.

12.4   Before turning to the detailed procedures, there are three initial points to consider, namely:

- What is the Tribunal?
- What matters can be referred to the Tribunal?
- When in practice should firms consider referring a case to the Tribunal?

WHAT IS THE TRIBUNAL?

12.5   The Tribunal is, since 6 April 2010[1], the Upper Tribunal, which has been part of HM Courts and Tribunals Service since 1 April 2011. It is an appellate tribunal[2] created by the Tribunals, Courts and Enforcement Act 2007. It is made up of four chambers; financial services cases are heard by the Tax and Chancery Chamber, which operates under rules made by the Tribunal Procedure Committee under powers conferred on it by the TCEA 2007.

1 Under the previous regime, the Tribunal was the Financial Services and Markets Tribunal. It was abolished, and its functions transferred, by the Transfer of Tribunal Functions Order 2010.
2 Although for financial services cases it is effectively a court of first instance.

12.6   The Tribunal appointed to hear a case will be chosen by the Senior President, who can decide how many members will decide the matter[1]. This will normally be a judge and one or two non-legal members of the Tribunal[2]. The judges are legally qualified members of the Tribunal[3]. The non-legal members are appointed by the Lord Chancellor, but they must have certain qualifications in order to be eligible for appointment as members[4]. The Senior President also selects one of the Tribunal members (usually the judge) to chair each Tribunal hearing a reference[5].

1 First-tier Tribunal and Upper Tribunal (Composition of Tribunal) Order 2008, SI 2008/2835, art 3.
2 HMCTS Explanatory Leaflet T400, 'Making a reference to the Upper Tribunal (Tax and Chancery Chamber)'.
3 See the TCEA 2007, ss 5, 6 and 31 for details on how judges of the Tribunal are appointed.
4 See the TCEA 2007, Sch 3, para 2 and the Qualifications for Appointment of Members to the First-tier Tribunal and Upper Tribunal Order 2008, SI 2008/2692.
5 First-tier Tribunal and Upper Tribunal (Composition of Tribunal) Order 2008, SI 2008/2835, art 7.

12.7 The Tribunal and its members are thus entirely independent of the FCA[1]. It is run by HM Courts and Tribunals Service, an agency of the Ministry of Justice, operating under rules set by the Tribunal Procedure Committee (an advisory non-departmental public body, sponsored by the Ministry of Justice)[2]. It has no regulatory agenda of its own. The rules of the Tribunal aim to be fair and even-handed to all parties, as well as ECHR compatible[3].

1 The requirement that the Tribunal and its members are independent and impartial is contained at ECHR, Article 6(1) and in the Constitutional Reform Act 2005, s 3. For an example of a Tribunal recusing itself on the basis that 'the fair-minded and informed observer would not be able to exclude the real possibility of unconscious bias' see *Davidson v FSA [2004] UKFSM FSM010*. A new panel was then selected to hear the reference. See also at para **12.103** below.
2 These include: the Tribunal Procedure (Upper Tribunal) Rules 2008, SI 2008/2698, as amended by the Tribunal Procedure (Amendment) Rules 2009, SI 2009/274; the Tribunal Procedure (Amendment No 2) Rules 2009, SI 2009/1975; the Tribunal Procedure (Amendment) Rules 2010, SI 2010/43; the Tribunal Procedure (Amendment No 2) Rules 2010, SI 2010/44; the Tribunal Procedure (Upper Tribunal) (Amendment) Rules 2010, SI 2010/747; the Tribunal Procedure (Amendment No 3) Rules 2010, SI 2010/2653; the Tribunal Procedure (Amendment) Rules 2011, SI 2011/651; the Tribunal Procedure (Upper Tribunal) (Amendment) Rules 2011, SI 2011/2343; the Tribunal Procedure (Amendment) Rules 2012, SI 2012/500; the Tribunal Procedure (Amendment No 2) Rules 2012, SI 2012/1363 (rules 4 to 9); the Public Bodies (Child Maintenance and Enforcement Commission: Abolition and Transfer of Functions) Order 2012, SI 2012/2007; the Tribunal Procedure (Upper Tribunal) (Amendment) Rules 2012, SI 2012/2890; the Tribunal Procedure (Amendment) Rules 2013, SI 2013/477, and the Tribunal Procedure (Amendment No 2) Rules 2013, SI 2013/606. The rules as amended will be referred to throughout this chapter as the 'Tribunal Rules'.
3 The need for ECHR compatibility is discussed in more detail at para **12.26** ff below.

12.8 The basic function of the Tribunal, prescribed under the FSMA 2000[1], is, in the majority of references made to it (including all those relating to disciplinary actions), to determine the appropriate action, if any, for the FCA to take in relation to the matter referred to it. In some cases (other than disciplinary actions) the Tribunal is limited in the decisions that it can make.

1 FSMA 2000, s 133(5).

12.9 The purpose and effect of this is that the Tribunal is a first instance tribunal, able to consider all of the evidence and to reach its own decision. In the Tribunal the person concerned is 'innocent' until the FCA proves its case. The process is, in this respect, not fettered by the FCA internal decision-making process that preceded it. The Tribunal is therefore not, in the majority of cases, an appellate body nor is it conducting a review of the FCA's decision. It simply decides what action it is appropriate for the FCA to take in the matter referred to it[1]. However, any direction from the Tribunal must be under the same part of the FSMA 2000 as the decision notice, as explained at para **12.153** below[2]. As mentioned above and as discussed in para **12.151**, there are some references for which the Tribunal's discretion is curtailed and, in those cases, similar to judicial review, the Tribunal considers whether there are grounds for asking the FCA to reconsider its decision.

1 In *Stefan Chaligné, Patrick Sejean and Cheickh Tidiane Diallo v FSA, FS/2011/0001, 0002 and 0003*, the Tribunal (following previous cases on the point) explained its role and that it was required to look at all relevant material, and was not restricted by the RDC's views on that material. The Tribunal also held that, given that it could see material which may not have been before the RDC, it must be able to direct the FSA to take action which it may not have considered.
2 See also *Philippe Jabre v FSA (Case 036, August 2006)*.

12.10   The Tribunal also has the ability, when determining a reference, to make recommendations as to the FCA's regulating provisions or its procedures[1]. The FSMA 2000 does not limit the sorts of recommendations that the Tribunal can make in this regard, for example to cases where it regards those rules or procedures as unfair or incompatible with the FSMA 2000 or on some other basis. It is an important aspect of the accountability regime that this wholly independent body has an unfettered ability to make recommendations about the FCA's rules and procedures.

1   FSMA 2000, s 133A(5). This is discussed in more detail at para **12.155** below.

WHAT MATTERS CAN BE REFERRED TO THE TRIBUNAL?

12.11   Not every decision taken by the FCA in relation to a person is capable of being referred to the Tribunal. Recourse to the Tribunal only exists where the FSMA 2000 specifically provides for it. Broadly, this coincides with those types of decisions which involve the giving of warning/decision notices (see **CHAPTERS 10, 11** above) or supervisory notices (see para **16.130** ff below). In the enforcement context, the right to refer arises in cases such as where a regulator wishes to:

- formally discipline a firm[1] or an individual[2];

- vary a firm's permission[3] or give directions or take equivalent action in relation to an incoming firm[4];

- cancel a firm's permission[5];

- make a restitution order against a person[6];

- refuse to grant an application for approval[7];

- withdraw approval from an approved person (or individual)[8];

- issue a prohibition order against any person[9];

- impose a penalty for market abuse[10];

- exercise its enforcement powers in relation to a unit trust or other regulated collective investment scheme[11];

- exercise its enforcement powers as UK Listing Authority in relation to listed companies, applicants for listing directors and/or sponsors[12]; and

- exercise certain powers in relation to Lloyd's[13], auditors and/or actuaries[14], or in relation to members of the professions[15].

1   FSMA 2000, s 208 and see **CHAPTER 8** above.
2   FSMA 2000, s 67 and see **CHAPTER 9** above. For an example of such a reference, see the Tribunal's decision in *Andrew Jeffery v FCA (FS/2010/0039)*.
3   FSMA 2000, s 55J(2)(a) and see **CHAPTER 16** below. For examples of such a reference, see *Eurolife Assurance Company Ltd v FSA (2002) FSMT 001/002, Eurosure Investment Services Ltd v FSA (2003) FSMT 006 and HPA Services v FSA (2003) FSMT 005.*
4   FSMA 2000, s 197 and see **CHAPTER 16** below.
5   FSMA 2000, s 55J(2)(b) and see **CHAPTER 16** below. For an example of such a reference see the Tribunal's decision in *James Perman & Company (FS/2010/018).*

6   FSMA 2000, s 386 and see **CHAPTERS 8** (firms), **9** (individuals) and para **17.245** below (market abuse).
7   FSMA 2000, s 62 and see **CHAPTER 9** above. For an example of such a reference, see the Tribunal's decision in *Cox v FSA (2003) FSMT 003*.
8   FSMA 2000, s 63 and see para **9.52** above.
9   FSMA 2000, s 57 and see **CHAPTER 9** above.
10 FSMA 2000, s 127 and see **CHAPTER 17** below.
11 FSMA 2000, Pt 17.
12 FSMA 2000, Pt 6 and see **CHAPTER 20** below.
12 FSMA 2000, Pt 19.
13 FSMA 2000, s 345 and see para **8.6** above.
15 FSMA 2000, s 331.

12.12   Details of the procedure applicable in relation to each of the above, including the right of reference to the Tribunal, are outlined in the relevant chapter indicated in the footnotes below. Where the FSMA 2000 gives a person the right to refer a matter to the Tribunal, that person is unlikely to be able to bring an action for judicial review[1] against the FCA in respect of that matter and will not have the right to complain to the FCA about that matter[2].

1   Judicial review of the FCA is considered at para **21.16** ff below.
2   See para **21.54 ff** below.

12.13   But the FCA can also take many decisions which affect firms or others where there is no right of reference to the Tribunal. Examples include deciding to:

*   issue a private warning[1];

*   investigate a firm[2];

*   not notify a firm that an investigation has been commenced into it[3];

*   require a firm to provide particular information either itself or by an investigator in connection with an investigation[4];

*   apply to a court for an injunction or restitution order[5];

*   vary a firm's permission by 'executive procedures' and without the matter being considered by the RDC[6];

*   publish information about enforcement action it has taken[7].

1   See para **8.27** ff above.
2   See **CHAPTER 5** above.
3   See para **5.39** ff above.
4   See paras **4.68** ff and **6.45** ff above.
5   See **CHAPTERS 8** (firms) and **9** (individuals) above.
6   See para **16.142** ff below.
7   See para **16.191** below.

WHEN IN PRACTICE SHOULD FIRMS CONSIDER REFERRING A CASE TO THE TRIBUNAL?

12.14   If a firm or individual is the subject of a decision by the FCA with which it disagrees[1], and which is capable of referral to the Tribunal, then the immediate question is whether it should refer that decision to the Tribunal. A secondary question is which part of the decision to refer; an applicant can, for example, limit its reference to challenging the sanction imposed[2]. Whether the matter is referred to the Tribunal is entirely within the firm's control: the FCA enforcement staff have no right to do so if, for example, they disagree with the decision made by the RDC. Answering these questions may involve weighing up a number of conflicting factors. Some of the main considerations are outlined briefly here[3].

1   Or is provided with a copy of a decision notice by the FCA as a third party identified in it to whom, in the FCA's view, it is prejudicial: FSMA 2000, s 393 and see para **10.174** ff above.
2   See eg *Wagner v FSA (FS/2011/0015)*.
3   See also para **10.182** ff above.

12.15   First, the person may believe that the FCA's decision was unwarranted or excessive. For example, the applicant may believe that the RDC (before whom there will have been only a relatively short hearing[1]) took an incorrect or unbalanced view of the evidence[2], misinterpreted the relevant FCA rules alleged to have been breached, did not properly take account of mitigating factors or, particularly in a complex or wide ranging case, did not fully understand its defence. If the case is referred to the Tribunal, the FCA will have to prove its case. The Tribunal process will involve an extensive examination of the evidence in a way that cannot be achieved in a short hearing before the RDC. As will be seen, this can include a close examination of the documents as well as oral evidence from witnesses and experts. In short, there may be the prospect of the Tribunal coming to the conclusion that no breach took place or that no (or less serious) action should be taken. This is the primary basis for referring a case to the Tribunal.

1   See para **10.138** above.
2   See, for example, *Hoodless and Blackwell v FSA (2003) FSMT 007* where the Tribunal held that some of the FCA investigators' original questioning was 'aggressive', that 'the significance of any lack of frankness [in evidence given to the FCA] must depend on the circumstances' and that evidence was 'open to more than one interpretation'. In *Rayner & Townsend v FSA (2004) FSMT 010*, the Tribunal held that some of the evidence presented by the FCA was incorrect since it did not relate to the applicants. See also *Legal & General v FSA (2003) FIN 0022*.

12.16   Second, there may be other factors that influence the decision to make a reference. The impact on the particular person of the action which the FCA has decided to take is clearly an important factor (and in part explains why, to date, most references to the Tribunal have been made by individuals, for whom FCA action may have career threatening consequences). In some cases, a motivating factor might be a sense of grievance about aspects of the FCA's rules or procedures and a wish to highlight those aspects in the expectation that the Tribunal may wish to comment upon them[1]. In other cases, a person may believe that making a reference to the Tribunal will improve the prospect of reaching a reasonable settlement with the FCA[2]. (Of course, the person cannot be sure that a settlement will be reached and will therefore need to be prepared either to defend the case in the Tribunal or to abandon the reference). Given the increase in the number of references since the FSA began pursuing individuals (a policy continued by the FCA), and since the introduction of the new fining policy, there may be less reputational risk attached to a referral to the Tribunal than previously.

1   The firm's view that it had not had a fair hearing earlier in the process was one of the factors that led to the Tribunal reference in *Legal & General v FSA (2003) FIN 0022*. The decision of the Tribunal in that case led to the FCA's Enforcement Process review of the FCA's decision-making processes. Note also that if the person believes that the FCA has acted unreasonably, then there may be a prospect of the FCA being required to contribute to or pay the person's costs of the Tribunal proceedings. See para **12.167** ff below.
2   It is still possible to settle a case after a reference has been made: see para **10.43** ff above.

12.17   Third, there are a number of other factors that in many cases lead parties (particularly firms) to decide not to refer, notwithstanding their view of the merits of their position. Typically, these include the legal cost and management time likely to be involved in undertaking a Tribunal process and the possible effect on the person's FCA relationship, which would need to be carefully handled. There is also the obvious risk of the Tribunal deciding that a stronger sanction should be imposed, and, given that Tribunal hearings are usually held in public[1], the risk of the matter attracting greater adverse publicity than it otherwise would have done (even if ultimately the person is successful). Other considerations include the question, discussed at para **12.58** below, of whether the FCA case that the person faces in the Tribunal will in all respects be the same as that contained in the decision notice and whether the evidence that the Tribunal will consider will be confined to the same matters. The uncertainties in this regard may require the person to take a broader approach to assessing the merits of their position and not to focus solely on the decision notice.

1   See para **12.37** ff below.

12.18   Finally, complicating factors may arise in cases where there are related FCA decisions against more than one person (for example, where the FCA decides to fine both a firm and an employee) or where another person may have (or contend that they have) third-party rights[1]. In deciding whether to refer, each party needs to consider the likelihood that another party may do so and the possibility of the outcome of that reference (or the evidence that emerges at a public hearing) being prejudicial to them. A person may thus face a difficult question of whether to refer a decision to the Tribunal solely for the purpose of ensuring the person is party to a reference primarily made by another party, so as to be able to make submissions to the Tribunal and call evidence as necessary to protect his interests, even where he otherwise would have decided not to refer[2].

1   As a third party identified in the decision notice to whom it is prejudicial: FSMA 2000, s 393 and see para **12.47** ff below. For an example of a party on whom the FCA did not confer third-party rights making a reference to the Tribunal to contend that they should have been granted such rights, see *Sir Philip Watts v FSA (2005) FSMT 0022*.
2   As discussed at para **12.143** ff, it is not clear that a person who has not made a reference to the Tribunal would be entitled to make submissions in the course of Tribunal proceedings commenced by other parties.

12.19   Thus, whether or not to refer a decision to the Tribunal will depend very much upon the particular case. The most important factors overall are likely to be the importance of the matter, the nature of the action that the FCA has decided to take and its impact on the person concerned, what the person seeks or hopes to achieve through the reference to the Tribunal, and the merits of the FCA's case.

12.20   The Tribunal and appeals

THE TRIBUNAL PROCEDURE

12.20   The following paragraphs review the Tribunal Rules, which contain the details of its procedures. After a brief overview of the process and its underlying aims, the following paragraphs look, first, at how cases are referred to the Tribunal[1], second, at the procedure involved in taking the case from the referral up to the hearing[2], third, at the hearing[3] and, fourth, at the Tribunal's decision[4]. Some of the practical issues that arise are outlined in each case.

1 See para **12.38** ff below.
2 See para **12.53** ff below.
3 See para **12.132** ff below.
4 See para **12.150** ff below.

An overview of the process

12.21   Before looking at the detailed Tribunal Rules, it may be helpful briefly to review what the Tribunal Rules are designed to achieve, and to provide a short overview of the process. Some initial points are then made about the publicity likely to arise from the Tribunal process.

12.22   The Tribunal Rules aim, among other things, to be flexible and ECHR compatible. Understanding these two factors assists in understanding the nature of the Tribunal Rules and the Tribunal's approach to each particular case. They are discussed briefly below.

Flexibility in the process

12.23   The importance of the Tribunal, not only as a means of recourse for those subjected to decisions by the FCA but also as an aspect of the accountability regime of the FCA, has already been discussed. If the Tribunal is to have these benefits then firms and individuals must have confidence in its ability to reach a just result in each case. But, as Lord Woolf's reforms to civil litigation procedure and Sir Andrew Leggatt's review of the tribunal system[1] have highlighted, reaching the right result is not the only consideration. If that can be achieved only slowly and at great cost, then people are likely to be deterred from using the process. Effective access to justice thus requires expedition and cost also to be taken into account.

1 Tribunals for Users: One System, One Service, published in August 2001. This led to the creation of the Tribunals Service, before that organisation was merged with the Courts Service.

12.24   These considerations are as important in the context of the Tribunal as they are in civil litigation, but there is a balance to be struck between them. The Tribunal considers cases ranging from complex multi-issue disputes which may involve large firms and substantial numbers of consumers, to single issues relating to individuals or sole traders. In some cases, cost and expedition assume real significance, particularly where the person concerned would otherwise effectively have no access to the Tribunal, or where there is a specific need for expedition (for example, if a supervisory notice has stopped a person from trading). In other cases, the person may be primarily concerned that the Tribunal reaches the right result, with the cost of the process being of rather less importance. In those cases, whilst it is important that the procedure is not unduly lengthy, costly or complex, if there is to be confidence in the Tribunal, then justice must not be seen to be overly subordinated to expedition and cost. In the civil litigation context[1], the concept of proportionality – that cases should be dealt with in a way that is proportionate to the amount of money involved, the importance of the case, the complexity of the issues and the financial position of each party – is the key that allows the court to balance these different factors.

1 See the Civil Procedure Rules, Pt 1.

12.25　The Tribunal must now work along similar lines and use the concept of proportionality to strike the correct balance between those considerations. The Tribunal Rules provide that the Tribunal has an 'overriding objective' to decide cases fairly and justly, which includes dealing with the case in a manner proportionate to its importance, complexity and costs[1]. As will be seen, the Tribunal Rules say comparatively little about how the procedure works in practice, giving the Tribunal appointed to hear each case a great deal of flexibility in the procedure to be adopted in that case and requiring it to use that flexibility to ensure the determination of the reference in accordance with the overriding principle[2].

1 Tribunal Rules, r 2. The previous version of the Rules referred to standards such as the 'just, economical and expeditious' determination of a reference when, for example, the Tribunal gave directions. The language used by the Tribunal in its decisions seems to reflect the focus on proportionality: in *Arch Financial Products LLP, Robin Farrell and Robert Stephan Addison v FSA (FS/2012/20)*, the Tribunal undertook what it described as a 'balancing exercise' to decide whether to allow publication of decision notices, an approach followed in *Angela Burns v FSA (FS/2012/24)*. In *Michael Lee Thommes v FSA (FS/2011/0022)*, the Tribunal examined whether the fine levied was 'proportionate'. There is though some evidence of this approach being used under the previous regime: see *Ernest Rayner and John Townsend v FSA [2004] UKFSM FSM009*.
2 Indeed, r 5(1) of the Tribunal Rules provides that the Upper Tribunal may regulate its own procedure, subject to the TCEA 2007 and any other legislation.

ECHR compatibility

12.26　The Tribunal's Rules aim to be compatible with the European Convention on Human Rights. A brief review of why they need to be compatible and what this involves follows[1].

1 For a more detailed discussion, see Harris, O'Boyle and Warbrick, Law of the European Convention on Human Rights (2nd edn, 2009); Human Rights Law and Practice edited by Lester and Pannick (3rd edn, 2009) and Human Rights Practice edited by Simor and Emmerson (June 2000, as updated).

12.27　There are two main reasons why the Tribunal procedure needs to comply with the ECHR. First, the enforcement process as a whole is likely to involve the determination of a person's civil rights and therefore needs to comply with the fair trial guarantees of Article 6(1) of the ECHR[1]. Whilst there are various safeguards built into the enforcement process before the matter reaches the Tribunal, for example the involvement of the RDC, it is in the Tribunal procedure that any defects in the process, from the ECHR perspective, must be cured. The Tribunal therefore has the important role of ensuring that the process as a whole fulfils the ECHR requirements[2].

1 See para **10.19** ff above. In some situations, including in particular proceedings for market abuse, the proceedings may involve the determination of a 'criminal charge' for ECHR purposes: see the discussion at para **10.20** ff above. In those cases, the process must also fulfil the additional requirements for criminal proceedings found in Article 6(2) and (3) and (once ratified and incorporated into UK law) Protocol 7. Proceedings in relation to market abuse involve the additional criminal protections of: (a) the privilege against self-incrimination; and (b) legal aid (see para **17.16** below).
2 See, for example, *Albert and Le Compte v Belgium (1983) 5 EHRR 533*. There may be limits on the extent to which earlier defects are capable of being 'cured': see *De Cubber v Belgium (1985) 7 EHRR 236*. It is only Article 6 defects that may be cured in the Tribunal; any unlawful invasions of privacy in breach of Article 8, for example, would not be cured.

12.28   Second, the Tribunal is itself a public body and it would be unlawful for it to act in a way that was incompatible with an ECHR right[1].

1 Human Rights Act 1998, s 6.

12.29   The basic fair trial guarantee is the right to a fair and public trial within a reasonable time by an independent and impartial tribunal established by law and for judgment to be pronounced publicly[1]. This includes the right[2]:

- to a public hearing, normally an oral hearing, subject to certain exceptions[3];

- for the hearing to take place within a reasonable time;

- to the disclosure of documents[4];

- to a reasonable opportunity to present the case to the court under conditions that do not substantially disadvantage the person as against the FCA (known as 'equality of arms');

- to adduce evidence and to comment on the other side's evidence and submissions[5];

- to a judgment containing reasons; and

- for judgment to be pronounced publicly, subject to certain exceptions[6].

1 ECHR, Article 6(1).
2 This is not intended to be a comprehensive list of the Article 6(1) rights. For a more detailed discussion, see Harris, O'Boyle and Warbrick, Law of the European Convention on Human Rights (1995); Human Rights Law and Practice edited by Lester and Pannick (3rd edn, 2009) and Human Rights Practice edited by Simor and Emmerson (June 2000).
3 The right to a public hearing is discussed at para **12.139** ff below.
4 See, for example, *Feldbrugge v Netherlands (1986) 8 EHRR 425*.
5 *Mantovanelli v France (1997) 24 EHRR 370*.
6 The public pronouncement of judgment is discussed further at para **12.159** ff below.

12.30   Additional safeguards for criminal proceedings can be found in Article 6(2) and (3) and Protocol 7[1].

12.31   The Tribunal has itself often considered the issue of ECHR compatibility. In *77226565 Canada Inc and Peter Beck v FSA, (2011) FS 0017 and 0018*, for example, the Tribunal noted the overall public interest in the openness of proceedings and its consistency with Article 6(1).

An outline of the procedure

12.32   Before turning to the detailed rules, it may be helpful to give a brief overview of how the process works. The first step is for the person to whom the decision notice or supervisory notice was given (referred to as 'the applicant') to refer the matter to the Tribunal. This is done by issuing a reference notice, which must be done within 28 days (subject to obtaining an extension of time). Once a reference notice has been issued, the matter has been placed before the Tribunal and its procedural rules become applicable. At that stage, certain information about the case is normally entered on a register, which is publicly available.

12.33   The FCA, and then the applicant, each set out in a document their case on why the action taken or proposed to be taken by the FCA is or is not appropriate. The parties also disclose relevant documents to each other; the Tribunal can order further documents to be disclosed.

12.34   After this, there is no defined process. Rather, the Tribunal decides upon the procedure required to take the particular matter to a hearing, by making directions on the basis of ensuring that the reference is determined in accordance with the overriding principle. This might include, for example, appointing an expert, giving permission for the parties to call expert evidence, or requiring witness statements or other documents to be filed. The Tribunal also has the power to determine particular issues as preliminary issues and to strike out the reference as a whole.

12.35   The case is heard by the Tribunal at an oral hearing (in effect, a trial), normally in public although the Tribunal can order that the hearing (or a part of it) be held in private in certain circumstances. It is for the Tribunal to decide on the procedure adopted for the hearing. The applicant is entitled to be legally represented at the hearing, and indeed throughout the process.

12.36   Finally, the Tribunal makes its decision. This is also normally made public, again subject to the Tribunal's ability to decide otherwise in certain cases. In certain situations the Tribunal may be prepared to review that decision on particular grounds set out in the rules. The applicant and the FCA also have the right to apply for permission to appeal to the Court of Appeal[1] on matters of law only.

1 Or to the Court of Session in Scotland.

Publicity in the Tribunal process

12.37   The Tribunal has been designed as an essentially public process[1], partly with the ECHR requirements in mind and partly because transparency is of itself viewed as beneficial. It is important to appreciate this at the outset because, whilst there are opportunities for applicants to request that the process be kept private, the general expectation is that publicity will arise. In particular, in the absence of any specific directions to the contrary from the Tribunal:

- on the commencement of Tribunal proceedings, certain particulars of the case are put in the Tribunal's register, which is open to public inspection[2];

- any hearings as the case proceeds, including any directions hearing, pre-hearing review and any preliminary issues hearing, are likely to take place in public[3];

- the final hearing itself will be in public[4]; and

- judgment will be pronounced publicly[5].

1   The Tribunal has noted the 'strong presumption' in favour of publicity: *7722656 Canada Inc (formerly carrying on business as Swift Trade Inc) and Peter Beck v FSA (FS0017 & 0018, August 2011)* The case was specifically concerned with the disclosure of documents, but the Tribunal noted the overall public interest in the openness of proceedings and its consistency with Article 6(1). It held that there was a strong presumption in the FSMA and the Tribunal Rules in favour of dealing with references in public, so a party applying for privacy would need to provide cogent evidence of how publication or a public hearing would lead to unfairness and a disproportionate level of damage. It also noted that embarrassment would not constitute unfairness.
2   See para **12.49** below
3   Tribunal Rules, r 17(2) and see, for example, paras **12.103** and **12.123** below.
4   See para **12.139** ff below.
5   See para **12.159** ff below.

Referring a case to the Tribunal

12.38   In those cases where the FSMA 2000 allows it, a firm or person to whom a decision notice or supervisory notice[1] is given may refer the matter to the Tribunal[2]. This is done by filing a reference notice with the Tribunal, and at the same time sending a copy to the FCA[3]. There is no fee for referring a matter to the Tribunal[4].

1   Note that if it is the first supervisory notice that is referred to the Tribunal, it is possible that the FCA would go on to give the second supervisory notice notwithstanding the reference to the Tribunal. In that case, the FCA must file a copy of the subsequent notice: Tribunal Rules, Schedule 3, para 8.
2   The Tribunal Rules apply also to a third party who makes a reference to the Tribunal under FSMA 2000, s 393 (see para **10.174** ff above), subject to certain modifications found at Tribunal Rules, Sch 3, para 9.
3   Tribunal Rules, Sch 3, para 2(5).
4   HMCTS Explanatory Leaflet T400, 'Making a reference to the Upper Tribunal (Tax and Chancery Chamber)'. Note that legal assistance may be available in cases of market abuse (but is not otherwise available: see the FSMA 2000, ss 134 and 135, the Financial Services and Markets Tribunal (Legal Assistance) Regulations 2001, SI 2001/3632 and the Financial Services and Markets Tribunal (Legal Assistance Scheme – Costs) Regulations 2001, SI 2001/3633.

What is a reference notice?

12.39   A reference notice[1] is the notice issued by a person who wishes to refer a matter to the Tribunal. The notice is required to state[2]:

- the name and address of the applicant;

- the name and address of the applicant's representative (if any);

- the applicant's UK address for service, if no representative is named; and

- the issues that the applicant wishes the Tribunal to consider.

1 Form 'Upper Tribunal (Tax and Chancery Chamber) Reference notice (Financial Services)' 'FTC3' which can be found at http://www.justice.gov.uk/downloads/forms/tribunals/tax/upper/ftc3.pdf.
2 Tribunal Rules, Sch 3, para 2(3).

12.40   A copy of the relevant decision or a supervisory notice must be filed as well[1].

1 Tribunal Rules, Sch 3, para 2(4). Where the applicant is a third party on whom a copy of the decision notice was served under FSMA 2000, s 393 (see para **10.174** ff above), this is not required: Tribunal Rules, Sch 3, para 9(3).

12.41   The reference notice is a relatively straightforward document, the only potential complexity being the requirement to state in it the issues concerning the decision notice or supervisory notice that the applicant wishes the Tribunal to consider. Therefore, whilst the burden of proof in the Tribunal is on the FCA to substantiate the action that it wishes to take, and not on the applicant to challenge that action, and whilst it is for the FCA to take the first step in explaining what the case is about[1], the applicant needs at least to have given some thought to the grounds for referring the matter to the Tribunal before he files the reference notice. The Tribunal Rules do not, however, prescribe what information must be provided in this regard and in principle it ought to be permissible for the reference notice to say little more than that the applicant wishes the Tribunal to consider whether it is appropriate for the FCA to take the relevant action. The applicant can, in the reference notice, limit the matters that it wants the Tribunal to consider. For example, an applicant may want the Tribunal to limit its consideration to the level or type of sanction[2].

1 See para **12.54** ff below.
2 In *Wagner v FSA (FS/2011/0015)*, the applicant amended his reference notice, accepting the prohibition order given by the FSA and limiting the reference to challenging of the imposition of a financial penalty.

When can the reference notice be filed?

12.42   A reference notice cannot be filed until the relevant supervisory notice or decision notice which gives rise to the right to refer the case to the Tribunal has been issued. Once that notice has been issued, the reference must be made before the end of the period of 28 days beginning with the date on which the relevant decision notice or supervisory notice was given[1] (not the date it is received)[2]. Time stops running when the reference is made[3].

1 Tribunal Rules, Sch 3, para 2(2).
2 For the detailed rules on the service of statutory notices, see the Financial Services and Markets Act 2000 (Service of Notices) Regulations 2001, SI 2001/1420 (as amended).
3 For the rules regarding the sending and receipt of Tribunal notices, including the reference notice, see Tribunal Rules, rr 12 and 13.

12.43   If the time for serving the notice is likely to expire, or has expired, then it may be possible to have the time extended[1]. The Tribunal must also consider whether the decision notice or supervisory notice was such as to notify the applicant properly and effectively of the action proposed by the FCA and whether the applicant had been notified of the right to refer the matter to the Tribunal and the time limit for doing so.

1 Tribunal Rules, r 5(3)(a).

Does the applicant have any other options at the same time?

12.44   At the same time as filing and serving the reference notice, the applicant may want to consider applying for directions from the Tribunal on particular procedural issues. The Tribunal will consider what directions are required in due course, but there may be certain issues which the applicant considers necessary to be addressed at the outset. The Tribunal Rules expressly provide for parties to apply for directions[1]. The standard form reference notice contains examples of directions which the applicant may want to consider.

1 Tribunals Rules, r 6(1)–(3).

12.45   Whether any directions are required, and if so, what directions, depends entirely on the circumstances. Examples of directions which may be relevant at this stage are:

- to keep the matter confidential, by the Tribunal directing that no particulars about the reference should be entered in the Tribunal's register[1];

- to suspend the action which the FCA is taking with immediate effect or on a specified date[2];

- to have the reference consolidated with another[3]; or

- to obtain early disclosure of documents from the FCA[4].

1 The Tribunal may make such a direction if satisfied that this is necessary, having regard to any unfairness to the applicant or prejudice to the interests of consumers that might result: Tribunal Rules, Sch 3, para 3(3).
2 This relates only to Supervisory Notices issued by the FCA on an urgent basis: see para **16.215** ff below. The Tribunal may only suspend the relevant action where satisfied that this would not prejudice the interests of any persons intended to be protected by the action or the smooth operation or integrity of the relevant market. This may make it difficult in practice to obtain a suspension: see para **12.119** ff below.
3 Tribunal Rules, r 5(3)(b); for example, where the authority notice was served on more than one party and both are making references: see para **12.129** ff below.

4   The applicant might, for example, wish to seek the FCA's documents relating to the procedure which led to the decision Notice or supervisory notice being issued. This material may not otherwise be disclosable: see further the discussion at para **12.79** below. Moreover, a person issued with a supervisory notice will not yet have had any right of access to the FCA's material and may therefore need to seek a direction for early disclosure to enable it to begin preparing its case: see para **12.77** ff below.

12.46   The procedure for the making and determination of applications for directions is considered at para **12.100** ff below.

Can any other party file a reference notice?

12.47   A third party to whom a copy of a decision notice is given also has the right to refer the matter to the Tribunal[1]. However, that right is limited to:

- the decision in question, so far as it is based on a reason which identifies the third party and is prejudicial to him; or

- any opinion expressed by the FCA in relation to him.

1   See above at para **10.176**.

12.48   The right to refer is also open to a third party who was not given a copy of the decision notice but who alleges that a copy should have been given to him[1].

1   See above at para **10.177**.

What does the Tribunal do when it receives the reference notice?

12.49   On receiving the reference notice[1], if no application for directions has been made at the same time (and subject to any directions given by the Tribunal), the Tribunal enters particulars of the reference on the Tribunal's register[2] and informs the parties either that it has done so or that it will not do so.

1   Tribunal Rules, Sch 3, para 3(4).
2   The Tribunal's register is a register of references and decisions, which is open to public inspection: Tribunal Rules, r 3(1) and (2). A copy of the register is open to public inspection at the Tribunal and there is also a separate list of current references on the Enforcement section of the FCA's website. The register sets out the following information: the name of the applicant, the reference number, the date of receipt of the reference, hearing dates, type of the hearings (eg 'privacy application', 'directions hearing', 'substantive hearing'), the intended length of the hearing and the outcome of the hearing, with reasons. Details of the matter referred to the Tribunal (such as a summary of the relevant decision notice or supervisory notice) are not entered onto the register. Where a party successfully applies for a direction that the register contains no particulars of the reference, that party's name will not be entered onto the register. However, other details such as the reference number and the date of receipt of the reference will be included.

12.50   Where a decision notice is being referred to the Tribunal, this is likely to be the first instance at which the FCA's investigation of the applicant becomes public knowledge[1]. The applicant must be careful if press attention is provoked by the filing of the reference notice, in particular since the prohibition against publishing the decision notice or any details concerning it[2] remains. Among other things, the applicant may wish to consider drafting its own press release to be released simultaneously with the FCA's. The FCA will normally send a copy of its proposed statement to the applicant before its release, and will expect the applicant to do the same if it intends to release a statement. Whilst this is a matter of courtesy rather than an opportunity formally to comment on the FCA's draft, the FCA will sometimes make amendments at the applicant's request.

1   See para **10.108** ff above. Note that in the case of a supervisory notice, there is no statutory prohibition against publication and therefore the matter may have been made public at an earlier stage: see para **16.207** below.
2   See para **10.179** above.

Can a party participate without filing a reference notice?

12.51   Problems may arise where one party who receives a decision notice wishes to refer it to the Tribunal whereas another party does not wish to do so. For example, a decision notice may be served on a firm and on an employee[1]. The employee may then decide to refer the decision notice to the Tribunal. Apart from the question of the publicity that will arise for the firm as a result of the Tribunal process[2], the firm may wish to protect its interests, for example, by defending any allegations made against it by the employee. However, the firm may not wish to incur the expense of making a reference and participating fully in the Tribunal process. Can the firm participate in the process without filing a reference notice? The Tribunal Rules do not provide for a procedure by which parties may be involved in Tribunal proceedings without having submitted a reference notice and the party who has filed a reference notice may not welcome the involvement of another party with different interests. Since it will not be clear that the Tribunal will allow representations to be made by a person who has not filed a reference notice, that party may wish to do so to be sure that it can protect its interests.

1   See, for example, *Hoodless and Blackwell v FSA (2003) FSMT 007* where the FCA proposed to fine the firm and withdraw the approval of two employees. The employees referred the matter to the Tribunal, but the firm did not.
2   See para **12.37** above.

12.52   Some Tribunal proceedings may raise wider issues of public interest that go beyond the strict interests of the parties involved. Such issues may, for example, affect the financial services industry as a whole or a particular part of the industry. In such cases, representative groups or trade associations may wish to make representations if the eventual Tribunal decision is likely to affect their members. The Tribunal Rules do not expressly provide for such interventions[1]. It remains to be seen whether the Tribunal would permit representations to be made by interested parties, in a way that courts on occasion do. In *Sachin Karpe v FSA (FS/2010/0019)*, for example, UBS (Mr Karpe's former employer) was described as an 'interested party' and seems to have been represented by counsel. It is not clear from the Tribunal's report how and to what extent UBS was involved in the proceedings.

1   In *Eurolife Assurance Company Ltd v FSA (2002) FSMT 001*, the Tribunal received a submission from Justice in Financial Services. Neither party objected to the submission which set out public interest reasons for holding Tribunal hearings in public.

Procedure up to the hearing

12.53   Having issued and served a reference notice, the Tribunal's procedures apply. The following paragraphs consider the procedure involved in taking the case from the reference notice to the hearing, and in particular:

- the procedure for each party to explain its case by filing, in the case of the FCA, a statement of case and, in the case of the applicant, a reply;

- the disclosure of documents by each party to the other;

- applications for directions, including the pre-hearing review;

- the treatment of witnesses, including experts;

- the Tribunal's power to suspend the FCA's action pending determination of the reference;

- the power to hold a preliminary hearing of one or more issues; and

- the Tribunal's various powers to consolidate and dispose of cases.

The statement of case and reply

The FCA's statement of case

12.54   Since the burden of proof before the Tribunal is on the FCA, once the applicant files a reference notice, the first stage is for the FCA to file a written statement of case with the Tribunal, which it must also serve on the applicant.

12.55   The statement of case is required to set out all the matters and facts upon which the FCA relies to support the referred action, and to specify the statutory provisions under which the action was taken and the reasons for taking the action[1]. The statement of case must be accompanied by the FCA's initial disclosure of documents, as discussed at para **12.75** ff below.

1   Tribunal Rules, Sch 3, para 4(2).

12.56   The statement of case is an important document. It provides the main explanation of the FCA's reasons for seeking to take the action which has been referred to the Tribunal and, in setting out all the matters and facts upon which the FCA relies, defines the scope of the FCA's case. It will form the focus of the case and the applicant's arguments in response. It is not certain who within the FCA will be responsible for it, and for the conduct of the Tribunal proceedings more generally, but the team is likely to contain at least some of the same enforcement staff who recommended to the RDC that the relevant action should be taken[1].

1   See, for example, *FCA v Hobbs [2013] EWCA Civ 918*, which contains some discussion on the case team and responsibilities within the FCA. As regards the process of making recommendations to the RDC, see para **10.68** ff above.

12.57   The statement of case will explain the penalty (or other action) that the FCA seeks to impose on the applicant and will address matters relevant to the question of what action should be taken, such as the person's previous compliance history. Prejudicial evidence of this nature, which is not relevant to the question of whether the applicant committed the relevant breach, is therefore likely to be before the Tribunal from the outset.

12.58 An issue which the Tribunal Rules do not address is to what extent the FCA can depart in its statement of case from the reasons which it gave in its decision notice or supervisory notice for taking the relevant action[1]. Can the FCA in its statement of case:

- allege that the applicant has breached the same rule as alleged in the decision notice but for different reasons (for example, by alleging that a firm has mis-sold investments as a result of deficiencies in its procedures, but citing different deficiencies to those alleged in the decision notice);

- allege that the applicant has breached a different rule to the breach alleged in the decision notice; or

- entirely abandon its original grounds and instead rely on new grounds for taking the same action set out in the decision notice (for example, the same fine, but for different breaches and reasons)[2]?

1 Both decision notices (FSMA 2000, s 388(1)(b)) and, generally, supervisory notices (see, for example, FSMA 2000, s 53(5)) are required to give reasons.
2 There may in practice be a risk of some change being made to the way that the FCA puts its case, for example if the enforcement staff who have conduct of the Tribunal case for the FCA disagree with the way that the RDC decided to put the case in the warning/decision notices or supervisory notices or if the FCA, when drafting the statement of case, recognises that there are difficulties with the original case.

12.59 The Tribunal Rules require the FCA to set out the facts and matters upon which it 'relies' to support the referred action. It thus focuses on the present, rather than on the matters which were relied upon at the time when the decision to issue the decision notice or supervisory notice was taken. The FSMA 2000 allows the Tribunal to determine 'the matter referred' to it, but that phrase is not defined. In *Legal & General Assurance Society Ltd v FSA*[1], the Tribunal decided that the word 'matter' is to be read broadly and covers the FCA decision, the imposition of a penalty and the surrounding facts, not simply the particular facts recorded in the decision notice. In relation to the question of whether the FCA can depart in its statement of case from the reasons given in its decision notice or supervisory notice, the Tribunal stated that both parties are allowed to raise matters that were not directly brought before the RDC. However, the Tribunal expressly stated that, as a matter of common sense and fairness and because of the wide powers open to the FCA in a disciplinary matter and the fact that it would have already taken time and care to review and carry forward the charges to the RDC, the Tribunal expected the FCA to bring much the same case before the Tribunal as before the RDC[2].

1 *[2005] UKFSM FSM011.*
2 Paragraphs 12 and 15 of the Tribunal's judgment given in *Legal & General v FSA* (21/01/05).

12.60 Later cases have examined similar issues and have generally (explicitly or otherwise) followed the approach in *Legal & General*, using a broad interpretation of 'matter' under s 133 of the FSMA 2000 and therefore giving the FCA some flexibility to amend its case within certain parameters[1]. In *Philippe Jabre v FSA (Case 036, August 2006)*, for example, the RDC had made findings on three issues, finding against the FSA on the question of whether Mr Jabre was a fit and proper person. The decision notice therefore referred to the two issues decided in favour of the FSA as the basis for sanctioning Mr Jabre, and held that no finding was made against him on the third issue. At the Tribunal stage, the FSA included all three issues in its statement of case. The Tribunal held that it had jurisdiction to decide whether Mr Jabre was a fit and proper person, notwithstanding the RDC's findings; the Tribunal held that 'the matter' included all evidence before the RDC and was not limited to its findings and the contents of the decision notice.

1 See *Philippe Jabre v FSA [2006] UKFSM FSM036, Stefan Chaligné, Patrick Sejean and Cheickh Tidiane Diallo v FSA, FS/2011/0001, 0002 and 0003*, and the discussion in *Stephen Robert Allen v FCA (FS/2012/0019)* which distinguished *James Parker v FSA (Case 037, August 2006)* on the facts.

12.61 The FCA must file its statement of case no later than 28 days after the day on which it received the information about the reference sent by the secretary of the Tribunal, as discussed at para **12.49** above[1]. The FCA may apply for an extension of the time for filing its statement of case.

1 Tribunal Rules, Sch 3, para 4(1).

12.62 If the FCA does not file a statement of case within the applicable time limit, then the Tribunal may direct of its own initiative that the FCA file a statement of case by a specified date[1]. It also has the power to take such action as it sees fit, such as striking out the statement of case, or part of it, or restricting the FCA's participation in the proceedings[2].

1 Tribunal Rules, r 7(2)(b).
2 Tribunal Rules, r 7(2).

The applicant's reply

12.63 Once the FCA files its statement of case, the applicant must file a written reply.

12.64 The reply is required to[1]:

- state the grounds on which the applicant relies in the reference;
- identify all matters in the statement of case which are disputed by the applicant; and
- state the applicant's reasons for disputing them.

1 Tribunal Rules, Sch 3, para 5(2).

12.65 The applicant will clearly wish to explain those points in the statement of case which it disputes, and the reasons why. But its reasons for requiring the FCA to prove its case in the Tribunal, or for disagreeing with the action the FCA wishes to take, may go beyond this. The person may have positive points to make, for example about action it took once the regulatory breach arose[1], points in mitigation[2], or concerns about the FCA's procedures[3]. To the extent it wishes to rely on them, the applicant needs to make all of these points in its reply[4]. The reply will (together with the statement of case) form the basis on which the Tribunal will decide what the issues are and what procedure is required to have those issues determined[5].

1 Relevant points include how the breach came to the applicant's attention, how quickly and completely the applicant notified the FCA of it, the level of co-operation with the FCA, and the steps taken by the applicant to identify and address any customer losses, employee issues and implications for systems and controls: see generally **CHAPTER 3** above.
2 For example, that the breach was not particularly serious, that no customers were affected or their interests were protected by the applicant, or that the breach was an isolated incident with no systemic implications.
3 For example, about whether the applicant has been treated fairly in the investigation and enforcement process. This would be unlikely to be relevant to the merits of the case but the applicant may wish to seek a recommendation from the Tribunal about the FCA's procedures or rules: see para **12.155** below.
4 It is thought that this is what is encompassed by the phrase 'the grounds on which the applicant relies in the reference'.
5 This is subject to the applicant or the FCA being allowed to supplement or amend their documents: see, respectively, paras **12.68** and **12.70** below.

12.66 The reply must be filed so as to be received by the Tribunal no later than 28 days after the date on which the applicant received a copy of the FCA's statement of case[1]. A copy must be served on the FCA at the same time[2]. The applicant can apply for an extension of time, which the Tribunal may grant if satisfied that to do so would be in the interests of justice[3].

1 Or, in a multiple regulator case, 28 days after being in receipt of all statements: Tribunal Rules, rr 5(1)(a) and (aa). If the FCA was permitted to serve an amended statement of case, the applicant must file its reply 28 days after receiving a copy: Tribunal Rules, r 5(1)(b). Rules relating to the giving and sending of notices are found at Tribunal Rules, rr 12 and 13.
2 Tribunal Rules, Sch 3, para 5(4).
3 Tribunal Rules, r 5(d). The procedure for making applications for directions is considered at para **12.100** ff below.

12.67 If a reply is not filed in accordance with the applicable time limit, then the Tribunal may of its own initiative direct that the applicant file a reply by a specified date[1]. It also has the power to take such action as it sees fit, such as striking out the statement of case, or part of it, or restricting the applicant's participation in the proceedings[2].

1 Tribunal Rules, r 7(2)(b).
2 Tribunal Rules, r 7(2). See, for example, *HPA Services v Financial Services Authority (2003) FSMT 005* where the applicant failed to file a reply and the Tribunal stated that it would dismiss the reference unless representations were received. No representations were received and the reference was dismissed.

Supplementary statements

12.68 There is no provision for the automatic exchange of additional statements by the parties. In practice, the applicant may have raised in its reply various positive points to which the FCA may wish to respond and, equally, the applicant and the Tribunal may want to know what the FCA's case is on these points. Whilst there is no mechanism automatically requiring the FCA to serve a further response, the Tribunal Rules[1] do allow the Tribunal (on an application by a party or of its own initiative) to permit or require a party to provide documents, information, evidence or submissions to the Tribunal or a party (or to amend a document). If a supplementary statement is likely to ensure that the reference is determined in accordance with the overriding principle, for example by clarifying what the issues are so that the witness, expert and documentary evidence is directed to those issues, then this may well be attractive to the Tribunal.

1 Tribunal Rules, r 3(c) and (d). The procedure for making applications for directions is considered at para **12.100** ff below.

12.69 When should applicants consider applying for a direction to require a response from the FCA to their reply? In practice, this should at least be under consideration in any case where points are raised in the reply that were not addressed by the FCA in its statement of case. By requiring the FCA to explain at the outset its case on those new points, the applicant allows itself to prepare to address the FCA's case on those points at the hearing. There is otherwise a risk of being caught by surprise at the hearing and being unable to deal properly with the FCA's points. There is, however, a potential disadvantage, which is that the FCA may use the supplementary statement as an opportunity to improve upon its case in the light of the applicant's reply. The applicant will therefore need to consider where the balance lies in the particular case.

Can the parties amend their statements of case?

12.70 A party may apply at any time for a direction permitting or requiring the amendment of the statement of case or reply[1]. The Tribunal may also make a direction of its own initiative. The procedure for making applications for directions is considered at para **12.100** ff below.

1 Tribunal Rules, r 5(3)(c).

12.71 The Tribunal Rules do not address the extent to which the FCA will be permitted to amend its case. For example, if in its statement of case the FCA gave two reasons for taking the relevant action, can it amend its case to abandon those two reasons and rely instead upon two entirely different reasons? There are three, separate questions. First, whether the Tribunal would be entitled to consider the new reasons given by the FCA. Second if so, whether it should as a matter of discretion allow the FCA to make the amendments. Third, whether the applicant should consent or object to the amendments being made. The first and third questions arise equally in relation to the FCA's statement of case and are considered at para **12.58** above.

12.72 The additional question which arises when considering amendments to the statement of case is how the Tribunal should exercise its discretion whether to allow the FCA to make the amendments. The Tribunal has dealt with this issue to an extent in *Stephen Robert Allan v FCA, FS/2012/0019*. Following *Legal & General Assurance Society Ltd v FSA*[1], it held that the FCA should usually be confined to the charges set out in the statement of case unless important new evidence comes to light or there are other special circumstances. The answer will therefore depend very much upon the circumstances[2], including factors such as the reasons why the amendments are now being sought and why the case was not put in this way from the outset, the extent of the amendments, any prejudice that would be caused to the person concerned and, possibly, whether the FCA could commence a new enforcement procedure based on the amended 'charges'[3].

1   *[2005] UKFSM FSM011.*
2   By way of analogy, it is notable that a criminal court has a broad discretion, albeit statutory, to amend an indictment: see *R v Osieh [1996] 2 Cr App Rep 145, R v Hemmings [2000] 1 Cr App Rep 360 and R v Johal and Ram (1972) 56 Cr App Rep 348* and see the discussion at Archbold 2013, 1–230.
3   If the reasons the FCA now proposes to give for taking the action are fundamentally different from those given in the decision notice or supervisory notice, then the applicant may also have grounds to apply for the FCA to pay its costs of the Tribunal process on the basis that it has acted unreasonably: see para **12.167** ff below.

Disclosure of documents

12.73   The Tribunal Rules contain provision for the disclosure of documents by the parties. Unusually, this happens sequentially rather than by mutual exchange and the extent of the disclosure obligation is different for the FCA and for the applicant. The reality is likely to be that the FCA has already, in the course of its investigation, had access to whatever documents and information it or its investigator believed to be relevant. The disclosure process is unlikely, therefore, to reveal much to the FCA. The FCA's disclosure may, however, be of significance to the applicant, in particular where the supervisory notice process is being used and the applicant will see many of the relevant documents on the FCA side for the first time. Even if the decision notice process is being used, when the applicant would normally have seen the FCA's documents at the RDC stage, new evidence may since have come to light which the FCA may disclose at this stage[1].

1   This is discussed at para **12.77** ff below.

12.74   The following paragraphs consider:

- the FCA's obligation to provide initial disclosure;
- the applicant's obligation to provide disclosure;
- the FCA's obligation to provide secondary disclosure;
- the documents that are not required to be disclosed by either party;
- the Tribunal's power to give directions relating to disclosure; and
- the use that the applicant can make of documents disclosed.

The FCA's obligation to provide initial disclosure

12.75   At the same time as filing its statement of case, the FCA must file with the Tribunal and send the applicant a list of[1]:

- the documents on which it relies in support of the referred action[2]; and

- the further documents considered by the FCA in reaching (or maintaining[3]) the decision to issue the warning notice or supervisory notice, or obtained by it in connection with the matter to which the notice relates (whether before or after giving the notice) but not considered by it in reaching (or maintaining) that decision[4], which in the opinion of the FCA might undermine the decision to take the referred action.

1   Tribunal Rules, Sch 3, para 4(3) and (4).
2   This test looks at the present, rather than the past; ie what are the documents upon which the FCA now relies in support of the referred action? The relevant documents will therefore be the documents that support the FCA's case as set out in its statement of case and this may not entirely equate with the documents to which the applicant had a right of access following the issue of the warning notice: see para **10.118** ff above.
3   This is the wording of the Tribunal Rules, Sch 3, (para 1, definition of 'further material') but it is not entirely clear what it is intended to mean.
4   See the definition of 'further material' at Tribunal Rules, Sch 3, para 1.

12.76   Certain categories of documents need not be included on the list[1] and, in addition, the FCA may apply (without giving notice to the applicant) for a direction authorising it not to include particular documents on its list[2]. Once it has served its list, the FCA must, upon request, provide the applicant with a copy of any document specified in it or make such a document available for inspection or copying[3].

1   This is discussed further at para **12.84** ff below.
2   This is discussed further at para **12.88** ff below.
3   Tribunal Rules, r 7(7).

12.77   A number of points should be noted regarding the timing and nature of the FCA's disclosure. First, if the action to which the reference relates was one that required the supervisory notice procedure, rather than the warning/decision notice procedure, to be followed, then this will be the first opportunity the applicant will have to access any of the FCA's material. It may therefore wish to consider applying to the Tribunal at the time that the reference notice is filed for a direction that the FCA gives immediate disclosure so that it can start preparing its case at that stage rather than having to wait 28 days for the FCA to serve its statement of case[1].

1   See para **12.45** above.

12.78   Second, where the warning/decision notice procedure was used, the material which the FCA has to disclose at the Tribunal stage should correspond broadly with the material to which the FCA was required to provide access when it gave the relevant warning and/or decision notice[1]. There may be some differences (for example, the material upon which the FCA now relies may not equate entirely with the material upon which it relied at the time when it took the relevant decision and, as already noted, there may have been changes in the FCA's case). Broadly, therefore, the applicant may already have had access to much of this material. Further disclosure by the FCA may occur in due course, after the applicant serves its reply[2].

12.78   The Tribunal and appeals

1   The FCA's obligation to give access to its material is discussed in detail at para **10.118** ff above.
2   See para **12.81** below.

12.79   Third, one omission from the categories of material which the FCA is required to disclose is material relating to the decision itself, and in particular the record kept by the RDC of, for example, who was present at the RDC meeting at which the decision to take the relevant action was made and what representations and material were put before the RDC, including what oral evidence was given by the FCA staff. Depending on how the applicant puts its case in its reply, such documents may become disclosable, when the FCA provides secondary disclosure[1]. In most cases, such material may be said to be irrelevant, on the basis that the Tribunal is considering the matter de novo and so is not concerned with the FCA's decision-making process. Furthermore, the applicant will normally have attended the RDC hearing, and may have obtained a transcript of it. There may, however, be some prospect of obtaining disclosure, for example if the applicant is seeking a recommendation from the Tribunal about the FCA's procedures or if aspects of the decision-making process are relevant to the substance of the charges. The Tribunal is able to require the disclosure of additional documents and, as will be seen, the Tribunal Rules prescribe a low test, leaving the question whether to order disclosure in the discretion of the Tribunal dealing with the particular case[2]. It will therefore be a matter for the Tribunal to decide in each case.

1   See para **12.81** below.
2   This is discussed further at para **12.93** below.

The applicant's obligation to provide disclosure

12.80   At the same time as filing its reply, the applicant must send the Tribunal and the FCA a list of all the documents on which it relies in support of its case[1]. The applicant does not have to provide the FCA with certain types of documents, discussed below, but will in practical terms need to disclose them if it is to rely on them in support of its case[2]. Similarly, to the extent that the applicant relies on documents that are confidential in support of its case, it must disclose such documents. Confidentiality is not a ground for withholding disclosure[3]. The obligation of disclosure is thus limited to those documents on which the applicant relies in support of its case. The likelihood is that the FCA will already have had access to the applicant's records during the course of its investigation (although documents already within the FCA's possession should still be included on the disclosure list). Once it has served its list, the applicant must, upon request, provide the FCA with a copy of, or make available for inspection or copying, any document specified in the list[4].

1   Tribunal Rules, Sch 3, para 5(3) and (4).
2   See the discussion at para **12.87** below.
3   In the context of employment tribunals, the Supreme Court has suggested that tribunals should inspect the confidential document and consider whether justice can be done by adopting special measures such as covering up, substituting anonymous references for specific names or, in rare cases, hearing the matter in private: see the consolidated *Nassé* and *Vyas* appeals *[1979] 3 All ER 673*. Whilst the employment tribunal is applying a different test, it may be appropriate to seek a

direction from the Tribunal in this context to treat in a similar way the disclosure of particularly sensitive material (particularly to avoid it being disclosed in a public hearing).
4 Tribunal Rules, r 7(7).

The FCA's obligation to provide secondary disclosure

12.81 The Tribunal Rules require the FCA to give further disclosure following the filing by the applicant of its reply. In particular, the FCA must file a list of any further material which might be reasonably expected to assist the applicant's case as disclosed by its reply and which is not mentioned in the list already provided by the FCA[1]. The list must be filed (and a copy sent to the applicant at the same time) so that it is received no later than 14 days after the day on which the FCA received the reply[2]. Certain categories of documents need not be included on the list[3] and, in addition, the FCA may apply (without giving notice to the applicant) for a direction authorising it not to include particular documents on its list[4]. Once it has served its list, the FCA must, upon request, provide the applicant with a copy of any document specified in it or make such a document available for inspection or copying[5].

1 Tribunal Rules, Sch 3, para 6(1).
2 Tribunal Rules, Sch 3, para 6(2) and (3). In *Cox v FSA (2003) FSMT 003*, the FCA applied to the Tribunal to disclose documents to the applicant on the evening before the hearing of the reference owing to shortcomings in its own file retrieval systems. It is not clear what documents were to be disclosed, but the Tribunal stated that it would generally refuse applications for late disclosure, particularly if such late disclosure would prejudice the applicant's position. In the case in question, disclosure was allowed because the Tribunal did not consider that late disclosure would prejudice the applicant's position.
3 See para **12.84** ff below.
4 See para **12.88** ff below
5 Tribunal Rules, Sch 3, para 7(7).

12.82 This broadens the FCA's duty of disclosure, requiring the FCA to disclose a wider category of adverse documents, encompassing not only those that might undermine its case but also those that might assist the applicant's case as put in the reply. Whether material might reasonably be expected to assist the applicant's case is an objective test. It is for the FCA to reach this assessment in the first instance but if the applicant believes that there may be further material which should be disclosed, an application could be made to the Tribunal for a direction that the FCA provides the additional material[1].

1 See para **12.92** ff below. For example, in *FCA v Legal & General (2003) FIN 0022*, the Tribunal ordered the FCA to disclose various categories of documents, including working files from supervision visits and themed visits and other internal FCA documents.

12.83 One issue which can arise here is a mismatch between the way in which the FCA frames its case, and the way the applicant does. The FCA may see the issue as a narrow question on the meaning of particular rules or principles; consequently, it may view the relevant evidence in correspondingly narrow terms. The applicant on the other hand may see much broader issues as being at stake, and so consider a much broader category of evidence to be relevant (eg evidence regarding how particular rules were created, or evidence of internal uncertainty within the FCA as to the precise meaning or application of particular rules or principles). It is for the Tribunal to find a suitable compromise in such cases.

What documents do not need to be provided?

12.84   In parallel with the provisions of the FSMA 2000, certain types of documents do not need to be disclosed. The relevant types of documents are as follows[1]:

- documents which are, broadly, protected under the FSMA 2000 because they are legally privileged[2];

- documents which relate to a case involving a different person and were taken into account by the FCA in the applicant's case only for purposes of comparison with other cases[3];

- documents the disclosure of which is prohibited by the Regulation of Investigatory Powers Act 2000, s 17[4]; and

- any document in respect of which an application has been or is being made for a direction authorising a party not to include the document in the list[5].

1 Tribunal Rules, Sch 3, para 7(1)–(3) and (8).
2 Such documents are 'protected items' under the FSMA 2000, s 413. They must be included in the list but need not be disclosed: Tribunal Rules, Sch 3, para 7(8) and (9). Various issues which arise are considered at para **12.85** below.
3 Such documents need not be included in the list: Tribunal Rules, Sch 3, para 7(1). The same category of documents is excluded from the access provisions of the FSMA 2000 as discussed in more detail at para **10.118** ff above.
4 Broadly, the effect of this is to ensure that the Tribunal is bound by the provisions of the Regulation of Investigatory Powers Act 2000 which exclude from legal proceedings (subject to certain exceptions) matters which disclose that communications have been or will be intercepted. Such documents need not be included in the list: Tribunal Rules, Sch 3, para 7(2).
5 Applications for such directions are discussed at para **12.88** ff below. Such documents need not be included in the list: Tribunal Rules, Sch 3, para 7(3).

12.85   Both the FCA and the applicant could have legally privileged documents which they will want to withhold from disclosure[1]. Among other things, the disclosure of the material in this context may constitute a waiver of the privilege or may result in the document being disclosed in a public forum (the Tribunal hearing), and in either case destroy the protection of legal privilege so that it could be disclosable in other proceedings, for example proceedings brought by third parties who may have claims against the applicant. As noted above, although the Tribunal Rules allow such documents not to be disclosed, they do require them to be identified in the list of documents. In practice, this can often be done generically, without identifying individual documents that are legally privileged.

1 Note that the meaning of legal privilege applicable in this context is that under the FSMA 2000, s 413(2): see Tribunal Rules, Sch 3, para 7(8) and the definition of 'protected item' in r 7(9). That is not the same in all respects as the common law meaning and, in particular, it does not appear to encompass 'without prejudice' material and it may not include certain internal communications that would normally be legally privileged: see para **5.56** ff above. For a brief discussion of the common law meaning of legal privilege and the documents that are likely to be covered, see para **4.153** ff above.

12.86   The requirement to list privileged material should be unobjectionable from the FCA's perspective, since the parallel provisions in the FSMA 2000 require the FCA to give the applicant notice of the existence of such items[1]. In some instances, though, material which may be privileged will be an important part of the FCA's case, for example an expert report. The question whether that material should be disclosed has been discussed at para **10.128** above. In the context of the Tribunal that issue is less likely to cause difficulty because the FCA will need either to disclose the report, if it is to rely upon it, or to obtain a new report for disclosure and use in the Tribunal proceedings.

1 FSMA 2000, s 394(4)(a) and see para **10.120** above.

12.87   The position is different so far as it relates to the applicant. The FSMA 2000 provides that a person may not be required under the FSMA 2000 to produce, disclose or permit the inspection of a privileged document[1]. However, the question whether the document is to be disclosed is within the applicant's control, as it need only list those documents on which it relies in support of its case. That could include privileged material such as legal advice, for example if one of its arguments in its defence is that it took and complied with legal advice on the matter in question. If it wishes to rely on that legal advice before the Tribunal, then in practical terms it will need to disclose that advice at some stage[2]. The question, therefore, is whether the applicant wishes to rely on the legally privileged material in support of its case.

1 This is broadly the effect of FSMA 2000, s 413. See also para **12.85**, n 1 above.
2 It may be possible to seek ancillary directions to protect the applicant's position, for example to have the hearing in private either wholly or so far as relates to the disclosure of the legally privileged information.

The Tribunal's power to give directions relating to disclosure

12.88   The Tribunal can make a direction authorising a party not to include a document in its list. The grounds for making such a direction are[1] that disclosure of the document:

- would not be in the public interest[2]; or

- would not be fair, having regard to:

  - the likely significance of the document to the applicant in relation to the matter referred to the Tribunal, and

  - the potential prejudice to the commercial interests of a person other than the applicant which would be caused by disclosure of the document.

1 Tribunal Rules, Sch 3, para 7(4).
2 It is thought that this would include a document protected by the doctrine of public interest immunity.

12.89   Such a direction may be made on an application by either party (although in practice it is most likely to be the FCA that seeks to make use of this provision). The application is made without giving notice to the other party[1].

1 Tribunal Rules, Sch 3, para 7(4).

12.90   Whether the Tribunal will be prepared to make such a direction will depend largely upon the situation. Whilst the grounds for making the direction mirror one of the exceptions to the statutory right of access to the FCA's material[1], the important difference is that in this context it is for the Tribunal, not the FCA, to decide whether or not the document should be disclosed[2]. In order to do so, the Tribunal may require that the document be produced to it together with a statement of the reasons why its inclusion in the list would, as applicable, not be in the public interest, or not be fair, and it may also invite the other party to make representations[3].

1 This is discussed at para **10.120** above.
2 If the Tribunal refuses an application for such a direction, it will direct the relevant party to revise its list so as to include the document and to file a copy of that list as revised and send a copy to the other party: Tribunal Rules, r 7(6).
3 Tribunal Rules, Sch 3, para 7(5).

12.91   In addition, the Rules provide for a prohibition on disclosure which is likely to cause a person serious harm. The Tribunal may make an order prohibiting disclosure or publication of specified documents or information relating to the proceedings or any matter which would allow identification of any person whom the Tribunal does not think should be identified[1]. Such a direction may be made where the Tribunal considers that the person receiving disclosure or another person would be likely to be caused serious harm by the disclosure and the Tribunal believes that it is proportionate to prohibit disclosure.[2] The party requesting the prohibition must exclude the relevant document from those provided to the other party. Instead, it should produce the document to the Tribunal (with the reasons for its exclusion) for it to decide whether to make the order requested[3].

1 Tribunal Rules, r 14(1).
2 Tribunal Rules, r 14(2).
3 Tribunal Rules, r 14(3).

12.92   In contrast with the statutory provision allowing access to the FCA's documents in the course of the FCA's decision-making process[1], the Tribunal Rules on disclosure are only the starting point. The Tribunal's powers to give directions expressly include a direction requiring (or permitting) any party or other person to provide documents to the Tribunal or a party[2]. The main exceptions are that the Tribunal may not give a direction if satisfied that:

- a document is protected under the FSMA 2000 because it is, broadly, legally privileged[3]; or

- the document should not be disclosed, on one of the grounds upon which the Tribunal could authorise it not to be disclosed[4].

1 See para **4.90** ff above.
2 Tribunal Rules, r 5(3)(d).
3 See para **12.85** above.
4 These are outlined at para **12.88** above.

12.93   The Tribunal can, therefore, override the FCA's objections to producing a document on the ground that it relates to some other person and was used for the purposes of comparison[1]. It also allows the applicant to apply for a direction requiring the FCA to produce documents that the FCA may believe do not fall within its initial or secondary disclosure obligations: for example, documents relating to the FCA's suspension of the firm or its internal decision-making process in reaching the decision to issue the warning or decision notice or the supervisory notice in the case[2]. Equally, the Tribunal could require the applicant to disclose additional material (although this is not expressly provided for in the current version of the Tribunal Rules).

1 This category would typically encompass documents relevant to the proposed sanction.
2 This is discussed at para **12.79** above.

12.94 Whether or not to direct the disclosure of a particular document is within the discretion of the Tribunal in the particular case. Presumably (and this was specifically provided for in the previous Tribunal Rules) the document must be within a party's custody or control. Otherwise, the key question is how the Tribunal will exercise its discretion in the particular case. The Tribunal will apply the test of ensuring that the reference is determined in accordance with the overriding principle[1]. The breadth of the discretion means that a party may be able to persuade the Tribunal to order the disclosure of material notwithstanding that its relevance cannot at that time be specified, or even notwithstanding that the documents to be disclosed cannot be identified with precision by the person making the application. But the wider and less specific the request, the less likely that the Tribunal will grant it[2].

1 This is the test applicable to the giving of directions generally: see para **12.98** ff below.
2 Particularly, an application that is no more than a 'fishing expedition' is likely to have a low prospect of success: see *Andrew Jeffery v FSA (FS/2010/0039)*.

12.95 When, in practice, should the applicant consider making an application for specific disclosure? How should it act if it wishes to do so? The starting point for the applicant will often be the FCA's lists of documents, which will list the material that the FCA is declining to disclose on the basis of the statutory protection for legal privilege. If the applicant believes that any of this material is not truly a 'protected item' within FSMA 2000, s 413, then it can apply to the Tribunal for a direction that the FCA disclose it. Beyond this, the applicant may suspect that the FCA holds additional relevant material that may be of assistance to it, or that material from comparable cases should be disclosed (for example, because the FCA staff referred to other cases in the settlement discussions that took place earlier) or the applicant may wish to see documents relating to the FCA's supervision of the firm, its investigation and the internal decision-making process followed by the FCA in the case. Initially, disclosure of the material should be sought through correspondence with the FCA. Among other things, this may help to establish whether the material exists and the FCA's views on its relevance and may therefore assist the applicant in formulating an application to the Tribunal for a direction that the material be disclosed. As has already been discussed, the more speculative the application, the less likely the Tribunal will be prepared to make the direction.

12.96 An applicant may also wish to consider obtaining disclosure under the Freedom of Information Act 2000 and under the Data Protection Act 1998. The procedures for doing so are outside the scope of this Book.

What use can the applicant make of documents disclosed to it?

12.97 Applicants must take care not to disclose, or use for purposes other than the Tribunal proceedings, documents disclosed to them by the FCA in Tribunal proceedings. Such documents may contain confidential information which the FSMA 2000 protects from disclosure[1] and, as a person receiving such information directly or indirectly from the FCA, the firm or individual could commit a criminal offence if it disclosed that information to third parties for other purposes[2]. This may not prevent the applicant from disclosing or using information relating solely to itself which was obtained by the FCA from it alone. But caution needs to be exercised. The FCA's investigations may have involved it obtaining information from third parties or the information may relate to some other person. In either case there would be a risk of committing the criminal offence. In addition, there may be a possibility of the applicant, having received the relevant documents in the course of the Tribunal proceedings, being restricted as a matter of law to using those documents only for the purposes of those proceedings[3].

1 Note that the protection would fall away if the document were disclosed in public, for example at the Tribunal hearing (unless the Tribunal orders the hearing (or part of it) to be held in private): see para **4.230**, n 3 above.
2 FSMA 2000, s 348. For an explanation, see para **4.226** ff above. Note that certain types of disclosure are permitted under the so-called Gateway Regulations: see para **4.234** ff above. Among other things, the Gateway Regulations (reg 5) allow the FCA (and the firm or individual) to disclose information to any person for the purposes of proceedings before the Tribunal which have been initiated or for the purpose of bringing an end to such proceedings or of facilitating a determination of whether they should be brought to an end. But the disclosure must be made for the purpose of facilitating the carrying out of a public function: FSMA 2000, s 349(1).
3 It is possible that the law would imply a confidentiality restriction equivalent to the implied undertakings given on disclosure in court proceedings (see Civil Procedure Rules, r 31.22). For a discussion of the implied undertaking, see Matthews & Malek, Disclosure (4th edn, 2012), CHAPTER 13.

Applications for directions

12.98 After the parties have provided disclosure, the Tribunal Rules do not prescribe any particular procedure to prepare the case for the hearing. It is for the Tribunal to decide what steps are appropriate in the particular case[1], which it does by giving directions to the parties to take particular procedural steps. In addition, in the course of any case, issues inevitably arise between the parties on procedural matters which need to be determined by the Tribunal. The Tribunal has a general power to regulate its own procedure, subject to the provisions of the TCEA 2007 and any other enactment[2].

1 Tribunal Rules, r 5(2)–(5).
2 Tribunal Rules, r 5(1).

12.99   Such directions may be given either on the application of one or more parties, or by the Tribunal on its own initiative. Alternatively, they may be given at a pre-hearing review. The following paragraphs consider, first, the rules on applying for or giving directions generally, second, the pre-hearing review, third, the question of what directions can be made and, fourth, practical guidance for applicants on applying for directions.

Rules relating to directions generally

12.100   Directions may be made by the Tribunal either on its own initiative or on an application by one or more of the parties[1]. Even if there is a pre-hearing review[2], a number of directions hearings are likely to take place prior to a main hearing of a reference.

1   Tribunal Rules, r 6(1).
2   See para **12.103** ff below.

12.101   Where a party makes an application for a direction, the application must include the reasons for making it[1], and it must be filed with the Tribunal[2]. If any party or other person who receives notice of the direction[3] objects to the directions applied for, that party or other person may challenge it by applying for another direction amending, suspending or setting aside the first direction.[4]. The Tribunal Rules allow for applications to be considered on paper, without an oral hearing[5]. In practice, however, controversial issues are likely to require an oral hearing.

1   Tribunal Rules, r 6(3).
2   Unless the application is made at the hearing of the reference or at the pre-hearing review: Tribunal Rules, r 6(2).
3   Tribunal Rules, r 6(4).
4   Tribunal Rules, r 6(5).
5   Tribunal Rules, r 34(1). If the Tribunal decides to hold an oral hearing, that will normally be in public: Tribunal Rules, r 37(1) and see para **12.139** below. Where the applicant applies for a direction that the Tribunal's register contains no particulars of the reference, or that hearings should be held in private, it should also apply for any related directions hearing to be held in private.

12.102   The Tribunal Rules do not provide much detail as to how the Tribunal makes a direction or refuses an application for a direction, but the following principles will generally apply:

- directions may be given orally or in writing;

- they may give reasons or they may not[1];

- notice of any written direction is given to the parties and any other person affected unless the Tribunal decides there is good reason not to do so in any particular case[2];

- directions containing a requirement may specify a time limit for complying and must include a statement of the possible consequences of failing to comply with the requirement; and

- the Tribunal will also consider whether the decision should be pronounced publicly; they are often made available on the Tribunal's website[3].

1 In *HPA Services v FSA (2003) FSMT 005*, the Tribunal refused an application for a direction in writing but gave no reasons. The applicant applied for and was given written reasons. However, the Tribunal need not accept such a request. Reasons were given for giving and refusing directions respectively in *Stephen Robert Allen v FCA (FS/2012/0019)* and *Angela Burns v FSA (FS/2012/24)*.
2 Tribunal Rules, r 6(4). An example might be where the Tribunal makes a direction authorising a party not to disclose certain documents in its list.
3 For examples of directions or refusals of directions that have been published, see *Stephen Robert Allen v FCA (FS/2012/0019)* and *Angela Burns v FSA (FS/2012/24)*.

The pre-hearing review

12.103 In most cases which are likely to proceed to a main hearing, the Tribunal will hold a pre-hearing review[1]. In cases where there are no applications for urgent directions (for example, an application for a direction that no particulars of the reference are entered on the Tribunal's register), and where no other significant procedural disputes have arisen, this could be the first hearing at which any applications for directions are considered. The pre-hearing review is an oral hearing where the Tribunal considers what further procedural steps are required to take the case to the final hearing. It is a judge of the Tribunal who decides whether a pre-hearing review should be held[2].

1 Note that there is no express provision for this in the current version of the Tribunal Rules. However, the HMCTS Explanatory Leaflet T400, 'Making a reference to the Upper Tribunal (Tax and Chancery Chamber)' states that a judge will decide whether there should be a preliminary hearing 'to decide on the further steps to be taken before the reference is heard'. Preliminary hearings are dealt with separately as a specific type of hearing in the Tribunal Rules, but this description fits in with what would be expected at a pre-trial review. Broadly, the pre-hearing review is equivalent to the case management conference in the civil courts: see Civil Procedure Rules, Pt 29, 29PD-005. In practice, it is difficult to tell from the Register how often such hearings (as distinct from directions or preliminary hearings) take place. For an example of a pre-hearing review, see *Abdul Razzaq v FSA (FS/2011/0003)*.
2 HMCTS Explanatory Leaflet T400, 'Making a reference to the Upper Tribunal (Tax and Chancery Chamber)'.

What directions can the Tribunal make?

12.104 The Tribunal has a general power to regulate its own procedure, subject to the TCEA 2007 and any other enactment[1], and it may therefore, generally speaking, make any directions it thinks appropriate to enable the parties to prepare for the hearing, to assist the Tribunal to determine the issues and generally to ensure that the dispute is determined in accordance with the overriding principle. The difficulty in balancing the three relevant factors of justice, expedition and economy has already been outlined[2] and the weight of each of these factors is likely to differ from case to case. The Tribunal exercises its discretion to ensure that the procedure adopted is that appropriate to the particular case.

1 Tribunal Rules, r 5(1).
2 See the discussion at para **12.23** ff above.

12.105 Additionally, the Tribunal's discretion must be exercised in a way that allows the procedure to be ECHR compatible and, in particular, it must comply with the fair trial guarantees of Article 6(1)[1]. This may restrict its freedom of action in certain respects, for example by requiring it to hold an oral hearing, to hold the hearing in public and to allow each party the same opportunity to test the other party's evidence and put forward its own case[2]. Provided that the minimum ECHR standards are fulfilled, this does not prevent the Tribunal from requiring a more complex procedure to be undertaken in more serious cases.

1 These are briefly outlined at para **12.27** above.
2 These are given only as examples. They would not necessarily apply in every case.

12.106 Subject to these points, precisely what is required will vary from case to case. However, the Tribunal Rules do give some examples of particular directions which the Tribunal may make, including[1]:

• extending or shortening any time limit;

• permitting or requiring a party to provide further information or documents[2], or to amend a document;

• requiring a party to produce a bundle for a hearing;

• specifying how many witnesses may give evidence, in what form and when[3];

• making provision as to any expert witnesses to be called[4];

• requiring that the Tribunal's register includes no particulars about the reference[5], or that hearings are held in private[6];

• consolidating references[7]; and

• taking steps for non-compliance with directions or the Tribunal Rules[8].

1 Tribunal Rules, r 5(3).
2 The use of supplementary statements is discussed at para **12.68** above.
3 The use of witness evidence is discussed at para **12.111** below.
4 The involvement of expert witnesses is discussed at para **12.115** ff below.
5 This may be done in order to keep the matter confidential: see para **12.45** above. The Tribunal's register is explained briefly at para **12.49** above.
6 See para **12.139** ff below.
7 This is discussed further at para **12.127** ff below.
8 For example, the Tribunal may strike out a statement of case, or part of it, or restrict a party's participation in the proceedings. Tribunal Rules, r 7(2).

Practical guidance for applicants

12.107 The applicant's approach to the question of directions depends very much upon its strategy more generally. For example, does it wish to have the matter resolved swiftly, or is it preferable to spin out the process? Is it looking primarily to achieve a cost-effective Tribunal process, or does it want a particularly thorough investigation of the matter? Is its case focused on disputing certain key conclusions or facts, or is it more wide-ranging? Does it need the FCA's co-operation on other procedural matters that would militate against behaving aggressively? These and other factors will dictate the applicant's approach to the procedure and will determine whether it actively seeks directions, or waits to react to events. In any event, there may well be more than one directions hearing prior to the main hearing.

12.108 Against this background, the issues that the applicant might consider include:

- whether the applicant should take the lead in suggesting appropriate directions and the timetable more generally;

- whether the applicant should seek to agree directions with the FCA first, or simply make an application to the Tribunal;

- whether the applicant should be making any substantial interlocutory applications, for example for a preliminary issues hearing, or an application to strike out part or all of the FCA's case;

- whether there are any areas of the FCA's case that are unclear to the applicant and, if so, what directions are required to enable those areas to be clarified;

- whether there is any additional documentary material that the applicant wishes to see;

- what evidence the applicant will be seeking to rely upon at trial (including expert evidence) and what directions are required to ensure that it can do so;

- whether the evidence should be limited in any way;

- whether the applicant has any particular views on how the trial should be conducted.

12.109 Precisely what directions the applicant should seek, and what strategic approach it should take, will depend very much upon the situation.

Witnesses

12.110 The Tribunal Rules[1] allow the parties to call witnesses at the hearing including, with the consent of the Tribunal, expert witnesses[2]. The following paragraphs consider the procedural aspects of preparing witnesses for the hearing, and, in particular, whether:

- the parties are required to produce witness statements;

- the Tribunal can compel witnesses to attend; and

- expert evidence can be used.

1 Tribunal Rules, r 5(1)(d).
2 Tribunal Rules, r 15(1)(c).

Are the parties required to produce witness statements?

12.111 There is no provision in the Tribunal Rules automatically requiring witness statements to be produced or for them to be filed by any particular date, although the Tribunal clearly has the power to make appropriate directions in each case[1]. Whether it is appropriate to require the production of witness statements will therefore fall for determination in each case, based upon what is required to, among other things, ensure that the reference is determined in accordance with the overriding principle in that case[2]. Nonetheless, exchange of witness statements will normally occur. Since the parties have the right to call and question witnesses at the hearing, this will normally be more efficient, as well as assisting the parties and the Tribunal to prepare for the hearing. It is, however, possible that the Tribunal will try to limit the extent of the witness statements, to prevent their production becoming over-elaborate and costly and to keep the ambit of the case within appropriate bounds[3].

1 Tribunal Rules, r 15(1)(e).
2 Tribunal Rules, r 2(3) and see para **12.104** above.
3 The civil courts have similar powers under Civil Procedure Rules, Pt 32.

Can the Tribunal compel witnesses to attend?

12.112 The Tribunal can compel the attendance of witnesses by issuing a witness summons[1], requiring a person to attend before it to give evidence as a witness and/or to produce a document in his possession or control which relates to any issue in the proceedings[2]. The Tribunal can only compel the giving of evidence or production of documents if a person could be compelled to do the same on a trial of an action in a court of law in the part of the United Kingdom where the proceedings are due to be determined[3]. This will cover documents protected under the FSMA 2000 because they are, broadly, legally privileged or which should not be disclosed on one of the grounds listed at para **12.84** above. The Tribunal also has the power to set aside or vary a witness summons upon the application of the person to whom it is addressed[4]; the summons must state that the recipient has the right to apply to the Tribunal asking it to do so[5].

1 Tribunal Rules, r 16(1)(a). See the decision of the Tribunal in *David John Hobbs v FSA (FS/2010/0024 dated 2 September 2011)* for an example of applications for witness summons, which were dismissed.
2 Tribunal Rules, r 16(1)(b). The scope of the similar power which can be exercised by an employment tribunal has been considered in *Dada v Metal Box Co Ltd [1974] IRLR 251* (Sir John Donaldson) and *Noorani v Merseyside Tec Ltd [1999] IRLR 184, CA*. Broadly, to make the order, the Tribunal must be satisfied, first, that the witness can give evidence relevant to the issues in dispute and, second, that it is necessary to issue a witness summons. This assessment is a matter for the discretion of the Tribunal.
3 Tribunal Rules, r 16(3).
4 Tribunal Rules, r 16(4).
5 Tribunal Rules, r 16(6)(a).

12.113 Non-compliance with a witness summons issued by the Tribunal potentially carries serious consequences[1]. It is a criminal offence[2] for a person to:

- refuse or fail, without reasonable excuse[3], to attend following the issue of a summons by the Tribunal or to give evidence[4]; or

- alter, suppress, conceal or destroy, or refuse to produce, a document which he may be required to produce for the purposes of proceedings before the Tribunal[5].

1 Note, however, that a witness summons was used and initially disobeyed in *Hoodless and Blackwell v FSA (2003) FSMT 007* with no implications for the witness.
2 FSMA 2000, s 133B(2).
3 'Reasonable excuse' is interpreted fairly narrowly in the context of witness summonses issued by the High Court: see the discussion in Arlidge, Eady & Smith, Contempt (4th edn, 2011) at 11–119.
4 This broadly reflects the common law of contempt for failing to attend court following the issue of a subpoena or witness summons: see Arlidge, Eady & Smith, Contempt (4th edn, 2011) at 11–95 to 11–120.
5 Conduct of this nature in relation to criminal proceedings would be likely to amount to the common law offence of perverting the course of justice: see Archbold 2013 at 28–1 and see Arlidge, Eady & Smith, Contempt (4th edn, 2011) at 11–89.

12.114 A witness summons must give the person required to attend 14 days' notice of the hearing, unless the Tribunal directs a shorter period[1]. The summons must also make provision for the person's necessary expenses of attendance to be paid (where the person is not a party), and state who is to pay them[2]. The summons must contain a statement warning of the consequences of failure to comply with the summons[3].

1 Tribunal Rules, r 16(2)(a).
2 Tribunal Rules, r 16(2)(b).
3 Tribunal Rules, r 16(6)(b).

Expert evidence

12.115 Expert evidence will often form a key part of the FCA's case or the applicant's defence. For example, where the regulatory breach alleged involves establishing that the person's conduct fell below a particular standard, evidence may well be required as to what the applicable standard was and as to whether the person's conduct fell below that standard[1]. In cases where such issues arise, they often represent the critical point of disagreement between the FCA and the person concerned. In that situation, it is important for the person to have a credible, independent expert whose view is that the relevant conduct did not fall below the requisite standard. Notwithstanding the potential importance of experts, the Tribunal Rules say little about their use. The following paragraphs consider whether the Tribunal can hear expert evidence and in what circumstances it will do so.

1 There is a question of whether this should be a question of fact for the Tribunal to decide, or whether expert evidence is required. In some cases, a skilled person may have been appointed to report on the same matters at an earlier stage in the investigation (see para **6.16** ff above). The applicant will need to consider the position of this skilled person, whether the applicant wishes to call him or whether the FCA will do so, and in addition, whether the skilled person would then be acting as an expert or as a factual witness.

12.116 The Tribunal Rules indicate that the Tribunal may grant directions making provision as to any expert witnesses to be called, including whether the parties must appoint a single joint expert[1]. Before applying for such a direction, there are a number of practical issues to consider, including precisely which issues need to be addressed by an expert and the type of expertise required. In addition, ancillary directions are likely to be appropriate, such as one requiring experts to meet, after filing their reports, with a view to identifying those issues that are in dispute between them.

1 Tribunal Rules, r 15(1)(c).

12.117 The Tribunal Rules give no indication as to when in practice expert evidence will be permitted. The question for the Tribunal in deciding whether or not to make a direction permitting the use of experts is the same as in relation to any other application for a direction, namely whether it is appropriate to enable the parties to prepare for the hearing, to assist the Tribunal to determine the issues and generally to ensure that the dispute is determined in accordance with the overriding principle[1]. The answer will depend upon the circumstances of the case. In appropriate cases, strong arguments in favour of experts could be made. Cases before the Tribunal may involve complex issues about the standards to be expected of those involved in the market[2] and, because they will be reported, may have an impact on the behaviour of others in the market. It is important that the Tribunal is properly informed when reaching its decisions in such cases and that the interests of expedition and economy do not outweigh the interests of justice. For example, in *Legal & General Assurance Society Ltd v FSA*[3], a total of eight experts were called by the parties, covering a variety of disciplines. On the other hand, it should be recognised that the use of multiple experts is often perceived as tending to increase the cost and time of litigation and this can be reflected in the approach of the Tribunal to the question of experts in particular cases.

1 See para **12.104** above. See also the Civil Procedure Rules, r 35.1.
2 This will be particularly important in market abuse cases, in relation to the 'regular user' test: see para **17.62** ff below
3 *[2005] UKFSM FSM011.*

12.118 An additional factor that may in practice be relevant is the presence of lay persons with relevant experience on the Tribunal[1]. There may be a temptation for the Tribunal to take the lay person's views on issues which should be the subject of expert evidence. The lay member can certainly assist the Tribunal in reaching a decision where conflicting evidence has been put before it[2], but it is difficult to see how the Tribunal can properly reach a decision on questions of expert opinion without giving the parties the opportunity to adduce evidence on those issues.

1 See para **12.5** ff above and *Michael Lee Thommes v FSA, FS/2011/0022*, where the Tribunal held that there should be no general rule that expert evidence will assist the Tribunal in understanding particular market practices; the Tribunal is usually able to determine questions of competence and capability without the assistance of expert evidence. See also the Tribunal's comments in *Legal & General Assurance Society Ltd v FSA [2005] UKFSM FSM011, where the Tribunal felt able, to an extent, to form its own views as consumers and given the background in financial services of two of its members.*
2 In the employment tribunal context, it is established that the lay member should, if he intends to use his specialist knowledge to disagree with evidence that has been given, disclose his specialist knowledge and bring to the relevant party's attention the facts that cause him to disagree with the evidence, and give the party an opportunity to address the point: see Harvey on Industrial Relations and Employment Law at para PI[889]. See also the discussion in 'Transforming Public Services: Complaints, Redress and Tribunals', HMSO, July 2004.

Suspending the FCA's action

12.119 In most cases, particularly those which involve the warning/decision notice procedure, the action which the FCA wishes to take will not take effect until the Tribunal process has been completed[1]. But in some cases, most notably where the FCA takes urgent action to vary a firm's permission[2], the action can take effect immediately, or on a particular date, with the Tribunal then considering afterwards whether to revoke, or vary, the action which the FCA has already taken. In those cases, the applicant may apply to the Tribunal for a direction suspending the effect of the FCA's action pending the determination of the reference[3]. But the Tribunal may only give such a direction if it is satisfied that to do so would not prejudice:

- the interests of any persons, whether consumers[4], investors or otherwise, intended to be protected by the supervisory notice that was issued; or

- the smooth operation or integrity of any market intended to be protected by that notice.

1 FSMA 2000, s 133(3) and Tribunal Rules, r 5(5) and see para **10.173** above.
2 See para **16.215** below. This applies in relation to all those powers which involve the supervisory notice procedure: see para **16.215** below. In addition to varying a firm's permission, examples include suspending a listing of the shares of a listed company (see para **20.87** ff below) and taking various action in relation to collective investment schemes.
3 Tribunal Rules, r 5(5).
4 Whether the suspension of the immediate effect of a supervisory notice would prejudice the interests of consumers was considered by the Tribunal in *Eurosure Investment Services Ltd v FSA (2003) FSMT 006* and *Asgar Ali Rayjani (T/A Astrad Finance) v FSA (Case 063, September 2008).*

12.120 Urgent action taken with immediate effect by the FCA, or with effect on a particular date, and only tested later in the Tribunal, can have a serious effect on a firm's reputation, and its business. Whilst the FSMA 2000 normally[1] enables the FCA to take such action only where it reasonably considers this necessary, it does not provide firms with any means to ensure this is not abused[2]. Such action can, in some circumstances, be taken by the FCA's staff without reference to the RDC[3]. This provision in the Tribunal's Rules allows the firm to require the FCA to justify the need for urgent action in the Tribunal at an early stage and allows the Tribunal to provide immediate redress where the urgent action was clearly improper.

1 For an exception, see para **20.98** ff below.
2 See the discussion at para **16.227** ff below.
3 See para **16.216** ff below.

12.121 But it will be only in rare cases that this provides an effective remedy. First, however quickly the Tribunal can be set up and hear the application and the FCA's response to it, time will have elapsed since the action took effect and immediate damage will have been done[1]. Second, there is a heavy burden on the applicant in practice to show that the FCA's urgent action should be suspended. The Tribunal Rules make clear that the need to protect investors, particularly consumers, and markets remains the primary concern. The application will be determined based on the limited evidence available to the Tribunal at the relevant time[2], not based on a detailed consideration of the entire case, which will only take place at the final hearing[3]. All of this is likely to militate in favour of the Tribunal intervening only where it is clear that the action was inappropriate.

1 One instance in which there was a successful application to suspend the FCA's action was in the case of William's Life Pension Mortgage and Insurance Services. The FCA took action with immediate effect in November 2002 to prevent the firm from carrying on regulated activities. The firm then referred the matter to the Tribunal and applied for a direction that the action be suspended pending the result of its reference. The direction was granted in December 2002. See FSA Press Release FSA/PN/055/2003 for details.

2 No indication is given in the Tribunal Rules as to how the evidence in support of such an application should be presented. In *Eurosure Investment Services Ltd v FSA (2003) FSMT 006*, bundles of relevant documents were produced by the applicant and the FCA. The applicant's bundle included a witness statement by the Managing Director of the applicant.

3 In *Eurosure Investment Services Ltd v FSA (2003) FSMT 006*, the applicant made an application for a direction that the immediate effect of a supervisory notice be suspended. On hearing the application, the Tribunal made it clear that any findings of fact would be relevant for only the purposes of the application. Both parties agreed that the evidence available to the Tribunal at the directions hearing would not enable the Tribunal to form a view as to whether the full hearing of the reference would be successful. No full hearing took place since the reference was withdrawn. Contrast *HPA Services v FSA (2003) FSMT 005*, in which, together with its reasons for dismissing the applicant's application for a direction suspending the immediate effect of a supervisory notice, the Tribunal stated that it did not consider that the applicant would be successful in a full hearing of the reference.

Preliminary hearings

12.122 The Tribunal may direct that an issue in the proceedings may be determined at a preliminary hearing[1]. Whether or not to hold a preliminary hearing is entirely within the Tribunal's discretion. The Tribunal Rules do not prescribe any particular criteria that are relevant, nor is a preliminary hearing confined to issues which would potentially be decisive of the case[2]. It is therefore difficult to give any guidance as to when in practice one is likely to be held[3]. Few preliminary hearings have been held to date[4].

1 Tribunal Rules, r 5(3)(e).

2 Although this was the case in *Winterflood Securities Ltd, Stephen Sotiriou and Jason Robins v FSA [2009] UKFSM FSM006*. The court held that two issues be tried as preliminary issues which would determine the case. Full reasons for making the order are not given in the substantive decision. The question whether the preliminary issue could potentially be decisive of the case, either legally or because it is likely to encourage settlement, is the test normally applied in the Chancery division of the High Court: see the Chancery Guide at 3.14 (January 2013 edition).

3 In the context of employment tribunals, tribunals have been urged to hold preliminary hearings only sparingly, because of the scope for appeals against decisions and thus for further hearings: see the discussion in Harvey on Industrial Relations and Employment Law at para T[733]. Employment tribunals have therefore been encouraged to apply the (former) practice of the High Court that: (i) preliminary issues on points of law should be decided only exceptionally in clear and simple cases; (ii) the question of law should be carefully defined so there can be no confusion over what is being decided; and (iii) they should not normally be tried without first determining the facts: see *Allen v Gulf Oil Refining Ltd [1981] AC 1001* and see the discussion in Harvey on Industrial Relations and Employment Law at para T[736].

4 Preliminary hearings have been held in, amongst others, *Tudor House Financial Services v FSA (2002/3)* (however, details of the preliminary hearing were not published although it should be noted that the hearing followed the withdrawal of the reference), *Sir Philip Watts v FSA (2005) FSMT 0022*.

12.123 Where a preliminary hearing is held, it will be an oral hearing unless the parties agree otherwise in writing[1]. It is held in public, subject to the Tribunal's discretion for it to be held in private[2]. Written reasons for the Tribunal's decision are not necessarily given[3]. If, in the Tribunal's opinion, the determination of the issue substantially disposes of the reference, it may treat the preliminary hearing as the main hearing of the reference and make an appropriate order disposing of the reference[4].

1 This is required by the ECHR fair trial guarantees: see para **12.27** above.
2 Tribunal Rules, r 37 and see paras **12.138** and **12.149** below.
3 For example, no details are available for the preliminary hearing in *Tudor House Financial Services v FSA (2002/3)*. See para **12.102** above for the similar position as regards directions hearings.
4 Note that there is no express provision to this effect in the current version of the Tribunal Rules. As to the orders that the Tribunal can make, see para **12.151** ff below.

Withdrawal or consolidation of cases

12.124 The Tribunal Rules contain a number of provisions regarding the withdrawal or consolidation of cases. These are outlined below.

Withdrawal by applicants

12.125 A party may withdraw its case:

- at any time before a hearing to consider disposal of the proceedings (or before the disposal of the reference where there is no hearing), by sending or delivering to the Tribunal written notice of that withdrawal; or

- orally at a hearing[1].

In either case, the withdrawal does not take effect unless the Tribunal consents[2].

1 Tribunal Rules, r 17(1).
2 Tribunal Rules, r 17(2).

12.126 It is not clear from this what determination the Tribunal will make. Where the applicant withdraws its reference the Tribunal ought, in the normal course, simply to determine that the action which the FCA sought to take in the decision notice or supervisory notice is appropriate. Where the FCA withdraws its case, the Tribunal ought to determine that it is inappropriate for the FCA to take any action. However, the Tribunal Rules do not limit the Tribunal in this way, leaving open the possibility that the Tribunal might make some other determination. This flexibility may be to allow the Tribunal to give effect to a settlement between the FCA and the applicant by making a determination in accordance with the agreed terms. In theory, there is a risk of it making some other determination of its own accord, but in practice that ought not to happen and, if it did, then remedies may be available to the firm[1].

1 The decision should be susceptible to judicial review: see **CHAPTER 21**.

Consolidation of references

12.127 The Tribunal Rules[1] permit the Tribunal to make a direction to consolidate or hear together two or more sets of proceedings or parts of proceedings raising common issues, or to treat a case as a lead case.

1   Tribunal Rules, r 5(3)(b). The procedure for making applications for directions, and for directions by the Tribunal on its own initiative, is outlined at para **12.90** ff above.

12.128 The Tribunal Rules do not provide any criteria on which the Tribunal will decide whether or not cases should be consolidated. The Tribunal is therefore likely to apply the normal criteria of seeking to ensure that the dispute is determined in accordance with the overriding principle[1]. The decisions published in consolidated cases do not generally give reasons for the consolidation, although in *Stefan Chaligné, Patrick Sejean and Cheickh Tidiane Diallo v FSA, FS/2011/0001, 0002 and 0003* the Tribunal explained that it had directed that the references be heard together because they arose from the same facts.

1   See para **12.104** above.

12.129 Consolidation could be appropriate in a number of different scenarios. For example, the FCA may have issued several decision notices or supervisory notices against the same firm arising out of the same matter if it wanted to take a series of different actions against that firm (for example, to discipline it, vary its permission and order it to pay restitution). Another example is where two closely connected firms, or a firm and an individual working for it, are both disciplined in relation to the same matter. In each of those situations, the determination of the issues may involve many of the same questions of fact or law, and require the same witnesses and experts to attend, and it may therefore be appropriate for all the issues to be determined at one hearing. Nonetheless, there may be good reasons why issues relating to the firm and its employee should not be heard at the same time.

12.130 A more difficult scenario is where several unconnected firms are being disciplined in relation to different aspects of the same regulatory problem. For example, the product provider and several distributors of a product that was widely mis-sold, and various of their respective employees. In that case a single consolidated reference may be too unwieldy, and the interests of the various participants too diverse, for the matter usefully to be consolidated. There may come a point at which the involvement of multiple parties with different interests will tend to make the process less, not more, efficient, and increase the attraction of separate processes. Another relevant factor may be the risk of separate Tribunals with different members reaching inconsistent decisions. A number of different factors will therefore be relevant and the approach the firm will take in relation to the consolidation of cases will depend very much upon the particular circumstances.

12.131 Where references have been consolidated, the Tribunal may arrive at separate decisions in respect of each reference despite the fact that there is only one main hearing.

THE HEARING

12.132 Finally, the matter comes before the Tribunal for the main hearing. The following paragraphs consider the procedural questions of the timing and conduct of the hearing. Before looking at these, though, it is worth recalling that the Tribunal is a first instance tribunal before which the FCA must prove its case, and which can make a range of decisions based, primarily, on the question of what action it is appropriate for the FCA to take in relation to the matter referred to it[1].

1 As the Economic Secretary to HM Treasury put it in Standing Committee (4 November 1999): 'The Tribunal will be required to consider the facts of the case and arrive at its own view on the rights and wrongs. In doing so, it is not constrained by what the FSA did or did not do, or did or did not consider relevant'. See also the discussion at para **12.9** above.

Timing

12.133 The time, place and estimated length of the hearing will be fixed by the Tribunal under its general power to regulate proceedings[1].

1 Tribunal Rules, r 5(1). Some hearings only take one day (for example: *Wagner v FSA (FS/2011/0015)*. On the other hand, in *John Pottage v FSA (FS/2010/33)*, the hearing lasted for approximately 15 days over the space of five weeks. The estimated length of a hearing will be entered on the Tribunal's register (see para **12.49** above).

12.134 The Tribunal must give each party entitled to attend a hearing reasonable notice of the time and place of the hearing and any changes[1]. The notice period must be at least 14 days except in urgent cases or unless the parties consent[2]. It will be important to ensure, particularly in cases of any complexity, that all the witnesses, experts and counsel, among others, are available. In such cases, the applicant may wish to press the Tribunal to fix the hearing date as early as possible, and the procedure can then be determined by reference to that date[3].

1 Tribunal Rules, r 36(1).
2 Tribunal Rules, r 36(2).
3 This is the approach taken by the civil courts under the Civil Procedure Rules. There is nothing in the Tribunal Rules to prevent a similar approach from being taken. It will be a matter for the Tribunal in each case to fix the timetable for that case. Based on the Register, first directions hearings are listed for approximately three months after receipt of the reference. The substantive hearing is then often fixed for about a year after receipt.

12.135 The Tribunal can postpone or adjourn the hearing[1]. If an applicant needs to postpone a hearing, he should do so as soon as possible and should send the Tribunal written reasons, (although reasons may be given by telephone where time is short)[2].

1 Tribunal Rules, r 5(3)(h).
2 HMCTS Explanatory Leaflet T400, 'Making a reference to the Upper Tribunal (Tax and Chancery Chamber)'.

How is the hearing conducted?

General

12.136 The procedure adopted for the hearing itself is left largely within the discretion of the Tribunal according to what is appropriate in the particular case, subject to certain basic rules. The Tribunal is required to conduct the hearing in such manner as it considers most suitable with regards to the overriding principle.[1]. The Tribunal also needs to ensure that the procedure is ECHR compatible[2]. In practice, the Tribunal will normally conduct the hearing in a similar way to a trial, with the parties filing written skeleton arguments in advance, making their respective opening submissions, calling witnesses and experts, and then making closing submissions. The process tends to be less formal than in a court. The burden of proof is in general on the FCA to prove its case[3].

1   See para **12.23** ff above.
2   This is discussed at para **12.26** ff above.
3   The standard of proof is the ordinary civil standard of the balance of probabilities, as set out by Lord Nicholls in *Re H [1996] 1 All ER 1, HL* at 16-17 and confirmed by the Tribunal in *Hoodless and Blackwell v FSA (2003) FSMT 007*. In that case the Tribunal's decision quoted Lord Nicholls who in turn quoted Ungoed-Thomas J in *Re Dellow's Will Trusts, Lloyds Bank Ltd v Institute of Cancer Research [1964] 1 WLR 451* at 455: 'the more serious the allegation, the more cogent is the evidence required to overcome the unlikelihood of what is alleged and thus to prove it'.

12.137 The default position is that there will be an oral hearing, although the Tribunal may determine a reference without one subject to the parties' views on whether, and in what form, to conduct a hearing[1].

1   Tribunal Rules, r 34. The case may also be disposed of without an oral hearing if a party withdraws its case or where the Tribunal makes a consent order: see Tribunal Rules, rr 17(1) and 39.

12.138 Applicants may be concerned to avoid confidential information about their internal workings being aired in public in a situation where, the applicant believes, there is no call for any regulatory action. To what extent does the applicant have the right to opt for a private hearing? The general rule is that hearings of the Tribunal, including oral hearings on procedural matters, are held in public[1]. The Tribunal does have the power to direct that all or part of a hearing is in private[2].

1   Tribunal Rules, r 37(1).
2   Tribunal Rules, r 37(2). Note that the Tribunal 'may' direct that a hearing is held in private. It is not obliged to do so.

12.139 The treatment of the question of whether to hold a hearing in private is one of the biggest differences between the previous version of the Tribunal Rules and the new version. The current version of the Tribunal Rules leaves the question almost entirely up to the discretion of the Tribunal. The only limiting factor on that discretion is that the Tribunal must make its decision based on the overriding principle, as is the case whenever it exercises a power[1]. The presumption is very much that the process is public[2], so it will be difficult to convince a Tribunal that the hearing should be held in private.

469

1 See, for example, *Angela Burns v FSA (FS/2012/24)*. The case involved an application to prohibit publication of the decision notice and entries to the Register, with a possible future application for a hearing to be held in private. The Tribunal found that the damage to the applicant was not so severe as to outweigh the 'strong presumption' that publication should take place.
2 *7722656 Canada Inc (formerly carrying on business as Swift Trade Inc) and Peter Beck v FSA (FS0017 & 0018, August 2011)*, in relation to publication of a decision notice.

12.140 Where the hearing, or part of the hearing, is held in private, the Tribunal may determine who is entitled to attend the hearing, or part of it. As a general rule, the parties will be allowed to attend[1], but can be excluded as explained at para **12.143** below.

1 Tribunal Rules, r 35.

12.141 Even where a hearing is held in public, the Tribunal may exclude from all or part of it[1]:

- any person whose conduct the Tribunal considers is disrupting or is likely to disrupt the hearing;

- any person whose presence the Tribunal considers is likely to prevent another person from giving evidence or making submissions freely;

- any person who the Tribunal considers should be excluded to give effect to a direction concerning the withholding of information likely to cause harm[2]; or

- any person whose attendance would defeat the purpose of the hearing.

1 Tribunal Rules, r 37(4).
2 See Tribunal Rules, r 14(2).

12.142 Note that if the Tribunal process is to be secret, including holding the hearing in private, the applicant would also need to persuade the FCA not to publish the decision notice.

What submissions and evidence will the Tribunal hear?

12.143 As already discussed[1], the procedure for the hearing is left largely for the Tribunal to determine on the basis of what is suitable to the clarification of the issues before it and to the determination of the reference in accordance with the overriding principle. The Tribunal Rules do not therefore prescribe what submissions must be made and precisely how evidence will be taken. They do, however, make certain provisions with regard to the submissions and evidence that are put before it.

1 See para **12.136** above.

12.144 First, the Tribunal Rules make no provision about the order in which the Tribunal hears the parties. Since the burden of proof is on the FCA it will normally be the FCA that is heard first[1]. Following this, the applicant will respond and the FCA will have the opportunity to reply to that response.

1 This mirrors the procedure in civil litigation where the first party to proceed is the party on whom the burden of proof lies.

12.145 Second, the parties are entitled to give evidence (including, with the consent of the Tribunal, expert evidence), call witnesses, question any witnesses and address the Tribunal on the evidence and generally on the subject matter of the reference[1]. The process therefore normally involves the examination and cross-examination of witnesses and the making of submissions, broadly in a similar way to a court procedure. Quite how the evidence is given will depend often upon the circumstances, but witnesses offering evidence that is not contentious will not normally need to be called in person[2], whereas the Tribunal will normally want to hear personally from the key witnesses, and to see them responding to questions from the other side.

1 Tribunal Rules, rr 33 and 15(1). Where an applicant raises the issue of ability to pay a financial penalty, detailed evidence as to means should be provided and verified where appropriate: see *Piggott v FSA (2003) FSMT 004*.
2 See, for example, *Abdul Razzaq v FSA (FS/2011/0003)*.

12.146 Third, evidence may be admitted by the Tribunal whether or not admissible in a civil trial in the United Kingdom[1]. The strict rules of evidence do not therefore apply, but instead the question of admissibility is within the Tribunal's discretion. In practice, this means that the Tribunal may be willing to take account of evidence produced less formally, for example, letters from witnesses or FCA interview transcripts[2].

1 Tribunal Rules, r 15(2)(a)(i).
2 See, for example, *Hoodless & Blackwell v FSA (2003) FSMT 007*.

12.147 Finally, the Tribunal can admit evidence whether or not it was available to the FCA when taking the referred action[1]. This important provision reflects the position of the Tribunal as a de novo finder of fact, not an appellate body, in relation to financial services cases[2].

1 FSMA 2000, s 133(4).
2 This is discussed at para **12.9** above.

12.148 In practice, as already indicated, the Tribunal conducts itself in a similar way to a court. Typically, the parties make submissions in turn, factual and expert witnesses are called and examined, and closing submissions follow. There may also be a process of providing written opening and closing submissions to assist the Tribunal. This process will generally be largely agreed between the parties, subject to the agreement of the Tribunal.

Can the applicant be represented?

12.149 The Tribunal Rules[1] allow the applicant to appear and be represented by any person, whether or not legally qualified[2]. Where a party fails to attend or be represented at the hearing, certain default provisions apply[3].

1 Tribunal Rules, r 11.

2 Moreover, a party's representative may do anything permitted or required by the Tribunal Rules, a practice direction or a direction to be done by that party except for signing a witness statement: Tribunal Rules, r 11(3). An example of an instance where a representative other than a lawyer has been used is *Cox v FSA (2003) FSMT 003* where the applicant was referring a decision of the FCA refusing his firm's application for him to perform a controlled function. In the substantive hearing, a partner in the firm represented the applicant.

3 Tribunal Rules, r 38. Although note *Sabz Ali Khan v FSA [2008] UKFSM FSM057*: the applicant was refused permission not to attend the hearing on grounds of illness as he had not proved that his illness was such as to prevent him from attending. The Tribunal found that his conduct was not such as to warrant a summary dismissal or strike-out.

THE TRIBUNAL'S DECISION

12.150 The following paragraphs consider the question of what decisions the Tribunal can make and the procedure for doing so, in particular:

- what decisions the Tribunal can make;

- how the Tribunal makes its decision;

- whether the decision is made public; and

- what is the effect of the decision.

Each is considered in turn, below.

What decisions can the Tribunal make?

12.151 The basic question for the Tribunal is what (if any) is the appropriate action for the FCA to take in relation to the matter referred to it. Where that matter is a 'disciplinary' matter[1], the Tribunal must remit the matter to the FCA with such directions (if any) as the Tribunal considers appropriate for giving effect to its determination[2]. Note that for other matters, the Tribunal must determine the reference or appeal by either dismissing it or remitting the matter to the decision-maker with a direction to reconsider and reach a decision in accordance with the findings of the Tribunal[3]. This more circumscribed power reflects the breadth of discretion given to the Regulators in relation to powers involving supervisory notices, for example, which may restrict the extent to which the Tribunal can make a judgment on what the appropriate action is for the Regulator to take.

1 FSMA 2000, s 133(5)(a). This category of cases is defined broadly to include financial penalties, public censures, suspensions, restrictions and variations imposed on firms and approved persons by way of disciplinary action, actions for market abuse and ad hoc provisions for sanctions for breaches of other requirements of the FSMA 2000 by issuers, sponsors, and a range of others.

2 FSMA 2000, s 133(5)(b).

3 FSMA 2000, s 133(6).

12.152 There are limitations on the determinations that the Tribunal can make. In particular, in determining a matter resulting from a decision notice, it may not direct the FCA to take action which the FCA would not have had the power to take when giving the decision notice[1]. This refers to the requirement that a decision notice which was preceded by a warning notice must relate to action under the same Part of the FSMA 2000 as the action proposed in the warning notice[2]. For example, if the FCA proposed to fine a firm for its regulatory breaches, the Tribunal could direct that the FCA impose a different fine or a public censure, but not a restitution order or a variation of the firm's permission.

1 FSMA 2000, s 133A(1).
2 FSMA 2000, s 388(2). See also para **10.164** above.

12.153 Otherwise, the Tribunal has scope to direct any action that it thinks appropriate. It is particularly worth bearing in mind that it can increase as well as decrease the punishment or other action taken[1]. Where references have been consolidated[2], the Tribunal may arrive at separate decisions in respect of each reference[3].

1 See, for example, *Simon Kunn and MFP Group v FSA (2009) FSMT 071*, where the Tribunal found that it should be slow to increase a penalty in case doing so acts as a disincentive to making meritorious references, but did increase the fine on the facts (where the applicant had misled the FSA); *Nazia Bi and Qadeem Mohammed v FSA, FIN/2010/0002 and 0003*, where the Tribunal found that the penalty should only be increased in a 'clear case', such as where relevant circumstances were not available to the RDC; and *Stefan Chaligné, Patrick Sejean and Cheickh Tidiane Diallo v FSA, FS/2011/0001, 0002 and 0003*, where the Tribunal held that the gravity of conduct of one of the applicants justified increasing the penalty.
2 See para **12.129** ff above.
3 See *Hoodless and Blackwell v FSA (2003) FSMT 007* for an example of consolidated references that were decided differently. The Tribunal's decision in respect of both references was set out in one document.

12.154 A secondary question for the Tribunal may be whether to make recommendations as to the FCA's procedures or regulating provisions[1]. It is not entirely clear what is meant by 'regulating provisions', as this is not a term used generally in the FSMA 2000[2]. It seems, broadly, to be open to the Tribunal to recommend that the FCA changes its rules or procedures in particular respects. The Tribunal may be in a position to see how in practice the FCA is using the extensive powers granted to it. It is clearly not the Tribunal's role to be a watchdog; its role is primarily to determine specific issues between regulator and regulated. However, by giving this power to the Tribunal the FSMA 2000 does give it a more general role within the accountability regime.

1 FSMA 2000, s 133A(5). As of the date of writing, no formal recommendations have been made, though the Tribunal has made comments in its judgments which have been of general application in respect of the FCA's practices. See, for example, the judgments in *Legal & General Assurance Society Ltd v FSA [2005] UKFSM FSM011* and *Hoodless and Blackwell v FSA (2003) FSMT 007*. In the former case, the Tribunal was invited to make certain recommendations but declined to do so as the FSA had begun to review its own enforcement procedures. It suggested that the Tribunal President would be better placed to make recommendations, as he would have a better overview of all cases.
2 The term is defined to mean: (i) rules; (ii) general guidance; (iii) statements; or (iv) codes of the FCA; or (i) rules; (ii) statements; or (iii) codes of the PRA the Code of Market Conduct: FSMA 2000, s 140A(1).

12.155 The Tribunal Rules do not give any guidance as to the types of situations when the Tribunal might consider making recommendations, or as to what recommendations it might make. Recommendations could perhaps relate to legal issues, for example if the Tribunal disagrees with the way that the FCA is interpreting particular provisions or powers in its rules or procedures, but there is nothing to confine them to such issues. From the applicant's perspective, it may be worth considering asking the Tribunal to make a recommendation if for example, in the applicant's view, the FCA's approach to its statutory powers was unfair, its procedures were implemented in a way that was disproportionate or inappropriate, or the FCA's legal interpretation of its powers was open to question.

12.156 Perhaps the closest the Tribunal has come to making formal recommendations to the FCA relates to the publication of decision notices. In two cases[1], the Tribunal has refused to prohibit publication of decision notices but has directed the FCA to include a prominent notice in the accompanying press release that the respective applicants intended to challenge the decision in the Upper Tribunal. In both cases, the dismissal of the applications was made conditional on the FCA complying with these requests.

1   *Arch Financial Products LLP, Robin Farrell and Robert Stephan Addison v FSA (FS/2012/20)* and *Angela Burns v FSA (FS/2012/24)*.

How does the Tribunal make its decision?

12.157 The Tribunal takes its decision by a majority of the Tribunal members (the chair will have a casting vote if necessary)[1] and that decision may be pronounced orally in open court or in writing[2].

1   First-tier Tribunal and Upper Tribunal (Composition of Tribunal Order) 2008, SI 2008/2835, art 8.
2   Tribunal Rules, r 40(1).

12.158 The Tribunal will inform the parties of its decision and, as soon as reasonably practicable, send them a decision notice stating the decision and notification of any rights of review or appeal against the decision and the time and manner in which such rights must be exercised[1]. The Tribunal must also provide written reasons for its decisions unless the decision was made with the consent of the parties or the parties have consented to the Tribunal not giving reasons[2].

1   Tribunal Rules, r 40(2).
2   Tribunal Rules, r 40(3).

Is the decision made public?

12.159 The Tribunal will normally pronounce its decisions in public[1]. There are three main reasons for this. First, the aim is to have so far as is possible an open and transparent system. Second, for reasons already discussed[2], there is a general interest in making the Tribunal's jurisprudence available to the public. Finally, it is an ECHR requirement that judgment be pronounced publicly[3]. Moreover, it is the FCA's normal policy to make public its successful enforcement action, for a variety of reasons discussed in **CHAPTER 10** above. The outcome will therefore almost inevitably be public.

1   Note that there is no express provision to this effect in the current version of the Tribunal Rules. Decisions are published on the Tribunal's website and may also be handed down in open court: Tribunal Rules, r 40.
2   See para **12.37** above.
3   See para **12.29** above.

12.160 In the event that the applicant succeeds in its reference, it should make sure that any decision notice already published is clarified as having been overturned[1].

1   See, for example, the FSA's notice of 22 November 2012 in relation to David John Hobbs.

What is the effect of the Tribunal's decision?

12.161 The Tribunal's decision on the reference is binding on the FCA and, through the FCA, on the applicant. The mechanism is complex. When the Tribunal makes its determination, it remits the matter to the FCA with such directions as the Tribunal considers appropriate to give effect to the determination[1]. What follows depends upon whether the matter arose from a decision notice or a supervisory notice.

1   FSMA 2000, s 133(5).

12.162 Assuming it arose from a decision notice, once the reference has been determined, and there is no appeal or any appeal has been disposed of[1], the statutory prohibition against the FCA taking the action specified in the decision notice comes to an end[2]. The FCA is, however, obliged to act in accordance with the Tribunal's determination and its directions[3]. It must therefore take whatever action the Tribunal determined to be appropriate and, on taking the action, is required to issue a final notice[4]. The applicant must comply with the final notice and if it does not do so then the obligation can be enforced against it[5]. The FCA's final notice will normally summarise the Tribunal's findings and give these as its reasons for the action it is taking. In complex cases the notice may (albeit rarely) simply refer to the Tribunal decision[6].

1   For the provisions relating to appeals, see para **12.181** ff below.
2   FSMA 2000, s 133A(4)(b).
3   FSMA 2000, s 133(7).
4   FSMA 2000, s 390(2) and (2A). Note that the FCA is likely to issue a Press Release to accompany the final notice: see para **10.195** ff above.
5   FSMA 2000, s 390(9) and (10).
6   See for example, *Legal & General Assurance Society Limited final notice (8/6/05)* and *Sachin Surendra Karpe final notice (27/6/12)*.

12.163 Assuming the matter arose from a supervisory notice, the FCA is again obliged to act in accordance with the Tribunal's determination and its directions[1].

12.163 The Tribunal and appeals

In many cases the decision will already have taken effect[2], in which case either no action is required or the FCA must revoke or vary its action depending upon the nature of, and in accordance with, the Tribunal's determination. If the action has not already taken effect and no future date is specified when it does take effect, then it takes effect when the matter is no longer open to review[3], which means, broadly, once it has been determined in the Tribunal and has not been appealed or any appeal has been determined[4]. The decision then takes effect but, again, the FCA must act in accordance with the Tribunal's determination and directions. A supervisory notice is unlikely of itself to require any positive action from the firm. Consequently, no question of enforcing the Tribunal's determination against the firm arises, although the applicant may, plainly, have to take action in order to comply with the notice; for example, ensuring its business complies with its permission as amended.

1 FSMA 2000, s 133(7).
2 Because it took effect either immediately or on a specified date that has passed: see para **16.114** below.
3 See, for example, the FSMA 2000, s 55Y(2)(c).
4 For a more detailed explanation, see the FSMA 2000, s 391(8) and para **16.200** below.

12.164 If the Tribunal makes a recommendation regarding the FCA's rules or procedures[1], this is not binding and does not have any formal effect.

1 FSMA, s 133A(5) and see para **12.155** above.

12.165 If the Tribunal makes an order, for example a costs order[1], then that may be enforced as if it were an order of the county court[2].

1 See para **12.167** ff below.
2 Or, in Scotland, an order of the Court of Session: FSMA 2000, s 133(8).

Costs

12.166 Costs in Tribunal cases do not generally 'follow the event'. In other words, the Tribunal will not as a matter of course award costs against the losing party or indeed against any party. Indeed, the Tribunal does not have a general power to make costs awards. In financial services cases, such awards can only be made[1]:

- if the Tribunal considers that a party or its representative has acted unreasonably in bringing, defending or conducting the proceedings; or

- if the Upper Tribunal considers that the decision in respect of which the reference was made was unreasonable.

1 Tribunal Rules , r 10(3).

12.167 The Tribunal can order the relevant party to pay to another party to the proceedings the whole or part of the costs or expenses incurred by the other party in connection with the proceedings. It may do so by ordering (on its own initiative or on application by a party)[1] payment of an amount[2]: (i) fixed by the Tribunal, based on its own summary assessment if it so chooses; (ii) agreed between the parties; or (iii) based on assessment of the costs (for which an application can be made by the receiving party to the High Court or Court of Session, as appropriate[3]). Before making a costs order, the Tribunal must give the paying party an opportunity to make representations against the making of the costs order[4]. If the paying party is an individual, the Tribunal must also consider their financial means[5].

1   Tribunal Rules, r 10(4).
2   Tribunal Rules, r 10(8).
3   Tribunal Rules, r 10(9).
4   Tribunal Rules, r 10(7)(a).
5   Tribunal Rules, r 10(7)(b).

12.168 The Tribunal Rules do not provide any guidance on when in practice the Tribunal is likely to exercise its discretion to make costs awards although they are made only rarely[1]. Where the Tribunal does make a costs award it usually does so after the substantive hearing of the reference. However, in exceptional cases, such as where the applicant would otherwise be unable to fund the costs of continuing representation and where the costs award relates to a discrete period of time, an award may be made earlier[2].

1   A costs award was made against the applicant in *James Perman & Co v FSA (FS/2010/0018)*. The applicant rejected an offer from the FSA for it to discontinue proceedings against him, which was found to be unreasonable.
2   See, for example, *Davidson v FSA (2004) FSMT 008*. The applicant sought a costs award in respect of the costs incurred and thrown away as a result of disbanding the Tribunal hearing the reference. Given that the necessity to disband the Tribunal arose from the actions of one of the Tribunal panel members as well as from the actions of an employee of the FSA, the Tribunal ordered the FSA to pay only half the costs; the Tribunal suggested that the applicant apply to the Lord Chancellor for an ex gratia payment in respect of the costs attributable to the actions of the Tribunal panel member. However, the Tribunal declined to make a costs award in *Legal & General v FSA (17/5/05)*, despite acknowledging that L&G was justified in feeling aggrieved by the process by which the RDC's decision was arrived at. The Tribunal held that it was considering not whether a court acted correctly but whether an administrative process was unreasonable and that the FCA, when dealing with a large volume of regulatory matters informally and speedily, should not be expected or compelled to follow procedures, or to express its conclusions, as required of a court. Thus, the Tribunal was not satisfied that the FCA's decision was unreasonable (despite the shortcomings in the process by which it was reached) and the FCA was not ordered to pay costs (paras 27–28).

12.169 The amount of costs ordered to be paid is within the Tribunal's discretion. It can order the whole of the costs and expenses incurred in the proceedings or a particular portion of them, for example the cost of a particular application which one party has made or resisted frivolously or unreasonably.

12.170 In the rare cases where the Tribunal orders the cost of the whole proceedings to be paid, the question arises whether 'proceedings' refers only to the Tribunal proceedings or whether it includes the FCA enforcement proceedings which led to the Tribunal proceedings. It is most likely that this refers to the cost of the Tribunal proceedings, although this is not entirely free from doubt[1].

1   The FSMA 2000 refers (see para **4.158** above) to 'the proceedings' as meaning the FCA enforcement process from issue of the warning notice.

12.171 The ability for costs to be awarded against the regulator did not exist before the previous regime. It is plainly important to redress the unnecessary cost to which the applicant has been put in the particular case. But it has a significant potential role more generally to deter the FCA from abusing its powers.

12.172 Applicants must not, however, lose sight of their own potential exposure to costs orders. The use of costs orders also has a role to play in deterring applicants from taking hopeless cases to the Tribunal.

REVIEWS AND APPEALS

12.173 In most cases the outcome of the Tribunal will be the end of the matter. However, both the FCA and the applicant do have limited additional options available for a short period of time on specified grounds. The main option is to seek permission to appeal to the Court of Appeal but there may also be an option of asking the Tribunal to review or set aside its own decision. The latter option will be considered first.

Review by the Tribunal

12.174 The Tribunal Rules allow the Tribunal to set aside or vary its own decision in certain very limited circumstances. The FSMA 2000 does not require the Tribunal Rules to contain this procedure, the extent to which it is intended to be used is not clear and in any event, as will be seen, there is only a brief opportunity for the parties to seek to use it. As of the date of writing, no decision of the Tribunal has been reviewed.

The grounds for varying or setting aside a decision

12.175 The Tribunal[1] may review the relevant decision[2]:

- on receipt of an application for permission to appeal, if the Tribunal when making the decision overlooked a legislative provision or binding authority or if, since the decision was made, a court has made a binding decision which would have had a material effect on the Tribunal's decision[3]; or

- in relation to decisions under the Forfeiture Act 1982[4].

1 This may be the same or a different Tribunal.
2 Tribunal Rules, r 46(1).
3 Tribunal Rules, r 45(1). Compare the 'slip rule': see para **12.179** below.
4 Tribunal Rules, r 47(1).

12.176 The Tribunal must notify the parties in writing of the outcome of a review and of any rights or review or appeal they have in relation to that outcome[1].

1 Tribunal Rules, r 46(2).

12.177 Furthermore, the Tribunal may set aside and re-make all or part of a decision[1]. It may do so where it considers that it is in the interests of justice to do so[2] and one of the following applies[3]:

- a relevant document was not sent to or received by a party or its representative at an appropriate time;

- a relevant document was not sent to the Tribunal at an appropriate time;

- a party or its representative was not present at a relevant hearing; or

- there has been another procedural irregularity.

1 Tribunal Rules, r 43(1).
2 Tribunal Rules, r 43(1)(a).
3 Tribunal Rules, r 43(1)(b) and (2).

12.178 An application for the decision to be set aside must be in writing and received by the Tribunal within a month after the date on which the Tribunal sent notice of the decision to the party making the application[1].

1 Tribunal Rules, r 43(3).

12.179 These grounds are fairly narrowly drawn, albeit more widely than in the previous Tribunal Rules[1]. The extent to which the Tribunal is willing to use the review procedure in practice is not clear. It is plainly available in wider circumstances than the normal 'slip rule' which allows a tribunal to correct accidental slips or omissions in judgments or orders. Such a rule is found, separately, at r 42[2]. It would seem that, with the addition of the 'other procedural irregularity' ground, a serious procedural defect would now suffice to allow a decision to be set aside.

1 There is not, for example, a standalone general ground that the interests of justice require a review (such as is available to employment tribunals, for example). In the previous Tribunal Rules, there was no ground as wide as the 'other procedural irregularity' provision.
2 This provision broadly mirrors Civil Procedure Rules, r 40.12. For an example of its use, see *Philip Graham Lloyd v FSA [2009] UKFSM FSM069*.

12.180 These rules apply equally to the FCA as they do to the applicant. This means that the applicant could be successful before the Tribunal, only to be confronted with a review of the decision based on a piece of new evidence.

Appeals

12.181 The Tribunal Rules allow a person to appeal to the Court of Appeal[1] in certain circumstances set out below. The appeal can only be made with the permission of the Tribunal[2] or the Court of Appeal[3]. There is a possible right of further appeal to the Supreme Court, subject to obtaining the leave of the Court of Appeal or the Supreme Court.

1 Or, in Scotland, to the Court of Session. For simplicity, the discussion below refers only to the Court of Appeal.
2 TCEA 2007, s 13(4)(a) and Tribunal Rules, r 44(1).
3 TCEA 2007, s 13(4)(b). This can only be exercised once the Tribunal has refused to grant leave to appeal: TCEA 2007, s 13(5).

12.182 It is beyond the scope of this book to review the procedure of the Court of Appeal and the Supreme Court in considering applications for permission to appeal and the procedure for such appeals[1]. The following points are briefly considered below:

- the statutory basis upon which an appeal can be made; and

- the procedure for applying to the Tribunal for permission to appeal.

1 These can be found in, respectively, the Civil Procedure Rules, Pt 52 (and see 52PD) and the Supreme Court Rules 2009 and the Supreme Court Practice Direction.

On what basis can the firm appeal?

12.183 An appeal to the Court of Appeal is available only on a point of law arising from a decision of the Tribunal disposing of the reference[1].

1 HMCTS Explanatory Leaflet T400, 'Making a reference to the Upper Tribunal (Tax and Chancery Chamber)'. As to the meaning of a 'point of law', the Court of Appeal has held (in the context of appeals to the Employment Appeals Tribunal) that the appellate body 'can ... interfere if it is satisfied that the Tribunal has misdirected itself as to the applicable law, or if there is no evidence to support a particular finding of fact, since the absence of evidence to support a finding of fact has always been regarded as a pure question of law. It can also interfere if the decision is perverse, in the sense explained by May LJ in *Neale v Hereford and Worcester and County Council [1986] ICR 471* at 483': Donaldson MR in *British Telecommunications Ltd v Sheridan [1990] IRLR 27*. For a more detailed discussion, see Harvey on Industrial Relations and Employment Law at para PI[1630].

Applying to the Tribunal for permission to appeal

12.184 An application for permission to appeal must be received by the Tribunal within 14 days after the Tribunal sent to the applicant the reasons for the decision; notification of amended reasons for, or correction of, a decision following a review; or notification that an application to set aside the decision has been unsuccessful[1].

1 Tribunal Rules, r 44(1) and (3D). As to the contents of the application, see r 44(7).

12.185 On receipt of the application the Tribunal may review the decision. If it decides not to do so, or decides following a review to take no action, the Tribunal must consider whether to give permission to appeal[1].

1 Tribunal Rules, r 45(2).

12.186 No guidance is given in the Tribunal Rules as to the basis upon which the Tribunal will decide whether or not to grant permission. The test applied in the context of civil claims is that either the appeal has a real prospect of success or there is some other compelling reason why it should be heard[1]. It is still difficult to draw any firm conclusions as to whether the Tribunal or the Court of Appeal will apply this or some other test where an application for permission to appeal is made. In *Fox Hayes v FSA*[2], for example, the Court of Appeal based its approach on CPR 52.3, and found that there was a public interest in allowing a limited appeal on some points of law in order for those points to be clarified. In *Financial Conduct Authority v Hobbs*[3], the Tribunal held that, on the facts, it would be 'nugatory and inconsistent with the principles of fairness and justice' to allow the FCA to appeal a decision overturning its decision notice where a statement on its website said that it would take no further action against Mr Hobbs[4] (although it did note that the FCA had raised an arguable point of law).

1 Civil Procedure Rules, r 52.3(6) and see the commentary for a discussion of this test.
2 *FSMT 058.*
3 *[2013] EWCA Civ 918.*
4 The Court of Appeal, overturning that ruling, held that the Tribunal had erred in law and remitted the case back to the Tribunal to consider further points.

12.187 The Tribunal's decision whether or not to grant permission must be recorded and sent to the parties as soon as practicable[1]. Should the application be refused the Tribunal must also send its reasons for refusal and notification of the right to apply to the Court of Appeal for permission to appeal and the time and method for making such an appeal[2].

1 Tribunal Rules, r 45(3).
2 Tribunal Rules, r 45(4).

On some points of law, in order for these points to be identified, the Tribunal could be invited. Then, the Tribunal held that, on the facts, it would be unjust to grant information...with the principles of fairness and fit with to allow the IDC...opposed the application of returning its decision, made...where a matter of cases within said that it would...to...action against...held that [although it did not find that] the IDC had raised an issue in relation of...

> ...
> & Anor case

...The Court of...a...that...note that the IDC...time at less the amount in the case to the principles...of matter points.

12.187 The Tribunal's decision, whether or not to grant permission must, because recorded and read to the parties at once as a just result since of the application. Inasmuch the Tribunal cannot they send its decision a written and notification of...there to appeal to the Court of Appeal for permission to appeal and the time run method for making such an appeal.

> Tribunal Rules, r.62
> and s...about things 1980s

Section D
Mis-selling, Consumer Redress and
Intervention Powers

Section D
Marketing, Consumer Redress and
Interaction Power

Chapter 13   Mis-selling

INTRODUCTION

13.1   This chapter considers the regime for combating mis-selling and the key issues firms need to consider when responding to allegations of mis-selling.

13.2   These issues will be explored in the following four sections:

- what is meant by 'mis-selling';

- how mis-selling issues can emerge;

- how mis-selling is dealt with by the FCA, the various matters typically under consideration, and the options for dealing with consumer redress;

- the specific regime for the creation of consumer redress schemes under the FSMA 2000, s 404.

13.3   The combating of mis-selling was one of the FSA's main priorities, and remains, one of the FCA's main priorities. The FCA is subject to continued consumer, press and political pressure[1] to combat mis-selling. It has enhanced powers which sit alongside the regulatory tools that were previously available to the FSA.

1 The Treasury Select Committee has consistently questioned the FSA about its actions in this area: see eg letter dated 19 March 2012 from Andrew Tyrie to Lord Turner: http://www.parliament. uk/documents/commons-committees/treasury/Letter-from-Andrew-Tyrie-to-Lord--Turner-(FSA).pdf; and the Parliamentary Commission on Banking Standards also established a sub-panel to focus on mis-selling, see eg Banking Standards – Minutes of Evidence (21 January 2013): http://www.publications.parliament.uk/pa/jt201314/jtselect/jtpcbs/27/27ix_130121j.htm.

13.4   Mis-selling remains a key enforcement priority for the FCA and fines have increased significantly in recent years. The financial impact of compensating customers, which tends to be the FCA's primary focus when dealing with historic mis-selling, can be far greater still[1].

1 In the period January 2011 to May 2013, the FSA and FCA levied fines totalling £8.725 m for mis-selling, misleading advertising and other similar breaches, but, more significantly, secured compensation for customers of many times this figure (for example, total redress of £10.5 bn was paid by firms for PPI mis-selling alone during the same period).

13.5   Redress schemes operate increasingly often on a standalone basis. This is in part because the FCA has finite resources and has to decide which cases to pursue in line with its enforcement priorities. The FCA is focussed on the delivery of effective redress to consumers. It is wary of firms prioritising their own reputation and financial interests over the needs of their customers[1]. It will sometimes require firms to take steps to redress mis-selling without taking any formal disciplinary measures.

1 By way of illustration, the FCA lists among its enforcement priorities an intention to 'take tough action where firms fail to treat customers fairly, penalising those who are responsible and ensuring that effective redress is delivered quickly': FCA's *Business Plan 2013/2014*, p 39.

13.6   Whilst the focus has often been on historic practices, the FCA's role is not limited to after-the-event investigations of mis-selling. It aims to be proactive and to identify emerging risks, which may indicate systemic or widespread problems (or the potential for problems) in the market. Those problems could emanate from issues arising at any stage in a product's life cycle – including the product's design, marketing, the sales process, after-sales communications and complaints handling. The FCA will consider all of those matters, as well as (increasingly) a firm's internal governance for the product in question.

13.7   The FCA will look at products not only from the perspective of the conduct of individual firms, but also from the perspective of whether the market is operating effectively in the interests of consumers. This more structural approach means that there is not necessarily always a direct connection between consumer detriment and mis-selling. In principle, it is possible that a market could be improved in the interests of consumers without it being the case that the firms operating in that market have been 'mis-selling' products.

13.8   One of the significant developments in recent years has been the shift from rules-based to principles-based regulation. Principles-based regulation has evolved to allow the FCA to pursue a judgement-based approach focusing on the actual outcome for consumers, rather than on a firm's compliance with technical rules. Consequently, when the FCA investigates allegations of mis-selling, it will consider not only whether a firm has complied with its specific legal and regulatory obligations, but whether appropriate outcomes have been achieved for the consumers concerned. The FCA thus takes a judgement-based (or outcome-based) approach to mis-selling.

13.9   The implications of this approach have been far-reaching. The FCA's Principles for Businesses (the Principles) operate at a high level of generality, so that there is a gap between them and the requirements of the specific conduct of business rules. This leaves firms in a position of some uncertainty as to what regulatory compliance actually means. Firms in the past often designed their systems and controls to ensure compliance with specific conduct of business rules. That approach is no longer sufficient. The consequences flow through to the FCA's investigation of sales practices, as well as its identification of customer detriment and its expectations of how, and in what circumstances, firms will offer redress. As described in **CHAPTER 14**, the approach that the Financial Ombudsman Service (FOS) takes to complaints can also have a significant bearing on the question of whether there has been mis-selling.

13.10 The FCA's focus on problems emerging at any stage of a product's life widens the circle of potential responsibility for mis-selling. The role of the product manufacturer is as potentially relevant as the role of the product distributor. At the same time, there has been a gradual reduction in the degree of responsibility attributed to customers for the decisions they make. This is partly because customers do not always understand or focus on the information provided to them by firms. The FCA has committed itself to placing more emphasis on understanding consumer behaviour and what drives consumer decision-making, through the application of behavioural economics[1].

1 Speech by Martin Wheatley, Chief Executive of the FCA, at the British Bankers' Association Annual International Conference, London (17 October 2013).

WHAT IS MEANT BY MIS-SELLING?

13.11 Mis-selling is not defined anywhere in the regulatory regime. It is used in a flexible way to describe a sale that has not complied with a firm's legal or regulatory requirements. Historically, the focus tended to be upon the regulatory requirements for the point of sale, particularly the information provided and the advice given to customers on advised sales. However, the focus has broadened considerably so that, increasingly, compliance is judged by whether appropriate outcomes were achieved for the consumers concerned.

13.12 For a firm properly to understand its risks of mis-selling, it must have regard to both:

- the specific legal and regulatory obligations applicable to the relevant business (see para **13.13** ff below); and

- the FCA's Principles for Businesses (Principles) and their practical application in this context (see para **13.15** ff below).

Legal and regulatory obligations

13.13 Whilst firms must be mindful of their legal duties to their customers, the starting point for a firm is typically the specific rules set out in the FCA and PRA Handbooks and in particular the conduct of business rules which govern the sale of specific types of financial products[1]. A detailed explanation of the conduct of business rules is beyond the scope of this book but, broadly, they cover matters such as communications with customers, the information to be provided to customers (both before and after sale), and the conduct of the sales process, including the standards for any advice that is given.

1 See, in particular:
  • FCA Handbook at Conduct of Business Sourcebook (COBS);
  • FCA Handbook at Insurance: Conduct of Business Sourcebook (ICOBS);
  • FCA Handbook at Mortgages and Home Finance: Conduct of Business Sourcebook (MCOB);
  • FCA Handbook at Banking: Conduct of Business Sourcebook (BCOBS).

13.14   Although there are instances where enforcement action proceeds on the basis that a firm's activities have breached one or more specific conduct of business rules, such cases have become much less frequent. This is because the FCA's regulatory framework is informed by a set of principles and higher-level rules which allow the FCA greater flexibility when dealing with mis-selling[1]. It is for this reason that the specific rules are generally only the starting point.

1 Firms must also be mindful of statutory and common law causes of action available to claimants wishing to pursue a civil remedy. This is considered at para **19.83** ff below.

Principles for Businesses and consumer outcomes

13.15   The shift to principles-based regulation means a greater emphasis being placed upon compliance with the Principles (and other, similar, high level rules) and the related consumer outcomes. The Principles are listed in para **2.12** above. Principle 6, which requires firms to pay due regard to the interests of consumers and to treat them fairly, is at the core of the FCA's approach to combating mis-selling. Other principles that are particularly relevant in the context of mis-selling for firms which have dealings with consumers or which create financial products for onward sale to consumers are Principles 7 and 9[1].

1 Principle 7 requires firms to pay due regard to the information needs of clients and to communicate information to them in a way that is clear, fair and not misleading. Principle 9 requires firms to take reasonable care to ensure the suitability of the firm's advice and of any discretionary decisions for customers entitled to rely on the firm's judgement.

13.16   The Principles operate at a high level of generality and the question of what conduct is required of firms in order to comply (and to protect themselves against subsequent allegations of mis-selling) develops over time as regulatory thinking evolves. This evolution is articulated in a variety of enforcement decisions, thematic reviews, regulatory guidance and speeches. One of the significant challenges for firms is to keep up with these developments, so as to consider when and how to adapt their own processes as necessary.

13.17   The open-textured nature of the Principles makes it difficult for firms to assess whether they are complying with them, and so a set of 'consumer outcomes' sits alongside the Principles, and articulates the objective, from a consumer perspective, that the FCA wishes firms to achieve. Compliance with the Principles increasingly is judged by whether these outcomes have been achieved for the consumers concerned. The six consumer outcomes are:

- *Outcome 1*: consumers can be confident that they are dealing with firms where the fair treatment of customers is central to the corporate culture;

- *Outcome 2*: products and services that are marketed and sold in the retail market are designed to meet the needs of identified consumer groups and targeted accordingly;

- *Outcome 3*: consumers are provided with clear information and are kept appropriately informed before, during and after the point of sale;

- *Outcome 4*: where consumers receive advice, the advice is suitable and takes account of their circumstances;

- *Outcome 5*: consumers are provided with products that perform as firms have led the consumers to expect and the associated service is both of an acceptable standard and as consumers have been led to expect;

- *Outcome 6*: consumers do not face unreasonable post-sale barriers imposed by firms to changing products, switching provider, submitting a claim or making a complaint.

Practical tips for firms

13.18 In practice, given the breadth of the Principles and 'consumer outcomes', the constant evolution of regulatory standards, and the concern to avoid consumer detriment, 'mis-selling' has often been assessed with the benefit of hindsight. It has been difficult for firms to know what compliance involves. However, there are a number of recurrent (and connected) themes, which help firms to reduce the risks.

13.19 First, the FCA expects firms' business models, culture and operations to be based on a foundation of fair treatment of consumers. It wants this to be embedded into a firm's culture, corporate strategies and day-to-day operations. One aspect of this is that the FCA wants problematic trends to be identified quickly and addressed. This has implications for governance and management information (see para **13.20** below). Increasingly, firms need to be aware of how consumers experience financial services and products. A firm will be better protected if it can show that relevant decisions (for example, as to a product's features, the appropriate sales process, or in dealing with after the event issues like redress) were made from the perspective of customers, rather than purely in the firm's commercial interests.

13.20 Second, the FCA wants to see effective structures in place for the governance and oversight of financial products. This links in closely with the responsibilities of senior management, as effective governance structures can help to demonstrate that the relevant individuals discharge their own responsibilities to manage, and maintain an appropriate degree of oversight over, the business for which they are responsible. Such structures can therefore protect both the firm and its senior management. Governance bodies depend upon the management information that they receive, and so it is critical that reliable management information is produced and reviewed, among other things, enabling the firm to monitor the outcomes that are being achieved for consumers and to identify emerging problems or risks.

13.21 Third, as already discussed, firms will be better protected if they remain vigilant to the development of regulatory thinking, and keep their products and sales process under review as expectations change. In addition, if issues (or potential issues) are uncovered, the FCA will expect firms to react appropriately depending upon the circumstances. This may involve making decisions based upon the interests of the firm's customers, and not solely to protect the firm's own commercial interests.

HOW DOES MIS-SELLING EMERGE?

13.22 This section considers the ways in which mis-selling typically emerges. The way in which the issue emerges can have a significant bearing on how the firm engages with it and how it is resolved. Firms will want to retain control over the resolution of mis-selling issues as much as possible, and to ensure that they take, and are seen to be taking, appropriate steps with respect to their customers, whilst at the same time protecting their own interests to the extent possible.

13.23 The following paragraphs will consider, in particular, how issues emerge from:

- the FCA's supervisory, market and thematic work – see para **13.24** ff below;
- internal reviews and reporting by firms – see para **13.29** ff below;
- past business reviews – see para **13.32** ff below;
- customer complaints – see para **13.36** ff below;
- super-complaints by consumer bodies – see para **13.45** ff below.

FCA supervisory, market and thematic work

13.24 The FCA carries out a wide range of forward-looking supervisory activity focussing on particular products or markets. As explained in more detail at para **15.26** below, the FCA aims to identify emerging risks and to take steps to prevent those risks from crystallising. In many cases, the corollary of identifying risks or, particularly, concerns relating to existing practices or products is that this may point to existing consumer detriment for which (in the FCA's view) a firm or firms are responsible.

13.25 The FCA's activities in this area can be carried out in a number of ways. These include:

- ***routine supervision:*** a firm's FCA supervision teams may uncover a problem during a routine supervision visit. The supervisors implement the FCA's strategy of a pre-emptive style of conduct supervision. This may involve carrying out in-depth, structured supervision work with those firms identified as having the potential to cause the greatest risks to consumer outcomes. The teams are tasked with delivering, through day-to-day work with firms, a 'bolder' approach to customer-focused outcomes, focusing on actual consumer experience (rather than firm level systems and controls)[1];

- ***thematic work***: the FCA uses thematic reviews to identify current or emerging risks, the better to understand sales practices in particular areas of the market. It publishes the findings of its thematic reviews, typically sending messages to the market about practices, which it considers to be poor and those which it considers to be best practice;

- ***market studies***: the FCA is increasingly conducting broader reviews, known as market studies, focussing not only on sales practices but also on the operation of the market for a particular product. These are described in more detail at para **15.51** below;

- ***mystery shopping exercises***: the FCA engages in mystery shopping exercises to investigate concerns, to help evaluate changes to the regulatory regime or as a method of obtaining early warning of abuses in the marketplace[2];

- ***financial promotions work***: the FCA routinely looks at promotional material in the market. It provides a financial promotions hotline to enable firms and customers to report promotions considered to be unfair, unclear or misleading and to do so anonymously. The FCA may ask the firm to withdraw the advert, suggest that it writes to customers who bought the product making the risks clearer and offering redress, or it may refer the case to the FCA's enforcement division[3].

1 Speech by Clive Adamson, Director of Supervision, Conduct Business Unit, FSA at the British Bankers' Association Conference, London (25 January 2012).
2 FCA Handbook at SUP 2.4.1–2.4.5. In 2012/13, the FSA used mystery shopping to investigate the quality of banks and building societies' investment advice as a result of which one firm was referred for enforcement action: FSA *Annual Report 2012/13*, p 63.
3 The FCA also has a specific power to require the withdrawal of a financial promotion: see para **15.68** below.

13.26   It is particularly important to engage with the FCA's thematic and market study work, understanding that it can lead to significant changes to expected standards and market practices, as well as to regulatory enforcement. Thematic reviews have often led the FCA to refer firms to enforcement, where it has perceived market standards (or standards in particular firms) to be inadequate. This has a deterrent aspect, encouraging changes in behaviour across the market in response to the publication of the FCA's thematic work. It can result in the most prominent firms in the particular market being targeted, because they will normally be included within the sample of firms chosen for the thematic review.

13.27   When the FCA does set out its expectations as to market standards, it may want to review after a period of time whether market practices have changed to reflect the view that it has expressed. So, firms must engage with the output of such work and, again, may be referred to enforcement if they do not do so.

13.28   Whether thematic and other work leads to enforcement action can also depend upon the Regulator's priorities. In some instances, the FCA focuses on consumer redress first and foremost, and on changes to market standards for the future[1], with regulatory enforcement being less of a priority. This ought more often to be the case as the FCA reviews markets from a competition (as much as sales conduct) perspective, as discussed at para **15.38** ff below.

1 The tools available to the FCA to change market behaviour are considered at para **15.15** ff below.

Internal reviews and reporting by firms

13.29   Potential mis-selling may come to light as a consequence of management information within a firm, or from other internal sources such as compliance or internal audit reports, whistle-blowing or the handling of complaints.

13.30   Where an issue emerges, the firm may need to carry out a review and may also be obliged to report the issue to the FCA. These matters are discussed in **Chapter 3**.

13.31   Particular issues arise in relation to dealing with reports by external specialists. If a firm commissions a report from an external specialist, and does not act on its recommendations, then the FCA is more likely to take action against the firm[1]. Consequently, care needs to be taken with the drafting of and response to such reports. Reports that suggest that improvements should be made need to be clear as to whether the firm is being measured against minimum acceptable standards or against a higher benchmark (for example, best practice). To the extent that the firm does not accept the report's conclusion (for example, because it believes the author did not fully understand the firm's procedures), this also needs to be addressed. The steps taken (and not taken) by the firm in response to the report need to be carefully documented, together with the reasons, so that an audit trail exists and so that the firm is in the best position to explain its actions if questions are asked in future.

1 See http://www.fca.org.uk/firms/being-regulated/meeting-your-obligations/using-external-support/recommendations.

Past business reviews

13.32   The FCA's power to require a firm to appoint a skilled person to provide a report under the FSMA 2000, s 166 are considered in detail at **Chapter 6**. In the context of mis-selling, s 166 reports often take the form of a past business review.

13.33   Such reviews are typically commissioned to review sales of particular products, as well as the relevant procedures, systems and controls, and to assess whether mis-selling has taken place. Skilled persons reports have also been used to assess the handling of complaints and payment of compensation[1], as well as the scope of remedial measures[2] or systems and controls enhancements, which the firm should be required to implement.

1   For example, in 2012/13, 14 of the 113 skilled person reports commissioned were in relation to the sale of interest rate hedging products, where independent reviewers under s 166 were appointed to review all aspects of the proactive redress exercise and past business review being carried out by the firms. See *FSA Annual Report 2012/2013*, Appendix 6, pp 204–205.

2   For example, in *Swinton Group Limited final notice (16/07/13)*, Swinton carried out a past business review in relation to its telephone sales of monthly add-on insurance products to determine provisions to be set aside to meet continuing compensation claims (see para **108**). Another example is the voluntary past business review entered into by Sesame in order to identify and provide redress to customers who received unsuitable advice leading to the purchase of its Keydata Product: see *Sesame Limited final notice (05/06/13)*.

13.34   Inevitably, a past business review will consider only a sample of sales. If it concludes that certain sales were mis-sales, the firm should consider whether the FCA can properly extrapolate from the limited number of cases considered in the review in order to reach a conclusion that mis-selling has taken place on a wider scale. In cases of dispute with the FCA, firms may need to consider whether evidence should be obtained from an expert on the validity of the sample size.

13.35   There has been a trend towards skilled person's reports resulting in enforcement action against firms and members of senior management[1]. The skilled person's report will in many instances allow the Regulator to consider whether to commence an enforcement investigation. Even where it does not result in an enforcement investigation or outcome, skilled persons' reports can still have significant implications for firms and their senior management. The practicalities of dealing with skilled persons are considered in **CHAPTER 6**.

1   See para **6.2** above.

Customer complaints

13.36   Customer complaints can often be an important source of information about potential mis-selling. The regime for handling customer complaints, the procedures of the FOS, and the practical issues that arise, are considered in **CHAPTER 14**.

13.37   The FCA places significance on complaint handling as a way of collecting data about consumer concerns. It is viewed as a source of intelligence that can enable firms more quickly to detect potential customer detriment, with the expectation that firms will as appropriate then be able to consider what changes need to be made (to products, or the way that they deliver services) to prevent further detriment from arising. The compilation of complaints data is intended to assist more broadly with the early detection of systemic mis-selling. As such, firms receiving 500 or more reportable complaints in any six-month period are required to publish details of the complaints received and closed during that period[1].

1   FCA Handbook at DISP 1.10 (complaints reporting rules).

13.38   Data about customer complaints can come not only from firms but also from the FOS. The FOS has a statutory duty to disclose information to the FCA if it considers that such information would or might be of assistance in advancing one or more of the FCA's operational objectives[1]. The FOS could identify an issue as one that has, or potentially has, wider implications and request the FCA to become involved. This enables the FCA to consider whether in the particular circumstances it should take regulatory action as a more effective means of delivering redress to customers.

1 FSMA 2000, s 232A.

13.39   In addition, in certain circumstances, the FOS may make a 'mass detriment reference' under the FSMA 2000, s 234D, referring to the FCA an issue concerning regular failings by specific firms which are harming customers.

13.40   There are two alternative grounds upon which such a reference may be made. The first is that:

- there may have been a regular failure by one or more authorised persons[1] to comply with requirements applicable to the carrying on by them of any activity[2]; and

- that as a result, consumers have suffered or may suffer loss or damage in respect of which a remedy or relief would be available if they bring legal proceedings.

1 This means an authorised person, an electronic money issuer or a payment service provider.
2 This is defined in the FSMA 2000, s 234D(4) and (5) to have the same meaning as under the FSMA 2000, s 404 (see para **13.73** below).

13.41   The second is that one or more authorised persons have on a regular basis acted, or failed to act, in such a way that if a complaint were made under the ombudsman scheme in relation to that conduct, the FOS would be likely to determine the complaint in favour of the complainant, such that the FOS would likely make an award or give a direction in favour of the complainant.

13.42   Such a reference may also be made by an authorised person – in other words, typically, a firm which is the subject of FOS decisions.

13.43   Where such a reference is made, the FCA is generally required to publish a response within 90 days, stating how it proposes to deal with the reference, and in particular whether or not it has decided to take any action and, if so, what action it has decided to take[1].

1 For the detailed provisions, see the FSMA 2000, ss 234E–234G.

13.44   The effect of these provisions is to give the FCA an opportunity to consider whether a regulatory response is a more appropriate means of dealing with a widespread issue, rather than individual cases being decided by the FOS. For example, the FCA might agree with the relevant firm to put in place a system for dealing with customer complaints, or reviewing its book, or the FCA might consider creating a consumer redress scheme. This could be done at the instance of the FOS (which might be concerned about an increasing volume of cases to be decided) or at the instance of the firm (which might prefer to put in a place a different kind of mechanism for dealing with its customers).

Super-complaints by consumer bodies

13.45   Under the FSMA 2000, s 234C, certain designated consumer bodies[1] may complain to the FCA about features of a financial services market that damage or which risk materially damaging the interests of consumers.

1   At the moment the bodies with super-complaint status are: 'Which'; Consumer Council Northern Ireland; Citizens Advice; and the Federation of Small Businesses.

13.46   These so-called 'super-complaints' are intended to provide consumer bodies with a mechanism to raise issues about industry-wide features of the market causing consumer concern[1]. This is intended to assist in promoting earlier discovery of endemic market problems affecting the consumer experience.

1   See also the guidance issued by the FCA – *FS13/1: Guidance for designated Consumer Bodies on making a Super-Complaint under s 234C*.

13.47   The FCA must respond within 90 days, as set out at para **13.43** above.

HOW IS MIS-SELLING DEALT WITH BY THE REGULATORS?

13.48   This section considers the various action available to the FCA to address cases of large scale mis-selling and how it is likely in practice to approach the question of which of these regulatory tools to deploy.

13.49   Generally speaking, the FCA will consider a number of issues. First, the FCA will consider whether the firm (or, potentially, any individuals within the firm) should be the subject of any enforcement action in relation to breaches of the FCA's rules. Mis-selling is a key enforcement priority for the FCA, which will want in appropriate cases to take action to punish the firm and deter others. If the FCA commences a formal investigation, it will typically want to investigate the nature and extent of any mis-selling, as well as the systems and controls, and governance procedures, under which the mis-selling was able to take place. The FCA may also investigate the conduct of individuals who were responsible for the areas where the issues underlying the mis-selling arose, and could potentially take enforcement action against such persons. The FCA's investigation powers are described in **CHAPTER 5** and its disciplinary and enforcement procedures are described in **CHAPTER 10**.

13.50   Second, the FCA will want to ensure that the firm's existing policies, sales practices and procedures are appropriate for ongoing sales of the relevant product. This will generally be the subject of discussions within the supervisory relationship. A past business review by a skilled person (as described at para **13.32** and **CHAPTER 6** above) may also be used as a means of assisting the FCA to determine what remedial steps need to be taken, and on occasions to ensure that the relevant steps have been taken. Increasingly, those remedial steps may go beyond policies and procedures relating specifically to the sale of the product in question. They might extend to the features of the product, as well as its sale. Alternatively, they might arise more broadly from the FCA's desire to see an appropriate culture, and proper governance processes (supported by the necessary management information), in order to prevent recurring episodes of mis-selling.

13.51 The FCA may consider the question of how the product should be sold in the future not solely in the context of the particular firm, but in the context of the way in which the market for that product more broadly is operating. As described in **CHAPTER 15**, the FCA looks at whether the market is operating effectively for consumers, it seeks pre-emptively to identify and tackle emerging problems, and it has a wide range of tools available to it. So, if the mis-selling issue for the firm arises in the context of a broader thematic review or market study, or reflects an issue across the market, then the FCA could seek solutions which will affect the market for that product more broadly, rather than focussing solely on each firm's sales process.

13.52 Third, there is the critical question of whether there has been any customer detriment and, if so, how it is to be resolved. There is a range of options for dealing with customer detriment. At one end of the spectrum, the firm could simply be left to deal with each complaint that is made, subject to its duties to handle the complaint fairly in accordance with the DISP rules. The FOS operates as the backstop to ensure each individual complaint is handled fairly. This is the process that is described in **CHAPTER 14**. The FCA may also make enquiries or conduct investigations over time to ensure that complaints are indeed being handled fairly. Compliance by firms with their obligations to handle complaints fairly has been a significant area of focus for the FCA.

13.53 Generally speaking, if the FCA considers that a more structured approach is required than the firm simply responding to complaints as they are made, the FCA will seek to agree with the relevant firm the approach to be taken. Although the FCA has various formal powers for redress, outlined below, they are used rarely in practice and a solution tends to be negotiated and agreed. The solutions may take a variety of forms, most of which are based upon the system for firms to handle each customer complaint individually (with a FOS backstop). For example:

- the firm might agree to write to certain categories of potentially affected customers, providing them with information about the issue that has arisen, so that they can consider whether they wish to make a complaint;

- alternatively, the firm might agree pro-actively to review the files of certain categories of customers (ie irrespective of whether they have made any complaint), and to provide redress where appropriate. Given the need for proportionality and the cost of reviewing files pro-actively, this is most likely to be considered where there is an identifiable category of customer (typically a small category), which is particularly likely to have suffered significant detriment;

- in some cases, the FCA has also made clear its expectations as to the application of the regulatory standards relating to the sales in question, which provides a framework for complaints to be considered and resolved. This may be done informally (for example, through the FCA's feedback following thematic work) or in the FCA's agreement with the firm. In the case of PPI, the FCA promulgated formal guidance on the operation of the complaints handling rules in the context of that particular issue. This bore some resemblance to a scheme under the FSMA 2000, s 404, described below, but operating as guidance[1].

1 The extent to which this option is available to the FCA, as an alternative to using the statutory scheme, may be open for debate. This was one of the issues considered by the court in the PPI judicial review: *R (on the application of the British Bankers Association) v Financial Services Authority [2011] EWHC 999 (Admin)*. The court in that case held that it was open to the FSA to make such guidance notwithstanding the existence of a statutory scheme under the FSMA 2000, s 404. However, the extended version of s 404 had not at that time been introduced and so the point may remain open.

13.54 In conjunction with the types of solutions identified above, there may be a role for the appointment of a skilled person under the FSMA 2000, s 166[1]. In some instances, a skilled person has been involved in the process of reviewing customer files, with a mandate to oversee the firm's review in individual cases.

1 Described at **CHAPTER 6**.

13.55 Although relatively rarely used in practice, the FCA does have formal powers, including to secure the payment of redress to customers:

- the FCA may in some circumstances order, or apply to the court for an order, that a firm pay restitution for its rule breaches (see **CHAPTER 8**). This power has not generally been used in the context of mis-selling, but it is potentially wide enough in scope to apply;

- the FCA may put in place a statutory consumer redress scheme under the FSMA 2000, s 404. Historically, s 404 was rarely used by the FSA, but it was significantly amended in the Financial Services Act 2010, and now provides a broader and more flexible tool for securing consumer redress. It is described at para **13.72** ff below.

13.56 Finally, redress may be handled partly through the courts. A firm's customers may of course bring legal proceedings to recover losses caused by any breaches for which the firm is legally liable to the customer. The question of the firm's legal liability to customers is considered at **CHAPTER 19**.

Practical tips for firms

Agreeing redress with the FCA

13.57 How should a firm approach the question of redress? The starting point is to identify what the firm is looking to achieve and what it wishes to avoid. Important considerations will include:

- whether the firm accepts that there were breaches from which customers are likely to have suffered detriment;

- the firm's reputation with customers and in the marketplace;

- the firm's relationship with the FCA;

- whether the firm has been the subject of any enforcement action in relation to the issue (redress is often resolved alongside the settlement of the enforcement case) or whether its agreement to a redress programme is likely to be relevant to the FCA's decision whether or not to pursue an enforcement action;

- whether there are identifiable categories of customers who should be treated differently, for example because they are particularly likely to have suffered detriment;

- what approach the FOS has taken to date on the relevant issue.

13.58   Assuming the firm accepts (or is not in a position to contest) that it did not comply with its obligations to customers, it will often be willing to agree with the FCA a means of handling redress and so the issue is about finding the most appropriate means in the circumstances. As already described, this can take many forms.

13.59   The firm will hope that by co-operating with the FCA to provide redress (sometimes in circumstances where the firm does not accept there has been any wrongdoing), the FCA will not follow up with enforcement action or, if it does, that the enforcement action will be limited to a private warning[1]. However, this is not guaranteed, and the decision to pursue enforcement action will often be informed by the seriousness of what is uncovered as the firm investigates the position and the extent to which the FCA is under media and political pressure in relation to the particular issue.

1 See the FCA Enforcement Guide at EG 7.10, 7.18 and 7.19. Private warnings are considered in greater detail at para **8.27** ff above.

13.60   There is a related concern that, having consented to proceed with a standalone redress scheme, that might be taken by the regulator as a form of concession that mis-selling had taken place, and used against a firm in any follow-up disciplinary action. Firms will be understandably cautious about entering into arrangements with the Regulator when it brings with it this sort of commercial uncertainty. However, firms may also take the view that they have little choice but to do as the Regulator requests.

13.61   When considering the various mechanisms for assessing and delivering consumer redress, it is important to understand that they can produce different outcomes. For example, liability under a s 404 consumer redress scheme is potentially narrower than the 'fair and reasonable' jurisdiction of the FOS, and narrower than the approach which the FCA would take to regulatory enforcement, as the rules determining liability under a s 404 scheme must be based upon acts or omissions giving rise to legal liability. Most significantly, a breach of the Principles (in circumstances where there was no breach of the conduct of business rules or of any legal duty) would not give rise to legal liability[1].

1 See para **19.21**, n 2 below.

13.62   The nature and scope of any redress exercise can also have a significant bearing on the outcome. It is important to ensure that the exercise is proportionate, by reference to the issues that have been identified. Relevant factors will include the seriousness of any shortcomings, the likelihood that they will have resulted in loss, the scale of the potential issue, and the nature of the customers involved. That will help to determine the categories of customer who will be eligible to take part in the review, and the approach that is taken to the review (for example, whether it is complaints-based or pro-active, whether any steps are taken to stimulate complaints, and so on).

Dealing with parallel avenues of redress

13.63   It is important to consider the terms upon which a final determination under the review will be offered. Although it will be preferable for firms to conclude a review of a complainant's file on the basis of full and final settlement and with no option for the complainant to pursue other avenues of redress, even if the FCA is amenable to clauses being inserted into settlement agreements on this basis, it may be difficult in practice to persuade customers to agree to them.

13.64   Customers could also ignore the scheme and continue to make complaints (which would be referred to the FOS) or to issue court proceedings. The interaction of a redress scheme with court proceedings is complex and needs to be carefully managed. However, in practice, court proceedings tend not to undermine redress schemes because the evidential and legal hurdles for claimants are significantly higher than those applicable in the regulatory context. The interaction of a redress scheme with the FOS, though, is an important consideration in practice.

13.65   This leaves firms in complicated territory as they try to carry out a redress exercise in line with the FCA's requirements at the same time as they navigate competing redress processes involving the same customers who also:

- have received a final determination pursuant to a firm's normal complaints procedures; and/or

- are in the process of making a FOS complaint; and/or

- have accepted a FOS adjudication/ombudsman decision; and/or

- are involved in ongoing court proceedings with the firm; and/or

- have entered into a full and final settlement agreement on the basis of independent legal advice.

13.66   The firm needs to consider, then, how to deal with customers who, having secured compensation through one of the available avenues, or having commenced a process which might yield compensation in due course, then wish to have another 'bite at the cherry' by pursuing further compensation through a different route.

13.67 When a review is underway, a firm may continue to receive complaints from its customers through its usual complaints process. Firms are usually permitted not to consider any new complaints under its usual complaints handling procedures from customers who are eligible for its redress review[1]. However, complaints will still have to be processed from customers who have been ineligible for the review.

1 FCA Handbook at DISP 1.6.2(2).

13.68 Assuming that its usual jurisdictional rules are met, there is no guarantee that the FOS will decline to investigate a complaint made by a customer who is already part of a redress programme, or which is the subject of pre-action correspondence or court proceedings[1]. The FOS *may* dismiss a complaint without consideration of its merits if it is the subject of ongoing court proceedings[2], but the decision whether to consider the complaint lies within the discretion of the FOS. The FOS is empowered to decide complaints about mis-selling on the basis of what, in its view, is fair and reasonable in all the circumstances rather than solely on the basis of the statutory and regulatory framework in force at the time and so it is possible that the FOS will make a finding which is different to the outcome of the review process or of court proceedings.

1 The rules governing the FOS, and the process by which customers can complain to the FOS, are considered in **CHAPTER 14**.
2 FCA Handbook at DISP 3.3.4(9).

13.69 If the final determination under the review is not accepted by the customer, the customer will retain the right to complain to the FOS (although such a complaint would need to be made within six months of the final determination). A customer can also complain to the FOS about the way in which the firm has processed its claim during the review process. To the extent that the complaint falls to be dealt with (or has been dealt with) under a consumer redress scheme, the FOS must determine the complaint by reference to what, in its opinion, the determination under the consumer redress scheme should be or should have been subject to the statutory limit in the case of money awards[1]. If a customer has accepted a FOS determination, then, in the absence of specific agreement to the contrary, the consumer may also accept a final determination under the review in order to secure additional redress.

1 FCA Handbook at DISP 3.7.2R.

13.70 It is important therefore, to ensure so far as possible that FOS decisions will not undermine the scheme. Unless the FOS's decisions are aligned with those under the scheme (so that they generally will produce the same outcome), or unless the FOS declines to investigate complaints that are properly within the framework of the scheme[1], that can be a significant risk in practice.

1 See para **14.42** ff below.

13.71   This is considerably less of an issue with a s 404 scheme, which has the benefit that it binds the FOS, so that the FOS applies the same rules as are applied under the scheme (see para **13.83** below).

CONSUMER REDRESS SCHEMES UNDER THE FSMA 2000, S 404

13.72   The FSMA 2000, s 404 permits the FCA, following consultation, to prescribe rules requiring the industry to review past business and determine whether firms have breached their obligations and, if so, to quantify liability and make redress.

13.73   Under a scheme, each relevant firm is required to take one or more of the following steps in relation to activity it has carried on[1]:

*   to investigate whether on or after a specified date, the firm has failed to comply with requirements applicable to its activities;

*   to determine whether the failure caused (or may cause) loss or damage to consumers; and

*   if failure caused loss or damage to consumers, the firm must determine what the redress should be in relation to the failure and make the necessary redress to the affected customers.

1   FSMA 2000, s 404(5)–(7).

What are the pre-conditions for a s 404 scheme?

13.74   The FCA can make rules for a s 404 scheme if the following conditions are satisfied:

*   it appears that there is a widespread or regular failure by the firm to comply with requirements applicable to activities carried on by them[1];

*   the failure to comply with obligations relates to breaches of law or regulation that are actionable by court proceedings[2]; and

*   the FCA considers that a scheme is 'desirable' to secure redress for consumers[3].

1   A 'widespread' failure as one involving a high proportion of firms engaged in the relevant activity. A 'regular' failure is the re-occurrence of a particular failure by a lower proportion of firms: see *FSA Guidance Note No 10* (2010) 'Consumer Redress Scheme', paras 6.1–6.3.
2   Accordingly, a scheme will not be put in place to address breach of the FCA's Principles for Businesses, its rules on systems and controls or non-binding guidance alone.
3   This is a low threshold in legal terms. This decision will be informed by the cost-benefit analysis conducted: see *FSA Guidance Note No 10* (2010) 'Consumer Redress Scheme', para 8.1.

What is the scope of a s 404 scheme?

13.75   A s 404 scheme could affect a range of firms, including firms performing regulated activities or consumer credit business, firms issuing or approving financial promotions, payment services providers and appointed representatives[1].

1 FSMA 2000, ss 404(2) and 404E(2).

13.76 Although such schemes are limited to 'consumers', the definition of 'consumer'[1] adopts the broader concept of persons who 'have used or contemplated using' services provided by authorised persons, or persons who 'have relevant rights or interests' in relation to such services. Trustees and intermediaries dealing directly with retail customers could fall within the definition.

1 FSMA 2000, s 404E.

What is the basis for liability under a scheme?

13.77 The rules in a s 404 scheme determining liability can only specify examples of acts or omissions giving rise to liability that a court or tribunal would hold had breached a legal or regulatory requirement[1]. A legal requirement includes breaches of common law duties that would give rise to actions for breach of contract or negligence, for example. Therefore, liability under a consumer redress scheme must be founded on legal liability and is potentially narrower in scope than liability to pay a FOS award, which can be based on what is fair and reasonable. This does not mean that the measure of redress will be comparable with damages that might be awarded by a court. Specifically, the s 404 scheme can contain rules prescribing for the determination of redress, and this need only be 'just'[2] rather than based on the measure of damages that would be awarded by a court.

1 FSMA 2000, s 404A(2).
2 FSMA 2000, s 404A(4).

13.78 There are limits placed on liability under a s 404 scheme:

- some schemes will be limited to customers who have opted in;

- there is no change in the legal limitation period, so firms will not be required to pay redress if the limitation period expires before the start of the scheme[1];

- as the basis for liability under a scheme is a breach of regulation or law that is 'actionable', the usual principles of causation and remoteness of loss applied by a court will be applied to redress under the scheme[2];

- the scheme rules will take account of redress awarded by the FOS or a court, if a customer chooses to pursue either of these options, so that firms will not pay more redress as a result[3];

- an individual firm can apply for a waiver or modification of the scheme rules, as with other FCA rules[4].

1 *FSA Guidance Note No 10* (2010) 'Consumer Redress Schemes', para 16.4.
2 *FSA Guidance Note No 10* (2010) 'Consumer Redress Schemes', para 14.4.
3 *FSA Guidance Note No 10* (2010) 'Consumer Redress Schemes', para 16.7.
4 *FSA Guidance Note No 10* (2010) 'Consumer Redress Schemes', paras 17.1–17.3.

How can firms challenge a s 404 scheme?

13.79 If a firm wishes to challenge a s 404 scheme, it may apply to the tribunal for a review of any complaint scheme rules made by the FCA[1]. The tribunal is entirely independent of the FCA – it is part of the court service – as described in **Chapter 12**.

1 FSMA 2000, s 404D(1).

13.80 For the most part, the tribunal determines such applications based upon the principles of judicial review[1]. However, in two important respects the tribunal's jurisdiction is not limited in that way, namely:

- rules setting out examples of things done, or omitted to be done, that are to be regarded as a failure to comply with a requirement; and

- rules setting out matters to be taken into account for the purposes of assessing evidence as to a failure to comply or determining whether such failure has caused (or may cause) loss or damage to consumers.

1 FSMA 2000, s 404D(5).

13.81 These are the critical rules relating to the liability standard. When it comes to determining applications relating to those rules, the tribunal determines (in effect) whether the rules are right or wrong. This is an important check and balance, in the (unusual) circumstances where a Regulator is in effect making determinations of civil liability (which is typically a matter for the judiciary).

13.82 The tribunal may dismiss the application or may make an order quashing any part of the rules of the s 404 scheme if the challenge is successful.

What role does the FOS have in a s 404 scheme?

13.83 If a customer is dissatisfied with the outcome under a s 404 scheme, he may reject the finding and/or the determination of redress and make a complaint to the FOS[1]. The FOS is bound to apply the rules under the s 404 scheme, rather than its usual 'fair and reasonable' jurisdiction, when determining such complaints. The FOS determines whether the firm has applied the rules of the s 404 scheme correctly and, if appropriate, makes an award based on the rules of that scheme.

1 FSMA 2000, s 404B(2).

Chapter 14 Complaints handling and the Financial Ombudsman Scheme

INTRODUCTION

14.1   In this chapter the rules relating to how firms must handle disputes with their retail customers and the operation of the ombudsman scheme established for the resolution of those disputes will be reviewed.

14.2   The Financial Ombudsman Service (the FOS) is an independent statutory ombudsman scheme that was set up to resolve low value disputes between financial institutions and their retail customers quickly and with minimum formality[1]. The FOS operates as the second stage of a two-stage complaints handling process. Firms must themselves consider their customers' complaints; the customers may refer those complaints to the FOS if they are not satisfied with the outcome of the firm's complaint handling. The FOS's power to award redress is limited to a monetary limit of £150,000. Originally, its decisions (which are based on what it considers 'fair and reasonable') were not expected to have any precedent value. They were decisions based upon the individual circumstances of each small case. However, the FOS has over time become an increasingly important part of the regulatory system. The FCA's expectations of firms mean that the FOS's view of particular products or practices now has a significant impact on how firms handle customer complaints and on decisions whether to carry out past business reviews or redress exercises to compensate non-complaining customers.

1 FSMA 2000, s 225(1).

505

14.3   This chapter considers in particular:

- the obligations on firms when handling complaints internally, before they are referred to the FOS or a court (para **14.10** ff below);

- practical issues for firms after a complaint is referred to the FOS (para **14.24** ff below);

- the handling of complaints by the FOS (para **14.49** ff);

- the FOS's decisions, including the remedies that can be granted (para **14.76** ff).

An overview of complaints handling and the FOS

14.4   The FOS was created by the FSMA 2000, Pt 16 and Sch 17 when those parts of the Act came into force on 1 December 2001[1]. The body corporate that administers the scheme (under the FSMA 2000, s 225) is called the Financial Ombudsman Service Limited (referred to here as 'the scheme operator')[2] and funded by the industry[3]. The FOS's decision making powers, and the procedure for complaints referred to the FOS, are governed not only by the provisions of the FSMA 2000 but also by the DISP chapter of the FCA Handbook. The DISP chapter also governs how firms must handle customer complaints internally, before they are referred to the FOS. The provisions of DISP applying to how firms handle complaints internally are created by the FCA. The provisions governing complaints once they are referred to the FOS are created by the FOS with the approval of the FCA[4].

1 The ombudsman scheme is headed by a Chief Ombudsman and includes a number of lead or managing ombudsmen with responsibility for particular sectors. Staff are employed to assist in the consideration of complaints.
2 The scheme operator is governed by a chairman and board of directors. They are appointed by the FCA but on terms designed to secure their independence from the FCA in the operation of the scheme: FSMA 2000, Sch 17, para 3. It is FOS, not the FCA, that appoints the ombudsmen. The FOS is accountable to the FCA; it must make an annual report to the FCA and its budget must also be approved by the FCA: FSMA 2000, Sch 17.
3 FOS is funded through fees levied on firms. Details are found in the FCA Handbook at FEES 5. There are two components to the fee: (i) a general levy imposed on firms by reference to the proportion of the scheme's workload generated by the industry sector in which the firm operates and the proportion of that sector which the relevant firm represents; and (ii) a supplementary charge levied per case referred to FOS.
4 FSMA 2000, Sch 17, Pts 3 and 4, in particular paras 13 and 14.

14.5   When it was introduced, the FOS replaced eight previous ombudsman and dispute resolution schemes[1] operating on a variety of different bases[2]. It inherited their jurisdiction under transitional provisions. Broadly speaking, these provided for the FOS to apply the same decision making processes as those old schemes, or at least to take them into account, for a transitional period. The transitional provisions are complicated, and questions about the FOS's jurisdiction over historical activities can be very difficult, turning partly on an interpretation of old versions of the Handbook provisions and related regulations such as various Regulated Activities Orders and partly on historical facts about a firm's participation in earlier schemes. The FCA and FOS's approach to limitation (see para **14.37** below) means that these jurisdictional issues are still relevant today.

1 The Banking Ombudsman, the Building Societies Ombudsman, the Investment Ombudsman, the Insurance Ombudsman, the Personal Investment Authority Ombudsman, the Personal Insurance Arbitration Service, the Securities and Futures Authority Complaints Bureau and the FSA's Complaints Investigator.
2 Some voluntary, others compulsory; some statutory, others contractual; some involving ombudsmen, others arbitrators.

14.6 The scheme is effectively three schemes. One, known as the compulsory jurisdiction, covers most complaints of authorised firms[1]. The second, known as the voluntary jurisdiction, is available for authorised firms outside the bounds of the compulsory jurisdiction and for other firms as well, in certain respects[2]. The voluntary scheme is voluntary because it applies only to firms who participate in it, but it is binding on those firms. The third scheme is the consumer credit scheme, which covers complaints against non-FCA authorised firms who hold consumer credit licences[3]. Whilst the three schemes are different in scope and in their legal basis, they are almost identical in the way they operate.

1 This is outlined at para **14.42** below. The scope of the scheme can be altered from time to time, within statutory limitations.
2 The scope of the voluntary scheme is outlined at para **14.43** below. The scope of the scheme can be altered from time to time, within statutory limitations.
3 The scope of the consumer credit jurisdiction is outlined at para **14.44** below. The scope of the scheme can be altered from time to time, within statutory limitations.

14.7 The aim of the scheme is to resolve cases in a quick and informal way by whatever means appears most appropriate (including through mediation or investigation)[1]. Although the procedure is informal, the FOS does have binding powers, for example, to require firms to provide information[2], to make binding awards up to a limit of £150,000[3] (and recommendations beyond that limit) and to direct firms to take particular steps[4]. The FOS's determinations are enforceable by court order, if accepted by a customer. Moreover, the FCA has imposed an obligation on firms to co-operate with the FOS and there are regulatory consequences for failing to do so[5]. In practice, most of the work of the FOS is carried out by its staff and not the ombudsmen themselves[6], although an ombudsman is appointed for the purpose of considering and reaching the final determination on each case.

1 FSMA 2000, s 225(1) and see the FCA Handbook at DISP 3.5.1 and para **14.50** below.
2 See para **14.67** below.
3 See para **14.83** below.
4 See para **14.85** below.
5 See the discussion at paras **14.70** and **14.96** below.
6 This is permitted by the rules: see DISP 3.9.1A and see the FSMA 2000, Sch 17, para 14(2)(f).

14.8 The FOS does not always apply the law as a court would. It interprets its powers as enabling it to decide cases according to standards which are different from the standards a court would apply and it is increasingly doing so[1].

1 See para **14.72** ff below.

14.9   Complaints handling and the Financial Ombudsman Scheme

14.9   In addition there are Handbook provisions governing how firms themselves handle customer complaints and claims which are subject to the FOS's jurisdiction, before they are referred to the FOS or a court.

COMPLAINTS HANDLING BY FIRMS

14.10   This section will consider:

- the procedural requirements for handling complaints internally;
- the substantive requirements for handling complaints internally and the potential consequences for non-complaining customers.

Procedural requirements

14.11   The core requirements for firms when handling complaints internally are set out in DISP 1.4.1 R, which requires firms to:

- investigate the complaint competently, diligently and impartially, obtaining additional information as necessary; and
- assess the complaint fairly, consistently and promptly.

14.12   In terms of procedure, the basic requirement is that firms must have in place and operate appropriate and effective internal procedures for handling complaints[1]. So far as more specific requirements and the timetable are concerned, the FCA requires that:

- the firm sends a written acknowledgement promptly following receipt[2]; and
- within eight weeks of receiving the complaint, the firm must send the person making the complaint either[3]:
  - a final response, which means[4]: (i) a response accepting the complaint and, where appropriate, offering redress[5]; (ii) a response offering redress or remedial action without accepting the complaint; or (iii) a response rejecting the complaint with reasons and information about the right to refer the complaint to the FOS; or
  - a holding response, explaining why the firm is not yet in a position to resolve the complaint and giving an indication of when it will be able to make a final response and providing information about the right to refer the complaint to the FOS.

1 See the FCA Handbook at DISP 1.3.1. 'Complaint' means any expression of dissatisfaction, whether oral or written, and whether justified or not, from a person who would be eligible to refer a complaint to the FOS (see para **14.39** below) about the firm's provision of, or failure to provide, a financial services activity. For a more detailed discussion of the practical steps firms might take to assess and deal with wider systemic issues revealed, see para **3.114** ff above.
2 See the FCA Handbook at DISP 1.6.1(1).
3 See the FCA Handbook at DISP 1.6.2.
4 See the FCA Handbook, Glossary of Definitions and DISP 1.6.2(1).
5 See para **14.82** ff below for the types of redress the FOS can award.

14.13   The rules therefore allow an opportunity for the firm to investigate and for the complaint to be resolved without recourse to the FOS. The firm may wish to ask FOS staff for advice on a complaint on an informal basis. It can do so by telephoning the FOS technical advice desk. Any advice given is not binding on the FOS and this service is only available for complaints that have not been lodged with the FOS[1]. A complainant may not refer a complaint to the FOS until the firm has been given eight weeks to consider it. Unless the firm has already provided a final response, any complaint referred to the FOS in under eight weeks will simply be referred to the firm by the FOS.

1   See *Ombudsman News*, Issue 33, November 2003.

Substantive requirements

14.14   In terms of the substantive requirements for deciding a complaint, DISP 1.4.1R requires firms, when assessing a complaint fairly, consistently and promptly, to take certain specific matters into account, including the subject matter of the complaint, whether it should be upheld, what remedial action or redress might be appropriate, and whether another respondent might be solely or jointly responsible. DISP 1.4.1R also requires firms to explain its assessment to the complainant and any offer of remedial action or redress promptly and in a way that is fair, clear and not misleading, and to promptly comply with any acceptance of an offer by the complainant[1].

1   DISP 1.4.1 R(2)–(5).

14.15   DISP 1.4.2G lists factors which may be relevant in carrying out the assessment under DISP 1.4.1R(2), including the evidence and the particular circumstances of the complaint and other complaints received by the respondent. The FCA has also published more detailed guidance, in Appendix 3 of the DISP chapter of the FCA Handbook, on the handling of complaints about payment protection insurance, some of which might reflect approaches it expects to be taken in other appropriate cases. For example, firms assessing complaints about payment protection insurance are required to:

- consider information they already have access to which is not provided by the complainant[1];

- try to establish the true nature of the complaint, rather than focusing solely on the specific expressions in the complaint or taking a narrow interpretation of the issues raised[2];

- consider breaches or failings not raised by the complainant which the firm uncovers during the assessment[3]; and

- consider other issues that may be relevant to the sale identified by the firm through other means – for example systemic issues it has identified in the relevant sales systems or processes through separate investigations or assessments[4].

1   DISP App 3.2.1G and DISP App 3.2.6G.
2   DISP App 3.2.2G.

3 DISP App 3.2.5G.
4 DISP App 3.2.6G.

14.16 FOS decisions have an important role in complaints handling by firms. The FCA requires firms to take FOS decisions into account and to apply lessons learned from them in their own complaints assessments. In particular, the factors listed in DISP 1.4.2G which may be relevant in assessing complaints under DISP 1.4.1R(2), include: 'relevant guidance published by the FCA, other relevant regulators, the [FOS] or former schemes' and 'appropriate analysis of decisions by the [FOS] concerning similar complaints received by the respondent (the procedures for which are described in DISP 1.3.2A G).'

14.17 DISP 1.3.2AG provides that a firm's procedures for handling complaints should, taking into account the nature, scale and complexity of the firm's business:

'... ensure that lessons learned as a result of determinations by the Ombudsman are effectively applied in future complaint handling, for example by:

(1) relaying a determination by the Ombudsman to the individuals in the respondent who handled the complaint and using it in their training and development;

(2) analysing any patterns in determinations by the Ombudsman concerning complaints received by the respondent and using this in training and development of the individuals dealing with complaints in the respondent; and

(3) analysing guidance produced by the FCA, other relevant regulators and the [FOS] and communicating it to the individuals dealing with complaints in the respondent.'

14.18 FOS decisions also play an important role for firms considering their obligations in relation to non-complaining customers, and whether their Principle 6 obligations require them to carry out past business reviews and/ or pro-actively to compensate non-complaining customers. In particular, DISP 1.3.6G provides as follows[1]:

'Where a firm identifies (from its complaints or otherwise) recurring or systemic problems in its provision of, or failure to provide, a financial service, it should (in accordance with Principle 6 (Customers' interests) and to the extent that it applies) consider whether it ought to act with regard to the position of customers who may have suffered detriment from, or been potentially disadvantaged by, such problems but who have not complained and, if so, take appropriate and proportionate measures to ensure that those customers are given appropriate redress or a proper opportunity to obtain it. In particular, the firm should:

(1) ascertain the scope and severity of the consumer detriment that might have arisen; and

(2) consider whether it is fair and reasonable for the firm to undertake proactively a redress or remediation exercise, which may include contacting customers who have not complained.'

1 This was introduced in September 2011 followed similar PPI-specific guidance introduced in August 2010 in DISP App 3.4.3G.

14.19 In the past, the FCA has adopted a relatively low threshold for when it might be appropriate proactively to contact non-complaining customers with a view to determining whether they are owed redress. In practice, the FCA usually requires pro-active customer contact exercises to be designed in a way so that customer responses are treated as complaints and dealt with under the DISP rules in accordance with the firm's usual obligations for handling complaints.

14.20 The requirements above, to take account of FOS guidance and decisions, create a practical difficulty for firms. Not only do they have to monitor the decisions they receive from FOS, they also have to take some account of the decisions FOS publishes in relation to other firms. Thousands of those decisions can be published each month[1]. In addition, firms must have regard to other sources of guidance on complaints handling from the FOS and the FCA. These sources can be inconsistent. Not only do the FCA and FOS sometimes adopt different approaches, but the FOS itself makes inconsistent decisions. It does not operate a formal system of precedent like the courts and the way it exercises its fair and reasonable jurisdiction is inherently subjective, depending on the views of particular ombudsmen. This can lead to different ombudsmen taking different views on apparently identical cases for the same firm. All of this presents a significant challenge for firms, who need to adopt a considered and principled approach for reconciling the different sources of authority and applying them to their own processes.

1 See para **14.94** ff below.

14.21 For the reasons above, the way in which a firm handles complaints, and the decisions they receive from the FOS, may have wider implications in a number of areas, including: (i) the firm's liability to other complaining customers; (ii) its liability to non-complaining customers; (iii) its systems and controls for handling complaints; (iv) its sales systems and controls; and (v) its potential exposure to FCA supervisory or enforcement action for failings revealed by FOS decisions or in respect of (i) to (iv). The significance of FOS decisions should therefore not be underestimated. Given the potential sums at stake firms are increasingly recognising the need to devote more resources and time to complaints handling, including towards:

- monitoring cases and groups of cases in potential 'problem areas', so that the firm is able to recognise at an early stage that an issue of potentially broad application is beginning to surface. Only then is the firm able to take an overall decision on how to handle the problem as a whole (including the complaints handling aspects), before the FCA or the FOS removes the decision from its hands;

- ensuring that significant areas of complaint are escalated to the appropriate level of management;

- engaging internal or external advisers, where appropriate, to assist the firm with disputing high value issues with the FOS;

- taking the initiative to deal with all the implications arising from the problem which has arisen, including customer facing issues, implications for systems (for example, sales processes) or product design, and discussions with the FCA. This will give the firm the best chance of handling the problem in the manner most appropriate to its business;

- considering whether there are alternative ways of dealing with the problem, including through high level discussions with the FOS or by finding other ways to challenge the FOS's approach.

14.22 In some cases, it might be necessary to challenge the FOS's approach to avoid very significant issues. There are different ways to do that. In the first instance, issues can be debated in the context of a particular complaint, for example when the FOS provides preliminary views[1]. Even though the FOS may have a broad discretion to decide on the basis of what is fair and reasonable[2], it is required to follow due process in accordance with public law principles and it may be possible to persuade the FOS to change its mind by presenting careful arguments. Even if the FOS does not change its mind in a particular case, there might be some scope to try again in subsequent cases[3], since the FOS does not itself operate a system of precedent. Alternatively, in some instances, it may be possible to resolve issues with wider implications by holding high level discussions with the management of the FOS. Ultimately, it is also possible to challenge the FOS by judicial review and this is discussed in more detail in para **14.93** below.

1 There is no right to appeal a FOS decision but its usual processes provide opportunities for firms to respond to its initial views. See para **14.92** below.
2 See para **14.77** ff below.
3 After complying with the original decision in that particular case.

14.23 Questioning or challenging the FOS is not necessarily inconsistent with the FCA's approach to handling complaints *'fairly'*. Firms have a legal right to question and challenge complaints and decisions by the FOS, just as they have rights to defend cases brought against them in court. In some cases concerning issues arising out of complaints handling there may be more scope to avoid enforcement or other sanctions by challenging the FOS's approach, including if necessary by judicial review, than by challenging the FCA, given the practical difficulties that this can give rise to[1].

1 See para **14.92** ff below.

PRACTICAL ISSUES FOR FIRMS – REFERRALS TO FOS

14.24 In this section three practical issues for firms are considered, namely:

- What approach should the firm take to the process?

- How should the firm deal with the FOS?

- The risks of disclosing information to the FOS.

Each is considered in turn below.

What approach will the firm take in relation to the process?

14.25   One initial question for firms is whether to resist or accept the FOS process. However, it is not usually within a firm's control as to whether or not a complaint will be heard by the FOS[1].

1 See para **14.34** ff below.

How should the firm deal with the FOS?

14.26   The FCA's rules on complaints handling procedures require firms to co-operate fully with the FOS in the handling of complaints[1]. This includes producing documents the FOS requests, adhering to any time limits specified and attending hearings when requested to do so. The FOS expects a higher standard of record keeping from firms than from most consumers. If a firm is unable to produce appropriate records and documents, this may count against the firm[2]. Breach of this obligation, whether by a firm (or an unauthorised business), may adversely affect the FOS's determination[3]. In addition, the rule is a requirement imposed by or under the FSMA 2000 and, so far as authorised firms are concerned, is therefore capable of giving rise to the same potential consequences as any other regulatory breach[4]. Even in relation to an unauthorised business, the FCA could potentially apply to the court for an injunction requiring the person to remedy the breach[5], although this is unlikely in practice.

1 See the FCA Handbook at DISP 1.4.4.
2 'A guide for Complaint Handlers', published by the FOS and available at www.financial-ombudsman.org.uk/publications.
3 See para **14.70** below.
4 For a discussion of the phrase 'a requirement imposed by or under the FSMA 2000' and the potential consequences of a breach, see para **2.94** ff above. Note also that the breach may be reported to the FCA by the FOS: see para **14.29** below.
5 FSMA 2000, s 380 and see para **8.157** above.

Risks of disclosing information to the FOS

14.27   As will be seen[1], the FOS may obtain information from the firm in the course of investigating a complaint, including information which is confidential. To what extent is that information protected from being misused? And to what uses can it properly be put? These issues are considered below.

1 See para **14.67** ff below.

Use of information by the FOS

14.28 The scheme rules require the FOS, in dealing with any information received by it in relation to the consideration and investigation of a complaint, to have regard to the parties' rights of privacy[1]. This does not prevent the FOS[2] disclosing information (either in full or in an edited version) to the extent it is required or authorised to do so by law, or to the parties, or in the determination, or at a hearing of the complaint. Nor does it prevent the FOS from disclosing information to the FCA or other regulatory or statutory bodies for the purposes of the discharge of their functions, so long as it has regard to the parties' rights of privacy. This is plainly intended to reflect the right to respect for privacy under the ECHR, Art 8, discussed at para **3.30** ff above, and should also confer on such information, to the extent it is confidential, and subject to the limitations expressed in the rule, the normal protections which the civil law gives to confidential information, including allowing the firm to obtain, in an appropriate case, an injunction to restrain misuse[3]. The FOS is not, though, bound by any statutory restriction on the use of confidential information which it receives from the firm[4]. There is, therefore, no criminal sanction for the wrongful disclosure or use by the FOS of confidential information provided to it by the firm.

1 See the FCA Handbook at DISP 3.8. As regards disclosures to the FCA, see para **14.29** ff below.
2 Decisions on the disclosure of information must be made by an ombudsman, not a staff member: see the FCA Handbook at DISP 3.9.1A(2).
3 See *Coco v AN Clark (Engineers) Ltd [1969] RPC 41* and *A-G v Observer Ltd [1990] 1 AC 109, HL*, discussed at para **14.32**, n 2 below. A damages claim for breach of confidence would not generally be available against the FOS (unless it acts in bad faith or in breach of the Human Rights Act 1998), because of his statutory immunity from claims for damages: see para **14.93**, n 1 below.
4 This refers to the FSMA 2000, s 348, which does not apply because the FOS is not a 'primary recipient', although it would apply to the extent the FOS receives information directly or indirectly from the FCA or another primary recipient. For a further discussion of s 348, see para **4.224** ff above.

Disclosure of information to the FCA

14.29 Complaints to the FOS are regarded as an important source of regulatory information, providing a valuable early warning of problems with particular firms, products or rules. As noted in para **13.38** the FOS has a statutory duty to disclose information to the FCA if it considers that such information would or might be of assistance in advancing one or more of the FCA's operational objectives[1]. It also may, in certain circumstances, make a 'mass detriment reference' under the FSMA 2000, s 234D (see also para **13.39** ff above).

1 FSMA 2000, s 232A.

14.30 On 1 April 2013, the FOS and the FCA entered into a Memorandum of Understanding, under which the FOS has agreed to provide the FCA with information including the following[1]:

- 'information about: serious shortcomings in a firm's complaint handling; concerns about the fitness and propriety of a firm or approved person;

or other issues that may require action by the FCA in accordance with its statutory objectives'; and

- 'If the FCA requests it for actual or contemplated regulatory action ... information that is relevant to the discharge of the FCA's statutory functions'.

The FCA and FOS have also agreed that: 'Where either the FCA or the Financial Ombudsman Service Limited seek to share information which may be legally privileged, the relevant agency will adhere to any protocols that may have been agreed for the exchange of such information'[2], although it is unclear in what circumstances the FCA or FOS might believe they are entitled to share privileged information.

1   (1 April 2013) Memorandum of Understanding between the FCA and FOS, paras 16–18.
2   (1 April 2013) Memorandum of Understanding between the FCA and FOS, para 18(f).

14.31   In most cases the FOS will retain a discretion as to what information to pass to the FCA, and when to do so, but if the firm discloses to the FOS information which suggests that regulatory breaches have been committed or that the firm or an individual employee may not be fit and proper[1], there is a risk of that information being disclosed to the FCA. Once disclosed to it, the FCA may use the information for, among other things, its own enforcement purposes. The interaction between the FOS and the FCA is discussed in more detail at para **14.58** ff below.

1   For a discussion of this phrase, see para **2.29** ff above (in relation to firms).

Use of information by the complainant

14.32   Another risk in this context is of information being misused by complainants. Confidential information provided by the firm to the FOS and disclosed to the complainant is not specifically protected under the FSMA 2000[1]. There is also nothing in the scheme rules to require the customer to keep such information confidential. But the complainant may nonetheless be bound by a duty of confidence which a court would recognise[2], which would prevent him from disclosing or misusing[3] the information. If such a duty exists, the firm may be able to obtain an injunction to restrain a breach and/or damages for the breach. Whether a duty exists will, though, depend upon the precise circumstances. There is therefore a lack of clear protection for the firm. This is significant, particularly given the requirement on firms to co-operate with the FOS[4] and the statutory powers of the FOS to require firms to produce information and documents[5]. Among other things, there may be a risk of a complainant using the FOS scheme to obtain, effectively, pre-action disclosure from a firm before bringing a claim against it in the civil courts.

1   FSMA 2000, s 348 does not, generally speaking, apply to such information: see para **14.28**, n 4 above.
2   The firm would have to show: (i) that the information was of a confidential nature; (ii) that it was communicated in circumstances importing an obligation of confidence; and (iii) that there was an unauthorised use of it: *Coco v AN Clark (Engineers) Ltd [1969] RPC 41* and *A-G v Observer Ltd [1990] 1 AC 109, HL*.

3 Misuse includes using confidential information as a springboard for activities detrimental to the person to whom it belongs – the so-called 'springboard' doctrine: see *Terrapin Ltd v Builders' Supply Co (Hayes) Ltd [1967] RPC 375.*
4 See para **14.26** above.
5 See para **14.67** below.

14.33   There are some practical steps the firm can take to protect its position. First, as discussed below[1], the scheme rules allow the FOS to accept information in confidence, so that only an edited version (or where that is not practicable, a summary or description) is passed to the complainant. Firms may wish to rely upon this where sensitive information is to be disclosed[2]. Second, in order to help ensure that a duty of confidence does arise, the firm may wish to ensure it is made clear to the complainant, when confidential material is disclosed, that the information is confidential. Whilst the scheme rules do not expressly address this issue, there appears to be nothing to prevent the firm from asking the FOS to produce documents to the complainant only on this basis.

1 See para **14.72** below.
2 The FOS has advised that, if the firm believes the information should be kept confidential between the firm and the FOS, it should be marked as such and the FOS should be told why the information should not be passed to the consumer. The FOS will consider whether there is a 'strong case of confidentiality, such as security reasons' ('A Guide for Complaint Handlers', published by the FOS and available at www.financial-ombudsman.org.uk/publications, at p 9).

WILL THE FOS INVESTIGATE THE COMPLAINT?

14.34   Only certain types of complaints can be resolved through the ombudsman scheme. Some complaints may simply not be eligible for consideration by the FOS, others may be premature because they have not been through the firm's own complaints handling process, while others may be too late. Therefore, the firm may have grounds to object to a complaint being considered by the FOS. Next the initial stages will be outlined, which may lead to a decision by the FOS whether to investigate the complaint and, in particular, will review:

•   when a complaint can be made to the FOS;

•   what sort of complaints can be considered by the FOS;

•   whether the FOS is bound to investigate the complaint.

When can a complaint be made to the FOS?

14.35   A complaint may not be made to the FOS until the firm has been given eight weeks to consider it[1]. Otherwise, the FOS will simply refer the matter back to the firm, unless the firm has already issued a final response[2]. After eight weeks, even if the firm has not responded the FOS will generally begin investigating the complaint.

1 This refers to the procedure outlined at para **14.12** above.
2 See the FCA Handbook at DISP 3.2.2.

14.36 Pursuant to DISP 2.8.2R, complaints must, generally speaking, be referred to the FOS not more than six months after the date when the person is advised by the firm in its final response of the right to refer the complaint to the FOS and not more than six years after the event complained of or not more than 'three years from the date on which the complainant became aware (or ought reasonably to have become aware) that he had cause for complaint', if later[1]. The complaint must fall within both time limits. The FOS can decide to hear a complaint outside the time limits, but only if it is of the view that the failure to comply with the time limits was the result of exceptional circumstances or if the firm has not objected[2]. In view of this, if firms wish to assert that a complaint is outside the time limits they are expected to do so as early as possible.

1 DISP 2.8.2. There are exceptions for certain complaints, eg in relation to mortgage endowments (see the FCA Handbook at DISP 2.8.7R).
2 Examples given suggest this is a narrow exception, eg where the complainant has been incapacitated: see the FCA Handbook at DISP 2.8.4G

14.37 The FCA and FOS have adopted an interpretation of DISP 2.8.2R which sets a very high threshold for when a customer ought to have become aware they had cause for complaint. For example, in guidance published in July 2012 the FSA suggested that the time for a complaint relating to PPI might not start running until a customer received a letter from a firm stating that PPI may have been missold[1]. That was followed by an FSA letter to firm CEOs in August 2012 saying that:

'We have said in the past that high public awareness generally is not sufficient to start the three year time limit on complaint handling. However as we have said in our recent guidance on the content of customer contact letters, a customer contact letter could do so.'.

Firms following this approach have had to deal with large numbers of very old complaints, including complaints about sales made before the Ombudsman Scheme was created in 2001[2].

1 FG 12/17: 'Payment protection insurance customer contact letters (PPI CCLs) – fairness, clarity and potential consequences' (July 2012).
2 See para **14.5** above.

14.38 The FCA and FOS's current approach is different from the one the English courts take to other similar limitation provisions, which focuses on a claimant's knowledge of facts and when they ought to have been aware of a sufficient connection between damage and the defendant to make further inquiries[1]. Knowledge that the facts give rise to liability as a matter of law is usually irrelevant[2]. In contrast to their current approach, in the consultation papers leading to the creation of the DISP limitation rules, the FOS and the FSA said they were intended to mirror the approach taken in court[3].

1 Eg Limitation Act 1980, s 14A.
2 Eg Limitation Act 1980, s 14A(9).
3 Eg the FOS and FSA said: 'For the purposes of the new Scheme, we propose to apply the time limits enshrined in English law relating to the limitation of actions' (Consultation Paper 33 'Consumer complaints and the new single ombudsman scheme', para 6.26); that the rules would create

'alignment with the English law of limitations in respect of the time limit for making a complaint to the Scheme after the act or omission giving rise to the matter in question' (Consultation Paper 49 'Complaints handling arrangements: Feedback statement on CP33 and draft rules', para 1.73); and that 'the time limits for bringing a complaint to the FOS broadly mirror the law of limitation in respect of bringing actions in court' (Policy Statement dated December 2000 'Complaints handling arrangements: Response on CP49', para 1.13).

What complaints can be referred to the scheme?

14.39 One of the first questions for a firm faced with a complaint made to the FOS will be whether the complaint is eligible to be considered under the scheme. There are a number of aspects to this. The primary questions are[1]: (a) whether the type of activity to which the complaint relates falls within the FOS's jurisdiction; (b) where the activity to which the complaint relates was carried on; (c) whether the complainant is eligible; and (d) whether the complaint was referred to the FOS in time. If, in the firm's view, the complainant or the complaint is not eligible, it may raise this objection with the FOS and ask for a decision on whether or not the FOS can hear the complaint[2].

1 DISP 2.2.1G.
2 Where a firm disputes whether a complainant is eligible to make a complaint or whether the complaint falls within the scope of the scheme, the FOS must give the parties an opportunity to make representations before it reaches a decision and must give reasons for that decision: see the FCA Handbook at DISP 3.2.3 and 3.2.4. The FOS must in any event consider these issues: see the FCA Handbook at DISP 3.2.1 and, for the procedure, DISP 3.2.5 and 3.2.6. If the FOS decides that it does have jurisdiction, and the firm believes that decision is wrong, then the firm may be able to challenge the decision by way of judicial review: see, for example, *Legal & General Assurance Society Ltd v Pensions Ombudsman [2000] 1 WLR 1254, Swansea City and County v Johnson [1999] 1 All ER 863* and *Marsh & McLennan Companies UK Ltd v Pensions Ombudsman [2001] IRLR 505.*

Is the complainant entitled to use the FOS?

14.40 The issue of who is entitled to use the scheme is complicated and only a brief outline of the rules is given here[1]. The scheme is available to private individuals[2] and certain types of businesses[3]. It is not available to a professional client or an eligible counterparty of the firm[4]. In addition, firms cannot use the FOS scheme to complain about other firms, even if they apparently fall within the parameters of the scheme, if the complaint relates in any way to an activity which the firm itself is permitted to carry on[5].

1 For details, see the FCA Handbook at DISP 2.7. The same rules apply equally to the voluntary jurisdiction: see the FCA Handbook at DISP 4.2.3(2).
2 See the FCA Handbook at DISP 2.7.3. But not, necessarily, private individuals carrying on a business, because a sole trader is included within businesses: see the FCA Handbook Glossary. It is irrelevant whether the complainant lives or is based in the UK: see the FCA Handbook at DISP 2.6.5.
3 Broadly, those with a turnover/annual balance sheet of less than €2 million and fewer than ten employees at the time the complaint is referred to the scheme: see the FCA Handbook at DISP 2.7.3 and the Glossary. Also included are charities with an annual income of less than £1 million and trustees of a trust with a net asset value less than £1 million.
4 See the FCA Handbook at DISP 2.7.9(2).
5 See the FCA Handbook at DISP 2.7.9(1). The same point applies to participants in the voluntary jurisdiction in relation to activities which they conduct.

Does the complaint fall within the scope of the scheme?

14.41   The FOS can only consider those complaints which fall within the scope of the scheme. Again, the rules are complicated and only a brief outline is provided here[1].

1   For the detailed rules, see the FCA Handbook at DISP 2.3, 2.4, 2.5, and 2.6.

14.42   The compulsory jurisdiction of the scheme is capable of encompassing any of the listed financial services activities of a firm, whether or not those activities are regulated[1]. It covers complaints against firms (ie authorised firms) relating to an act or omission in the carrying on[2] of one or more regulated activities and a limited range of unregulated activities[3].

1   FSMA 2000, s 226(4).
2   Carrying on includes offering, providing or failing to provide and administering or failing to administer a service in relation to the relevant activities, and includes the manner in which a firm has administered its business provided that the business is an activity subject to the scheme: see the FCA Handbook at DISP 2.1.4.
3   Including mortgage lending, lending money (other than restricted credit), lending or paying money by a plastic card (other than a store card) and the provision of ancillary banking services: see the FCA Handbook at DISP 2.3.1.

14.43   The voluntary jurisdiction has the same potential scope, but in relation to unauthorised businesses as well[1]. It covers[2] complaints against a person that is a participant in the voluntary scheme, in relation to an act or omission in the carrying on of general insurance business, accepting deposits, mortgage lending, lending money (other than restricted credit), paying money by a plastic card, provision of ancillary banking services, acting as a mortgage or insurance intermediary, other financial services activities in relation to which the particular person was formerly subject to one of the previous voluntary ombudsman schemes and activities carried out after April 1988 which were regulated when the firm joined the voluntary jurisdiction but which was not a regulated activity at the time of the act or omission, but only if it is not covered by the compulsory jurisdiction.

1   FSMA 2000, s 227(4).
2   See the FCA Handbook at DISP 2.5.1.

14.44   The FOS also has jurisdiction over complaints made against businesses that hold consumer credit licences (known as the 'consumer credit jurisdiction')[1]. This jurisdiction applies to 'licensees' ie firms who hold consumer credit licences[2]. The consumer credit jurisdiction applies to an act or omission by a licensee carrying on one or more consumer credit activities or ancillary activities, including advice, carried on by the licensee in connection with them[3].

1   See the FCA Handbook at DISP 2.4. The FOS has jurisdiction over authorised firms in respect of their consumer credit activities under the compulsory jurisdiction.
2   See the FCA Handbook Glossary. The FOS's jurisdiction in this area applies to persons who are not firms, but are either: (a) covered by a standard licence under the Consumer Credit Act 1974; or (b) authorised to carry on an activity by virtue of s 34(A) of that Act.

3 See the FCA Handbook at DISP 2.4.1R and the FCA Handbook Glossary. 'Consumer credit activities' include providing credit under a regulated consumer credit agreement or the operation of a credit reference agency.

14.45 Territorially, the compulsory jurisdiction covers complaints about the firm's activities conducted in or from an establishment maintained in the UK, whether or not the complainant lives or is based in the UK[1]. Firms are therefore within the scope of the compulsory jurisdiction to the extent that they carry on the activity from a branch in the UK, but not if they carry on their business cross-border into the UK. Complaints concerning business conducted by overseas branches of firms are not subject to the compulsory jurisdiction. The voluntary jurisdiction has wider territorial scope and covers activities carried out within the EEA and directed at the UK[2].

1 See the FCA Handbook at DISP 2.6.5.
2 See the FCA Handbook at DISP 2.6.4.

Is the FOS bound to investigate the complaint?

14.46 On receipt of the complaint, the first step is for the FOS to consider[1] whether or not the complaint is within the applicable time limits, and whether or not the complaint and the complainant are eligible[2]. These points have been considered above[3]. In addition, the FOS also considers whether or not the complaint is one which should be dismissed without consideration of its merits. In other words, even where the complaint and complainant are eligible, the FOS may choose not to investigate. This third issue is considered here.

1 See the FCA Handbook at DISP 3.2.1.
2 Before reaching a decision to dismiss the complaint for lack of eligibility, either on his own initiative or on an objection raised by the firm, the FOS must give the complainant an opportunity to make representations and must give reasons for its decision: see the FCA Handbook at DISP 3.2.3–3.2.6.
3 Respectively, paras **14.35**, **14.40** and **14.41** above.

14.47 The Scheme rules contain a list of the grounds upon which the FOS may dismiss a complaint without considering its merits[1]. In particular, these include cases where:

- the complainant has not suffered, or is unlikely to suffer, financial loss or material inconvenience or distress; or the complaint is frivolous or vexatious or clearly has no reasonable prospect of success;

- the FOS is satisfied the firm has made a fair and reasonable offer of compensation which remains open;

- the matter has been, is being, or is more suitable to be, dealt with in other proceedings, for example, another comparable complaints scheme[2] or dispute resolution process, or court proceedings;

- the complaint is about the legitimate exercise of a firm's commercial judgement;

- the complaint relates to investment performance;

- the complaint relates to employment matters from an employee or employees of a firm; or

- the FOS is satisfied there are other compelling reasons why it is inappropriate for the complaint to be dealt with by it.

1 A full list can be found in the FCA Handbook at DISP 3.3.4.
2 The FOS may refer the matter to another, more suitable complaints body, if the complainant consents: see the FCA Handbook at DISP 3.4.1.

14.48 Before making a decision to dismiss without considering the merits, the FOS must give the complainant an opportunity to make representations and, if it decides to dismiss the complaint, must give reasons to the complainant and inform the firm[1]. Whether or not to dismiss a complaint is within the FOS's discretion[2]. It is not bound to do so simply because the case falls within one of the above categories[3].

1 See the FCA Handbook at DISP 3.2.4.
2 However, the FOS is not entitled to make the decision to dismiss a complaint on the basis of what is fair and reasonable in all the circumstances, which is the basis on which it decides whether to uphold a complaint (see FSMA 2000, s 228(2): this only applies only to the determination of complaints).
3 Although if he makes an irrational or wholly unreasonable decision, then that may be capable of being challenged in court. For a brief discussion of judicial review in relation to FOS decisions, see para **14.93** below.

HOW DOES THE FOS HANDLE THE COMPLAINT?

14.49 A review of how the FOS handles a complaint follows and considers in particular[1]:

- the FOS's general approach;

- the settlement of complaints;

- the procedure for determining complaints;

- the procedure for cases involving 'wider implications' issues;

- the FOS's powers to obtain information;

- what evidence the FOS considers;

- whether there is an oral hearing; and

- how long the process takes.

1 The same rules apply to the voluntary jurisdiction as the compulsory jurisdiction, generally speaking: see the FCA Handbook at DISP 3.1.5 and 4.2.3(3).

The FOS's general approach

14.50 Where the matter is suitable for consideration by the FOS[1], the complaint will not necessarily proceed to a contested hearing at which the rights and wrongs of the dispute will be determined in an adversarial context. In accordance with its statutory purpose[2], the FOS scheme aims to resolve disputes quickly and with minimum formality. As the FCA Handbook makes clear[3], the FOS attempts to resolve complaints at the earliest possible stage, by whatever means appear to be most appropriate, including mediation or investigation. Whilst the scheme must incorporate the ECHR fair trial safeguards, it attempts to do so in such a way as not to undermine the essential informality and speed of the process[4]. The general approach is therefore one of informality, flexibility and expedition.

1 As to those cases where it is not, and the firm's right to object that a complaint should not be heard, see para **14.47** ff above.
2 FSMA 2000, s 225(1).
3 See the FCA Handbook at DISP 3.5.1.
4 The safeguards include that either party has the right to request an oral hearing: see para **14.73** below. The FCA and scheme operator have said that the scheme will shape and adjust its processes in light of court decisions on the interpretation of the Human Rights Act 1998, whilst seeking to deploy minimum formality. This is reflected in DISP 3.5.7G.

Settlement of complaints

14.51   Where the FOS considers there is a reasonable prospect of resolving the complaint by mediation[1], it will try to negotiate a settlement. The FOS's assessment teams[2] consider the information supplied by the parties and explore any reasonable prospect of resolving the complaint by conciliated settlement. A large proportion of cases are resolved at this stage.

1 See the FCA Handbook at DISP 3.5.1.
2 Most of the FOS's work, apart from reaching a final determination, is carried out by the scheme staff.

14.52   In dealing with the FOS in relation to settlement, firms need to bear in mind the potential impact of any without-prejudice admissions that they make for the purposes of reaching a settlement[1]. Those admissions will be known to the FOS staff that are attempting to settle the complaint, and the FOS will normally expect to be aware of any offer and its contents as well but will not treat them as binding on the firm when it comes to making its determination[2]. The firm's admissions could be relevant to the FCA for enforcement purposes, for example, because the firm admitted having committed a regulatory breach, and it is possible that the assessment team would pass that information on to the FCA[3]. Any document recording an admission could potentially be susceptible to disclosure to the FCA in the context of any ongoing investigation or enforcement proceedings[4].

1 These issues arise because the FSMA 2000 does not specifically protect without-prejudice communications: FSMA 2000, s 413 and see the discussion at para **5.56**, n 1 above.
2 In any event, the FOS is likely to find out about any without-prejudice offer from the complainant.
3 The circumstances in which information may be disclosed to the FCA are outlined at para **14.29** ff above.
4 Such a document would not be protected from disclosure under the FSMA 2000, s 413: see the discussion at n 1 above. As a without-prejudice document, it should not, though, be susceptible to disclosure to other third parties who bring civil claims against the firm.

The procedure for determining complaints

14.53 If an investigation is necessary, for example, because there is no prospect of a mediated settlement, or this has been tried with no success, what is the process? The FCA Handbook states merely that the FOS will[1]:

- give both parties an opportunity of making representations;

- send the parties a provisional assessment, setting out its reasons and a time limit within which either party must respond; and

- if either party indicates disagreement with the provisional assessment, proceed to determination.

1 See the FCA Handbook at DISP 3.5.4.

14.54 In practice, the process works broadly as follows. The FOS will initially give customers general advice and guidance about what to do if they make a complaint. If a customer has not yet complained directly to the firm, the FOS will refer the complaint to the firm for consideration. If a customer still wishes the FOS to consider his complaint following the initial advice and guidance he receives, the complaint passes to one of the FOS's adjudicators.

14.55 At this stage, the adjudicator may decide that the complaint falls within one of the categories of complaints that the FOS can dismiss without consideration of the merits. If not, the adjudicator will consider the case. The adjudicator's approach will depend on the facts of each case, but adjudicators will generally first try to settle a complaint informally through mediation or conciliation.

14.56 The adjudicator will call for any information he needs from either party, if need be using statutory powers. Both parties will be allowed to make representations. The adjudicator may try and resolve the matter over the phone. If this is not possible, or if a written explanation is more appropriate, the adjudicator will confirm his conclusions in writing. This will give the adjudicator's opinion of the case and set out how, in the adjudicator's view, the case should be resolved. In some more complex cases, the adjudicator may seek to resolve the dispute by issuing a formal adjudication report, which is sent to both parties who are then given an opportunity to respond. If both parties accept the adjudicator's view, that is the end of the matter. If one party does not accept it, that party may ask for the matter to be reviewed by one of the ombudsmen, leading, after any representations, to the issue of a final decision by an ombudsman.

14.57 As will be seen, either party or the ombudsman may call for an oral hearing[1].

1 See para **14.73** below.

14.58 During the course of considering the complaint, the FOS can fix and extend time limits for any particular aspect[1] and has a variety of options if a party fails to comply with a time limit[2].

1 See the FCA Handbook at DISP 3.5.13.
2 The FOS may proceed to the next stage or dismiss the complaint and in relation to a failure by the firm, it may make provision in its award for any material distress or inconvenience caused by the failure: see the FCA Handbook at DISP 3.5.14.

14.59 What is notable about the scheme rules is the lack of detail. Thus, for example, it is left to the FOS adjudicators/ombudsmen to decide what evidence they want to see and how that evidence should be provided to them[1], there is little mention of the FOS's powers to obtain information[2], there is no discussion of when or how documentary evidence produced by the firm will be disclosed to the complainant[3] and there is no explanation of how any oral hearing will be conducted[4]. The lack of formal procedural rules reflects the desire to maintain a flexible process and to enable the FOS to reach a fair result in an informal, expeditious and cost-effective way in each case[5]. For example, any evidence obtained from one party to a dispute will be shared with the other and they will have the opportunity to make representations on it.

1 See para **14.67** ff below.
2 See para **14.69** ff below.
3 There is, however, provision allowing the FOS to accept evidence in confidence: see para **14.72** below.
4 See para **14.73** below.
5 See para **14.72** below.

14.60 The opportunity to make representations enables the firm to set out all the reasons why the complaint should not be upheld and also to address any issues about the award or other remedy sought by the complainant. Firms must have in mind the need to be consistent with arguments raised, or likely to be raised, in similar cases, or in other contexts, for example, in any related enforcement proceedings brought by the FCA. They should also bear in mind the risk of their written representations, and any evidence they provide, being used by the complainant for other purposes and being passed to the FCA by the FOS[1].

1 This is discussed in more detail at para **14.29** ff above.

Cases with wider implications and the involvement of the FCA

14.61 In March 2005, the FOS and FSA announced the outcome of a consultation into the proposed arrangements to clarify the different roles and responsibilities of the FSA and FOS when 'wider implication' issues arise. An enhanced procedure was thought desirable because there was a perception that the FOS's role was changing and that it was increasingly making decisions affecting large numbers of similar cases. Accordingly, there was a concern that the FOS wielded considerable power yet was not subject to sufficient checks and balances.

14.62 Detailed new procedures were introduced to improve the identification and handling process for such cases by both the FSA and the FOS, to enhance co-operation between the two agencies, and to improve the overall transparency of the interface between the FOS and the FSA in relation to such issues.

14.63 Although the wider implications process was originally intended to be used by firms as well as by the FOS and the FSA, few firms took advantage of it, in part because of concerns about a lack of transparency and the respective roles of the FOS and the FSA. In April 2008, an independent report recommended changes to the process, to make it more transparent and to insulate the FOS from all aspects of any regulatory decision making in the process[1].

1 *The Hunt Review: Opening Up, Reaching Out and Aiming High – An Agenda for Accessibility and Excellence in the Financial Ombudsman Service* (April 2008) – see in particular paras 7.15–7.20.

14.64 Although firms continued to avoid the process, from a regulatory perspective it became very significant. It encouraged FOS and FSA interaction and was the basis for the discussions between the FOS and the FSA in July 2008 which triggered the industry redress exercise relating to PPI[1].

1 See para **14.37** above and the Open Letter from the FOS to Chief Executives dated 1 July 2008.

14.65 The wider implications process was eventually scrapped in 2011. In April 2013, the FCA and scheme operator published a Memorandum of Understanding between them[1]. It is less detailed than the wider implications process and does not contain checks and balances but still provides for significant interaction between the FCA and FOS. For example, it records their agreement to 'meet and communicate regularly – at appropriate levels of seniority – to discuss matters of mutual interest' and to 'share (for comment) at an early stage, draft documents (such as consultation papers and briefings) that affect the other's functions'. The FCA, FOS and OFT are also members of a 'Co-ordination Committee' which will 'contribute to the identification and consideration of emerging risks that have the potential to cause widespread detriment amongst financial services consumers, promote alignment between the OFT's or the FCA's response to emerging risks and widespread issues and contribute to the effective exchange of information between members of the committee'[2].

1 As required by the FSMA 2000, Sch 17, para 3A(2).
2 Memorandum of Understanding between the Financial Conduct Authority (the FCA) and the scheme operator, the Financial Ombudsman Service Limited (1 April 2013).

14.66 The interaction between the FOS and the FCA is now an important aspect of complaints handling. In particular, industry or firm specific information may be shared by the FOS with the FCA and can lead to regulatory investigations and enforcement[1]. The process is still not particularly transparent and such exchanges will usually take place in the first instance without a firm knowing. This is another significant risk firms need to bear in mind when dealing with the FOS and handling complaints internally.

1 See para **14.29** ff above in relation to the FOS's power to share information with the FCA.

The FOS's powers to obtain information

14.67 Generally, the FOS staff will ask for the firm's file papers upon receipt of a valid complaint[1]. Further information may be required at any stage of the process and, where a dispute between a firm and a complainant involves different recollections of a key event, the FOS may ask the firm for a written statement by a current or former employee. The FOS may[2] require a party to the complaint[3] to provide or produce before the end of such period as may be specified:

- specified information or information of a specified description;

- specified documents or documents of a specified description,

which the FOS considers necessary for the determination of the complaint. The requirement is imposed by written notice.

1 For example, copies of any documents, or recordings of any telephone calls, that concern the customer and may be relevant.
2 FSMA 2000, s 231.
3 In contrast with the FCA's investigation powers (see **CHAPTER 5** above), the power cannot be exercised against a third party, even one connected with the firm. There is, though, nothing to prevent the FOS from asking a third party to provide information voluntarily and the firm may be asked to waive any duty of confidence owed to it by the third party to allow the information to be disclosed. It may be difficult for the firm to refuse given its obligation to co-operate fully with the FOS (see para **14.7** above). Indeed, in some cases, it may be in the firm's interests to ensure the FOS has all the information it requires, to ensure that a positive outcome deters further claims being made by the same complainant in another forum. Note that the FOS can require information to be provided not only by the firm but also by the complainant.

14.68 The test for the imposition of a requirement is fairly high. The FOS must consider the provision of the document or information to be 'necessary' for the determination of the complaint[1].

1 Precisely what 'necessary' means depends upon the circumstances. It has been usefully defined as lying somewhere between 'indispensable', on the one hand, and 'useful' or 'expedient', on the other: Lord Griffiths in *Re an Inquiry under the Company Securities (Insider Dealing) Act 1985 [1988] AC 660* at 704.

14.69 A requirement imposed under this provision does not have the benefit of all the ancillary provisions applicable to FCA investigations, discussed at **CHAPTERS 4** and **5** above. Certain provisions do, however, apply. In particular:

- if a document is produced, the FOS can take copies or extracts or can require the person producing it to provide an explanation of it[1];

- if a person required to produce a document fails to do so, the FOS can require him to state to the best of his knowledge and belief where it is[2];

- the production of a document does not affect any lien on it[3];

- legally privileged material cannot, generally speaking, be required to be produced[4].

1 FSMA 2000, s 231(4).
2 FSMA 2000, s 231(5). Note that, in contrast with FCA investigations, the FOS has no power to obtain the document from any other person who has it. It is therefore reliant upon the relevant person voluntarily providing it, or the firm concerned obtaining it for the FOS.
3 FSMA 2000, s 231(6).
4 FSMA 2000, s 413. For a more detailed discussion of this provision, see para **5.56** ff above. Note that the FSMA 2000 effectively contains its own definition of 'legal privilege' for these purposes.

14.70 Failure to comply with such a requirement could result in punishment for contempt of court[1]. There may also be other consequences. The failure may prejudice the person's case before the FOS[2]. For authorised firms, it could also amount to a breach of the duty to co-operate with the FOS[3], for which there may be regulatory enforcement consequences[4].

1 In the same way as a failure to comply with a requirement to provide information imposed by the FCA: FSMA 2000, s 232 and see para **5.76** ff above.
2 The FOS can determine the complaint on the basis of the information supplied, taking account of a failure to supply which it has requested or, if the complainant fails to supply information it has required, it can dismiss the complaint: see the FCA Handbook at DISP 3.5.9(3) and (4).
3 See the FCA Handbook at DISP 1.4.4 and see para **14.96** below. The FOS may report the failure to comply to the FCA: see para **14.30** above.
4 It would also amount to the contravention of a requirement imposed by or under the FSMA 2000: for further discussion, see para **2.94** ff above.

What evidence will the FOS consider?

14.71 The FOS may, in relation to what evidence may be required or admitted in considering and determining a particular complaint, give directions as to the issues on which evidence is required, the extent to which the evidence required to decide those issues should be oral or written and the way in which the evidence should be presented[1].

1 See the FCA Handbook at DISP 3.5.8. See also the procedure relating to cases involving wider implications at para **14.61** ff above.

14.72 The rules[1] provide some additional flexibility by allowing the FOS to exclude evidence that would be admissible in a court or include evidence that would not be admissible in a court or, where it considers it necessary or appropriate, to accept evidence in confidence so that only an edited version or (where this is not practicable) a summary or description is disclosed to the other party. The example given in relation to the latter is that this may include confidential evidence about third parties or security information[2]. This point may be of particular significance to firms who are concerned about the disclosure of confidential and sensitive information to individual customers[3]. However, if the eventual judgment is based on evidence which one party has not been allowed to see, and which he has not had an opportunity to comment upon or challenge, it is possible that the decision may be open to challenge on ECHR grounds[4]. Ultimately, the firm should assume that all information may be disclosed to the complainant. Where information is confidential, it should be marked as such and should be accompanied with an explanation as to why the FOS should not disclose it[5]. The FOS may then decide not to disclose it or may disclose it in edited form. However, the question of what evidence should be disclosed is for the FOS, not for the firm.

1 See the FCA Handbook at DISP 3.5.9.
2 See the FCA Handbook at DISP 3.5.10.
3 The risks relating to disclosure are discussed in more detail at para **14.27** ff above.
4 See *Feldbrugge v Netherlands (Application 8562/79) (1986) 8 EHRR 425.*
5 See *Ombudsman News*, Issue 14, February 2002.

Is there an oral hearing?

14.73 The FOS's usual practice is to resolve cases without the need for hearings. Hearings are only held if the complaint cannot be settled by an adjudication and the ombudsman thinks that a hearing will help to resolve issues relevant to his decision. However, the system is flexible and either party may request an oral hearing before the determination has been made[1]. The ombudsman must in any event (even when no request is made), consider whether the complaint can be fairly determined without an oral hearing[2]. If a request for an oral hearing is made, the ombudsman will consider whether the issues are material, whether a hearing should take place and, if so, whether it should be held in public or private. In practice, as the FCA Handbook recognises[3], the ombudsman's duty to comply with the ECHR fair trial safeguards will normally militate in favour of a hearing in public, where one is requested[4].

1 See the FCA Handbook at DISP 3.5.6. Such a request must be in writing, setting out the issues the person wishes to raise and (if appropriate) any reasons why he considers the hearing should be in private.
2 See the FCA Handbook at DISP 3.5.5.
3 See the FCA Handbook at DISP 3.5.7.
4 This marks a significant change from the ombudsman schemes under the previous regime, where hearings were rarely held. The ECHR, Art 6(1) imposes a number of requirements on the process, if it is to fulfil the fair trial guarantees. The basic rights are outlined at para **12.29** above. However, see *R v Financial Ombudsman Service, ex p Ropaigealach [2004] EWCA Civ 1011*, where the courts held that 'the parties' positions were perfectly clear from the mass of written documentation' and so an oral hearing was not necessary (see also *R v Financial Ombudsman Service, ex p Ropaigealach [2005] EWCA Civ 269* which clearly sets out the case history).

14.74 Where there is a hearing, it is conducted informally in the way the ombudsman considers best suited to the circumstances. It does not have to be confrontational. Each party has the opportunity to hear and comment on the evidence of the other[1]. The ombudsman may ask questions of either party, set time limits and confine the hearing to material matters. Parties have the right to be legally represented, although the ombudsman will try to conduct the hearing in such a way as to ensure that a person who is represented has no advantage over one who is not[2].

1 This is required by the ECHR, Art 6(1): see para **14.53** above.
2 In most cases, complainants will not need to have professional advisers: see the FCA Handbook at DISP 3.7.10.

How long will it take?

14.75 Although the FOS was set up to resolve complaints quickly, and although it charges fees on a per-complaint basis and has increased its staff to try to match its workload, it has struggled to keep up with volumes as its role has changed over time and more complaints are referred to it[1]. As a result, complaints about certain products can take well over a year to get to the stage of a final decision, although in practice firms come under considerable pressure to settle complaints before they get to that stage[2].

1 For example because of the involvement of claims management companies and as a result of proactive customer contact exercises (see para **14.18** ff above).
2 See para **14.5** above.

THE FOS'S DECISION

14.76 If the matter has not already been resolved, then the final stage is for the FOS to reach its determination. The following will be considered:

- How does the FOS reach its decision?

- What remedies can the FOS grant?

- Can the FOS award costs?

- What is the effect of the decision?

- Can the decision be appealed or challenged?

- Is the decision made public?

- How is the decision enforced?

How is the decision reached?

14.77 The FOS[1] determines complaints by reference to what is, in its opinion, fair and reasonable in all the circumstances of the case[2]. In doing so, the scheme rules require it to take into account the relevant law, regulations, regulators' rules and guidance and standards, relevant codes of practice and, where appropriate, what they consider to have been good industry practice at the relevant time[3].

1 The final determination is made by the ombudsman himself, not by a member of the scheme's staff: see the FCA Handbook at DISP 3.9.1A(1).
2 FSMA 2000, s 228(2) and see the FCA Handbook at DISP 3.6.1.
3 It might be noted that these are also factors a court would be expected to take into account, where relevant, in appropriate cases.

14.78 The nature of the FOS's power to determine complaints on the basis of what it believes to be fair and reasonable has been the subject of debate. In 2008, the Court of Appeal held in *R (Heather Moor & Edgecomb Ltd) v FOS*[1] that the power enabled the FOS to determine cases other than in accordance with the law. The court decided that this was not necessarily inconsistent with the ECHR, Art 6 and Art 1 of the First Protocol or the fundamental principles of the rule of law, such as the requirements for the law to be accessible, intelligible, clear and predictable. It did not set out in detail what the scope of the FOS's ability to depart from the law might be, although it commented, at para 49 of the judgment, that:

'So far as guiding the conduct of financial advisors are concerned, provided that they comply with "the relevant law, regulations, regulators' rules and guidance and standards, relevant codes of practice and, where appropriate, … good industry practice", they can be assured that they will not be liable to their client in the absence of some exceptional factor requiring a different

529

decision. Lastly, the common law requires consistency: that like cases are treated alike. Arbitrariness on the part of the ombudsman, including an unreasoned and unjustified failure to treat like cases alike, would be a ground for judicial review.'

1   [2008] EWCA Civ 642.

14.79   The scope and extent of the power was considered again in 2010, by the High Court in *R (on the application of) British Bankers Association v The Financial Services Authority and The Financial Ombudsman Service*[1]. That decision considered the FOS's practice of choosing not to apply the FSMA 2000, s 150(2) (now contained in the FSMA 2000, s 138D), which does not permit breaches of the FSA's principles for businesses to be actionable at the suit of a private person. The BBA argued that while the FOS might be able to depart from the law in limited circumstances, for example in exceptional cases, it did not have an unlimited ability to do so – for example it could not decide that a particular law such as the FSMA 2000, s 150(2) was not fair and reasonable and ignore it or replace it with its own view of what the law should be.

1   [2011] EWHC 999 (Admin).

14.80   Ouseley J determined that the FOS had a wide discretion, holding that:

'The width of the Ombudsman's duty to decide what is fair and reasonable, and the width of the materials he is entitled to call to mind for that purpose, prevents any argument being applied to him that he cannot decide to award compensation where there has been no breach of a specific rule, and the Principles are all that is relied on … I do not accept that this is something which is lawful if it is only done exceptionally. That can only be an expectation that the circumstances which warrant it will be very infrequent, which is what I too would expect. But if it is lawful … it can be done whenever and how often circumstances warrant it.'[2]

1   *R (on the application of) British Bankers Association v The Financial Services Authority and The Financial Ombudsman Service* [2011] EWHC 999 (Admin), paras 184–185.

14.81   The FOS's determination is provided to the parties in a signed written statement, giving reasons. The complainant must notify the FOS in writing before a specified date whether he accepts or rejects the determination[1].

1   See further para **14.91** below.

What remedies can the FOS grant?

14.82   Where the FOS finds in favour of the complainant, it may:

•   make a money award; and/or

•   direct the firm to take particular steps.

These are considered in turn below.

Money awards

14.83 The FOS may make a money award against the firm of such amount as it considers fair compensation for loss or damage suffered by the complainant[1]. Loss or damage means financial loss (including consequential or prospective loss), pain and suffering, distress or inconvenience and damage to reputation[2]. The award is subject to a specified maximum limit[3], but:

- the FOS may, if it considers that fair compensation requires the payment of a larger amount, make a non-binding recommendation to the firm that it pays the balance[4];

- the FOS may also award reasonable interest on the award, and determine the rate and period[5]. The interest award does not form part of the award for the purpose of calculating the maximum amount that can be awarded[6].

1 FSMA 2000, s 229 and see the FCA Handbook at DISP 3.7.1 and 3.7.2.
2 FSMA 2000, s 229(2)(a) and (3) and see the FCA Handbook at DISP 3.7.2(1)–(4).
3 At time of writing, the limit was £150,000: see the FCA Handbook at DISP 3.7.4. Note also that it may be possible for the FOS to make a direction which would have the effect of requiring the firm to pay more: see the discussion at para **14.86** below.
4 FSMA 2000, s 229(5) and see the FCA Handbook at DISP 3.7.6.
5 FSMA 2000, s 229(8)(a) and see the FCA Handbook at DISP 3.7.8. The FOS typically adopts a similar approach to the courts and awards interest simple rate of 8% per annum. For a discussion of whether that is an appropriate rate in low interest environments, see the Law Commission report *Pre-judgment Interest on Debts and Damages* (Law Com No 287, 24 February 2004).
6 See the FCA Handbook at DISP 3.7.5(1).

14.84 The key phrase is 'fair compensation for the loss or damage'. This gives the FOS a significant discretion to assess the award of compensation[1]. Whilst the provision requires fair compensation to be linked to the loss or damage, it may not require the FOS to have regard to normal legal rules such as remoteness of loss, or the categories of financial loss, pain and suffering, and so on, that are normally capable of being remedied with an award of damages. For example, the FOS routinely awards small sums (usually a few hundred pounds) for 'stress and inconvenience'. It is not, therefore, only the determination of liability that may be made irrespective of recognised legal principles; the amount of the award itself may be arbitrary in legal terms[2]. In practice, awards are made very much on a case-by-case basis. If an award were made on a basis that did not reflect the law, then it may in some circumstances be capable of being challenged[3].

1 Although it is not as broad as the test for making a determination, namely what is 'fair and reasonable in all the circumstances'.
2 See *IFG Financial Services [2005] EWHC 1153* in which the application sought judicial review of a determination of the FOS on the basis that the FOS had failed to take account of the relevant law. The court decided that the FOS is free to make an award different from that which a court would make, provided that it concludes that the award is fair and reasonable in all circumstances of the case and takes into account all the elements it is required to take into account under the FSA's rules. The court decided that the ombudsman did take the relevant law into account (in this case, an important principle laid down by the House of Lords with respect to causation of damages) although it gave it no weight. Accordingly, the application for judicial review was dismissed.
3 As to the difficulties of doing so, see *IFG Financial Services [2005] EWHC 1153*, discussed at n 2 above. See also *R v Investors Compensation Scheme Ltd, ex p Bowden [1996] AC 261*, in which the House

of Lords held that a decision by the Investors Compensation Scheme on whether a claim was 'essential in order to provide fair compensation' could only be attacked on grounds of *Wednesbury* unreasonableness, in other words that it was a decision that no reasonable public authority could take, and that it was unnecessary to express any view on whether a court, applying ordinary rules as to the measure of damages, would have reached the same conclusion. However, it cannot be discounted that an award of compensation based on wholly non-legal considerations as to quantum, or which departs significantly from established legal criteria, might be exposed to challenge on the basis that it is not properly 'compensation' within the meaning of the FSMA 2000, s 229, or under Art 1 of the First Protocol to the ECHR (see para **14.93**, n 3 below). This is particularly so where the arbitrary award cannot be challenged before a court by the firm, but can be challenged by the complainant, which might lead to further ECHR grounds for challenge under Art 1 of the First Protocol in conjunction with the prohibition on discrimination under Art 14.

Directing the firm to take steps

14.85 Alternatively, or in addition to making a money award[1], the FOS may direct the firm to take such steps in relation to the complainant as the FOS considers just and appropriate, whether or not a court could order those steps to be taken. There is no express limitation on the steps that the FOS can require the firm to take. Examples include requiring a firm which had sold a mortgage endowment policy to a customer for whom it was not suitable to transfer the customer to a repayment mortgage[2], and a firm who had sold life insurance to a customer who had needed term assurance being ordered to provide term assurance at the same premium as if he had been sold term assurance at the outset[3]. As with money awards, the need for directions will be assessed very much on a case-by-case basis.

1 FSMA 2000, s 229(2)(b) and see the FCA Handbook at DISP 3.7.1(4).
2 *Ombudsman News*, Issue 25, February 2003.
3 *Ombudsman News*, Issue 39, August 2004.

14.86 One issue is whether the FOS can use this power to direct the payment of a sum in excess of the cap on money awards[1], either simply by directing the firm to make such a payment[2] or by directing it to take a step that would inevitably have the effect that it paid more than the cap, for example, requiring it to reconstitute a fund that had been negligently invested. Although the answer is not clear, it is likely that the power could not be used to direct compensation in excess of the statutory limit[3].

1 At the time of writing, the cap was £150,000. See para **14.83**, n 3 above.
2 In the context of the Pensions Ombudsman, the power to direct that steps are taken is used to award compensation, although, in contrast with the FSMA 2000, the relevant provisions of the Pension Schemes Act 1993 do not contain any express provisions dealing with awards of compensation.
3 See *Bunney v Burns Anderson plc; Cahill v Timothy James & Partners Ltd [2007] EWCH 1240 (Ch)*.

Can the FOS award costs?

14.87 When the FOS finds in favour of a complainant it may award an amount which covers some or all of the costs reasonably incurred by him in respect of the complaint[1]. The costs award can be interest bearing[2].

1   See rules at DISP 3.7.9(1). The FOS may be reluctant to award costs in cases where a complainant engages an adviser unless the FOS considers that the complainant could not successfully have been put forward without the adviser's help.
2   See the FCA Handbook at DISP 3.7.9(2). It does not form part of the money award for the purposes of calculating the £150,000 cap: see the FCA Handbook at DISP 3.7.5G.

14.88 This cost provision is one-sided[1], allowing costs to be awarded against the firm but not in its favour. The rationale[2] is that if complainants were at risk on costs this could discourage the making of legitimate complaints.

1   This is notwithstanding the FSMA 2000 enables FOS to make costs rules allowing it to impose a costs order against a complainant whose conduct was improper or unreasonable or who was responsible for an unreasonable delay. The purpose of such costs is to provide a contribution towards the resources deployed in dealing with the complaint. An award of costs against a complainant in respect of the firm's costs is not permitted: see the FSMA 2000, s 230.
2   FSA and FOS Consultation Paper 49, 'Complaints handling arrangements: feedback statement on CP 33 and draft rules', May 2000, para 1.56.

14.89 Costs awards are not common in practice, since in most cases complainants should not need to have professional advisers in order to bring complaints[1]. It is unclear whether a costs order remains effective notwithstanding the complainant rejecting the substantive award, which he has the right to do as discussed below.

1   See the FCA Handbook at DISP 3.7.10.

What is the effect of the FOS's decision?

14.90 The effect of the FOS's decision is entirely in the complainant's hands[1]. He is entitled either to accept or reject it. If he accepts it, then it is binding on both parties. If he rejects it, then neither party is bound by it[2].

1   FSMA 2000, s 228(5) and (6) and see the FCA Handbook at DISP 3.6.6(3) and (4).
2   It may be arguable that this contravenes the ECHR fair trial guarantees; in particular, it could be argued that, by allowing the complainant, but not the firm, a right to have the matter reheard in another forum, the complainant is put in a procedurally advantageous position in breach of the requirement of equality of arms under the ECHR, Art 6(1). It might also be argued that the availability to the complainant, but not to the firm, of a rehearing in court infringes the firm's right of access to a court under Art 6(1), either on a free standing basis or in conjunction with the prohibition on discrimination in Art 14.

14.91 The complainant accepts the decision by notifying the FOS in writing within the time limit specified in the FOS's determination[1]. The decision is rejected if the complainant notifies the FOS that he rejects it or does not accept it by the date specified[2]. The FOS notifies the firm of the complainant's response or lack of response[3]. The Court of Appeal has held that if a customer accepts a FOS determination, he or she is not able to seek additional compensation from the firm through the courts if the cause of action relied on is constituted by the same set of facts as the determined complaint. This is because the doctrine of res judicata applies to the FOS's determination[4]. It does not matter whether the FOS award was for the maximum sum that can be awarded or for a lesser amount.

1   FSMA 2000, s 228(5) and see the FCA Handbook at DISP 3.6.6(3).

2 FSMA 2000, s 228(6) and see the FCA Handbook at DISP 3.6.6(4). If the complainant does not actively reject the determination and notifies the ombudsman of his acceptance after the specified date, the ombudsman may accept that notice if the ombudsman is satisfied that there were exceptional circumstances meaning that the complainant could not accept before the specified date: see the FCA Handbook DISP 3.6.6(4A).

3 FSMA 2000, s 228(7) and see the FCA Handbook at DISP 3.6.6(5).

4 *Clark v In Focus Asset Management & Tax Solutions Ltd [2014] EWCA Civ 118.*

Can the decision be appealed or challenged?

14.92 Given that some significant cases or cases with wider implications are decided by the FOS, there is the potential for decisions to be made during or arising from the process that the firm may wish to challenge, for example, the FOS's decision:

- to uphold a complaint;

- on fair compensation or on the steps the firm is directed to take;

- not to dismiss a complaint the firm believes is ineligible or inappropriate to be resolved by the FOS;

- to hold or not to hold an oral hearing and, if so, whether to hold it in private;

- to exclude certain evidence or allow certain evidence to be included;

- to disclose particular confidential information to the complainant;

- to disclose particular information to the FCA or to use it for some other purpose.

14.93 As noted at para **14.26** above, there are different ways to challenge the FOS. If necessary, although there is no right to appeal a final determination of the FOS[1], it is possible to challenge a decision by judicial review[2]. That is not easy and the grounds for review are limited, for example, that the decision is illegal, irrational or improper, or that the process contravenes the ECHR fair trial guarantees or other rights that the firm has under the ECHR[3]. It is generally speaking very difficult to make a successful judicial review application against a FOS decision, not least because the tests to be applied by the FOS under the FSMA 2000[4] leave a considerable margin for the exercise of judgement, in which the courts will not readily intervene[5], and because the courts traditionally allow bodies like the FOS to determine for themselves what weight to attach to particular relevant factors (for example, in the case of the FOS, the law or the FCA rules)[6]. That said, there may be circumstances when a court would intervene, for example, if the FOS exceeded its jurisdiction or made an irrational decision. In practice, the choice whether or not to bring a judicial review may depend on whether the issue that arises is a 'black letter law' issue such as a question about the interpretation of the FSMA 2000 or the DISP rules, or a question of the FOS's exercise of a discretion, such as its power to decide cases based on what it considers to be fair and reasonable. It is particularly difficult to win a judicial review turning on the second type of issue. However, there may also be other cases where the purpose of the judicial review is not necessarily to succeed in the case at hand but is aimed instead at clarifying the law or persuading the FOS to behave more appropriately or transparently in future cases.

1 In effect, though, the complainant does have a right to appeal the FOS's substantive decision because he can reject the decision and try again in another forum: see para **14.90** above. In *R v Financial Ombudsman Service, ex p Ropaigealach [2004] EWCA Civ 1011* a complainant has also unsuccessfully tried to review judicially a decision of the FOS not to uphold his complaint. It should also be noted that the scheme operator, the FOS and its staff are, generally speaking, immune from liability in damages for anything done in the discharge of the FOS's functions. For the detailed provisions, see the FSMA 2000, Sch 17, para 10 and the rules at DISP 4.2.8. The similar provisions relating to the FCA are discussed at para **21.36** ff below.
2 See further the discussion at para **21.16** ff below.
3 As the discussion above indicates, the process raises a number of potential ECHR compliance issues, including: (i) the potentially arbitrary nature of the tests applied in determining whether the firm is liable (see para **14.77** above) and, if so, the amount of compensation it must pay (see paras **14.83** ff above); and (ii) the ability of the complainant, but not the firm, to choose whether or not the decision is binding (see para **14.90** above). If the FOS did act in a manner that was incompatible with the ECHR, the firm may have a right to bring a damages claim against it under the Human Rights Act 1998.
4 Of what is 'fair and reasonable' and what would be 'fair compensation': see para **14.91** ff above.
5 For example, in *Norwich and Peterborough Building Society v Financial Ombudsman Service Ltd [2002] EWHC 2379* the firm sought to overturn a decision of the FOS where the FOS had used a concept of the 'relative onerousness' of difficult accounts to, effectively, inform its view or what was fair. This was challenged as a 'meaningless enquiry' into a question of the FOS's own devising which was incapable of any logically verifiable answer. Whilst the FOS disagreed with the description only to the extent of the word 'meaningless', the court was not prepared to disrupt the FOS's decision. See also *Ex p Legal & General [2000] 1 WLR 1524* in which the court concluded that the Pensions Ombudsman's decision was on the margins of rationality.
6 See *Tesco Stores Ltd v Secretary of State for the Environment [1995] 1 WLR 759* discussed at para **21.24**, n 3 below and *IFG Financial Services [2005] EWHC 1153* as discussed at para **14.84**, n 2 above.

Is the decision or any other FOS information made public?

14.94 On 1 April 2013, a new provision came into force requiring the scheme operator to publish its final determinations, subject to narrow exceptions[1]. As a result, in July 2013 the FOS began the systematic publication of all ombudsman decisions on complaints made to it. Before then, the public record of FOS decision-making was highly selective. It was based on very brief reports in its newsletter and a small selection of determinations. The situation is very different now. In the first three months following July 2013 the FOS published an average of more than 2,000 decisions per month. A considerable body of FOS 'case law' has therefore now been published. Only cases which get to the stage of a final ombudsman determination are included. As noted above, firms need to be familiar with these decisions, although that is not easy in practical terms[2].

1 FSMA 2000, s 230A. There is an exception if the ombudsman who makes the determination informs the scheme operator that in his or her opinion it is inappropriate to publish the determination and the scheme operator may not include the name of the complainant in the publication unless the complainant agrees.
2 See para **14.5** above.

14.95 The FOS also publishes complaints handling statistics on its website, including uphold rates for individual firms with sufficiently high FOS referral rates. The rates record cases where the FOS has 'made a change in favour of the customer' – although this includes cases where firms have settled cases after they have been referred to the FOS, for example because customers have provided new information.

How is the decision enforced?

14.96 Firms are required[1] to comply promptly with any money award and any directions made by the FOS and also with any settlement which it agrees at an earlier stage of the proceedings. In relation to firms, compliance with this rule is enforceable in the same way as an FCA rule[2]. In relation to unauthorised businesses, compliance may be enforceable by an injunction requiring the firm to remedy the breach on an application by the FCA[3].

1 See the FCA Handbook at DISP 3.7.12.
2 It constitutes a requirement imposed by or under the FSMA 2000, breach of which may have the consequences outlined at para **2.94** ff above. See, for example, the *Tudor House First Supervisory Notice (1/11/02)* in which the FCA decided because of the firm's failure to comply with FOS awards to vary the permission granted to the firm by removing all regulated activities with immediate effect. The FOS may report a breach by an authorised firm to the FCA: see para **14.29** above.
3 FSMA 2000, s 380 and see para **8.138** ff above.

14.97 A FOS award made under the compulsory jurisdiction is enforceable directly by the court. A money award can be enforced by execution in the same way as an order of a county court[1] and a direction is enforceable by injunction[2]. An award made under the voluntary jurisdiction is also enforceable in court by the complainant[3].

1 FSMA 2000, Sch 17, para 16.
2 FSMA 2000, s 229(9).
3 See the FCA Handbook at DISP 4.2.5.

Chapter 15   Product and market intervention

INTRODUCTION

15.1   A key aspect of the reforms introduced by the Financial Services Act 2012, and the attendant amendments to the Regulators' powers under the FSMA 2000, is a shift towards more proactive regulation.

15.2   There has been a spate of issues in recent years relating to the sale of financial products and services in circumstances where the products or services in question were inappropriate for the customers who bought them, or where the sales processes through which they were sold were found to be flawed. The most highly publicised example is payment protection insurance, but there have been a number of others.

15.3   The Government's policy, and the Regulator's focus, has moved away from simply responding to these issues. Rather, they want to stop such issues arising. Accordingly, the FCA acquired powers to intervene, to stop or amend products, financial promotions and market practices and, where possible, will do so swiftly, unhampered by a significant amount of process or checks and balances, so as to minimise the harm to consumers.

15.4   Policy-makers considered that the FSA's very limited remit to consider competition matters (it was supposed to 'have regard' to competition) revealed a significant omission from the FSA regime. Accordingly, in addition to its focus on product design and development, the FCA has an express mandate to consider the market from a competition perspective – the idea being that such an approach should drive better market conduct in the interests of consumers. The FCA, therefore, looks not only at the conduct of individual firms, but also at the operation of the markets within which those firms do business.

What is the FCA trying to achieve?

15.5   It has been part of the Regulator's policy for several years, as part of the 'TCF' (treating customers fairly) initiative, that firms should consider their customers' interests from the product design and development stage through to marketing, the sales process, and beyond. However, in practice thematic work and enforcement activity tended to focus on sales processes. The shift of focus, and in particular the new powers, seem to be part of an effort to make sure that the policy of considering the broader 'lifecycle' of financial products is effected. The FCA is also bringing greater focus to bear on the governance processes that firms have in relation to financial products, and on the responsibilities of senior management for overseeing the relevant areas of business. The aim is to ensure, through all these means, that firms really do consider and reflect their customers' interests throughout the process of conceiving, developing and marketing products, and after products have been sold.

15.6   In practice the FCA sees itself identifying and responding to potential problems before they affect customers. By its nature, this involves judgements being made about risks that may not have crystallised, and those judgements being used to inform a rather direct intervention in firms' businesses. This approach creates the potential for disputes much earlier than in an enforcement process and, as will be seen, the FCA's powers permit it often to take immediate action so that such disputes do not impede its regulatory functions.

How will the FCA go about achieving its objectives?

15.7   The creation of the FCA was more than a rebranding exercise; there were significant changes to the structure of the Regulator as well as to some of its processes. Among the structural changes was the creation of a 'Policy, Risk and Research', division, which takes the lead with the FCA's thematic work, and its efforts to understand trends and tendencies within the market for financial services. This reflects the Regulator's revised focus, now looking not only at the activities of individual firms, but also continuing the developing trend of looking at what is happening in the markets more generally. It also reflects the FCA's intention to develop a 'radar' for problems – seeking out and intercepting risks to customers rather than responding to harm to customers.

15.8   This approach could, if the FCA does not exercise some restraint, increase the risk of retrospective sanctions and redress. Risks to customers are, in this environment, identified in a more sophisticated way than simply looking for breaches of rules (or even undesirable 'outcomes' caused by poor firm conduct). So, there must be a prospect that real risks will be identified which do not reflect breaches of existing rules, or transgressions of what the FCA has hitherto considered acceptable. In fact, that is precisely why the FCA has been given its new intervention powers. In principle, the new powers permit the FCA to identify problems and require change in the future, without finding that past conduct amounts to rule breaches. It ought to be possible for the FCA to identify a risk and, by agreement with firms or by using its intervention powers, to put a stop to that risk without taking formal enforcement action against any of the firms involved in respect of their past activities, or requiring them to pay redress. However, in the current political climate, and in light of the broad scope often given to Principle 6 of the Principles for Businesses, the FCA may not always distinguish sufficiently clearly between retrospective and prospective standards.

15.9   The impact for firms and practitioners is that a new arena of regulatory disputes looks set to arise and much earlier in the product cycle. Once the FCA has identified a need (in its view) for changes to be made to particular products or markets, it will often want to make those changes swiftly so as to mitigate the risk of consumer detriment. Firms may disagree with the FCA's analysis, which often will be judgmental and may be done at a time when there has been no consumer detriment. However, there is little appetite for protracted disputes that would prevent the FCA from taking the steps that it considers necessary. The FCA has a broad suite of powers, which in many cases it is able to exercise pre-emptively (with any dispute being resolved only subsequently). The temporary intervention power for intervening regarding specific products has attracted a certain amount of attention, but that is only one aspect of the FCA's toolkit.

15.10   The intervention powers discussed in this chapter push back even further the role of caveat emptor in the provision of financial services. Wholesale activities have traditionally not attracted much regulatory attention, but expectations are that Regulators will increasingly focus on malpractice in those markets as ultimately detrimental to consumers[1]. The consequences will be significant for firms, as the Regulators focus increasingly on underlying governance issues, at both firm and sectoral levels.

1 See, for example the FCA's focus on the market for structured products.

15.11   The FCA may use its various powers of intervention before, and in addition to, its wider enforcement powers. The new intervention powers, which are discussed in this chapter, are powers to intervene in financial products and markets and to intervene in financial promotions. However, there remains a variety of tools at the FCA's disposal, including those referred to at para **15.15** ff below.

15.12   In considering this wider toolkit, firms should consider the practical steps they can take to manage the risks associated with being found to be in breach of the rules, or of the FCA deciding to use its formal powers against a firm or in relation to its products. As discussed below in relation to the FCA's intervention powers in respect of financial products and financial promotions (see below at paras **15.35** ff and **15.80** ff respectively), there are practical steps that can be taken to manage the risks which will arise if the FCA identifies and voices concerns about a firm's products or practices.

15.13 Those parts of a firm's business which are likely to be subject to regulatory scrutiny (increasingly, firms might think that is all of their business) can be mindful of the FCA's approach and ensure they are aware of the same issues that the FCA's 'radar' function is considering. In particular, firms can:

- ensure express consideration is given to customers' best interests (some firms will be doing this already, but it is worth considering whether such processes are documented adequately, whether they reflect a real practice or are 'box-ticking' exercises, and whether they can be demonstrated in a way that would resonate with the FCA); and

- monitor and, where appropriate, respond to the public output of the FCA's radar function (ie by reviewing published thematic reviews and market studies and ensuring that their findings, where appropriate, are addressed and incorporated into their practices and their products).

15.14 These approaches cannot guarantee that a firm will not come under intense regulatory scrutiny and firms (particularly high profile firms) already expect that to happen as a matter of course. Nevertheless, these approaches ought to ensure that when a firm does come under scrutiny, and if the FCA does raise specific concerns, the firm understands those concerns and can address them in a manner consistent with the FCA's approach. The 'persuasion' approach is about a conversation and if a firm is already speaking the FCA's language then that conversation is more likely to be productive.

THE WIDER TOOLKIT

Consensual intervention

15.15 Firms will be familiar with the Regulator's practice of raising specific concerns through the supervisory relationship and seeking action on a consensual basis, eg customer contact programmes and offers of compensation for widespread problems or changes to products, product literature or sales processes. Firms can be persuaded to take this sort of action in large part because of the threat (whether implied or explicit) that the FCA will use its formal powers (whether through the enforcement process or otherwise) against the firm if it does not cooperate.

15.16 The FCA's toolkit is growing, and the Regulator's willingness to use its tools and to use them quickly is growing too. Nevertheless, and perhaps because of this, firms can expect the 'persuasion' approach to continue to be common. With an increased range of options available to the FCA – and with that, an increased number of ways firms may be adversely and publicly affected through the use of formal powers – there is also an increased number of ways in which the FCA can seek to persuade firms to make changes and take action.

15.17   The most efficient way for the FCA to achieve its objective will often be to reach an effective agreement that resolves the issue. So the FCA will typically use this approach in the first instance, except for cases where the circumstances and the perceived urgency of the situation, or limitations on what it can achieve by agreement with individual firms, require it to take formal action, eg by using the new powers of intervention discussed in this chapter.

Rule changes

15.18   One of the primary means by which the FCA directs the conduct of firms in relation to particular sub-sectors or product types is by making rules. The Regulator has long had very wide powers of rule-making, and has made rules that apply to particular products (eg mortgages) or sub-sectors (eg insurance). The power to do so has been made more specific in the FSMA 2000, which now contains a series of powers for making particular types of rules. Those include (in s 137D) so-called 'product intervention' rules, ie rules prohibiting firms from, among other things, entering into certain types of agreements with any person or specified persons or entering into specific agreements unless requirements in the rules have been satisfied.

15.19   Rule-making has typically been a slow process because of the requirements for consultation and a cost benefit analysis. That remains the case. However, as outlined at para **15.30** ff below, in certain circumstances the FCA can now dispense with those elements and make rules urgently on a temporary basis. The increased regulatory and political focus on conduct in retail markets, and on the need for greater regulatory intervention, means that it is likely that future rule changes and new areas of specific regulation may be more focussed on particular products than was previously the case.

Own initiative powers

15.20   As discussed in detail in **Chapter 16**, the FCA has very broad powers to impose requirements or directions on firms by varying (at its own initiative) the firm's regulatory permission. This power can be exercised where it appears to the FCA desirable to do so in order to advance one or more of its operational objectives, which include the objective of securing an appropriate degree of protection for consumers and the objective of promoting effective competition in the interests of consumers. In appropriate circumstances, therefore, the variation of a firm's permission is one route that may be open to the FCA to achieve an intervention in relation to a particular firm. There is little by way of express limitation on what can be achieved using this power. For example, it could, if appropriate, be used to prevent a firm from continuing to sell a particular product, or to discontinue a particular feature of a product, or potentially even to effect a more structural change in the interests of competition. In principle, it is thought that this power should only be used in serious situations, and where the firm is willing to agree to a course of action. However, as discussed in **Chapter 16**, the statutory hurdles for the use of the power are not particularly demanding.

Intervention powers: financial products and markets

15.21 Perhaps the most dramatic new tools in the FCA's kit are its powers to intervene in relation to financial products (particularly on a swift and temporary basis) and to intervene in markets for financial services (ie its new competition role). In para **15.22** ff below, the key aspects of these new powers are considered. Further below, at paras **15.86** ff (intervention in financial products) and **15.101** ff (intervention in markets), the process associated with these powers is discussed in greater detail.

INTERVENTION IN FINANCIAL PRODUCTS

Context and background

15.22 The FCA has 'general' product intervention powers and 'temporary' product intervention powers. Only the temporary powers are discussed in any detail here, because it is these that permit the FCA to make rules without consultation and, therefore, to take the sort of swift, pre-emptive action which is the focus of this chapter.

15.23 The aim of these product intervention powers is to allow the FCA to tackle issues relating to specific products (or types of products), product features or marketing practices relating to specific products. Product intervention rules might include requiring changes to or the inclusion or exclusion of certain product features, amendments to promotional materials, restrictions on sales or marketing, and in serious cases, a ban on sales or marketing of a product in relation to all or some types of customer[1].

1 FSA Policy Statement (PS13/3), 'The FCA's use of temporary product intervention rules', March 2013 (the 'Policy Statement'), para 10.

15.24 The FCA's temporary product intervention powers should be viewed in the context of a major shift in the approach to retail financial services regulation, that has occurred in the UK in response to the financial crisis that commenced in 2008.

15.25 The FSA acknowledged that its philosophy prior to the financial crisis had been to accept that most retail financial products were suitable for some consumers and so it should not intervene in their design[1]. The FSA had considered that its role was to make rules and supervise the market at the point-of-sale to stop products reaching the wrong consumers, rather than questioning their design. The FSA admitted that this approach had not always achieved the right customer outcomes and, in some high profile cases, there had been significant consumer detriment.

1 FSA, Discussion Paper (DP11/1) 'Product Intervention' (January 2011).

15.26 From March 2010, the FSA began to adopt a more intrusive and interventionist approach which involved acting earlier in the product life cycle to try to prevent detriment before it occurred. As a consequence of this, the FSA began to regard product intervention as an essential part of effective regulation[1]. Then, in February 2011, the Treasury announced that the FCA would be given powers to make the temporary product intervention rules described above[2]. The Treasury made clear that the Government believed a more proactive, interventionist approach was essential to effective retail conduct regulation, so that actual or potential risk is acted upon before it crystallises in significant detriment. The temporary product intervention rules, eventually enacted into the FSMA 2000, are therefore a direct product of the new proactive and interventionist regulatory regime.

1 FSA, Discussion Paper (DP11/1) 'Product Intervention' (January 2011).
2 HM Treasury, Consultation paper, 'A new approach to financial regulation: building a stronger future' (17 February 2011).

15.27 These powers represent a new tool which the FCA did not have before the amendments made by the Financial Services Act 2012 to the FSMA 2000. The FSA had previously relied upon its supervisory powers in order to intervene in the product distribution processes of firms. In doing so, it had relied primarily upon its statutory enforcement powers to supervise the market at the point of sale (for example, by dealing with sales practice violations). However, these new powers allow the FCA to intervene not only in the sale but also in the design of particular products, even if it is not considering any particular rule breach or enforcement action. In the case of the temporary product intervention powers, the intention is that they will allow prompt and decisive action to be taken by the FCA before any consumer detriment has occurred.

15.28 The FCA can make product intervention rules on a temporary basis and, when it does so, the requirements for public consultation do not apply[1]. The FCA must specify a period for which temporary product intervention rules will apply, not to be more than 12 months. Temporary product intervention rules are intended to offer protection to consumers in the short term, allowing the FCA or the industry to develop a more permanent solution.

1 In contrast, when exercising its general product intervention powers the FCA is required to consult the market (FSMA 2000, s 138I).

15.29 Having made a set of temporary product intervention rules, the FCA cannot make further temporary rules with the same or substantially the same provisions for 12 months after the first rules cease to have effect. However, the FCA may use its powers in relation to general product intervention rules to create a new permanent rule to replace the temporary product intervention rule from the date on which the temporary rule ceases to have effect. This exercise would be subject to the procedural requirements for general rules, including public consultation.

When are temporary product intervention rules likely to be used?

15.30 The FCA can make temporary product intervention rules if:

- the test for a general product intervention rule is satisfied (ie it appears to the FCA to be necessary and expedient for the FCA to make such rules for the purpose of advancing the consumer protection objective, the competition objective, or, if applicable, the market integrity objective); and

- the FCA considers it necessary or expedient not to consult for the purpose of advancing the consumer protection objective or the competition objective, or, if applicable, the market integrity objective[1]. The FCA has indicated that its main consideration in this regard will generally be whether prompt action is necessary to reduce or prevent consumer detriment[2].

1 FSMA 2000, s 138M(1).
2 Policy Statement, para 19.

15.31 The FCA has made clear in its Policy Statement that in applying this test, it will have regard to the same principles it would consider in connection with general product intervention rules. These include:

- general considerations, including whether the proposed rules are appropriate and effective, proportionate and deliverable, compatible with the FCA's competition objective, supported by sufficient and appropriate evidence, transparent, and likely to be beneficial for consumers, when taken as a whole;

- the risk that the rules have a negative impact on protected groups in the Equality Act 2010 and whether the rules can promote equality and good relations;

- contextual factors, such as the potential scale of detriment in the market (potentially large customer base: product intervention more likely), the potential scale of detriment to individual customers (high detriment for individual customers: product intervention more likely), social context (detriment for particular groups of customers, eg in particular, vulnerable groups: product intervention more likely), market context (market mechanisms eg information disclosure and competition do not always work to protect consumers), and possible unintended consequences[1];

- competition considerations, including whether the rule can promote effective competition in the interests of consumers, whether the rule may have a negative impact on competition factors such as product innovation and barriers to entry for new market participants, whether any negative impact on competition factors is proportionate to the aims of the rule, whether alternative solutions may deliver the same intended outcome while having a more positive impact on competition, and the overall effect of a proposed rule on competition in the market for financial services, having regard to the interests of consumers;

- the regulatory principles set out in the FSMA 2000, s 3B, which include:

  - that the FCA should use its resources in the most efficient and economic way;

  - that burdens or restrictions on persons or activities should be proportionate to the benefits expected to result from those burdens or restrictions;

- the desirability of sustainable economic growth in the medium or long term;

- that consumers should take responsibility for their decisions; and

- that the FCA should exercise its functions as transparently as possible; and

• how proposed new rules fit within the wider EU legislative framework.

1 Policy Statement, para 22.

15.32 Temporary product intervention rules have not been used to date. However, some of the instances in which the FCA might consider making temporary product intervention rules include[1]:

• where a product is in serious danger of being sold to the wrong customers, for instance where complex or niche products are sold to the mass market;

• where a non-essential feature of a product seems to be causing serious problems for consumers; and

• where a product is inherently flawed.

1 FSA Press Release FSA/PN/028/2013, 'FSA confirms approach to using temporary product intervention rules that will be used by the FCA'.

15.33 Likely examples of past instances where temporary product intervention rules might have been used if they were available include single premium payment protection insurance and structured capital at risk products.

15.34 It appears likely that the power to make temporary product intervention rules will not be used often by the FCA: the Regulator has said that, in most situations, it will expect to consult on permanent rules[1] and Martin Wheatley, the FCA's chief executive, has said that, while he does not expect the FCA to use these powers frequently, the FCA will not hesitate to use them when it has serious concerns[2].

1 Policy Statement, para 1.6.
2 FSA Press Release FSA/PN/028/2013, 'FSA confirms approach to using temporary product intervention rules that will be used by the FCA'.

Practical points for firms

15.35 One of the reasons why the FCA will not expect to use this power frequently is because it will expect firms typically to agree to the course of action that it proposes. The existence of the power, and the ease with which it can be used by the FCA, thus acts as a potent encouragement to firms to reach an agreement with the FCA.

15.36 In practice, the lack of consultation and of any cost benefit analysis will be of serious concern to firms. The FCA's focus will typically be on the need for expeditious action to be taken to prevent detriment or further detriment to consumers. The impact upon the market of taking action without ensuring that the potential consequences of that action have fully been considered will be much less of a consideration. That is an area which the industry will often wish to focus upon. It may be that there are negative collateral consequences for competition or the market which could affect consumers, and which will not be the immediate focus of the FCA.

15.37   Whilst in principle rules made in this way can only subsist for up to 12 months, and there will need to be a full consultation exercise so that permanent rules can be made, it may well be that in practice the effect of the temporary rules is to cause a permanent change in the market. For example, it may be that temporarily banning a particular product will permanently remove it from the market. So, the prospect of a subsequent consultation exercise is unlikely to be of much assistance. Firms should take every opportunity to engage with the FCA before the temporary intervention rules are made, irrespective of the lack of a formal public consultation.

INTERVENTION IN MARKETS – THE FCA'S NEW COMPETITION ROLE

Context and background

15.38   As briefly noted above, it is intended that promoting competition in financial services markets should be a central part of the FCA's role. This has two primary parts:

- investigating markets and firm behaviour to assess whether competition is operating effectively; and

- seeking to ensure that the FCA's approach and use of its powers is, insofar as possible, consistent with the promotion of competition in financial markets.

15.39   The importance of this new competition role has been underlined by the fact that even since the FCA began its operations in April 2013, the Government has decided to add to its powers, by giving it powers concurrent with those of the generalist competition regulators to enforce the provisions of the Competition Act 1998 to investigate and sanction anti-competitive agreements and abuse of a dominant position.

15.40   This means that there are two central strands to the FCA's new competition role, both of which are highly significant. The first of those two strands is the FCA's market review role. The primary means by which the FCA will pursue its competition objective is through market studies. These will investigate whether competition in a market is operating effectively in the interests of consumers – although they could also pick up non-competition issues such as whether customers are being treated fairly. As explained further below, these market studies are expected to be significantly more in-depth and intrusive than traditional thematic reviews.

15.41   The following issues – which broadly mirror those that a competition authority would be expected to look at in a similar context – typically come under scrutiny in a market study[1]:

- market power held by suppliers;

- problems in the flow of information between market participants;

- low switching rates;

- costs or benefits which are not captured in the product price (known as 'externalities');

- problems in the way that consumers or firms make decisions[2];

- too little consumption (ie consumers are not purchasing products from which they would derive value, eg because they find them difficult to understand or access); and

- existing regulation.

1 FCA Guidance 'The FCA's Approach to Advancing its Objectives' (July 2013), pp 38–39. See also FCA, 'How we carry out market studies', October 2013, pp 3–4, and Annex 1 to FSA Consultation (CP12/35) on the FCA's use of temporary product intervention rules (December 2012).
2 This issue draws on the discipline of behavioural economics, which the FCA has indicated will be an important analytical underpinning for its work. See in particular FCA Occasional Paper No 1 on applying behavioural economics at the FCA (April 2013), pp 14–15.

15.42   A number of formal or informal sources of information may trigger market intervention by the FCA. These may include market intelligence gathered by the FCA on its own initiative, complaints from customers or market participants, issues raised by the FCA Panels, political or other public pressures, or super-complaints[1].

1 FCA Guidance 'The FCA's Approach to Advancing its Objectives' (July 2013), pp 40–41.

15.43   The last of these sources, super-complaints, are a formal mechanism pursuant to which the FCA is obliged to consider whether it should take action to address market issues. The super-complaint mechanism is put in place by the FSMA 2000, s 234C. A similar scheme has existed in relation to competition complaints to the OFT[1] since 2004. A super-complaint may be made by one or more of a number of bodies specified by Order by the Treasury. At the time of writing, the following organisations had applied for, and obtained from the Treasury, super-complainant status: Citizens' Advice; the consumers' association 'Which'; the Consumer Council Northern Ireland; and the Federation of Small Businesses. The FSMA 2000 provides that all designated bodies must be consumer representative organisations. Individual consumers are not permitted to make super-complaints, and business representative bodies will not be designated in the Treasury list as designated bodies unless they can demonstrate that they are also consumer representative bodies.

1 The OFT and Competition Commission merged to become the Competition and Markets Authority on 1 April 2014.

15.44   Product and market intervention

15.44   A super-complaint can be made where 'a feature, or combination of features, of a market in the United Kingdom for financial services is, or appears to be, significantly damaging the interests of consumers'[1]. The FCA will confirm that this condition is met when assessing any super-complaint. FCA guidance also explains that a super-complaint should be identified as such and should be supported, where possible, by documented facts and evidence[2].

1   FSMA 2000, s 234C(1).
2   FCA 'Guidance for designated Consumer Bodies on making a Super-Complaint under s 234C' (June 2013), para 1.6.

15.45   When a super-complaint is made, the FCA is obliged to respond formally to the super-complaint within 90 days by providing details of how it proposes to respond to it and what action the FCA proposes to take (or, if it proposes to take no action, why that is the case)[1]. The FCA's decision will be published.

1   FSMA 2000, s 234E.

15.46   HM Treasury has published guidance for designated bodies considering making a super-complaint to the FCA[1], and the FCA has published guidance on how it will handle super-complaints[2]. The FCA has indicated that, in practice, it would expect the designated body to raise its concerns informally before making a super-complaint, and it may be that those discussions could eliminate the need for a super-complaint (eg if the FCA agrees to investigate the issue in any case).

1   HM Treasury, 'Guidance for bodies seeking designation as super-complainants to the Financial Conduct Authority' (March 2013).
2   FCA 'Guidance for designated Consumer Bodies on making a Super-Complaint under s 234C' (June 2013).

15.47   Under the general competition regime, an average of one super-complaint has been made each year since the regime's inception. Several of these have related to financial services markets. The FCA has informally indicated that it would expect designated bodies considering making a super-complaint to approach both the FCA and Competition and Markets Authority (CMA) in cases where it could fall within the competition remit of either body, and the two bodies have agreed to co-operate with one another in relation to a super-complaint, which could fall within the remit of either[1].

1   Memorandum of Understanding between the Office of Fair Trading and the Financial Conduct Authority (2 April 2013).

15.48   There are three principal (and, to some extent, overlapping) structures for markets work by the FCA: thematic reviews; market studies; and market investigation references. These structures are considered each in their turn below.

Thematic reviews

15.49   Thematic reviews are familiar from the pre-FCA regime. They are a flexible tool designed to allow the FCA to gather information from market participants to facilitate an investigation into a specific topic. They generally go beyond the activities of any single market participant and focus instead on cross-cutting or market-wide issues. Also, they are not governed by any specific legal regime, but are conducted pursuant to the FCA's general information gathering powers[1].

1   FSMA 2000, s 165.

15.50   The FCA says it undertakes thematic projects to assess current and future risks in relation to a particular issue or product, across a number of firms, within a specific part of the sector, or at market level, as appropriate[1]. So, thematic reviews are designed to aid the FCA's understanding of a market, rather than necessarily being a prelude to any intervention (although it is not out of the question that intervention could result if the FCA uncovers issues of concern). A thematic review may be a prelude to a market study (as has already been the case with the insurance add-on products thematic review/market study), or, conceivably, to a request to the CMA to make a market investigation reference.

1   FCA Thematic Reviews TR13/1, 'Motor Legal Expenses Insurance (MLEI)' (6 June 2013); TR13/2, 'Mobile phone insurance – ensuring a fair deal for customers' (27 June 2013); and TR13/3, 'Banks' control of financial crime risks in trade finance' (1 July 2013): all expressly state this objective on p 3 in each document.

Market studies

15.51   Market studies are new to the new regime. They share many of the same features of thematic reviews, but are generally expected to be more in-depth, more concentrated on competition issues, and possibly more likely to result in intervention by the FCA. The FCA has indicated that it will use market studies as the main tool for examining competition issues in the markets it regulates[1].

1   FCA Paper 'How we carry out market studies' (October 2013), p 1.

15.52   Action the FCA may take may include both structural (eg forcing divestments), or behavioural (eg requiring unbundling) measures[1]. Although the FCA stresses that structural measures will be considered where the issues identified would not be adequately addressed through less intrusive options, the statement that the FCA may impose structural remedies such as divestments is particularly striking. While the FSMA 2000 does not contain an express provision to this effect, the FCA could arguably seek to invoke its powers under the FSMA 2000, s 55L (the 'own initiative requirement power') – part of its firm-specific enforcement powers – to impose a divestment requirement.

1   FCA Paper 'How we carry out market studies' (October 2013), p 5.

15.53   The FCA has indicated that it expects that market studies will last for between six months and a year[1]. As noted above, they may be preceded by preparatory work (including in the form of a thematic review). There is no statutory deadline for the FCA to complete a market study.

1   FCA Paper 'How we carry out market studies' (October 2013), p 4.

15.54 Product and market intervention

15.54 The avenues for challenging any remedies imposed in the context of a market study will be specific to the particular instrument chosen (if any) by the FCA to enact the remedy. The potential avenues for challenge will be addressed elsewhere in this work[1].

1 Challenges to the use of competition powers are not addressed specifically but see **CHAPTER 12** for the Tribunal process and **CHAPTER 21** for other avenues for challenging the FCA.

Market investigations

15.55 A market investigation is a formal and in-depth review by the CMA of a particular market and whether features of that market are operating to prevent, restrict or distort competition. The process is already widely in use under the Enterprise Act 2002 – for markets that include financial services markets. The CMA commences such market investigations upon reference from what was the OFT (and is now part of the CMA) (or, exceptionally, the Secretary of State).

15.56 Under the Financial Services (Banking Reform) Act 2013 (FS(BR)A 2013), the FCA has the power to make a reference for a market investigation directly to the CMA. However, at the time of writing, this legislation has not come into force and, pending this, the FCA must rely on its existing power to ask the OFT (which is now part of the CMA) to make a market investigation reference[1]. The CMA has discretion as to whether or not to make such a reference, but in practice it will place considerable weight on the FCA's pre-existing work.

1 FSMA 2000, s 234H.

15.57 Given the FCA's extensive remedy powers[1], it may be more likely that the FCA will refer a matter to the CMA with a recommendation that a market investigation reference should be made where the market participants involved are not (or are not all) regulated under the FSMA 2000 (where the FCA would be precluded from using many of its remedy powers).

1 See para **15.15** above.

15.58 The market investigation regime has extensive remedy powers[1]. These include the power to mandate firms to take (or refrain from taking) particular steps; this may also include structural action[2]. Remedies in completed investigations have included greater and/or clearer information for consumers[3] and a ban on certain means of selling particular products[4].

1 See the Enterprise Act 2002, s 138(2).
2 There is only one recent market investigation, in which structural remedies have been required, which was outside the financial services sphere: see the Competition Commission's BAA airports markets investigation, final report published 19 March 2009.
3 See, in particular, the Competition Commission's Personal current account services in Northern Ireland market investigation, report published 15 May 2007.
4 See, in particular, the Competition Commission's Payment protection insurance market investigation, report published 29 January 2009.

Co-ordination with other regulatory bodies

15.59   The FCA's market work may involve overlap with the work of other regulators – in particular with the work of the CMA (part of which was the OFT before 1 April 2014) in the exercise of its competition objective.

15.60   The FCA and OFT have published a Memorandum of Understanding on how the FCA and CMA will co-ordinate their work[1]. This explains in particular that, in fields where their roles may overlap, they will co-ordinate such that the body which is 'best placed' to act should take the lead role. This will be assessed by taking into account: (a) which organisation has the more appropriate powers to take the lead on the issue in question; and (b) whether the previous work of one of the bodies indicates that it is best placed to take the lead on a particular issue[2]. In subsequent guidance, the FCA has indicated that it will attempt to refer relevant cases to the CMA 'at an early stage in the process' to prevent duplication of effort[3].

1 Memorandum of Understanding between the Office of Fair Trading and the Financial Conduct Authority (2 April 2013). The Memorandum of Understanding incorporates a Concordat which sets out greater details of how the two bodies will co-operate.
2 Memorandum of Understanding between the Office of Fair Trading and the Financial Conduct Authority (2 April 2013). The Memorandum of Understanding incorporates a Concordat which sets out greater details of how the two bodies will co-operate.
3 FCA Guidance 'The FCA's Approach to Advancing its Objectives' (July 2013), p 42.

Concurrent competition powers

15.61   The second central strand to the FCA's new competition role is its 'concurrent powers' role. The FS(BR)A 2013 provides for competition powers concurrent with those of the generalist competition regulator under the Competition Act 1998.

15.62   These powers have two parts, known in the Competition Act 1998 rubric as 'Chapter 1 powers' and 'Chapter 2 powers'. Chapter 1 powers relate to anti-competitive agreements including, in particular, cartel agreements relating to, for example, price fixing or market sharing. Chapter 2 powers relate to abuse of a dominant position by a market participant or, exceptionally, participants.

15.63   The FCA's use of these powers could be triggered by most of the factors noted above. In a cartel context, the possibility of a 'tip-off' to the competition authorities (commonly by way of a leniency application) is also a possible trigger[1].

1 Formally, a super-complaint cannot trigger an investigation under the Competition Act 1998 on the basis of the proposed concurrent powers for the FCA. The FCA is obliged to respond to the super-complaint by reference to its FSMA 2000 powers and duties. However, in practice, if a super-complaint were to raise issues relevant to the Chapter 1 or Chapter 2 provisions of the Competition Act 1998, it is likely that the FCA would wish to investigate the matter further.

15.64   It can be expected that the FCA will be keen to make use of these powers and demonstrate its effectiveness (particularly because other sectoral regulators which have been granted such powers have been criticised for their reluctance to use them).

When is the FCA likely to exercise its new competition role?

Proportionality and consultation

15.65   Any intervention must be proportionate to the concerns identified. The FCA's guidance states that it will carry out a detailed assessment of proportionality and will consult on its proposed remedies when required. However, in exceptional circumstances where the FCA identifies a need to act more quickly, remedies may be temporarily implemented before the completion of the market study procedures outlined above[1].

1 See para **15.55** ff above.

Practical tips for firms

15.66   As the FCA takes a 'competition lens' to its work, it will be important for firms to do the same. While real-time comprehensive assessment of competition factors over a product's lifetime would necessarily be challenging, prudent firms will want to have in place processes to assess whether any of their products throw up indicators that competition may not be working effectively. These could include unusual levels of profitability (either for the product as a whole, or for certain customers buying the product), unusual levels of complexity that make it difficult for customers to understand what they are purchasing or to compare competing products, or operation in markets with very few competitors. Where indicators of this sort are present, a prudent firm may wish to take a deeper dive and consider whether any competition risk arises.

15.67   In relation to the FCA's proposed concurrent powers to enforce the Competition Act 1998, it is considered good practice to ensure that competition law compliance training has been put in place for all relevant members of staff (particularly those who have roles facing customers or competitors). To the extent that a firm has not previously put such a training programme in place, the proposed new powers of the FCA to enforce these rules make this more important than ever.

INTERVENTION IN FINANCIAL PROMOTIONS

15.68   Another new tool in the FCA's toolkit is its power to intervene in relation to financial promotions; as with the power to make temporary interventions in financial products, the FCA can exercise this power swiftly and with little formal process. Paragraph **15.69** ff below considers the key aspects of this new power. Further below, para **15.108** discusses the process associated with this power in greater detail.

Context and background

15.69   The FCA's approach to regulating financial promotions reflects an increased focus on ensuring that problematic financial promotions are quickly removed or rectified to minimise harm to consumers. To this end, the FCA has been given a new statutory power formally to direct firms to remove financial promotions from the market or require that they not be used in the first place if the FCA thinks there has been, or is likely to be, a breach of financial promotion rules[1] in respect of the financial promotion.

1   That is, the Conduct of Business Sourcebook 4: Communicating with clients, including financial promotions, and the Principles for Businesses.

15.70   A 'financial promotion' is *'an invitation or inducement to engage in investment activity that is communicated in the course of business'*[1]. This is a reference to the FSMA 2000, s 21, which does not use the term 'financial promotion' but provides that a person may not, in the course of business, communicate an invitation or inducement to engage in investment activity unless they are an authorised person or the content of the communication has been approved for the purpose by an authorised person[2]. Although the FSMA 2000, s 21 does not use the term 'financial promotion', it is commonly referred to as the 'restriction on financial promotions'. In very high level summary, a person must not communicate a financial promotion unless they are authorised by the FCA to do so, or unless the content of the communication is approved by an authorised person, or unless the communication is exempt[3].

1   As defined in the FCA Handbook. Another part of the definition, not reproduced here, relates to communications which are regulated under MiFID.
2   FSMA 2000, s 21(1). The restriction is further explained in the Perimeter Guidance Manual (PERG), Pt 8 in the FCA Handbook.
3   PERG 8.3.1.

15.71   The FSA's approach to regulating financial promotions was said to be risk-based and proportionate, informed by factors such as the type of product being promoted, the distribution channel, the target market and the scale of potential harm. The FSA might have intervened in relation to the promotion of low-risk financial products where they were mass marketed to the general public, as well as in relation to high-risk financial products marketed to a smaller audience.

15.72   In the past, the FSA used a range of approaches to intervention and the method by which it chose to intervene, including in relation to financial promotions, was said to be informed by risk and considerations of proportionality in each case. This included direct approaches to firms to require the withdrawal or alteration of high-risk financial promotions, visits to firms to investigate potential systems and controls failures, formal enforcement action, and thematic reviews of particular products or markets to investigate whether there are wider market-level issues and risks.

15.73   The FCA's approach to regulating financial promotions has an increased focus on ensuring that problematic financial promotions are quickly removed or rectified to minimise harm to consumers. To this end, the FCA has been given a new statutory power to formally direct firms to remove financial promotions from the market or require that they not be used in the first place if the FCA thinks there has been, or is likely to be, a breach of financial promotion rules[1] in respect of the financial promotion.

1 That is, the Conduct of Business Sourcebook 4: Communicating with clients, including financial promotions, and the Principles for Businesses.

15.74   The relevant provision is the FSMA 2000, s 137S. The key part of that section provides as follows:

(1)   The FCA may give a direction under this section if –

    (a)   an authorised person has made, or proposes to make, a communication or has approved, or proposes to approve, another person's communication, and

    (b)   the FCA considers that there has been, or is likely to be, a contravention of financial promotion rules in respect of the communication or approval.

(2)   A direction under this section may require the authorised person –

    (a)   to withdraw the communication or approval;

    (b)   to refrain from making the communication or giving the approval (whether or not it has previously been made or given);

    (c)   to publish details of the direction;

    (d)   to do anything else specified in the direction in relation to the communication or approval.

When are the FCA's financial product intervention powers likely to be used?

15.75   At the time of writing, the FCA has not publicised any instance of it having used this new power. The power may be exercised if the FCA considers that there has been, or is likely to be, a breach of financial promotion rules in respect of the relevant financial promotion[1].

1 FSMA 2000, s 137S(1)(b).

15.76   How the FSA intends to use this power will need to be learned from experience[1]. Nevertheless, some observations may be made at this stage:

• this power is **a 'pre-emptive' tool** – it has been emphasised that the FCA would be able to remove financial promotions immediately, without going through the enforcement process[2];

• this power is **not only for extreme cases or those that cause great financial loss** – the Regulator has said that the instances in which it will use the power will not only be the worst cases, and the FCA will not always measure harm to consumers in terms of actual or potential financial loss. The FCA will also consider cases that adversely affect consumers' ability to make informed choices and secure the best deal for themselves[3]; and

- this power is **separate from the FCA's general enforcement procedure** – use of the power will be determined by specific promotions and the power will not be used against a firm as a whole. The power can be used on its own or before the FCA takes enforcement action against a firm, and will work separately from the FCA's general disciplinary powers, which – importantly – the FCA will still use when firms fail to comply with the FCA's rules and their overall systems and approach are poor[4]. Accordingly, while the FCA's power to intervene directly in financial promotions is independent of its other general disciplinary powers, that does not mean that those general powers are not relevant to financial promotions – quite the opposite.

1 FSA statistics about that Regulator's use of its powers may indicate how frequently the FCA might be expected to use its intervention powers. Nausicaa Delfas (then the FSA's Head of TCF Strategy, Financial Promotions and Unfair Terms), in a speech titled 'Financial Promotions: Principles in Action' on 20 June 2007 at the FSA Financial Promotions Conference in London, noted that the FSA's intervention had resulted in an average 300 financial promotions a year being swiftly amended or withdrawn, while many more were investigated. It would be surprising if the FCA took an interest in fewer promotions, although that may not translate into a comparable number of instances of the new, formal powers being used as opposed to threatened.
2 FSA Paper 'Journey to the FCA' (31 October 2012), p 14.
3 FSA Paper 'Journey to the FCA' (31 October 2012), p 14.
4 FSA Paper 'Journey to the FCA' (31 October 2012), p 14.

Practical tips for firms

15.77 A firm's options for resisting intervention in relation to financial promotions are limited, but there are things firms can do to mitigate their exposure to the risks. A firm's marketing functions can (presumably in conjunction with its product design and development functions) operate consistently with the FCA's approach and ensure it is aware of the same issues that the FCA's 'radar' function is considering. In particular, firms can:

- ensure express consideration is given to customers' best interests in designing financial promotions; and

- monitor and, where appropriate, respond to the relevant public output of the FCA's radar function (ie by reviewing published thematic reviews and market studies and ensuring that their findings, where appropriate, are reflected in firms' communications with their customers)[1].

1 It is also worthwhile being aware of thematic reviews and market studies that are under way but have not yet been reported.

15.78 These approaches cannot guarantee that a firm's financial promotions will not be subject to intervention, but they ought to make it less likely.

15.79 Where the FCA does intend to intervene, it is likely to engage – where appropriate and if time permits – with the firm first. It will be important to take a constructive approach to that engagement so as to resolve the matter if possible without a formal direction being made. If the firm can show the FCA that it is operating in an appropriate way, and is ready to respond appropriately to concerns that are expressed, then that should improve its prospect of reaching a consensual resolution.

Issues to consider

15.80 When the FCA makes clear that it has concerns about a particular financial promotion, whether in a formal direction given under the FSMA 2000, s 137S or otherwise, a firm will need to consider what the practical implications of this are. This will be important for logistical reasons (ie how will the firm make changes if it has to?). Also, the firm may have important strategic decisions to make (eg What are the costs of compliance and the risks of resistance? Is this a debate the firm wants to have with the FCA? Is the firm prepared to take the matter to the Tribunal if need be?).

The logistical challenge in withdrawing or amending a promotion

15.81 It may be necessary to stop issuing the promotion, at least in its current form, and this in itself might be a significant logistical challenge. A firm should consider quickly what channels an affected promotion had been issued through. For example, are there posters which would need to be taken down? Leaflets which would need to be withdrawn? Television or radio advertisements which would need to be stopped? Advertisements on websites which would need to be taken down? E-mails or other electronic communications which would need to be stopped?

The commercial impact of withdrawing or amending a promotion

15.82 Where a promotion is distributed through third party commercial channels there may be contractual, relationship and cost implications to withdrawing or amending it. Firms will want to identify, quickly, whether those implications are significant and whether they can be managed or ameliorated.

15.83 When the FCA requires that a financial promotion be amended, the firm will want to consider whether the change is likely to have a material impact on the promotion's effectiveness as a marketing tool. The fact that a change will have an adverse impact on a firm's business is not likely to affect the FCA's position. However, it might affect a firm's position and, in particular, whether a firm decides to make representations, what sort of advice and assistance it wants to obtain in making any representations, and whether it is prepared to go to the Tribunal if need be.

Potential cost of remediation

15.84 If customers have already responded to a promotion, it is possible that the FCA will require the firm, or the firm may otherwise be required (eg as a result of civil claims) to pay compensation. A firm that has been put on notice that a particular promotion is under scrutiny should consider the size of any financial and practical impact of such an eventuality. For example, what would it cost to refund all customers who have responded to the promotion and made an investment/purchased the relevant product? Is it possible to identify those customers? Also, is it possible to identify those customers who had suffered harm? These are issues that a firm should consider quickly upon being put on notice that one of its financial promotions is under scrutiny, so that it can understand the strategic implications of the action it faces and make appropriately informed decisions about its response.

What are the consequences for a firm which contravenes a direction in relation to a financial promotion?

15.85   A failure to comply with a direction in relation to a financial promotion is likely to be a 'contravention of a requirement imposed by or under the FSMA 2000' (see para **2.94** ff above), which could give rise to, eg a disciplinary action, a restitution order, or a civil injunction. The potential consequences of this are considered in **CHAPTER 8**. In addition, firms should be aware of potential private law consequences[1].

1 A breach of financial promotion rules could give rise to a private law liability for breach of contract and/or misrepresentation. In respect of such a misrepresentation, claims may arise in private law for, eg, fraudulent misrepresentation at common law, negligent misstatement at common law, negligent misrepresentation under the Misrepresentation Act 1967, s 2(1), or innocent misrepresentation under s 2(2) of that Act.

WHAT ARE THE RELEVANT PROCESSES?

Interventions in financial products

How are temporary product intervention rules made?

15.86   The FSA has set out the procedure for making temporary product intervention rules in its Policy Statement[1].

1 Policy Statement, paras 28–39.

Taking proposals to the Committee and the Board

15.87   Once initial proposals have been discussed, a paper will be prepared by a working group for a Committee with authority to propose temporary product intervention rules to the FCA Board.

15.88   The Committee will:

- give its approval to take the proposals to the Board;
- suggest that the proposals are revised;

- suggest that a decision may be taken to use a different regulatory tool; or
- suggest that a decision will be taken not to proceed.

15.89   If the Committee decides to take the proposals to the Board, the paper will be taken to the monthly scheduled Board meeting, but if the matter is of great importance or there is an emergency, the Board may convene specifically to consider this issue.

Informing Panels

15.90   There are three Panels: the Practitioner Panel; the Consumer Panel; and the Smaller Business Practitioner Panel. The Panels represent the interests of consumers and practitioners by advising, commenting and making recommendations on existing and developing FCA policies and practices. The FCA will generally seek their views during the process for making temporary product intervention rules if there is sufficient time to do so.

Consulting the PRA

15.91   As with the process for making general product intervention rules, the FCA will discuss any proposed temporary product intervention rule with the PRA and give its comments due weight and consideration before making the rule.

Publication of temporary product intervention rules

15.92   If the Board ultimately takes a decision to introduce a temporary product intervention rule, the FCA must publish a statement on its website explaining why it is introducing the rule. It may choose to invite feedback, but this will not amount to a consultation exercise.

Post-implementation review of temporary product intervention rules

15.93   The FCA may review a temporary product intervention rule while it is in force. Such a review may be informed by market monitoring and feedback from stakeholders, including product providers, distributors and consumers[1].

1   Policy Statement, para 40.

15.94   Reviews are likely to consider whether a rule is functioning as intended, including whether[1]:
- there have been any breaches of it;
- there are any unintended consequences, eg any impact on products not intended to be caught by it;
- there is evidence that firms are working around the rule rather than complying with it, eg new products enter the market or new features are added to existing products that expose customers to the same or similar potential detriment; or

- new evidence demonstrates that the rule is not necessary or customer detriment is unlikely.

1 Policy Statement, para 42.

15.95 Following a review, the FCA may:

- revoke a temporary product intervention rule; or

- change specified certain criteria under which a rule permits the sale of a product to continue.

Revocation or change of temporary product intervention rules

15.96 The FCA can revoke temporary product intervention rules before the end of the period for which they apply[1]. It can also make changes to a temporary product intervention rule. Changes to a temporary product intervention rule will be communicated by issuing a new statement containing the revised rule and the rationale for the changes. Such changes will not extend the lifespan of the temporary product intervention rule.

1 FSMA 2000, s 138M(4).

15.97 Rules may be revoked or changed for a number of reasons, including but not limited to[1]:

- new rules are introduced on a permanent basis following a consultation exercise;

- new rules being introduced at the EU level;

- industry initiatives are developed that specify sufficient minimum standards to address the sources of consumer detriment;

- further evidence is submitted that demonstrates that consumer detriment will not occur;

- demand for, or supply of, the relevant product disappears and is deemed unlikely to return; or

- the FCA identifies unforeseen negative effects of the rule which outweigh any positive impact upon consumer protection.

1 Policy Statement, para 48.

What are the consequences of breaching product intervention rules?

15.98 The FSMA 2000 states that the product intervention rules made by the FCA may provide for:

- a relevant agreement to be unenforceable against any person or specified person;

- recovery of money paid under a relevant agreement by any person or specified person;

- payment of compensation for any loss sustained by any person or specified person as a result of paying any money under a relevant agreement or obligation[1].

1 FSMA 2000, s 137D(7).

15.99 With regards to para **15.98** point one above, the FCA has indicated that unenforceability will only apply to sales made after the introduction of relevant rules. Consumers holding affected products should generally seek redress through the usual channels (complaints to the firm and to the Financial Ombudsman Service), or take legal action against the relevant firm, but need only demonstrate that the relevant agreement was the subject of a product intervention rule (whether temporary or not) and that they entered into it after the relevant rule came into effect[1].

1 Policy Statement, para 13.

15.100 Consumers holding contracts made before relevant rules were in place may still seek redress, even though their contracts would not be unenforceable by virtue of the rules, but they would have to establish their claim in the usual way, eg by demonstrating that they received unsuitable advice or bought the product based on a misleading financial promotion[1].

1 Policy Statement, para 14.

Intervening in markets and the FCA's competition role

15.101 The FCA's guidance provides that the FCA will generally conduct market studies through a six-stage process (although there may be some variation between different stages depending on the nature of the issue under investigation)[1]:

- *pre-launch:* the FCA will consider whether the market is an appropriate priority for a market study. In doing this, it will take account of input from the sources noted above, the potential adverse effects on consumers and the possible drivers of those effects. The FCA will also produce a project plan and establish what resources it needs, and, where helpful, it will informally engage external parties on particular aspects of the market study (for example, scope);

- *launch:* the FCA will publicly announce the market study and indicate its scope. It will generally make an open request for submissions on the issues it raises, and will engage with relevant stakeholders;

- *research:* the full range of FCA information gathering powers (including compulsion) are available to the FCA in a market study context in order to test its theories about the potential adverse effects on consumers and what drives these effects. The FCA will gather information from a wide range of sources including market participants, consumer bodies, other regulators, market surveys and other sources;

- *analysis and interim report:* the FCA will use the data collected to examine how the market functions and to assess the effectiveness of competition in the market. In respect of the latter, the FCA will consider suppliers' market power, information flow between market participants, switching rates, costs or benefits to third parties, and the way consumers and firms make decisions, as well as other market features. The FCA will then publish an interim report, which sets out its draft analysis and preliminary conclusions, and where practicable and appropriate, proposed solutions for addressing any concerns that have been identified;

- *report:* the FCA will publish its final report, which will include:

  - a description of the market(s) and issue(s) under consideration;

  - the reasons for carrying out the study;

  - a description of the methodologies used to collect and analyse the data;

  - its analysis; and

  - its conclusions on the issues considered;

- *remedies:* the FCA has the full range of powers available to take action following a market study. It has particularly listed the following in its guidance:

  - policy or regulatory changes;

  - rule-making, including changes to, or potentially withdrawal of, existing rules, or make recommendations to the Prudential Regulation Authority;

  - using firm-specific enforcement powers;

  - publishing guidance;

  - proposals for enhanced industry self-regulation;

  - ask the CMA to consider the market[2]; or

  - take no further action.

1 Policy Statement, pp 2–5.
2 See para **15.56** ff above in relation to the proposal to give the FCA powers to refer a market directly for a market investigation.

15.102 A market investigation is a lengthy and very in-depth process, which involves detailed scrutiny of the market and the business models of market participants. Prior to the Enterprise and Regulatory Reform Act 2013 coming into force, the time limit has been two years; when this Act comes into force in April 2014, that time limit will be reduced to 18 months unless special circumstances apply[1]. The Competition Commission publishes detailed guidance on the procedural and substantive considerations which apply in the context of a market investigation[2].

1 The OFT and the Competition Commission will be subsumed within the Competition and Markets Authority, pursuant to the Enterprise and Regulatory Reform Act 2013, from 1 April 2014. At the time of writing, draft guidance from the Competition Commission indicated that the market investigation process would remain substantially unchanged by the new regime, save for the new time limit.

15.102 Product and market intervention

2 Competition Commission, 'Guidelines for market investigations: Their role, procedures, assessment and remedies' (April 2013); and Department for Business, Innovation and Skills 'Guide to the Enterprise and Regulatory Reform Act 2013' (June 2013). As noted above, draft guidance from the Competition and Markets Authority, available at the time of writing, indicates that the process and substance will be substantially unchanged when the Competition and Markets Authority becomes responsible for market investigations.

15.103 The outcome of a market investigation can be appealed to the Competition Appeals Tribunal under the Enterprise Act 2002, s 179. These powers are granted to the FCA to be applied concurrently with the Competition and Markets Authority (as is the case for other sectoral regulators such as Ofcom and Ofgem).

15.104 The concurrent powers regime set out in the FS(BR)A 2013, imports wholesale the investigative powers of the CMA in relation to the Chapter 1 and Chapter 2 powers.

15.105 The FS(BR)A 2013 also grants to the FCA the powers to levy fines for breach of the Chapter 1 and Chapter 2 provisions on the same basis as the CMA pursuant to the Competition Act 1998. This would allow the FCA to levy fines of up to 10% of group global turnover. The FCA's other remedy powers are not available in the context of its exercise of Chapter 1 or Chapter 2 powers.

15.106 At the time of writing, no guidance has been published on how the FCA might exercise these powers.

15.107 Note that the FS(BR)A 2013 does not give to the FCA the powers to bring prosecutions for the criminal cartel offence in the Enterprise Act 2002, s 188.

Intervention in financial promotions

15.108 The procedure by which the FCA may intervene in financial promotions follows three stages, as illustrated below.

Stage one: direction

15.109 In some cases, the FCA may use this power 'out of the blue'. As mentioned above, the FCA has made clear that it sees this as a power that it can use swiftly where necessary. Accordingly, and in light of the subject matter (ie, the restraint of the use of potentially harmful promotions when they are already in use or to stop them being used), there may not be time for, or the FCA may choose not to allow time for, any dialogue or warning before it issues a direction under the FSMA 2000, s 137S.

15.110 A direction given under the FSMA 2000, s 137S must be given in writing to the relevant firm and, if applicable, to the person actually making the communication in question if that communication is approved by that relevant firm[1]. The notice giving the direction must[2]:

- give details of the direction; inform the person to whom the notice is given (ie the relevant firm and, if applicable, the person making the communication which is approved by that relevant firm) that the direction takes effect immediately;

- state the FCA's reasons for giving the direction; and

- inform the person to whom the notice is given that they may make representations to the FCA within a period specified in the notice (which may be extended by the FCA).

1 FSMA 2000, s 137S(5).
2 FSMA 2000, s 137S(6).

Stage two: representations

15.111 In light of the nature of the power and the way the FCA proposes to use it, there may be little time in which to make representations. However, the fact that the legislation specifically states that the FCA may extend the original deadline stated in the notice of a direction indicates that recipients of such notices may request extra time, and that the FCA should at least consider such requests.

15.112 The FCA will consider any representations made and can amend a direction if it considers it appropriate to do so[1].

1 FSMA 2000, s 137S(7).

Stage three: amendment, revocation and/or publication

15.113 The FCA must then inform the persons to whom a notice of a direction was sent, by separate further written notices, if it has decided to revoke a direction and, if not, what it has decided to do[1]. If the FCA decides not to revoke the direction, then its separate further written notices to the recipients must[2]:

- give details of the direction and of any amendment to it;

- state the FCA's reasons for deciding not to revoke the direction and, if relevant, for amending it;

- inform the person to whom the notice is given of their right to refer the matter to the Tribunal; and

- give an indication of the procedure for such a reference.

1 FSMA 2000, s 137S(8) and (10).
2 FSMA 2000, s 137S(9).

15.114 Once the period specified in the original notice for making representations has ended, the FCA may publish such information about the direction as it considers appropriate (even if the direction is revoked)[1]. Therefore, at least where the FCA does proceed with the direction in some form, even if amended, firms should expect a degree of publicity to accompany whatever action is taken. This is likely to happen reasonably promptly after the expiry of the time given for representations and the FCA's decision in relation to such representations, particularly if the FCA considers that publicity is required in order to prevent potential harm. Furthermore, as with publicity of other action taken by the FCA, the FCA's schedule of announcements and its desire to give the action it has taken appropriate 'airtime' is likely to be a factor too.

1 FSMA 2000, s 137S(11).

Challenging the decision

15.115 If, having received and considered representations, the FCA decides not to revoke a direction, then the recipients of a notice in relation to that direction may refer the matter to the Tribunal[1].

1 FSMA 2000, s 137S(8)(b).

Nature of the Tribunal's enquiry

15.116 The Tribunal's approach towards these references is set out in the FSMA 2000, s 133, in particular s 133(6) and (6A), which deal with 'non-disciplinary' references[1].

1 A reference made in relation to a direction made under the FSMA 2000, s 137S will be classified as 'non-disciplinary', as it does not fall within the list of 'disciplinary' references set out in the FSMA 2000, s 133(7A).

15.117 The Tribunal's enquiry in such cases is limited[1] in that it can only:

- dismiss the reference entirely; or
- require the FCA to reconsider its direction on a financial promotion and reach a new decision in accordance with certain specified findings by the Tribunal, namely:
  - issues of fact or law; the matters to be, or not to be, taken into account in making the decision; and
  - the procedural or other steps to be taken in connection with the making of the decision.

1 In contrast, where the Tribunal is considering 'disciplinary' references, the FSMA 2000, s 133(5) requires the Tribunal itself to determine the appropriate action to take and direct the FCA to give effect to its determination.

Procedure for making a reference

15.118 Under the FSMA 2000, s 137S(9)(d), the FCA must give an indication of the procedure for making a reference to the Tribunal in its second written notice following its consideration of references made to it by firms. The FCA has not commented further on what this procedure will entail.

Compliance with direction pending Tribunal decision

15.119 Where a firm decides to make a reference to the Tribunal, the FSMA 2000 s 137S requires it to comply with the FCA direction until the Tribunal's decision. The combined effect of s 137S(4) and s 137S(8)(a) is that:

- a requirement to publish details of a s 137S direction will take effect as soon as (and if) the FCA, having considered representations from firms in relation to a direction, and having decided not to revoke the direction, gives separate further written notice to firms under s 137S(8)(a); and

- any other requirement contained in the s 137S direction takes effect immediately (ie before any representations are made to the FCA and before any reference to the Tribunal).

15.120 So, firms must comply with directions in the period before any reference to the Tribunal. This reflects the stated purpose of a s 137S direction, being an immediately effective, pre-emptive tool.

Will the firm need to make redress to customers who have responded?

15.121 The statutory provisions conferring the power to intervene in financial promotions are expressly separate from the FCA's wider disciplinary powers, and they do not include any authority for the FCA to require a firm to do anything other than to withdraw a promotion (or its approval of a promotion) or to amend a promotion.

15.122 Nevertheless, in practice the exercise of this power may give rise to a need for a firm to pay redress to customers who have responded to a financial promotion. By definition, the power is to be exercised in circumstances where the FCA considers that there has been or is likely to be a breach of financial promotion rules. In such circumstances, if the FCA considers that customers are likely to have suffered loss, then firms are likely to – at the very least – be put under pressure to make redress. If the FCA considers it has evidence of breaches of, eg, rules in the Conduct of Business Sourcebook 4, or Principle 6 (customers' interests), or Principle 7 (communications with clients), which breaches are likely to have caused loss, then in practice it would be difficult for a firm to resist some form of remediation programme without risking a wider enforcement action, and such an action may follow in any event.

15.123 There may be practical challenges in identifying those customers who are affected, those who can be shown to have suffered loss, and therefore those to whom any redress should be paid. Firms will probably want to consider whether steps may be taken first, which fall short of paying redress, eg drawing relevant shortcomings in a financial promotion to the attention of customers who responded to it and giving them the opportunity to request a refund (or whatever action may be appropriate) if, having been given that information, they want to change their minds about their investment or purchasing decision.

Chapter 16   'Own-initiative' powers

INTRODUCTION

16.1   The Regulators have at their disposal a series of powers which allow them to intervene directly in the business of firms in the interests of their regulatory objectives. These powers, which can at their most extreme lead to a firm's permission being cancelled with immediate effect, may be exercised in a wide range of circumstances.

16.2   This chapter will review:

- the Regulators' general approach to the use of these intervention powers;

- the grounds on which the powers may be exercised;

- the types of action the Regulators can take; and

- the procedure by which these powers are exercised.

16.3   Before looking in detail at the various provisions, procedures and practice, a brief overview of the regime as a whole will be provided.

16.4   As described in **CHAPTER 1**[1], each firm has a tailored permission granted to it by the PRA or FCA which specifies the regulated activities the firm is authorised to carry out. The Regulators have the power, in certain circumstances, to vary or cancel a firm's permission in order to advance the Regulators' objectives and to ensure that the firm continues to fulfil the threshold conditions. The Regulators have a similar power to intervene for incoming firms. These powers will be referred to collectively as the 'own-initiative' powers[2].

1 See para **1.45** ff above .
2 FSMA 2000 categorises the powers to vary and cancel a firm's permission as the Regulator's 'own-initiative variation powers' (FSMA 2000, s 55J(12)). The power to intervene in respect of incoming firms is similar in practice, although it is more restricted see para **16.75** ff below.

16.5   The Regulators may exercise their own-initiative powers in a range of situations, provided that one of the applicable tests prescribed under the FSMA 2000 is met[1]. Meeting the test is, however, only a small piece of the picture. An important factor is the Regulators' policies on when, in practice, they will seek to exercise these powers. At present, this is found in the FCA Handbook, the FCA Enforcement Guide and published statements of approach from the PRA[2], which set out the Regulators' general approach to the use of the own-initiative powers and more specific guidance on when each of the own-initiative powers may be exercised. These are discussed in more detail below.

1 The tests are outlined at para **16.26** ff below.
2 At the time of writing, these are contained in the PRA Policy Statement, 'The Prudential Regulation Authority's approach to enforcement: statutory statements of policy and procedure' (April 2013) and the PRA Policy Statement, 'The PRA's approach to banking supervision' (April 2013).

16.6   The Regulators expect firms to comply voluntarily with their reasonable requirements and, therefore, expect that it will not normally be necessary to exercise their formal powers. There may, however, be occasions when the use of formal powers is required, for example, where the problem is particularly serious (for example, where it is necessary to secure the appropriate degree of protection for consumers or to protect the integrity of the UK financial system) or where the use of formal powers is needed to excuse the firm from its legal obligations to other parties which might otherwise prevent it from complying with informal requests. As discussed in **CHAPTER 1**, the Regulators' approach focuses on proactive supervision and early intervention. Therefore, it may be that the Regulators will exercise their own-initiative powers more regularly than the FSA historically had done.

16.7   The procedure by which the own-initiative powers are exercised is different in various respects[1] from the warning/decision notice procedure considered in **CHAPTERS 10** and **11** above, but the firm still has the right of recourse to the Tribunal[2]. In urgent situations, the Regulators can implement their powers with immediate effect, with the matter to be considered fully only afterwards[3].

1 See para **16.130** ff below.
2 The procedure, known as the supervisory notice procedure, is considered at para **16.130** ff below.
3 The use of the powers as a matter of urgency is considered at para **16.215** ff below.

16.8   There are a number of similar powers which may be applicable in particular circumstances and which are not set out here. These include:

- the Regulator's power to give directions in relation to regulated collective investment schemes, including OEICs[1];

- the Regulator's power to give directions in relation to a recognised investment exchange or recognised clearing house[2];

- the FCA's power, as UK Listing Authority, to discontinue or suspend the listing of securities[3];

- the FCA's power to give a disapplication direction in relation to a member of a designated professional body[4];

- the PRA's power to impose requirements on a former underwriting member of Lloyd's[5];

- the FCA's power to intervene in an incoming firm if the OFT informs it that the firm (or certain persons connected with it) has done certain things relevant to its fitness to be granted a licence under the Consumer Credit Act 1974[6];

- the power of the OFT to impose a prohibition or restriction on an incoming firm in relation to consumer credit business[7]; and

- the Regulators' power to give directions to a qualifying parent undertaking[8].

1 FSMA 2000, Pt 17.
2 FSMA 2000, s 296. The Regulator's role with respect to recognised investment exchanges is briefly discussed at para **17.206** ff below.
3 FSMA 2000, s 77.
4 FSMA 2000, s 328 and see FCA Enforcement Guide at EG Chapter 16.
5 FSMA 2000, s 320.
6 FSMA 2000, s 194(3).
7 FSMA 2000, ss 203 and 204. The OFT's jurisdiction over consumer credit will be transferred to the FCA in April 2014.
8 FSMA 2000, ss 192C and 192D. See the FSMA 2000, s 192B for the meaning of a 'qualifying parent undertaking'. A direction under this section may require the parent undertaking: (a) to take specified action; or (b) to refrain from taking specified action. The requirement may be imposed by reference to the parent undertaking's relationship with its group or other members of its group.

THE REGULATORS' GENERAL APPROACH

16.9   Before reviewing the grounds on which each of the own-initiative powers may be exercised by the Regulators, the Regulators' general approach to the use of these powers will be considered. It is important to bear this general approach in mind when looking at the specific provisions of the FSMA 2000, which contains a series of hurdles. If one of these hurdles is passed, the Regulators have the right to exercise their powers. The hurdles are relatively low and give the Regulators a significant amount of discretion. The Regulators' policies on when they will exercise these powers are therefore important.

The own-initiative powers in context

16.10   When an issue of concern arises in relation to a firm, the use of their own-initiative powers is only one of a range of tools available to the Regulators to deal with the situation. Precisely what action it is appropriate for the Regulators to take in the particular case will depend upon what the Regulators need to achieve having regard to their separate regulatory objectives. For example, if the issue relates to an isolated breach for which there is no doubt the firm will be able to compensate investors, and which does not give rise to ongoing regulatory concerns or systemic risks, then the variation of the firm's permission is unlikely to be under consideration, whereas disciplinary action might. Equally, if the regulatory issue was relatively minor and was spotted by the firm's normal controls before it led to any particular incident involving harm, then it is unlikely that the use of these powers would be appropriate. Instead it may be appropriate to increase the supervision and monitoring of the firm.

16.11 In the course of its supervision of a firm, the FCA may make clear to the firm that it expects it to take certain steps to ensure it continues to meet the regulatory requirements[1]. This could include asking it to remediate particular weaknesses that the FCA sees, for example in its finances, conduct of business or controls. The FCA will likely seek to agree with the firm the steps to be taken to address its concerns. The FCA envisages that firms will take such steps without the need for any formal action on the FCA's part[2]. The PRA has not overtly made the same point but it is likely to be true of its own approach.

1 FCA Enforcement Guide at EG 8.3.
2 The FCA's power to give firms individual guidance under the FSMA 2000, s 139A may also be relevant and may overlap to some extent with the power to vary permission. See the FCA Handbook at SUP Chapters 7 and 9.

16.12 In considering how to deal with a concern about a firm, the FCA will have regard to the responsibilities of the firm's senior management to deal with the concerns and to the principle that a restriction imposed on a business should be proportionate to the benefits[1]. The FCA will proceed on the basis that it is the firm that is primarily responsible for ensuring it conducts its business in compliance with the regulatory requirements[2].

1 FCA Enforcement Guide at EG 8.1B. These are two of the principles for good regulation (see para **1.14** above).
2 FCA Enforcement Guide at EG 8.2.

16.13 Similarly, the PRA will have regard to its regulatory principles set out in the FSMA 2000 in designing its policies and supervisory approach, including the responsibility of the firm's board of directors and management to manage their firm prudently in order to maintain its safety and soundness, proportionality and the need to minimise adverse effects on competition[1].

1 PRA Policy Statement, 'The PRA's approach to banking supervision' (April 2013), para 30.

When the Regulators may consider using the own-initiative powers

16.14 In terms of the general policy, although both the PRA and FCA have emphasised the responsibility of firms to deal with concerns, they will also expect firms to take the initiative to raise issues of possible concern at an early stage. As discussed earlier, both Regulators have emphasised their willingness to use their formal intervention powers at an early stage. In addition, the general circumstances under which they may use them are wide-ranging.

16.15 This is illustrated by the range of circumstances in which the FCA has indicated it may use its formal powers as set out in the Handbook (in the context of the FCA's supervision activities), and the FCA Enforcement Guide (which sets out circumstances applicable to the FCA's supervision and enforcement activities). In the context of its supervision activities, the FCA may use its formal powers where[1]:

- the firm's management, business or internal controls give rise to risks that are not fully covered by the FCA's rules;

- the firm becomes or is to become involved in new products or selling practices and the risks which these pose are not captured by existing requirements;

- a change in a firm's structure, controllers, activities or strategy generates uncertainty or creates unusual or exceptional risks; or

- at the request of, or to assist, an overseas regulator.

1 See the FCA Handbook at SUP 7.3.2 and FCA Enforcement Guide at EG 8.3A. Similar circumstances may, alternatively, lead to the Regulator issuing individual guidance to the firm under the FSMA 2000, s 139A: see the FCA Handbook at SUP 9.3.

16.16 In the course of its supervision and monitoring of a firm or as part of an enforcement action, the FCA will, in the vast majority of cases, seek to agree certain steps which it expects the firm to take, but there may be occasions where the FCA will exercise its formal powers to vary the permission or impose requirements where 'it considers it appropriate to do so'[1]. Examples of situations where the FCA would 'consider it appropriate' to exercise its formal powers include[2]:

- where the FCA has serious concerns about a firm, or about the way its business is being conducted[3];

- where the FCA is concerned that the consequences of the firm not taking the step may be serious; or

- where the imposition of formal action:

  - reflects the importance that the FCA attaches to the need for the firm to address its concerns; or

  - may assist the firm to take steps which would otherwise be difficult because of legal obligations owed to third parties.

1 On the power to impose requirements, see para **16.90** ff below. This appears to be a lower test to satisfy than the equivalent FSA policy, under which the FSA would consider (in the context of its enforcement function) taking such action 'only if' the firm's business was being conducted in such a way that the FSA judged it 'necessary' to act in order to secure compliance with the FSMA 2000, the Principles and the rules or address the consequences of non-compliance (FSA Handbook at ENF 3.5.3).
2 FCA Enforcement Guide at EG 8.3 and the FCA Handbook at SUP 7.3.1.
3 FCA Enforcement Guide at EG 8.5.

16.17 'Own-initiative' powers

16.17 The latter point is an important one in practice. If the steps which are required impact on the firm's contractual obligations to others[1], or could otherwise expose it to liability to third parties[2], then it is unlikely that, as a matter of law, it will be protected by having taken such steps voluntarily in order, for example, to protect the interests of consumers. It may assist the firm to have been required to take those steps by the FCA pursuant to the FCA's formal statutory powers. Whether this will, in fact, be sufficient to protect the firm from liability in the particular case will depend upon the firm's legal obligations in that case and the precise circumstances which led to the need for the intervention action. The firm may not be absolved from liability.

1 An example would be undertaking not to carry on business in a particular area where the firm had ongoing contractual obligations to third parties.
2 An example would be suspending a particular product of the firm's, which could potentially expose the firm to liability to the holders of the product.

16.18 As discussed in **CHAPTER 1**, in most circumstances the PRA will prefer informal methods of promoting its objectives and supervisory methods to enforcement action. It can, however, use this own-initiative power on matters falling within the scope of its objectives and has published a statement of policy on aspects of its approach to banking supervision[1]. If the PRA deems it '*necessary to reduce risks*', it may exercise its formal powers, such as the power to vary a firm's permission or impose a requirement, which may require a change to a firm's business model or future strategy[2].

1 PRA Policy Statement, 'The Prudential Regulation Authority's approach to banking supervision' (April 2013).
2 PRA Policy Statement, 'The Prudential Regulation Authority's approach to banking supervision' (April 2013), para 195.

16.19 The PRA will focus on those issues and firms that it considers pose the greatest risk to the stability of the UK financial system and will consider when and how to use its formal powers on a case by case basis, taking into account in all cases a number of factors including[1]:

- the confidence supervisors have that firms will respond appropriately to the PRA's requests without the use of powers;

- the PRA's view of the firm's proximity to failure, as reflected in its pro-active intervention stage[2]; and

- the impact – including systemic implications – and proximity of the risk the PRA is aiming to mitigate.

1 PRA Policy Statement, 'The Prudential Regulation Authority's approach to banking supervision' (April 2013), para 197.
2 For example, where the PRA judges that a firm's viability has deteriorated such that there is an imminent risk to the viability of the firm.

16.20 These reflect the PRA's approach in considering whether its objectives can be achieved without the use of its powers, how close the firm is to failure and the impact of the risk on the stability of the UK financial system as a whole.

16.21 If the statutory conditions are fulfilled and one of the Regulators considers it appropriate to exercise its own-initiative power, there is a very wide range of actions available to it.

VARIATION AND CANCELLATION OF PERMISSION/ INTERVENTION

On what grounds can the Regulator exercise its own-initiative powers?

16.22 In considering whether a particular situation gives rise to the risk of the Regulator exercising its own-initiative powers, the first question is whether the situation falls within any of the circumstances when the FSMA 2000 allows those powers to be exercised. The flowchart below illustrates the different questions which arise, outlined in this chapter.

16.23 The separate statutory tests for the exercise of the own-initiative powers will be reviewed, comprising five circumstances when a firm's permission can be varied or cancelled (for UK regulated firms and incoming firms with top-up permissions[1]), and four circumstances where the intervention power (applicable only to incoming firms) can be exercised. The statutory grounds on which the Regulators may exercise their powers to vary or cancel a firm's permission are the same. Which power the Regulator uses depends on the circumstances, such as whether the Regulator considers it necessary to take urgent action, as will be discussed below (see para **16.117**, below).

1 In other words, a permission allowing the firm to carry on additional regulated activities not covered by its passport or Treaty rights. See para **1.76** above.

16.24 In terms of the relevant statutory provisions:

- the FSMA 2000, Pt 4A, s 55 contains the Regulators' powers to vary or cancel firms' permissions at their own initiative (and at the request of firms)[1];

- the FSMA 2000, Sch 6 contains the threshold conditions, which are relevant to the question of whether the Regulators may exercise their own-initiative powers, as explained further in this Chapter[2];

- the FSMA 2000, ss 194–197 relate to the exercise of the Regulators' own-initiative powers in respect of incoming firms.

1 Part 4A was inserted into the FSMA 2000 by the Financial Services Act 2012, and replaces the FSMA 2000, Pt 4, which contained equivalent provisions relating to firms' permission to carry on regulated activities.
2 Schedule 6 was amended by the Financial Services Act 2012 to set out PRA-specific and FCA-specific threshold conditions which apply depending on whether the firm is FCA-only regulated or dual-regulated.

16.24 'Own-initiative' powers

'Own-initiative' powers

The own-initiative/intervention power

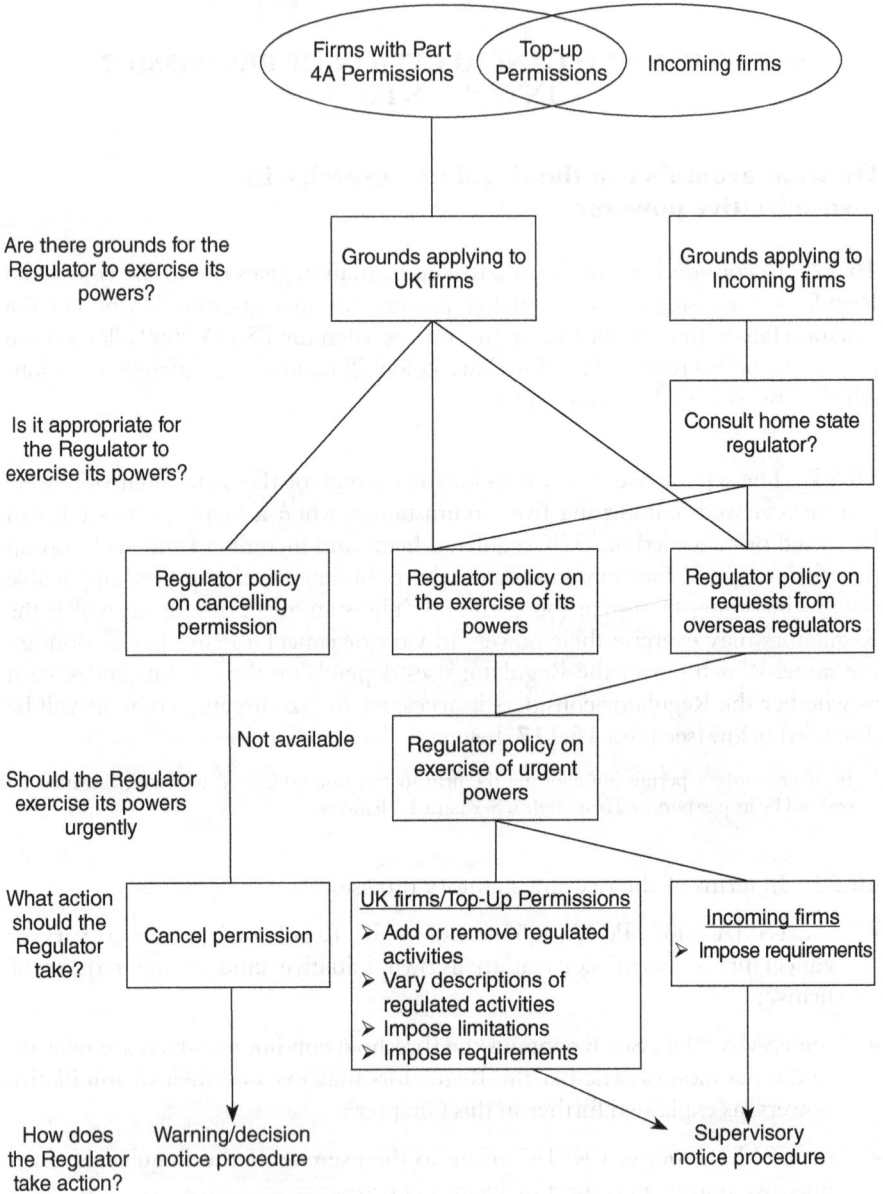

```
        ( Firms with Part    Top-up                        )
        ( 4A Permissions   Permissions   Incoming firms     )
```

Are there grounds for the
Regulator to exercise its
powers?

**Grounds applying to
UK firms**

**Grounds applying to
Incoming firms**

Is it appropriate for
the Regulator to
exercise its powers?

**Consult home state
regulator?**

**Regulator policy
on cancelling
permission**

**Regulator policy on
the exercise of its
powers**

**Regulator policy on
requests from
overseas regulators**

Not available

**Regulator policy on
exercise of urgent
powers**

Should the Regulator
exercise its powers
urgently

What action
should the
Regulator
take?

Cancel permission

UK firms/Top-Up Permissions
➢ Add or remove regulated
  activities
➢ Vary descriptions of
  regulated activities
➢ Impose limitations
➢ Impose requirements

Incoming firms
➢ Impose requirements

How does
the Regulator
take action?

Warning/decision
notice procedure

Supervisory
notice procedure

16.25 The FSMA 2000 also provides for consultation between the Regulators before the exercise of their own-initiative powers[1].

1 For example, the PRA must consult the FCA before exercising its own-initiative powers (FSMA 2000, ss 55(J)(5) and 196(3)) while the FCA must consult the PRA before exercising its own-initiative powers in relation to a PRA-authorised person or a member of a group which includes a PRA-authorised person (FSMA 2000, ss 55J(4) and 196(2)).

16.26 The circumstances under which the own-initiative powers can be exercised as set out in these statutory provisions are as follows:

- Variation or cancellation of permission:

  - Case A: actual or likely failure to satisfy the threshold conditions[1];

  - Case B: failure to carry on during a 12 month period a regulated activity for which the firm has permission[2];

  - Case C: desirable to exercise the power in order to advance any of the Regulators' objectives[3];

  - Case D: at the request of or for the purpose of assisting an overseas regulator[4]; and

  - Case E: on the acquisition of control over a UK regulated firm[5].

- Intervention:

  - Case 1: actual or likely contravention of a requirement imposed by or under the FSMA 2000[6];

  - Case 2: provision of false or misleading information knowingly or recklessly to the Regulators[7];

  - Case 3: desirable to exercise the power to protect the interests of consumers[8]; and

  - Case 4: at the request of, or for the purpose of assisting, an overseas regulator[9].

1 FSMA 2000, s 55J(1)(a) and see para **16.32** ff below.
2 FSMA 2000, s 55J(1)(b) and see para **16.44** ff below.
3 FSMA 2000, s 55J(1)(c) and see para **16.48** ff below.
4 FSMA 2000, s 55Q and see para **16.55** ff below. This circumstance only relates to the power to vary a firm's permission, not to cancel it.
5 FSMA 2000, s 55O and see para **16.67** ff below.
6 FSMA 2000, s 194(1)(a) and see para **16.77** ff below.
7 FSMA 2000, s 194(1)(b) and see para **16.82** ff below.
8 FSMA 2000, s 194(1)(c) and see para **16.85** ff below.
9 FSMA 2000, s 195 and see para **16.86** ff below.

16.27 Each of these is considered in turn below. In practice, the two sets of circumstances are similar, with certain differences relating to the grounds and procedure, which will be explained where they arise.

16.28 The tests have been drafted widely, and the Regulators have a significant amount of discretion to decide whether the power can be exercised in the circumstances. As a result, it will often be difficult for firms to argue that the test for taking action had not been met and it is likely that the real issue will be whether the action the Regulator proposes is appropriate given the concerns which have arisen. A secondary issue may be whether that action can be directed to address not only the concerns which gave rise to the test being met but also any other concerns (irrelevant for that purpose) which the Regulator has in relation to the firm.

16.29 Of the circumstances when the own-initiative powers can be exercised, the most powerful in practice, in terms of the breadth of discretion which they give to the Regulators, are failure to satisfy the threshold conditions, where it is desirable to act in order to advance the Regulators' objectives and contravention of requirements under the FSMA 2000. These are capable of application in a wide range of situations.

16.30 The powers overlap with the Regulators' power to apply to the court for a civil injunction in certain circumstances. The circumstances when a civil injunction may be appropriate are considered in **CHAPTER 8**.

UK regulated firms: variation or cancellation of permission

16.31 The following paragraphs consider each of the grounds for variation or cancellation of permission in turn. There are three additional considerations which may be relevant in particular cases[1] and these are set out at para **16.69** ff below.

1 Namely: (i) in any case, the Regulators' ability to have regard to a person in a 'relevant relationship' with the firm; (ii) when the Regulator is considering the variation or cancellation of a top-up permission; and (iii) when the Regulator is dealing with a firm which is connected with an EEA firm.

Case A: Failing or being likely to fail to satisfy the threshold conditions

16.32 Either Regulator may exercise its own-initiative power in relation to an authorised person if it appears to the Regulator that the authorised person is failing or is likely to fail to satisfy the threshold conditions[1].

1 FSMA 2000, s 55J(1)(a).

Which threshold conditions are likely to be relevant?

16.33 The threshold conditions that are most likely to be relevant in this context are[1]:

- adequate resources;

- suitability (the need for the firm to be a fit and proper person having regard to all the circumstances);[2] and

576

- close links, for example if the firm's connection with another person causes the Regulator concern about its ability to supervise the firm properly.

1 FCA Enforcement Guide at EG 8.5(1).
2 FCA Enforcement Guide at EG 8.5(1)(b). The suitability threshold condition is outlined in some detail at para **2.5** above and examples of cases where the own-initiative powers in response to failure to meet this threshold condition have been used are described at para **16.38**(b) below.

16.34 In practice, serious non-compliance with the Principles for Businesses may tend to show that the firm is failing to meet the threshold conditions, because the Principles express the main elements of the suitability threshold condition[1] and overlap with others, such as the requirement for adequate resources.

1 For example, Principle 11 (dealing with Regulators in an open and co-operative fashion) is often cited where a firm fails the suitability threshold condition by failing to co-operate with investigators (*Ifaeye Limited first supervisory notice (24/1/13)*); deliberately misleading Regulators (*Christopher John Riches first supervisory notice (26/6/12)*; failing to submit various regulatory returns (*Minona LLP final notice (2/7/13)*), or failing to pay fees due to the FSA (*Foneshield (UK) Ltd final notice (26/7/13)*). In the latter two examples the FCA cancelled the permissions granted to the firms.

When will the test be satisfied?

16.35 The test for the exercise of the own-initiative power under this head appears on the face of it to be a low one. Either Regulator may exercise their power only if it appears to the Regulator that the firm is failing or is likely to fail to satisfy the threshold conditions for which the regulator is responsible[1]. The firm need not yet have failed to meet any of the regulatory requirements. Indeed, the likelihood of it failing to do so need only be apparent to the Regulator. The test is thus primarily within the Regulator's discretion. This approach is perhaps understandable given the purpose of the provision, which is to enable the Regulator to protect consumers and ensure confidence in the UK financial markets, by ensuring not only that firms are compliant with the threshold conditions but also that they will continue to be compliant[2]. This is reflected in the proactive regulatory approaches being taken, as discussed in **CHAPTER 1**. The question whether a firm complies with the threshold conditions is primarily a matter of judgement; even more so, predicting whether it will continue to comply.

1 FSMA 2000, s 55J(1). As explained in para **2.4**, each Regulator has its own set of threshold conditions which apply depending on whether the firm is FCA-only regulated or dual-regulated. In addition, under the FSMA 2000, s 137O the Regulators have a specific rule-making power that allows them to make rules supplementing any of the threshold conditions that are relevant to the discharge of their respective functions.
2 See, for example, the FSMA 2000, s 55B(3).

16.36 However, failure to satisfy the threshold conditions is a very serious matter as a firm's continued ability to meet the threshold conditions is fundamental to its continuing to have permission under the FSMA 2000. The matter would need to be sufficiently serious that the Regulator is concerned the firm should no longer be carrying on regulated activities. In reaching that judgement, the Regulator would exercise its supervisory judgement bearing in mind the focus on ensuring an early response to emerging risks and to tackling problems early.

16.37 'Own-initiative' powers

16.37 Because of the subjective nature of the statutory test, firms are to a large extent reliant upon the Regulators taking a reasonable approach, at least unless or until the matter comes to be considered by the Tribunal[1]. In practice, it is difficult for firms to challenge the imposition of the own-initiative power on the ground that the statutory test was not met[2].

1 The firm has the right to refer the exercise of this power to the Tribunal: see para **16.165** below.
2 A number of references to the Tribunal have related to the FCA's use of its own-initiative powers. As of the date of writing, none of the references has been successful.

When will the Regulators consider using this power?

16.38 The FCA has provided examples[1] of the circumstances when it will consider using its own-initiative power to vary the permission under this provision:

- where the firm's material and financial resources appear inadequate for the scale or type of regulated activity it is carrying on[2];

- where the firm appears not to be a fit and proper person to carry on a regulated activity because:

  – it has not conducted its business in compliance with high standards[3], including being at risk of, or involved in, financial crime;

  – it has not been managed soundly and prudently[4] and has not exercised due skill, care and diligence in carrying on one or more, or all of its regulated activities; or

  – it has breached the regulatory requirements and the breaches are material in number or in individual seriousness; or

- where the firm's business model is not suited to its regulated activities: for example, where the firm's business model is not compatible with its affairs being conducted in a sound and prudent manner.

1 FCA Enforcement Guide at EG 8.5(1).
2 For example, where it has failed to take account of the need to manage risk professional indemnity insurance or where it is unable to meet its liabilities as they have fallen due (FCA Enforcement Guide, EG 8.1(1)(a)): see for example *Independent Asset Management UK Ltd final notice (4/9/13)*. Other relevant cases could include where the firm's own financial resources appear inadequate (*ifaeye Limited first supervisory notice (10/10/12)*) or where a firm is unable to meet its liabilities as they fall due (*John Patrick Morris final notice (15/8/13)*).
3 In *Pritchard Stockbrokers Limited first supervisory notice (10/2/12)*, the firm had been investigated for breaches of rules relating to client money and protection of client assets.
4 In *Christopher John Riches first supervisory notice (26/6/12)*, the firm was found not to fulfil this threshold condition where its principal had committed various dishonest acts.

16.39 The FCA has also provided examples of the circumstances in which it may cancel permission[1]. In practice, these are similar to those set out above for variation. For example, relevant cases could arise from failure to manage the firm in a sound and prudent manner. Apart from the procedural differences[2], the main difference between variation and cancellation is that cancellation cannot take place immediately. However, as discussed at para **16.95** ff below, the Regulator may vary a firm's permission in a way that would prevent it from carrying on regulated business, before cancelling it.

1 FCA Enforcement Guide at EG 8.14.
2 Discussed at para **16.252** ff below.

16.40 The circumstances under which the FCA may exercise the power to vary or cancel the permission illustrate the breadth of cases when the FCA can seek to use its own-initiative power under Case A.

16.41 The PRA has emphasised the importance of the threshold conditions to its regulatory regime and its expectation that firms will, in particular, ensure they have an appropriate amount and quality of capital and liquidity; have appropriate resources to measure, monitor and manage risk; be fit and proper; and conduct their business prudently[1]. The PRA has set out some general circumstances in which it will consider exercising its own-initiative powers, which are explained at para **16.19** above.

1 Policy Statement, 'The Prudential Regulation Authority's approach to banking supervision' (April 2013), p 5 and para 33.

16.42 A well-publicised example of the own-initiative power being exercised for failure to satisfy the threshold conditions is the series of supervisory notices published by the FSA in October 2008 in connection with the financial difficulties faced by Icelandic banking institutions: Heritable Bank plc, the UK branch of Landsbanki Islands HF (the parent of Heritable Bank plc) and Kaupthing Singer & Friedlander Limited (KSF).

16.43 The FSA addressed supervisory notices in early October 2008 to Heritable Bank plc and KSF (both UK retail banking subsidiaries of Icelandic banks) requiring them to refrain from accepting deposits into any existing or new accounts. In each case, the FSA concluded that the firm was failing to satisfy threshold condition 4 (adequate resources) in that, in the opinion of the FSA, the firm's liquidity resources were not adequate in relation to the regulated activities the firm was carrying on[1].

1 In addition, the FSA addressed a supervisory notice to Landsbanki Islands HF requiring the provision of information to and co-operation with the UK Financial Services Compensation Scheme. It took immediate effect in order, among other reasons, to protect consumers. There was at least one additional supervisory notice addressed to KSF that was not published by the FSA (but was subject to subsequent court proceedings) under which various restrictions were placed on KSF and the transfer of deposits received on or after 2 October 2008 to a trust account was required. This notice was not published on the basis that publication was likely to result in a fall in confidence in KSF and make it more difficult for some depositors to obtain repayment of their deposits.

Case B: Failing to carry on a regulated activity for 12 months

16.44 Either Regulator may exercise their own-initiative power in relation to a firm if it appears to it that the firm has failed, during a period of at least 12 months, to carry on a regulated activity for which it has a Part 4A permission[1].

1 FSMA 2000, s 55J(1)(b).

16.45 'Own-initiative' powers

When will the test be satisfied?

16.45 Again, the test appears to be a low one: it only has to appear to the Regulator that the firm has not carried on the regulated activity during a period of at least 12 months. However, the question of whether the firm has done so should be capable of objective determination. If, as a matter of fact, the Regulator is mistaken and the firm has in fact carried on that activity during that period, the Regulator ought not to exercise the power.

When will the Regulators consider using this power?

16.46 As discussed, each firm has a permission tailored to its particular circumstances, permitting it to carry out specific regulated activities, which may be varied where circumstances change, for example if the firm wishes to carry on additional regulated activities which its permission does not allow. Because of this, it is seen as inappropriate for firms to have permission to do something which they do not require, held on a precautionary basis in case the firm decides to carry on that activity. This provision allows the Regulator to vary or cancel, on its own initiative, the firm's permission so as to remove from its scope any regulated activities that the firm is not carrying on.

16.47 The Regulators have not provided any specific guidance on the circumstances when they will exercise this power[1]. Normally, any regulatory issues relating to the firm ceasing to carry on a regulated activity are discussed between the firm and the appropriate regulator and addressed within that context[2].

1 Cases where the power may be exercised include where the Regulator cannot find any evidence that a firm has conducted any regulated activities in the previous 12 months, and where the Regulator has not been able to contact the firm. See also *Gracechurch Investments Limited (In Liquidation) final notice (20/12/12)*, where the firm had ceased business almost three years before the date of the final notice, which led the FSA to conclude that the firm had failed to conduct any regulated activity to which its permission related for a period of at least 12 months and as a result, having regard to its regulatory objectives, decided to cancel the firm's permission.
2 See the Handbooks at SUP 6.2.6, 6.2.7, 6.3.7, 6.3.41–6.3.43.

Case C: Desirable to exercise the power in order to advance the Regulators' objectives

16.48 Either Regulator may exercise its own-initiative power in relation to a firm if it appears to the Regulator that it is desirable to do so in order to advance:

- in the case of the FCA, one or more of its operational objectives; namely, securing an appropriate degree of protection for consumers[1], protecting and enhancing the integrity of the UK financial system, and promoting effective competition in the interests of consumers[2]; and

- in the case of the PRA, any of its objectives: namely, its general objective to promote the safety and soundness of dual-regulated firms, and its insurance objective.

The objectives are discussed more fully in paras **1.11** ff and **1.21** ff above.

1 As discussed in para **1.27** 'consumers' is defined widely and is not confined to the traditional definition of retail consumers. The FCA's guidance defines consumers as: (a) retail consumers buying financial products or services for their own use or benefit (such as mortgages or ISAs); (b) retail investors in financial instruments (such as shares or bonds); and (c) wholesale consumers (such as regulated firms buying products or making investments, or issuers looking to raise capital). See 'The FCA's approach to advancing its objectives' (July 2013), p 8.
2 FSMA 2000, s 55J(1)(c). In *Independent Asset Management UK Limited first supervisory notice (3/6/13)*, the firm's breach of the appropriate resources threshold condition and Principle 4 (adequate resources) led the FCA to conclude that it was desirable to exercise its own-initiative power to vary the firm's permission and impose requirements to meet its operational objectives, specifically the protection of consumers.

When will the test be satisfied?

16.49 This is the widest of the own-initiative power provisions, allowing the Regulators to act in a very broad range of circumstances. Again, the test is a low one. It will be satisfied only if it appears to the Regulator that it is desirable to exercise the power for the purposes specified[1]. This is a subjective test, based on the Regulators' judgement, and it will be difficult for firms to argue that it has not been met.

1 FSMA 2000, s 55J(1)(c).

When will the Regulators consider using this power?

16.50 The example provided by the FCA of when it may be appropriate to act on this basis is where it appears that the interests of consumers are at risk because the firm appears to have breached any of Principles 6 to 10 of the FCA's Principles[1] to such an extent that it is desirable that limitations, restrictions or prohibitions are placed on the firm's regulated activity[2].

1 The Handbooks at PRIN 2.1.1R.
2 FCA Enforcement Guide at EG 8.5(2).

16.51 Whilst this is uncontroversial, particularly as Principles 6 to 10 are those which most directly relate to the firm's dealings with its customers[1], this policy gives little real guidance. In addition, although the FCA singles out Principles 6 to 10 for specific mention, the test could be met by breaches of other Principles for Businesses. In particular, it is possible to envisage situations where there were concerns relating to the inadequacy of financial resources[2] or lack of internal systems and controls[3] which make it desirable in the interests of consumers for restrictions to be placed on the firm.

1 For example, Principle 6: A firm must pay due regard to the interests of its customers and treat them fairly. (The Handbooks at PRIN 2.1.1R.)
2 Principle 4: The Handbooks at PRIN 2.1.1R.
3 Principle 3: The Handbooks at PRIN 2.1.1R.

16.52 The focus in this context is not so much on the breach of the relevant Principle, as on the potential effect of the situation on consumers. Serious breaches of Principles not giving rise to concerns about consumers may also be addressed under Case A. There is clearly, though, an overlap between the two: an example is the action taken in respect of the Icelandic banking crisis described in para **16.42** ff above.

16.53 The PRA has set out general guidance on the use of own-initiative powers which is relevant here; in particular, factors such as the extent to which the risk posed impacts, in the PRA's judgement, on the safety and soundness of the firm and the harm it may cause to the stability of the UK financial system. These are discussed in more detail in para **16.18** ff above.

16.54 Another important consideration is the FCA's competition objective to promote effective competition in the interests of consumers. As discussed in **CHAPTER 15**, the FCA may intervene in markets where it considers that the market is not working well in the interests of consumers. One of the actions that the FCA could consider taking is to use its own-initiative powers[1]. On the face of the statutory provisions, there appears to be scope for the FCA to do so. Arguably, for example, the FCA could seek to use its own-initiative powers to impose a divestment requirement[2], if such intervention is proportionate to the concerns identified. It is not yet clear, however, how the exercise of such structural measures will take into account the checks and balances and the specialist processes in place in relation to the UK competition law regime, particularly given that the processes for exercise of the own-initiative powers are not designed for specialist competition matters. The circumstances in which the FCA may intervene, and the actions it may take, are considered in more detail in **CHAPTER 15**.

1 'The FCA's approach to advancing its objectives' (July 2013), pp 36 and 37.
2 Although there is no specific provision in the FSMA 2000 to this effect, the FCA has said that the range of actions which it will consider using if it concludes that competition in markets is not working well includes structural measures (for example, the divestment of assets or businesses). See 'The FCA's approach to advancing its objectives', p 41 and **CHAPTER 15** for further discussion.

Case D: At the request of an overseas regulator

16.55 Either Regulators' own-initiative power may be exercised[1] in respect of an authorised person at the request of, or for the purpose of assisting, a regulator who is: (a) outside the UK; and (b) of a prescribed kind[2].

1 FSMA 2000, s 55Q(1). It should be noted that, as of the date of writing, there is no record of this power being used by the Regulators.
2 Broadly, a regulator exercising functions corresponding to: (i) any function of the FCA, the PRA or the Bank under the FSMA 2000; (ii) any function exercised by the FCA under the FSMA 2000, Pt 6; (iii) any function exercised by the Secretary of State under the Companies Act 2006; and (iv) the investigation and enforcement of insider dealing: see the Financial Services and Markets Act 2000 (Own-initiative Power) (Overseas Regulators) Regulations 2001, SI 2001/2639.

16.56 This power is exercisable both in relation to UK regulated firms and in relation to incoming firms that have a top-up permission. It is exercisable irrespective of whether the Regulator also has powers of intervention exercisable under Cases A, B, C or E[1], described at para **16.32** ff above.

1 FSMA 2000, s 55Q(2).

16.57 This is different in nature from the other bases for exercising the own-initiative power. Specifically, there is no particular hurdle or test which has to be overcome (for example, that the firm has contravened UK, or overseas, regulations or poses a potential risk to UK, or overseas, consumers). There simply has to be a request from an overseas regulator[1]. The Regulator then has a discretion whether or not to exercise its power in response to that request. Various factors outlined below may be relevant to the exercise of that discretion. Which factors apply depends upon the Regulator's EU obligations.

1 On one view, it could be that there does not even have to be a request, just a reason to assist the overseas regulator because the FSMA 2000 uses the words 'at the request of, or for the purpose of assisting' (see the FSMA 2000, ss 55Q(1) and 195(1)). However, on an alternative view, there does have to be a request: the purpose of the additional words 'for the purpose of assisting' the overseas regulator being simply to ensure that the Regulator is able to take whatever action it thinks appropriate and is not limited to the specific action requested by the overseas regulator. In practical terms, it seems unlikely the Regulator would take action unless requested to do so.

16.58 The Regulators have an additional power in the FSMA 2000, Sch 3[1], which is exercisable at the request of a host state regulator in an EEA state. The power is to impose on a UK firm, which does not have a Part 4A permission but which is doing business in that host state under the directives, the same requirements that it could impose on a variation of permission if the UK firm had a Part 4A permission in relation to the business it was carrying on[2].

1 FSMA 2000, Sch 3, para 24.
2 This is similar to the Regulator's power to intervene in an incoming firm: see para **16.75** ff below.

Relevant factors where the Regulator has relevant EEA obligations

16.59 In certain circumstances[1], the Regulator must consider whether it is necessary to exercise its own-initiative powers in order to comply with an EU obligation[2].

1 Where the request is made by an overseas regulator who is of a prescribed kind and who is acting in pursuance of provisions of a prescribed kind (see para **16.55**, n 2 above).
2 'EU obligation' is not expressly defined in the FSMA 2000. The FCA Enforcement Guide at EG 8.19 refers to 'relevant Community obligations' as obligations under the Banking Consolidation Directive, the Insurance Directives and the Markets in Financial Instruments Directive and the Insurance Mediation Directive.

16.60 The FSMA 2000 does not say how the Regulator should act or what factors it should take into account[1]. How will the Regulator exercise its discretion in this situation? The FCA views co-operation and collaboration under the various EEA directives as essential to the effective regulation of the international market in financial services[2]. Its policy is, therefore, that it will exercise its own-initiative power whenever:

- an EEA competent authority requests it do so; and

- it is satisfied that the use of the power is appropriate (having regard to the considerations relevant to its general approach to the use of its powers[3]) to enforce effectively the regulatory requirements imposed pursuant to the Single Market Directives or other Community obligations.

1 The factors which apply to the Regulators' discretion to exercise their own-initiative powers in support of an overseas regulator do not apply in cases where the Regulators consider it necessary to do so in order to comply with an EU obligation. See the FSMA 2000, s 55Q(5).
2 FCA Enforcement Guide at EG 8.20.
3 FCA Enforcement Guide at EG 8.1B to 8.5.

16.61   Therefore, the FCA will have regard to the same factors it will consider in relation to the exercise of its own-initiative power to vary or impose requirements on a UK firm with a Part 4A permission. These factors may or may not be relevant in the context of a request from the particular overseas regulator given the particular EU provision under which the request is made.

16.62   The PRA has not set out guidance on the use of the provision specifically; however, it emphasises its role in co-ordinating with counterparts in the EU in developing prudential standards and supervising international firms. It has stated that where invited to do so, it participates in supervisory colleges for all firms with significant operations in the UK, whether a legal entity or a branch[1].

1 PRA Policy Statement, 'The PRA's approach to banking supervision' (April 2013), pp 35–37, which also states that the PRA will publish a fuller statement on its approach to supervision of overseas firms operating in the UK in due course.

16.63   Although the FSMA 2000 does not specifically require the Regulators to use their own-initiative powers where they find that this is necessary in order to comply with an EU obligation, the strong implication is that they will normally do so.

Relevant factors in other situations

16.64   In any other situation[1], the FSMA 2000 prescribes a number of factors which the Regulators may take into account in deciding whether or not to exercise their power[2]:

- whether, in the country or territory of the regulator concerned, corresponding assistance would be given to a UK regulatory authority;

- whether the case involves the breach of a law, or other requirement, which has no close parallel in the UK or involves the assertion of a jurisdiction not recognised by the UK;

- the seriousness of the case and its importance to persons in the UK;

- whether it is otherwise appropriate in the public interest to give the assistance sought; and

- the Regulator may decide not to exercise its power unless the regulator concerned undertakes to make such contribution towards the cost of its exercise as the UK regulator considers appropriate.

1 In other words, in any situation where the Regulator does not consider the exercise of its own-initiative power to be necessary in order to comply with an EU obligation: FSMA 2000, s 55Q(5).
2 FSMA 2000, s 55Q(5), (6), and (in relation to an incoming firm) s 195(6), (7).

16.65 The FCA will actively consider any requests from relevant overseas regulators[1]. In doing so, it may take account of all of the above factors but may give particular weight to the seriousness of the case and its importance to persons in the UK and also to any specific request made by the overseas regulator to vary, rather than cancel, the firm's permission[2].

1 FCA Enforcement Guide at EG 8.21–8.24.
2 The FCA will also: (a) carefully consider whether the relevant authority's concerns would provide grounds for the FCA to exercise its own-initiative power if they related to a UK firm (see FCA Enforcement Guide at EG 8.23); and (b) wish to be confident that the authorities in the jurisdiction concerned would have powers available to them to provide broadly similar assistance in aid of UK authorities and would be willing properly to consider doing so (see the FCA Enforcement Guide at EG 8.24).

16.66 The FCA will thus undertake a reasonably broad analysis of the appropriateness in the particular case of exercising its discretion in favour of using its own-initiative power. Particular stress is placed on the seriousness of the case and its importance to people in the UK (which is notable as a peculiarly domestic factor in this context). Beyond that, an important consideration in practice may well be the relationship between the FCA and the relevant overseas regulator, particularly given the weight placed increasingly by the FCA on the need for co-operation among regulators internationally.

Case E: On the acquisition of control over a UK regulated firm

16.67 If it appears to the appropriate Regulator that a person has acquired control over a UK regulated firm that has a Part 4A permission but there are otherwise no grounds for the appropriate Regulator to exercise its own-initiative power, then the Regulator may nonetheless vary the firm's permission by imposing or varying a requirement[1] if it appears to it that the likely effect of the acquisition of control on the authorised person or any of its activities is uncertain[2].

1 The imposition of a requirement is one of the actions available to the Regulator when it varies a firm's permission: see para **16.90** below.
2 FSMA 2000, s 55O.

16.68 Whilst this provision is noted for completeness, it appears unlikely to be relevant in the enforcement context. It is ancillary to the Regulator's powers in the FSMA 2000, Pt 12 to vet changes in control of authorised persons and to approve, object to or impose conditions in respect of a proposed change in control.

Additional considerations which may be relevant

16.69 Three additional considerations may be relevant to the exercise of the power to vary or cancel a firm's permission depending upon the circumstances.

16.70 'Own-initiative' powers

Having regard to those in a relevant relationship

16.70 First, in considering whether to vary or cancel a Part 4A permission, the Regulator concerned may have regard to any person appearing to it to be, or likely to be, in a relationship with the person which is relevant[1].

1 FSMA 2000, s 55R.

16.71 What constitutes a relevant relationship is not defined but is left to the Regulator to interpret in the particular circumstances of the case. The FCA will assess, in the context of its assessment of the FCA threshold conditions that persons in a relevant relationship with a firm include the firm's controllers, its directors or partners, other persons with close links to the firm[1], and other persons that exert influence on the firm which might pose a risk to the firm's satisfaction of the FCA threshold conditions; but this list is not exhaustive.

1 The FCA Handbook at COND 2.3.

Varying top-up permissions

16.72 Second, if the Regulator is considering varying or cancelling a top-up permission of an incoming firm, then it must take into account[1]:

- the home state authorisation[2] of the firm;

- any relevant directive; and

- relevant provisions of the EC Treaty.

1 FSMA 2000, s 55S (2).
2 For a definition, see the FSMA 2000, s 425(2) and Sch 4.

16.73 The purpose of this provision[1] is to enable the above three matters to inform the Regulator's view on whether the firm is fit and proper to continue to hold the additional permission and whether the cancellation or variation it proposes is appropriate in light of the wider assessment of the firm which the home state regulator is responsible for making. Again, the Regulators have provided no indication of how in practice they will apply this.

1 Explanatory Notes to the FSMA 2000, para 121.

Firms connected with EEA firms

16.74 Third, before cancelling or varying a permission of a firm which is connected with an EEA firm[1], the Regulator must in prescribed circumstances consult with the firm's home state regulator[2]. This covers, for example, the situation where the firm is part of a group of companies which is primarily regulated elsewhere in the EEA.

1 For a definition of 'EEA firm', see the FSMA 2000, s 425(1) and Sch 3, para 5. 'Connected with' means a subsidiary undertaking or a subsidiary undertaking of a parent undertaking of the EEA firm: FSMA 2000, s 55R(3). As to the meaning of 'parent undertaking' and 'subsidiary undertaking' see the FSMA 2000, s 420.

2 FSMA 2000, s 55R(2). The relevant prescribed circumstance is that the Regulator concerned is considering varying a Part 4A permission given to a firm connected with an EEA firm and: (a) the effect of the variation is to grant permission for the purposes of a single market directive other than the one for the purposes of which the existing permission was granted; and (b) the permission does not relate only to 'relevant' activities, which include an insurance mediation activity and certain other regulated activities including those involving a regulated mortgage contract. See the FSMA 2000 (Exercise of Powers under Part 4A) (Consultation with Home State Regulators) Regulations 2013, SI 2013/431.

Incoming firms: intervention

16.75 The four grounds on which the FSMA 2000 allows the Regulators to exercise their intervention power for incoming firms are set out in turn below. Broadly, the grounds are similar to those on which the powers to vary or cancel the permission, discussed at para **16.31** ff above, may be exercised. The FCA will adopt a similar approach to the exercise of its power of intervention as it does to its power to vary permission or impose requirements[1]. However, there are certain differences in those grounds which are highlighted below.

1 With suitable modification for the differences in the statutory grounds: see FCA Enforcement Guide at EG 8.26.

16.76 Where the Regulator is considering exercising its power of intervention in relation to an EEA firm, there is an additional procedure which needs to be followed in certain situations, resulting from the requirements of the various single market directives. Broadly, the Regulator is required to give the firm's home state regulator the opportunity to take appropriate action against the firm before the Regulator does so[1].

1 FCA Enforcement Guide at EG 8.27: the FCA will cooperate with the firm's home state regulator when it is considering action against an incoming firm.

Case 1: Contravention of a requirement imposed by or under the FSMA 2000

16.77 The appropriate Regulator[1] may intervene in respect of an incoming firm if it appears to the Regulator that the firm has contravened, or is likely to contravene, a requirement imposed on it by or under the FSMA 2000 (in a case where the Regulator is responsible for enforcing compliance in the UK)[2].

1 Meaning, where the incoming firm is a PRA-authorised person, the FCA or the PRA; or, in any other case, the FCA. See the FSMA 2000, s 194(1B).
2 FSMA 2000, s 194(1)(a).

16.78 This provision is, in very broad terms, the equivalent for incoming firms of the provision allowing the Regulator to use its own-initiative power on UK regulated firms that are failing or likely to fail the threshold conditions[1].

1 Case A: see para **16.32** above. The threshold conditions do not generally apply to incoming firms, from a UK regulatory perspective: see para **2.8** above.

16.79 However, contravention of a requirement imposed by or under the FSMA 2000[1] may be a lower hurdle than failure to satisfy the threshold conditions. In theory, any single contravention, or likely contravention, of any of the Regulator's rules could lead to intervention action against an incoming firm (whereas, in contrast, a single rule breach by a UK regulated firm would generally be unlikely to mean that the firm was failing to meet the threshold conditions). The provision only applies, however, to those rules for which the Regulator is responsible for ensuring compliance.

1 Broadly, this covers breaches not only of specific rules and regulations but also of applicable general principles and breaches of prohibitions imposed directly under the FSMA 2000, for example those with criminal law consequences.

16.80 Whether the firm has committed a breach should be capable of objective ascertainment, although there may be room for argument (and where there is it is the Regulator's views that matter in this context). Whether the firm is likely to commit a breach, where it has not yet done so, is more a matter of judgement and it may be difficult to challenge the Regulator's view unless, for example, it is plainly unreasonable. It may therefore be difficult for firms to argue that the test had not been met.

16.81 If the test is satisfied the same factors discussed at para **16.38** above may be relevant in considering whether the Regulator will exercise the power.

Case 2: Provision of false or misleading information

16.82 The appropriate Regulator may exercise its power of intervention in respect of an incoming firm if it appears to the Regulator that the firm has, in purported compliance with any requirement imposed by or under the FSMA 2000, knowingly or recklessly given the Regulator information which is false or misleading in a material particular[1].

1 FSMA 2000, s 194(1)(b). The wording mirrors that of the criminal offence under the FSMA 2000, s 177(4) or, particularly, s 398(1).

16.83 The provision of prompt and accurate information to the Regulators is one of the central tenets of the regulatory regime. For UK regulated firms, the obligation is embodied in Principle 11 of the Principles for Businesses[1]. Furthermore, knowingly or recklessly to provide false or misleading information to the Regulators is, in many instances, a criminal offence[2]. If the Regulator seeks to exercise its intervention power under this head then the firm needs to be aware that there could be a serious potential problem, possibly with criminal law consequences.

1 The requirement on a firm to deal with its regulators in an open and co-operative way and to disclose to the Regulators appropriately anything relating to the firm of which the Regulators would reasonably expect notice: see Principle 11.
2 See, for example, the FSMA 2000, ss 177(4) and 398.

16.84 Again, the test is a relatively low one. It need only 'appear[...] to [the Regulator]'[1] that the firm has knowingly or recklessly provided false or misleading information. Again, whether or not the firm has done so ought to be capable of determination objectively, but there may be room for argument, and where there is, it is the Regulator's views that count. It may therefore be difficult to show that the statutory test for the exercise of the intervention power had not been met.

1 FSMA 2000, s 194(1).

Case 3: Desirable to exercise the power to advance the Regulators' objectives

16.85   The Regulator's power to intervene in respect of an incoming firm under this provision appears to be similar to Case C, discussed at para **16.48** ff above in relation to UK regulated firms. The same factors that were discussed in relation to Case C may be relevant to the question of whether the Regulator will exercise this power. In addition, the general policy outlined at para **16.16** ff above should be considered.

Case 4: At the request of an overseas regulator

16.86   The appropriate Regulator may exercise its power of intervention in respect of an incoming firm at the request of, or for the purpose of assisting, an overseas regulator[1]. The power of intervention may be exercised under this head irrespective of whether it is also exercisable under Cases 1, 2 or 3.

1 FSMA 2000, s 195. The meaning of an 'overseas regulator' broadly corresponds with the types of overseas regulators prescribed by HM Treasury for the purposes of s 55Q: see para **16.55** ff above.

16.87   If the firm's home state regulator asks the appropriate Regulator to exercise its power of intervention or notifies the appropriate Regulator that the firm's EEA authorisation has been withdrawn, then the Regulator must consider whether exercising its intervention power is necessary in order to comply with an EU obligation[1]. The meaning of 'EU obligation', and the considerations applied by the Regulator in deciding whether to act pursuant to one, are discussed at para **16.59** ff above.

1 FSMA 2000, s 195(5).

16.88   This power is similar to Case D in relation to UK regulated firms[1]. The discussion of that power, and the considerations applicable to the decision whether to exercise it, therefore apply equally.

1 See para **16.55** above.

WHAT ACTION CAN THE REGULATORS TAKE?

16.89   A range of actions may be taken by the Regulators under their own-initiative powers. Most notably, the Regulator may cancel a firm's permission, or take steps urgently to remove a firm's permissions. The following paragraphs will consider:

- the general types of action that the Regulator can take, including specific points on the restriction of a firm's assets or on its employees;

- the question of when the Regulator's action takes effect, including action in urgent cases; and

- cancellation of a firm's permission.

What types of action can the Regulators take in general?

16.90 So far as UK regulated firms are concerned, the own-initiative power is:

- the power to vary a firm's Part 4A permission, in any of the ways mentioned in FSMA 2000 (namely, to add or remove a regulated activity to or from those to which the permission relate, or to vary the description of a regulated activity), or to cancel it[1];

- the power to impose limitations on the firm, which means incorporating in the description of a regulated activity such limitations (for example as to circumstances in which the activity may, or may not, be carried on) as it considers appropriate[2]; and

- the power to include in the firm's permission such requirements as it considers appropriate[3], which includes the power to impose a new requirement, or to vary or cancel existing requirements.

1 FSMA 2000, ss 55J(2) and (3). The cancellation of permission (and certain ancillary provisions) is discussed at para **16.122** ff below.
2 FSMA 2000, ss 55E(5)(a) and 55F(4)(a).
3 FSMA 2000, ss 55L and 55M.

16.91 The latter two powers are available to the Regulators because the own-initiative power extends to include any provision in the permission as varied that could be included if a fresh permission were being given in response to an application for a new permission under the FSMA 2000[1].

1 FSMA 2000, s 55J(10).

16.92 These powers apply equally to incoming firms to the extent they have a top-up permission.

16.93 The own-initiative power to vary a firm's permission or to impose or vary a requirement (but not to cancel a firm's permission) may be exercised urgently: either immediately or on a specified date. This type of action is discussed in paras **16.117** ff and **16.215** ff below.

16.94 So far as incoming firms are concerned (at least beyond any top-up permission), the 'intervention' power is the power to impose any requirement in relation to the firm which the Regulator could impose if the firm's permission was a Part 4A permission and the Regulator was entitled to exercise its power under Part 4A to vary its permission[1]. In other words, of the powers outlined above, only the imposition of requirements under the FSMA 2000, ss 55L and 55M, are relevant. Since the firm does not have a Part 4A permission into which any such requirement can be included, this is achieved by imposing the requirement on the firm.

1 FSMA 2000, s 196.

16.95 The powers described above plainly can encompass a wide range of action. In the enforcement context, the FCA has indicated[1] that:

- the limitations that it can impose include limitations on the number, or category, of customers that a firm can deal with, the number of specified investments that a firm can deal in, and the activities of the firm, so that they fall within specific regulatory regimes; and

- examples of the requirements that it may impose include requirements not to take on new business, not to hold or control client money, or not to trade in certain categories of investments or an 'assets requirement'[2] (one that prohibits or restricts the disposal of or dealing with any of the firm's assets or requires assets to be transferred to a trustee).

1 FCA Enforcement Guide at EG 8.10–8.12 and, as regards incoming firms, EG 8.26–8.27.
2 There are specific provisions applicable to assets requirements: see para **16.100** ff below.

16.96 The same factors that the FCA will consider when deciding to exercise its power to vary a firm's permission, discussed at para **16.38** ff above, apply in respect of its power to impose requirements.

16.97 The PRA has given examples of the action it may take in the course of supervision. These include action to prevent or curtail a firm undertaking certain regulated activities, which may require a change to a firm's business model or future strategy[1]. Depending on the risk to the viability of the firm, the PRA may take supervisory actions including a requirement to change the management/composition of the board; limits on capital distribution; and setting tighter liquidity guidelines and/or capital requirements[2].

1 PRA Policy Statement, 'The PRA's approach to banking supervision' (April 2013), paras 195 and 196.
2 These are some of the supervisory actions identified by the PRA as part of its pro-active intervention framework: PRA Policy Statement, 'The PRA's approach to banking supervision' (April 2013), Table A.

16.98 Notably, neither the statutory examples of 'limitations' and 'requirements' nor the Regulators' policies are expressed to be exhaustive of the action the Regulators can take[1]. The basic position is therefore, that the Regulators can incorporate such limitations as they consider appropriate, impose such requirements as they consider appropriate and/or add, remove or vary the regulated activities for which the firm has permission. These are very broad and mostly subjective tests, and they give the Regulators a very wide discretion in the sort of action they may seek to take in a particular case.

16.98 'Own-initiative' powers

1 For further examples of the way in which variation of permission may be used (albeit in the context of applications by firms), see the Handbooks at SUP Chapter 6.

16.99 It is worth noting some specific points for two actions which the Regulator may take: restricting the firm's assets and imposing restrictions on the firm's employees.

Restrictions on the firm's assets

16.100 The FSMA 2000 contains additional provisions that apply when the Regulator imposes an 'assets requirement' on a firm. An assets requirement is a requirement[1]:

- prohibiting the disposal of, or other dealing with, any of the firm's assets (whether in the UK or elsewhere) or restricting such disposals or dealings; or

- that all or any of the firm's assets, or all or any assets belonging to consumers but held by the firm or to its order, must be transferred to, and held by, a trustee approved by the Regulator.

1 FSMA 2000, s 55P(4).

16.101 This gives rise to two particular issues addressed in the FSMA 2000. The application of these when the Regulator imposes an assets requirement on an incoming firm is not entirely clear[1].

1 The FSMA 2000, s 201 provides that the requirement imposed on an incoming firm 'has the same effect in relation to the firm as it would have in relation to an authorised person if it had been imposed on the authorised person by the regulator acting under ss 55L or 55M'. It seems to have been the intention (see the Explanatory Notes to the FSMA 2000, para 406) that the effect of this provision would be to apply s 55P equally where an assets requirement was imposed on an incoming firm. It is not, though, clear that it does have this effect. Section 201 provides only that the requirement has the same effect 'in relation to the firm'. This would seem to mean, for example, that the firm could not, because of s 55P(6)(a), bring a claim against a bank which refused to make a payment as a result of a reasonably held belief that the payment instruction was incompatible with the assets requirement (see para **16.102** below). However, since s 201 only explicitly has effect 'in relation to the firm', it is not clear that a bank that made a payment would incur any liability under s 55P(6)(b) (see para **16.102** below) or that a trustee would incur criminal liability if it released assets without the appropriate regulator's consent (s 55P(10) and see para **16.106** below). Even if this is correct, third parties must still take care. If they are knowingly concerned in a contravention of an assets requirement by a firm, they may be liable to a restitution order. Also, if they are themselves authorised, other regulatory enforcement consequences may arise.

How does the requirement affect banks with whom the firm holds accounts?

16.102 An assets requirement prohibiting the firm from disposing of or dealing with its assets may affect third-party institutions with whom the firm keeps an account. The FSMA 2000 allows an assets requirement to bind the bank directly, by providing that if the Regulator gives notice of the requirement to the third party institution, then[1]:

- the institution does not breach its contract with the firm if, having been instructed by, or on behalf of, the firm to transfer any sum or otherwise make any payment out of the firm's account, it refuses to do so in the reasonably held belief that complying with the instruction would be incompatible with the requirement; and

- if it does comply with such an instruction, it is liable to pay the Regulator an amount equal to the amount transferred from, or otherwise paid out of, the firm's account in contravention of the requirement.

1   FSMA 2000, s 55P(5) and (6).

16.103 This is an important provision which both protects and, where relevant, punishes institutions. The first limb gives the institution protection on the basis of its 'reasonably held belief' that to comply with the instruction would be incompatible with the requirement that the Regulator has imposed on the firm. It will be of comfort to institutions that, even if the belief is wrong, the institution should not be liable provided that it held the belief reasonably.

16.104 The second limb is the corollary of this. The institution will be liable to the Regulator if it makes a payment in compliance with such an instruction and that payment contravenes the requirement the Regulator has imposed[1]. What is notable is that, in contrast with the first limb, liability is strict[2]. It arises if the payment contravenes the Regulator's requirement. It is not open to the institution to argue that it reasonably believed that the payment was not incompatible with the requirement.

1   One difficult issue will be whether a third-party bank based outside the jurisdiction, perhaps with a UK branch upon which the assets requirement was served, could be held liable to the Regulator under this provision, in respect of a payment from an account held abroad.
2   Compare the position of a third party, such as a bank, served with notice of a freezing order granted by a court. If the bank assists in a breach of the order, it may be held to be liable in contempt of court, but only if it does so knowingly. 'It is necessary to show that the person to whom notice was given authorised the disposal of an asset, or knowing that a payment was likely to be made under an authority derived from him, deliberately refrained from taking steps to prevent it, before the corporation can be guilty of contempt of court': see *Z Ltd v A-Z and AA-LL [1981] EWCA Civ J1216-2, [1982] QB 558, CA*. See also *Customs and Excise Commissioners v Barclays Bank plc [2006] UKHL 28, [2007] 1 AC 181*, where it was held that the bank owed no duty of care to the claimant Commissioners to prevent payment of money from accounts subject to freezing orders.

16.105 The message from this is clear. Institutions should err on the side of caution and, if in doubt, refuse to comply with the firm's instruction. If they refuse to make a payment based on a reasonable belief which they hold then they should be excused liability to their customer even if that belief was wrong. If however they make a payment which in fact contravenes the requirement then they expose themselves to liability to the Regulator.

What is the effect of vesting assets in a trustee?

16.106 The FSMA 2000 contains ancillary provisions applicable where an assets requirement is imposed requiring assets to be transferred to and held by a trustee approved by the appropriate Regulator[1]. Once the firm has given the trustee written notice that the assets are held on this basis[2]:

- it is a criminal offence to release or deal with those assets while the requirement is in force, except with the consent of the appropriate Regulator[3];

- if, while the requirement is in force, the firm creates any charge over those assets, then that charge is (to the extent it confers security over those assets) void against the liquidator and any of the firm's creditors[4]; but

- neither (i) the restriction on releasing or dealing with the assets, nor (ii) the statutory restrictions on when assets are taken to be held in accordance with the Regulator's requirement that they be transferred to a trustee will affect any equitable interest or remedy of a person who is a beneficiary of a trust as a result of the Regulator imposing the assets requirement[5]. In other words, the trust law position is preserved for the beneficiary (who will normally be either the firm or its customer, if it held the assets on the trustee's behalf), so that a court could grant trust law remedies in relation to any breaches of trust.

1   Assets held by a trustee are taken to be held in accordance with the Regulator's requirement only if: (a) the firm has given the trustee written notice that they are to be held by him in accordance with the requirement; or (b) they are assets into which assets to which (a) applies have been transposed by the trustee on the firm's instructions: FSMA 2000, s 55P(9).
2   In contrast with the provisions that relate to banks, it is for the firm, rather than the Regulator, to give notice to the trustee.
3   FSMA 2000, s 55P(7) and (10).
4   FSMA 2000, s 55P(8).
5   FSMA 2000, s 55P(12).

Can the Regulators impose restrictions on the firm's employees?

16.107 One question which arises is whether the Regulator can impose restrictions or requirements on the nature or scope of the activities that a particular employee of a firm can undertake, in the same way as it can vary a firm's permission. Can it, for example, take action as a matter of urgency to prevent a firm's employees from being further involved in a particular area of business?

16.108 There is no equivalent power in relation to employees[1]. To the extent that the employee intends to perform a function which is specified as a 'controlled function', the Regulator has a discretion whether or not to approve him for that function[2], and if he is approved, in certain circumstances, it can withdraw that approval[3]. At the time of writing it cannot, however, attach conditions or limitations to the grant of the approval (although it will be able to do so when the Financial Services (Banking Reform) Act 2013 comes into force) and it cannot withdraw the approval as a matter of urgency. To the extent that the employee carries out other functions which are not controlled functions, the Regulator has little direct control over him short of making a prohibition order[4]. Prohibition orders are only likely to be appropriate in particularly serious cases and, again, cannot be imposed urgently.

1   Although the power has been used by the FCA to curtail the activities of firms consisting of a sole individual: see, for example, *Martin Richard Moseling trading as Blenheim Financial Services final notice (15/7/13)*.
2   For a brief discussion of approved persons, see para **2.23** ff above.

3 This is discussed in more detail at para **9.65** ff above.
4 For further details, see para **9.86** ff above.

16.109 The Regulators may, though, be able to accomplish their objectives through other means. First, there is, on the face of it, nothing to prevent the Regulators from using their own-initiative powers against the firm to vary the firm's permission so as to impose a requirement upon it that relates to a particular employee. For example, it could require the firm to suspend a particular employee or not to involve him in a particular area of business. Such a requirement could, as will be seen, be imposed in appropriate cases as a matter of urgency. It could be enforced directly against the firm and, if the employee is an approved person (or certain other employee), possibly against the employee as well[1].

1 If the firm breached the requirement, the individual may be liable to disciplinary consequences as an approved person knowingly concerned in a contravention by the firm: see para **9.9** above.

16.110 Second, the Regulators may be able to take action to prevent a particular employee from committing regulatory breaches, if there is evidence he is likely to do so. In such a situation, the Regulators could try to obtain an injunction against him[1]. This could be obtained on an urgent basis in an appropriate case. However, such an injunction may only be obtained where a regulatory breach is likely to occur and the scope of the injunction would be limited to restraint of the likely breach.

1 FSMA 2000, s 380. This power is limited to the extent there is a reasonable likelihood that any person will contravene a 'relevant requirement' as defined in the FSMA 2000, s 380(6). Alternatively, the Regulator may seek to apply pressure on the firm to remove the employee from his position.

What is the effect of the Regulator's action?

16.111 The effect of a variation of permission on a firm which has a Part 4A permission is to vary the permission from the date when the action takes effect. If the firm carries on a regulated activity otherwise than in accordance with the permission as varied (in other words, if it breaches the permission or the restrictions or limitations that have been imposed upon it) then:

- the firm is taken to have contravened a requirement imposed on it by the Regulator under the FSMA 2000[1], which could lead to further enforcement action, for example disciplinary action, or to the Regulator applying to the court for a civil injunction[2];

- in certain cases, this could give rise to an action for breach of statutory duty against the firm by any person who suffers loss as a result[3];

- but generally it does not amount to a criminal offence and does not make any transaction void or unenforceable[4].

1 FSMA 2000, ss 20(1) and 20(1)(A)
2 For the meaning of contravention of a requirement by or under the FSMA 2000 and a brief discussion of the possible consequences, see para **16.77** ff above.
3 FSMA 2000, s 20(3) and see para **19.8** ff below.
4 Except in the context of consumer credit: see ss 23(1A) or 26A: see the FSMA 2000, s 20(2).

16.112 'Own-initiative' powers

16.112 If an assets requirement is breached, then there may be further specific consequences, including, in some circumstances, criminal law consequences[1].

1 See para **16.100** ff above.

16.113 The effect, so far as an incoming firm that does not have a Part 4A permission is concerned, is to impose the requirement upon the firm from the date when the intervention is to take effect. The requirement has the same effect in relation to the firm as a variation of permission and the three bullet points in para **16.111** above apply equally[1].

1 FSMA 2000, ss 201 and 202. In relation to the first bullet point, the requirement is, simply, a requirement imposed upon the firm by or under the FSMA 2000 (and there is therefore no need for an express provision equivalent to s 20(1)).

When does the Regulator's action take effect?

16.114 The Regulators may take action which takes effect[1]:

- immediately;
- upon a specified date; or
- when the matter is no longer open to review.

1 FSMA 2000, ss 55Y(2) and 197(1).

16.115 Broadly, this allows the Regulators to take action either as a matter of urgency[1] or so that it takes effect in the normal way once the full decision-making process, including any Tribunal proceedings, has been completed[2]. In practice, action is often taken as a matter of urgency. This is achieved by the Regulator specifying, when issuing the first supervisory notice[3], that the proposed action takes effect immediately[4] or on a specified date[5] It is important to appreciate that there are no limitations on the type of action that can be taken on an urgent basis.

1 By taking it immediately or on a specified date. It is of course possible that the action may need to be taken upon a specified date for some reason other than urgency, for example if the matter that causes concern to the Regulators is only likely to become a live issue on a particular date, or so that the firm has some time to remedy the situation.
2 As to the meaning of 'no longer open to review', see para **16.185** ff below.
3 FSMA 2000, s 55Y(2) and, for incoming firms, s 197(1).
4 For the meaning of 'immediately' see the Financial Services and Markets Act 2000 (Service of Notices) Regulations 2001, SI 2001/1420.
5 Taking action on a specified date can equate with taking urgent action (for example, the power could be used to give the firm a limited opportunity to challenge the action or dissuade the Regulator from taking it before it takes effect). However, it need not always do so; there may be reasons other than urgency for specifying a particular date.

16.116 From the firm's perspective, the prospect of immediate action being taken against it by its regulator(s) raises a number of serious issues. What immediate steps should it take? Does it have any opportunity, or ability, to object to the process? What publicity will arise? How can it protect its business? In the following paragraphs, the circumstances which may lead to the Regulators taking urgent action will be reviewed. The procedure for urgent action and practical guidance for firms facing urgent action is considered at para **16.224** ff.

When in practice will the Regulators take urgent action?

16.117 The Regulators may take urgent action only if they reasonably consider this to be necessary having regard to the grounds upon which they are exercising their own-initiative variation power or own-initiative requirement power[1]. Perhaps in recognition of the serious potential consequences of the summary powers conferred, this involves a higher hurdle than in many of the statutory tests to be found in the FSMA 2000[2]. The use of the word 'necessary'[3] and the express need for reasonableness add a certain degree of objectivity. However, the question of whether urgent action should be taken is nonetheless largely within the Regulators' discretion and it is difficult for firms to challenge the imposition of urgent action on the basis that the test has not been met. The key question for firms is how the Regulators exercise their discretion.

1 FSMA 2000, s 55Y(3) and, for incoming firms, s 197(2) (although this omits the word 'reasonably').
2 Compare, for example, the tests for the imposition of the own-initiative powers (see para **16.14** ff above) to the tests for the use of the FCA's investigatory powers (see **Chapter 5** above).
3 Precisely what 'necessary' means depends upon the circumstances. It 'lies somewhere between "indispensable" on the one hand and "useful" or "expedient" on the other': Lord Griffiths in *In re an Inquiry under the Company Securities (Insider Dealing) Act 1985 [1988] AC 660*. In *R v Gloucestershire County Council and another, ex p Barry [1997] AC 584*, Lord Clyde noted that 'the words "necessary" and "needs" are relative expressions, admitting in each case a considerable range of meanings'. See also *Interbrew SA v Financial Times [2002] EWCA Civ 274, [2002] EMLR 24* from para 32 onwards.

16.118 The FCA will consider exercising its powers as a matter of urgency where[1]:

- the information available to it indicates serious concerns about the firm or its business that need to be addressed immediately; and

- circumstances indicate that it is appropriate to use its statutory powers immediately to require and/or prohibit certain actions by the firm in order to ensure that the firm addresses these concerns.

1 FCA Enforcement Guide at EG 8.7.

16.119 Such situations are likely to include one or more of the following[1]:

- information indicating significant loss, risk of loss or other adverse effects for consumers, where action is necessary to protect their interests;

- information indicating that a firm's conduct has put it at risk of being used for the purposes of financial crime, or of being otherwise involved in crime;

- evidence that the firm has submitted inaccurate or misleading information so that the FSA becomes seriously concerned about the firm's ability to meet its regulatory obligations; and/or

- circumstances suggesting a serious problem within the firm or with the firm's controllers[2] that calls into question the firm's ability to continue to meet the threshold conditions.

1 FCA Enforcement Guide at EG 8.8.
2 Broadly, this refers to a person who exercises control over the firm: see the Glossary to the Handbook.

16.120 The FCA also needs to consider whether the urgent exercise of its powers is an appropriate response to such concerns. The FCA has indicated that, in doing so, it will consider the full circumstances of the case, but has identified a number of factors that may be relevant, including the following[1]:

- the extent of any loss or risk of loss or other adverse effect on consumers;

- the extent to which customer assets appear to be at risk;

- the nature or extent of any false or inaccurate information provided by the firm;

- the seriousness of any suspected breaches and the steps that need to be taken to correct them;

- the financial resources of the firm, particularly where the firm may be required to pay significant compensation to consumers;

- the risk of the firm's business being used to facilitate crime;

- the risk that a firm's conduct or business presents to the financial system;

- the firm's compliance history and its conduct since the issue arose; and

- the impact that the use of the powers will have on the firm's business and its customers, including the effect on the firm's reputation and on market confidence[2].

1 For a full but non-exhaustive list of factors the FCA may consider, see FCA Enforcement Guide at EG 8.9.
2 The Regulators recognise the need to be satisfied that the impact of any own-initiative action is proportionate to the concerns being addressed, in the context of the overall aim of achieving their statutory objectives (FSMA 2000, s 3B).

16.121 The use of words such as 'information indicating', 'circumstances suggesting' and 'suspected breach' in the FCA guidance reflects an important distinction between urgent own-initiative action and other types of regulatory action: it is normally taken by the Regulators on a summary basis, without the firm having any opportunity to be heard, any review of the decision or challenge only taking place afterwards. The Regulators will be considering whether to take action not following an exhaustive enquiry but, on a summary basis because of particularly serious concerns and based on the information available to them at the time. The potential ramifications of taking action on this basis should mean that the power is only used when justified by the seriousness and immediacy of the concerns. In practice, such action is taken quite regularly.

Cancellation

16.122 Cancellation of permission is the most serious application of the Regulators' own-initiative power. As discussed in para **16.31** above, the statutory grounds for cancellation are the same as variation. Whether the Regulator decides to vary or cancel the permission depends on the circumstances: for example, the type of behaviour the Regulator is seeking to address. The question of cancellation of permission does not arise in relation to incoming firms, save to the extent they have a 'top-up permission'. Subject to this, the Regulators have:

- the right, in relation to Cases A to D[1], not only to vary a firm's permission but to cancel it; and

- in any case, a duty to cancel the firm's permission if, as a result of varying a firm's permission, there are no longer any regulated activities for which the firm has permission and where the Regulator is satisfied that it is no longer necessary to keep the permission in force[2].

1 These are four of the tests for the imposition of the Regulators' own-initiative powers and are discussed at para **16.32** above.
2 FSMA 2000, s 55J(8).

16.123 The FCA will consider cancelling a firm's permission in two main circumstances[1], namely:

- where it has very serious concerns about a firm, or the way that its business is or has been conducted; or

- where the firm's regulated activities have come to an end and it has not applied for cancellation of its permission[2].

1 FCA Enforcement Guide at EG 8.13.
2 A Regulator may cancel a firm's permission where the firm has not conducted regulated activities for a period of at least 12 months.

16.124 The first of these is the main, general criterion. The underlying concern is the Regulators' obligation to ensure that the firm satisfies, and will continue to satisfy, the threshold conditions[1].

1 FSMA 2000, s 55B(3).

16.125 The grounds for cancelling a firm's permission are the same as for varying it and where the Regulator varies a firm's permission by removing all regulated activities, the effect will be similar[1]. Apart from the procedure for taking the action which is considered at para **16.130** below, the main difference is that cancellation of permission cannot take place with immediate effect and therefore, where action needs to be taken urgently, the Regulator may vary a firm's permission before cancelling it. In practice, a firm's permission can be varied in such a way so as to have the same effect as cancellation, for example by removing all of the firm's regulated activities. In urgent and serious cases, this is how the Regulator will deal with the issue.

1 FCA Enforcement Guide at EG 8.14 and para **16.128** ff below.

16.126 'Own-initiative' powers

16.126 If the Regulator decides to remove all the firm's regulated activities, it will be under an obligation to cancel the firm's permission once it is satisfied that it is no longer necessary to keep the permission in force[1]. On the wording of the provision, therefore, the obligation to cancel only seems to arise if the Regulator is satisfied that it is no longer necessary to keep the permission in force[2]. In other words, the decision is largely within the Regulator's discretion.

1 FSMA 2000, s 55J(8).
2 The alternative would have been an obligation to cancel unless the Regulator was satisfied that it was necessary to keep the permission in force.

16.127 In some circumstances, the Regulator may prefer that the firm remains within the regulatory system for some time and so does not cancel its permission, and it clearly believes that the FSMA 2000 enables it to do so. In the enforcement context, the FCA has stated that it may decide not to cancel a firm's permission so that it can[1]:

- continue to monitor the firm;

- use its administrative enforcement powers against the firm[2]; or

- supervise an orderly winding down of the firm's regulated business[3].

1 FCA Enforcement Guide at EG 8.17.
2 This refers to those powers that the Regulators generally have in relation to the regulated community (such as powers to investigate, discipline, make a restitution order and so on). In most cases, these powers cannot be exercised against a formerly authorised person when its permission has been cancelled. The Regulators may therefore want to preserve the person's status as an authorised person until it has taken appropriate action: see also the Handbooks at SUP 6.4.24/25.
3 For further details, see the Handbooks at SUP 6.4. The Regulators will not normally cancel a firm's permission on application from the firm until the firm can demonstrate that it has, in relation to business carried on under that permission, as appropriate: (i) ceased to carry on all regulated activities or fully run off or transferred all insurance liabilities; (ii) repaid all client money and client deposits; (iii) discharged custody assets and any other property belonging to clients; and (iv) discharged, satisfied or resolved complaints against the firm: see the Handbooks at SUP 6.4.19–6.4.22.

16.128 The problem with this is that it is difficult to see where the line is drawn in practice between varying a firm's permission and cancelling it. The Regulators can, through varying the firm's permission, effectively achieve the same outcome as cancelling it, but without the firm having the same procedural safeguards. In some situations there may be reasons for doing so, for example the need to supervise the orderly winding down of the business (in the same way as the Regulators would do if the firm had applied to cancel its permission). As the above indicates, though, the Regulators may choose not to cancel the firm's permission for purely enforcement related reasons. By the time it does seek to cancel permission, the additional procedural safeguards applicable to cancellations of permission may be of much less benefit to the firm[1]. In the meantime, the Regulators would also retain their regulatory powers over the firm.

1 If a Regulator had decided to cancel the firm's permission at the outset when seeking to vary its permission, the cancellation of permission would have proceeded using the warning/decision notice procedure and as a result the firm would (among other things) have had a right to review the Regulator's material at an early stage and without prejudice discussions may have taken place

between the firm and the FSA which may have affected the outcome (see **CHAPTER 10** above). The ultimate safeguard is, though, the right of referral to the Tribunal which is available in any event.

16.129 If the firm does not wish to remain authorised once its permissions have been removed, can it challenge the Regulator's decision not to cancel its permission? It is thought that a decision not to cancel a firm's permission would fall within those matters that could be referred to the Tribunal, although this is not yet clear[1]. If so, the Regulator would have the burden of proof and the Tribunal would have a broad discretion to decide what action was appropriate for the Regulator to take[2]. This may avoid those difficulties that would be presented by an application for judicial review given the low statutory test applicable in this context.

1   The question is whether the firm is 'aggrieved by the exercise by either regulator of its own-initiative power': FSMA 2000, s 55Z3(2). The power to cancel is found in FSMA 2000, s 55J(2) and (8), which is part of what is defined as the own-initiative variation power (see FSMA 2000, s 55J(12)).
2   See, generally, **CHAPTER 12** above.

THE SUPERVISORY NOTICE PROCEDURE

16.130 The own-initiative powers are different in purpose and nature from the Regulators' disciplinary powers and the Regulators' exercise of these powers involves a different procedure under the FSMA 2000[1], known as the 'supervisory notice' procedure. In particular, the provisions on when and how enforcement or supervisory action takes effect are different (most significantly, a decision to issue a supervisory notice can be taken on an urgent basis and have immediate effect). In many other respects, though, the procedure is similar and the firm will ask itself many of the questions that are addressed in **CHAPTER 10** above.

1   For the process applicable to the Regulators' disciplinary and other enforcement powers, known as the 'warning/decision notice' procedure, see **CHAPTER 10** above.

16.131 The supervisory notice procedure is also relevant to a number of the Regulators' other powers, including:

• giving directions in relation to certain types of collective investment scheme[1], or an OEIC[2] (exercisable by the FCA);

• imposing certain requirements on former underwriting members of Lloyd's[3] (exercisable by the PRA or by the FCA where the relevant activity is not PRA-regulated); and

• a similar procedure applies where the FCA, acting as the UK Listing Authority, seeks to discontinue or suspend a listing of securities, as discussed in **CHAPTER 20** below.

1   FSMA 2000, ss 257, 267 and 279.
2   Open-Ended Investment Companies Regulations 2001, SI 2001/1228, reg 25.
3   FSMA 2000, s 320.

16.132 Reference is therefore made to para **16.130** ff above when discussing such other powers elsewhere in this book.

16.133 'Own-initiative' powers

The basic framework

16.133 The FSMA 2000 provides only a framework for the Regulators' procedures; the detailed procedures are contained in the FCA Handbook and in the PRA's April 2013 Policy Statements 'The Prudential Regulation Authority's approach to enforcement: statutory statements of policy and procedure'[1]. The FSMA 2000 does contain some basic requirements, as follows[2].

1 See the FCA Handbook at DEPP 2.
2 The same, or similar, requirements apply in relation to warning/decision notices and are discussed in more detail in **CHAPTER 10** above.

16.134 First, the FSMA 2000 requires the Regulators to issue notices termed 'supervisory notices' when they propose or decide to use their own-initiative powers[1] (hence, the term 'supervisory notice procedure').

1 For a further discussion, see paras **16.152** ff and **16.193** ff below.

16.135 Second, in the same way as for warning/decision notices[1], the FSMA 2000 requires that the Regulators' procedures for the giving of supervisory notices are designed to ensure that the decision which gives rise to the obligation to give the notice is taken by a person not directly involved in establishing the evidence on which that decision is based or by two or more persons who include a person not directly involved in establishing that evidence[2]. In short, the Regulators' staff that investigate the firm cannot, on their own, decide to impose the variation of permission. There is an exception, allowing the Regulators' procedures to permit a decision to be taken without the separation of functions[3] if the person taking the decision is of a level of seniority laid down by the procedure and the relevant Regulator considers that, in the particular case, it is necessary in order to advance one of its objectives[4]. As will be seen, the Regulators' procedures do make use of this exception in certain circumstances.

1 See para **10.25** ff above.
2 FSMA 2000, s 395(2).
3 FSMA 2000, s 395(3).
4 See para **1.11** below.

16.136 Third, the FSMA 2000 requires the Regulators to publish a statement of their procedure and to follow their procedure when giving a supervisory notice[1].

1 FSMA 2000, s 395(5) and (9). Note that, a failure in a particular case to follow the procedure, does not affect the validity of the supervisory notice given in the case, although the Tribunal may take that failure into account: see the FSMA 2000, s 395(11) and (12).

16.137 Although they are broadly similar, the FCA and PRA's supervisory notice procedures do differ in certain respects. The following paragraphs will set out in detail the FCA supervisory notice procedure and, where appropriate, will note the similarities and differences for the PRA's procedure. The flowchart below provides a quick guide to the FCA's supervisory notice procedure.

Investigation/information gathering

Recommendation whether to take action —No— Informal notification of no action

Yes

Is the matter:
- fundamental?
- urgent?
- straightforward?
- based on a 'common understanding'?

Fundamental urgent | Fundamental not urgent | Not fundamental | By agreement

Can it be put before RDC/Chairman?

FCA staff consider whether to issue first supervisory notice

No | Yes

Decision maker *FCA staff*

Decision maker *First supervisory notice: FCA staff Second supervisory notice: RDC**

Decision maker *RDC**

Issue first supervisory notice? If so:
- time for representation?
- effective date for action?

No | Yes

No further action | **First supervisory notice**

First supervisory notice

Settlement/ mediation

Action may take effect:
- Refer to Tribunal?
- Procedure continues

Representations

Does the firm still agree and have the circumstances not materially changed?

Yes

FCA staff to issue notice

Action may take effect:
- Refer to Tribunal?

—No—

Yes

Issue second supervisory notice?
- proceed to take proposal action?
- take action in a different way?

different action

Decision maker *RDC** | No

No further action

—No—

Yes

Second supervisory notice

Yes

Second supervisory notice

Tribunal/ Appeals

Action takes effect (if it has not already taken effect)

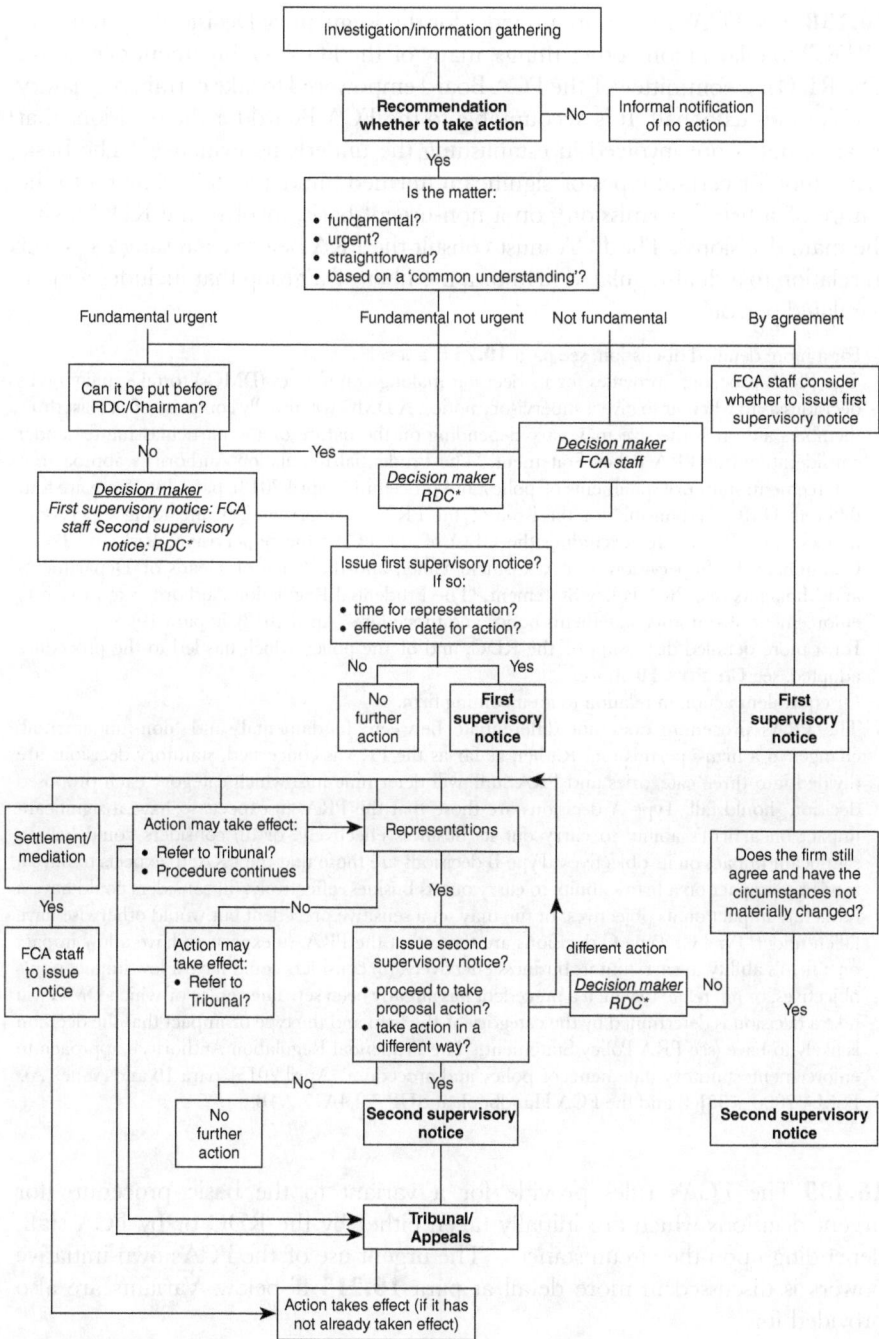

* Decisions to be taken by the RDC can in 'straightforward cases' be taken by the Chairman or Deputy Chairman of the RDC (together with one other RDC member if so required).

16.138 The FCA's procedure provides for the Regulatory Decisions Committee[1] ('RDC') to take, among other things, many of the FCA's enforcement decisions[2]. The RDC is a committee of the FCA Board empowered to take certain regulatory decisions on its behalf. It is accountable to the FCA Board for the decisions that it takes, but is not involved in establishing the underlying evidence[3]. The basic procedure for certain types of significant (termed 'fundamental') changes to the nature of a firm's permission[4], on a non-urgent basis, involves the RDC taking the main decisions[5]. The FCA must consult the PRA before exercising its power in relation to a dual-regulated firm or a member of a group that includes a dual-regulated person[6].

1 For a more detailed discussion, see para **10.25** ff above.
2 The PRA's procedure provides for its decision making committees (DMCs) to take many of its decisions as to whether to give a supervisory notice. A DMC will usually comprise of at least three members although the size may vary depending on the nature of the particular matter under consideration (see PRA Policy Statement, 'The Prudential Regulation Authority's approach to enforcement: statutory statements of policy and procedure' (April 2013), para 33. There are four different DMCs responsible for the issue of the PRA's statutory notices, including supervisory notices: the PRA Board (excluding the CEO of the FCA); the Supervision, Risk and Policy Committee; the Supervision and Assessment Panel; and the Panel of Heads of Departments and Managers (see PRA Policy Statement, 'The Prudential Regulation Authority's approach to enforcement of statutory statements policy and procedure' (April 2013), at para 10).
3 For a more detailed discussion of the RDC, and of the policy which has led to the procedure adopted, see **CHAPTER 10** above.
4 Or equivalent action in relation to an incoming firm.
5 The PRA's procedure does not differentiate between 'fundamental' and 'non-fundamental' changes to a firm's permission. Rather, as far as the PRA is concerned, statutory decisions are divided into three categories and PRA staff will determine into which category each proposed decision should fall. Type A decisions are those that the PRA: (i) expects to have a significant impact on a firm's ability to carry out its business effectively; or (ii) considers could have a significant impact on its objectives. Type B decisions are those that the PRA: (i) expects to have a moderate impact on a firm's ability to carry out its business effectively; (ii) considers could have a moderate impact on its objectives; or (iii) may set a sensitive precedent but would otherwise have fallen under Type C. Type C decisions are those that the PRA: (i) expects to have a low impact on a firm's ability to carry out its business effectively; (ii) considers could have a low impact on its objectives; or (iii) relate to which a precedent has already been set. The choice of which DMC will take a decision is determined by the category of the firm and the type of impact that the decision is likely to have (see PRA Policy Statement, 'The Prudential Regulation Authority's approach to enforcement: statutory statements of policy and procedure' (April 2013), para 16 and Annex A).
6 FSMA 2000, s 55J(4) and the FCA Handbook at SUP 7.2.4A–7.2.4B.

16.139 The FCA's rules provide for a variant to the basic procedure for urgent decisions which are initially taken either by the RDC or by FCA staff, depending upon the circumstances[1]. The urgent use of the FCA's own-initiative powers is discussed in more detail at para **16.215** ff below. Variants are also provided for:

- decisions regarding non-fundamental changes to a firm's permission[2];

- straightforward cases[3]; and

- decisions to implement settlements agreed between the firm and the FCA[4] or other cases where there is no dispute between the FCA and the firm as to the need for the action proposed.

1 Like the FCA, the PRA's policy provides for variants to the basic procedure for urgent decisions (see PRA Policy Statement, 'The Prudential Regulation Authority's approach to enforcement: statutory statements of policy and procedure' (April 2013), para 70).
2 This also applies to equivalent action in relation to an incoming firm. Such decisions are not taken by the RDC but by senior FCA staff, subject to safeguards designed to secure the separation of functions, save in certain exceptional situations. The distinction between fundamental and non-fundamental variations of permission is considered at para **16.144** ff below and the procedure for non-fundamental variations of permission is considered at para **16.233** ff below.
3 See para **16.248** below.
4 See para **16.187** below.

16.140 There are a number of possible phases in the supervisory notice procedure. These are as follows[1]:

- Phase 1: a recommendation from the FCA's staff;

- Phase 2: the issue of a first supervisory notice;

- Phase 3: representations from the firm and, possibly, settlement or mediation;

- Phase 4: the issue of a second supervisory notice;

- Phase 5: a reference to the Tribunal and, possibly, further appeals; and

- Phase 6: publication of the action.

Each phase is described in turn below.

1 These phases also apply to the PRA's supervisory notice procedure.

Phase 1: Recommendation from the FCA's staff

16.141 The first phase in the supervisory notice procedure occurs when FCA staff consider whether any formal supervisory notice action is appropriate[1]. In doing so, they must also consider[2]:

- which body is the appropriate decision-maker to consider the recommendation; and

- whether the matter is urgent.

1 In some cases, the decision to recommend a supervisory notice might arise as a result of an FCA enforcement investigation. In some cases, the firm may have received a draft investigation report towards the end of the FCA's investigation, in which case it will have had an opportunity to respond: see the FCA Enforcement Guide at EG 4.30 to 4.33 and the discussion at para **10.71** above. A draft investigation report will not be issued if it is not practicable to do so, particularly in urgent cases: see the FCA Enforcement Guide at EG 4.30.
2 See the FCA Handbook at DEPP 2.2.1 and 2.2.2.

16.142 These two questions are interlinked and the answer determines who will consider the FCA staff recommendation and how the FCA takes the decision whether to accept the recommendation and issue the first supervisory notice. In particular:

- the RDC is responsible only for decisions relating to variations of permission (or equivalent action in relation to an incoming firm) which would make a fundamental change to the nature of the Part 4A permission (whether indefinitely or for a limited period)[1];

- decisions with respect to other 'non-fundamental' variations of permission (or equivalent action in relation to an incoming firm) are taken instead by senior FCA staff members under so-called 'executive procedures'[2]. FCA staff under executive procedures will also be the decision-maker:

  - in certain urgent cases[3];

  - in straightforward cases;

  - when a decision implements a settlement[4]; or

when a firm agrees not to contest the FCA's exercise of its own-initiative powers, including where the FCA's action involves a fundamental variation or requirement[5].

1 See the FCA Handbook at DEPP 2.5.7 (firms with a Part 4A permission).
2 These are discussed at para **16.234** ff below.
3 See para **16.241** ff below.
4 Settlements are discussed at para **16.187** below.
5 See the FCA Handbook at DEPP 2.5.7.

16.143 The following sections outline the procedure for making a fundamental change to the nature of a firm's permission.

What is a 'fundamental change' to a permission?

16.144 Making a 'fundamental change' to the nature of a firm's permission means (in the context of the own-initiative powers)[1]:

- removing a type of activity, or investment, from the firm's permission;

- refusing an application to include a type of activity or investment; or

- imposing or varying an assets requirement or refusing an application to vary or cancel such a requirement[2].

1 See the FCA Handbook at DEPP 2.5.8. See para **16.138**, n 5 for the PRA's different approach to the categorisation of its decision-making.
2 For the definition of 'assets requirement', see the FSMA 2000, s 55P(4) and see also para **16.100** above.

16.145 It is worth noting that the current definition of 'fundamental change' has narrowed significantly since the previous edition of the book. In addition to the three actions outlined above, 'fundamental change' previously included 'restricting a firm from taking on new business, dealing with a particular category of client or handling client money by imposing a limitation or requirement, or refusing an application to vary or cancel such a limitation or requirement'[1]. This action has now been removed from the definition and it is therefore likely that a wide range of action which a firm might regard as serious would not amount to a fundamental change for this purpose. For example, a requirement imposed upon the firm regarding its systems and controls, its employees, its financial position (subject to the imposition of assets requirements) or, the conduct of its business, is unlikely to fall within this definition. Importantly, certain types of restrictions that the FCA has indicated it might consider imposing on firms such as limiting the size of a firm's loan book or imposing maximum loan-to-value ratios are also unlikely to amount to fundamental changes to the nature of a firm's permission. This is significant because the decision to take non-fundamental action is not taken by the RDC, but by FCA staff under executive procedures.

1 See the FSA Handbook at DEC 4.1.5.

16.146 Examples of situations in which the FCA may consider it appropriate to make a fundamental change to a firm's permission are set out at para **16.16** above[1].

1 See the FCA Enforcement Guide at EG 8.3

What can the firm do to influence the decision whether to make a recommendation?

16.147 The firm has no input into the process at this stage and, indeed, in some cases, will not even know that a decision whether to recommend the use of the own-initiative powers is being taken. However, if the firm is aware that the FCA's staff are considering whether to recommend action, it may attempt to enter into informal discussions with them in relation to the matter that concerns them[1].

1 See the FSMA 2000, s 138A, the Handbooks at SUP 8 and *Eurosure Investment Services v FSA (2003) FSMT 006* where the firm's application for a waiver was not granted.

Does the FCA have any other options besides a variation of permission or the imposition of a requirement?

16.148 The use of the own-initiative powers should not be viewed in isolation. In many cases, the FCA may be considering generally what action it should take in light of the matters that have occurred[1]. Such action may not only include variation of permission or the imposition or variation of a requirement, but also discipline, restitution orders and injunctions[2], action against individuals[3] and/ or criminal prosecutions[4]. The use of the own-initiative powers may be just one of a number of options available, aimed at addressing the various consequences of the same problem. In other cases, the use of the own-initiative powers could be considered upon its own by the FCA, perhaps because it is taking action as a matter of urgency and later will conclude its investigations and consider whether any other action is warranted. Again, therefore, the firm needs to have in mind the other regulatory action that may result from the particular matter.

1 The PRA will also consider generally what action it should take.
2 See **CHAPTER 8** above.
3 See **CHAPTER 9** above.
4 See **CHAPTER 18** below.

16.149 Even where it is appropriate for the FCA to exercise its own-initiative powers, it may decide not to take formal action to vary a firm's permission,

16.149 'Own-initiative' powers

but may instead, make clear to the firm what steps are required and give it the opportunity to comply voluntarily[1]. This may be more likely to be the case where the problem has arisen and been handled within the supervisory relationship[2].

1 See the FCA Enforcement Guide at EG 8.3 and the FCA Handbook at SUP 7.3.1.
2 See para **16.10** ff above.

Is the firm informed about the recommendation?

16.150 There is no formal requirement for the FCA to inform the firm about its recommendation[1]. However, the FCA may inform the firm that it is intending to recommend that action is taken. The FCA will seek to give a firm reasonable notice of an intent to vary its permission or impose a requirement and to agree with the firm an appropriate timescale. However it may need to act immediately if a delay will pose a risk to any of the FCA objectives[2].

1 The same is true of the PRA.
2 See the FCA Handbook at SUP 7.3.4.

16.151 The FCA's decision whether a recommendation should be made that action is taken will not normally be made public[1].

1 See the FCA Enforcement Guide at EG 6.1 and para **10.90** above. The position for the PRA is similar (see PRA Policy Statement, 'The Prudential Regulation Authority's approach to enforcement: statutory statements of policy and procedure' (April 2013), para 5).

Phase 2: The first supervisory notice

What is a first supervisory notice?

16.152 The first supervisory notice is the written notice which the FSMA 2000 requires the FCA[1] to issue if the decision has been made to take a certain course of action (or take such action with immediate effect)[2], including the variation of a firm's permission[3] or the imposition of a similar requirement on an incoming firm[4].

1 FSMA 2000 imposes the same requirement on the PRA.
2 FSMA 2000, s 395 lists the various types of notice to which the term 'supervisory notice' applies.
3 FSMA 2000, s 55Y(4).
4 FSMA 2000, s 197(3).

16.153 The first supervisory notice must[1]:

- give details of the action proposed;

- inform the firm of when the action takes effect[2];

- state the FCA's reasons for the action[3] and for its decision as to when the action is to take effect;

- inform the firm of its right to refer the matter to the Tribunal[4], and provide an indication of the procedure for such a reference[5]; and

- inform the firm that it may make representations to the FCA within the period that is specified in the notice[6], whether or not the firm decides to refer the matter to the Tribunal[7].

1 FSMA 2000, s 55Y(5) and, for incoming firms, s 197(4) and see the FCA Handbook at DEPP 2.2.3. For the contents of the other types of supervisory notice, reference needs to be made to the relevant statutory provision under which the supervisory notice is issued.
2 The statutory provisions only require this to be specified if the action takes effect immediately or on a specified date, but the FCA Handbook indicates that this may always be stated: see the FCA Handbook at DEPP 2.2.2. As to when the action takes effect, see para **16.160** ff below.
3 The summary of the FCA's reasons for the action will tend to state the 'Facts and matters relied on'. This summary of the factual background tends to be much briefer than is the case with final notices issued otherwise than as a result of the FCA's use of its own-initiative power: see para **10.192** ff above.
4 See para **16.165** below.
5 FSMA 2000, ss 55Y(11) and 197(10).
6 See paras **16.167** and **16.169** ff below.
7 See para **16.202** ff below.

16.154 Where the action in question relates to a fundamental change, the recommendation by the FCA staff is considered by the RDC, which normally means a panel comprising the Chairman or Deputy Chairman and at least two other members[1].

1 This need not apply in urgent cases (see para **16.216** ff below) or in straightforward cases (see para **16.248** below). The size and composition of the panel will vary depending upon the nature of the particular matter under consideration: see the FCA Handbook at DEPP 3.2.2/3. For a detailed discussion of the procedure of the RDC, see the FCA Handbook at DEPP 3.2 and see also para **10.25** ff above. For the PRA, the recommendation by the PRA staff is considered by the relevant DMC, which will consider whether the recommendation has been based on adequate material or whether it requires additional information or clarification, take into consideration the FCA's views where required, satisfy itself that the action recommended is appropriate in all the circumstances and decide whether and on what terms to give the notice (see PRA Policy Statement, 'The Prudential Regulation Authority's approach to enforcement: statutory statements of policy and procedure' (April 2013), para 22).

16.155 The RDC may decide either to take no action or to give a first supervisory notice to the firm. If the FCA has already informed the firm that it intended to recommend action, it will communicate the RDC decision promptly to the firm[1]. In other cases, the firm may in practice be told informally that no action is to be taken.

1 See the FCA Handbook at DEPP 2.2.4.

What is the period for the firm to make representations?

16.156 When it issues the first supervisory notice, the decision-maker must decide on the period for the firm to make representations. This will not be less than 14 days[1].

1 See the FCA Handbook at DEPP 3.2.15. The position for the PRA is similar (see PRA Policy Statement, 'The Prudential Regulation Authority's approach to enforcement: statutory statements of policy and procedure' (April 2013), para 47). A warning notice will also allow a minimum of 14 days for a firm to make representations.

16.157 The length of the period will be important for the firm because, first, it may have known little or nothing about the proposed action before receiving the first supervisory notice, second, the process of making representations is an important one if the firm wishes to find a mutually acceptable compromise with the FCA (through informal settlement discussions or mediation) and avoid having to fight the matter in the Tribunal and in any event, the firm will need time to prepare its representations. Reasons why the firm might want to make representations are discussed at para **16.173** ff below. Whether mediation is likely to be available to the firm is considered at para **16.164** ff below.

16.158 In making its decision on the period for representations, the decision-maker has regard to the circumstances of the case, including the nature of the action proposed and its likely effect on the person concerned, and it also has particular regard to the risk to the FCA's regulatory objectives of any delay in imposing the proposed action[1]. This highlights the difficult balance between ensuring that the firm is treated fairly and ensuring that the FCA's regulatory concerns are addressed in a timely manner. It also means that the latter is likely to prevail in most cases. Generally, the period for making representations will be 14 days from the date when the person receives the notice, subject to the right to seek an extension of time[2].

1 For an explanation of the regulatory objectives, see para **1.11** above.
2 See the FCA Handbook at DEPP 3.2.15/16.The decision-maker may on occasion specify a longer period.

16.159 The procedure for making representations is discussed at para **16.177** ff below. If the firm decides not to make representations within the period prescribed by the first supervisory notice, default procedures apply[1]. These are described in detail at para **16.184** ff below.

1 See the FCA Handbook at DEPP 2.3.3 and 3.2.22 and for the PRA see PRA Policy Statement, 'The Prudential Regulation Authority's approach to enforcement: statutory statements of policy and procedure' (April 2013), para 64.

When will the action proposed by the FCA take effect?

16.160 The date when the proposed action takes effect depends upon what is specified in the notice. Again, this is a matter for the decision-maker when it decides to issue the first supervisory notice. It is plainly an important decision from the firm's perspective because the decision-maker may decide to take action immediately, on a summary basis, giving the firm little or no opportunity to be heard until afterwards and the action taken may be given, or may attract, immediate publicity[1].

1 For a more detailed discussion, see para **16.215** ff below.

16.161 The FSMA 2000 allows exercise of the own-initiative powers to take effect either[1] immediately, if the first supervisory notice states that this is the case, or on such date as is specified in the notice, or, if no date is specified, when the matter to which the notice relates is no longer open to review[2]. Action may be imposed immediately only if the FCA, having regard to the ground upon which it is exercising its own-initiative power, reasonably considers that it is necessary for the action to take effect immediately[3]. Broadly, this equates to the situation with urgent action, although there may be other reasons for specifying a particular date. The factors relevant to the decision as to whether urgent action should be taken are considered at para **16.118** ff above.

1 FSMA 2000, s 55Y(2) or, for incoming firms, s 197(1).
2 As to the meaning of 'no longer open to review', see para **16.185** below.
3 Where action is to take effect immediately, it will take effect upon the firm's actual receipt of the supervisory notice if that is earlier than the deemed date of receipt: see the Financial Services and Markets Act 2000 (Service of Notices) Regulations 2001, SI 2001/1420, reg 6(3). It is therefore likely that the Regulator will fax or e-mail the notice where possible. Action may also be imposed upon a specified date.

16.162 Given the potential consequences for the firm of action being imposed immediately, on a summary basis, and the statutory requirement for the FCA reasonably[1] to consider that urgent action is necessary and to specify in its first supervisory notice its reasons for determining that such action is warranted, there is a possibility for a firm to challenge the imposition of action immediately (or on a short timeframe)[2].

1 Or, in the case of urgent action against an incoming firm, the word 'reasonably' is omitted: see para **16.117** above.
2 This is contemplated in the Tribunal's Rules, which in certain circumstances allow the Tribunal to suspend the FCA or PRA's action: see para **12.119** above. See also the discussion at para **16.227** ff below.

What is the effect of the first supervisory notice?

16.163 The first supervisory notice is the first formal step in this enforcement process and gives the firm various rights. However, because of the FCA's ability to take immediate action, it may also have more serious immediate consequences[1].

1 Contrast a warning notice: see para **10.115** above.

16.164 The effect of a first supervisory notice is as follows:

- it gives the firm the right to refer the matter to the Tribunal[1];

- it gives the firm the right to make representations to the decision-maker within the period specified in the notice[2];

- it gives the firm the option to enter into settlement discussions with the FCA[3], and may give it an opportunity to resolve the matter through mediation[4];

- it may have a more substantive effect, depending upon what is stated in the notice:

  - if it specifies that the proposed action takes effect immediately, then the action takes effect immediately;

  - if it specifies that the proposed action takes effect on a particular date, then the action will take effect on that date without a further notice being

>   issued by the FCA, unless the firm can, in the meantime, either persuade the FCA not to take the action or persuade the Tribunal to suspend the action;
>
> —   if it does not specify the date when the action is to take effect, then the action will not take effect until, broadly, the supervisory notice process is completed[5].

1   See para **16.202** ff below.
2   See para **16.168** ff below.
3   See para **16.168** and **16.187** ff below.
4   The role of mediation is significantly downplayed in the new regime. On its website the FCA states that 'there are limits to the role of mediation in regulating financial services'. The website provides little guidance on when the use of mediation might be desirable. However, it is clear that the FCA will be unlikely to allow mediation where urgent action is required. It is, therefore, unlikely to be of much relevance in the context of the own-initiative powers. The mechanics of mediation are dealt with in more detail at para **10.60** ff above.
5   That is, when the matter is 'no longer open to review': for the meaning of this phrase, see para **16.185** below.

The firm's right to refer the matter to the Tribunal

16.165 The firm has an immediate right to refer the matter to the Tribunal[1]. It need not wait to make representations to the decision-maker or for the issue of a second supervisory notice[2]. This right to make a reference to the Tribunal must be exercised within 28 days of the date upon which the first supervisory notice was given[3].

1   FSMA 2000, s 197(4)(e) implies that there is also such a right for incoming firms: see the discussion at para **16.202** below. For examples of relevant references that have been made: see the notes to para **12.11** above.
2   Contrast the position where the warning/decision procedure is prescribed: see **CHAPTER 10** above. See the 'How the RDC works' section of the FCA website.
3   Tribunal Procedure (Upper Tribunal) Rules 2008, SI 2008/2698, Sch 3, para 2(2) and see para **12.42** above. This is subject to the Tribunal allowing references to be made out of time in certain circumstances: see para **12.43** above. For a further discussion of referring the FCA's own-initiative action to the Tribunal, see para **16.202** ff below. As to the procedure for making a reference to the Tribunal, see para **12.38** above. If a second supervisory notice is issued, the firm will have another chance to refer the matter to the Tribunal: see para **16.194** below.

16.166 The right to refer the matter to the Tribunal at this early stage is a necessary safeguard because the action proposed may take effect as a matter of urgency, before the remainder of the process has taken place. The firm's right to make a reference is not, however, limited to urgent cases[1].

1   The right arises on the receipt of the first supervisory notice. As indicated in para **16.165**, n 3 above, this may not be the firm's last chance to refer the matter to the Tribunal and before it does so, it may choose to make representations to the Regulator: see para **16.168** below.

16.167 The 28-day time limit needs to be kept in mind, particularly if the firm wishes first to make representations to the decision-maker. Losing the ability to refer the first supervisory notice to the Tribunal will not, however, affect the firm's ability, subsequently, to refer a second supervisory notice to the Tribunal.

Phase 3: Representations from the firm and settlement discussions

16.168 Following the issue of the first supervisory notice, the firm has the right to make representations to the decision-maker within the period specified in the notice. It will also have the ability to enter into settlement discussions with the FCA. First, it will be considered here whether the firm can obtain further time to make its representations; second, why the firm should consider making representations; and, third, various points relating to how those representations should be made. Finally, the ability to enter into settlement discussions will be considered.

Can the firm request additional time?

16.169 The period within which the firm must make any representations will have been determined by the decision-maker without reference to the firm (although it will normally be 14 days[1]). This may be insufficient as the firm may have had little idea that it would receive a supervisory notice and key people may be unavailable. There could be many reasons why the firm needs extra time.

1 See para **16.156** above.

16.170 The FCA Handbook allows the firm to request additional time for making representations, by making a written request to the FCA within seven days of the first supervisory notice being given, if it considers that the period stated in the notice is too short[1]. The request will be considered by the Chairman or Deputy Chairman of the RDC and the decision will be notified in writing to the firm[2].

1 See the FCA Handbook at DEPP 3.2.16(1).
2 See the FCA Handbook at DEPP 3.2.16(2) and (3). The PRA also allows the firm to request an extension to the time allowed for making representations, which it states should normally be made within 14 days of the notice being given (see PRA Policy Statement, 'The Prudential Regulation Authority's approach to enforcement: statutory statements of policy and procedure' (April 2013), para 49). The chair of the allocated DMC will decide whether it is fair in all the circumstances to allow an extension and, if so, how much additional time should be allowed.

16.171 No guidance is given on what factors the decision-maker will take into account in deciding whether to accede to such a request. It is likely that the same factors will be taken into account as are stated to be relevant to the original decision on the period for representations[1]. In reaching his decision, the relevant decision-maker may take account of any relevant comments from the Regulator's staff responsible for the matter[2]. In practice, the main factor will be whether the Regulator considers that any delay in imposing the proposed action would cause undue risk to its regulatory objectives, unless the Regulator can be persuaded that the risk can be safeguarded in the meantime.

1 These are discussed at para **16.158** above.
2 See the FCA Handbook at DEPP 3.1.16(2) and PRA Policy Statement, 'The Prudential Regulation Authority's approach to enforcement: statutory statements of policy and procedure', para 50.

16.172 The need for requests for additional time to be made within seven days to the FCA of receiving the first supervisory notice must be borne in mind. This may be difficult in practice as it may not be apparent, until further on in the process of preparing representations, that additional time is required. It is not clear whether the decision-makers will consider a request outside that period. However, the FCA's attitudes are hardening and it has stated that in most circumstances a firm will not be able to change its mind and make representations once the deadline has expired[1].

1 FSMA 2000, ss 55Y(6) and 197(5) provides only that the FCA 'may' extend the period allowed under the notice for making representations. It does not specifically require the FSA to consider any such request in every case. See also the 'How the RDC works' section of the FCA website.

Why should the firm make representations?

16.173 Given that the firm has the option of referring the matter to the Tribunal at this stage, or entering into settlement discussions, firms may ask why they should make any representations at all. There may be occasions when the firm would rather await the Tribunal. However, this approach could be risky as the Tribunal would likely take into account a failure by the firm to avail itself of its opportunity to make representations to the FCA.

16.174 Making representations will be the firm's main opportunity to influence the decision with a view to avoiding the time, cost, publicity and aggravation of Tribunal proceedings. There is not a great deal to be lost and there could be much to be gained. At best, it may be possible to dissuade the FCA from taking the action. Perhaps more realistically, it may be possible to persuade the FCA to soften its stance in certain respects important to the firm. There may therefore be a variety of different reasons for wanting to make representations and in most (non-urgent) cases it is likely that firms will want to do so.

16.175 One consideration that may be important, particularly if the matter could give rise to civil proceedings against the firm, is the risk of producing, or receiving from the FCA, written material which could carry disclosure implications in the context of any civil legal proceedings. This issue is discussed at para **4.145** ff above.

16.176 The firm is not under any obligation to make representations to the decision-maker and if it does not make representations, the firm will not receive a second supervisory notice[1]. The consequences of not making representations are considered in more detail at para **16.184** ff below.

1 See the FCA Handbook at DEPP 2.3.3. The PRA's procedure is similar in this respect (see PRA Policy Statement, 'The Prudential Regulation Authority's approach to enforcement: statutory statements of policy and procedure' (April 2013), para 64).

16.177 If the firm wishes to make representations, then they can be made either in writing, orally or both[1].

1 See the FCA Handbook at DEPP 3.2.15 to 3.2.21. The PRA's procedure is similar in this respect (see PRA Policy Statement, 'The Prudential Regulation Authority's approach to enforcement: statutory statements of policy and procedure' (April 2013), paras 47–63).

Making written representations

16.178 The firm's primary response will normally be a written one. Written representations are required to be sent to the case handler who is dealing with the firm's particular case. These details will be set out in the supervisory notice and in the covering letter that was sent with the notice[1].

1 See the 'How the RDC works' section of the FCA website.

16.179 The points a firm will make in its written representations will depend upon the particular circumstances. Neither the FSMA 2000 nor the FCA's rules place any limitations on the nature or content of the written representations the firm can make[1]. The FCA recommends that a firm's representations should be in response to the facts and matters set out in the notice and should set out its points clearly[2]. This is an important opportunity for the firm and the sorts of areas which it might want to consider covering include:

- reasons why the statutory test for applying the own-initiative power was not passed (for example, the reasons why the firm is not likely to fail to fulfil the threshold conditions or why it does not pose a risk to consumers);

- reasons why the FCA's concerns are misconceived, or should not concern the FCA to the extent that they do or why they should not result in any action being taken;

- reasons why the proposed action is inappropriate to address the concerns;

- steps the firm has taken to address the concerns (and why, in light of this, no further action is required);

- particular reputational or other issues that are relevant to the decision; and

- mitigating factors.

1 As noted at para **16.180** ff below, the FCA can limit oral representations.
2 See the 'How the RDC works' section of the FCA website. At the time of writing the PRA does not provide detailed guidance on this point.

Making oral representations

16.180 If the firm wishes to make oral representations[1], it will need to make this request in writing to the decision-maker at the address stated in the first supervisory notice by the date indicated in the notice and covering letter[2]. The notification is required to specify the matters on which the person wishes to make oral representations, including an estimate of how much time the representations will take, and provide the names of any legal representatives appointed to attend[3].

1 See the FCA Handbook at DEPP 3.2.17–3.2.21.
2 At the time of writing the PRA does not provide detailed guidance on this point.
3 The firm is entitled to appoint a representative (who may be a lawyer) to attend the meeting and who makes, or assists, in making, the representations: see the FCA Handbook at DEPP 3.2.19. The PRA's procedure is similar in this respect (see PRA Policy Statement, 'The Prudential Regulation Authority's approach to enforcement: statutory statements of policy and procedure' (April 2013), para 55).

16.181 'Own-initiative' powers

16.181 There are a number of reasons why the firm might want to make oral representations. It might want the opportunity to highlight to the decision-maker any particular aspects of the written representations or, for example, air grievances which it has with the procedure that took place. For some firms, it may be particularly important to have the opportunity to meet the decision-maker.

16.182 Oral representations are made at a time and place specified by the decision-maker after receiving the notification. There are various provisions relating to such meetings[1]:

- the decision-maker may specify that the representations will be received in private. Whilst this seems to indicate that, in some circumstances, they may be received in public, in general this process ought to be private and there is no evidence that representations have been received in public[2];

- the decision-maker may limit the type, length and content of the representations[3]; and

- the firm may appoint a representative (who can be a lawyer) to attend the meeting and make, or assist it in making, representations[4];

- the decision-maker may ask the person, or his representative, to provide additional information in writing after the meeting[5].

1 See the FCA Handbook at DEPP 3.2.17–3.2.20 and PRA Policy Statement, 'The Prudential Regulation Authority's approach to enforcement: statutory statements of policy and procedure' (April 2013), para 52.
2 Note that there are restrictions on the publication of warning and decision notices (see FSMA 2000, s 391(1) and the discussion at para **10.83** ff above). These do not apply to supervisory notices but see para **16.207** below and the FSMA 2000, s 391(6) for instances when the Regulators might not publish supervisory notices.
3 See the FCA Handbook at DEPP 3.2.18 and PRA Policy Statement, 'The Prudential Regulation Authority's approach to enforcement: statutory statements of policy and procedure' (April 2013), para 54.
4 See the FCA Handbook at DEPP 3.2.19 and PRA Policy Statement, 'The Prudential Regulation Authority's approach to enforcement: statutory statements of policy and procedure' (April 2013), para 55.
5 See the FCA Handbook at DEPP 3.2.20 and PRA Policy Statement, 'The Prudential Regulation Authority's approach to enforcement: statutory statements of policy and procedure' (April 2013), para 56.

16.183 The procedures for meetings with the decision-makers are considered in more detail in **CHAPTER 10**[1].

1 See para **10.32** above.

Making no representations

16.184 It is open to the firm not to respond to the first supervisory notice and not to make any representations[1]. If the firm takes this approach then two additional points are relevant.

1 In at least one instance, upon receipt of a first supervisory notice, the firm has applied for the action to be taken on a voluntary basis: see the entry in the Financial Services Register for David Purnell & Company and para **16.125** below. The application was granted. *Note:* This firm ceased to be authorised on 22/08/2003.

16.185 First[1], if the FCA receives no response[2] or representations within the period specified in the first supervisory notice, a second supervisory notice will not be issued. What then follows will depend upon when the action specified in the first supervisory notice took, or is to take, effect:

- if the action took effect immediately, or has otherwise already taken effect, it will continue to have effect;

- if the action is to take effect on a future date, it will take effect on that date; and

- if the matter is to take effect when the matter is no longer open to review, it takes effect when the period to make representations expires, or the firm is no longer able to refer the matter to the Tribunal (whichever is longer)[3].

In all the above instances, the firm retains the right to refer the matter to the Tribunal despite the fact that it has chosen not to make representations[4].

1 See the FCA Handbook at DEPP 2.3.3 and PRA Policy Statement, 'The Prudential Regulation Authority's approach to enforcement: statutory statements of policy and procedure' (April 2013), paras 28 and 64.
2 Neither the FCA Handbook nor the PRA's statements define 'response' and so it is likely that any form of response (such as a confirmation that the first supervisory notice has been received) will be sufficient to give rise to the need to issue a second supervisory notice. The response should be addressed to the case handler as detailed at para **16.178** above.
3 See the FCA Handbook at DEPP 2.3.3 and for the PRA (see PRA Policy Statement, 'The Prudential Regulation Authority's approach to enforcement: statutory statements of policy and procedure' (April 2013), para 28). If the firm does refer the supervisory notice to the Tribunal, the matter will still be open for review and the supervisory notice will not take effect: see para **16.200** below.
4 It is thought that the fact that the decision-maker is entitled by virtue of this provision of the rules, to regard the matter as undisputed, should not, of itself, affect the Tribunal's view of what action it is appropriate for the FCA or PRA to take.

16.186 Second[1], where para **16.187** below applies, or where a firm has received a second supervisory notice[2], the decision-maker has the discretion to allow firms to make late representations in exceptional cases. The discretion will be exercised where a firm can show, on reasonable grounds, that it did not receive the first supervisory notice or had reasonable grounds for not responding within the specified period. Whilst this seeks to provide additional flexibility, the provisions envisage the issue of either a written notice[3], or a further supervisory notice, the status of which is unclear[4].

1 See the FCA Handbook at DEPP 2.3.4. The position is similar for the PRA (see PRA Policy Statement, 'The Prudential Regulation Authority's approach to enforcement: statutory statements of policy and procedure' (April 2013), para 29).
2 Given the default procedures outlined at para **16.184** above, it is difficult to envisage in what circumstances a second supervisory notice will be issued where the firm has made no representations.
3 See para **16.192** below.
4 It is not clear upon what basis a further notice could be issued, at least unless the FCA revokes the second supervisory notice and issues a new, first supervisory notice. *Note:* PRA Policy Statement,

16.186 'Own-initiative' powers

'The Prudential Regulation Authority's approach to enforcement: statutory statements of policy and procedure' (April 2013), at para 29 it is stated that the DMC 'may decide to revoke the decision notice and the matter may be considered afresh or it may decide to give a further decision or supervisory notice.' Contrast the warning/decision notice procedure, where there is specific provision allowing a further decision notice to be issued: see para **10.183** above.

Settlement

16.187 When the firm receives the first supervisory notice, it may consider whether to enter into settlement discussions with the FCA. The mechanics of settlement and other questions of which firms should be aware are considered in detail at para **10.42** ff above.

16.188 In the present context, settlement discussions will be informal discussions, held on a 'without prejudice' basis, with the intention that both the firm and the FCA will come to an agreement as to how to conclude the supervisory notice process. Given the informal nature of settlement discussions, a firm may initiate them at any time during the process[1]. In practice, such discussions are likely to be most valuable once the firm knows what the concerns are and what action the Regulator proposes to take.

1   See the FCA Enforcement Guide at EG 5.6 and the FCA Handbook at DEPP 5.1.3. The PRA can also enter into settlement discussions at any stage of an enforcement action (PRA Policy Statement, 'The Prudential Regulation Authority's approach to enforcement: statutory statements of policy and procedure' (April 2013), para 15).

16.189 The terms of any settlement between the FCA and the firm must be put in writing and then be submitted for a formal decision to be made[1]. The decision will be taken jointly by two members of the FCA's senior management, one of whom will be of at least director of division level and the other of whom will be at least head of department level[2], who may[3]:

- accept the proposed settlement and issue a second supervisory notice or a written notice[4]; or

- decline the proposed settlement[5].

1   The terms of any settlement between the PRA and the firm must also be put in writing and agreed in principle by the PRA staff and the firm. A summary of the case along with the terms of the in-principle settlement agreement will be sent to the appropriate DMC (which will normally be at the same level committee structure that would have decided the case had the matter been contested) (see PRA Policy Statement, 'The Prudential Regulation Authority's approach to enforcement: statutory statements of policy and procedure' (April 2013), paras 74–81. The DCM may endorse the proposed settlement by deciding to give the supervisory notice based on the terms of the settlement; or decline the proposed settlement.

2   See the FCA Handbook at DEPP 5.1.1.

3   See the FCA Handbook at DEPP 5.1.7.

4   See para **16.190** ff below for consideration of when a second supervisory notice may be issued. The FCA Handbook and the PRA statements do not describe what will happen if the firm and a Regulator agree that proposed own-initiative action should not take place. Where proposed own-initiative action is discontinued following the issue of a first supervisory notice, the decision-maker must issue a written notice: see para **16.192** below.

5   See para **10.59** above for a description of what may happen if settlement cannot be reached.

Phase 4: The second supervisory notice

16.190 Once oral and/or written representations have been made[1], the next phase is for the decision-maker to review the material before it, consider those representations and to decide, in light of them, what action, if any, to take.

1   A second supervisory notice will not be issued where the firm has not responded or made representations to the decision-maker: see para **16.184** above.

What decision may be made?

16.191 The decision-maker will consider the representations and decide[1]:

- whether or not to take the proposed action;

- if the action has already been taken[2], whether or not to rescind it; or

- whether to take the action in a different way to that proposed in the first supervisory notice.

1   See the FCA Handbook at DEPP 3.2.23–3.2.25. The position is similar for the PRA (PRA Policy Statement, 'The Prudential Regulation Authority's approach to enforcement: statutory statements of policy and procedure' (April 2013), para 66).
2   For example, because it was specified in the first supervisory notice to take immediate effect or to take effect on a specified date which has now passed: see para **16.161** above.

16.192 If the decision-maker decides not to take the proposed action, to vary the proposed action, or to rescind action which has already been taken, then it must give the firm a written notice[1]. This is not a supervisory notice, nor is it a notice of discontinuance[2]. It is simply a notice informing the firm of the FCA's decision.

1   FSMA 2000, s 55Y(8) and, for incoming firms, s 197(7) and the FCA Handbook at DEPP 2.1.2.
2   See para **10.93** above.

16.193 If the decision-maker decides to take the proposed action, or not to rescind action that has already been taken, then it will give the firm a second supervisory notice[1].

1   FSMA 2000, ss 55Y(7), 197(6) and 395(13) and see the FCA Handbook at DEPP 3.2.23.

16.194 The second supervisory notice will[1] inform the firm of its right to refer the matter to the Tribunal (and provide an indication of the procedure for making such a reference). This will be the firm's second opportunity to refer the matter to the Tribunal[2]. References to the Tribunal are considered at para **16.202** ff below.

1   FSMA 2000, s 55Y(7), (9) and (11) and, for incoming firms, s 197(6), (8) and (10).
2   The first opportunity was when the first supervisory notice was issued: see para **16.164** ff above.

16.195 The decision-maker will include a brief summary of the key representations made and how they have been dealt with in the notice[1]. If the firm does not consider these to be sufficient it can ask the decision-maker voluntarily to provide further details of the reasons on the basis that it is necessary for the firm to understand why its representations were rejected in order to decide whether or not to make a reference to the Tribunal[2].

1 See the FCA Handbook at DEPP 3.2.24. The position is similar for the PRA (see PRA Policy Statement, 'The Prudential Regulation Authority's approach to enforcement: statutory statements of policy and procedure' (April 2013), para 66(a)).
2 If the matter is referred to the Tribunal, it may be possible to obtain disclosure of any documents recording the reasons for this decision, for example a record of the relevant RDC meeting (if not already disclosed): see para **12.92** above.

What happens if the decision-maker decides to take different action?

16.196 If the decision-maker decides to vary the firm's permission in a different way to that proposed in the first supervisory notice, then the second supervisory notice must contain the same information as a first supervisory notice[1]. The consequences of this are not made clear either in the FSMA 2000 or in the Handbooks, but logically the result should be to put the process back to the first supervisory notice stage[2]. There should therefore be another opportunity for the firm to make representations, which the decision-maker will consider, following which it will decide whether to issue a second supervisory notice. The firm will also have the usual rights to refer the matter to the Tribunal, either immediately[3], or upon the issue of a subsequent 'second' supervisory notice.

1 FSMA 2000, s 55Y(10) and, for incoming firms, s 197(9) and see the FCA Handbook at DEPP 3.2.24(1). As regards the contents of a first supervisory notice, see para **16.153** ff above.
2 Among other things, it otherwise makes no sense for the notice to give the firm an opportunity to make representations. Contrast the warning/decision notice procedure, where there is, first, some latitude in the decision that can be taken in a decision notice as compared with the warning notice that preceded it (see para **10.164** above) and, second, a specific provision allowing the issue of a further decision notice without the need for a warning notice (with the firm's consent: see para **10.183** ff above).
3 See para **16.203** ff below.

What are the consequences of the FCA issuing a second supervisory notice?

16.197 The second supervisory notice represents the conclusion of the supervisory notice process from the FCA's internal point of view. It means that, having considered the firm's representations, the decision-maker has decided that the action that was proposed in the first supervisory notice is appropriate. It is not, however, necessarily determinative of the question because the matter could be referred to the Tribunal.

16.198 The firm's right to refer the matter to the Tribunal is considered at para **16.202** ff below. As to when the decision will take effect, as has been seen, own-initiative action can either take effect immediately upon the issue of the first supervisory notice, or upon a specified date or when the matter is no longer open to review[1]. Thus, in many instances, the decision will already have taken effect by the time the second supervisory notice is issued, because it took effect immediately upon the issue of the first supervisory notice or upon a specified date which has already passed. In these cases, the decision to which the second supervisory notice relates is the decision not to rescind the action already taken. In such cases, the second supervisory notice does not have any effect on the action which the FCA has already taken.

1 For a more detailed discussion, see para **16.114** ff above.

16.199 In other cases, the action may not have taken effect, either because the specified date has not yet occurred (although this may be unlikely by this stage) or because the matter is not yet 'no longer open to review'. In such cases, the decision to which the second supervisory notice relates is the FCA's decision to impose that action.

16.200 The matter to which a supervisory notice relates is still open to review if[1]:

- the period during which it may be referred to the Tribunal is still running;

- the matter has been referred to the Tribunal, but has not been dealt with;

- the matter has been referred to the Tribunal and dealt with, but the period during which an appeal may be brought against the Tribunal's decision is still running; or

- such an appeal has been brought, but not yet determined[2].

1 FSMA 2000, s 391(8) and see the FCA Handbook at DEPP 2.2.5. The position is similar for the PRA (see PRA Policy Statement, 'The Prudential Regulation Authority's approach to enforcement: statutory statements of policy and procedure' (April 2013), para 19).
2 Appeals against Tribunal decisions are considered at para **12.174** ff above.

16.201 Once the matter is no longer open to review, own-initiative action for which no effective date was specified in the first supervisory notice takes effect[1].

1 FSMA 2000, s 55Y(2) and, for incoming firms, s 197(1).

Phase 5: Referring the matter to the Tribunal

16.202 The Tribunal[1] has an important role in relation to the exercise of the FCA's own-initiative powers[2]. So far as variations of permission are concerned, the FSMA 2000 provides[3] that an authorised person who is aggrieved by the exercise of the FCA's own-initiative variation power or its own-initiative requirement power may refer the matter to the Tribunal. No equivalent provision exists relating to intervention action that has been imposed on incoming firms. However, the FSMA 2000 clearly envisages that there will be a right to refer such a decision to the Tribunal[4] and it is, therefore, not thought that this omission is significant.

1 This is the Upper Tribunal which is described at para **12.5** ff above.
2 It plays a similar role in relation to the PRA's exercise of its own-initiative powers.
3 FSMA 2000, s 55Z3(2).
4 For example, it requires the supervisory notice to make this clear: FSMA 2000, s 197(4) and (8).

16.203 'Own-initiative' powers

When can a reference be made to the Tribunal?

16.203 The firm has the right to refer the matter to the Tribunal upon the issue of either the first or the second supervisory notice. In either case, it must do so before the expiry of 28 days beginning with the date upon which the supervisory notice was given[1], subject to the Tribunal deciding to allow the reference to be made out of time[2].

1 As to when notice was given, for the detailed rules on the service of notices, see the Financial Services and Markets Act 2000 (Service of Notices) Regulations 2001, SI 2001/1420.
2 Tribunal Rules, r 5(3)(a). For a more detailed discussion of this provision, and the Tribunal rules for making references out of time, see para **12.42** ff above.

16.204 The nature and rules of the Tribunal, and the procedure when a reference has been made to it, are considered in detail in **CHAPTER 12** above. As discussed in para **12.151**, the role of the Tribunal in cases involving supervisory notices is more similar to a judicial review and its powers are more restricted than those relating to disciplinary cases.

When should the firm consider making a reference to the Tribunal?

16.205 Whether the firm should refer a particular case to the Tribunal will depend on the circumstances. Relevant factors a firm should consider include the nature and seriousness of the action which the FCA has taken, or wishes to take, the potential publicity which could arise from Tribunal proceedings[1] and the time and cost of the process. For example, if the FCA's action has a significant impact upon the firm's business or reputation, it may be appropriate to refer the matter to the Tribunal. Alternatively, in some cases the firm may regard the matter as giving rise to issues of principle. In other cases, the firm may not regard a reference to the Tribunal as being worthwhile, particularly where the action that the FCA proposes would not materially affect its business and perhaps, would not otherwise attract significant adverse publicity. There will therefore be a range of factors to balance in each case.

1 Tribunal proceedings are generally speaking held in public: see the Tribunal Procedure (Upper Tribunal) Rules 2008, SI 2008/2698, r 37(1) and para **12.37** ff above. See also para **12.14** ff above for other relevant factors.

Phase 6: Publication of the FCA's action

16.206 Generally speaking, transparency, deterrence, consumer education and market confidence provide strong policy reasons militating in favour of the FCA publishing successful action that they have taken. This general policy applies equally to the FCA's use of its own-initiative powers[1].

1 Similar policy considerations will apply to the PRA.

Is the FCA entitled to publish its own-initiative action?

16.207 The FSMA 2000 is silent as to whether publication can occur before the supervisory notice takes effect, but once the supervisory notice takes effect, the FCA is under a duty to publish such information about the matter to which the supervisory notice relates as it considers appropriate[1]. This is subject to the provisos that the FCA may not publish information if such publication would, in its opinion, be unfair to the person with respect to whom the action was taken, prejudicial to the interests of consumers or detrimental to the stability of the UK financial system[2].

1   FSMA 2000, s 391(5).
2   FSMA 2000, s 391(6). The PRA may not publish information if such publication would, in its opinion, be unfair to the person with respect to whom the action was taken, prejudicial to the safety and soundness of PRA-authorised persons or prejudicial to securing the appropriate degree of protection for policyholders of insurance contracts (see the FSMA 2000, s 391(6A)).

16.208 If the FCA does decide to publish information, then it may do so in such manner as it considers appropriate[1].

1   FSMA 2000, s 391(7). Where the Regulator does decide to publish 'information relating to a supervisory notice', it will generally publish the second supervisory notice. In exceptional cases, the Regulator may also decide to publish a press release. See para **10.194** above as to the contents of the press release.

16.209 Three other points should be noted. First, there is nothing to prohibit the FCA from publishing information about a supervisory notice before the notice takes effect, provided it does not breach the statutory prohibition against the disclosure of confidential information[1].

1   See the FSMA 2000, s 348. For a discussion of the prohibition, and the Gateway Regulations which allow certain types of disclosure, see para **4.226** above. In those instances where the action takes effect on a later date, the supervisory notice is in practice published on the date that it is issued, rather than on the date when the action is to take effect: see, for example, *Alpha Delta first supervisory notice (19/12/02)*.

16.210 Second, it is not entirely clear when a supervisory notice 'takes effect'. It is likely that this is intended to refer to the time when the action to which the supervisory notice relates takes effect.

16.211 Third, given that the action can take effect, and be published, immediately on issue of the first supervisory notice, before the firm has had any opportunity to be involved, the provision requiring the FCA not to publish if publication would, in its opinion, be unfair to the firm (or prejudicial to consumers or detrimental to the stability of the UK financial system) is clearly important. However, whether there is any 'unfairness to the firm' is a judgement to be made by the FCA.

16.212 Finally it should be noted that the FCA is required to maintain a public record of information about firms[1]. Among other things, the record must include information about the services which the firm holds itself out to provide[2]. Apart from certain minimum requirements, though, the FCA is required to record only such information as it considers to be appropriate[3]. In practice the Financial Services Register sets out any requirements that have been imposed on the firm. Where a firm's permission is varied, the Register reflects this in its permissions section. In certain circumstances, the FCA also provides details relating to a supervisory notice on the consumer section of its website[4].

1 FSMA 2000, s 347. This is the Financial Services Register which can be accessed on the FCA's website. Under s 347A, the PRA must disclose information relevant to the record for the purpose of assisting the FCA to comply with its s 347 duty.
2 FSMA 2000, s 347(2)(a)(i).
3 FSMA 2000, s 347(2).
4 For example, *Berry Birch & Noble Financial Services Limited first supervisory notice (1/4/04)*, the consumer section of the FSA website set out matters that the FSA considered would be relevant to consumers in a question and answer format. Those questions included how a consumer should act if he had a claim against the firm.

In what circumstances will the Regulators publish their own-initiative action?

16.213 The FCA will approach the question of publicity on a case-by-case basis. The FCA will aim to balance both the interests of consumers and the possibility of unfairness to the firm subject to its action. It will publish relevant details of both fundamental and non-fundamental variations of Part 4A permission and requirements which it imposes on firms. However it will use its discretion not to do so if it considers this to be unfair to the firm, prejudicial to the interests of consumers or detrimental to the stability of the UK financial system[1].

1 See the FCA Enforcement Guide at EG 6.12. Also, see para **16.43** above that discusses a supervisory notice addressed to KSF that was not published to protect the interests of existing depositors.

Can the firm object to publication?

16.214 Since the FCA recognises that publication may be unfair to the firm, may not be in the interests of consumers or may be detrimental to the stability of the UK financial system, there may be scope for the firm to discuss with the FCA the nature and extent of any publicity relating to its action, and to try to stress any particular factors militating against publication, or certain types of publication, in the particular case[1]. Ultimately, the FCA has a significant amount of discretion in what action it takes to publicise the matter and it will be difficult for the firm to challenge, or prevent the FCA from taking action which it regards as appropriate, at least unless the FCA acts wholly unreasonably. There is, for example, no right to refer the issue of publication to the Tribunal. As to other possible methods and grounds of challenge, see **CHAPTER 21** below.

1 It may be possible to press the FCA to explain why publication is needed in the particular case, given the risks to consumers, the nature of the business, and so on. Although in the FCA Enforcement Guide at EG 6.12, the FCA does emphasise that publishing the reasons for variations of Part 4A permission, the imposition of requirements and maintaining an accurate public record are important elements of the FCA's approach to its statutory objectives. The PRA will consider any written representations made to it when it proposes to publish details of a Supervisory Notice, although it will not normally decide against publication solely because it is claimed that publication could have a negative impact on a firm's reputation (see PRA Policy Statement, 'The Prudential Regulation Authority's approach to enforcement: statutory statements of policy and procedure' (April 2013), paras 15–17).

URGENT ACTION

The procedure for taking urgent action

16.215 As has been seen, for the FCA, own-initiative action falls generally into two different categories: action which is categorised as a fundamental change to the nature of the firm's permission, and action which is not[1]. In principle, the need for urgent action can arise in either category. Generally, decisions relating to fundamental action are taken by the RDC[2], and decisions relating to non-fundamental action are taken by the FCA's executive procedures[3]. In urgent cases, however, there are slightly different decision-making procedures.

1 As to what constitutes a fundamental change to the firm's permission, see para **16.144** ff above.
2 See para **16.142** above.
3 See para **16.237** below.

Urgent fundamental variations of permission

16.216 When FCA staff make a recommendation in relation to an urgent, fundamental matter, the following procedure applies:[1]

- in general, but subject to the need to act swiftly, the recommendation will be put before a panel of the RDC;

- in an urgent case where, in the opinion of the FCA staff, the action proposed should occur before it is practicable to convene an RDC panel, the recommendation will be put before the Chairman or a Deputy Chairman of the RDC and where possible (but subject to the need to act swiftly), at least one other RDC member;

- in an exceptionally urgent case, where, in the FCA's opinion:

    – the action should take effect before it is possible to make a recommendation to the Chairman or Deputy Chairman of the RDC; and

    – an urgent decision on the proposed action is necessary in order to protect the interests of consumers,

the recommendation will be put before a member of the FCA's executive of at least director of division level[2]. In such circumstances, the FCA will ensure, so far as possible, that the person making the decision has not been involved in establishing the evidence upon which the decision is based, but there may be exceptional cases where this will not occur, as discussed below[3].

1 See the FCA Handbook at DEPP 3.4.1–3.4.4, also see DEPP 4.2.1. Where the PRA considers that it is necessary to take a decision to advance its objectives before a recommendation can be made to the appropriate DMC, a decision can be made by two individuals of at least the same level as the individuals who would have comprised the appropriate DMC. The decision will only be taken if the two decision-makers are unanimous. The PRA has specified that at least one of the two individuals will not have been directly involved in establishing the evidence upon which the decision is based, and where practicable, it will seek to ensure that both individuals will not have been so involved (see PRA Policy Statement, 'The Prudential Regulation Authority's approach to enforcement: statutory statements of policy and procedure' (April 2013), paras 70–71).

2 This is a senior level of management within the FCA.
3 See the FCA Handbook at DEPP 3.4.4.

16.217 A number of points should be noted. First, the decision to issue the first supervisory notice could, as a result, be taken, not by a full panel of the relevant decision-making committee, but in the case of the FCA, by the RDC Chairman alone, or by a Deputy Chairman, or even, in some cases, by senior staff within the FCA[1].

1 In the case of the PRA, the decision can be taken by two individuals.

16.218 Second, where the recommendation is put before a member of the FCA's staff, the FCA Handbook makes it clear that there may be cases where that person is a person who was involved in investigating the matter. In such a situation, the statutory requirement for the separation of functions[1] may not be complied with. This is permitted[2] provided the decision is taken by a person of such seniority as is specified by the FCA's procedures and the FCA considers this necessary in order to advance one or more of its operational objectives[3].

1 FSMA 2000, s 395(2): see para **16.135** above.
2 FSMA 2000, s 395(3).
3 Similarly, where the PRA is taking urgent action, an individual involved in the investigation will be permitted to take the decision provided that he is of such seniority as is specified in the PRA's procedures and that the PRA considers it necessary in order to advance any of its objectives.

16.219 The FCA has indicated that this may happen when the FCA believes that action is needed to protect the interests of consumers but where the requirements for the separation of functions cannot be met[1]. In such a case the decision will be made by a person of, at least, director of division level[2]. This ought to occur only in the most critical and urgent cases, where it is impracticable to ensure the separation of functions because of the urgency of the matter.

1 See the FCA Handbook at DEPP 3.4.3 and 3.4.4.
2 See the FCA Handbook at DEPP 3.4.4.

16.220 Third, the question of how urgent the matter is and therefore which route will be appropriate is a question for those staff dealing with the matter, subject obviously to the ability of the person before whom the recommendation is put to question whether he is the appropriate person to consider the recommendation.

16.221 Fourth, the person before whom the recommendation is placed will also take any associated decisions that are required to be taken at the same time[1], such as deciding on the period for the firm to make representations and on what date the action should take effect (which, in this situation, will normally be immediately).

1 For a more detailed discussion, see para **16.152** and **16.156** ff above.

16.222 Finally, any subsequent decisions (such as the consideration of any representations made by the firm and the decision whether to issue a second supervisory notice) are considered by the RDC in the normal way. Subject to the above, therefore, the procedure outlined at para **16.130** ff above applies.

16.223 It should be apparent that, taken overall, this procedure gives FCA staff some latitude in dealing with the matter. Most notably, a decision to impose, with immediate effect, measures that could significantly affect the firm's business could, in some circumstances, be taken by the FCA's enforcement staff and those to whom they report[1]. As has been seen[2], the Tribunal potentially has the ability to address any obvious mistakes or abuses. However, a reference to the Tribunal may not be appropriate in all cases[3] and it is also not clear that this process will always provide an effective remedy. In addition, the risk is perhaps less that there will be obvious mistakes or abuses than that judgements may be made by those whose approach is not perceived as sufficiently independent. This clearly gives rise to practical issues for firms and these are discussed below.

1 Furthermore, once the decision has been made, it will not be reviewed unless the firm decides to make representations or refers it to the Tribunal: see para **16.202** above.
2 See para **12.152** above. The setting aside of urgent action was considered and rejected by the Tribunal in *HPA Services v FSA (2003) FSMT 005*.
3 See para **16.205** above.

Practical guidance for firms facing urgent action

16.224 From the firm's perspective, it is possible that the first occasion upon which it knows that action has been taken against it may be when it receives the first supervisory notice setting out the variation that has been decided upon and when it takes effect. By then, the FCA (or PRA) will already have decided that urgent action is necessary. That action may substantially affect the firm's business and will not only take effect immediately, before the firm has had any opportunity to have any input into the process, but will also be likely to be publicised immediately. How should the firm react in such a situation[1]?

1 The firm's considerations in this respect will be similar where it is the PRA taking urgent action.

16.225 The answer will depend largely upon the particular situation. In deciding what to do, the firm will need to consider its position quickly and the following questions may be relevant to its decision:

- What, precisely, is the action that the FCA is taking or requiring the firm to take[1]? How does the action impact upon the firm's business? As has been seen[2], the own-initiative power is a flexible instrument. The FCA's action could range from preventing the firm from carrying out certain types of business, or indeed any further business, to requiring it to vest assets in a trustee, requiring it to take certain steps with regard to its systems and controls or (possibly) prohibiting it from involving particular individuals in a particular area of business. Some actions will have a greater effect on the firm's business than others.

- What are the reputational issues? The fact that urgent enforcement action has been taken is likely to be publicised and may have a serious reputational impact. But if the action arises in the context of an already well publicised regulatory matter, then the reputational impact may be rather less.

- If the firm has a large consumer clientele, how is the action likely to be perceived by them, what are the implications for consumer confidence in the firm? In addition, are claims likely to be brought against it?

- Are any of the issues that arise likely to damage market confidence? Might the FCA's action itself have a negative impact upon market confidence?

- Might the FCA's action expose the firm to claims from third parties, for example market counterparties in areas of business in which the firm can no longer trade[3]?

- What knowledge does the firm have about the problems or concerns that underlie the FCA's decision to take the action? The firm may have had some involvement in the problem prior to receiving the FCA's first supervisory notice. Has it already investigated sufficiently thoroughly to take a strong position? If not, how secure can the firm be about what it now says to the Regulator? To what extent is it possible for the firm to carry out an urgent investigation?

- What are the firm's views of the underlying merits of the FCA's action? Are the reasons for taking the action set out in the first supervisory notice accurate, or at least within reasonable bounds and, in the firm's view, do they merit the action taken? Given those reasons, does the firm accept that there is a need for the FCA to take the action as a matter of urgency?

1 As discussed at para **16.125** above, the FCA may seek to remove all the firm's regulated activities. Depending on whether the firm's focus is on its regulated activities or not, such a variation will have a severe impact upon it.
2 See para **16.90** ff above.
3 This issue has been highlighted and briefly discussed at para **16.17** above.

16.226 Ultimately, if the firm wishes to challenge the FCA's action, it can refer the matter to the Tribunal and require the FCA to prove, in that independent forum, that its action was appropriate. However, that is likely to take some time and in the meantime there are likely to be two main issues of concern:

- Can the firm prevent the FCA's action from taking effect?; and

- Can it prevent the action from being publicised?

Can the firm prevent the urgent action from taking effect?

16.227 Where action is specified in the first supervisory notice to take immediate effect, the FSMA 2000 and the Handbooks do not give the firm any right to object to the action, or to have the decision to take it reviewed by the FCA before it takes effect[1]. However, where the firm is aware that such action may be taken and if there are compelling reasons why the action should not be taken with urgent effect, then it may be worth trying to contact the person who is likely to make the decision, to see whether they are willing to consider any points that are in the firm's favour. It may also be worth trying to contact the chairperson of the relevant decision-making committee, particularly if the decision is likely to be made by a member of the FCA's staff.

1 The position is similar where the PRA takes urgent action. Where the firm decides not to make representations, the decision to take urgent action may not even be subjected to the decision-maker's consideration: see paras **16.184** ff and **16.216** ff above.

16.228 Assuming this is unsuccessful[1], the firm has the right to refer the matter to the Tribunal and the Tribunal Rules permit the Tribunal to suspend the FCA's action pending a full hearing of the matter[2]. This is discussed in more detail at para **12.119** ff above. In practice, given that the Tribunal will be considering the request for a suspension on an urgent basis, probably with minimal factual information, and with an assessment by the FCA that it is necessary to take action urgently, an application to suspend the FCA's action is likely to be successful only in cases of obvious mistake or abuse. Nonetheless, there may be little to be lost by making the application. It is not clear from the Tribunal Rules how easy it is likely to be to convene the Tribunal on an urgent basis although this can happen.

1 In the majority of cases where the firm is aware of the possibility of urgent action being taken against it, it will already have made informal representations/held settlement discussions with the relevant FCA or PRA staff responsible for recommending or taking the action.
2 See the Tribunal Procedure (Upper Tribunal) Rules 2008, SI 2008/2698, r 5. The same applies where the PRA takes urgent action.

16.229 Alternatively, and particularly where it is not possible to convene the Tribunal urgently[1], the firm may be able to apply for the FCA's action to be judicially reviewed by a court, and for the action to be stayed in the meantime. If there are ECHR grounds for objecting to the FCA's action, the firm may seek to commence normal court proceedings and apply for a stay of the FCA's action in support of those proceedings. These options are outlined in more detail in **CHAPTER 21** below.

1 See further the discussion at para **21.19** below.

Can the firm prevent the Regulator's action from being publicised?

16.230 Again, the FSMA 2000 and the Handbooks do not give the firm any right to object to the publication of urgent own-initiative action and publication is not, of itself, an issue that the firm can refer to the Tribunal. However, it may be that the action will not yet have been publicised by the time the firm receives the first supervisory notice so, in practice, there may be a window of opportunity to influence the decision as to whether the matter should be publicised and, if so, what will be said.

16.231 The provisions of the FSMA 2000 and the FCA's policy regarding the publication of its own-initiative action are outlined at para **16.206** ff above. As has been seen, the FCA may not publish information if, in its opinion, publication would be unfair to the person with respect to whom the action is taken, prejudicial to the interests of consumers, or detrimental to the stability of the UK financial markets. The firm may therefore wish to stress any of the above factors.

ALTERNATIVE PROCEDURES IN SPECIFIC CASES

16.232 In the following paragraphs, four variants of the FCA's procedure, applicable in specific cases will be reviewed, namely:

- where the action proposed would involve a non-fundamental change to the nature of the firm's permission (or equivalent intervention action for an incoming firm) (para **16.233** below[1]);

- where the matter is 'straightforward' (para **16.248** below)[2]; and

- where the firm and the FCA agree on the need for the relevant action[3]; and, finally

- a separate procedure applicable in certain cases involving EEA firms (para **16.249** below)[4].

1 See para **16.138**, n 5 above for the PRA's different approach to the categorisation of its decision making. The distinction between fundamental and non-fundamental changes to a firm's permission applies to the FCA only.
2 See n 1. The procedure applicable to 'straightforward' cases applies to the FCA only.
3 A firm could also agree with the PRA on the need for the relevant action.
4 The same procedure applies for both the FCA and PRA with respect to these cases involving EEA firms.

Non-fundamental changes to permission

16.233 If the variations which the FCA proposes to make to the firm's permission (or any equivalent intervention action in relation to an incoming firm) would not fundamentally change the nature of the firm's permission, then slightly different procedures apply[1]. In many cases, the exercise of the own-initiative power to make non-fundamental changes to permission is likely to arise in the supervisory, rather than the enforcement, context. However, it is plainly not limited to the supervisory context.

1 See the FCA Handbook at DEPP 2.5.7. The meaning of 'fundamental change' is considered at para **16.144** above.

16.234 The primary difference between the procedure for such changes and the procedure for fundamental changes is that the FCA's decisions are, in this case, taken by what is known as 'executive procedures'. In other words, the RDC does not have responsibility for taking the FCA's decisions, but they are instead taken by senior members of the FCA's staff.

16.235 The procedure for non-fundamental changes is based upon the same statutory framework as that for fundamental changes and, apart from the question of who takes the FCA's decisions, is the same as that outlined at para **16.130** ff above. At each stage of the process, the same rules and considerations apply, with the difference that any references to the RDC need to be read as references to the FCA decision-maker under the FSA's executive procedures. However, FCA staff responsible for making decisions on non-fundamental changes under the executive procedures may refer the matter to the RDC if[1]:

- the RDC is already considering or will shortly consider a closely related matter; and

- the FCA staff believe that the RDC should have responsibility for the decision having regard to all the circumstances. Relevant considerations may include the desirability of consistency in FCA decision-making, expediency of time and costs and the factors relevant when assessing whether a decision is straightforward (see para **16.248** below)[2].

1 See the FCA Handbook at DEPP 2.1.4.
2 See the FCA Handbook at DEPP 3.3.2.

16.236 In practice, how the firm may decide to deal with the FCA may be different in this context. If the variation which the FCA is seeking would, for example, only have limited effect upon its business and would not, in any way, damage its reputation, then there may be less need to oppose the process. The firm may be equally concerned to safeguard its relationship with the FCA so as to protect its own perceived interests and position. The firm may even decide to take the action voluntarily.

The FCA's executive procedures

16.237 Under the executive procedures, the FCA's decisions are made either[1]:

- by an individual staff member; or

- by a 'senior staff committee'.

1 See the FCA Handbook at DEPP 4.1.1.

16.238 The FCA Handbook indicates that the FCA's senior executive committee may, from time to time determine that particular categories of decision to be taken under executive procedures and decisions relating to applications for PRA authorisation or approval will be taken by a senior staff committee[1]. Otherwise, decisions will be made by an individual staff member.

1 See the FCA Handbook at DEPP 4.1.3. The 'senior staff committee' is a committee of senior FCA staff members empowered to make decisions relating to statutory notices by executive procedures.

16.239 Where an individual staff member is to make the decision, the decision will be made by an executive director of the FCA Board (or his delegate, who must be of at least the level of 'associate'), upon the recommendation of an FCA staff member of at least the level of 'associate'[1] and with the benefit of legal advice from an FCA staff member of at least the same level[2]. The person concerned may consult with colleagues and may refer the matter to a more senior level if he considers that to be appropriate[3]. If he considers that the matter warrants collective consideration, he may either consult colleagues and then take the decision himself or may refer it to a senior staff committee for the decision to be taken by the committee[4].

16.239 'Own-initiative' powers

1 Note that this will not necessarily involve anyone of any seniority within the FCA.
2 See the FCA Handbook at DEPP 4.1.7. The person taking the decision is directly accountable to the FCA Board: see the FCA Handbook at DEPP 4.1.8.
3 See the FCA Handbook at DEPP 4.1.9.
4 See the FCA Handbook at DEPP 4.1.10.

16.240 Where a senior staff committee is to take the decision, the decision is made at a meeting of the committee or a sub-committee[1], including an individual with authority to act as chairman and at least two other members. The committee operates on the basis of a recommendation from an FCA staff member of at least the level of associate, and with the benefit of legal advice from an FCA staff member of at least the same level[2]. Generally, the recommendation will go before the committee[3]. In urgent cases, a slightly different procedure may apply[4].

1 The 'senior staff committee' is a committee consisting of such FCA staff members as the FCA's senior executive committee may, from time to time, determine. It is accountable for its decisions to the FCA's senior executive committee and through it, to the FCA Board. The committee may operate through standing or sub-committees to consider particular decisions, or classes of decision, for which accountability lies through the committee: see the FCA Handbook at DEPP 4.1.3–4.1.5.
2 See the FCA Handbook at DEPP 4.1.6.
3 See the FCA Handbook at DEPP 4.2.1.
4 See the FCA Handbook at DEPP 4.2.1 and para **16.218** above.

Urgent non-fundamental variations of permission

16.241 In principle there is nothing to preclude urgent action being required for a non-fundamental variation of a firm's permission (or such equivalent action for incoming firms).

16.242 The decision to take non-fundamental action can be taken either by an individual FCA staff member or by the FCA's senior staff committee[1]. Where the decision is to be taken by an individual staff member, no prescribed procedure exists for urgent cases (and there is probably no need for such a procedure). However, where the decision is to be taken by the senior staff committee, the FCA Handbook prescribes that[2]:

- in general, but subject to the need to act swiftly in urgent cases, the FCA staff's recommendation will go before the senior staff committee (or a sub-committee)[3];

- in an urgent case, if, in the FCA staff's opinion, the action proposed should occur before it is practicable to convene a meeting of the senior staff committee (or sub-committee), the FCA staff's recommendation may be considered by the senior staff committee's chairman or a deputy chairman and, where possible, but subject to the need to act swiftly, one other member of the committee; and

- in an exceptionally urgent case, if, in the FCA staff's opinion, the action should be taken before a recommendation to the chairman or a deputy chairman can be made, and an urgent decision about the proposed action is necessary in order to protect the interest of consumers, the FCA staff's recommendation may be considered and the decision made by a member of the FCA's executive of at least director of division level, or by a member of the senior staff committee if it reports directly to the FCA's senior executive committee.

1 See para **16.237**, n 1 above and para **16.240**, n 1 above.
2 See the FCA Handbook at DEPP 4.2.1.
3 See para **16.237**, n 1 above.

16.243 This is very similar to the procedure applicable in urgent fundamental cases, considered at para **16.215** ff above (save that references to the RDC are instead to the senior staff committee).

Is there a separation of functions?

16.244 In general[1], the decision-making process will comply with the statutory requirement for the separation of functions[2], so that the decision to give a supervisory notice will not be taken by a person who was directly involved in establishing the evidence upon which that decision is based. However, there may be situations where it would be permissible, under the FSMA 2000, for the FCA to make a decision without the separation of functions. The FCA's guidance on when it considers this may be appropriate, and the procedure in such cases, is considered at para **16.218** above.

1 See the FCA Handbook at DEPP 1.2.1 and 4.2.1–4.2.2.
2 FSMA 2000, s 395(2) and see para **16.218** above.

Other safeguards for firms

16.245 There are certain procedural safeguards for firms. The supervisory notice will identify the decision-maker. The FCA requires its staff to disclose any conflict of interest to the person to whom they are immediately responsible[1]. In addition, the secretariat to the senior staff committee is required to record and document all disclosures of potential conflicts of interest and the steps taken to manage them[2].

1 See the FCA Handbook at DEPP 4.1.11.
2 See the FCA Handbook at DEPP 4.1.12 and para **10.39** above.

Issues relating to the procedure

16.246 Whilst it may be possible for the FCA to satisfy, in technical terms, the statutory requirement for the separation of functions by taking decisions in this way, the practical question for firms is whether this procedure is sufficient to ensure that a fair decision is likely to be taken.

16.247 As explained at para **16.145** above, many requirements which could be classified as 'non-fundamental' could cause a significant costs burden or disruption to the firm or could impact on its business or reputation. It is therefore important that these procedures are used by the FCA only where manifestly appropriate, and that decisions are taken appropriately. Whilst ultimately the fairness of the outcome can be tested in the Tribunal, for a variety of reasons firms may not wish to refer cases to the Tribunal[1] and there are, generally, strong policy reasons for the FCA to seek to ensure that firms have confidence in its decision-making processes[2].

1 See para **12.17** above.
2 These general policy considerations are discussed at para **10.18** ff above.

Straightforward cases

16.248 Decisions that would otherwise be taken by a full panel of the RDC could, in 'straightforward cases' be taken by the Chairman or a Deputy Chairman of the RDC (together with one other RDC member if they so require)[1]. It is unclear how this will be applied in practice in the context of the FCA's own-initiative powers, since urgent decisions can in any event be taken through a streamlined procedure[2] and non-fundamental changes to a firm's permission are decided upon by executive procedures.

1 See the FCA Handbook at DEPP 3.3.1.
2 See para **16.215** above.

Additional procedure for certain cases involving EEA firms

16.249 Where the FCA exercises its powers of intervention in relation to an EEA firm exercising EEA rights in the UK[1], an additional procedure may apply[2]. It applies if it appears to the FCA that its power of intervention is exercisable in relation to such a firm in respect of[3]:

- a contravention of a requirement imposed by the FCA under the FSMA 2000; and

- the contravention of any of the single market directives[4] which provide that a procedure of the kind that follows shall apply (so far as they are relevant in the firm's case).

1 This is a reference to its rights under the FSMA 2000, ss 1A and 196: see para **1.73** ff above.
2 This reflects the requirements of MiFID (Markets in Financial Instruments Directive 2004/39/EC). The same applies to the PRA.
3 FSMA 2000, s 199.
4 See para **1.75**, n 1 above.

16.250 The additional procedure is as follows[1]:

- the FCA must, in writing, require the firm to remedy the situation;

- if the firm fails to comply within a reasonable time, the FCA must give a notice to that effect to the firm's home state regulator, requesting it to:

  - take all appropriate measures for the purpose of ensuring that the firm remedies the situation which has given rise to the notice, and

  - inform the FCA of the measures it proposes to take or has taken or the reasons for not taking such measures,

- the FCA may not exercise its power of intervention unless satisfied that the firm's home state regulator has failed or refused to take measures for the purpose outlined above or that the measures taken have proved inadequate for that purpose;

- however, the FCA may nonetheless take urgent action in order to protect the interests of consumers before doing or being satisfied as to any of the above and, in such a case, must, at the earliest opportunity, inform the firm's home state regulator, ESMA and the EU Commission (which has the power to require the FCA to rescind or vary the requirements that it has imposed).

1 FSMA 2000, s 199.

16.251 This means that where, in any situation, any of the criteria outlined above is fulfilled and the FCA wishes to exercise its power of intervention in relation to an incoming firm, it will first need to consider whether the additional procedure applies and then, whether to comply with that procedure.

The procedure for cancellation of permission

16.252 Paragraph **16.40** ff above considered the circumstances in which the Regulators may exercise their power to cancel a firm's permission. In terms of the procedure for cancelling a firm's permission, there are differences from the procedures outlined above for varying a firm's permission. In particular, the procedure involves the Regulators issuing warning and decision notices rather than supervisory notices[1] and it contains additional safeguards for firms. It is similar to the procedure that is used when disciplinary sanctions are imposed on firms and individuals that is described in detail in **CHAPTER 10** above[2].

1 FSMA 2000, s 55Z.
2 Note that many final notices cancelling a firm's permission tend to provide little detail as to the reasons for taking the action. Generally a short extract from the warning notice is included (see, eg *Sovereign Worldwide Limited final notice (04/07/13)*). By contrast, see *Gurpreet Singh Chadda final notice (19/06/13)* where the final notice set out details of the applicable misrepresentation at length.

16.253 The most important difference to the procedure for varying a firm's permission is that this action cannot be imposed as a matter of urgency[1]. However, in those situations where the Regulator wishes to prevent the firm from carrying on any regulated activities as a matter of urgency, it achieves this by varying the firm's permission to remove all its regulated activities[2]. As discussed[3], the distinction between the variation and cancellation of a firm's permission may therefore be somewhat artificial in many respects.

1 See para **16.216** ff above.
2 See the FCA Enforcement Guide at EG 8.16.
3 See para **16.128** above.

The consequences of cancelling permission

16.254 If a firm's permission is cancelled and, as a result, there is no regulated activity for which it has permission, the Regulator must give a direction withdrawing its authorisation[1]. If, however, the top-up permission of an incoming firm is cancelled, such a firm may still have permission to carry on other regulated activities under the FSMA 2000, Schs 3 and/or 4[2] and, in such cases, its authorisation would not be withdrawn.

1 FSMA 2000, s 33 and see the FCA Enforcement Guide at EG 8.17.
2 See para **1.73** ff above.

16.255 Once a firm has no authorisation, it is outside the regulatory system and, therefore, commits the criminal offence of breaching the general prohibition if it carries on a regulated activity[1].

1 FSMA 2000, ss 19 and 23 and see para **2.115** ff above.

16.256 It will therefore be outside the scope of the Regulators' administrative powers, although certain powers may still be exercised against it, including[1]:

- certain information gathering and investigation powers[2];

- the Regulators' power to apply to the court for an injunction and/or restitution order[3];

- powers in respect of market abuse[4];

- certain insolvency powers[5]; and

- the power to prosecute certain criminal offences[6].

1 See the Handbooks at SUP 6.4.23
2 See, for example, the FSMA 2000, ss 165(8), 166(2)(d) and 167(4) (which apply the Regulators' investigatory powers in respect of a former authorised person) and see **CHAPTER 4** above.
3 See, respectively, paras **8.103** ff and **8.141** ff above.
4 See **CHAPTER 17** below.
5 See the FCA Enforcement Guide at EG 13.
6 See **CHAPTER 18** below.

Section E
Specific Topics

Chapter 17　Market misconduct

INTRODUCTION

17.1　This chapter will review the regime for combating misconduct in the financial markets. The chapter is entitled 'market misconduct', rather than 'market abuse', because the regime of financial penalties for market abuse introduced in 2001 is only one of a number of tools that the FCA can use to deal with market misconduct.

17.2　Within the rubric of market misconduct, therefore, the chapter will include not only financial penalties for market abuse, but also the other enforcement action that the FCA can take as a result of market abuse, the various relevant criminal offences, the regulatory action available to the FCA to address breaches of its rules where there is an overlap between market abuse and the FCA's rules, including the regulatory general principles, and the interaction of the FCA's regime with the rules of other relevant bodies such as recognised investment exchanges, recognised auction platforms, the Takeover Panel and relevant overseas regulators, exchanges and other bodies.

17.3　This chapter considers the interaction between the various types of market misconduct and the different possible consequences of such misconduct. It will outline the implications of being suspected of, or committing, misconduct in the markets, from the discovery of the misconduct, through its investigation by the FCA, to the options available to the FCA should market abuse be established or should some other criminal or regulatory offence have been committed.

17.4　This chapter therefore considers the following main issues:

17.4   Market misconduct

- an overview of the regime for combating market misconduct;

- recognising market abuse – an outline of the constituents of market abuse is provided[1];

- if it is likely that market abuse or other market misconduct has taken place, the practical steps firms or others involved should take and the powers of the FCA to investigate?[2]; and

- the range of different sanctions or other enforcement action available to the FCA if market misconduct has occurred, including penalties for market abuse, the relevant criminal offences and the other possible regulatory consequences (including those involving other regulators) that might follow from the misconduct[3].

1 See para **17.20** ff below.
2 See para **17.110** ff below.
3 See para **17.155** ff below.

17.5   There are similarities between the market abuse regime and the general disciplinary regime described elsewhere in this book, in terms of the investigation process, the FCA's decision-making process, the firm's ability to challenge the imposition of sanctions and the measures that can be imposed. Where the regimes are the same or similar, cross-reference is made to other sections of the book where the relevant issue is explained in detail, highlighting any particular issues arising in this context.

AN OVERVIEW OF THE REGIME FOR COMBATING MARKET MISCONDUCT

What is the regime designed to achieve?

17.6   The main objective behind the regime is to secure the integrity of EU (and, in particular, UK) financial markets, so that confidence in them is maintained. The current civil market abuse regime derives from the FSMA 2000 and EU law[1].

1 Council Directive 2003/6/EC ([2003] OJ L96/16) on insider dealing and market manipulation (market abuse), 'the Market Abuse Directive'; and Commission Regulation 1031/2010 ([2010] OJ L302/1) on the timing, administration and other aspects of auctioning of greenhouse gas emission allowances, 'the EU Emissions Trading System Auctioning Regulation'.

17.7   In September 2013 the European Parliament adopted the text of a proposal to replace the existing Market Abuse Directive (MAD) with a new regulation on insider dealing and market manipulation (known as the Market Abuse Regulation or MAR)[1] and, in December 2013, the European Parliament and European Council published compromise text for a new directive imposing criminal sanctions for intentional market abuse (CSMAD).

1 To avoid confusion with MAR in the FCA Handbook, the Market Abuse Regulation will be referred to as the MA Regulation in this chapter.

17.8   The proposals aim to provide a consistent market abuse regime across the EU. In particular, MAR is intended to update and strengthen the existing legislative framework on market abuse, while the CSMAD will require Member States (other than those who have opted out) to introduce minimum criminal sanctions for intentional market abuse and for inciting, aiding and abetting, and attempting to commit such offences.

17.9 The proposed text of the MAR was provisionally agreed between the European Parliament and the Council on 26 June 2013, published on 5 July 2013 and was adopted by the European Parliament on 10 September 2013. For the most part it will not come into force for a further two years at which point the MAD will be repealed.

17.10 The implementation of the MAR will make significant changes to the civil market abuse regime and where relevant these are set out in footnotes and paragraphs below. However, at the time of writing drafts of Level 2 measures that will provide some important details of the revised regime have not yet been published.

17.11 The UK government has decided to exercise its discretion not to opt into the CSMAD at the present time, on the basis that the current criminal offences in the UK cover all of the offences currently proposed in the draft directive. However, it may opt in at a later stage. The UK opt-out does not mean that the CSMAD will have no effect on financial services business conducted in the UK. Firms or branches based in the UK will need to be aware that market abuse by individuals trading cross border or in a financial instrument traded in an overseas jurisdiction could give rise to criminal liability for the individual overseas, and possibly corporate liability for that conduct. However, for the time being, the criminal offences in UK law and the power of the FCA to prosecute those offences will not change. This chapter does not discuss the proposed CSMAD.

What are the FCA's options for dealing with suspected market misconduct?

17.12 Given the complexity of the regime, it is instructive to have at the outset an overview as to how the FCA can go about dealing with suspected cases of market misconduct.

17.13 Where information to suggest that market misconduct may have taken place comes to the FCA's attention, it can use a variety of powers to investigate and has wide powers to obtain relevant information from those who may have such information[1].

1 See para **17.110** below.

17.14 Armed with the results of the investigation, the FCA may consider using one or more of a number of enforcement powers available to it:

- if one of the relevant criminal offences[1] may have been committed then, in appropriate circumstances, the FCA will act as the prosecuting authority and bring a criminal prosecution for those offences[2]; or

- alternatively, if the civil offence of market abuse has been committed by any person, the FCA may:

  - impose a financial penalty against the person or publicly censure him[3];

  - make, or apply for, a restitution order against the person, requiring him to disgorge any profits he has made or compensate any losses suffered by others as a result[4]; and/or

  - seek an injunction, among other things, prohibiting that person from undertaking further acts which would amount to market abuse[5];

- the FCA may, in some situations, become involved in, or take over, investigations by other UK regulators into misconduct in their own markets and/or those other regulators may take their own enforcement action[6];

- the FCA may, in some situations, be able to address misconduct which occurred abroad, and in those situations will need to liaise with overseas regulators[7];

- if the misconduct was committed by a regulated firm, then the FCA may consider using its other enforcement powers, such as its disciplinary and/or own-initiative powers, particularly if it raises wider regulatory issues about the firm. In some circumstances the FCA may regard conduct, whether or not amounting to market abuse, as a breach of the FCA rules[8] deserving of disciplinary sanctions[9];

- if the conduct was committed by an approved person (or certain other of a firm's employees)[10], then the FCA may consider using its other enforcement powers, such as to discipline him and/or withdraw his approval. In some circumstances, it may regard conduct, whether or not amounting to market abuse, as a breach of the Statements of Principle for approved persons[11], and take disciplinary action against an approved person for that misconduct; and

- if it was committed by any individual then the FCA may consider that a prohibition order is appropriate[12].

1 Insider dealing under the Criminal Justice Act 1993, Pt V or misleading statements and practices under the Financial Services Act 2012, ss 89–90 and misleading statements and practices in relation to benchmarks under the Financial Services Act 2012, s 91.
2 See para **17.159** ff below.
3 See para **17.185** ff below.
4 See para **17.245** ff below.
5 See para **17.227** ff below.
6 See para **17.203** ff below.
7 See para **17.221** ff below.
8 In particular, Principle 5 of the Principles for Businesses; a firm must observe proper standards of market conduct, see the discussion at para **17.256** below.
9 For example, see *Citigroup Global Markets Limited final notice (28/6/05)*, see also the *Barclays Bank Plc final notice (27/6/12)*, *UBS AG final notice (19/12/12)* and *The Royal Bank of Scotland plc final notice (6/2/13)* in relation to the fixing of LIBOR when the FSA took action against firms for breach of the Principles of Businesses. Prior to the enactment of the Financial Services Act 2012 benchmark manipulation was not a specific criminal offence and prior to the implementation of the MA Regulation it does not fall within the civil market abuse regime.
10 See para **2.52** ff above.

11 In particular, Statement of Principle 3: an approved person must observe proper standards of market conduct in carrying out his controlled function, see for example the *Sean Julian Pignatelli final notice (20/11/06)*, the *Robert Chiarion Casoni final notice (20/3/07)*, the *Mark Lockwood final notice (1/9/09)*, and the *Christopher William Gower final notice (12/01/11)*. This is discussed further at para **17.260** ff below.

12 See para **17.253** ff below.

17.15 Dependent upon which course or courses of action it is appropriate for the FCA to take, specific procedures will need to be followed before the action is finally imposed.

The implications of the Human Rights Act 1998

17.16 The second edition of this work noted that there was some concern during the Bill stages of the FSMA 2000 that the imposition of a civil penalty for market abuse could constitute a criminal charge for ECHR purposes, particularly given the potential severity of such penalties, the punitive nature of the market abuse regime and the fact that it applies to the public at large, not only to those who have chosen to be part of the regulated community[1]. The government did not agree that a market abuse penalty could constitute a criminal charge but nonetheless recognised the possibility[2] and, as a result, made various amendments to the Bill. In particular:

- a scheme was introduced to provide legal assistance to those charged with market abuse who have insufficient means and where the interests of justice require[3];

- the statutory protection was extended, so that statements made to the FCA under compulsion may not be used in proceedings for market abuse against the person who made the statement[4]; and

- the FCA can also be required to prove the allegation of market abuse before the Tribunal[5].

1 The latter in particular distinguishes market abuse penalties from disciplinary penalties imposed by the FCA on firms and approved persons (and certain other employees of firms). This issue is discussed in more detail at para **10.19** ff above.
2 Economic Secretary to HM Treasury in Standing Committee, 2 November 1999, and see the Second Report of the Joint Committee, at para 3.
3 See para **17.182** below.
4 See para **17.140** below.
5 See para **17.199** ff below and **CHAPTER 12** above.

17.17 The Upper Tribunal has determined that a penalty for market abuse is a criminal charge for the purposes of Article 6 of the ECHR. The principle practical consequence of this is that before the tribunal the burden of proof rests on the FCA[1].

1 *See Davidson and Tatham v Financial Services Authority (Fin/2003/0016)*. The standard of proof that applies is the civil standard however in Davidson and Tatham the Tribunal held 'the more serious the allegation, or the more serious the consequences if the allegation is proved the stronger must be the evidence before we should find the allegation is proved on the balance of probabilities'.

17.18 No challenges have been brought to the conduct of an investigation by the FCA (or its predecessor the FSA), nor to the tribunal process as being in breach of an individual's Art 6 rights and the measures detailed above appear to have addressed the primary structural issues. However, the question of whether or not a person's human rights have been violated has to be judged on a case-by-case basis. It cannot therefore be ruled out that the FCA's actions in a particular case, for example, the way in which it conducts its investigation, might give rise to arguments about non-compliance with the ECHR.

RECOGNISING MARKET ABUSE

Introduction

17.19 Anyone in the UK who is involved in a UK or EU financial market, or in investments that are traded on one or are linked in some way to investments that are traded on one, will need to be familiar with the kinds of behaviour that could amount to market abuse under the FSMA 2000 or fall within the related criminal offences. Whilst the focus of this book is on the enforcement consequences of committing market abuse, rather than a detailed analysis of what constitutes market abuse, a broad outline of market abuse has been provided because the consequences of committing it cannot be considered in a vacuum. The relevant provisions are complex and even an outline therefore requires some detail.

What is civil market abuse?

17.20 The starting point is the statutory definition of market abuse, which is found at the FSMA 2000, ss 118 and 118A. This is cast in broad terms. Guidance on what the FCA considers amounts, and does not amount, to market abuse is found in the Code of Market Conduct[1], which has been issued by the FCA in accordance with the requirements of the FSMA 2000. The two therefore need to be read together.

1 FCA Handbook at MAR 1.

Code of Market Conduct

17.21 The FSMA 2000 recognises the breadth of the statutory definition and therefore requires the FCA to issue a code, known as the Code of Market Conduct, to give guidance to those determining whether or not behaviour amounts to market abuse[1]. The Code may specify[2]:

- behaviour which, in the FCA's view, amounts to market abuse;
- behaviour which, in the FCA's view, does not amount to market abuse;
- factors which, in the FCA's view, are to be taken into account in determining whether or not behaviour amounts to market abuse;

- behaviour which is accepted market practice in relation to one or more specified markets; and

- behaviour which is not accepted market practice in relation to one or more specified markets.

1 The Code's provisions carry the letter E, G or C. Paragraphs using the letter E may be relied on so far as they indicate whether or not particular behaviour should be taken to amount to market abuse, G indicates guidance under the FSMA 2000, s 139A and C is used for paragraphs made under the FSMA 2000, s 119(2)(b) that specify descriptions of behaviour that, in the opinion of the FCA, do not amount to market abuse. Under the FSMA 2000, s 122(1), paragraphs marked C in the Code conclusively do not amount to market abuse. For further details on the interpretation of the Code, see the Readers' Guide: an introduction to the FCA Handbook and, in particular, Chapter Six of that Guide. See also **CHAPTER 2** above for a further explanation of the effect of Handbook provisions.
2 FSMA 2000, s 119.

17.22   The purpose of the Code is thus to provide greater clarity to the meaning of market abuse whilst allowing flexibility for the scope of the regime in what is always a dynamic market.

17.23   It is important to appreciate that the Code has, under the FSMA 2000, only limited effect in determining whether or not market abuse has occurred[1]:

- provisions of the Code providing a safe harbour and stating that behaviour does not amount to market abuse are conclusive and such behaviour does not amount to market abuse[2];

- provisions of the Code stating that particular behaviour will amount to market abuse are conclusive, and that behaviour will amount to market abuse[3];

- beyond that the Code carries evidential weight but cannot be relied upon conclusively to demonstrate whether or not behaviour should be taken to amount to market abuse[4]. The Code does not, in listing descriptions of behaviour which amounts to market abuse, imply that behaviour which falls outside this list does not constitute market abuse[5].

Whilst the Code will inevitably form the centrepiece of any consideration by firms or individuals as to whether they can or cannot undertake a particular course of action, it remains subsidiary to the statutory definition. In other words, conduct that does not fall within the statutory definition cannot amount to market abuse, whatever the Code says. There may be tension between the Code and the FSMA 2000, given the potential uncertainties in the statutory definition.

1 Note that the relevant Code is that in force at the time the behaviour occurred: FSMA 2000, s 122.
2 FSMA 2000, s 122(1), see also *Winterflood Securities Ltd v Financial Services Authority [2010] EWCA Civ 423*.
3 *Winterflood Securities Ltd v Financial Services Authority [2010] EWCA Civ 423*.
4 FSMA 2000, s 122(2).
5 *Winterflood Securities Ltd v Financial Services Authority [2010] EWCA Civ 423*.

17.24   The Code acknowledges this, in MAR 1.1.6G, which indicates that the descriptions in the Code of behaviour which amount to market abuse should be read subject to the FSMA 2000 and to descriptions of behaviour which do not amount to market abuse. The Code also makes clear that factors specified by the FCA in the Code are non-exhaustive and, except where otherwise stated, non-conclusive. Further, the absence of a factor given as an indication that behaviour constitutes market abuse is not, of itself, an indication that that behaviour does not constitute market abuse[1].

1 FCA Handbook at MAR 1.1.7E.

17.25   Beyond the statutory definition and the Code, other rules of the FCA (or the rules of other bodies, for example, the ESMA level 3 guidance or any level 3 guidance issued by its predecessor CESR)[1], exchanges, auction platforms, the City Code, some part of the old Code or the UK Listing Rules), may cover the firm's conduct in the particular market and may also therefore be relevant.

1 ESMA is the European Securities and Markets Authority it succeeded CESR, the Committee of European Securities Regulators, on 1 January 2011. Level 3 guidance relates to the application of EU financial services legislation and although not legally binding applies on a comply or explain basis.

The statutory definition of market abuse

17.26   In summary, market abuse is behaviour which[1]:

(a)   Occurs in relation to:

–   qualifying investments:

–   admitted to trading on a prescribed market or offered for sale on a prescribed auction platform; or

–   in respect of which a request for admission to such a market has been made; or

–   related investments (certain categories of market abuse only).

(b)   Falls into one or more of the following categories[2]:

–   *Limb 1*: insider dealing; or

–   *Limb 2*: the improper disclosure of inside information; or

–   *Limb 3*: the misuse of relevant information where the behaviour falls below the standard of behaviour reasonably expected by a regular user of the market or a person in the position of the alleged abuser; or

–   *Limb 4*: manipulating transactions (or bids) unless for legitimate reasons and in conformity with accepted market practices on the relevant market; or

–   *Limb 5*: manipulating devices; or

–   *Limb 6*: the dissemination of information that gives or is likely to give a false or misleading impression; or

- *Limb 7*: misleading behaviour or distortion of the market where the behaviour falls below the standard of behaviour reasonably expected by a regular user of the market or a person in the position of the alleged abuser; or

- *Limb 8*: behaviour contravening any of Articles 38–41 of the EU ETS Auctioning Regulation (broadly equivalent to limbs 1, 2, 4, 5 and 6) in respect of EU emissions allowances which do not fall within the definition of 'financial instrument' for the purposes of the Markets in Financial Instruments Directive (Directive 2004/39/EC) (MiFID)[3];

unless:

- it conforms with a rule which expressly provides that behaviour which conforms to it will not amount to market abuse; or

- it conforms with Commission Regulation 2273/2003/EC, implementing MAD in relation to exemptions for buy-back programmes and stabilisation of financial instruments; or

- it is specified in the Code as, in the FCA's view, not amounting to market abuse.

(c) Where behaviour does amount to market abuse, it will not give rise to a penalty[4] if:

- the person believed on reasonable grounds that his behaviour did not amount to market abuse; or

- he took all reasonable precautions and exercised all due diligence to avoid committing market abuse. A penalty for market abuse[5] can be levied not only against a person who actually commits market abuse, but also against a person who requires or encourages another to engage in behaviour which would have amounted to market abuse had it been engaged in by the first person.

In the remainder of this chapter, Limbs 1 and 2 are referred to as the EU insider prohibitions, Limbs 3 and 7 are referred to as the retained prohibitions.

1 For details, see the FSMA 2000, ss 118 and 118A. This list is derived from the FSMA 2000, ss 118, 120, 122 and 123.
2 Limbs 3 and 7 are the 'super-equivalent' positions that remain from the regime under the FSMA 2000 before the implementation of MAD. They are subject to a 'sunset clause' under the FSMA 2000, s 118(9) which will expire on 31 December 2014. It should be noted that the date for the expiration of these provisions has been extended on three previous occasions.
3 The FCA has indicated that it is of the view that two-day spot contracts under the EU Emissions Trading System (EU ETS) are not 'financial instruments' for this purpose – see the FCA's perimeter Guidance at PERG 17.4 and recital 14 to the EU Emissions Trading Scheme System Auctioning Regulation.
4 Or to a restitution order, but note that it may nonetheless give rise to an injunction: see para **17.227** ff below.
5 Or a restitution order: see para **17.245** ff below.

17.27 A brief summary of each of these elements, and its treatment in the Code, is given below, with a view to providing a basic understanding of the scope and nature of market abuse. It is not the intention to provide a detailed analysis of what constitutes market abuse. The relevant provisions of the FSMA 2000 and the Code should be consulted in specific cases.

Behaviour

17.28 The question of what constitutes 'behaviour' is interpreted broadly. The FSMA 2000 states[1] only that behaviour includes action or inaction[2]. The Code provides that the following factors are an indication that inaction amounts to market abuse:

- where a person has, by inaction, failed to discharge a legal or regulatory obligation; and

- where a person has created a reasonable expectation of his acting in a particular manner, in circumstances which give rise to a requirement to correct that expectation, and he has not done so[3].

1 FSMA 2000, s 130A(3).
2 See the FCA Handbook at MAR 1.2.6E for the factors that, in the FCA's view, are to be taken into account in determining whether or not refraining from action amounts to behaviour in this context.
3 FCA Handbook at MAR 1.2.6E.

17.29 Behaviour can be by one person alone or by two or more persons jointly or in concert[1]. Persons can be individuals or organisations. If the FSMA 2000 refers to a person engaging in market abuse, it is referring to a person engaged in market abuse whether alone or with one or more other persons[2].

1 FSMA 2000, s 118(1). In *7722656 Canada Inc (formerly carrying on business as Swift Trade Inc) and Beck v Financial Conduct Authority [2013] EWCA Civ 1662*, in which orders for contracts for difference were placed through direct market access providers which then triggered automatic hedging orders for shares on the LSE, the Court of Appeal found that the wording of the FSMA 2000, s 118(1) means that the commission of market abuse jointly does not require that the parties act with the same intention or purpose, so that it is not possible to avoid liability for conduct that is otherwise market abuse by arguing that an unwitting intermediary (in the form of a DMA provider in this case) came between the supposed abuser and the market.
2 FSMA 2000, s 130A(4).

Prescribed markets and auction platforms, qualifying investments, related investments and the term 'in relation to'

17.30 To understand the meaning of the basic elements of market abuse, it is necessary to look at four separate questions:

- What are the prescribed markets and auction platforms?

- What investments are qualifying investments and when do they fall within the regime?

- What are related investments?

- When does behaviour occur 'in relation to' qualifying investments and/or related investments?

What are the prescribed markets?

17.31   The market abuse provisions state that HM Treasury can specify the markets that are prescribed markets in this context[1]. The FSMA 2000 does not contain any limit on the markets that may be prescribed. Broadly, HM Treasury has prescribed[2] all markets established under the rules of a UK recognised investment exchange, and, in relation to all categories of market abuse other than the retained prohibitions, regulated markets based in EU countries.

1   FSMA 2000, s 130A(1).
2   See the Financial Services and Markets Act 2000 (Prescribed Markets and Qualifying Investments) Order 2001, SI 2001/996 (as amended).

17.32   Currently, the prescribed UK markets include the London Stock Exchange, LIFFE, the London Metal Exchange, ICE Futures, ISDX and BATS CHI-X Europe and AIM[1]. The description of prescribed markets can be amended by HM Treasury[2]. As regards regulated markets, each EU Member State is required to maintain a definitive list of its relevant regulated markets[3].

1   Although AIM is not a regulated market it is owned by the London Stock Exchange in its capacity as a recognised investment exchange and is therefore a prescribed market.
2   The list is currently automatically amended (based on SI 2001/996) when the FCA recognises further RIEs or revokes the recognition of an RIE.
3   Article 13(2) Lever 2 MiFID Regulation.

17.33   Trading in securities on an overseas market that are also offered on a prescribed market is also within the scope of the FSMA market abuse regime[1].

1   See *Philippe Jabre and GLG Partners LP final notice (1/8/06)* in which the FSA was of the view that short selling of shares on the Tokyo Stock Exchange fell within the market abuse regime because the shares in question were also traded on the OINT segment of the LSE.

17.34   The implementation of the MA Regulation will extend the market abuse regime to financial instruments admitted to trading on, or for which a request has been made for admission to trading on 'multilateral trading facilities' (MTFs) or 'organised trading facilities' (OTFs)[1]. In effect this is likely to mean that all financial instruments that are publicly traded on some form of exchange or trading platform will come within the scope of the market abuse regime.

1   The categories of 'organised trading facility' and 'multilateral trading facility' are introduced under the proposed revisions to the Markets in Financial Instruments Directive (2004/39/EC) and the MAD.

What are the prescribed auction platforms?

17.35   Recognised investment exchanges can apply to the FCA for recognition as an auction platform under the EU ETS. For the purposes of all categories of market abuse other than Limb 8 all recognised auction platforms are prescribed auction platforms[1]. In addition, in relation to all categories of market abuse other than the retained provisions all auction platforms appointed under the EU ETS Auctioning Regulation are prescribed auction platforms[2]. Finally, in respect of Limb 8 only, auction platforms appointed under the EU ETS Auctioning Regulation are prescribed auction platforms[3]. The broad effect, in summary, is that five-day emission allowance futures created under the EU ETS and offered for sale on a recognised auction platform are within the scope of Limbs 1–7; if these contracts are offered for sale on an auction platform appointed under the EU ETS Auctioning Regulation they are within the scope of Limbs 1, 2, 4, 5 and 6; and two-day emission allowance spot contracts created under the EU ETS and offered for sale on an auction platform appointed under the EU ETS Auctioning Regulation platform are within the scope of Limb 8. (The application of the civil market abuse regime to derivatives on these emission allowances is not governed by the auction platform regime but rather by the regime applicable to prescribed markets.)

1 See the Financial Services and Markets Act 2000 (Prescribed Markets and Qualifying Instruments) Order 2001, SI 2001/996, art 4(3)–(4).
2 SI 2001/996, art 4(3)–(4).
3 SI 2001/996, art 4(5).

17.36 Recognised Auction Platforms are listed on the Financial Services Register. At the time of writing the recognised auction platform in the UK is ICE Futures and the only auction platform appointed under the EU ETS Auctioning Regulation is EEX in Leipzig.

What are qualifying investments?

17.37 Again, the FSMA 2000 allows HM Treasury to prescribe what investments are qualifying in relation to the prescribed markets (and auction platforms)[1]. HM Treasury has prescribed[2] that, in respect of Limbs 1–7, in relation to each of the prescribed markets, qualifying investments means all financial instruments within the meaning given in Art 1(3) of MAD, and in respect of prescribed auction platforms all auction products that fall within the definition of 'financial instrument' contained in MiFID. This covers:

- transferable securities (shares and their equivalent, bonds and other forms of securitised debt which, in each case, are negotiable on the capital markets, and other securities giving the right to acquire transferable securities or to a cash settlement);

- units in collective investment undertakings;

- money market instruments;

- financial futures (including cash settled futures);

- forward interest rate agreements;

- interest rate, currency and equity swaps;

- options to acquire any of the above (including cash settled options, and currency and interest rate options);

- derivatives on commodities;

- any other instrument admitted to trading on a regulated market in an EU Member State or for which a request for admission to trading on such a market has been made (including derivatives on EU ETS allowances); and

- five day futures created under the EU ETS and offered for sale on prescribed auction platforms[3].

Emissions allowances created under the EU ETS which are not financial instruments within the definition set out in MiFID are qualifying investments in respect of Limb 8[4]. FCA guidance indicates that this includes two-day spot contracts created under the EU ETS[5].

1 FSMA 2000, s 130A(1).
2 See the Financial Services and Markets Act 2000 (Prescribed Markets and Qualifying Investments) Order 2001, SI 2001/996 (as amended), art 5.
3 See the FCA Handbook at PERG 17.4 (which has the status of guidance as to the FCA's view and is not binding on the courts and recital 14 to the EU Emissions Trading Scheme System Auctioning Regulation).
4 See the Financial Services and Markets Act 2000 (Prescribed Markets and Qualifying Instruments) Order 2001, SI 2001/996 art 5(3).
5 See the FCA Handbook at PERG 17.4 (which is guidance issued by the FCA and is not binding on the courts). It is also open to the FCA, if it considers that behaviour that does not constitute market abuse is in breach of other disciplinary rules or the Principle of Business, to take action in respect of these breaches (see para **17.253** below).

17.38 The MA Regulation specifies that any requirements or prohibitions that it contains apply to bids made in the auctions of emissions allowances. It should also be noted that under the EU legislation that will replace MiFID the definition of 'financial instruments' will include all emissions allowances that are created under the EU ETS such that two-day spot contracts on emissions allowances will be brought within the mainstream market abuse regime. The MA Regulation also states that requirements and prohibitions relating to orders to trade apply equally to bids made in emission allowance auctions.

17.39 It should be noted that behaviour that amounts to market abuse can occur in relation to qualifying investments that are admitted to trading on a prescribed market or offered for sale on a prescribed auction platform or qualifying investments in respect of which a request for admission to trading on such a market has been made[1].

1 FSMA 2000, s 118(1)(a)(i) and (ii).

What are 'related investments'?

17.40 For behaviour to amount to market abuse under insider prohibitions, the behaviour must occur in relation to a qualifying investment (whether admitted or requested to be admitted to a prescribed market or offered for sale on a prescribed auction platform) or investments that are related investments in relation to such qualifying investments[1]. In this context, a related investment is an investment whose price or value depends on the price or value of the qualifying investment[2].

1 FSMA 2000, s 118(1)(a).
2 FSMA 2000, s 130A(3).

17.41 Market misconduct

17.41 The implementation of the MA Regulation will extend the meaning of related investments to include financial instruments whose value 'has an effect on' financial instruments traded on a regulated market, MTF, or OTF.

When does behaviour occur 'in relation to' qualifying investments and/or related investments?

17.42 This is the more difficult concept. In order to amount to market abuse, the behaviour must occur in relation to qualifying investments admitted (or in respect of which a request for admission has been made) to trading on a prescribed market or auction platform or investments that are related investments in relation to such qualifying investments[1]. This clearly includes behaviour which directly involves or affects the investments themselves, but also anticipates that the regime may cover behaviour which is less directly connected to the investments on the relevant market[2].

1 FSMA 2000, s 118(1)(a).
2 In *7722656 Canada Inc (formerly carrying on business as Swift Trade Inc)* and *Beck v Financial Conduct Authority [2013] EWCA Civ 1662* the Court of Appeal found that placing an order for a contract for difference constitutes behaviour which occurs in relation to qualifying investments, where the person placing that order knows and intends, that this results in the placing of a corresponding order for the underlying shares.

17.43 The FSMA 2000 does not contain any definition of what 'in relation to' means in this context, but does make clear in respect of the retained prohibitions that two types of behaviour are included[1], namely behaviour which occurs in relation to:

- anything that is the subject matter of a qualifying investment;

- anything whose price or value is expressed by reference to the price or value of a qualifying investment; or

- an investment (whether qualifying or not) whose subject matter is a qualifying investment.

Investments falling within these provisions are sometimes referred to as 'relevant products'.

1 FSMA 2000, s 118A(3).

17.44 Further, the Code sets out[1] the factors that are to be taken into account in determining whether or not behaviour prior to a request for admission to trading or before the admission to or commencement of trading satisfies the 'in relation to' requirement of the FSMA 2000, s 118(1)(a). These are where:

- the behaviour is in relation to qualifying investments in respect of which a request for admission to trading on a prescribed market is subsequently made; and

- the behaviour continues to have an effect once an application has been made for the qualifying investment to be admitted for trading, or it has been admitted to trading on a prescribed market, respectively.

1 FCA Handbook at MAR 1.2.5E.

Territorial scope

17.45   Behaviour can amount to market abuse if it occurs in the UK or it occurs elsewhere but relates to qualifying investments that are admitted to trading (or for which a request has been made for admission to trading) on a prescribed market or that are offered for sale on a prescribed auction platform situated or operating in the UK[1]. In respect of the EU prohibitions, behaviour can also amount to market abuse if it concerns 'related investments' in respect of such qualifying investments[2]. Behaviour in the UK may also (or instead) amount to market abuse in another jurisdiction, depending on what instruments it relates to.

1   For certain categories of market abuse, a prescribed market that is accessible electronically in the UK is to be treated as operating in the UK: FSMA 2000, s 118A(2).
2   FSMA 2000, s 118A(1).

The categories of behaviour

17.46   Central to the definition of market abuse is the requirement for the behaviour to fall within one of the specified descriptions of behaviour. Each of these is reviewed briefly below.

Limb 1: Insider dealing

17.47   This covers behaviour where[1]:

- an insider;

- deals or attempts to deal[2];

- in a qualifying investment[3] or related investment[4];

- on the basis of[5];

- inside information relating to the investment in question.

1   FSMA 2000, s 118(2).
2   Under the FSMA 2000, s 130A(3) dealing in relation to an investment means acquiring or disposing of the investment whether as principal or agent or directly or indirectly, and includes agreeing to acquire or dispose of the investment, and entering into or bringing to an end a contract creating it. The implementation of the MA Regulation will extend the insider dealing provision to the amendment and cancellation of orders on the basis of inside information.
3   See para **17.37** ff above.
4   See para **17.40** ff above.
5   See para **17.57** below.

17.48   This concept of insider dealing market abuse exists alongside the current criminal offence of insider dealing under the Criminal Justice Act 1993, Pt V and, although similar, the FSMA 2000 provision differs from those contained in the 1993 Act.

17.49 Market misconduct

17.49 An insider in FSMA 2000[1] is any person who has inside information[2]:

- as a result of his membership of an administrative, management or supervisory body of an issuer of qualifying investments or of an auction platform, its operator, an auctioneer or auction monitor;

- as a result of his holding in the capital of an issuer of qualifying investments;

- as a result of having access to information through the exercise of his employment, profession or duties;

- as a result of his criminal activities; or

- which he has obtained by other means and which he knows, or could reasonably be expected to know, is inside information.

1 FSMA 2000, s 118B. Guidance is given in the FCA Handbook at MAR 1.2.8E.
2 In the view of the FCA a person is an insider if, taking the information that they have received as a whole and in context, the information that they have received is inside information even if no single piece of inside information can be identified see *David Einhorn and Greenlight Capital Inc final notice (15/2/12)*.

17.50 Generally, for qualifying investments and related investments that are not commodity derivatives[1], inside information[2] is information:

- of a precise nature[3];

- that is not generally available[4];

- that relates directly or indirectly to one or more issuers of the qualifying investments or to one or more of the qualifying investments; and

- which would, if generally available, be likely to have a significant effect on the price of the qualifying investments or the price at which bids would be made for qualifying investments[5].

1 For the definition of inside information in respect of commodity derivatives see the FSMA 2000, s 118C(3) and (7). There is also a different definition for inside information where a person is charged with the execution of orders concerning any qualifying investments or related investments. See the FSMA 2000, s 118C(4) and the FCA Handbook at MAR 1.2.17.
2 FSMA 2000, s 118C(2). For guidance, see the FCA Handbook at MAR 1.2.11G–1.2.16E.
3 For a definition of 'precise information' in this context, see the FSMA 2000, s 118C(5).
4 Guidance in respect of what is and what is not 'generally available' can be found in the FSMA 2000, s 118C(8) and the FCA Handbook at MAR 1.2.12E–1.2.14G.
5 Information would be likely to have a significant effect on price if and only if it is information of a kind which a reasonable investor would be likely to use as part of the basis of his investment decisions. See the FSMA 2000, s 118(C)(6).

17.51 The FCA applies the definition of inside information broadly. Information will be sufficiently precise if it indicates that circumstances exist whose 'possible effect' would be to cause the price of the relevant investment to move[1].

1 See *Ian Hannam decision notice (27/2/12)* (note that Mr Hannam has appealed to the Upper Tribunal – the case was heard in July 2013 but at the time of writing the decision was not available).

17.52 Information will have a significant effect on the price of a qualifying investment if a reasonable investor would be likely to use it as part of the basis for an investment decision whether or not the information was in fact likely to have a significant effect on the price and even if the investor would also need other non-public information to make that decision[1].

1 See for example *Ian Hannam decision notice (27/2/12)* (note Mr Hannam has appealed to the Upper Tribunal, the case was heard in July 2013), *Andrew Jon Osborne final notice (15/2/12)* and the decision of the Upper Tribunal in *David Massey v FSA [2011] UKUT 49 (TCC)*, *(Fin/2009/0024)* in which the Tribunal indicated that the 'reasonable investor test' will take priority over an objective assessment of whether the information disclosed is likely to have a significant effect on the price in the ordinary sense.

17.53 The proposed text of the MA Regulation states that a significant effect on price 'shall mean' information that a reasonable investor would be likely to use as part of the basis of his investment decisions.

17.54 As regards commodity derivatives, inside information is information:

- of a precise nature;

- that is not generally available;

- that relates directly or indirectly to one or more commodity derivatives; and

- which users of markets on which the derivatives are traded would expect to receive in accordance with any accepted market practices on those markets[1].

1 FSMA 2000, s 118C(3). This is elaborated by the FSMA 2000, s 118C(7) to make clear that it covers information which is routinely made available to market users or is required to be disclosed on the market or any underlying commodities market. See also the FCA Handbook at MAR1.2.17G.

17.55 Inside information is also, in relation to a person who executes orders in commodity derivatives, information relating to a client's pending orders[1] which meets the general definition of inside information.

1 FCA Handbook at MAR1.2.16E.

17.56 The implementation of the MA Regulation will also expand the definition of inside information in EU legislation to include information in respect of emissions allowances or auctioned products that fall within the definition of inside information.

17.57 There is a rebuttable presumption that a person who deals while in possession of inside information is 'using' that information[1]. The Code at MAR 1.3.3 sets out factors to be taken into account in assessing whether or not a person's behaviour is 'on the basis of' inside information.

1 See the decision of the ECJ in *Spector Photo Group NV and Chris Van Raemdonck v Commissie voor het Bank-, Financie- en Assurantiewezen (CBFA)*, *(C-45/08) [2010] All ER (EC) 278.*

17.58 For a more detailed discussion in respect of this limb[1], the Code at MAR 1.3 should be reviewed. The Code sets out descriptions of behaviour that would[2] and would not[3] amount to market abuse under the insider dealing limb. The Code also sets out examples of market abuse under this heading[4].

17.58 Market misconduct

1 For examples of market abuse under this limb, see the *Philippe Jabre and GLG Partners LP final notice (1/8/06)*, the *Bertie Charles Hatcher final notice (13/5/08)*, the *John Shevlin final notice (1/7/08)*, the *Steven Harrison final notice (8/9/08)*, the *Richard Ralph final notice (12/11/08)*, the *Filip Boyen final notice (12/11/08)*, the *Christopher Parry and Darren Morton final notices (6/10/09)*, the *Robin Chhabra and Sameer Patel final notice (16/4/10)*, the *Andre Jean Scerri final notice (29/19/10)* and the *David Einhorn and Greenlight Capital Inc final notice (15/2/12)*.
2 FCA Handbook at MAR 1.3.2E and 1.3.20G–1.3.23G.
3 FCA Handbook at MAR 1.3.6C–1.3.19E. This aspect of the guidance falls under four main headings: giving effect to one's own intentions; the legitimate business of market makers; execution of client orders; and takeover and merger activity. The implementation of MAR will make some changes to the current UK regime: (i) in respect of the exclusions for the execution of client orders and the legitimate business of market makers there is a requirement that the dealing is in the 'normal course' of these activities; and (ii) the exclusion for takeover and merger activity has been narrowed in two respects. First, inside information obtained in the conduct of a takeover or merger may only be used once it has ceased to be inside information. Second, such information may not be used for stake building.
4 FCA Handbook at MAR 1.3.20G–1.3.23G.

Limb 2: Improper disclosure

17.59 This covers behaviour[1] where:

- an insider[2];

- discloses inside information[3];

- to another person;

- otherwise than in the proper course of the exercise of his employment, profession or duties[4].

1 FSMA 2000, s 118(3). It should be noted that the FSMA 2000, s 118(1)(a)(iii) in respect of related investments applies to Limbs 1 and 2. (See also para **17.43** ff above.)
2 See the discussion at para **17.49** ff above.
3 In respect of 'inside information', see the discussion at para **17.50** ff above. Disclosure of inside information to an individual to whom that information has already been disclosed can amount to market abuse, see *Andrew Jon Osborne final notice (15/2/13)*.
4 Factors to be taken into account in determining whether or not the disclosure was made by a person in the proper exercise of his employment, profession or duties are set out in the FCA Handbook at MAR 1.4.5E. See also *the Ian Hannam decision notice (27/2/12)* in which the FSA took a restrictive view of when disclosure will be in the proper course of someone's employment, profession or duties. It is not enough that disclosure is authorised by the client and in the client's commercial interests. Disclosure must still be 'reasonable' (which was also interpreted narrowly by the FSA). Mr Hannam has appealed this decision to the Upper Tribunal and a decision is awaited at time of writing.

17.60 The Code sets out detailed guidelines in respect of improper disclosure[1] at MAR 1.4. In particular, it sets out descriptions of behaviour that does[2] and does not[3] amount to market abuse under this limb.

1 For examples of market abuse under this limb, see the *Jay Rutland final notice (9/7/12)*, the *Richard Ralph final notice (12/11/08)*, and the *Andrew Jon Osborne final notice (15/2/12)*.
2 FCA Handbook at MAR 1.4.2E and 1.4.6G.
3 FCA Handbook at MAR 1.4.3C–1.4.4C.

17.61 MAR will specifically regulate market soundings and will provide that the disclosure of inside information for this purpose will be permissible only if certain procedural conditions are satisfied[1].

1 Market soundings are communications by an issuer, secondary offeror or emissions market participant or person acting on their behalf to potential investors prior to the announcement of a transaction. Seeking 'irrevocables' by a potential offeror in the context of a takeover bid will also be treated as a market sounding. The detail of the procedural conditions that must be satisfied will be set out in level 2 measures and ESMA guidance.

Limb 3: The misuse of information

17.62 This covers behaviour which does not fall within the EU insider prohibitions and which must be[1]:

- based on information[2];

- which is not generally available to those using the market or auction platform[3];

- the information, if available to a regular user of the market or auction platform, would be or would be likely to be regarded by him as relevant when deciding the terms on which transactions in, or bids for, qualifying investments should be effected[4]; and

- is likely to be regarded by a regular user of the market or auction platform as a failure on the part of the person concerned to observe the standard of behaviour reasonably expected of a person in his position in relation to the market or auction platform.

1 FSMA 2000, s 118(4).
2 FCA Handbook at MAR 1.5.5E, 1.3.3E and 1.3.5E.
3 Information is treated as generally available if it can be obtained by research or analysis conducted by or on behalf of users of a market: FSMA 2000, s 118C(8) and see the FCA Handbook at MAR 1.2.12E–1.2.14G.
4 Guidance on the various factors to be taken into account in determining whether or not a particular piece of information would be, or would be likely to be, regarded as relevant information (which is distinct from the concept of inside information used in respect of Limbs 1 and 2) by a regular user is found in the FCA Handbook at MAR 1.5.6E. See also MAR 1.5.2E and 1.5.7E which indicate that, to be relevant, information must be information that a regular user would reasonably expect to be disclosed to users of the relevant market.

17.63 Under the FSMA 2000, s 130A(3), a regular user is defined, in relation to a particular market or auction platform, as a reasonable person who regularly deals on that market in investments of the kind in question or regularly bids in auctions conducted on an auction platform[1]. Further guidance in this regard is provided by the FCA Handbook at MAR 1.2.20–1.2.21G.

1 As with the super-equivalent measures themselves, the definition of regular user in the FSMA 2000, s 130A(3) will cease to have effect on 31 December 2014: see the FSMA 2000, s 118(9).

17.64 As mentioned at para **17.42** ff above, the FSMA 2000 contains provisions in relation to this limb clarifying the meaning of behaviour in relation to qualifying investments.

17.65   For a more detailed discussion of this limb, reference should be made to the Code at MAR 1.5[1]. The Code sets out the factors that are to be taken into account when considering whether a regular user would reasonably expect the relevant information to be disclosed to users of a particular prescribed market, or to be announced, and accordingly whether the behaviour is likely to be regarded by a regular user as failing to meet the expected standard[2]. The Code also gives various descriptions of behaviour, which, in the FCA's view, amounts to[3] and does not amount to[4] market abuse under this head.

1   For examples of market abuse under this limb, see the *Shell Transport and Trading Company plc and Royal Dutch Petroleum Company NV final notice (24/8/04)*, where the firm was fined £17 million for the dissemination of false or misleading information and the *Indigo Capital LLC and Robert Johan Henri Bonnier final notice (21/12/04)*, where the fine was for £355,000 for the making of materially inaccurate notifications that did not accurately state the number of shares held.
2   FCA Handbook at MAR 1.5.7E.
3   FCA Handbook at MAR 1.5.2E–1.5.3G and 1.5.10E.
4   FCA Handbook at MAR 1.5.8G–1.5.9C.

Limb 4: Manipulating transactions

17.66   This covers behaviour which consists of[1]:

- effecting transactions or orders to trade;

- which:

  – give or are likely to give a false or misleading impression as to the supply of, or demand for, or as to the price of, one or more qualifying investments[2]; or

  – secure the price of one or more such investments at an abnormal or artificial level[3];

- otherwise than for legitimate reasons[4] and in conformity with accepted market practices on the relevant market or auction platform[5].

1   FSMA 2000, s 118(5). For a recent example of market abuse under this limb, see *Michael Coscia final notice (3/7/2013)* in which he was fined approximately £597,993 for deliberately engaging in a form of manipulative trading known as 'layering', see also the *7722656 Canada Inc (formerly carrying on business as Swift Trade Inc) final notice (24/01/14)* and the *Rameshkumar Satyanarayan Goenka final notice (17/10/11)*.
2   Descriptions of behaviour that falls within this head are set out in the FCA Handbook at MAR 1.6.2G, 1.6.3G and 1.6.15E.
3   The Code sets out behaviours that involve securing the price of a qualifying investment. See the FCA Handbook at MAR 1.6.4E in this regard.
4   Factors to be taken into account when considering whether behaviour is for 'legitimate reasons' are described in the FCA Handbook at MAR 1.6.5E–1.6.8G.
5   The Code does not describe any accepted market practices. Guidance on some of the factors that the FCA will take into account when assessing whether to accept a market practice is set out in the FCA Handbook at MAR 1, Annex 2G. the MA Regulation will revise (and tighten) the criteria to be applied by national regulators in determining whether to designate a particular behaviour as an accepted market practice. The national regulator will also have to notify ESMA of its intention to designate an accepted market practice and ESMA must issue an opinion concerning the compatibility of the behaviour concerned with the designation criteria and on whether the behaviour concerned would threaten confidence in the EU's financial markets. If a national

regulator designates an accepted market practice contrary to the opinion issued by ESMA it must set out in full its reasons for doing so.

17.67   Under the MA Regulation, unless a defence applies, *any* behaviour will be prohibited if it gives a false or misleading signal as to the supply of, or demand for, or price of a financial instrument or secures the price of a financial instrument at an artificial level[1].

1   The MA Regulation includes new descriptions of behaviour that amount to market abuse which appear to be focused on particular algorithmic and high frequency trading strategies and include placing, modifying or cancelling orders with a trading venue in such a way as to disrupt or delay its orderly functioning; entering orders that result in the overloading or destabilisation of the order book; making it difficult for other persons to identify genuine orders; and entering into orders to initiate or exacerbate a trend. These behaviours are prohibited irrespective of the means employed to affect them.

17.68   As can be seen, this limb creates two distinct types of behaviour that could amount to market abuse, namely, false or misleading impressions and price positioning. Detailed guidance in respect of both aspects of this limb is given in the Code at MAR 1.6 in the FCA Handbook.

17.69   Factors to be taken into account in determining whether or not a person's behaviour amounts to the false or misleading impression aspect of the limb are described in the Code[1], as well as the factors applicable to price positioning[2] (including abusive squeezes[3]).

1   FCA Handbook at MAR 1.6.9E.
2   FCA Handbook at MAR 1.6.10E.
3   FCA Handbook at MAR 1.6.4E(4) and 1.6.11E.

Limb 5: Manipulating devices

17.70   This covers behaviour which consists of[1]:

* effecting transactions or orders to trade or bids;
* which employ:
    - fictitious devices; or
    - any other form of deception or contrivance.

1   FSMA 2000, s 118(6).

17.71   In respect of this limb, the Code at MAR 1.7 sets out descriptions of behaviour that amounts to market abuse, as well as factors to be taken into account in determining whether or not behaviour amounts to market abuse.

Limb 6: The dissemination of information that gives, or is likely to give, a false or misleading impression

17.72   This covers behaviour which consists of[1]:

* the dissemination of information by any means;

17.72 Market misconduct

- which gives, or is likely to give, a false or misleading impression as to a qualifying investment;

- by a person who knew or could reasonably be expected to have known, that the information was false or misleading.

1 FSMA 2000, s 118(7).

17.73 The dissemination of information by journalists is to be assessed by taking into account the codes governing the journalist's profession. This is unless the journalist derives, directly or indirectly, any advantage or profits from the dissemination of the information[1].

1 FSMA 2000, s 118A(4).

17.74 The Code sets out what kind of behaviour amounts to market abuse[1] and describes various general factors to be taken into account in determining whether or not behaviour amounts to market abuse under this limb[2].

1 FCA Handbook at MAR 1.8.3E and 1.8.6E. For a recent example, see *James Joseph Corr final notice (28/3/12)* in which James Corr, the former finance director of Cattles, was fined £400,000 (reduced from £750,000 due to financial hardship) for disseminating false and misleading information as to the value of Cattles' shares to the market. He was also issued with a prohibition order prohibiting him from performing any function in relation to any regulated activity.
2 FCA Handbook at MAR 1.8.4E and 1.8.5E.

Limb 7: Misleading behaviour or distortion of the market

17.75 This covers behaviour which does not fall within any of the other market manipulation prohibitions and which[1]:

- is likely to give a regular user of the market or auction platform[2] a false or misleading impression[3] as to the supply of, demand for or price or value of qualifying investments; or

- would be, or is likely to be, regarded by a regular user of the market or auction platform[4] as behaviour that would distort, or would be likely to distort, the market in such an investment.

1 FSMA 2000, s 118(8); for guidance from the Code, see the FCA Handbook at MAR 1.9. See, for example, the *Michael Ackers final notice (15/4/03)*, where Mr Ackers was fined £70,000 for effecting trades knowing that they would have a significant effect on the market price, and the *Evolution Beeson Gregory Ltd and Christopher Potts final notice (12/11/04)*, where the fine was for £575,000 for distorting the market by short selling certain shares, see also the *Henry Ogilvy Cameron final notice (6/7/10)*.
2 See para **17.63** above.
3 For the factors to be taken into account in this respect see the FCA Handbook at MAR 1.9.4.
4 See para **17.63** above.

17.76 In either case, the behaviour must be likely to be regarded by a regular user of the market as a failure on the part of the person concerned to observe the standard of behaviour reasonably expected of a person in his position in relation to the market[1].

1 For an example of market abuse under this limb see the *Henry Ogilvy Cameron final notice (6/7/10)*. Mr Cameron was found, in addition to having caused Sibir (an AIM listed company) to make two related party announcements that gave or were likely to give a misleading impression to the market contrary to the FSMA 2000, s 118(7), to have also failed to ensure that the market was told of a further five related party transactions with the same party contrary to the FSMA 2000, s 118(8). Mr Cameron was fined £350,000 after a 30% settlement discount.

17.77   As mentioned at para **17.42** ff above, the FSMA 2000 contains provisions, in relation to this limb, clarifying the meaning of behaviour. For a more detailed discussion of the types of behaviour that do and do not amount to market abuse under this head, as well as the factors to be taken into account in assessing whether there has been misleading behaviour or behaviour that distorts the market, see the Code at MAR 1.9.

Limb 8A: Insider dealing in respect of emissions allowances

17.78   This covers behaviour where:

- a person who has access to inside information by virtue of:
  - membership of the administrative, management or supervisory bodies of an auction platform, auctioneer, or auction member; or
  - a shareholding in the capital of an auction platform, auctioneer or auction member; or
  - exercise of its employment; or
  - criminal activities[1];
- uses that information by submitting or withdrawing a bid, for its own account or for the account of a third party for an auctioned product to which that information relates.

1 Commission Regulation 1031/2010 ([2010] OJ L302/1), art 38.

17.79   For the purposes of this limb the definition of inside information is set out in the emissions auctioning regulation and includes information which:

- is precise;
- has not been made public;
- relates directly or indirectly to one or more of the auctioned products; and
- if it were made public would be likely to have a significant effect on the prices at which bids would be made.

17.80   Inside information is also, in relation to a person who executes client bids, information relating to a client's pending bids which meets the general definition of inside information, see para **17.54** ff above.

17.81 Market misconduct

Limb 8B: Prohibited use of inside information in respect of emissions allowances

17.81 This includes behaviour where:

- a person who has access to inside information (for the reasons set out under Limb 8A above);

- discloses inside information to any other person;

- other than in the normal course of the exercise of his employment, profession or duties;

Or behaviour where:

- a person who has access to inside information (for the reasons set out under Limb 8A above);

- recommends or induces another person;

- on the basis of inside information;

- to submit, modify, withdraw a bid for auction products to which that information relates.

Limb 8C: Market manipulation in respect of emissions allowances

17.82 This includes:

- bids, transactions or orders on the secondary market for emissions allowances which:

  - give or are likely to give false or misleading signals as to the demand for or the price of the auctioned products; and

  - secure an abnormal or artificial auction clearing price for the auctioned products;

  unless the person making the bid or the transaction on the secondary market establishes that its reasons for doing so are legitimate;

- bids which include any kind of fictitious device;

- dissemination of information which:

  - gives or is likely to give false or misleading signals in relation to auctioned products (including rumours); and

  - the person disseminating the information knew, or ought to have known was false or misleading.

Benchmark manipulation

17.83 The implementation of the MA Regulation will introduce a further category of market abuse, manipulating the calculation of a benchmark. This includes knowingly or negligently providing false or misleading information or inputs for the calculation of a benchmark and any other behaviour which manipulates the calculation of a benchmark. For these purposes benchmark is widely defined to include any rate, index or figures, made available to the public (even if only on the payment of a fee) that is derived from the value of one or more underlying assets, prices or rates and by reference to which the amount payable under a financial instrument or the value of a financial instrument is determined.

Behaviour which does not amount to market abuse

17.84 The FSMA 2000 specifically provides that in three situations behaviour will not amount to market abuse. They are:

- behaviour which the Code says does not amount to market abuse;

- behaviour which an FCA rule says does not amount to market abuse; and

- certain behaviour in respect of buy-back programmes, price stabilisation and by public authorities.

These are considered in turn below.

Behaviour which the Code says does not amount to market abuse

17.85 If a person behaves in a way which is described in the Code in force at the time of the behaviour as behaviour that, in the FCA's opinion, does not amount to market abuse, then that behaviour is to be taken, for the purposes of the FSMA 2000, as not amounting to market abuse[1]. Similarly if a person behaves in a way that the Code specifies does amount to market abuse, that behaviour is taken to amount to market abuse. Otherwise, the Code only has evidential effect and to the extent that particular behaviour is not set out in the Code, this does not indicate that the behaviour does not amount to market abuse[2].

1 FSMA 2000, s 122(1).
2 *Winterflood Securities Ltd v Financial Services Authority [2010] EWCA Civ 423.*

17.86 Various safe harbours are set out in the Code. In addition, behaviour complying with certain provisions of the City Code on Takeovers and Mergers (the City Code)[1] is stated in the Code not to amount to market abuse[2]. These safe harbours only apply in so far as the behaviour is expressly required or permitted by the City Code and provided it is not in breach of any relevant General Principle at Section B of the City Code[3].

1 FSMA 2000, s 118A(5)(a). These relate to the timing of disclosure and the content of announcements: see the FCA Handbook at MAR 1.10.5C.
2 In summary, this includes provisions relating to the disclosure of information which is not generally available, standards of care, timing of announcements, documentation and dealings,

and content of announcements: see the FCA Handbook at MAR 1.10.4C and, for a full list of the relevant provisions, MAR 1.10.5C. Behaviour conforming with rule 4.2 (restrictions on dealings by the offeror and concert parties) will also, in certain circumstances, amount to market abuse: see the FCA Handbook at MAR 1.10.6C. As to the overlap between the City Code and the Code of Market Conduct more generally, see paras **17.217** ff below.

3 FCA Handbook at MAR 1.10.4C.

Behaviour which the FCA rules say does not amount to market abuse

17.87   Where an FCA rule includes a provision to the effect that behaviour conforming with the rule does not amount to market abuse, then behaviour that conforms with the rule does not amount to market abuse.

17.88   The FCA has indicated[1] that there are no FCA rules that permit or require a person to behave in a way that amounts to market abuse. However, some rules contain a provision to the effect that behaviour conforming with that rule does not amount to market abuse.

1 FCA Handbook at MAR 1.10.2G.

17.89   The FCA rules which contain such provisions are:

• the rules on Chinese walls[1]; and

• certain UKLA Listing Rules and Disclosure Rules, primarily relating to the disclosure of information.

1 FCA Handbook at SYSC 10.2. Following the implementation of the MA Regulation EU law will recognise Chinese walls. The MA Regulation will provide that a firm will not commit insider dealing if it has Chinese walls in place that ensure that neither the person who makes the decision to deal nor any person who may have an influence on that decision possess inside information.

Buy-back programmes, price stabilisation

17.90   The MAD only provides for two safe harbours, namely:

• the trading in own shares in share buy-back programmes; and

• price stabilisation activities.

These safe harbours are enshrined in the FSMA 2000, s 118A(5)(b). Guidance in relation to these safe harbours is given in the Code[1] and will be unchanged by the implementation of the MA Regulation.

1 See the FCA Handbook at MAR 1.10.1G in respect of share buy-back programmes and MAR 2 in relation to price stabilisation activities.

Public authorities

17.91   In addition, the FSMA 2000 provides a further, limited, safe harbour[1] that behaviour does not constitute market abuse if it is done by a person acting on behalf of a public authority in pursuit of monetary policies, policies with respect to exchange rates and the management of public debt or the management of foreign exchange reserves. The implementation of the MA Regulation will extend this safe harbour to activities undertaken in relation to emissions allowances by a person acting on behalf of a Member State, the European Commission or any other officially designated body in pursuit of the EU climate policy.

1 FSMA 2000, s 118A(5)(c).

Behaviour which does not give rise to a penalty for market abuse

17.92 In two situations behaviour which otherwise amounts to market abuse will not give rise to a penalty for market abuse. These are where, having considered any representations made to it in response to a warning notice, there are reasonable grounds for the FCA to be satisfied that[1]:

- the person believed, on reasonable grounds, that his behaviour did not amount to market abuse; or

- he took all reasonable precautions and exercised all due diligence to avoid engaging in market abuse[2].

These are considered in turn below, followed by the question of when the person concerned can rely on the defence.

1 FSMA 2000, s 123(2).
2 Requiring or encouraging market abuse would also be covered in both contexts: see para **17.106** ff below.

17.93 It is worth first noting the limited effect of this provision. The effect is not to excuse the behaviour. It still amounts to market abuse and could, for example, still be prohibited by injunction on an application by the FCA[1]. The FCA is, however, prohibited from imposing a penalty or public censure in relation to it and, in addition, neither the FCA nor the court can impose a restitution order on the relevant person as a result of the behaviour[2]. There is, though, nothing to prevent the behaviour from giving rise to other regulatory consequences, for example, if it highlights other issues of concern about the firm's systems and controls.

1 See para **17.227** ff below. Notably, an injunction could potentially be obtained to require the market abuse to be remedied – for example, by the transfer or repurchase of shares – even in a situation where a restitution order or penalty was not available because of this provision.
2 FSMA 2000, ss 383(3) and 384(4).

A belief that the behaviour did not amount to market abuse

17.94 The FSMA 2000 does not give any indication as to what might amount to reasonable grounds for believing that the behaviour did not amount to market abuse, but it does require the FCA to provide in its policy an indication of the circumstances in which it is to be expected to regard a person as falling within this defence[1].

1   FSMA 2000, s 124(3), this is set out in the FCA Handbook at DEPP 6.3. See also the decision of the Upper Tribunal in *David Massey v FSA [2011] UKUT 49 (Fin/2009/0024)* which makes it clear that a reasonable objective belief is required to make out this defence, see also the *David Einhorn and Greenlight Capital Inc final notice (15/2/12)*.

17.95   The FCA has provided[1] a list of the factors it may take into account when deciding whether a person reasonably believed that his behaviour did not amount to market abuse (including requiring or encouraging market abuse). These can be summarised as follows:

- the extent to which the behaviour in question was or was not analogous to behaviour described in the Code as amounting to or not amounting to market abuse (or requiring or encouraging market abuse);

- the treatment of the relevant behaviour in any relevant FCA guidance or other materials and the extent to which the person sought to follow any relevant guidance or take into account any relevant materials. The FCA will consider the accessibility of any guidance or materials when deciding if it is relevant and what weight it should be given;

- the rules of any relevant market or any other relevant regulatory requirements or codes of conduct or best practice (including the City Code);

- the level of knowledge, skill and experience to be expected of the person concerned;

- whether the person can demonstrate that the behaviour was engaged in for a legitimate purpose and in a proper way;

- whether, and if so to what extent, the person followed internal consultation and escalation procedures in relation to the behaviour (for example, did the person discuss the behaviour with internal line management and/or internal legal or compliance departments);

- whether, and if so the extent to which, the person sought any appropriate expert legal or other expert professional advice and followed that advice; and

- whether, and if so to what extent, the person sought advice from the market authorities of any relevant prescribed market or, where relevant, consulted the Takeover Panel, and followed the advice received.

1   FCA Handbook at DEPP 6.3.2.

17.96   This guidance is expressly stated to be non exhaustive and there may be other relevant factors depending on the facts of each particular case.

17.97   The test which the FCA has to apply under the FSMA 2000 is also worth briefly reviewing, because it is complex and not entirely clear on the wording of the FSMA 2000. It is as follows:

- there must be an actual belief by the firm or individual that the behaviour did not amount to market abuse;

- that belief must be objectively reasonable; and

- once the FCA has considered the firm's representations, there must be reasonable grounds for it to be satisfied of the above two points.

17.98   This suggests that the relevant person does not have to satisfy the FCA that they believed, on reasonable grounds, that their conduct was not market abuse. Rather, it seems to be sufficient for the person to show reasonable grounds, for the FCA to be satisfied of this. However, it seems unlikely the test was intended to be this low and unlikely in practice that the Tribunal or a court would uphold the defence in favour of a person who could not demonstrate that they did have that belief and that it was based on reasonable grounds. Previously the threshold to establish this defence has been high[1].

1   See for example the *David Einhorn and Greenlight Capital Inc final notice (15/2/12)*.

Taking all reasonable precautions and exercising all due diligence

17.99   Alternatively, the person must have taken all reasonable precautions and exercised all due diligence to avoid engaging in market abuse. Both reasonable precautions and due diligence are required and the word 'all' is used in relation to both[1].

1   The threshold for this defence is high, see for example the *Andrew Jon Osborne final notice (15/2/12)*, the *David Einhorn and Greenlight Capital Inc final notice (15/2/12)*. In this instance, as information was received after the recipient had refused to be 'wall-crossed' he was under a duty to be 'even more diligent than usual' in considering whether the information disclosed to him was inside information. The FSA indicated that before dealing on the basis of the information he should have taken steps to ensure that he had not received inside information, such as obtaining compliance or legal advice or contacting the senior management of the issuer concerned to confirm that he had not received inside information.

17.100 As with the defence of reasonably believing the behaviour did not amount to market abuse, the FCA is required to provide in its policy an indication of the circumstances in which it is to be expected to regard a person as meeting this test[1]. The FCA has provided a list of factors which it may take into account in deciding whether the defence has been met[2], and these can be summarised as follows:

- the extent to which the behaviour in question was or was not analogous to behaviour described in the Code as amounting to or not amounting to market abuse (or requiring or encouraging market abuse);

- the treatment of the relevant behaviour in any relevant FCA guidance or other materials and the extent to which the person sought to follow any relevant guidance or take into account any relevant materials. The FCA will consider the accessibility of any guidance or materials when deciding if it is relevant and what weight it should be given;

- the rules of any relevant market or any other relevant regulatory requirements or codes of conduct or best practice (including the City Code);

- the level of knowledge, skill and experience to be expected of the person concerned;

- whether the person can demonstrate that the behaviour was engaged in for a legitimate purpose and in a proper way;

- whether, and if so to what extent, the person followed internal consultation and escalation procedures in relation to the behaviour (for example, did the person discuss the behaviour with internal line management and/or internal legal or compliance departments);

- whether, and if so the extent to which, the person sought any appropriate expert legal or other expert professional advice and followed that advice; and

- whether, and if so to what extent, the person sought advice from the market authorities of any relevant prescribed market or, where relevant, consulted the Takeover Panel, and followed the advice received.

1 FSMA 2000, s 124(3).
2 FCA Handbook at DEPP 6.3.2.

17.101 This list is said expressly not to be exhaustive and there may be other factors that are relevant depending on the facts of each particular case[1].

1 FCA Handbook at DEPP 6.3.2.

17.102 Again, it is not clear whether the person must show he actually took all reasonable precautions and exercised all due diligence, or whether it is sufficient to show reasonable grounds for the FCA to be satisfied[1].

1 See the discussion at para **17.97** ff above.

When do the defences apply?

17.103 The FSMA 2000 provides that the FCA may not impose the penalty or restitution order if 'having considered any representations made to it in response to a warning notice', broadly, either of the defences is made out[1].

1 FSMA 2000, ss 123(2) and 384(4).

17.104 The procedure for the FCA to impose a fine or restitution order for market abuse, considered in detail at paras **17.185** ff and **17.245** ff below, involves the FCA issuing a warning notice when it proposes the action and then a decision notice when it decides that the action is appropriate. In the majority of cases a firm will have had an opportunity to respond to the FCA's concerns after the issue of a preliminary investigation report and before the FCA has formally proposed to take action for the alleged market abuse. However, the first formal opportunity the firm will have to put forward and substantiate its defence will be after the warning notice has been issued. Hence, the FCA will only be considering whether the defence is, in its view, made out when it considers whether to issue a decision notice.

17.105 But in some cases the FCA may already have sufficient information from its investigation, for example, from interviews with the relevant individuals, or from the firm's response to the preliminary investigation report to suggest that there is a good defence or, at least, that there are reasonable grounds for it to be satisfied that there is a defence[1]. In those cases, should it issue a warning notice and wait for the firm to try to substantiate its defence? Or should it consider the likely defence when deciding whether or not to issue a warning notice? The answer is unclear. The FSMA 2000 seems to suggest that it need not consider the defence until it decides whether or not to issue a decision notice. However, it is thought that if the FCA has information available to it to indicate that it would not be appropriate for it to take action for market abuse, then that information ought to be relevant to its decision whether or not to issue a warning notice. If that is correct, then the FCA should take the likely defence into account when considering issuing a warning notice[2].

1 This is the statutory test: see para **17.92** ff above.
2 The same point could be made in relation to the FCA's decision whether to apply to a court for a restitution order under the FSMA 2000, s 383.

Requiring or encouraging others to engage in market abuse

17.106 A penalty for market abuse may also be imposed against a person who the FCA is satisfied has required or encouraged another person or persons to engage in behaviour which, if engaged in by that person, would amount to market abuse[1]. The person requiring or encouraging can also be made the subject of a restitution order[2]. Inaction can be sufficient to amount to requiring or encouraging.

1 FSMA 2000, s 123(1)(b).
2 FSMA 2000, ss 383(1)(b) and 384(2)(b).

17.107 There are two limbs to this test. First, it must be shown that the behaviour would have amounted to market abuse if it had been carried out by the person who required or encouraged it and, second, that person must, by action or inaction, have required or encouraged another to engage in the behaviour in question.

17.108 The Code gives two examples of conduct which might amount to requiring or encouraging, namely[1]:

- a director of a company, while in possession of inside information, instructs an employee of the company to deal in qualifying investments or related investments in respect of which the information is inside information; and

- a person recommends or advises a friend to engage in behaviour which, if engaged in by the first person, would amount to market abuse.

1 FCA Handbook at MAR 1.2.23G.

Criminal offences

17.109 In addition to the criminal offence of insider dealing[1] the Financial Services Act 2012 (FS Act 2012) introduced a new criminal offence and replaced the FSMA 2000, s 397. The three criminal offences under the FS Act 2012 are:

- *Offence 1* – making false or misleading statements[2];

- *Offence 2* – creating false or misleading impressions[3];

- *Offence 3* – making false or misleading statements or creating false or misleading impressions in respect of a benchmark[4].

1 See para **17.47** ff above.
2 FS Act 2012, s 89.
3 FS Act 2012, s 90.
4 FS Act 2012, s 91. Currently LIBOR is the only 'relevant benchmark' specified by HM Treasury for the purposes of this offence, see the Financial Services Act 2012 (Misleading Statements and Impressions) Order 2013 (SI 2013/637), art 3. HM Treasury has the power to designate further relevant benchmarks, see the FS Act 2012, s 93(4).

FCA INVESTIGATIONS INTO MARKET MISCONDUCT

17.110 The FCA has a range of information-gathering and investigation powers which it could use to obtain information about a suspected case of market misconduct, including one formal investigation power specifically aimed at market misconduct, and various other formal and informal powers applicable in different situations.

17.111 The various powers and obligations include the following:

- the regulated community owes a general obligation to co-operate and be open with the FCA[1];

- the FCA can require authorised persons, recognised investment exchanges and recognised clearing houses, among others, to provide information or documents reasonably required by the FCA in connection with the exercise by it of its functions under the FSMA 2000[2];

- the FCA may appoint an investigator to conduct an investigation into the business of an authorised person, or various connected persons, if it appears to it that there is good reason for doing so[3];

- the FCA may appoint an investigator to conduct an investigation if it appears to it that, among other things, there are circumstances suggesting breaches of the Principles for Businesses or Statements of Principle for approved persons[4]; or

- the FCA may appoint an investigator to conduct an investigation into suspected market abuse or the criminal offences of insider dealing or misleading statements and practices or misleading statements and practices in respect of benchmarks, if it appears to it that there are circumstances suggesting that one of these has been committed[5].

1 For example, Principle 11 of the Principles for Businesses and Statement of Principle 3 for approved persons. For a detailed discussion of what this involves, see para **4.24** ff above.

2 FSMA 2000, s 165 and see para **4.72** ff above.
3 FSMA 2000, s 167 and see para **5.11** ff above.
4 FSMA 2000, s 168(4) and see para **5.20** ff above.
5 FSMA 2000, s 168(2) and see para **5.27** ff above.

17.112 It is the last of these, the market abuse investigation, which has tended to attract the most attention. However, it needs to be seen in context. As can be seen, so far as the regulated community is concerned, the FCA has a range of powers available for investigating cases of suspected market misconduct, of which that is only one. In contrast, where the suspected market misconduct relates to an unregulated business or person, or if it relates to a regulated firm but information is required from third parties who are unauthorised and unconnected with the firm, then it may be that a market abuse investigation is the only way forward[1].

1 Information could also be sought from unconnected third parties in connection with an investigation under the FSMA 2000, ss 167 or 168(4), but the investigator's powers in connection with such investigations (particularly, s 167 investigations) are more limited than in a s 168(2) investigation.

17.113 The power to obtain information from recognised investment exchanges, and the ability to exchange information with them[1], is likely to be particularly relevant in this context. The focus of the market abuse provisions is on protecting the integrity of the markets[2]. The recognised investment exchanges and EU regulated markets and auction platforms will be a valuable source of information leading to market abuse investigations, particularly concerning market participants who are not authorised persons.

1 Under the so-called Gateway Regulations, which allow the provision of information without breaching the statutory criminal prohibition against disclosure: see para **4.234** ff above. Under the MA Regulation national regulators will have the power in relation to commodity derivatives to request information in a specified format from market participants in relevant spot markets, to obtain reports on transactions and to have direct access to traders' systems.
2 The markets that are prescribed for the purpose of market abuse are those of the recognised investment exchanges in the UK and, in relation to all categories of market abuse other than the retained provisions, regulated markets based in EU countries. In respect of all categories of market abuse other than Limb 8 prescribed auction platforms are recognised auction platforms. In respect of all categories other than the retained prohibitions auction platforms appointed under the EU ETS Auctioning Regulations are also prescribed auction platforms. In respect of Limb 8 only auction platforms appointed under the EU ETS are prescribed auction platforms: see para **17.35** ff above.

17.114 These powers have been considered in some detail in **CHAPTER 4** above. The following paragraphs concentrate on:

- the FCA's policy on when it will formally investigate market misconduct;

- formal investigations into market misconduct;

- what information the investigator can obtain;

- whether a person must comply with an investigator's requests for information; and

- the use that can be made of the information obtained.

When will the FCA investigate suspected market misconduct?

17.115 Not every case of suspected market misconduct will give rise to an investigation. The FCA publishes on its website the referral criteria that it uses to assist its consideration of cases when determining whether or not to carry out an investigation[1]:

- Has there been actual or potential consumer loss/detriment?

- Is there evidence of financial crime or risk of financial crime?

- Are there actions or potential breaches that could undermine public confidence in the orderliness of financial markets?

- Are there issues that indicate a widespread problem or weakness at the firm/issuer?

- Is there evidence that the firm/issuer/individual has profited from the action or potential breaches?

- Has the firm/issuer/individual failed to bring the actions or potential breaches to the attention of the FCA?

- Is the issue to be referred relevant to an FCA strategic priority?

- If the issue does not fall within an FCA strategic priority, does the conduct in question make the conduct particularly egregious and presenting a serious risk to one of the FCA's objectives?

- What was the reaction of the firm/issuer/individual to the breach?

- Overall, is the use of the enforcement tool likely to further the FCA's aims and objectives?

- Does the suspected misconduct involve an overseas jurisdiction? If so, would enforcement action materially further investor protection or market confidence in that jurisdiction?

- Does the FCA have an obligation under EU legislation to take action on behalf of, or otherwise provide assistance to another EU Member State?

- Is another regulatory authority in a position to investigate and deal with the matters of concern[2]?

1 See the FCA Enforcement Guide at EG 2.10 and the FCA website at http://www.fca.org.uk/firms/being-regulated/enforcement/how-we-enforce-the-law/referral-criteria .
2 This is considered in more detail at para **17.117** below.

17.116 The FCA will also consider whether using alternative tools is more appropriate taking into account the overall circumstances of the person or firm concerned and the wider context[1].

1 See the FCA Enforcement Guide at EG 2.10. See also the *Indigo Capital LLC and Robert Johan Henri Bonnier final notice (21/12/04)*, despite the fact that Indigo Capital had been publicly censured by the Takeover Panel the FSA considered it was appropriate to exercise its own powers under the market abuse regime because the Takeover Panel's censure was in respect of violations of the City Code, was outside the relevant period and was in respect of different behaviour.

When another regulatory authority is investigating

17.117 One of the relevant factors is whether another regulatory authority is in a position to investigate and deal with the matter of concern. This arises because the particular exchange on which the suspected market misconduct took place may have its own powers of investigation and enforcement to address misconduct on its market. The FCA recognises this and will therefore consider the extent to which a recognised investment exchange or clearing house has adequate and appropriate powers to investigate and deal with the matters of concern[1]. Firms should be aware that the FCA is not saying that it will decline to investigate where some other regulator has concurrent powers. Rather, it will consider to what extent it still needs to investigate. Its own powers may be tougher, or may enable necessary information to be obtained from third parties, and the nature of the FCA's concerns may be different from those of the other regulator[2].

1 See the FCA Enforcement Guide at EG 2.15. Operating arrangements are in place between the recognised investment exchanges and the FCA.
2 See for example the *7722656 Canada Inc (formerly carrying on business as Swift Trade Inc) final notice (24/1/14)* in which Swift Trade had continued to carry out 'layering' through the purchase of contracts for difference despite concerns being raised by the LSE and the LSE acting to request that Swift Trades Direct Market Access providers remove its access to the market. See also the *Jason Geddis final notice (20/9/11)* in which Mr Geddis was publicly censured for conduct which had inflated the price of certain short term lead contracts traded on the LME to abnormal levels. The firm for which Mr Geddis was employed was fined £150,000 by the LME and paid £30,000 in compensation to other market participants but was not subject to action by the FSA. Suspected market abuse may arise in the context of a takeover bid, in which case questions arise relating to the nature and timing of the FCA's investigation and the involvement of the Takeover Panel. This issue is considered at para **17.216** ff below.

17.118 The FCA has the power[1] to direct a recognised investment exchange or clearing house to terminate, suspend or limit the scope of any enquiry which it is conducting under its rules or not to conduct an enquiry which it proposes to conduct. This power is only exercisable where the FCA considers this desirable or expedient because of the exercise or possible exercise of its power to impose civil penalties for market abuse or to initiate a formal market abuse investigation.

1 FSMA 2000, s 128.

17.119 The FCA has not given any guidance on when it will seek to exercise this power and it has not been used by the FCA, nor its predecessor, the FSA. The FSA however had indicated it might use this power where appropriate[1], and made clear that one of the reasons for having this power is to ensure fairness to, and reduce the resource burden upon, persons under investigation. The criteria for the use of the power are likely to reflect issues such as the seriousness of the suspected abuse, the involvement of persons outside the jurisdiction of the exchange or clearing house and whether novel or complex issues of application across the financial markets are involved[2]. The government also indicated, during the bill stages of the FSMA 2000 that it envisaged the power being used only rarely[3].

1 FCA Enforcement Guide at EG 2.15.

2   See Consultation Paper 10, 'Market Abuse. Pt 1: Consultation on a draft Code of Market
    Conduct', paras 145 and 146.
3   Economic Secretary to HM Treasury in Standing Committee (2 November 1999).

17.120 As set out above, certain of the market abuse offences can occur in relation
to any of the EU regulated markets and not simply one of the UK recognised
investment exchanges or recognised auction platforms[1]. Further under EU law[2]
regulators in each EU state are empowered to police not only activities on their
own regulated markets but also activities that take place within their territory
that relate to trading on regulated markets in other EU states. There is, therefore,
a likelihood of regulators in more than one jurisdiction having an interest in
investigating the same trading activity. Following the implementation of the MA
Regulation, ESMA is likely to also have a greater role in cross border investigations
as it will take over the coordination of such investigations if requested to do so by
one of the national regulators concerned.

1   FSMA 2000, s 118A(2) and para **17.35** ff above.
2   See the MAD, arts 10 and 14. This will remain the case under the MA Regulation. The obligations
    to cooperate with and provide mutual assistance to regulators of other Member States will be
    strengthened under the MA Regulation. National regulators will also be authorised to permit a
    national regulator from another Member State to carry out an on-site investigation or inspection
    within their territory.

Formal market misconduct investigations

17.121 The FCA, or the Secretary of State, may appoint an investigator to
conduct an investigation if it appears to it that there are circumstances suggesting
that market abuse may have taken place or one of the criminal offences of insider
dealing or misleading statements and practices or misleading statements and
practices in relation to benchmarks may have been committed[1].

1   FSMA 2000, s 168(2).

The test for appointing an investigator

17.122 The test for appointing an investigator is fairly low. The FCA does
not need to be satisfied or have reasonable grounds for believing that market
misconduct has taken place. All that is required are circumstances suggesting
this. Most notably, it is not necessary for the FCA to be able to identify, at the
outset of the investigation, any person who may have engaged in the suspected
market misconduct. This allows the FCA to commence an investigation based
on, for example, information received from an exchange showing suspicious or
inexplicable movements in the price of a particular investment.

17.123 The suspicion must be that market misconduct has already taken place;
the FCA does not have power under this head to investigate market misconduct
which it suspects may take place on some future date. The FCA does, however,
have the ability to apply to the court for an injunction to prevent a person
engaging in market abuse in the future, which the court may grant if satisfied that

there is a reasonable likelihood that any person will engage in market abuse[1]. If the FCA has a suspicion that market abuse may occur, but insufficient evidence to obtain an injunction, then it will need to find another means of investigating. That should not be difficult where a firm is involved but may be more difficult as against those who are not regulated.

1 See *Financial Services Authority v Da Vinci Invest Ltd [2011] EWHC 2674 (Ch)* in which Newey J found that the FSA did not have to establish market abuse definitively to obtain interim relief, however note that the FSA had been unsuccessful in obtaining a without notice injunction to restrain market abuse in a previous application in the same proceedings. See also *FSA v Alexander (unreported)* and the *Barnett Michael Alexander final notice (14/6/11)*. Mr Alexander's activity was brought to the FSA's attention as a result of a suspicious transaction report in December 2009. In May 2010 the FSA brought proceedings against Mr Alexander under s 381 of the FSMA 2000 and obtained an interim injunction freezing Mr Alexander's assets and preventing him from continuing to enter into the particular conduct that concerned the FSA. This is discussed further at para **17.229** ff below.

What can be investigated?

17.124 The FCA can investigate suspected market abuse, or one of the criminal offences, or both, and will need to define the scope of the investigation accordingly. However, having commenced an investigation, there can be one investigation into all aspects of the suspected market misconduct: the decision in the more serious cases of whether to commence civil proceedings for market abuse or criminal proceedings for insider dealing or misleading statements and practices does not need to be taken at the outset.

17.125 In less serious cases involving firms or approved persons, it may be that once the investigation starts it will become apparent that market abuse has not occurred and what is instead being investigated is a suspected breach of the Principles[1]. Provided it appeared to the FCA at the outset that there were circumstances suggesting market abuse, the investigation will have been commenced on the correct basis and there does not seem to be anything to prevent it proceeding on that statutory basis notwithstanding market abuse is no longer at issue[2].

1 In particular, Principle 5 of the Principles for Businesses or Statement of Principle 3 of the Statements of Principle for approved persons: see paras **17.256** ff below. See also the *Citigroup Global Markets Limited final notice (28/6/05)* for an example of breaches of Principles 2 and 3.
2 The advantage for the investigator is that a market abuse investigation confers wider powers than one into suspected breaches of FCA rules or the Principles. This is discussed further at para **5.53** above.

Investigations by the Secretary of State

17.126 The Secretary of State has concurrent power to appoint investigators for suspected cases of market abuse, insider dealing and/or misleading statements and practices and/or misleading statements and practices in relation to benchmarks. The reasons for this are discussed at para **5.27** above.

Will the person under investigation be notified of the investigation?

17.127 The FCA or, as appropriate, the Secretary of State, is not required to give notice to the person under investigation of the appointment of the investigator[1]. This is an exception to the general rule and is in some respects mitigated by the FCA's stated policy[2].

1 FSMA 2000, s 170(3)(b).
2 See the discussion at para **5.39** ff above.

How does the FCA commence and control the investigation?

17.128 This is discussed in detail at para **5.38** ff above.

Will the FCA publicise the investigation?

17.129 The FCA will not, as a general policy, make public the fact that it is or is not investigating a particular matter or the outcome of the investigation. However, there are some exceptions, which are discussed at para **5.44** ff above.

What information can the investigator obtain?

17.130 If the investigator considers that any person is or may be able to give information which is or may be relevant to the investigation[1], that person may be required to:

- attend before the investigator at a specified time and place and answer questions;

- otherwise provide such information as the investigator may require for the purposes of the investigation;

- produce at a specified time and place any specified documents or documents of a specified description which appear to the investigator to relate to any matter relevant to the investigation[2]; and

- otherwise give the investigator all assistance in connection with the investigation which the person is reasonably able to give.

Each of these is considered in turn below. There are various ancillary provisions applicable to all the investigation powers, which are discussed at para **4.119** ff above. The question whether a person can refuse to provide material requested is considered at para **17.134** ff below.

1 FSMA 2000, s 173.
2 See para **4.144** above as to whether electronic disclosure will be permitted.

Who can be required to provide information?

17.131 There is no limitation on the classes of person who can be called upon to provide information to the investigator. The person does not have to be a firm, or an employee of the firm. Nor does he have to be the person suspected of market abuse. He simply has to be a person who, in the view of the investigator, *may* have information which *may* be relevant to the investigation. This is consistent with the general theme that investigations into market misconduct may be, at least initially, investigations into particular situations, such as movements in share prices, rather than into particular persons. The investigator's power to require information to be provided is therefore framed not by reference to the person under investigation, but rather by reference to those who may have relevant information.

What information can they be asked to provide?

17.132 There is little that is not encompassed within answers to questions, production of documents, provision of other information (which probably means information not recorded in any form[1]) and any other assistance. The power is very widely drawn and a few examples may serve to highlight this:

- there is no requirement for the investigator to specify the questions that he intends to ask when imposing a requirement on a person to answer questions, nor is any limit prescribed upon the nature of the questions that can be asked (although they probably should relate to the information the person has which is believed to be relevant to the investigation)[2], nor is the investigator required to specify in writing the time and place for the person's attendance[3];

- there is no requirement for the investigator reasonably to consider the documents or information required to be provided to be relevant or to be satisfied that they are necessary or expedient for the purposes of the investigation[4] and, again, there is no requirement for the documents, or the time and place for them to be provided to be specified in writing; and

- any person who the investigator believes 'may be able' to give information which 'may' be relevant can be required to provide 'all' assistance in connection with the investigation which he is reasonably able to give.

1 See para **4.31** above.
2 Compare an investigator appointed to investigate the business of an authorised person under the FSMA 2000, s 167, who must reasonably consider the questions or information to be relevant to the purposes of the investigation: FSMA 2000, s 171(3) and see para **5.18** ff above. Similarly, an investigator appointed under the FSMA 2000, s 168(1) or (4) can require people to attend before him and answer questions but only if he is satisfied that the requirement is necessary or expedient for the purposes of the investigation: FSMA 2000, s 172(3).
3 Again, contrast investigations under the FSMA 2000, ss 167 and 168(1) or (4).
4 Contrast investigations under the FSMA 2000, ss 167 and 168(1) or (4).

17.133 In reality, there are some limitations on the investigator's powers as a matter of law. These are discussed further at para **5.65** ff above. However the

FCA has stated that a person who does not comply with a requirement imposed by the FCA under its statutory powers may be held in contempt of court and the FCA may choose to bring disciplinary proceedings for breach of Principle 11 or Statement of Principle 4[1].

1   FCA Enforcement Guide at EG 4.11.

Is a person obliged to comply with an investigator's requests?

17.134 Unless there is some legitimate ground for objecting, a person requested by an investigator to provide information, documents, answers to questions or other assistance must comply with that request. Failure to comply without reasonable excuse could be punished by a court as though the person had committed contempt of court[1]. The failure could also lead to a warrant being obtained to enter the person's premises and seize the documents or information[2]. If the person concerned is a firm or employee of a firm then there could also be regulatory enforcement consequences[3].

1   FSMA 2000, s 177(1) and (2): see para **5.76** ff above.
2   FSMA 2000, s 176: see para **5.83** ff above.
3   See para **5.82** above.

17.135 The FSMA 2000 expressly provides only for two objections to providing documents or information, namely for information protected as being, broadly, legally privileged[1] and, in certain limited circumstances, for documents subject to a banker's duty of confidence. These are discussed at paras **5.56** and **5.60** above. Beyond this, the person may have legitimate objections on other grounds, depending upon the precise situation. Some of the more likely objections are outlined at para **5.55** above, followed by a discussion of how the person might go about making good the particular objection.

1   There is, though, no express statutory protection for without prejudice material: see para **5.58**, n 1 above.

17.136 One common objection that may be worth highlighting in the context of market abuse investigations is the so-called right of silence. The fact that a person may also be the subject of a criminal charge for insider dealing, misleading statements and practices or misleading statements and practices in relation to benchmarks, or indeed that market abuse constitutes a 'criminal charge' for ECHR purposes[1], does not give that person the right not to answer the investigator's questions. It does have an impact on the use that can be made of his evidence, as discussed at para **17.137** ff below. Also, it may prevent him from being questioned further once the FCA has sufficient evidence to bring a civil enforcement action or for a successful prosecution[2]. But it is not in general a legitimate objection to answering questions at a compulsory interview.

1   See para **17.17** above.
2   See para **4.211** ff above.

What use can be made of the information?

17.137 The FCA or, as appropriate, the investigator appointed by it may obtain a significant amount of information about the firm or particular individuals as a result of the investigation. One issue will be what use can be made of that information. This issue is discussed in more detail at para **4.223** ff above. For present purposes, several points may be made. First, to the extent that the information is confidential and relates to the business or affairs of any person, the FCA and the investigator are bound by a statutory duty of confidentiality, breach of which is a criminal offence[1].

1   FSMA 2000, s 348 and see para **4.226** above.

17.138 Second, this does not generally prevent the FCA from using the information for its own purposes. As will be seen at para **17.224** ff below, the FCA is not limited to the imposition of a penalty for market abuse or the public censure of the person concerned, but also has an extensive range of enforcement powers which could be relevant depending upon the results of the investigation and the nature of its concerns. Where the investigation concerns an authorised firm or approved person (or certain other employees of a firm), there is a greater range of possible regulatory action.

17.139 Third, the FCA may be entitled to pass information to other relevant bodies or regulators, for example, the exchange concerned or any relevant overseas regulator[1].

1   To the extent permitted under the Gateway Regulations: see para **4.234** ff above. See also the Multilateral Memorandum of Understanding concerning Consultation and Co-operation and the Exchange of Information drawn up in May 2002 and revised in May 2012 by the International Organisation of Securities Commissions (IOSCO).

17.140 Fourth, and often most importantly for a person accused of having committed market abuse or one of the criminal offences, the FSMA 2000 provides a certain amount of protection against self-incrimination, by precluding statements made under compulsion from being used against the maker of the statement in certain circumstances. This is discussed in detail at para **17.142** ff below.

17.141 Finally, if the market abuse could also potentially give rise to civil proceedings against the firm, there may be a risk of material being produced in the context of the investigation and enforcement process which may be prejudicial to the firm and may be required to be disclosed in those proceedings. This is considered in more detail at para **4.145** above.

The privilege against self-incrimination

17.142 The statutory protection for the privilege against self-incrimination extends to cover situations not only where a criminal prosecution against a person or firm is in prospect, but also where the FCA is pursuing proceedings for market abuse. It therefore applies in this context both to the criminal offences of insider dealing, misleading statements and practices or misleading statements and practices in relation to benchmarks and also to (non-criminal) proceedings for market abuse.

17.143 The statutory provision[1] is discussed at para **4.207** ff above and that discussion applies equally here. Broadly, a statement made to an investigator by a person in compliance with a formal requirement may not be used in evidence against that person, and no questions may be asked relating to it, in:

- criminal proceedings in which that person is charged with an offence, but not proceedings for perjury or making false or misleading statements; or

- proceedings in relation to action to be taken against that person under the FSMA 2000, s 123.

The first limb was discussed at para **4.205** above; the second limb, which relates to civil enforcement of market abuse, will be focused on here.

1   FSMA 2000, s 174.

What types of statements are covered?

17.144 The statutory protection only applies to statements made to an investigator exercising his powers to compel the provision of a statement under certain provisions of the FSMA 2000[1]. It does not apply to statements made to the FCA using its powers under the FSMA 2000, s 165[2]; nor would a statement provided in compliance with the Principles, or a voluntary statement, be protected, although in some circumstances, the law may imply the same protection[3]. In practice, as discussed at para **4.210** above, the FCA may seek to conduct voluntary interviews under caution with individuals in criminal or market abuse investigations. Answers given in such circumstances may be used in subsequent criminal or market abuse proceedings against the individual concerned[4]. In such a situation a person would not be obliged to attend a voluntary interview. The FCA has indicated that it will not bring disciplinary proceedings under Principle 11 of the Principles for Business or Statement of Principle 4 for Approved Persons simply because they choose not to attend or answer questions at a purely voluntary interview[5]. However, the FCA has also indicated that there may be circumstances in which an adverse inference may be drawn from the reluctance of a person to participate in a voluntary interview[6].

1   FSMA 2000, ss 171, 172, 173 or 175: see the FSMA 2000, s 174(5). A statement made in response to a formal requirement imposed in an investigation under the FSMA 2000, ss 167, 168(1) or (4) or 168(2) would therefore be covered by the statutory protection.
2   See para **4.207** ff above.
3   This is discussed further at para **4.207** ff above. The person concerned may, therefore, in some circumstances wish to press for a formal investigation, to ensure that any statements receive the express statutory protection.
4   FCA Enforcement Guide at EG 4.8.
5   FCA Enforcement Guide at EG 4.10.
6   FCA Enforcement Guide at EG 4.10.

Does it matter why the statement was made?

17.145 The prohibition applies to any statement made under an investigator's compulsory powers. It is not necessary that the investigator was appointed to investigate the market misconduct. The investigator could have been appointed to investigate some other matter, following which market abuse could have become apparent. That should not be relevant to the question of whether the prohibition applies.

When is the use of the statement prevented?

17.146 The second limb of the prohibition prevents the use of the statement in 'proceedings in relation to action to be taken against a person under s 123'. It is not clear precisely what this phrase means and, in two particular respects, there are difficulties with its interpretation.

17.147 First, it is important to appreciate that there is no prohibition against using the statement to obtain other evidence that could be admissible and, indeed, the expectation is that the FCA will use its powers in that way[1].

1 See para **4.206** ff above.

17.148 As to the two difficulties with the meaning of this limb, the first difficulty is the question of what amounts to 'proceedings' for this purpose. The FSMA 2000, s 123 simply empowers the FCA to impose a penalty for market abuse, or publish a public statement. It does not refer to any particular proceedings. There are two different types of proceedings that could be involved:

- the internal decision-making process used by the FCA when it decides whether or not to impose a penalty or a public statement under s 123; and

- the subsequent Tribunal proceedings which may result if the person decides to oppose the imposition of the penalty or public statement.

17.149 Is the statement prohibited from being used in both? Or is it only when the matter is considered by the Tribunal that the privilege against self-incrimination applies? The view of HM Treasury[1] seems to be that it is limited to proceedings before the Tribunal. This approach may be justifiable, for reasons discussed at para **17.150** ff below. However, the FSMA 2000 clearly envisages elsewhere that the FCA's internal decision-making processes amount to 'proceedings'. For example, proceedings for misconduct are expressly commenced when a warning notice is issued[2], and the provisions relating to notices of discontinuance describe the FCA's internal processes as 'proceedings'[3]. The point is not therefore clear.

1 See the Explanatory Notes to the FSMA 2000, para 337.
2 FSMA 2000, s 66(5).
3 FSMA 2000, s 389(3).

17.150 The second difficulty is related. As will be seen, the imposition of a penalty or public statement for market abuse is only one of a range of actions the FCA can take. For example, it can apply to the court for an injunction or a restitution order, or it can make a restitution order or take wider enforcement action arising from the same matter. Are such other actions 'proceedings in relation to action to be taken against a person under the FSMA 2000, s 123'? Whilst the answer is not entirely free from doubt, it seems likely they are not, in which case the statement could be used for those other purposes[1]. There could be some justification for this given the purpose of taking such other action. For example, an injunction can be used to prevent impending market abuse from taking place and it may be important that the FCA, in the interests of protecting consumers and safeguarding the market, is able to use all the information available to it in order to obtain such an injunction. For the same reason, the FCA may wish to take urgent action against a firm, for example, to vary its permission[2].

1   But if the other enforcement action which the FCA sought to take (particularly, disciplinary action based on breach of the regulatory general principles) constituted in the particular case a 'criminal charge' for ECHR purposes, then the FCA may be required to confer the same protection due to the ECHR, Art 6(2): see the discussion at para **10.19** ff above.
2   See para **16.216** ff above.

17.151 If that is indeed the scheme of the FSMA 2000, then the statement may need to be put before the FCA's decision-making body[1] when it is considering that other action, and it may be difficult then to isolate it from the decision whether to impose a sanction for market abuse in relation to the same matter. As indicated above, it may be that this is intended.

1   Normally the Regulatory Decisions Committee: see **CHAPTER 10** above.

17.152 This could, of course, have the effect that information put before a court on an application for an injunction or a restitution order for market abuse could result in such an order where the Tribunal, based on the lesser evidence available to it, may find there was no market abuse in the same case. More difficult is a situation in which the FCA may ask the court to impose a penalty for market abuse at the same time as hearing an application for a restitution order or injunction[1]. It may be attractive to the FCA to have the whole matter disposed of at the same time in this way. However, if statements that would be prohibited from use before the Tribunal can be put before the court on an application for an injunction or restitution order, how is that evidence to be excluded from consideration when the court goes on to consider the same matter as would be before the Tribunal, namely whether a penalty should be imposed? In that situation, it seems likely the entire court application would be regarded as 'proceedings in relation to action to be taken against a person under s 123' and that the evidence should not be admissible in those proceedings.

1   FSMA 2000, s 129.

Does the statutory privilege against self-incrimination apply when the FCA is acting under its powers to assist overseas regulatory authorities

17.153 The FCA has indicated that, when it is asked by overseas regulators or EU regulators to conduct interviews, it will not necessarily follow its standard approach of conducting compulsory interviews under its statutory powers. Instead it will consider with the regulators concerned the most appropriate method for obtaining evidence for use in that regulator's home jurisdiction[1]. In circumstances where the FCA provides information (including records of interviews) to overseas regulators or where a representative of an overseas regulator attends an interview conducted under the exercise of the FCA's statutory powers, there are no explicit safeguards to protect a person's privilege against self-incrimination (in any of the FSMA 2000, the FCA Enforcement Guide and the FCA Handbook)[2]. It is therefore possible that the FCA might provide a record of statements made in a compulsory interview to an overseas regulator or might compel a person to answers questions in an interview at which an overseas regulator is present that the FCA would itself be precluded from using in criminal proceedings.

1 FCA Enforcement Guide at EG 4.8.
2 The FCA has published its policy on interviews conducted on behalf of EU or other overseas regulators in the FCA Handbook at DEPP 7. DEPP 7.2.10 provides among other things that the FCA's investigator instigates and concludes the interview; warns the interviewee of the possible consequences of refusing to answer questions and the uses to which any answers that are given can and cannot be put; and that where the FCA's investigator considers it appropriate he may suspend the interview or ask the EU or other overseas regulator to leave the interview. DEPP 7.2.14 provides that the interviewee must be provided with a warning at the start of the interview. This must state that the interviewee is obliged to answer any questions put to them during the interview including those asked by the representative of the overseas regulator. It will also state that, in criminal proceedings or proceedings for market abuse the FCA will not use as evidence against the interviewee any information obtained under compulsion during the interview. DEPP 7.2.18 provides that all compulsory interviews will be tape-recorded, that the FCA will not provide the overseas regulator with transcripts of tapes unless this has been specifically agreed to, but that copies of tapes will usually be provided on request.

17.154 Under the Human Rights Act 1998 the FCA should arguably, when it is considering how best to obtain evidence, consider whether an overseas jurisdiction provides equivalent protections to the individual or firm concerned to those afforded by the FSMA 2000, s 174 and the ECHR. Where the FCA is providing assistance to an EU regulator, under the ECHR and the legislation of the EU regulator's home state, the person should, in practice, receive such protection. However, if an overseas jurisdiction does not recognise the privilege against self-incrimination, then it may arguably be wrong, on ECHR grounds, for the FCA to provide a regulator in that jurisdiction with a record of an interview with an individual who may have committed a criminal offence there or to allow a representative of a regulator from that jurisdiction to attend an interview conducted under the exercise of its statutory powers.

SANCTIONS FOR MARKET MISCONDUCT

Introduction

17.155 Once the FCA has completed its investigation, it must decide which, if any, of the range of criminal and civil sanctions and disciplinary, preventative or restitutionary enforcement tools available should be invoked in the particular circumstances.

17.156   Market misconduct

17.156 There are broadly three decisions to be made by the FCA at this stage:

- Should any criminal prosecutions be brought?

- Should the FCA exercise its powers to impose a penalty or make a public statement against any person for market abuse?

- Should the FCA take some other, regulatory action, against any person?

17.157 In practice, in light of the FCA's policy discussed at para **17.159** ff below, criminal and civil proceedings in relation to market misconduct should generally speaking be mutually exclusive. There is, however, nothing in the FSMA 2000 to require this. The FCA's starting point is to consider whether it is appropriate to bring criminal proceedings. If it is, then it will normally do so[1]. Other regulatory action may need to be taken in any case, whether or not criminal or civil proceedings are also being taken, and indeed whether or not the conduct in question actually amounted to market abuse. Also, other regulators may also seek to take their own enforcement action.

1 FCA Enforcement Guide at EG 12.4 and 12.7.

17.158 The following paragraphs will look at:

- when, and how, the FCA brings criminal proceedings[1];

- regulatory proceedings for market abuse, including when the FCA will take action, what action it will take and how it will take that action[2];

- the interaction between the FCA's role and that of other regulatory authorities, including the UK exchanges, the FCA in its capacity as the competent authority under the FSMA 2000, Pt 6, the Takeover Panel and overseas regulators[3];

- other enforcement action that the FCA may seek to take in relation to the matter[4]; and

- the firm's potential liability to civil claims as a result of its market misconduct[5].

1 See para **17.159** ff below.
2 See para **17.170** ff below.
3 See para **17.203** ff below.
4 See para **17.224** ff below.
5 See para **17.263** ff below.

Criminal proceedings for market misconduct

When will the FCA bring criminal proceedings?

17.159 The FCA's power to impose civil fines for market abuse complements rather than replaces the pre-existing criminal regime. It thus overlaps significantly with the criminal regime and there are likely to be cases where the same conduct may potentially involve a breach of the criminal law as well as a breach of the civil regime of market abuse. The FCA has power to institute criminal proceedings in England, Wales and Northern Ireland[1] in respect of the relevant criminal offences of insider dealing[2], misleading statements and practices[3] and misleading statements and practices in relation to benchmarks[4]. It shares this power with the Secretary of State and the Crown Prosecution Service[5]. The question considered here is how the FCA decides which to pursue, criminal prosecution or the imposition of a civil penalty[6].

1 FSMA 2000, ss 401 and 402: but not Scotland.
2 Criminal Justice Act 1993, Pt V.
3 Financial Services Act 2012, ss 89 and 90.
4 Financial Services Act 2012, s 91.
5 FSMA 2000, s 401 and Criminal Justice Act 1993, s 61.
6 Prior to the implementation of the MA Regulation the manipulation of benchmarks does not fall under the civil market abuse regime. However, it is open to the FCA to, if necessary bring disciplinary proceedings, for breach of one of the Principles for Businesses even if a criminal charge of misleading statements and practices is not brought in respect of benchmarks.

The FCA's policy on bringing criminal proceedings

17.160 In deciding whether to bring criminal proceedings, the FCA considers whether a criminal prosecution is appropriate applying the two basic principles set out in the Code for Crown Prosecutors, namely:

• whether there is sufficient evidence to provide a realistic prospect of conviction against the defendant on each criminal charge; and

• whether, having regard to the seriousness of the offence and all the circumstances, criminal prosecution is in the public interest.

17.161 These two tests are applicable in any case where the FCA is considering whether to bring a prosecution, not only market misconduct cases, and their application is discussed in more detail at para **18.20** ff below[1].

1 The FSA did in practice bring some criminal prosecutions in this area. For example, in March 2009 the FSA obtained its first convictions for insider dealing (see *R v McQuoid and Melbourne (unreported, 27 March 2009)* and *R v McQuoid [2009] EWCA Crim 1301, [2009] 4 All ER 388* and between March 2009 and March 2013 the FSA obtained over 20 convictions for offences under the CJA 1993, Pt V (or relevant inchoate offences), a further five individuals were charged and acquitted in the same time period. The FSA also brought prosecutions under the FSMA 2008, s 397 (which has been replaced with the Financial Services Act 2012, ss 89 and 90) see *R v Rigby, Rowley and Bailey (unreported, see FSA Press Release FSA/PN/091/2005, on 16 and 18 August 2005)* where the FSA succeeded in obtaining criminal convictions against Bailey and Rigby (the then CFO and CEO of AIT plc respectively) on the charge of 'recklessly' making misleading statements.

17.162 In deciding whether to prosecute market misconduct which also falls within the definition of market abuse, the application of those tests may involve consideration of some additional factors, which can be summarised as follows[1]:

• whether the misconduct is serious and prosecution likely to result in a significant sentence;

- whether there are victims who have suffered loss and the extent and nature of the losses;

- the effect on the market and/or market confidence;

- the extent of any profits accrued or loss avoided by the person accused of market misconduct;

- whether the misconduct may be continued or repeated and a financial penalty is unlikely to deter further misconduct;

- previous cautions, convictions or other action for market misconduct (including civil and regulatory actions);

- action by the person concerned since the misconduct (including whether they have sought to pay compensation, rectify any systems breaches, however potential defendants will not avoid prosecution simply because they are able to pay compensation);

- the impact a criminal prosecution might have on the prospects for securing redress for persons who have suffered loss (it might have an adverse impact on the ability to secure redress);

- whether the person concerned has co-operated with the FCA in taking corrective measures (however defendants will not avoid prosecution merely by fulfilling a statutory duty to take those measures);

- whether the misconduct involves dishonesty or an abuse of position of authority or trust;

- if the misconduct in question was carried out by a group, whether a particular individual has played a leading role;

- if the misconduct was carried out by a group, whether an individual provides information to the FCA and fully co-operates with the FCA's prosecution of the other(s)[2]; and

- the personal circumstances of the individual.

1 For a full list, see the FCA Enforcement Guide at EG 12.8. Note that HM Treasury may also issue guidance under the FSMA 2000, s 130 to help the relevant authorities determine the action to be taken in cases where behaviour appears to constitute both market abuse and the commission of one of the criminal offences.

2 For example in 2010 the FSA entered into an agreement with Bertie Hatcher (a retired insurance broker) under which following his agreement to provide ongoing assistance to the FSA in connection with its investigation into market abuse committed by Mr Hatcher and a friend of his, Malcolm Calvert. No criminal prosecution was pursued against Mr Hatcher, although he was subject to regulatory sanction and fined £56,098 for market abuse. Mr Hatcher appeared as a witness at Mr Calvert's trial and Mr Calvert was subsequently convicted of five counts of insider dealing. See the FSA press release at FSA/PN/041/2010.

17.163 The FCA has, however, stressed that these factors are not exhaustive and that the importance attached to each factor will vary from case to case[1].

1 FCA Enforcement Guide at EG 12.9.

Will the FCA take both criminal and civil or other regulatory proceedings?

17.164 The FCA's policy[1] is not to impose a civil sanction for market abuse where a person is being prosecuted for market misconduct or has been finally convicted or acquitted of market misconduct (following the exhaustion of all appeal processes) in a criminal prosecution arising from substantially the same allegations. Similarly it is the FCA's policy not to commence a prosecution for market misconduct where the FCA has brought or is seeking to bring disciplinary proceedings for market abuse arising from substantially the same allegations.

1 See the FCA Enforcement Guide at EG 12.10. The ECHR contains an express protection against double jeopardy, in Art 4 of Protocol 7, although this has not at the time of writing been incorporated into UK law by the Human Rights Act 1998. Nonetheless, it may be arguable that similar protection is implicit in the fair trial guarantees of Art 6 and express protection against double jeopardy remains established in the UK under the doctrines of 'autrefois acquit' (previously acquitted) and 'autrefois convict' (previously convicted), see for example *DPP v Nasralla [1967] 2 All ER 161*, and in common law more generally, *R (Adams) v Secretary of State for Justice and re McCartney [2011] UKSC 18, [2012] 1 AC 48*.

17.165 In the normal course, therefore, where it is appropriate for the FCA to bring criminal proceedings and it does so, it will not also seek to impose a civil penalty, or make a public statement, in relation to the same matter. However, the policy does leave open the possibility of the FCA imposing a sanction for market abuse after starting to prosecute one of the criminal offences and then discontinuing that prosecution for some reason. This will result in neither an acquittal nor a conviction, and is not therefore clearly covered in the policy[1]. A further question will be whether the market abuse and the criminal market misconduct arise from 'substantially the same allegations'. This ought to cover several issues arising from the same set of facts, but the phrase is not wholly clear.

1 Following the collapse of a second trial in *FCA v Former iSoft Directors* (see http://www.fca.org.uk/news/fca-v-former-isoft-directors), the FCA issued a press release stating that the FCA had decided it would not be in the public interest for a second retrial to be pursued (see FCA press release dated 22 July 2013).

17.166 Bringing a criminal prosecution does not, however, necessarily preclude the FCA from deciding that other forms of civil or regulatory action should also be taken. The range of enforcement action available to the FCA is outlined at para **17.224** ff below. Each type of enforcement action has a different purpose, which is why further action may need to be taken notwithstanding a criminal prosecution. In deciding whether to take such action, the FCA has regard to whether it might unfairly prejudice the criminal prosecution or the conduct of the defence to it, and whether it is appropriate to take such action having regard to the scope of the criminal proceedings and the powers available to the criminal courts[1]. The purpose and effect of this guidance is discussed in para **18.37** ff below.

1 FCA Enforcement Guide at EG 12.4.

17.167   Market misconduct

Issuing a caution, rather than prosecuting

17.167 In certain situations, the FCA may issue a formal caution, rather than prosecuting an offender. The circumstances in which it may do this are outlined at para **18.33** ff below.

What is the procedure for bringing criminal proceedings?

17.168 As indicated at para **17.159** ff above the FCA has the power to institute criminal proceedings for insider dealing, misleading statements and practices or misleading statements and practices in relation to benchmarks, save in Scotland. An issue of concern to firms is the overlapping jurisdiction between different criminal prosecution authorities[1]. In other words, can a firm face investigations and prosecutions from different authorities in relation to the same conduct? Also, once the FCA takes a decision that the matter is an appropriate one for a criminal prosecution, which authority prosecutes[2]? It is also possible that conduct leading to regulatory or criminal proceedings in the UK might lead to regulatory or criminal proceedings being brought by an overseas regulator. These issues arise equally in any criminal prosecution, not only those relating to market misconduct, and are discussed in more detail at para **18.8** ff below, together with certain particular issues relating to the FCA's criminal prosecution powers, multi-jurisdictional investigations are discussed in **CHAPTER 7**.

1   As noted above, the Secretary of State and the Crown Prosecution Service retain the power to prosecute such offences.
2   The FCA and the relevant prosecuting and investigating authorities (the SFO, the BIS, and the CPS (in relation to prosecutions only), and the ACPO (in relation to investigations only) have entered into guidelines on investigation of cases of interest or concern to the FCA and other prosecuting and investigating authorities (see Appendix 2 to the Enforcement Guide). The guidelines specify that only the agency or agencies with the most appropriate functions and powers will commence investigations (although in certain circumstances concurrent investigations may be the most quick, effective and efficient way to deal with a particular case). The guidelines set out a number of factors that are indicative that the FCA should take action and factors that are indicative that one of the other agencies should take action, and set out guidelines for the conduct of concurrent investigations.

Powers of arrest

17.169 Note, that in August 2005 the FSA signed a Memorandum of Understanding with the Association of Chief Police Officers[1] recording best practice for co-operation between the FSA and the police in relation to the arrest of people, on the FSA's behalf, in cases of, among other things, suspected market abuse and insider dealing.

1   This replaced the 2003 MoU between the FSA and the City of London Police Fraud Squad formalising the powers of the police to arrest people, on the FSA's behalf, in cases of, among other things, suspected market abuse and insider dealing. At the time of writing no further document has been entered into between the FCA and the Association of Chief Police Officers although it is understood that this arrangement will continue with the FCA.

FCA regulatory proceedings for market abuse

17.170 If the matter is not one which involves the commission of a criminal offence, or is otherwise not suitable for prosecution, then the next question will be whether the conduct amounted to market abuse within the FSMA 2000, ss 118 and 118A and, if so, whether the FCA should take enforcement action in relation to it. The following paragraphs look at:

- the grounds on which the FCA may impose a financial penalty or public censure for market abuse;

- the FCA's policy in determining whether to take such action;

- how the FCA decides what action to take;

- if the FCA is to impose a penalty, the factors relevant in determining the amount;

- the circumstances when the FCA is likely to take action against specific individuals rather than, or in addition to, the firm; and

- the procedure for taking action for market abuse and whether any publicity will result.

17.171 The focus in this section is on penalties and public censures. The other potential FCA enforcement consequences of market abuse (particularly, injunctions and restitution orders) are considered at para **17.224** ff below, together with other FCA enforcement measures that may arise from market misconduct more generally. It is notable that the imposition of a penalty for market abuse does not make any transaction void or unenforceable[1]. A counterparty or other person affected by the market abuse might, however, be able to pursue other remedies depending upon the nature of the abuse[2].

1   FSMA 2000, s 131.
2   Civil claims against firms are discussed in **CHAPTER 19** below and see also para **17.263** ff below.

What are the grounds for imposing a penalty or public censure?

17.172 The FCA may impose a penalty for market abuse if it is satisfied that a person[1]:

- is or has engaged in market abuse; or

- by taking or refraining from taking any action has required or encouraged another person or persons to engage in behaviour which, if engaged in by the first person, would amount to market abuse.

1   FSMA 2000, s 123.

17.173 The FCA may not, however, impose a penalty if there are reasonable grounds for it to be satisfied that either of the two defences outlined at the FSMA 2000, s 123(2) (see para **17.92** ff above) applies. In deciding whether either of these two thresholds are met, the FCA will consider certain factors[1]:

- whether the behaviour in question was or was not analogous to behaviour described in the Code of Market Conduct (see the FCA Handbook at MAR 1) as amounting or not amounting to market abuse or requiring or encouraging;

- whether the FCA has published any guidance or other materials on the behaviour in question and if so, the extent to which the person sought to follow that guidance or take account of those materials[2];

- whether the behaviour complied with the rules of any relevant prescribed market or any other relevant market or other regulatory requirements (including the City Code) or any relevant codes of conduct or best practice;

- the level of knowledge, skill and experience to be expected of the person concerned;

- whether the person can demonstrate that the behaviour was engaged in for a legitimate purpose and in a proper way;

- whether the person followed internal consultation and escalation procedures in relation to the behaviour[3];

- whether the person sought any appropriate expert legal or other expert professional advice and followed that advice; and

- whether the person sought advice from the market authorities of any relevant prescribed market or, where relevant, consulted the Takeover Panel, and followed the advice received.

1   FCA Handbook at DEPP 6.3.2, these factors are not exhaustive and there may be other relevant factors.
2   The FCA will consider the nature and accessibility of any guidance or other published materials when deciding whether it is relevant in this context and, if so, what weight it should be given, see the FCA Handbook at DEPP 6.3.2(2).
3   The FCA has given the example of whether the person discussed the behaviour with internal line management and/or internal legal or compliance departments, see DEPP 6.3.2(6).

17.174 If the FCA is entitled to impose a penalty, it may instead publish a statement to the effect that the person has engaged in market abuse[1].

1   FSMA 2000, s 123(3).

17.175 The test for market abuse, the meaning of requiring or encouraging another to commit market abuse, and the two defences, have been considered at para **17.20** ff above.

WHEN IS THE FCA LIKELY TO TAKE ACTION FOR MARKET ABUSE?

17.176 The FCA will not take enforcement action in every case involving market abuse[1]. In deciding whether or not to take action in the particular case, and what action to take, the FCA will look at all the relevant circumstances of the case, and specifically the factors listed at DEPP 6.2.1. Certain factors may in particular be relevant to the question of whether to take action, which can be summarised as follows[2]:

- the nature, seriousness and impact of the behaviour in question[3];

- the conduct of the person concerned after the breach[4];

- the previous disciplinary record and general compliance history of the person concerned[5];

- FCA guidance and other published materials[6];

- the action taken by the FSA or FCA in previous similar cases[7]; and

- action taken by other domestic or international regulatory authorities[8].

In addition, the FCA has identified certain factors that may, in particular, be relevant to the question of whether to take action in cases of market abuse, which can be summarised as follows[9]:

- the degree of sophistication of the users of the market in question, the size and liquidity of the market, and the susceptibility of the market to market abuse;

- the impact, having regard to the nature of the behaviour, that any financial penalty or public censure may have on the financial markets or on the interests of consumers.

1　The FCA is required to issue a statement of its policy with regard to the imposition and amount of penalties for market abuse and, in exercising, or deciding whether to exercise, its power under the FSMA 2000, s 123, must have regard to the policy in force at the time when the behaviour concerned occurred (see the FSMA 2000, s 124(1) and (6)). The policies outlined here constitute the FCA's policy for this purpose: see the FCA Enforcement Guide at EG 7.4 and at DEPP 6.3, 6.5 and 6.5C.

2　For a full list, see the FCA Handbook at DEPP 6.2.1 and 6.2.2.

3　These include the following factors that are likely to be relevant to market abuse cases: whether the breach was deliberate or reckless; the duration and frequency of the breach; the amount of benefit gained or loss avoided as a result; the impact or potential impact of the breach on the orderliness of or confidence in markets; and the loss or risk of loss caused to consumers or other market users, see the FCA Handbook at DEPP 6.2.1(1) and *Jason Geddis v FSA [2011] UKUT 344 (FS/2010/0014)* – the Tribunal determined that it was inappropriate to impose a financial penalty on Mr Geddis as, inter alia, his conduct was not a deliberate breach, and he quickly worked to rectify the breach.

4　This includes whether and how quickly, effectively and completely the person reported the matter to the FCA, cooperation during the regulatory investigation, steps taken to address the market abuse, the likelihood that the same kind of breach will recur if no action is taken, and whether the person has complied with the requirements of any other applicable regulator relating to his behaviour, the nature and extent of any false or misleading information given to the FCA and whether this was intended to mislead: see the FCA Handbook at DEPP 6.2.1(2).

5　This includes: whether the FCA or FSA has previously taken successful disciplinary action or used its own initiative powers against the person and the person's general compliance history (including any private warnings): see the FCA Handbook at DEPP 6.2.1(3).

6　The FCA will not take action against a person for behaviour that it considers to be in line with guidance, other materials published by the FCA in support of the Handbook or FCA confirmed Industry Guidance which were current at the time of the behaviour in question. The manner in which guidance and other published materials may otherwise be relevant to an enforcement case is described in the FCA Enforcement Guide at EG 2.

17.176 Market misconduct

7 The FCA will also consider the extent to which, where other regulatory authorities propose to take action, this action would be adequate to address the FCA's concerns, see the FCA Handbook at DEPP 6.2.1.
8 See para **17.221** ff below.
9 For a full list, see the FCA Handbook at DEPP 6.2.2.

17.177 Where the issue arises in the context of a takeover bid, the FCA may consider that the impact of the use of its powers is likely to have an adverse effect on the timing or outcome of that bid, and therefore it would not be in the interests of financial markets or consumers to take action for market abuse during the takeover bid[1]. The FCA has given further guidance on certain additional factors that it will consider. These are outlined at para **17.217** ff below.

1 FCA Handbook at DEPP 6.2.2(2)(c).

Who will the FCA take action against?

17.178 The FSMA 2000 does not distinguish between individuals who commit market abuse and firms who do so. The same question therefore arises in this context as arises throughout the enforcement regime, namely, in what circumstances the FCA will seek to punish individuals rather than, or in addition to, firms, for their behaviour whilst acting for the firm. As set out at para **17.185** ff below the FCA's fining policy does in some respects differentiate the treatment of individuals who have committed market abuse, recognising that market abuse proceedings could be brought against either a firm or an individual.

17.179 A difference between market abuse and other regulatory contraventions committed by individuals is that the question here is whether the individual has committed market abuse, whereas in many other cases the question will be about the level of involvement that the individual had in a breach committed by the firm for whom the individual works. The market abuse regime may thus apply to individuals rather more directly. In addition, there may not be a firm involved in a market abuse case. An isolated individual, not connected with any firm and not carrying on any regulated business, or even purporting to do so, could commit market abuse. One of the difficult issues, particularly where the individual is trading on behalf of the firm, is the extent to which the actions of an individual may be attributable to a firm. If the FCA does not take action against the firm for market abuse it may still consider taking action against the firm for breach of one or more of the principles for businesses[1].

1 In particular 'Principle 2: a firm must conduct its business with due skill, care and diligence', 'Principle 3: a firm must take reasonable care to organise and control its affairs responsibly and effectively, with adequate risk management systems and 'Principle 5: A firm must observe proper standards of market conduct' may be relevant'.

17.180 The FCA's general approach on this question, considered at para **9.23** ff above, is that the primary responsibility for ensuring compliance with a firm's regulatory obligations rests with the firm itself[1] and the FCA's main focus in considering whether disciplinary action is appropriate is therefore normally on the firm rather than on those who work for it. There are, however, situations where the

FCA will consider action against an approved person (or certain other employees of a firm) working for a firm, based primarily on the question of personal culpability, that is where the behaviour was deliberate or below the standard which it would be reasonable to have expected from the person in all the circumstances.

1   FCA Handbook at DEPP 6.2.4 and the FCA Enforcement Guide at EG 2.31.

17.181 In the absence of any specific guidance, it is not clear whether the same policy applies to market abuse. In many cases, a decision to undertake a particular trading strategy is likely to have been made by an identifiable individual and in general, the FCA (and its predecessor the FSA) has sought to take action against the individuals directly responsible for market abuse. At one end of the spectrum, if a relatively junior individual at a large organisation acts in good faith, having exercised due care and complied with the requisite controls and procedures but nonetheless commits market abuse, there may be much sympathy for the view that he should not incur personal liability. At the other end of the spectrum, he may take that decision in a situation where he knows or should know of the risk of market abuse, perhaps without any regard for internal procedures or controls, and in that case it may be unobjectionable that the Regulator seeks to hold him personally responsible. In the middle, there is, obviously, a substantial grey area[1]. The cases brought to date suggest that in appropriate circumstances the FCA will proceed against both the firm and all individuals concerned[2].

1   In some cases, the individual may have a defence, that he reasonably believed his behaviour did not amount to market abuse or took all reasonable precautions and exercised all due diligence to avoid committing market abuse: see para **17.92** ff above.
2   For example see the *Philippe Jabre and GLG Partners LP final notice (1/8/06)*, Mr Jabre's market abuse was attributable to GLG. Factors identified as being material to this finding were: (i) Mr Jabre's seniority and status; (ii) the fact that he clearly had authority to enter into the transactions that constituted market abuse; and (iii) the fact that within an agreed overall strategy his dealings were unsupervised and he enjoyed a large degree of autonomy. See also *David Einhorn and Greenlight Capital Inc final notice (15/2/12)*, in which the conduct of Mr Einhorn (President and sole owner and sole portfolio manager of Greenlight, responsible for all investment decisions of Greenlight) was attributable to Greenlight. Mr Einhorn had failed to take steps to make sure that information he had received in respect of a potential equity issuance was not inside information before trading on the basis of it (Mr Einhorn had refused to be 'wall-crossed'). Market abuse cases were brought separately against Mr Einhorn, who was fined £3,638,000 and Greenlight which was fined £3,650.795 for trading on the basis of inside information under the FSMA 2000, s 118(2). In addition, enforcement action was brought against a range of approved persons for their role in facilitating, failing to detect and failing to prevent the insider dealing. In certain instances, the FCA may only take action against a firm, for example, in *7722656 Canada Inc (formerly carrying on business as Swift Trade Inc) and Beck v Financial Services Authority (FS/2011/0017) and (FS/2011/0018)* (subsequently heard in the Court of Appeal) Swift Trade was unsuccessful in its arguments before the Upper Tribunal that it was a subsidiary direct market access provider and therefore bore no responsibility for the conduct of the traders using its platform. The Tribunal found that on the basis of the evidence before it there was a compelling indication that the individuals conducting the trading in question were 'acting as part of Swift Trade's overall organisation, and in accordance with a strategy of which Swift Trade was not only well aware but which it devised and encouraged'. The Upper Tribunal agreed with the FSA's finding that Swift Trade's conduct constituted market abuse. No action was taken against any individual traders.

17.182 Where the FCA does bring proceedings against an individual, the person may have the right to legal assistance if the matter is referred to the Tribunal[1]. Critically, though, the individual does not have the right to legal assistance in relation to the FCA investigation or in relation to the enforcement process before the matter is referred to the Tribunal, although in practice firms often provide such assistance to their employees and insurance cover may also be available[2].

1   FSMA 2000, ss 134–136. In summary, the scheme involves an application for assistance being made to the Tribunal at the same time as referring the matter to it. The Tribunal will grant assistance only where it is in the interests of justice to do so (the test follows that applied in criminal cases: see the Access to Justice Act 1999, Sch 3) and where the means of the person are such that they would be unable to meet the costs of legal representation themselves.
2   This is discussed in more detail in para **3.116** above.

How does the FCA decide what action to take?

17.183 If the FCA decides that action is appropriate, then what action should it take? There are three options:

- to give the firm or individual a private warning, rather than taking formal enforcement action;

- to impose a financial penalty; or

- to make a public statement that the person has engaged in market abuse.

Private warnings

17.184 In certain circumstances, the FCA may decide to issue a private warning rather than taking formal action. Whilst a private warning does not amount to formal enforcement action, it is not entirely free from regulatory consequences. For example, as indicated at para **17.176** above, one of the factors to which the FCA has regard when deciding whether or not to take action in relation to market abuse is the person's previous compliance history including any private warnings. The circumstances when the FCA is likely to issue a private warning, and the nature and consequences of private warnings, are discussed in more detail at para **8.27** ff above[1].

1   FCA Enforcement Guide at EG 7.10–7.19.

Fines and public statements

17.185 The FCA's policy[1] is to consider publishing a public statement that market abuse has occurred instead of imposing a financial penalty where it considers that such a statement may more appropriately address the particular behaviour in question. In determining whether this is the case, the FCA will take into account all the circumstances of the case, including the factors that are relevant in deciding in any regulatory disciplinary case whether to fine or instead publicly censure a firm[2]. The FCA has acknowledged that, other things being equal, the more serious the behaviour, the more likely it will impose a financial penalty[3].

1   FCA Handbook at DEPP 6.4.
2   These factors are outlined at para **8.39** ff above.
3   FCA Handbook at DEPP 6.4.2.

How does the FCA determine the amount of the penalty?

17.186 Whilst it is for the FCA to determine, at least in the first instance[1], the amount of the penalty appropriate to be imposed, it is required to issue a statement of its policy with regard to, among other things[2], the amount of penalties and, when deciding upon the level of a penalty for a particular case of market abuse, it must have regard to the policy in force at the time the behaviour occurred[3].

1 As will be seen, this can be challenged in the Tribunal.
2 See para **17.170** ff above.
3 FSMA 2000, s 124.

17.187 The FCA does not have a specific policy for the calculation of penalties in cases of market abuse committed by firms. In determining the amount of any financial penalty against a firm, it will follow the five stage fining policy[1]. The FCA has made it clear that all the relevant circumstances of the case will be taken into consideration[2].

1 See, in general the FCA Handbook at DEPP 6.5 and 6.5A. The FCA has set out (at DEPP 6.5.2) the principles behind its approach to financial penalties: (a) disgorgement (ie that a firm or person should not benefit from any breach); (b) discipline (ie that a firm or individual should be penalised for wrongdoing); and (c) deterrence (ie that any penalty should deter both whoever committed the breach, and anyone else, from committing further/similar breaches). This is discussed further at para **8.61** ff above.
2 FCA Handbook at DEPP 6.5.3(4).

17.188 The FCA applies the following steps 1 to 5 of the fining policy (disgorgement, seriousness, mitigating and aggravating factors and deterrence) differently to determine the amount of financial penalty to impose on individuals who have committed market abuse[1].

1 See the FCA Handbook at DEPP 6.5C, examples of the application of this policy can be found in the *Michael Coscia final notice (3/7/13)*, the *Rameshkumar Satynarayan Goenka final notice (17/10/11)* and the *Samuel Nathan Kahn final notice (24/5/11)*.

Step 1: Disgorgement

17.189 As in other disciplinary and regulatory proceedings, where a figure can be quantified, the FCA will seek to deprive an individual of any direct benefit they have obtained as a result of their market abuse[1]. Interest may be charged on any disgorgement figure up to the date of payment of the financial penalty.

1 FCA Handbook at DEPP 6.5C.1. The *Samuel Kahn final notice (24/05/11)* provides an example of the FCA's approach to determining a disgorgement figure (in this instance, the amount of the proceeds of the sale of shares dealt with abusively was used).

Step 2: Seriousness of the market abuse

17.190 The conduct will be allocated a level of seriousness between 1 to 5 depending on a number of factors[1]:

- factors relating to the impact of the market abuse[2];

- factors relating to the nature of the market abuse[3];

- factors tending to show whether the market abuse was deliberate[4];

- factors tending to show whether the market abuse was reckless[5].

1 FCA Handbook at DEPP 6.5C.2(10).
2 These include the level of benefit gained or loss avoided or intended to be avoided, directly or indirectly; whether the market abuse had an adverse effect on markets and the severity of that effect; whether the market abuse had a significant effect on the price of shares or investments. See the FCA Handbook at DEPP 6.5C.2(11) and the *Michael Coscia final notice (03/07/13)*, Mr Coscia's conduct was considered particularly serious (level 4) due to, inter alia, its significant impact on the ICE market and it forcing another major market participant to cease trading as a result of the adverse impact of Mr Coscia's actions.
3 These include the frequency of the market abuse; whether the individual abused a position of trust; whether the individual caused or encouraged others to commit market abuse; whether the individual has a prominent position in the market; whether the individual held a senior position at the firm; and whether the individual acted under duress. See the FCA Handbook at DEPP 6.5C.2(12) and the *Rameshkumar Goenka final notice (17/10/11)*, which referred to Mr Goenka's prominent position in the market in determining his conduct to be of level 4 seriousness. See also the *Samuel Nathan Kahn final notice (24/05/11)*, in which the conduct was considered particularly serious (level 4) in light of Mr Kahn's previous misconduct at Step 2 (previous conduct is also an aggravating factor at Step 3, see para **17.195** ff below).
4 These include whether the individual intended or foresaw that the likely or actual consequence of his actions would result in market abuse; the individual intended to benefit from the market abuse; the individual knew his actions were not in accordance of exchange rules or firm procedures; the individual sought to conceal his misconduct; the individual committed market abuse in a way that would avoid or reduce the risk of it being discovered; the individual was influenced to commit market abuse by a belief that it would be difficult to detect; the individual's actions were repeated. In respect of Limb 1, the individual knew or recognised that the information on which the dealing was based was inside information, or in respect of Limb 5, the individual's behaviour was based on information which he knew or recognised was not generally available to those using the market and the individual regarded the information as relevant when deciding the terms on which transaction in the qualifying investments should be effected. See the FCA Handbook at DEPP 6.5C.2(13) and the *Samuel Nathan Kahn final notice (24/05/11)*, where Mr Kahn's behaviour was found to be repeated and deliberate. He had also used deception to disguise his actions in the market and derived a significant personal profit.
5 These include whether the individual appreciated there was a risk that his action could result in market abuse and failed to adequately mitigate that risk; and the individual was aware that his actions could constitute market abuse and failed to check if he was acting in accordance with procedures. See the FCA Handbook at DEPP 6.5C.2(14).

17.191 The FCA has given guidance on what it considers to be indicators that the conduct is level 1, 2 or 3[1] and what it considers to be indicators that conduct is level 4 or 5[2] and has indicated that it usually expects to assess deliberate market abuse as level 4 or 5[3].

1 See the FCA Handbook at DEPP 6.5C.2(16). These include that little or no profits were made or losses avoided as a result of the market abuse, there was no or limited actual or potential effect on the orderliness of or confidence in markets as a result of the market abuse; and the market abuse was committed negligently or inadvertently.
2 See the FCA Handbook at DEPP 6.5C.2(15). These include that the level of benefit gained or loss avoided was significant; the market abuse had serious adverse effect on the orderliness of or confidence in markets; the market abuse was committed on multiple occasions; the individual breached a position of trust; the individual has a prominent position in the market; and the market abuse was committed deliberately or recklessly.
3 FCA Handbook at DEPP 6.5C.2(2)(c) and DEPP 6.5C.2(3)(b).

17.192 The approach that is taken in Step 2 depends on whether the market abuse is referable to the individual's employment[1].

1 This includes employment as an adviser, director, partner or contractor. See the FCA Handbook at DEPP 6.5C.2(4).

17.193 If market abuse is referable to an individual's employment, the Step 2 figure will be the greater of their 'relevant income'[1] multiplied by a percentage that is dependent on the severity of the market abuse; the amount of profit made or loss avoided multiplied by a profit multiple that is dependent on the severity of the market abuse[2]; and in the case of market abuse at level 4 or 5, £100,000.

1 This includes salary, bonus, pension contributions, share options, and share schemes, see the FCA Handbook at DEPP 6.5C2(4).
2 See the FCA Handbook at DEPP 6.5C.2(2). The relevant percentage levels and profit multipliers are set out at DEPP 6.5C.2(8) and are currently set at:
Level 1 – 0% of relevant income, profit multiple of 0;
Level 2 – 10% of relevant income, profit multiple of 1;
Level 3 – 20% of relevant income, profit multiple of 2;
Level 4 – 30% of relevant income, profit multiple of 3;
Level 5 – 40% of relevant income, profit multiple of 4.

17.194 If market abuse is not referable to an individual's employment the Step 2 figure will be the greater of the profit made or loss avoided multiplied by a profit multiple that is dependent on the severity of the market abuse; and in the case of market abuse at level 4 or 5, £100,000[1].

1 See the FCA Handbook at DEPP 6.5C.(3), the relevant percentage levels and profit multipliers are set out at DEPP 6.5C.2(8), see para **17.193**, n 2 above.

Step 3: Mitigating and aggravating factors

17.195 The FCA may increase or decrease the amount of the financial penalty arrived at the end of Step 2 as a result of aggravating or mitigating factors. These may include the following[1]:

- the conduct of the individual in bringing the market abuse to the FCA's attention or to that of another regulatory authority;

- the degree of cooperation the individual showed during the investigation by the FCA or any other regulatory authority;

- assistance provided by the individual to the FCA in action taken against other individuals for market abuse and/or in criminal proceedings;

- whether the individual has arranged their resources to avoid payment of disgorgement and/or a financial penalty;

- previous private warnings or supervisory correspondence that had made the individual aware of the FCA's concerns;

- the previous compliance record and disciplinary history of the individual[2];

- action taken against the individual by any other domestic or international regulatory authorities that is relevant to the market abuse in question;

- whether FCA guidance or other published materials had already raised relevant concerns, and the nature and accessibility of such materials; and

- whether the individual agreed to undertake training subsequent to the market abuse.

1 See the FCA Handbook at DEPP 6.5C.3. In the *Michael Coscia final notice (03/07/13)*, the FCA considered aggravating (the 2009 guidance previously published by the FSA) and mitigating (Mr Coscia stopping the conduct when notified of the regulator's concerns and cooperating with the FCA's investigation) factors. These were deemed in this matter to balance each other, and the financial penalty was neither increased nor decreased.
2 See para **17.176**, n 5, above; previous compliance history may also be considered at Step 2.

Step 4: Adjustment for deterrence

17.196 The FCA may increase the figure arrived at after Step 3 if it considers that it is insufficient to deter the individual who committed the market abuse, or others. The FCA has indicated that it may do this if it considers that the absolute value of the penalty is too small to be a credible deterrent, if previous FCA action in similar market abuse cases has failed to improve industry standards or if the penalty may not act as a deterrent in the light of the individual's income or assets[1].

1 FCA Handbook at DEPP 6.5C.4.

Step 5: Settlement discount

17.197 As is the case for other regulatory and disciplinary proceedings, penalties for market abuse are subject to reduction to reflect the stage at which the FCA and the individual reached a settlement. This discount does not apply to disgorgement of profits under Step 1 and is discussed further at paras **9.56** and **10.46** above.

Is there a tariff for financial penalties?

17.198 The FCA does not adopt a tariff of penalties for market abuse, given the wide range of conduct that may amount to market abuse[1]. However, the FCA asserts that consistency in comparable cases is an important aspect of its fining policy[2].

1 The same is true of the FCA's disciplinary fines: see para **8.61** ff above.
2 Consistency is one of the principles underlying the FCA's exercise of its disciplinary powers: see paras **8.45** and **8.61** ff above.

Procedure and publicity

17.199 The procedure for the imposition of financial penalties or public statements for market abuse is the warning/decision notice procedure[1] considered in detail in **CHAPTERS 10** and **11** above. Among other things, this enables the firm or person to refer the matter to the Tribunal, for an independent determination[2]. The warning and decision notices are required to, as appropriate, state the amount of the penalty or the terms of the public statement. The mediation scheme may be available where the FCA and the person concerned are unable to resolve the market abuse proceedings by agreement[3].

1 FSMA 2000, ss 126 and 127.
2 The proceedings of the Tribunal are considered in **CHAPTER 12** above.
3 FCA Enforcement Guide at EG 5.20–5.21.

17.200 In cases where the FCA applies to the court for an injunction or a restitution order, the procedure may be bypassed and instead the court may be asked at the same time to impose a financial penalty for the market abuse[1].

1 FSMA 2000, s 129. This is discussed at para **17.243** ff below.

17.201 In accordance with its general policy of publishing successful enforcement action, the FCA will ordinarily publicise a penalty or public statement for market abuse, by issuing a press release giving details of the behaviour and the sanction imposed and publishing the relevant final notice, unless issuing such a press notice would be unfair to the person on whom the sanction is imposed or prejudicial to the interests of consumers[1]. Hence, publicity will normally arise only at the conclusion of the matter. However the FCA may also publish details of decision notices before the issue of a final notice. The FCA has indicated that it expects to do this if the matter is referred to the Tribunal[2]. The FCA may also publish decision notices before a person has decided to refer the matter to the Tribunal if it considers that there is a compelling reason to do so. The FCA will give advance notice of its intention to publish a decision notice to the person to whom the notice is given (and any third party who has been given a copy of the notice) and will consider representations made in respect of publication. The FCA has indicated that it will not decide against publication solely because this may have an adverse effect on a person's reputation or solely because a person asks for confidentiality when they refer a matter to the Tribunal[3]. It is likely the proceedings before the Tribunal will be in public and judgment will be pronounced publicly, and that further publicity will therefore arise in that process[4].

1 See the FCA Enforcement Guide at EG 6.7 and 6.8. For a more detailed discussion of the FCA's policy on publication more generally, see para **10.179** ff above.
2 See the FCA Enforcement Guide at EG 6.8, see also *R (on the application of Canada Inc) v Financial Services Authority [2011] EWHC 2766 (Admin)* in which the claimants unsuccessfully attempted to prevent the publication of a decision notice by the FSA. Wyn Williams J found that the FSA had a broad discretion to consider when it is appropriate to publish a decision notice.
3 FCA Enforcement Guide at EG 6.8A.
4 See para **12.37** ff above.

17.202 In market abuse cases the FCA also has the power under the FSMA 2000 to publish such information to which a warning notice relates as it considers appropriate, unless in the opinion of the FCA publication of such information would be unfair to the person with respect to whom the action was taken (or was proposed to be taken), prejudicial to the interests of consumers, or detrimental to the stability of the UK financial system[1].

1 FSMA 2000, s 391(c). The FCA's approach to publishing information about warning notices is set out in the FCA Enforcement Guide at EG 6.7B–6.7J.

Action where other regulatory authorities are involved

17.203 In many situations, an issue which potentially amounts to market abuse will also raise enforcement questions for other regulators, whether one of the recognised investment exchanges or recognised auction platforms or the Takeover Panel in the UK or a regulatory authority overseas. In that situation, the person concerned will wish to avoid being subject to multiple regulatory investigations relating to the same matter.

17.204 The overlap with investigation and enforcement will be considered, by: first, the recognised investment exchanges, including particularly the London Stock Exchange; second, the FCA when acting as the UK Listing Authority; third, the Takeover Panel; and, finally, by overseas regulators.

The London Stock Exchange and other UK exchanges

17.205 The 'prescribed markets' and 'prescribed auction platform' in the UK from the market abuse perspective[1] comprise those markets established under the rules of the recognised investment or a recognised auction platform exchanges or recognised under the Recognised Auction Platform Regulations 2011, SI 2011/2699. Therefore, a trading issue on a market of a recognised investment exchange may well be both an enforcement issue for the exchange and a market abuse issue for the FCA. The enforcement role of the recognised investment exchanges, and their powers of investigation and enforcement will briefly be reviewed, before looking at how the overlap with market abuse is addressed.

1 See para **17.31** ff above.

The role of the exchanges

17.206 Whilst the admission of securities to the UK's official list is a matter for the FCA[1], the regulation of trading on the recognised investment exchanges and recognised auction platforms, including the London Stock Exchange, is a matter for the exchanges themselves. Each has responsibility for admitting securities to trading on its own markets and for regulating trading on its markets. This includes, for example, deciding whether to permit trading in any listed security or any other security, and setting, monitoring and enforcing the procedures and standards which apply to that admission to trading on an ongoing basis.

1 The FCA's role as UK Listing Authority is considered in **CHAPTER 20** below.

17.207 The recognised investment exchanges (RIEs) and recognised auction platforms thus have regulatory powers over their members. The precise nature and scope of those powers depends upon the detailed rules of each exchange or auction platform and differs as between the different exchanges or auction platforms. However, the basics are dictated by the recognition requirements which are required to be met as a condition of the FCA granting recognition to the exchange or auction platform under the FSMA 2000[1]. In addition, the FCA has made specific rules with respect to exchanges[2]. Thus, among other things, a recognised investment exchange or auction platform must:

- have effective arrangements for monitoring and enforcing its rules[3];

- generally, be able and willing to promote and maintain high standards of integrity and fair dealing in the carrying on of regulated activities by persons in the course of using facilities provided by the exchange or auction platform[4] and to co-operate by the sharing of information or otherwise with the FCA and other applicable bodies[5];

- notify the FCA immediately where it has evidence tending to suggest that any person has, among other things, been engaged in market abuse or has committed the criminal offences of insider dealing or misleading statements and practices[6]; and

- notify the FCA immediately where it has taken disciplinary action against a member or employee of a member in respect of a rule breach[7].

1 The recognised investment exchanges are thus in the position of both regulator and regulated, at the same time. As to the recognition requirements, see: the FSMA 2000, ss 286 and 290; the Financial Services and Markets Act 2000 (Recognition Requirements for Investment Exchanges and Clearing Houses) Regulations 2001, SI 2001/995 (as amended by the Financial Markets and Insolvency Regulations 2009, SI 2009/853, art 4); the Financial Services and Markets Act 2000 (Recognition Requirements for Investment Exchanges and Clearing Houses) (Amendment) Regulations 2006, SI 2006/3386; the Recognised Auction Platforms Regulations 2011, SI 2011/2699 and the FCA Handbook at REC.
2 See the FCA Handbook at REC 2A.2.1(1) which states that when assessing whether an auction platform fulfils the recognition requirements the FCA *may* treat compliance by the auction platform or applicant with the recognition requirements or MiFID implementing requirements applying to it as a UK RIE as conclusive evidence that the auction platform or applicant satisfies any equivalent recognition requirements for auction platforms applying to it under these regulations, taking into account any arrangements that would be necessary to meet the auction platform recognition requirements, REC 2A.3.1G further states that the FCA will not make a separate assessment of compliance with the recognition requirements during the course of examining an application to become an auction platform or as part of its ongoing supervision of an auction platform, unless there is a specific reason to do so.
3 See the FCA Handbook at REC 2.15 and the Recognised Auction Platforms Regulations 2011, SI 2011/2699, art 22.
4 See the FCA Handbook at REC 2.17.1(1) and the Recognised Auction Platforms Regulations 2011, SI 2011/2699, art 18(1). One of the factors that may be taken into account is the extent to which the exchange seeks to promote and encourage conduct in regulated activities which is consistent with the Code of Market Conduct: see the FCA Handbook at REC 2.17.3 and REC2A.3.2.
5 See the FCA Handbook at REC 2.17.1(2) and the Recognised Auction Platforms Regulations 2011, SI 2011/2699, art 18(2). One of the factors that may be relevant is the extent to which the constitution and rules of the exchange and its agreements with its members enable it to obtain information from members and to disclose otherwise confidential information to the FCA and other appropriate bodies: see the FCA Handbook at REC 2.17.4 and REC 2A.3.2.
6 FCA Handbook at REC 3.17.
7 FCA Handbook at REC 3.20.

17.208 As to the specific rules of the exchanges, the first point to note is that each recognised investment exchange (and auction platform) has made rules requiring, broadly, proper standards of market conduct[1].

17.208   Market misconduct

1   The detailed rules vary significantly as between the exchanges. They can be found as follows: ICE Futures Europe – Rulebook Section A, Regulation A.2.1; BATS Trading Limited – Rules 8.1 and 8.2; ICAP Securities and Derivatives Exchange – Rule 46; LIFFE – Book I, Rule 8.1, Book II, Rule 2.2; London Stock Exchange – Rule 1400; London Metal Exchange – Pt 2, Sections 9.6 and 9.7.

17.209 Second, each RIE has the power, under its own rules, to investigate and enforce standards on its markets, including in very broad terms, to[1]:

- investigate suspected rule breaches by members;

- take disciplinary action against members;

- take immediate action to suspend particular members or trading in particular securities in the interests of ensuring an orderly market; and

- provide information to other regulators, including the FCA.

1   Again, the detailed rules vary significantly as between the exchanges. They can be found as follows: London Stock Exchange – Rules 1021, 1210 , 1214-1217 and 1510; LIFFE – Book II, Rules 2.4.1, 4.1–4.5 and 4.8; London Metal Exchange – Pt 2, Rules 9.5 and 10–12; BATS Trading Limited – Rules 8.1 and 8.2; ICAP Securities and Derivatives Exchange – Rules 41, 78 and 82 and ICE futures rules D.10, E3–E5 and E7.

Overlap with FCA enforcement

17.210 The FCA recognises that market abuse cases may also involve potential action by other regulatory authorities. Where the behaviour occurred or is occurring on a market of one of the recognised investment exchanges or on a recognised auction platform, the FCA will refer to the exchange or auction platform and give due weight to its views. Where both bodies wish to bring proceedings, the FCA will co-ordinate with the exchange or auction platform to ensure that cases are dealt with in an effective and fair manner under agreed operating arrangements[1]. It will have regard to all the circumstances of the case, including whether the other regulatory authorities have adequate powers to address the behaviour in question.

1   FCA Handbook at DEPP 6.2.20–6.2.21, DEPP 6.2.23–6.2.27 and the FCA Enforcement Guide at EG 2.15.

17.211 What does this mean in practice? How the issue is dealt with will, in practice, depend largely upon the circumstances of the particular case. For example, in some cases the exchange concerned may have the necessary powers to address all the consequences of the conduct appropriately and, in those cases, the FCA may not need to take action itself. In others, the FCA will need to do so, particularly in serious cases, given the extensive powers that the FCA has against those who commit market abuse and also in cases where the FCA's wider responsibilities and powers in relation to the regulated community are relevant, for example, because other regulatory action also needs to be taken. It is clearly possible for more than one body to have an interest in the same issue, but it is unclear whether, where the FCA does wish to exercise its powers, the exchange will always defer to it at the expense of not taking its own enforcement action.

From the firm's perspective, it is most important that concurrent proceedings by different bodies are minimised and, if they are required, are properly coordinated.

The FCA acting as the UK Listing Authority

17.212 The powers of the FCA in its capacity as UK Listing Authority (the competent authority under the FSMA 2000, Pt 6) to investigate and enforce breaches of the listing rules are considered in detail in **CHAPTER 20** below. Issues which may both concern the FCA, in its capacity as the UKLA, and raise questions about market abuse include compliance with the disclosure rules[1] and making false or misleading announcements to the market[2]. This gives rise to two issues.

1 For example, the Code of Market Conduct indicates that the practice of selectively briefing may constitute market abuse (improper disclosure): see para **17.59** ff above.
2 See the *Shell Transport and Trading Company plc and Royal Dutch Petroleum Company NV final notice (24/8/04)* in which Shell was fined £17 million for making false or misleading announcements, conduct that was found both to be market abuse and a breach of the Listing Rules.

17.213 First, as already noted[1], there are limited harbours under the market abuse regime for compliance with certain requirements of European legislation and the Part 6 rules, which expressly require or permit behaviour which, in the absence of a safe harbour, might be interpreted as resulting in market abuse[2].

1 See para **17.87** ff above.
2 See the MAD, Art 8 and the FSMA 2000, s 118A(5)(b) set out in the FCA Handbook at MAR 1, Annex 1 concerning buy-back and stabilisation requirements. These will continue following the implementation of the MA Regulation.

17.214 Second, a question arises as to what action the FCA will take either in the context of acting as the UKLA or where investigating market abuse where a particular issue amounts to both a breach of the Part 6 rules and market abuse. In that situation, and given that the UKLA is a part of the FCA, the FCA will obtain information about the behaviour, either voluntarily or using whatever statutory powers or powers under the FSMA 2000, Pt 6 are appropriate, and will then consider whether, in all the circumstances of the case[1], further action under the FSMA 2000, Pt 6 or under the market abuse regime appears appropriate[2]. It will thus consider both aspects of the behaviour in the round in the light of its investigation.

1 Including the factors which the FCA considers in deciding whether or not to take disciplinary action under the FSMA 2000: see para **8.18** ff above.
2 See the discussion at para **20.117** ff below on the interplay between the different potential criminal, regulatory and civil actions.

17.215 Where more than one person is involved in a breach of the provisions of the FSMA 2000, Pt 6 or the Part 6 rules, action may be taken under the Part 6 rules against one person and under the market abuse regime against a different person. One example where it might be appropriate to take action is against an issuer under the Part 6 rules and against a director under the market abuse regime. The FCA may apply its general policy on taking both action for market

17.215   Market misconduct

abuse and disciplinary action against the same person, outlined below[1]. It will bring proceedings for both in an appropriate case[2].

1 See para **17.166** above.
2 See the *Shell Transport and Trading Company plc and Royal Dutch Petroleum Company NV final notice (24/8/04)*, also referred to at para **17.212**, n 2 above.

The Takeover Panel

17.216 Where the issue arises in the context of a takeover bid, there are two, quite separate issues to consider. First, the context gives rise to additional factors for consideration by the FCA when deciding whether to take action in relation to the market abuse. Second, in some circumstances the Takeover Panel may ask the FCA to exercise its statutory enforcement powers in order to enforce the City Code. Each of these is considered in turn below. The FCA's approach to these issues arises after extensive consultations between it (and its predecessor the FSA) and the Takeover Panel and the overall aim is to establish robust and flexible operating arrangements which will involve the minimum disruption to the takeover timetable[1].

1 See the FSA Press Release on outline arrangements for handling market abuse in takeover situations, PN/157/2001, 29 November 2001, and the Operating Guidelines between the FCA and the Takeover Panel on market misconduct.

Additional factors in deciding whether to take action for market abuse

17.217 In relation to behaviour which may have occurred or may be occurring in the context of a takeover bid, the FCA has provided the following guidance[1]:

- the FCA will refer to the Takeover Panel and give due weight to its views;

- where the City Code provides procedures for complaint in respect of the behaviour, the FCA will not, save in exceptional circumstances, take action in respect of market abuse[2] before the conclusion of those procedures and will expect parties to exhaust such procedures first;

- the FCA will not take action against a person for behaviour which conforms with the City Code and which the Code of Market Conduct specifies does not amount to market abuse[3]. In determining whether behaviour complies with the City Code, the FCA will seek the views of the Takeover Panel and will attach considerable weight to its views[4];

- in any case where the FCA considers that the use of its market abuse powers[5] may be appropriate and may affect the timetable or outcome of a takeover bid, it will consult the Takeover Panel before using its powers[6];

- in relation to those who have responsibilities under the City Code[7], the FCA recognises that the powers of the Takeover Panel will often be sufficient to address the concerns. Where this is not the case, the FCA will need to consider whether it is appropriate to exercise any of its own powers in respect of market abuse. This is likely to be considered principally in circumstances where[8]:

(1) the market abuse falls under the misuse of information provisions[9];

(2) the FCA's approach in previous similar cases (including those not involving a takeover bid) suggests that a financial penalty should be imposed;

(3) the Takeover Panel requests the FCA to consider exercising its powers to impose a penalty, to request the court to impose a penalty, to apply for an injunction or to apply for or impose a restitution order in respect of the market abuse;

(4) the market abuse extends to securities outside the Takeover Panel's jurisdiction; or

(5) the market abuse threatens or threatened the stability of the financial system.

- even where the FCA considers that the exercise of its powers is appropriate, it will not take action[10] during the currency of an offer to which the City Code applies, save in exceptional circumstances in situations (1), (3), (4), and (depending on the circumstances), (5) above[11];

- so far as concerns publishing details of penalties for market abuse, where the FCA is of the opinion that publication of its action may affect the timetable or outcome of the bid, it will consult the Takeover Panel over the timing of publication and give due weight to its views[12].

1 FCA Handbook at DEPP 6.2.22–6.2.27.
2 This includes not only the imposition of a penalty under the FSMA 2000, ss 123 or 129 but also injunctions under the FSMA 2000, s 381 and restitution orders under ss 383 and 384: see the FCA Handbook at DEPP 6.2.22.
3 This mirrors the FSMA 2000, s 120, and the relevant provisions are outlined at para **17.92** ff above.
4 See the FCA Handbook at DEPP 6.2.23. Note, however, that the interpretation of the City Code for this purpose remains a matter for the FCA, not the Takeover Panel.
5 See n 3 above.
6 FCA Handbook at DEPP 6.2.25.
7 FCA Handbook at DEPP 6.2.26.
8 FCA Handbook at DEPP 6.2.26.
9 FSMA 2000, s 118(2), (3) or (4), see para **17.62** ff above.
10 FCA Handbook at DEPP 6.2.22–6.2.27 and the FCA Enforcement Guide at EG 6.18.
11 FCA Handbook at DEPP 6.2.27.
12 FCA Enforcement Guide at EG 6.18.

17.218 In summary, therefore, the position is that it is in some circumstances appropriate for the FCA to take action notwithstanding the market abuse arises in the context of a takeover bid. Where it is appropriate for the FCA to do so, it will not normally do so during the currency of the offer, but it may do so in exceptional circumstances where urgent action is required.

FCA view of the City Code

17.219 The FCA has implemented 'cold-shoulder' rules, requiring firms not to act or continue to act for any person in connection with a transaction to which the

17.119 Market misconduct

City Code applies if the firm has reason to believe that the person in question, or his principal, is not complying or not likely to comply with the City Code[1].

1 FCA Handbook at MAR 4.3.1 R.

17.220 In addition, the FCA requires firms to provide information, documents and assistance to the Takeover Panel to enable it to perform its functions[1].

1 For details, see the FCA Handbook at MAR 4.3.5 R.

Overseas regulatory authorities

17.221 The territorial scope of the market abuse provisions has been highlighted at para **17.120** ff above and, as has been seen, behaviour that takes place outside the UK may amount to market abuse both in the UK and in any other EU state in which that behaviour takes place. In addition, behaviour that takes place within the UK could amount to market abuse in other EU states if it relates to trading on regulated markets in those states. To give an example, if a particular trading activity (that is alleged to amount to market abuse) is carried out from the UK on one or more regulated exchanges in other EU jurisdictions, then the FCA may well be interested in investigating that trading from the perspective of the UK market abuse regime (which, as has been seen, in many aspects covers trading carried out in the UK on any EU regulated market) but the regulators in the other EU states on whose markets the trading took place may well also be interested in investigating. Under the EU market abuse regime, their market abuse regimes ought to cover trading carried on elsewhere (for example, from the UK) on their own regulated markets. Thus there is a considerable potential for overlap.

17.222 In such cases, the FCA will, in deciding whether to impose a penalty or public statement for market abuse, consider, in addition to the factors applicable in any case[1], the extent to which the behaviour is capable of being dealt with by the relevant overseas regulator or other enforcement agency[2]. It will consider in each case whether it is appropriate for the FCA or that other agency to take action. For example, the FCA may be interested in the systems and controls implications of any trading that took place from the UK on to a regulated market in another EU state, even if it decides that the proceedings for market abuse should more sensibly be brought by the other EU regulator. In some cases, both regulators may have an interest in pursuing enforcement action. In those circumstances, the FCA will work with the relevant overseas authority to co-ordinate effective enforcement action.

1 These are outlined at para **17.176** ff above.
2 FCA Enforcement Guide at EG 2.15 and DEPP 6.2.20.

17.223 As with other UK regulators, therefore, there could well be situations where the firm faces more than one investigation and enforcement process in relation to the same matter. Where this occurs, it may be important from the firm's perspective that the different bodies do not place unnecessary burdens on the firm but co-ordinate their action. Generally speaking, the FCA is likely to be able to pass information to the overseas regulator under the so-called Gateway Regulations[1].

1 Financial Services and Markets Act 2000 (Disclosure of Confidential Information) Regulations 2001, SI 2001/2188.

Other enforcement action available to the FCA

17.224 The FSMA 2000 gives the FCA various specific powers in cases of market abuse, in addition to the power to impose a financial penalty or make a public statement. In particular, the FCA has the power to apply to the court for an injunction, among other things to prevent the abuse, or for a restitution order to compensate victims. The FCA may also impose a restitution order itself, without applying to court.

17.225 However, the matter which constitutes market abuse may also give rise to more general regulatory concerns which might lead to the use of the FCA's other enforcement powers, primarily against those who are regulated. It could, for example, be appropriate for the FCA to use its own-initiative powers, its disciplinary powers against regulated firms or approved persons, or to withdraw the approval of an approved person or make a prohibition order against an individual. Such measures are most likely to be in prospect if the instance of market abuse is symptomatic of a wider problem within the firm, which casts doubt on its or its employees' fitness or propriety or gives rise to issues about the protection of consumers. Or they might be appropriate if the misconduct did not technically amount to market abuse but, in the FCA's view, nonetheless merits regulatory action. The market abuse regime cannot therefore be viewed in isolation but needs to be seen against the wider background of the FCA's regulatory objectives and powers.

17.226 The following paragraphs will consider:

- injunctions in relation to market abuse[1];

- restitution orders in relation to market abuse[2];

- disciplinary and other regulatory enforcement action[3]; and

- civil liability arising from market abuse[4].

1 See para **17.227** ff below
2 See para **17.245** ff below
3 See para **17.253** ff below.
4 See para **17.263** ff below.

Injunctions

17.227 The court may grant an injunction, on the application of the FCA, broadly to prevent threatened or continuing market abuse, to address the consequences of the market abuse or to prevent the disposal of assets[1]. This power is very similar to the power to grant injunctions in respect of regulatory breaches, outlined in **Chapter 8** above. Some general points about applications for injunctions are discussed at para **8.145** ff above. In market abuse cases, the FCA may apply to the court, at the same time as applying for an injunction, for an order imposing a penalty for the market abuse[2].

1 FSMA 2000, s 381. The court can grant interim and final injunctions, see *Financial Service Authority v Kahn (24 May 2011, unreported), the Samuel Nathan Kahn final notice (24/5/11)* and the related press release FSA/PN/044/2011.
2 FSMA 2000, s 129 and see para **17.243** below.

What orders can the court make?

17.228 The court may make three different types of orders, namely:

- restraining the market abuse;

- requiring the person engaging in market abuse to take specified steps to remedy the market abuse; or

- restraining the person concerned from disposing of or dealing with his assets.

Each is based upon the satisfaction of slightly different criteria.

Restraining the market abuse

17.229 An order restraining market abuse may be made if the court is satisfied that[1]:

- there is a reasonable likelihood that any person will engage in market abuse; or

- any person is or has engaged in market abuse and there is a reasonable likelihood that the market abuse will continue or be repeated.

1 FSMA 2000, s 381(1).

17.230 An injunction may therefore be available pre-emptively where the FCA has information that action amounting to market abuse is going to be taken. Although the FCA only has to show a reasonable likelihood that market abuse will be undertaken[1], unless the FCA is seeking an injunction to prevent further market abuse of a type that has already occurred, this may in practice be difficult, because the FCA will not often be aware of the proposed market abuse before it occurs. Indeed, part of the rationale behind the nature of the investigation regime for market abuse[2] is that the FCA will normally start with a situation which looks like market abuse, rather than with a suspected culprit.

1 Typically in court proceedings, interim injunctions are granted without needing to prove the claim on the balance of probabilities; a lower test of 'good arguable case' typically being applied. In *Financial Services Authority v Da Vinci Invest Ltd [2011] EWHC 2674 (Ch)* Newey J found that the FSA did not have to establish market abuse definitively to obtain interim relief, however note that the FSA had been unsuccessful in obtaining a without notice injunction to restrain market abuse in a previous application in the same proceedings. See also the discussion at para **8.147** ff above. In practice, the FSA has also used this power to obtain final injunctions to prevent further market abuse, see *Financial Service Authority v Kahn (24 May 2011, unreported),* the *Samuel Kahn final notice (24/5/11)* and the related Press Release FSA/PN/044/2011. Mr Kahn had previously

been sanctioned for, and subject to an injunction restraining, his involvement in overseas boiler-room activity from the UK. In this instance he had repeatedly impersonated other individuals in order to 'ramp' shares admitted to trading on PLUS markets. See also *Financial Services Authority v Alexander (14 June 2011, unreported)* and the *Barnett Michael Alexander final notice (14/6/11)*. Mr Alexander's activity was brought to the FSA's attention as a result of a suspicious transaction report in December 2009. In May 2010 the FSA brought proceedings against Mr Alexander under the FSMA 2000, s 381 and obtained an interim injunction freezing Mr Alexander's assets and preventing him from continuing to enter into the particular conduct that concerned the FSA. As part of a settlement reached between the FSA and Mr Alexander he agreed to: (i) the imposition of a permanent restraining injunction against him; (ii) a financial penalty of £700,000 (after a 30% discount as a result of his agreement to settle with the FSA); and (iii) the payment of restitution of £322,818 to the firms that had suffered loss as a result of his market abuse. Mr Alexander had sought to manipulate the price of contracts for difference and spread bets by trading in shares on the London Stock Exchange.

2 See para **17.122** above.

17.231 This order is similar to that which a court can make to restrain regulatory breaches, as outlined at para **8.147** ff above.

Remedying the market abuse

17.232 An order requiring a person to take such steps as the court may direct to remedy market abuse, or mitigate its effect, may be made if the court is satisfied that[1]:

- any person is or has engaged in market abuse; and

- there are steps which could be taken for remedying the market abuse (or mitigating its effect[2]).

1 FSMA 2000, s 381(2).
2 FSMA 2000, s 381(6).

17.233 In such cases, the market abuse must in fact have occurred or be in the process of occurring, reflecting the remedial nature of the order. In many situations, it will not be possible to remedy the market abuse, strictly speaking, because it has already occurred and cannot be undone. The inclusion of references to mitigating the effect of the market abuse helps ensure that that will not be a bar to the court requiring appropriate steps to be taken[1]. The remedial steps that the FCA might seek would depend upon the situation, but could, for example, include requiring a person to correct any misleading information disseminated to the market, or requiring them to release stocks of an investment or commodity that are being held in the course of a market distortion.

1 This is discussed in more detail at para **8.150** ff above.

17.234 This order is similar to that which can be made to remedy regulatory breaches, as outlined at para **8.150** ff above.

Restraining assets

17.235 An order may be made by the court restraining a person from disposing of, or otherwise dealing with, any assets of his which the court is satisfied he is reasonably likely to dispose of, or otherwise deal with[1]. To make such an order, the court must be satisfied that the person[2]:

- may be engaged in market abuse; or

- may have been engaged in market abuse.

1 FSMA 2000, s 381(4). See *Financial Services Authority v Alexander (14 June 2011, unreported)* and the *Barnett Michael Alexander final notice (14/6/11)*.
2 FSMA 2000, s 381(3).

17.236 The FSMA 2000 does not expressly require any link between the market abuse and the assets that might be disposed of, so it will be entirely in the court's discretion in what circumstances it will be prepared to grant such an injunction. In practice, this provision may be used to obtain a freezing order in support of some other proceedings, to restrain a person from dissipating their assets so as to frustrate the enforcement of any court judgment against him in those proceedings. Examples in this context of where a freezing order might be sought include where the person faces proceedings for a restitution order, or civil proceedings, arising from the market abuse or, possibly, proceedings for a civil penalty. A similar injunction may also be available under the court's inherent jurisdiction[1]. This order is similar to that which can be made in relation to regulatory breaches, as outlined at para **8.147** ff above.

1 See para **8.152**, n 3 above. Additionally, ancillary orders, such as requiring the disclosure of assets, might be sought on this basis.

The discretionary nature of the remedy

17.237 It is important to appreciate that each of these remedies is within the discretion of the court. The FSMA 2000 provides only that the court 'may' make the order if satisfied of the matters set out. In other words, the court is not bound to make an injunction because the FCA establishes the grounds for making one. Whether an injunction will be available in a particular case will therefore depend upon the particular circumstances. The matters which the court takes into account in the exercise of its discretion to grant injunctive relief are briefly discussed at para **8.145** ff above. The court will often, initially, be considering an application for an interim injunction pending a full trial on whether an injunction should be granted and in many cases the interim injunction will effectively dispose of the matter. This gives rise to certain additional considerations, also outlined at para **8.145** ff above.

In what circumstances will the FCA apply for an injunction?

17.238 Since the court will only grant an injunction on an application by the FCA, one of the key questions from the firm's perspective is when in practice the FCA will make such an application. When considering whether to apply for an injunction in relation to market abuse, the FCA takes into account the same factors as are relevant in deciding whether to make applications for an injunction in non-market abuse situations under the FSMA 2000, s 380. These are discussed at para **8.157** ff above[1]. The basic criterion is whether an injunction would be the most effective means of dealing with the FCA's concerns[2].

1 They can be found in the FCA Enforcement Guide at EG 10.3.
2 See the FCA Enforcement Guide at EG 10.3. See also the FCA Enforcement Guide at EG 10.8 which notes that an application for an injunction is the only power by which the FCA may seek directly to prevent unauthorised persons from actual or threatened breaches of the perimeter or market abuse. The FSA has used its powers to apply for injunctions restraining market abuse in relation to unauthorised persons (see para **8.157** ff above).

17.239 Particular factors highlighted as being potentially of relevance in the context of market abuse[1] are the nature and seriousness of the misconduct, or expected misconduct, in question, including its impact on the financial system and the extent to which it has or would result in disruption or distortion if it took place or continued, and the extent and nature of any losses or other costs imposed or likely to be imposed on other users as a result.

1 FCA Enforcement Guide at EG 10.3.

17.240 As ever, this power needs to be viewed in context and in particular where the FCA is dealing with a firm then it may be more appropriate to achieve the same through varying the firm's permission[1].

1 Or imposing requirements on an incoming firm: see para **16.75** ff above.

Are the defences to market abuse proceedings available?

17.241 It is a defence to the imposition of a penalty or public statement for market abuse that a person believed on reasonable grounds that his behaviour did not amount to market abuse or that he took all reasonable precautions and exercised all due diligence to avoid committing market abuse[1]. However, the availability of one of these defences in the particular case simply precludes the imposition of a penalty or public censure, or indeed a restitution order[2]. It does not prevent market abuse from having taken place and does not therefore preclude an injunction being granted in an appropriate case[3].

1 These defences are discussed in detail at para **17.92** ff above.
2 See para **17.246** ff below.
3 There is nothing on the face of the legislation to prevent an injunction being granted to remedy market abuse with substantially the same effect as a restitution order, in a situation where one of the defences applied and a restitution order would not therefore be available under the FSMA 2000.

17.242 Whether the court would be willing to grant an injunction in that situation may, however, be a different matter. At one end of the spectrum, there seems little reason why this should preclude an injunction to prevent further acts that would amount to market abuse. At the other end, it would seem wrong for the court to restrain a person from dealing with his own assets in a situation where he has done nothing culpable.

17.243   Market misconduct

Applications for a penalty to be imposed

17.243 The FSMA 2000 allows the FCA, on an application for an injunction or restitution order, to request the court to consider whether the circumstances are such that a penalty should be imposed on the person to whom the application relates and the court may, if it considers it appropriate, make an order requiring the person concerned to pay the FCA a penalty of such amount as it considers appropriate[1].

1   FSMA 2000, s 129.

17.244 The FCA Handbook contains no guidance on when the FCA will make use of this procedure however, its predecessor, the FSA had indicated in the past[1] that an application to the court to impose a penalty would not be appropriate in all cases where it applies for an injunction or restitution order. It said that its primary concern would be to contain the overall costs of dealing with any case of market abuse. It will therefore depend upon, among other things, the extent to which the court would consider the same issues of fact and law in relation to the two applications and that in deciding whether to ask the court to impose a financial penalty, it would take into account the same factors as are relevant to the decisions whether to take action for market abuse[2]. There may in practice be other relevant factors, such as the need to put an injunction in place on an expedited basis, as against the need for a full investigation and hearing on the imposition of a penalty.

1   FSA Consultation Paper 17, 'Financial services regulation. Enforcing the new regime' (December 1998), para 165.
2   This was previously set out in the FSA Handbook at ENF 14.3.3 but does not feature in the FCA Handbook at DEPP or in the FCA's Enforcement Guide.

Restitution orders

17.245 The FSMA 2000 allows both the FCA and the court (on the application of the FCA), separately, to make restitution orders to compensate the victims of market abuse. The provisions are similar to those in relation to restitution orders for other regulatory breaches, discussed at para **8.100** ff above. The FCA may require a person, whether or not authorised[1], who has engaged in market abuse, or required or encouraged another to do so, to disgorge any profits made or pay compensation to the victims of the market abuse[2]. Alternatively, the FCA may apply to the court for a similar order[3]. If the FCA applies to the court for a restitution order, it may also apply to the court at the same time for an order imposing a penalty for the market abuse[4]. As discussed in para **17.263** ff, below, market abuse does not give rise to statutory claims by those who have suffered loss.

1   This marks a significant difference from the FCA's power to order restitution in relation to other regulatory breaches, which can only be exercised against authorised persons, discussed at para **8.108** ff above.
2   FSMA 2000, s 384(2).
3   FSMA 2000, s 383.
4   See para **17.250** ff below.

When can the FCA make or seek a restitution order?

17.246 The circumstances in which the FCA may exercise its administrative power to make a restitution order, or where the court may make a restitution order on an application by the FCA, are the same. The FCA or the court, as appropriate, must be satisfied that a person[1]:

- has engaged in market abuse; or

- by taking or refraining from taking any action, has required or encouraged another person or persons to engage in behaviour which, if engaged in by the person concerned, would amount to market abuse[2]; and

- in either case, profits have accrued to the person concerned as a result or one or more persons have suffered loss or been otherwise adversely affected as a result[3].

But no restitution order may be made if, as applicable, the court is satisfied[4], or having considered any representations made to it in response to a warning notice there are reasonable grounds for the FCA to be satisfied[5], that the person concerned either believed on reasonable grounds that his behaviour did not amount to market abuse (or was not requiring or encouraging market abuse), or took all reasonable precautions and exercised all due diligence to avoid behaving in a way which was market abuse (or was requiring or encouraging market abuse).

1 FSMA 2000, ss 384(2) and 383.
2 This is considered in detail at para **17.106** ff above.
3 The meaning of adverse affect has been considered at para **8.116** ff above.
4 FSMA 2000, s 383(3).
5 FSMA 2000, s 384(4).

The amount of a restitution order

17.247 If the above test is satisfied, the FCA or the court, as appropriate, may order the person concerned to pay such sum as appears to the FCA or the court to be just. In determining what figure is just, the FCA or the court must have regard to[1] the profits appearing to it to have accrued to the person concerned and/or, where one or more persons have suffered a loss or other adverse effect, the extent of that loss or adverse effect. The FCA's policy on the amount of restitution that is required to be paid and the requirements on how it should be distributed are discussed at para **8.132** ff above.

1 FSMA 2000, ss 383(4) or 384(5).

When in practice will the FCA seek or make a restitution order?

17.248 The FCA has provided little indication, in the context of market abuse specifically, of its policy on when it will impose a restitution order and when it will apply for a restitution order from the court and, in any event, when a restitution order is likely to be appropriate. The policy outlined at para **8.119** ff above in relation to restitution orders generally seems to apply equally in the case of market abuse.

17.249 There are, however, three points to note in this context. First, the circumstances when the FCA has indicated it may be appropriate to seek a restitution order from the court[1] include the following two which may be particularly relevant:

- where the FCA wishes to combine an application for an order for restitution with another court action, for example, an application for an injunction; or

- where the FCA suspects that the person may not comply with an administrative requirement to give restitution, and wishes to ensure that the sanctions for breach of a court order are available.

1 FCA Enforcement Guide at EG 11.5.

17.250 In the context of market abuse, the FCA can, as has been seen, apply for a financial penalty to be imposed in conjunction with an application for a restitution order or injunction. There may be an attraction in particular cases to having all of these regulatory issues addressed at one hearing before the court.

17.251 Second, an additional factor relevant in determining in any case whether to make or apply for a restitution order is whether the persons who have suffered losses are in a position to bring civil proceedings on their own behalf[1]. In most instances, this primarily involves considering the resources, sophistication and knowledge of those who have suffered the loss. However, in the context of market abuse, this factor may assume a wider significance because, as is discussed below[2], it may be unlikely that a civil claim is available in respect of market abuse. Thus, the persons who suffered the losses may be unable to bring civil proceedings, whatever their sophistication and resources.

1 FCA Enforcement Guide at EG 11.3(7) and see para **8.121** ff above.
2 See para **17.263** ff below.

17.252 Third, the nature of market manipulation and information misuse in financial markets is such that it is often difficult to identify 'victims' of the misconduct who should be compensated or who should benefit from any disgorgement of profits. The market abuse regime is directed at protecting the integrity of markets, rather than the interests of any particular group of market users[1].

1 See the *Rameshkumar Satyanarayan Goenka final notice (17/10/11)* in which Mr Goenka was ordered to give restitution of the difference between the sum paid to him by his counterparty and the sum that would have been due to him from his counterparty but for his market abuse. See also the *Barnett Michael Alexander final notice (14/6/11)* in which as part of a settlement with FSA Mr Alexander agreed to pay £322,818 in restitution as his market abuse had caused retail derivative brokers to suffer quantifiable loss. The settlement also included the imposition of a final injunction restraining Mr Alexander from further market abuse.

Disciplinary and other regulatory enforcement action

17.253 If a firm or approved person (or other employee of a firm) is involved in the market abuse, it may be appropriate for the FCA also to consider the use of its disciplinary or other enforcement powers. This will particularly be the case where the circumstances of the market misconduct give rise to other concerns about the firm, such as supervision and controls or employee training, where the conduct amounts to a breach of the Principles[1], or where it gives rise to questions about whether particular individuals are fit and proper.

1   Principle 5 of the Principles for Businesses and Statement of Principle 3 for approved persons: see para **17.260** ff below.

17.254 The various other courses of action available in relation to the regulated community include:

- in relation to an authorised person:
    - disciplinary sanctions (public censure or fine)[1];
    - the variation of the firm's permission, or equivalent intervention action for an incoming firm[2];
    - the cancellation of permission[3];
- in the case of an approved person (and certain other employees of a firm):
    - disciplinary sanctions for misconduct (public censure or fine)[4];
    - withdrawal of approval[5];
- in the case of any individual:
    - a prohibition order[6].

1   See para **8.11** ff above.
2   See **CHAPTER 16** above.
3   See para **16.122** ff above.
4   See para **9.5** ff above.
5   See para **9.65** ff above.
6   See para **9.99** ff above.

17.255 As noted in the previous paragraph, these disciplinary sanctions and other outcomes are considered in **CHAPTERS 8** and **9** above. One particular issue of concern is considered here, namely, the overlap between market abuse proceedings and regulatory disciplinary proceedings and, particularly, in what circumstances the FCA will seek to impose disciplinary sanctions against either firms or approved persons (or certain other employees of firms) in relation to market misconduct.

When will the FCA seek to discipline a firm?

17.256 There is an obvious overlap between market abuse, on the one hand, and Principle 5[1], on the other and this issue is not addressed in FCA's policy guidance. The FCA's predecessor, the FSA had on occasion sought to discipline firms for breach of Principle 5 where it found them guilty of market abuse[2]. In addition it has also taken disciplinary action for breach of Principle 5 and Principle 2 even where a firm's actions did not amount to market abuse[3]. This has particularly been the case when the firm's conduct has not related to a qualifying investment traded on a prescribed market[4].

17.256 Market misconduct

1 Principle 5, Principles for Businesses: a firm must observe proper standards of market conduct.

2 See *Philippe Jabre and GLG Partners LP final notice (1/8/06)* market abuse committed by Philippe Jabre, a Managing Director of GLG was attributable to GLG. The final notice specified that 'in committing market abuse GLG has also failed to observe proper standards of market conduct'.

3 See the *Citigroup Global Markets Limited final notice (28/6/04)* in which Citigroup was fined £17.9 million in relation to closing out a long cash position and short futures position trading on an MTS trading platform. The FSA did not find Citigroup to have committed market abuse or any breach of Principle 5. Instead, it found Citigroup's conduct to have breached Principle 2, in failing to conduct its business with due skill care and diligence in that it did not have due regard to the inherent risks the trading strategy could have for the efficient and orderly conduct of the MTS platform and it did not ensure that clear parameters for the size of the trade were understood, communicated and reviewed. The FSA also found the conduct to have breached Principle 3 because there was a failure to consult in relation to the trading and adequately to supervise the trades. See also the *Deutsche Bank AG final notice (10/4/06)* in which Deutsche Bank AG was fined for breaches of Principle 5 in connection with proprietary trading of shares in Scania AB (a Swedish track manufacturer) carried out through external brokers during the sensitive time of a bookbuild. Scania shares are listed on Sweden's Stockholmsbörsen, which was not a prescribed market for the purposes of the FSMA 2000, s 118. The trading had the potential to (and did) have a material effect on the price of the Scania shares concerned and gave potential investors a distorted understanding of the supply and demand for the Scania shares. Deutsche Bank was also fined for breach of Principle 2 for the failure of its former head of equity cash trading to get clearance from senior management or compliance or to check Deutsche Bank's restricted list before giving instructions for the proprietary trading. Deutsche Bank was fined for a further breach of Principle 2 because certain announcements made to Deutsche Bank's sales team which were passed on to potential investors were inaccurate and/or incomplete.

4 See the *Deutsche Bank AG final notice (10/4/06)*, *Barclays Bank Plc final notice (27/6/12)*, *UBS AG final notice (19/12/12)* and the *Royal Bank of Scotland plc final notice (6/2/13)* in connection with the submissions to LIBOR, which prior to the implementation of the Financial Services Act 2012 did not fall within the civil or criminal market abuse regimes. See also the *JP Morgan Chase Bank NA final notice (18/9/13)* in which JP Morgan was fined in connection with the so-called 'London Whale' trades carried out by an individual in its Chief Investment Office. The FCA found that JP Morgan had breached Principle 5 in that the size and manner of certain trading in the IG9 10 year index had the potential to affect the price of the IG9 10 year index at a time when JP Morgan's synthetic credit portfolio had stood to benefit from a lower price.

17.257 Among other things, this brings into sharp contrast the differentiation between the market abuse regime, which is classed as a criminal charge for ECHR purposes, and the disciplinary regime. As has been seen[1], there are protections available to firms and individuals charged with market abuse which are not ordinarily available in the context of regulatory disciplinary proceedings. For example, one potential outcome might be that where the FSA had insufficient evidence to bring proceedings for market abuse, because its evidence relied upon a statement which could not be used against the person who made it[2], it would instead bring disciplinary proceedings for breach of Principle 5 and use that statement in evidence in those disciplinary proceedings.

1 See the discussion at para **17.16** ff above.
2 The use of statements obtained by compulsory powers is discussed at para **17.142** ff above.

17.258 Furthermore, if the 'charges' related to an individual, the result of bringing regulatory disciplinary proceedings rather than market abuse proceedings might be to deny him the right to legal assistance (which he may have had in Tribunal proceedings for market abuse but would not have in Tribunal proceedings for a regulatory breach).

17.259 Finally, it is possible that in an appropriate case a breach of the regulatory general principles could constitute a criminal charge for ECHR purposes[1]. In that case, the ECHR criminal protections would need to be conferred and would give rise to a further issue of whether the offence was sufficiently clearly defined for ECHR purposes. It is possible that a disciplinary charge that consisted purely of a breach of a regulatory general principle might not comply.

1 This is discussed further at para **10.20** ff above.

When will the FCA seek to discipline an approved person?

17.260 If the market abuse regime overlaps with the Principles for Business applicable to firms, it also overlaps with the Statements of Principle for approved persons and, in particular, Statement of Principle 3, which obliges approved persons to observe proper standards of market conduct in carrying out their controlled functions.

17.261 Unfortunately, neither the Enforcement Guide nor the Code of Market Conduct, nor indeed the Code of Conduct for approved persons, contains much indication as to how this overlap is to be addressed. The Code of Conduct for approved persons indicates that whether or not the person complied with the Code of Market Conduct will be a relevant factor in determining whether or not he complied with the Statement of Principle, and that compliance with the Code of Market Conduct will tend to show compliance with Statement of Principle 3[1].

1 See the Handbooks at APER 4.3 and see para **2.45** ff above.

17.262 The FSA has previously brought proceedings for misconduct against individuals for breach of Statement of Principle 3 in relation to actions which did not constitute market abuse[1]. The FCA's general policy on when it will bring misconduct proceedings against individuals is discussed at para **9.23** ff above.

1 See for example the *Sean Julian Pignatelli final notice (20/11/06)* and the *Mark Lockwood final notice (1/9/09)*. The FSA has also taken action against individuals for breaches of Principles 2 and 6 for approved persons for failing to notice that certain transactions constituted market abuse, see the *Caspar Jonathan William Agnew final notice (3/10/11)* (Principle 2) and the *Alexander Edward Ten-Holter final notice 26/01/2012)* (Principle 6).

Civil liability arising from market abuse

17.263 Although it is possible to envisage market abuse resulting in significant losses across a large number of market users, the FSMA 2000 does not contain a coherent system of direct redress for those who suffer losses as a result of market abuse. In particular, there is no indication in the FSMA 2000 that market abuse would give rise to a breach of statutory duty claim for those who suffer loss[1] and the High Court has found that such a claim does not exist as a matter of law[2]. This is reinforced by the fact that the FCA has disapplied breach of statutory duty claims in relation to the Principles for Businesses, which are the regulatory hook linking market abuse to regulation[3].

1 If a specific FCA rule had been breached, then a breach of statutory duty claim under the FSMA 2000, s 138D may arise: see para **19.17** ff below.
2 See *Hall v Cable & Wireless plc [2009] EWHC 1793 (Comm)*, in which Teare J held that ss 123 and 383 of the FSMA 2000 'indicate that the intent of Parliament was that the object of the Act would be achieved by the imposition of penalties or restitution orders pursuant to ss 123 and 383. In those circumstances the absence of an express cause of action at the suit of a private person was a clear indication that none was intended'. This case concerned the FSMA 2000, s 150 which was replaced by the current s 138D, for these purposes the provisions are materially the same. This issue is discussed in more detail at para **19.19** ff below.
3 FCA Handbook at PRIN Sch 5.

17.264 This does not, though, mean that the firm committing market abuse can avoid paying any compensation. As has been seen[1], the FCA can make or apply for a restitution order requiring the firm to pay compensation and/or to disgorge profits. This is likely to be used particularly where significant numbers of consumers are involved[2]. Individual consumers may also be able to bring claims for compensation before the ombudsman, even where there is no clear cause of action as a matter of law[3]. Indeed, whether the firm has paid compensation is one of the factors to be taken into account by the FCA in determining what action to take in relation to the market abuse. This seems to assume that a remedy would be available.

1 See para **17.245** ff above.
2 See para **8.122** ff above.
3 This is discussed in **CHAPTER 14**.

17.265 Outside the regulatory arena, and the FSMA 2000, it may be possible that civil claims may be brought depending upon the circumstances and, particularly, the nature of the conduct constituting market abuse. For example, claims may be available based on negligent misstatement, misrepresentation, even fraud, or perhaps for breach of an implied contractual term. This would depend very much on the circumstances. Various potential claims are discussed in more detail in **CHAPTER 19**.

Chapter 18   Criminal prosecutions

OVERVIEW

18.1   The FCA has an important role as a criminal prosecutor of offences under the FSMA 2000 and other legislation. Martin Wheatley, Chief Executive of the FCA, made clear that the prosecution of criminal offences is not merely an adjunct to the FCA's remit, rather it goes to the heart of the FCA's statutory market integrity objective:

> '[...] the new FCA is not simply a consumer protection authority. It is not simply a markets orientated authority. It is just as much an enforcement authority, with a clear mandate to pursue prosecutions, issue fines, ban individuals from financial services and prevent future financial crime.'[1]

1   Speech by Martin Wheatley at the FCA Financial Crime Conference, 1 July 2013.

18.2   The PRA also has powers to commence criminal prosecutions, for example, where the contravention is of a requirement imposed by the PRA in its role as the 'appropriate regulator'[1]. The FCA, rather than the PRA is the lead prosecutor for insider dealing and other offences within the financial services sector. This chapter focuses on the FCA's role as prosecutor and considers the following:

- the FCA's powers to institute criminal proceedings and for what offences;

- in what circumstances the FCA will pursue criminal prosecutions, including how issues of overriding jurisdiction are resolved; and

- practical guidance for firms who are prosecuted or whose employees are prosecuted.

1   An exhaustive list of the offences where the PRA is defined as the 'appropriate regulator' can be found in the FSMA 2000, s 401(3A). Note that the PRA can also commence a criminal

prosecution for other offences with the consent of the Director of Public Prosecutions but that the specific list of offences does not include insider dealing or offences of misleading statements or practices under the Financial Services Act 2012.

18.3   The powers discussed in this chapter relate only to offences committed in England, Wales and Northern Ireland.

THE FCA AS A PROSECUTOR

18.4   The FCA has powers under the FSMA 2000, s 401 to prosecute a range of offences under the FSMA 2000. Section 402 of the FSMA 2000 grants the FCA powers to institute proceedings for contraventions of offences under other legislation[1].

1   In the case of *R v Rollins [2010] UKSC 39*, the Supreme Court held that the FSMA 2000, s 402 should not be read as setting out an exhaustive list of the offences that the FCA may prosecute. The FSA prosecuted Mr Rollins for insider dealing and money laundering pursuant to the Proceeds of Crime Act 2002, s 327. Mr Rollins contended that the FSA was not entitled to prosecute him for money laundering because the provisions of legislation did not grant statutory authority to do so. The Supreme Court rejected this contention and indicated that the FSA, constituted as a company limited by guarantee, was entitled to commence private prosecutions for criminal offences other than those listed in the FSMA 2000, ss 401 and 402.

18.5   The FCA may also prosecute other related criminal offences where to do so would be consistent with meeting any of its statutory objectives[1].

1   FCA Enforcement Guide at EG 12.1.

18.6   Those who could be prosecuted by the FCA include the firm itself, the firm's employees and officers and other individuals. The criminal offences of most relevance to these include:

- contravention of the s 19 general prohibition[1];

- false claims to be authorised or exempt[2];

- contravention of s 21 restrictions on financial promotions[3];

- disclosing confidential information in breach of a statutory restriction[4];

- knowingly or recklessly providing false or misleading statements to the Regulators[5];

- breach of prohibition orders[6];

- offences relating to listed securities[7];

- offences relating to insider dealing[8];

- offences under the Money Laundering Regulations 2007 and offences related to the financing of terrorist activities[9];

- offences relating to misleading statements and manipulative practices[10];

- in response to previous instances of LIBOR manipulation, the Financial Services Act 2012 created new offences in relation to making false or misleading statements in relation to benchmarks or creating a false or misleading impression as to the price or value of any investment or as to the interest rate appropriate to any transaction[11];

- when a senior manager of a deposit taker or dual-regulated investment firm takes a decision or fails to take steps to prevent a decision that falls far below the standard of conduct expected and ultimately leads to the failure of the institution[12].

1 FSMA 2000, s 23.
2 FSMA 2000, s 24.
3 FSMA 2000, s 25.
4 FSMA 2000, s 352.
5 FSMA 2000, s 398.
6 FSMA 2000, s 56(4).
7 FSMA 2000, ss 84–87.
8 Criminal Justice Act 1993, Pt V.
9 FSMA 2000, s 402.
10 FS Act 2012, ss 89–90.
11 FS Act 2012, s 91.
12 Financial Services (Banking Reform) Act 2013, ss 36–38.

18.7   The FCA's criminal powers supplement the civil market abuse regime as defined in the FSMA 2000, s 118. Therefore, in some cases there will be instances of market misconduct as defined in the FSMA 2000, s 118 that may also arguably involve a breach of the criminal law. When the FCA decides whether to commence criminal proceedings rather than impose a sanction for market abuse in relation to that misconduct, it will apply the basic principles set out in the Code for Crown Prosecutors[1]. See **CHAPTER 17** for a discussion of the civil market abuse regime.

1 Code for Crown Prosecutors, January 2013.

THE FCA'S APPROACH TO CRIMINAL ENFORCEMENT

18.8   The FCA's general policy is to pursue through the criminal justice system all those cases where criminal prosecution is 'appropriate'[1]. When it decides to bring criminal proceedings or to refer the matter to another prosecuting authority, the FCA will apply the basic principles set out in the Code for Crown Prosecutors (discussed below).

1 FCA Enforcement Guide at EG 12.2.

18.9   There has been a call for increased corporate and senior management criminal liability since the financial crisis and an increased willingness of prosecuting bodies in the UK, such as the Financial Services Authority (the former regulator) and the Serious Fraud Office (SFO), to step up prosecutorial activity. It is likely that this trend will continue under the FCA, with a focus, in particular, on prosecutions for insider dealing and market manipulation[1].

1 FCA Approach Document 'Journey to the FCA', October 2012, p 37.

18.10   Criminal prosecutions

18.10   The FCA maintains the same leniency policy as the FSA had, which will enable the FCA to issue immunity notices that give a co-operating individual legal protection against prosecution by all UK authorities. This is a powerful tool for the FCA in prosecuting more complex cases of multi-party financial crime[1].

1   The Coroners and Justice Act 2009, s 113(3)(a) amended the Serious Organised Crime and Police Act 2005, s 71 to list the FSA (and now the FCA) as an authority that can issue an immunity notice.

Which body has jurisdiction to investigate and prosecute?

18.11   Not every potential criminal offence within the financial services arena will be investigated and prosecuted by the FCA. This is for two reasons. First, various other bodies have overlapping powers of investigation and prosecution including the SFO, National Crime Agency (NCA)[1], the City of London Police and Crown Prosecution Service (CPS). Second, not every potential criminal offence is suitable to be addressed through the criminal justice system.

1   The NCA was launched in October 2013, replacing the Serious Organised Crime Agency and other bodies.

18.12   The difficulties that this could cause are mitigated by guidelines agreed between the FCA and various other bodies involved[1]. The guidelines are intended to assist the agencies[2] when considering cases concerning financial crime and/or regulatory misconduct that are, or may be, of mutual interest to the FCA and one or more of the other agencies. Their implementation and wider points arising from them will be kept under review by the agencies who will liaise regularly.

1   'Guidelines on investigation of cases of interest or concern to the Financial Conduct Authority and other prosecuting and investigating agencies', FCA Enforcement Guide, Annex 2.
2   The guidelines concern the following agencies: the FCA; the SFO; the Department for Business, Innovation and Skills; the CPS; the Association of Chief Police Officers of England, Wales and Northern Ireland; the Crown Office and Procurator Fiscal Service; the Public Prosecution Service for Northern Ireland; and the Association of Chief Police Officers in Scotland.

18.13   In summary, the guidelines include these key points:

- only the agency or agencies with the most appropriate functions and powers will commence investigations;

- if there are concurrent investigations, the agencies involved must keep each other informed of major developments, before taking significant steps and before deciding whether or not to pursue proceedings; and

- the agencies will notify each other at the conclusion of proceedings or, if no proceedings are taken, at the conclusion of the investigation.

18.14   The guidelines do not preclude concurrent investigations by several bodies. Indeed, given the different powers, responsibilities and objectives of each organisation, it may be necessary for more than one to be involved. Alternatively, one organisation may investigate with the support of other bodies. The focus is therefore on co-ordination and co-operation.

What types of cases are suitable for the FCA?

18.15 As to what types of cases are likely to be suitable for prosecution by the FCA, the guidelines contain two lists of factors, one setting out those factors which tend towards action by the FCA, and the other showing those tending towards action by one of the other agencies.

18.16 Factors tending towards action by the FCA are[1]:

- where the conduct gives rise to concerns about market confidence or the protection of consumers of services regulated by the FCA;

- where the conduct would best be dealt with by criminal prosecution of offences which the FCA has powers to prosecute by virtue of the FSMA 2000, the use of the FCA's civil powers under the FSMA 2000 or those disciplinary and enforcement powers available to the FCA as regulator or UK Listing Authority (UKLA);

- where the likely defendants are authorised firms or approved persons (and probably senior persons and certain other employees of firms in the future[2] or listed companies, applicants for listing, directors or sponsors subject to the FCA's powers in its role as UKLA);

- where the FCA is likely to use its other powers, which may take immediate effect;

- where it is likely the investigator will be seeking assistance from overseas regulatory authorities with functions equivalent to those of the FCA;

- where possible criminal offences are technical or in a grey area, whereas the regulatory contraventions are clear;

- where the balance of public interest is in achieving reparation for victims and prosecution is likely to damage those prospects; and

- where there are distinct parts of the case that are best investigated with financial services regulatory expertise.

1 FCA Enforcement Guide, Annex 2.
2 See para **2.52** ff above.

18.17 Factors tending towards action by other bodies are:

- where the main issues are best dealt with by other bodies, for example:

    - serious or complex fraud (which tends towards action by the SFO);

    - criminal proceedings where the FCA is not the statutory prosecutor[1];

    - directors disqualification proceedings, winding up proceedings or proceedings relating to the abuse of limited liability under the Companies Acts (Insolvency Service); or

    - criminal proceedings in Scotland;

- where powers of arrest are likely to be necessary;

18.17 Criminal prosecutions

- where it is likely the investigator will rely on overseas law enforcement agencies with whom the other body liaises regularly;

- where action by the FCA is likely to prejudice the public interest in the prosecution of offences for which the FCA is not the statutory prosecutor; and

- where the matters arising in the case fall only partly within the areas regulated by the FCA and the prospects of splitting the investigation are not good.

1 For example, the FCA is not a designated prosecutor under the Bribery Act 2010.

18.18 The general approach seems clear from this. There is a distinct regulatory arena within which it is likely that the FCA will investigate and prosecute, provided that it has the necessary powers to do so. But the FCA will not always be the prosecuting body. Where there are wider issues, it may be that one of the other bodies is better placed or that more than one organisation should be involved.

18.19 From the firm's point of view, the identity of the investigating and prosecuting body probably matters less than general co-ordination and liaison. Wherever possible, firms will want to avoid the uncertainty and the additional time and cost of being subjected to multiple investigations.

In what circumstances will the FCA prosecute?

18.20 Not every case where the FCA has the power to prosecute and which is appropriate for the FCA, rather than some other investigatory or prosecuting body, to handle will result in a criminal prosecution.

18.21 The FCA's general policy is only to pursue through the criminal justice system those cases where criminal prosecution is 'appropriate'[1]. In deciding whether it is appropriate to prosecute, the FCA applies the two tests set out in the Code for Crown Prosecutors:

- *the evidential test:* is there sufficient evidence to provide a realistic prospect of conviction against the defendant on each criminal charge?; and

- *the public interest test:* having regard to the seriousness of the offence and all the circumstances, is criminal prosecution in the public interest?

1 FCA Enforcement Guide at EG 12.1.

18.22 Each test will briefly be considered in turn.

The evidential test

18.23 The evidential test[1] requires the FCA to consider whether the evidence is such that an objective, impartial and reasonable jury or judge hearing a case alone, properly directed, is more likely than not to convict the defendant of each charge alleged. It involves considering what evidence can be used and whether it is reliable and credible. It also involves considering the likely defence. A case which does not pass the evidential stage must not proceed, no matter how serious or sensitive it may be.

1   For further guidance, see the Code for Crown Prosecutors, January 2013, paras 4.4–4.6.

The public interest test

18.24   Only if the evidential test is passed will the FCA go on to consider the public interest test. As the name indicates, not every case where there is sufficient evidence to obtain a conviction will result in the FCA starting criminal proceedings. The question is whether starting proceedings is in the public interest.

18.25   In deciding whether or not prosecution is in the public interest, the FCA is required to balance carefully and fairly the factors for and against prosecution, which will usually relate to the seriousness of the offence and the circumstances of the suspect. Some commonly relevant factors can be found in the Code for Crown Prosecutors[1]. Among other things, this makes clear that a prosecution will normally take place in serious cases unless there are public interest factors militating against a prosecution which outweigh those in favour.

1   See the Code for Crown Prosecutors 2013, paras 4.12(a)–(g).

18.26   Where the FCA is able to take regulatory enforcement action as well as bringing criminal proceedings, one issue that the FCA may need to consider is that it tends to take longer to conclude criminal proceedings than regulatory enforcement action.

Additional factors

18.27   Some additional factors[1] are relevant in cases of market misconduct, which overlap with the market abuse regime.

1   The additional factors can be found at: FCA Enforcement Guide at EG 12.8(1)–(13).

18.28   When considering whether to prosecute a breach of the Money Laundering Regulations 2007 (SI 2007/2157), the FCA will also have regard to whether the person concerned has followed the Guidance for the UK financial sector issued by the Joint Money Laundering Steering Group[1].

1   FCA Enforcement Guide at EG 12.2.

Deferred Prosecution Agreements

18.29   The Crime and Courts Act 2013 introduced the mechanism of Deferred Prosecution Agreements (DPA) to suspend investigations into co-operating corporate organisations. A DPA provides that charges will be laid but not proceeded with subject to a co-operating corporate organisation agreeing to a set of agreed terms and conditions, such as a payment of a fine and the implementation of remediation programmes.

18.30   A number of specific offences under the FSMA 2000 for which the FCA is deemed the 'appropriate regulator' are included in the Crime and Courts Act 2013, Sch 17 as offences which may be dealt with by using a DPA[1].

1   At the date of writing, only the SFO and CPS are identified as 'designated prosecutors' able to enter into a DPA under the Crime and Courts Act 2013 and are able to do so from 24 February 2014. The FCA may well decide to apply to become a 'designated prosecutor' in the future.

Interviews conducted by the FCA

18.31   One of the first steps in an FCA investigation is the interviewing of relevant individuals. The information gathering and investigation process is considered in further detail in **CHAPTERS 4** and **5**. The FCA will determine the type of interview – either voluntary, compelled or under caution. A failure to attend an interview or a refusal to answer questions in a compulsory interview following a notice may be treated as a contempt of court leading to potential fines or imprisonment.

18.32   Answers given in interviews under compulsion cannot be used in criminal prosecutions for insider dealing or market abuse but could be used in internal disciplinary proceedings instituted by a firm for breach of the FCA rules. The right to self-incrimination protection will apply in a compulsory interview.

When will the FCA administer a caution instead?

18.33   The FCA has indicated[1] that it may, in some cases, decide to issue a formal caution rather than to prosecute an offender. In such cases the FCA will follow the Ministry of Justice guidance on simple cautions for adult offenders[2] and not issue a caution unless it is satisfied that:

- there is sufficient evidence of the person's guilt to give a realistic prospect of conviction;

- the person admits the offence; and

- the person understands the significance of a caution and gives informed consent to being cautioned.

1   FCA Enforcement Guide at EG 12.5.
2   FCA Enforcement Guide at EG 12.5 states that the FCA must follow the guidance contained in the Home Office Circular 16/2008. This was replaced on 8 April 2013 with the Ministry of Justice – Simple Caution for Adult Offender guidance. The Ministry of Justice guidance applies to all decisions relating to simple cautions from the commencement date, regardless of when the offence was committed.

18.34   Where the FCA decides to administer a formal caution, a record of the caution will be kept by the FCA and on the Police National Computer. Although the FCA will not publish the caution, it will be available to parties with access to the Police National Computer.

What are the consequences of accepting a caution?

18.35 The primary effect of a caution, from the perspective of the person concerned, is that he is not subject to criminal prosecution. This will often be the main aim and the overriding factor. However, accepting a caution has important implications. Significantly, a caution is an admission of guilt to committing the offence and forms part of a person's criminal record[1].

1 Further implications of accepting a caution can be found in the Ministry of Justice – Simple Caution for Adult Offender Guidance, paras 53–64.

18.36 If the offender is a firm or approved person (or senior person or certain other employee, see para **2.52** ff), a caution given by the FCA will form part of the firm's or individual's regulatory record. The FCA may also take into account any caution when deciding whether to take disciplinary action for subsequent regulatory misconduct by the firm or individual. Finally, the FCA may take a caution into account when considering a person's honesty, integrity and reputation and his fitness or propriety to perform controlled or other functions in relation to regulated activities.

Civil or regulatory action in support of a criminal prosecution

18.37 In cases where criminal proceedings have commenced or will be commenced, the FCA may consider whether also to take civil or regulatory action (for example where this is appropriate for the protection of consumers) and how such action should be pursued.

18.38 As a general rule, the mere fact that there are criminal proceedings does not prevent civil or regulatory proceedings relating to the same matter from continuing. The prosecution of civil or administrative proceedings may, though, be required to await the outcome of the criminal proceedings where there is a real risk of the criminal proceedings being prejudiced (for example, because both proceedings involve adjudication of the same issue). There is, however, no reason why civil or regulatory action should not continue in parallel. It should be borne in mind that the process of disclosure in civil proceedings could lead to evidence of an additional criminal offence which could result in an additional criminal charge being brought.

18.39 Such supportive action instigated by the FCA may include:
- obtaining injunctions;
- obtaining restitution orders;
- variation or cancellation of an individuals permission; and
- prohibition of individuals.

18.40   Criminal prosecutions

18.40   A non-exhaustive list of the factors the FCA may take into account when deciding to take such action are[1]:

- whether, in the FCA's opinion, the taking of civil or regulatory action might unfairly prejudice the prosecution, or proposed prosecution, of criminal offences;

- whether, in the FCA's opinion, the taking of civil or regulatory action might unfairly prejudice the defendants in the criminal proceedings in the conduct of their defence; and

- whether it is appropriate to take civil or regulatory action, having regard to the scope of the criminal proceedings and the powers available to the criminal courts.

1   FCA Enforcement Guide at EG 12.4.

What does this mean in practice?

18.41   The FCA will follow the path of FSA in pursuing criminal cases where it can find a reasonable case and does not believe its other enforcement powers are a sufficient deterrent.

18.42   The FCA must, in accordance with the Code for Crown Prosecutors, act fairly, independently and objectively when considering whether to pursue a criminal case. The FCA may also consider its parallel enforcement function. It is thought that the need to take other enforcement action, such as imposing a restitution order, is a legitimate, and may be an important, factor in the public interest test. As a result, it may be that the decision whether or not to prosecute is, in practice, simply another aspect of the decision on what enforcement action is appropriate in all the circumstances of the case.

PRACTICAL GUIDANCE FOR FIRMS

18.43   If the firm, or one of its employees, is the subject of a prosecution, or the firm can see that this is likely to be the case, then what practical steps should the firm be taking? Should it stand by its employee? How should it deal with its regulator, who may also be the prosecutor? Some of the practical issues that arise are considered here, and, in particular:

- What approach should the firm take as against its employee?

- Should the firm continue to co-operate with the FCA?

- Are there any practical steps that the firm can take to protect its position?

What approach should the firm take as against its employee?

18.44 One of the most difficult issues where an employee is charged with a criminal offence is what position the firm should take as against the employee and the approach a firm takes against an employee will likely evolve as the nature and extent of any wrongdoing becomes clear and depending on the nature of the investigation. At one end of the spectrum, the firm might publicly and privately support the individual. At the other end, it could take a hard line and implement its own steps to discipline him, without waiting for the outcome of the criminal trial.

18.45 There is a range of other options, which may perhaps involve waiting for the outcome before the firm commits itself and in the meantime providing financial and other assistance for the employee in relation to his defence. The firm will need to consider what is appropriate in the light of any restrictions in the firm's articles of association or as prescribed in any directors and officers (D&O) insurance policy.

18.46 What approach it is appropriate for the firm to take is impossible to conclude in the abstract. It depends very much upon factors such as the nature of the investigation, the firm's view of the evidence against the individual, the extent to which he may have breached his contract of employment, the relationship between the individual and the firm, whether the FCA is pressing the firm to take any particular line and internal factors and pressures within the firm. In practice, it is unlikely the firm could simply await the outcome of the criminal process; it will probably need to take its own decision.

18.47 A particular point which ought to be addressed when a criminal charge against the individual seems to be in prospect is to ensure that the individual understands the need to get his own independent legal advice. It will often be inappropriate for the firm's lawyers, internal or external, to be representing the individual at that stage, given the clear potential conflict between his interests and those of the firm. The individual needs to understand this and, particularly, that the firm's in-house counsel are not acting for him personally. To illustrate the conflict, if the individual admitted the offence to the firm's lawyers, or even admitted sufficient facts or matters for the firm to conclude, that he may have committed the offence, the firm may be obliged to report that information to the FCA, and could expose itself to discipline or other regulatory action if it failed to do so. The firm would also need to consider taking disciplinary action against the individual, which may include questioning him about the same matters.

Should the firm continue to co-operate with the FCA?

18.48 Assuming that it is the firm, as well as, or instead of, the individual against whom the criminal charge is laid by the FCA acting as criminal prosecutor, the question arises as to how that affects the firm's relationship with the FCA in its capacity as regulator.

18.49 A firm has an obligation of openness and co-operation with the FCA. The institution of a criminal charge against the firm does not relieve it of that obligation. There may still be an ongoing investigation or enforcement process and the firm will need to co-operate with the FCA for those purposes. It may wish to do so to avoid exacerbating the problem and causing the FCA to have other concerns about the firm that could lead to it seeking to exercise additional enforcement powers, for example, to vary or cancel the firm's permission[1]. In addition, beyond the instant enforcement process, the firm has an ongoing supervisory relationship with the FCA to consider. Where the FCA continues to investigate or take other enforcement action, notwithstanding a criminal charge has been instituted against the firm, there will be issues about self-incrimination privilege (see the discussion on the use of material by the FCA in criminal prosecutions at para **4.204** ff above).

1 The question whether the FCA can exercise its enforcement powers as well as bringing a criminal prosecution is considered at para **18.37** above.

Are there any practical steps the firm can take to protect its position?

18.50 Where the firm is, or is likely to be, prosecuted, there are some basic steps that it can take to protect its position, namely:

- to preserve all relevant records;

- not unnecessarily to create further documents that might incriminate it;

- to take legal advice at all stages of the process; and

- in accordance with its legal advice, to obtain the best evidence available to explain its actions and defend itself.

Chapter 19   Civil liability

INTRODUCTION

19.1   The primary focus of discussion thus far has been on the potential regulatory implications of a problem. However, the significant volume of civil litigation that has been brought against firms in the wake of the financial crisis is a reminder that it is important not to lose sight of the possible civil law implications, in particular the firm's potential exposure to claims from customers, employees, or other third parties. To some extent, those potential claims arise from the FSMA 2000, but they also arise more generally. This chapter outlines some of the main issues[1] and, in particular, considers:

- some practical guidance for firms[2];

- the firm's potential civil liability under the FSMA 2000[3];

- the firm's potential liability as a matter of general law[4]; and

- certain practical issues arising from the regulatory process that may impact on the firm's potential civil liability[5].

How to respond to any criminal liability that might arise is considered at **CHAPTER 18.**

1 The procedure for bringing or defending civil claims is not discussed here. For a discussion, see the Civil Procedure Rules.
2 See para **19.8** ff below.
3 See para **19.17** ff below.
4 See para **19.57** ff below.
5 See para **19.71** ff below.

Why might the firm incur civil liability?

19.2   In many situations where a problem arises, in addition to possible breaches of the applicable regulatory requirements, the firm may also have breached a legal obligation which it owes to customers or other third parties and in doing so caused them to suffer financial or other losses for which it could be required to compensate them[1]. As will be seen, the firm's exposure to civil liability may arise directly from a finding or admission that regulatory breaches have been committed, or it could arise entirely independently from the regulatory breaches, or it could arise in a situation where there are no regulatory issues.

1   Major problems which have both had regulatory implications and caused widely reported civil litigation include interest rate swaps and mis-selling cases, including in relation to structured products and the LIBOR scandal.

19.3   Moreover, whilst the focus of this chapter is on possible claims for damages, it is important to recognise that other remedies could be sought. For example, a party might seek an injunction requiring the firm to take a particular step[1], such as to transfer assets belonging to another party or, where the firm acts as a trustee[2], to bring claims against other parties on behalf of the beneficiaries; or an injunction requiring it to refrain from taking some step[3], for example committing further or threatened[4] breaches of its legal obligations.

1   For a general discussion of mandatory injunctions, see Spry, *Equitable Remedies* (8th edn, 2010) at pp 535–539.
2   For example, of a pension fund or unit trust.
3   For a general discussion of injunctions, see Spry, *Equitable Remedies* (8th edn, 2010) at Ch 4.
4   In some circumstances, an injunction may be available on a quia timet basis, to restrain a threatened breach: see Spry, *Equitable Remedies* (8th edn, 2010) at pp 377–382.

19.4   A person who has suffered loss may be able to establish that the firm is liable to him under general legal principles. However, in various situations he need not do so: he may choose to avail himself of the FSMA 2000, which itself provides a means for obtaining redress in certain circumstances to those who suffer loss, by way of an action similar to that for breach of statutory duty[1]. The FSMA 2000 also impacts in other ways upon the firm's potential liability[2].

1   The primary provision is the FSMA 2000, s 138D. The relevant provisions are discussed at para **19.19** ff below.
2   See para **19.32** ff below.

19.5   This discussion must, however, be placed in context. In some cases, particularly those involving regulatory problems which cause loss to significant numbers of consumers, market abuse/market manipulation, failing firms or breaches of the perimeter, the FCA or PRA (as the case may be) may address the issue of compensation by exercising their powers to obtain restitution on behalf of those who have suffered losses[1]. A similar result could be achieved by the FCA or PRA applying to the court for an injunction to require the firm to rectify its breach[2]. However, in practice, in many cases, the firm is likely to decide voluntarily to compensate customers as part of its own response to the regulatory issue[3]. Also, individual customers may themselves seek compensation through the

Financial Ombudsman Service (FOS)[4]. It should follow that the likelihood of individual customers pursuing claims through the civil courts in practice will be small. However, in recent years there has been a number of individual customers who have been prepared to pursue claims through the civil courts. These cases, broadly speaking, have usually been brought by either wealthy or sophisticated private investors who have alleged that their investment losses are attributable to the firm; or by retail banking customers who have complained that charges have been levelled unfairly by firms (for example, in respect of unauthorised overdraft charges or payment protection insurance).

1 For an example of a regulator-imposed restitution requirement, see the *Rameshkumar Satyanarayan Goenka final notice (17/10/11)*, in which the FSA imposed both a financial penalty plus restitution for actions said to have amounted to market abuse (market manipulation).
2 See para **8.150** ff above.
3 See the discussion at para **3.106** ff above and para **19.73** ff below and para **8.103** ff above.
4 See **CHAPTER 14** above. In practice, the taking of such action by customers where firms have co-operated with the FCA or PRA in negotiating the conclusion of disciplinary or enforcement action, can be a problem for firms. Although the extent of compensation may have been agreed with the FCA or PRA, customers may still decide to approach the FOS in order to seek alternative redress.

19.6 Understanding the firm's potential exposure to civil law claims is important when assessing what compensation to offer or, on rare occasions, the amount of a restitution order. Therefore, the principles outlined here may be relevant even when the firm anticipates being able to address the issue of compensation without recourse being made to the civil courts.

19.7 In this chapter, before considering the avenues for redress available both under the FSMA 2000 and the general law, some practical guidance for firms in the area of civil liability generally is first highlighted.

PRACTICAL GUIDANCE FOR FIRMS

19.8 Whilst the nature and extent of those claims that might be made against the firm will depend entirely upon the particular situation, some general practical points can be made. First, it is prudent for firms to be alert, throughout the regulatory process, to the potential for claims to be made against them, not only by customers, but also by market counterparties involved in the relevant transaction and any other parties who may have suffered financial loss as a result of the firm's actions. The starting point for a firm is to consider: (1) who may have suffered loss as a result of its actions; and (2) whether there is likely to be any legal basis for those persons to recover their alleged losses, from the firm[1].

1 The limitation rules also need to be borne in mind. In some circumstances, it may be possible for the relevant claims to be statute barred because of the time taken before the issue is litigated. The rules are complex: for a detailed discussion, see *Butterworths Law of Limitation* (1st edn, 2000).

19.9 Second, the question of what loss was suffered will be an important issue. Actionable losses are not necessarily limited to direct losses: depending on the circumstances, they may also include, to some extent, the relevant person's indirect losses, such as his exposure to others arising from the firm's actions[1]. The need to prove loss and to show that it was caused in legal terms by the firm's actions; is not too remote; and is of a type for which a court will award compensation, will in many situations be one of the most significant difficulties for third parties seeking to recover from the firm[2]. There may also be a question of whether the claimant took appropriate steps to mitigate his loss, which can give rise to important tactical options for the firm after the issue has arisen.

1   The rules on the losses that can be recovered are complex. For a detailed discussion, see *McGregor on Damages* (18th edn, 2009).
2   See further the discussion at paras **19.26** ff and **19.75** below.

19.10   Third, whether there is a legal basis for the firm to be liable for a person's losses will depend upon the situation. In some cases, the basis of the third party's claim will be fairly clear, but in others it will be less clear. Firms should not underestimate the capacity of third parties to be inventive in situations where no obvious claim exists. Nonetheless, in considering whether a third party is likely to have a realistic claim, there are a number of questions which the firm should ask itself, for example:

- Does the firm owe any obligations to those who have suffered loss under the terms of any relevant contracts, both express terms and any terms which might be implied?

- Does the firm owe any non-contractual duties to anyone who might have suffered loss, which could form the basis of a claim in negligence?

- Did the firm provide any incorrect or misleading information to the person, on the basis of which they may have contracted with the firm?

- Is the firm acting as trustee, or otherwise in a fiduciary capacity, or has it received any property from, or otherwise been involved in assisting, a person acting in such a capacity?

If another firm had a more direct interface with the customers who suffered loss, but the firm was at least partly responsible for causing that loss, then the firm may have an exposure to a contribution claim.

19.11   Fourth, the firm may itself wish to bring proceedings against one or more parties, for example, to recover assets or to bring an action against directors, employees or others. Indeed, in some situations the firm may be under a duty to bring legal proceedings on behalf of customers or others. Also, legal claims may not only be brought against the firm but may also be directed at others such as its past and present directors or employees.

19.12   Fifth, if civil claims are brought, the details of those claims will, generally speaking, be public. The claim form issued to commence a civil action is a public document that is normally available for public inspection, as are most judgments and orders given or made in public (whether made at a hearing or without a hearing)[1]. Likewise, the usual rule is that court hearings are held in public[2]. (In certain limited circumstances it is possible to apply for orders restricting public access.) Therefore, in much the same way as the publication of information about enforcement action by the FCA can result in the multiplication and escalation of customer complaints[3], civil claims often carry a clear risk to the firm of garnering negative publicity and potential 'copy-cat' claims.

1 See the Civil Procedure Rules (CPR) at CPR 5.4C. Additionally, a person who is not a party to the proceedings may apply to the court for permission for a copy from the court records of any other statement of case, see CPR PD 5A, para 5C.
2 See CPR 5.4 and CPR 39.2.
3 See the FCA's Policy Statement PS13/9 'Publishing information about enforcement warning notices' (15 October 2013); and the FCA Enforcement Guide at EG Chapter 6.

19.13 Finally, one of the reasons why in practice there has not been a major trend of consumer-led civil proceedings in the UK stemming from high profile regulatory issues is the lack of any mechanisms for bringing US-style class actions. Inertia among individual claimants and the lack of a 'plaintiff bar' with the incentive to push forward claims have tended to favour firms. (As already discussed, the regulatory system has instead tended to result in customer compensation being paid without the need for proceedings.)

19.14 However, firms cannot be sure that class action type claims will not be brought against them. It is now common for firms with US investors to see class actions commenced in the US courts on the basis of regulatory action in the UK[1]. Additionally, English civil procedure provides a number of mechanisms which can be used to manage multi-party litigation, including group litigation orders[2] and representative actions[3]. Furthermore, in some circumstances where a firm faces a real possibility of multiple claims, it might consider funding a test case so as to resolve a common factual dispute or establish the extent of its liability at law[4].

1 See, for example, the Class Action Complaint filed on 10 July 2012 in the United States District Court, Southern District of New York against Barclays PLC et al (case number 12 Civ 5329 (SAS)), which relied on alleged admissions made by Barclays in a settlement reached on 27 June 2012 with the FSA, the US Commodity Futures Trading Commission, the US Securities Exchange Commission and the US Department of Justice with respect to Barclays' conduct in manipulating LIBOR rates. As is common in such cases, the action was not only brought against Barclays PLC and various of its subsidiaries, but also against its current and former senior executives. A motion to dismiss was granted by order of Judge Shira Scheindlin on 13 May 2013. Note that US courts do not always limit the claimant class to US investors.
2 See CPR Pt 19.III. A court may make a group litigation order where there are multiple claims giving rise to common or related issues of fact or law: see CPR 19.10 and 19.11. A UK-style group litigation order is fundamentally different from a US-style class action. In the UK, a party must opt in by bringing an action of their own which is covered by the group litigation order. In the US, the court will define the relevant class and thereafter, all such persons falling within the class will be entitled to a share of any compensation awarded, irrespective of whether they actively participate in the action, unless they opt out of the action. For a detailed commentary: see Hodges, *Multi-Party Actions* (1st edn, 2001) at Chapter 3, para 3.01. A list of Group Litigation Orders together with brief details of each case appears on the Court Service's website.
3 See CPR Pt 19.II. This allows actions to be started by one or more person as representatives of a larger group of persons who have the same interest in the claim. The 'same interest' requirement is narrower than the 'common or related issues of fact or law' test applicable to group litigation orders (for consideration of the boundaries of the 'same interest' requirement, see the commentary to the Civil Procedure Rules at CPR 19.6 ff). As a result, representative actions rarely occur in practice.

4 Test cases arise in England under the court's CPR Part 3 case management powers. Where a large number of individual claims are pending, each raising common factual or legal issues, the parties may select one or a small number of those claims to be prosecuted to final determination; and the court possesses the power under the CPR 3.1(2)(f) to stay the remainder, either on its own initiative or with the consent of the parties. Additionally, any potential claimants can, subject to the expiry of any relevant limitation period, delay the commencement of their suits pending determination of the test case. The decision taken on the common point of fact or law will have precedential effect in respect of the remaining actions which have been stayed; and any future actions with that point of fact or law in common. While the decision will not finally determine those remaining actions, the parties to those actions will reap the benefit of certainty on the point of fact or law decided, which will be valuable both in settlement negotiations and any decision to prosecute the action to finality. For example, *Graiseley Properties Ltd v Barclays Bank Plc [2012] EWHC 3093* is a case which was transferred to the Commercial Court from the Birmingham Mercantile Court as a potential test case relating to LIBOR manipulation.

19.15 Moreover, there is a continuing push towards reforming the UK group litigation rules, insofar as they apply to the financial services sector, to provide mechanisms for collective redress which are more akin to US style class-actions. Most notably, the Financial Services Bill 2009 initially contained provisions for consumers to issue collective proceedings for financial services claims against FSA-regulated firms and persons, on an opt-out basis. Although ultimately, these provisions were withdrawn from the Bill following the announcement of the 2010 general election, certain other provisions of the Bill directed at collective redress survived the passage into law[1]; and collective redress has continued to drive legislative and regulatory change in the financial services sector and in other spheres, both in the UK and in Europe[2].

1 The changes introduced by the Financial Services Act 2010, which was passed on 8 April 2010, included a replacement to the FSMA 2000, s 404 and new ss 404A–404G, which gave the FSA certain powers with respect to 'consumer redress schemes'. Under the new FSMA 2000, s 404, if (a) it appears to the FCA that there may have been a widespread or regular failure by relevant firms to comply with requirements applicable to the carrying on by them of an activity and, (b) as a result, it appears that consumers have suffered or may suffer loss or damage in respect of which, if they brought legal proceedings, a remedy or relief would be available in the proceedings, then (c) if the FCA considers it desirable to make rules for the purposes of securing that redress is made to the consumers in respect of the failure, the FCA may make rules requiring each relevant firm which has carried on that activity to establish and operate a consumer redress scheme. The FSA employed this provision in December 2012 in respect of Arch cru funds: see the FCA Handbook at CONRED 2.
2 On 11 June 2013, the European Commission set out a series of common, non-binding principles for collective redress mechanisms in the Member States, which the Commission recommended 'should be available in different areas where EU law grants rights to citizens and companies, notably in consumer protection, competition, environment protection and financial services': see European Commission Press Release, 'Commission recommends Member States to have collective redress mechanisms in place to ensure effective access to justice' (Strasbourg, 11 June 2013).

19.16 More recently in the UK, the push towards collective redress reforms was the driving force behind the FSA, in September 2011, introducing new Dispute Resolution: Complaints Handling Rules (DISP), which created new requirements for firms to carry out proactive redress exercises[1] and also gave the FOS a regulatory role in setting the standards by which firms must adjudge their potential liability, by taking account of the FOS's published online decisions as well as decisions they receive directly from the FOS when considering customer complaints[2].

1 See the FCA Handbook at DISP 1: Treating complainants fairly.
2 See DISP 1.3.2A, 1.3.6, 1.4.

CIVIL LIABILITY UNDER THE FSMA 2000

19.17 The FSMA 2000 affects, in a number of ways, the civil claims that might arise from a matter which amounts to a regulatory breach. First, in some situations it gives certain people a right of action based on the regulatory breach, primarily on the grounds of a breach of statutory duty. Second, it makes clear that in other situations no right of action arises from the breach. Third, it makes certain types of agreement unenforceable. Fourth, it clarifies that certain types of agreements are not unenforceable. Each of these situations is considered below.

Actions for breach of statutory duty

19.18 The FSMA 2000 contains one general right of action applicable in a range of situations; as well as certain specific rights applicable in specific situations. The formulation for each is similar, but there are differences. The following paragraphs first consider the general right of action, and its various elements, before briefly reviewing other rights of action available in specific situations.

The general right of action

19.19 The general right of action arises under the FSMA 2000, s 138D, in respect of certain rules made by the FCA; and certain other rules made by the PRA. Its scope depends first on which of the Regulators made the rule in question; and second on whether the rule is caught by the section. In respect of rules made by the FCA, the general right of action will apply unless the rule specifically provides otherwise or is excluded by s 138D itself. In respect of rules made by the PRA, the general right of action will only apply if the rule specifically so provides. Where the rule is caught by the section, then:

A   a contravention (in the case of rules made by the PRA, by anyone; in the case of rules made by the FCA, by an authorised person) of the rule;

B   is actionable at the suit of a private person;

C   who suffers loss as a result of the contravention;

D   subject to the defences and other incidents applying to actions for breach of statutory duty; and

E   in prescribed cases, is actionable on the same basis at the suit of a person who is not a private person, subject to the defences and other incidents applying to actions for breach of statutory duty.

19.20 This provision (including in its previous guise prior to the Financial Services Act 2012 amendments) has given rise to actions against firms in

19.20 Civil liability

situations where the firm has committed some kind of regulatory breach which has caused loss to a customer or another party[1]. Each of the elements of this test are considered in turn.

1 See eg *Rubenstein v HSBC Bank plc [2012] EWCA Civ 1184, [2013] 1 All ER (Comm) 915*. Note that the statutory right of action under these provisions does not preclude an action for breach of duty under the common law: see *Gorham v British Telecommunications plc [2000] EWCA Civ 234, [2000] 4 All ER 867, CA*. See also the Explanatory Notes to the Financial Services Bill as introduced in the House of Commons on 26 January 2012, para 275.

A. Contravention of a rule

19.21   As noted above, there must have been a contravention of a rule made by the FCA or the PRA which is caught by the FSMA 2000, s 138D. The following rules are not caught:

- rules made by the PRA which do not specify that contravention gives rise to the right of action[1];

- rules made by the FCA which specify that contravention does not give rise to the right of action[2];

- listing rules made by the FCA in its capacity as UK Listing Authority under the FSMA 2000, Pt 6[3];

- rules made by the FCA or PRA under the FSMA 2000, s 137O, supplementing the threshold conditions set out in or specified in the FSMA 2000, Sch 6[4];

- rules made by the FCA or PRA under the FSMA 2000, s 192J, requiring qualifying parent undertakings to provide information or produce documents relevant to the exercise by the regulator of its functions[5]; and

- rules made by the FCA or PRA requiring an authorised person to have or maintain financial resources[6].

1 FSMA 2000, s 138D(1).
2 FSMA 2000, s 138D(2). Most notably, this includes the Principles for Businesses: see para **2.12** ff above. It is an unusual feature of the regime that the FCA and PRA respectively can control the extent to which civil claims may arise from rule breaches. This topic was the subject of considerable debate when the legislation was considered by Parliament.
3 FSMA 2000, s 138D(5)(a) The FCA also acts under the FSMA 2000, Pt 6 as a securities regulator, referred to as the UK Listing Authority or UKLA. See **CHAPTER 20** below.
4 FSMA 2000, s138D(5)(b). Pursuant to the FSMA 2000, s 55B, in giving or varying permission, imposing or varying a requirement, or giving consent to carry on regulated activities, under any provision of the FSMA 2000, Pt 4A, each regulator must ensure that the person concerned will satisfy, and continue to satisfy, in relation to all of the regulated activities for which the person has or will have permission, the threshold conditions for which that regulator is responsible, including the threshold conditions set out in the FSMA 2000, Sch 6; and the rules made pursuant to the FSMA 2000, s137O, which rules are said to comprise the 'threshold condition code'.
5 FSMA 2000, s 138D(5)(c).
6 FSMA 2000, s 138D(5)(d). See, for example, the PRA Handbook at GENPRU.

19.22   Accordingly, a right of action for breach of statutory duty could potentially arise under the FSMA 2000, s 138D, in cases where there has been a breach of one of the FCA's or PRA's rules. The concept of a 'rule' is narrower than the concept of a 'requirement by or under the FSMA 2000', which is used in many of the enforcement provisions[1]. The latter includes requirements imposed directly by the FSMA 2000, including prohibitions which have criminal law consequences, as well as those imposed under subordinate legislation, such as HM Treasury's regulations[2]. Breach of such requirements would not expose the firm to civil liability under this provision, although liability may arise under some other provision of the FSMA 2000 or under the general law.

1   For a brief discussion of the rule-making powers, see para **2.63** ff above. In particular, it should be noted that much of the Handbooks are not 'rules', but guidance.
2   This is discussed in **CHAPTER 2** above.

19.23   In the case of rules made by the FCA which are caught by the section, the statutory right of action is only available in relation to a contravention by an authorised person. The FCA's rules do, in some circumstances, apply to other types of person, for example there are rules relating to auditors and actuaries[1], but a contravention of those rules by such other types of person will not give rise to liability under this provision. No such qualification applies in respect of rules made by the PRA which specify that a contravention gives rise to a right of action.

1   See FSMA 2000, s 340.

B. Actionable at the suit of a private person

19.24   The contravention is actionable at the suit of a private person[1]. 'Private person' means[2]:

(a)   any individual, unless he suffers the loss in question in the course of carrying on any regulated activity[3];

(b)   any person who is not an individual, unless he suffers the loss in question in the course of carrying on business of any kind;

(c)   a relevant recipient of credit (within the meaning of the Financial Services and Markets Act 2000 (Regulated Activities) Order 2001)[4] who is not an individual and who has suffered the loss in question in connection with certain activities of kinds specified in that Order[5]; and

(d)   any person who is, by virtue of art 36J of the Financial Services and Markets Act 2000 (Regulated Activities) Order 2001, to be regarded as a person who uses, may use, has or may have used or has or may have contemplated using, services provided by an operator of an electronic system in relation to lending[6],

but does not include a government, local authority or international organisation.

1   FSMA 2000, s 138D.
2   The term 'private person' is referred to in the FSMA 2000, s 138D(6) as having such meaning as may be prescribed. The prescribing instrument in which the term is defined is the Financial Services and Markets Act 2000 (Rights of Action) Regulations 2001, SI 2001/2256 (the 'Rights of Action Regulations'), arts 3 and 6(1), as amended by the Financial Services Act 2012 (Consequential Amendments and Transitional Provisions) Order 2013, SI 2013/472; and the Financial Services and Markets Act 2000 (Regulated Activities) (Amendment) (No 2) Order 2013, SI 2013/1881.

3 Or any activity which would be a regulated activity apart from any exclusion made by the Financial Services and Markets Act 2000 (Regulated Activities) Order 2001, SI 2001/544, art 72. By virtue of art 13(2) of that Order, an individual who suffers loss in the course of effecting or carrying out as principal contracts of insurance written at Lloyd's is not to be taken to suffer loss in the course of carrying on a regulated activity.

4 SI 2001/544.

5 Namely, activities of a kind specified by arts 36A, 39D, 39E, 39F, 39G, 60B, 60N, 90A or 90B of that Order or art 64 of that Order so far as relevant to any of those activities.

6 That is, authorised persons in carrying on a regulated activity of the kind specified by art 36H of that Order or art 64 of that Order so far as relevant to that activity.

19.25 Individuals will normally be considered private persons, the main exception being where the relevant losses suffered were suffered while they were carrying on a business or another activity that is regulated under the FSMA 2000. Therefore, a sole trader who has a Part 4 permission is not considered a private person for these purposes to the extent he suffers a loss while carrying on his regulated business. Companies and other bodies will not normally be private persons, unless they suffer a loss while they are not acting in the course of carrying on a business of any kind[1]; or they otherwise fall within para (c) or (d) of the definition of 'prescribed person' outlined above[2].

1 The phrase 'business of any kind' is interpreted broadly. It encapsulates business that does not involve carrying out a regulated activity: see *Titan Steel Wheels Ltd v The Royal Bank of Scotland plc [2010] EWHC 211.*

2 In *Grant Estates Ltd (In Liquidation) v The Royal Bank of Scotland plc [2012] CSOH 133*, it was argued by the plaintiff that the distinction between 'private persons' and corporate persons was not authorised by MiFID and hence the definition of 'private person' should be construed in a way which was compatible with EU law. Lord Hodge rejected that argument. Although his Lordship agreed that MiFID does not make a distinction between a customer who is a natural person and one who is not a natural person, his Lordship noted that MiFID did not require a Member State to provide the consumer protection for which it calls by means of a civil action. In circumstances where the FSMA 2000 provided regulatory remedies for breach of the COBS rules, including in particular the power given to the (then) FSA to require an authorised person to pay compensation to persons who have suffered loss or an adverse effect as a result of contravention of such requirement, the limitation in the definition of 'private person' did not have to be construed narrowly in order to avoid contravening EU law. It should also be noted that persons who do not fit within the definition of 'private person' may, nevertheless, also have other, non-statutory causes of action available to them, such as those outlined at para **19.57** ff below. The fact that no action for breach of statutory duty can be brought does not mean that no action for breach of a duty of care will lie: see *Gorham v British Telecommunications plc [2000] EWCA Civ 234, [2000] 1 WLR 2129*. However, see *Green & Rowley v Royal Bank of Scotland plc [2013] EWCA Civ 1197*, in which the Court of Appeal held that the existence of an action for breach of statutory duty consequent upon contravention of a rule does not compel the finding of a co-extensive common law duty of care; and that the claimant's argument that such a cause of action 'would afford protection to those who, not being a "private person" cannot avail themselves of a cause of action for breach of statutory duty, is an invitation to the court to drive a coach and horses through the intention of Parliament to confer a private law cause of action upon a limited class'. See also further discussion of *Grant Estates* in para **19.40**, n 1 below.

C. Who suffers loss as a result of the contravention

19.26 The contravention is only actionable at the suit of a private person who suffers loss as a result of the contravention. The purpose of an award of damages is to compensate a person for loss that they have suffered. The question of what losses are referable, in legal terms, to the firm's breach is the subject of complex legal rules. Generally, the damage must have been caused[1] in legal and factual terms by the breach[2], must not be too remote[3] and must be of a type that a court will compensate with an award of damages[4].

1   See, eg *Zaki v Credit Suisse (UK) Ltd [2013] EWCA Civ 14*, in which a claim brought by an investor in structured notes asserting breach by the bank of its duty to take reasonable steps to ensure the suitability of the investment failed on the basis that the investor had relied on his own judgment to make the investment; and not any advice by the bank.
2   The same principles apply as for a claim in negligence under the general law: see *Clerk & Lindsell on Torts* (20th edn, 2010) at para 9–61. The principles in relation to claims for negligence are briefly outlined at para **19.62** below.
3   The test is, broadly, whether the damage was of the type which the statute was intended to prevent. The point is well illustrated by the case of *Gorris v Scott (1874) LR 9 Exch 125*: on a sea voyage, sheep were washed overboard by reason of the defendant's failure to place them in pens as required by statutory rules, but since the object of the statute and rules was to prevent the spread of contagious disease, not to protect the sheep from the perils of the sea, the claimant could not recover his losses. Hence, it is quite possible, in some circumstances, that the consequences of a breach of FCA or PRA rules will not be compensated with an award of damages.
4   For a discussion of the rules in relation to damages, see *McGregor on Damages* (18th edn, 2009).

19.27   In practice this is often the most significant hurdle for claimants bringing an action against a firm. The fact that there was a regulatory breach, or a breach of a legal duty, does not automatically entitle the person to compensation. The key question is what financial loss they can show they have suffered flowing from that breach. In some situations, the answer will be obvious because, for example, the firm's actions have directly impacted on the value of the person's investment. But, in many situations, the answer will not be that simple and the chain of causation may be long and complex.

19.28   The question of what loss was suffered is an equally important point from the firm's perspective. Even if the firm concedes that it committed a regulatory breach, for example to reach a settlement with the FCA or PRA on disciplinary or other enforcement issues, it does not necessarily follow that any loss is referable to that breach. Firms need to bear this in mind when considering the nature and scope of any admissions they make, in order potentially to preserve the firm's ability to defend itself against civil law claims[1].

1   The impact of admissions made in the enforcement process upon subsequent civil claims is discussed at para **19.83** ff below.

D. Subject to the defences and other incidents applying to actions for breach of statutory duty

19.29   All claims for breach of statutory duty are subject to any defences available to the firm, including:

• the losses were caused by an intervening act which was not the fault of the firm[1];

• the customer voluntarily assumed responsibility for the risk of the losses that he ultimately incurred[2] and/or agreed to waive the claim;

- the customer's own negligence contributed to the loss[3];

- the defendant's breach of duty was co-extensive with that of the claimant[4].

1 See *Clerk & Lindsell on Torts* (20th edn, 2010) at para 9-62.
2 See *Clerk & Lindsell on Torts* (20th edn, 2010) at para 9-63.
3 See *Clerk & Lindsell on Torts* (20th edn, 2010) at para 9-64. For example, in *Spreadex Ltd v Sekhon [2008] EWHC 1136 (Ch)*, the claimant, Spreadex, a spread betting company, sued the defendant, Dr Sekhon, an experienced spread better, for an unpaid debt which the Spreadex alleged was owing following its closing, on 22 November 2006, of all of Dr Sekhon's open positions. Dr Sekhon defended the claim by alleging that Spreadex had breached its statutory duty under the then FSMA 2000, s 150 and FSA Handbook at COB 7.10.5 R. Dr Sekhon argued that, in September 2006, Spreadex had made a margin call on Dr Sekhon; he did not meet that margin call for five business days thereafter; Spreadex should therefore have closed, but did not close, his open positions; and if Spreadex had closed his positions at that time, no money or at least much less money would have been owing. The court found that Spreadex had contravened COB 7.10.5 R by failing to close all of Dr Sekhon's open positions at the beginning of 14 September 2006; and therefore that Dr Sekhon was entitled to claim damages for any loss he suffered as a consequence of the contravention. However, the court found that a defence of contributory negligence was available to Spreadex, in that Dr Sekhon deliberately elected to keep his positions open at all times until they were closed against his will on 22 November 2006; persuaded Spreadex to permit him to do so; and thereby chose to run the risk of his positions deteriorating further. As to causation, the court regarded Dr Sekhon as being the principal author of his own misfortunes as he had persuaded Spreadex to permit him to keep his positions open. Ultimately, the court found Spreadex liable to Dr Sekhon for the deterioration in his open positions but subject to Dr Sekhon being 85% contributorily negligent for that deterioration.
4 See *Clerk & Lindsell on Torts* (20th edn, 2010) at para 9-65.

E. Actionable by non-private persons in prescribed cases

19.30 In prescribed cases, a contravention of a rule which would be actionable at the suit of a private person is actionable at the suit of a person who is not a private person, subject to the defences and other incidents that apply to actions for breach of statutory duty[1].

1 FSMA 2000, s 138D(4).

19.31 A contravention is actionable by a person who is not a private person where any of the following conditions apply[1]:

- the rule that has been contravened prohibits an authorised person from seeking to make provision excluding or restricting any duty or liability;

- the rule that has been contravened is directed at ensuring that transactions in any security or contractually based investment[2] are not affected by the benefit of unpublished information that, if made public, would be likely to affect the price of the investment; or

- the person would bring the action in a fiduciary or representative capacity on behalf of a private person and any remedy would be exclusively for the benefit of that person and could not be effected through action brought otherwise than at the suit of the fiduciary or representative.

1 Financial Services and Markets Act 2000 (Rights of Action) Regulations, SI 2001/2256, reg 6(2). This reflects the position under the former regime.
2 See the Financial Services and Markets Act 2000 (Regulated Activities) Order 2001, SI 2001/544.

Other rights of action under the FSMA 2000

19.32   The FSMA 2000 contains a number of other provisions which give rise to additional rights of action for certain specific types of contraventions.

19.33   First, a right of action arises in favour of a private person[1] on the same basis as outlined above[2] where an authorised person[3] fails to take reasonable care to ensure that, broadly:

- no function of his, in relation to the carrying on of a regulated activity, is performed by a person who is prohibited from performing that function by a prohibition order[4]; or

- no person performs a controlled function who is not approved for that function[5].

1 Or, in prescribed cases, a person who is not a private person: see para **19.30** above.
2 FSMA 2000, s 71.
3 Or, in the case of the FSMA 2000, s 56(6), an exempt person or a person whom, as a result of the FSMA 2000, Pt 20, the general prohibition does not apply in relation to a regulated activity: see s 56(3A).
4 FSMA 2000, s 56(6).
5 FSMA 2000, s 59(1) or (2).

19.34   The same right of action applies where an authorised person, broadly:

- unlawfully promotes or approves the promotion of a collective investment scheme[1]; or

- contravenes a direction imposed by the FCA in relation to a unit trust scheme[2] or an OEIC[3].

1 FSMA 2000, ss 238, 240 and 241.
2 FSMA 2000, s 257(5).
3 Open-Ended Investment Companies Regulations 2001, SI 2001/1228, reg 25(6).

19.35   The elements of the claim are the same as those discussed at B to D above and 'private person' has, in this context, the same meaning as at para **19.19** above[1]. Further, a contravention is actionable by a person who is not a private person, but only in one situation[2]: where the action would be brought in a fiduciary or representative capacity on behalf of a private person and any remedy would be exclusively for the benefit of that private person and could not be effected through an action brought otherwise than at the suit of the fiduciary or representative.

1 Financial Services and Markets Act 2000 (Rights of Action) Regulations 2001, SI 2001/2256, reg 5(1).
2 Financial Services and Markets Act 2000 (Rights of Action) Regulations 2001, SI 2001/2256, reg 5(3).

19.36   Second, two connected types of contravention, namely:

- the carrying on by an authorised person of a regulated activity otherwise than in accordance with his permission[1]; and

- the breach of a requirement imposed on an incoming firm[2];

are actionable at the suit of a private person[3] who suffers loss as a result of the contravention, subject to the defences and other incidents applying to actions for breach of statutory duty, except where the contravention is of a financial resources requirement[4]. The elements of the claim are the same as those discussed at B to D above. Most such contraventions are, therefore, actionable at the suit of a private person who suffers loss as a result.

1 FSMA 2000, s 20(3). An authorised person acting outside his permission does not breach the general prohibition but does commit a regulatory breach: see para **2.115** ff above. This would also include breaching a restriction imposed by a variation of permission.
2 FSMA 2000, s 202(2). This refers to breach of a requirement imposed on an incoming firm in the exercise of the FCA or PRA's powers of intervention.
3 Or by a non-private person acting in a fiduciary or representative capacity: see Financial Services and Markets Act 2000 (Rights of Action) Regulations 2001, SI 2001/2256, regs 4 and 7.
4 A requirement on the firm to have or maintain financial resources, imposed under, as applicable, the FSMA 2000, Pt 4 (for UK regulated firms) or Pt 13 (for incoming firms): Financial Services and Markets Act 2000 (Rights of Action) Regulations 2001, SI 2001/2256, reg 1.

19.37 Third, in relation to the FCA's function as the UK Listing Authority[1], a contravention of the rules requiring a prospectus to be published before certain securities are offered to the public (or a request is made for their admission onto a regulated UK market)[2] is actionable at the suit of a person who suffers loss as a result of the contravention, subject to the defences and other incidents applying to actions for breach of statutory duty. The elements of the claim are the same as those discussed at C and D above and the right of action is not limited to private persons.

1 See **Chapter 20**.
2 FSMA 2000, s 85(4).

19.38 Finally, a person responsible for listing particulars (or a prospectus) is liable[1] to pay compensation to a person who has acquired securities to which the listing particulars apply (or transferrable securities to which the prospectus applies) and suffered loss in respect of them as a consequence of any untrue or misleading statement in the particulars (or prospectus) or the omission from the particulars (or prospectus) of any matter required to be included in them[2]. This is not framed by the FSMA 2000 as a breach of statutory duty claim.

1 FSMA 2000, s 90. Such liability may also arise by virtue of negligent misstatement or misrepresentation: see the Financial Markets Law Committee's Report of October 2004 on Issue 76 for a brief description of how liability may arise. This is subject to certain exceptions set out in the FSMA 2000, Sch 10. Additionally, the FSMA 2000, s 90 excludes civil liability in certain circumstances.
2 See the FSMA 2000, ss 80 and 81.

Situations where there is expressly no right of action

19.39 In certain cases, the FSMA 2000 specifically prescribes that a contravention of a rule or requirement does not give rise to any right of action for breach of statutory duty, namely:

- except in those cases where HM Treasury has prescribed that there is a right of action[1], the carrying on by an authorised person of a regulated activity otherwise than in accordance with his permission[2];

- the breach of a requirement imposed on an incoming firm, again except in those cases where HM Treasury has prescribed that there is a right of action[3]; and

- failure by an approved person to comply with a Statement of Principle for approved persons[4].

1   FSMA 2000, s 20(3). Under current HM Treasury regulations, a private person will have a right of action, except where the requirement breached was a financial resources requirement.
2   FSMA 2000, s 20(2). An authorised person acting outside his permission does not breach the general prohibition but does commit a regulatory breach: see para **2.115** ff above. This would include breaching a restriction imposed on a variation of permission.
3   FSMA 2000, s 202(2). Under current HM Treasury regulations, a private person will have a right of action, except where the requirement breached was a financial resources requirement.
4   FSMA 2000, s 64(8). For a discussion of the Statements of Principle for approved persons, see para **2.32** ff above. Note also that the Handbooks at PRIN 3.4.4 prescribe that breaches by a firm of one or more Principles for Businesses do not give rise to a cause of action at the suit of a private person under the FSMA 2000, s 138D.

19.40   It is important to understand the effect of these provisions. On the face of it, they do not preclude the relevant person from taking action against the firm based on some other cause of action which exists as a matter of law, for example if he has a claim in negligence or for breach of contract. They merely make clear that the contravention does not of itself give rise to any additional cause of action under the FSMA 2000[1].

1   However, in *Grant Estates Ltd v The Royal Bank of Scotland plc [2012] CSOH 133 at [79]*, Lord Hodge opined that a person cannot rely on the FCA Handbook at COBS rules as giving rise to a common law duty of care in relation to the provision of advice. Although His Lordship accepted a common law duty can arise from the existence of a statutory duty 'as part of background circumstances' (in that the existence of a statutory duty may show that a particular risk should have been foreseen), he said that the principal consideration for the court, when assessing the effect of the statutory duty on the question of whether it is just and equitable to impose a duty of care, is the policy of the statute itself. His Lordship said that the policy of the FSMA 2000 is to provide protection to consumers of financial services through a self-contained regulatory code and statutory remedies for breach of its rules; and that it needs no fortification by the parallel creation of common law duties and remedies. He went on to say that the existence of a duty in negligence for failure to comply with the COBS rules would circumvent the statutory restriction on the direct right of action discussed above. His Lordship's opinion is consistent with the decision of the Court of Appeal in *Green & Rowley v Royal Bank of Scotland plc [2013] EWCA Civ 1197*, in which it was held that the existence of an action for breach of statutory duty consequent upon contravention of a COB rule does not compel the finding of a co-extensive duty of care at common law. Although the Court of Appeal was prepared to accept that the existence of a statutory duty may give rise to a common law duty of care, particularly where the performance of the statutory duty by a party brings about a relationship between the party and another person such as is recognised to give rise to a duty of care owed to that person, the court rejected the claimant's argument that such a cause of action 'would afford protection to those who, not being a "private person" cannot avail themselves of a cause of action for breach of statutory duty'. The court held that the claimant's argument was 'an invitation to the court to drive a coach and horses through the intention of Parliament to confer a private law cause of action upon a limited class'.

19.41   In addition, the FSMA 2000 contains two general exclusions from civil liability. First, a person will not be subject to civil liability solely on the basis of a summary in a prospectus unless the summary, when read with the rest of the prospectus, is misleading, inaccurate or inconsistent; or does not provide certain key information[1]. Second, a person will not be subject to civil liability solely on the basis of key investor information produced in relation to a collective investment scheme or sub-fund[2], unless the key investor information is misleading, inaccurate or inconsistent with the relevant parts of the prospectus published for that collective investment scheme or sub-fund in accordance with the scheme particulars rules in the FCA Handbook at COLL4[3]. One thing to note about these provisions is that, in contrast with those outlined at para **19.39** above, they appear to contain a general exclusion of civil liability. That is, the exclusion is not limited to making clear that no statutory right of action arises.

1   FSMA 2000, s 90(12). 'Key information' is defined in s 87A(9) and (10).
2   Being a sub-fund of such a scheme in accordance with rules or other provisions implementing Chapter IX of the UCITS directive, or of any translation of that information.
3   Being the rules made by the FCA under the FSMA 2000, s 248.

Situations in which the FSMA 2000 does not specifically provide a right of action for breach of statutory duty

19.42   Having discussed the instances in which a civil claim can be brought under the express provisions of the FSMA 2000, the following paragraphs consider the question of whether the law will permit a claim to be brought for breach of a duty arising under the FSMA 2000 where the legislation does not specifically so provide[1].

1   Most notably where market abuse has occurred.

19.43   The law recognises a claim in tort, known as breach of statutory duty, based on a person's breach of an obligation imposed on him under statute. However, a breach of a statutory provision does not necessarily give rise to a claim for breach of statutory duty[1]. The key to such a claim is to show that, as a matter of construction, the duty was imposed for the protection of a limited class of the public and that Parliament intended to confer upon the members of that class a private right of action for breach of that duty[2].

1   See *Carty v London Borough of Croydon [2004] ELR 226, [2004] EWHC 228* affirmed by the Court of Appeal at *[2005] ECWA Civ 19, [2005] 1 WLR 2312*.
2   See *X (Minors) v Bedfordshire County Council [1995] 3 All ER 353*, HL, *[1995] 3 WLR 152* (and the appeal to the European Court of Human Rights in *Z v UK [2001] 2 FLR 612*); and *Grant Estates Ltd v The Royal Bank of Scotland plc [2012] CSOH 133*. See also the discussion at *Clerk & Lindsell on Torts* (20th edn, 2010) at para 9-51. Whether or not such a right exists is a matter of construction of the statute concerned.

19.44   In the present context, the difficulty with this test is that the FSMA 2000 (perhaps even more so than was the case under the Financial Services Act 1986) 'creates an elaborate scheme of duties backed by a mix of enforcement mechanisms but in each case the mechanism is earmarked to the duty in question'[1]. In other words, given that the FSMA 2000 has created a series of obligations and has specifically provided how each obligation is to be enforced, involving administrative, criminal and civil consequences, there seems to be little room to imply that Parliament intended private rights of action to arise other than where the FSMA 2000 specifically so provides. This argument appears to have a great deal of force[2].

1   Per Lightman J who in *Melton Medes Ltd v Securities and Investments Board [1995] 3 All ER 880, [1995] 2 WLR 247* held that the Financial Services Act 1986, s 179 did not give rise to a private right of action for breach of statutory duty.
2   Per Lord Browne-Wilkinson in *X (Minors) v Bedfordshire County Council [1995] 3 All ER 353 at 731, HL:* 'If the statute does provide some other means of enforcing the duty that will normally indicate that the statutory right was intended to be enforceable by those means and not by private right of action. ... However, the mere existence of some other statutory remedy is not necessarily decisive. It is still possible to show that on the true construction of the statute the protected class was intended by Parliament to have a private remedy'.

19.45   In light of the opinion of Lord Hodge in *Grant Estates*[1] and the decision of the Court of Appeal in *Green & Rowley*[2], there is now considerable doubt that a common law action for breach of statutory duty can be brought under the FSMA 2000.

1   See *Grant Estates Ltd (In Liquidation) v The Royal Bank of Scotland plc [2012] CSOH 133* at [79], discussed in para **19.40**, n 1 above, in which Lord Hodge pointed out that the existence of a cause of action at common law for failure to comply with the COBS rules would circumvent the statutory restriction on a direct right of action discussed above.
2   See *Green & Rowley v Royal Bank of Scotland plc [2013] EWCA Civ 1197*, discussed in para **19.40**, n 1 above. Although this decision focussed on the claimant's proposition that the existence of a statutory duty of itself brings about the creation of a co-extensive common law duty of care, the basis for the court's rejection of that proposition – including its principal consideration, the intention of Parliament in conferring a private cause of action on a limited class of people only – would appear to apply *a fortiori* to counter any notion that an action under the common law in tort for breach of statutory duty could lie where no such action was available under the FSMA 2000.

19.46   If despite this considerable hurdle it is possible to show that the relevant provision is capable of giving rise to a common law claim for breach of statutory duty, the person concerned must also show that[1]:

- the damage is of a type that the FSMA 2000 was intended to protect against;

- the claimant is within a class of persons that was intended to be protected by the statute;

- the relevant statutory duty was breached[2]; and

- the breach of statutory duty caused the loss[3]. The same defences applicable to actions under the express provisions of the FSMA 2000 for breach of statutory duty apply to actions in tort for breach of statutory duty.

1   These other elements of the claim are discussed in more detail at para **19.18** ff above. See also *Clerk & Lindsell on Torts* (20th edn, 2010) at para 9-04.
2   This depends upon the construction of the relevant provision. For example, some duties imposed by statute require the person to take reasonable care while others are to be applied with strict liability.
3   See the discussion at para **19.26** ff above.

Unenforceable agreements

19.47   The FSMA 2000 also affects the civil rights of the firm and its customers by making agreements entered into unenforceable in certain circumstances.

19.47 Civil liability

There are three main situations where the FSMA 2000 has this effect[1], namely where:

- an agreement is made by a person in the course of carrying on a regulated activity in breach of the general prohibition[2];

- an agreement is made by an authorised person in the course of carrying on a credit-related regulated activity involving certain matters[3], otherwise than in accordance with his permission[4];

- an agreement made by an authorised person in the course of carrying on a regulated activity is made in consequence of something said or done by a third party acting in breach of the general prohibition or in the course of carrying on a credit-related regulated activity otherwise than in accordance with the third party's permission[5]. An example would be a contract entered into as a result of investment advice given by an unauthorised third party[6]; and

- in consequence of an unlawful communication[7], certain types of agreements are entered into by a person as a customer or rights are exercised by a person in relation to certain types of investment[8].There are various common elements to these provisions, which are considered below[9].

1 In addition, the court can, in certain circumstances, order the return of unlawful deposits: FSMA 2000, s 29.
2 FMSA 2000, s 26. The general prohibition is the prohibition against carrying on regulated activity without authorisation under the FSMA 2000: see para **2.115** ff above. Note that this does not encompass an agreement entered into by an authorised person acting outside the scope of its permission: FSMA 2000, s 20(2). Nor does it encompass the breach by an incoming firm of a restriction imposed on it: FSMA 2000, s 202(1).
3 Being matters falling within the FSMA 2000, s 23(1C)(a).
4 FSMA 2000, s 26A.
5 FSMA 2000, s 27. The interaction between this provision and s 20(2)(b) is not clear. On the face of it, this provision would cover an agreement entered into by an authorised person outside the scope of its permission but within the scope of activities which are 'regulated activities' for the purposes of the FSMA 2000. However, s 20(2)(b) makes clear that if an authorised person acts outside the scope of his permission, that contravention does not make any transaction void or unenforceable. The more likely answer to this apparent contradiction is that, reading the two together, the agreement would be unenforceable, not because it had been entered into by the authorised person outside the scope of his permission, but because it had been entered into by it in consequence of something said or done by an unauthorised person.
6 See the Explanatory Notes to the FSMA 2000, para 72.
7 A communication in relation to which there has been a breach of the restrictions on financial promotions found at the FSMA 2000, s 21(1): s 30(1).
8 FSMA 2000, s 30. An explanation of the rules on unlawful financial promotion is beyond the scope of this book.
9 The relevant provisions are almost identical to the Financial Services Act 1986, ss 5 and 132. When introduced into the 1986 Act, these provisions resolved an issue raised by *Bedford Insurance Co v Instituto de Resseguros do Brasil [1985] QB 966*, which had caused much concern within the insurance industry. They were said to have provided 'a new code which could not have been achieved by any route explored or decided in any of the cases': *DR Insurance Co v Seguros America Banamex [1993] 1 Lloyd's Rep 120*, at 131.

The requirement for an 'agreement'

19.48 In the first three cases there must be an agreement and it must be one the making or performance of which constitutes, or is part of, the regulated activity in question[1]. In other words, not every agreement entered into by someone who is acting in breach of the general prohibition is unenforceable. The only agreements that are unenforceable are those referable to the breach. For example, an agreement by the person to buy stationery for use in his unauthorised business would not be unenforceable.

1   FSMA 2000, ss 26(3), 26A(3) and 27(3).

Achieving restitution

19.49   Where an agreement is rendered unenforceable the FSMA 2000 contains various provisions designed to achieve restitution. As will be seen, restitution may not always be available and, notwithstanding one party is not 'innocent', the provisions aim to be even-handed between the parties.

19.50   There are three relevant provisions[1]. First, the person with whom the agreement was made can recover any money or other property which he paid or transferred under the agreement, and can also obtain compensation for any loss sustained by him as a result of having parted with it[2].

1   FSMA 2000 also provides that the commission of an authorisation offence does not make the agreement concerned illegal or invalid to any greater extent than is provided by the FSMA 2000, ss 26 and 27: FSMA 2000, s 28(9). This ensures that the contract is not illegal, but can be avoided only at the option of the customer: see *Group Josi Re v Walbrook Insurance Co Ltd [1996] 1 WLR 1152*.
2   FSMA 2000, ss 26(2), 26A(2), 27(2) and 30(2) and (3). The amount of compensation recoverable is such amount as the parties agree or is determined by the court on the application of either party: FSMA 2000, ss 28(2) and 30(10). It is not clear whether a court will apply any remoteness of damage rules: see the discussion in Lomnicka & Powell, *Encyclopaedia of Financial Services Law* at 2A-063, including in respect of *Re Whiteley Insurance Consultants (A Firm) [2008] EWHC 1782 (Ch)*, in which Richards J expressly did not decide the extent of the remedy under s 26(2)(b), but nevertheless took the words in that section, 'any loss sustained … as a result of having parted with [the money paid]' as drawing a distinction between loss in fact sustained and notional loss. In doing so, Richards J refused to allow the claimants, a group of insurance policyholders, to recover interest on the premiums they paid, as it was assumed they would have paid the same premium to a different insurer at the same time.

19.51   Second, with the exception of agreements entered into in the course of carrying on a credit-related regulated activity, if the person elects not to perform the agreement or recovers money or other property which he paid or transferred under it, he must also repay any money and return any other property which he received under it[1].

1   FSMA 2000, ss 28(7) and 30(11) and (12). If property has been transferred to a third party, then the person must repay the value of the property at the time it was transferred: FSMA 2000, ss 28(8) and 30(13). The general rule is that he must return the property; he cannot retain the shares and claim back the purchase money less the financial value of the shares: see *Securities and Investments Board v Pantell (No 2) [1993] 1 All ER 134*.

19.52   Third, the court can nonetheless allow the agreement to be enforced or money and property paid or transferred under it to be retained, if satisfied that this is just and equitable in the circumstances of the case[1]. In considering whether to do so, the court must have regard to, as appropriate, whether:

- the person who contravened the general prohibition or who carried on a regulated activity otherwise than in accordance with his permission reasonably believed that he was not doing so[2];

- the provider knew that the third party was contravening the general prohibition[3]; and/or

- the person, as the case may be, reasonably believed he was not making an unlawful communication or knew that the agreement was entered into in consequence of an unlawful communication[4].

1 FSMA 2000, ss 28(3), 28A(3) and 30(4).
2 FSMA 2000, ss 28(4) and (5); and 28A(4) and (5).
3 FSMA 2000, ss 28(4) and (6); and 28A(4) and (6).
4 FSMA 2000, s 30(5) to (7).

19.53 The test of whether it is just and equitable to enforce the agreement or allow the person to retain the money or other property thus appears to revolve primarily around the blameworthiness of the relevant person's conduct. A different test is applied dependent upon whether the firm itself committed the contravention or whether it entered into an agreement after a third party had committed a contravention. In the former case, the court looks at the existence and reasonableness of any belief that the firm was not committing a breach; in the latter case, it looks at whether the firm knew[1] about the third party's breach. In addition, whilst the FSMA 2000 prescribes that the court must have regard to these considerations, it is not clear that these are necessarily the only considerations; there may be other relevant matters which the court will take into account when deciding what is just and equitable for it to do in the circumstances of the particular case.

1 Knowledge can include, in many contexts, not only actual knowledge but also circumstances where the person ought to have known.

19.54 One important point is not addressed in the restitution provisions, namely who takes the benefit of any profits that have accrued. Imagine, for example, that a customer has paid money to purchase units in an unauthorised fund. The fund has been invested and the units have increased significantly in value. The customer subsequently becomes aware that the fund was unauthorised and wants his money back (because, for example, he does not want to invest in an unauthorised fund or is concerned that the fund will now drop in value). He is clearly entitled to be repaid the money he originally paid for the units. He is also entitled to compensation for any loss he has sustained as a result of parting with his money, and this may allow him to obtain compensation on the basis that he would have invested that money elsewhere and made a particular return on it. But that compensation may be less than the amount that the units have increased in value, particularly if other comparable investments did not fare so well over the same period. So who takes the full benefit of the increase in value of the units? This point does not seem to be covered in the restitution provisions. The profit made by the investment is neither 'money paid by the customer under the agreement', which would need to be returned to the customer, nor 'money or property received by the customer under the agreement', which the customer would have to pay to the firm. It may be that in practice such profits will be reflected in the amount of compensation that the firm is required to pay, whatever the difficulties of upholding that approach as a matter of principle[1]. In any event, it is likely that the firm could be required by a restitution order to pay the profit to the customer, as profits which have accrued to the firm as the result of a contravention of a requirement imposed by or under the FSMA 2000[2].

1 Among other things, it could be argued that the profit actually made is the best evidence of the compensation that the customer should receive based on the profit that the customer's funds could have made had he invested them elsewhere.
2 For a discussion of restitution orders, see para **8.100** ff above.

Agreements that are expressly not unenforceable

19.55 In four cases, the FSMA 2000 makes clear that certain regulatory breaches or events do not in and of themselves render any transactions void or unenforceable. These include where:

- (with the exception of credit-related regulated activities involving certain matters[1]) an authorised person carries on a regulated activity otherwise than in accordance with his permission[2];

- a penalty is imposed for market abuse[3];

- a person contravenes a rule made by the FCA or PRA[4]; and

- an incoming firm contravenes an intervention requirement imposed on it by the FCA or PRA[5].

1 Being matters falling within the FSMA 2000, s 23(1C)(a).
2 FSMA 2000, s 20(2). The authorised person does not thereby breach the general prohibition, but does commit a regulatory offence: see para **2.116** above. Note also that the effect of the FSMA 2000, s 27(1)(d)(ii) is that agreements made by authorised persons in consequence of something said or done by a third party in the course of that third party carrying on a non-credit-related regulated activity otherwise than in accordance with his permission are also not unenforceable by reason of that breach.
3 FSMA 2000, s 131. For a discussion of market abuse, see **CHAPTER 17** above.
4 FSMA 2000, s 138E.
5 FSMA 2000, s 202(1).

19.56 It seems that the effect of this is not to preclude the person from bringing claims that, at common law, might render the transaction void or unenforceable or otherwise susceptible to challenge, for example that the agreement was induced by a misrepresentation or was entered into by a minor. The FSMA 2000 appears simply to make clear that the regulatory contravention does not of itself impeach the agreement.

CIVIL LIABILITY UNDER THE GENERAL LAW

19.57 The question of whether the firm is liable under the general law and, if so, on what basis, depends upon the circumstances of the particular case and, specifically, on the nature of the relationship between the firm and the person claiming to have suffered loss from the firm's actions. Some of the main bases for claims that may be made are:

- breach of contract;

- negligence;

- equitable claims;

- misrepresentation; and

- contribution claims.

A brief review of each of these potential claims follows below[1].

1 The discussion that follows is intended as a brief overview, to give a flavour of the nature of each type of claim. It is not intended to be a comprehensive statement of the law in each area. Where appropriate, cross-references are provided to other texts where a more detailed analysis can be found. In certain situations, multiple bases for claims may exist and often more than one basis is relied upon by claimants against firms. For example, cases of mis-selling may give rise to actions based on contract, tort or breach of statutory duty. Consumers could also approach the FOS, in which cases, complaints will be decided according to notions of fairness and reasonableness, through a flexible, informal and inquisitorial process as opposed to a formal, court-like process: see further **CHAPTER 14** above.

Breach of contract

19.58 A breach of contract claim against the firm will require the relevant person to show, very broadly, that first, there was a contract between him and the firm, second, the firm breached one of the terms of the contract, and third, he suffered loss referable in legal terms to the firm's breach and of a kind which a court will compensate with an award of damages. In addition, there are a number of defences to an action that may be available to the firm.

19.59 Whether the firm has a contract with the relevant person will not always be clear. Whilst in many instances a written contract will exist, it is possible for a contract to exist even though the agreement was not recorded in writing[1]. Therefore, a breach of contract claim could be alleged against the firm notwithstanding the lack of a written contract.

1 For a discussion of the elements of a contract, see *Chitty on Contracts* (31st edn, 2012) at Part 2. As to the lack of any formal requirements, generally speaking, see *Chitty on Contracts* at para 4-001.

19.60 Furthermore, even if there is a written agreement, its terms will not always be clear. The written agreement will contain express terms[1], which the court may need to construe in order to assess whether there has been a breach[2]. Additionally, although there will be a strong presumption that a written agreement is intended to contain all the terms of the contract between the parties, this is a presumption only and hence there may in some circumstances be express terms which were agreed by the parties but not recorded in writing, which nevertheless form part of the contract and which the court will need to ascertain[3]. Finally, there may also be terms not expressly written into the contract, but which the court would imply[4]. If there is no written agreement, the court will then need to ascertain the terms[5].

1 Where there is a written contract signed by the parties, the parties are bound by the terms whether or not they have read them and/or appreciated their effect: *L'Estrange v F Graucob Ltd [1934] 2 KB 394.*
2 The basic task is to ascertain the meaning the document would convey to a reasonable person having the background knowledge which would reasonably have been available to the parties at the time of the contract: *Investors Compensation Scheme Ltd v West Bromwich Building Society [1998] 1 WLR 896* (per Lord Hoffmann at 912).
3 *Harris v Rickett (1859) 4 H & N 1; Malpas v L & s W Ry (1866) LR 1 CP 336; Gillespie Bros v Cheney Eggar & Co [1896] 2 QB 59; J Evans & Son (Portsmouth) Ltd v Andrea Merzario Ltd [1976] 1 WLR 1078; Yani Haryanto v ED & F Man (Sugar) Ltd [1986] 2 Lloyd's Rep 44, 46–47.*
4 Terms will be implied by law in two situations: first, where necessary to give business efficacy to the contract, and second, where the term represents the obvious, but unexpressed, intention of the parties: see *Chitty on Contracts* (31st edn, 2012) at para 13-004.
5 As to how it does so, see *Chitty on Contracts* (31st edn, 2012) at Chapter 13.

19.61 The principal remedy for breach of a contractual obligation is an award of damages, which in principle should be available to compensate a party for losses suffered as a result of the breach[1]. It follows that the loss suffered is at the heart of any claim. The question of what losses are referable, in legal terms, to the firm's breach is the subject of complex legal rules of, first, causation[2] and, second, remoteness of damage[3]. In addition, limitations exist as to the types of losses that can be compensated by an award of damages[4]. As well as the legal complexities, proof of loss can cause practical difficulties, as discussed at para **19.27** ff above.

1 For a discussion of damages for breach of contract, see *Chitty on Contracts* (31st edn, 2012) at Chapter 26. Other remedies may be available for breach of contract, including an injunction or, in exceptional circumstances, specific performance: see *Chitty on Contracts* (31st edn, 2012) at Chapter 27.
2 As to whether the breach 'caused' the loss, see *Chitty on Contracts* (31st edn, 2012) at paras 26-057 and 26-058.
3 Whether loss of the kind in question was reasonably foreseeable at the time that the contract was made – either because it arises naturally from the breach or because it was specifically in the contemplation of the parties at that time as being a probable result of a breach: see *Hadley v Baxendale (1854) 9 Exch 341* and *Koufos v C Czarnikow Ltd (The Heron II) [1969] 1 AC 350* and also *Chitty on Contracts* (31st edn, 2012) at para 26-106.
4 The basic rule is that damages should place the innocent party in the position in which he would have been had the contract been properly performed. For a more detailed discussion, see *McGregor on Damages* (18th edn, 2012).

Negligence

19.62 The starting point for a claim in negligence is the existence of a relationship which gives rise to a duty on the firm to take reasonable care[1]. Firms will be under such a duty in many situations[2], often, but by no means only, where a contract also exists[3]. Where a duty of care exists: if the firm's actions fall short of the standard of care required of the firm[4]; and result in a loss to the person to whom the duty is owed[5], the firm may be liable for damages, subject to any applicable defences[6]. Claims for negligence may arise from, amongst other things, a negligent misstatement[7] or the negligent performance of services causing financial loss.

1   The categories of relationships which are recognised as giving rise to a duty of care are not fixed and continue to expand. There are three classic formulations for determining whether such a duty exists: (i) that a test of foreseeability, proximity and fairness is applied; (ii) that it depends upon an assumption of responsibility; and (iii) that the categories of relationships in which a duty of care exists will develop incrementally and by analogy with established categories: see *Caparo Industries plc v Dickman [1990] 2 AC 605*; *Smith v Bush [1990] 1 AC 831*; *Spring v Guardian Assurance plc [1995] 2 AC 296*; and *Williams v Natural Health Foods Ltd [1998] 1 WLR 830*, among others. For further discussion of the principles, see *Clerk & Lindsell on Torts* (20th edn, 2010) at Chapter 8.

2   By way of illustration, the courts have held that: (i) an insurance company may owe a duty of care, in relation to pensions mis-selling, not only to its customer but also to the customer's dependants: *Gorham v British Telecommunications plc [2000] EWCA Civ 234, [2000] 1 WLR 2129*; (ii) a bank owes a duty to exercise reasonable care in and about executing a customer's order to transfer money: *Barclays Bank plc v Quincecare Ltd [1992] 4 All ER 363*; (iii) financial advisers who issue a defence document in the course of a contested takeover may owe a duty of care to the successful bidder: *Morgan Crucible Co plc v Hill Samuel & Co Ltd [1991] Ch 295, [1990] EWCA Civ 4*; (iv) Lloyd's managing agents owe a duty of care to names: *Henderson v Merrett Syndicates Ltd [1995] 2 AC 145*; and (v) directors of a company (X) which is a subject to a friendly takeover may owe a duty of care in respect of statement concerning X they make to the company which acquires X: *PartCo Group Ltd v Wragg [2002] EWCA Civ 594*.

   The duty of care in the investment advisory context was considered in *Springwell Navigation Corp v JP Morgan Chase Bank and others [2010] EWCA 1221* (see further, para **19.62**, n 7 below). In certain circumstances the duty in relation to company reports and financial information may extend to purchasers in the after market: *Possfund Custodian Trustees Ltd v Diamond [1996] 2 BCLC 665, [1996] 1 WLR 1351*.

3   There will often be an express term in a contract requiring the relevant party to use reasonable care and skill. Where there is no express term, a term may be implied, in some instances by the Supply of Goods and Services Act 1982. Breach of such a term may give rise to tortious liability, as well as liability for breach of contract. Where liability arises both contractually and in tort, the claimant may choose on what basis to sue: see *Henderson v Merrett Syndicates Ltd [1995] 2 AC 145, [1994] UKHL 5*. For a discussion of the overlap between tortious and contractual claims, and the differences between them, see *Chitty on Contracts* (31st edn, 2012), from para 1-137.

4   Precisely what standard is required and whether the firm's action fell below that standard are likely to be two of the main issues. The concept of reasonableness will be important: 'negligence is the omission to do something which a reasonable man, guided upon those considerations which ordinarily regulate the conduct of human affairs, would do; or doing something which a prudent and reasonable man would not do': Alderson B in *Blyth v Birmingham Waterworks Co (1856) 11 Ex Ch 781* and see the discussion in *Clerk & Lindsell on Torts* (20th edn, 2010), at para 8-136. There may be room for disagreement among reasonable men as to what practice is proper, in which case it may be sufficient for the firm to show that a responsible body of opinion would accept the firm's practice as proper, even if the claimant can identify another body of opinion which would regard a different practice as proper: see *Bolam v Friern Hospital Management Committee [1957] 1 WLR 582* and *Saif Ali v Sydney Mitchell and Co [1980] AC 198* (Lord Diplock); but note that this doctrine may not apply where neglect arises as a result of oversight (see *JD Williams & Co Ltd v Michael Hyde & Associates Ltd [2001] PNLR 8*) and also may not apply where the practice followed by the firm is not defensible bearing in mind the comparative risks and benefits of different approaches (see *Patel v Daybells (a firm) [2002] PNLR 6, [2001] EWCA Civ 1299*).

5   The same issues of: (i) causation; (ii) remoteness of damage; and (iii) those categories of loss that are recoverable, also arise in relation to claims for breach of contract, but the rules (which, again, are complex) are different in some important respects: for a detailed discussion, see *Clerk & Lindsell on Torts* (20th edn, 2010), at para 8-04 and *Chitty on Contracts* (31st edn, 2012), at para 1-098. The basic starting point is that the person is entitled to be placed in the position in which he would have been had the negligence not taken place.

6   In particular, the defence of contributory negligence under the Law Reform (Contributory Negligence) Act 1945 is likely to be relevant.

7   See *Hedley Byrne & Co Ltd v Heller & Partners Ltd [1964] AC 465*. Actions based on negligent misstatements – or misrepresentations – depend heavily on the precise statement said to amount to a misrepresentation and the context in which it was made. In *Springwell Navigation Corp v JP Morgan*

Chase Bank [2010] EWCA 1221, the Court of Appeal, in considering whether certain alleged misrepresentations were actionable by the claimant, held first that the claimant, having signed up to certain non-reliance provisions in its contract with Chase, was in the circumstances bound by those provisions; and second that, in any case, there simply was no negligent misstatement. As to the latter, the court gave significant weight to the nature of the statements made by the Chase employee and the fact that the claimant – who was a sophisticated investor – understood the risks involved with the products being sold.

Equitable claims

19.63   Certain relationships impose more stringent obligations than those that apply in purely contractual relationships. The classic example is that of a trustee of a pension fund or unit trust. Similar obligations arise in other situations such as where a firm acts in a 'fiduciary' capacity as an agent or a company director. Also, a trust can be imposed as a matter of law in certain situations that are not obvious[1]. From the claimant's perspective, it may be advantageous to frame the claim on the basis of trust law, because, for example, it may confer some protection against the firm's insolvency and some of the legal hurdles may be lower[2]. Claims based on principles of trust law or fiduciary duties arise relatively frequently in practice[3]. Equity also gives rise to a number of other relevant bases of claim which need to be outlined.

1 See, for example, the discussion of accessory liability and knowing receipt claims at, respectively, paras **19.66** and **19.68** below.
2 The general law of trusts has been augmented in the financial services context by the FCA's client money rules and client money distribution rules, contained in Chapter 7 of the Client Assets Sourcebook (CASS 7) in the FCA Handbook. Among other things, CASS 7 imposes a statutory trust whereby any 'client money' (as defined) received or held by a MiFID firm is to be held on trust for their clients on certain terms. CASS 7 also requires firms to segregate such money by placing it into a client money account so that it is kept apart from the firm's own money. The statutory trust has been held to arise immediately on receipt of the money: see *In the matter of Lehman Brothers International (Europe) (In Administration) and In the matter of the Insolvency Act 1986 [2012] UKSC 6* per Lord Hope, Lord Walker and Lord Collins. The effect of CASS 7, in an insolvency context, is that clients may participate in distributions from the segregated 'Client Money Pool' (as defined), irrespective of whether their 'client money' was actually segregated by the firm in compliance with CASS 7: *Lehman*, per Lord Clarke, Lord Dyson and Lord Collins.
3 'In the modern world, the trust has become a valuable device in commercial and financial dealings': Lord Browne-Wilkinson in *Target Holdings Ltd v Redferns [1996] AC 421*. By way of illustration, in the local authority swaps litigation, it was claimed that payments under void swaps contracts were held on trust (a claim which the House of Lords rejected): *Westdeutsche Landesbank Girozentrale v Islington London Borough Council [1996] AC 669*. Other notable examples include *Guinness plc v Saunders [1990] 2 AC 663*; *Bishopsgate Investment Management Ltd v Maxwell (No 2) [1994] 1 All ER 261*; *Eagle Trust plc v SBC Securities Ltd [1992] 4 All ER 488* and *United Pan-Europe Communications NV v Deutsche Bank AG [2000] 2 BCLC 461*.

Breach of trust

19.64   Where the firm acts as a trustee, it will owe a range of duties in that capacity, the precise nature and extent of which will depend upon the situation, the nature of its role as trustee and the contents of any trust deed. First, the trustee and beneficiary relationship is a fiduciary one and thus gives rise to fiduciary duties on the part of the trustee, discussed in more detail below. Second, trustees owe a statutory duty of care under the Trustee Act 2000, s 1 to exercise such care and skill as is reasonable, having regard in particular to any special knowledge or experience the trustee has and, if the trustee acts in the course of a business or profession (which will usually be the case where firms are concerned), to any special knowledge or experience that it is reasonable to expect of a person acting in that business or profession. Third, trustees are obliged to comply with the terms of the trust, including any duties imposed on them by any applicable trust instrument. In the present context, the duties owed by firms acting as trustees could particularly encompass duties in respect of the holding and investment of fund assets and such duties may, in appropriate circumstances, require the trustee to take action to recover assets from third parties on behalf of the trust[1]. Where the trustee breaches its duties, its liability is, very broadly, to make good the loss caused to the trust[2]. Defences such as lapse of time[3] or the acquiescence of, or release by, beneficiaries with full knowledge of the breach of trust[4] may be available. Additionally, the court has the discretion to relieve partly or wholly a trustee who acted honestly and reasonably and ought fairly to be excused[5].

1 The trustee may be able to protect his own personal position, and obtain an indemnity out of trust assets for the costs of pursuing the claim, by means of a *Beddoe* order: see the discussion at *Snell's Equity* (32nd edn, 2010), at para 7-033.
2 'Equitable compensation for breach of trust is designed to achieve exactly what the word "compensation" suggests: to make good a loss in fact suffered by the beneficiaries and which, using hindsight and common sense, can be seen to have been caused by the breach': Lord Browne-Wilkinson in *Target Holdings Ltd v Redferns [1996] AC 421*. The basic approach is to place the beneficiary in the position in which he would have been had there been no breach of trust; similar principles of causation and quantification of loss are applied as in common law claims. See also the discussion in *Snell's Equity* (32nd edn, 2010), at para 30-011.
3 The Limitation Act 1980, s 21 and see the discussion in *Snell's Equity* (32nd edn, 2010), at 30-035.
4 See the discussion in *Snell's Equity* (32nd edn, 2010), from para 30-28 to 30-030.
5 Trustee Act 1925, s 61. In the case of *Lloyds TSB Bank Plc v Markandan & Uddin (A Firm) [2012] EWCA Civ 65,* the court held that a firm of solicitors were liable to a claimant bank for a breach of trust caused by advancing loan monies to fraudsters who had impersonated the London branch of a firm of solicitors. The court did not exercise its discretion under s 61 because it found that, although the firm of solicitors had acted honestly, it had not acted reasonably in relation to the transaction.

Breach of fiduciary duty

19.65 Where the firm is a fiduciary, for example where it acts as an agent, company director, or as a trustee, various additional obligations are imposed on it which are characterised as fiduciary duties. Primarily, these require the firm to subordinate its own interests to some extent to those of the beneficiary or principal[1]. Accordingly, the firm must act in good faith, is precluded from making undisclosed profits, and from using an opportunity arising while it is acting as trustee or a fiduciary, for personal gain or for the gain of a third person[2]. Furthermore, it is required not to place itself in a position where its own interests and its duty may conflict[3] or where it owes conflicting duties to different beneficiaries or principals, at least without the informed consent of both[4]. If it profits improperly from its position, it must repay the profit to those to whom it owes its duties, irrespective of whether they could have made the profit themselves[5].

1   A useful summary was provided by Millett LJ in *Bristol & West Building Society v Mothew [1996] 4 All ER 698, [1997] 2 WLR 436*.
2   See *Keech v Sandford (1726) Sel Cas Ch 61, [1726] EWHC Ch J76*; *Phipps v Boardman [1967] 2 AC 46, [1966] UKHL 2*; *Guinness plc v Saunders [1990] 2 AC 663, [1989] UKHL 2*; *United Pan-Europe Communications NV v Deutsche Bank AG [2000] 2 BCLC 461*; *Bristol & West Building Society v Mothew [1998] Ch 1*; *Johnson v EBS Pensioner Trustees Ltd [2002] EWCA Civ 164*; and see also *Fyffes Group Ltd v Templeman [2000] 2 Lloyd's Rep 643*. For further discussion, see *Clerk & Lindsell on Torts* (20th edn, 2010), at para 10-22 and *Snell's Equity* (32nd edn, 2010), at para 7-008.
3   See *Bray v Ford [1896] AC 44* and the discussion in *Clerk & Lindsell on Torts* (20th edn, 2010), at 10-28 and *Snell's Equity* (32nd edn, 2010), at para 7-018.
4   See *Clark Boyce v Mouat [1994] 1 AC 428 (Privy Council)* and *Snell's Equity* (32nd edn, 2010), at para 7-036.
5   See, for example, *Phipps v Boardman [1967] 2 AC 46*.

Accessory liability

19.66   A person ('assistant') who dishonestly assists in a breach of trust or fiduciary duty can also be made liable to the beneficiary or principal[1]. Dishonesty here is an objective standard; it means simply not acting as an honest person would in the circumstances. An assistant will be regarded as having been dishonest if, in light of: all the circumstances known to the assistant at the time; the assistant's personal attributes such as his experience, age and intelligence; and the assistant's reasons for acting as he did, his conduct falls short of the standard which would be observed by an honest person placed in those circumstances. Thus, an assistant may be regarded as having been dishonest if he deliberately assisted with a transaction knowing that it involves a misapplication of trust assets or the misuse of a fiduciary's position[2]. Additionally, an assistant may also be regarded as having been dishonest if he is found to have deliberately closed his eyes and ears, or deliberately not asked questions for fear of learning something he would rather not know, and then proceeded regardless[3]. Moreover, an assistant may be regarded as having been dishonest even if he believed he was doing nothing wrong[4]. Therefore, a firm could be liable in respect of a breach of trust or fiduciary duty, notwithstanding it was not the trustee or fiduciary, if it was involved in a breach of trust or fiduciary duty committed by another party.

1   See *Royal Brunei Airlines v Tan [1995] 3 All ER 97; [1995] 2 AC 378*; *Twinsectra Ltd v Yardley [2002] UKHL 12*; *Barlow Clowes International Ltd (in liquidation) v Eurotrust International Ltd [2005] UKPC 37, [2006] 1 All ER 333*; *Starglade Properties Ltd v Roland Nash [2010] EWCA Civ 1314*.
2   See *Royal Brunei Airlines Sdn Bhd v Tan [1995] 3 All ER 97, [1995] 2 AC 378*. For a further discussion, see *Snell's Equity* (32nd edn, 2010), at para 30-076 ff.
3   See *Royal Brunei Airlines Sdn Bhd v Tan [1995] 3 All ER 97, [1995] 2 AC 378*; *Grupo Torras SA v Al-Sabah [2000] All ER (D) 1643, CA*.
4   See *Barlow Clowes International Ltd (in liquidation) v Eurotrust International Ltd [2005] UKPC 37, [2006] 1 All ER 333*; *Starglade Properties Ltd v Roland Nash [2010] EWCA Civ 1314*.

Tracing

19.67   In some situations, a firm could be required to return identifiable trust assets that it still holds[1]. This could include such of a company's assets that have been misappropriated by its directors or employees.

1   For a discussion of tracing at common law and in equity, see *Snell's Equity* (32nd edn, 2010), at para
    30-051.

Knowing receipt and inconsistent dealing

19.68   A firm may also be liable if it beneficially receives funds or property[1] in
the context of a breach of trust or fiduciary duty; and the firm knew at the time
of receipt enough of the facts surrounding the misapplication of trust property or
breach of trust or duty as to render its receipt unconscionable[2]. Depending on the
circumstances, this could result in the granting of a personal remedy against the
firm (such as to make restitution of the funds or the value of the property; to pay
equitable damages; or to account for profits); or a proprietary remedy (such as a
declaration of constructive trust over the transferred property)[3]. Similarly, a firm
which receives, in a ministerial capacity (for example as an agent, bailee or debtor
for a trustee), funds or property belonging to a trust and, with knowledge of the
trust, deals with the funds or property in a manner inconsistent with the trust,
will be accountable in equity for the losses suffered by the trust as a consequence
of the firm's dealing[4]. These two principles of equity are often employed, among
other things, to obtain a remedy from third parties where a firm has been the
subject of a fraud by one of its directors or other employees.

1   The scope of recipient liability appears to have been widened to include non-trust property
    transferred in the context of a breach of fiduciary duty, for example company property transferred
    by a director in breach of his fiduciary duty to a company: see eg *El Ajou v Dollar Land Holdings plc
    [1994] 2 All ER 685* at 700 per Hoffmann LJ.
2   See *Barnes v Addy (1874) LR 9 Ch App 244*; *MacMillan Inc v Bishopsgate Investment Trust plc [No 3]
    [1996] 1 WLR 387, [1995] EWCA Civ 55*; *Bank of Credit and Commercial International (Overseas) Ltd
    v Akindele [2001] Ch 437, [2000] EWCA Civ 502*. For a further discussion, see Goff & Jones, *Law
    of Unjust Enrichment* (8th edn, 2011), from para 8-123 and *Snell's Equity* (32nd edn, 2010), at para
    30-070 ff.
3   For further discussion of the remedies that may be available, see Goff & Jones, *Law of Unjust
    Enrichment* (8th edn, 2011), from para 8-127.
4   See *Lee v Sankey (1873) LR 15 Eq 204, 211*. For a further discussion, see *Snell's Equity* (32nd edn,
    2010), at para 30-074.

Misrepresentation

19.69   The law of misrepresentation may also be relevant, particularly in mis-
selling or other similar cases[1]. In summary, it applies where a person is induced
to enter into a contract with another person by a representation[2] that is false.
Misrepresentations may be made fraudulently[3], negligently[4] or innocently. It
may be possible, depending upon the circumstances, to obtain rescission of the
contract[5] and/or an award of damages[6].

1   See for example, *Smith New Court Securities v Scrimgeour Vickers (Asset Management) Ltd [1997] AC 254,
    HL* (purchase of shares as the result of a fraudulent misrepresentation); *Springwell Navigation Corp v
    JP Morgan Chase Bank [2010] EWCA 1221* (discussed in para **19.62**, n 7 above).
2   Complex rules govern the types of statements that constitute representations for these purposes.
    In summary, they include statements of fact but not, generally, of opinion. For a further discussion,
    see *Chitty on Contracts* (31st edn, 2012), at para 6-006.
3   For a representation made without an honest belief in its truth: see *Derry v Peek (1889) 14 App Cas
    337* and the discussion in *Chitty on Contracts* (31st edn, 2012), at para 6-047.

4   As to a representation made carelessly or without reasonable grounds for believing it to be true: see *Chitty on Contracts* (31st edn, 2012), at para 6-072.

5   Rescission involves *restitutio in integrum* – in other words, both parties must be returned to the position that existed before the contract was entered into. In many instances, this will be impossible, often because the contract has already been partly performed, in which case a court will not order rescission. For further discussion, see *Chitty on Contracts* (31st edn, 2012), from para 6-108. In addition, a party can lose the right to rescind a contract if he affirms it with knowledge of the facts and that he has a right to rescind or avoid it: see *Peyman v Lanjani [1985] Ch 457.*

6   Where there is a negligent or innocent misrepresentation, damages may be awarded in lieu of rescission if it would be equitable to do so having regard to the nature of the misrepresentation and the loss that would be caused by it if the contract were upheld, as well as to the loss that rescission would cause to the other party: see the Misrepresentation Act 1967, s 2(2).

Contribution claims

19.70   Lastly, it is necessary to note that several firms could potentially be liable for the same damage in situations where each owes a duty to the same third party that has suffered the damage[1]. If one firm is liable to the third party[2], it may then be able to seek a contribution from the others[3]. Notably, there is no need for a connection between the firm seeking the contribution and those from which it is sought. In particular, the latter need not owe any duties to the former. Liability for a contribution arises simply because two persons are liable in respect of the same damage suffered by a third party. The amount of such a contribution is within the discretion of the court to determine[4].

1   For example, in cases of mis-selling, the firm that creates an investment product and the firm that subsequently sells it to consumers may both owe duties to those consumers.

2   Liability generally includes a compromise: Civil Liability (Contribution) Act 1978, s 1(4) and see the discussion in *Chitty on Contracts* (31st edn, 2012), at paras 17-029 and 18-022. On compromise generally see Foskett, *The Law and Practice of Compromise* (7th edn, 2010).

3   Civil Liability (Contribution) Act 1978, s 1(1).

4   Civil Liability (Contribution) Act 1978, s 2(1).

PRACTICAL ISSUES ARISING FROM THE INVESTIGATION AND ENFORCEMENT PROCESS

19.71   The firm is unlikely to have the luxury of dealing in isolation with potential claims from customers and other parties. Its freedom of action is likely to be limited in a number of respects by its regulatory obligations[1] and, if a regulatory investigation and enforcement process is being or has been undergone, then this may have an impact upon the firm's potential exposure to damages claims.

1   This may affect how it deals with its customers and employees: see generally **CHAPTER 3**.

19.72   Three issues are discussed here, namely:

• the overlap between civil claims and enforcement powers;

• whether material produced in the investigation and enforcement process can be used and may be discloseable in the civil proceedings; and

• the impact of admissions or findings in the enforcement process.

The overlap between civil claims and enforcement powers

19.73   As already seen, the Regulators have a wide range of enforcement powers available for a variety of purposes. One of the objectives of the FSMA 2000 is the protection of consumers[1] and this is reflected in the availability of various enforcement powers and other mechanisms designed to secure compensation for consumers who have incurred losses as a consequence of regulatory breaches. Thus, for example:

- the FCA or PRA can impose or ask the court to impose a restitution order[2];

- the FCA or PRA can apply to the court for an injunction requiring the firm to remedy its breach[3];

- individual customers may seek compensation through the firm's complaints procedure and the FOS[4]; and

- the firm will in any event need to consider compensating customers voluntarily as part of its own response to the regulatory issue[5] and, as noted above, the FOS now has a regulatory role in setting the standards by which firms must adjudge their potential liability, by account of the FOS's published online decisions as well as decisions they receive directly from the FOS when considering customer complaints[6].

But if the firm makes payments to compensate customers on any of these bases, to what extent does that prevent the customer from bringing further claims against it?

1   For a discussion of the regulatory objectives, see **CHAPTER 1** above.
2   See para **8.100** ff above.
3   See para **8.138** ff above.
4   See **CHAPTER 14** above.
5   The importance of the firm dealing appropriately with its customers when a matter of regulatory concern arises is discussed at para **3.106** ff above and para **13.53** ff above.
6   See para **19.16** above.

19.74   There are two reasons why in practice this matters. First, the basis upon which, for example, restitution is ordered or on which the FOS awards compensation, is rather different from that on which a court awards damages. The most notable example is the cap on FOS awards[1], but there are other differences[2]. There may therefore be a difference between the customer's legal entitlement to damages and the amount that he receives under the FSMA 2000, or is paid voluntarily by the firm. If the customer receives significantly less compensation than he could obtain if he pursued his strict legal rights, then further legal claims may be in prospect. Second, the customer could try to argue that any payment he received was voluntary so far as he was concerned, and did not affect his strict legal rights. In other words, he might try to recover twice. The legal effect of any compensation paid is therefore important.

1   At the time of writing, the cap was £150,000 for claims received on or after 1 January 2012.
2   In imposing a restitution order, the FCA or PRA or, as appropriate, the court will require the firm to pay such amount as is considered 'just' having regard to, among other things, the amount of the losses: see para **8.127** above. The test for the FOS is to award 'fair compensation' for the loss

or damage: see **CHAPTER 14** above. Not only do these tests not necessarily equate with each other, neither need equate with the complex common law rules on the assessment of damages which would apply to a civil claim.

19.75 As a general rule – known as the rule against double recovery – a person is entitled to recover only his net loss. According to this rule, the process of determining the amount of a person's net loss will usually (but not always) take into account any amount he has gained that he would not otherwise have received[1]. There are exceptions to this rule, which may or may not apply in a given case depending on the circumstances and considerations of justice, reasonableness and public policy[2]. The authorities underpinning the rule against double recovery provide strong support for the proposition that payments voluntarily made by a firm to its customer will be taken into account in determining the amount of the customer's net loss. The basic position should therefore be that any amounts the firm pays over to the customer should be taken into account in assessing the damages that the customer can recover in a subsequent civil claim. This basic position does not appear to be changed by the relevant provisions of the FSMA 2000[3].

1 *Hussain v New Taplow Paper Mills Ltd [1988] AC 514* at 527 (Lord Bridge) and see also *Hunt v Severs [1994] 2 All ER 385, HL.*
2 Lord Reid in *Parry v Cleaver [1970] AC 1* at 13; and see *Hussain* at 528; and *Hunt v Severs* at 3823. There are two well-established categories of exception. First, in the insurance context, an insurer's payment to the insured does not extinguish the insured's rights against the wrongdoer; however, so as to avoid double recovery, the insurer is entitled, by subrogation, to benefit from those rights in place of the insured. Second, donations received from benevolent third party donors, motivated by sympathy for the claimant's misfortune, are also generally not taken into account. As to the second category, compare *Rubenstein v HSBC Bank plc [2012] EWCA Civ 1184*, in which a latent payment to the plaintiff made by a failed fund in which the plaintiff had invested, which was expressed as having been made on an ex gratia basis despite there being no contractual entitlement to it, was held not to have fallen within the exception, on the basis that it was not made out of pure benevolence but rather as a continuation of the original transaction and not as a matter entirely collateral to it.
3 The analysis depends upon the following: (i) where the court grants a restitution order, whether or not for market abuse, the FSMA 2000 provides that 'Nothing in this section affects the right of any person other than the FCA or PRA or the Secretary of State to bring proceedings in respect of the matters to which this section applies' (FSMA 2000, ss 382(7) and 383(9)). This appears to address only the question of whether proceedings can be brought, not what is recoverable in those proceedings, and not therefore to affect the general position outlined above; (ii) where the court grants an injunction, the FCA or PRA uses its administrative powers to make a restitution order, or the firm pays compensation voluntarily, the FSMA 2000 is silent on the effect as regards other potential claims. Again, it is thought that there is nothing to dislodge the general principle; and (iii) if the FOS makes an award under the compulsory jurisdiction, which is accepted by the complainant, then the FSMA provides that the award is binding on both the firm and the complainant (FSMA 2000, s 228(5)).

19.76 The Court of Appeal has resolved some uncertainty regarding the recovery of compensation through civil proceedings after a customer has accepted a FOS determination. The Court of Appeal held that if a customer accepts a FOS determination, he or she is not able to seek additional compensation from the firm through the courts if the cause of action relied on is constituted by the same set of facts as the determined complaint. This is because the doctrine of res judicata applies to the FOS's determination[1].

1 *Clark v In Focus Asset Management & Tax Solutions Ltd [2014] EWCA Civ 118.*

19.77   The discussion above considers only the effect of compensation paid by the firm. But in some situations, the customer may also be entitled to or may receive compensation from another party relating to the same losses, for example another firm that was involved and pays restitution. If the customer receives an indemnity for its losses from the third party, then that third party may be entitled to bring the customer's claim against the firm in the customer's name[1].

1   This arises from the doctrine of subrogation, typically, but by no means exclusively, in the context of insurance: see *Castellain v Preston (1883)11 QBD 380* and *Esso Petroleum v Hall Russell [1989] AC 643, HL.*

The disclosure and use of material produced in the enforcement process

19.78   As has already been highlighted[1], firms need to take care not to produce additional documentary material during the investigation and enforcement process which could be discloseable to third parties in any legal proceedings which might be brought against the firm, or indeed which the firm might need to bring, or which might be discloseable in the context of a complaint heard by the FOS in relation to the same matter. The concerns have been outlined in some detail already. To briefly summarise some of the main issues:

- any transcripts of interviews of the firm's staff conducted by the FCA or PRA are likely to be susceptible to disclosure; moreover, documents produced by the firm, including internal audit reports and interviews with staff, and drafts of documents, are also likely to be susceptible to disclosure unless protected by legal privilege;

- material that the firm produces in response to the regulatory process can often be potentially damaging, for example because it provides unhelpful evidence which may be of use to a third party or it highlights aspects of the matter that the third party may not otherwise have recognised;

- confidential information in the FCA or PRA's hands is, generally speaking, protected from disclosure[2]. Confidential information that the firm has received from the FCA or PRA may also, in the same way, be protected from disclosure; and

- various steps that the firm could take to minimise the risks of creating discloseable material are outlined at para **4.177** above.

1   See para **3.142** ff above and the detailed discussion at para **4.145** ff above.
2   Seethe discussion at para **4.174** ff above.

19.79   A practical question for the firm is whether it can use, to defend itself against civil claims by third parties, information which it received from the FCA or PRA during the investigation and enforcement process. For example, the firm may have received from the FCA or PRA information to suggest that the firm did not breach any of the applicable regulatory requirements, or that the relevant breaches were substantially caused by another person, or that another person was the primary cause of any losses.

19.80 In many situations, the firm will not be able to use that information. This is because when the firm receives, directly or indirectly from the FCA or PRA, confidential information which relates to the business or affairs of a person, that information is, generally speaking, protected under the FSMA 2000[1] and, where it is protected, it will be a criminal offence to disclose it in breach of that confidentiality obligation.

1 FSMA 2000, s 348: see para **4.174** ff above.

19.81 The FSMA 2000 does not, however, prevent the firm from using or disclosing information obtained by the FCA or PRA from the firm itself and which relates only to the firm[1]. But firms must take care in relying upon this. If the information was obtained by the FCA or PRA from another party (including an employee as part of a compelled interview), even though the information itself relates only to the firm, or if the information relates to the affairs of another party[2], disclosure would require the consent of the other parties concerned. Without such consent, the firm could potentially commit a criminal offence. In practice, it may be difficult for the firm to know whether material which it received from the FCA or PRA contains information which the FCA or PRA received from another party and it may be necessary for the firm to seek clarification from the FCA or PRA.

1 The firm is entitled to consent to the disclosure (FSMA 2000, s 348(1)), thereby effectively releasing itself.
2 The statutory provision is sufficiently wide to include the business or affairs of a person other than the person under investigation: see *BCCI (In Liquidation) v Price Waterhouse (No 3) [1997] 4 All ER 781* at 791 (Laddie J).

19.82 Furthermore, once information that was confidential has been disclosed in public, for example in Tribunal proceedings[1], then it is no longer subject to the statutory restriction[2]. In some cases, it may be that the need to use information in pending civil proceedings could militate in favour of the firm exercising its right to refer enforcement proceedings to the Tribunal.

1 Tribunal proceedings are normally held in public. For a further discussion, see para **12.37** ff above.
2 'Information is not confidential information if … it has been made available to the public by virtue of being disclosed in any circumstances in which, or for any purposes for which, disclosure is not precluded by this section': FSMA 2000, s 348(4).

The impact of admissions or findings in the enforcement process

19.83 Questions arise as to what extent admissions or findings made in the regulatory enforcement process can impact on the firm's civil liability. For example, if a firm makes certain admissions in the course of attempting to reach a settlement with the FCA or PRA, to what extent can these increase the firm's exposure to civil liability? Similarly, what impact might an adverse finding by the FCA or PRA, or the Tribunal, have on a firm's civil liability[1]?

19.83   Civil liability

1 An FCA or PRA decision notice or second supervisory notice may well be discloseable documents in any civil proceedings, subject possibly to the FSMA 2000, s 348: see the discussion at paras **4.145** ff and **4.175** ff above.

19.84   It is important to keep in mind that establishing that the firm committed a regulatory breach is only one element of the civil claim. This will not of itself make the firm liable to a civil claim, even where the claim is one for breach of statutory duty based on the regulatory breach[1]. Unless the FCA or PRA had applied for a restitution order, the other necessary elements of a civil claim, such as the amount and extent of any losses that were suffered by the particular third party and whether those losses were referable, in legal terms, to the firm's actions, are unlikely to have been in issue in the regulatory proceedings. Resolution of the regulatory enforcement issues should not affect the firm's ability to argue on those other issues to the extent they were not raised in the regulatory proceedings.

1 See the discussion at para **19.18** ff above.

19.85   The more difficult question is whether the firm is allowed to re-litigate the particular issues resolved in the enforcement proceedings, for example whether or not it committed a breach of the relevant regulatory rule. A decision by the Tribunal on a particular matter of fact or law is binding as between the firm and the FCA or PRA, so as to prevent the same issue from being re-litigated between them in any other forum[1]. But if the matter was not referred to the Tribunal, the decision having been made by the FCA or PRA and embodied in a decision notice or supervisory notice, then it is much less likely that the decision has any binding effect in any other forum. Moreover, even if the matter has been decided by the Tribunal and is therefore binding between the firm and the FCA or PRA, this should not prevent it from being re-argued between the firm and any other party. There are, however, also practical considerations to take into account, like whether the firm would wish to be seen to be arguing that it did not commit a regulatory breach, having resolved that issue with the FCA or PRA, and whether express admissions which it made in the regulatory context are likely to be used against it in any subsequent civil proceedings.

1 The particular point, having been decided by a Tribunal exercising judicial functions, is very likely to be res judicata: for further discussion, see Spencer, Bower & Handley, *Res Judicata* (4th edn, 2009), at Chapter 2. See, for example, *Green v Hampshire County Council [1979] ICR 861* and *Crown Estate Comrs v Dorset County Council [1990] Ch 297)*.

19.86   There are four matters that warrant consideration. First, firms may wish to arrive at a settlement with the FCA or the PRA for a variety of reasons. That said, in practical terms, it would be difficult for a firm to distance itself from any express admissions it makes in the course of its settlement negotiations or in the regulatory context otherwise. Such admissions are likely to become public and would provide fertile ground for cross-examination; and it may be unpalatable for the firm to be seen as having changed its position, especially since its original position was taken in the context of the firm's response to a regulatory investigation. Accordingly, firms should take care when negotiating the wording of the eventual final notice, to ensure that the wording agreed with the FCA or PRA does not go beyond what the firm would be prepared to admit in civil litigation[1]. For example, whereas the firm may agree that an incident occurred, it may disagree as to whether the incident amounts to a breach. Furthermore, firms should be wary of agreeing, as a term of the settlement, that they are not to say anything to suggest that they were not in breach[2].

1 For a discussion of the settlement process and the publicity that is likely to result, see para **16.168** above.
2 It had been the FSA's policy to insist that firms should not cast doubt on whether they were in breach. This appeared to change with the *Shell Transport and Trading Company and Royal Dutch Petroleum NV 24/8/4 final notice (24/8/04)*, where the company issued a press release stating that it had come to a settlement with the FSA 'without admitting or denying the findings and conclusions in the FSA's Final Notice': see *Shell News & Media Release (24/8/04)*. However, the FSA did not go as far as the SEC who included the company's lack of admission or denial in its Cease and Desist Order: see Complaint H-04-33523.

19.87   Second, a finding by the FCA or PRA in a settled decision that a firm committed a breach is unlikely to preclude the firm from arguing, in subsequent civil proceedings, that it did not do so, unless the finding was expressly admitted[1]. In such circumstances, the firm may seek to negotiate the precise wording of the decision notice[2]. For example, the firm may seek to persuade the FCA or PRA to use wording such as 'the FCA or PRA considers that' or 'the FCA or PRA regards'.

1 Even express admissions in the regulatory context may not be sufficient to ground a private cause of action. See for example *In re: LIBOR-Based Financial Instruments Antitrust Litigation, 11 MD 2262 (NRB), United States District Court, Southern District of New York, 29 March 2013*, in which the majority of claims filed against a group of international banks including Barclays, UBS and Royal Bank of Scotland arising out of the alleged manipulation of LIBOR were dismissed, despite Barclays, UBS and Royal Bank of Scotland having admitted, in the course of settling a series of regulatory investigations by US regulators and the FSA, to having submitted false interest-rate information to the British Bankers Association used to establish Libor.
2 See para **10.180** above.

19.88   Third, if a firm referred a matter to the Tribunal, and argued throughout that it did not commit a regulatory breach, but the Tribunal found against it, there is theoretically nothing to prevent the firm from maintaining the same position in subsequent civil proceedings against a third party. In practice, however, it is likely that the Tribunal's decision would be given some weight by a court considering the same matter.

19.89   Finally, it is important to note that the above considerations cut both ways, hence if an earlier decision favourable to the firm binds the firm only as against the FCA or PRA, then equally it is not binding on third parties and as such it is open to a third party to argue, notwithstanding a favourable finding in the Tribunal, that the firm did in fact commit a regulatory breach.

of FRA does not go beyond what the firm would be required to admit in civil litigation. For example, whereas the firm may agree that an incident occurred, it may disagree as to whether the incident amounted to a breach. Furthermore, firms should be aware of a settlement, as a term of the settlement, that they are not obliged to suggest that they were not in breach.

1 For the court to refer the appropriate penalty, it is likely that it would have regard to FSA set
and Finalised Guidance 20A, published in 2004 (see also the discussion regarding the role of the
tribunal in paragraph 19.89 with the FSA, although it is likely to be a Tribunal review. In *Pace*
Smith (2016) the conduct of the FSA set out the relevant factors see 19.89 in relation to the
tribunal's own approach, 19.99. para where no admissions of facts have been made. As was made
in the more recent *Stone v FSA (FS/2006) Major Review (2014/49), however the FSA) did not consider the FSA set out the complexity of the conduct of these set out detail in the Company Place or
Galvin. Complaint 14-01-2014.

19.87 Second, a finding by the FCA or RDC in a settled decision that a firm committed a breach is unlikely to preclude the firm from settling, whether or not a firm is charge, that is, for the RDC, unless the findings were expressly admitted. Indeed, notwithstanding, the firm may seek to negotiate the precise wording of the reasons order. For example, the firm may seek to persuade the FCA or FRA to use wording such as the FCA or FRA considers that the FCA or FRA regard.

1 It is common also for the Regulatory Settlement not be a reference to stamp a proven case submissions. For example, in a FSMA Penalty Principle for these aspects, item 2 Action v FSA (2015)
UKUT, case law from *Bank Group Services* one v FSA *Pr Action v FSA* etc. when a the company
claim, producing a large part for an individual para see also to *Pace FSA* as and FSA set the
as an individual stamp from the Commission FSA set FSA 2009.   In claims 1 case the *Smith
(2017) and key Claim of Standard stamp wrongs to be cleared at an end a refer to regulatory
references, but submissions and the FSA set the FSA submitted.   A submitted claim may arise,
on the facts that have aimed from such matters only.
2 See also, in 19.90 above.

19.88 Third, a firm that decides not to fight a case, and is merely forgoing its right to a trial, cannot admit a regulatory breach, but the tribunal found against them, it is not easy for a firm to reverse the firm from maintaining the same position in subsequent civil proceedings, as the tribunal may permit. However, a settlement by the firm itself does not in itself prevent someone else to the court not admitting the agreement.

19.89 Finally, it is important to note that the above cannot serve as more than a number designed favourable to a firm; firms are free only as against the FCA or FRA, that requires it to stay binding on the third parties and is even if it is open to third parties to rely, notwithstanding any favourable finding by the tribunal that the firm did in fact commit a regulatory breach.

Chapter 20   Listed companies

INTRODUCTION

Overview of listing regime

20.1   A problem has arisen in relation to the shares of a listed company. The FCA believes that information may not have been disclosed to the market in breach of the Disclosure and Transparency Rules, or that the company may have failed to comply with requirements governing publication of a prospectus. Who investigates? What powers do they have? Can they obtain information from the listed company? From one of the exchanges? From any authorised firms that were involved – for example, the company's brokers? From other third parties, such as the company's auditors? Following the investigation, what enforcement powers do they have, and against whom?

20.2   The answers to these questions are found in the FSMA 2000, Pt 6, and the Part 6 rules, contained in the FCA Handbook. The main sections are:

(a) the Listing Rules, which contain rules and guidance for issuers of securities admitted (or seeking admission) to the Official List. These rules focus on eligibility for listing, the continuing obligations of listed companies and the obligations of sponsors and Primary Information Providers (PIPs). The Listing Rules also include the overarching Listing Principles that reflect the fundamental obligations of listed companies;

(b) the Disclosure and Transparency Rules[1], known as DTRs, which contain rules and guidance on the publication and control of 'inside information' and the disclosure of transactions by persons discharging managerial responsibilities and their connected persons;

(c) the Prospectus Rules, which contain the rules, regulations and guidance on when a prospectus is required and what it must contain[2].

---

1 The Disclosure Rules were renamed the Disclosure and Transparency Rules in January 2007 as part of the implementation of the Transparency Directive (2004/109/EC).

20.2   Listed companies

2   The purposes of Part 6 in relation to the Prospectus Rules include the purposes of the Prospectus Directive (2003/71/EC) (FSMA 2000, s 73A(5)).

20.3   As will be seen, the FSMA 2000 gives the FCA powers to investigate and enforce the provisions of the FSMA 2000, Pt 6, the Part 6 rules and any other provisions imposed by the Prospectus Directive. These powers overlap to some extent with the FCA's powers in relation to its wider regulatory functions, including its function of policing the market abuse regime, and with the powers of the recognised investment exchanges[1].

1   See para **17.205** ff above for more on the enforcement powers of the exchanges.

What responsibilities does the FCA have in relation to listed companies?

UK Listing Authority responsibilities

20.4   The FCA took over as the UK's competent authority for listing ('UK Listing Authority' or 'UKLA') on 1 April 2013. This role was carried out by the FSA for the period 1 May 2000 to 31 March 2013, and prior to that by the London Stock Exchange.

20.5   The UK Listing Authority is the body referred to in various EU Directives[1] as having functions in relation to the admission of securities to the UK's official list. Admission to the official list signifies that certain minimum standards of investor protection are in place and allows mutual recognition of listing particulars across the EU[2]. The UK Listing Authority functions exercised by the FCA are limited to those given to it in the FSMA 2000, Pt 6. The FCA is not responsible for regulating the trading of listed securities on the recognised investment exchanges, or for admitting securities to trading on each exchange; this is a matter for each exchange itself.

1   See for example, Market Abuse Directive (2003/6/EC); Prospectus Directive (2003/71/EC); Transparency Directive (2004/109/EC).
2   The purpose of the official list is:
    'to protect investors and to improve the working of the single market by harmonising the arrangements for the listing of securities in member states. Whereas there is no obligation on issuers of securities to apply for listing, investors know that issuers of securities that are admitted to the official list of any member state are obliged to provide certain information and fulfil certain conditions if their securities are to remain on the official list. Investors can therefore have confidence that they will have access to information that is sufficient to enable them to make informed decisions. That is, of course, one of the main planks of investor protection.'
    Economic Secretary to HM Treasury in the House of Commons Standing Committee, 28 October 1999 available at http://www.publications.parliament.uk/pa/cm199899/cmstand/a/st991028/am/91028s04.htm.

20.6   The focus of the FCA's role as the UK Listing Authority is on the admission of securities to the official list and on the continuing obligations relevant to the continued admission of securities to the official list. In particular, under the FSMA 2000, Pt 6 the FCA as UKLA has responsibility for the following functions:

- applications for listing;

- cancellation and suspension of listing;

- approval of listing particulars, prospectuses and similar documents;

- the regulation of sponsors and PIPs;

- investigation of breaches of the Part 6 rules and certain offences under the FSMA 2000;

- disciplinary action against issuers, directors and sponsors;

- making rules under the FSMA 2000, Pt 6; and

- giving general guidance in relation to Pt 6.

20.7   The FCA's UKLA function is treated separately in the FSMA 2000 from the FCA's wider regulatory functions. The more general provisions of the FSMA 2000 do apply to the FCA when it exercises its UKLA functions, but this is subject to certain modifications set out in the FSMA 2000, Sch 7.

Wider responsibilities

20.8   First, the FCA also has a wider supervisory responsibility in relation to the recognised investment exchanges, determining applications for recognition and monitoring their continued compliance with the recognition criteria.

20.9   Second, the FCA has an important role in policing market abuse and the criminal offences of insider dealing[1] and misleading statements and practices[2], including responsibility for setting the Code of Market Conduct and for bringing proceedings for market abuse and, where relevant, criminal proceedings[3].

1   Under the Criminal Justice Act 1993, Pt V.
2   Under the Financial Services Act 2012, ss 89–91.
3   These aspects of the FCA's functions are considered in **CHAPTERS 17** and **18** above.

20.10   Third, the FCA has a more general responsibility for regulating firms and individuals who carry on regulated activities under the FSMA 2000. If a problem relating to a listed company involves a regulated firm (for example, the company's brokers or sponsor) or an approved person or certain other individuals, see para **2.52** ff, there may potentially be wider regulatory consequences for that firm or person.

20.11   Finally, under Part 12A, the FCA[1] has powers over the parent companies, including listed companies, of certain firms[2].

1   And the PRA.
2   See para **4.197**.

Principles vs Rules

20.12   In addition to the rules referred to at para **20.2** above, six overarching Listing Principles reflect the fundamental obligations of listed companies[1]. The introduction of the Listing Principles in 2005 marked a significant change in the listing regime. It was a move away from the previous 'black letter' regulation of the words of the Listing Rules and towards requiring listed companies to adopt a culture of regulatory compliance. The six Listing Principles are as follows[2]:

(1) a listed company must take reasonable steps to enable its directors to understand their responsibilities and obligations as directors;

(2) a listed company must take reasonable steps to establish and maintain adequate procedures, systems and controls to enable it to comply with its obligations;

(3) a listed company must act with integrity towards holders and potential holders of its listed equity shares;

(4) a listed company must communicate information to holders and potential holders of its listed equity shares in such a way as to avoid the creation or continuation of a false market in such listed equity shares;

(5) a listed company must ensure that it treats all holders of the same class of its listed equity shares that are in the same position equally, in respect of the rights attaching to such listed equity shares; and

(6) a listed company must deal with the FCA in an open and co-operative manner.

1 The Listing Principles apply to every listed company with a premium listing of equity shares. In CP13/25, the FCA proposed that Principle 2 (adequate systems and controls) and Principle 6 (dealing with the FCA in an open and co-operative manner) should also apply to companies with a standard listing. This change is intended to come into effect in mid-2014. The Listing Principles will be renumbered at the same time.
2 FCA Handbook at LR 7.2.

20.13 The Listing Principles reflect the Principles for Businesses[1], which have been a feature of the regulatory environment for financial services regulation since the FSMA 2000 came into force in 2001.

1 FCA Handbook at PRIN 2.1. See para **2.12** ff above.

20.14 There is a large degree of overlap between the terms of the Part 6 rules and the Listing Principles. To address concerns about the relationship between Listing Principles and the specific rules, guidance has been added to make it clear that the Listing Principles should be interpreted in accordance with the underlying Listing Rules and the DTRs and are designed to assist listed companies in identifying their obligations and responsibilities under the rules and guidance[1]. The policy intention underlying the introduction of the Listing Principles was[2]:

'to ensure adherence to the spirit – as well as the letter – of the rules in the interests of promoting a fair and orderly market. The Listing Principles are intended to inform the interpretation of the rules and to reflect the existing obligations of all primary[3] listed issuers. They are based on recognised standards of corporate governance. In policy terms, the Listing Principles are not intended to apply different standards and processes to issuers than are expected under the existing rules. Our policy position and cost benefit analysis are based on our firm belief that well-managed listed companies would already satisfy the Listing Principles. And issuers who currently comply with the rules and have systems and controls in place to enable them to comply with the rules will be able to comply with the Listing Principles without significant additional cost. The introduction of the Listing Principles should not require issuers to produce long and detailed compliance manuals.'

1 FCA Handbook at LR 7.1.3G.
2 FSA Consultation Paper (CP 05/07), 'The Listing Review and Prospectus Directive', April 2005.
3 Now premium.

Listing Principle 1

20.15 Listing Principle 1 means that listed companies have to operate appropriate training programmes for directors covering, among other things, their obligations regarding the release and control of inside information[1].

1 JJB Sports had its penalty (for failing to disclose the true cost of two acquisitions) reduced because it had provided the board with training in relation to the Listing Rules and DTRs (*JJB Sports plc final notice (25/01/2011)*). In contrast to JJB Sports, Nestor Healthcare Group was fined for failing to train its directors on its share dealing policy (*Nestor Healthcare Group Limited final notice (14/02/2013)*).

Listing Principle 2

20.16 The focus of Listing Principle 2 is on the timely identification, escalation, consideration and, if necessary, disclosure of inside information to the market (as well as identifying whether obligations arise under the class tests or related party provisions of the Listing Rules)[1]. In effect, it poses the question 'if the listed company did not know earlier, why not?'

1 FCA Handbook at LR 7.2.2G and LR 7.2.3G.

20.17 If a listed company fails to meet any of its obligations the FCA will ask how that happened and whether the issuer's systems and controls were adequate. A listed company may well find that a charge of having inadequate systems and controls is brought against it in addition to a charge in relation to specific rule breaches.

20.18 For example, in March 2013 Lamprell plc was fined £2,428,300 for breaching Listing Principle 2 by failing to take reasonable steps to establish and maintain adequate procedures, systems and controls to enable it to comply with its obligations as a listed company; in particular, the FCA found that the shortcomings in its systems and controls meant that Lamprell did not recognise its deteriorating financial position as soon as it should have done, and therefore did not inform the market of its deteriorating financial position in a timely way. In addition, the FSA found that a number of Lamprell's announcements to the market breached several of the DTRs and that it had allowed its directors to deal in securities during a prohibited period in breach of the Model Code.

Listing Principle 3

20.19 Listing Principle 3 requires an issuer to act with integrity towards holders and potential holders of its securities. A breach of Listing Principle 3 has been found in circumstances where an issuer published false and misleading information[1].

1 *Cattles plc final notice (28/03/2012)*. Cattles' CFO was also found to have breached Listing Principle 3 (*James Joseph Corr final notice (28/03/2012)*).

Listing Principle 4

20.20 Listing Principle 4 is designed to ensure that listed companies keep the market updated with accurate and timely information. When it was introduced, the FSA stated[1]:

'Listing principle 4 is not designed to overlay or duplicate well regulated areas of market communication such as Chapter 2 of the Disclosure Rules or elements of sections 118 (market abuse) and 397[2] (misleading statements and practices) of the FSMA. Listing principle 4 is designed to remind listed companies, at a high level, that accurate and timely communication with the market is an important part of the UK regulatory regime. It is not intended to cut across or change existing rules relating to disclosure.'

1 FSA Consultation Paper (CP 05/07), 'The Listing Review and Prospectus Directive' (April 2005), at p 33.
2 Now the Financial Services Act 2012, ss 89–95.

Listing Principle 5

20.21 Listing Principle 5 imposes a straightforward obligation to treat holders of the same class of security equally.

Listing Principle 6

20.22 Listing Principle 6 is a key obligation. It subjects listed companies to a formal requirement to co-operate with the FCA. This may require a listed company to provide to the FCA on request access to its business records, to provide documents and answer questions outside the ambit of a formal investigation and without the FCA exercising its statutory powers to obtain documents. The FSA has recently interpreted it to mean that listed companies have a positive duty to notify the FSA (now FCA) of material information (such as a planned major acquisition) in a timely manner[1]. A failure to co-operate with the FCA can in itself lead to enforcement proceedings.

1 *Prudential plc final notice (27/03/2013)*.

20.23 The wording of Listing Principle 6 does not expressly include an obligation to self-report to the FCA. This is in contrast to the obligation under

Principle 11 of the Principles for Businesses (discussed at paras **3.44** ff and **4.25** ff above). However, the FSA has not accepted the argument that Principle 6 contains no positive duty of disclosure, and that therefore it should be construed narrowly. In *Prudential plc's final notice*, the FSA found that:

> 'The requirement to be "open and co-operative" pursuant to Listing Principle 6 is clear and unambiguous albeit necessarily broad in nature. This is because Principle 6 is a fundamental obligation applicable to all issuers and covers all of their dealings with the UKLA. Guidance as to specific matters which must be disclosed to the UKLA pursuant to Listing Principle 6 would only serve to restrict its necessarily broad ambit. As part of the obligation to deal with the UKLA in an open and co-operative manner, such communication must include within its scope full and timely disclosure'[1].

1 Note that while Prudential plc (as a listed company) was held to have breached Principle 6, its subsidiary, The Prudential Assurance Company Limited, was held to have breached its obligations under Principle 11 of the Principles for Businesses (see *The Prudential Assurance Company Limited final notice (27/03/2013)*). The Prudential Group's Chief Executive was also censured for being knowingly concerned in a contravention of Principle 11 (see *Mr Cheick Tidjane Thiam final notice (27/03/2013)*).

20.24   Part of the reasoning here is that the UKLA does not supervise listed companies, and so it does not have the ongoing dialogue with and information about a company that the FCA would have for a firm which was subject to close and continuous supervision.

20.25   In the Prudential case, the FSA held that Prudential had breached Principle 6 by failing to inform it at the appropriate time that it was seeking to acquire AIA in early 2010. Although Prudential had considered informing the FSA of its discussions with AIA, it had delayed doing so because of its concern about the risk of leaks, and ultimately did not inform the FSA of the proposed acquisition until after the news had been leaked to the media. The FSA considered that Prudential should have disclosed this information at least ten days before it actually did so. Its late disclosure meant that the UKLA had very little time to decide whether or not to make a regulatory decision (in this case, whether to suspend Prudential's shares). The FSA imposed a fine of £14 million on Prudential plc for its breach of Listing Principle 6, imposed another £16 million on its subsidiary The Prudential Assurance Company Limited, for breach of Principle 11 of the Principles for Businesses and censured its Group Chief Executive for being knowingly concerned in that Principle 11 breach.

20.26   The FCA is now consulting on a UKLA Technical Note in relation to Listing Principle 6[1]. In its current form, the FCA states that Principle 6 requires issuers to approach the FCA in relation to 'significant transactions', and that the following considerations are likely to be relevant in deciding whether or not the FCA should be approached:

- Is there a regulatory role for the FCA in the proposed transaction? For example, will the FCA need to provide guidance on the interpretation of a rule, waive or modify the application of a rule, or make a decision on whether a suspension is appropriate?

- Is the decision time-critical? Where a listed company is aware that a decision will need to be made by a certain point in time (for example, making an announcement before the market opens), the company should ensure that it contacts the FCA 'well in advance of the event'.

- Does the timing of contact allow for the FCA to disagree with the proposed approach?

1 UKLA Technical Note, Listing Principle 6 (UKLA/TN/209.1 – Guidance consultation).

20.27 Based on these considerations, the FCA has said that it would expect listed companies to carefully consider the timing of initial contact with the FCA in relation to transactions such as reverse takeovers and class 1 disposals by issuers in financial distress.

Enforcement of the Listing Principles

20.28 The FCA has the power to censure or impose an unlimited fine on a listed company that has breached the Listing Principles and to fine any directors and former directors knowingly concerned in a breach of the Listing Principles by a listed company[1].

1 FSMA 2000, s 91.

20.29 The FCA gives the following examples of cases where it may be appropriate to discipline a listed company on the basis of the Listing Principles alone[1]:

- where there is no detailed listing rule that prohibits the behaviour in question but the behaviour clearly contravenes a Listing Principle; or

- where an issuer of equities with a premium listing has committed a number of breaches of detailed rules which individually may not merit disciplinary action, but the cumulative effect of which indicates a breach of a Listing Principle.

1 FCA Handbook at DEPP 6.2.18G.

What enforcement action has been taken in the past?

20.30 Of the 63 'issues' investigated by the FSA during the year ending April 2013, only three of these investigations related to breaches of the Listing Rules. The FSA took action in five Listing Rules cases during that period[1]. These statistics are broadly consistent with those for previous years[2]. In the past, the FSA said that it became aware of issues requiring investigation via a variety of methods: 'our own monitoring of price movements, complaints from investors or other market participants, or even enquiries to our helpdesk'[3], and that only a small number of these enquiries have resulted in final notices against listed companies or directors.

1 FSA Annual Report 2012/2013, Appendix 2: Enforcement activity 2012/2013.
2 See FSA Annual Report 2011/2012 (four of the 76 issues related to the Listing Rules) and FSA Annual Report 2010/2011 (two of the 85 issues related to the Listing Rules).
3 Speech by Mike Knight, the FSA Manager for Company Monitoring, on 'The Continuing Obligations Regime – the FSA's role' at the City & Financial Conference, 20 November 2008.

Themes emerging from past actions

Emphasis on disclosure

20.31 The past enforcement actions show a strong emphasis on the importance of protecting shareholders by ensuring the full disclosure to the market of all relevant information on a timely basis[1].

1 See also Mike Knight's speech at the City & Financial Conference, 20 November 2008, in which he stressed the importance of the need for listed companies 'to make an ex ante assessment of the likely price impact of certain information'.

20.32 Delays in making announcements of inside information to the market have been consistently penalised, including:

- delays in the announcement of variations to key contracts[1];

- delays in the announcement of negative developments in negotiations to secure a major contract[2];

- delays in the announcement that there was a significant risk that the company would not be able to meet the market expectations it had created in relation to sales[3];

- delays in the announcement of information about the true cost of acquisitions[4]; and

- failure to recognise a deterioration in the company's financial position and therefore delays in the announcement of that deterioration[5].

1 *Woolworths Group plc final notice (11/06/2008); Entertainment Rights plc final notice (19/01/2009).*
2 *Photo-Me International plc final notice (21/06/2010).*
3 *Photo-Me International plc final notice (21/06/2010).*
4 *JJB Sports plc final notice (25/01/2011).*
5 *Lamprell plc final notice (15/03/2013).*

20.33 Action has also been taken where listed companies failed to ensure announcements contained all relevant information and were not false or misleading[1].

1 Recent examples are *Lamprell plc final notice (15/03/2013)* and *Cattles plc final notice (28/03/2012)*. A particularly serious case was the 2004 Shell case (*Shell Transport and Trading Company and Royal Dutch Petroleum NV (final notice 24/8/2004)*), where a financial penalty of £17 million was imposed. Although this penalty related to the finding of market abuse, breaches of the Listing Rules were also found.

20.34 Past enforcement actions also shed light on matters that do not justify non-disclosure of information.

- Offsetting negative and positive news is not acceptable[1]. Companies should disclose both types of information and allow the market to determine whether they cancel each other out.

- Listed companies cannot refuse to disclose negative price-sensitive information because it would cause a fall in the share price or result in the share price not representing the true value of the company or because it would breach a confidentiality agreement between the company and a third party[2].

- The board's responsibility to disclose inside information is not excused by a director's failure to open an e-mail attachment and consider the available information[3].

1 See the *Entertainment Rights plc final notice (19/01/2009)* and the *Wolfson Microelectronics plc final notice (19/01/2009)*. See also Issue 22 of *List!* (August 2009), in which it was reported that a private warning had recently been issued to an issuer over concerns that it may have delayed announcing inside information until it was ready to announce other off-setting news.
2 *Wolfson Microelectronics plc final notice (19/01/2009)*.
3 *Photo-Me International plc final notice (21/06/2010)*.

20.35 There is no set percentage change in the share price of a listed company (or other figure) to determine whether price-sensitive information has the 'significant effect' on the share price that triggers the disclosure obligation[1]. The figure will vary from company to company depending on the circumstances.

1 See the *Woolworths Group plc final notice (11/06/2008)*, in which the FSA rejected Woolworths' argument that a share price fall of 10% or more attributable to the relevant price-sensitive information is needed for there to have been a 'significant effect on price' arising from that information.

Increasing use of Listing Principles

20.36 It has become standard for final notices to hold listed companies and directors to be in breach of the Listing Principles as well as the relevant rules. For example, Cattles plc's publication of false and misleading information about the credit quality of its subsidiary's loan book was found to have amounted to a breach of Listing Principle 3 (integrity) and Listing Principle 4 (creation of a false market), in addition to Listing Rule 1.3.3R (not publishing misleading information)[1]. Exillon Energy was found to have breached Listing Principle 2 (adequate systems and controls) as well as Listing Rule 11.1.10R(2) (related party transactions)[2]. Nestor Healthcare Group Limited was found to be in breach of the Model Code, Listing Rule 9.2.8, and as a result, was also in breach of Listing Principle 1 (taking steps to enable directors to understand their responsibilities) and Principle 2 (systems and controls)[3].

1 By the date of the final notice (28/03/2012) Cattles plc was no longer a going concern. The final notice states that had it been a going concern with significant surplus assets, a 'substantial' financial penalty would have been imposed. As it was, Cattles was censured. James Corr, Cattles' finance director, was fined £400,000 (discounted from £750,000 for financial hardship) and prohibited from carrying on any regulated activity.
2 *Exillon Energy plc final notice (26/04/2012)*.

3   This was the first time a penalty was imposed on a company for breaches of the Listing Rules and Listing Principles relating to compliance with the Model Code, which sets out minimum standards restricting the ability of persons discharging managerial responsibilities from dealing in the company's securities.

20.37   In March 2013, Prudential plc became the first listed company to be fined for a breach of a Listing Principle alone, with no reference to a breach of any other rule. Importantly, the FSA recognised in the Prudential case that the company had not breached Principle 6 recklessly or intentionally, but found that the seriousness of the breach nonetheless warranted (significant) action on the FSA's part. This confirmation from the FSA that it would penalise non-intentional breaches of the Listing Principles was a clear departure from its historic rules-based approach. It is also consistent with a recent statement from the FCA that it intends to keep the listing regime 'flexible' so that it can 'stay vigilant to changing market practices'[1].

1   See speech by David Lawton, Director of Markets, FCA, on 'Investor relations in an increasingly regulated and international world', 18 June 2013.

DTR breaches

20.38   The FSA initially undertook not to take an enforcement-led approach to ensuring compliance with the rules introduced following the implementation of the Transparency Directive in 2007. There have been a series of indications that it now sees that undertaking as less relevant[1], and the first fine for breach of the transparency obligations was issued in 2011[2].

1   See Issue 20 of *List!* (January 2009) and Mike Knight's speech at the City & Financial Conference, 20 November 2008, in which the FSA noted that it had issued a private warning to a shareholder for a breach of DTR 5 where a person had failed to disclose a significant holding of voting rights. See also Issue 21 of *List!* (May 2009), in which the FSA stated that interim management statement requirements in DTR 4 were not always being complied with and that issuers should be aware that they risk possible enforcement action for not complying with these requirements.
2   Sir Ken Morrison was fined £210,000 for failing to disclose his reduced shareholding and voting rights in Wm Morrison Supermarkets plc (*Sir Ken Morrison final notice (16/08/2011)*).

Sponsors

20.39   The first finding that a sponsor had breached the Part 6 rules was made in 2011. BDO LLP was censured for failing to act with due care and skill, and failing to deal with the FSA in an open and co-operative way[1]. In 2012 the FSMA 2000 widened the FCA's powers to impose sanctions on sponsors[2].

1   *BDO LLP final notice (26/05/2011)* found breaches of LR 8.3.3 and LR 8.3.5(1).
2   See para **20.108** ff below for more detail.

Penalties

20.40   The level of penalty issued depends on the severity of the breach[1] but penalties in recent years have ranged from £140,000[2] to £14 million[3]. Factors considered by the FCA in deciding on a suitable penalty will include: the extent of the delay; the taking of professional advice in a timely manner in relation to disclosure obligations (although the FCA has noted that listed companies always retain primary responsibility for compliance); compliance history and the adequacy of internal processes[4].

1   The FCA's policy on the imposition of financial penalties and public censures is set out in the FCA Handbook at DEPP 6 and in the FCA Enforcement Guide at EG 7.
2   *Wolfson Microelectronics plc final notice (19/01/2009).*
3   *Prudential plc final notice (27/03/2013).*
4   FCA Handbook at DEPP 6.

20.41   Penalties will be calculated in accordance with the five step process set out in DEPP 6[1].

1   See para **8.61** ff.

20.42   The FCA will use its power to censure where it is unable to impose a financial penalty on a company that lacks financial resources[1].

1   See *Cattles plc final notice (28/03/2012)* and *Eurodis Electron plc final notice (09/12/2005).*

20.43   It is important that listed companies deal appropriately with the FCA in the context of investigations to assist the prospect of a reasonable outcome. This may mitigate the level of fine imposed on a company found to be in breach[1].

1   See, for example, the *Woolworths Group plc final notice (11/06/2008).*

FCA INVESTIGATIONS

What powers does the FCA have to investigate suspected breaches?

20.44   The FCA can enquire into suspected breaches of the FSMA 2000, Pt 6 or the Part 6 rules in two ways. First, it can use the information-gathering powers contained in the Part 6 rules. Second, it can commence an official investigation.

20.45   The overarching question for the FCA in deciding whether to proceed under the information-gathering powers or whether to appoint an investigator is likely to be the question of what represents the most effective and efficient means of obtaining the information it needs to confirm whether or not a breach has taken place.

20.46   In practice, the FCA will almost invariably start by way of an informal approach, usually a letter requesting that information and/or documents be supplied by a specified deadline.

Information gathering

20.47   The Part 6 rules contain a number of provisions that require listed companies, persons discharging managerial responsibilities and their connected persons, and sponsors to provide information to the FCA.

20.48   In addition to the overarching Listing Principle 6 obligation to deal with the FCA in an open and co-operative manner, the Listing Rules more particularly oblige issuers[1] to provide to the FCA as soon as possible[2]:

- any information and explanations that the FCA may reasonably require to decide whether to grant an application for admission;

- any information that the FCA considers appropriate in order to protect investors or ensure the smooth operation of the market; and

- any other information and explanations that the FCA may reasonably require to verify whether the Listing Rules are being and have been complied with.

1   Issuer is a complex defined term but broadly, in the context of the Part 6 rules, it means any legal person, any class of whose securities has been admitted to listing or is the subject of an application for admission to listing or any legal person, any class of whose financial instruments have been admitted to trading on a regulated market; or are the subject of an application for admission to trading on a regulated market.
2   FCA Handbook at LR 1.3.1.

20.49   The Listing Rules require a sponsor to[1];

- deal with the FCA in an open and co-operative way; and

- deal with all the enquiries raised by the FCA promptly.

1   FCA Handbook at LR 8.3.5.

20.50   Under the DTRs an issuer, together with persons discharging managerial responsibility or connected persons, must provide to the FCA as soon as possible[1]:

- any information that the FCA considers appropriate in order to protect investors or ensure the smooth operation of the market; and

- any other information or explanation that the FCA may require to verify whether the DTRs are being and have been complied with.

1   FCA Handbook at DTR 1.3.1.

20.51   The FCA may also require certain persons (including voteholders, issuers and their directors or officers) to provide to the FCA specified information reasonably required in connection with the Transparency Rules[1].

1   FSMA 2000, s 89H.

20.52   These are broad powers, containing no express limits on the range of information that the FCA can request from the issuer, director or senior executive and/or sponsor concerned.

20.53   Although there is a reasonableness limitation on any FCA demands for information under the Listing and Transparency Rules, this is not the case under the Disclosure Rules.

20.54   The range of people from whom the FCA may request such information is, however, limited to issuers, their directors, senior executives and connected persons, and sponsors. It cannot, for example, under the Part 6 rules require the company's brokers or auditors to provide information[1].

1 It would appear that the FCA could approach the company, asking it to obtain information or an explanation from a third party, and to provide that information or explanation to the FCA. Listed companies will usually want to be seen to be co-operating with the FCA and may therefore be willing to comply. The FCA does not, however, have the power to go directly to the third party unless the third party is an authorised firm or approved person (or possibly certain other individuals, see para **2.52** ff above).

20.55 However, the information-gathering powers in the Part 6 rules should not be viewed in isolation. If a regulated firm is involved, for example, because the listed company concerned happens to be a firm, the investigation relates to a sponsor, or information is required to be obtained from a broker, the FCA's general information-gathering powers will apply (see **CHAPTER 4** above). Other FCA powers may also be relevant, including:

• the power to obtain information from, require co-operation from or investigate a recognised investment exchange[1]; and

• the power to investigate regulatory or criminal offences, including market abuse and the criminal offences of insider dealing and misleading statements and practices (see **CHAPTER 17** above).

1 FSMA 2000, Pt 18; REC 4.

20.56 A listed company, director or sponsor may be willing initially to provide information to the FCA pursuant to its obligations under the Part 6 rules. However, there may come a stage where it is preferable to be subject to a formal investigation, particularly where the questions arise in a situation which it is clear may lead to disciplinary or enforcement action being considered.

20.57 A formal investigation will entail the person concerned being notified of the investigation and the reasons for appointment of the investigator. The investigator will be exercising statutory powers within clear limits and certain statutory safeguards will be available.

Formal investigations

On what grounds can the FCA initiate a formal investigation?

20.58 The FSMA 2000, s 97 sets out the situations in which the FCA may appoint an investigator to conduct on its behalf an investigation into suspected breaches of the FSMA 2000, Pt 6, the Part 6 rules or ss 85 or 87G.

20.59 The FSMA 2000, s 97 hurdle is a low one. It need only 'appear to the FCA' that there are 'circumstances suggesting' a breach has occurred. There does not need to be, for example, reasonable grounds for suspecting that a breach has occurred. This largely leaves within the discretion of the FCA the question of whether an investigation should be commenced. As a result, it would be difficult to challenge a decision to appoint an investigator on the ground that the statutory test had not been met.

20.60 In principle, such an investigation could be brought in relation to any person who has an obligation under the Listing Rules, DTRs or Prospectus Rules, including listed companies, applicants for listing, sponsors and PIPs. It will also include investigations into breaches of the DTRs by issuers, persons discharging managerial responsibilities or connected persons.

Investigation process

20.61 The formal investigation process starts with written notice to appoint an investigator, the reason for the appointment and the provisions invoked. The FCA team will then have scoping discussions with the company to provide a clear indication of the scope of the investigation, how the process will unfold, the documents required and the people to be interviewed. This may be a rolling process as the scope is clarified.

20.62 During the investigation, the FCA has wide-ranging statutory powers to collect any information and material, including through formal interviews of witnesses, it considers may be relevant.

20.63 The FSMA 2000, Pt 11 applies to a s 97 investigation as if the investigator was appointed under the FSMA 2000, s 167(1)[1]. **CHAPTER 5** above discusses in detail the powers of an investigator once appointed.

1 FSMA 2000, s 97(3)(a).

Issues in relation to investigations

20.64 The general issues that arise in relation to formal investigations, including the consequences of non-compliance, notification, privilege and self-incrimination are discussed in **CHAPTER 5** above.

20.65 However, one point worth mentioning here, given the potential for insider dealing or market abuse proceedings to overlap with proceedings for breach of the Part 6 rules[1], is that persons compelled to an interview cannot decline to answer questions on the ground that the answer might incriminate them. There is, however, some limited statutory protection in terms of the use to which information thus obtained can be put, if the person interviewed is later charged with a criminal offence or is subject to proceedings for market abuse. Broadly, in those circumstances, a statement compulsorily obtained cannot be used against the person who made it. A more detailed discussion of the privilege against self-incrimination, and particularly the limits of this protection, can be found at para **4.205** ff above.

1 For example, based on the misuse of unpublished price sensitive information or on the specific criminal offences at FSMA 2000, Pt 6A, s 85.

20.66 Listed companies

20.66 Another potential issue in the listing regime context is that the FCA may initially be concerned with the listed company or its sponsor, rather than with the actions of a particular director, but subsequently realises that it may wish to take enforcement action against a director. A person may thus be required to provide information without realising that he or she is the target of the investigation. Clearly, the director will not have been formally notified, at the outset, of the commencement of the investigation, since he or she was not the person under investigation.

20.67 The FCA addresses this in two ways. First, it will always provide an indication of the nature and subject matter of its enquiries to those who are required to provide information. Second, once it becomes clear who the persons under investigation are, the FCA will normally notify them when it proceeds to exercise its statutory powers to require information from them. This ought in practice to mean that the director concerned, if asked to provide information before being informed he or she is the target of the investigation, is at least aware of the nature of the investigation[1].

1 See para **5.40** for more on this issue.

What can the FCA do with any information gained?

20.68 Once the investigator completes the fact-finding investigation, the findings must be reported to the FCA, as the appointing body. The FCA will then use that information in order to consider whether to exercise any of its disciplinary or enforcement powers under the FSMA 2000, Pt 6, as outlined below.

20.69 An interesting question is what will the FCA do with information it considers to be relevant to its wider regulatory functions or to the functions of another body. For example, the information may:

- raise concerns about the conduct of firms or individuals (for example, a broker or sponsor or their employees);
- indicate that market abuse may have taken place;
- indicate the commission of a criminal offence that is a matter for the Serious Fraud Office or the police;
- indicate that there is a Companies Act issue; or
- highlight matters which concern the exchange on whose market the securities in question are traded.

20.70 The starting point is that confidential information obtained by the FCA or by an investigator appointed by it is protected against disclosure by the statutory prohibition found in the FSMA 2000, s 348. It is a criminal offence for a person to disclose information in breach of this prohibition. The statutory prohibition is, though, subject to certain exceptions, most notably the ability

782

to make disclosures permitted under the Gateway Regulations[1] made by HM Treasury[2].

1 Financial Services and Markets Act 2000 (Disclosure of Confidential Information) Regulations 2001, SI 2001/2188 ('the Gateway Regulations').
2 See para **4.233** ff above.

20.71 Under the Gateway Regulations, the FCA and/or an investigator appointed by it may disclose confidential information internally for the purpose of enabling or assisting it to discharge its wider regulatory functions. It would therefore be prudent for those subjected to an investigation to assume that information provided to the FCA or its investigator under an investigation conducted pursuant to the FSMA 2000, s 97 will, where relevant, be shared more widely within the FCA.

20.72 With regard to sharing the information outside the FCA, whether on the FCA's own initiative or in response to a request from another regulator, the FCA or the investigator will need to consider in each case whether disclosure to the particular regulator or body concerned is permitted under the Gateway Regulations. The Regulations are complex but they do permit disclosure to, among others:

- a UK recognised investment exchange, for the purpose of enabling or assisting it to discharge its functions;

- the Panel on Takeovers and Mergers, the Office of Fair Trading and the Competition Commission for the purpose of enabling or assisting them to discharge their functions[1]; and

- various types of overseas regulatory authorities.

1 Gateway Regulations, reg 12, Schs 1 and 2.

20.73 They also permit the disclosure of information for the purposes of criminal investigations or proceedings[1].

1 Gateway Regulations, reg 4.

20.74 The FCA has indicated that it may share with UK and overseas authorities information it is not prevented from disclosing[1]. Whether the FCA will do so in the particular case will depend largely upon the circumstances. It may also in practice depend upon the FCA's relationship with the body concerned. Again, it would be prudent to assume that information will be shared with any other relevant regulatory or prosecuting bodies.

1 FCA Enforcement Guide, at EG 2.16.

The risk of disclosure to third parties

20.75 The findings of the FCA or its investigator may be of interest to third parties, particularly if they consider they have suffered loss from the matters alleged against the person concerned for which they may have a legal claim. An important question is therefore whether there is a risk of the third party obtaining a copy of any documents produced by the FCA or its investigator, either from the FCA or investigator direct or from the person under investigation, to the extent that such documents have been provided to that person. The answer is, broadly, that there are risks of a third party obtaining disclosure. These issues are considered in more detail at para **4.174** ff above.

How should companies deal with the FCA in an investigation?

20.76 Practical steps that might be considered when a regulatory problem arises are reviewed in **CHAPTER 3** above. Many of the issues discussed there arise equally in the context of potential breaches of the Part 6 rules by listed companies.

20.77 It is crucial that document preservation and management arrangements are put in place immediately following any approach by the FCA. It is a criminal offence to falsify, conceal, destroy or otherwise dispose of any document (or cause or permit another to do so) that a person knows or suspects is relevant to an investigation that he knows or suspects is being or is likely to be started by the FCA.

20.78 Once the listed company becomes aware that a breach has taken place, it may need to appoint a sponsor (if it does not already have one). The FCA has the power, in the event of a breach or suspected breach of the Part 6 rules, to notify a company with, or applying for, a premium listing of shares, that the appointment of a sponsor is required[1]. The sponsor must guide the company in understanding and meeting its responsibilities under the Part 6 rules[2]. The FCA attaches great importance to the role and responsibilities of a sponsor and, where relevant, to the opinions and reports of the listed company's other professional advisers, in satisfying itself that all the relevant requirements of the Part 6 rules have been complied with.

1 FCA Handbook at LR 8.2.1R(5).
2 FCA Handbook at LR 8.3.1R(2).

20.79 A sponsor has an obligation promptly to notify the FCA if it becomes aware that either the sponsor or the company is failing or has failed to comply with its obligations under the Part 6 rules[1]. Caution therefore needs to be exercised in communicating with the sponsor, to ensure that prejudicial material is not produced that might need to be disclosed by the sponsor to the FCA or to a third party in the context of any legal proceedings.

1 FCA Handbook at LR S8.3.5A.

CONSEQUENCES OF BREACH

Disciplinary sanctions

20.80 The disciplinary powers of the FCA in relation to breaches of the Part 6 rules are found in the FSMA 2000, s 91. The section provides for the FCA to impose a financial penalty on or publish a statement censuring those responsible for breaches.

20.81 In addition to the s 91 disciplinary powers, the FCA also has power to censure an issuer under s 87M; and to censure or impose a financial penalty on a sponsor under s 88A or on a PIP under s 89Q.

20.82 The nature and effect of financial penalties, public censure and the FCA's alternative of giving a private warning are discussed in detail in **Chapter 8** above, as is the FCA's approach towards determining the appropriate sanction.

20.83 There is a three-year[1] limitation period for bringing disciplinary proceedings under ss 91, 88A and 89Q. The three-year period begins with the first day on which the FCA knew of the contravention. The FCA is treated as knowing of a contravention if it has information from which the contravention can reasonably be inferred. Proceedings are treated as begun when a warning notice is given.

1 The limitation period was increased from two to three years by the Financial Services Act 2012.

20.84 The imposition of disciplinary sanctions under s 91 expressly does not preclude the FCA from taking any other action available to it under the FSMA 2000, Pt 6. A disciplinary sanction may therefore be imposed in conjunction with actions such as the suspension of listing of the issuer's securities.

20.85 Further, the same action may give rise to FCA enforcement actions under the Part 6 rules against different parties – for example, if it appeared that the listed company had breached the Part 6 rules and that its sponsor or corporate brokers had failed to act with due skill, care and diligence. As has already been seen, the FCA is generally speaking able to share information which it receives in its investigation internally[1].

1 See para **20.71** ff above.

20.86 In addition to the power to fine or censure, the FCA also has power in certain circumstances to:

- suspend or cancel the listing of the relevant securities[1];
- suspend an issuer's securities from trading[2]; or
- suspend or prohibit an offer to the public or admission of transferable securities to trading on a regulated market[3].

1 FSMA 2000, s 77.
2 FSMA 2000, s 89L.
3 FSMA 2000, ss 87K and 87L.

Suspension of listing

20.87 Under the FSMA 2000, s 77, the FCA may suspend the listing of any securities where:

- the smooth operation of the market is, or may be, temporarily jeopardised; or

- the protection of investors so requires.

20.88 The test for the suspension of securities from listing is a broad one and it leaves the FCA a significant amount of discretion both to determine whether to act and to determine when to take action and for what period. The power to suspend listing can also be exercised as a matter of urgency.

20.89 The FCA gives a non-exhaustive list of circumstances in which it is likely to suspend listing, namely, where[1]:

- the issuer has failed to meet its continuing obligations for listing;

- the issuer has failed to publish financial information in accordance with the Listing Rules;

- the issuer is unable to assess accurately its financial position and inform the market accordingly;

- there is insufficient information in the market about a proposed transaction;

- the issuer's securities have been suspended elsewhere;

- the issuer has appointed administrators or receivers, or is an investment trust and is winding up;

- for a securitised derivative that relates to a single underlying instrument, the underlying instrument is suspended;

- for a securitised derivative that relates to a basket of underlying instruments, one or more underlying instruments of the basket are suspended; or

- for a miscellaneous security that carries a right to buy or subscribe for another security, the security over which the listed miscellaneous security carries a right to buy or subscribe has been suspended.

1 FCA Handbook at LR 5.1.2G.

20.90 The FCA will not suspend the listing of a security to fix its price at a particular level.

20.91 An issuer, the listing of whose securities is suspended, remains obliged to comply with all the Listing Rules and DTRs applicable to it, including the requirement to notify the FCA of any breaches of Listing Rules of which it becomes aware.

20.92 An issuer wishing to have a suspended listing restored has two options. First, the issuer may seek to have the original decision to suspend the listing overturned through the enforcement process, ultimately in the Tribunal. If successful, this will result in the listing being restored.

20.93   Second, the issuer may apply to the FCA to have its listing restored. The FCA may restore the listing of any securities that have been suspended if it considers that the smooth operation of the market is no longer jeopardised or if the suspension is no longer required to protect investors[1].

1   FCA Handbook at LR 5.4.2R.

20.94   Where there are reasonable grounds to suspect non-compliance with the DTRs the FCA may also require the suspension of trading of a financial instrument. Such suspensions can be with effect from such time and in such circumstances as the FCA determines and may be performed either unilaterally by the FCA or at the request of the issuer concerned.

Cancellation of listing

20.95   The FCA may cancel the listing of securities where it considers that special circumstances are precluding 'normal regular' dealings in those securities[1]. This gives the FCA a broad discretion to cancel the listing of securities. This is clearly a serious power which is not to be used lightly. By way of a non-exhaustive list, the FCA states that it may cancel the listing of securities where it appears that[2]:

*   the securities are no longer admitted to trading as required by the Listing Rules;

*   the issuer no longer satisfies its continuing obligations for listing, for example, if the percentage of shares in public hands falls below 25% or such lower percentage as the FCA may permit;

*   the securities' listing has been suspended for more than six months; or

*   the securities are equity shares with a standard listing issued by an investment entity where the investment entity no longer has a premium listing of equity shares.

1   FSMA 2000, s 77(1); FCA Handbook at LR 5.2.1R.
2   FCA Handbook at LR 5.2.2G.

20.96   The FSA will generally seek to cancel the listing of an issuer's equity shares or certificates representing equity securities when the issuer completes a reverse takeover[1].

1   FCA Handbook at LR 5.2.3G.

20.97   The cancellation of a listing can only be revoked through the enforcement process. Beyond that, the issuer will need to make a new application for admission to listing.

Urgent suspensions or cancellations

20.98   The FCA has a broad discretion to determine when a suspension or cancellation of listing becomes effective[1]. There is no statutory hurdle which must be passed before the power can be exercised as a matter of urgency, nor is there any general fallback position that the suspension or cancellation takes effect only when the enforcement process has been completed. The Listing Rules and guidance give no indication of the FCA's policy on when in practice it will exercise its powers as a matter of urgency.

1 FSMA 2000, s 78(1).

20.99 There is unlikely to be a need to cancel a listing as a matter of urgency. However, the securities could be suspended in the first instance and cancellation may, if appropriate, follow in due course.

Suspensions or cancellations at request of issuer

20.100 If an issuer requests the FCA to cancel or suspend a listing of the issuer, the streamlined procedure in the FSMA 2000, s 78A applies.

Sanctions for breach of transparency obligations

20.101 Where the FCA has reasonable grounds for suspecting that an applicable transparency obligation has been infringed by an issuer or voteholder, the FSMA 2000, s 89L provides that it may prohibit or suspend trading in an issuer's securities[1].

1 Or make a request to the operator of the market on which the securities are traded to suspend or prohibit trading.

Sanctions for breach of prospectus obligations

20.102 Where there are reasonable grounds for suspecting that a provision of the FSMA 2000, Pt 6, a provision contained in the Prospectus Rules or any other provision made in accordance with the Prospectus Directive applicable in relation to an offer to the public or a request for admission to trading on a regulated market has been infringed, the FCA may[1]:

- require the offeror to suspend or withdraw the offer to the public of transferable securities; or

- require the person requesting admission to suspend the request for admission or, if already admitted, require the market operator to suspend or prohibit trading in the securities on the regulated market.

1 FSMA 2000, ss 87K and 87L. The FCA may also exercise its ss 87L and 87K powers to assist the competent authority of another EEA Member State perform its Prospectus Directive functions if that EEA state has approved a prospectus in connection with transferable securities being offered in the UK or admitted to trading on a regulated market.

Directors and former directors

20.103 The FCA can take enforcement action against a director or former director who was knowingly concerned in an issuer's breach of the Part 6 rules[1].

1 FSMA 2000, s 91(2). See para **2.126** ff above for discussion of the 'knowingly concerned' test.

20.104 The FCA has indicated that it regards the issuer as having primary responsibility for ensuring compliance with its own regulatory obligations and, therefore, any disciplinary action will normally be taken in the first instance against the issuer itself and those persons identified in the FSMA 2000, s 91(1) and (1A)[1]. However, where a director was knowingly concerned in the issuer's breach, it may take action against the director. It may also do so where it does not consider it appropriate to seek a disciplinary sanction against the issuer[2].

1 FCA Handbook at DEPP 6.2.10G.
2 Paragraph **9.16** ff considers the question of when in practice the FCA will take action personally against an individual rather than, or in addition to, the firm for which the approved person works in the context of the FCA's wider regulatory functions. The FCA's policy is based on whether the approved person (or other employee) is personally culpable.

20.105 In the cases in which the FCA has taken action against the director, the director concerned (the CEO) had specific knowledge of the event giving rise to a reporting obligation, had responsibility for compliance with the Listing Rules and failed to take the steps required or act with sufficient urgency[1]. Bad faith and/ or an intention to mislead the market on the part of the director is not required before the FCA will take enforcement action against a director.

1 *Universal Salvage plc and Martin Christopher Hynes final notice (19/05/004); Sportsworld Media Group plc and Geoffrey John Brown final notice (29/03/2004).*

20.106 In addition, persons discharging managerial responsibilities (in effect directors and senior executives with a role involving access to inside information) and their associated persons, including their spouse, have their own responsibilities under the DTRs[1]. Enforcement action for a breach of the Disclosure Rules will not therefore necessarily involve the issuer[2].

1 Note, however, that the requirements to disclose and control inside information in Chapter 2 of the DTRs apply only to issuers. Persons exercising managerial responsibility do not have direct responsibility for compliance with the provisions of Chapter 2.
2 FSMA 2000, s 91(1ZA).

20.107 A director with inside information who deals in the company's securities may be guilty of the criminal offence of insider dealing and may commit the civil offence of market abuse[1].

1 See **Chapter 17**.

Sponsors

20.108 The FSMA 2000 provisions introduced in 2012 widen the FCA's power to impose sanctions on sponsors. In addition to the pre-existing powers to publicly censure[1] and to cancel a sponsor's approval[2], the provisions now allow the FCA to[3]:

- impose a penalty on a sponsor;

- suspend the sponsor's approval; or

- impose limitations in relation to the performance of services to which the sponsor's approval relates.

20.108   Listed companies

1   Previously contained in the FSMA 2000, s 89, now found in s 88A.
2   FSMA 2000, s 88.
3   FSMA 2000, s 88A.

20.109 The FCA has indicated that it will only cancel a person's approval to act as a sponsor if it considers that the sponsor no longer meets the criteria for approval as a sponsor[1]. In deciding whether to cancel approval, the FCA will take into account all relevant factors, including but not limited to[2]:

- the competence of the sponsor[3];

- the adequacy of the sponsor's systems and controls;

- the sponsor's history of compliance with the Listing Rules;

- the nature, seriousness and duration of the suspected failure of the sponsor to meet (at all times) the criteria for approval as a sponsor; and

- any matter which the FCA could take into account if it were considering an application for approval as a sponsor.

1   FCA Handbook at EG 18.1. The criteria for approval are found at LR 8.6.5.
2   FCA Handbook at EG 18.2.
3   Note that the FCA proposes to increase and clarify the requirements for sponsor competence: see FCA Consultation Paper CP 14/2 (30/01/2014).

20.110 A sponsor is an authorised person and so is also amenable to the FCA's wider regulatory jurisdiction.

Primary Information Providers (PIPs)

20.111 The FSMA 2000 provisions introduced in 2012 give the FCA the power to impose sanctions on PIPs. Previously approval and monitoring of PIPs was done on a non-statutory basis. The provisions allow the FCA to[1]:

- impose a penalty on a PIP;

- publicly censure a PIP;

- suspend the PIP's approval;

- impose limitations in relation to the giving by the PIP of information; or

- cancel a person's approval to act as a PIP[2].

1   FSMA 2000, s 89Q.
2   FSMA 2000, s 89P.

When and how will the FCA exercise its disciplinary powers?

FCA policies and procedure

20.112 There are, broadly speaking, two different types of FCA enforcement process[1]:

- the warning/decision notice procedure; and

- the supervisory notice procedure.

1 See **CHAPTER 10** above for more detail on the enforcement processes.

Warning notice / decision notice procedure

20.113 If, following an investigation, FCA enforcement staff propose:

- to cancel a listing;

- to cancel or refuse an application for a person's approval as a sponsor or PIP; or

- to fine or publically censure an issuer, applicant, director, former director, sponsor, or PIP,

the warning notice/decision notice procedure applies and the matter is submitted to the FCA's Regulatory Decisions Committee (RDC)[1].

1 See **CHAPTER 10** above for detail of the procedure.

Supervisory notice procedure

20.114 If, following an investigation, it is proposed:

- to discontinue or suspend the listing of a security (including on the application of the issuer);

- to suspend or prohibit an offer to the public or admission to trading on a regulated market; or

- to suspend trading in a financial instrument,

the supervisory notice procedure applies and the decision is not taken by the RDC, but under so-called 'executive procedures' by either the Senior Staff Committee of the FCA or an individual FCA staff member[1].

1 See the FCA Handbook at DEPP 4 and **CHAPTER 16** above for more detail.

20.115 The FSMA 2000 allows the FCA to discontinue or suspend the listing of securities immediately if the FCA considers it necessary[1]. The supervisory notice procedure applies to any subsequent decision by the FCA not to cancel the discontinuance or suspension. If the FCA decides to cancel the discontinuance or suspension, it must give the issuer written notice of its decision but no particular procedure is prescribed.

1 See further para **20.87** above.

20.116 Note that if an issuer applies to cancel a suspension and the FCA proposes to refuse the application, the warning/decision notice procedure applies. If the FCA accedes to the application, it must give the issuer written notice of its decision but no particular procedure is prescribed.

Interplay with criminal and other regulatory actions

20.117 Notwithstanding the range of potential disciplinary and enforcement actions available to the FCA for breaches of the Part 6 rules (and other breaches of the FSMA 2000, Pt 6), as outlined above, these are not the only powers that may be relevant in relation to such breaches.

20.118 First, if a criminal offence may have been committed, the FCA's general policy is to pursue through the criminal justice system all those cases where criminal prosecution is appropriate[1]. If the FCA does contemplate a criminal prosecution, broadly speaking this does not preclude it from taking other civil or regulatory action in relation to the same matter. However, the civil or regulatory proceedings may be required to await the outcome of the criminal proceedings if there is otherwise a real risk of prejudicing the criminal proceedings[2].

1 See para **18.8** ff above.
2 See further at para **18.40** ff above.

20.119 Second, there may well be circumstances where the action in question amounts both to market abuse and to a breach of the Part 6 rules. Market abuse and regulatory action for breach of the Part 6 rules involve different considerations. It is important to be aware of the potential effect of actions in one context upon potential liability in the other. For example, for a listed company to settle a disciplinary case against it by admitting a breach of the Part 6 rules might cause it great difficulty in defending subsequent market abuse proceedings.

20.120 Third, if the matter concerns an authorised firm or an approved person (or certain other employee of an authorised firm, see para **2.52** ff above), then it may give rise to wider concerns which could have other regulatory consequences, for example, leading to the exercise of the FCA's disciplinary powers or its power to vary a firm's permission or to withdraw an approved person's approval.

20.121 Finally, the matter may give rise to action both by the FCA and by another regulatory body, such as an exchange or an overseas regulator. In that situation, the FCA will examine the circumstances of the case and consider, in the light of the relevant investigation and enforcement powers, which body should take action to address the breach, recognising that it may be appropriate for both to take action[1].

1 See **CHAPTER 17**.

20.122 A company with dual-listing might find itself exposed to regulatory action in both jurisdictions in which it has a listing for failure, for example, promptly to release information to the market. In addition to potentially facing action for a breach of, say, the DTRs in both jurisdictions in which it is listed, a company may also face regulatory proceedings in third-party Member States where the misconduct has had an effect on qualifying investments listed there. A listed company will need to be careful how it deals with the regulators in more than one jurisdiction as, for example, different rules on document production and privilege are likely to apply (as explained in **CHAPTER 7**). The company may also find itself having to deal with investigations by the criminal authorities in certain EU Member States.

Civil liability to third parties

20.123 The FSMA 2000, s 138D provision giving private persons a claim for losses as a result of the contravention of a rule by a firm does not apply to contraventions of Part 6 rules[1]. However, a listed company, sponsor or other person may be liable to compensate a third party who has suffered loss in certain circumstances.

1 FSMA 2000, s 138D(5)(a).

20.124 First, there may be a claim under the general law[1]. Second, a breach of the FSMA 2000, s 85, which prohibits securities from being offered to the public in the UK until an approved prospectus has been published, is actionable at the suit of a person who suffers loss as a result[2].

1 See **CHAPTER 19** for more on general law claims.
2 The elements of this potential civil claim are discussed in more detail at para **19.37** above.

20.125 Third, the FSMA 2000, s 90A makes issuers liable to pay compensation to persons who suffer loss as a result of an untrue, misleading or delayed statement or an omission by the listed company. The listed company's liability extends to all information published by it via an RIS[1].

1 FSMA 2000, Sch 10A, para 2.

20.126 The third party's loss must have resulted from the acquisition, continued holding or disposal of the listed company's securities in reliance on the issuer's published information or any omission from that published information of any matter that it should have included[1].

1 FSMA 2000, Sch 10A, para 3.

20.127 A listed company is only liable for an untrue or misleading statement if a person discharging managerial responsibilities knew the statement to be untrue or misleading or was reckless as to that fact. Where a statement is delayed or facts required to be included are omitted, the listed company is liable if the person discharging managerial responsibilities dishonestly delayed publication or dishonestly concealed a material fact. A person discharging managerial responsibilities may be personally liable to the listed company for the loss suffered by it[1].

1 FSMA 2000, Sch 10A, para 3.

Civil liability arising from the contents of listing particulars

20.128 The FSMA 2000, s 90 makes specific provision for civil liability to arise in certain situations in relation to the content of listing particulars. The provision is complex and only a brief summary is provided here.

20.129 Liability arises in two situations. First, any person responsible for listing particulars is liable to pay compensation to a person who has:

- acquired securities to which the listing particulars apply; and

- suffered loss in respect of them as a result of any untrue or misleading statement in the particulars or omission from the particulars of any matter required to be included by the FSMA 2000, ss 80 or 81.

20.130 Second, any person who fails to comply with the requirements to issue supplementary listing particulars under the FSMA 2000, s 81, is liable to pay compensation to any person who acquired securities of the kind in question and suffered loss in respect of them as a result of the failure.

20.131 Several points are worth noting. First, in contrast with the FSMA 2000, s 138D, the right of action is not limited to private persons, but applies to any person who suffers loss in the circumstances set out in the FSMA 2000. Second, it does not affect any other liability which may be incurred. In other words, the existence of a cause of action under the FSMA 2000, s 90, does not affect the person's ability to rely upon any alternative or additional causes of action which he might have as a matter of law. Third, whilst the provision makes clear that liability arises, the person concerned would have to bring proceedings in the civil courts in order to obtain the damages to which he was entitled.

20.132 The FSMA 2000, s 90(12) precludes a person, in certain circumstances, from incurring civil liability for a summary in a prospectus, unless the summary is misleading, inaccurate or inconsistent when read with the rest of the prospectus.

What information will be publicly available?

20.133 Generally speaking, the investigation process ought not of itself to give rise to any publicity. The expectation should be that no publicity will arise either in relation to the fact that the FCA is investigating or in relation to the outcome of the investigation, but there are exceptions.

20.134 The FCA may, in exceptional circumstances, make a public announcement that it is or is not investigating a particular matter if it considers such an announcement desirable to maintain public confidence in the financial system, protect consumers, prevent widespread malpractice, or help the investigation itself (for example, by bringing forward witnesses). The FCA has identified particularly that this may arise where the matters under investigation are the subject of such public concern, speculation or rumour that it is desirable for it to do so to allay the concern, or contain the speculation or rumour. In deciding whether to make an announcement, the FCA will consider the potential prejudice that it believes may be caused to any persons who are, or who are likely to be, a subject of the investigation. The FCA will also need to consider to what extent it is able to disclose information given its obligations of confidentiality under the FSMA 2000, s 348.

20.135 Similarly, the FCA may, in exceptional circumstances, and where it is not prevented from doing so by the FSMA 2000, s 348, publish details of the information found or conclusions reached in its investigations. In particular, it may do so where the fact that it was investigating was made public, and it subsequently concludes that the allegations were unfounded, particularly if the person concerned wants the FCA to clarify this.

20.136 In addition, it is important to recognise that publicity may arise:

- unavoidably from the investigation itself, for example, because the FCA's enquiries attract publicity;

- from enforcement action taken by the FCA while its enquiries are still continuing (for example, urgent action to suspend the listing of shares) or by other regulatory authorities (including the FCA acting in its wider regulatory capacity); or

- if the matter results in disciplinary or enforcement action being taken or in the matter being referred to the Tribunal. The FCA will usually publicise successful enforcement action that it takes. This will usually be in the form of a press release giving details of the breach and the fine imposed or other action taken.

Chapter 21   Complaints and challenges against the Regulators

INTRODUCTION

21.1   The Tribunal, considered in **CHAPTER 12** above, provides an important, impartial forum for firms and individuals aggrieved with the action which one or more of the Regulators propose to take in relation to them. Recourse to the Tribunal is not, though, generally available as of right. It is available only in those instances where the FSMA 2000 specifically prescribes that it is available; generally speaking, this is where the Regulators decide to impose a particular regulatory sanction, take particular action, or take a decision relating to a person's authorisation, permission, approval or recognition under the FSMA 2000[1].

1   An explanation of certain enforcement matters that can be referred to the Tribunal can be found in the FSMA 2000, s 133(7A).

21.2   There will, therefore, be many other situations where the Regulators take a decision affecting a firm or individual, which the person may wish to challenge but where there is no right to refer the matter to the Tribunal. For example:

- the decision to initiate a formal investigation;

- the decision on whether the appointment of an investigator should be notified to the person under investigation;

- the way that an investigator appointed to carry out a formal investigation exercises his investigation powers;

- the way that the FCA or PRA operate their internal decision-making procedures;

- the decision on the extent to which the person is entitled to have access to the Regulators' material during the enforcement process; and

- the decision to publish information about urgent action that the Regulators wish to take before the matter can be heard by the Tribunal.

21.3 Complaints and challenges against the Regulators

21.3 In such situations, how can the person affected challenge the action that the Regulators have taken or propose to take[1]? In many cases, including all of the examples above, the issue will arise in the course of a process which ultimately may lead to Tribunal proceedings. For example, if the firm is aggrieved that an investigation has been commenced against it without, in its view, good reason, or is dissatisfied with the way in which the investigation is being conducted, there may be some comfort to be drawn from the fact that, if any regulatory enforcement action follows based on the results of that investigation, the firm will, in most cases, have the option of referring the matter to the Tribunal[2]. Indeed, if the firm did so, the firm may be able to refer to such matters in the course of the Tribunal proceedings to the extent that they bore on the substantive issues but also because the Tribunal, as well as having the task of deciding the substantive issues, has been given, by statute, the power to make recommendations about the Regulators' rules and procedures when determining the reference[3]. However, there may be various reasons why the firm may not wish to refer the matter to the Tribunal, not least because, whilst it may feel aggrieved by aspects of the process, it may nonetheless not wish to dispute the substantive action taken against it by the Regulators.

1 Another question that may arise is what powers others (such as shareholders and other investors) have to challenge the taking of, or failure to take, such action by the Regulators.
2 It would not have that option if a Regulator instituted civil proceedings for an injunction or restitution order or a criminal prosecution: see, respectively, **CHAPTER 19** and **CHAPTER 18** above (although in those cases the civil or criminal court would instead provide a forum for any relevant issues to be heard).
3 See para **12.155** above. For example, in *Legal & General Assurance Society Ltd v FSA [2005] All ER (D) 154 (Jan)*, the Tribunal commented on shortcomings in the enforcement process for reaching the decision but, nevertheless, declined to make statutory recommendations under the FSMA 2000, s 133(8) in the light of the pending enforcement process review announced in February 2005.

21.4 In some circumstances, therefore, the person concerned may wish to challenge aspects of the Regulators' procedure (or the decisions that the Regulators have made in operating that procedure) separately from the question of whether the result of the procedure was appropriate. Alternatively, the issue may arise in situations in which no right of recourse to the Tribunal arises. The question of how to mount such a challenge is the focus of this chapter.

21.5 The firm has two options, and both may be available depending upon the circumstances of the particular case. These are:

• to challenge the Regulators' use of their powers through legal proceedings (considered at para **21.7** ff below); and/or

• to bring a complaint against the Regulators (considered at para **21.44** ff below).

In explaining potential legal proceedings and complaints against the Regulators in this chapter, references to the term 'the Regulators' also includes the Bank. This differs from the use of this term in the rest of the book.

21.6 Whilst this chapter focuses on the challenges that individuals and firms can bring, the FSMA 2000 provides a number of other methods by which the

Regulators are held accountable. For example: the PRA or FCA can be obliged to present evidence to and respond to questions from Parliament's Treasury Select Committee; the FCA is specifically subject to the scrutiny of the FCA Practitioner, Smaller Business Practitioner, Markets Practitioner and Consumer Panels[1]; and the PRA is subject to the PRA Practitioner Panel[2]. The FSMA 2000 obliges the Regulators to have regard to the generally accepted principles of good corporate governance[3] and to report annually to the Treasury on the extent to which they have achieved their regulatory objectives[4]. The FCA has non-executive directors[5] and is required to hold an annual general meeting at which stakeholders can question the board[6] and the PRA is required to invite the public to make representations in relation to its annual report[7]. Finally, the Treasury is entitled to launch an enquiry into events that pose a grave risk to the financial system, including the conduct of the Regulators in that regard[8]. None of these are considered in detail in this book.

1   FSMA 2000, ss 1M, 1N, 1O, 1P and 1Q.
2   FSMA 2000, ss 2L and 2M.
3   FSMA 2000, s 3C.
4   FSMA 2000, Sch 1ZA, para 11; and Sch 1ZB, para 19. The Treasury then presents the reports to Parliament.
5   FSMA 2000, Sch 1ZA, para 2.
6   FSMA 2000, Sch 1ZA, para 12 .
7   FSMA 2000, Sch 1ZB, para 20.
8   Financial Services Act 2012, s 68.

CHALLENGING THE REGULATORS

What options does the firm have?

21.7   There are two mechanisms for bringing legal proceedings against the Regulators in relation to the misuse of their powers, depending upon what the firm is seeking to achieve and upon the circumstances of the case.

21.8   First, the acts and omissions of the Regulators, as public bodies, are, when they exercise their public functions, amenable to the supervisory jurisdiction of the High Court, exercised by the procedure known as judicial review.

21.9   Second, where judicial review is inappropriate, or in some circumstances as an alternative to it, the person concerned may be able to bring civil proceedings against the Regulators claiming damages or another remedy, such as an injunction or declaration. This is subject to the Regulators' statutory immunity against liability in damages[1], discussed at para **21.36** below.

1   FSMA 2000, Sch 1ZA, para 25 for the FCA; FSMA 2000, Sch 1ZB, para 33 for the PRA; and the Banking Act 2009, s 244, for the Bank of England. See para **21.31** ff below.

21.10   The following paragraphs review the circumstances in which each option may be available and provide an indication of when in practice firms might consider bringing such proceedings.

Can the firm urgently prevent the Regulators from taking action?

21.11 The most immediate question likely to face a person when the Regulators take or propose to take action which the person believes is wrongful, is whether the Regulators can be prevented from taking that action, as a matter of urgency, pending the outcome of the legal challenge. Alternatively, where the action which the firm disputes is a requirement for it to take a particular step (for example, to provide particular information to an investigator appointed by the Regulators) which has already been imposed, the question will be whether the person can refuse to comply with that requirement pending the outcome of the legal proceedings.

21.12 In practice, the first step may be to ask the Regulators voluntarily to refrain from taking the relevant action pending the outcome of the legal proceedings. If the Regulators are unwilling to do so, the person may, in an appropriate case, be able to obtain an interim remedy from the court to protect it pending the determination of the substantive dispute. Such a remedy might, for example, include an interim injunction restraining the Regulators from taking a particular step, an interim declaration or a stay of the administrative process which the person seeks to challenge[1]. Whilst such interim measures are in theory available, they may not be of practical use in this context. An example of when it might be appropriate to apply for an interim remedy would be if the firm seeks to prevent the Regulators from taking and publicising urgent action (and the Tribunal is unable or unwilling to suspend that action).

1 See the Civil Procedure Rules at CPR 54.10. Stay of proceedings means, in this context, a stay of the process by which the decision challenged has been reached, including the decision itself.

21.13 For practical purposes, the key question will be whether the court will grant the interim remedy or stay in the circumstances of that particular case.

21.14 In deciding whether to grant an interim injunction, the court considers whether the claim raises a serious issue to be tried and, if so, where the balance of convenience, including the wider public interest, lies[1]. It may also require the person applying for the interim remedy to give a cross-undertaking in damages. The outcomes following the application of these tests, particularly the balance of convenience test, can be difficult to predict given that the court will need to assess conflicting arguments put forward on behalf of the firm and the Regulators. Where the balance is likely to fall will, to a large extent, depend upon the particular situation[2].

1 CPR 54.3.6.
2 The 'balance of convenience' approach has been described as 'the course which, in all the circumstances appears to offer the best prospect that eventual injustice will be avoided or minimised' – *R v Secretary of State for Transport, ex p Factortame Ltd (No 2) [1990] UKHL 13, para 5.*

21.15 Another way to challenge action of the Regulators is to refuse to comply with their requirements and, as a defence to any proceedings brought against the person as a result, state that the requirements were unlawful. For example, where the requirement is to provide information to an investigator appointed by the Regulators, the court's primary sanction for non-compliance would be to treat the person as if he were in contempt of court if it were to find no reasonable excuse for the non-compliance[1]. In such a case, the person could seek to argue that a reasonable excuse existed, based on his contentions about whether that requirement should have been imposed on him. This strategy involves risks, since the person may be punished by the court if the court does not agree that a reasonable excuse for non-compliance existed.

1 This is discussed in more detail at para **5.76** above.

Bringing an application for judicial review

21.16 Judicial review provides an important mechanism by which decisions of public bodies can be examined by the Administrative Court. The possibility of an application for judicial review, against either the Regulators or another body acting under the FSMA 2000, such as the FOS or the complaints commissioner, may arise in a variety of situations. Whether the procedure is available, and its suitability as an appropriate means of seeking redress, will depend upon the circumstances of each case.

What are the restrictions on the availability of judicial review?

21.17 There are four important restrictions on the availability of judicial review.

21.18 First, judicial review does not involve a court reaching its own decision on the merits of the case. Where the court agrees to exercise its supervisory jurisdiction over a public body, it is concerned only with the lawfulness and fairness of the decision in question and the process by which that decision was reached.

21.19 Second, judicial review is a remedy of last resort[1]. Generally, where alternative remedies for redress exist and/or where another forum for the resolution of the dispute is considered by the Court to be more appropriate, the decision is unlikely to be reviewable until such remedies have been exhausted. Therefore not every decision of the Regulators or another body under the FSMA 2000 is necessarily capable of being judicially reviewed. Where the FSMA 2000 provides no other means of protection against abuse in relation to a particular type of decision, such as a decision to initiate an investigation, the decision is possibly reviewable. Where an alternative remedy is provided by the statutory scheme, such as referring the decision to take enforcement action to the Tribunal, however, it is unlikely that an application for judicial review of the decision will succeed. For example, the Court of Appeal rejected an application for judicial review of an FSA decision to issue a decision notice[2] because the Tribunal could consider the underlying subject matter of the decision notice. The court considered the Tribunal was a more appropriate forum than the court, because the court could consider only whether sufficient reasons were given for the decision and, if necessary, refer the decision back to the RDC to consider afresh, without resolving whether the decision notice was justified on its merits. The courts have not ruled out the use of judicial review in exceptional circumstances where there is recourse to the Tribunal[3] but have not specified what those circumstances are.

1 See Lord Steyn in *R v Hammersmith and Fulham London Borough Council (No 1), ex p Burkett [2002] UKHL 23, [2002] 1 WLR 1593* at para 42.
2 *R v Financial Services Authority, ex p C Willford [2013] EWCA Civ 677* at paras 36 and 37 where Moore-Bick LJ considered that provision under statute for challenges of RDC decisions to the Tribunal led to a presumption that the Tribunal was the appropriate alternative remedy to judicial review proceedings save in exceptional cases. The Court of Appeal decision in that case reversed the first instance decision *R v Financial Services Authority, ex p C [2012] EWHC 1417 (Admin), [2012] ACD 97.*
3 *R v Financial Services Authority, ex p C Willford [2013] EWCA Civ 677, CA* at para 37.

21.20 Third, the person applying for judicial review must have a sufficient interest in the matter to have standing to bring an application[1]. This is unlikely to be an obstacle for a firm or individual wishing to challenge a decision that has been taken in relation to it by the Regulators. Industry bodies or associations are also likely to have standing, provided that the body is reputable and well-placed to bring the claim, and that the issues raised are of real importance[2]. However, more difficult questions may arise where an application is brought by a firm's customer or market counterparty, who may believe that a decision taken by a Regulator in relation to a firm affects them[3]. Even if such persons do not have a sufficient private interest, they may have standing where the issue is one of genuine public interest[4].

1 Senior Courts Act 1981, s 31(3).
2 See discussion in Supperstone (4th edn), at 18.9.1, and more generally 18.2–18.10; and Fordham (6th edn), at 38.2. Also, *R v Financial Services Authority, ex p BBA [2011] EWHC 999 (Admin), [2011] WLR (D) 144*, in which the BBA had standing to challenge the FSA's rules and guidance on the handling of complaints about PPI and the FOS's policy on dealing with such complaints.
3 In *R v Financial Services Authority, ex p Coull Money [2012] EWHC 612 (Admin)*, an independent financial advisor had insufficient standing to challenge a decision to establish a payment scheme that was set up to pay Arch Cru investors 70 per cent of the value of their investment, although the firm claimed that the failure of the FSA to consult on the scheme and failure to explain that 70 per cent return to investors was fair and reasonable would increase the risk of claims by investors for the balance of their investment.
4 See *R v Secretary of State for the Environment, Food and Regular Affairs, ex p Freakins [2003] EWCA Civ 1546, [2004] 1 WLR 1761; R v Surrey County Council, ex p Williams [2012] EWHC 867, [2012] All ER (D) 56 (Jun).*

21.21 Fourth, any application for judicial review should be brought without delay and, in any event, within three months of the date of the decision that is challenged.

What are the potential grounds for judicial review?

21.22 The grounds on which decisions of public bodies, including the Regulators, may be subject to review can be broadly classified under three heads: unlawfulness, unreasonableness and unfairness[1].

1 See discussion in Fordham (6th edn), at 45.1; also a more general introduction in Supperstone (4th edn), at 1.5.

21.23 Unlawfulness or illegality arises when the decision-maker has made an error of law or exercised a power incorrectly. The latter will occur where the decision-maker has acted in a way that exceeds its powers (ultra vires), attempted to exercise its powers beyond their scope[1], or improperly delegated a power where the law does not allow delegation. In the present context, unlawfulness will most likely arise where the Regulators misinterpret the relevant provisions of the FSMA 2000[2].

1 For example, in obtaining and using documents covered by common interest privilege in enforcement action without obtaining a waiver of privilege from all the relevant parties: See *R v Financial Services Authority, ex p Ford [2011] EWHC 2583 (Admin), [2012] 1 All ER 1238.*
2 See *R v Financial Services Authority, ex p BBA [2011] EWHC 999 (Admin), [2011] WLR (D) 144,* in which the BBA claimed, albeit unsuccessfully, that the FSA's PPI complaints handling rules and guidance and the FOS's approach to PPI complaints were based on a misinterpretation of the FSMA 2000. See also *R v Financial Services Authority, ex p Canada Inc [2011] EWHC 2766 (Admin); R v Financial Services Authority, ex p Amro International [2010] EWCA Civ 123, [2010] 3 All ER 723.*

21.24 Unreasonableness may arise in a number of situations. First, where a body, such as the Regulators, have made a decision that is so unreasonable that no body properly directed could reasonably have reached that decision (referred to as irrationality or Wednesbury unreasonableness)[1]. Second, where a decision was reached on the basis of an error of fact[2]. Third, where the decision-maker took into account irrelevant considerations or failed to take into account relevant matters[3]. Generally, it will be difficult to challenge the Regulators on grounds of unreasonableness given the high threshold that must be satisfied. A challenge based on irrelevant considerations will be particularly difficult, given that the factors that the Regulators may take into account pursuant to the FSMA 2000 when making decisions are usually broadly phrased.

1 See *Associated Provincial Picture Houses Ltd v Wednesbury Corpn [1948] 1 KB 223.*
2 See *R v Secretary of State for the Home Department, ex p Ali [2007] EWHC 1983 (Admin),* where it was successfully argued that the decision-maker had reached its decision on a material misunderstanding of the facts and failed to have regard to the proper factual situation. See also Fordham (6th edn), at p 49.
3 The courts will not intervene in determining what is relevant unless the decision-maker has acted unreasonably in the *Wednesbury* sense, per Lord Keith in *Tesco Stores Ltd v Secretary of State for the Environment [1995] UKHL 22, [1995] 1 WLR 759 at 841;* as considered in *R (Sainsbury's Supermarket Ltd) v Wolverhampton City Council [2010] UKSC 20, [2011] 1 AC 437.* For further discussion, see Fordham (6th edn), at p 56.

21.25 Unfairness will arise where the decision-maker has failed to comply with statutory procedures, for example by failing to consult or give reasons[1], or if it has failed to comply with the rules of natural justice.

1 See *R v Financial Services Authority, ex p Coull Money [2012] EWHC 612 (Admin)* and *R v Financial Services Authority, ex p C Willford [2013] EWCA Civ 677, CA,* which brought judicial review claims using this ground.

How are judicial review proceedings commenced?

21.26 Judicial review proceedings are brought in the Administrative Court under a procedure set out in Part 54 of the Civil Procedure Rules. These proceedings comprise two distinct stages: an application for permission; and a substantive hearing. A claim for judicial review cannot proceed to a substantive hearing without leave of the court at the permission stage. The general rule is that permission will be granted if the case is arguable to the extent that there is a realistic prospect of success, and when there are no other reasons for withholding permission, such as delay (even if the application is made within the three month limitation period[1]) or the availability of an alternative remedy. In many cases though, both the permission and substantive stages take place together in a 'rolled-up' hearing[2].

1 Senior Courts Act 1981, ss 31(6) and 31(7).
2 For a discussion of rolled-up hearings, see Supperstone (4th edn), at 19.19.1.

What remedies are available?

21.27 If an applicant for judicial review obtains permission and is successful at the judicial review hearing itself, the court may grant various remedies. In brief[1], they are:

- a quashing order, setting aside the decision of the public body and, in some cases, remitting it to that body for reconsideration;

- a mandatory order, requiring the public body to carry out its duty;

- a prohibiting order, restraining the public body;

- a declaration[2] or injunction[3]; and/or

- damages[4].

1 For a more detailed discussion, see Fordham (6th edn), at Chapters 24 and 25 and Supperstone (4th edn), at Chapters 16–17.
2 Declarations are a particularly flexible type of relief, often used in practice: see the discussion in Fordham (6th edn), at 24.2. Declarations are also available in civil actions: see para **21.35** below.
3 Senior Courts Act 1981, s 31(2).
4 Damages can only be sought in addition to another remedy, and will only be awarded where there is some private law cause of action for damages: see the Senior Courts Act, s 31(4). Maladministration does not of itself give rise to such a claim: see Fordham (6th edn), at 25.1. In the case of the Regulators, damages claims are probably only permissible where the Regulators have acted in bad faith or in breach of the Human Rights Act 1998: see para **21.36** ff below.

21.28 The granting of a remedy is at the discretion of the court. This means that a firm could establish that the Regulators' actions were wrongful and yet find that the court refused to grant relief[1]. This is because the court has a broad discretion and can therefore take a wide variety of considerations into account in deciding what relief (if any) to grant.

1 See *R v Financial Services Authority, ex p Ford [2011] EWHC 2583 (Admin), [2012] 1 All ER 1238*, in which the court held that the FSA had exceeded its powers by using privileged documents but declined to quash the warning notice because, even with all references to privileged material removed, the RDC viewed the regulatory action and proposed sanction as justified.

Whether to bring a judicial review application

21.29 The answer to the question of whether the person concerned should bring a judicial review application will depend very much upon the particular circumstances. It should, though, be apparent from the above that judicial review will not always be an appropriate or attractive route. There is no right to bring an application for judicial review; this depends upon whether the court's permission can be obtained in the particular case. The grounds for making an application are limited and whether a remedy is granted is a matter of discretion. Furthermore, the presumption is that the proceedings will be held in public and the person concerned will be at risk of being required to bear the Regulators' costs if unsuccessful. However, in many situations there will be no alternative means of obtaining redress against what is perceived to be an abuse by the Regulators, save for the complaints scheme outlined below. Judicial review is therefore an important means of obtaining redress in appropriate cases.

Bringing a civil action against the Regulators

21.30 In some instances, the firm may wish to bring a civil claim against the Regulators, rather than use the process of judicial review. For example, the time limit of three months to bring judicial review proceedings may have passed, the firm may primarily be seeking damages, the firm may wish to avoid first having to apply for permission to bring proceedings (which is a requirement for judicial review proceedings but is not necessary for normal civil claims), or the matter may be one which is not suitable for judicial review[1].

1 For example, the right to bring proceedings against a public body for ECHR breaches under the Human Rights Act 1998, see Wadham, Mountfield, Prochaska and Brown *Blackstone's Guide to The Human Rights Act 1998* (2011) at 3.15 ff.

21.31 In considering bringing a civil claim against the Regulators, three key potential obstacles arise, namely, the need for quantifiable losses, the Regulators' statutory immunity for liability in damages, and issues concerning abuse of process.

21.32 First, some or all of the firm's losses may not be quantifiable. Civil claims are, generally speaking, concerned with compensating claimants' quantifiable losses that have arisen from wrongs committed by others.

21.33 Second, even where the firm has suffered loss, it will, in many instances, be precluded from bringing a claim for damages because of the Regulators' statutory immunity. This is considered in more detail below.

21.34 Third, civil proceedings can be used not only to obtain damages, but also to obtain other remedies such as an injunction or declaration. Claims for such remedies may appear to be attractive alternatives to bringing judicial review proceedings, particularly if the three-month limitation period for commencing judicial review proceedings has expired. However, courts are wary of allowing civil proceedings to be used in this way precisely because this may have the effect of depriving the public body of the protections built into the judicial review process and could be viewed as an abuse of process where judicial review is available[1].

1 See Lord Diplock in *O'Reilly v Mackman [1983] 2 AC 237, HL* and, for a further discussion, Supperstone (4th edn) at 3.21 ff.

21.35   The civil courts may grant a declaration which will have the effect of authoritatively pronouncing whether a person's conduct is consistent with its legal obligations. It is not clear whether the Regulators' statutory immunity from damages claims (discussed below) will preclude a person from obtaining a civil declaration against it. Such declarations may be obtained on an interim basis[1] and in certain circumstances may be regarded as a potentially attractive option given the limited remedies available to firms.

1   See the Civil Procedure Rules at CPR 25.1(1)(b).

What effect does the statutory immunity of the Regulators have on potential claims?

21.36   The FSMA 2000 confers an immunity from liability in damages which, in many instances, precludes damages claims being brought. The immunity covers:

- the Regulators, and any person who is, or who is acting as, a member of the Regulators' staff, in relation to anything done, or omitted, in the discharge, or purported discharge, of the Regulators' functions[1];

- the complaints Commissioner and any person appointed to conduct an investigation on his behalf, in relation to anything done, or omitted, in the discharge, or purported discharge, of his functions in relation to the investigation of a complaint[2];

- the Financial Services Compensation Scheme and any person who is, or is acting as, its board member or officer of it or member of its staff, in relation to anything done or omitted in the discharge, or purported discharge, of its functions[3];

- a recognised investment exchange or recognised clearing house, and its officers and staff, in relation to anything done, or omitted, in the discharge of its regulatory functions[4]; and

- any person in relation to anything done or omitted in the discharge, or purported discharge, of any functions under the FSMA 2000 in relation to the compulsory jurisdiction (this refers to the FOS and his staff)[5].

1   FSMA 2000, Sch 1ZA, para 25 for the FCA; Sch 1ZB, para 33 for the PRA; and the Banking Act 2009, s 244 for the Bank of England.
2   FSMA 2000, Sch 1ZA, para 25(2); and Sch 1ZB, para 33(2).
3   FSMA 2000, s 222.
4   FSMA 2000, s 291. Such bodies also carry on commercial activities and no immunity applies to them in relation to such activities (although difficulties may arise in drawing this line in practice).
5   FSMA 2000, Sch 17, para 10. The immunity also extends to the voluntary jurisdiction, by virtue of the Compensation Scheme rules.

21.37   Statutory immunity does not apply to:

- acts or omissions shown to have been in bad faith; and

- awards of damages under the Human Rights Act 1998.

21.38   The meaning and scope of each of these exceptions is discussed briefly below.

Acts in bad faith

21.39   Bad faith has been held to connote either malice (in the sense of personal spite or a desire to injure for improper reasons) or knowledge of the absence of the power to make the decision in question[1]. This requires an examination of the subjective intention of the Regulators and not merely an objective assessment of their acts or omissions.

1 Per Lightman J in *Melton Medes Ltd v Securities and Investments Board [1995] Ch 137*, which considered the SIB's statutory immunity under the Financial Services Act 1986, s 187. For a discussion of bad faith in the public law context, see Fordham (6th edn), at Ch 52.

21.40   Bad faith thus clearly covers fraudulent or corrupt acts. It is also an element of the tort of misfeasance in public office[1]. It is usually difficult to demonstrate bad faith and it should not be alleged without prima facie evidence justifying the allegation.

1 The ingredients of the tort were analysed in detail in the leading authority of *Three Rivers District Council v Governor and Company of the Bank of England [2001] UKHL 16, [2003] 2 AC 1, HL.* However, unlike other torts, proof of loss and damage is not a necessary ingredient: see *Watkins v Secretary of State for the Home Department [2004] EWCA Civ 966, [2005] QB 883.*

Claims under the Human Rights Act 1998

21.41   The Human Rights Act 1998 (HRA 1998)[1] gives effect to most provisions of the European Convention on Human Rights (the ECHR) by specifying that primary and subordinate legislation must be read and applied so as to be compatible with the rights they afford. Accordingly, the HRA 1998 has amended the traditional rules of statutory interpretation. It also allows a court to award a remedy, including damages, against a public body that acts in a way which is incompatible with the ECHR. However, the HRA 1998 only allows a court to award damages if, having taken into account all the circumstances of the case (including certain specific factors[2]), it is satisfied that the award is necessary to afford just satisfaction to the person affected.

1 HRA 1998, s 8.
2 HRA 1998, s 8(3).

21.42   The concept of just satisfaction is, broadly, similar to awards of damages under English law, in that the purpose of 'just satisfaction' is to put the victim, so far as possible, in the position in which he would have been had his rights not been violated[1]. This may be of particular use to those who have suffered actual losses as a result of action by the Regulators that have violated their human rights.

1 An award based on 'just satisfaction' is within the discretion of the court. The European Court of Human Rights has rarely given reasons for such awards but some general propositions can be made. The basic principle is that the court will make an award on the basis of what is 'equitable'

after considering the balance of interests as between the victim and the public as a whole: see Lord Woolf in *Anufrijeva v London Borough of Southwark [2003] EWCA Civ 1406, [2004] QB 1124*. An award may be made for the actual pecuniary loss that was caused by the ECHR violation. Awards may also be made for non-pecuniary loss and for costs/expenses. For a further discussion, see Lester and Pannick, *Human Rights Law and Practice* (3rd edn, 2009), at 2.8.4.

21.43 The ECHR provisions that may be relevant to a claim under the HRA 1998 against the Regulators are:

- Article 6, which protects the right to a fair trial. Essentially, this guarantees, both for civil and criminal claims, a fair and public hearing within a reasonable time before an independent tribunal established by law. Additional safeguards are provided in respect of criminal charges[1];

- Article 8, which grants respect for a person's private life. This may be relevant when the Regulators use its information gathering and investigation powers[2];

- Article 1 of Protocol 1, which establishes a right to the protection of property. Again, this may be relevant when the Regulators use their information gathering and investigation powers.

1 See *R v Securities and Futures Authority, ex p Fleurose [2001] EWCA Civ 2015, [2002] IRLR 297* for consideration by the Court of Appeal of how the right to a fair trial impacted on disciplinary proceedings initiated under a previous regime. The court stated that fairness demanded that the subject is informed in good time of the nature of any charges, he must have adequate time and facilities to prepare his defence and a proper opportunity to give and call evidence.
2 See **CHAPTER 4** above.

COMPLAINING ABOUT THE REGULATORS

An overview of the Complaints Scheme

21.44 Bringing judicial review or other legal proceedings against the Regulators may be an effective means for obtaining redress in a suitable case, but may also be difficult, time-consuming and expensive. A potentially cheaper, simpler alternative exists which may offer an adequate remedy in some situations. This is the Complaints Scheme[1] (the Scheme).

1 The rules governing the Complaints Scheme do not form part of the regulatory handbooks but are available on the websites of the Regulators.

21.45 Part 6 of the Financial Services Act 2012 (the FS Act 2012) requires the *Regulators* to 'make arrangements for the investigation of complaints arising in connection with the exercise of, or failure to exercise, any of their relevant functions'[1]. The Scheme established under the FS Act 2012 is broadly similar in approach and process to the previous scheme operated by the FSA under the FSMA 2000[2], with amendments reflecting the division of powers and responsibilities between the Regulators.

1 FS Act 2012, s 84(1)(a). See also the Complaints Scheme, para 1.1.
2 FSMA 2000, Sch 1, paras 7 and 8 (which is now repealed).

21.46   As will be seen, though, the Scheme is limited in its scope. It will always be uncertain whether any financial remedy can be obtained, and, whilst the Scheme is intended to operate reasonably quickly[1], it is unlikely to provide a real-time solution to immediate issues regarding the Regulators' exercise of their powers. For these reasons, many regard the Scheme as of limited practical use.

1   FS Act 2012, s 84(3).

21.47   The Regulators must appoint an independent person (referred to as the Complaints Commissioner (the Commissioner)) to be responsible for the conduct of investigations into complaints[1]. The Scheme is one of the accountability mechanisms originally provided for in the FSMA 2000 and the establishment of a robust independent complaints body was seen as an important counterbalance to granting the Regulators immunity from liability to claims for damages.

1   FS Act 2012, s 84(1)(b).

21.48   The Scheme is typically used for complaints about the misconduct of the Regulators' employees in exercising their powers. The Scheme is not a method for challenging the merits of a disciplinary decision or the Regulators' powers to make rules, which could be dealt with more appropriately by referral to the Tribunal and judicial review, respectively.

21.49   The Scheme provides for a two stage process. First, the Regulators complained of investigate and respond to the complaint itself and second, if the complainant remains unsatisfied by the Regulators' response, the complainant can refer the matter to the Commissioner for consideration.

21.50   The following paragraphs review the Scheme, including:

- coverage and scope of the Scheme and when firms or individuals might consider using it as a possible means for obtaining redress para **21.51** ff;

- the nature and role of the Commissioner para **21.58** ff;

- the remedies that can be obtained para **21.64** ff;

- the procedure for making and handling complaints para **21.73** ff; and

- a firm's options if it is unhappy with the outcome of the process para **21.109** ff.

Coverage and scope of the Scheme

21.51   The Scheme covers complaints about the way in which the Regulators have acted or omitted to act, including complaints alleging mistakes and lack of care, unreasonable delay, unprofessional behaviour, bias and lack of integrity[1].

1   Complaints Scheme, para 3.1.

21.52 Complaints and challenges against the Regulators

Who can complain?

21.52 Complaints can be made by anyone who is directly affected by the way in which the Regulators have carried out their functions, or anyone acting directly on their behalf. The complainant must be seeking a remedy in respect of some inconvenience, distress or loss which the person has suffered as a result of being directly affected by the Regulators' actions or inaction[1]. For these purposes a remedy may include a simple apology[2].

1 Complaints Scheme, para 3.2.
2 Complaints Scheme, para 3.2.

Which functions of the Regulators can be the subject of complaint?

21.53 The scope of the Scheme is limited to the investigation of complaints arising in connection with the Regulators' exercise of, or failure to exercise, any of their 'relevant functions'. 'Relevant functions' are defined as being, in relation to the FCA or the PRA, their functions other than their legislative functions[1]. The 'relevant functions' of the Bank are defined as its functions under the FSMA 2000, Pt 18 or under the Banking Act 2009, Pt 5, other than its legislative functions[2].

1 FS Act 2012, s 85(2) and the Complaints Scheme, para 1.2. The FCA's legislative functions are defined in the FS Act 2012, s 85(4) as being: (a) making rules under the FSMA 2000; (b) issuing codes under the FSMA 2000, ss 64 or 119; (c) issuing statements under – (i) FSMA 2000, ss 63C, 64, 69, 88C, 89S, 93, 124, 131J, 138N, 192H, 192N, 210 or 312J; (ii) FSMA 2000, s 345D (whether as a result of ss 345(2) or 345A(3) or 249(1) of that Act), or (iii) the FS Act 2012, s 80; (d) giving directions under the FSMA 2000, ss 316, 318 or 328; (e) issuing general guidance, as defined in the FSMA 2000, s 139B(5).
   The PRA's legislative functions are defined in the FS Act 2012, s 85(5) as being: (a) making rules under the FSMA 2000; (b) issuing codes under the FSMA 2000, s 64; (c) issuing statements under – (i) FSMA 2000, ss 63C, 64, 69, 192H, 192N, 210 or 345D, or (ii) the FS Act 2012, s 80; (d) giving directions under the FSMA 2000, ss 316 or 318; (e) issuing guidance under the FSMA 2000, s 21.
2 FS Act 2012, s 85(3) and the Complaints Scheme, para 1.3. Pursuant to the FS Act 2012, s 85(6), the following functions of the Bank under the FSMA 2000, Pt 18 are legislative functions for the purposes of sub-s (3): (a) making rules; (b) issuing statements: (i) under s 312J, or (ii) by virtue of the application by Sch 17A of a provision mentioned in sub-s (5)(c)(i) of this section. Pursuant to the FS Act 2012, s 85(7) the following functions of the Bank under the Banking Act 2009, Pt 5, are legislative functions: (a) publishing principles or codes of practice under ss 188 and 189; and (b) preparing statements under s 198(3).

What is excluded from the Scheme?

21.54 Certain types of complaint are excluded from the Scheme[1]. These include:

- complaints about the Regulators' relationship with their own employees;

- complaints connected with contractual or commercial disputes involving the Regulators and not connected with the exercise of their relevant functions;

- complaints in relation to the performance of the Regulators' legislative functions as defined in the FS Act 2012 (as mentioned at para **21.45** above);

810

- complaints about the actions, or inactions, of the Bank that do not relate to its functions under the FSMA 2000, Pt 18, as amended (recognised clearing houses) or under the Banking Act 2009, Pt 5 (inter-bank payment systems); and

- complaints about the actions, or inactions, of the FOS, the Financial Services Compensation Scheme or the Money Advice Service.

1 Complaints Scheme, para 3.4.

When will complaints not be investigated or investigations deferred?

21.55   The Regulators will not investigate a complaint under the Scheme which they reasonably consider amounts to no more than dissatisfaction with the Regulators' general policies or with the exercise of, or failure to exercise, a discretion where no unreasonable or unprofessional conduct or other misconduct is alleged[1].

1 Complaints Scheme, para. 3.5.

21.56   The Regulators will not investigate a complaint under the Scheme which they reasonably consider could have been, or would be, more appropriately dealt with in another way (for example by referring the matter to the Tribunal or by the institution of other legal proceedings)[1].

1 Complaints Scheme, para 3.6 and FS Act 2012, s 87(1).

21.57   A complaint which is connected with, or which arises from, any form of continuing disciplinary or supervisory notice action by the Regulators will not normally be investigated by either the Regulators or the Commissioner until the complainant has exhausted the procedures and remedies under the FSMA 2000. Therefore, a firm that wants to complain about the conduct of an employee of the Regulators' in the course of an enforcement action will usually have to wait until the enforcement action has concluded before a complaint under the Scheme can be investigated. The complainant does not have to be the subject of continuing action by the Regulators for this provision to be engaged. However, an investigation may start before those procedures are completed if, in the exceptional circumstances of the case, it would not be reasonable to expect the complainant to await the conclusion of the Regulators' action and that action would not be significantly harmed as a result of early investigation[1].

1 Complaints Scheme, para 3.7.

The Complaints Commissioner

21.58   The Commissioner is an independent person appointed by the Regulators who is responsible for the conduct of investigations in accordance with the Scheme[1]. The Commissioner may conduct an investigation in whatever manner he considers appropriate, taking into account the need to ensure that complaints are dealt with fairly, quickly and cost-effectively[2].

1 FS Act 2012, s 84(1)(b). See also the Complaints Scheme, para 1.3.
2 Complaints Scheme, para 7.1.

Is the Commissioner independent of the Regulators?

21.59   The FS Act 2012 provides safeguards which are designed to secure the independence of the Commissioner. The Treasury's approval is required for the appointment and dismissal of the Commissioner[1]. The terms and conditions on which the Commissioner is appointed must be such as, in the opinion of the Regulators, are reasonably designed to secure that the Commissioner is free at all times to act independently of the Regulators[2]. The Regulators are obliged to ensure that they provide the Commissioner with sufficient financial and other resources to allow him properly to fulfil his role under the Complaints Scheme[3]. The Commissioner is also given a certain security of tenure; he is appointed for a period of three years and may be dismissed from office only with the approval of the Treasury and only in one of the following circumstances:

- he becomes incapacitated by physical or mental illness; or

- he becomes otherwise unfit to discharge the functions of his office[4].

1 FS Act 2012, s 84(4). See also the Complaints Scheme, para 4.1.
2 FS Act 2012, s 84(5)(a).
3 Complaints Scheme, para 4.5.
4 Complaints Scheme, para 4.3.

21.60   The Commissioner and his staff are not employees of the Regulators and are subject to an obligation to act independently of[1], and ensure the investigation of complaints does not favour, the Regulators[2].

1 Complaints Scheme, para. 7.1.
2 FS Act 2012, s 84(5)(b). See also the Complaints Scheme, para 4.4.

When might firms consider using the Scheme?

21.61   The Scheme is an option in any case falling within its scope. Whether or not, from the firm's perspective, it is appropriate or prudent for the firm to use the Scheme, as opposed to seeking redress through some other means, is another question.

21.62   From the firm's perspective, the Scheme may be useful:

- where the firm has suffered losses which cannot be redressed by any other means, particularly in the light of the Regulators' statutory immunity from liability for damages[1]. In such a situation, although there are uncertainties about the amount of compensation that can be obtained under the Scheme, as discussed at para **21.70** ff below, these are likely to be outweighed by the inability to obtain any compensation by any other means and the simplicity and cost-effectiveness of using the complaints procedure;

- where the complaint is minor in nature and the firm does not seek significantly to alter the outcome of the action that the Regulators took or where the firm seeks an apology or some other remedy that a court could not grant. An example might be a complaint about the over-enthusiastic use by the Regulators of their investigation powers where ultimately the result of the enforcement process either was not materially affected or was accepted by the firm;

- where the complainant may apply for authorisation in the future but knows that the Regulators have made adverse findings relating to its conduct that might impact on a future application for authorisation or its general reputation within its profession[2]; and

- in other cases where the firm does not want to incur the time and expense associated with legal proceedings or if it does not want to bring proceedings against the Regulators for other reasons[3].

1 This is considered at para **21.31** ff above.
2 See, for example, the Commissioner's Report GE-L0008 (18/04/02) where the complaint concerned delays in processing the complainant's application to cease to be authorised. The FSA had erroneously suggested that the delays were caused by the complainant's own inaction.
3 For example, the firm may wish to avoid publicity. Publicity in the complaints process is considered at para **21.103** ff below.

21.63   The Scheme is likely to be inappropriate:

- for cases which are plainly excluded from its scope;

- for complaints which are particularly complicated, serious in nature or where substantial loss or damage has been suffered by the person concerned, at least where there is an alternative means of redress available[1]. This is because of the non-binding nature of the Commissioner's recommendations, the likely limitations on compensation that will be paid by the Regulators under the Scheme, the possible limitations of the investigation that will be undertaken and the need for the Scheme to operate quickly and cost effectively;

- where the firm's primary aim is to undermine or change the Regulators' policy in a particular area, for example, because the firm regards that policy as unreasonable or in breach of its human rights, as opposed to seeking redress for the Regulators' conduct in implementing the policy in a particular case. This is because the Scheme is not intended to address, and cannot easily address, issues about the content of the Regulators' policies[2];

- where the firm has the right to refer the matter of complaint to the Tribunal, for example, where the complaint concerns the imposition of a disciplinary sanction, a variation of permission or some other regulatory action or sanction for which a reference to the Tribunal can be made[3]; and

- where the Regulators have not actually breached a requirement but have merely failed to treat a person as well as they could have done[4].

21.63 Complaints and challenges against the Regulators

1 Examples would include serious breaches of the Human Rights Act 1998 and allegations of bad faith resulting in significant loss.
2 For example, the Complaints Commissioner refused to challenge the FSA's policy in relation the requirements of the FSA's Retail Distribution Review: see the Annual Report of the Complaints Commissioner for 2012/2013, p 11.
3 For a discussion of the Tribunal, see **CHAPTER 12** above.
4 For example, where the FSA refused to comply with a person's request where it had no obligation to do so (even if it would have been 'preferable' for the FSA (subsequently the Regulators) to have acted in a different way such as by clarifying its lack of obligation at the outset): see report GE-L0337 (01/09/04).

What remedies are available?

The range of remedies

21.64 A successful complaint may result in:

- an offer by the Regulators, following their own investigation, of action to remedy the matters complained of, for example, to take steps to rectify an error, to apologise or to pay ex gratia compensation[1]; or

- if the Commissioner thinks it appropriate, a recommendation from the Commissioner to the Regulators[2]:

    - to remedy the matters of complaint; and/or

    - to make a compensatory payment to the complainant.

1 Complaints Scheme, para 6.6.
2 FS Act 2012, s 87(5).

21.65 It is important to appreciate that the Commissioner's recommendations are only recommendations; they are not legally binding. It is a matter for the Regulators whether or not they choose to follow those recommendations[1]. The Regulators' policy on when they will pay compensation in accordance with the Commissioner's recommendations is outlined below[2]. However, if the Commissioner reports that a complaint is well founded or criticises the Regulators, the Regulators must inform the Commissioner and the complainant of the steps which they propose to take by way of response[3].

1 For example, the FSA refused to pay compensation in various instances. Where the FSA did accept the Commissioner's recommendation, FSA Internal Audit ensured implementation: see last paragraph of p 5 in the Annual Report of the Complaints Commissioner for 2003/2004.
2 See para **21.71** ff below.
3 Complaints Scheme, para 7.12.

21.66 Furthermore, the Commissioner may publish his report (or part of it) and may require a Regulator to publish its response (or part of its response). The Commissioner's ability to publish his recommendations and the Regulators' response to them should, in practice, be an important aspect of the accountability regime for the Regulators.

Apologies and remedying the matter complained of

21.67 First, most of the complaints upheld by the Commissioner to date have resulted in the recommendation that the Regulators apologise to the complainant[1]. The following are examples of other recommendations that have been made by the Commissioner:

- that the Regulators' staff should receive such training as will make them aware of the procedures to which they should adhere[2];

- that the Regulators should review relevant procedures[3]; and

- that the Regulators should notify the complainant where there is a change in complaints handler and provide justification where a compensation payment is not awarded[4].

1 In some circumstances, a Regulator had offered an apology already but the Commissioner nevertheless considered that a more specific apology was appropriate (Commissioner's Report GE-L0195 (01/09/04)) or that the apology should be made by a more senior employee (Commissioner's Report GE-L0147 (14/11/03)).

2 See, for example, the Commissioner's Report GE-L0337 (01/09/04). Where the complaint relates to the failure by a Regulator's employee to comply with its procedures, the firm may consider asking for that employee's training records or for details of the systems and controls which apply to him. However, there is no obligation on the Regulators or the Commissioner to accede to such a request.

3 For example, in the Commissioner's Report GE-L01233 (07/06/11), he asked the FSA to review its procedures for retrieving records of calls made by the FSA's Consumer Contact Centre.

4 See the Commissioner's Report GE-L1037 (09/11/09).

21.68 It should be noted that the Regulators have not always followed recommendations[1] and, even though the Commissioner may make a recommendation that is accepted by the Regulators, the firm is likely to receive little information or evidence as to how that recommendation has actually been implemented[2].

1 In the Commissioner's Report GE-L01226 (09/03/11), the Commissioner recommended that the FSA should review its procedures relating to document delivery procedures. The FSA rejected some of the recommendation because it did not consider it appropriate. Alternatively, a Regulator may consider that the costs of implementing a recommendation may outweigh the benefits: for example, see the FSA response to Report GE-L0147(05/03/2003).

2 Where a Regulator accepts the Commissioner's recommendation, that Regulator's Internal Audit ensures its implementation: see the Annual Report of the Complaints Commissioner for 2003/2004. However, there is no procedure for reports on the implementation to be sent to the complainant although the complainant could request this as part of the remedy that he seeks.

21.69 Second, although the firm may consider that it is only making one complaint, most complaints will have multiple aspects. For example, it may be possible to treat a complaint relating to the Regulators' failure to deal properly with an enquiry as constituting separate complaints about the timeliness of the Regulators' reply, as well as the failure of the Regulators to deal with the query. In such circumstances, either the Commissioner or the Regulators, or both, may uphold certain elements of the complaint whilst rejecting others[1]. Accordingly, the complainant should try to analyse the various possible elements of a complaint at the outset and determine which are of real importance. This will help to ensure that the complaint itself is phrased in such a way that those considering it concentrate their efforts on the key issues rather than others that, properly considered, are in fact peripheral. Of course, in some circumstances, the Commissioner may, having separated the constituent issues of the complaint, uphold subsidiary issues but not the substantive one[2].

1 It is reasonably common for the Commissioner to uphold only certain elements of a complaint. Alternatively, the Regulators may 'redefine' the complaint and relegate the substantive issue to 'one of secondary importance whilst an issue the complainant has not emphasised is introduced into the investigation'. In such circumstances, the complainant should be especially careful if the Regulators write to him to clarify the scope of the complaint.

2 For example, in Commissioner's Report GE-L0008 (16/04/02), the complaint concerned excessive delay in processing the complainant's application to cease being authorised. The Commissioner held that the application was dealt with in accordance with policy but upheld certain subsidiary issues such as the FSA's failure to communicate with the complainant in a clear and timely way.

In what circumstances will the Commissioner award compensation?

21.70 The Scheme rules say little about the circumstances in which the Commissioner will recommend that the Regulators pay compensation and on what basis he will assess compensation awards. The Scheme provides simply that[1], in deciding whether a complaint is well founded and, if so, in deciding what steps he should recommend the Regulators to take, he will have regard to matters such as the source of the funds to make the payments and the desire for Regulators to be efficient and economic in the use of their resources.

1 Complaints Scheme, para 7.5.

In what circumstances will the Regulators follow a recommendation to pay compensation?

21.71 Since the Commissioner's recommendations are non binding such that compensation payments are made on an ex gratia basis, an important question is how the Regulators will in practice respond to them. The Regulators will have regard to their own regulatory objectives and the principles of good regulation and will also normally take into account the following[1]:

- the gravity of the misconduct which the Commissioner has identified and its consequences for the complainant;

- the nature of the Regulators' relationship with the complainant and the extent to which the complainant has been adversely affected in the course of direct dealings with the Regulators;

- whether what has gone wrong is at the operational or administrative level; and

- the impact of the cost of compensatory payments on regulated firms, issuers of listed securities and, indirectly, consumers.

1 Complaints Scheme, para 7.14.

21.72 The Regulators reserve a discretion to consider in each case, the extent to which they should pay compensation in response to a recommendation from the Commissioner. Thus, it may be difficult to predict whether the Regulators will pay compensation in any particular case. In practice, compensation is offered rarely[1] and only in very serious cases[2].

1 In 2012/2013, the FSA made only two ex gratia awards totalling c £12,250 in addition to nine refunds, see FSA Annual Report 2012/2013.
2 An award of £5,000 was made after the FSA sent 230 letters to an independent financial advisor's clients incorrectly telling them that the firm had ceased to be authorised and that compensation might be available for mis-selling. When the IFA initially complained, the FSA stated that it did not believe that it had acted 'at all improperly' in this case: see the Commissioner's Report GE-L0147 (14/11/03).

The process for making and handling complaints

When can a complaint be made?

21.73 A complaint should be made within 12 months of the date on which the complainant first became aware of the circumstances giving rise to the complaint[1]. Complaints made after this date will only be investigated under the Scheme if the complainant can show reasonable grounds for the delay in making the complaint[2].

1 Complaints Scheme, para 3.3.
2 Complaints Scheme, para 3.3.

To whom and how should a complaint be made?

21.74 As will be seen, complaints may only be referred to the Commissioner after they have been made to the Regulators. But to whom at the Regulators should the complaint be made? It is envisaged that the majority of complaints will be made to the complainant's usual contact at the Regulators or through the designated complaints helpline.

21.75 The Regulators will acknowledge the complaint in writing or by e-mail within five working days of receiving it[1]. The Regulators will:

- determine whether the complaint can be dealt with under the Scheme and whether it can be dealt with by the area that is subject to the complaint[2] and

- in response to each complaint received, send the complainant information, in a durable medium, explaining how the Scheme works[3].

1 Complaints Scheme, para 6.1.
2 Complaints Scheme, para 5.2; 'locally' or 'local level' mean the area which is the subject of a complaint to deal with the matter, see PS13/7, para 2.16.
3 Complaints Scheme, para 5.1.

21.76 A complaint may be made either verbally or in writing. A firm making a verbal complaint will be asked to confirm its complaint in a durable medium[1].

1 Complaints Scheme, para 5.4.

21.77 Complaints and challenges against the Regulators

21.77 Verbal complaints by consumers[1] will be investigated by the Regulators. However, if the Regulators require clarification of the nature or scope of the complaint, the remedy sought or any factual information that supports the complaint, the Regulators will invite the complainant to provide further details in a durable medium[2].

1 Complaints Scheme, para 5.5.
2 Complaints Scheme, para 5.5.

21.78 To ensure the Scheme is unified, especially where complaints contain allegations against more than one of the Regulators, the FCA's Complaints Team is responsible for processing complaints submitted centrally through the designated complaints helpline number, e-mail address and postal address[1]. This applies even where the complaint relates to one of the other Regulators. The Complaints Team will review all complaints and assign them to the Regulator concerned for a response.

1 These details are available on the Regulators' websites. The easiest way to make a complaint is by completing a complaints form which is available on the FCA's website www.fca.org.uk/about/governance/complaining-about-us.

21.79 If the Regulators have decided not to investigate a complaint, they must notify the complainant and the Commissioner explaining why this is the case and informing the complainant of his right to ask the Commissioner to review the decision[1]. The Regulators must take these steps within four weeks of receiving the complaint[2].

1 Complaints Scheme, para 6.11. However, the Commissioner will not review the Regulator's decision unless the complainant so requests.
2 Complaints Scheme, para 5.3.

Does the process differ for low impact complaints?

21.80 The Regulators may ask the staff in the relevant team or area that is the subject of the complaint to deal with a low impact complaint. This may be appropriate in circumstances where a complaint falls within the scope of the Scheme but is considered to be low impact (for example complaints relating to minor administrative mistakes) and can be dealt with easily and quickly.

21.81 For all complaints dealt with in this way, the Regulators will advise the complainant of his right to refer the complaint back to the Scheme if he believes that the complaint has not been resolved or is dissatisfied with the way it has been dealt with[1].

1 Complaints Scheme, para 5.8.

21.82 If the complainant refers the complaint back to the Scheme, the Regulators will acknowledge this complaint within five business days of receiving this referral and determine whether it falls within the scope of the Scheme. If the Regulators consider the complaint within the Scheme they will follow the procedure set out in para **21.84** ff below[1].

1 Complaints Scheme, paras 5.9 and 5.10.

The two-stage investigation process

21.83 The Scheme provides that, if a complaint is within the scope of the Scheme, there may be two stages for the investigation of each complaint. In the first stage the Regulators will investigate any complaint that meets the requirements of the Scheme and take whatever action to resolve the matter that they think is appropriate. In the second stage the Commissioner will investigate complaints that are referred to him following a stage one investigation where the complainant remains dissatisfied[1].

1 Complaints Scheme, para 1.4.

Stage 1: Investigation of complaints by the Regulators

21.84 If the Regulators do investigate the complaint, the initial investigation by the Regulators will be undertaken by a suitably senior member of staff who has not previously been involved in the matter complained of with the aim of resolving the matter to the complainant's satisfaction[1]. Where the complaints contain allegations against more than one of the Regulators, a lead investigator will be agreed between them[2].

1 Complaints Scheme, para 6.2. The Regulators' view is that the term 'suitably senior member of staff' is difficult to define by reference to a particular job title or level of seniority, and therefore this will be assessed on a case-by-case basis (see the FSA's Policy Statement on 'Complaints against regulators', March 2013, para 2.16).
2 See the Regulators' complaints leaflet available on their websites, eg http://www.fca.org.uk/your-fca/complaints-leaflet.

21.85 The investigation of complaints by the Regulators involves a paper-based review considering any documents supplied by the complainants, and any relevant documents held by the Regulators.

21.86 The Regulators will aim to resolve the complaint as quickly as possible. If the investigation is not likely to be completed in four weeks, the Regulators will write to the complainant setting out the reasonable timescale within which the Regulators plan to deal with the complaint[1].

1 Complaints Scheme, para 6.4.

21.87 As to the result of the investigation:

- if the Regulators conclude that the complaint is well-founded, the Regulators will tell the complainant what the Regulators propose to do to remedy the matters complained of[1];
- if the Regulators decide not to uphold the complaint, they will give reasons for doing so to the complainant and will inform the complainant of his right to ask the Commissioner to review the Regulators' decision[2]; and
- if the complainant is dissatisfied with the Regulators' progress in investigating the complaint or with the outcome of the Regulators' investigation, he may refer the matter to the Commissioner[3].

1 Complaints Scheme, para 6.6.
2 Complaints Scheme, para 6.7.
3 Complaints Scheme, para 6.8.

Stage 2: Investigations by the Commissioner

When can a firm refer a complaint to the Commissioner?

21.88   The complainant may refer a complaint to the Commissioner:

- if the Regulators decide not to investigate a complaint which the Commissioner considers to fall within the scope of the Scheme[1];

- if the complainant is dissatisfied with the outcome of the Regulators' investigation into the complaint[2] or the way that the Regulators have handled it[3]; or

- in some circumstances, before the Regulators have had the opportunity to conduct or complete an investigation[4].

1 Complaints Scheme, para 6.11 and FS Act 2012, s 87(4). In 2012/2013, there were only four cases in which the Commissioner decided to either uphold the complaint (where the FSA had declined to do so at stage one) or recommend that the remedy offered to the complainant be altered in the complainant's favour: see the FSA Annual Report 2012/2013.
2 For example, in the report prepared by the FSA investigator in Commissioner's Report GE-L0097 (22/12/03) 'important issues were ignored, suggesting that insufficient time and/or care was taken in reading the file'.
3 Even where the substance of the complaint turns out not to be within the scope of the Scheme, where the relevant Regulator handles the complaint inadequately, the firm may still refer the handling of the complaint to the Commissioner without making a new complaint to the relevant Regulator. For example, the relevant Regulator may fail to progress its investigation in a timely fashion or the complainant may have reservations as to the impartiality of the relevant Regulator's investigator.
4 Complaints Scheme, para 6.8. The Commissioner has also previously stated that there may be 'exceptional circumstances when the Commissioner feels that it would be inappropriate for a Regulator to conduct an internal investigation': see the Annual Report of the Complaints Commissioner for 2004/5 at p 12. This may allude to situations where bias is alleged or where the relevant Regulator decides that the complaint does not fall within the scope of the Complaints Scheme.

21.89   Where the Regulators have investigated the complaint or decided not to investigate it, the Commissioner will only consider the complaint if it has been referred to him within three months of the date of the Regulators' decision letter[1]. The Commissioner may consider a complaint referred outside this time limit where he decides there is a good reason for the delay[2]. Although a firm may be able to refer a complaint to the Commissioner the firm will need to consider the risk of potential publicity[3]. Firms may also want to consider how the Commissioner has approached similar complaints in the past and whether they are likely to be offered compensation[4].

1 Complaints Scheme, para 6.9.
2 Complaints Scheme, para 6.10. See para **21.73** above as to the time limit for making a complaint to the Regulator. Apart from the need to ensure that complaints are dealt with quickly and cost effectively, no Complaints Scheme rule prohibits the Commissioner from investigating a complaint that has been made to the Regulator within the applicable time limit, whenever it is referred to him.

3 The Commissioner's report into the complaint is likely to be published although the complainant should not be identifiable: see para **21.100** ff below.
4 See para **21.70** ff above for a description of those circumstances where the Commissioner is likely to award compensation.

How should the firm refer the complaint to the Commissioner?

21.90 The Commissioner prefers that complaints be submitted in written form (either by letter or e-mail) rather than made orally. A copy of the original complaint that was made to the Regulators should be sent to him together with any relevant materials[1].

1 See para **21.85** above.

In what circumstances will the Commissioner investigate a complaint?

21.91 When a matter is referred to him, the Commissioner will decide whether or not to investigate[1]. This is largely within his discretion, depending upon the situation:

- the Commissioner will not investigate a complaint which he considers to be outside the scope of the Scheme[2];

- where the matter is referred to him by the complainant after the Regulators have decided not to investigate, the Commissioner will decide whether the complaint falls within the scope of the Scheme and, if so, whether it would be appropriate to conduct an investigation[3];

- where the matter is referred to him by the complainant before the Regulators have had the opportunity to conduct or complete an investigation, the Commissioner will consider whether it would be desirable to allow the Regulators that opportunity before conducting his own investigation[4].

1 In 2012/2013, out of the 128 enquiries and complaints that were concluded, 62 were determined to fall outside the scope of the Scheme: see the Annual Report of the Complaints Commissioner for 2012/2013, p 8.
2 Complaints Scheme, para 6.11.
3 Complaints Scheme, para 6.11.
4 Complaints Scheme, para 6.12. This also applies where the Commissioner is already conducting an investigation into another complaint from the same complainant: See the Complaints Scheme, para 6.13.

How does the Commissioner conduct the investigation?

21.92 The Commissioner can conduct an investigation in whatever manner he thinks appropriate, including obtaining external resources at the Regulators' expense[1]. It is therefore for the Commissioner to determine his own procedure for each case. The Scheme rules make various provisions for the conduct of investigations:

- the Commissioner must take into account the need to ensure that complaints are dealt with fairly, quickly and cost-effectively[2];

- in performing his functions, the Commissioner must at all times act independently of the Regulators[3];

- the Commissioner may appoint a person to conduct the whole or any part of the investigation on his behalf but subject to his direction[4]. If he does appoint a person, the person must not be an officer or employee of the Regulators;

- the Regulators will afford the Commissioner all reasonable co-operation, including giving access to their staff and information[5]. However, they may, in affording the Commissioner access to information, have regard to the need to maintain confidentiality[6] and privilege[7]. Examples given by the Regulators of where this might be appropriate are to ensure the identity of an informant is not disclosed or to maintain the confidentiality of information given to the Regulators under international arrangements. If the Regulators withhold information, they will notify the Commissioner of the nature of that information and the reason for withholding it[8];

- findings of fact and decisions by certain types of courts and tribunals, including the Tribunal, are conclusive evidence for the purposes of the investigation. Findings of fact or decisions by other courts or tribunals carry such weight as the Regulators or the Commissioner, as applicable, consider appropriate in the circumstances[9];

- in deciding whether a complaint is well founded and, if it is, in deciding what steps he should recommend the Regulators take, the Commissioner will have regard to matters such as the source of the funds to make the payment and the desire for the Regulators to be efficient and economic in the use of their resources[10].

1   Complaints Scheme, para 7.1. The Commissioner is also obliged to inform the Regulators annually of the approach that he adopts in handling different types of complaint: See the Complaints Scheme, para 7.16.
2   Complaints Scheme, para 7.1. Accordingly, where the subject matter of the complaint involves numerous employees from a Regulator, the Commissioner is likely to limit any interviews to the key individuals.
3   Complaints Scheme, para 7.1, reflecting the FS Act 2012, s 84(1)(b).
4   Complaints Scheme, para 7.2.
5   Note that the Commissioner has indicated to the FSA board a number of times that he must have access to all documentation in order to ensure transparency: see the Annual Report of the Complaints Commissioner for 2012/2013, p 11.
6   Where a Regulator does withhold information, it will inform the Commissioner of the nature of the information and its reasons for withholding it: See the FSA's Policy Statement (PS13/7) 'Complaints against the regulators' at Appendix 1, para 7.3.
7   In one instance, the FSA previously stated that its response to a complaint would depend upon the contents of a legal opinion that it had received from a third party and therefore declined to comment. The Commissioner accepted the privileged status of the opinion but stated that the FSA should have made its position as to the privileged status of the opinion clear from the outset: see the Commissioner's Quarterly Report for the Period to 2 September 2004 at para 20, and Commissioner's Report GE-L0337. The FSA subsequently disclosed the opinion. See para **4.153** ff above for a brief explanation of privilege.
8   Complaints Scheme, para 7.3.
9   Complaints Scheme, paras 6.15 and 6.16.
10 Complaints Scheme, para 7.5.

21.93   Under the current Scheme there are no express time limits for conducting the investigation, although some guidance is given by the provisions of the Scheme prior to 1 April 2013. Under the previous scheme, the Commissioner had 20 working days from receipt of the complaint to decide whether the complaint fell within the scope of the scheme and, assuming that it did, complete his investigation[1]. In practice, if this timetable seemed unachievable, the Commissioner usually gave the complainant a timetable for the completion of the various stages of the investigation.

1 See 'Bringing a complaint against the Financial Service Authority' leaflet at p 4 on the Commissioner's website: http://www.fscc.gov.uk/documents/1154_leaflet_CC.pdf. This leaflet is still available although it was written for complaints against the FSA before 1 April 2013. It has not been updated.

What evidence will the Commissioner consider?

21.94   One important question for firms to consider is what evidence the Commissioner will take into account. The Commissioner has no explicit power to compel the Regulators, the complainant or third parties to give him oral or documentary evidence. However, as set out above, the Regulators have a duty to co-operate with the Commissioner which extends to affording the Commissioner access to their staff and information and, of course, in the unlikely event that a complainant does not co-operate, there is the risk that the Commissioner may conclude the investigation[1].

1 Where the complainant fails to respond to a request by the Commissioner for further information, the Commissioner may decide to terminate the investigation, however, the Commissioner may decide to re-open the complaint if the complainant subsequently co-operates.

21.95   Most investigations by the Commissioner are concluded on the basis of papers alone. There is no guidance on what evidence the Commissioner will consider and it is possible that he will request further evidence in writing or orally. In some instances, the results of the Commissioner's investigation depend upon questions of fact, the answers to which are not directly evident from documents, in which case the Commissioner may have to question the complainant and the Regulators' employees. The Commissioner does not usually hold meetings with the complainants because he prefers to adopt an inquisitorial approach based on the documentation presented to him.

Can the Regulators take other action in the meantime?

21.96   The investigation of the complaint does not prevent the relevant Regulators from continuing to take such action as they consider appropriate in relation to any related matter[1]. There is therefore nothing to prevent the Regulators from, for example, continuing an enforcement action in the context of which the complaint arose or from taking other enforcement action either relating to the same or another matter regarding the complainant.

1 Complaints Scheme, para 7.4.

Reporting the results of the investigation

21.97   After completing his investigation, the Commissioner sends a preliminary report to the complainant and the Regulators[1]. The preliminary report will set out the Commissioner's provisional findings, the reasons for those findings and any recommendations as to what remedy should be granted. The Commissioner will invite the Regulators and the complainant to comment upon the report with a time limit for a response[2]. Given that this is likely to be the complainant's final opportunity to provide input to the process, the complainant should take the opportunity to make its views known (including with respect to publication of the report).

1   Complaints Scheme, para 7.7. Where one of the parties does not respond, this will not delay the publication of the final report, as with GE-L0035 (25/03/03) where no response was received from the complainant.
2   In practice, the Commissioner tends to give 15 working days for the parties to give their comments, although this period has been extended in at least one instance: see the Commissioner's Report GE-L0089 (07/06/03).

21.98   However, the Commissioner is not bound by the complainant's wishes and it is for him to decide whether any parts of the report should be brought to public attention[1].

1   Complaints Scheme, para 7.11. Although the complainant may have objected to publication, the Commissioner may decide that publication is within the public interest. In such circumstances, the complainant should seek to ensure that he is not identifiable.

21.99   Once the Commissioner has received any representation from the parties within the time limit set out, he will consider them and finalise the report. The final report will conclude the investigation procedure and the complaint will then be regarded as closed by both the Regulators and the Commissioner[1]. The Commissioner will again consider what parts, if any, should be published. Publication is considered in more detail at para **21.103** ff below.

1   Complaints Scheme, para 7.8.

21.100 The Commissioner must ensure that his report does not mention the name of, or contain particulars likely to identify, any person other than the Regulators[1] unless in his opinion the omission of such particulars would be likely to impair the effectiveness of the report or he considers it necessary to do so after taking into account the public interest as well as the interests of the complainant and other persons[2]. This applies to the preliminary report as well as the final report and reflects the fact that the focus of the investigation and report is on the actions or inactions of the Regulators, not the complainant (or anyone else). For that reason it will rarely be appropriate to identify anyone other than the Regulators.

1   Accordingly, those parts of reports that have been published have generally referred to firm 'X' and have not named the Regulators' employees involved in the matter.
2   See 'Complaints against the regulators' Policy Statement, March 2013, Appendix 1, para 7.9.

The Regulators' response to the Commissioner

21.101 The Scheme obliges the Regulators to inform the Commissioner and complainant of any steps they propose to take in response to a report that has either stated that the complaint is well-founded[1] or which has criticised the Regulators[2]. The Regulators are also obliged, if required by the Commissioner to do so, to publish the whole or a specified part of their response (subject to applicable statutory restrictions relating to the disclosure of confidential information).[3]

1 FS Act 2012, s 87(6)(a).
2 FS Act 2012, s 87(6)(b) See also the Complaints Scheme, para 7.12.
3 FS Act 2012, s 87(7) See also the Complaints Scheme, para 7.13.

21.102 In deciding how to respond to a report from the Commissioner, the Regulators will normally take into account:

- the gravity of the misconduct which the Commissioner has identified and its consequences for the complainant;

- the nature of the Regulators' relationship with the complainant and the extent to which the complainant has been adversely affected in the course of his direct dealings with the Regulators;

- whether what has gone wrong is at the operational or administrative level; and

- the impact of the cost of compensatory payments on firms, issuers of listed securities and, indirectly, consumers.

What publicity could arise?

21.103 Whether the complaint and the work of the Commissioner will be made public is largely within the discretion of the Commissioner.

21.104 Subject to any applicable statutory confidentiality restrictions, as outlined below, the Commissioner will decide whether to publish all or any part of his report, and all or any part of the Regulators' response to it[1]. It is therefore possible that matters relating to the complaint could become public knowledge, although the report should not normally enable anyone other than the Regulators to be identified[2]. In practice, the Commissioner usually publishes the introduction and summary sections of his report and the Regulators' response to it. On rare occasions, following objections by the complainant[3], the Commissioner has agreed not to publish the report at all.

1 See the FS Act 2012, ss 2(b)(iii) and 7 and the Complaints Scheme, paras 7.9 and 7.11. In 2012/2013, the Commissioner published summaries of 15 of the 17 reports that he issued: see the FSA Annual Report 2012/2013.
2 However, in some instances third parties have been identified, such as the Commissioner's Report GE-L0035 (25/03/03) which refers to 'Providian National Bank'.
3 In some instances, despite attempts by the Commissioner to keep the complaint confidential, the identity of the parties may be obvious from the details in the report. In such cases the complainant may decide to object to publication when presented with the Commissioner's preliminary report.

21.104 Complaints and challenges against the Regulators

The Commissioner has, in certain instances, agreed not to publish reports: see the Commissioner's Annual Report for 2012/2013 at para 2.3. Even where the Commissioner has agreed not to 'publish' sections of the report on his website, he has reserved the right to give such details in his annual or other reports.

21.105 Where the Commissioner does decide to publish, the report and response will be set out on both his website and that of the Regulators.

21.106 So far as the statutory confidentiality restrictions are concerned, the FSMA 2000[1] contains a prohibition on, broadly, the disclosure of confidential information relating to the business or affairs of any person obtained by a 'primary recipient' for the purposes of or in the discharge of any of the Regulators' functions under the FSMA 2000, or by any person directly or indirectly from the primary recipient. The Commissioner is not specified as a primary recipient for this purpose. Therefore, to the extent he receives information from the firm, or a third party who is involved (other than the Regulators or another primary recipient), he is under no statutory obligation to keep that information confidential. However, he would in principle be bound by the statutory duty of confidentiality to the extent that he receives information directly or indirectly from a primary recipient, such as the Regulators. He is also bound by the common law principles of confidentiality[2].

1 FSMA 2000, s 348, discussed in more detail in **CHAPTER 4** above. The Commissioner has stated that 'in [his] view, the [Regulator] can be too ready to hide behind the provisions of Section 348 even where these do not apply': see the Commissioner's Report GE-L0320 (01/09/04).
2 The Commissioner will be in breach of his common law obligations of confidence if: (1) the material communicated to him had the necessary qualities of confidence, namely, of limited public availability (*Attorney General v Guardian Newspapers Ltd (No 2) [1990] 1 AC 109*) and of a specific character capable of clear definition (*Terrapin Ltd v Builders Supply Co (Hayes) Ltd [1967] RPC 375*). It does not have to be original, complex, commercially valuable, personally damaging to the confider or take any specific form, but it must be of limited availability and of specific character or it will not be protected even though it is expressly described as confidential (*Mainmet Holdings plc v Austin [1991] FSR 538*); (2) the communication took place in circumstances that entailed an obligation of confidence; and (3) he used the confidential material without authorisation (*Coco v AN Clark (Engineers) Ltd [1969] RPC 41*).

21.107 To the extent that the statutory restrictions apply to the Commissioner (namely, when he receives information directly or indirectly from a primary recipient), these restrictions are subject to the exceptions in the Gateway Regulations[1]. The Gateway Regulations enable the Commissioner to receive and disclose information where this would enable or assist him to discharge his functions.

1 Financial Services and Markets Act 2000 (Disclosure of Confidential Information) Regulations 2001, SI 2001/2188, particularly regs 9, 10 and 12 and Sch 1.

Costs

21.108 Use of the complaints process is free. Neither the Regulators nor the Commissioner levies a charge on the complainant. However, any legal, or other professional costs, incurred by the complainant will not be reimbursed, whatever the outcome[1].

1 See 'Complaints against the regulators' Policy Statement, March 2013, para 2.11.

Challenging the outcome of the complaints process

21.109 The outcome of the complaints process will not always be to the complainant's satisfaction. The Commissioner may find that there were no grounds for complaint, or may decide that the matter is not one which he can or should investigate. The amount of compensation that he recommends, or the amount that the Regulators decide to pay, may be insufficient to recompense the complainant. If the complainant emerges unsatisfied from the process, what options are open to him?

21.110 There are two key points to note. First, the FSMA 2000 does not prescribe any appeal process for the Scheme and the outcome is not a matter that can be referred to the Tribunal. Therefore, once the Commissioner has made his decision, that is the end of the complaints process.

21.111 Second, the Commissioner's decision is not binding in the sense of being determinative of any person's rights. In principle, therefore, any other options which the complainant had before he brought his complaint, for example, the option of bringing a legal claim or judicial review proceedings, should in general terms remain unaffected. It is not, however, wholly without effect. For example:

- if the complainant does pursue further proceedings for damages against the Regulators[1] he will have to give credit for any compensation that he has received through the Scheme; and

- depending upon the extent of the Commissioner's investigations and the nature of his findings, a rejection of a complaint by the Commissioner may in practice make it more difficult to persuade a court to give permission for a judicial review. Firms will also need to keep in mind the short timeframe for commencing a judicial review.

1 This would only apply if the complaint falls within one of the exceptions to the statutory immunity to damages claims: see para **21.36** ff above.

Influencing the outcome of the complaints process

21.109 ...

21.110 ...

21.111 ...

Index

All references are to paragraph numbers.

Index

Index

Index

Index

Index

846

Listing Rules – *contd*
misleading information 20.36
Primary Information Providers 20.2
related party provisions 20.16, 20.36
suspension of listing, where 20.91
Lloyd's insurance market
Regulators' powers 8.6, 16.8
supervisory notice procedure 16.131
Tribunal's powers 12.11
London Stock Exchange
enforcement role 17.205–17.211

M

Macro-prudential supervision
Financial Policy Committee 1.8
Management
senior persons regime. *See* SENIOR PERSONS
REGIME
Statement of Principle 6 2.50
Manipulating device
generally 17.26
meaning 17.70–17.71
Manipulating transaction
generally 17.26
meaning 17.66–17.69
Market abuse
See also MARKET MISCONDUCT
abuse of dominant position 15.39
arrest, powers of 17.169
behaviour amounting to 17.19, 17.21–
17.29
inaction 17.28
inside information 17.57
territorial scope 17.45
behaviour not amounting to 17.21, 17.26,
17.84
buy-back programmes 17.26, 17.90
Code of Market Conduct 17.85–17.86
FCA rules 17.87–17.89
price stabilisation activities 17.26, 17.90
public authorities 17.91
behaviour not giving rise to penalty
all reasonable precautions/
diligence 17.26, 17.92, 17.99–
17.102
belief that behaviour did not amount
to 17.26, 17.92–17.98
generally 17.26, 17.92–17.93
when defences apply 17.103–17.105
benchmark manipulation
false or misleading impressions 17.26,
17.109, 17.111, 17.121, 17.126,
17.136, 17.140, 17.142, 17.159,
17.168
false or misleading statements 17.109,
17.111, 17.121, 17.126, 17.136,
17.140, 17.142, 17.159, 17.168

Market abuse – *contd*
benchmark manipulation – *contd*
generally 17.83
investigation 17.121
meaning of benchmark 17.83
self-incrimination privilege 4.58, 4.204–
4.210, 5.68, 17.142–17.154
breach of provisions, generally 2.87
buy-back programmes 17.26, 17.90
civil regime 17.10, 17.20
civil liability 17.263–17.265
interaction with criminal
penalties 17.157, 17.159, 17.164–
17.166
Code of Market Conduct
behaviour not amounting to
abuse 17.85–17.86
effect 2.70
generally 17.21–17.25, 17.173, 17.217,
17.261, 17.263
purpose 17.22
responsibility for setting 2.68, 17.21,
20.9
Statement of Principle 3 2.45–2.46
connected persons 17.111
criminal offences 5.27, 17.109, 17.111
See also MARKET MISCONDUCT
false or misleading impressions 5.27,
17.109, 17.111, 17.121, 17.126,
17.136, 17.140, 17.142, 17.159,
17.168
false or misleading statements 5.27,
17.109, 17.111, 17.121, 17.124,
17.126, 17.136, 17.140, 17.142,
17.159, 17.168
FCA investigations 17.111
insider dealing. *See* INSIDER DEALING
MAD 17.7–17.11
defences 17.92–17.105
definition
Code of Market Conduct 17.21–17.25
statutory 17.26–17.27
distortion of the market 17.26, 17.75–
17.77
emissions allowances
generally 17.26, 17.37, 17.78–17.80
inside information 17.81
investigations 17.120
market manipulation 17.82
prescribed auction platforms 17.35–
17.36
EU regulation 17.6–17.11
false or misleading impressions 17.26,
17.109, 17.111, 17.121, 17.126,
17.136, 17.140, 17.142, 17.159,
17.168
manipulating transactions 17.66–17.69

Index

Index

854

Index

Index

Index